The Oxford Handbook of

Chinese Psychology

The Oxford Handbook of **Chinese Psychology**

Edited by

Michael Harris Bond

Chair Professor of Psychology
Department of Applied Social Sciences
Hong Kong Polytechnic University
Hung Hom, Kowloon
Hong Kong S.A.R.
China

OXFORD
UNIVERSITY PRESS

Great Clarendon Street, Oxford OX2 6DP

Oxford University Press is a department of the University of Oxford.
It furthers the University's objective of excellence in research, scholarship,
and education by publishing worldwide in

Oxford New York

Athens Auckland Bangkok Bogotá Buenos AiresCalcutta
CapeTown Chennai Dar es Salaam Delhi Florence Hong Kong Istanbu
Karachi Kuala Lumpur Madrid Melbourne Mexico City Mumbai
Nairobi Paris São Paulo Singapore Taipei Tokyo Toronto Warsaw
with associated companies in Berlin Ibadan

Oxford is a registered trade mark of Oxford University Press
in the UK and in certain other countries

Published in the United States by
Oxford University Press Inc., New York

British Library Cataloguing in Publication Data

Data available

Library of Congress Cataloguing in Publication Data

Data available

ISBN 978-0-19-954185-0

10 9 8 7 6 5 4 3 2 1

Typeset in Minion
by Glyph International, Bangalore, India
Printed in Great Britain
on acid-free paper by
CPI Antony Rowe

Contents

List of Figures

List of Tables

List of Contributors

Ali, Farhan
.
Department of Organismic and Evolutionary Biology
Harvard University
USA

Au, Wing-Tung
区永东
Department of Psychology
The Chinese University of Hong Kong
Hong Kong

Blowers, Geoffrey
Department of Psychology
University of Hong Kong
Hong Kong

Chan, Agnes S-Y.
陈瑞燕
Department of Psychology
The Chinese University of Hong Kong
Hong Kong

Chan, Charles C.
陈清海
Department of Applied Social Sciences
The Hong Kong Polytechnic University
Hong Kong

Chan, Darius K-S.
陳鈞承
Department of Psychology
The Chinese University of Hong Kong
Hong Kong

Chang, Lei
张雷
Department of Educational Psychology
The Chinese University of Hong Kong
Hong Kong

Chen, Chao C.
.
Business School
Rutgers University
USA

Chen, Sylvia Xiaohua
陈晓华
Department of Applied Social Sciences
The Hong Kong Polytechnic University
Hong Kong

Chen, Xinyin
.
Department of Psychology
University of Western Ontario
Canada

Cheng, Cecilia
郑思雅
Department of Psychology
The University of Hong Kong
Hong Kong

Cheng, Sheung-Tak
.
Department of Psychological Studies
Hong Kong Institute of Education
Hong Kong

Cheng, Zi Juan
成子娟
Department of Educational Psychology
The Chinese University of Hong Kong
Hong Kong

Cheung, Fanny M.
张妙清
Department of Psychology
The Chinese University of Hong Kong
Hong Kong

Cheung, Him
张谦
Department of Psychology
The Chinese University of Hong Kong
Hong Kong

Cheung, Mei-Chun
张美珍
Institute of Textiles and Clothing
The Hong Kong Polytechnic University
Hong Kong

Cheung, Shu-Fai
张树辉
Department of Psychology
University of Macau
Macau

Chio, Jasmine H.M.
赵骞雯
Department of Psychology
The University of Hong Kong
Hong Kong

Chiu, Chi-Yue
赵志裕
Department of Psychology
University of Illinois at Urbana-Champaign
USA
and
Nanyang Business School
Nanyang Technological University
Singapore

Chiu, Ming Ming
趙明明
Department of Learning and Instruction,
Graduate School of Education
State University of New York at Buffalo
USA

Chua, Zhiren
.
Department of Psychology
National University of Singapore
Singapore

Farh, Jiing-Lih
.
Department of Management of Organizations
Business School, Hong Kong University of
Science and Technology
Hong Kong

Feng, Bing
.
Chinese Centre for Contemporary Chinese
Discourse Studies
Zhejiang University
China

Fong, Yui-Chi
方蕊慈
Department of Psychology
The Chinese University of Hong Kong
Hong Kong

Fung, Helene H.
.
Department of Psychology
The Chinese University of Hong Kong
Hong Kong

Guo, Tieyuan
郭铁元
Department of Psychology
Queen's University
Canada

Han, Kuei-Hsiang
韓貴香
Center for General Education and Core
Curriculum
Tamkang University
Taiwan

Hau, Kit-Tai
侯傑泰
Department of Educational Psychology
The Chinese University of Hong Kong
Hong Kong

Ho, Connie Suk-Han
.
Department of Psychology
University of Hong Kong
Hong Kong

Ho, Irene T.
何德芳
Department of Psychology
The University of Hong Kong
Hong Kong

Hong, Jiewen
洪洁雯
Department of Marketing
Business School, Hong Kong University of
Science and Technology
Hong Kong

Hong, Ying-Yi
康萤仪
Department of Psychology
University of Illinois at Urbana-Champaign
USA
and
Nanyang Business School
Nanyang Technological University
Singapore

Hui, Chin-Ming
許展明
Department of Psychology
Northwestern University
USA

Hwang, Kwang-Kuo
黃光國
Department of Psychology
National Taiwan University
Taiwan

Ji, Li-Jun
纪丽君
Department of Psychology
Queen's University
Canada

Kember, David
University of Hong Kong
Hong Kong

Kulich, Steve J.
顾力行
SISU Intercultural Institute
Shanghai International Studies University
China

Kwan, Virginia S-Y.
Department of Psychology
Arizona State University at Tempe
USA

Lee, Albert
李启聪
Department of Psychology
Queen's University
Canada

Lee, Hing-Chu
李慶珠
Hong Kong Sports Institute
Hong Kong

Lee, Peter W-H.
李永浩
Department of Psychiatry
University of Hong Kong
Hong Kong

Leung, Hildie
梁晓迪
Department of Psychology
The Chinese University of Hong Kong
Hong Kong

Leung, Kwok
梁觉
Department of Management
City University of Hong Kong
Hong Kong

Leung, Patrick W.-L.
梁永亮
Department of Psychology
The Chinese University of Hong Kong
Hong Kong

Leung, Winnie W.
梁穎文
Neuropsychology Laboratory
Department of Psychology
The Chinese University of Hong Kong
Hong Kong

Li, Mei-Chih
张树辉
National Chengchi University
Taiwan

Li, Ping
李 平
Department of Psychology and Center for Language Science
Pennsylvania State University
USA

Liao, Yuan
廖原
Faculty of Business Administration
Simon Fraser University
Canada

Lin, Dan
林丹
The Chinese University of Hong Kong
Hong Kong

Lin, En-Yi
林恩意
Centre for Social and Health Outcomes Research and Evaluation
Massey University
New Zealand

Liu, James
刘豁夫博士
Department of Psychology
Victoria University of Wellington
New Zealand

Liu, Wai-Sum
廖慧心
Department of Psychology
The Chinese University of Hong Kong
Hong Kong

Lo, Barbara C.Y.
罗传意
Department of Psychology
The University of Hong Kong
Hong Kong

Lonsdale, Chris
School of Physiotherapy and Performance Science
University College Dublin
Ireland

Lu, Luo
陸洛
Department of Business Administration
National Taiwan University
Taiwan

Mak, Winnie W.S.
麦颖思
Department of Psychology
The Chinese University of Hong Kong
Hong Kong

McBride-Chang, Catherine
The Chinese University of Hong Kong
Hong Kong

McGee, James A.
Princeton University
USA

Ng, Isabel Wing-Chun
.
Tuck School of Business
Dartmouth College
USA

Ng, Theresa T-T.
吳 姉 庭
Department of Psychology
The Chinese University of Hong Kong
Hong Kong

Ni, Yu-Jing
倪玉菁
Department of Educational Psychology
The Chinese University of Hong Kong
Hong Kong

O, Jiaqing
.
Department of Psychology
National University of Singapore
Singapore

Penney, Trevor B.
Department of Psychology
National University of Singapore
Singapore

Shek, Daniel Tan-Lei
石丹理
Department of Applied Social Sciences
The Hong Kong Polytechnic University
Hong Kong

Shi-Xu
施旭
Centre for Contemporary Chinese Discourse Studies
Zhejiang University
China

Shu, Hua
舒华
School of Psychology
Beijing Normal University
China

Si, Gang-Yan
姒刚彦
Hong Kong Sports Institute
Hong Kong

Smith, Peter B.
School of Psychology
University of Sussex
United Kingdom

Stewart, Sunita Mahtani
Department of Psychiatry
University of Texas Southwestern Medical Center at Dallas
USA

Tang, Catherine So-kum
.
Department of Psychology
National University of Singapore
Singapore

Tao, Rongrong
陶蓉蓉
Department of Psychiatry
University of Texas Southwestern Medical Center at Dallas
USA

Thomas, David C.
Faculty of Business Administration
Simon Fraser University
Canada

Wang, Qian
王茜
Department of Psychology
The Chinese University of Hong Kong
Hong Kong

Ward, Colleen
Department of Psychology
Victoria University of Wellington
New Zealand

Watkins, David
Faculty of Education
University of Hong Kong
Hong Kong

Wyer, Robert S. (Jr.)
Department of Business Administration
University of Illinois at Urbana-Champaign
USA

Yang, Yung-Jui
杨永瑞
Department of Psychology
University of Illinois at Urbana-Champaign
USA

Yap, Foong-Ha
叶凤霞
Department of English
The Hong Kong Polytechnic University
Hong Kong

Yik, Michelle
Division of Social Science
Hong Kong University of Science and Technology
Hong Kong

Yip, Virginia
叶彩燕
Department of Linguistics and Modern Languages
The Chinese University of Hong Kong
Hong Kong

Yue, Xiao-Dong
.
Department of Applied Social Studies
City University of Hong Kong
Hong Kong

Zhang, Jianxin
张建新
Institute of Psychology
Chinese Academy of Science
China

Zhang, Rui
张睿
Department of Psychology
University of Alberta
Canada

INTRODUCTION

Reaching this stage in studying the psychology of the Chinese people

Michael Harris Bond

All things bear the shade on their backs
and the sun in their arms;
By the blending of breath
from the sun and the shade
equilibrium comes to the world.

Tao te ching (The way of virtue), poem 42 by Lao Tzu, trans. 1955 by R. N. Blakney

As I begin this introduction to *The Oxford handbook of Chinese psychology*, it is 27 April 2008. The first drafts of this handbook's chapters are due at the end of this May, so now seems an apt time to express my hopes for this academic project. I will then assess their realization some ten or so months down the road, when I draft my conclusion and submit the final package for publication to Oxford University Press.

I have been associated with three Oxford publications on the psychology of the Chinese people. In 1986 I edited *The psychology of the Chinese people*. That collection went to twelve impressions, was in print for two decades and sold more than 10,000 copies. In 1991 I wrote a trade book as an introduction to Chinese psychology titled *Beyond the Chinese face*. That paperback has gone to fourteen impressions, and is still in print. In 1996 I edited *The handbook of Chinese psychology*, a collection of scholarly chapters integrating the research in thirty-two content areas of Chinese psychology. That hardcover resource for research was reprinted once, selling over 2,000 copies before it was taken out of print in 2006.

Clearly, there has been, and continues to be, a considerable demand for intellectual material on the psychology of the Chinese people. This curiosity is fueled by a host of factors: China's longevity as a coherent cultural tradition over 4,000 years old; China's size, geographically and demographically; the distinctiveness of Chinese language systems, both written and spoken; China's gradual emergence onto the world's political stage, heralded by the meeting of Richard Nixon with Mao Zedong in 1972; Chinese economic dynamism following the introduction of the socialist market reform policies instituted by Deng Xiaoping; and an emerging recognition of China's central role in the management of those crucial global interdependencies that will determine our planetary survival in the twenty-first century.

China is all these things, and more—it is different from the West in its cultural legacy, and, as Boulding (1970) reminds us, it is perceived by Westerners as different, very different. But how do these differences play themselves out in the psychology of its cultural legatees, the contemporary Chinese people found across the globe, particularly in China, Hong Kong, Singapore, and Taiwan, where persons claiming a Chinese heritage constitute the numerical majority in those political entities? It is these persons who will be enacting the Chinese drama in their daily lives and who will, together, be ushering us further into the twenty-first century. Who are they?

Emerging answers to that question will help us grow in our understanding of who we all are. It is obvious that individuals become most aware of their culturedness when they encounter another person of a different culture. The manifest differentness of this other person, at first physiognomically, then behaviorally in terms of dress, deportment, language, non-verbal performance, and interpersonal style, commends itself to our attention by contradicting our routine expectations and thereby provoking our curiosity. As a concept, then later as a word, 'culture' was probably invented initially to capture that arresting apprehension of human differentness, and became a verbal *léger de main* for 'explaining' such observed differences.

Of course, such an explanation is empty until it is given some scientific substance. What exactly is culture, and how does it exercise its impact in molding the lives of those individuals born into that tradition and socialized by its institutions? It is our happy work as behavioral scientists to mine this rich seam of culture's impact. Corporately, we began this academic journey into culture through initial encounters with a people from a manifestly different culture. These early encounters and attempts at understanding were initiated by anthropologists at the turn of the twentieth century, most notably E. B. Taylor, and continue today in the many branches of the social sciences that have sprung up in the United States since the Second World War. Leading the Allies, the Americans won that war and emerged in 1945 with their social institutions mostly intact, so that academia and its personnel survived the damage of that collective savagery. Indeed, the GI Bill with its provision for subsequent higher education of serving military personnel fueled the development of higher education in the United States. Since then, the American intellectual heritage and the revolutionary Greco-Roman heritage upon which it is founded have shaped the discourse in the behavioral sciences.

In psychology, the recentering of the discipline from Europe to America throughout the twentieth century has meant that most attempts to understand culture and its impact on human socialization have originated from America, by Americans, and mostly for Americans attempting to address the American social mandate to incorporate ethnic diversity in politically correct ways. Supporting this dynamic have been a relative few, mostly American-trained, psychologists who practice cross-cultural psychology. Many have taken their acquired skills abroad, often back to their country of origin, researching psychological processes in the nooks and crannies of their particular specialties.

They become cross-cultural psychologists by necessity: if they do their research only with locals in their culture of practice, they will inevitably be challenged by reviewers when they attempt to publish their work: 'How generalizable are your findings?' 'Do the results you present for scientific consideration need to be put into cultural context before they can be incorporated into our growing understanding of the processes you study?' These questions are rarely asked of American or other Western social scientists doing their research within their own country and culture, but they are routinely asked of researchers working in non-Western cultural traditions. And today, more than ever before, academics everywhere must 'publish or perish'. To publish and flourish, they must be able to answer such reviewer challenges about possible 'culture-of-origin effects', as psychologists in marketing refer to the phenomenon.

It is a salutary challenge: if culture matters psychologically, then behavioral scientists must be pushed out of their intellectual comfort zone to show how, when, and why it matters. This is not an easy process, and has gone through a number of stages bringing us to our present level of understanding about culture and its influence on psychological constructs and dynamics (Bond, 2009). It began, however, in the research encounter with difference, simple differences at first, but differences demanding an explanation by social scientists.

With the wisdom of hindsight, these initial explanations now appear simplistic. But their very inadequacy provoked a continued assault of applied intelligence to the job of 'unpackaging culture' to reveal its modes of psychological operation (Bond & van de Vijver, in press). This process required the discovery of differences to stimulate the demand for better explanations of culture's impact. Publication of evidence for those initial differences in psychological constructs and process began with psychologists working in Africa during the 1960s, but slowly shifted to the Far East, especially to Japan and Taiwan in the 1970s. Cross-cultural work then surged, especially with the arrival of Hong Kong as an exporter of comparative psychological data in the 1980s. Singapore and recently China have joined the colloquy, so we in Chinese psychology find ourselves now positioned at the spearhead of the psychological discourse on how culture shapes human behavior.

It thus appears to me that the future of culture in psychology, and our halting attempts to understand our shared humanity by encompassing cultural factors, will emerge out of the renaissance in Chinese psychology and its integration into our disciplinary discourse. Chinese culture provides the necessary degree of presumed difference to the Western, particularly American, cultural tradition; psychologists have researched and will research its legacy as socialized into the lives of Chinese persons more than they have done or will do for members of any other distinctive cultural tradition; with Stanford's president, John Hennessy, averring that five of China's universities are about to join the world's top twenty-five academic institutions, we may assume with some confidence that the resources and personnel are in place to make Chinese culture the beachhead for future developments in cross-cultural psychology.

With some of these thoughts in mind, in 2007 I approached the world's best scholars in their subdisciplines to draft an integrative chapter for a handbook of Chinese psychology. I compiled the resulting list of about thirty-five chapter titles and prospective authors, approaching Oxford University Press to assess its interest in continuing its identification with such 'things Chinese'. The commissioning editor accepted with alacrity. Subsequently, I added a few more authors and their topic areas, inviting all senior authors to bring in other competent co-authors as each saw fit. This *Oxford handbook of Chinese psychology*, with its forty content chapters, is the result. I hope that it makes an important addition to the intellectual resources of our twenty-first century.

> The myriad creatures carry on their backs the *yin*
> and hold in their arms the *yang*,
> taking the *ch'i* in between as harmony.
>
> *Tao te ching*, poem 42, trans. 1989 by D. C. Lau

References

Bond, M. H. (2009). Circumnavigating the psychological globe: From *yin* and *yang* to starry, starry night … In A. Aksu-Koc & S. Beckman (eds), *Perspectives on human development, family and culture.* Cambridge, England: Cambridge University Press.

Bond, M. H. & van de Vijver, F. (in press). Making scientific sense of cultural differences in psychological outcomes: Unpackaging the *magnum mysterium.* In D. Matsumoto & F. van de Vijver (eds), *Cross-cultural research methods.* New York: Oxford University Press.

Boulding, K. E. (1970). *A primer on social dynamics: History as dialectics and development.* New York: Free Press.

CHAPTER 1

The continuing prospects for a Chinese psychology[1]

Geoffrey H. Blowers

While the Chinese have traditionally linked the subject matter of psychology with the long-standing teachings of Confucius, Mencius, Laozi, and their followers, the modern discipline that emerged out of Euro-America only began to make an impact in the first two decades of the twentieth century. Chinese philosophers had not made any special study of mind–body problems, nor had they sought their empirical analysis using the tools of European enlightenment science. From the traditional viewpoint, this indifference was based on the assumptions that the mind performed a natural evaluative role, including the making of sensory distinctions, all in accordance with how one should act in relation to others. These understandings have generally framed the Chinese intellectual outlook and help explain why there has been no theory of mind to explain the 'soul' and seemingly no need to distinguish between conscious and unconscious thought (Mote, 1971; Munro, 1969; Petzold, 1987).

Like other sciences from nineteenth-century Europe, the emerging modern psychological discipline was unrecognizable to the Chinese, who had to discover, adopt and adapt it along with other strange new things from the West (Reardon-Anderson, 1991, p. 6). On the path to its current standing as an academic discipline and topic of popular discourse, modern psychology in China has been buffeted by enormous political upheavals, and these have had a very strong and very mixed influence. Chinese psychology, or rather, psychology in China, thereby stands as an acute example of a discipline peculiarly sensitive to ideological influence (Jing & Fu, 2001).

For a variety of reasons China regarded psychology as a foreign discipline, initially European and American, with much of it coming through Japan (Blowers, 2000), later Marxist, and later still, Soviet. In the second decade of the People's Republic of China, it became progressively Maoist in outlook, only to be outlawed as a bourgeois discipline (Munro, 1977). Over the last thirty years it has re-emerged with a broadened scope and aims as China, once again, has become receptive to new ideas from inside and outside the culture.

It is also clear from even a casual perusal of the growing research literature that modern accounts of 'Chinese psychology' render the term ambiguous. This ambiguity lies deeply rooted in the variety of ways psychologists, East and West, have come to regard their subject matter, and is a succinct indication of its current state. No longer considered a unified and coherent discipline in some Western quarters, psychology is perhaps best thought of as psychological studies (Koch, 1993), separate and parallel activities arising largely as a result of the crisis of confidence over what are the subject's aims, objects, and modes of enquiry. At issue are the means for establishing the validity of its findings and determining their truth value, as well as the social, political, and cultural positions from which different researchers report their findings.

Partly as a reaction to these developments, and partly in ignorance of them, many Western and some Chinese psychologists are continuing to seek universal concepts for understanding mental phenomena, and have sought validation by employing non-Western subjects for their research studies. Here, the use of Chinese subjects in Western research studies has become the sole and sufficient criterion for classifying them as studies in Chinese psychology. This development prompts an examination of the question of what a Chinese psychology might be.

What is Chinese psychology?

Broadly defined, Chinese psychology can be taken to mean a discipline—Eurocentric in origin—practiced in its many forms within regions of a geographical space—China—and also as something by and for a specified culture with its own distinct philosophical traditions. The latter meaning is sometimes described as 'indigenous psychology' and contrasted with the former, but this contrast is misleading, as Danziger (2006a, 2006b) has made clear. For, while the recognition of indigenous psychology as a field of psychology would appear to be a relatively recent phenomenon, it is only its labeling and identifying which are new. Indigenization of modern psychology began as various ways of envisioning human subjectivity emanating from regions of Europe—German experimental psychology, British evolutionary biology, and French psychiatry—each with its own distinctive research tradition, first made their way to America.

Each was transformed in the process. An American psychology with a strong research tradition in experimental work including experimental psychology emerged, but its original object—individual consciousness—was dropped from the research agenda quite quickly. This development led in turn to various applications of psychology in the creation of sub-fields and alternative local perspectives on what was to count as experimental science, most notably in the development of what came to be known as Behaviorism. Thus, for most of the modern period, indigenization—the making over for local purposes of what was imported from elsewhere—has been occurring if we understand this as a term for a whole complex of processes including defining psychological concepts, disciplinary boundaries, and involving student exchanges, the setting up of new institutions and departments, international conferences and dialogue.

China is no exception to this set of indigenizing processes. Its intellectual culture from the time of the May 4th Movement has been caught between (a) widespread mimesis of Euro-American sciences, including psychology, by students studying abroad, and/or from their reading, interpreting, and translating its literature; and (b) a need to preserve elements of what was being debated as uniquely Chinese. The discussions which ensued at this time were conducted both within academia itself, along lines which already partly decided what was to count as psychology, and more widely in the debates conducted within an emerging publication culture in which a growing number of intellectual and literary magazines and journals began in the early days of the Republic. A re-examination of some of this output shows how the multiplicity of viewpoints from which they were conducted led to 'Chinese psychology' becoming a contested space—a legacy it has yet to resolve (see Blowers, Cheung, & Han, 2009).

Even to talk of China and Chinese psychology, we have to be clear whether we are referring to mainland China, Taiwan, Hong Kong, Singapore, or elsewhere. We can, of course, assume that the studies done within these regions as a whole constitute, by dint of their geographical location and the ethnicity of their participants, an indigenous psychology de facto. But this would be to dismiss the enormous historical and socio-political differences between these regions and extend the meaning of the term to include any research studies in the psychological sphere involving ethnic Chinese as subjects.

Such an extension disguises real differences between the modes of transmission of knowledge arising out of very real differences in power relations (see, for example, Moghaddam, 1987, 2006; Staeuble, 2004, 2006). Euro-American psychology has dominated the others due to the massive export of its products to virtually all parts of the globe. Some have viewed this development as a success (e.g. Sexton and Hogan, 1992), while others err on the side of caution or voice opposition (e.g. Ho, 1988). The transfer of this knowledge to regions beyond the borders of its origins both highlights and disguises differences between how it is perceived and the reactions to it and out of which other indigenous psychologies are thought to have arisen, as Danziger (2006a, 2006b) has succinctly noted. Psychology from the First World has spread as both a science and a discipline which to some extent mutually define each other. Scientific psychology is seen as trying to derive causal laws of phenomena thought to be applicable everywhere to all people; the discipline works with scientific forms of enquiry and findings and disregards other approaches to the subject matter as 'unscientific', and therefore illegitimate.

The discipline also confers a professional identity on its practitioners, with its own institutional forms of training via accredited curricula, journals, professional societies, conferences, and, crucially, its audience, largely students in training and other professional psychologists. Its knowledge does not directly impact upon the common man or woman. This scientific-disciplinary complex has been transplanted to many parts of the world, often as an extended by-product of colonialism, its aim being to foster educated elites in the countries of the colonized to serve the colonizers' interests (Staeuble, 2006). This has resulted in shared understandings of the project, but the findings from this activity which can be said to constitute its knowledge claims may be far removed from the colonized inhabitants' own world views, beliefs, and values which help to shape their understanding of humankind.

Another sense of indigenous psychology applied to the Chinese is the application of psychological methods culled from the West to culturally specific practices, such as calligraphy, acupuncture, *qi gong* (Wang, 1989; Xie, 1988), even the Chinese language itself (Chen & Tzeng, 1992). The metaphysical assumptions which lie behind these practices shape the culture in terms of its health beliefs, aesthetic preferences, etc., and generally frame the way it is perceived by its inhabitants.

The indigenous psychology movement of which Yang Kuo Shu writes has gained prominence in the last thirty years (see Lock, 1981, and below), and psychologists in many parts of the Third World have voiced objections to the suitability of Western (American) psychology for meeting the needs and understandings of their own peoples (Yang, 1993, 1995, 1999, 2006). However, many of these objections, especially those from Asia, have regarded the problematic of this complex as lying in the content of Western psychology rather than its scientific approach to the subject matter. It has been left to others to examine the nature of science often seen as a monolith, to point out its various and varied practices in social contexts, (see for example, Harding, 1988; Pickering, 1992; Ziman, 2000).

Compounding these viewpoints is the long-running debate over whether culturally isolated practices should be studied using a conventional cross-cultural set of methods, given that these have been developed in cultures other than those which are usually the objects of study (e.g. Berry, 1989; Jahoda, 1977). These methods and the belief systems which inform them are on the agenda of those involved in the study of indigenous Chinese psychology, for they highlight a conflict over intention, often expressed as a debate over cultural vs. universal features of mind. The conundrum has been well expressed by Lock (1981, p. 184):

> When one proposes some basic universal dimensions from one cultural perspective and finds an apparent fit of other cultural systems to these dimensions, one has not proposed universals at all. Rather, one has constructed a translation and classificatory system which enables one to gain some understanding of an alien culture by locating elements of their systems within the hermeneutic circle of one's own.

While many traditionalists in the discipline would not share this understanding, it does clarify the pro-indigenous case. Those who would advocate the study of universal features of mind are, from this viewpoint, already engaged in the proclamation of an indigenized psychology, viz. their own. It is the hallmark of those cultures which celebrate the centrality of the individual in society, and whose authoritative, dominant, intellectual mode champions the cause of rationality over superstition. Its origins lie in the European Enlightenment.

Psychology comes to China

Problems of translation. There was a curiosity and interest in what this new subject had to offer China, ignited in 1899 by the first psychology book to appear there, Joseph Haven's *Mental philosophy*, translated by Y. K. Yen (Yan Yongjing). Sponsored by the American church mission in Shanghai,

Yan had studied at Kenyon College, Ohio, where he acquired an enthusiasm for the philosophy of the mind, and subsequently taught the subject at church schools in China as part of a general moral education program (Kodama, 1991). Haven's book dealt with the nature of mental science and the analysis and classification of mental 'power', couched in the language of the faculty psychology of its day. It had chapters on consciousness, attention and conception (thinking), memory and imagination, synthesis (generalization) and analysis (reasoning); its last section was devoted to existence, the nature of intuition, and the understanding of the beautiful and the right. It concluded with a discussion of human wisdom being greater than that of animals, and of the brain and the nervous system, and their effects on psychological functioning.

Yan used the text not so much for his students to understand the mind's workings per se, but rather to foster the notion of a healthy mind which would instigate correct patterns of behavior. Psychological knowledge could thus underpin the importance of Confucian values in the curriculum. In this respect, it shared with many other texts from the West in the last two decades of the nineteenth century its being introduced to enhance 'self-strengthening' by way of the *ti-yong* principle, the Chinese characters *ti* (體) meaning 'essence' and *yong* (用) 'utility'. The term was commonly used to suggest that there was an underlying structure to Chinese philosophical and moral values, which gave continuity to its civilization, and the implication that adaptation to all sorts of Western practices did not fundamentally threaten its cultural core (Spence, 1999).

In being the first psychology text to be translated, it was the first to encounter the difficulty of translating psychology—of finding appropriate equivalent terms in Chinese which do not distort the original meanings. Having no prior terms as foundation, Yan chose three characters not previously conjoined, *xin ling xue* (心靈學), which translates back into English as 'pneumatology', the study of spirit, a far remove from the contemporary understanding of psychology! His choice of the character *ling* (靈), for spirit, may have been informed by his reading of Aristotle's *De Anima* and Bain's journal, *Mind*. It may also be that the theme of Haven's book, that behavior is a derivative of the soul, and the fact that in Chinese culture the soul is considered a primary element of mind and nature, exhausted all possible interpretations (Zhao, 1983).

The next prominent Western psychology text to come to China was Harald Hoffding's *Outline of psychology* in 1907, which introduced a broad range of psychological topics in vogue at the time of the book's original 1882 appearance in Danish.[2] Hoffding presented a view of psychology as a new experimental science using subjective methods and psychophysical principles. It ran through ten editions in Chinese translation until 1935, and was enormously influential as a basic psychology text. The translator of this text probably relied on the Japanese translation for psychology, *xin li xue* (心理學), with *li* (理), the term in effect today, replacing *ling*. While the current, simple back-translation renders this phrase as 'knowledge of the heart', both *xin* and *li* have long histories of meaning, including, from the time of Mencius, ethical principles of conduct arising out of competing views on human nature, and from the Confucian ethic of intrinsic goodness, to the heart's propensity for evil, in the writings of Xun Zi (荀子) (Creel, 1954).

The heart-mind performed a natural evaluative role. While this activity included the making of sensory distinctions, all evaluations would appear to be made in accordance with how one should act in relation to others. These understandings have generally framed the Chinese intellectual outlook, as other commentators (e.g. Munro, 1969, 1977; Petzold, 1987) have noted. They also help to explain why, traditionally, there has been no sophisticated philosophical or psychological system of mind, or why it is unnecessary to distinguish conscious from unconscious thought.

This beginning, then, marks two developments for Western psychology into China: the selective borrowing of a psychological literature for utilitarian purposes, rather than for a general philosophical orientation, and the reshaping of its meaning through translation difficulties. In selecting texts with concepts for which there were no Chinese equivalents, decisions were arbitrarily taken to coin new terms by borrowing Chinese characters with similar, but by no means identical, semantic features. Translation of texts thus marked an indigenizing process common to many foreign subjects, which only became apparent after the trickle of translated academic books at the end of the nineteenth century turned into a flood in the early part of the twentieth.

The initial impetus

China's defeat in its military engagements with France in 1894 and Japan in 1895 prompted the Qing court to introduce educational reforms along the lines of those introduced earlier into Japan following the Meiji restoration. Included were a form of compulsory education for a specified number of years, a de-emphasis on educating an elite for government service, the formation of an Imperial University in Peking, and opportunities for large numbers of Chinese to study overseas. A further consequence of these reforms was the setting up of a large number of teachers' colleges or normal universities in which psychology figured prominently in the curriculum, with much reliance on Japanese textbooks and teachers (Abe, 1987; Blowers, 2000).

The establishment of the Republic in 1912 led to improvements in higher education due to both the *Bai Hua* movement to raise the vernacular Chinese language to a literary form and in 1919 the May 4th student movement against the Versailles settlement of previous German possessions in Shandong being handed over to Japan. These movements led to calls for a universal education, importing of more foreign ideas, and making textbooks and teaching materials relevant to everyday life (Lutz, 1971). Out of these developments there emerged a number of journals and magazines in which modern Western knowledge in a variety of fields including psychology and psychoanalysis was reviewed and discussed. Chief amongst these were the *Jiaoyu Zazhi* (Education Journal), *Dongfang Zazhi* (Eastern Journal), and *Xin Qing Nian* (New Youth), which employed a more popular and less scholarly style. However, in 1921, arising out of a new initiative in the formation of the Chinese Psychological Society, the journal *Xinli* (Psychology) under the editorship of Zhang Yaoxiang was established. Amongst its aims Zhang outlined in the first issue was the proposition that psychology 'is the most useful science in the world. Not only can it be applied to education, but also to business, medicine, fine arts, law, the military and daily life ...' (Zhao, 1992, p. 48). Zhang encouraged readers and contributors to focus on three areas of study: first, the revival of older ideas in the historical literature of the country; second, the study of newer material from other countries; third, striving to develop new theories and experiments out of a synthesis of the first two. Between 1922 and 1940 some 370 books on psychology were published (Pan, Chen, Wang, & Chen, 1980).

Early institutional developments

The first laboratory was established at Peking National University in 1917, at the urging of the democratic reformer Cai Yuanpei, who had studied under Wundt in Leipzig (Petzold, 1987). Many of the intellectuals of this period had studied abroad in Europe or America, and many of the first generation of Chinese psychologists were American-trained. The first psychology department was opened at Southeastern University in Nanking in 1920. Within ten years, other departments opened at universities in Canton, Shanghai, Qinqhua, Amoy, and Tientsin (Chou, 1927a, 1927b, 1932). By 1928 the Institute of Psychology was founded within the Chinese Academy of Sciences. A Chinese Psychological Society was formally established in 1921.

These developments did not pose any threat to fundamental values, since they were seen as tools in the service of the greater good for Chinese society. The Behaviorism and Functionalism which the American-educated students brought back to China with them could be accommodated within the new pragmatic view of the need for Western science, even if their essentially deterministic conceptions could, arguably, be seen as a challenge to Confucian notions of mind. This leniency was not accorded to psychoanalysis, however. Here Chinese intellectuals trod warily through some of the more radical aspects of the theory, as they attempted to exalt Freud for the purposes of education and social reform. Some translations of Freud resulted in layers of censorship introduced by his translators in order to downplay what they took to be his pan-sexualism and make his ideas more palatable to Chinese cultural prescriptions. Oedipal theory, for example, was subverted into a social theory of family conformity (Blowers, 1997; Zhang, 1992).

By the end of the twenties and early thirties, not only universities but also many teacher colleges were instructing their pupils in the ideas of Freud, Watson, McDougall, Piaget, Lewin, and Kohler, using translated texts and critical essays (Bauer & Hwang, 1982). There was very little experimental work in this period, however. The dominant form of practice was the psychometric variant of the group study with its emphasis on educational testing. This had arisen out of the widespread belief in education as 'a means of solving the many social, moral and political problems of the nation', as one outside observer had noted after an official visit in the 1920s (Monroe, 1922, p. 29). A need had been seen to test children of all ages for educational purposes, and adults for recruitment into appropriate forms of military and other service. This had led to serious enquiry into the nature of testing, and to a journal and society devoted to these ends. However, those who employed educational tests—a combination of psychologists and educators—were more concerned about public demonstrability than internal validity, with most published studies being reports of surveys, testing children for classroom placement, or teacher evaluation. Trying to be socially accountable through the widespread use of tests in the 1930s yielded a poor outcome, as beyond the academy few graduates armed with this new knowledge could get jobs because of a lack of development of social science professions. This contrasted with other areas of the social sciences, notably economics and sociology, which had received a boost to their development through initiatives funded by the Rockefeller Foundation to support research into rural reconstruction (Chiang, 2001).

In spite of the fact that it had been a period of openness during which different viewpoints were widely discussed in journal articles (Dikotter, 2008), no clear intra-disciplinary directive or any developed policies for social administration emerged that impacted directly upon psychology. The concerns of Chinese psychologists remained largely confined to the pages of their journals, where the intellectual work was carried on of deciding what features of psychology, substantial and methodological, were best for tackling psychological problems with Chinese characteristics. To this extent indigenization was benign and proceeded along a liberal trajectory but, after the formation of the People's Republic of China in 1949, it was to alter course, assuming a much narrower focus and a rigidly applied political orthodoxy, discussed next.

Psychology in the People's Republic of China

Redefining the discipline. Following the founding of the People's Republic in 1949, a broad program of socialist reform was ushered in. At this time it was widely held that psychology, based upon Western ideas, had to be revised to fit better into the new social and political milieu. Like other intellectuals, psychologists had to study Marxist philosophy, and their discipline had to be practiced in accordance with two principles: that psychological phenomena are a product or function of the brain, and that mind is a reflection of outer reality. These were drawn from Lenin's theory of reflection in his *Materialism and empirio-criticism* and Mao Zedong's *On contradiction* and *On practice* (Ching, 1980). Soviet psychology had to be studied, and Western psychology, in its various schools, had to be critically examined for its various failings (Lee & Petzold, 1987).

Thus, 1949 brought a halt to the teaching and practice of Western psychology in the mainland (Chin & Chin, 1969). Most of the allowable textbooks in psychology were translations from the Russian (Petzold, 1984). Russian educationalists came to China in the early fifties to teach in Beijing, advocating a new foundation for the acquisition of knowledge. Inspired by the work of Vygotsky, Luria, and Leont'ev, dialectical materialism became the central philosophy underlying all permissible psychology. From this position consciousness was a historically and developmentally formed mental product, so that its objects could not be thought of as separate from the reflection process, *fan she* (反射), which brings them into being. This contrasted with certain idealist tendencies in Western psychology which were predicated upon a separation of subject and object, or of mental image and objective reality.

An effect of this position was to introduce a new term for consciousness, *tzuchueh neng tungli* (自覺能動力) (active consciousness), which is formed out of the activities of people in society undertaking concrete actions. Mental processes, it was argued, could not be studied apart from the contexts in which they occur. Consciousness was seen as the supreme force governing human behavior unchallenged by, and therefore granting no status to, competing forces such as the preconscious or unconscious. It was capable of self-reflection, that is, awareness of its own changes, and by all of its activities it increased its knowledge, the process being known as *ren shi* (認識) (recognition). Ding Zuan (Ting Tsang), the secretary of the Chinese Psychology Society re-formed in 1955, wrote that there was little room within this framework for Freud's 'mysterious sexual drives' (Ding, 1956). Paradoxically, psychotherapy, a direct offshoot of Freud's theory, gained respectability only when its theoretical justification was presented in Pavlov's system as an ordering of reflexes responding to verbal stimuli.

In spite of the tendency to theorize about all psychological activity in terms of Pavlovian reductionism, Chinese psychologists, following the reopening of the Psychological Society, fought for their own views. This was made possible in the brief period of liberal reform which became known as the One Hundred Flowers Movement of 1957. It was during this period that psychologists questioned the status of much reductionist psychology, arguing that it was becoming divorced from reality (Zhao, Lin, & Zhang, 1989), and should assume a practical or applied component. This led many psychologists to give up laboratory work and seek out applications in factories, hospitals, and schools.

Early suppression. However, this period of open debate and questioning was quickly counteracted by the Anti-rightist or Criticism Movement which followed in August of 1958. Psychology was banned as 'bourgeois pseudoscience' and many psychologists were persecuted. The political justification of this suppression was as follows: by concentrating on the biological foundations of behavior and the experimental isolation of variables, psychologists were guilty of abstracting entities from their social context. By so doing, psychology remained too 'academic' and therefore played into the hands of class enemies of the state. As the study of consciousness, psychology was class-bound, and psychologists were criticized as dehumanizing the class nature of their activities by failing to take into account the social nature of their subject matter. This line of thinking denied the possibility of there being any common or universal features of the mind that were worthwhile objects of study.

Following the failure of the Great Leap Forward, these criticisms were stopped a year later, and discussions amongst psychologists led to an integration of the viewpoints that psychology was both a natural and a social science (Cao, 1959). In the early 1960s, educational and developmental psychology became the most productive areas of the discipline, so that by 1963, at the first annual meeting of the Chinese Psychological Society, they comprised over three-quarters of the 203 papers presented. Other papers were in the applied areas of personnel and clinical psychology.

Later suppression. This burgeoning of productivity was short-lived, however, as attacks on the discipline soon came from students and young cadres in the course of the Cultural Revolution. Following a general line taken by Mao, the country's youth was encouraged to engage in anarchic activities against the more progressive elements of the Party which had been content to accord a certain amount of autonomy to intellectuals, whom Mao believed would lead the country to failure. Attacks on many academic disciplines occurred. Psychology became especially targeted by a leading figure of the party, Yao Wenyuan. As minister of propaganda, and writing an editorial under a pseudonym in *Renmin Ribao*, Yao attacked an article on color and form preferences in children by Chen Li and Wang Ansheng, for much the same reasons that had motivated the outbursts during the earlier Criticism Movement: the experiments abstracted from the lived realities of people in actual social contexts, and were not therefore legitimate objectives of research (Blowers, 1998). Because of Yao's influential position, his editorial fueled the flames of a growing attack on the discipline as a whole, forcing it to be shut down by 1966, with the banning of psychology books and journals and the ceasing of its teaching in universities and research institutes.

Rehabilitation. A full twelve years later, at the Third Plenary session of the Party Congress in 1978, however, the discipline became respectable again. The first meeting of the Chinese Psychological Society held during this period re-elected Pan Shu as its president. Along with a contemporary of his generation, Gao Juefu, Pan was invited to write histories of Chinese and Western psychology (Gao, 1985; Pan & Gao, 1983). At the meeting there were also many opportunities for the denunciation of the previous injustices perpetrated by Yao Wenyuan, led by Chen Li himself (Blowers, 1998; Chen & Wang, 1981; Petzold, 1987). In this more favorable post-Mao climate, psychologists were called upon to contribute to the modernization program, as China, once again, became receptive to the West. Intellectuals of various persuasions began visiting, and exchanges were, and continue to be, encouraged.

The outlook. There was an enormous gap in continuity of education created by the closing of university doors for over ten years. Despite the loss of intellectual development for a whole generation of actual and potential students, this hiatus has been more than compensated by dramatic developments in psychology due to a change in attitude of the Chinese government (Clay, 2002). It is claimed there are today over 150 psychology departments and institutes at Chinese universities, running approximately 130 master's programs and thirty doctoral programs. There are approximately 10,000 undergraduates, 2,000 master's-level, and 300 doctoral-level graduate students studying psychology (Zhang, 2007).

Dialogue with Western psychologists continues through visits and reciprocal arrangements for study periods. Since 1980, China has been a member of the International Union of Psychological Science (IUPS) and in 2004 hosted the International Congress of Psychology, which attracted over 6,000 local and overseas participants. Other international conferences on the psychology-related topics of mental health and psychotherapy are also regularly held. The Chinese Psychology Society has over 6,000 members, each of whom has to have 'at least a master's degree in psychology or relevant research experience in psychology' (Zhang, 2007 p. 175). The government has recognized that with its booming market economy, it is encountering social problems for which psychological services are now very much needed, particularly in the areas of counseling (now a government-approved job category), human resources, and health psychology (Clay, 2002; Shanghai Mental Health Center, 2008).

However, the development of an appropriate theoretical perspective for Chinese psychology has yet to emerge. From an historical viewpoint, one thing seems clear. While much present-day Western psychology is welcomed for its utilitarian value, there is little evidence that the metaphysical assumptions of its rigid determinism, as evidenced in radical behaviorism and psychoanalysis, and its individualism, as evidenced in personality and intellectual assessment, are embraced in any fundamental way by Chinese people. Western psychology is seen to provide skills training in helping society solve a myriad of problems in child and adult development, health, and industry, but all in the service of an authoritarian, collectivist culture.

This practice provides all the more reason, therefore, for the Chinese themselves to develop a specifically Chinese framework for future study (Pan, 1980). Whether this framework will ultimately materialize will depend upon the kind of curriculum encompassed within the departments and the type of research question setting the research agendas as well as in professional training about what might constitute good practice. As one psychologist on the scene has recently observed:

> What China needs now are highly qualified psychologists for both research and education. Although psychology departments are flourishing in China, only a small number of psychologists have published research papers in journals with high international reputations. Most Chinese psychologists have never had the opportunity to attend an international conference, let alone to join international research teams.
>
> Han, 2008

Psychology in other Chinese regions

Institutional developments. Unlike the recent rapid expansion into higher education that China has promoted, Taiwan, Hong Kong, and even Singapore have been developing their psychological studies unimpeded by the political uncertainties characterizing China over the latter half of the twentieth century. Prior to that period, psychology in each of these regions sprang from humble, pre-war, colonial beginnings. In Taiwan under Japanese rule, it was taught in Japanese by the Department of Literature at Taipei Imperial (now National Taiwan) University. That legacy was richly endowed with many hundreds of translations and secondary source writings in Japanese on Western psychological topics. Japanese psychology in the thirties and forties was dominated by the Gestalt school, with the result that the early stages of experimental research in Taiwan were concerned with problems of perception.

In Hong Kong under the British, psychology was taught in English in the Faculty of Arts at the University of Hong Kong as an adjunct to philosophy. It remained there until the annexation of those departments in 1967 when the Faculty of Social Sciences was formed. In Taiwan, psychology's emergence from the Department of Literature came in 1949 when, following the declaration of the Republic by Chiang Kai Shek (Jiang Jieshi) and the implementation of Mandarin as the medium of instruction, it became a separate department housed in the Faculty of Sciences. In Taiwan and Hong Kong, each psychology department, once separated, made great strides in its development, and shortly thereafter other departments at other institutions in these regions sprang up (Blowers, 1987; Fu, 2002; Hsu, 1987).

The discipline of psychology is relatively new in Singapore. It was first taught in the National University of Singapore (NUS) within the Department of Social Work in 1952, from which it emerged as a separate department in 1995. Since then, it has also become an integral part of programs in two other publicly funded universities, Nanyang Technological University and Singapore Management University, as well as at some of the polytechnics, which provide pre-university education in Singapore, and various privately run schools. Programs at both undergraduate and graduate level are offered, and NUS's department has become research-intensive, its work in psychology focusing upon 'basic psychological processes with a particular emphasis on how those processes play out in the context of culture', Singapore being an ideal locale given its diverse ethnic composition of Chinese, Malay, and Indian (Bishop, 2008; Long, 1987).

The investment in research. Economic growth from the fifties onwards made for closer ties to Britain in the cases of Hong Kong and Singapore, and to America in the case of Taiwan, with educational curricula tailored to each tradition. These changes affected the kind of psychology that was taught and the psychological problems investigated. The general intellectually liberal climate that prevailed at the tertiary level enabled many exchanges with overseas academics and the fostering of closer intellectual ties. Research activity flourished. Of significance was the formation in Hong Kong in 1972 of the International Association for Cross-Cultural Psychology (IACCP), an organization devoted to the testing of hypotheses in different cultures, in all aspects of the discipline, using samples of 'Western' (usually American) subjects as a baseline for cross-cultural comparison.

An outgrowth of this endeavor was the gathering in 1986 of research data in several areas in social psychology, psychopathology, language, personality, etc. into a single edited volume entitled *The psychology of the Chinese people* (Bond, 1986). This was shortly followed by a volume compiled by Ho, Spinks, and Yeung (1989) of abstracts of experimental research that has used Chinese subjects, be they from the mainland, Taiwan, Hong Kong or elsewhere, and which had been written in English. The current volume is the second edition of a handbook on Chinese psychology (Bond, 1996), and provides evidence for the continuing influence of this endeavor.

While the scope of the compilation by Ho et al. (1989) was extensive, the editors noted that many of the papers were poorly written, methodologically unsound, and lacked insight or theoretical rigor. They laid the blame at the blind copying of Western studies by Chinese psychologists and the fact that not enough steps had been taken to ensure impartial peer review and editorial responsibility in Chinese journals. At the same time they commented favorably upon the Sinicization conference held in Taiwan in 1980 at which criticisms were voiced about the continual use of Western models for the study of psychological processes in the Chinese (Yang & Wen, 1982). Similar conclusions were reached by Hsu in his review of psychology in Taiwan to 1982 (Hsu, 1987). He commented that while Taiwan may advocate a policy of Sinicization with its emphasis upon Chinese traditions and culture, Taiwan's psychologists remained adamant in their adherence to the 'empirical stance, to objective data, and to the operational definition of concepts. Thus the results of any such policy [will] be limited to changes in *content*, without innovation in basic concepts and methods' (p. 135) though there are signs this approach might be changing (see e.g. Lu, this volume).

This position encapsulates a widely held attitude, namely that psychology is science, akin to natural sciences, even if the study of its subject matter, its 'objects', may not be undertaken independently of the manner in which they are conceived. This view, however, has been seriously challenged in the West, and the future of any psychological studies, perceived as indigenous or otherwise, will depend upon the extent to which communities of psychologists meet this challenge, outlined next.

The postmodern turn

In the last thirty years or so, psychology in the West has taken a self-critical turn. An earlier generation of psychologists in the thrall of Kuhn's *The structure of scientific revolutions* (1970) had debated the consequences of whether areas of their own discipline were paradigmatic or pre-paradigmatic science. What was generally not at issue, however, were the rules to be adopted for determining what counted as legitimate forms of enquiry, valid data, or appropriate method. Appeals to universal certainty were justified in the name of unprejudiced observation, tried and tested. While abstractions from data were always on shaky ground and liable to sudden replacement, the means for deciding upon the truth of any abstraction invoked the cardinal rules of the game. Psychology was science, and science proceeded by the empirical methods of operationalism, hypothesis testing, and the prioritizing of observation over theory.

Increasingly, however, the notion of truth came to be seen not as a foundation to knowledge but as a perspective, and therefore as a product of social exchange built, as Gergen (1992) eloquently argued, into systems of communication and relationship. From this position, it follows that 'What passes as knowledge within the sciences may properly be seen as the result of social processes within the culture of science' (p. 21). Far from transparently revealing an already constituted subject matter, the languages of science are, in tandem with other languages, narratives, employing a variety of rhetorical devices for persuading us about the world. As such, they resonate with the valuational biases of their authors, and with the literary forms and styles of the historical and cultural moment of their genesis.

The earlier view, namely the presumption of the independence of objects from the means of their description, can only be upheld by masking its metaphysical and ideological commitments. For example, the notion that there are universal properties of mind maintains credibility only at the expense of leaving unchallenged the 'peculiarly Western ontology of the person' (Gergen, 1992, p. 24), for not all cultures attribute cognitive processes to persons. This universalist fiction promotes the idea of a person as a private decision maker in charge of his or her own fate. Enquiries into the social realm remind us that our languages are a product of interaction, not isolation, and that our ways of speaking about minds are precisely that: culturally endorsed ways of speaking.

The focus of much new-look psychology in the West has thus turned the emphasis to discourse and its analysis, and to the social construction of our knowledge base with two important implications. The first is that it will no longer be legitimate to prioritize some methods over others, since the notion that methods are linked to truth claims is unwarranted and misleading; the goal is no longer a claim to truth, but to the exploration of a perspective and all that is entailed by the assumption of that perspective. The second is that, if cultural specificity is to become the central feature of study, the search for universals will have to be (temporarily) abandoned. There have already been hints in the literature that the search for understanding at the cultural level should precede any judgements of transcultural understanding, especially in the rash fitting of data to overarching theory where the fit is often far from smooth (Jahoda, 1992, 1994; Ongel & Smith, 1994). Understanding in this context would then have to take account of the social, political, and historical forces that shape cultural phenomena, and would cast the psychologist in the role of cultural critic, a human rather than natural scientist.

The future for Chinese psychology

In spite of this challenge, it may be that Hsu's (1987) forecast, above, will prevail. Chinese psychologists, following fundamental cultural imperatives, have been interested in the pursuit of knowledge more for its relation to conduct and action than for the elaboration of specific forms of analytical self-reflection (Munro, 1967, 1977). This agenda has probably contributed to the tendency to see psychology as an applied discipline and to evaluate it only with respect to its utility: in education as an adjunct to teacher training; in industrial sectors as a spur to productivity; and in the medical sphere as a preliminary to clinical diagnosis, although this last use is still relatively rare.

In some areas of the discipline, most notably social psychology, the justification for pursuing indigenous lines of research is strong, given the cultural influence over social processes (see Chen & Farh; Hwang & Han; Ji, Lee, & Guo; Lu; Smith; all this volume). In areas more traditionally aligned to natural sciences, for example experimental and cognitive psychology, Chinese psychologists are continuing to imitate their Western counterparts. Funding for experimentally based projects continues from China itself and from grants abroad. Given how funding is often tied to academic exchanges amongst those with mutual interests, there will likely be a tendency to develop more studies in partnership with psychologists in the West, and therefore to strengthen more traditional areas of the discipline. These financial considerations will continue to affect Chinese psychologists both in and outside China.

Some factors are also likely to influence the possibility of an indigenous psychology emerging in the near future. Given the propensity to judging the worth of the discipline for its applications, many students and young academics weighing their future prospects see professional development not as a lifelong commitment to intellectual enquiry but as a job opportunity, one amongst many. Nonetheless, the expansion of the universities over the last ten years or so, the opening up of more psychology departments and the teaching of psychology as an adjunct to other disciplines, coupled with the increasing number of joint degree programs being offered with universities overseas, have led to an increasing number of professionals teaching psychology.

Not all, however, are fully committed to doing research (Han, 2008). This is because there remain problems of writing research reports and papers in one's second language of English, an activity which is necessary for the advancement of the discipline in the international community, as well as for the academic promotion of the individual. This requirement poses an added strain, since one's English standard will have to be good enough to pass muster in the editorial offices of leading overseas journals. But, since writing academic psychology can be seen as the exhibition of one's latest conjectures, it poses a problem for those exceptionally concerned about negative evaluations. A typical solution to this problem leads many to adopt an ultra-conventional style of writing as seen, for example, in the format of the experimental report, with its attention to technical detail at the expense of conjecture and reflection, and it's often 'variable vague' view of the behavior of its studies' participants (Billig, 1994). This solution encourages a movement away from writing more freely and speculatively about one's own culture and its influences.

However, from this standpoint one can also see how some are driven through zeal and commitment to write about cultural experience in their own language of Chinese. In so doing there is often the need to borrow terms derived from Western psychology, and therefore to deal with the problems posed by translation as mentioned earlier. Terminological borrowing cuts both ways, however, as Western psychologists may begin to show interest in translating Chinese texts into English in order to learn more about the social processes that may be distinctively Chinese.

Against the albeit slim possibility of a Chinese cultural view of psychology emerging must be countered the impact of the cross-cultural psychology movement, which has been slow to meet this challenge. Retaining for the most part a modernist view of the discipline as a progressively evolving natural science, it has continued to pursue cultural enquiry by referencing measures of cultural difference with respect to criteria culled from primarily North American university student populations. With its emphasis on quantitative differences with respect to reference group criteria, and its reliance on cultural stereotypes to explain those differences, often in post-hoc fashion, 'Chinese psychology' becomes, almost by definition, nothing other than the employment of Chinese subjects in (any) comparative psychological studies. Such research activity proliferates, even if most of its cultural content has been confined to pan-cultural abstractions, such as 'individualism-collectivism'. This kind of work has been undergoing critical re-evaluation even from adherents to this movement (e.g. Brewer & Chen, 2007; Jahoda, 1994; Ongel & Smith, 1994; Smith, this volume), and it is to be hoped that it will encourage a widening of perspective and critique.

Unless and until psychology curricula in tertiary institutes in the West include evaluation of the knowledge base of psychology as a core activity, and cultural critique and interpretative stance become the accepted tools of the trade, Chinese psychologists are likely to continue emulating what they believe to be the still-dominant, positivist mode of mainstream Western psychology. But, as this brief historical excursion into China's relations with the discipline has shown, a distinctive Chinese view informing the discipline is unlikely to be forthcoming in the near future. Unlikely, that is, unless Chinese psychologists grow sufficiently confident to challenge their own long-held assumptions about the ways of doing psychology, and Western psychologists become overwhelmingly postmodern in outlook and encourage Chinese psychologists in similar ways.

Chapter notes

1 Over the years this work has been supported by funds from the Department of Psychology and the Conference and Research Grants Committee of the University of Hong Kong. I remain grateful to Chan Wing-man for her help in compiling and translating material for this chapter.

2 The text was translated by Wang Guo Wei, who used the English translation by Loundes.

References

Abe, H. (1987). Borrowing from Japan: China's first modern education system. In R. Hayhoe (ed.), *China's education and the industrialized world* (pp. 57–80). Armonk, NY: Sharpe.

Bauer, W. & Hwang, S. C. (1982). *German impact on modern Chinese intellectual history.* Wiesbaden, Germany: Franz Steiner Verlag.

Berry, M. W. (1989). Imposed etics-emics-derived etics: The operationalising of a compelling idea. *International Journal of Psychology, 24*, 721–735.

Billig, M. (1994). Repopulating the depopulated pages of social psychology. *Theory and Psychology, 4*, 307–335.

Bishop, G. D. (2008). Psychology in Singapore. *APS Monitor, 21* (5). At http://www.psychologicalscience.org/observer/getArticle.cfm?id=2343

Blowers, G. H. (1987). To know the heart: Psychology in Hong Kong. In G. H. Blowers, G. H. & Turtle, A. M. (eds), *Psychology moving East: The status of Western psychology in Asia and Oceania* (pp. 139–162). Boulder, CO: Westview Press.

Blowers, G. H. (1997). Freud in China: The variable reception of psychoanalysis. *China Perspectives 10*, March/April, 33–39.

Blowers, G. H. (1998). Chen Li: China's elder psychologist. *History of Psychology, 1*, 315–330.

Blowers, G.H. (2000). Learning from others: Japan's role in bringing psychology to China. *American Psychologist, 55*, 1433–1436.

Blowers, G., Cheung, B. T., & Han, R. (2009). Emulation vs. indigenization in the reception of Western psychology in Republican China: An analysis of the content of Chinese psychology journals (1922–1937). *Journal of the History of the Behavioural Sciences*, 45, 21–33.

Bond, M. H. (ed.) (1986). *The psychology of the Chinese people.* Hong Kong: Oxford University Press.

Bond, M. H. (ed.) (1996). *The handbook of Chinese psychology.* Hong Kong: Oxford University Press.

Cao, R. C. (10 June 1959). *Canjia Xinlixue xueshu taolun de tihui.* (Experiences learned from the symposium on Psychology) *Renmin Rebao*, p. 6. (in Chinese)

Brewer, M. B. & Chen, Y. R. (2007). Where (who) are collectives in collectivism? Toward conceptual clarification of individualism and collectivism. *Psychological Review, 114*, 133–151.

Chen, H. C. & Tzeng, O. J. L. (eds) (1992). *Language processing in Chinese.* Amsterdam, The Netherlands: Elsevier.

Chen, L. & Wang, A. S. (1981). Hold on to scientific explanation in psychology. In L. B. Brown (ed.), *Psychology in contemporary China* (pp. 151–156). New York: Pergamon.

Chiang, Y. C. (2001). Social engineering and the social sciences in China, 1919–1949. Cambridge, England: Cambridge University Press.

Chin, R. & Chin, A. L. S. (1969). *Psychological research in Communist China 1949–1966.* Cambridge, MA: MIT Press.

Ching, C. C. (Jing Qicheng) (1980). Psychology in the People's Republic of China. *American Psychologist, 35*, 1084–1089.

Chou, S. G. K. (1927a). Trends in Chinese psychological interest since 1922. *American Journal of Psychology, 38*, 487–488.

Chou, S. G. K. (1927b). The present status of psychology in China. *American Journal of Psychology, 38*, 664–666.

Chou, S. G. K. (1932). Psychological laboratories in China. *American Journal of Psychology, 44*, 372–374.

Clay, R. A. (2002). Psychology around the world: 'Seizing an opportunity' for development: Chinese psychology moves from 'pseudo-science' to an increasingly accepted field. *Monitor on Psychology, 33*, No. 3, March. At http://www.apa.org/monitor/mar02/seizing.html

Creel, H. G. (1954). *Chinese thought from Confucius to Mao Tse Tung.* London: Eyre and Spottiswoode.
Danziger, K. (2006a). Universalism and indigenization in the history of modern psychology. In A. Brock (ed.), *Internationalizing the history of psychology* (pp. 208–225). New York: New York University Press.
Danziger, K. (2006b). Comment. *International Journal of Psychology 41* (4) 269–275.
Dikötter, F. (2008). *The age of openness: China before Mao.* Hong Kong: Hong Kong University Press.
Ding, Z. (Ting Tsang). (1956). *Qaichan wuquoyishu toshan qiqi goshu xingji.* (Developing a program in Chinese medical psychology). *Zhunghua xienjen goshu zashi, 4,* 322–325. (in Chinese)
Fu, W. (2002). *The public image of psychologists in Hong Kong: An historical and cultural perspective.* Unpublished doctoral thesis, University of Hong Kong.
Gao, J. F. (ed.) (1985). *Zhongguo Xinlixueshi* (History of psychology in China). Beijing: Renmin Jiaoyu Chubanshe. (in Chinese)
Gergen, K. J. (1992). Towards a postmodern psychology. In S. Kvale (ed.), *Psychology and postmodernism* (pp. 17–30). London: Sage.
Han, S. H. (2008). Bloom and grow: My view of psychological research in China. *APS Monitor,* 21 January. At http://www.psychologicalscience.org/observer/getArticle.cfm?id=2284
Harding, S. (1988). *Is science multicultural? Postcolonialisms, feminisms, and epistemologies.* Bloomington: IN: Indiana University Press.
Ho, D.Y.F. (1988). Asian psychology: A dialogue on indigenization and beyond. In A.C. Paranjpe, D.Y.F. Ho, & R.W. Rieber (eds), *Asian contributions to psychology* (pp. 53–77). New York: Praeger.
Ho, D. Y. F., Spinks, J. A., & Yeung, C. S. H. (1989). *Chinese patterns of behaviour: A sourcebook of psychological and psychiatric studies.* New York: Praeger.
Hsu, J. S. Z. (1987). The history of psychology in Taiwan. In G. H. Blowers & A. M. Turtle (eds), *Psychology moving East: The status of Western psychology in Asia and Oceania* (pp. 127–138). Boulder, CO: Westview Press.
Jahoda, G. (1977). In pursuit of the emic-etic distinction: Can we ever capture it? In Y. H. Poortinga (ed.), *Basic problems in cross-cultural psychology* (55–63). Lisse, The Netherlands: Swets and Zeitlinger.
Jahoda, G. (1992). *Crossroads between culture and mind: Continuities and change in theories of human nature.* London, England: Harvester/Wheatsheaf.
Jahoda, G. (1994). Review of P. B. Smith and M. H. Bond's 'Social psychology across cultures', *The Psychologist, 7,* 174– 175.
Jing, Q. C. & Fu, X. L. (2001). Modern Chinese psychology: Its indigenous roots and international influences. *International Journal of Psychology 36,* 408–418.
Koch, S. (1993). 'Psychology' or 'The psychological studies'? *American Psychologist, 48,* 902–903.
Kodama, S. (1991). Life and work of Y. K. Yen, the first person to introduce Western psychology to modern China. *Psychologia, 34,* 213–226.
Kuhn, T. (1970). *The structure of scientific revolutions.* Chicago, IL: University of Chicago Press.
Lee, H. W. & Petzold, M. (1987). Psychology in the People's Republic of China. In G. H. Blowers & A. M. Turtle (eds), *Psychology moving East: The status of Western psychology in Asia and Oceania* (pp. 105–125). Boulder, CO: Westview Press.
Lock, A. (1981). Indigenous psychology and human nature: A psychological perspective. In P. Heelas & A. Lock (eds), *Indigenous psychologies: The anthropology of the self* (pp. 183–201). London, England: Academic Press.
Long, F. Y. (1987). Psychology in Singapore: Its roots, context and growth. In G. H. Blowers & A. M. Turtle (eds), *Psychology moving East: The status of Western psychology in Asia and Oceania* (pp. 223–248). Boulder, CO: Westview Press.
Lutz, J. G. (1971). *China and the Christian colleges 1850–1950.* Ithaca, NY: Cornell University Press.
Moghaddam, F. M. (1987). Psychology in the three worlds: As reflected in the crisis in social psychology and the move towards indigenous Third World psychology. *American Psychologist, 42,* 912–920.
Monroe, P. (1922). *A Report on education in China.* Institute of International Education: New York.
Mote, F. (1971). *Intellectual foundations of China.* New York: Knopf.
Munro, D. J. (1969). *The concept of man in early China.* Stanford, CA: Stanford University Press.
Munro, D. J. (1977). *The concept of man in contemporary China.* Ann Arbor, MI: The University of Michigan Press. Ongel, U. & Smith, P. B. (1994). Who are we and where are we going? JCCP approaches its 100th issue. *Journal of Cross-Cultural Psychology, 25* (1), 25–53.
Pan, S. (1980). On the investigation of basic theoretical problems of psychology. *Chinese Sociology and Anthropology, 12,* 24–42.
Pan, S., Chen, L., Wang, J. H., & Chen, D. R. (1980). Weilian Fengte yu Zhongguo xinlixue (Wilhelm Wundt and Chinese psychology), *Xinli Xuebao, 12,* 367–376. (in Chinese)
Pan, S. & Gao, J. F. (eds) (1983). *Zhongguo gudai xinlixue sixiang yanjiu* (The study of psychology in ancient China). Nanshong: Jiangxi Renmin Chubanshe. (in Chinese)
Petzold, M. (1987). The social history of Chinese psychology. In M. G. Ash & W. R. Woodward (eds), *Psychology in twentieth-century thought and society* (pp. 213–231). Cambridge, England: Cambridge University Press.
Pickering, A. (1992). *Science as practice and culture.* Chicago, IL: Chicago University Press.
Reardon-Anderson, J. (1991). *The study of change: Chemistry in China 1849–1949.* Cambridge, England: Cambridge University Press.

Sexton, V. S. and Hogan, J. D. (1992). *International psychology: Views from around the world.* Lincoln, NB: University of Nebraska Press.
Shanghai Mental Health Center, (2008). At: http://211.144.96.8:8080/submain.asp?maincolumnid=61&subcolumnid=101
Spence, J. (1999). *The search for modern China.* New York: Norton.
Staeuble, I. (2004). De-centering Western perspectives: Psychology and the disciplinary order in the First and Third World. In A. Brock, J. Louw, & W. van Hoorn (eds), *Rediscovering the history of psychology: Essays inspired by the work of Kurt Danziger.* New York: Kluwer.
Staeuble, I (2006). Psychology in the Eurocentric order of the social sciences: Colonial constitution, cultural imperialist expansion and postcolonial critique. In A. Brock (ed.), *Internationalizing the history of psychology* (pp. 183–287). New York: New York University Press.
Wang, J. S. (1989). *Zhonguo Qigong xinlixue* (Psychology of Chinese *Qi gong*). Beijing: Shehui Kexue Chubanshe. (in Chinese)
Xie, H. (1988). *Scientific basis of Qi gong.* Beijing: Beijing Institute of Technology Press.
Yang, K. S. & Wen, C. I. (eds) (1982). The Sinicization of social and behavioural science research in China. *Institute of Ethnology Academia Sinica Monograph Series*, B, 10.
Yang, K. S. (ed.) (1993). *Bentu xinlixue yanjiu.* (Indigenous psychological research in Chinese societies) Vol.1. Taipei: Gueiguan. (in Chinese)
Yang, K. S. (1995). Chinese social orientation: An integrative analysis. In W. S. Tseng, T. Y. Lin, & Y. K. Yeh (eds), *Chinese societies and mental health* (pp. 19–39).Hong Kong: Oxford University Press.
Yang, K. S. (1999). Towards an indigenous Chinese psychology: A selected review of methodological, theoretical, and empirical accomplishments. *Chinese Journal of Psychology*, *41*, 181–211.
Yang, K. S. (2006). Indigenized conceptual and empirical analyses of selected Chinese characteristics. *International Journal of Psychology*, *41*, 298–303.
Zhao, L. R. (1983). *Youguan xinlinxue yi shudi yanjiu.* (Pneumatology: A Chinese translation of Joseph Haven's 'Mental Philosophy') *Xuebao*, *15*, 380–388. (in Chinese)
Zhao, L. R., Lin, F., & Zhang, S. Y. (1989). *Xinli xueshi.* (History of psychology) Beijing, China: Tungyi Chubanshe. (in Chinese)
Zhang, J. Y. (1992). *Psychoanalysis in China: Literary transformations 1919–1949.* Ithaca, NY: East Asia Program, Cornell University.
Zhang, K. (2007). Psychology in China and the Chinese Psychological Society. *Japanese Psychological Research*, *49*, 172–177.
Zhao Liru (1992). *Xhonggua Xiandai xinlixue de qi yuan he fa zhan* (The origin and development of modern psychology in China) *Xinlixue Dongtai* (Current state of psychology). *Quarterly Journal of the Institute of Psychology*, Academia Sinica. (in Chinese)
Ziman, J. M. (2000). *Real Science: What it is, and what it means.* Cambridge, England: Cambridge University Press.

CHAPTER 2

What is Chinese about Chinese psychology? Who are the Chinese in Chinese psychology?

Ying-yi Hong, Yung Jui Yang, and Chi-yue Chiu

The two-pronged objectives of this chapter are (1) to engage Chinese psychology researchers in a critical examination of the assumptions about Chineseness in their enquiry, and (2) to suggest an expansion of the research agenda for Chinese psychology to include the psychology of Chinese identity. We will review several possible referential meanings of the term *Chinese psychology*. We will also discuss how identity politics plays a role in the debates over the term's referential meaning and influences the choice of the criteria that are used to evaluate the validity of knowledge about Chinese psychology. Through this review, we invite investigators of Chinese psychology to expand their current research agendas so as to position this burgeoning research area as an integral part of psychological science in an increasingly globalized world.

Multiple meanings of Chinese psychology

We begin our analysis with an examination of the semantic meanings of *Chinese psychology*. *Chinese* is both a noun and an adjective. According to Merriam-Webster Dictionary, as a noun *Chinese* refers to (1) a native or inhabitant of China, (2) a person of Chinese (ethnic or cultural) descent, and (3) the language(s) spoken by the Chinese. In its adjectival form, it can be used to characterize anything *about/on*, *of*, *among*, *by*, *with*, *within*, *from*, and *for* China, the Chinese people, Chinese culture, the Chinese language. That is, *Chinese psychology* can be psychology (1) about the Chinese, Chinese culture, China, (2) belonging to the Chinese, China, (3) originating from China, the Chinese traditions, (4) practiced, created, and consumed by the Chinese, (5) practiced within China and among the Chinese, (6) constructed with the use of Chinese stimuli, research materials, research participants, (7) exported from China, and (8) created for the benefits of or consumption by China or the Chinese. Interestingly, all these usages of the term can be found in the *Handbook of Chinese Psychology* (Bond, 1996).

In addition, *Chinese psychology* has different meanings depending on how it is translated into Chinese. For example, two common Chinese translations of the term *Chinese people* are *Zhongguoren* (中國人) and *Huaren* (華人). The two terms differ in their relative stress on national and cultural memberships, and the choice between these two terms in Chinese psychology publications hides an unsettling political dispute over the ownership of the Chinese identity. Wei-ming Tu (1994) astutely points out the nuances between these two terms: '*Huaren* is not geopolitically centered, for it indicates a common ancestry and a shared cultural background, whereas *Zhongguoren* necessarily evokes obligations and loyalties of political affiliation, and the myth of the Central Country' (p. 25). Overseas Chinese can claim ownership of the *Huaren* identity by virtue of their Chinese ancestry and cultural background, but not necessarily ownership of the *Zhongguoren* identity. Consistent with Tu's observation, a recent study (Yang, Wu, & Hong, 2008) showed that college students in Taiwan see the *Huaren* identity as a cultural identity defined by one's Chinese cultural heritage and ethnic ancestry, which is different from the regional/political identities of Taiwanese Chinese and mainland Chinese. Moreover, to Taiwanese college students, both Taiwanese Chinese and mainland Chinese are *Huaren*.

For the definition of Chineseness to go beyond *Huaren* and *Zhongguoren*, Tu (1994) provides 'Cultural China' as an alternative. Cultural China involves the 'interaction of three symbolic universes: (1) mainland China, Taiwan, Hong Kong, and Singapore; (2) overseas Chinese communities throughout the world (the 'Chinese diaspora'); and (3) 'the international communities of scholars, students, officials, journalists, and traders who provide a global forum for China-related matters' (p. vii).

If the notion of Cultural China is used to define Chineseness, Chinese psychology will be an inclusive discipline, consisting of scientific activities directed to understanding the psychological foundations and consequences of engaging in Cultural China. We favor this definition, and forecast that a successful Chinese psychology will be one that adopts an international (vs. regional) outlook; one that does not allow arbitrary geographical or intellectual boundaries to restrict creative expansion of research ideas; and one that strives to craft a global identity with a Chinese character by engaging the international academic communities in developing communicable theories of the Chinese sociality (Chiu, 2007). However, the adoption of such an inclusive definition of Chinese psychology would likely meet many obstacles, some of which cannot be removed without understanding the complexity of Chinese identity politics.

Identity politics and the definition of Chineseness

The tension created by the Central Country (Middle Kingdom) myth (中國謎思) that Tu refers to provides an illustration of the power struggle in Chinese identity politics. The Central Country myth refers to a false sense of continuity from 'the Han and Tang dynasties, as if their greatness still provides practicable standards for contemporary Chinese culture and politics' (Tu, 1994, p. 4). On the one hand, this myth has created a basis for Chinese people to take pride in being the 'children of the Yellow Emperor' (黃帝子孫) or the 'descendents of the Dragon' (龍的傳人). On the other hand, it may make it psychologically difficult for the leadership in China's politics or cultural domains to abandon its sense of superiority as the center and to allow inclusion of other seemingly less central groups. In reality, however, the seemingly less central groups, including overseas Chinese communities and international communities of scholars on China-related matters, have continuously exerted important influence on the discourse of Chineseness. As a result, 'China, or Chinese culture, has never been a static structure, but rather a dynamic, constantly changing landscape' (Tu, 1994, p. 4).

Discourses on the Chinese diaspora reveal dual loyalty as another major political concern in defining the Chinese identity. Broadly speaking, diaspora is a coherent unit of geographically dispersed people bounded by sentiment, culture, and history (McKeown, 1999). The issue of dual loyalty emerges because overseas Chinese (華僑) desire both the security and opportunities available in their countries of settlement as well as a continuing bond with Chinese culture and the Chinese in other countries. Thus, overseas Chinese are often confronted with the crisis of dual loyalty, oscillating between competing concerns with loyalty to their host land and homeland, and occasionally exhibiting patriotic resistance to assimilation (Cohen, 1996).

From the perspective of the Chinese state, the definition of the Chinese identity is a matter of national interest. The overseas Chinese as a formidable economic network is a major economic power. Before China started to actively participate in the global economy during the 1980s, the

Chinese state was indifferent to whether overseas Chinese had assimilated to their countries of settlement (Ong, 1999). When China started its economic transformation in the 1980s, however, the Chinese state's indifference to the loyalty of the Chinese diasporic communities turned into ambivalence. On the one hand, the Chinese state values financial investments of overseas Chinese in China, their rich transnational experiences, as well as their emotional attachment to their motherland, characterizing overseas Chinese as 'married-out daughters who still have feelings for home' (Ong, 1999). On the other hand, the Chinese state has prevailing concerns over the promiscuous opportunism of overseas Chinese capitalism and the contaminating influence of social systems and lifestyles infecting the overseas Chinese communities.

These concerns fuel the search for a new Chinese identity that would confront and accommodate to the globalizing forces simultaneously. Against this context enters Confucianism. As Aihwa Ong (1999, pp. 40–1) puts it:

> As more and more Chinese reject the statist production of socialist truth and appropriate the newly valorized signs of sex, individualism, fashions, and pleasure that come with consumer market, academic elites are reviving Confucianism (*rujia sixing*) as a moral force 'that can serve as a single source for building a new culture.' This revival and deployment of Confucianist discourse also renews the cultural and ethnic continuities between mainland and overseas Chinese, of whom the latter are viewed as the embodiments of diffuse, enduring solidarity rooted in shared cultural traits ... As the boundaries between socialism and capitalism, and between China and overseas-Chinese communities, become blurred, Confucianism can be usefully invoked, with fruitful ambiguity, to simultaneously suggest the interbraiding of 'Chinese' essence with the far-flung overseas-Chinese networks that accumulate capital throughout the region.

In these new discourses on the Chinese identity, Confucianism is transformed from being a feudalist ideology decried in the Cultural Revolution to a dynamic force of modernity in contemporary China. Such transformation can be seen in some intellectual works (Chinese Culture Connection, 1987; Redding, 1993), and is particularly evident in the indigenous Chinese psychology movement in Taiwan, Hong Kong, mainland China, and Singapore (C. F. Yang, 1993; K. S. Yang, 1993). For example, under the influence of this movement, paternalism becomes a defining feature of Chinese capitalism and leadership (Farh & Cheng, 2000; see also Chen & Farh, this volume).

Implications for Chinese psychology

Similar identity politics have significantly influenced the development of Chinese psychology. It fuels the debates on what constitutes 'authentic' conceptualizations of the Chinese psyche, as opposed to imported (and hence distorted) conceptualizations or imaginations of it from Western psychology. These identity politics have also shaped the determination of validity criteria in Chinese psychology: what type of knowledge generation process would likely produce valid characterizations of Chinese psychology? Advocates of the major intellectual traditions in Chinese psychology (e.g. indigenous Chinese psychology, cultural psychology, and cross-cultural psychology) have vigorously debated the issue of what constitutes valid knowledge about Chinese psychology. This is a legitimacy issue as much as a scientific one, since each tradition has its own strong views on what is the appropriate (and hence legitimate) subject matter for the field, what the appropriate (legitimate) inclusion and exclusion criteria for Chinese research participants are, and who has the (legitimate) authority to represent the Chinese in Chinese psychology (see a special section on this topic published in the *Journal of Psychology in Chinese Society, 2000, Volume 1*, pp. 125–58). All attempts to address these issues will ultimately take us back to the same two questions: what is Chinese about Chinese psychology; who are the Chinese in Chinese psychology?

From our perspective, what constitutes Chineseness is not a definitional issue that can be satisfactorily resolved with analytical reasoning alone. Critical reflectivity on how our preferred approaches to Chinese psychology are symptoms (or victims) of Chinese identity politics can help clarify the value commitment of our current engagement in Chinese psychology. Thus, we invite Chinese psychology investigators to answer two hard questions: who are the Chinese in *your* Chinese psychology;

what is Chinese about *your* Chinese psychology? Their answers to these questions will guide the selection and framing of the research problems they explore in Chinese psychology. More important, answering these two questions will also increase their awareness of and sensitivity to the identity politics informing Chinese psychology. The issue at stake is: what is *Chinese* psychology?

When engaging in these reflections, it would be useful to debunk the Central Country myth and be reminded that, like other cultural identities, the Chinese identities are 'not something which already exist, transcending place, time, history, and culture ... Far from being eternally fixed in some essentialized past, they are subject to the continuous "play" of history, culture, and power' (Hall, 2003, p. 236).

Summary

In summary, with the globalization of academia, research institutions in Greater China increasingly feel incentives and pressure to be connected with and accepted into the global academic community. The globalization of Chinese psychology has intensified the need to negotiate the meanings of Chineseness in Chinese psychological research. New Chinese identities (e.g. cultural Chinese, bicultural Chinese, cosmopolitan Chinese, pan-Chinese) and variants of Chinese psychology (*Huaren* psychology, bi-cultural psychology, cosmopolitan psychology, pan-Chinese psychology) have emerged.

Chinese psychology has also responded to the scientific trends in psychology. For example, the biological revolution in psychology has set forth the possibility of locating distinctive Chinese patterns in the brain (cf. Han & Northoff, 2008; see also Ali & Penney, this volume). These developments further complicate the character of Chinese psychology. As Chinese psychology researchers gather new insights through this dialogue and reach new heights in their explorations, the same identity issue continues to press for possible answers: what gives these expeditions their Chinese character, and who are the Chinese in these expeditions?

As mentioned, while many Chinese psychology researchers are preoccupied with crafting an identity for Chinese psychology, numerous people around the globe who are given or feel entitled to the Chinese identity are managing the same identity politics. These shareholders and stakeholders in Chinese identity negotiate the meanings of Chinese identity and contest the inclusion and exclusion criteria of being Chinese. If Chinese psychology is also a psychology *for* the Chinese, the discipline has not given enough consideration to the identity needs of its constituents. Perhaps the mountaineers are the last to behold the mountain's panoramic view: the *Handbook of Chinese Psychology* (Bond, 1996) does not even have a chapter on Chinese identity!

Although science cannot determine what Chineseness is, it can be applied to understanding how people in Cultural China construct and negotiate their cultural identities within a certain historical, cultural, and political context (see e.g. Bond, 1993; Bond & Mak, 1996; Weinrich, Luk, & Bond, 1996). Such an analysis can reveal the social psychology of Chinese identity politics and hence provide useful materials for critical reflection (see also Liu, Li, & Yue, this volume). Space does not permit a comprehensive review of the pertinent literature. In the next section, we will focus on a few empirical phenomena that are particularly germane to the above discussions on Chinese identity politics in this continuously changing, transnational, and globalizing environment. These phenomena include management of dual identities, the psychological benefits of multiculturality, and psychological reactions to globalizations.

The social psychology of identity politics in multicultural Chinese communities

Management of dual identities

Today, many Chinese live in multicultural communities. A major identity issue confronting these individuals is dual identity management. For example, among Hong Kong Chinese, some may interpret the *Zhongguoren* identity as a political identity grounded in identification with the Chinese state. To these individuals, *Zhongguoren* identification conflicts with their allegiance to their city of settlement, a city with a distinctive modern, post-colonial culture. Among these individuals, some may choose to pledge their allegiance to the Hong Konger identity only. Choice of the Hong Konger identity over the *Zhongguoren* identity has been found to be associated with the tendency to seek positive distinctiveness of the Hong Konger identity by displaying attitudinal, linguistic, and behavioral biases against mainland Chinese (Lam, Chiu, Lau, Chan, & Yim, 2006; Tong, Hong, Lee, & Chiu, 1999). Other Hong Kong Chinese may choose to pledge their allegiance to the *Zhongguoren* identity only. Those who make this identity choice tend to cherish pro-China attitudes and welcome the return of Hong Kong's sovereignty to mainland China (DeGolyer, 1994; Ho, Chau, Chiu, & Peng, 2003). There are also individuals who endorse both the Hong Konger and *Zhonggouren* identities and switch between them across situations, acting more Chinese in the presence of a Westerner and less Chinese in the presence of a mainland Chinese. For example, in one study (Yang & Bond, 1980), Hong Kong Chinese participants were asked to complete an attitude survey. For some participants, the researcher was a Westerner and the participants completed the survey in English. For others, the researcher was a Chinese and the participants completed the survey in Chinese. Participants in the Western researcher condition endorsed Chinese attitudes more strongly than did the participants in the Chinese researcher condition, suggesting that the participants were trying to affirm their Chinese identity in front of a Westerner. Conversely, the participants in the Chinese researcher condition endorsed Western attitudes more strongly than did the participants in the Western researcher condition, suggesting that the participants were trying to differentiate themselves from the Chinese (see also Bond & Cheung, 1984).

Interestingly, a sizeable proportion of Hong Kong Chinese have managed to construe *Zhongguoren* as a cultural category that includes all ethnic Chinese who share the heritage tradition of historical China as well as the responsibility for China's future well-being (Lam et al., 2006; Lam, Lau, Chiu, Hong, & Peng, 1999). These individuals are comfortable with the Hong Kong Chinese identity, a dual identity that entails allegiance both to the Chinese cultural tradition and to their region of settlement (cf. Brewer, 1999).

Similar identity negotiation phenomena have also been observed among Chinese Americans in North America. Some Chinese Americans feel that they cannot be Chinese and American at the same time—the two identities are perceived to be incompatible. These individuals tend to report greater conflicts between their ethnic and national identities (Benet-Martinez & Haritatos 2005; Benet-Martinez, Leu, Lee, & Morris, 2002; Kramer, Lau-Gesk, & Chiu, in press). In addition, when cues in the immediate environment remind these individuals of their Chinese identity, they feel that they are not Chinese enough and tend to inhibit prototypic Chinese responses to the situation. For example, upon seeing some iconic images of Chinese culture, they tend not to make situational inferences from behavioral cues—a characteristic attribution style found among the Chinese. Likewise, when environmental cues prime their American identity, they feel that they are not American enough and tend to inhibit prototypic American responses. Upon seeing some iconic images of American culture, they tend not to make dispositional inferences from behavioral cues—a characteristic inferential practice among European Americans (Benet-Martinez et al., 2002; see also No et al., 2008).

A major factor that predicts individual variations in the management of dual identities is people's assumption about the nature of personal qualities and racial categories. Some people believe that every person is a certain kind of person and nothing can change a person's core character. These individuals, referred to as entity theorists (Dweck, Chiu, & Hong, 1995), tend to attribute essential qualities to the individuals who make up a social category (Hong et al., 2003). Thus, to entity theorists, a social category consists of individuals with a certain defining essence, and a person's group membership reflects the person's deep, unalterable traits.

In contrast, some individuals tend to believe that human qualities are malleable. These individuals, referred to as incremental theorists (Dweck et al., 1995), believe that groups are formed based on shared historical experiences and future imaginations. Thus, with effort, people can earn membership in a certain cultural group; they can learn to become members of this group by adopting its shared goal and acquiring its defining experiences. In this view, individuals who have acquired the qualifying experiences of multiple groups can comfortably claim membership in these groups. Thus, incremental personality theorists do not feel that a person's group identity is indicative of the person's deep, unchangeable personal traits (Hong et al., 2003).

Not surprisingly, entity theorists, who believe that a group identity reflects the unchangeable, core attributes of the self, are more likely than incremental theorists to feel strongly attached to their identity choice, as evident in the identity politics in Hong Kong during the political transition, when Hong Kong would soon become an administrative region of the People's Republic of China. The identity issue was: should the Hong Konger identity be assimilated into the *Zhongguoren* identity, or should the Hong Konger identity remain one that is positively distinctive from the *Zhongguoren* identity? During this time, individuals who subscribed to an entity theory had a pronounced tendency to use their identity endorsement to construct other aspects of their personal identities and to guide their interactions with mainland Chinese. For example, entity theorists who chose the Hong Konger identity were particularly likely to exhibit estrangement (vs. integration) toward mainland Chinese (Hong et al., 2003).

In contrast, those who subscribed to the incremental theory displayed very different responses during the political transition. These individuals did not believe that group membership reflected deep, unalterable traits. Instead, they saw cultural identities as fluid, transforming and historical. Accordingly, they were not as psychologically attached to their identity choice, and tended not to display an identity-driven intergroup orientation toward mainland Chinese (Hong et al., 2003).

Lay theorization of the nature of race occupies center stage in the public discourse on inter-ethnic relations in the United States, and the lay construction of race as a fixed, essential category versus a historical, transforming one affects dual identity management among Chinese Americans. When people view individuals of the same race as having the same biologically determined and unalterable traits, they also tend to see racial boundaries as impermeable. From the perspective of these individuals, because the defining essence of a race cannot be acquired or altered, individuals cannot pass through racial boundaries: if a person does not possess the essential qualities of a certain race, this person cannot be a member of that race (Hong, Chao, & No, 2009). Inasmuch as a fish can never become a bird, a Chinese American, being a cultural hybrid, can never be an authentic American. Because they are not comfortable with their dual cultural identities, they find it difficult to switch between the two cultural identities; it is also stressful for them to discuss their bicultural experiences, as reflected by increased skin conductance when they engage in such discussions (Chao, Chen, Roisman, & Hong, 2007, Study 2).

These individuals' rigidity in switching between cultural frames was also reflected in their response times in a lexical decision task (Chao et al., 2007, Study 1), where participants were required to identify on each trial whether a string of letters was a word or non-word. In this task, if the string of letters was a word, it referred to a core American value, a core Chinese value, or a culture-neutral word. In addition, the participants were exposed briefly to a pictorial icon of Chinese culture, a pictorial icon of American culture, or a culture-neutral image before each string of letters appeared. Among Chinese Americans who subscribed to an essentialist theory of race, seeing a Chinese cultural icon slowed down their responses to core American values, and seeing an American cultural icon slowed down their responses to core Chinese values, indicating difficulty in switching between the American and Chinese cultural frames. Chinese Americans who did not believe in racial essentialism did not display this response pattern.

Aside from having difficulty in switching between cultures, Asian Americans who hold stronger essentialist beliefs are less identified with American culture (No et al., 2008), probably because of a lack of motivation to cross cultural boundaries. Furthermore, Asian Americans' lay beliefs about race also predict the ways they process race- or ethnicity-related information: Asian Americans who hold stronger essentialist belief more readily use race to categorize people and are quicker in detecting covariation between skin color (a racial cue) and membership in an artificial group (see Hong et al., 2009).

In summary, the Chinese can view the Chinese identity as a fixed, static, and non-historical entity. Alternatively, they can view it as a fluid, transforming, and historical concept. The research reviewed above shows that the Chinese who hold these two views of Chineseness manage their dual identities in very different ways: Relative to those who hold a static view, those who hold a fluid view of Chinese identity are more comfortable with claiming both Chinese identity and the identity of their region of settlement, and can comfortably switch between cultural frames. As we will argue in the next section, being comfortable with one's dual cultural identities can confer important psychological benefits.

The psychological benefits of multiculturality

One concern that fuels identity politics in multicultural Chinese communities is the fear that contact with foreign cultures will inevitably lead to erosion and contamination of the Chinese culture and destroy the Chinese identity. This concern underlies many Chinese people's resistance to intercultural learning. At the turn of the twentieth century, confronted with the military and economic might of the Western powers, China saw an urgent need to modernize the country in order to counter Western imperialism in China. Yet, the concern over Western contamination of Chinese culture had driven Chinese reformers to accept modernization while containing the spread of Western culture in China. The concern over spiritual pollution in the pre-Deng Xiaoping era had caused the People's Republic of China to close its door on Western influence. More recently, Cheng-gang Rui, an anchorman of China Central Television (CCTV), argued in an essay on his blog (http://blog.sina.com.cn/s/blog_4adabe27010008yg.html) that the presence of Starbucks Coffee in Beijing's Imperial Palace Museum demeaned Chinese culture. This essay incited strong nationalistic sentiment in China, which led to the eventual removal of Starbucks Coffee from the Museum. The fear of cultural contamination and erosion can also be found in post-colonial Hong Kong: although Chinese college students in Hong Kong embrace values that support modernization (e.g. creativity, will power), they are not enthusiastic in accepting Western moral values (e.g. individuality, democracy) (Fu & Chiu, 2007; see also Bond & King, 1985).

Despite the seeming pervasiveness of fears surrounding globalization, scholars have argued that globalization actually proliferates rather than destroys cultures (see Chiu & Hong, 2006). First, individuals who are exposed to two cultures gradually acquire insider knowledge of both cultures and can discriminatively apply knowledge of the two cultures to cope with changing cultural demands in the situation (Chiu & Hong, 2005; see also Berger & Huntington, 2002). For example, Hong Kong Chinese or Chinese Americans, by virtue of living in both Chinese and Western or American cultures, have acquired insider knowledge of both cultures. They can act like Chinese in response to environmental reminders of Chinese cultural knowledge and can act like Americans or Westerners in response to environmental reminders of American and Western cultural knowledge.

There is considerable evidence that exposure to Western cultures increases the behavioral flexibility of bicultural Chinese (Hong, Chiu, & Kung, 1997; Hong, Morris, Chiu, Benet-Martinez, 2000; Hong, Benet-Martinez, Chiu, & Morris, 2003). For example, in one experiment, Hong Kong Chinese were exposed to (primed with) either Chinese icons (e.g. pictures of the Chinese dragon, the Great Wall) or American icons (e.g. pictures of the Statue of Liberty, Capital Hill). After being primed with Chinese (American) cultural icons, the participants were more inclined to interpret an ambiguous event in a typically Chinese (American) way. They made more group attributions (a more typical attribution style among the Chinese) and fewer individual attributions (a pattern more typical of Americans). Similar cultural priming effects have been found among Chinese Americans, and across dependent measures in different psychological domains, such as spontaneous self-construal (Ross, Xun, & Wilson, 2002), cooperative behaviors (Wong & Hong, 2005), and memory of significant others (Sui, Zhu, & Chiu, 2007). The culture priming effect has been replicated in studies using different bicultural Chinese samples (e.g. Chinese Canadians, Chinese Americans, and Singaporeans), and with a variety of cultural primes (e.g. language, experimenter's cultural identity; Ross et al., 2002).

These spontaneous behavioral shifts in response to cultural cues are discriminating responses rather than knee-jerk reactions to situational cues; bicultural individuals use environmentally cued cultural knowledge to guide their response only when such knowledge and enactments are appropriate in the context. For example, cueing Chinese culture would increase the Hong Kong Chinese tendency to make more group (vs. individual) inferences only when they are required to explain an event where the tension between the individual and the group is salient (Hong et al., 2003), or when the situation calls for a normative rather than an idiosyncratic response (Fu et al., 2007). Similarly, cueing Chinese culture would increase the cooperative behavior of Hong Kong Chinese only in interactions with friends (where cooperation is expected) but not in interactions with strangers (where cooperation is not expected) (Wong & Hong, 2005).

In summary, exposure to Western cultures, instead of destroying the Chinese culture or one's cultural resources, can increase response flexibility. Moreover, these findings attest to the dynamic nature of cultural processes. Again, culture does not rigidly determine human behaviors, nor are individuals passive recipients of their cultural environment. Instead, individuals flexibly shift their responses and use culture as a cognitive resource for optimizing their experiences.

Aside from increasing behavioral flexibility, exposure to Western cultures can enhance Chinese individuals' creativity, particularly when Western knowledge traditions are treated as intellectual resources (Maddux, Leung, Chiu, & Galinsky, 2009). For many kinds of problems, Chinese and Western cultures prescribe markedly different ways of identifying and defining problems, as well as finding and evaluating solutions. Thus, familiarity with both Chinese and Western cultures affords opportunities for novel combinations of seemingly non-overlapping concepts and practices from different cultures (see individual chapters throughout this volume). Such a conceptual combination process has previously been found to enhance creative performance (Wan & Chiu, 2002; Leung & Chiu, in press) and integrative complexity (Tadmor, Tetlock, & Peng, 2009). The creative outcomes of this process may also result in the emergence of new fusion cultures (Cheng, Sanchez-Burks, & Lee, in press).

Thus, the concern that exposure to Western cultures could destroy Chinese culture seems largely unjustified. Exposure to Western cultures seldom results in erosion of Chinese culture. On the contrary, it offers opportunities to increase the response flexibility and creative performance of Chinese people. Instead of contaminating Chinese culture, exposure to Western cultures creates variations of Chinese culture (fusion cultures) that do not necessarily displace the original form of Chinese culture.

The social psychology of globalization and reactions to foreign cultures

If globalization and exposure to world cultures do not destroy Chinese culture, how do we explain the Chinese anxiety over cultural contamination and erosion? Globalization scholars agree that globalization has resulted in compression of time and space; it has brought cultures from different geographical localities and historical epochs together. As a result, in the same globalized space, people will find symbols of East and West, and of traditional and modern.

The visual contrasts between symbols of East and West, and those of traditional and modern often draw the perceiver's attention to the contrasts between the cultures these symbols stand for. There is consistent evidence that following incidental exposure to symbols of two dissimilar cultures, people tend to direct their attention to the differences between the two cultures (Chiu, Mallorie, Keh, & Law, 2009). Following simultaneous exposure to two cultures, the presence of situational cues that activate the motivation to protect the integrity of one's heritage culture will evoke strong nationalistic sentiments (Chiu & Cheng, 2007). An example of such situational cues is reminders of intercultural or international competition: people reminded of intercultural or international competition may view foreign countries and their cultures as threats to the integrity of their own culture. Another example of such situational cues is reminders of mortality: when reminded of their mortality, people experience existential anxiety, which they can manage by adhering to and defending their cultural world view because doing so can confer a sense of symbolic immortality—as a part of the imperishable culture, the self is immortal. Fear of cultural erosion and contamination underlies the evoked nationalistic sentiments, which can fuel exclusionary reactions toward foreign cultures (Chao & Hong, 2007; Chiu & Cheng, 2007).

In summary, nationalistic, exclusionary reactions to foreign cultures are typically not based on realistically grounded fears. Instead, they come from the interaction or co-presence of symbols from contrastive cultures (a perceptual feature in a globalized space that draws the perceiver's attention to cultural differences), and a situation-induced motivation to protect the integrity of one's cultural tradition. Thus, these hot reactions to foreign cultures are often based on imagined rather than real threats of cultural diffusion. Perceptions of cultural threats, even if they originate from the perceiver's imagination, could create tensions between cultures and hamper the individual's learning from other cultures, which in turn dampens their flexibility in responding adaptively to an increasingly multicultural world.

Conclusion

In the first of part of this chapter, we reviewed identity politics in Chinese psychology. In the second part, we reviewed the social psychology of identity politics in multicultural Chinese communities. Although the psychological processes underlying the identity politics of lay Chinese may differ from those underpinning identity politics in Chinese psychology, lay Chinese persons and Chinese psychology scholars face similar identity issues. As globalization proceeds, both groups of people need to face global competition. The Chinese and Westerners can learn from each other to increase their global competitiveness. Similarly, Chinese psychology scholars and 'mainstream' psychology scholars can learn from each other to identify universal principles of human behavior and their cultural variations (see Smith, this volume). Globalization affords opportunities for boundary spanning, enhancement of creativity, and proliferation of new cultures. Globalization of Chinese psychology affords opportunities for creative conceptual expansions and generation of new knowledge.

However, identity politics continue and intensify as globalization proceeds. In multicultural Chinese communities, compression of space and time enhances the perceptual contrasts between cultures; situational evocation of the motivation to preserve the integrity of the heritage culture fuels exclusionary reactions. In Chinese psychology, motivated by the search for an authentic Chinese voice, the quest for an authentic Chinese psychology, and by resistance to the intellectual hegemony of 'Western' psychology, Chinese psychology has been selective in appropriating ideas from Western research traditions (see Blowers, this volume). Such selectivity often motivates the rejection of an inclusive definition of Chineseness in Chinese psychology.

The goal of this chapter is not to evaluate the 'validity' of the different strategies for defining 'Chineseness' in Chinese psychology. In fact, given unequal power and status of Chinese and Western psychology, selective appropriation of Western theories and ideas may be necessary to ensure that at least some Chinese voices will be heard in the global auditorium. Instead, the goal of this chapter is to invite Chinese psychology scholars to reflect on the political matrix that underlies identity politics in the discipline, on the political forces that shape their definitions of Chineseness in their enquiry, and on the intellectual consequences of their identity choices.

Authors' note

Preparation of this chapter is partially supported by a grant from Nanyang Business School (reference number RCC6/2008/NBS) awarded to the first-named author. Correspondence related to this paper should be sent to Ying-yi Hong, Nanyang Business School, SMO, Nanyang Avenue, Singapore 639798; email: yyhong@ntu.edu.sg.

References

Benet-Martinez, V. & Haritatos, J. (2005). Bicultural Identity Integration (BII): Components and psychosocial antecedents. *Journal of Personality, 73*, 1015–1050.

Benet-Martinez, V., Leu, J., Lee, F., & Morris, M.W. (2002). Negotiating biculturalism: Cultural frame switching in biculturals with oppositional versus compatible cultural identities. *Journal of Cross-Cultural Psychology, 33*, 492–516.
Berger, P. L. & Huntington, S. P. (eds) (2002). *Many globalizations: Cultural diversity in the contemporary world.* Oxford and New York: Oxford University Press.
Bond, M. H. (1993). *Between the 'yin' and the 'yang': The identity of the Hong Kong Chinese.* Professorial inaugural lecture, Chinese University of Hong Kong.
Bond, M. H. (1996). *Handbook of Chinese psychology.* Hong Kong: Oxford University Press.
Bond, M. H. & Cheung, M. K. (1984). Experimenter language choice and ethnic affirmation by Chinese trilinguals in Hong Kong. *International Journal of Intercultural Relations, 8*, 347–356.
Bond, M. H. & King, A. Y. C. (1985). Coping with the threat of Westernization in Hong Kong. *International Journal of Intercultural Relations, 9*, 351–364.
Bond, M. H. & Mak, A. L. P. (1996). Deriving an inter-group topography from perceived values: Forging an identity in Hong Kong out of Chinese tradition and contemporary examples. *In Proceedings of the Conference on Mind, Machine and the Environment: Facing the challenges of the 21st century* (pp. 255–266). Seoul, Korea: Korean Psychological Association.
Brewer, M. B. (1999). Multiple identities and identity transition: Implications for Hong Kong. *International Journal of Intercultural Relations, 23*, 187–198.
Chao, M., Chen, J., Roisman, G., & Hong, Y. (2007). Essentializing race: Implications for bicultural individuals' cognition and physiological reactivity. *Psychological Science, 18*, 341–348.
Chao, M. & Hong, Y. (2007). Being a bicultural Chinese: A multilevel perspective to biculturalism. *Journal of Psychology in Chinese Societies, 8*, 141–157.
Cheng, C. Y., Sanchez-Burks, J., & Lee, F. (in press). Increasing innovation through identity integration. *Psychological Science.*
Chinese Culture Connection (1987). Chinese values and the search for culture-free dimensions of culture. *Journal of Cross-Cultural Psychology, 18*, 143–164.
Chiu, C. (2007). How can Asian social psychology succeed globally? *Asian Journal of Social Psychology, 10*, 41–44.
Chiu, C. & Cheng, S. Y. (2007). Toward a social psychology of culture and globalization: Some social cognitive consequences of activating two cultures simultaneously. *Social and Personality Psychology Compass, 1*, 84–100.
Chiu, C. & Hong, Y. (2005). Cultural competence: Dynamic processes. In A. Elliot & C. S. Dweck (eds), *Handbook of motivation and competence* (pp. 489–505). New York: Guilford.
Chiu, C-y. & Hong, Y. (2006). *Social psychology of culture.* New York: Psychology Press.
Chiu, C., Mallorie, L., Keh, H-T., & Law, W. (2009). Perceptions of culture in multicultural space: Joint presentation of images from two cultures increases ingroup attribution of culture-typical characteristics. *Journal of Cross-Cultural Psychology, 40*, 282–300.
Cohen, R. (1996). Diasporas and the nation-state: From victims to challengers. *International Affairs, 72*, 506–520.
DeGolyer, M. E. (1994). Politics, politicians, and political parties. In D. H. McMillen & S. W. Man (eds), *The other Hong Kong report 1994* (pp. 75–101). Hong Kong: The Chinese University Press.
Dweck, C. S., Chiu, C., & Hong, Y. (1995). Implicit theories and their role in judgments and reactions: A world from two perspectives. *Psychological Inquiry, 6*, 267–285.
Farh, J. L., & Cheng, B. S. (2000). A cultural analysis of paternalistic leadership in Chinese organizations. In J. T. Li, A. S. Tsui, & E. Weldon (eds), *Management and organizations in the Chinese context* (pp. 84–127). London: MacMillan.
Fu, H. & Chiu, C. (2007). Local culture's responses to globalization: Exemplary persons and their attendant values. *Journal of Cross-Cultural Psychology, 38*, 636–653.
Fu, H., Morris, M. W., Lee, S-l. Chao, M., Chiu, C., & Hong, Y. (2007). Epistemic motives and cultural conformity: Need for closure, culture, and context as determinants of conflict judgments. *Journal of Personality and Social Psychology, 92*, 191–207.
Hall, S. (2003). Cultural identity and diaspora. In J. Evans & A. Mannur (eds), *Theorizing diaspora* (pp. 233–246). Malden, England: Blackwell.
Han, S., & Northoff, G. (2008). Culture-sensitive neural substrates of human cognition: A transcultural neuroimaging approach. *Nature Review Neuroscience, 9*, 646–654.
Ho, D. Y. F., Chau, A. W. L., Chiu, C-y., & Peng, S. Q. (2003). Ideological orientation and political transition in Hong Kong: Confidence in the future. *Political Psychology, 24*, 403–413.
Hong, Y., Abrams, D., & Ng, S. H. (1999). Social identifications during political transition: The Hong Kong 1997 experience. *International Journal of Intercultural Relations, 23*, 177–185.
Hong, Y., Benet-Martinez, V., Chiu, C., & Morris, M. W. (2003). Boundaries of cultural influence: Construct activation as a mechanism for cultural differences in social perception. *Journal of Cross-Cultural Psychology, 34*, 453–464.
Hong, Y., Chan, G., Chiu, C., Wong, R. Y. M., Hansen, I. G., Lee, S-l., Tong, Y., & Fu, H. (2003). How are social identities linked to self-conception and intergroup orientation? The moderating effect of implicit theories. *Journal of Personality and Social Psychology, 85*, 1147–1160.
Hong, Y., Chao, M., & No, S. (2009). Dynamic interracial/intercultural processes: The role of lay theories of race. *Journal of Personality, 77*, 1283–1309.

Hong, Y., Chiu, C., & Kung, M. (1997). Bringing culture out in front: Effects of cultural meaning system activation on social cognition. In K. Leung, U. Kim, S. Yamaguchi, & Y. Kashima (eds), *Progress in Asian social psychology*, Vol.1. (pp. 139–150) Singapore: Wiley.

Hong, Y., Morris, M., Chiu, C., & Benet, V. (2000). Multicultural minds: A dynamic constructivist approach to culture and cognition. *American Psychologist, 55*, 709–720.

Kramer, T., Lau-Gesk, L., & Chiu, C. (in press). Biculturalism and mixed emotions: Managing cultural and emotional duality. *Journal of Consumer Psychology.*

Lam, S. F., Chiu, C., Lau, I. Y., Chan, W., & Yim, P. (2006). Managing intergroup attitudes among Hong Kong adolescents: The effects of social category inclusiveness and time pressure. *Asian Journal of Social Psychology, 9*, 1–11.

Lam, S., Lau, I., Chiu, C., Hong, Y., & Peng, S. (1999). Differential emphases on modernity and traditional values in social categorization. *International Journal of Intercultural Relations, 23*, 237–256.

Leung, A. K. & Chiu, C. (in press). Multicultural experiences, idea receptiveness, and creativity. *Journal of Cross-Cultural Psychology.*

Leung, A. K., Maddux, W. W., Galinsky, A. D., & Chiu, C. (2008). Multicultural experience enhances creativity: The when and how? *American Psychologist, 63*, 169–181.

Maddux, W. M., Leung, A. K., Chiu, C., & Galinsky, A. (2009). Just the beginning of a more complete understanding of the link between multicultural experience and creativity. *American Psychologist, 64*, 156–158.

McKeown, A. (1999). Conceptualizing Chinese diasporas, 1842 to 1949. *Journal of Asian Studies, 58*, 306–337.

No, S., Hong, Y., Liao, H., Lee, K., Wood, D., & Chao, M. (2008). Lay theory of race affects and moderates Asian Americans' responses toward American culture. *Journal of Personality and Social Psychology, 95*, 991–1004.

Ong, A. (1999). *Flexible citizenship: The cultural logics of transnationality.* Durham, NC: Duke University Press.

Redding, G. (1993). *The spirit of Chinese capitalism.* Berlin, Germany: De Gruyter.

Ross, M., Xun, W. Q. E., & Wilson, A. E. (2002). Language and the bicultural self. *Personality and Social Psychology Bulletin, 28*, 1040–1050.

Sui, J., Zhu, Y., & Chiu, C. (2007). Bicultural mind, self-construal, and recognition memory: Cultural priming effects on self- and mother-reference effect. *Journal of Experimental Social Psychology, 43*, 818–824.

Tadmor, C. T., Tetlock, P. E., & Peng, K. (2009). Acculturation strategies and integrative complexity: The cognitive implications of biculturalism. *Journal of Cross-Cultural Psychology, 40*, 105–139.

Tong, Y., Hong, Y., Lee, S., & Chiu, C. (1999). Language as a carrier of social identity. *International Journal of Intercultural Relations, 23*, 281–296.

Tu, W. (1994). Cultural China: The periphery as the center. In W. M. Tu (ed.). *The living tree: The changing meaning of being Chinese today.* (p. 1–34). Stanford, CA: Stanford University Press.

Wan, W. & Chiu, C. (2002). Effects of novel conceptual combination on creativity. *Journal of Creative Behavior, 36*, 227–241.

Weinreich, P., Luk, C. L., & Bond, M. H. (1996). Ethnic stereotyping in a multicultural context: Acculturation, self-esteem and identity diffusion in Hong Kong Chinese University students. *Psychology and Developing Societies, 8*, 107–169.

Wong, R. Y-M. & Hong, Y. (2005). Dynamic influences of culture on cooperation in the Prisoner's Dilemma. *Psychological Science, 16*, 429–434.

Yang, C. F. (1993). How to root indigenous Chinese psychology: A critical review of current development. *Journal of Indigenous Psychological Research in Chinese Societies, 1*, 122–183. (in Chinese)

Yang, K. S. (1993). Why indigenous psychology for the Chinese? *Journal of Indigenous Psychological Research in Chinese Societies, 1*, 6–88. (in Chinese)

Yang, K. S. & Bond, M. H. (1980). Ethnic affirmation by Chinese bilinguals. *Journal of Cross-cultural Psychology, 11*, 411–425.

Yang, Y. J., Wu, C. M., & Hong, Y. (2008). *The identifications of Taiwanese people.* (unpublished data: University of Illinois at Urbana-Champaign.)

CHAPTER 3

The cultured brain: interplay of genes, brain, and culture

Farhan Ali and Trevor B. Penney

The brain is perhaps the most complex phenotype, but it is, nonetheless, plastic. It can be cultured evolutionarily and developmentally across genetic and neuroanatomical levels. In this chapter, we provide a brief overview of how recent advances in molecular biology and genetics may be used to inform future cross-cultural psychological research. Specifically, we discuss the interaction of genes and culture in shaping the brain and its functions, with specific reference to Chinese psychology, and how one might begin to establish a genetically informed, cross-cultural psychology.

The Chinese peoples: a brief genetic history

Understanding how different populations and ethnic groups are related provides a context in which to test ideas about putative cultural differences in psychology and behavior. Moreover, in studies uncovering group relationships, a rough measure of time can be obtained, potentially providing information as to the rate of cultural and psychological change among human populations. Traditionally, inferring origins and ethnic group relationships depended primarily upon archaeology (e.g. Bellwood, 1997) and linguistic analyses (e.g. Greenberg, 1966). Although these methods have produced an interesting picture of the relationships among populations of humans from all over the world, they have drawbacks such as the reliance on fragmentary fossil records and the presence of extensive borrowing of lexicons, processes that can cloud actual inter-group relationships.

Moreover, when psychologists discuss cross-cultural differences, the cultural groupings are often very broad. For example, the title of the present edited volume is *The Oxford handbook of Chinese psychology*, but given that the political entity known as China has fifty-six officially recognized ethnic groups and over 200 linguistic groups (Cavalli-Sforza, 1998), one may wonder whether the eventual goal of any cross-cultural psychology involving the Chinese will be to describe the psychology of the Chinese *peoples*. Alternatively, given the extensive admixture of genes over thousands of years in the region of what is modern China, the problem of uncovering the population history of the Chinese people, or peoples, is very much complicated.

However, because all genes have a history, anthropologists and geneticists have been able to uncover the history of populations (Cavalli-Sforza, 1998). The past decade has seen active application of advances in genetic techniques to shed light on the origins and relationships of the populations that comprise modern China. Like comparative linguistics and archaeology, anthropological genetics uses clustering techniques on variations found within and among populations to reconstruct tree-like genealogies. However, because the data used are DNA sequences, the interpretations of the data are somewhat less susceptible to subjective influences. In the following, we first outline some assumptions about the origins of the Chinese peoples that have been challenged or confirmed by genetic studies, especially more recent large-scale studies, and then discuss the implications of these findings in the context of the psychology of the Chinese peoples.

Before the advent of modern anthropological genetics, there were two prevailing views of how Chinese populations originated. First, modern *Homo sapiens* populations in China were believed to have evolved locally from *Homo erectus*. This view was based primarily on cranial features of fossils uncovered in modern China (reviewed in Etler, 1996). However, genetic analyses provide a more nuanced picture of the origins of the Chinese. Since the classic paper by Cann et al. (1987), which posited a relatively recent origin (about 200,000 years ago) of modern humans all over the world, many subsequent studies have challenged the local-origin theory of modern humans in China (reviewed in Jin & Su, 2000), and strong evidence now points to modern *Homo sapiens* in East Asia originating from a recent migration out of East Africa (Jin & Su, 2000).

The second prevailing view was that the Northern and Southern Chinese populations were distinct, although it was controversial whether they were descended from the same population or if one group descended from the other (Z. B. Zhang, 1988). Indeed, since ancient times the Chinese populations have been subdivided into north and south, shaped by the somewhat separate histories and climates of these two geographical areas (Eberhard, 1965). This view received subsequent support from research using various genetic markers, such as particular Y-chromosome sequences and mitochondrial DNA sequences, that show there are indeed two distinct genetic groups, the Northern and Southern Chinese (Chu et al., 1998). The most recent large-scale analyses using genome-wide data confirmed the North–South genetic gradient (Li et al., 2008). However, according to Chu et al (1998), and contrary to previous hypotheses, the Northern Chinese descended from populations in the South including those from Southeast Asia (for a review, see F. Zhang, Su, Zhang, & Jin, 2007).

Findings from anthropological genetics have implications for the study of cultural psychology. First, it has been found quite consistently that genetic variation within a group accounts for over 80 per cent of total genetic variation in humans (Li et al., 2008). As such, it is quite unlikely that any robust psychological-level differences between two cultures can be explained convincingly by genetic differences alone. This conclusion, however, does not preclude the possibility of more subtle genetic effects (see below) among groups. Second, in the genealogies of populations, or commonly called phylogenies, of different Chinese populations, some Southern Chinese have been shown to be more closely related genetically to other Southeast Asian populations than to the Northern Chinese (for a review, see F. Zhang, Su, Zhang, & Jin, 2007). Moreover, recent studies argue against classifying all of the Han Chinese into one group given their considerable differences in genetic make-up (Yao, Kong, Bandelt, Kivisild, & Zhang, 2002). Such evidence challenges the concept of unity of the Han Chinese that defines the identity of the major group of Chinese in China.

This result indicates that, with respect to genetic complement, it may be worthwhile for cultural psychologists to consider more than a person's self-reported cultural group identity. For example, genetic analyses open the possibility for cross-cultural psychologists to test whether group effects differ when the grouping is based on particular genetic markers. Differences in results based on these two approaches to grouping participants can potentially shed light on the extent of contributions from genetics and self-reported cultural background to cognition and behavior.

Brain, genes, and culture

A genomic approach

The preceding discussion briefly reviewed anthropological genetics evidence for the relationships amongst various cultural groups that are commonly assumed to be Chinese. However, many of those studies used genetic markers that mutate neutrally, meaning that they are genetic differences not likely to be functional and not directly correlated with group differences in phenotypes. Yet the class of functional genetic markers is likely to be of greater interest to psychologists attempting to explain group differences in behavior and psychology. Hence, in this section, we focus on the more functional aspects of genetics, highlighting both similarities and differences across cultures.

Moreover, the rapidly advancing field of molecular genetics has opened up new possibilities of uncovering a more nuanced description of the interaction between genes, brain, and culture. We present an overview of some recent large-scale genetic surveys showing that members of apparently distinct cultures do not necessarily differ with respect to the complement of alleles associated with the brain and cognitive phenotypes that they possess. The implications of these null findings for the interpretation of putative cultural differences in brain and cognition will be discussed.

Linking genetics and cross-cultural differences is fraught with difficulties and has ignited much controversy. Indeed, many psychologists, for both scientific and political reasons, are wary of research efforts that attempt to correlate supposed ethnic differences in intelligence with genetic differences (e.g. Herrnstein & Murray, 1996; Rushton, 1995). For example, Herrnstein & Murray (1996) and Rushton (1995) failed to show any empirical evidence that different ethnic groups do in fact differ in allele frequencies relevant to intelligence, cognition, or the brain itself.

One less well-known report that claimed a connection between a particular allele and a cultural practice is a study of the members of a linguistic group in Papua New Guinea, the Fore, who have a high preponderance of protective alleles for kuru, an infectious neurodegenerative disease (Mead et al., 2003). This finding was linked to their widespread practice of cannibalism, such that members of the group were subject to selective pressure for individuals with alleles to protect against neurodegenerative infections arising from cannibalism. However, the original study has been criticized for making both methodological and statistical errors (Kreitman & Rienzo, 2004), so the status of its findings is at present uncertain.

Moreover, very recent genomic studies have questioned the extent of functional human genetic variation related to brain and cognition across different cultural groups (Barreiro, Laval, Quach, Patin, & Quintana-Murci, 2008; Jakobsson et al., 2008; Sabeti et al., 2007; Voight, Kudaravalli, Wen, & Pritchard, 2006; Williamson et al., 2007). A key problem in such genomic studies is the identification of putative population differences in functional genes that were driven by natural selection rather than merely a consequence of neutral mutations.

Many analytical methods have been pioneered to overcome this problem, yet the key message from these recent studies is clear: few differences among present human populations are functionally driven by natural selection, and even fewer of such differences are directly related to brain and cognitive phenotypes. For example, although some candidate genes that can explain morphological differences in hair, pigmentation, and disease prevalence among different human populations (e.g. Europeans vs. East Asians) have been identified, Sabeti et al (2007) found that none was related to brain and cognitive phenotypes.

However, two studies (Voight et al., 2006; Williamson et al., 2007) reported that at least thirteen different genes related to sensory development and Alzheimer's disease differ across human populations. For example, *SV2B*, a gene that is related to brain development, was shown to be positively selected, meaning that it was evolving at a rate faster than neutral expectations, in an African-American sample (Williamson et al., 2007), while *SLC6A4*, a serotonin transporter gene, exhibits signals of selection in East Asians and Europeans (Voight et al., 2006). Nonetheless, many more candidate genes for positive selection have been found for which the functions are either unrelated to the brain or are unknown.

Such large-scale genomic scans have a number of advantages. They set an unbiased baseline for genetic differences among human populations and cultures that can potentially explain phenotypic differences related to the brain by using large amounts of data that sample almost the whole human genome. However, in spite of over 3 million nucleotide differences in over 20,000 genes and many more in the non-coding regions, only a few polymorphisms related to brain and cognitive phenotypes are believed to be functional. Some of these candidate genes might also be false positives, further reducing the number of potential functional genetic differences across cultures. For each remaining promising candidate, experimental verification from functional studies is needed to confirm the relevance of the genome scan results. For example, it is not clear what phenotypic difference between African-American and other populations can be correlated with the selection of the brain development gene *SV2B*. Until further studies of genetic association that correlate phenotype with *SV2B* polymorphisms are done, it is premature to identify these genes as responsible for putative cross-cultural differences in brain and behavior.

The candidate gene approach

The genome-wide approach takes advantage of recent advances in molecular techniques that allow for large-scale, rapid screening of polymorphisms in the human genome, but these statistical studies lack a functional basis. A complementary approach that has gained popularity recently is closer examination of specific genes combined with correlation of those genes to particular brain and cognition phenotypes. Such studies have been conducted in non-human primates as well as among different human populations.

One gene that has garnered much interest is the *ASPM* (abnormal spindle microcephaly associated) gene, mutated forms of which cause reduced brain size in humans (Bond et al., 2002). This gene has evolved rapidly in *Homo sapiens*, where brain size has increased tremendously in the past 1 million years (Evans et al., 2004; Kouprina et al., 2004; J. Z. Zhang, 2003), as well as in other primates that have undergone major changes in cerebral cortex size (Ali & Meier, 2008). An early study reported that a particular genetic variant in *ASPM* had a distinct geographical distribution that seemingly correlated with brain size in human populations (Mekel-Bobrov et al., 2005). However, subsequent studies that correlated the gene with normal human brain size variability and measures of intelligence failed to uncover a functional relationship (Dobson-Stone et al., 2007; Rushton & Vernon, 2006; Timpson, Heron, Smith, & Enard, 2007; Woods et al., 2006).

Although these null findings are complicated by their use of the relatively imprecise phenotype of whole brain size instead of the cerebral cortex, the brain region where *ASPM* is thought to act (Bond et al., 2002), they imply that the *ASPM* gene may influence phenotypes other than the brain itself. One hypothesis is that *ASPM* is involved in a language phenotype, specifically tonal perception (Dediu & Ladd, 2007). Dediu and Ladd (2007) found that there was a strong correlation between population frequencies in two *ASPM* alleles and whether or not tone is used in the languages of those populations. For example, in the population of native speakers of Mandarin, a tone language and the most common Chinese dialect, the *ASPM*-D allele has low frequency, whereas in the population of native speakers of non-tone languages there are very high *ASPM*-D allele frequencies.

The example of *ASPM* is very instructive for a nascent, genetically based cross-cultural psychology. First, it shows how data from evolutionary studies of multiple species can inform human research, particularly as applied across populations. Second, it shows that correlations between genes and phenotypes can be found at the level of psychological phenotypes in addition to the physical brain itself. Moreover, the study by Dediu and Ladd (2007) is also intriguing because it provides an alternative methodology for uncovering genotype–phenotype correlations across cultures.

Dediu and Ladd (2007) argue that researchers should correlate genes with specific psychological or behavioral phenotypes combined across many cultures. Adopting this approach permits researchers to better control for other, potentially confounding, effects that are associated with different cultural groups, and to focus solely on whether a particular gene is associated with a particular psychological phenotype. It is also noteworthy that Dediu and Ladd's (2007) study suggests testable hypotheses regarding the influence of genes on language features. One such hypothesis is that the *ASPM*-D allele is somehow less efficient in supporting the production or perception of tone in speech, something that can be empirically tested through, for example, training speakers who have different *ASPM* alleles in artificial languages with and without tones. Combined with brain imaging measures, such a study could reveal how genes influence language phenotypes.

Conclusion

While cultural psychologists usually use simple measures of group membership such as self-identification for psychological studies, it is important to recognize the anthropological genetic evidence that argues against a simple categorization of groups such as the Chinese. Recent studies that use advances in molecular biology and genetic analyses support the idea that future research in cross-cultural psychology can benefit from the tools and insights of genetics. However, the fluid nature of gene flow in evolutionary history substantially complicates the interpretation of the relationships among genes, the brain, culture, and behavior. One result of this additional layer of complication is that many studies have failed to find strong evidence that genes underlie group differences in brain and cognitive phenotypes. We believe that testing more complex interactions between genes and cognitive phenotypes both within and across cultures offers a promising avenue of discovery for cultural psychology.

References

Ali, F. & Meier, R. (2008). Positive selection in *ASPM* is correlated with cerebral cortex evolution across primates but not with whole brain size. *Molecular Biology and Evolution, 25*, 2247–2250.

Barreiro, L. B., Laval, G., Quach, H., Patin, E., & Quintana-Murci, L. (2008). Natural selection has driven population differentiation in modern humans. *Nature Genetics, 40*, 340–345.

Bellwood, P. (1997). *Prehistory of the Indo-Malaysian Archipelago.* Honolulu, HI: University of Hawaii Press.

Bond, J., Roberts, E., Mochida, G. H., Hampshire, D. J., Scott, S., Askham, J. M. et al (2002). *ASPM* is a major determinant of cerebral cortical size. *Nature Genetics, 32*, 316–320.

Cann, R., Stoneking, M., & Wilson, A. (1987). Mitochondrial DNA and human evolution. *Nature, 325*, 31–36.

Cavalli-Sforza, L. L. (1998). The Chinese Human Genome Diversity Project. *Proceedings of the National Academy of Sciences of the United States of America, 95*, 11501–11503.

Chu, J. Y., Huang, W., Kuang, S. Q., Wang, J. M., Xu, J. J., Chu, Z. T. et al (1998). Genetic relationship of populations in China. *Proceedings of the National Academy of Sciences of the United States of America, 95*, 11763–11768.

Dediu, D. & Ladd, D. R. (2007). Linguistic tone is related to the population frequency of the adaptive haplogroups of two brain size genes, *ASPM* and *Microcephalin. Proceedings of the National Academy of Sciences of the United States of America, 104*, 10944–10949.

Dobson-Stone, C., Gatt, J. M., Kuan, S. A., Grieve, S. M., Gordon, E., Williams, L. M. et al (2007). Investigation of *MCPH1* G37995C and *ASPM* A44871G polymorphisms and brain size in a healthy cohort. *Neuroimage, 37*, 394–400.

Eberhard, W. (1965). Chinese regional stereotypes. *Asian Survey, 5*, 596–608.

Etler, D. A. (1996). The fossil evidence for human evolution in Asia. *Annual Review of Anthropology, 25*, 275–301.

Evans, P. D., Anderson, J. R., Vallender, E. J., Gilbert, S. L., Malcom, C. M., Dorus, S. et al (2004). Adaptive evolution of ASPM, a major determinant of cerebral cortical size in humans. *Human Molecular Genetics, 13*, 489–494.

Greenberg, J. H. (1966). *The languages of Africa* (2nd edn). Bloomington, IN: Indiana University Press.

Herrnstein, R. J. & Murray, C. (1996). *The bell curve: Intelligence and class structure in American life.* New York, NY: Free Press.

Jakobsson, M., Scholz, S. W., Scheet, P., Gibbs, J. R., VanLiere, J. M., Fung, H. C. et al (2008). Genotype, haplotype and copy-number variation in worldwide human populations. *Nature, 451*, 998–1003.

Jin, L. & Su, B. (2000). Natives or immigrants: Modern human origin in East Asia. *Nature Review Genetics, 1*, 126–133.

Kouprina, N., Pavlicek, A., Solomon, G., Gersch, W., Yoon, Y. H., Collura, R. et al (2004). Accelerated evolution of the ASPM gene controlling brain size begins prior to human brain expansion. *PLoS Biology, 2*, 653–663.

Kreitman, M. & Rienzo, A. D. (2004). Balancing claims for balancing selection. *Trends in Genetics, 20*, 300–304

Li, J. Z., Absher, D. M., Tang, H., Southwick, A. M., Casto, A. M., Ramachandran, S. et al (2008). Worldwide human relationships inferred from genome-wide patterns of variation. *Science, 319*, 1100–1104.

Mead, S., Stumpf, M. P., Whitfield, J., Beck, J. A., Poulter, M., Campbell, T. et al (2003). Balancing selection at the prion protein gene consistent with prehistoric kurulike epidemics. *Science, 300*, 640–643.

Mekel-Bobrov, N., Gilbert, S. L., Evans, P. D., Vallender, E. J., Anderson, J. R., Hudson, R. R. et al (2005). Ongoing adaptive evolution of ASPM, a brain size determinant in *Homo sapiens. Science, 309*, 1720–1722.

Rushton, P. (1995). *Race, evolution, and behavior: A life history perspective.* New Brunswick, NJ: Transaction Publishers.

Rushton, P. & Vernon, P. (2006). No evidence that polymorphisms of brain regulator genes Microcephalin and ASPM are associated with general mental ability, head circumference, or altruism. *Biology Letters, 3*, 157–160.

Sabeti, P. C., Varilly, P., Fry, B., Lohmueller, J., Hostetter, E., Cotsapas, C. et al (2007). Genome-wide detection and characterization of positive selection in human populations. *Nature, 449*, 913–918.

Timpson, N., Heron, J., Smith, G. D., & Enard, W. (2007). Comment on papers by Evans et al and Mekel-Bobrov et al on evidence for positive selection of *MCPH1* and *ASPM*. *Science, 317,* 1036.

Voight, B. F., Kudaravalli, S., Wen, X. Q., & Pritchard, J. K. (2006). A map of recent positive selection in the human genome. *PLoS Biology, 4,* 446–458.

Williamson, S. H., Hubisz, M. J., Clark, A. G., Payseur, B. A., Bustamante, C. D., & Nielsen, R. (2007). Localizing recent adaptive evolution in the human genome. *PLoS Genetics, 3,* 901–915.

Woods, R. P., Freimer, N. B., De Young, J. A., Fears, S. C., Sicotte, N. L., Service, S. K. et al (2006). Normal variants of *Microcephalin* and *ASPM* do not account for brain size variability. *Human Molecular Genetics, 15,* 2025–2029.

Yao, Y. G., Kong, Q. P., Bandelt, H. J., Kivisild, T., & Zhang, Y. P. (2002). Phylogeographic differentiation of mitochondrial DNA in Han Chinese. *American Journal of Human Genetics, 70,* 635–651.

Zhang, F., Su, B., Zhang, Y. P., & Jin, L. (2007). Genetic studies of human diversity in East Asia. *Philosophical Transactions of the Royal Society of London B—Biological Sciences, 362,* 987–995.

Zhang, J. Z. (2003). Evolution of the human *ASPM* gene, a major determinant of brain size. *Genetics, 165,* 2063–2070.

Zhang, Z. B. (1988). An analysis of the physical characteristics of modern Chinese. *Acta Anthropologica Sinica, 7,* 314–323.

CHAPTER 4

Socio-emotional development in Chinese children

Xinyin Chen

Developmental researchers have observed considerable individual differences in children's socio-emotional functioning (e.g. Rothbart & Bates, 2006; Rubin, Bukowski, & Parker, 2006). Whereas some children are sociable and cooperative and tend to engage in positive social interactions, others exhibit hostile and defiant behaviors, such as aggression-disruption in social settings. In addition, children who are shy and socially inhibited often display wary and vigilant behaviors, showing a high level of anxiety when faced with challenging situations. It has been found in Western societies that sociability and cooperation are associated with indexes of social, school, and psychological adjustment such as peer acceptance, teacher-rated competence, academic achievement, and emotional well-being. In contrast, aggression-disruption is associated with peer rejection, school dropout, and juvenile delinquency. Finally, shyness-inhibition may contribute to difficulties in peer relationships and adjustment problems of an internalizing nature, such as loneliness and depression (see Dodge, Coie, & Lynam, 2006; Coplan, Prakash, O'Neil, & Armer, 2004; Rubin, Burgess, & Coplan, 2002).

Socio-emotional development is likely to be affected by social and cultural context. Culture may promote or weaken the exhibition of specific aspects of socio-emotional functioning through facilitation or suppression processes (e.g. Weisz et al., 1988). Moreover, cultural norms and values may define the functional meanings of socio-emotional characteristics by providing guidance for social interpretation and evaluation of these characteristics, and eventually shape their developmental patterns (Benedict, 1934; Chen & French, 2008). Thus, socio-emotional development is a complex phenomenon that needs to be understood with social and cultural factors taken into account.

In the past twenty years, socio-emotional development in Chinese children has received increased attention from researchers in psychology, anthropology, and health science (e.g. Camras et al., 1998). It has been argued that the social and cultural conditions in Chinese society exert a pervasive impact on children's early behaviors, emotion expressivity and regulation, and interaction styles (e.g. Chen, 2000; Stevenson, 1991). Among various contextual factors, cultural beliefs, norms, and values concerning socialization and social relationships appear to be particularly relevant to socio-emotional development. In this chapter, I first discuss some theoretical issues and a conceptual framework concerning culture and socio-emotional development. Then I review the work on Chinese children's dispositional characteristics in the early years and socio-emotional functioning in childhood and adolescence, mainly from a cross-cultural perspective. Researchers have recently conducted several studies examining the implications of macro-level social, economic, and cultural changes in China for socialization and children's socio-emotional functioning. I review the findings of these studies in the next section. The chapter will conclude with a discussion of future directions in the study of socio-emotional development in Chinese children.

Culture and socio-emotional development: a social contextualist perspective

The role of culture in human development has been explored from several major perspectives. Among them, Bronfenbrenner's ecological theory (Bronfenbrenner & Morris, 2006) is concerned with how culture affects individual development as a part of the socio-ecological environment. According to this theory, the beliefs, values, and practices that are mostly endorsed within a cultural group play a significant role in human development. In addition to its direct effects, culture may affect development through organizing various social settings, such as community services and school and day-care arrangements (Bronfenbrenner & Morris, 2006; Super & Harkness, 1986). Another major perspective, represented by socio-cultural theory (Rogoff, 2003; Vygotsky, 1978), focuses on the transmission or internalization of external symbolic systems such as language, concepts, signs, and symbols, along with their cultural meanings, from the social or interpersonal level to the intrapersonal level. During development, children master these systems and use them as psychological tools to perform mental processes, such as remembering and recalling. An important mechanism of internalization is collaborative or guided learning in which more experienced peers or adults, as skilled tutors and representatives of the culture, assist the child to understand and solve cognitive and other problems (Cole, 1996; Wang & Chang, this volume).

Chen and his colleagues (e.g. Chen & French, 2008; Chen, Wang, & DeSouza, 2006a) have recently proposed a social contextualist perspective on culture and children's socio-emotional functioning. The perspective is reflected by a conceptual framework concerning cultural values and major aspects of socio-emotional characteristics, and a process model concerning how social evaluations and responses in interactions are guided by cultural values and, at the same time, regulate individual behavior and development.

According to Chen et al (2006a), social initiative and self-control, as manifestations of the fundamental temperamental dimensions of reactivity and regulation (Rothbart & Bates, 2006) in social domains, are two distinct systems that may account for individual and group differences in socio-emotional functioning (see Figure 4.1). *Social initiative* refers to the tendency to initiate and maintain social interactions, as indicated by reactions to challenging social situations. Whereas high social initiative is driven by the child's approach motive in these situations, internal anxiety or inhibition may impede spontaneous engagement in social participation, leading to a low level of social initiative (Asendorpf, 1990). *Self-control* represents the regulatory ability to modulate behavioral and emotional reactivity. This dimension is closely related to maintaining the appropriateness of behaviors during social interactions.

Chinese and Western societies may place different values on social initiative and norm-based behavioral control in children and adolescents (e.g. Chen et al., 2006a). In Western self-oriented or individualistic cultures where acquiring autonomy and assertive social skills is an important socialization goal, social initiative is viewed as a major index of social maturity; the display of vigilant and inhibited behavior is often considered socially incompetent (Greenfield, Suzuki, & Rothstein-Fisch, 2006). On the other hand, although self-regulation and control are encouraged, the cultural emphasis on individual decision making, self-assertion, and free will allows individuals to maintain a balance between the needs of the self and those of others (Maccoby & Martin, 1983). Consequently, behavioral control is regarded as less important, especially when it is in conflict with the attainment of individual goals (Triandis, 1995).

In Chinese group-oriented society, social initiative may be less appreciated or valued because it may not facilitate harmony and cohesiveness in the group (see Leung & Au, this volume). To maintain interpersonal and group harmony, individuals need to restrain personal desires in an effort to address

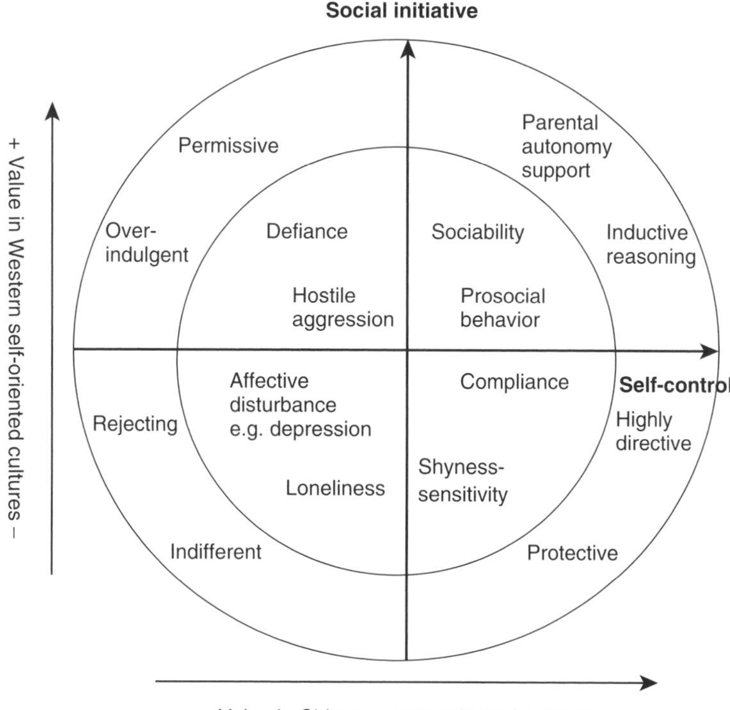

Fig. 4.1 A contextual model concerning socio-emotional functioning (inner circle) and parenting styles (outer circle) in relation to social initiative and self-control and their value in Western, self-oriented vs. Chinese, group-oriented cultures.

the needs and interests of others (Tamis-LeMonda et al., 2008; Triandis, 1995). Thus, self-control is emphasized in a more consistent and absolute manner; the lack of control is considered a serious problem in children and adolescents (Ho, 1986).

Cultural values of social initiative and self-control may have a direct impact on the social interpretations and evaluations of specific aspects of socio-emotional functioning, including aggression-disruption (based on high social initiative and low control), shyness-sensitivity (based on low social initiative and adequate control to constrain behavioral and emotional reactivity toward self), sociable and pro-social-cooperative behaviors (active social participation with effective control), and internalizing symptoms such as depression (disregulated emotions and feelings). According to the social process model (Chen, Chung, & Hsiao, 2009), peers and adults may evaluate socio-emotional characteristics in manners that are consistent with cultural belief systems prevalent throughout the society. Moreover, in social interactions, peers and adults in different cultures may respond differently to these socio-emotional characteristics and express different attitudes (e.g. acceptance, rejection) toward children who display these characteristics (Wang & Chang, this volume). Social evaluations and responses, in turn, may regulate the targeted children's behaviors and, ultimately, their socio-emotional development. Cultural norms and values, which are themselves changing, provide a basis for the social processes (Chen et al., 2009). At the same time, children actively engage in social interactions through expressing their reactions to social influence and through participating in constructing cultural norms for social evaluations and other group activities (Corsaro & Nelson, 2003). Thus, the social processes are bi-directional and transactional in nature.

Socio-emotional functioning in Chinese children: prevalence, meanings, and developmental patterns

Chinese children may display distinct dispositional characteristics in the early years. These characteristics constitute a major developmental origin of socio-emotional functioning in childhood and adolescence. Social evaluations and attitudes, which are guided by cultural values, are important factors in shaping the experiences (e.g. peer acceptance, emotional adjustment) and developmental trajectories of Chinese children with specific social-behavioral qualities.

Early socio-emotional characteristics

Among early socio-emotional characteristics, Chinese children have been found to differ from Western children on emotional expressivity and communication (Camras et al., 1998; Freedman & Freedman, 1969), sociability (Chen, DeSouza, Chen, & Wang, 2006), and impulsivity (Ho, 1986). For example, Camras and her colleagues (1998) found that Chinese infants and toddlers were more emotionally restrained than their North American counterparts in the laboratory setting. The relatively low level of emotional expressivity in Chinese children seems to be related to their skills at emotion communication and emotion knowledge in the later years (e.g. Wang, 2003). According to Chen et al (2006a), the differences between Chinese and Western children in the early years may be characterized systematically by the dimensions of initiative and control in social situations.

Social initiative and self-control. Researchers have long noticed that Chinese children have a lower level of social initiative, due to their higher reactivity to challenging situations, than do North American children (e.g. Kagan, Kearsley, & Zelazo, 1978). In a recent study of behavioral inhibition, Chen et al (1998) observed behaviors of Chinese and Canadian two-year-olds in a variety of activities, including mother–child free play and interaction with a stranger. The results indicated that, compared with Canadian toddlers, Chinese toddlers were more inhibited, vigilant, and reactive in stressful and challenging situations. Specifically, Chinese toddlers stayed closer to their mothers and were less likely to explore the environment. When interacting with the stranger, Chinese toddlers displayed more anxious and fearful behaviors, as indicated by their higher scores on the latency of approaching the stranger and touching the toys when they were invited to do so.

Inhibited behavior in challenging situations is considered a dispositional characteristic that may be biologically rooted (Kagan, 1998). Some initial evidence has indicated that Chinese and European-American children and adults differ on serotonin transporter genetic polymorphisms (5HTTLPR), cortisol reactivity, and the function of the autonomic nervous system, such as heart rate and heart rate variability in stressful settings (Kagan et al., 1978; Tsai, Hong, & Cheng, 2002). It has been found that these biological/physiological measures are associated with behavioral inhibition and anxiety in Western children (e.g. Fox, Henderson, Marshall, Nichols, & Ghera, 2005; Kagan, 1998; Lesch et al., 1996). However, no research has been conducted to examine the links in Chinese children. Thus, any conclusions about the links between biological factors and early inhibition at the national level need to be made with caution.

Chinese and North American children also display different levels of self-control in early childhood (Ho, 1986). Chen et al (2003) found that, in a clean-up session in which the child was asked to put the toys into a basket, Chinese children were more likely than Canadian children to maintain their compliant behaviors without adult intervention, indicating committed and internalized control. In contrast, Canadian children tended to exert control based on situational requirements, such as parental requests. Moreover, during a delay task in which the experimenter told the child to wait before playing with a packet of attractive crayons until she returned to the room, Chinese toddlers waited for significantly longer time than did Canadian toddlers. Consistent with the results of this study, Sabbagh, Xu, Carlson, Moses, and Lee (2006) found that Chinese preschoolers performed more competently than their US counterparts on tasks of executive function assessing self-control abilities that are associated with the prefrontal cortex of the brain.

Social attitudes and responses. Cultural norms and values may be reflected in adults' and children's attitudes toward socio-emotional functioning. Chen et al (1998) found that, whereas children's inhibited behavior was associated with parental punishment orientation, disappointment, and rejection in Canada, it was associated with parental warmth and accepting attitudes in China. In a study concerning how children responded to inhibited behaviors, Chen, DeSouza et al (2006) found that, when making passive and low-power social initiations, relative to others, inhibited children received fewer positive responses and more rejection from peers in Canada. However, inhibited children who displayed the same behavior were more likely than others to receive positive responses and support in China. These results indicated the role of culture in determining social attitudes and responses toward children's inhibited behavior.

Cultural values are also reflected in social expectations and attitudes about self-control. Compared with Canadian parents, Chinese parents expected their toddlers to maintain a higher level of behavioral control (Chen et al., 2003). When children failed to do so, Chinese parents were more likely to express negative attitudes, such as dissatisfaction and concern. Similarly, Kohnstamm et al (1998) found that when the researcher asked parents to describe their children, relative to parents in Western countries, Chinese parents had significantly higher proportions of descriptors about child conscientiousness (careless or diligent) and were more concerned about the lack of control in their children. The expectation of and socialization for control may be observed in various aspects of daily-life parent–child interaction. For example, many Chinese parents start toilet training when their children are under one year old. Chen et al (2003) found that most Canadian children, particularly boys, wore diapers at the age of two years, whereas virtually all the Chinese toddlers had finished toilet training.

Socio-emotional functioning and adjustment in childhood and adolescence

Early dispositional characteristics, culturally directed parental child-rearing attitudes and peer evaluations, and their interactions determine, to a large extent, how children develop in socio-emotional areas. Among the major aspects of socio-emotional functioning in childhood and adolescence, researchers have been interested in pro-social and sociable behaviors, aggression-disruption, shyness-sensitivity, and affective disturbance. In the following section, I focus on the exhibition of these aspects of socio-emotional functioning and their significance for social, school, and psychological adjustment in the Chinese cultural context.

Pro-social and sociable behaviors. Pro-social orientation and sociability represent two main aspects of social competence in children (e.g. Chen, Li, Li, Li, & Liu, 2000). Whereas sociability refers to the capacity to engage in social interactions, pro-social-cooperative behavior, including helping, cooperating, and caring or taking responsibility for another, taps into children's attitudes and acts that are based on the consideration of the interests of others in social interactions.

Pro-social-cooperative behavior is highly encouraged in Chinese culture because it is considered essential to collective well-being. In the traditional Confucian view, human beings are innately endowed with empathic feelings, compassion, or 'human-heartedness', and the sense of concern for others, which constitute the 'root' of *ren* (virtue). The cultivation and strengthening of these feelings and interpersonal concerns are believed to result in a harmonious society (Luo, 1996). Consistent with this view, children in Chinese schools are required to receive moral education in which children are taught to cooperate with each other in the group. Children are also encouraged to display pro-social behaviors in a variety of group activities that are organized by student organizations.

Compared with Western children, Chinese children tend to display more pro-social and cooperative behaviors (e.g. Orlick, Zhou, & Partington, 1990; Rao & Stewart, 1999). Orlick et al (1990), for example, found remarkable differences in cooperation between Chinese and Canadian children; 85 per cent and 22 per cent of the social behaviors displayed by kindergarten children were cooperative in China and Canada, respectively. Similar results have been reported by Navon and Ramsay (1989). In social interactions involving resource possession, relative to their American counterparts, Chinese preschoolers displayed more cooperative behaviors and were more likely to redistribute materials to ensure that others had equal amounts (see also Au & Leung, this volume).

Chinese children may differ from Western children not only in the prevalence of pro-social-cooperative behavior, but also in their understanding of and motivation to perform such behavior. Pro-social behavior is often seen in Western cultures as a personal decision based on such factors as how much one likes the target person(s) (Eisenberg, Fabes, & Spinrad, 2006; Greenfield et al. 2006). In societies that emphasize group harmony and social relationships, there is great pressure on children to regard pro-social behavior as obligatory. Miller (1994) argues that individuals in sociocentric societies view responsiveness to the needs of others as a fundamental commitment and responsibility, whereas individuals in Western societies attempt to maintain a balance between pro-social concerns and individual freedom of choice and action. Consistent with Miller's argument (1994), Fung (1999, 2006) found that parents in Taiwan often use shaming practices in child rearing to help children develop pro-social behavior. Fung (2006) argues that shaming practices are based on a strong group concern because the experience of shame may lead to self-examination and repentance, which in turn may facilitate the internalization of rules and social responsibility. It will be interesting in the future to examine the implications of different understandings and motivations of pro-social behavior for intercultural interactions (see Thomas & Liao, this volume).

Pro-social behavior is associated with, and predictive of, social and school adjustment in Chinese children. Chen, Li et al (2000), for example, found that pro-social behavior made a significant contribution to peer acceptance, leadership status, and school achievement in China. Moreover, a pro-social orientation served as a protective factor for children who experienced social and psychological difficulties. Caring and helping behaviors that pro-social children display likely lead to mutual assistance from peers in social and school performance (Eisenberg et al., 2006). At the same time, these behaviors help improve the quality of social relationships with others, which, in turn, may change children's feelings and beliefs about the world (see Leung, this volume).

Compared with pro-social behavior, sociability is not so highly valued in Chinese culture. Although children are encouraged to interact and to maintain relationships with others, it is believed that social interactions and activities must be guided by pro-social orientations (Ho, 1986; Luo, 1996). It has been reported that Chinese children and adolescents appear less sociable than their Western counterparts (e.g. Chan & Eysenck, 1981; Gong, 1984). Moreover, sociability does not make clear contributions to social and school adjustment in Chinese children. In a longitudinal study conducted in China, Chen, Li et al (2000) found that sociability positively predicted social impact or salience in the peer group, but not social acceptance or preference. Moreover, after its overlap with pro-social behavior was controlled, sociability did not predict social or academic outcomes, and *positively* predicted later externalizing problems.

Nevertheless, sociability in Chinese children was found to contribute significantly and positively to social affiliation and integration in early adulthood during periods of life transition (Chen et al., 2002). Moreover, sociability was associated positively with self-regard and negatively with internalizing symptoms, such as loneliness. It appears that active social participation facilitates the formation of interpersonal support systems. As a result, sociable children may use these support systems to cope with emotional difficulties under adverse circumstances. Therefore, although sociable behavior is not as valued as pro-social behavior and may not predict social status and educational attainment, sociability and extensive social contact may be beneficial to psychological adjustment in Chinese children (see also Bond, Kwan, & Li, 2000).

Aggression-disruption. Bond (2004) argues that aggression is judged based on the norms that are established by the society to solve resource allocation problems and is related to the extent to which the culture emphasizes the control or regulation of coercive behavior. The hierarchical structure of Chinese society and the heightened concern about social harmony make it necessary to form social and cultural systems that prohibit individual antisocial, aggressive, and defiant behavior (Ekblad, 1989). Materials such as illegal drugs and guns that can be used in antisocial behaviors are generally unavailable to children and adolescents. Indeed, Chinese children and adolescents seldom engage in extreme forms of antisocial behaviors, such as drug use, theft, murder, and robbery. Violent or delinquent behaviors in the form of large groups or gangs are also rare. From a developmental perspective, children in China are required from the early years to learn how to control or suppress their impulsivity, frustration, and anger (Ho, 1986; Yang, 1986), a socialization practice which results in relatively low levels of aggression (Zhou et al., 2007). Empirically, Ekblad and Olweus (1986) reported that Chinese children were less aggressive than Western children. Navon and Ramsay (1989) found that Chinese children reacted less aggressively than American children to possession-related disputes. In a study of social behaviors in Canadian school-age children with Chinese and European backgrounds, Chen and Tse (2008) found that Chinese-Canadian children were rated by peers as less aggressive and disruptive than were European-Canadian children.

In Western cultures, despite the general discouragement of aggression, aggressive children and adolescents may receive social support from peers and are sometimes even perceived as 'stars' in their groups (e.g. Cairns & Cairns, 1994; Rodkin, Farmer, Pearl, & van Acker, 2000). As a result, aggressive children often have biased self-perceptions, overestimate their social competence, and do not report internalizing psychological problems (Asher, Parkhurst, Hymel, & Williams, 1990). Unlike their Western counterparts, aggressive children in China experience extensive social and psychological difficulties including low social status, poor quality of peer relationships, negative self-perceptions, and feelings of loneliness and depression (e.g. Chen, Rubin, & Li, 1995a; Chen et al., 2004). The psychological problems of aggressive children in China may be related to the regular collective and public evaluations in schools. During these activities, children are required to evaluate themselves in a group setting in terms of whether their behaviors reach the school standards and whether they have made improvement over time. Peers and teachers provide feedback on the child's self-evaluations. This public interactive process makes it difficult for aggressive children to develop inflated or 'biased' self-perceptions of their competence and social status (Oettingen, Little, Lindenberger, & Baltes, 1994).

Shyness-sensitivity. Shyness-sensitivity is a wary, restrained, and anxious reaction to stressful social situations or social evaluations (Rubin & Asendorpf, 1993). In Western cultures, because children are expected to be increasingly assertive and self-directed, shy and sensitive behavior is viewed as socially incompetent, immature, and deviant (Rubin et al., 2002). It has been found in Western, particularly North American, societies that children who display shy and sensitive behavior are likely to experience difficulties in peer relationships and school performance (Asendorpf, 1991; Coplan et al., 2004; Gazelle & Ladd, 2003). Moreover, when they realize their difficulties in social situations, shy-sensitive children may develop negative self-perceptions of their social competence and self-worth and other psychological problems, such as social dissatisfaction and depression (e.g. Coplan et al., 2004; Rubin, Chen, McDougall, Bowker, & McKinnon, 1995). Longitudinal research has also indicated that shyness in childhood contributes to later life adjustment problems in such areas as educational attainment and career stability (e.g. Caspi, Elder, & Bem 1988; Rubin et al., 2002).

In traditional Chinese culture, sensitive, wary, and restrained behavior is viewed as an indication of social maturity and mastery (Chen, 2000). Shy-sensitive behavior is thought to be associated with virtuous qualities, such as modesty and cautiousness; shy-sensitive children are often perceived as well behaved and understanding. This cultural endorsement may help shy children obtain social support in interactions, develop self-confidence, and achieve positive adjustment outcomes. Findings of empirical studies conducted in China have indicated that shy-sensitive children are accepted by peers and viewed as competent by teachers, and perform well in academic areas (Chen, Rubin, & Sun, 1992; Chen, Rubin, & Li, 1995b). Shy children are also more likely than others to acquire leadership status and the award of distinguished studentship in the school (e.g. Chen et al., 1995b). Moreover, shy children do not feel lonely or depressed, or develop negative perceptions of their competence (Chen et al., 1995a; Chen et al., 2004). Finally, results from longitudinal projects have shown that shyness-sensitivity in childhood predicts social competence, school achievement, and psychological well-being in adolescence (e.g. Chen, Rubin, Li, & Li, 1999). Thus, shy-sensitive Chinese children continue to adjust well in later years.

It should be noted that the construct of shyness-inhibition is different from those representing various types of social withdrawal, such as social solitude, social disinterest, and unsociability, e.g. 'kids who are often alone' or 'would rather be alone'. Social disinterest and preference for solitude or aloneness are inconsistent with the collectivistic orientation. Children who prefer solitude and intentionally stay away from the group may be regarded as selfish or anti-collective, perceptions likely to elicit negative reactions from others in group-oriented cultures. Indeed, it has been found that children who are socially solitary or withdrawn are clearly rejected by peers and experience socio-emotional problems in China, a finding similar to what has been found in Western cultures (Chang et al., 2005; Chen, 2008).

Finally, Chen and Tse (2008) recently found that Chinese children, particularly girls, in Canada (both Canadian born and immigrant) were more shy-sensitive in the school than children of European background. The differences were consistent according to the evaluations of European-Canadian and Chinese-Canadian children, as well as children from other cultural backgrounds (e.g. non-Chinese Asian, South American). Similar results have been reported based on a study conducted with Asian-American and European-American adults (Lee, Okazaki, & Yoo, 2006). Interestingly, Chen and Tse (2008) found that shyness was associated with social problems, such as peer rejection and victimization in European-Canadian children, but the associations were non-significant or significantly weaker in Chinese-Canadian children.

The results appear similar to those found in China (e.g. Chen et al., 1992). However, the processes involved in the relations may not necessarily be the same because the cultural contexts are different in Canadian and Chinese schools. It is possible that some Chinese cultural practices help children develop skills to cope with adverse outcomes of their shy-sensitive behavior. For example, the regulatory skills that Chinese children develop in the early years may allow them to express their shyness-sensitivity in a relatively acceptable manner (e.g. engaging in parallel play activities: Asendorpf, 1991) and to minimize the negative consequences of their shy behavior. It is also possible that the group stereotypical reputation (e.g. 'Chinese are shy') serves to protect shy-sensitive Chinese children in Canada from developing social difficulties in cross-ethnic peer interactions and thereby reducing their adjustment problems.

Affective disturbance. In traditional Chinese culture, the moderation or suppression of individual emotional reactions and feelings is regarded as necessary for achieving interpersonal and intrapersonal harmony (Bond, 1993; Bond & Hwang, 1986; Kleinman, 1980, 1986). According to Solomon (1971), Chinese people think of the expression of emotions and feelings, particularly negative ones, as 'dangerous' or shameful to self and family. This may be particularly the case in children and adolescents because they are expected to concentrate on their social and school performance. Children's internalizing emotional symptoms, such as depressed affect and loneliness, are considered to indicate a lack of control over personal feelings and are sometimes treated as medical or political-ideological problems, especially when they are associated with interpersonal problems (Chen, 2000).

Compared with their North American counterparts, Chinese children and adolescents experience an equal, or even higher, level of affective disturbance (Chen et al., 1995a; Crystal et al., 1994; Dong, Yang, & Ollendick, 1995; Lee et al., 2006). They also seem to have more somatic complaints (Chen & Schwartzman, 2001). The somatic complaints about physical symptoms, such as headaches, stomach pains, chronic fatigue, and sleep problems, have a strong psychological basis because they are associated with stress and depressed mood. In addition, a high rate of suicide in adolescents has been reported in the Chinese literature and in the media. According to Li (2002), the suicide rate in China was about 10.63 per 100,000 for adolescents (15–24 years of age) in 1998, which was one of the highest in the world. The rate was higher for female than male adolescents (15.96 vs. 8.67 per 100,000), particularly in rural areas (see also Stewart, Lee, & Tao, this volume).

Several studies conducted in China (e.g. Chen et al., 1995a; Chen & Li, 2000) have shown that affective disturbance influences social and school adjustment. In these studies, depression was found to be moderately stable over time (e.g. $r = .40$s from age twelve years to age fourteen years), suggesting that children who reported depression likely continued to suffer emotionally later. Moreover, early depression predicted social and school adjustment problems, including social isolation, low social status, and school underachievement. These findings indicate a similar maladaptive nature of affective disturbance in Chinese and Western cultures, which contradicts the argument that personal emotions and feelings are irrelevant to social relationships and adjustment in Chinese culture (Potter, 1988).

Multiple factors may contribute to affective problems in Chinese children and adolescents. Among these factors, parent–child relationships, particularly maternal acceptance and rejection, are associated robustly with depression. In a study concerning the effects of family environment on adolescent depression in Hong Kong, Lau and Kwok (2000) found that parent–child relationships were significantly associated with the major aspects of adolescent depression (emotionality, lack of positive experience, and physiological irritation). Similarly, Chen, Liu and Li (2000) found that maternal warmth had unique and negative effects in predicting later depression in children after the stability effect was controlled (see also Stewart, Rao, Bond, McBride-Chang, Fielding, & Kennard, 1998). Chen, Rubin and Li (1997) found that maternal acceptance and academic achievement interacted in the prediction of depression. Children who had academic difficulties and were rejected by their mothers were likely to develop depression; however, children who had low academic achievement but were accepted by their mothers were not depressed at the later time. Thus, maternal acceptance appeared to be a buffering factor that protected children who had academic difficulties from developing depressive symptoms. Another familial factor that had a similar buffering function was the quality of marital relationship (Chen & He, 2004). For children from families in which there was high marital conflict, poor academic achievement was associated with later depression. However, academic difficulties were not related to later depression for children from families in which marital relationship was harmonious.

The implications of social and cultural changes for children's socio-emotional development

Chinese society has changed dramatically since the early 1980s, particularly in the past fifteen years. During this period, China has carried out a full-scale reform towards a market economy that allows for the adoption of many aspects of capitalism. The rapid expansion of the market system to a range of different sectors has led to increased variations in individual and family income, massive movement of population, decline in government control of social welfare, and a rapid rise in economic competition and the unemployment rate (e.g. Zhang, 2000). At the same time, individualistic values such as liberty and individual freedom have been introduced into the country from Western societies (see Kulich, this volume). The dramatic changes in social structure and the introduction of Western values have exercised a profound influence on socialization beliefs and practices and children's socio-emotional functioning.

Parenting beliefs and practices in a context of chang

The primary socialization goal in traditional Chinese society is to help children develop attitudes and behaviors that are conducive to collective well-being, such as interdependence within the family, orientation to the larger group, and obedience to legitimate authority (Tamis-LeMonda et al., 2008). It has been argued that Chinese parents are concerned more with training children to maintain appropriate behaviors and less with encouraging children to be independent and exploratory (Ho, 1986). Compared with Western parents, Chinese parents have been found to be more controlling and power-assertive, and less responsive and affectionate in child rearing (e.g. Chao, 1994; Chen et al., 1998; Kelley, 1992). Chinese parents are less likely to use reasoning and induction and are more authoritarian and punishment-oriented than Western parents (Chen et al., 1998; Wu, 1981, 1996).

The traditional child-rearing beliefs, attitudes, and practices of Chinese parents are, however, changing in the market-oriented society. Social and behavioral qualities, such as expression of personal opinions, self-direction, and self-confidence, are required for adaptation to this new social environment, and it is important for parents to help children develop these qualities (Yu, 2002). Liu et al (2005) found that, although Chinese mothers had higher scores on encouragement of relatedness and lower scores on autonomy support than did Canadian mothers, mothers in both samples had significantly higher scores on encouragement of autonomy than on encouragement of relatedness.

Chen and Chen (in press) recently examined the similarities and differences in child-rearing attitudes between parents of elementary school children in two cohorts (1998 and 2002) in Shanghai. The parents completed a parenting measure assessing four major dimensions: *parental warmth*, e.g. 'My child and I have warm, good times together', 'I comfort my child when he/she is upset or afraid', 'I like to play with my child'; *power assertion*, e.g. 'I do not allow my child to question my decisions', 'I believe physical punishment to be the best method of discipline'; *encouragement of autonomy and independence*, e.g. 'I let my child make many decisions for him/herself', 'When my child gets into trouble, I expect him/her to handle the problem mostly by him/herself'; and *encouragement of achievement*, e.g. I encourage my child always to do his/her best'. The results indicated no differences between the cohorts on encouragement of academic achievement. However, both mothers and fathers in the 2002 cohorts gave significantly higher scores on parental warmth and lower scores on power assertion than did those in the 1998 cohort. Mothers in the 2002 cohort also gave significantly higher scores on autonomy support than did mothers in the 1998 cohort. These results suggest that parents in China are increasingly coming to realize the importance of socio-emotional well-being and the role of affective parent–child communication in promoting children's social competence. Moreover, parents now tend to place a greater value on independence, and encourage their children to learn initiative-taking skills.

Finally, Chen and Chen (in press) found that in both the 1998 and 2002 cohorts, parents' scores on encouragement of autonomy and independence were higher for girls than for boys, indicating that parents were more likely to encourage girls than boys to develop independent behaviors. Although the gender differences in parental attitudes did not change during the period from 1998 to 2002 in this study, the results are still interesting because they are inconsistent with the traditional gender stereotype in both Chinese and Western societies in which girls are socialized to be more communal and less independent than boys (e.g. Chen & He, 2004; Ho, 1986). The stronger emphasis on autonomy for girls in China over the past decade may be due, in part, to the one-child family policy that was implemented in the 1970s. Parents may feel greater pressure to change their gender-stereotypical attitudes and to encourage their daughters, as the 'only hope' of the family (Fong, 2004), to develop independent and assertive skills.

Children's socio-emotional functioning and adjustment in a context of change

Comprehensive reform in China may have altered the socialization beliefs and values of parents as well as other socialization agents. Following the 'Outline of the Educational Reform' from the Ministry of Education of China (Yu, 2002), for example, many Chinese schools have changed their education goals, policies, and practices to facilitate the development of social skills. A variety of strategies, e.g. encouraging students to engage in public debate and to propose and implement their own plans about extra-curricular activities, has been used to help children master these skills. Relative to some other aspects of socio-emotional functioning, shyness-sensitivity seems to be particularly susceptible to the influence of the macro-level changes in China (Chen, Wang, & DeSouza, 2006). Shy-sensitive behavior that may impede exploration and self-expression is incompatible with the requirements of the contemporary, more competitive society; the emphasis on initiative and assertiveness in school education and other activities is likely to lead to decline in the adaptive value of shy-sensitive behavior. Consequently, shy children may be at a disadvantage in obtaining social approval, and come to experience difficulties in social and psychological adjustment (Hart et al., 2000).

Chen, Cen, Li, and He (2005) examined the relations between shyness and peer relationships and adjustment in urban China at different times of this societal transition. Data on shyness and adjustment were collected in three cohorts (1990, 1998, and 2002) of elementary school children. Whereas children in the 1990 cohort experienced relatively limited influence of comprehensive reform and children in the 2002 cohort were socialized in an increased self-oriented cultural context, the 1998 cohort was raised during an intermediate phase in which children might have mixed socialization experiences.

The analysis revealed significant cross-cohort differences in the relations between shyness and adjustment variables. Whereas shyness was positively associated with peer acceptance, leadership, and academic achievement in the 1990 cohort, it was negatively associated with peer acceptance and school adjustment and positively associated with peer rejection and depression in the 2002 cohort. The relations between shyness and peer relationships and adjustment variables were non-significant or mixed in the 1998 cohort. The results indicated an ongoing process in which social and historical transition in China influences individual attitudes and behaviors. By the early part of the twenty-first century, as the country became more deeply immersed in a market economy, shy-sensitive children, unlike their counterparts in the early 1990s, were perceived as incompetent and problematic by teachers, rejected by peers, displayed school problems, and reported high levels of depression.

An interesting finding of Chen et al's study (2005) was that shyness was positively associated with both peer acceptance and peer rejection in the 1998 cohort. The analysis of the sociometric classification revealed that, whereas shy children were more popular in the 1990 cohort and more rejected in the 2002 cohort than others, shy children in the 1998 cohort received mixed reports: they were liked and disliked by peers at the same time. These results indicate the ambivalent attitudes of peers toward shy-inhibited children, which, to some extent, may reflect the conflict between imported Western values of initiative compatible with emerging economic pressures and traditional Chinese values of self-control.

Another interesting finding was that, in the 2002 cohort, shyness was associated with negative peer, teacher, and self-attitudes and evaluations, but not with school performance, such as distinguished studentship and academic achievement. Thus, the macro-level social changes may affect different aspects of socio-emotional functioning and adjustment in a steady and cumulative fashion. The finding also supports the argument that social attitudes and relationships serve as a major mediator of contextual influence on individual development (Chen & French, 2008; Chen, French, & Schneider, 2006; Silbereisen, 2000).

Urban-rural differences in socio-emotional functioning and adjustment

The massive social and economic reform in China, such as the opening of stock markets, has been largely limited to urban centers and cities. There are substantial regional, particularly urban–rural, differences in social and economic development. In general, families in rural China have lived mostly agricultural lives, and rural children do not have as much exposure as urban children to the influence of the market economy. In many rural areas, traditional Chinese values, such as family responsibility and self-control, are highly emphasized (Fuligni & Zhang, 2004; Shen, 2006). Rural parents use child-rearing practices that are consistent with traditional values, such as filial piety, respect for elders, and self-sacrifice for the family (e.g. Shen, 2006). Social interaction processes among rural children may still be regulated largely by these more traditional values.

Urban–rural differences in children's social experience and adjustment have been found in several studies. Guo, Yao, and Yang (2005) reported that, based on teacher evaluations and self-reports, relative to urban children, rural children were more group-oriented, displayed greater social responsibility, and were less likely to pursue individual interests. Chen and his colleagues (Chen & Chen, in press; Chen, Wang, & Wang, 2009) found in samples of rural children in 2004 to 2006 that shyness was associated with indexes of social, school, and psychological adjustment, such as leadership and teacher-rated competence. Thus, like their urban counterparts in the early 1990s, shy rural children are not yet regarded as problematic; these children still obtain approval from peers and adults and achieve success in social and academic areas. It is important to note that many rural regions of China are currently undergoing rapid changes. Urban and Western values increasingly influence socialization beliefs and practices and socio-emotional development in rural children. It will be interesting to investigate how rural children adapt to the changing socio-economic environment, particularly as the Chinese government attempts to 'develop the countryside'.

Conclusions and future directions

Chinese children may display distinct characteristics in the early years. These early-appearing characteristics constitute the major temperamental basis for the development of socio-emotional functioning such as pro-social behavior, aggression, shyness, and depressed affect. Through socialization and social interaction processes, the cultural norms and values in Chinese society are involved in determining the exhibition and significance of socio-emotional functioning. The dramatic macro-level changes in the country also have pervasive implications for children's socio-emotional development.

Researchers have been increasingly interested in socio-emotional development in Chinese children in the past two decades. However, studies in this area have been conducted mostly in mainland China. It will be important to examine whether the findings can be generalized to other regions or societies such as Hong Kong, Taiwan, and Singapore where traditional Chinese culture has exerted an extensive influence on human development. Furthermore, China is a large country with fifty-six recognized ethnic groups. However, most research on Chinese children has been conducted with the Han nationality. The social, economic, and cultural backgrounds of ethnic minorities may have a unique impact on social behaviors and psychological well-being of children in these ethnic groups. In addition to ethnicity, social class and other demographic conditions may be important factors in socio-emotional development. The diversities in Chinese society provide challenges as well as rich opportunities for researchers to study how personal and contextual factors contribute to human development. Hopefully, more developmental research will be conducted by researchers residing both in and outside China.

In this chapter, I focus mainly on two fundamental dimensions of socio-emotional functioning, social initiative and control, and the social behaviors that are formed based upon these key dimensions. There are other important areas of socio-emotional development, such as early parent-child relationships, children's and adolescents' friendships, and self and social understanding. Unfortunately, little is known about the development of Chinese children in these areas, as relatively little research is currently being conducted in developmental psychology generally. It will be crucial to build upon current initiatives but expand our knowledge about other aspects of socio-emotional functioning in various Chinese cultural contexts.

According to the social contextualist perspective (Chen & French, 2008), social and cultural influence on individual behavior is a dynamic process in which children play an active role in their own development. This active role may be reflected in the ways in which children participate in social interactions, e.g. the choices of playmates, settings and activities, and react to social influence (Edwards, Guzman, Brown, & Kumru, 2006). How social interaction processes serve to transmit and construct cultures in socio-emotional development in Chinese children need to be examined further in the future.

Finally, research on socio-emotional development in Chinese children has been conducted using both the cross-cultural and within-cultural approaches. Moreover, researchers have started to explore the processes in which cultural factors are involved in socio-emotional development through socialization and social interaction (e.g. Chen, DeSouza et al., 2006). Nevertheless, cultural influence on individual behaviors and relationships is a complex phenomenon, involving personal and contextual factors at multiple levels (Bond & van de Vijver, in press). It is crucial to engage in continuous exploration of the issues in the area in order to achieve a more thorough understanding of the processes underpinning socio-emotional development in the Chinese cultural context.

References

Asendorpf, J. B. (1990). Beyond social withdrawal: Shyness, unsociability, and peer avoidance. *Human Development, 33,* 250–259.

Asendorpf, J. B. (1991). Development of inhibited children's coping with unfamiliarity. *Child Development, 62,* 1460–1474.

Asher, S., Parkhurst, J. T., Hymel, S., & Williams, G. A. (1990). Peer rejection and loneliness in childhood. In S. R. Asher & J. D. Coie (eds), *Peer rejection in childhood* (pp. 253–273). New York: Cambridge University Press.

Benedict, R. (1934). Anthropology and the abnormal. *Journal of General Psychology, 10,* 59–82.

Bond, M. H. (1993). Emotions and their expression in Chinese culture. *Journal of Nonverbal Behavior, 17,* 245–262.

Bond, M. H. (2004). Culture and aggression—From context to coercion. *Personality and Social Psychology Review, 8,* 62–78.

Bond, M. H. & Hwang, K. (1986). The social psychology of the Chinese people. In M. H. Bond (ed.), *The psychology of Chinese people* (pp. 213–266). Hong Kong: Oxford University Press.

Bond, M. H., Kwan, V. S. Y., & Li, C. (2000). Decomposing a sense of superiority: The differential social impact of self-regard and regard-for-others. *Journal of Research in Personality, 34,* 537–553.

Bond, M. H. & van de Vijver, F. (in press). Making scientific sense of cultural differences in psychological outcomes: Unpackaging the *magnum mysterium.* In D. Matsumoto & F. Van de Vijver (eds), *Cross-cultural research methods.* New York: Oxford University Press.

Bronfenbrenner, U. & Morris, P. A. (2006). The bioecological model of human development. In W. Damon (series ed.) & R. M. Lerner (vol. ed.), *Handbook of child psychology: Vol 1. Theoretical models of human development* (pp. 793–828). New York: Wiley.

Cairns, R. B. & Cairns, B. D. (1994). *Lifelines and risks: Pathways of youth in our time.* New York: Cambridge University Press.

Camras, L. A., Oster, H., Campos, J., Campos, R., Ujiie, T., Miyake, K., Wang, L., & Meng, Z. (1998). Production of emotional facial expressions in European American, Japanese, and Chinese infants. *Developmental Psychology, 34,* 616–628.

Caspi, A., Elder, G. H., Jr, & Bem, D. J. (1988). Moving away from the world: Life-course patterns of shy children. *Developmental Psychology, 24,* 824–831.

Chan, J. & Eysenck, S. B. G. (1981). *National differences in personality: Hong Kong and England.* Paper presented at the joint IACCP-ICP Asian Regional Meeting, National Taiwan University, Taipei, Taiwan, August.

Chang, L., Lei, L., Li, K. K., Liu, H., Guo, B., Wang, Y. et al (2005). Peer acceptance and self-perceptions of verbal and behavioral aggression and withdrawal. *International Journal of Behavioral Development, 29,* 49–57.

Chao, R. K. (1994). Beyond parental control and authoritarian parenting style: Understanding Chinese parenting through the cultural notion of training. *Child Development, 65,* 1111–1119.

Chen, X. (2000). Social and emotional development in Chinese children and adolescents: A contextual cross-cultural perspective. In F. Columbus (ed.), *Advances in psychology research, Vol. I* (pp. 229–251). Huntington, NY: Nova Science Publishers.

Chen, X. (2008). Shyness and unsociability in cultural context. In A.S. LoCoco, K. H. Rubin, & C. Zappulla (eds), *L'isolamento sociale durante l'infanzia (Social withdrawal in childhood)* (pp. 143–60). Milan, Italy: Unicopli.

Chen, X., Cen, G., Li, D., & He, Y. (2005). Social functioning and adjustment in Chinese children: The imprint of historical time. *Child Development, 76,* 182–195.

Chen, X. & Chen, H. (in press). Children's social functioning and adjustment in the changing Chinese society. In R. K. Silbereisen & X. Chen (eds), *Social change and human development: Concepts and results.*

Chen, X., Chung, J., & Hsiao, C. (2009). Peer interactions, relationships and groups from a cross-cultural perspective. In K. H. Rubin, W. Bukowski, & B. Laursen (eds), *Handbook of peer interactions, relationships, and groups* (pp. 432–451). New York, NY: Guilford.

Chen, X., DeSouza, A., Chen, H., & Wang, L. (2006). Reticent behavior and experiences in peer interactions in Canadian and Chinese children. *Developmental Psychology, 42,* 656–665.

Chen, X. & French, D. (2008). Children's social competence in cultural context. *Annual Review of Psychology, 59,* 591–616.

Chen, X., Hastings, P., Rubin, K. H., Chen, H., Cen, G., & Stewart, S. L. (1998). Childrearing attitudes and behavioral inhibition in Chinese and Canadian toddlers: A cross-cultural study. *Developmental Psychology, 34,* 677–686.

Chen, X. & He, H. (2004). The family in mainland China: Structure, organization, and significance for child development. In J. L. Roopnarine & U. P. Gielen (eds), *Families in global perspective* (pp. 51–62). Boston, MA: Allyn and Bacon.

Chen, X., He, Y., De Oliveira, A. M., Lo Coco, A., Zappulla, C., Kaspar, V., Schneider, B., Valdivia, I. A., Tse, C. H., & DeSouza, A. (2004). Loneliness and social adaptation in Brazilian, Canadian, Chinese and Italian children. *Journal of Child Psychology and Psychiatry, 45,* 1373–1384.

Chen, X. & Li, B. (2000). Depressed mood in Chinese children: Developmental significance for social and school adjustment. *International Journal of Behavioral Development, 24,* 472–479.

Chen, X., Li, D., Li, Z., Li, B., & Liu, M. (2000). Sociable and prosocial dimensions of social competence in Chinese children: Common and unique contributions to social, academic and psychological adjustment. *Developmental Psychology, 36,* 302–314.

Chen, X., Liu, M., & Li, D. (2000). Parental warmth, control and indulgence and their relations to adjustment in Chinese children: A longitudinal study. *Journal of Family Psychology, 14*, 401–419.

Chen, X., Liu, M., Rubin, K. H., Cen, G., Gao, X., & Li, D. (2002). Sociability and prosocial orientation as predictors of youth adjustment: A seven-year longitudinal study in a Chinese sample. *International Journal of Behavioral Development, 26*, 128–136.

Chen, X., Rubin, K. H., & Li, B. (1995a). Depressed mood in Chinese children: Relations with school performance and family environment. *Journal of Consulting and Clinical Psychology, 63*, 938–947.

Chen, X., Rubin, K. H., & Li, B. (1997). Maternal acceptance and social and school adjustment in Chinese children: A four-year longitudinal study. *Merrill-Palmer Quarterly, 43*, 663–681.

Chen, X., Rubin, K. H., Li, B., & Li. Z. (1999). Adolescent outcomes of social functioning in Chinese children. *International Journal of Behavioral Development, 23*, 199–223.

Chen, X., Rubin, K. H., & Li, Z. (1995b). Social functioning and adjustment in Chinese children: A longitudinal study. *Developmental Psychology, 31*, 531–539.

Chen, X., Rubin, K. H., Liu, M., Chen, H., Wang, L., and Li, D., Gao, X., Cen, G., Gu, H., & Li, B. (2003). Compliance in Chinese and Canadian toddlers. *International Journal of Behavioral Development, 27*, 428–436.

Chen, X., Rubin, K. H., & Sun, Y. (1992). Social reputation and peer relationships in Chinese and Canadian children: A cross-cultural study. *Child Development, 63*, 1336–1343.

Chen, X. & Swartzman, L. (2001). Health beliefs, attitudes and experiences in Asian cultures. In S. S. Kazarian & D. R. Evans (eds), *Handbook of cultural health psychology* (pp. 389–410). New York: Academic Press.

Chen, X. & Tse, H. C. (2008). Social functioning and adjustment in Canadian-born children with Chinese and European backgrounds. *Developmental Psychology, 44*, 1184–1189.

Chen, X., Wang, L., & DeSouza, A. (2006). Temperament and socio-emotional functioning in Chinese and North American children. In X. Chen, D. French, & B. Schneider (eds), *Peer relationships in cultural context* (pp. 123–147). New York: Cambridge University Press.

Chen, X., Wang, L., & Wang, Z. (2009). Shyness-sensitivity and social, school, and psychological adjustment in rural migrant and urban children in China. *Child Development, 80*, 1499–1513.

Cole, M. (1996). *Cultural psychology*. Cambridge, MA: Harvard University Press.

Coplan, R. J., Prakash, K., O'Neil, K., & Armer, M. (2004). Do you 'want' to play? Distinguishing between conflicted-shyness and social disinterest in early childhood. *Developmental Psychology, 40*, 244–258.

Corsaro, W. A. & Nelson, E. (2003). Children's collective activities and peer culture in early literacy in American and Italian preschools. *Sociology of Education*, 76, 209–227.

Crystal, D. S., Chen, C., Fuligni, A. J., Hsu, C. C., Ko, H. J., Kitamura, S., & Kimura, S. (1994). Psychological maladjustment and academic achievement: A cross-cultural study of Japanese, Chinese, and American high school students. *Child Development, 65*, 738–753.

Dodge, K. A., Coie, J. D., & Lynam, D. (2006). Aggression and antisocial behavior in youth. In N. Eisenberg (ed.), *Handbook of child psychology: Vol. 3. Social, emotional, and personality development* (pp. 719–88). New York: Wiley.

Dong, Q., Yang, B., & Ollendick, T. H. (1994). Fears in Chinese children and adolescents and their relations to anxiety and depression. *Journal of Child Psychology and Psychiatry, 35*, 351–363.

Edwards, C. P., Guzman, M. R. T., Brown, J., & Kumru, A. (2006). Children's social behaviors and peer interactions in diverse cultures. In X. Chen, D. French, & B. Schneider (eds), *Peer relationships in cultural context* (pp. 23–51). New York: Cambridge University Press.

Eisenberg, N., Fabes, R. A., & Spinrad, T. L. (2006). Prosocial development. In N. Eisenberg (ed.), *Handbook of child psychology: Vol. 3. Social, emotional, and personality development* (pp. 646–718). New York: Wiley.

Ekblad, S. (1989). Stability in aggression and aggression control in a sample of primary school children in China. *Acta Psychiatrica Scandinavia, 80*, 160–164.

Ekblad, S. & Olweus, D. (1986). Applicability of Olweus' Aggression Inventory in a sample of Chinese primary school children. *Aggressive Behavior, 12*, 315–325.

Fong, V. L. (2004). *Only hope: Coming of age under China's one-child policy*. Stanford, CA: Stanford University Press.

Fox, H. A., Henderson, H. A., Marshall, P. J., Nichols, K. E., & Ghera, M. M. (2005). Behavioral inhibition: Linking biology and behavior within a developmental framework. *Annual Review of Psychology, 56*, 235–262.

Freedman, D. G. & Freedman, N. C. (1969). Behavioral differences between Chinese-American and European-American newborns. *Nature, 224*, 1227.

Fuligni, A. J. & Zhang, W. X. (2004). Attitudes toward family obligation among adolescents in contemporary urban and rural China. *Child Development, 74*, 180–192.

Fung, H. (1999). Becoming a moral child: The socialization of shame among young Chinese children. *Ethos*, 27, 180–209.

Fung, H. (2006). Affect and early moral socialization: Some insights and contributions from indigenous psychological studies in Taiwan. In U. Kim, K. S. Yang, & K. K. Hwang (eds), *Indigenous and cultural psychology: Understanding people in context* (pp. 175–196). New York: Springer.

Gazelle, H. & Ladd, G. W. (2003). Anxious solitude and peer exclusion: A diathesis-stress model of internalizing trajectories in childhood. *Child Development, 74*, 257–278.

Gong, Y. (1984). Use of the Eysenck Personality Questionnaire in China. *Personality and Individual Differences, 5*, 431–438.

Greenfield, P. M., Suzuki, L. K., & Rothstein-Fisch, C. (2006). Cultural pathways through human development. In K. A. Renninger & I. E. Sigel (eds), *Handbook of child psychology: Vol. 4. Child psychology in practice* (pp. 655–699). New York: Wiley.
Guo, L., Yao, Y., & Yang, B. (2005). Adaptation of migrant children to the city: A case study at a migrant children school in Beijing. *Youth Study, 3*, 22–31.
Hart, C. H., Yang, C., Nelson, L. J., Robinson, C. C., Olson, J. A., Nelson, D. A., Porter, C. L., Jin, S., Olson, S. F., & Wu, P. (2000). Peer acceptance in early childhood and subtypes of socially withdrawn behavior in China, Russia and the United States. *International Journal of Behavioral Development, 24*, 73–81.
Ho, D. Y. F. (1986). Chinese pattern of socialization: A critical review. In M. H. Bond (ed.), *The psychology of the Chinese people* (pp. 1–37). Hong Kong: Oxford University Press.
Kagan, J. (1998). Temperament and the reactions to unfamiliarity. *Child Development, 68*, 139–143.
Kagan, J., Kearsley, R. B., & Zelazo, P. R. (1978). *Infancy: Its place in human development.* Cambridge, MA: Harvard University Press.
Kelley, M. L. (1992). Cultural differences in child rearing: A comparison of immigrant Chinese and Caucasian American mothers. *Journal of Cross-Cultural Psychology, 23*, 444–455.
Kleinman, A. (1980). *Patients and healers in the context of culture.* Berkeley, CA: University of California Press.
Kohnstamm, G. A., Halverson, C. F. Jr, Mervielde, I., & Havill, V. L. (1998). *Parental descriptions of child personality: Developmental antecedents of the Big Five?* Mahwah, NJ: Erlbaum.
Lau, S. & Kwok, L. K. (2000). Relationship of family environment to adolescents' depression and self-concept. *Social Behavior and Personality, 28*, 41–50.
Lee, M. R., Okazaki, S., & Yoo, H. C. (2006). Frequency and intensity of social anxiety in Asian Americans and European Americans. *Cultural Diversity and Ethnic Minority Psychology, 12*, 291–305.
Lesch, K. P., Bengel, D., Heilis, A., Sabol, S. Z., Greenberg, B. D., Petri, S., Benjamin, J., Muller, C. R., Hamer, D. H., & Murphy, D. L. (1996). Association of anxiety-related traits with a polymorphism in the serotonin transporter gene regulatory region. *Science, 274*, 1527–1531.
Li, J. (2002). The importance of research on adolescent suicide in China. *China Youth Study, 22*, 46–50.
Liu, M., Chen, X., Rubin, K. H., Zheng, S., Cui, L., Li, D., Chen, H., & Wang, L. (2005). Autonomy- vs. connectedness-oriented parenting behaviors in Chinese and Canadian mothers. *International Journal of Behavioral Development, 29*, 489–495.
Luo, G. (1996). *Chinese traditional social and moral ideas and rules.* Beijing, China: The University of Chinese People Press. (in Chinese)
Maccoby, E. E., & Martin, C. N. (1983). Socialization in the context of the family: Parent–child interaction. In E. M. Hetherington (ed.), *Handbook of child psychology: Vol.4. Socialization, personality and social development* (pp. 1–102). New York: Wiley.
Miller, J. G. (1994). Cultural diversity in the morality of caring: Individually oriented versus duty-based interpersonal moral codes. *Cross-Cultural Research, 28*, 3–39.
Navon, R. & Ramsey, P. G. (1989). Possession and exchange of materials in Chinese and American preschools. *Journal of Research on Childhood Education, 4*, 18–29.
Oettingen, G., Little, T. D., Lindenberger, U., & Baltes, P. B. (1994). Causality, agency and control beliefs in East versus West Berlin children: A natural experiment in the control of context. *Journal of Personality and Social Psychology, 66*, 579–595.
Orlick, T., Zhou, Q. Y., & Partington, J. (1990). Co-operation and conflict within Chinese and Canadian kindergarten settings. *Canadian Journal of Behavioural Science, 22*, 20–25.
Potter, S. H. (1988). The cultural construction of emotion in rural Chinese social life. *Ethos, 16*, 181–208.
Rao, N. & Stewart, S. M. (1999). Cultural influences on sharer and recipient behavior: Sharing in Chinese and Indian preschool children. *Journal of Cross-Cultural Psychology, 30*, 219–241.
Rodkin, P. C., Farmer, T. W., Pearl, R., & van Acker, R. (2000). Heterogeneity of popular boys: Antisocial and prosocial configurations. *Developmental Psychology, 36*, 14–24.
Rogoff, B. (2003). *The cultural nature of human development*. New York: Oxford University Press.
Rothbart, M. K. & Bates, J. E. (2006). Temperament. In N. Eisenberg (ed.), *Handbook of child psychology: Vol. 3, Social, emotional, and personality development* (pp. 99–166). New York: Wiley.
Rubin, K. H., Bukowski, W., & Parker, J. G. (2006). Peer interactions, relationships, and groups. In N. Eisenberg (ed.), *Handbook of child psychology: Vol 3. Social, emotional, and personality development* (pp. 571–645). New York: Wiley.
Rubin, K. H., Burgess, K. B., & Coplan, R. J. (2002). Social withdrawal and shyness. In P. K. Smith & C. H. Hart (eds), *Blackwell handbook of childhood social development* (pp. 330–352), Malden, MA: Blackwell Publishers.
Rubin, K. H., Chen, X., McDougall, P., Bowker, A., & McKinnon, J. (1995). The Waterloo Longitudinal Project: Predicting adolescent internalizing and externalizing problems from early and mid-childhood. *Development and Psychopathology, 7*, 751–764.
Sabbagh, M. A., Xu, F., Carlson, S. M., Moses, L. J., & Lee, K. (2006). The development of executive functioning and theory of mind: A comparison of Chinese and U.S. preschoolers. *Psychological Science, 17*, 74–81.
Shen, R. (2006). Problems and solutions for child education for migrant rural worker families. *Journal of China Agricultural University (Social Science Edition), 64*, 96–100.

Silbereisen, R. K. (2000). German unification and adolescents' developmental timetables: Continuities and discontinuities. In L. A. Crockett, & R. K. Silbereisen (eds), *Negotiating adolescence in times of social change* (pp. 104–22). Cambridge, England: Cambridge University Press.

Solomon, R. H. (1971). *Mao's revolution and the Chinese political culture.* Berkeley, CA: University of California Press.

Stevenson, H. W. (1991). The development of prosocial behavior in large-scale collective societies: China and Japan. In R. A. Hinde & J. Groebel (eds), *Cooperation and prosocial behaviour* (pp. 89–105). Cambridge, UK: Cambridge University Press.

Stewart, S. M., Rao, N., Bond, M. H., McBride-Chang, C., Fielding, R., & Kennard, B. (1998). Chinese dimensions of parenting: Broadening western predictors and outcomes. *International Journal of Psychology, 33*, 345–358.

Super, C. M. & Harkness, S. (1986). The developmental niche: A conceptualization at the interface of child and culture. *International Journal of Behavioral Development, 9*, 545–569.

Tamis-LeMonda, C. S., Way, N., Hughes, D., Yoshikawa, H., Kalman, R. K., & Niwa, E. (2008). Parents' goals for children: The dynamic co-existence of collectivism and individualism in cultures and individuals. *Social Development, 17*, 183–209.

Triandis, H. C. (1995). *Individualism and collectivism.* Boulder, CO: Westview Press.

Tsai, S. J., Hong, C. J., & Cheng, C. Y. (2002). Serotonin transporter genetic polymorphisms and harm avoidance in the Chinese. *Psychiatric Genetics 12*, 165–168.

Vygotsky, L. S. (1978). *Mind in society: The development of higher psychological processes.* Cambridge, MA: Harvard University Press.

Wang, Q. (2003). Emotion situation knowledge in American and Chinese preschool children and adults. *Cognition and Emotion, 17, 5*, 725–746.

Weisz, J. R., Suwanlert, S., Chaiyasit, W., Weiss, B., Walter, B. R., & Anderson, W. W. (1988). Thai and American perspectives on over- and under-controlled child behavior problems: Exploring the threshold model among parents, teachers, and psychologists. *Journal of Consulting and Clinical Psychology, 56*, 601–609.

Wu, D. Y. H. (1981). Child abuse in Taiwan. In J. E. Korbin (ed.), *Child abuse and neglect: Cross-cultural perspectives* (pp. 139–165). Los Angeles, CA: University of California Press.

Wu, D. Y. H. (1996). Chinese childhood socialization. In M. H. Bond (ed.), *The psychology of the Chinese people* (pp. 143–154). Hong Kong: Oxford University Press.

Yang, K. S. (1986). Chinese personality and its change. In M. H. Bond (ed.), *The psychology of the Chinese people* (pp. 106–170). Hong Kong: Oxford University Press.

Yu, R. (2002). On the reform of elementary school education in China. *Educational Exploration, 129*, 56–57.

Zhou, Q., Hofer, C., Eisenberg, N., Reiser, M., Spinrad, T. L., & Fabes, R. A. (2007). The developmental trajectories of attention focusing, attentional and behavioral persistence, and externalizing problems during school-age years. *Developmental Psychology, 43*, 369–385.

CHAPTER 5

Parenting and child socialization in contemporary China

Qian Wang and Lei Chang

The ostensible peculiarities, as well as similarities, of parenting and child socialization in China vis-à-vis Western countries such as the United States have been capturing intellectual curiosity and creating debate among investigators in the past few decades (for representative reviews, see Chao & Tseng, 2002; Ho, 1986; Lau, 1996; Wu, 1996). Drawing on relatively recent empirical research in three major Chinese societies (mainland China, Hong Kong, and Taiwan), we attempt in this chapter to depict a state-of-the-art picture of parenting and child socialization in contemporary China. Particular attention will be paid to the growing body of research conducted with only children in urban areas of mainland China, given that they constitute a substantial proportion of the youth population in contemporary Chinese societies.

In reviewing the extant literature, we search for answers to three questions that have been of enduring or burgeoning interest to investigators. First, how do Western frameworks characterizing parenting and child socialization apply in China, a culture commonly believed to be interdependence-oriented, in contrast to many Western cultures, such as the United States, commonly believed to be independence-oriented (e.g. Greenfield, Keller, Fuligni, & Maynard, 2003; Sorkhabi, 2005)? Second, what are the notions of parenting and child socialization indigenous to Chinese culture that may be absent or under-examined in the existing Western frameworks? Third, how does the portrait of typical Chinese parenting as hierarchical, authoritarian, and gender-unequal (see Chao & Tseng, 2002; Ho, 1986; Lau, 1996) hold, given the drastic economic, societal, and cultural changes that have been rapidly taking place in contemporary Chinese societies, particularly in mainland China (e.g. Chan, Ng, & Hui, this volume; Chen, this volume; Kulich, this volume)? We conclude with our insights into these issues and discuss emerging and future directions for research on Chinese parenting and child socialization.

Contemporary Chinese parenting scrutinized under Western frameworks

There are many apparent discrepancies across different investigators' theoretical articulations, terminologies, and operational definitions of the constructs characterizing parenting and child socialization (for summaries of key elements of parenting commonly studied in Western cultures, see Barber, Stolz, & Olsen, 2006; Nelson, Nelson, Hart, Yang, & Jin, 2006; Stewart & Bond, 2002). Nevertheless, decades of research in Western cultures have attested to the significance of an assortment of parental behaviors and affect toward children that are well captured by two major frameworks: Baumrind's authoritative–authoritarian parenting typologies (Baumrind, 1971; see also Maccoby & Martin, 1983), and Rohner's parental acceptance–rejection theory (Rohner, Khaleque, & Cournoyer, 2007).

Authoritative parenting entails that parents are warm, responsive, and supportive to children, use reasoning and induction with children, grant children autonomy and encourage democratic participation by children, yet maintain appropriate monitoring of children and set reasonable rules for children. These components of parenting convey parents' acceptance of and care for children, and have positive consequences for children's development. In contrast, authoritarian parenting involves that parents use punitive disciplinary techniques rather than reasoning and induction with children, impose physical punishment and coercion upon children, and are verbally hostile and psychologically controlling toward children. These components of parenting convey parents' rejection of and lack of care for children, and have negative consequences for children's development. As reviewed below, there is convergent evidence for similar meanings and functional relevance to those documented in Western cultures of all the aforementioned aspects of parenting in contemporary Chinese societies, despite divergent evidence due to methodological issues.

Convergent evidence for the applicability of Western frameworks to Chinese parenting

Meanings of Western parenting practices in China. Taking a qualitative approach, Chang and colleagues (see Chang, 2006) presented, in individual interviews, items from Western measures of authoritative and authoritarian parenting to a sample of parents in Beijing, China. Authoritative parenting encompassed the dimensions of warmth, easy-going responsiveness, inductive reasoning, and democratic participation, while authoritarian parenting encompassed the dimensions of authoritarian directiveness, non-reasoning, verbal hostility, and physical punishment. All items were endorsed by the parents as meaningful and relevant, indicating the applicability of the Western authoritative–authoritarian framework to Chinese parenting.

Such applicability is also evident in quantitative studies. Chang and colleagues (see Chang, 2006) examined samples of primary- and secondary-school children and their mothers in Beijing and Shanghai, China. Mothers rated their child-rearing behaviors on Likert scales in response to the items tapping authoritative and authoritarian parenting used in the above-mentioned qualitative study. Confirmatory factor analyses of mothers' responses revealed factor structures that were consistent with those found in Western cultures. Wu and colleagues (2002) examined samples of mothers of preschoolers in Beijing and in an urban area in the United States. Two-group confirmatory factor analyses were conducted to directly compare Chinese and American mothers' ratings of their child-rearing behaviors, in response to items from Western measures of authoritative and authoritarian parenting. The revealed factor structures were invariant between the two countries.

Similar evidence has been found in studies with adolescents. Supple and colleagues (2004) asked a sample of adolescents in Beijing, ranging in age from twelve to nineteen years, to rate their parents' behaviors in response to items based on Western frameworks that tapped support, autonomy granting, monitoring, punitiveness, and love withdrawal. Confirmatory factor analyses of children's responses revealed factor structures for these parenting dimensions that were similar to those found in Western cultures. Wang, Pomerantz, and Chen (2007) examined samples of early adolescents in Beijing, China and Chicago, the United States at the beginning and end of seventh grade. At both times of data collection, children rated their parents' behaviors along the dimensions of psychological control, autonomy support, and behavioral control, with most of the items adopted from Western measures. Two-group confirmatory factor analyses revealed measurement equivalence across country and across time for these parenting dimensions. Taken together, findings from the foregoing studies suggest that aspects of parenting derived from Western frameworks are meaningful and equivalent in capturing Chinese parenting.

Functional relevance of aspects of Western parenting in China. There is also evidence for similar functional relevance in China of those aspects of parenting that were originally identified in Western cultures. In the quantitative studies by Chang and colleagues (see Chang, 2006), authoritative parenting was consistently found to be positively associated with children's academic performance, favorable self-concept, and pro-social leadership, but negatively associated with children's social withdrawal. In contrast, authoritarian parenting was consistently found to be negatively associated with children's academic performance, favorable self-concept, and pro-social leadership, but positively associated with children's aggression. These findings are similar to those documented in Western cultures, and replicate those from a study conducted a decade earlier with a sample of primary-school children and their parents in Beijing (Chen, Dong, & Zhou, 1997). The negative effects of several specific dimensions of authoritarian parenting on the development of Chinese children are also similar to those found in Western cultures. For example, harsh parenting in terms of physical coercion and psychological control has been linked to heightened aggression among both preschool children in Beijing (Chang, Schwartz, Dodge, & McBride-Chang, 2003; Nelson, Hart, Yang, Olsen, & Jin, 2006) and primary-school children in Hong Kong, China (Chang, Lansford, Schwartz, & Farver, 2004; Chang, Stewart, McBride-Chang, & Au, 2003). The associations between parents' physical discipline and children's heightened anxiety and aggression have been found among children of various ages, ranging from middle childhood to late adolescence, in Beijing (Lansford, Chang, Dodge, Malone, Oburu, Palmérus et al., 2005).

In the study by Supple and colleagues (2004; see also Peterson, Cobas, Bush, Supple, & Wilson, 2004) with a sample of adolescents in Beijing, parental support, autonomy granting, and monitoring were found to be associated with children's heightened self-esteem and more positive orientation toward academics, in line with findings from Western cultures. In addition, the foregoing three aspects of parenting were found to be related to heightened conformity of children to parents' expectations, a developmental outcome relatively less examined in prior work. In contrast, parental punitiveness was found to be associated with undesirable developmental outcomes among children, such as dampened self-esteem, diminished conformity to parents' expectations, and less positive orientations toward academics. Also consistent with findings from Western cultures, a longitudinal study by Shek (2007) with a sample of early adolescents in Hong Kong showed detrimental effects of parental psychological control, such that psychological control was associated with a dampened sense of mastery, lower life satisfaction, and lower self-esteem but a heightened sense of hopelessness among children, both concurrently and one year later.

Further evidence for cross-cultural similarities has emerged from several studies that directly compared samples in China and the United States. In a study of eleventh graders in Tianjin, China and the greater Los Angeles area, the United States, Greenberger, Chen, Tally, and Dong (2000) found that parental warmth and acceptance predicted dampened depression among both Chinese and American adolescents, with a stronger effect in China. In another study of seventh and eighth graders in Beijing and Taipei, China and those of Chinese versus European descent in southern California, the United States, Chen, Greenberger, Lester, Dong, and Guo (1998) found that parent–child relations lacking parental warmth and monitoring were associated with heightened misconduct among adolescents, regardless of their cultural origins or residential regions. A more recent multination study by Barber, Stolz, and Olsen (2006) showed significant relations of parental support to heightened social initiative and dampened depression, of parental psychological control to heightened depression, and of parental behavioral control to dampened antisocial behavior among school-going urban adolescents in both China and the United States, as well as in a number of other countries.

The study by Wang, Pomerantz, and Chen (2007) of early adolescents in Beijing and Chicago at the beginning and end of seventh grade moved beyond prior work in that it was both longitudinal and cross-cultural. Negative effects of parental psychological control on children's emotional functioning, positive effects of parental autonomy support on children's emotional as well as academic functioning, and positive effects of parental behavioral control on children's academic functioning were documented over time in both China and the United States. Interestingly, whereas the effects of psychological and behavioral control were of similar strength in the two countries, those of autonomy support were generally stronger in the United States. This finding is consistent with the idea that autonomy is valued to a greater extent in independence-oriented cultures, such as the United States, than in interdependence-oriented cultures, such as China (e.g. Greenfield et al., 2003). To summarize, the foregoing body of research indicates that aspects of parenting derived from Western frameworks generally play similar roles in Chinese children's development.

Divergent evidence for the applicability of Western frameworks to Chinese parenting

Yet there is a handful of research showing different effects on Chinese children's (versus their Western counterparts') development of some of the aforementioned aspects of parenting. Notably, most of this research was conducted with Chinese immigrant children in the United States (e.g. Chao, 2001; Dornbusch, Ritter, Leiderman, Roberts, & Fraleigh, 1987; Steinberg, Lamborn, Darling, Mounts, & Dornbusch, 1994), and revealed no effects of authoritative or authoritarian parenting on Chinese-American children's academic achievement. This is different from the findings that authoritative parenting has beneficial effects whereas authoritarian parenting has detrimental effects on the academic achievement of European-American children. In contrast, the positive effects of authoritative parenting and the negative effects of authoritarian parenting on children's socio-emotional functioning were similarly evident among children of diverse ethnicities, including Chinese, in the United States (Steinberg, Mounts, Lamborn, & Dornbusch, 1991).

Rather than entirely attributing the foregoing differences in the effects of authoritative and authoritarian parenting on the academic achievement of Chinese- versus European-American children to their different cultural origins, several investigators have emphasized the role of immigrant status. For instance, immigrant status may highlight the utility of academic achievement (Sue & Okazaki, 1990) and the negative consequences of academic failure (Steinberg, Dornbusch, & Brown, 1992) to Chinese-American children. Such factors may have significant impact on Chinese-American children's academic achievement and render the effects of parenting different from those on European-American children. We join these investigators as well as others (e.g. Phinney & Landin, 1998) in recognizing the confounding of immigrant status and culture in research with immigrant Chinese parents and children residing in Western countries.

A few studies of children residing in Chinese societies also reported effects different from those found in Western cultures of some aspects of parenting derived from Western frameworks. For example, McBride-Chang and Chang (1998) found no relations of either authoritative or authoritarian parenting to children's school performance in a sample of Chinese adolescents in Hong Kong. However, when analyses were conducted at the group rather than the individual level, it was found that parents of children from schools with higher achievement levels were more authoritative and less authoritarian than parents of children from schools with lower achievement levels. Thus, the authors sensibly acknowledged that it might be premature to invalidate the applicability of authoritative and authoritarian parenting in predicting Chinese children's academic achievement. In a cross-cultural study of adolescents in Hong Kong, the United States, and Australia, Leung, Lau, and Lam (1998) employed items from Western measures tapping authoritative and authoritarian parenting, and further divided each along the general versus academic dimension. They found that in Hong Kong, neither general nor academic parental authoritativeness was associated with children's school performance, while parents' academic authoritarianism was negatively but general authoritarianism was positively associated with children's school performance. In contrast, in the United States and Australia, parents' general authoritativeness was positively and general authoritarianism was negatively associated with children's school performance, consistent with previous findings in these Western cultures. In addition, in the United States and Australia, parents' academic authoritarianism was negatively associated with, but academic authoritativeness was unrelated to, children's school performance.

In the study by Supple and colleagues (2004) of adolescents in Beijing, it was found that parental love withdrawal (a major component of psychological control) was unrelated to developmental outcomes, such as self-esteem, orientation toward academics, and conformity to parents' expectations. These findings are different from those by other investigators in both China and Western cultures (e.g. Barber et al., 2006; Wang et al., 2007). Both Leung et al (1998) and Supple et al (2004) concluded that certain aspects of child-rearing behaviors derived from Western frameworks might not be applicable to Chinese parenting. However, a closer look at these studies suggests that caution is warranted in drawing such conclusions, because the measures employed seem to be somewhat lacking in terms of their psychometric properties. For example, in the study by Leung and colleagues (1998), after further dividing authoritative and authoritarian parenting along the general and academic dimension, the measures of the four constructs under examination consisted of no more than four items and Cronbach's α, which indicates internal consistency of the measures, fell below .60 in most cases. In the study by Supple and colleagues (2004), the measure of parental love withdrawal consisted of only two items after omitting items that were cross-loaded on other constructs under examination. As Stewart and Bond (2002) have argued, when adapting Western measures of a given parenting construct for use in non-Western cultures, it is essential to include items that cover a reasonably wide range, are closely related to one another, and emerge as coherent in factor analyses. Falling short of these criteria may preclude any definite conclusions from being drawn, as with the studies by Leung et al (1998) and Supple et al (2004).

Contemporary Chinese parenting reflected in indigenous notions

The notion of *guan*

While significant endeavors have been made to investigate the meanings and functional relevance in Chinese societies of the key aspects of parenting derived from Western frameworks, notable research has also been conducted to uncover aspects of parenting that may be of particular significance in Chinese culture, yet are unidentified or under-studied in prior work in Western cultures. One of such aspects is *guan* (training), introduced by Chao (1994). *Guan* taps into the sense of responsibility endorsed by Chinese parents in their child rearing. Central to this responsibility is that parents 'govern' and 'train' children through providing close monitoring, firm directives, and high demands to help children develop into well-functioning members of society. Chao (1994) made the case that Chinese parenting would be better understood in terms of child-rearing ideologies and practices associated with *guan*, rather than by using constructs derived from Western frameworks, such as authoritative and authoritarian parenting. It was expected that *guan* ideologies and practices would be endorsed by Chinese parents to a greater extent than by Western parents, and be more predictive of Chinese children's functioning, particularly academic achievement, than would aspects of parenting derived from Western frameworks.

Indeed, immigrant Chinese parents in the United States were found to endorse child-rearing ideologies associated with *guan*—e.g. 'Mothers should do everything for their child's education and make many sacrifices'—to a greater extent than did European-American parents (Chao, 1994; Chao, 2000; Jose, Huntsinger, Huntsinger, & Liaw, 2000). However, Chinese parents in Taiwan and European-American parents endorsed such ideologies to a similar extent (Jose et al., 2000); so did Chinese parents in Hong Kong in comparison with their counterparts in the United Kingdom (Pearson & Rao, 2003). Moreover, no association was found between parents' *guan* ideologies and children's academic achievement in a sample of Chinese adolescents in Hong Kong (McBride-Chang & Chang, 1998), nor were mothers' *guan* ideologies found to be related to their preschoolers' peer competence in either Hong Kong or the United Kingdom (Pearson & Rao, 2003).

Stewart and colleagues (1998; 2002) conducted a series of studies examining the relations of parental *guan* to children's overall well-being. They employed a measure of parenting practices associated with *guan* based on Chao's (1994) questionnaire of *guan* ideologies, measures of parenting practices in terms of warmth and restrictive control, and measures of well-being in terms of perceived health and life satisfaction, tailored to Chinese culture. Stewart, Rao, Bond, McBride-Chang, Fielding, & Kennard (1998) found positive relations of parental *guan* to the well-being of late adolescent girls in Hong Kong. *Guan* was also positively related to parental warmth, but unrelated to parental restrictive control. After adjusting for the effects of parental warmth and restrictive control on children's well-being, the contribution of parental *guan* to children's well-being became non-significant.

Intriguingly, there is also evidence that Chinese parents' ideologies and practices associated with *guan* are positively related to both authoritative and authoritarian parenting (Chen & Luster, 2002; Pearson & Rao, 2003). In a study by Stewart, Bond, Kennard, Ho, & Zaman (2002), the above-mentioned measure of *guan* was administered to late adolescent girls in Hong Kong, Pakistan, and the United States. Supporting the 'exportability' of the Chinese notion of *guan* to other cultures, these investigators found comparable internal consistency of the *guan* measure, similar positive associations between parental *guan* and parental warmth, and similar positive relations of parental *guan* to children's well-being in all three cultural groups.

Other indigenous notions

In the study by Wu and colleagues (2002), mothers of preschoolers in Beijing and in an urban area in the United States were administered measures of parenting practices that were deemed particularly important in China, based on relevant literature and focus-group interviews with Chinese parents. Such parenting practices included encouragement of modesty, protection, maternal involvement, shaming/love withdrawal, and directiveness. Meaningful factor structures for measures of these parenting practices emerged that were invariant in China and the United States. Yet, as expected, Chinese mothers endorsed these practices to a greater extent than did American parents, except for maternal involvement, which was endorsed at similar levels.

Lieber and colleagues (2006) administered to samples of parents of preschoolers in Hong Kong and Taiwan a questionnaire consisting of a comprehensive set of items that tap aspects of parenting documented by both Chinese (e.g. Chao, 1994; Fung, 1999) and Western investigators (e.g. Baumrind, 1971; Maccoby & Martin, 1983). They identified four key dimensions of Chinese child-rearing beliefs: training, shame, autonomy, and authoritativeness. Training was based on Chao's (1994) idea of *guan*, representing an essential aspect of parenting that was assumed to be unique to Chinese culture; so was shaming, which was believed to be typically used by Chinese parents as an effective socialization tool to teach children lessons about 'right and wrong', and to motivate children to constantly engage in self-improvement (Fung, 1999). The autonomy and authoritativeness dimensions both seemed to involve parental promotion of children's exploration of the environment, expression of themselves, and self-esteem. Indeed, these two dimensions were found to be closely related to each other. Furthermore, training was found to be positively related to the authoritative and autonomy dimensions.

Chang and colleagues took a refreshing 'bottom-up' approach that did not limit the aspects of parenting under study to those assumed in prior literature to be particularly relevant to either Chinese or Western cultures (see Chang, 2006; Wang & Chang, 2008). In their ongoing work, they conducted unstructured interviews with a sample of parents with children of all ages in Beijing, and derived from the interviews aspects of parenting that were of concern to these parents from diverse educational and socioeconomic backgrounds. Interestingly, in addition to expressing concerns over their children's psychological and emotional well-being as much as their Western counterparts would, the Chinese parents interviewed, who mostly had only one child, expressed substantial concerns over their children's physical and material well-being. Moreover, consistent with the observation that Chinese parenting is focused on promoting children's educational attainment (see Chao & Tseng, 2002; Ho, 1986; Lau, 1996; Wu, 1996), when the Chinese parents interviewed talked about being controlling with their children, their reported exercise of control was almost exclusively over their children's academic work.

Based on these insights into Chinese parenting, Chang and colleagues developed items tapping child-rearing practices that address parental concerns over children's physical and material well-being as well as capture parental control in the academic arena. These items include: 'We do everything we can to make sure our child is healthy' (physical warmth), 'Within our financial abilities, we will satisfy most of our child's material needs' (material warmth), 'We punish our child physically if s/he does not do well in school' (physical academic authoritarianism), and 'We take away our child's material privileges if s/he does not do well in school' (material academic authoritarianism). These items together with items adopted from Western measures tapping authoritative and authoritarian parenting were administered to mothers of primary- and secondary-school children in Beijing and Shanghai. Information on a variety of developmental outcomes in children of these mothers was also collected.

Confirmatory factor analyses evidenced the construct validity of parental physical-material warmth and parental physical-material academic authoritarianism. These constructs were associated with authoritative and authoritarian parenting in expected ways, i.e. physical-material warmth was positively associated with authoritative parenting but negatively associated with authoritarian parenting, while physical-material academic authoritarianism was negatively associated with authoritative parenting but positively associated with authoritarian parenting. More importantly, structural equation modeling revealed that these two additional aspects of parenting made unique contributions to Chinese children's development. After adjusting for the relations of authoritative and authoritarian parenting to the developmental outcomes in children, parental physical-material warmth still significantly predicted children's heightened academic performance and dampened aggression, while its positive relation to children's favorable self-concept became non-significant. Intriguingly, the positive relation of physical-material warmth to children's pro-social leadership became negative after taking into account its shared variance with authoritative and authoritarian parenting. The negative relations to children's academic performance and favorable self-concept as well as the positive relations to children's aggression and withdrawal of parental physical-material academic authoritarianism remained significant after taking into account the role of authoritative and authoritarian parenting. However, the negative relation to children's pro-social leadership of parental physical-material academic authoritarianism became non-significant once its shared variance with authoritative and authoritarian parenting was adjusted.

Summary

To summarize, a burgeoning body of research is revealing interesting aspects of parenting that have not been the focus of previous work in Western cultures. Notably, although the new or additional aspects of parenting examined in the studies reported above may be unidentified or under-studied in Western cultures, they may not be completely distinct from those aspects of parenting originally identified and widely studied in Western cultures, nor may they be unique to Chinese culture. For example, *guan* has been found to be quite closely related to parental warmth, and its 'exportability' to Western cultures has been demonstrated (Stewart et al., 1998; Stewart et al., 2002). In Wu and colleagues' work (2002), the parenting practices deemed as particularly emphasized in China were found to be more or less associated with authoritative and authoritarian parenting. Moreover, these 'Chinese' parenting practices were found to be meaningful to American parents as well. Chang and colleagues (see Chang 2006; Wang & Chang, 2008) also found significant relations between authoritative and authoritarian parenting and the physical and material dimensions of parental warmth and academic control identified in their research with Chinese parents.

These 'additional' dimensions of parenting actually have captured the attention, albeit fleeting, of a few Western investigators (e.g. Roe & Siegelman, 1963; see Wang & Chang, 2008). It is particularly noteworthy that research on the functional relevance of these indigenous Chinese aspects of parenting is still quite limited. For example, evidence for the effects of *guan* on various arenas of children's development is only emerging. The effects on children's development of the parenting practices and beliefs identified by Wu et al (2002) and Lieber et al (2006), as well as of the physical and material dimensions of parental warmth and academic control documented by Chang and colleagues (see Chang, 2006; Wang & Chang, 2008), need to be further investigated in both Chinese and Western cultures.

Persistent themes in Chinese parenting revisited

Relationships and interactions between parents and children in Chinese culture have been typically portrayed as hierarchical and authoritarian, gender-unequal, and academically focused (see Chao & Tseng, 2002; Ho, 1986; Lau, 1996). Below we draw on relatively recent research to appraise the current relevance of these persistent themes.

Is Chinese parenting authoritarian?

Mixed evidence from comparative research. Wu and colleagues (2002) found that Chinese mothers of preschoolers in Beijing endorsed physical coercion toward children to a greater extent and endorsed warmth toward children and children's democratic participation to a lesser extent than did their American counterparts. Pearson and Rao (2003) found that, compared with their English counterparts in the United Kingdom, Chinese mothers of preschoolers in Hong Kong reported themselves as engaging in higher levels of authoritarian parenting and similar levels of authoritative parenting. In an observational study Jose and colleagues (2002) found that Chinese mothers of preschoolers in Taiwan were more direct, but no less warm, when interacting with their children than were their American counterparts.

Research on parenting adolescents also yields findings that are not entirely consistent. Chen and colleagues (1998) documented higher levels of warmth among European-American parents than among Chinese parents in Beijing and Taipei, as reported by their adolescent offspring. However, in a study by Greenberger and colleagues (2002), Chinese adolescents in Tianjin reported higher levels of parental warmth than did American adolescents. The study by Wang et al (2007) revealed higher levels of psychological control but lower levels of autonomy support as well as lower levels of behavioral control among Chinese parents in Beijing than among American parents in Chicago, as reported by their early adolescent offspring. In terms of parents granting children autonomy in making decisions over a variety of issues in daily life, e.g. 'How much TV I watch' and 'Who I make friends with', Chinese early adolescents reported having less say in such decision making than did their American counterparts (Qin, Pomerantz, & Wang, 2008). Also focusing on daily-life issues, Feldman and Rosenthal (1991) found that Chinese adolescents in Hong Kong expected to make decisions on their own at an older age than did their counterparts in the United States and Australia. Interestingly, such later autonomy expectations of adolescents of Asian descent (including Chinese) versus those of Western descent were evident among adolescents attending the same international school in Hong Kong (Deeds, Stewart, Bond, & Westrick, 1998).

Reasons for the apparent inconsistency in this relatively small body of comparative research may include differences across studies in the specific constructs under examination, specific measures employed, and specific characteristics of the samples recruited. Nevertheless, the lack of convergent evidence for a depiction of Chinese parents as hierarchical and authoritarian is noteworthy. Such a potential stereotype may be better understood through alternative lenses.

Rethinking Chinese parental authoritarianism. One alternative is to pay due attention to within- rather than cross-culture comparisons. Indeed, when Chinese parents' authoritarian and authoritative beliefs and practices in child rearing are compared against each other, instead of being compared with those of their Western counterparts, there is substantial evidence that Chinese parenting is quite authoritative. For example, in a study by Xu and colleagues (2005), a sample of Chinese mothers of two-year-olds in Shanghai reported on their authoritarian and authoritative parenting practices on a five-point Likert scale where 1 = strongly disagree and 5 = strongly agree. While the mean rating of authoritarian parenting in this sample was 2.9, just below the middle point of 3 (= neither disagree nor agree), that of authoritative parenting was 4.3 (for similar findings, see Chen et al., 1997; Pearson & Rao, 2003). In the study by Wang et al (2007), early adolescents in Beijing reported on their parents' exertion of psychological control and autonomy support on a five-point Likert scale (1 = not at all true, 5 = very true). While the mean rating of parental psychological control in this sample was 2.8, falling between 2 (= a little bit true) and 3 (= kind of true) on the scale, that of parental autonomy support was 3.5, falling between 3 (= kind of true) and 4 (= pretty true) on the scale (for similar findings, see Barber et al., 2006). In addition, there is evidence for considerable input of Chinese children in making decisions over issues in their daily life, either by children making decisions on their own or by children making decisions together with their parents, rather than parents unilaterally deciding for their children (Qin et al., 2008; Xia, Xie, Zhou, DeFrain, Meredith, & Combs, 2004).

As mentioned earlier, Chang and colleagues identified additional aspects of parenting not focused on in previous work in Western cultures, i.e. physical-material warmth and physical-material academic authoritarianism (see Chang, 2006; Wang & Chang, 2008). This work provides a second alternative to 'stereotyping' Chinese parenting as authoritarian. It was found that Chinese parents endorsed to a considerable extent (i.e. above 4.0 on a five-point Likert scale where 1 = strongly disagree, 5 = strongly agree) child-rearing practices in terms of physical-material warmth, suggesting that prior work focusing only on psychological-emotional warmth may have underestimated Chinese parents' warmth toward their children. Moreover, it was found that Chinese parents' control was almost exclusively over children's academic work. This finding echoes both parenting researchers' recognition of educational achievement as a major concern of Chinese parents in raising their children (e.g. Chao & Tseng, 2002; Ho, 1986; Wu, 1996), and motivation researchers' recognition of parenting as a major influence on Chinese children's educational achievement (e.g. Hau, this volume; Pomerantz, Ng, & Q. Wang, 2008; Stevenson, Lee, C. Chen, Stigler, Hus, & Kitamura, 1990).

Indeed, Ng and colleagues (2008) found that Chinese mothers of primary-school children in Hong Kong were more likely to view parents trying their best to motivate and help children in schoolwork as reflecting parental love, whereas their American counterparts were more likely to view it as reflecting parental duty. Wang and Pomerantz (2008a) found that over the course of early adolescence, decrements in children's school performance were predictive of Chinese, but not American, parents' increased levels of psychological control. Cheung and Pomerantz (2008) found that Chinese, but not American, parents' psychological control was positively associated with their involvement in their children's schoolwork. These findings suggest that Chinese parents' authoritarianism, which tends to be centered on children's schoolwork, is more likely to reflect parents' intentions to assist their children in achieving academically than to reflect lack of love and warmth.

Yet such well-meant parenting may, unfortunately, backfire (for an account of how such well-meant parenting backfires in Western cultures, see Grolnick, 2003). As mentioned earlier, Wang and Chang (2008) found that parental physical-material academic authoritarianism had negative effects on a number of aspects of Chinese children's development, including academic performance. Wang and Pomerantz (2008a) found that increases in Chinese parents' psychological control, which were associated with decrements in their children's school performance, predicted subsequently worse rather than improved performance among children.

Is Chinese parenting gender-unequal?

Besides heightened parental control and the centering of parenting on children's educational achievement, another common perception of Chinese parenting and child socialization concerns gender differentiation, whereby males are favored over females due to the tradition of patrilineage and associated son preference (see Ho, 1986; Lau, 1996). In terms of the aspects of parenting commonly studied in extant research, however, there is relatively little systematic examination of Chinese parents' differential treatment of their male versus female offspring.

The few studies that have paid attention to the issue of gender surprisingly showed gender differences in favor of girls. In a study by Chang and colleagues (2003) of a sample of kindergarteners and their parents in a southern Chinese city, fathers of boys reported themselves as engaging in higher levels of harsh parenting than did fathers of girls, while mothers of boys and girls reported themselves as engaging in similar levels of harsh parenting. In a study by Chen and colleagues (2000) of a sample of primary-school children in Shanghai, boys and girls reported similar levels of maternal and paternal warmth and indulgence, while boys reported higher levels of paternal control than did girls. In a study by Wang and Pomerantz (2008b) of a sample of early adolescents in Beijing, boys and girls reported similar levels of parental autonomy support, behavioral control, and involvement in their schoolwork, while boys reported higher levels of parental psychological control than did girls. A study by Shek (2007) of Chinese adolescents in Hong Kong also found that boys reported their parents to be more psychologically controlling than did girls. Notably, although the foregoing handful of research appears to support a generally gender-equal depiction of Chinese parenting and child socialization, caution is advised against drawing a blanket conclusion, because gender differences may exist in other aspects of parenting, such as encouragement of children's gender-typed activities and career choices (Cheung, 1996).

Summary

In sum, our appraisal of the relevant research indicates that Chinese parents are generally quite warm and authoritative toward their children, with their love and care particularly being manifest in their efforts to ensure and promote their children's physical and material well-being. When it comes to children's academic work, Chinese parents tend to exert their authority and exercise heightened control, believing that such authoritarianism benefits children. Chinese parents also appear to be generally gender-egalitarian, parenting boys and girls quite similarly.

Future directions

Based on the foregoing inspection of the extant literature, we reach the following answers to the three questions raised at the beginning of this chapter. First, there is convergent evidence for the applicability of major Western frameworks tapping parenting (i.e. the authoritative-authoritarian parenting typologies and parental acceptance-rejection theory) to Chinese culture. Measures of various aspects of parenting derived from these frameworks have been shown not only to be meaningful and equivalent in Chinese samples, but also predictive of a range of developmental outcomes among Chinese children in ways similar to what has been found in Western cultures. Second, a number of aspects of parenting that were not the focus of previous work in Western cultures have been identified as of particular salience in Chinese culture. There is evidence that these aspects of parenting are also applicable in Western cultures. Third, a closer examination of recent research portrays Chinese parents as generally warm, authoritative and gender-equal toward their male and female offspring, while they tend to be authoritarian when it comes to their children's academic work. These conclusions help us better gauge the directions for future research on Chinese parenting and child socialization.

Differentiating levels of analysis

As noted by several investigators (Bond, 2009; Bond & van de Vijver, 2009; Rovwe, Vazsonyi, & Flannery, 1994; Wang et al., 2007), one important future direction is to draw the distinction between levels of analysis when comparing child-rearing beliefs and practices across cultural groups. Cross-cultural comparisons focusing on the means of certain aspects of parenting in each cultural group under study represent analyses at the mean level ('the positioning effect of culture' or 'level-oriented studies' see Bond, 2009; Bond & van de Vijver, 2009). Differences across cultural groups at the mean level reflect different salience and norms of the aspects of parenting under examination in different cultural groups; they do not necessarily indicate that those aspects of parenting have different meanings or functional relevance across cultures. For example, Chinese parents are less autonomy granting in comparison with their American counterparts, but this mean-level difference does not mean that parental autonomy granting has different functional relevance to Chinese children's development. For another example, American parents emphasize modesty to a lesser extent in comparison with their Chinese counterparts, but this does not mean that modesty is of little relevance to child socialization in the United States.

Cross-cultural comparisons focusing on the presence and strength of associations between certain aspects of parenting and certain aspects of children's development in each cultural group under study represent analyses at the relational level ('the linking or moderating effect of culture' or 'structure-oriented studies' see Bond, 2009; Bond & van de Vijver, 2009). The presence of a certain association in one cultural group but its absence or lesser strength in another may be indicative of different functional relevance of the aspect of parenting under study across cultures. Differences in the strength of a certain association in different cultural groups may suggest somewhat different mechanisms through which the aspect of parenting affects the aspect of children's development under study. For example, Wang and Pomerantz (2009) found that parental autonomy support was beneficial to early adolescents' emotional functioning in both China and the United States, with such effects being weaker in China. Moreover, the effect of parental autonomy support was completely mediated by children's feelings of autonomy in China, but only partially mediated in the United States. These differences suggest that there may be other mechanisms in addition to children's feelings of autonomy underlying the link between parental autonomy support and children's emotional functioning in the United States.

Notably, in research comparing parenting and child socialization in Chinese versus Western cultures on aspects of child rearing derived from Western frameworks, the positioning effect of culture has long been a focus, with emerging work treating culture as a moderating variable (e.g. Wang et al., 2007). Future research may also examine indigenous Chinese notions of parenting across cultures in terms of both the positioning and moderating effects of culture (for preliminary studies along these lines, see Pearson & Rao, 2003; Stewart et al., 2002). Moreover, multi- rather than bi-cultural comparisons may be particularly valuable in answering important questions, such as whether cross-cultural differences in parenting account for cross-cultural differences in children's development (see Pomerantz et al., 2008).

Taking a dynamic and multidimensional approach to culture

Another future direction is to view culture as a dynamic system, whose past legacies do take on new meanings as society progresses, rather than treating culture as a static entity. Cross-cultural comparisons should be made along multiple and changing cultural dimensions. The simplistic contrast between East Asian Confucianism and collectivism on the one hand, and Western Protestantism and individualism on the other (see Oyserman, Coon, & Kemmelmeier, 2002), may cloud parenting research which, as reviewed in this chapter, shows both similarities and differences between the East and the West. Instead, the dynamic and multidimensional approach is to 'unpackage' culture (Bond, 2009; Bond & van de Vijver, 2009) or to treat culture as multiple proximal influences on parenting and child development. In other words, patterns of parenting and child socialization in China are unlikely to be determined by monolithic and unchanging traditions, such as Confucianism, that render notions of independence, autonomy, and gender egalitarianism irrelevant. Rather, traditions including Confucianism, which are admittedly influential on many aspects of social lives in China, have also been affected by dramatic economic, societal, and cultural changes that have been rapidly taking place in contemporary Chinese societies (see Hwang & Han, this volume; Kulich, this volume; Ng, this volume).

Mainland China, for example, has undergone four extraordinary changes. The first is Westernization, which appeared first in the form of colonialization and continues in the form of technological advances, globalization, and economic, political, and social reforms. The second is the imported Communist ideology that reached its apex during the Cultural Revolution and attempted to eradicate Confucianism together with many other Chinese cultural traditions. The third is China's ongoing rapid economic development, with double-digit annual GDP growth for over twenty consecutive years. The fourth is the single-child policy, which commenced in the late 1970s, and has resulted in a generation of urban Chinese children raised in the absence of siblings. The fusion of these four remarkable changes has transformed Chinese culture into one that seems to be characterized by its willingness to embrace the new and, for now at least, also to initiate some oblivion of the old.

Put in this proximal cultural context, the state-of-the-art depiction in this chapter of contemporary Chinese parents as being generally warm, authoritative, and gender-egalitarian yet authoritarian over children's academic work may not be surprising. Modernization and Westernization as well as the single-child policy may have led Chinese parents to increasingly value independence, autonomy, and gender egalitarianism, and may also have heightened the utility of education; in turn, Chinese parents may engage in child-rearing practices that they believe are conducive to the realization of these values (for an anthropological account, see Fong, 2004).

Notably, the economic, societal, and cultural changes may have been happening less rapidly and dramatically in rural than urban areas. For example, the single-child policy seems not to have been consistently and strictly enforced in rural areas. Moreover, large and increasing numbers of rural residents have been migrating into urban areas as a labor force. This results in special groups of children who live with their migrant-worker parents in usually undesirable conditions in urban areas, or who are left behind in rural areas with substitute caregivers such as grandparents. There is an obvious paucity of research on parenting and child development among Chinese rural populations (for much needed exceptions, see Fuligni & Zhang, 2004; Zhang & Fuligni, 2006), or the emerging migrant-worker population. It remains an open question whether the conclusions we have drawn in this chapter, based almost exclusively on research with families in urban areas, hold for these 'neglected' populations.

In capturing the dynamic and multidimensionality of culture, it would also be fruitful to examine parenting beliefs and practices that may be antecedents of documented cross-cultural differences in adults' psychological functioning. For instance, differences in attachment styles (e.g. Schmitt, Alcalay, Allensworth, Allik, Ault, Austers et al., 2004), regulatory focus (for a review, see Wyer, 2009), and coping strategies (for a review, see Cheng, Lo, & Chio, this volume) have been identified among adults in China versus Western cultures. There is emerging research relating parenting to such psychological functioning in which cross-cultural differences are already evident among children (e.g. Ng, Pomerantz, & Lam, 2007; Xu, Farver, Chang, Yu, & Zhang, 2006).

Conclusions

To conclude, relationships and interactions between parents and children in contemporary Chinese societies (i.e. urban areas in mainland China, Hong Kong, and Taiwan) are generally warm, authoritative, and gender-egalitarian, with parental warmth particularly manifesting itself in parents' concern over children's physical and material well-being. Yet Chinese parents are rather authoritarian and controlling when it comes to their children's schoolwork, reflecting the utmost value of educational achievement as well as parents' assumption of great responsibility in promoting such achievement in their children.

It seems that Chinese parents nowadays typically endorse socialization goals, child-rearing beliefs, and parenting practices reflecting both traditional Chinese and modern Western values. Notably, despite some mean-level differences in Chinese versus Western parents' endorsement of certain goals, beliefs, and practices, the functional relevance of those parenting aspects to children's development is quite similar in Chinese and Western cultures. Specifically, authoritative parenting, which conveys parents' acceptance of children and respects children's sense of self, has positive effects on various dimensions of children's development. In contrast, authoritarian parenting, which conveys parents' rejection of children and violates children's sense of self, has negative impacts, even if it is only conditional, for example, when children do not do well in school.

References

Barber, B. K., Stolz, H. E., & Olsen, J. A. (2006). Parental support, psychological control, and behavioral control: Assessing relevance across time, culture, and method. *Monographs of the Society for Research in Child Development, 70, Serial No. 282*, 1–137.

Baumrind, D. (1971). Current patterns of parental authority. *Developmental Psychology Monograph, 4*, 1–103.

Bond, M. H. (2009). Circumnavigating the psychological globe: From *yin* and *yang* to starry, starry night ... In A. Aksu-Koc & S. Beckman (eds), *Perspectives on human development, family and culture*. Cambridge, England: Cambridge University Press.

Bond, M. H. & van de Vijver, F. (2009). Making scientific sense of cultural differences in psychological outcomes: Unpackaging the *magnum mysterium*. In D. Matsumoto & F. van de Vijver (eds), *Cross-cultural research methods*. New York: Oxford University Press.

Chang, L. (2006). *Confucianism or confusion: Parenting only children in urban China*. Keynote address at the 19th biennial convention of the International Society for the Study of Behavioral Development. Australia: Melbourne, July.

Chang, L., Lansford, J. E., Schwartz, D., & Farver, J. M. (2004). Marital quality, maternal depressed affect, harsh parenting, and child externalizing in Hong Kong Chinese families. *International Journal of Behavioral Development, 28*, 311–318.

Chang, L., Schwartz, D., Dodge, K. A., & McBride-Chang, C. (2003). Harsh parenting in relation to child emotion regulation and aggression. *Journal of Family Psychology, 17*, 598–606.

Chang, L., McBride-Chang, C. Stewart, S., & Au, E. (2003). Life satisfaction, self-concept, and family relations in Chinese adolescents and children. *International Journal of Behavioral Development, 27*, 182–190.

Chao, R. K. (1994). Beyond parental control and authoritarian parenting style: Understanding Chinese parenting through the cultural notion of training. *Child Development, 65*, 1111–1119.

Chao, R. K. (2000). The parenting of immigrant Chinese and European American mothers: Relations between parenting styles, socialization goals, and parental practices. *Journal of Applied Developmental Psychology, 21*, 233–248.

Chao, R. K. (2001). Extending research on the consequences of parenting styles for Chinese Americans and European Americans. *Child Development, 72*, 1832–1843.

Chao, R. K. & Tseng, V. (2002). Parenting of Asians. In M. H. Bornstein (ed.), *Handbook of Parenting: Vol. 4. Social Conditions and Applied Parenting* (pp. 59–93). Mahwah, NJ: Lawrence Erlbaum.

Chen, C., Greenberger, E., Lester, J., Dong, Q., & Guo, M.-S. (1998). A cross-cultural study of family and peer correlates of adolescent misconduct. *Developmental Psychology, 34*, 770–781.

Chen, F.-M. & Luster, T. (2002). Factors related to parenting practices in Taiwan. *Early Child Development and Care, 172*, 413–430.

Chen, X., Dong, Q., & Zhou, H. (1997). Authoritative and authoritarian parenting practices and social and school performance in Chinese children. *International Journal of Behavioral Development, 21*, 855–873.

Chen, X., Liu, M., & Li, D. (2000). Parental warmth, control, and indulgence and their relations to adjustment in Chinese children: A longitudinal study. *Journal of Family Psychology, 14*, 401–419.

Cheung, C. S. & Pomerantz, E. M. (2008). *Changes in parents' involvement in children's schooling during early adolescence in the US and China: Implications for children's learning strategies*. Poster presented at the 20th biennial meeting of the International Society of the Study of Behavioral Development. Germany: Würzburg, July.

Cheung, F. M. C. (1996). Gender role development. In S. Lau (ed.), *Growing up the Chinese way: Chinese child and adolescent development* (pp. 45–67). Hong Kong: The Chinese University Press.

Deeds, O., Stewart, S. M., Bond, M. H., & Westrick, J. (1998). Adolescents in between cultures: Values and autonomy expectations in an international school setting. *School Psychology International, 19*, 61–77.

Deutsch, F. M. (2006). Filial piety, patrilineality, and China's one-child policy. *Journal of Family Issues, 27*, 366–389.

Dornbusch, S. M., Ritter, P. L., Leiderman, P. H., Roberts, D. F., & Fraleigh, M. J. (1987). The relation of parenting style to adolescent school performance. *Child Development, 58*, 1244–1257.

Feldman, S. S. & Rosenthal, D. A. (1991). Age expectations of behavioral autonomy in Hong Kong, Australian, and American youth: The influences of family variables and adolescents' values. *International Journal of Psychology, 26*, 1–23.

Fong, V. L. (2002). China's one-child policy and the enpowerment of urban daughters. *American Anthropologist, 104*, 1098–1109.

Fong, V. L. (2004). *Only hope: Coming of age under China's one-child policy*. Stanford, CA: Stanford University Press.

Fuligni, A. J. & Zhang, W. (2004). Attitudes toward family obligation among adolescents in contemporary urban and rural China. *Child Development, 74*, 180–192.

Fung, H. (1999). Becoming a moral child: The socialization of shame among young Chinese children. *Ethos, 27*, 180–209.

Greenberger, E., Chen, C., Tally, S. R., & Dong, Q. (2000). Family, peer, and individual correlates of depressive symptomatology among U S and Chinese adolescents. *Journal of Consulting and Clinical Psychology, 68*, 209–219.

Greenfield, P. M., Keller, H., Fuligni, A., & Maynard, A. (2003). Cultural pathways through universal development. *Annual Review of Psychology, 54*, 461–490.

Grolnick, W. S. (2003). *The psychology of parental control: How well-meant parenting backfires*. Mahwah, NJ: Lawrence Erlbaum.

Ho, D. Y. F. (1986). Chinese patterns of socialization: A critical review. In M. H. Bond (ed.), *The psychology of the Chinese people* (pp. 1–37). New York: Oxford University Press.
Jose, P. E., Huntsinger, C. S., Huntsinger, P. R., & Liaw F.-R. (2000). Parental values and practices relevant to young children's social development in Taiwan and the United States. *Journal of Cross-Cultural Psychology, 31*, 677–702.
Lansford, J. E., Chang, L., Dodge, K. A., Malone, P. S., Oburu, P., Palmérus, K. et al (2005). Physical discipline and children's adjustment: Cultural normativeness as a moderator. *Child Development, 76*, 1234–1246.
Lau, S. (1996). *Growing up the Chinese way: Chinese child and adolescent development.* Hong Kong: The Chinese University Press.
Leung, K., Lau, S., & Lam, W.-L. (1998). Parenting styles and academic achievement: A cross-cultural study, *Merrill-Palmer Quarterly, 44*, 157–172.
Lieber, E., Fung, H., & Leung, P. W. (2006). Chinese child-rearing beliefs: Key dimensions and contributions to the development of culture-appropriate assessment. *Asian Journal of Social Psychology, 9*, 140–147.
McBridge-Chang, C., & Chang, L. (1998). Adolescent–parent relations in Hong Kong: Parenting styles, emotional autonomy, and school adjustment. *Journal of Genetic Psychology, 159*, 421–436.
Maccoby, E. E. & Martin, J. A. (1983). Socialization in the context of the family: Parent–child interaction. In P. H. Mussen (series ed.) & E. M. Hetherington (vol. ed.), *Handbook of child psychology: Vol. 4, Socialization, personality, and social development* (4th edn, pp. 1–101). New York: Wiley.
Nelson, D. A., Hart, C. H., Yang, C, Olsen, J. A., & Jin, S. (2006). Aversive parenting in China: Association with child physical and relational aggression. *Child Development, 77*, 554 – 572.
Nelson, D. A., Nelson, L. J., Hart, C. H., Yang, C., & Jin, S. (2006). Parenting and peer-group behavior in cultural context. In X. Chen, D. C., French, & B. H. Schneider (eds), *Peer relationships in cultural context* (pp. 213–246). New York: Cambridge University Press.
Ng, F.-F., Pomerantz, E. M., & Lam S. F. (2008). *Chinese and American parents' beliefs about children's achievement: Indigenous Chinese notions and their implications for parents and children.* Symposium paper presented at the 20th biennial meeting of the International Society of the Study of Behavioral Development. Germany: Würzburg, July.
Oyserman, D., Coon, H. M., & Kemmelmeier, M. (2002). Rethinking individualism and collectivism: Evaluation of theoretical assumptions and meta-analyses. *Psychological Bulletin, 128*, 3–72.
Pearson, E. & Rao, N. (2003). Socialization goals, parenting practices, and peer competence in Chinese and English preschoolers. *Early Child Development and Care, 173*, 131–146.
Peterson, G. W., Cobas, J. A., Bush, K. R., Supple, A., & Wilson, S. M. (2004). Parent–youth relationships and the self-esteem of Chinese adolescents: Collectivism versus individualism. *Marriage and Family Review, 36*, 173–200.
Phinney, J. S. & Landin, J. (1998). Research paradigms for studying ethnic minority families within and across groups. In V. C. McLoyd, & L. Steinberg (eds), *Studying minority adolescents: Conceptual, methodological, and theoretical issues* (pp. 89–109). Mahwah, NJ: Lawrence Erlbaum.
Pomerantz, E. M., Ng, F. F., & Wang, Q. (2008). Culture, parenting, and motivation: The case of East Asia and the United States. In M. L. Maehr, *Advances in motivation and achievement* (Vol. 15, pp. 209–240). Bingley, England: Emerald Group Publishing.
Qin, L., Pomerantz, E. M., & Wang, Q. (2008). *Changes in early adolescents' decision-making autonomy in the US and China: Implications for their emotional functioning.* Poster presented at the biennial meeting of the Society for Research on Adolescence. USA: Chicago, March.
Roe, A. & Siegelman, M. (1963). A parent–child relations questionnaire. *Child Development, 34*, 355–369.
Rohner, R. P., Khaleque, A., & Cournoyer, D. E. (2007). *Introduction to parental acceptance–rejection theory, methods, and evidence.* Retrieved November, 2007 from University of Connecticut, Center for the Study of Parental Acceptance and Rejection website: http://www.cspar.uconn.edu.
Rowe, D. C., Vazsonyi, A. T., & Flannery, D. J. (1994). No more than skin deep: Ethnic and racial similarity in developmental process. *Psychological Review, 101*, 396–413.
Schmitt, D. P., Alcalay, L., Allensworth, M., Allik, J., Ault, L., Austers, I. et al (2004). Patterns and universals of adult romantic attachment across 62 cultural regions: Are models of self and of other pancultural constructs? *Journal of Cross-Cultural Psychology, 35*, 367–402.
Shek, D. T. L. (2007). A longitudinal study of perceived parental psychological control and psychological well-being in Chinese adolescents in Hong Kong. *Journal of Clinical Psychology, 63*, 1–22.
Sorkhabi, N. (2005). Applicability of Baumrind's parent typology to collective cultures: Analysis of cultural explanations of parent socialization effects. *International Journal of Behavioral Development, 29*, 552–563.
Steinberg, L., Dornbusch, S. M., & Brown, B. B. (1992). Ethnic differences in adolescent achievement: An ecological perspective. *American Psychologist, 47*, 723–729.
Steinberg, L., Lamborn, S. D., Darling, N., Mounts, N. S., & Dornbusch, S. M. (1994). Over-time changes in adjustment and competence among adolescents from authoritative, authoritarian, indulgent, and neglectful families. *Child Development, 65*, 754–770.
Steinberg, L., Mounts, N. S., Lamborn, S. D., & Dornbusch, S. M. (1991). Authoritative parenting and adolescent adjustment across varied ecological niches. *Journal of Research on Adolescence, 1*, 19–36.

Stevenson, H. W., Lee, S.-Y., Chen, C., Stigler, J. W., Hsu, C.-C., & Kitamura, S. (1990). Contexts of achievement: A study of American, Chinese, and Japanese children. *Monographs of the Society for Research in Child Development, 55 (1–2, Serial No. 221).*

Stewart, S. M. & Bond, M. H. (2002). A critical look at parenting research from the mainstream: Problems uncovered while adapting Western research to non-Western cultures. *British Journal of Developmental Psychology, 20,* 379–392.

Stewart, S. M., Bond, M. H., Kennard, B. D., Ho, L. M., & Zaman, R. M. (2002). Does the Chinese construct of *guan* export to the West? *International Journal of Psychology, 37,* 74–82.

Stewart, S. M., Rao, N., Bond, M. H., McBride-Chang, C., Fielding, R., & Kennard, B. D. (1998). Chinese dimensions of parenting: Broadening Western predictors and outcomes. *International Journal of Psychology, 33,* 345–358.

Sue, S. & Okazaki, S. (1990). Asian-American educational achievements: A phenomenon in search of an explanation. *American Psychologist, 45,* 913–920.

Supple, A. J., Peterson, G. W., & Bush, K. R. (2004). Assessing the validity of parenting measures in a sample of Chinese adolescents. *Journal of Family Psychology, 18,* 539–544.

Wang, Q. & Pomerantz, E. M. (2008a). *Transactions between early adolescents' achievement and parents' psychological control: A longitudinal investigation in China and the US.* Symposium paper presented at the 20th biennial meeting of International Society of the Study of Behavioral Development. Germany: Würzburg, July.

Wang, Q. & Pomerantz, E. M. (2008b). *Chinese early adolescents' relationships with their parents: Investigating gender differences in a contemporary urban sample.* Paper presented at the International Conference on Gender and Family in East Asia. Hong Kong.

Wang, Q. & Pomerantz, E. M. (2009). *How does parents' autonomy support contribute to early adolescents' emotional functioning? An investigation in the US and China.* Symposium poster presented at the biennial meeting of the Society for Research in Child Development.

Wang, Q., Pomerantz, E. M., Chen, H. (2007). The role of parents' control in early adolescents' psychological functioning: A longitudinal investigation in the United States and China. *Child Development, 78,* 1592–1610.

Wang, Y. & Chang, L. (2008). Multidimensional parental warmth and its relations to pupils' social development: A comparison between paternal and maternal parenting (in Chinese). *Journal of Psychology in Chinese Societies, 9,* 121–147.

Wu, D. Y. H. (1996). Chinese childhood socialization. In M. H. Bond (ed.), *Handbook of Chinese psychology* (pp. 143–154). New York: Oxford University Press.

Wu, P., Robinson, C. C., Yang, C., Hart, C., Olsen, S. F., Porter, C. L. et al (2002). Similarities and differences in mothers' parenting of preschoolers in China and the United States. *International Journal of Behavioral Development, 26,* 481–491.

Wyer, R. S. (2009). Culture and information processing: A conceptual integration. In R. S. Wyer, C.-Y. Chiu, & Y.-Y. Hong (eds) *Understanding culture: Theory, research and application.* New York: Psychology Press.

Xia, Y. R., Xie, X., Zhou, Z., DeFrain, J. Meredith, W. H., & Combs, R. (2004). Chinese adolescents' decision-making, parent–adolescent communication and relationships. *Marriage and Family Review, 36,* 119–145.

Xu, Y., Farver, J. M., Chang, L., Yu, L., Zhang, Z. (2006). Culture, family contexts, and children's coping strategies in peer interactions. In X. Chen, D. C., French, & B. H. Schneider (eds), *Peer relationships in cultural context* (pp. 264–280). New York: Cambridge University Press.

Xu, Y., Farver, J. A. M., Zhang, Z., Zeng, Q., Yu, L., & Cai, B. (2005). Mainland Chinese parenting styles and parent–child interaction. *International Journal of Behavioral Development, 29,* 524–531.

Zhang, W. & Fuligni, A. (2006). Authority, autonomy, and family relationships among adolescents in urban and rural China. *Journal of Research on Adolescence, 16,* 527–537.

CHAPTER 6

Language and the brain: computational and neuroimaging evidence from Chinese

Ping Li and Hua Shu

These are exciting times for psychological, cognitive, and linguistic sciences. According to some, the understanding of the nature of mind and the nature of intelligence is paralleled in history perhaps only by the searches for the origin of life and the evolution of the universe (Estes & Newell, 1983). Within only a few decades, the field of cognitive science (counting from 1956; Gardner, 1985) has progressed from the mind-as-a-computer metaphor to the integration of mind, brain, behavior, and culture at multiple levels of analysis and with multiple, convergent tools and methodologies. In particular, the interface between cognitive science and neuroscience has provided fertile ground for transformative research and revolutionary thinking, yielding perspectives that allow for fundamental scientific discoveries and rapid paradigm shifts (Kuhn, 1970). The study of language, a unique human capacity, has played an important role in this scientific movement.

A large body of knowledge has accumulated on the cognitive and neural mechanisms underlying language representation and language acquisition. Much of this knowledge, however, has come from studies of Indo-European languages, in particular, English. Recent interest in Asian languages, particularly Chinese, has revived some of the age-old debates on linguistic universals and linguistic specificity. The universality perspective, reflected most clearly in Chomsky's theory of language (e.g. Chomsky, 1957), has dominated much of linguistics and psycholinguistics since the cognitive revolution in the 1950s. A contrasting perspective, championed by many scholars doing crosslinguistic, comparative research (e.g. Bates & MacWhinney, 1989), has emphasized how linguistic specificity and variation can impact upon the course of language acquisition, language representation, and language use.

While the debate is far from being over, in recent years computational and neuroimaging studies have provided significant insights into the issue of how language-specific experience shapes the mind and behavior of the language user. These studies have led to accumulating evidence that starts to change our conceptualization about linguistic experience and linguistic behavior, and, more specifically, new ways of thinking about the relationships between language, brain, and culture. On the one hand, computational modeling has allowed us to demonstrate the developmental dynamics in which the learning agent interacts with the learning environment in complex, non-linear ways during the acquisition and representation of language. Neuroimaging research, on the other hand, has enabled us to gain a better understanding of how language-specific properties and the linguistic experiences therein shape the cognitive neural systems of the speaker and the language learner.

The Chinese language provides a particularly important testing ground for theories of language and for understanding the cognitive and neural substrates of language behavior.[1] Spoken by one-quarter of the world's population, Chinese differs significantly from most Indo-European languages and offers distinct features in its orthographic, phonological, lexical, and grammatical structures. First, on the orthographic level, Chinese uses characters rather than alphabetic letters as the basic writing unit, in square configurations that map onto meaningful morphemes rather than onto phonemes in the spoken language. On a phonological level, Chinese uses a tonal system to distinguish lexical items, and although the modern language relies more and more on disyllabic words, traditionally, monosyllables have dominated the language in forming the basic meaning units, and, even with tonal distinctions, homophones are still pervasive. On a grammatical level, Chinese does not have devices that indicate differences in tense, number, gender, or case; in other words, grammatical functions and relations for sentence constituents are not linked by morphological associations. Scholars have begun to examine in detail how these distinctive features influence and impact language behaviors, including some of our own comparative, crosslinguistic studies (e.g. Li, Bates, & MacWhinney, 1993; Li, 1996; Li & Bowerman, 1998). The recent *Handbook of East Asian psycholinguistics* has showcased this line of crosslinguistic research from a large number of scholars (see Li, Tan, Bates, & Tzeng, 2006 for overviews and reviews).

In this chapter, we focus on the computational mechanisms and neural signatures based on our recent crosslinguistic computational and neural studies. These studies examine the acquisition, representation, and processing of spoken and written Chinese in the context of both native speakers and second-language learners. Our results demonstrate that the dynamic interactions between language-specific properties, linguistic experiences, and characteristics of learning directly affect the course and outcome of the acquisition and the representation of both native and non-native languages. Findings from our research will also contribute in general to the understanding of the relationships between brain, language, and cognition.

Computational studies

Significant advances have been made in the language sciences during the last three decades, thanks in large part to the use of computational models and tools for the study of the processing and acquisition of words and sentences by children and adults. Empirical studies, especially of young children, are typically constrained by the limited degrees of freedom in terms of direct, parametrical manipulations of the learning environment. By contrast, computational models provide flexible and powerful tools for the understanding of the detailed processes of how language speakers and learners handle one language or multiple languages. For example, one cannot directly manipulate the language input in terms of quantity, rate, or frequency of occurrence of the words to which children are exposed. These parameters, e.g. quantity, rate, frequency, undoubtedly influence the speed and accuracy of language acquisition in children. In computational modeling these parameters can be treated as independent variables and be flexibly controlled in an experimental design. By doing so, we can use these models for the testing of specific hypotheses regarding whether and how a given variable will influence the course of language processing (hence identification of causal relationships). More important, the models can make predictions based on simulation findings, according to which new empirical studies can be designed and evaluated. Finally, computational modeling also allows for an explicit specification of the necessary mechanisms responsible for learning and processing. Such mechanisms minimally include association (e.g. associating sound with meaning), competition (e.g. multiple meanings competing for memory retrieval), and organization (e.g. multiple sound–meaning pairs grouping into sensible clusters).

Using these powerful and flexible computational models, we have been able to model the dynamic changes that occur in the language learner and the dynamic interactions that occur in the competing language systems over the course of learning. In particular, our research attempts to identify the computational mechanisms and the cognitive structures that characterize the interactive dynamics underlying the learning of one or more multiple lexical systems, e.g. words acquired early by children and by Chinese–English bilinguals. Approaching this goal, we developed the DevLex model, a self-organizing model that captures the development of the lexicon in the learning of first and second languages. The specific class of models that we have used in this research is called 'neural network models' or 'connectionist models'. These models utilize the notions of a large assembly of neurons, parallel distributed processing, and non-linear learning rules (see Rumelhart, McClelland, & the PDP Group, 1986). The human brain consists of a massive network of billions of neurons working together, often in parallel. As such, neural network models are more biologically motivated than models from classical cognitive science: multiple processing units, activation, and connection weights provide better neurally plausible constructs to conceptualize human information processing than do traditional discrete symbols, rules, linguistic true structures, and the like. Crucially, computational models built on these constructs are ideally suited for modeling the complex and interactive processes underlying language acquisition and representation.[2]

Modeling lexical organization in development

A fundamental puzzle for the researcher of language acquisition is how the child manages to acquire a large vocabulary with apparent ease and rapid speed during the first few years of life. While a great deal has been learned about how the child makes the initial form–meaning mapping (e.g. learning to connect the sound /kæt/ with the white furry animal), relatively little is known about how the child mentally organizes various mapped items into a coherent whole and how the mental organization changes over time in the process of development. Although words may be learned individually one by one, they are not put together haphazardly into the child's mental representation, i.e. the mental dictionary or mental lexicon. Once a significant number of words is learned, children start to organize them into meaningful categories that would form what linguists call nouns, verbs, and adjectives, and within each of these categories, further organize them into clusters that naturally group together, e.g. food, clothing, toy, etc. within the noun category. In fact, looking at any normally developing child's early vocabulary, we can see that the earliest words from the child form clear meaningful clusters by just a few months into his or her word production process (e.g. Bates et al., 1994; Dale & Fenson, 1996).

What computational mechanisms allow children to organize words into meaningful representations? Researchers have only just begun to address this question. Our research has made efforts to unravel the computational mechanisms of organization in the context of the representation of the lexicon as a structured whole. The DevLex model has been proposed to explicitly capture lexical organization during vocabulary development (Li, Farkas, & MacWhinney, 2004; Li, Zhao, & MacWhinney, 2007). It uses an architecture of unsupervised, self-organizing, neural networks (the self-organizing maps or SOM: Kohonen, 1982, 2001) for deriving the typographical organization of word meaning and word form over time. The model connects multiple maps (SOMs)[3] via Hebbian learning rules in order to simulate learning in different modalities and the connections between different modalities, e.g. comprehension and production.

There is a number of distinct advantages to the DevLex structure in learning a lexicon (see Li, 2003; Li et al., 2004, 2007), the most important of which being that the model can capture the developing structure over time, and show how the mental lexicon may change as a function of the system's learning of an expanding vocabulary. Figure 6.1 presents an example of how meaningful patterns might emerge over time in the representation of the lexicon by monolingual children during the early stages of vocabulary acquisition. The example shows that at the earliest stage when the model has learned only fifty words, the vocabulary consists primarily of nouns, but at the end when the model has learned 500 words, clear categories and categorical boundaries have emerged for nouns, verbs, and adjectives. In between, the size of the vocabulary continuously expands and the boundaries shift as a function of the system's learning additional vocabulary.

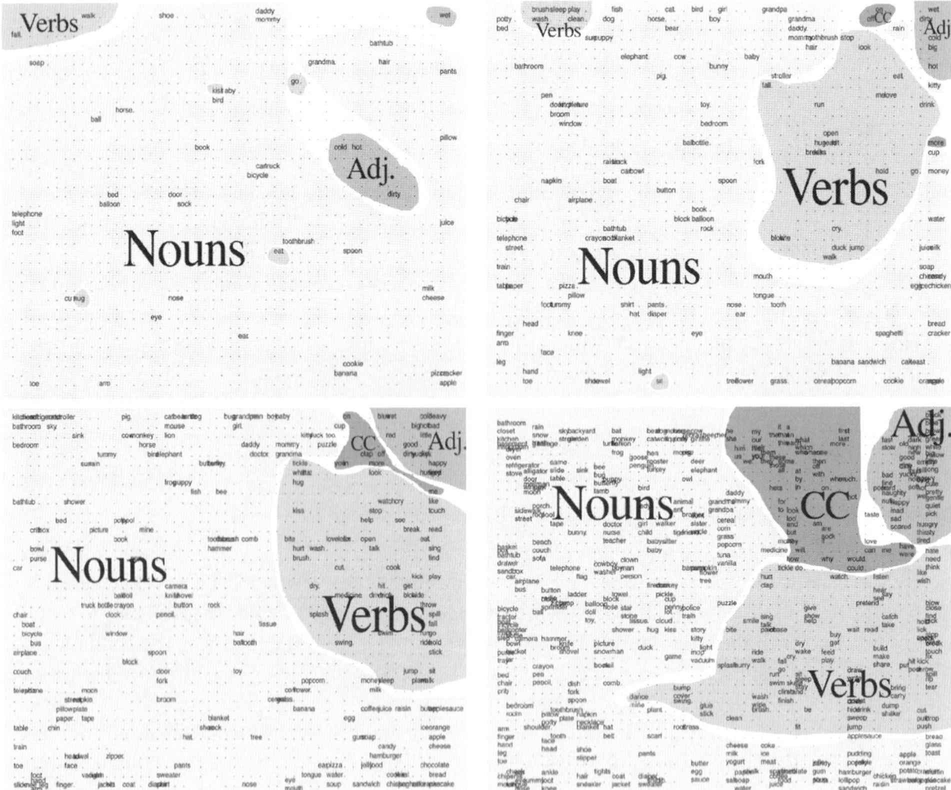

Fig. 6.1 Snapshots of DevLex across different developmental stages: Stage 1 (50 words—upper left), Stage 3 (150 words—upper right), Stage 5 (250 words—lower left) and Stage 10 (all 500 words—lower right). The sequence of images illustrates the nature of changes underlying the developmental process, as a result of the expanding vocabulary and the changing/enriched word representations. DevLex clearly separates the four major lexical categories (and the semantic subcategories within each category) toward the final stage. Because of the large number of words involved in each map, the individual words are not legible in this figure. (Reprinted from Hernandez, Li, & MacWhinney, 2005, with permission from Elsevier.)

How does DevLex derive the meaningful categories of nouns, verbs, and adjectives incrementally to capture the process of lexical organization in development? Our computational model relies on the use of two simple but powerful learning principles: self-organization and Hebbian learning, in artificial neural networks (Hebb, 1949; Kohonen, 1982; Miikkulainen, 1993). It has been designed to examine mechanisms of association, organization, competition, and plasticity in the development and representation of the lexicon (see Li, 2006; Li et al., 2004, 2007, for technical descriptions of the model). The model has been applied successfully to capture both monolingual and bilingual lexical development. Figure 6.2 presents a diagrammatic sketch of the model that learns both the Chinese and the English lexicon in simulating the situation of simultaneous bilingual language acquisition (see Li & Farkas, 2002; Zhao & Li, 2007).

The architecture of the model is built upon a number of considerations concerning the limitations of existing connectionist language models. Our model is inspired by the idea that mental organization of the lexicon occurs without explicit instruction and corrective feedback, viz. it is a self-organizing process, and thus relies on unsupervised, self-organizing processes to learn (Li, 2003;

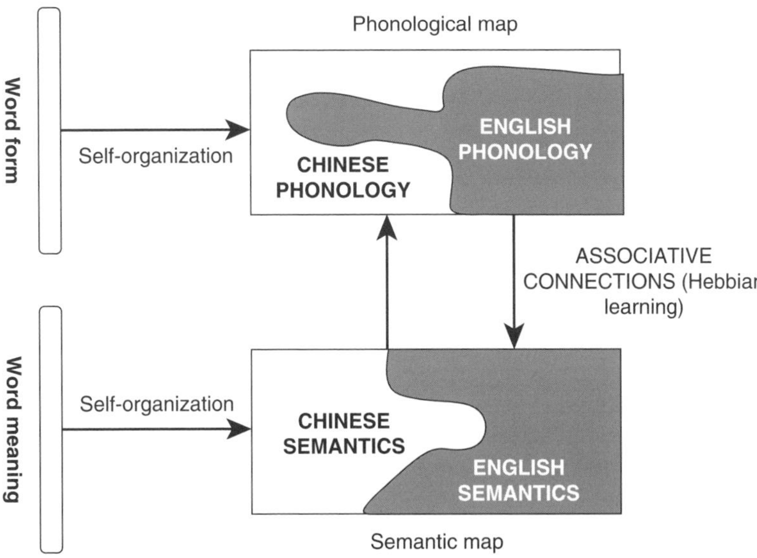

Fig. 6.2 A sketch of the DevLex bilingual model. Each of the two self-organizing maps (SOMs) receives the lexical input and organizes the phonological and semantic information of the lexicon, respectively, for both language inputs. The associative connections between maps are trained by Hebbian learning. (Based on Li & Farkas, 2002.)

MacWhinney, 2001). SOM-based self-organization has been motivated by topography-ordering characteristics that can be found in many parts of the brain (Kohonen, 2001; Miikkulainen, Bednar, Choe, & Sirosh, 2005). Its distinctive features of gradual formation of categories with soft boundaries make this type of model ideally suited to the study of mechanisms of language learning (Li, 2003, 2006). Over the past years, we have taken advantage of these features and applied the model to examine a number of issues in monolingual and bilingual contexts.

As indicated in Figure 6.1, our model is able to capture how structured representation might evolve over time. Early on, the representation tends to be a relatively random collection of items, mostly nouns that refer to objects. Gradually, a more organized structure emerges for the major linguistic categories of nouns, verbs, adjectives, and closed-class words. Interestingly, the development of lexical organization does not proceed identically across languages. For example, English-speaking children's early vocabulary shows a clear 'noun bias' (Gentner, 1982), a preponderance of nouns compared to other categories of words. However, this noun bias has been found to be weak or non-existent in some East Asian languages, for example, Chinese and Korean (Choi, 2000; Tardif, 1996, 2006). One of the major goals of our research is to account for the dynamic interaction of the learner with the learning environment. Given the characteristics of our model in capturing realistic data in children's vocabulary acquisition, it seems reasonable to assume that the model should be able to provide an account of how cross-language similarities and differences occur in the development of the early lexicon.

A consistent feature of our model is its use of linguistically and developmentally realistic data. The model acquires lexical items and develops lexical organizations based on the corpus of child-adult speech interactions (from the CHILDES database; MacWhinney, 2000). In Figure 6.2, the input to the model was based on CHILDES parental speech in a bilingual learning situation (mother's speech in Chinese and father's speech in English; Yip & Matthews, 2001). The model, taking sentences word by word, was able to derive meaningful categories and groups, building independent lexical representations for each language. In other cases, we combined CHILDES parental input with information from the MacArthur–Bates Communicative Development Inventory (CDI; Bates et al., 1994; Dale & Fenson, 1996), so that we can model the earliest 500–600 words that children actually produce. Grounding our input and learning targets to the CHILDES and the CDI gives our model the opportunity to handle realistic learning situations rather than artificial simulations. Below we provide a few examples that illustrate our model's capabilities in the crosslinguistic context.

Modeling crosslinguistic differences in lexical development

In empirical research there have been suggestions that factors such as parental input and language-specific properties of the lexicon might be key in accounting for crosslinguistic patterns in early vocabulary development. For example, Tardif (2006) argued that there is a prevalence of verbs in adult Chinese as compared with adult English, and that verbs occur more frequently in child-directed parental speech in Chinese than in English. Thus, the linguistic input to the two groups of children might be different from the outset. If this is indeed the case, we can introduce Chinese and English early vocabularies to our model for learning to identify how specific characteristics of the linguistic input can affect the developmental time course.

To validate the hypothesis that there are input differences in child-directed parental speech, we first conducted a corpus analysis of the CHILDES database (Liu, Zhao, & Li, 2008). We examined the developmental patterns for nouns, verbs, adjectives, and closed-class words in both children's speech and the corresponding caregivers' speech in the CHILDES database for English, Mandarin Chinese, and Cantonese. The data were divided into eight different age groups from thirteen to sixty months according to the age of the child at which the data were collected. Our analyses are highly consistent with the hypotheses that language-specific differences in the linguistic input strongly influence children's vocabulary development. As can be seen in Figure 6.3, the percentages of nouns, verbs, and adjectives in children's productive vocabularies at different stages vary greatly across the three languages, most notably between English on the one hand and Mandarin and Cantonese on the other. For English, nouns dominate the early stages, as reflected in the high noun-verb ratios up to 31–36 months, whereas for both Mandarin and Cantonese, nouns are more frequent for only the earliest stage (13–18 months), and then become similar in proportion with verbs for later stages. Moreover, these cross-language differences are also reflected in the adult speech, in that English adults show a high noun–verb ratio whereas Chinese adults show a more balanced profile for the two categories.

Given this finding, we further trained DevLex to learn the early vocabularies based on CDI (Fenson & Dale, 1996 for English, and Tardif et al., 2002 for Chinese). Our model received the input of 500 words each for English and Mandarin Chinese. These words were then treated in the standard DevLex procedure for phonological, phonemic, and semantic representations (see Li et al., 2007; Zhao & Li, 2007, 2008). Two sets of networks with identical simulation parameters were run separately, one for each language. During a simulation, words from the training lexicon (Chinese or English) were presented to the model one by one, according to a word's frequency of occurrence in the parental speech of the CHILDES database. Figure 6.4 presents the average number of words correctly produced by the model for three major grammatical categories as a function of the network's expanding vocabulary size.

These results are highly consistent with patterns from our corpus-based analysis. First, for both English and Chinese, during most stages of vocabulary learning (represented by the total number of learned words), our model can correctly produce more nouns than verbs, and more verbs than adjectives. This overall noun advantage in our network's productive vocabulary for both languages runs counter to the argument that verbs dominate over nouns in early Chinese vocabulary (Tardif, 1996), but is consistent with our corpus-based results. Second, clear differences exist in the lexical composition of English and Chinese. Comparing Figure 6.4a and Figure 6.4b, we can see that the network generally produced more nouns in English than in Chinese, and more verbs in Chinese than in English, across most stages. In English, nouns always dominated over verbs in number, whereas in Chinese nouns overtake verbs in number only later.[4] In general, our network displayed a much stronger noun bias in English than in Chinese.[5]

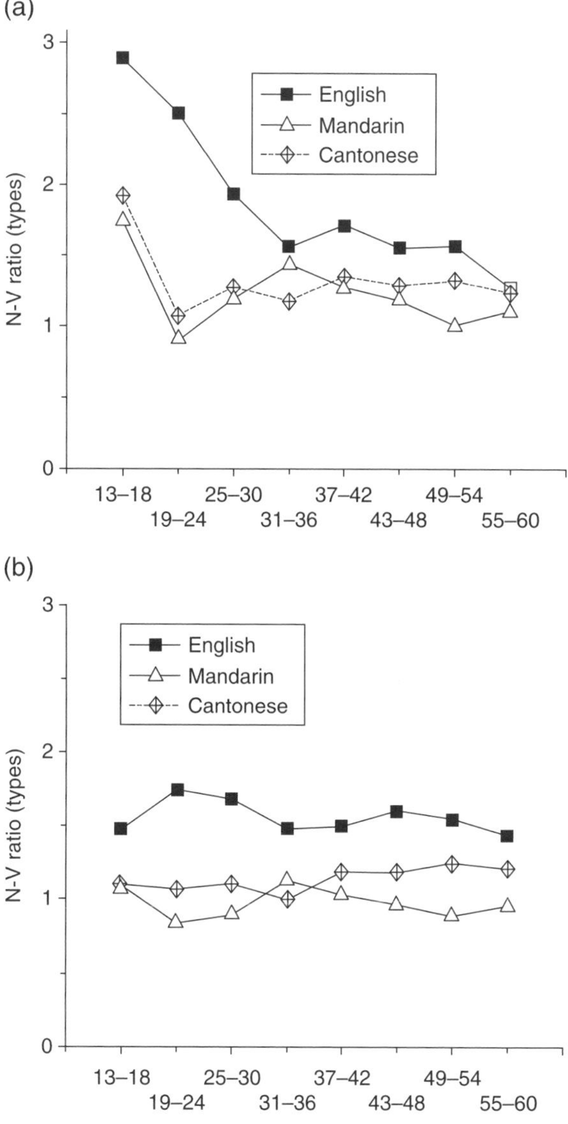

Fig. 6.3 Noun–verb ratio (in types) as a function of age for English, Mandarin, and Cantonese: (A) children, (B) adults. (Based on Liu, Zhao, & Li, 2008).

Using identical simulation parameters, our model derived different patterns in vocabulary growth, and this is strong evidence that the learning outcomes must be due to characteristics of the input to the model. In a post-hoc analysis of the 500 input words in each language, we found that the nouns and verbs in the two languages differ along a number of dimensions, most clearly in word length and word frequency. Compared to nouns, most verbs in Chinese are shorter, and more than 40 per cent are monosyllabic. In English, nouns and verbs overlap more closely in word length. Thus, the monosyllabic nature of Chinese is more clearly reflected in verbs than in nouns.[6] With regard to word frequency, we found that more verbs have higher frequencies in Chinese than in English when comparing the Chinese and the English parental speech in the CHILDES corpus (see Zhao & Li, 2008 for details). Consequently Chinese verbs may be generally easier to learn than nouns. From these

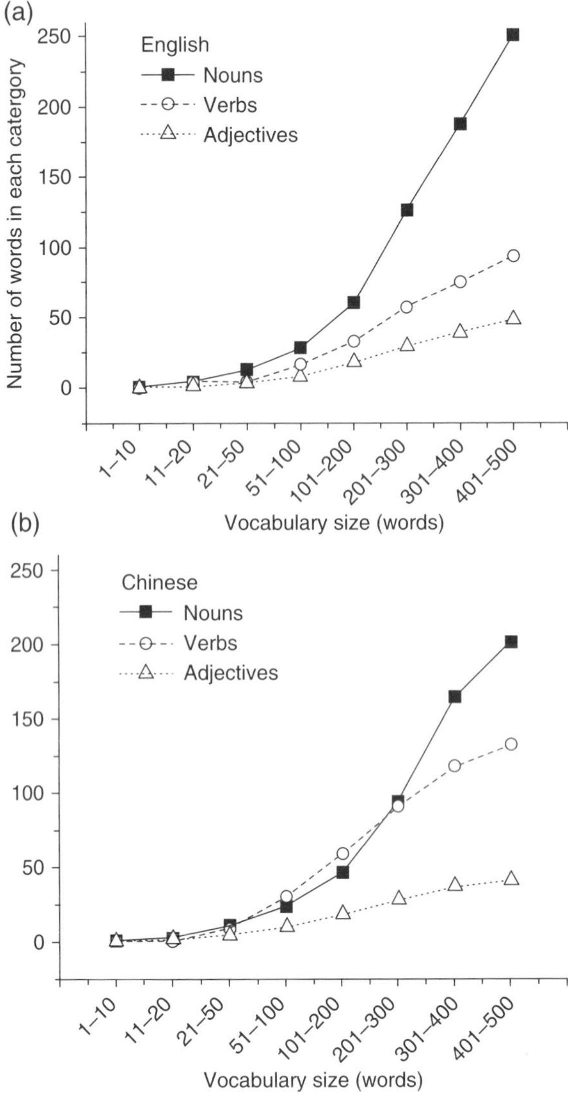

Fig. 6.4 Mean number of nouns, verbs, and adjectives learned by DevLex-II at different developmental stages for (A) Chinese and (B) English. Results are averaged across ten simulation trials (see Zhao & Li, 2008).

analyses we can suggest that children, as well as our network, capitalize on the linguistic characteristics of the lexicon in acquiring early vocabulary, and in this process, verbs may be relatively more advantaged in Chinese as compared with English and other languages. In sum, our simulated results indicate clear crosslinguistic differences in early vocabulary development, and analyses of the properties of the input to the model shed light on the sources of such differences.

Modeling bilingual language acquisition

Our ability to acquire not only a first (L1) but also a second (L2) language, or more, has been a fascinating topic for scientists and laymen alike (see Cheung, this volume). Recent computational and neuroimaging studies have begun to reveal important mechanisms about how we learn and represent two or more languages in one brain. Computational studies are particularly insightful in this respect, given their flexibility in parameter variation and ability to test hypotheses. In empirical studies it is hardly possible to control for the great number of variables such as timing, rate, frequency, and quantity of L1 versus L2 input, whereas computational models provide the necessary tools for dealing with these variables systematically.

How does our model contribute specifically to the understanding of fundamental issues of bilingual language acquisition and representation? In the discussion above, we trained two separate models that received the discussion above inputs from two different languages and then compared the two models to infer sources of differences in learning outcomes. In this section, we discuss bilingual models that take inputs from different languages together (see Figure 6.2 for an example). Our model has so far focused on the effects of the timing (age of acquisition) and the amount of L2 input on the learning process. In particular, we focus on how the two lexical systems compete during the acquisition of L2, as compared with the acquisition of L1. Traditionally, the age of acquisition issue has attracted more research attention in the study of second-language acquisition (SLA), whereas the issue of lexical representation has attracted more attention in bilingual memory research. Our computational work has attempted to link these two issues, that is, to argue that the mental representation of the bilingual lexicon depends on the age of acquisition, or that age effects also appear in bilingual lexical representation. In making this connection we see SLA and bilingual processing as two sides of the same coin, especially as we take a developmental perspective toward the evolving representations during learning.

As shown earlier in Figure 6.2, the network was able to receive and self-organize input from both Chinese and English, and derived meaningful semantic and phonological representations for both languages. What is more interesting for our purpose is how the representational structures can develop and change as a function of the learning history. To understand the emergence of lexical categories across languages, we manipulated the onset time of L2 learning relative to that of L1 learning. We varied the vocabulary onset time in three scenarios: (1) simultaneous learning, in which the two target lexicons from Chinese and English are learned together; (2) early learning, in which the L2 (Chinese) lexicon is learned after the L1 (English) lexicon has started; and (3) late learning, in which the L2 lexicon is learned after the L1 lexicon has been consolidated in learning. By manipulating vocabulary onset time for L2 relative to that of L1, our model allows us to see clearly how the consolidation of lexical organization in one language impacts lexical representation in the other language. We hypothesized that the representational structure for the two lexicons in our model would differ as a function of this age of acquisition manipulation.

Figure 6.5 presents snapshots of the results from the three learning situations in our simulations. In the simultaneous learning situation, we can see clear and distinct lexical representations emerging for both L1 (English) and L2 (Chinese) at both the phonological and the semantic levels and within each language. The results are similar to Li and Farkas's (2002) previous work, and the network's ability to develop distinct representations for each language shows that simultaneous learning of two languages allows the system to easily separate the lexicon during learning (see also French & Janquet, 2004).

In the case of sequential acquisition, however, the results are not so clear-cut. If L2 was introduced into learning early on, then the lexical organization patterns were similar (though not identical) to those found in simultaneous acquisition, as shown in Figure 6.5c and Figure 6.5d. The differences are reflected as the slightly smaller spaces occupied by the L2 words (Chinese, the dark areas on each map) as compared to the lexical space occupied by L1, and more dispersed and fragmented distributions of L2 on the phonological map (Figure 6.5d) as compared to simultaneous learning results (Figure 6.5b). Finally, if L2 was introduced into learning late, the lexical organization patterns were significantly different from those found in simultaneous acquisition, as shown in Figure 6.5e and Figure 6.5f. L2 representations appeared to be parasitic on those of L1 words: the L2 words were dispersed throughout the map and did not form any large independent groups.

Why is late L2 learning so different from the other two situations? We believe that this is due to the significant difference in developmental changes as a function of learning history. In the late learning

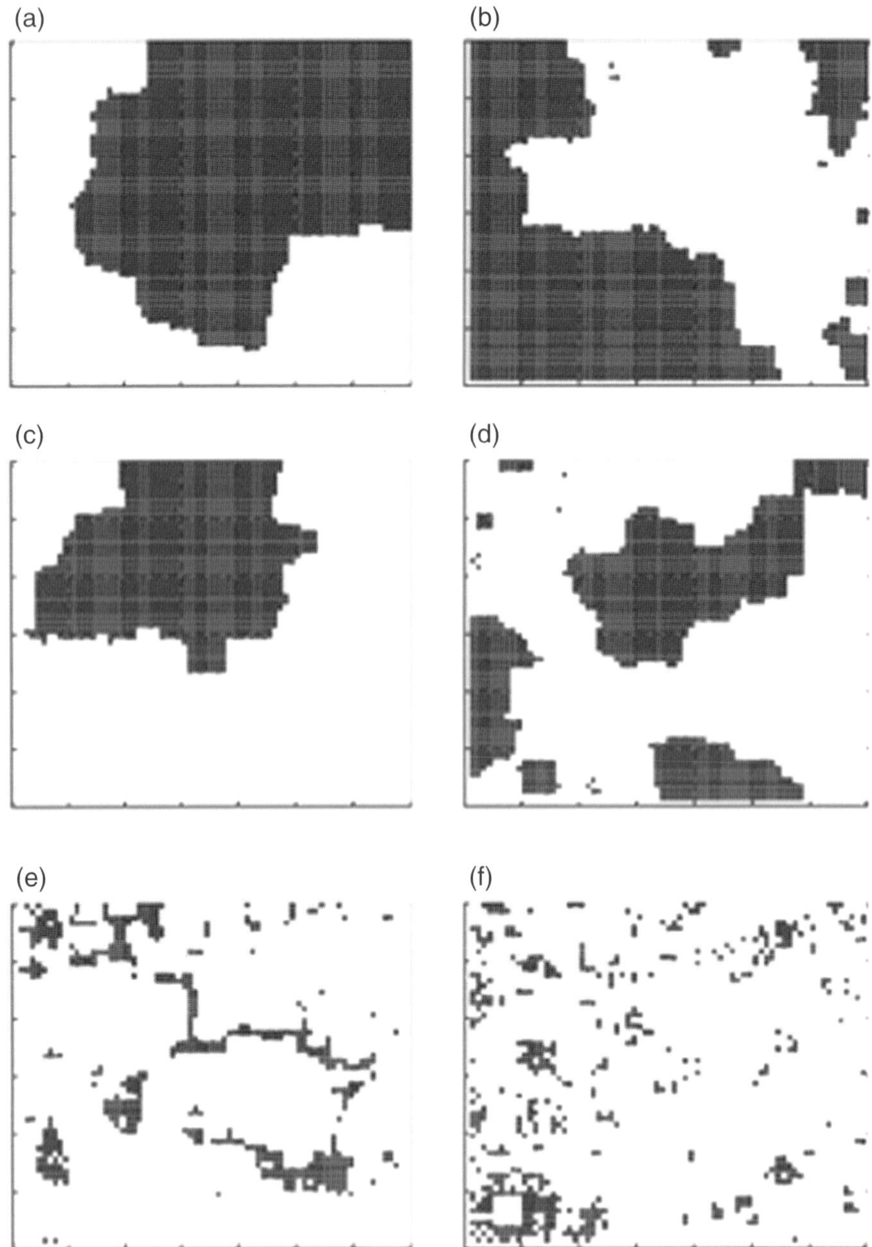

Fig. 6.5 Examples of bilingual lexical representations on the semantic map and the phonological map. Dark areas correspond to L2 (Chinese) words; (a, b): simultaneous learning; (c, d): early L2 learning; (e, f) late L2 learning (see Zhao & Li, 2007).

situation, L2 is introduced at a time when the learning system has dedicated its resources and representational structure to L1, and L1 representations are consolidated, such that L2 can only use existing structures and associative connections that are already built by the L1 lexicon. This is because the network's re-organizational ability (plasticity) has been significantly weakened as its functional connections become specified. In contrast, for the early L2 learning, the network still has a significant degree of plasticity and can continually reorganize the lexical space for L2. Rather than becoming parasitic on the L1 lexicon, early learning allows the increase of the L2 lexicon to present a significant competition against the L1 lexicon. Our simulations here provide further insights into the relationships between competition, entrenchment, and plasticity in the learning of L1 and l2 lexicons together, either simultaneously or sequentially. These findings allow us to see how two competing language systems interact with each other, and the effects of this interaction on the organization and representational structure of the bilingual lexicon.

Modeling Chinese character acquisition

In an effort to extend the computational modeling to the acquisition of Chinese orthography, we used a self-organizing, connectionist model to simulate character acquisition by school-aged children (Xing, Shu, and Li, 2002, 2004; Yang et al., 2006). There have been only a few computational models for the processing of Chinese characters (e.g. Chen & Peng, 1994; and Perfetti, Liu, & Tan, 2005), but no model has examined character acquisition prior to our work. In contrast to the dearth of computational research, there has been a wealth of knowledge gained from experimental and corpus-based studies of how Chinese children learn characters (see for example Shu et al., 2000).

We aimed our connectionist model of character acquisition at two goals: (1) to test the usefulness of self-organizing neural networks in orthographic processing, and, more importantly, (2) to evaluate the degree to which connectionist models can inform us of the complex structural and processing properties of the Chinese orthography. The most serious obstacle to this second goal was the faithful representation of the complex orthographic similarities of Chinese characters. To overcome this obstacle, we analyzed a large-scale character database, the UCS Chinese character database (Standards Press, 1994), and examined the strokes, components, and structures for each of the 20,902 characters in the database. On the basis of this analysis, our character representation system incorporated the component features, shapes, stroke structures, radical positions, and stroke numbers, encoded in a 60-unit vector representation of the 20,902 characters. For example, component features include single, separate, crossing, and connecting; radical positions included top, bottom, left, right, middle, inner, etc. (see Xing, Shu, & Li, 2004, 2007 for details).

To simulate children's acquisition of characters, we selected the input characters from the school Chinese corpus that consists of 2,570 characters from elementary school textbooks used in Beijing (Shu, Chen, Anderson, Wu, & Xuan, 2003). Our model was trained on three batches of roughly 300 characters each, which occurred in Grades 1, 3, and 5 in the corpus. The training progressed by pairing the orthographic representations of these characters in one map with their phonological representations in the other (i.e. the PatPho representations of Chinese; see Li & MacWhinney, 2002; Xing et al., 2004). Once the train was completed, the model was tested with novel words for character naming, and the testing words varied in their frequency (high vs. low), regularity (regular vs. irregular), and consistency (consistent vs. inconsistent).

Our simulations revealed several interesting patterns. First, the model developed clearly structured representations for Chinese characters, indicating the validity of both the representational method and the effectiveness of the self-organizing learning process. Second, the tests with novel characters in our model showed both frequency effects and regularity effects in character acquisition, and more importantly, the interaction between the two: regularity effects were only marginal for high-frequency characters, but were pronounced for low-frequency characters and novel characters. Figure 6.6 presents the effects of regularity, frequency, and consistency in character naming by our model. Such interaction effects have been found to be robust in empirical studies (e.g. Yang & Peng, 1997), and our model captures these interactions faithfully. We further conducted analyses on the naming errors produced by the model and found that the model's 'awareness' of regularity increased with the training grade: in Grade 2, the network tended to read novel characters as totally irrelevant characters, but in Grades 4 and 6, it became more likely to read the character in the pronunciation of its phonetic part or as another character having a similar phonetic part. These developmental

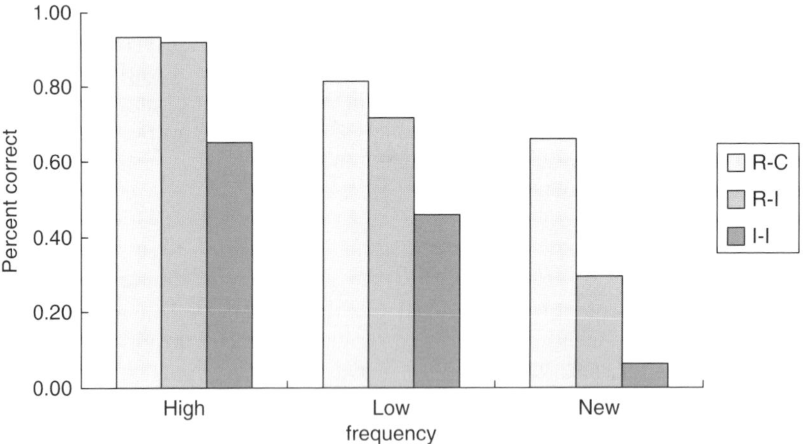

Fig. 6.6 Interaction between regularity, frequency, and consistency in the model's character naming (R-C = regular consistent, R-I = regular inconsistent, I-I = irregular inconsistent). Both regularity effects and consistency effects are stronger for low-frequency and new items than for high-frequency items (see Xing, Shu, & Li, 2004).

patterns match up well with empirical observations, for example, as reported by Shu, Anderson, and Wu (2000).

While these simulations represent only an initial step in modeling the acquisition of Chinese characters, they should make a good starting point for fertile explorations of the computational mechanisms underlying the acquisition of logographic orthographies. It is our hope that this type of work will also serve as a catalyst for future comparative studies of language learning in the monolingual and bilingual contexts. In particular, experience with the target language characteristics—for example, Chinese characters and the Chinese lexicon—might differentially impact upon the learning process and the cognitive and neural representations of the language user (see Perfetti, Liu, Fiez, Nelson, Bolger, & Tan, 2007). One might reasonably speculate that an English learner will have significantly different experiences when learning Chinese as a second language versus learning Spanish as a second language, given the differences between English and Chinese and the overlaps between English and Spanish with respect to both the written and spoken characteristics of the two target languages. Future computational explorations of language-specific properties and their impact on language acquisition should lead to important discoveries in both the monolingual and the bilingual context.

Neuroimaging studies

While computational modeling has significantly advanced our understanding of the cognitive mechanisms underlying language, neuroimaging techniques, particularly functional Magnetic Resonance Imaging (fMRI), have swiftly revolutionized our view of the relationships between language, brain, and culture. The explosion of research projects and publications that have relied on the fMRI method in the last decade has been unprecedented. The non-invasiveness of the technique has allowed researchers to peek into the workings of the human mind via the functions of the brain. Specifically, fMRI provides the so-called BOLD (blood-oxygen-level-dependent) signals in pinpointing the functional activities occurring in various cortical regions of the brain. Through comparing BOLD signals due to various tasks in cognitive processing versus those from a baseline task, researchers can infer the role that each cortical region plays in a given task, for example in processing of the prosody, phonology, or semantics of words or sentences.

Although mature fMRI technology has been made available to psychologists and linguists only recently, it has quickly found its way into the cognitive study of language representation and language acquisition. It has also been successfully applied to the study of Chinese: for example, dyslexia in Chinese-speaking children, and Chinese–English bilingual representation (see Chee, 2006; Siok et al., 2004; and Tan & Siok, 2006, for reviews). In what follows, we discuss a few recent studies from our laboratories that have examined language processing in Chinese using fMRI methodology.

Processing of nouns and verbs in Chinese

A central issue in the cognitive neuroscience of language has been how the brain represents linguistic categories, such as nouns and verbs. This issue is directly related to our major themes about the development of lexical organization and the emergence of lexical categories. In English, it has been shown that nouns and verbs elicit distinct cortical responses, in that nouns activate the posterior brain systems encompassing temporal-occipital regions, while verbs activate the prefrontal and frontal-temporal regions (e.g. Damasio & Tranel, 1993; Martin, Haxby, Lalonde, Wiggs, & Ungerleider, 1995; Pulvermüller, 1999). Neuropsychological data from patients with brain injuries first showed this verb–frontal, noun–posterior dissociation (e.g. Bates, Chen, Tzeng, Li, & Opie, 1991; Caramazza & Hillis, 1991; Miceli, Silveri, Nocentini, & Caramazza, 1988). However, more recent evidence suggests that this view might be overly simplistic (see e.g. Pulvermüller, 1999; Tyler et al., 2001). Researchers have pointed out a number of problems with the presumed noun–verb dissociation, suggesting that the specific task and the actual word stimuli used in the experiments could all contribute to whether a clear-cut noun–verb distinction can be found in the brain.

Chinese linguists have long debated whether a clear-cut noun–verb distinction can even be observed in the language (Kao, 1990; Hu, 1996). In Indo-European languages, nouns are marked for definiteness, case, gender, and number, whereas verbs are marked for aspect, number, and tense. The Chinese language does not have similar morphological markers (with the exception of aspect markers). In addition, many nouns can occur freely in sentence predicates and verbs in subject positions, involving no morphological changes. Furthermore, the Chinese language has a large number of class-ambiguous words that can be used as nouns and as verbs (like *paint* in English), but unlike their counterparts in English and other languages, these ambiguous words involve no morphological changes when used in the sentence as either nouns or verbs. Linguists call these 'words of dual membership', identical in pronunciation and writing but only related in meaning.[7] Although such ambiguous words are also possible in other languages, they may not occur as frequently or may involve morphological changes.

A natural question to ask is how these language-specific properties affect representations in the brain. Do speakers of typologically different languages have different neural representations for nouns and verbs? One prediction, based on such differences, is that nouns and verbs in Chinese do not involve distinct neural representations as they do in English or other Indo-European languages. A different prediction would be that nouns and verbs in Chinese, although not marked grammatically as such, should still show differences in neural representations, due to the conceptual and linguistic differences between the two categories in denoting objects and actions.

Li, Jin, and Tan (2004) tested these predictions in an fMRI study, and found evidence that confirms the first prediction. Native Chinese speakers from Beijing were asked to read lists of nouns, verbs, and class-ambiguous words and make lexical decisions in a scanner, and their functional images were acquired while they performed the lexical decision task (see Li et al., 2004 for technical details). The results showed that unlike in English and Indo-European languages, nouns and verbs in Chinese similarly activate a wide range of overlapping brain areas, in both the left and the right hemisphere. We found no statistically significant differences between nouns, verbs, and class-ambiguous words in brain activation patterns. Compared with baseline fixations, nouns, verbs, and ambiguous words all elicited brain activities in inferior frontal, middle temporal, and the cerebellum areas. Figure 6.7 presents the averaged brain activations for the three categories versus the baselines.

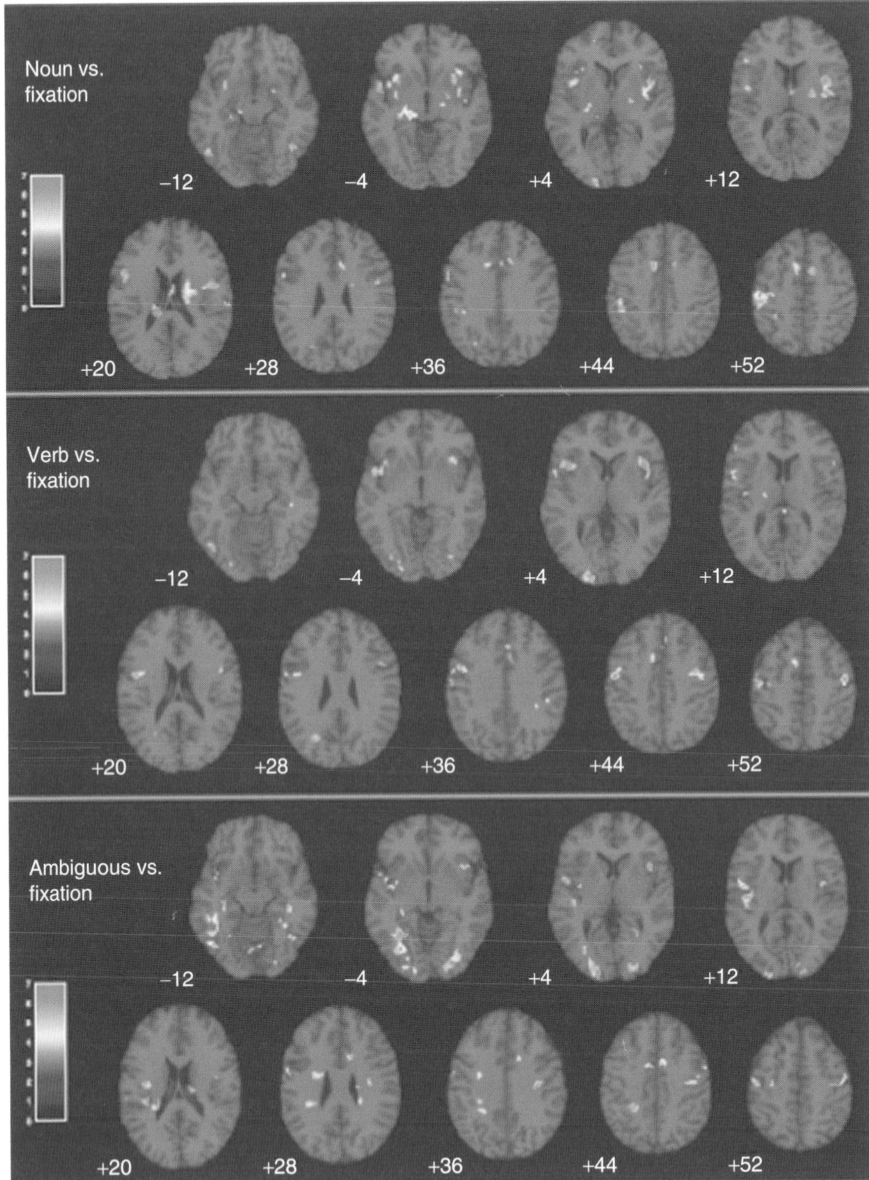

Fig. 6.7 Averaged brain activations for nouns versus fixations, verbs versus fixations, and class-ambiguous words versus fixations. No significant differences were found between nouns, verbs, and ambiguous words. Reprinted from Li et al., 2004, with permission from Elsevier.

If the cortical patterns in the processing of nouns and verbs in Chinese are due to the language user's experiences with language-specific properties of the lexicon and the grammar, as we propose here, how do speakers who have experiences with both Chinese and English represent nouns and verbs in the bilingual brain? Would nouns and verbs from Chinese and English be represented and processed in the same way as in one language, or would they exhibit specific patterns of response according to the specific language? In a follow-up study, we examined the neural patterns of noun versus verb representations in a group of early bilingual learners in Hong Kong who started to learn English between the ages of three and five. Participants were asked to read lists of nouns and verbs in Chinese and English, and their fMRI images were acquired while they performed lexical decision tasks (see Chan et al., 2008 for details).

The results showed that nouns and verbs generated distinct cortical response patterns in the bilinguals' two languages. For Chinese, nouns and verbs activated a wide range of overlapping brain areas, distributed in frontal, parietal, occipital areas as well as the cerebellum; this pattern is consistent with findings from the monolingual study discussed above. For English, however, nouns and verbs showed significant differences in a number of cortical regions, including the left putamen, cerebellum, supplementary motor area, and the right visual cortex. These regions are implicated in motor and sensory functions such as the coordination of speech articulation, and activation in these areas may be due to the action and movement valence denoted by verbs.

Our findings from the bilingual fMRI study are also consistent with the argument that linguistic experiences with language-specific properties shape the neural systems of language representation, as discussed for the monolingual study. By contrast, our findings are at odds with the proposal that there is a common neural system for bilingual language representation, as suggested by a number of scholars who have applied neuroimaging techniques to the bilingualism and second-language acquisition research (e.g. Abutalebi & Green, 2007; Chee et al., 1999; Klein et al., 1995; Kim et al., 1997; Perani et al., 1998). Our study instead suggests that the form of representation in the bilingual brain is weighted by properties of the particular target languages and may have distinct underlying neural correlates. When the key properties of the two language systems differ more widely, the neural systems involved show greater differentiation.

Cortical competition during language discrimination

The frontiers of cognitive neuroscience have quickly moved from identifying the functions of individual cortical regions to the understanding of the brain as a dynamical system of coordinated neural networks involved in information processing or problem solving. In particular, it is important to understand the interactive dynamics that lead to the recruitment of complementary and competing cortical regions, depending on the task demand or the nature of the problem.

In what follows we will illustrate this new direction of research with a study that examines the discrimination of languages by native speakers of Chinese.[8] Our study shows that the perception and discrimination of language in a single task are the result of joint contributions from a network of multiple brain regions, each being weighted by the validity of the corresponding cues being processed. Again, neural representations are dependent on the specific experience of the language user, though this time involving a coordinated system of several regions rather than individual regions.

As is the case with nouns and verbs, typologically different languages tend to highlight different aspects of the linguistic system, leading to the idea that the same linguistic cues (e.g. morphology, syntax, semantics) may have different validities for speakers of different languages. According to the competition model of Bates and MacWhinney (1982, 1987, 1989), different linguistic cues compete with each other during language processing and language acquisition, and the cues that have higher validities tend to win the competition, leading to faster processing and earlier acquisition. Within the lexicon, there are at least the following cues that learners can attend to: phonemes (phonetic repertoire of a language), phonotactics (regularities underlying phonemic co-occurrences), prosody (e.g. rhythm, stress, tone), and the semantic content of words. Ramus and Mehler (1999) considered phonetic repertoire, phonotactics, and prosody as the 'prelexical' cues that listeners can use in discriminating between different languages, which differ from 'lexical' knowledge that contains semantic and conceptual representations, which listeners also undoubtedly use in language discrimination.

How different prelexical and lexical cues compete and interact during early language perception has been a topic of much empirical research. Previous studies in language discrimination, however, have focused on prelexical cues, and have not examined how both prelexical and lexical cues compete during language processing. In particular, we are interested in identifying the underlying neural mechanisms, that is, how patterns of cue competition translate into patterns of cortical competition.

Previous neuroimaging research has provided evidence that prosodic and phonological processing versus lexical semantic processing are subserved by separate brain regions with overlapping boundaries (see e.g. Bookheimer, 2002; Price 2000; Vigneau et al., 2006 for reviews). For example, phonological processing is associated with neural activities in the left hemisphere in inferior frontal, superior temporal, and supramarginal areas (BA44/22/40: Brodmann's areas), whereas processing of intonation and tones is often associated with activities in the right hemisphere in the anterior superior temporal gyrus (BA22) and the inferior frontal gyrus (operculus, BA44). By contrast, lexical semantic processing involves a stronger role of the temporal lobe, including the inferior temporal gyrus (BA20) and middle temporal gyrus (BA21) in the left hemisphere. What has not become clear is how the different brain regions may interact and compete with each other during the same processing task.

In our fMRI study we provided native Chinese listeners in Beijing with both synthesized and natural speech from familiar (L1, Chinese and L2, English) and unfamiliar languages (Japanese and Italian). Participants were asked to decide if two successively presented sentence stimuli belong to the same language (see Zhao et al., 2008 for details). Anatomical and functional images were acquired while the participants performed the task. Figure 6.8 presents the contrasting patterns of brain activation elicited by familiar (Chinese and English) and unfamiliar languages (Japanese and Italian).

The results illustrate clearly how prelexical and lexical cues compete and how such competitions are reflected as cortical activities. First, when processing unfamiliar languages such as Italian and Japanese, native Chinese listeners can only rely on prelexical cues, including prosodic and phonological information, given that lexical semantic information is not accessible to the participants. Thus, the left inferior frontal gyrus (along with superior temporal gyrus, not shown here) associated with phonological and prosodic processing becomes highly activated. In contrast, when processing

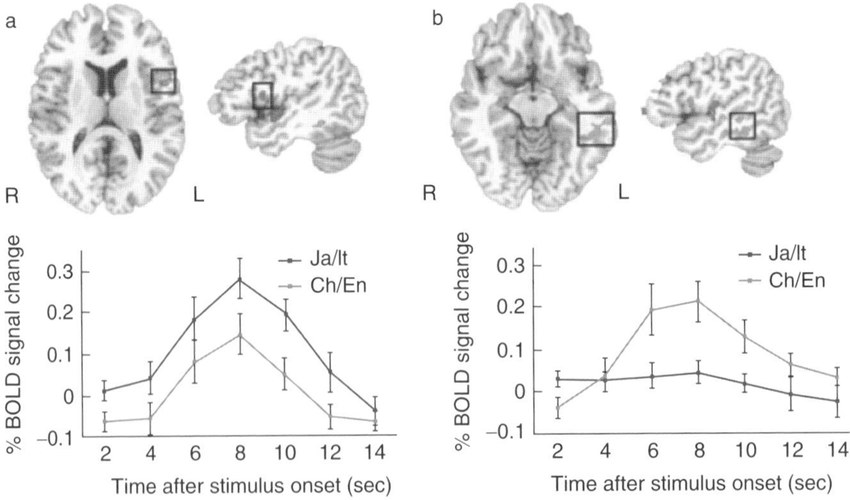

Fig. 6.8 Selected brain regions showing significant activation differences between familiar (Chinese/English) and unfamiliar (Italian/Japanese) stimulus conditions in the language discrimination task. Activation maps and time-course results indicate that (a) unfamiliar languages elicited stronger activations than familiar languages in the left inferior frontal gyrus (IFG), while (b) familiar languages elicited stronger activations than unfamiliar languages in the left inferior temporal gyrus (ITG). Error bars indicate standard errors of the mean (reprinted from Zhao et al., 2008, with permission from Elsevier).

familiar languages of the L1 and L2, listeners can use both prelexical and lexical semantic knowledge, and thus the left inferior temporal gyrus associated with semantic processing, as well as the left inferior frontal gyrus, becomes activated. These patterns of activation indicate that complementary brain regions relevant to the processing task are recruited.

Second, comparing Figure 6.8a and Figure 6.7b, we can see that when lexical semantic cues are available and semantic analysis is possible, as in the Chinese–English case, the brain regions associated with phonological or prosodic processing become less activated, as compared with the situation when only prelexical cues are available. This weaker activation is clearly the result of cue competition, given that lexical semantics carry higher cue validities as compared to prelexical cues for language discrimination. Finally, our comparison of the results from synthesized versus natural speech (see Zhao et al., 2008) indicates that cortical activities tend to work 'additively' for prelexical cues (more activation for more cues), while prelexical and lexical cues together show the 'competitive' patterns discussed above. This progression from 'additive' to 'competitive' patterns of neural response could have significant implications for understanding the child–adult differences in language acquisition, given that infants first attend to prelexical cues (prosody, rhythm, tones, and intonation) and then acquire lexical semantic information, while adults have to deal with both prelexical and lexical cues at the same time in learning a second language.

Idiom processing in Chinese

If we have to name the one most prominent feature of the Chinese language, we probably have to say that Chinese differs from all modern languages in its reliance on a two-thousand-year culture and tradition. No modern language reflects its sociocultural history as strongly as does Chinese, and this reflection is most clearly seen in its use of the large number of idioms that are grounded in its past history and literature. For example, many idioms, such as 叶公好龙 (*ye gong hao long*, 'Mr Ye likes dragons'), are deeply grounded in the context of a historical event, a legendary story, a play, or a description in a novel.[9] Such figurative meanings deviate greatly from the literal meanings of the words in the idioms, a feature significantly different from most idioms in Western languages.

Idiom processing has generated interesting empirical research and has led to theoretical debates regarding the role of the left versus the right hemisphere in the processing of idioms. According to the classical RH theory (Burgess & Chiarello, 1996), the right hemisphere is particularly important in reading idioms, due to its role in accessing meanings that are dependent on pragmatic and social contexts. This hypothesis was supported by early neuropsychological evidence, such as patients' lack of understanding of the figurative meanings of idioms—these patients typically suffer from right hemisphere injuries (Van Lancker & Kempler, 1987; Kempler et al., 1999). Recent neuroimaging studies, however, have shown evidence contradicting this theory: brain activations were found in inferior frontal gyrus and middle temporal gyrus (Zempleni et al., 2007) and in dorsolateral prefrontal cortex (Rizzo et al., 2007), in both hemispheres in figurative comprehension of idioms. Other studies have found that the left hemisphere may even play a more important role in processing idioms (Papagno et al., 2004; Cacciari et al., 2006; Fogliata et al., 2007; Mashal et al., 2008).

The massive number of idioms in Chinese provides an ideal opportunity for identifying the neural substrates of idiom processing.[10] In our fMRI study, participants were asked to read four-character idioms, and determine if there was any character in the idiom that was in italic font (see Liu et al., 2008, for details). This was an implicit semantic processing task, and participants pressed two different response buttons to indicate their yes and no choices. Three types of the materials were used in our experiment: (1) figurative idioms, such as 叶公好龙 (*ye gong hao long*, 'Mr Ye likes dragons'), in which the figurative meaning is based on sociocultural or literary contexts (see above), (2) literal idioms, such as 鹅毛大雪 (*e mao da xue*, 'feature-like big snow'), in which the figurative meaning can be derived from the literal meaning, and (3) regular phrases, such as 飞机起飞 (*fei ji qi fei*, 'plane takes off'), in which no figurative meaning is possible. Figure 6.9 presents the activation differences in terms of the percentage of BOLD signal changes that the three types of stimuli elicited.

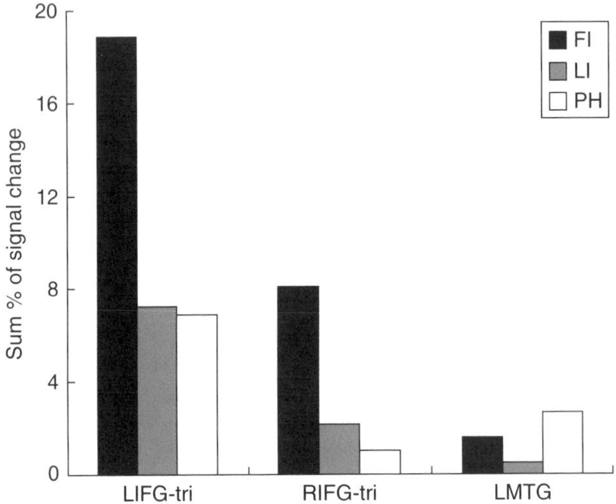

Fig. 6.9 The sum percentage change of signal intensity in three brain regions for the three types of stimuli. LIFG-tri: left inferior frontal gyrus (p. triangularis); RIFG-tri: right inferior frontal gyrus (p. triangularis); LMTG: left middle temporal gyrus. FI: figurative idiom; LI: literal idiom; PH: regular phrases.

Several brain regions have been found to show significantly different patterns for the three types of stimuli. The inferior frontal gyrus appears to be heavily involved in idiom processing. In the left inferior frontal gyrus, the sum signal intensity of figurative idioms was significantly greater than that of literal idioms and regular phrases. Planned comparisons showed that the level of activation for figurative idioms was significantly greater than that for literal idioms and phrases, but that there was no significant difference between the later two conditions. Moreover, in the right inferior frontal gyrus, there was clearly a graded effect of the sum signal intensity across figurative idioms, literal idioms, and phrases, suggesting that this region may be particularly involved in idiom processing. Planned comparisons showed that the activation for figurative idioms was significant greater than for literal idioms and regular phrases, and activation for literal idioms was significantly greater than for regular phrases. In sum, the results show bilateral neural substrates for idiom processing, with the right inferior frontal gyrus playing the most important role. This role might be particularly due to the involvement of the right inferior frontal gyrus in the retrieval of long-term, episodic, memory (see Wiggs et al., 1999), given that the Chinese figurative idioms require special efforts in organizing and completing a knowledge-based story comprehension (i.e. the sociocultural background of the idioms).

General discussion

In this chapter we have provided an overview of the research from our laboratories in computational and neuroimaging studies of the Chinese language. In light of the increasing interest in Chinese from a comparative perspective, in the past decade we have conducted many studies that look into the dynamics and neural substrates underlying language processes. The various studies reviewed here have been designed to identify the computational and neural mechanisms responsible for the acquisition, representation, and processing of languages from a crosslinguistic perspective. On the one hand, we hope to show that the Chinese language presents unique opportunities for the study of language by cognitive neuroscientists, and on the other, we also hope that our studies, however preliminary, will stimulate new research in the domain, given that so many interesting issues remain unexplored.

A general theme that runs through our various studies is that the linguistic brain is highly plastic and hence highly sensitive to distinctive features of particular languages. This applies to both language acquisition and language representation, and in both the monolingual and the bilingual situation. Our computational research indicates clear differences between Chinese and English in the acquisition of nouns and verbs. Our neuroimaging research shows clearly that nouns and verbs are represented differently in the Chinese brain versus in the Western brain, and that bilingual speakers of both types of language display distinct patterns in response to the specific characteristics of the language that they have experience using.

Other published studies provide evidence consistent with our claim regarding language specificity and linguistic experience (see for example Chen et al., 2007; Tan & Siok, 2006; Wang, Sereno, & Jongman, 2006; Zhang & Wang, 2007). Given these data, and the recent Whorfian renaissance (e.g. Levinson et al., 2002; Gentner & Goldin-Meadow, 2003), should we be arguing that these data provide support to the Sapir–Whorf hypothesis that language determines thought? Rather than making such an argument, we propose that our data are best interpreted in the context of a dynamical systems perspective on language, according to which it is the complex nonlinear interactions between the linguistic environment, the language experience, and the characteristics of the adaptive brain that determine the course and outcome of language acquisition and representation.

One particular focus that has emerged from our research is the understanding of the interactive dynamics involved in the language learning process. In particular, our DevLex model is geared towards understanding how early learning impacts upon later development, more specifically, how early learning leads to dedicated cognitive and neural structures that affect or shape the process and outcome of later development. For example, in the case of lexical acquisition in a first language, earlier-learned words establish a basic semantic framework or structure upon which later word learning can be built, leading to vocabulary spurt (see Li et al., 2007). In the case of bilingual lexical representation, previously established lexical structure in a first language often acts to impede optimal learning and representation of a second-language lexicon. This is particularly true when the structural consolidation in L1 has reached a point where further reorganization becomes difficult or impossible; if the learning of L2 occurs at this point, a fundamentally different structure will result for the representation of the L2 lexicon. Our analyses in Figure 6.5 indicate clearly how the reduced plasticity of learning can result in compressed space, fragmented structure, and a parasitic lexicon overall. Understanding of such developmental dynamics is important, and is easy to see once the dynamics are fleshed out mechanistically in a model, such as the DevLex in which learning outcomes and developmental trajectories are determined by the joint forces of learner and learning variables, e.g. the timing of the learning, characteristics of the input, and resources and capacity available for the learning.

Although we have presented the computational findings and the neuroimaging findings separately, it is possible to make some connections and comparisons between the two types of data. For example, in the monolingual case, our modeling results indicate that, given the same learning parameters, the model produces different profiles of nouns and verbs in early vocabulary, depending on which language provides the initial input; in the bilingual case, the nature of lexical representation may be fundamentally different depending on whether L2 is introduced early or late into the acquisition. In our neuroimaging study, all the bilingual speakers were early learners, and therefore they were able to build an English lexical representation system strong enough to compete with their L1 lexicon from early on. Thus, their distinct patterns of neural response match well with the modeling patterns due to age-of-acquisition effects.

If late language learning is so fundamentally different from early language learning, what dimensions of learning might be responsible for such differences? One hypothesis, based on the available neural and computational evidence so far, is the sensorimotor integration hypothesis (see Hernandez & Li, 2007, for discussion). This hypothesis stipulates that sensorimotor learning is privileged early on for linguistic and musical skills, as this type of learning taps more directly into the acoustic, auditory, and phonological, as opposed to semantic and conceptual, codes of language during early stages.

This early-acoustic and later-semantic sequence may turn out to be significant for explaining age-related effects in language acquisition. Our cortical competition findings from the language discrimination study shed some light on this issue, given that we see an additive pattern of cortical activation for the prelexical cues, while competitive patterns of cortical response when both lexical and prelexical cues are being processed. It is likely that children are particularly privileged early on by focusing on sensorimotor integration and working on auditory and acoustic processing, taking advantage of the gradual, 'additive' neural effects of prelexical cues in building up the early preverbal linguistic representation. That is, in infancy through young childhood, the learner builds up language from the ground up, acquiring and using lower-level information such as rhythmic, intonational, and other prosodic cues first, and segmental and phonological cues second, before they acquire lexical semantic contents of words. In contrast, in adulthood the learner faces the language task through exposure and experiences with prelexical and lexical, suprasegmental and segmental, and syntactic and semantic, cues, all competing at once for learning. Our findings suggest that cortical competition might take very different forms in infants, children, and adults for language discrimination, and consequently in the learning of a new language.

Finally, our research suggests that language acquisition and language representation cannot and should not be studied without looking into the intricate relationships between language, cognition, culture, and the brain. Modern research in cognitive science and cognitive neuroscience has been actively exploring such relationships. Computational and neuroimaging methods have provided us with powerful tools for identifying such relationships, and the Chinese language provides us with unique opportunities to study such relationships.

Authors' note

Preparation of this article was supported by grants from the National Science Foundation (#BCS-0642586) to Ping Li, Natural Science Foundation of China (#60534080, #30625024) to Hua Shu, and the Fund for Foreign Scholars in University Research and Teaching Programs (B07008) to PL and HS. We would like to thank Igor Farkas, Youyi Liu, Brian MacWhinney, Li Hai Tan, Hongbing Xing, Jingjing Zhao, and Xiaowei Zhao for their comments, discussions, and collaborations over the years.

Correspondence concerning this article should be addressed to Ping Li, Department of Psychology, Pennsylvania State University, PA 16802, USA; email: pul8@psu.edu. This article was completed while he was working for the National Science Foundation. The opinions expressed in this article are those of the authors and do not necessarily reflect the views of the National Science Foundation.

Chapter notes

1 In this chapter we take a broad definition of 'Chinese' and use it to refer to all dialectal variations of the Chinese language, including Mandarin Chinese and Cantonese.

2 It is beyond the scope of this chapter to provide a detailed discussion of connectionist models, but we have elsewhere provided introductions to which readers can refer (see Li, 2003, 2006). Readers interested in further details should consult Anderson (1995), Dayhoff (1990), Ellis & Humphreys (1999), and Rumelhart, McClelland, and the PDP Group (1986).

3 A 'map' can be considered an independent network, which handles a particular type of linguistic information, e.g. phonology, orthography, or lexical semantics. A 'model' in our case often consists of several maps linked together via Hebbian learning rules (see Li et al., 2004, 2007).

4 In a more recent formulation, Tardif (2006) does not argue for a 'verb bias' but rather suggests that nouns and verbs show parallel growth patterns in Chinese, with perhaps only a marginal verb advantage at the very earliest stages.

5 Interestingly, the simulation patterns are not identical to those from our corpus analyses. In the corpus data, child-directed adult speech in Chinese is rather uniform in terms of noun-verb ratio, whereas children's speech shows a weak verb advantage at the earliest stages. In the model, there is also a slight verb advantage at the 100–200-word level. It might be that the child and the model have capitalized on particular characteristics of verbs early on in the acquisition process.

6 According to Wang (1994), 1,337 out of 3,000 (45 per cent) most frequently spoken Chinese words are monosyllabic. And according to Sun et al. (1996), among the 8,822 words used by the Chinese government to evaluate students' vocabulary levels, 22 per cent are monosyllabic.

7 According to one estimate (Guo, 2001), about 17 per cent of the high-frequency Chinese words have dual-membership status. Another estimate, specifically on nouns and verbs, indicates that regardless of frequency, between 13 per cent and 29 per cent (depending on test criteria) of Chinese monosyllabic and disyllabic words can be used as nouns and as verbs (Hu, 1996).

8 In China, experienced listeners can readily differentiate the seven major dialects spoken in various parts of the country, and in the United States and many parts of the world, speakers can often distinguish southern from northern dialects. This ability to distinguish dialects based on phonological characteristics similarly works in discriminating between familiar and unfamiliar languages, due to listeners' use of a variety of phonological and prosodic cues, e.g. Chinese listeners differentiating Japanese from Italian sentences upon hearing them spoken in a restaurant. Language discrimination can broadly refer to the process of distinguishing between different languages or dialects by the use of prosodic, phonological, and lexical information.

9 The idiom 叶公好龙 (*ye gong hao long*, literally 'Mr Ye likes dragons'), for example, comes from a story in the book by Liu Xiang in the Han Dynasty (25–220 AD), which describes a man who claimed to be fond of dragons, with paintings and carvings of dragons all over his house, but was scared to death when a real dragon came into his house. The four-character idiom has since been used to refer to a situation when someone claims to love something but does not really love it or is in fact afraid of it.

10 By our own estimate, the Chinese language has more than ten thousand items that can be considered idioms.

References

Anderson, J. A. (1995). *An introduction to neural networks*. Cambridge, MA: MIT Press.

Abutalebi, J. & Green, D. (2007). Bilingual language production: The neurocognition of language representation and control. *Journal of Neurolinguistics, 20*, 242–275.

Bates, E., Chen, S., Tzeng, O., Li, P., & Opie, M. (1991). The noun–verb problem in Chinese aphasia. *Brain and Language, 41*, 203–233.

Bates, E. & MacWhinney, B. (1982). Functionalist approaches to grammar. In E. Wanner & L. Gleitman (eds), *Language acquisition: The state of the art*. New York: Cambridge University Press.

Bates, E. & MacWhinney, B. (1987). Competition, variation, and language learning. In B. MacWhinney (ed.), *Mechanisms of language acquisition*. Hillsdale, NJ: Lawrence Erlbaum.

Bates, E. & MacWhinney, B. (1989). Functionalism and the Competition Model. In B. MacWhinney & E. Bates (ed.), *The crosslinguistic study of sentence processing*. New York: Cambridge University Press.

Bates, E., Marchman, V., Thal, D., Fenson, L., Dale, P. S., Reznick, J. S., Reilly, J., & Hartung, J. (1994). Developmental and stylistic variation in the composition of early vocabulary. *Journal of Child Language, 21*, 85–123.

Bookheimer, S. (2002). Functional MRI of language: New approaches to understanding cortical organization of semantic processing. *Annual Review of Neuroscience, 25*, 151–188.

Burgess, C. & Chiarello, C. (1996). Neurocognitive mechanisms underlying metaphor comprehension and other figurative language. *Metaphor and Symbol. 11*, 67–84.

Cacciari, C., Reati, F., Colomboc, M. R., Padovani, R., Rizzo, S., Papagno, C. (2006). The comprehension of ambiguous idioms in aphasic patients. *Neuropsychologia, 44*, 1305–1314.

Caramazza, A. & Hillis, A. E. (1991). Lexical organization of nouns and verbs in the brain. *Nature, 349*, 788–790.

Chan, A., Luke, K., Li, P., Li, G., Yip, V., Weekes, B., & Tan, L. (2008). Neural correlates of nouns and verbs in early bilinguals. *Annals of the New York Academy of Sciences, 1145*, 30–40.

Chee, M. W. L. (2006). Language processing in bilinguals as revealed by functional imaging: a contemporary synthesis. In Li, P., Tan, L. H, Bates, E., & Tzeng, O. (2006). *Handbook of East Asian Psycholinguistics* (Vol.1: Chinese). Cambridge, UK: Cambridge University Press.

Chee, M. W. L., Tan, E. W. L., & Thiel, T. (1999). Mandarin and English single word processing studied with fMRI. *Journal of Neuroscience, 19*, 3050–3056.
Chen, L., Shu, H., Liu, Y., Zhao, J., & Li, P. (2007). ERP signatures of subject–verb agreement in L2 learning. *Bilingualism: Language and Cognition, 10*, 161–174.
Chen, Y. & Peng, D. (1994). A connectionist model of recognition and naming of Chinese characters. In H.-W. Chang, J.-T. Huang, C.-W. Hue, & O. Tzeng (eds), *Advances in the study of Chinese language processing* (Vol.1, pp. 211–240). Taipei: National Taiwan University Press.
Choi, S. (2000). Caregiver input in English and Korean: Use of nouns and verbs in book-reading and toy-play contexts. *Journal of Child Language, 27*, 69–96.
Chomsky, N. (1957). *Syntactic structures.* The Hague: Mouton & Co.
Dale, P. S. & Fenson, L. (1996). Lexical development norms for young children. *Behavior Research Methods, Instruments, & Computers, 28*, 125–127.
Damasio, A. & Tranel, D. (1993). Nouns and verbs are retrieved with differently distributed neural systems. *Proceedings of the National Academy of Sciences, 90*, 4957–4960.
Dayhoff, J. (1990). *Neural network architectures.* New York: Van Nostrand Reinhold.
Ellis, R. & Humphreys, G. (1999). *Connectionist psychology: A text with readings.* East Sussex, UK: Psychology Press.
Estes, W. K. & Newell, A. (1983). Report of the Research Briefing Panel on Cognitive Science and Artificial Intelligence. Washington, DC: National Academy Press.
Fogliata, A., Rizzo, S., Reati, F. Miniussi, C., Oliveri, M., & Papagno, C. (2007).The time course of idiom processing. *Neuropsychologia*, 45, 3215–3222.
French, R. M. & Jacquet, M. (2004). Understanding bilingual memory. *Trends in Cognitive Science, 8*, 87–93.
Gardner, H. (1985). *The mind's new science: A history of the cognitive revolution.* New York: Basic Books.
Gentner, D. (1982). Why nouns are learned before verbs: Linguistic relativity versus natural partitioning. In S. A. Kuczaj (ed.), *Language development (Vol. 2. Language, thought and culture)* (pp. 301–334). Hillsdale, NJ: Lawrence Erlbaum Associates.
Gentner, D. & Goldin-Meadow, S. (2003). *Language in mind: Advances in the study of language and thought.* Cambridge, MA: MIT Press.
Guo, R. (2001). *Hanyu cilei huafen de lunzhen* (On the classification of lexical classes in Chinese). *Zhongguo Yuwen* (Chinese Language), *6*, 494– 507.
Hebb, D. (1949). *The organization of behavior: A neuropsychological theory.* New York, NY: Wiley.
Hernandez, A., Li, P., & MacWhinney, B. (2005). The emergence of competing modules in bilingualism. *Trends in Cognitive Sciences, 9*, 220–225.
Hernandez, A. & Li, P. (2007). Age of acquisition: its neural and computational mechanisms. *Psychological Bulletin, 133*(4), 638–650.
Hu, M. Y. (1996). *Cilei wenti kaocha* (A study of lexical categories). Beijing, China: Beijing Language Institute Press.
Kao, M. K. (1990). *Guanyu hanyu de cilei fenbei* (On the differentiation of lexical classes in Chinese). In: M. K. Kao (ed.), *Kao MK yuyanxue lunwenji* (Linguistic Essays of Kao Ming Kai), pp. 262–272. Beijing, China: Commercial Press.
Kempler, D., Van Lancker, D., Merchman, V., & Bates E. (1999). Idiom comprehension in children and adults with unilateral brain damage. *Developmental Neuropsychology, 15*, 327–349.
Kim, K., Relkin, N., Lee, K., & Hirsh, J. (1997). Distinct cortical areas associated with native and second languages. *Nature, 388*, 171–174.
Klein, D., Milner, B., Zatorre, R. J., Meyer, E., & Evans, A. C. (1995). The neural substrates underlying word generation: A bilingual functional-imaging study. *Proceedings of the National Academy of Sciences, 92*, 2899–2903.
Kohonen, T. (1982). Self-organized formation of topologically correct feature maps. *Biological Cybernetics, 43*, 59–69.
Kohonen, T. (2001). *Self-organizing maps* (3rd edn), Berlin & New York: Springer.
Kuhn, T. S. (1970). *The structure of scientific revolutions.* Chicago, IL: University of Chicago Press.
Levinson, S. C., Kita, S., Huan, D. B. M., & Rasch, B. H. (2002). Returning the tables: Language affects spatial reasoning. *Cognition, 84*, 155–188.
Li, P. (1996). The temporal structure of spoken sentence comprehension in Chinese. *Perception and Psychophysics, 58*, 571–586.
Li, P. (2003). Language acquisition in a self-organising neural network model. In P. Quinlan (ed.), Connectionist models of development: *Developmental processes in real and artificial neural networks.* Hove & New York: Psychology Press.
Li, P. (2006). In search of meaning: The acquisition of semantic structure and morphological systems. In J. Luchjenbroers (ed.), *Cognitive linguistics investigations across languages, fields, and philosophical boundaries.* Amsterdam, Holland: John Benjamins, Inc.
Li, P., Bates, E., & MacWhinney, B. (1993). Processing a language without inflections: A reaction time study of sentence interpretation in Chinese. *Journal of Memory and Language, 32*, 169–192.
Li, P. & Bowerman, M. (1998). The acquisition of grammatical and lexical aspect in Chinese. *First Language, 18*, 311–350.
Li, P. & Farkas, I. (2002). A self-organizing connectionist model of bilingual processing. In R. Heredia & J. Altarriba (eds), *Bilingual sentence processing.* North-Holland: Elsevier Science Publisher.
Li, P., Farkas, I., & MacWhinney, B. (2004). Early lexical development in a self-organizing neural networks. *Neural Networks, 17*, 1345–1362.

Li, P., Jin, Z., & Tan, L. (2004). Neural representations of nouns and verbs in Chinese: An fMRI study. *NeuroImage, 21*, 1533–1541.

Li, P. & MacWhinney, B. (2002). *PatPho*: A phonological pattern generator for neural networks. *Behavior Research Methods, Instruments, and Computers, 34*, 408–415.

Li, P., Tan, L.-H., Bates, E., & Tzeng, O. (2006). *Handbook of East Asian Psycholinguistics* (*Vol. 1: Chinese*). Cambridge, UK: Cambridge University Press.

Li, P., Zhao, X., & MacWhinney, B. (2007). Dynamic self-organization and early lexical development in children. *Cognitive Science, 31*, 581–612.

Liu, S., Zhao, X., & Li, P. (2008). Early lexical development: A corpus-based study of three languages. In B. C. Love, K. McRae, & V. M. Sloutsky (eds), *Proceedings of the 30th Annual Conference of the Cognitive Science Society*. Austin, TX: Cognitive Science Society.

MacWhinney, B. (2000). *The CHILDES project: Tools for analyzing talk*. Hillsdale, NJ: Lawrence Erlbaum.

MacWhinney, B. (2001). Lexical connectionism. In P. Broeder, & J. M. Murre (eds), *Models of acquisition: Inductive and deductive approaches*. Oxford, UK: Oxford University Press.

Martin, A., Haxby, J. V., Lalonde, F. M., Wiggs, C. L., & Ungerleider, L. G. (1995). Discrete cortical regions associated with knowledge of color and knowledge of action. *Science, 270*, 102–105.

Mashal, N., Faust, M., Hendler, T., & Jung-Beeman, M. (2008). Hemispheric differences in processing the literal interpretation of idioms: Converging evidence from behavioral and fMRI studies. *Cortex*. (in press).

Miceli, G., Silveri, M. C., Nocentini, U., & Caramazza, A. (1988). Patterns of dissociation in comprehension and production of nouns and verbs. *Aphasiology, 2*, 351–358.

Miikkulainen, R. (1993). *Subsymbolic natural language processing: An integrated model of scripts, lexicon, and memory*. Cambridge MA: MIT Press.

Miikkulainen, R., Bednar, J., Choe, Y., & Sirosh, J. (2005). *Computational maps in the visual cortex*. New York: Springer.

Papagno, C., Tabossi, P., Colombo, M. R., Zampetti, P. (2004). Idiom comprehension in aphasic patients. *Brain and Language*, 89, 226–234.

Perani, D., Paulesu, E., Sebastian-Galles, N., Dupoux, E., Dehaene, S., Bettinardi, V. et al (1998). The bilingual brain: proficiency and age of acquisition of the second language. *Brain, 121*, 1841–1852.

Perfetti, C. A., Liu, Y., Fiez, J., Nelson, J., Bolger, D. J., & Tan, L. H. (2007). Reading in two writing systems: Accommodation and assimilation of the brain's reading network. *Bilingualism: Language and Cognition, 10*, 131–146.

Perfetti, C. A., Liu, Y., & Tan, L. H. (2005). The Lexical Constituency Model: Some implications of research on Chinese for general theories of reading. *Psychological Review, 112*(1), 43–59.

Price, C. J. (2000). The anatomy of language: contributions from functional neuroimaging. *Journal of Anatomy, 197*, 335–359.

Pulvermüller, F. (1999). Words in the brain's language. *Behavioral and Brain Sciences, 22*, 253–336.

Ramus, F. & Mehler, J. (1999). Language identification with suprasegmental cues: A study based on speech resynthesis. *Journal of the Acoustical Society of America, 105*, 512–521.

Rizzo, S., Sandrini, M., & Papagno, C. (2007). The dorsolateral prefrontal cortex in idiom interpretation: An rTMS study. *Brain Research Bulletin*, 71, 523–528.

Rumelhart, D. E., MeClelland, J. L. & the PDP Research Group. (1986). Parallel Distributed Processing, Explorations in the Microstructure of Cognition (Vol.1). Cambridge, MA.: The MIT Press.

Standards Press of China (1994). *Information Technology—UCS: Universal Multiple-Octet Coded Character Set* (Part 1: Architecture and Basic Multilingual Plane). Beijing.

Shu, H., Anderson, R., & Wu, N. (2000). Phonetic awareness: Knowledge on orthography-phonology relationship in character acquisition of Chinese children. *Journal of Educational Psychology, 92*, 56–62.

Shu, H., Chen, X., Anderson, R., Wu, N., & Xuan, Y. (2003). Properties of school Chinese: Implications for learning to read. *Child Development, 74*, 27–47.

Siok, W. T., Perfetti, C. A., Jin, Z., & Tan, L. H. (2004). Biological abnormality of impaired reading is constrained by culture. *Nature, 431*, 71–76.

Sun, H.L., Sun, D.J., Huang, J.P., Li. D.J. & Xing, H.B. (1996). "现代汉语研究语料库"概述. In Luo, Z.S. & Y.L. Yuan (eds), *Studies of Chinese language and characters in a computer era* (pp, 283–294). Beijing, China: Tsinghua University Press.

Tan, L. H. & Siok, W. T. (2006). How the brain reads the Chinese language: Recent neuroimaging findings. In P. Li, L. H. Tan, E. Bates, & O. Tzeng (eds), *Handbook of East Asian Psycholinguistics (Vol. 1: Chinese)*. Cambridge, UK: Cambridge University Press.

Tardif, T. (1996). Nouns are not always learned before verbs: Evidence from Mandarin speakers' early vocabularies. *Developmental Psychology, 32*, 492–504.

Tardif, T. (2006). The importance of verbs in Chinese. In P. Li, L. H. Tan, E. Bates, & O. Tzeng (eds), *Handbook of East Asian Psycholinguistics* (*Vol. 1: Chinese*). Cambridge, UK: Cambridge University Press.

Tardif, T., Fletch, P., Liang, W. L, & Zhang, Z. X. (2002). Nouns and verbs in children's early vocabularies: A cross-linguistic study of the MacArthur Communicative Developmental Inventory in English, Manadarin, and Cantonese. Poster presented at the *Joint Conference of International Association for the Study of Child Language and Society for Research in Communication Disorders*. Madison, WI, July 2002.

Tyler, L. K., Russell, R., Fadili, J., & Moss, H. E. (2001). The neural representation of nouns and verbs: PET studies. *Brain, 124*, 1619–1634.
Van Lancker, D. & Kempler, D. (1987). Comprehension of familiar phrases by left but not by right hemisphere damaged patients. *Brain and Language, 32*: 265–277.
Vigneau, M., Beaucousin, V., Herve, P. Y., Duffau, H., Crivello, F., Houde, O., Mazoyer, B. & Tzourio-Mazoyer, N. (2006). Meta-analyzing left hemisphere language areas: Phonology, semantics, and sentence processing. *NeuroImage, 30*, 1414–1432.
Wang, Y., Sereno, J., & Jongman, A. (2006). L2 acquisition and processing of Mandarin tones. In P. Li, L. H. Tan, E. Bates, & O. Tzeng (eds), *Handbook of East Asian Psycholinguistics (Vol. 1: Chinese)*. Cambridge, UK: Cambridge University Press.
Wiggs, C. L., Weisberg, J., & Martin, A. (1999). Neural correlates of semantic and episodic memory retrieval. *Neuropsychologia, 37*, 103–118.
Xing, H., Shu, H., & Li, P. (2002). A self-organizing connectionist model of character acquisition in Chinese. In W. D. Gray & C. D. Schunn (eds), *Proceedings of the Twenty-Fourth Annual Conference of the Cognitive Science Society* (pp. 950–955). Mahwah, NJ: Lawrence Erlbaum.
Xing, H., Shu, H., & Li, P. (2004). The acquisition of Chinese characters: Corpus analyses and connectionist simulations. *Journal of Cognitive Science, 5*, 1–49.
Yang, H. & Peng, D. L. (1997). How are Chinese characters represented by children? The regularity and consistency effects in naming. In H. C. Chen (ed.). *The cognitive processing of Chinese and related Asian Languages*. Hong Kong: The Chinese University Press.
Yang, J., Zevin, J., Shu, H., McCandliss, B., & Li, P. (2006). A triangle model of Chinese reading. In R. Sun & N. Miyaki (eds), *Proceedings of the 28th Annual Conference of the Cognitive Science Society* (pp. 912–917). Mahwah, NJ: Lawrence Erlbaum.
Yip, V. & Matthews, S. (2000). Syntactic transfer in a Cantonese–English bilingual child. *Bilingualism: Language and Cognition, 3*, 193–208.
Zempleni, M., Haverkort, M., Renken, R., & Stowe, L. A. (2007). Evidence for bilateral involvement in idiom comprehension: An fMRI study. *NeuroImage, 34*, 1280–1291.
Zhang, Y. & Wang, Y. (2007). Neural plasticity in speech acquisition and learning. *Bilingualism: Language and Cognition, 10*, 147–160.
Zhao, J., Shu, H., Zhang, L., Wang, X., Gong, Q., & Li, P. (2008). Cortical competition during language discrimination. *NeuroImage, 43*, 624–633.
Zhao, X. & Li, P. (2007). Bilingual lexical representation in a self-organizing neural network. In D. S. McNamara & J. G. Trafton (eds), *Proceedings of the 29th Annual Conference of the Cognitive Science Society* (pp. 755–760). Austin, TX: Cognitive Science Society.
Zhao, X. & Li, P. (2008). Vocabulary development in English and Chinese: A comparative study with self-organizing neural networks. In B. C. Love, K. McRae, & V. M. Sloutsky (eds), *Proceedings of the 30th Annual Conference of the Cognitive Science Society*. Austin, TX: Cognitive Science Society.

CHAPTER 7

Language and literacy development in Chinese children

Catherine McBride-Chang, Dan Lin, Yui-Chi Fong, and Hua Shu

Studies of Chinese children's reading have focused both on development and impairment of literacy skills. In this chapter, we will first survey the basics of Chinese literacy development, considering the environments in which reading and writing are taught across Chinese societies, as these may differ in languages and scripts used, among other things. These differences in languages and scripts are reflected in the fact that our examples throughout the remainder of the chapter alternate between traditional and simplified script and Mandarin, or Putonghua, and Cantonese speech. Following this review of these macro-level variables, we will highlight those cognitive/linguistic skills that appear to be important for early Chinese reading acquisition and implicated in Chinese developmental dyslexia, including phonological processing, morphological awareness, and visual-orthographic skills (see also Ho, this volume).

Our next focus will be on parents and home literacy practices in relation to reading and writing achievement in Chinese children. Very early literacy experiences likely pave the way for subsequent literacy development, and a few relatively new studies on Chinese home environments help to illustrate this point.

In the next section, we will overview more specifics about Chinese characters, particularly the components that constitute these characters, and discuss how knowledge of these components might affect literacy development and expertise as children grow into fluent readers.

Finally, we will briefly discuss reading comprehension in Chinese children. The ultimate developmental transition in relation to literacy progresses from learning to read to reading to learn. Fluent reading comprehension marks this achievement, and we will review some necessary components of this process in this last section.

Basics of Chinese literacy

Chinese children learn to read under quite different circumstances in different Chinese societies. One striking difference across societies is found in the existence of two different Chinese scripts, traditional and simplified. Traditional characters are used in Taiwan and Hong Kong, whereas simplified characters are used in mainland China as well as Singapore. In 1956, the mainland Chinese government decided to make many of the traditional Chinese characters easier to read and write, so they were changed in various ways over time. For example, the traditional character 廣 (broad) was simplified into 广 by eliminating the whole character 黃.

Traditional character	Simplified character	English translation
廣	广	broad
電	电	electricity
嗇	啬	stingy
園	园	garden
塵	尘	dust
書	书	book
備	备	preparation
滿	满	full
豐	丰	abundant
義	义	righteousness

Fig. 7.1 Examples of Chinese characters in traditional and simplified script.

Some other examples of simplified and traditional characters are given in Figure 7.1. These demonstrate the varied techniques used for simplifying the characters. In example 3, for instance, the simplified character 啬 (stingy) was created from a simplification of the traditional form, 嗇, by removing some strokes from the original. Another example is simplification by phonetic borrowing. In one such case, the traditional character 園 (garden) was replaced by 园, because both the components 元 and 袁 share a similar sound (phonetic feature), but the former is simpler in structure. However, sometimes the traditional characters were entirely replaced by new, simpler characters, such as 義 (righteousness) and 义 in example 10.

In mainland China, teachers tend to discourage their pupils from using traditional characters, and would consider a pupil's writing incorrect if it were done using traditional characters (Cheung & Ng, 2003). There is relatively little empirical research on the extent to which these different scripts are easier or more difficult to read. In one study comparing children from the mainland (Xiangtan, China) and Hong Kong on character recognition in relation to various cognitive skills, mainland Chinese children were stronger across all visual skills tested than were the Hong Kong Chinese children (McBride-Chang, Chow, Zhong, Burgess, & Hayward, 2005). This finding was a bit surprising given that the Hong Kong children were higher in all other skills tested, including phonological awareness, speeded naming, and character recognition itself.

Given these results, we speculated that perhaps simplified Chinese characters make relatively greater demands on basic visual attention and perception in beginning readers than do traditional characters, primarily because traditional characters include more strokes by which to distinguish them. That is, from a basic cognitive perspective, traditional characters contain more varied visual features that help to differentiate across them for naïve readers, compared to simplified characters. Given this result and other work (M. J. Chen & Yuen, 1991) focusing on differences between traditional and simplified Chinese characters, it may be the case that for beginning readers, traditional characters are easier to recognize, i.e. read, and more difficult to write than are simplified characters for the same reason, viz. their numbers of strokes. Simplified characters comprise fewer strokes, making them more difficult to distinguish relative to traditional characters. However, in practice, the extent to which this distinction can be made is probably impossible to test empirically given the other environmental differences in literacy training across different Chinese societies.

Another such environmental difference across Chinese societies in relation to literacy skills is the use of phonological coding systems for teaching reading. Mainland China and Singapore use the Pinyin system, whereas Taiwan uses the Zhuyin Fuhao system; Hong Kong does not use a phonological coding system to teach Chinese character recognition. Examples of Pinyin and Zhuyin are shown in Figure 7.2. The Pinyin system adopted in China is an auxiliary alphabet used to transcribe Mandarin speech. The system is regarded as alphabetic in the sense that the letters of Pinyin represent individual phonemes. In contrast, in the Zhuyin system, symbols represent either syllable onsets or rimes. That is, the vowel and coda components within the rime are not separately coded. At the

Character	Pinyin	Zhuyin Fuhao	English translation
電單車	diàndānchē	ㄉㄧㄢˋㄉㄢˉㄔㄜˉ	motorcycle
兒子	érzi	ㄦˊㄗ˙	son
危險	wēixiǎn	ㄨㄟˊㄒㄧㄢˇ	danger

Fig. 7.2 Examples of *Pinyin* and *Zhuyin Fuhao*.

(Note: the diacritical marks e.g. ' ˉ ', ' ˇ 'are applied to indicate the tone of each character. Sometimes tones are demonstrated by numbers instead of marks, such that *1* = ' ˉ ', *2* = 'ˊ', *3* = ' ˇ ', *4* = 'ˋ'. For example, the Pinyin 'diàndānchēcan be written as 'dian*4*dan*1*che*1*'.

same time, both phonological coding systems provide shorthand ways for students to decode, or more aptly to recognize, characters or words with which they are not yet familiar. Most Chinese textbooks include the phonetic representation of the newly introduced character or word alongside its representation in Chinese characters.

Researchers interested in literacy development from alphabet-reading societies will recognize phonological coding as essential for learning to read. Knowing that T makes the /t/ sound helps a child to recognize the word *top*, for example. In Chinese coding systems, the speech sound information is marked using phonological symbols equivalent to letters or rhymes in words. In addition, lexical tonal information, which is nonexistent in many alphabetic languages, is marked (see Figure 7.2).

Lexical tone is a fundamental feature of Chinese spoken languages. Lexical tone refers to the pitch of speech that is used to distinguish minimal word pairs that are not differentiated by segmental information (Yiu, van Hasselt, Williams, & Woo, 1994.) Because Putonghua is the most common language of instruction in mainland China, Singapore, and Taiwan, the tonal information presented in Figure 7.2 all maps onto Putonghua. That is, both Pinyin and Zhuyin are used to transcribe Putonghua only. Putonghua has four main tones (i.e. high-level, rising, dipping, and falling tone), together with a fifth, 'neutral', tone. Lexical tone is described in more detail elsewhere in works on the Chinese language, but it is important to mention here that phonetic transcriptions of Chinese include not just consonant and vowel information but also lexical tone information.

By contrast, in Hong Kong no coding system is used to introduce new Chinese characters. Instead, children must learn to recognize these characters using the principle of 'look and say', which basically involves rote memorization of the character and its pronunciation. In addition, Cantonese has more and more varied tones, with estimations ranging from six to twelve (Cheung & Ng, 2003), as compared to Putonghua. In Hong Kong, therefore, character pronunciations are directly associated with the unanalyzed visual images of the characters. Although some teachers might attempt to demonstrate to pupils that many characters are actually decomposable, e.g. that the phonetics in some complex characters could function as effective sound cues, these individual attempts tend to be scattered and unsystematic, because the Education Bureau of Hong Kong has not promoted the method by developing any concrete guidelines for character decomposition (Cheung & Ng, 2003).

This difference in teaching methods for introducing new Chinese characters and words, i.e. making use of a phonetic transcription system vs. none, across Chinese societies might be quite important for how Chinese children learn to read and write, though research on such differences is sparse. What is clear from previous research, however, is that Hong Kong's lack of phonological coding system is associated with weak phonological awareness, or sensitivity and access to the sound system of one's language, as compared to that of children in all other Chinese societies (Holm & Dodd, 1996; Huang & Hanley, 1995). In most research on alphabetic languages, this weak phonological awareness tends to be associated with poorer reading skills. However, the extent to which phonological awareness matters for reading in Chinese remains debatable at present, a topic to which we will return when we consider cognitive components of early reading development.

Along with script and phonological coding system differences across societies, perhaps an even more fundamental aspect of learning to read is the language onto which the script is mapped. The linguistic environment represents a fundamental difference across Chinese societies. In mainland China, Putonghua, or Mandarin, is the language of school instruction across the country. In many places in China, such as Beijing, Putonghua is indeed the only language spoken either at school or at home by the majority of the residents. In other areas, such as Shanghai, other Chinese languages or dialects are commonly spoken at home, though Putonghua remains the language of instruction at school. Putonghua is also the language of instruction in Taiwan and Singapore. In contrast, Cantonese is spoken both at home and at school by the majority of children in Hong Kong. At the same time, however, even in Hong Kong, written Chinese typically follows the grammar and basic structure of Putonghua. This can be somewhat problematic for Cantonese speakers in Hong Kong, because both vocabulary and grammar can have different spoken and even written forms when considered in Putonghua vs. Cantonese (e.g. Chow, McBride-Chang, Cheung, & Chow, 2008). The problem arises because Cantonese, as it has evolved, is currently a somewhat more informal language than Putonghua, and both its spoken and written forms have developed somewhat differently from those of Putonghua.

Cognitive linguistic development

A great deal of research has been devoted to identifying those cognitive skills that are particularly important for children learning to read in different orthographies. Identification of such skills can contribute to our understanding of the development of reading, and difficulties in mastering such skills sometimes signal risks for reading difficulties in children. Thus, understanding the cognitive components most important for learning to read is both theoretically and practically useful.

The cognitive components of most interest for those reading alphabetic orthographies tend to be phonological processing skills. Phonological processing skills are abilities that make use of speech-sound awareness, because learning to read an alphabet typically involves mapping a written symbol, i.e. a letter of the alphabet, to an oral speech sound. For example, knowing that B makes a /b/ sound helps in reading words such as *bed* or *bone*. However, the unique orthographic structure of Chinese is remarkable for its many distinctive features, not the least of which is the fact that phonological correspondences of written symbols are tenuous at best (Shu, Chen, Anderson, Wu, & Xuan, 2003). Thus, a focus on phonological processing skills alone is likely not enough to understand fully reading development and impairment in Chinese. Below, we review some of these cognitive skills, beginning with phonological processing, such as phonological awareness and speeded naming, and proceeding on to morphological awareness and visual-orthographic skills.

Numerous studies on Chinese children's reading development (Ho & Bryant, 1997; McBride-Chang & Kail, 2002; Siok & Fletcher, 2001) and impairment (Chung, McBride-Chang, Wong, Cheung, Penney, & Ho, 2008; Ho & Ma, 1999; Ho, Law, & Ng, 2000) have demonstrated that phonological awareness, or access to the sound system of a language, is associated with Chinese character recognition. This is true across Chinese societies whether or not a phonological coding system is used to teach reading.

For example, Ho and Bryant (1997) demonstrated that early phonological sensitivity was associated with subsequent reading of Chinese words in young Hong Kong Chinese children four years later, even with mothers' educational levels and children's IQ scores statistically controlled. In another study, we showed that syllable awareness in Hong Kong Chinese children was longitudinally predictive of subsequent skill in Chinese word reading, even with the autoregressive effects of Chinese reading in the first year controlled (Chow, McBride-Chang, & Burgess, 2005). The study further demonstrated a bidirectional association between syllable awareness and Chinese character recognition, with syllable awareness at time 2 being explained by Chinese character recognition even with time 1 levels of syllable awareness statistically controlled as well. At the same time, however, we have found that phoneme awareness tends not to be as strongly associated with skill in Chinese word reading as is syllable awareness, even in mainland China, which uses the Pinyin system highlighting onset phonemes (McBride-Chang, Bialystok, Chong, & Li, 2004). We have also demonstrated the importance of lexical tone, one aspect of phonological sensitivity in Chinese, for word reading in Chinese for both mainland China (Shu, Peng, & McBride-Chang, 2008) and Hong Kong, (McBride-Chang, Tong, Shu, Wong, Leung, & Tardif, 2008).

One might summarize recent work on phonological awareness in relation to Chinese word reading by noting its importance particularly for early reading acquisition and also the fact that the aspects of phonological awareness that are especially important tend to represent larger units, or grain sizes (Ziegler & Goswami, 2005), than those most often used to explain reading development in alphabetic scripts.

Speeded naming is at least in part a phonological processing skill as well (Wagner & Torgesen, 1987), because it involves lexical access to symbols. In tasks of speeded naming, children are asked to identify pictures or symbols as quickly as possible, when they are presented on a sheet of paper. Most such tasks repeat a small subset of these pictures or symbols several times, and errors on the tasks are minimal. The measure of interest is usually simply the speed with which children can identify these presented stimuli. Denckla and Rudel (1976) were among the first to demonstrate a high association between slowness in naming speed and word reading ability in English. They noted that this slowness is an important clinical marker of reading difficulty. Such findings have been replicated in studies of Chinese children (e.g. Ho & Ma, 1999; Ho, Chan, Tsang, & Lee, 2002). Indeed, in studies of Chinese children with and without dyslexia, slow naming speed tends to be among the best tasks for distinguishing those with reading difficulties, both in Hong Kong (Ho et al., 2002) and mainland China (Shu, McBride-Chang, Wu, & Liu, 2006). Conclusions from researchers as to the precise nature of speeded naming, i.e. what it does and does not measure, have been varied.

In some ways, speeded naming involves many of the same skills required for reading itself. Manis, Seidenberg, and Doi (1999) pointed out that in many ways speeded naming tasks tap part of the 'arbitrariness' aspect of word recognition in English. Learning to pronounce some English words is somewhat based on memorization of spelled words, particularly irregular-sounding words, the pronunciations of which could not be predicted from their spellings, such as *psyche*, *know*, or *meant*.

Given how irregular the correspondences between pronunciations and written forms of Chinese characters are, one might expect that the arbitrariness factor in learning to read Chinese might even be even higher than it is in English. Speeded naming, too, requires a mapping of individual symbols or pictures to oral labels, and naming these aloud is another kind of arbitrariness. Indeed, some researchers have argued that because of this particular arbitrariness in Chinese, learning visual–verbal paired associates, which involves learning to identify new visual symbols using new verbal labels, might be a good marker of reading disability in Chinese children as well (Ho, Chan, Tsang, Lee, & Chung, 2006).

In one study (H. Li, Shu, McBride-Chang, & Xue, 2009), we indeed found that performance in learning visual–verbal paired associates explained unique variance in reading of irregular, but not regular, Chinese words in children with and without dyslexia. Moreover, with this measure of paired-associates learning included in the model, the speeded naming component was no longer a significant correlate of reading. Thus, it is possible that the arbitrariness of associations in speeded naming tasks may be one factor in its importance for identifying those at risk for reading difficulties. Regardless of the explanation for the importance of speeded naming for word recognition in Chinese, speeded naming is clearly an important indicator of early reading and reading disability.

Apart from phonological processing variables, morphological awareness has been a particularly important aspect of research on the acquisition of Chinese reading in the past ten to fifteen years or so. Definitions of morphological awareness vary widely, in part because certain aspects of morphological awareness may involve oral language, print, or both, and the extent to which this is the case may differ by orthography. In our own research, we have tended to conceptualize morphological awareness as awareness of and access to the meaning structure of words comprising morphemes, with a morpheme being the smallest unit of meaning in language. However, Shu and Anderson (1997) have also talked about the understanding of semantic radicals as a form of morphological awareness in print in previous work. In some ways, it is indeed difficult to characterize morphological awareness in Chinese in ways that conform to definitions emerging from Indo-European languages because of the unique writing system of Chinese. In the present section, we will outline research on morphological awareness primarily at the level of oral language in relation to reading acquisition. Morphological awareness in relation to print is best considered under our section on children's understanding of features of print, because awareness of semantic radicals is fundamental to this concept.

Morphological awareness is particularly interesting to explore in a Chinese–English contrast. In English, a morpheme can be represented as a single letter (e.g. the *s* in *hills* indicates that the word is plural), a syllable (e.g. *tree*, *frog*), or a multi-syllable word (e.g. *lettuce*). By contrast, in Chinese, in almost every instance, a morpheme is a single syllable that can also be represented by a single Chinese character. Thus, there is a virtually perfect 1 (syllable) to 1 (morpheme) to 1 (character) correspondence of phonological, morphological, and orthographic representations with one another in Chinese. Moreover, in Chinese, most words comprise two or more morphemes, and these morphemes are often combined in multiple ways via lexical compounding. Thus, the words *fruit* (水果), *apple* (苹果), and *mango* (芒果) all share the common morpheme indicating *fruit* (果).

The fact that there is so much lexical compounding in Chinese as compared to English, where compound words are common but less so than in Chinese, might be a clue to reading development in Chinese children as well (McBride-Chang, Shu, Zhou, Wat, & Wagner, 2003). As children learn individual morphemes both orally and in print, they might make use of their knowledge of these morphemes to generalize them to new words. For example, in English, we can find the morpheme *snow* in *snowstorm* and *snowman* as well, and identifying *snow* in these words might facilitate reading them. This facilitation might be even more important in Chinese, where there are many more homophones.

We tested the extent to which knowing how morphemes fit together in Chinese to conform to the rules of the language (e.g. in English, one can say *snowman* but not *mansnow*) would be associated with reading. We found that both morphological sensitivity and homophone sensitivity, two aspects of morphological awareness, were uniquely associated with Chinese character recognition (e.g. McBride-Chang et al., 2003). Morphological awareness has also been demonstrated to be associated with the reading of Chinese words in other studies (e.g. X. Chen, Hao, Geva, Zhu, & Shu, 2008; McBride-Chang, Cho, Liu, Wagner, Shu, Zhou, Cheuk, & Muse, 2005). Moreover, morphological awareness distinguishes children with and without dyslexia, both in mainland China (e.g. Shu et al., 2006) and in Hong Kong (Chung et al., 2008). In another study, parents who trained their children in games of morphological awareness tended to have children who could read better twelve weeks later as compared to those who did not (Chow et al., 2008). Thus, overall, morphological awareness in the form of lexical compounding, either inclusive of or separate from, homophone awareness, is important for reading Chinese.

Finally, visual skills have been linked to reading in Chinese in some studies. Given the complexity of Chinese characters, researchers have long considered visual skills to be important for early learning of Chinese. However, results testing this speculation are mixed. When researchers combine visual and orthographic skills, the relevance of such skills increases greatly. This is because orthographic knowledge by definition involves knowledge about the writing system in question, and print knowledge tends to predict print knowledge. However, when pure visual skills are considered only, the connection is less clear.

Overall, there is mixed evidence for a unique contribution of visual skills and Chinese character recognition. Some demonstrate such an association (e.g. Huang & Hanley, 1995; Lee, Stigler, & Stevenson, 1986; Siok & Fletcher, 2001) and some do not (e.g. Hu & Catts, 1998; Huang & Hanley, 1997). We found some early longitudinal contribution of visual skills to subsequent Chinese character recognition in mainland China and Hong Kong in one study (McBride-Chang et al., 2005), but only at the earliest stages of reading. Moreover, when some other cognitive skills thought to be important for reading, such as speeded naming and phonological awareness, were additionally included, these associations were not always stable. Thus, despite the fact that Chinese characters are indeed more visually complex than in English (e.g. H. C. Chen, 1996) or perhaps any other orthography, the importance of pure visual analysis skills, such as shape comparison or visual line memorization for recognition, in reading Chinese remains unclear. Rather, the most important cognitive skills for very early reading development in Chinese children at this point appear to be speeded naming and morphological awareness. However, the area of cognitive skills in relation to Chinese literacy development is still relatively new, and more studies may change this conclusion in future work.

The importance of parents in fostering language and literacy skills

Given the importance of individual cognitive skills for reading development, we must acknowledge the equally important consideration of the environment in which such skills develop. One immediate proximal environment in which this development takes place from the earliest age is the home. Parents play an important role in setting the stage for children's approaches to literacy development, both in terms of the cognitive skills learned, including reading and writing themselves, and also in terms of influencing children's attitudes towards all acts of literacy. That is, parents provide a natural context through which literacy skills are or are not encountered and enjoyed (e.g. Vygotsky, 1978). Well before children can read, their parents often facilitate children's overall concepts about print, books, and reading (e.g. Clay, 1979). Scaffolding is an important aspect of these experiences.

Through the use of scaffolds, mother–child interactions mediate language and literacy development within children's 'zone of proximal development' (Vygotsky, 1978). Activities such as joint book reading in early childhood (Levy, Gong, Hessels, Evans, & Jared, 2006; Senechal, 2006) and collaborative parent–child writing (Aram & Levin 2001; Aram & Levin, 2002; Aram & Levin, 2004) can facilitate children's progress in literacy development. Although most studies on parent–child interactions in relation to literacy development were conducted in Western cultures, some recent studies have demonstrated the importance of parents for early Chinese literacy development as well (e.g. Chow & McBride-Chang, 2003; Chow, McBride-Chang, Cheung, & Chow, 2008; Fung, Chow, & McBride-Chang, 2005; Lin, McBride-Chang, Aram, Levin, Cheung, Chow, & Tolchinsky, 2009). These studies highlight the importance of parents' approaches to shared storybook reading and even early writing in facilitating children's development of literacy skills.

One of the clearest results of this research is the importance of parents' interaction strategies for reading with their children. The idea of dialogic reading, a way of reading with children in which the children are encouraged to interact with parents in talking about the books they are reading together, emerged from a series of studies undertaken by Grover Whitehurst and colleagues in the United States (e.g. Zevenbergen & Whitehurst, 2003). We adopted this technique for Hong Kong parents by training them on ways to talk with their children about books. This approach emphasizes the importance of asking open-ended questions about stories. In this approach, questions should ideally not require one-word answers; rather, they should be questions that require children to think about the stories and explain and elaborate on answers.

The focus is not so much on correctness of answers (e.g. what color is the bunny, how many carrots do you see, where is the frog, etc.). Indeed, particularly for Chinese parents, who tend to be highly motivated to teach their children at every opportunity, asking these types of right/wrong questions comes fairly naturally. Rather, this technique focuses on children's anticipation of events, opinions, and other ideas coming from the story that might generate conversation. Questions such as, 'What do you think will happen next?' or 'What would you do if you were in that situation?' would be more encouraged using this technique.

In three separate studies in Hong Kong, new books were provided each week to participating families, during the study for the dialogic and typically reading families, but following the study for the control group. Children whose parents were trained and encouraged to use the dialogic reading technique outscored both those whose parents were encouraged to read as they typically did and those serving as a control group during the research period, which lasted from eight to twelve weeks across studies (Chow & McBride-Chang, 2003; Chow, McBride-Chang, Cheung, & Chow, 2008; Fung, Chow, & McBride-Chang, 2005). Moreover, parents tended to enjoy the dialogic reading technique and to view it as motivating and interesting for their children; most reported adopting the technique for storybook reading with their children following the study as well. These studies illustrate the importance of Chinese parents in encouraging their children's very early reading interest and cognitive skills.

In addition to the finding that parent–child reading is helpful in children's language development, a result that is widely noted across cultures, we have begun exploring the extent to which parent–child writing is also useful for children's literacy development. The study by Lin et al. (2009) was among the first to look at mother–child joint writing in relation to reading skills in young Chinese children. This study of Hong Kong Chinese children was run at three grade levels—second year kindergarten (K2), third year kindergarten (K3), and first grade (P1). Twenty-two two-character words were given to mothers, initially using pictures. Mothers were asked to help their children write these words, 'as you see fit'. With these instructions, we hoped to examine some natural variability in approaches to writing across families. The twenty-two words selected were designed to be relatively common words but not ones that the children already knew how to write. The words also shared some overlap in various features, e.g. the words for *bee* (蜜蜂) and *honey* (蜂蜜) in Chinese, both of which were included on this list, consist of the same two characters, but the characters are reversed across the two words. Such a selection gave mothers various opportunities to make comparisons and connections across words for their children. The writing processes in all dyads were videotaped.

We observed at least six strategies that mothers used with their children to try to help them to write. One basic technique was simply to ask the children to copy whatever the mothers wrote. Some mothers would even hold the pen or pencil with the child in order to write together. A second approach taken by mothers was to dictate what strokes should be placed where, so as to create the entire character and word. A third approach was to use visualization. In this technique, children were told that a certain character looked like a 'picturable' object. For example, part of the character for 車 /che1/ (vehicle) looks like a box. Another approach to writing was to segment the characters into radicals, or components. Many of the characters had semantic or phonetic radicals that could be identified independently, and mothers sometimes asked the children to recall how to write a particular radical, e.g. the mouth radical in *eat*, and write that radical before continuing on with writing the rest of the character and word. A less common technique was to identify the phonetic radical of the word. This approach focused the children on the sound of the character and the radical within a given character that made that sound. Unlike most alphabetic languages, where speech-sound information tends to be prominent in parents' focus on writing (e.g. Aram & Levin, 2004), this strategy was the least used of all the strategies noted in our study. Finally, mothers frequently made use of morphological structure within and across words and characters. For example, at the word level, mothers might point out that in order to write *honey* one can simply use the same two characters as those used in *bee*, but reverse the two characters (e.g. 蜜蜂 vs. 蜂蜜). At the character level, mothers sometimes also made observations about semantic radicals within characters based on meaning. For example, in the word for *bee*, one character includes a radical that means insect (虫). In this instance, mothers sometimes explained that that radical was important to show that a bee is one type of insect.

Results showed strong developmental trends for mothers' strategy usage. Chinese mothers tended to use primarily copying and stroke order strategies in K2, decreasing their use in K3 and P1, whereas mothers tended to use more morphologically focused strategies to teach characters to the P1 children as compared to the kindergartners. Apart from these age-related trends, however, strategy use by mother–child dyads was strongly associated with children's ability to read Chinese words independently. In particular, copying strategies were found to be negatively associated with reading skill, even statistically controlling for age and grade level. In addition, a prevalence of morphologically based strategies was found to be positively associated with reading skill, independent of age and grade level. Although both longitudinal studies and experiments examining parent–child interactions in relation to shared writing and subsequent literacy skills will be essential before any conclusions regarding parent–child interactions and long-term literacy development can be drawn, this study demonstrates another way in which parents are potentially important for promoting Chinese children's early reading and writing skills.

Given the importance of parents for Chinese children's literacy development, one might wonder about whether parental literacy-related practices differ across Chinese societies. H. Li and Rao (2000) examined this question in a correlational study of preschoolers in Beijing, Hong Kong, and Singapore. They had parents across these cities complete a series of questionnaires about literacy practices, and also administered to their children a battery of reading and writing tests. They found striking differences in home literacy environments across the three cities. For example, only about one-third of Beijing parents reported teaching their preschool children to write Chinese characters at home, whereas 52 per cent of Hong Kong parents and 48 per cent of Singapore parents did. However, most Beijing parents (over 60 per cent), but fewer than 45 per cent of Hong Kong and Singapore parents, reported buying or borrowing Chinese books for their children at least monthly. They also found some correlations between parents' reported practices and children's performances. Specifically, the age of the children when parents began teaching them to read predicted unique variance in children's performances on a task of character acquisition, even after controlling for mother's educational level and child's age.

The categories and typical structures of Chinese characters

With this general background on very early Chinese reading and writing development, we turn now to more concrete details on the Chinese writing system. As children develop, they become increasingly aware of the structures of Chinese characters, both within the characters themselves and across Chinese words (e.g. McBride-Chang & Chen, 2003). The basic unit of writing in Chinese is the character. Across Chinese languages and societies, Chinese is famous for having many homophones per syllable, on average five per syllable in Mandarin and approximately four per syllable in Cantonese (e.g. Chow et al., 2008; Shu et al., 2003). These homophones are often disambiguated in writing, because many homophones are represented by unique characters in text.

A study by Perfetti and Zhang (1995) of the Modern Chinese Dictionary (1995) suggested that 10 per cent of present-day used characters were simple characters. Simple characters are not further divisible into distinct components. Some of them can indicate the shapes of referents. For example, 山 (mountain) indeed looks like its referent. However, many of these characters are relatively simple but not obvious pictorial representations, e.g. 天 (sky), 见 (see), and 立 (stand).

The most frequent (80 per cent of modern characters) type of Chinese character is usually referred to as a compound character. Compound characters are composed of two functionally independent compounds: a semantic radical and a phonetic radical. For example, in 洋 (sea, pronounced */yang4/*), the left radical 氵 (water) indicates the meaning, and the right one, which is 羊'(goat), indicates the pronunciation, because it is pronounced as */yang4/.* The numbers of semantic and phonetic radicals in Chinese are approximately 200 and 800 respectively (Hoosain, 1991). Semantic radicals often give some indication of meaning within the character, whereas phonetic radicals sometimes give an indication of the character's pronunciation. However, the association between these radicals and the meanings and sounds of each character is far from reliable.

The reliability of phonetic radicals has been explored extensively, particularly in Mandarin. Shu et al. (2003) found that 39 per cent of compound characters are regular, such that the phonetic radical gives reliable information about a character's pronunciation, e.g. 逗 */dou4/*, with the phonetic 豆 */dou4/.* Approximately 26 per cent of compound characters are described as semi-regular in relation to the phonetic. This is to say, in these characters, the phonetic radical gives partial information about the pronunciation of its character. For example, 桃 */tao2/* and the phonetic 兆 */zhao4/* share the same rime but different onset and tone, i.e. some partial sound information in common. Moreover, the character 坝 */ba4/* and its phonetic 贝 */bei4/* are pronounced with a different rime but share the same onset and tone; this is another example of the semi-regular character. Finally, the character 烂 */lan4/* is also semi-regular because it shares the same onset and rime as its phonetic 兰 */lan2/* but a different tone. According to Shu et al. (2003), there are approximately 15 per cent irregular characters, i.e. characters for which the phonetic radical gives no information about the pronunciation of a character. When children realize the extent to which phonetics may be useful in providing information about the pronunciations of characters, using their knowledge of phonetic radicals, they may have an easier time in mastering written Chinese (e.g. McBride-Chang & Chen, 2003).

As in the case of phonetic radicals, semantic radicals can also be categorized as transparent, semi-transparent, and semantic opaque; estimated percentages of each of these categories in written Chinese for children are 58 per cent, 30 per cent, and 9 per cent respectively (Shu et al., 2003). Semantically transparent Chinese characters are those in which the semantic radical indicates the conceptual category of a character, e.g. 姐 (sister) with the semantic radical 女 (female) or is directly related to the character meaning, e.g. 树 (tree) with the radical 木 (wood). Semi-transparent characters are those in which the semantic radical indirectly suggests the character's meaning, e.g. there is an animal radical 犭 in 猎 (hunt). Semantically opaque characters are ones in which the radical provides no semantic information about the character, e.g. the animal radical 犭 in 猜 guess.

All these semantic or phonetic radicals may be further divided into about 648 sub-components (e.g. 十, 口) (Fu, 1989). The smallest unit of the Chinese writing system is the stroke. These components or sub-components are combined to form hundreds and thousands of characters. The inter-structure and position of components within characters are considered to be important in character recognition. Different patterns of the same strokes represent different characters, such as 工 (work), 土 (soil), 士 (soldier) and 上 (up). In addition, different configurations of the same components form different characters, such as 呆 (dull) and 杏 (apricot). Most radicals have a fixed position within compound characters. For example, the semantic radical 氵 typically occupies the position on the left of a character.

As children learn more about the writing system of Chinese, they gain in understanding of the systematic nature of Chinese character and words structures. Although many Chinese schoolchildren may not be explicitly taught about the underlying structures of Chinese characters in relation to radicals or positions of radicals within characters, they gradually learn about these structures with experience. Moreover, they can use this knowledge to learn new characters or even pseudo-characters (i.e. nonsense characters comprising phonetic and semantic radicals) fairly efficiently (McBride-Chang & Chen, 2003). Some examples of this learning are reviewed below.

How Chinese children develop an understanding of character features

What information do children extract when they read and write Chinese characters? Orthographic knowledge in Chinese refers to the knowledge of specific locations, structures, and functions of semantic and phonetic radicals in Chinese characters. Children tend to develop initial orthographic or positional knowledge at an early age and gradually acquire more specific orthographic knowledge, e.g. internal structure of radicals, positional frequency knowledge, according to their reading experience (Cheng & Huang, 1995; J. Li, Fu, & Lin, 2000; Peng & Li, 1995; Shu & Anderson, 1999). In Shu and Anderson's (1999) study, first-, second-, fourth-, and sixth-grade Chinese children were first asked to make lexical decisions about real characters, pseudo-characters (with a radical in a common position), and two types of non-characters. Results showed that even very young children exhibited solid positional knowledge, but children's awareness of the internal structure of radicals had developed relatively late.

Orthographic knowledge is also important for children's character writing. Qian (2002) analyzed children's accuracy and errors in a delayed copy task in first-, second-, and fourth-grade children. The results revealed that first graders made a large proportion of stroke-related errors related to memorization, whereas fourth graders made far fewer stroke-related errors and relatively more radical errors. Thus, with experience, older children tend to write characters based on knowledge about radical units, thereby indicating the ability to use orthographic knowledge.

Studies have also demonstrated the importance of phonetics knowledge in early Chinese character identification. Using a learning–testing task, Anderson, Li, Ku, Shu, and Wu (2003) and Shu, Bi, and Wu (2003) asked fourth-grade children with Mandarin as their home language to learn three types of novel characters: (1) characters with phonetics providing full information, e.g. regular character (same onset, rime and tone); (2) characters with phonetics providing partial information, e.g. tone-different characters (same onset and rime) or onset-different characters (same rime and tone); (3) characters with phonetics providing no information, e.g. irregular characters. Children found it easiest to learn regular characters and most difficult to learn irregular characters; characters with phonetics with partial information were intermediate in difficulty. However, even the semi-regular characters showed differences across categories: Children performed better on tone-different, semi-regular characters than on onset-different characters. These results suggest that children effectively make use of partial information in semi-regular characters and are sensitive to different degrees of partial information. Anderson et al. (2003) further demonstrated that children as young as second grade made good use of phonetic information in reading novel compound Chinese characters. Moreover, older and higher-ability readers tend to make better use of this information than do younger and less able readers (Chan & Siegel, 2001; Shu, Anderson, & Wu, 2000). Indeed, sensitivity to phonetic information in the form of recognizing phonetic consistency across characters increases at least through eighth grade and college (Shu, Zhou, & Wu, 2000). Thus, Chinese children appear to develop phonetic awareness even during the very early stages of reading development, but their awareness of the consistency/inconsistency principle of Chinese characters develops relatively late.

For another important feature of Chinese characters, the semantic radical, there is no analogy in alphabetic scripts. This part of Chinese characters, indicating something about meaning, is sometimes considered a unique aspect of morphological awareness, as discussed above. Shu and Anderson (1997), using a radical identification task, demonstrated that children from third grade onwards performed much better for morphologically transparent characters than for opaque ones, especially in low-frequency characters, suggesting that transparent radical information is helpful for facilitating children's reading from an early age. Indeed, Cheng and Huang (1995) found that even first graders tended to match semantically related characters together based on semantic radicals.

The effectiveness of semantic radicals was also documented in character writing tasks. Meng, Shu, and Zhou (2000) examined both the effects of semantic and phonetic radicals in a writing task in fourth graders. The results demonstrated a significant interaction between semantic transparency and phonetic regularity. Children's writing performance was better for regular characters (e.g. 倒) than irregular (e.g. 跌) and bound phonetic characters (e.g. 鳞); but for irregular and bound phonetic characters, semantic transparent characters were written better than opaque characters, indicating that phonetic and semantic radical information are both important for writing characters.

Understanding of semantic radicals likely facilitates literacy skills at all levels. For example, Shu and Anderson (1997) found that good readers were more aware of the relationship between a semantic radical and the meaning of a character among Chinese children in primary school. Moreover, Ku and Anderson (2001) also found that Chinese children's reading of passages was strongly related to children's knowledge of semantic radicals. Thus, understanding of semantic radicals may be important for reading comprehension as well as lower-level reading skills.

Reading comprehension

Although reading comprehension is the ultimate goal of educators and families, very little is known about this area relative to the other, more easily measurable areas of word reading and writing. The consensus appears to be that reading comprehension should represent a similar process in Chinese as in other languages (e.g. H. C. Chen, 1996). As outlined by Snow (2002), reading comprehension brings with it characteristics of the text, reading activity, and reader characteristics. Reader characteristics presumably include all of those discussed in our section on cognitive skills and word reading, such as phonological and morphological awareness, as well as speed in reading. Other characteristics perhaps more relevant to text reading as compared to word recognition include working memory, inference-making, background knowledge, and metacognition.

Of these components, studies on Chinese children have particularly found working memory and metacognition to be associated with reading comprehension in some studies (e.g. Chan & Law, 2003;

Leong, Tse, Loh, & Hau, 2008; McBride-Chang & Chang, 1995). Memory skills were among the strongest correlates of reading comprehension in two studies of primary school children, one in mainland China (McBride-Chang & Chang, 1995) and one in Hong Kong (Leong et al. 2008). Chan and Law (2003) focused specifically on two aspects of metacognition, beliefs and strategies, in their study of sixth graders in Hong Kong. They found that metacognitive beliefs were relatively strongly associated with inferential comprehension, underscoring the importance of this aspect of metacognition, or thinking about thinking, for advanced reading comprehension. In both this and a previous study (McBride-Chang & Chang, 1995), vocabulary knowledge was also a strong correlate of reading comprehension.

In addition to these aspects of the individual reading, text characteristics may also be important. It is possible that somehow characteristics of the text might affect comprehension, potentially even across languages. For example, the vocabulary and syntax of Chinese may make reading of Chinese text relatively easy or difficult depending upon context (H. C. Chen, 1996). In addition to these considerations, the structure of the text should fit the reader. A text that is too easy or too difficult for a given child will not be a good fit with the reader. H. Li and Rao (2000) point out that, compared to English-reading children, Chinese children need more years of scaffolding by parents in order to read some texts simply because the process of learning Chinese characters goes on for such a long time. Many characters may be difficult to identify even at a relatively advanced level for Chinese readers, and these characters cannot always be accessed and comprehended without a seasoned adult to explain them.

The third aspect of reading comprehension identified by Snow (2002) is the nature of the reading activity involved. For example, children will read differently for enjoyment as compared to reading for the purpose of doing well on an exam. Children may also gauge their approach to reading at a more surface level, e.g. memorization, as compared to a deeper level, which might involve some analysis of the text (see Kember & Watkins, this volume). Presumably, different reading activities may encourage readers to make use of different individual reader characteristics, such as working memory for more surface-level understanding or metacognitive monitoring for more in-depth analysis.

Both the extent to which children themselves enjoy reading and whether or not their peers enjoy reading are positively associated with their actual reading comprehension across cultures among adolescents (Chiu & McBride-Chang, 2006). Thus, development of reading comprehension, as for all other facets of literacy development, involves a combination of individual characteristics, such as working memory skill, vocabulary knowledge, and metacognitive skills, and environmental aspects, such as whether or not children have peers who enjoy reading or types of texts and contexts in which children are reading.

Conclusion

Although our stated focus has been literacy development in Chinese children as broadly defined, the vast majority of our coverage has been on character and word recognition, rather than on text processing. This mismatch between word-level and text-level research in children is not unique to research on the Chinese language. Indeed, reading comprehension is such an all-encompassing topic that it is difficult to begin to study it because of the numerous components involved.

However true this assessment is of research across the world's languages, it is likely that research on the development of Chinese literacy is even more skewed in this respect simply because Chinese orthography is unique but much less thoroughly studied than alphabetic reading, particularly in children. Thus, there has been a great deal to understand in this field, and there is much more to do, even at the word level.

Nevertheless, what we have learned about Chinese literacy development thus far is relatively comprehensive. We know that there are some universal aspects of this development, such as the importance of environment, particularly home environment, for early literacy development. We also know that Chinese orthography is special in a number of ways, including its different scripts, languages mapped onto these scripts, and importance of lexical tone for distinguishing across words. At a more specific level, the characteristics of Chinese characters and words in how they are structured make the challenges, including cognitive abilities important for the process of learning Chinese, unique in some ways. Understanding the roles, forms, and positions of semantic and phonetic radicals within characters is particularly striking in this regard. Overall, the study of Chinese literacy affords psychologists exciting opportunities to understand many of the most important aspects of Chinese culture, including both cognitive and social influences within and across societies.

References

Anderson, R. C., Li, W., Ku, Y. M., Shu, H., & Wu, N. (2003). Use of partial information in learning to read Chinese characters. *Journal of Educational Psychology, 95*, 52–57.

Aram, D. & Levin, I. (2001). Mother–child joint writing in low SES: Sociocultural factors, maternal mediation and emergent literacy. *Cognitive Development, 16*, 831–852.

Aram, D. & Levin, I. (2002). Mother–child joint writing and storybook reading: Relations with literacy among low SES kindergartners. *Merrill Palmer Quarterly, 48*, 202–224.

Aram, D. & Levin, I. (2004). The role of maternal mediation of writing to kindergartners in promoting literacy achievements in second grade: A longitudinal perspective. *Reading and Writing: An Interdisciplinary Journal. 17*, 387–409.

Chan, C. K. K. & Law, D. Y. K. (2003). Metacognitive beliefs and strategies in reading comprehension for Chinese children. In C. McBride-Chang, & H. C. Chen (eds), *Reading development in Chinese children* (pp. 171–182) Westport, CT: Praeger.

Chen, H. C. (1996). Chinese reading and comprehension: A cognitive psychology perspective. In M. H. Bond (ed.), *The handbook of Chinese psychology* (pp. 43–62). Hong Kong: Oxford University Press.

Chen, M. J. & Yuen, J. C.-K. (1991). Effects of pinyin and script type on verbal processing: Comparisons of China, Taiwan, and Hong Kong experience. *International Journal of Behavioral Development, 14*, 429–448.

Chen, X., Hao, M., Geva, E., Zhu, J., & Shu, H. (2008). The role of compound awareness in Chinese children's vocabulary acquisition and character reading. *Reading and Writing.*

Cheung, H. & Ng, K. H. (2003). Chinese reading development in some major Chinese societies: An introduction. In C. McBride-Chang & H.-C. Chen (eds), *Reading development in Chinese children.* Westport, CT: Greenwood.

Chiu, M. M. & McBride-Chang, C. (2006). Gender, context, and reading: A comparison of students in 41 countries. *Scientific Studies of Reading, 10*, 331–362.

Chow, B. W. Y. & McBride-Chang, C. (2003). Promoting language and literacy through parent–child reading. *Early Education and Development, 14*, 233–248.

Chow, B. W.-Y., McBride-Chang, C., & Burgess, S. (2005). Phonological processing skills and early reading abilities in Hong Kong Chinese kindergarteners learning to read English as an L2. *Journal of Educational Psychology, 97*, 81–87.

Chow, B. W.-Y., McBride-Chang, C., Cheung, H., & Chow, C. (2008). Dialogic reading and morphology training in Chinese children: Effects on language and literacy. *Developmental Psychology, 44*, 233–244.

Chung, K. K. H., McBride-Chang, C., Wong, S. W. L., Cheung, H., Penney, T. B., & Ho, C. S.-H. (2008). The role of visual and auditory temporal processing for Chinese children with developmental dyslexia. *Annals of Dyslexia, 58*, 15–35.

Clay, M. M. (1979). *Reading: The patterning of complex behavior.* Auckland, New Zealand: Heinemann.

Denckla, M. B. & Rudel, R. G. (1976). Rapid 'automatized' naming (RAN): Dyslexia differentiated from other learning disabilities. *Neuropsychologia, 14*, 471–479.

Fu, Y. H. (1989). A basic research on structure and its component of Chinese character. In Y. Chen (ed.), *Information analysis of used character in modern Chinese language* (pp. 154– 186). Shanghai, China: Shanghai Educational Press.

Fung, P. C., Chow, W. Y., & McBride-Chang, C. (2005). The impact of a dialogic reading program on deaf and hard-of-hearing kindergarten and early primary school-aged students in Hong Kong. *Journal of Deaf Studies and Deaf Education, 10*, 82–95.

Ho, C. S.-H., Chan, D. W., Tsang, S.-M., Lee, S.-H., & Chung, K. K. H. (2006). Word learning deficit among Chinese dyslexic children. *Journal of Child Language, 33*, 145–161.

Ho, C. S.-H., Chan, D. W.-O., Tsang, S.-M., & Lee, S.-H. (2002). The cognitive profile and multiple deficit hypothesis in Chinese developmental dyslexia. *Developmental Psychology, 38*, 543–553.

Ho, C. S.-H., Law, T. P.-S., & Ng, P. M. (2000). The phonological deficit hypothesis in Chinese developmental dyslexia. *Reading and Writing: An Interdisciplinary Journal, 7*, 171–188.

Ho, C. S.-H. & Ma, R. N.-L. (1999). Training in phonological strategies improves Chinese dyslexic children's character reading skills. *Journal of Research in Reading, 22*, 131–142.

Ho, C. S.-H. & Bryant, P. (1997). Learning to read Chinese beyond the logographic phase. *Reading Research Quarterly, 32*, 276–289.

Holm, A. & Dodd, B. (1996). The effect of first written language on the acquisition of English literacy. *Cognition, 59*, 119–147.

Hoosain, R. (1991). *Psycholinguistic implications for linguistic relativity: A case study of Chinese.* Hillsdale, NJ: Erlbaum.
Hu, C. F. & Catts, H. W. (1998). The role of phonological processing in early reading ability: What we can learn from Chinese. *Scientific Studies of Reading, 2,* 55–79.
Huang, H. S. & Hanley, J. R. (1995). Phonological awareness and visual skills in learning to read Chinese and English. *Cognition, 54,* 73–98.
Huang, H. S. & Hanley, J. R. (1997). A longitudinal study of phonological awareness, visual skills, and Chinese reading acquisition among first graders in Taiwan. *International Journal of Behavioral Development, 20,* 249–268.
Ku, Y. M. & Anderson, R. C. (2001). Chinese children's incidental learning of word meanings. *Contemporary Educational Psychology, 26,* 249–266.
Lee, S.-Y., Stigler, J. W., & Stevenson, H. W. (1986). Beginning reading in Chinese and English. In B. R. Foorman & A. W. Siegel (eds), *Acquisition of reading skills: Cultural constraints andcognitive universals* (pp. 93–115). Hillsdale, NJ: Erlbaum.
Leong, C. K., Tse, S. K., Loh, H. Y., & Hau, K. T. (2008). Text comprehension in Chinese children: Relative contribution of verbal working memory, pseudoword reading, rapid automatized naming, and onset-rime segmentation. *Journal of Educational Psychology, 100,* 135–149.
Levy, B. A., Gong, Z., Hessels, S., Evans, M. A., & Jared, D. (2006). Understanding print: Early reading development and the contributions of home literacy experiences. *Journal of Experimental Child Psychology, 93,* 63–93.
Li, J., Fu X. L., & Lin, Z. X. (2000). Study on the development of Chinese orthographic regularity in school children. *Acta Psychologica Sinica, 32,* 121–126. (in Chinese)
Li, H. & Rao, N. (2000). Parental influences on Chinese literacy development: A comparison of preschoolers in Beijing, Hong Kong and Singapore. *International Journal of Behavioral Development, 24,* 82–90.
Li, H., Shu, H., McBride-Chang, C., & Xue, J. (2009). Paired associate learning in Chinese children with dyslexia. *Journal of Experimental Child Psychology, 103,* 135–151.
Lin, D., McBride-Chang, C., Aram, D., Levin, I., Cheung, R. Y. M., Chow, Y. Y. Y., & Tolchinsky, L. (2009). Maternal mediation of writing in Chinese children. *Language and Cognitive Processes, 24,* 1286–1311.
Manis, F. R., Seidenberg, M. S., & Doi, L. M. (1999). See Dick RAN: Rapid naming and the longitudinal prediction of reading subskills in first and second graders. *Scientific Studies of Reading, 3,* 129–157.
McBride-Chang, C., Bialystok, E., Chong, K., & Li, Y. P. (2004). Levels of phonological awareness in three cultures. *Journal of Experimental Child Psychology, 89,* 93–111.
McBride-Chang, C. & Chang, L. (1995). Memory, print exposure, and metacognition: Components of reading in Chinese children. *International Journal of Psychology, 30,* 607–616.
McBride-Chang, C. & Chen, H. C. (eds) (2003). *Reading development in Chinese children.* Westport, CT: Praeger.
McBride-Chang, C., Cho, J.-R., Liu, H., Wagner, R. K., Shu, H., Zhou, A., Cheuk, C. S.-M., & Muse, A. (2005). Changing models across cultures: Associations of phonological and morphological awareness to reading in Beijing, Hong Kong, Korea, and America. *Journal of Experimental Child Psychology, 92,* 140–160.
McBride-Chang, C., Chow, B. W.-Y., Zhong, Y.-P., Burgess, S., & Hayward, W. (2005). Chinese character acquisition and visual skills in two Chinese scripts. *Reading and Writing: An Interdisciplinary Journal, 18,* 99–128.
McBride-Chang, C. & Kail, R. (2002). Cross-cultural similarities in the predictors of reading acquisition. *Child Development, 73,* 1392–1407.
McBride-Chang, C., Shu, H., Zhou, A., Wat, C.-P., & Wagner, R. K. (2003). Morphological awareness uniquely predicts young children's Chinese character recognition. *Journal of Educational Psychology, 95,* 743–751.
McBride-Chang, C., Tong, X. L., Shu, H., Wong, A. M.-Y., Leung, K.-W., & Tardif, T. (2008). Syllable, phoneme, and tone: Psycholinguistic units in early Chinese and English word recognition. *Scientific Studies of Reading, 12,* 1–24.
Meng, X. Z., Shu, H., & Zhou, X. L. (2000). Character structural awareness of children in character production processing. *Psychological Science, 23,* 260–264. (in Chinese)
Peng, D. L. & Li, Y. P. (1995). *Orthographic information in identification of Chinese characters.* Paper presented to the 7th International Conference on Cognitive Aspects of Chinese Language. University of Hong Kong, June.
Perfetti, C. A. & Zhang, S. (1995). Very early phonological activation in Chinese reading. *Journal of Experimental Psychology: Learning, Memory, and Cognition, 21,* 24–33.
Qian, Y. (2002). The visual units in copying characters by Chinese children. Master degree thesis. Beijing Normal University.
Senechal, M. (2006). Testing the home literacy model: Parent involvement in kindergarten is differentially related to grade 4 reading comprehension, fluency, spelling, and reading for pleasure. *Scientific Studies of Reading, 10,* 59–87.
Shu, H. (2003). Chinese writing system and learning to read. *International Journal of Psychology, 38,* 274–285.
Shu, H. & Anderson, R. C. (1997). Role of radical awareness in the character and word acquisition of Chinese children. *Reading Research Quarterly, 32,* 78–89.
Shu, H. & Anderson, R. C. (1999). Learning to read Chinese: The development of metalinguistic awareness. In J. Wang, A. W. Inhoff, & H.-C. Chen (eds), *Reading Chinese script: A cognitive analysis* (pp. 1–18). Mahwah, NJ: Lawrence Erlbaum.
Shu, H., Bi, S. M., & Wu, N. N. (2003). The role of partial information a phonetic provides in learning and memorizing new characters. *Acta Psychologica Sinica, 35,* 9–16. (in Chinese)

Shu, H., Chen, X., Anderson, R. C., Wu, N., & Xuan, Y. (2003). Properties of school Chinese: Implications for learning to read. *Child Development, 74*, 27–47.

Shu, H., McBride-Chang, C., Wu, S., & Liu, H. Y. (2006). Understanding Chinese developmental dyslexia: Morphological awareness as a core cognitive construct. *Journal of Educational Psychology, 98*, 122–133.

Shu, H., Peng, H., & McBride-Chang, C. (2008). Phonological awareness in young Chinese children. *Developmental Science, 11*, 171–181.

Shu, H., Zhou, X., & Wu, N. (2000). Utilizing phonological cues in Chinese characters: A development study. *Acta Psychologica Sinica, 32*, 164–169. (in Chinese)

Siok, W. T. & Fletcher, P. (2001). The role of phonological awareness and visual-orthographic skills in Chinese reading acquisition. *Developmental Psychology, 37*, 886–899.

Snow, C. (2002). *Reading for understanding: toward a research and development program in reading comprehension.* Berkeley, CA: RAND Corporation.

Vygotsky, L. S. (1978). *Mind in society: The development of higher psychological processes*. Cambridge, MA: Harvard University Press.

Wagner, R. K. & Torgesen, J. K. (1987). The nature of phonological processing and its causal role in the acquisition of reading skills. *Psychological Bulletin, 101*, 192–212.

Yiu, E. M., van Hasselt, C. A., Williams, S. R., and Woo, J. K. S. (1994). Speech intelligibility in tone language (Chinese) laryngectomy speakers. *European Journal of Disorders of Communication, 29*, 339–347.

Zevenbergen, A. & Whitehurst, G. (2003). Dialogic reading: A shared picture book. Reading intervention for preschoolers. In A. van Kleeck, S. Stahl, & E. Bauer (eds) *On reading books to children: Parents and teachers* (pp. 177–200). Mahwah, NJ: Erlbaum.

Ziegler, J. C. & Goswami, U. (2005). Reading acquisition, developmental dyslexia, and skilled reading across languages: A psycholinguistic grain size theory. *Psychological Bulletin, 131*, 3–29.

CHAPTER 8

Understanding reading disability in the Chinese language: from basic research to intervention

Connie Suk-Han Ho

Reading disability, also called developmental dyslexia, has been studied for over a century in countries using alphabetic writing systems. Generally speaking, around 3 to 5 per cent of the school population in a Western country has reading disability, a severe and persistent difficulty in reading and spelling, which is not a result of any apparent intrinsic or extrinsic causes. Delayed and inappropriate intervention often results in learning, emotional, and behavioral problems in these children. The early belief was that developmental dyslexia was only a problem for Western people. Although early observations and surveys (e.g. Kline, 1977; Kuo, 1978; Makita, 1968) reported a very low incidence of reading disability among Asian populations, viz. Chinese, Japanese and Korean, we know today that Asian children also have difficulties in reading (e.g. D. W. Chan, Ho, Tsang, Lee, & Chung, 2007; Hirose & Hatta, 1988; Stevenson, Stigler, Lucker, Hsu, & Kitamura, 1982).

It is only during the last ten to twenty years that we have begun to study reading disability in Chinese, the major non-alphabetic language with the largest reader population in the world. Chinese has been described as a logographic and morphosyllabic writing system which has unique linguistic, phonological, orthographic and morphological characteristics that are different from those of alphabetic languages (see also Him, Yap, & Yip, this volume; McBride-Chang, Lin, Fong, & Shu, this volume). The Chinese language, therefore, is a very good case for examining the issue of cultural/linguistic universality and specificity in reading disability.

In this chapter, I will first give a review of research literature on reading disability in alphabetic languages. Then I will introduce the characteristics of the Chinese writing system; highlight some research projects on Chinese reading disability; and explore how these findings may be applied to the identification of and intervention for Chinese children with reading disability.

Reading disability in alphabetic languages

There is convergent evidence showing that the core problem of reading disability in alphabetic languages, given their close connection between script and sound, lies in the difficulties of phonological processing (e.g. L. Bradley & Bryant, 1978; Hulme & Snowling, 1992; Mc-Bride-Chang et al., this volume; Olson, Rack, & Forsberg, 1990; Shankweiler, Liberman, Mark, Fowler, & Fischer, 1979). These dyslexic children normally perform poorly in phoneme segmentation and non-word reading.

Researchers believe that it is the abstract, grapheme–phoneme association required in learning alphabetic languages that makes English difficult to learn, while other non-alphabetic languages, like Chinese and Japanese, may rely on learning a less abstract level of grapheme–syllable or grapheme–morpheme association. However, Gleitman (1985) has suggested that Chinese characters are easy to start acquiring but hard to finish acquiring, because Chinese children need to memorize a lot more grapheme–sound mappings than do alphabetic readers.

Apart from phonological difficulties as the core deficit in developmental dyslexia, researchers have found that some dyslexic children also have difficulties in rapid naming and orthographic processing. Studies have shown that dyslexic readers are impaired in the rapid recognition and retrieval of visually presented linguistic materials (e.g. Ackerman & Dykman, 1993; Badian, 1995; Bowers & Wolf, 1993; Denckla & Rudel, 1976a, 1976b). The naming-speed deficit may be an indication of the disruption of the automatic processes involved in the extraction and induction of orthographic patterns. This hypothesis is supported by Bowers, Sunseth, and Golden (1999), who maintain that more accurate but slower readers have less knowledge of orthographic patterns.

Orthographic deficit has been a neglected factor in dyslexia research in the past. The use of orthographic information, e.g. the frequency of letter sequences, alters the unit of perception by enabling the reader to move from processing individual letters to processing letter sequences. Some research findings show that orthographic deficit is also one of the causes of reading failures with some children. For instance, Hultquist (1997) reported that the dyslexic readers in his study performed significantly worse than the reading-level controls on several orthographic measures.

Characteristics of the Chinese writing system

The basic graphic unit in Chinese is a character. There are about 3,000 Chinese characters in daily use in mainland China (Foreign Languages Press Beijing, 1989), and about 4,500 frequently used characters in Taiwan (Liu, Chuang, & Wang, 1975). Chinese characters are made up of different strokes. Strokes are combined to form stroke-patterns, also called radicals, that act as basic orthographic units. The number of strokes in a Chinese character is a measure of its visual complexity. The average number of strokes of 2,000 commonly used Chinese characters is 11.2 for the traditional script used in Hong Kong and Taiwan, and 9.0 for the simplified script used in mainland China (M. Y. Chan, 1982). Chinese characters are therefore visually compact and complicated.

All Chinese characters are monosyllabic. In consequence, there are many homophones at the character level. To avoid the problem of homophones, the majority of words are multi-syllabic, and about two-thirds of them are bi-syllabic (Taylor & Taylor, 1995). Chinese is not, however, as logographic as people think. Only a small percentage of Chinese characters convey meaning by pictographic or ideographic representation (Hoosain, 1991). According to Kang (1993), about 80 per cent to 90 per cent of Chinese characters are ideophonetic compounds, each comprising a semantic and a phonetic radical.

In general, the semantic radical in a Chinese character signifies the semantic category of the character. There are different degrees of transparency for the semantic implications of different semantic radicals. A transparent semantic radical gives a reliable cue for the meaning of a character, e.g. the semantic radical 女 'female' in the character 媽 'mother', while an opaque semantic radical does not, e.g. the semantic radical 土 'soil' in the character 增 'increase'. A semantic radical typically occupies a habitual position in a Chinese character—left or top.

Unlike the case of an English word in which the sound is encoded in all letters, only one part of a Chinese character, i.e. the phonetic radical, encodes or specifies the sound of the character. This part-to-whole conversion rule is called the 'orthography–phonology correspondence' rule (Ho & Bryant, 1997) or the 'phonetic principle' (Anderson, Li, Ku, Shu, & Wu, 2003). The phonetic radical provides a sound cue for an ideophonetic compound character either by 'direct derivation' or by 'analogy'. The sound of a Chinese character can be derived directly from its phonetic radical, e.g. deriving the sound of 碼 [ma]5 'yard' from its phonetic 馬 [ma]5, or indirectly by making an analogy with other characters having the same phonetic radical, e.g. associating the sound of 碼 [ma]5 'yard' with 螞 [ma]5 'ant'. The former is analogous to the regularity effect in English, while the latter reflects a consistency effect.

There are different degrees of semantic and phonological regularity/consistency in Chinese characters. According to some statistical analyses, the predictive accuracy of the pronunciation of an ideophonetic compound character from its phonetic radical is about 40 per cent (Shu, Chen, Anderson, Wu, & Xuan, 2003; Zhou, 1980; Zhu, 1987). This figure drops to between 23 per cent and 26 per cent if tone is taken into consideration (Fan, Gao, & Ao, 1984; Shu et al., 2003; Zhou, 1980). Overall, semantic radicals are functionally more reliable than phonetic ones.

The orthographic rules in Chinese are rather complicated with all the above characteristics, e.g. having a large number of orthographic units and many homophones, different degrees of positional, semantic, and phonological regularities for radicals. Many of these rules are not formally taught in school. We believe that it would take children a long time to acquire complete orthographic knowledge in Chinese. Based on our research findings, we have proposed a model of orthographic knowledge development in Chinese (Ho, Yau, & Au, 2003). As suggested by this model, Chinese children acquire various types of orthographic knowledge in the sequence of character configuration knowledge, structural knowledge, radical information knowledge, positional knowledge, functional knowledge, and complete orthographic knowledge. It takes children nearly all the years of their elementary school education to acquire a complete orthographic knowledge in Chinese. It appears that children learning an alphabetic script may reach the 'consolidated alphabetic phase', with consolidated orthographic representations and automatic activation of whole word spellings, earlier than do their Chinese counterparts (e.g. Ehri, 1980, 1994, 1998).

Apart from being monosyllabic, each Chinese character also represents a morpheme, the smallest unit of meaning. Many words in Chinese are formed by combining different morphemes, e.g. 'football', 'basket-ball', 'hand-ball', etc., so that Chinese readers may derive the meaning of the whole word from knowing its constituent morphemes. Given the characteristics of many homophones, homographs, and word compoundings in Chinese, awareness of morphemes is particularly important in learning to read Chinese (McBride-Chang, Wagner, Muse, Chow, & Shu, 2005). One obvious advantage of this logographic and morphosyllabic nature of the Chinese language is that the same script can be used in a large population where people speak different dialects.

Comparisons with Japanese and Korean

It is interesting to note that Chinese characters (around 2,000) are also used in two other languages, namely Japanese and Korean. About half of Japanese vocabularies are Sino-Japanese words. The Japanese language is written in Kanji (i.e. Chinese characters), Hiragana and Katakana (two forms of Japanese syllabary). Kanji are used for most Sino-Japanese words and for many Japanese native-content words. Hiragana are used to write frequent grammatical morphemes, such as postposition after nouns. Katakana are used to write less frequent items such as foreign loan words.

Kanji readings are complicated. A Kanji may be pronounced in a Kun reading (Japanese native reading) or an On reading (Chinese reading), or in both. Despite this complication, the logographic Kanji are retained because they are useful. First, Kanji help to differentiate the abundant homophones in the Japanese language. Second, Kanji convey meanings quickly and their presence in a text makes silent reading efficient. Third, the Kanji for Sino-Japanese morphemes are highly productive and readily combine to form compound words.

For Korean, there are also two kinds of scripts: Hangul, an alphabetic syllabary, and Hancha, i.e. Chinese characters. Each Hangul letter represents a phoneme, and thus is alphabetic. A Hangul letter is always written in combination with other letters to form a syllable block. So Hangul is used like a syllabary in reading and writing. All words can be written in Hangul, but only Sino-Korean words can be written in Hancha. As in Chinese, semantic and phonetic components of a character and multi-character compound words in Hancha are also taught in Korean schools.

Given the above linguistic similarities and differences with Chinese, researchers have reported that phonological awareness is more important for reading in English and Korean than in Chinese, whereas morphological awareness is more important for reading Chinese and Korean than reading in English (McBride-Chang et al., 2005). Phonological deficit has also been found in Japanese dyslexic children and phonological awareness has been shown to be important for the learning of

Japanese Kana (Seki, Kassai, Uchiyama, & Koeda, 2007). However, the role of morphological awareness in reading Japanese has not yet been reported.

Reading disability in Chinese

Reading-related cognitive deficits

Given the different linguistic characteristics of the Chinese language listed above, individuals with dyslexia show a cognitive profile somewhat different from that of dyslexic readers using alphabetic languages. With the multidimensional method, we have identified seven sub-types of reading disability in Chinese: global deficit, orthographic deficit, phonological memory deficit, mild difficulty, and three other sub-types with rapid naming-related deficits (Ho, Chan, Lee, Tsang, & Luan, 2004). Ho et al. (2004) have reported that rapid naming deficit (in 57 per cent of the dyslexic sample) and orthographic deficit (in 42 per cent of the dyslexic sample) are the major reading-related cognitive deficits in Chinese reading disability, figures that confirm earlier findings (Ho, Chan, Tsang, & Lee, 2002). Rapid-naming deficit in Chinese dyslexic children may also reflect their problems in developing a stable and strong orthographic representation that allows rapid retrieval.

Ho et al. (2004) have suggested that orthographic-related difficulties may be the crux of the problem in Chinese developmental dyslexia. Such orthographic-related deficits may reflect poor orthographic representations and weak linkage between orthographic and phonological processors of Chinese dyslexic readers. As described above, the orthographic rules in Chinese are rather complicated, so that the acquisition of orthographic skills becomes a hurdle for many dyslexic Chinese children.

Apart from orthographic-related deficits, other studies show that morphological deficit may be another salient feature of reading disability in Chinese. Morphological awareness has recently been found to be an important predictor of reading success and failure in Chinese (Luan & Ho, in preparation; McBride-Chang et al., 2005; Shu, McBride-Chang, Wu, & Liu, 2006). Given the large frequency of homophones and word compounding in Chinese, morphological awareness is even more important in learning to read Chinese than in learning to read alphabetic languages (McBride-Chang et al., 2005). Morphological awareness has been found to contribute significantly and uniquely to Chinese character reading in kindergarten and Grade 2 children, even after controlling the effects of age, phonological awareness, speeded naming, speed of processing, and vocabulary (McBride-Chang, Shu, Zhou, Wat, & Wagner, 2003). Chinese dyslexic children were found to perform significantly less well than age controls in morpheme production and judgment (Shu, McBride-Chang, Wu, & Liu, 2006).

Different cognitive profiles for different Chinese populations

Dyslexic children reading different orthographies may exhibit different cognitive profiles. Based on the above review, the core problem for alphabetic dyslexic readers is related to phonological processing difficulties, whereas that for Chinese dyslexic readers is associated with morphological and orthographic-related problems. However, different Chinese populations with differences in spoken dialects, scripts, and instructional methods may also show different cognitive profiles.

We have conducted a study comparing the cognitive profile of dyslexic readers in Beijing and Hong Kong (Luan & Ho, in preparation). Children in Beijing speak Putonghua (the official spoken language in mainland China), read the simplified version of Chinese script, and learn to read Chinese characters using the Pinyin system from the age of six. On the other hand, children in Hong Kong speak Cantonese, a dialect that has the largest number of tones and is mainly used by people in Guangdong, southeastern Guangxi, Hong Kong, and Macau, read the traditional Chinese script, and learn to read Chinese characters with a look-and-say method from the age of three. It was found that difficulties in morphological awareness (in 29.6 per cent of the sample), phonological awareness (in 27.6 per cent of the sample), and rapid naming (in 27.6 per cent of the sample) are the three most dominant types of cognitive deficits in dyslexic children from Beijing. Similarly, rapid naming (in 52 per cent of the sample), morphological deficit (in 26.5 per cent of the sample), and orthographic deficit (in 24 per cent of the sample) are dominant in dyslexic children from Hong Kong.

The most striking differences between the cognitive profiles of Beijing and Hong Kong dyslexic children lie in their proportions of deficits in phonological awareness (27.6 per cent vs. 12 per cent) and rapid naming (27.6 per cent vs. 52 per cent). This result is likely due to the differences in instructional method practiced in these two locations. Pinyin is an alphabetic system, like English, that emphasizes grapheme–phoneme conversions. Therefore, weakness in phonological awareness would hinder Beijing dyslexic children from learning to read Chinese characters using Pinyin. On the other hand, the look-and-say method used by Hong Kong teachers emphasizes rapid retrieval of the name of Chinese characters. Slow naming speed in Hong Kong dyslexic children is an indicator of the disruption of the automatic processes involved in the extraction and induction of orthographic patterns. Good paired-associate learning skills and automatic recognition and retrieval of visual stimuli are essential in the look-and-say method of learning. In sum, different instructional methods place different demands on learning to read and hence produce different cognitive profiles of reading disability, even in the same language system.

Comparing the cognitive profile of Chinese reading disability and other developmental disorders

As reviewed above, the findings from most past research suggest that phonological deficit is unique to reading disability insofar as alphabetic languages are concerned. We have conducted a study to investigate the existence of any similarly unique, reading-related cognitive deficits associated with reading disability in Chinese as compared with other types of developmental disorders or learning disabilities (Ho, Chan, Leung, Lee, & Tsang, 2005). Chinese children with different types of developmental disorders or learning difficulties, including reading disability (RD), attention deficit/hyperactivity disorder (ADHD), developmental coordination disorder (DCD), and borderline intelligence (BI) have been tested on literacy, rapid naming, phonological, orthographic, and visual processing skills.

We have found that (a) the comorbidity rates among these developmental disorders were high; (b) the RD-only group was most impaired in rapid naming and orthographic processing, performing significantly worse than other 'pure' groups, i.e. groups with a single disability; (c) the ADHD-only and DCD-only groups performed very close to the average normal range in literacy and cognitive domains; and (d) the cognitive profile of the RD+ADHD group resembled that of the RD-only group, while that of the RD+DCD group resembled some characteristics of both the pure groups.

Based on these findings, we conclude that rapid-naming deficit and orthographic deficit are unique marker deficits of reading disability in Chinese, a finding that is different from the case of alphabetic languages. These different patterns are probably due to differences in the linguistic features between Chinese and alphabetic languages. The high comorbidity rates among various developmental disorders in Chinese highlight the need for developing standard screening procedures for practitioners to identify overlapping conditions.

Chinese preschool children at risk for reading disability

There is strong evidence showing that reading disability is both familial and heritable, e.g. Pennington et al. (1991). When there is an affected parent, an offspring's risk of having reading disability increases from two to eighty times over population expectancies, based on various estimates (Gilger et al., 1991). We understand that untimely and inappropriate intervention often results in learning, emotional, and behavioral problems in dyslexic children. It is evident that early identification and early intervention help to alleviate the problems in these children. It would therefore be helpful if we could identify at-risk children at preschool levels and understand their early difficulties.

We have conducted a three-year longitudinal study to examine whether Chinese preschool children of high and low familial risk differed in language, phonological, print-related, and other reading-related cognitive skills (Ho, Leung, & Cheung, submitted). Our findings show that Chinese preschool children at family risk for reading disability have early difficulties in articulation, oral language, phonological awareness, and print-related skills, like their alphabetic counterparts (e.g. Hindson et al., 2005). Based on the present findings, we suggest that early problems in articulation and oral language, particularly vocabulary and verbal expression, may be considered as an early screener of potential reading difficulties in Chinese, especially for those with family risk. To better understand the causes and nature of family risk of reading disability in Chinese, we are currently undertaking a behavioral genetic study on language and literacy development and a molecular genetic study on reading disability.

These basic research studies provide a solid foundation for evidence-based practice in education. Many of the findings inform us how to develop tools for the identification of Chinese children with reading disability, and guide the development of effective intervention methods and curriculum materials.

The need for early identification and early intervention

Before I describe the tools that we have developed for the identification and intervention of reading disability in Chinese, I would like to reiterate the need for early identification of and early intervention with children with reading disability. First, the problem of reading disability in Chinese is much more common than one expects, at least among the Chinese school population in Hong Kong. We have examined the prevalence rate of reading disability in Hong Kong using a representative stratified random sample (D. W. Chan, Ho, Tsang, Lee, & Chung, 2007). Our findings show that 9.7 per cent of the sample had reading disability (with 6.2 per cent, 2.2 per cent, and 1.3 per cent having mild, moderate, and severe difficulties respectively). Of course, the prevalence rate always depends on how stringent the cut-off criteria are made. However, our findings show at least that the problem of reading disability is common in Hong Kong, a Cantonese-speaking Chinese population, and that the percentage of children with severe literacy difficulties is close to the same figure for children learning alphabetic languages.

Second, the problem of reading disability is persistent. For instance, 74 per cent of children who were found to be poor readers in third grade remained poor readers in ninth grade (Francis et al., 1996). Some of the persisting difficulties include poor phonological memory, e.g. in remembering names, difficulty with sequence, e.g. ordering days of the week, poor spelling, and difficulty in learning foreign languages. Reading disability is indeed a lifelong challenge!

Given that reading disability is common and persistent, early identification and early intervention become important. They help to improve the success rate of intervention, prevent the reading problem from continuing into higher grades, and avoid the development of emotional and behavior problems or poor self-esteem associated with poorer academic performance (W. S. Chan, 2002; see also Hau, this volume). Overseas experiences also suggest that schools need to invest more teaching time if teachers help the children later than earlier in their school life (two hours per day at fourth grade vs. 0.5 hours per day at kindergarten) (Hall & Linch, 2007).

A two-stage model for identifying reading disability

As early identification of reading disability is important, how are we going to identify children with reading disability? We would like to propose a two-stage model for efficient and effective identification of children with reading disability. The first stage is a quick and economical screening stage requiring the development of some standardized and user-friendly behavior checklists for parents and teachers. These checklists help parents and teachers identify quickly and at a low cost those children at risk for reading disability. Parents and teachers may then give initial attention and assistance to these at-risk children. If their progress in reading is not satisfactory, their problems may need to be better examined in order to identify and provide more appropriate intervention.

The second stage of identification requires a comprehensive assessment. Normally, professional psychologists administer standardized psychological tests in order to ascertain the degree and areas of difficulties experienced by a child. Assessment at this stage aims at making a diagnosis and collecting diagnostic information for more intensive intervention. We have developed some standardized screening and assessment tools, i.e. behavior checklists and assessment batteries, for the identification of Chinese individuals with reading disability in Hong Kong. I will describe these tools in the following sections.

Chinese behavior checklists

Our research team has developed three standardized behavior checklists for screening of Chinese individuals of various ages with learning disability in Hong Kong, namely: The Hong Kong Learning Behavior Checklist for Preschool Children (Parent Version) (Wong, Ho, Chung, Chan, Tsang, & Lee, 2006); The Hong Kong Specific Learning Difficulties Behavior Checklist (for Primary School Pupils), (Ho, Chan, Tsang, & Lee, 2000); and The Hong Kong Reading and Writing Behavior Checklist for Adults (Ho, Leung, Cheung, Leung, & Chou, 2007). Currently, we are developing a new checklist for the identification of Chinese adolescents in secondary schools with learning disability.

The idea of these checklists is to ask the informant (parents for the preschool checklist, teachers for the primary school checklist, and individuals for the adult checklist) to rate how frequently some behavioral indicators of learning and reading disabilities occur. Behavioral indicators are developmental. That is, oral language and motor problems may be an indicator of learning disability in preschool children, but not for adults. On the other hand, poor organization skills may be more indicative of learning disability in adults than in young children. Therefore, different domains of items are included in the checklists for different age groups. For instance, there are eight domains of items in the preschool checklist, namely oral language skills, general learning ability, writing performance, attention, memory, sequence, spatial, and motor coordination.

It is noteworthy that there is considerable behavioral overlap between ordinary children and children with learning disabilities. The two groups of children are very much alike in many aspects of their daily behavioral repertoires. Information based on a behavior checklist therefore could not be perfectly accurate. However, the three Chinese checklists evidence a satisfactory discriminative power. The degree of accuracy in discriminating or predicting those who have reading disability and those who do not ranges from around 70 per cent to 85 per cent. These behavior checklists are widely used by parents, teachers, and psychologists for screening individuals with learning disabilities in Hong Kong.

Chinese assessment batteries

There have been controversies regarding the procedures for determining reading disability. The use of IQ score-achievement discrepancy as a primary determining practice for identifying reading disability has been criticized (e.g. Vaughn & Klingner, 2007). With more research findings, we have come to understand that dyslexic individuals often show certain more specific cognitive deficits that could be used as one of the diagnostic criteria, e.g. phonological impairment for alphabetic dyslexic readers.

Our research team has developed two standardized assessment batteries for diagnostic assessment of Chinese primary school and secondary school students with reading disability in Hong Kong, namely The Hong Kong Test of Specific Learning Difficulties in Reading and Writing for Primary School Students, 2nd edition (HKT-P(II)) (Ho, Chan, Chung, Tsang, Lee, & Cheng, 2007), and The Hong Kong Test of Specific Learning Difficulties in Reading and Writing for Junior Secondary School Students (HKT-JS), (Chung, Ho, Chan, Tsang, & Lee, 2007). Development of the sub-tests for these assessment instruments is based on the findings of our own and others' studies on the cognitive profile of Chinese reading disability reviewed above. In other words, we suggest that apart from low attainment in reading and spelling, Chinese children with reading disability also exhibit specific cognitive difficulties, especially in the areas of orthographic processing and rapid naming, diagnostic areas that should be included in the diagnostic criteria.

Take the test battery for primary school students as an example. There are twelve sub-tests in this test battery, three on literacy and nine on reading-related cognitive skills. Since word decoding is the core problem of children with reading disability, the three literacy sub-tests focus mainly on word-level processing, namely Chinese word reading, word dictation, and one-minute word reading. Research evidence has shown that rapid naming deficit and orthographic deficit are the major reading-related cognitive deficits in Chinese reading disability (Ho et al., 2004). Therefore, there are four sub-tests measuring rapid naming and orthographic skills.

Our other studies also show that Chinese dyslexic children have greater difficulties in phonological awareness and phonological memory than do ordinary children (e.g. Ho, Law, & Ng, 2000). As such, there are also five sub-tests measuring these phonological skills in the primary school test battery. With local norms on these sub-tests, the test battery helps to identify Chinese children with reading disability in Hong Kong. Apart from helping to make the diagnosis, the information on the relative strengths and weaknesses of the children may suggest areas for intervention.

At the time we published the first edition of the primary school test battery in 2000, not much had been reported about the important role of morphological awareness in reading development in Chinese, and we did not include any measures on morphological awareness. However, we did add two morphological measures when we developed the secondary school test battery later. Apart from the three word-level tasks, we have also included sub-tests on reading comprehension and writing in the secondary school test battery to examine text-level literacy processing of adolescents. These standardized Chinese test batteries are now widely used by professional psychologists for diagnostic assessment of reading disability in Hong Kong.

A Chinese three-tiered response-to-intervention model

It has been a challenge to develop an evidence-based approach for teaching students with reading disability, and such programs are rare in Chinese learning settings. Traditional approaches often identify and help students with reading disability using a 'wait-to-fail' model rather than an early prevention model. The response-to-intervention (RTI) approach has received growing attention in recent years and its effectiveness has been established in studies conducted in North America (see a comprehensive review in Haager, Klingner, & Vaughn, 2007). RTI has also been specified as 'the most promising method' for identifying individuals with learning disabilities (R. Bradley, Danielson, & Hallahan, 2002).

This approach is based on monitoring students' progress, by means of curriculum-based measures, over the course of their participation in appropriate interventions. Students who make little progress are deemed to require a more intensive and specific intervention, and those with continuous non-responsiveness to intervention may be considered as having a learning disability.

In one of our ongoing projects, we are developing a Chinese, three-tiered RTI model as an alternative to traditional methods used for identifying and teaching students with reading disabilities. This is an evidence-based and prevention-focused model. In this model, Tier 1 is whole-class, quality core reading instruction provided to all general education students. Those who fall below the benchmarks receive more intensive intervention. Tier 2 is small-group supplemental instruction, and Tier 3 is individualized intensive instruction. Progressions along the different tiers depend on students' responsiveness to the preceding interventions. In general, Tier 1 instruction should meet the needs of around 70 to 80 per cent of learners. The lowest 20 to 30 per cent of students may require additional support with Tier 2 intervention, and around 5 to 10 per cent may need more intensive support from the Tier 3 intervention.

In our current research project, we tried out Tier 1 instruction in three primary schools in Hong Kong last academic year (2006–7), and are experimenting with Tier 2 intervention this academic year (2007–8). A control school receiving no intervention was recruited for comparison. A total of 573

Grade 1 pupils participated, matched in age and IQ across schools. Some initial findings on Tier 1 intervention will be reported later in this chapter. There are three important elements in Tier 1: (1) a core reading program based on scientific research findings, (2) benchmark testing and progress monitoring to determine instructional needs, and (3) professional development for teachers to ensure that students receive quality instruction in reading.

A core reading curriculum in Chinese, and teacher training

The RTI model provides only a general framework for structuring human resources, grouping students, and gauging the intensity of intervention. What to teach depends very much on what the important skills are for reading a particular language. Based on research findings, a consensus has emerged about the essential components of core reading instruction in English. They are the Big Five: phonemic awareness, phonics, fluency, vocabulary, and text comprehension (National Reading Panel, 2000). Research findings about the cognitive profile of Chinese reading disability reviewed above suggest what to teach when developing a core reading instructional curriculum in Chinese. Specifically, phonological awareness is not as important in reading Chinese as in alphabetic languages, whereas orthographic skills and morphological awareness are significant predictors of reading success or failure in Chinese. This is especially the case when Hong Kong teachers mainly use the look-and-say method instead of Pinyin to teach children reading Chinese characters.

In our Chinese reading curriculum, the eight core components include oral language (vocabulary and verbal expression), morphological awareness, orthographic skills, word recognition skills, syntactic knowledge, reading comprehension, fluency, and writing. For each component, we have designed a sequence of training topics arranged from basic to more advanced levels. Taking orthographic skills as an example, topics include Chinese character structure, functions of semantic radicals, different forms and positions of semantic radicals, and functions of phonetic radicals. Since this is the first program of its kind, we have included as many core components as have been indicated by various research findings in Chinese.

Training on the theoretical background and teaching strategies of these core components was presented in several teacher seminars. There were also bi-weekly lesson preparation meetings with the teachers, and teaching materials were provided by our research team. Regular class observations by our team members were carried out to ensure that the teachers understood the curriculum and teaching method and implemented them appropriately in their classrooms.

Assessment and progress monitoring

Assessment in the tiered intervention model serves three functions: (1) screening of children that may require more attention, (2) progress monitoring for entry and exit decisions, and (3) assessment for informing instructional planning. Benchmark assessments, preferably three times a year, help in early identification of students at risk for reading problems. For those who are not making good progress, teachers may combine Tier 1 instruction with Tier 2 or Tier 3 intervention to satisfy students' learning needs. The data on ongoing progress monitoring help teachers in adjusting their instruction to ensure students' academic growth.

However, there is no benchmark assessment as such in Hong Kong to serve the purpose of screening and assessment. We have developed some experimental tasks for each core reading component to serve the first and second functions. These experimental tasks were administered three times a year in Tier 1. Some five-minute class assessments were administered by the teachers after teaching each core component to determine instructional effectiveness, i.e. to serve the third function.

Preliminary findings

To ensure that our core components were selected appropriately, regression analyses were carried out. The results show that (1) oral language, morphological awareness and orthographic skills make significant, unique contributions to Chinese word reading and dictation; and (2) syntactic awareness makes significant unique contributions to reading comprehension, reading fluency and simple writing, even after controlling all demographic, word reading, and word-level cognitive–linguistic measures. Therefore, oral language, morphological awareness, orthographic skills, and syntactic awareness are significant reading-related cognitive–linguistic skills in mastering Chinese.

In a review paper, Marston (2005) has indicated that the effectiveness of tiered intervention programs has been measured in three ways. First, effectiveness is reflected in measures of student growth. For instance, the average gain in words ranged from thirty per term (Tilly, 2003) to sixty (Vaughn, 2003). The second indicator is the contrasts among student performances. Research findings generally show significant differences in student performance between program schools and control schools in each tier. The third indicator is placement outcomes. For instance, Tilly (2003) reported a decrease in special education placement rate from 55 per cent in kindergarten to 19 per cent in Grade 3 in schools with tiered intervention programs.

The present study employed contrasts of student performance as a measure of program effectiveness. After the Tier 1 intervention in our study, the program schools showed significantly greater improvement in all word-level and text-level components, except for morphological awareness, when compared with the control school. We also analyzed data of sixty-one children at the bottom of their class in Chinese from the three program schools. Results showed that their improvement rates in orthographic skills, morphological awareness, syntactic knowledge, Chinese word reading, and fluency were significantly higher than those of their peers in the same grade. Therefore, Tier 1 intervention was found to be effective in promoting the children's reading-related cognitive skills and literacy performance; it was especially beneficial for beginning readers who are struggling.

Based on all these findings, we propose that the 'Big Six' of core reading components in Chinese are oral language, including vocabulary and verbal expression, morphological awareness, orthographic skills, syntactic knowledge, text comprehension, and fluency. This list of proposed core components overlaps with three of the Big Five in English, namely vocabulary, text comprehension, and fluency. The dissimilar core components reflect the different cognitive demands needed for reading diverse orthographies: phonological training is essential for learning to read English, whereas morphological and orthographic training is significant for reading success in Chinese.

We have also found that syntactic knowledge is one of the most important predictors of text-level processing in Chinese. Chinese syntax is known to be non-inflectional, and there are no clear word boundaries. Sensitivity to word order and word segmentation is therefore important. There are also large discrepancies in the use of vocabularies and word order between spoken Cantonese and written Chinese. Ordinary children may be able to acquire these complicated and elaborate rules for syntax through exposure to language and print. However, our findings show that struggling Chinese readers may require explicit and systematic instruction on syntax in order to enhance their reading comprehension. We therefore propose this to be one of the core components in any Chinese reading curriculum.

Conclusion and future directions

This chapter takes the position that well-planned and systematic research in reading disability is essential for developing effective evidence-based identification and intervention approaches for children with reading disability. Given the different linguistic characteristics of Chinese and alphabetic languages, basic research in Chinese is necessary for developing effective identification and intervention methods that are suitable for Chinese children. Research findings so far indicate that the core problem of Chinese dyslexic readers derives from morphological and orthographic-related problems, which are different from the phonological processing difficulties of dyslexic readers of alphabetic languages. Knowledge of the cognitive profile of Chinese reading disability has facilitated our development of Chinese-appropriate assessment instruments and reading curriculum. The overlaps and divergence between the Big Five in English and the Big Six in Chinese suggest that there are areas of both language-universal and language-specific demands in reading different orthographies.

Since the above conclusion is largely based on research data collected in Hong Kong, where the children speak Cantonese and learn to read the traditional Chinese script with a look-and-say method, future research may extend intervention programs to other Chinese populations speaking Mandarin and reading the simplified Chinese script with the use of Pinyin to validate the Big Six in Chinese.

Author's note

The author would like to thank the support of the Research Grants Council (grants #HKU7150/02H and #HKU7212/04H), the Hong Kong Jockey Club, and the Quality Education Fund in Hong Kong, whose support has helped us in producing the work reported in this chapter. Many of the projects reported in this chapter have been the collaborative effort of the Hong Kong Specific Learning Difficulties Research Team and the Read and Write Team.

The author may be contacted at the Department of Psychology, The University of Hong Kong, Pokfulam Road, Hong Kong, China, or by email at shhoc@hkucc.hku.hk.

References

Ackerman, P. T. & Dykman, R. A. (1993). Phonological processes, confrontational naming, and immediate memory in dyslexia. *Journal of Learning Disabilities, 26*, 597–609.

Anderson, R. C., Li, W., Ku, Y.-M., Shu, H., & Wu, N. (2003). Use of partial information in learning to read Chinese characters. *Journal of Educational Psychology, 95*, 52–57.

Badian, N. A. (1995). Predicting reading ability over the long-term: The changing roles of letter naming, phonological awareness and orthographic processing. *Annals of Dyslexia, XLV*, 79–86.

Bowers, P. G., Sunseth, K., & Golden, J. (1999). The route between rapid naming and reading progress. *Scientific Studies of Reading, 3*, 31–53.

Bowers, P. G. & Wolf, M. (1993). Theoretical links among naming speed, precise timing mechanisms and orthographic skill in dyslexia. *Reading and Writing, 5*, 69–85.

Bradley, L. & Bryant, P. (1978). Difficulties in auditory organization as a possible cause of reading backwardness. *Nature, 271*, 746–747.

Bradley, R., Danielson, L., & Hallahan, D. P. (2002). *Identification of learning disabilities: Research to practice.* Mahwah, NJ: Lawrence Erlbaum Associates.

Chan, D. W., Ho, C. S.-H., Tsang, S.-M., Lee, S.-H., & Chung, K. K.-H. (2007). Prevalence, gender ratio and gender differences in reading-related cognitive abilities among Chinese children with dyslexia in Hong Kong. *Education Studies, 33*, 249–265.

Chan, M. Y. (1982). Statistics on the strokes of present-day Chinese script. *Chinese Linguistics, 1*, 299–305. (in Chinese)

Chan, W. S. (2002). *The concomitance of dyslexia and emotional/behavioral problems: A study on Hong Kong children.* Unpublished master's thesis, The University of Hong Kong.

Chung, K., Ho, C. S.-H., Chan, D., Tsang, S.-M., & Lee, S.-H. (2007). *The Hong Kong Test of Specific Learning Difficulties in Reading and Writing for Junior Secondary School Students (HKT-JS).* Hong Kong: Hong Kong Specific Learning Difficulties Research Team.

Denckla, M. B. & Rudel, R. (1976a). Naming of objects by dyslexics and other learning-disabled children. *Brain and Language, 3*, 1–15.

Denckla, M. B. & Rudel, R. (1976b). Rapid 'automatised' naming (RAN): Dyslexia differentiated from other learning disabilities. *Neuropsychologia, 14*, 471–479.

Ehri, L. C. (1980). The development of orthographic images. In U. Frith (ed.), *Cognitive processes in spelling* (pp. 311–338). London: Academic Press.

Ehri, L. C. (1994). Development of the ability to read words: Update. In R. B. Ruddell, M. R. Ruddell, & H. Singer (eds), *Theoretical models and processes of reading* (pp. 323–358). Newark, DE: International Reading Association.

Ehri, L. C. (1998). Grapheme–phoneme knowledge is essential for learning to read words in English. In J. L. Metsala & L. C. Ehri (eds), *Word recognition in beginning literacy* (pp. 3–40). Mahwah, NJ: Erlbaum.

Fan, K. Y., Gao, J. Y., & Ao, X. P. (1984). Pronunciation principles of the Chinese character and alphabetic writing scripts. *Chinese Character Reform, 3*, 23–27.

Foreign Languages Press Beijing. (1989). *Chinese characters.* Beijing, China: Foreign Languages Press.

Francis, D. J., Shaywitz, S. E., Stuebing, K. K., Shaywitz, B. A., & Fletcher, J. M. (1996). Developmental lag versus deficit models of reading disability: A longitudinal, individual growth curves analysis. *Journal of Educational Psychology, 88*, 3–17.

Gilger, J. W., Pennington, B. F., & Defries, J. C. (1991). Risk for reading disability as a function of parental history in three family studies. *Reading and Writing: An Interdisciplinary Journal*, 3, 205–217.
Gleitman, L. R. (1985). Orthographic resources affect reading acquisition—if they are used. *RASE: Remedial and Special Education, 6*, 24–36.
Haager, D., Klingner, J., & Vaughn, S. (2007). *Evidence-based reading practices for response to intervention.* Baltimore, MD: Brookes.
Hall, S. & Linch, T. (2007, November). Implementing response to intervention. Paper presented at the Annual Conference of International Dyslexia Association, Dallas, TX.
Hindson, B., Byrne, B., Fielding-Barnsley, R., Newman, C., Hine, D. W., & Shankweiler, D. (2005). Assessment and early instruction of preschool children at risk for reading disability. *Journal of Educational Psychology*, 97, 687–704.
Hirose, T. & Hatta, T. (1988). Reading disabilities in modern Japanese children. *Journal of Research in Reading, 11*, 152–160.
Ho, C. S. H. & P. Bryant (1997). Phonological skills are important in learning to read Chinese. *Development Psychology, 33*, 943–951.
Ho, C. S.-H., Chan, D., Chung, K., Tsang, S.-M., Lee, S.-H., & Cheng, R. W.-Y. (2007). *The Hong Kong Test of Specific Learning Difficulties in Reading and Writing for Primary School Students, 2nd edn (HKT-P(II)).* Hong Kong: Hong Kong Specific Learning Difficulties Research Team.
Ho, C. S.-H., Chan, D., Leung, P. W.-L., Lee, S.-H., & Tsang, S.-M. (2005). Reading-related cognitive deficits in developmental dyslexia, attention deficit/hyperactivity disorder, and developmental coordination disorder among Chinese children. *Reading Research Quarterly, 40*, 318–337.
Ho, C. S.-H., Chan, D., Tsang, S.-M., & Lee, S.-H. (2000). *The Hong Kong Specific Learning Difficulties Behavior Checklist (for primary school pupils).* Hong Kong: Hong Kong Specific Learning Difficulties Research Team.
Ho, C. S.-H., Chan, D., Tsang, S.-M., & Lee, S.-H. (2002). The cognitive profile and multiple-deficit hypothesis in Chinese developmental dyslexia. *Developmental Psychology, 38*, 543–553.
Ho, C. S.-H., Chan, D., Tsang, S.-M., Lee, S.-H., & Luan, V. H. (2004). Cognitive profiling and preliminary subtyping in Chinese developmental dyslexia. *Cognition, 91*, 43–75.
Ho, C. S.-H., Law, T. P.-S., & Ng, P. M. (2000). The phonological deficit hypothesis in Chinese developmental dyslexia. *Reading and Writing, 13*, 57–79.
Ho, C. S.-H., Leung, M.-T., & Cheung, H. (submitted). *Early difficulties of Chinese preschool children at familial risk for dyslexia: deficits in oral language, phonological processing skills, and print-related skills.* Manuscript submitted for publication.
Ho, C. S.-H., Leung, K. N.-K., Cheung, H., Leung, M.-T., & Chou, C. H.-N. (2007). *The Hong Kong Reading and Writing Behavior Checklist for Adults.* Hong Kong: The University of Hong Kong and The Chinese University of Hong Kong.
Ho, C. S.-H., Yau, P. W.-Y., & Au, A. (2003). Development of orthographic knowledge and its relationship with reading and spelling among Chinese kindergarten and primary school children. In C. McBride-Chang & H.-C. Chen, *Reading development in Chinese children (pp. 51–71).* London: Praeger.
Hoosain, R. (1991). *Psycholinguistic implications for linguistic relativity: A case study of Chinese.* Hillsdale, NJ: Lawrence Erlbaum Associates.
Hulme, C. & Snowling, M. (1992). Phonological deficits in dyslexia: A 'sound' reappraisal of the verbal deficit hypothesis? In N. N. Singh & I. L. Beale (eds), *Progress in learning disabilities* (pp. 270–301). New York: Springer Verlag.
Hultquist, A. M. (1997). Orthographic processing abilities of adolescents with dyslexia. *Annals of Dyslexia, 47*, 89–114.
Kang, J. S. (1993). Analysis of semantics of semantic–phonetic compound characters in modern Chinese. In Y. Chen (ed.), *Information analysis of usage of characters in modern Chinese* (pp. 68–83). Shanghai, China: Shanghai Education Publisher. (in Chinese)
Kline, C. L. (1977). Orton Gillingham methodology: Where have all of the researchers gone? *Bulletin of the Orton Society, 27*, 82–87.
Kuo, W. F. (1978). *Assessing and identifying the development and educational needs of the exceptional individual.* Paper presented at the World Congress on Future Special Education, Stirling, Scotland.
Liu, I. M., Chuang, C. J., & Wang, S. C. (1975). *Frequency count of 40,000 Chinese words.* Taiwan, Taipei: Lucky Books.
Luan, V. H. & Ho, C. S.-H. (in preparation). Morphological and other reading-related cognitive deficits in Chinese dyslexic children: A regional comparison between Beijing and Hong Kong.
Makita, K. (1968). The rarity of reading disability in Japanese children. *American Journal of Orthopsychiatry, 38*, 599–614.
Marston, D. (2005). Tiers of intervention in responsiveness to intervention: Prevention outcomes and learning disabilities identification patterns. *Journal of Learning Disabilities, 38*, 539–544.
McBride-Chang, C., Shu, H., Zhou, A., Wat, C. P., & Wagner, R. K. (2003). Morphological awareness uniquely predicts young children's Chinese character recognition. *Journal of Educational Psychology, 95*, 743–751.
McBride-Chang, C., Wagner, R. K., Muse, A., Chow, W. Y. B., & Shu, H. (2005). The role of morphological awareness in children's vocabulary acquisition in English. *Applied Psycholinguistics, 26*, 415–435.
National Reading Panel (2000). *Teaching children to read: An evidence-based assessment of the scientific research literature on reading and its implications for reading instruction.* Washington, DC: National Institute of Child Health and Human Development.

Olson, R. K., Rack, J. P., & Forsberg, H. (1990, September). *Profiles of abilities in dyslexics and reading-level-matched controls.* Poster presented at the Rodin Remediation Academy meeting at Boulder, CO.

Penninton, B. F., Gilger, J. W., Pauls, D., Smith, S. A., Smith, S. D., & DeFries, J. C., (1991). Evidence for major gene transmission of developmental dyslexia. *JAMA: The Journal of American Medical Association, 266,* 1527–1534.

Shankweiler, D., Liberman, I. Y., Mark, L. S., Fowler, C. A., & Fischer, F. W. (1979). The speech code and learning to read. *Journal of Experimental Psychology: Human Learning and Memory, 5,* 531–545.

Shu, H., Chen, X., Anderson, R. C., Wu, N., & Xuan, Y. (2003). Properties of school Chinese: Implications for learning to read. *Child Development, 74,* 27–47.

Shu, H., McBride-Chang, C., Wu, S., & Liu, H. (2006). Understanding Chinese developmental dyslexia: Morphological awareness as a core cognitive construct. *Journal of Educational Psychology, 98,* 122–133.

Stevenson, H. W., Stigler, J. W., Lucker, G. W., Hsu, C. C., & Kitamura, S. (1982). Reading disabilities: The case of Chinese, Japanese, and English. *Child Development, 53,* 1164–1181.

Taylor, I. & Taylor, M. M. (1995). *Writing and literacy in Chinese, Korean and Japanese.* Philadelphia, PA: John Benjamins.

Tilly, W. D. (2003, December). *How many tiers are needed for successful prevention and early intervention? Heartland Area Education Agency's evolution from four to three tiers.* Presented at the National Research Center on Learning Disabilities Responsiveness-to-Intervention Symposium, Kansas City, MO.

Vaughn, S. (2003, December). *How many tiers are needed for response to intervention to achieve acceptable prevention outcomes.* Presented at the National Research Center on Learning Disabilities Responsiveness-to-Intervention Symposium, Kansas City, MO.

Vaughn, S. & Klingner, J. (2007). Overview of the three-tier model of reading intervention. In D. Haager, J. Klingner, & S. Vaugh, S. (eds), *Evidence-based reading practices for response to intervention* (pp 3–19). Baltimore, MD: Brookes.

Wong, E. Y.-F., Ho, C. S.-H., Chung, K., Chan, D., Tsang, S.-M., & Lee, S.-H. (2006). *The Hong Kong Learning Behavior Checklist for Preschool Children (Parent Version).* Hong Kong: Hong Kong Specific Learning Difficulties Research Team.

Zhou, Y. K. (1980). *Precise guide to pronunciation with Chinese with Chinese phonological roots.* Jilin: Jilin People's Publishing Co. (in Chinese)

Zhu, Y. P. (1987). Analysis of cuing functions of the phonetic in modern China. Unpublished paper, East China Normal University. (in Chinese)

CHAPTER 9

Chinese bilingualism

Him Cheung, Foong Ha Yap, and Virginia Yip

Overview

In this chapter we will discuss three aspects of Chinese bilingualism. First, we are interested in the cognition and neuro-cognition of language as well as general processing in bilingual people who speak Chinese as either their dominant or subordinate language. In this section we focus on how bilingual processing may impact on their other aspects of cognition, whether their two languages share one common computational/neuro-cognitive substrate or are based upon separate processing mechanisms, how the bilingual verbal memories are organized, and the interaction between their two languages. Second, we will examine young children's acquisition of Chinese (Mandarin or Cantonese) together with another language in different contexts. Third, we will look at language use at a pragmatic level in the bilingual population under broad sociolinguistic contexts, discussing socio-cultural factors that impact on the bilingual's verbal behavior.

Cognitive and neuro-cognitive processing

Learning two languages is a complex task. This is particularly true if the two languages are dissimilar. Chinese bilinguals are therefore faced with a real challenge, because Chinese differs greatly from Indo-European languages, which are popular second languages, in terms of many aspects including phonology, morphology, and writing. Such differences inevitably impact on how Chinese speakers and readers process their second languages.

The Chinese language

The syllable. In Chinese, virtually every syllable has a meaning and the smallest phonological unit that can carry meaning is the syllable. Hence there is a near one-to-one correspondence between syllables and meaning. These syllables are therefore usually co-extensive with lexical morphemes. Chinese syllables are simple in that they do not allow consonant clusters, and many of them are open syllables. Consonantal codas are relatively rare and, by and large, unreleased. The fact that Chinese syllables do not allow consonant clusters and have only a few possible codas that are unreleased, and hence perceptually not too distinct from the preceding vowel, gives rise to the result that perceptually Chinese syllables are whole units that are not readily separable into phonemes. This has been shown to impact on young Chinese-speaking children's explicit analysis of syllables into phonemes compared to their English-speaking counterparts (Cheung, Chan, Lai, Wong, & Hills, 2001; see also McBride-Chang, Lin, Fong, & Shu, this volume).

Tones. Chinese syllables must carry tones which constitute a contrastive dimension producing differentiation in meaning. The actual number of tones varies from language to language. For instance, Mandarin has four tones whereas Cantonese has six. Like phonemes, tones are not coded in writing. Some previous evidence has shown that tones are not just one aspect of prosody. For instance, Gandour et al. (2003) showed that while the pitch contours associated with intonation are processed by the right hemisphere, those associated with tones are processed by the left hemisphere in Chinese listeners.

Tones are also perceived categorically, like phonemes (Francis, Ciocca, & Ng, 2003). Chinese infants typically start reorganizing tone perception between six and nine months of age; this parallels the reorganization of vowels in Western babies (Kuhl, 1993; Mattock & Burnham, 2006). Tones are at least partially acquired before two years (Lee, Chiu, & van Hasselt, 2002); then a steady developmental trend is observed from three up to ten years, when children perceive tones as accurately as do adults (Ciocca & Lui, 2003; Wong, Schwartz, & Jenkins, 2005).

Morphology. Chinese morphology is characterized by extensive compounding, which refers to combining morphemes to form words having meanings that are rather predictable from their component morphemes. An example would be combining the 'fly' and the 'machine' morphemes to form the word 'plane'. Such morphological transparency gives rise to a particularly strong correlation between children's word learning (i.e. vocabulary) and their awareness of the function of morphemes in word formation, or 'morphological awareness' (McBride-Chang, Cho, Liu, Wagner, Shu, Zhou, Cheuk, & Muse, 2005; McBride-Chang, Shu, Zhou, Wat, & Wagner, 2003). On the other hand, Chinese words can be described as morphologically simple from a grammatical point of view, because grammatical inflections are minimal.

Writing. The basic unit of Chinese writing is the character, which is a spatially marked pattern of strokes phonologically realized as a full syllable and in most cases semantically interpreted as having a complete meaning. Unlike written English, only characters, not words, are marked by space in writing and print. Because any characters are pronounceable as syllables and most syllables are lexicalized (i.e. meaningful), what we see are regular one-to-one correspondences among meaning (morpheme), sound (syllable), and writing (character). These correspondences distinguish Chinese from the majority of the world's languages, rendering it a unique language system.

Chinese characters are further decomposable into radicals, which are of two broad types. Phonetic radicals are themselves pronounceable characters; they therefore necessarily carry meaning, but as radicals they provide sound information about the pronunciations of their host characters, and their meanings are suppressed. On the other hand, semantic radicals are not necessarily full characters and therefore not necessarily pronounceable. They provide meaning information about their host characters. The same stroke pattern can function as either a phonetic or a semantic radical, depending on its position in relation to other components within the host character. Evidence has shown that skilled readers are capable of identifying the radicals and making use of the information they carry appropriately when attempting to derive character meaning and pronunciation (Cheung, Chan, & Chong, 2007).

Chinese bilingualism and cognition

Given the features described above, what are the impacts on cognitive processing of being able to speak Chinese plus an additional language? Generally speaking, Chinese-speaking bilinguals' cognitive and meta-cognitive skills are found to be enhanced by their bilingualism. In an early paper, Ho (1987) argued that Chinese-English bilingual students have an advantage over their monolingual counterparts in the development of general cognition, including variables that are of great educational concern, such as divergent or creative thinking. Hsieh and Tori (1993) found that Chinese-English bilingual children aged nine to twelve years had a higher level of IQ than their monolingual English-speaking counterparts. The bilinguals' sequential abilities were also shown to be superior.

Ruan (2004) examined the use of meta-cognitive skills by Chinese-English bilingual first graders in a story-composing task. Results showed that their story-writing performance was associated with many meta-cognitive utterances during story composing, and that was attributable to their ability to use two languages. Goetz (2003) compared the theory-of-mind performances of three- and four-year-old English monolinguals, Chinese monolinguals, and Chinese-English bilinguals. Theory of mind was assessed through a perspective-taking test and a variety of false-belief tasks. In addition to an age main effect, the bilingual children were found to outperform both of the monolingual groups. The author argued that the bilinguals' heightened performance was attributable to their stronger meta-linguistic understanding and a greater sensitivity to sociolinguistic interactions. Overall, the bilinguals' enhanced meta-cognitive and meta-linguistic skills appear to be explainable by the fact that the bilingual can always think about one of their languages via the other language. They can also engage themselves in complex cognitive computation using two languages instead of one, a skill that promotes perspective shifting.

Unitary organization or two separate systems?

The unitary view. Does the Chinese bilingual rely on one single or two separate neuro-cognitive systems for their two languages? Weekes, Su, Yin, and Zhang (2007) examined the impairment to written-word comprehension and oral reading by aphasic patients who spoke Mongolian and Mandarin-Chinese as their first (L1) and second (L2) language respectively. The purpose was to investigate the effect of written-language differences (Mongolian and Chinese employ very different scripts) on impairment to written-language processing. The authors demonstrated only minimal differences in the pattern of written-word comprehension and reading between the two languages. It was therefore concluded that there was no need to hypothesize independent cognitive systems or brain regions to account for the processing of the two languages.

Using a cross-language picture-word interference task, Guo and Peng (2006) studied the parallel activation of translation equivalents in the Chinese-English bilinguals' speech production. In this paradigm, one looks at the activation of an item in the non-target language when the participant is asked to orally produce the translation equivalent of that item in the target language. Guo and Peng (2006) demonstrated such parallel activation despite the fact that Chinese and English are written with very different scripts. This finding is consistent with the hypothesis that the two languages of the Chinese-English bilingual are processed by one neuro-cognitive system.

Li and Yip (1998) had Chinese speakers and Chinese-English bilinguals identify Chinese and across-language homophones within sentence context. Sentence context helped disambiguate homophone identity to similar extents in the monolingual and bilingual situation. Processing of the two languages by the Chinese-English bilingual was thus seen to be based on distributed, parallel activations of the same set of neural units rather than being based in two distinct cognitive systems.

Li (1996) asked Chinese-English bilinguals to recognize code-switched (English) words in Chinese speech. The availabilities of phonological, structural, and contextual information were manipulated. Results showed that the amount of information needed for successful recognition did not differ significantly from that needed by monolingual English speakers for recognizing English target words. In other words, switching between the two language codes in the bilingual situation did not incur extra cognitive costs in target recognition, and therefore it appears that processing of the two languages was based upon the same set of neural units.

Gandour et al. (2007) employed the functional magnetic resonance imaging (fMRI) technique to investigate whether Chinese-English bilinguals' judgments about some prosodic characteristics in the two languages are associated with similar or different areas of brain activation. The prosodic phenomena in question were sentence focus, which referred to a contrast in stress at the sentence-initial versus sentence-final position, and sentence type, which involved prosodic contours suggesting a declarative versus an interrogative mode. The participants were asked to make speeded discrimination judgments about sentence focus and sentence type in both languages.

Results showed that judgments in the L1 and L2 elicited a large amount of overlapping activations in the frontal, temporal, and parietal lobes. For sentence-type discrimination, no differences were found in activation areas between the two languages. For sentence focus, some between-language differences were found, which were nevertheless attributable to cross-language differences in the actual phonetic manifestation of sentence focus. It was therefore concluded that the two languages of the Chinese-English bilingual are mediated by one single, unitary neural system.

Li, Peng, Guo, Wei, and Wang (2004) employed the event-related potential (ERP) technique to investigate Chinese-English bilinguals' processing of sentence-final words in relation to the prior-sentence context. The sentence-final words could be either lexically consistent or inconsistent, and semantically congruent or incongruent with the prior context. Semantic integration of sentence-final words into sentence context could be either within- or between-language. Very similar ERP responses to Chinese and English sentence-final words were obtained, indicating a common semantic representation for both languages.

The separate-system view. On the other hand, some previous studies have shown that the L1 and L2 of the Chinese-English bilingual may be processed by separate neuro-cognitive systems. For instance, Rusted (1988) argued that Chinese and written English are inherently different in processing terms, because the two writing systems represent speech and meaning differently. Her results showed that access to meaning was more rapid with the Chinese than with the English script. While pictures interfered with Chinese processing more at the semantic decision stage, the locus of its interference with English processing was more likely to lie at the stage of response selection. Reading Chinese was also shown to be more comparable to processing pictures than to reading English.

At a neurological level, Cheung, Chan, Chan, and Lam (2006) argued that, in normal Chinese-English bilinguals, written English shows more left hemispheric lateralization, whereas written Chinese tends to be processed by both hemispheres. For bilingual patients suffering from left temporal lobe epilepsy, therefore, part of the English reading capacity has to be taken up by the right hemisphere, resulting in a shift toward bi-hemispheric lateralization. This should contrast with right temporal lobe epilepsy patients, whose English word reading should remain left-lateralized. The pattern was actually demonstrated, supporting the view that Chinese and English reading in the bilingual are lateralized to different degrees.

Using fMRI, Ding, Perry, Peng, Ma, Li, Xu, Luo, Xu, and Yang (2003) showed that English word reading in the bilingual was associated with more right hemispheric activation than was Chinese word reading, which stands in contrast with Cheung et al's (2006) findings. While the discrepancy can be explained by the different English proficiencies of the bilinguals used in the two studies, both sets of data are consistent with the hypothesis that the two languages of the Chinese-English bilingual are processed by separate neural mechanisms. Chee, Soon, and Lee (2003) examined the fMRI signals from Chinese-English bilinguals engaged in a word-repetition task. Repetitions were either within- or between-language. Changes in fMRI signals were found to be greater when the participant was asked to repeat words from different languages than from the same language. This result suggests that on top of the shared semantic network, there exist language-specific neural components subserving the respective languages.

Liu and Perfetti (2003) and Perfetti and Liu (2005) argued that in the Chinese-English bilingual, reading in the two languages correlates with different time courses and also different brain areas of activation. Liu and Perfetti (2003) demonstrated an earlier activation of the word-frequency effect in Chinese reading than in English reading. Reading high-frequency English words resulted in left occipital activation, whereas Chinese character reading produced more bilateral activation. On the other hand, low-frequency English words were associated with more bilateral activation. Hence, it appears that the two languages of the Chinese-English bilingual require support from at least some separate, language-specific neural circuits. The exact neural configuration seems to depend on L2 proficiency.

The bilingual verbal memory

How is the bilingual verbal memory organized, in relation to the underlying conceptual system? Overall, previous research has shown that communication between the L1 and L2 lexicons is possible, either through a direct word association link between translation equivalents or an indirect route mediated by the common underlying meaning shared by the translation equivalents. The former direct route has come to be known as word association, whereas the latter is called concept mediation (Kroll & Stewart, 1994). Furthermore, the L1 is generally seen to be more strongly connected to the underlying conceptual system than is the L2; the L2 is more strongly connected to the L1 than underlying concepts.

In other words, presenting L1 items to the bilingual would result in quick and strong activation of the underlying meaning, whereas presenting L2 items would most likely initially activate their L1 translations, instead of the underlying concepts. This phenomenon is known as L1–L2 asymmetry, and is readily observable in a word translation task (Kroll & Stewart, 1994). Translation from L1 to L2, or forward translation, is expected to be indirect and must be mediated by meaning. Hence it may take longer and could be affected by meaning variables. In contrast, L2 to L1, or backward, translation is done through a direct L2-to-L1 lexical route; hence it is faster and unaffected by meaning variables (Kroll & Stewart, 1994).

The asymmetry model is generally applicable to Chinese-English bilingualism. Chen, Cheung, and Lau (1997) replicated the translation asymmetry effect in Chinese-English bilinguals. The authors also showed that other variables such as response production time, concept retrieval time, and L2 proficiency were at work in word translation and category-matching tasks. The asymmetry effect was later replicated by Cheung and Chen (1998) and Jiang (1999).

Cheung and Chen (1998) further argued that although the L2-to-concept link is generally weak, as stipulated by the asymmetry model, the actual strength of the link is qualified by the familiarity of the L2 items in question. Familiar L2 items are more closely connected to their underlying meaning than are unfamiliar items. Generally speaking, as the bilingual's L2 proficiency increases, more L2 word items would become familiar, and thus the L2 lexicon becomes more strongly connected to the underlying conceptual system. Therefore, L2 proficiency correlates positively with the degree of concept mediation and negatively with word association; balanced bilinguals are expected to display similar levels of concept mediation for the L1 and L2, resulting in a much reduced degree of asymmetry.

Cross-language transfer

How do the two languages of the Chinese-English bilingual interact with each other? L1–L2 interaction can be viewed from the traditional perspective of language transfer (Odlin, 1989). The basic idea is that because the L1 is usually the stronger language, the bilingual may extend their L1 knowledge and processing strategies to help in L2 processing whenever possible. Such L1 knowledge and processing strategies are said to have transferred to L2 processing. The result is that some relevant L1 characteristics may become observable in the bilingual's L2 output.

In the area of bilingual reading, for instance, Cheung and Lin (2005) argued that while the L1 system for written-word recognition is very automatic because of high L1 proficiency, the corresponding L2 system is much less automatic and modular. So it is subject to influences, i.e. transfer from both the L1 word recognition system and a language-neutral central system which entails effortful, conscious processing strategies. As L2 proficiency increases, the L2 word recognition system becomes more automatic and modular, and therefore is more insulated from transfers from the L1 word recognition and the central system.

The qualifying effect of L2 proficiency on L1-to-L2 transfer was also reported in performance domains other than word recognition. For example, Liu, Bates, and Li (1992) asked their Chinese-English bilingual participants to make judgments about sentences. In Chinese, the animacy of a noun phrase, that is, whether the noun phrase refers to a living thing, is an important cue to the possible grammatical role of that noun phrase in a sentence. But animacy is not a useful cue in English, in which word order is more important. Liu et al's (1992) results showed that use of animacy as cue, which was presumably due to L1-to-L2 transfer, was much more prominent in the late bilinguals whose L2 was relatively weak. The pattern was less clear with the early bilinguals whose English was fluent.

Basnight-Brown, Chen, Hua, Kostic, and Feldman (2007) compared the performances of monolingual English speakers, Serbian-English and Chinese-English bilinguals on processing English verb inflections, both regular and irregular, using the priming paradigm. It was reported that while a facilitatory priming effect due to prime-target overlap of verb stems (e.g. 'draw' and 'drawn') was observed with the Serbian-English bilinguals, no such priming was observed with the non-proficient Chinese-English bilinguals. Presumably the total lack of verb inflection in Chinese gave rise to a certain negative transfer effect, viz. a lack of sensitivity to inflectional rules, so that the Chinese-English bilinguals were not benefiting from prime-target relationships based on inflectional regularities in English, compared to the Serbian-English bilinguals whose L1 entailed verb inflections.

Perhaps the most widely studied aspect of between-language interaction in the Chinese-English bilingual has to do with transfer effects due to orthographic differences (Jackson, Lu, & Ju, 1994). As mentioned above, the Chinese orthography differs significantly from alphabetic systems in several ways. First, phonemes are not represented in written Chinese; the smallest phonological unit that is coded in the system is the syllable. Second, the sound cues (i.e. phonetic radicals) available in compound characters may provide only an approximate indication of how the characters may be pronounced. Sometimes the radical and its host character share the same syllable, while at other times they may share only the rime, onset, tone, or any combinations of these dimensions. There are no regularities regarding in what situation which of these dimensions associated with the radical are useful in guessing character pronunciation. Third, compound characters may contain semantic radicals which provide categorical information about the referents of their host characters, independent of phonology. Fourth, characters, syllables, and morphemes correspond with one another. Fifth, only characters are marked by space; there are no clear word boundaries in writing and print (see also McBride-Chang et al., this volume).

How would extensive reading experience with such a writing system impact on L2 reading and general processing? Tan et al. (2003) used the fMRI to investigate Chinese-English bilinguals' brain-activation patterns in reading Chinese words versus English words. In one experiment it was shown that, in Chinese character reading, a neural system involving left, middle-frontal and posterior-parietal gyri was uniquely activated. This same system in the bilinguals was also highly activated when they were required to perform a phonological task using English words, while the usual areas of maximal activation in monolingual English speakers reading English words were shown to display only weak activity. The authors therefore concluded that the bilinguals were applying their neural system for reading L1 to L2 reading, which is consistent with the notion of cross-language transfer.

Rayner, Li, Williams, Cave, and Well (2007) examined the eye-movement patterns of Chinese-English bilinguals and monolingual English-speakers in reading and other visual tasks. The Chinese speakers typically displayed more numerous but shorter fixations than the English speakers in counting Chinese characters in text, viewing faces, and nonverbal scenes. Such differences were attributed to the Chinese speakers' extensive experience in reading Chinese as an L1.

Finally, Chinese-English bilinguals not only process English differently from monolingual English speakers but also assess it differently. In an interesting study by Aaronson and Ferres (1986), monolingual English speakers and Chinese-English bilinguals were asked to rate English words on their contribution to the structure and meaning of sentences. Results showed that overall the bilinguals rated English words as contributing more to the both the meaning and structure of sentences than did the monolinguals. Specifically, the bilinguals rated English content words as contributing more to sentence structure and function words as contributing more to sentence meaning than did the monolinguals. It was concluded that the differences were attributable to the bilinguals' experience with Chinese as their L1, which entails a processing experience that is quite different from that in English.

Chinese-English bilingual acquisition in childhood

How do children acquire two languages in the first years of their life? What if the languages are as different as Chinese and a European language? To address this question, we will focus on studies of childhood bilingualism involving the acquisition of Chinese (Mandarin or Cantonese) and English. Taking a historical perspective, we will go back in time to look at the earliest studies on record and then move on to more recent case studies.

Some early studies

The earliest studies of Chinese-English bilingual development (Smith, 1931, 1935) were based on diary records of eight children kept by their mothers from the birth of the eldest child in China until their return to America. From birth, the children were exposed to English from their missionary parents and Mandarin Chinese from their servants. At this period, it was widely assumed that bilingual children must be linguistically confused and even mentally disadvantaged (Baker, 2001, p. 136). Consistent with the prevalent view, Smith found that the English vocabulary of the bilingual children was significantly less rich than that of a monolingual child of the same age, while language mixing was common and treated as a sign of confusion. Against this anachronistic view, current thinking points to cognitive and meta-linguistic advantages associated with the acquisition of two languages in children (Bialystok, 2001).

In the first case study of Cantonese-English bilingual development, Light (1977) described the language of his daughter Claire, which he termed *Clairetalk*. The child grew up in a Cantonese-dominant household before arriving in the United States at sixteen months. Light attributed several features of Claire's Cantonese to the influence of English in her new linguistic environment. At the phonological level, the shift in dominance from Cantonese to English led to 'disintegration'of the Cantonese tonal system. In (1), non-target high level tones are assigned to the first person pronoun *ngo5* (which has a low rising tone) and the intensifier *hou2* (high rising), while the high-level tone on the adjective *gwaai1* is realized as a falling tone, reflecting the English sentence-final intonation pattern (Light, 1977, p. 265):

(1) Ngō hōu gwàai.
I very good
I'm very good.

At the level of grammar, Light (1977, p. 267) noted overgeneralization of the classifier *go3* as a determiner before a noun such as *syu1* 'book' as in (2):[1]

(2) *Go3 Maa1mi4 tai2 go3 syu1.* (Claire 1;8[2])
CL Mommy read CL book
Mommy is reading.

This non-target use of *go3* is attributed to exposure to the English article system. From age 4;0 to 6;6 Claire also overextended the benefactive marker *bei2* 'give/for' as in (3): (Light, 1977, p. 269)

(3) *Keoi5 sai2 wun2 bei2 ngo5.*
he wash bowls give me
He washes the bowls for me.

Two aspects of this utterance are attributed to English influence: the use of *bei2* 'for/give' as an equivalent of the English benefactive preposition *for* (adult Cantonese would use *bong1* 'help') and the non-target word order, whereby the benefactive prepositional phrase *bei2 ngo5* 'for me' comes after the verb, whereas it would precede the verb in Cantonese as in *Keoi5 bong1 ngo5 sai2 wun2.* Similar cases of post-verbal prepositional phrases under English influence are described in Yip and Matthews (2007a).

Chinese bilingual acquisition in Singapore

In a case study from Singapore, Kwan-Terry (1986, 1989, 1991, 1992) describes aspects of the Cantonese-English bilingual development of her child, Elvoo, from age 3;6 to 5;0. The parents spoke primarily Cantonese, often mixed with English, while English input came from an older sister and a Filipino maid. Transfer from Cantonese to English was observed in several grammatical domains, including *wh*-in-situ interrogatives where English *wh*-words were not preposed, following the Cantonese word order (Kwan-Terry, 1986, p. 23):

(4) You are doing what? (Elvoo 3;6)

Conversely, when the child began to prepose *wh*-words in English, his Cantonese was affected and he produced non-target interrogatives with fronted *wh*-words like (5):

(5) *Mat1je5 lei5 zung1ji3?* (Elvoo 4;9)
what you like
What do you like?

Elvoo also produced many English questions with *or not*:

(6) Let me see you have or not?

Such sentences are based on the Southern Min polar interrogative construction, reinforced by the English *or not* pattern. Since the child did not actually speak a Min dialect, such as Hokkien or Teochew, this linguistic form may be a substrate feature of Singapore Colloquial English (SCE) as acquired by the child, rather than a case of direct transfer from the child's developing Chinese grammar. Similarly, Kwan-Terry suggested that the use of Cantonese sentence final particles in English could be attributed to exposure to SCE, since 'only those particles which have been identified in Colloquial Singapore English found their way to Elvoo's English' (Kwan-Terry, 1991, p. 181). A case in point is the particle *ho2* which serves to solicit agreement and support:

(7) Patsy bad girl *ho2*. I don't like Patsy. (Elvoo 4;9)

Gupta (1994) provides a detailed description of four Singapore children's longitudinal development of SCE (1;3 to 7;8) as one of their first languages, embedded in a rich discussion of the social factors affecting children's language acquisition in a multilingual environment. She discusses a number of Chinese-influenced structures in their English, including *wh*-in-situ interrogatives similar to (4) and polar questions with *or not* like (6). Another feature described by Gupta (1994) involves conditional sentences formed without explicit conjunctions or conditional markers:

(8) Why I talk no sound one?
Why is there no sound when/if I talk? (YG 3;6)

The development of conditionals in SCE and Singapore Colloquial Mandarin (SCM) in bilingual preschool children (2;10 to 6;6) was investigated in an experimental study by Chen (2003). In elicited imitation tasks, children as young as three were found to command a range of conditional constructions. In addition to 'bare' conditionals like (8), Chen identifies the pattern seen in (9), where the child's version marks conditionality by using *then* in the main clause, rather than *if* in the subordinate clause, as in the experimenter's model sentence:

(9) Experimenter: If you see Piglet, come and tell Pooh.
Child: You have see Piglet, *then* you tell Pooh. (YJ 4;6)

This pattern is based on the Chinese conditional construction where a conjunction (*jiu* 'then' in Mandarin) introduces the main clause.

Chinese bilingual acquisition in Hong Kong

Many of the features identified in Singapore bilingual children are also confirmed in children's acquisition of Cantonese and English in Hong Kong. Yip and Matthews (2000, 2007a) argue for systematic transfer and a high degree of interactivity in Cantonese-English bilingual development. The data come from six children represented in the Hong Kong Bilingual Child Language Corpus (1;5 to 4;6), deposited at the Child Language Data Exchange System (CHILDES; MacWhinney, 2000). The children grew up in one-parent, one-language families where the parents were native speakers of either Cantonese or English. In the case of the researchers' own three children, the recordings were supplemented by diary data. The analysis showed qualitative and quantitative differences between bilingual and monolingual development as well as pervasive transfer effects in three areas of English grammar:

(i) *wh*-in-situ interrogatives, where the child fails to prepose the *wh*-word:

(10) You go to the what? (Timmy 2;5)

(ii) null objects, where the object of a transitive verb is omitted:

(11) You get, I eat ... [father takes chocolates off shelf] (Timmy 2;02;03)

(iii) prenominal relatives, where a relative clause precedes the noun it modifies:

(12) Where's the Santa Claus give me the gun? (Timmy 2;07;05) [i.e. the gun Santa Claus gave me]

The transfer of the Chinese relative clause structure to English as in (12) was discussed in relation to typological universals and processing factors by Matthews and Yip (2002) and Yip and Matthews (2007b). Comparable relative clauses are not attested in monolingual children, while other transfer-based structures such as *wh*-in-situ (10) and null objects (11) are also found in monolinguals, but are substantially less frequent.

Whereas influence from Cantonese on English is strong due to the dominance of Cantonese over English in the majority of children studied, the cross-linguistic influence is not unidirectional. English influence on Cantonese in certain 'vulnerable domains' of grammar (Müller, 2003, Yip & Matthews, 2007a) results in non-target structures, such as prepositional phrases following the verb (13) and double object constructions with *bei2* 'give' (14):

(13) *Keoi5 sik6 min6-min6 hai2 po4po2 go2dou6 aa3.* (Alicia 3;11;17)
She eat noodle-noodle at grandma there SFP
She's eating noodles at Grandma's.

(14) *Je4sou1 bei2 ngo5 cin2 aa3.* (Sophie, 2;05;02)
Jesus give me money SFP
Jesus gave me money.

The orderverb–indirect object–direct object [V–IO–DO] in (14) deviates from the usual adult order [V–DO–IO]. Chan (in press) found that the non-target structure (14) also occurs in monolingual Cantonese children. She argues that there is some ambiguity in the input data which makes the target [V–DO–IO] structure inherently difficult and hence a vulnerable domain for both monolingual and bilingual children. In the bilingual subjects' Cantonese, however, the structure persists until age six and beyond, apparently due to the influence of English which instantiates the [V–IO–DO] order. In a related study, Gu (in press) considers the relationship between double object and prepositional dative constructions in the same children. The bilingual children are shown to follow a developmental path distinct from that of monolingual children.

To summarize these findings on grammatical development in Hong Kong Chinese children, the influence from Cantonese as the dominant language to English is pervasive and striking, as in the case of *wh*-in-situ and prenominal relative clauses, while the influence from English to Cantonese is relatively subtle, largely affecting the frequency and productivity of structures for which there is already a precedent in Cantonese. Nevertheless, the fact of bi-directional influence argues for a high degree of interaction between the child's developing grammars. Investigation of the reverse dominance patterns, i.e. children for whom English is the dominant language, may be expected to produce parallel, contrasting results.

Much research in the field of bilingual, first-language acquisition has been focused on the question of whether bilingual children begin with a unitary system, as suggested by Volterra and Taeschner (1978).

Current evidence suggests that bilingual children are able to divide the input into two separate systems from early on (e.g. De Houwer, 1990; Genesee, Nicoladis, & Paradis, 1995; Meisel, 2001); the remaining question is how early the differentiation is evident in the acquisition of phonology, lexicon, and syntax.

There are divergent views regarding the question of when differentiation is achieved in phonological systems, ranging from total undifferentiation at two years old to partial or total differentiation by age two (Paradis, 2001; Lleó and Kehoe, 2002). Experimental evidence shows that four-to-five-month-old bilingual infants have the perceptual ability to distinguish two rhythmically close languages, Spanish and Catalan (Bosch & Sebastián-Gallés, 2001). In terms of production, there is evidence that French-English bilingual infants develop differentiated systems during the babbling stage around twelve months (Poulin-Dubois & Goodz, 2001). Yip and Matthews (2003) argue for early phonological differentiation based on data from two bilingual children whose syllable-final stops were found to exhibit language-specific features, being unreleased in Cantonese but optionally released or even over-released in English.

In terms of lexical differentiation, evidence is sought in the degree of overlap in the vocabularies of each language. If the child has translation equivalents for the same word, such as both a German and an English word for *car*, this is taken as evidence for two separate lexicons (Pearson & Fernandez, 1995; Lanvers, 1999). Yip and Matthews (2008) found that two Cantonese-English bilingual children were regularly using two words, one from each language, to refer to the same object or concept from the earliest recordings, i.e. 1;03 (Alicia) and 1;06 (Sophie). The results are consistent with the application of the principle of contrast within each language: there are two differentiated lexicons with translation equivalents. Evidence for growth spurts is identified in the lexical development of Cantonese, the children's dominant language, while no clear evidence for a spurt is found in English, the weaker language.

Immigrant and adopted children

Immigrant children who move from Chinese-speaking communities to an English-speaking country or vice versa will have the opportunity to develop childhood bilingualism. Li and Lee (2002), investigating the development of Cantonese in British-born Chinese-English bilinguals, report delayed and stagnated development of Cantonese due to incomplete learning of their L1 Cantonese combined with the influence of English, a dominant language in the environment. For example, the children showed overuse of the general classifier *go3* and failure to acquire the full system of classifiers, as described by Light (1977) in the case study described above.

Jia (2006) discusses the L2 acquisition of English in Chinese children in immigration settings, suggesting that younger learners tended to switch their dominant language from L1 to L2 while leaving certain features of English morphology and syntax unacquired. In particular, such learners often fail to fully acquire morphological features, such as plurals and verb agreement, as well as articles (Jia, 2006, p. 67). Jia and Aaronson (2003) address the issue of switch of dominant language in younger learners and language maintenance by older learners in a longitudinal study where the age of arrival of Chinese children ranged between five and sixteen.

Another category of children who are drawing increasing attention from the international academic community is that of adopted children, whose language development before and after adoption has become an intriguing domain of inquiry. Recent years have seen the number of international adoptions rising, with China the number-one source of children adopted into the United States. Many children adopted into American families leave China before age two or three and have to acquire a 'second first language' (Pollock, Price, & Fulmer, 2003; Roberts, Pollock, Krakow, Price, & Wang, 2005). In monolingual English-speaking homes, it is likely that these children's first language, Chinese, will gradually be lost while English takes the place of Chinese as their first language (Nicoladis & Grabois, 2002). For those adopted into homes where Chinese is regularly spoken and English spoken in the community, some form of bilingualism is likely to develop, with both Chinese and English acquired together. Questions arise as to whether these constitute cases of bilingual or child second language acquisition.

Conclusions and future studies

Studying the bilingual acquisition of Chinese and English has helped to address questions such as interactive development, language dominance and mechanisms of transfer. Questions for future studies include: how do different dominance patterns shape development in different language pairs? What are the effects of factors, such as age of first exposure, imbalance, interruption or temporary deprivation of input? What are the qualitative and quantitative differences between bilingual and monolingual acquisition? How is the simultaneous acquisition of two languages similar to and different from the successive acquisition of two languages in childhood? To what extent is the difference between the bilingual child's dominant and non-dominant languages similar to that between a first and second language in childhood second-language acquisition?

Apart from longitudinal corpus data based on case studies, experimental data are called for to investigate unexplored territory in the areas of language perception, production, and comprehension. Studies of language differentiation in phonology, in terms of segmental and supra-segmental features, including tone and prosody, are lacking especially when compared to the growing research in the study of development of bilingual lexicon and syntax. The acquisition of tone in bilingual children is one area where studies of Chinese languages can contribute to the overall understanding of bilingual development (see Chu, 2008, for a discussion of the tonal development of Cantonese in bilingual children). Another area of research that is unique to bilingual contexts and which awaits investigation in the Chinese context involves code-mixing patterns of bilingual children (Lanza, 1997) and the emergence of structural constraints against code-mixing (Paradis, Nicoladis, & Genesee, 2000).

The findings reviewed here have all been based on children acquiring English and either Mandarin or Cantonese. Studies investigating childhood bilingualism pairing a Chinese language with a language other than English will be important in extending the empirical database and addressing theoretical issues related to language contact and cross-linguistic interaction. Childhood bilingualism will be better understood when investigated against a rich background of linguistic diversity involving Chinese and other Asian languages, such as Japanese and Korean.

The sociolinguistic aspect

Bilingualism has also been extensively studied from a social perspective. These studies investigate issues related to language contact, language attitude, and language choice, with implications for language change at the societal level. For example, bilingualism sometimes gives rise to shifts in language dominance, and potentially to issues such as language maintenance, language death, and language revitalization. In China, given the increasingly important role of Putonghua (Standard Mandarin) in various domains including government (*officialtalk*), media (*newstalk*), entertainment (*celebritytalk*), education (*schooltalk*) and friendship (*peertalk*), there is a strong tendency for each new generation to contribute to shifts in language dominance, in some cases even in the home (*familytalk*). Whether such shifts need to be accompanied by official efforts to maintain or revitalize the local languages or dialects often becomes an issue for public debate.

Present-day Hong Kong provides a good illustration of such debates. In the post-1997 decade, upon the return of Hong Kong from British to Chinese rule, many schools officially switched their medium of instruction from English to mother-tongue Cantonese in the late 1990s; ten years later, some of these schools were thinking of reversing this decision. A concurrent issue being debated throughout this period is the status of the local Cantonese dialect in light of the increasing prominence of Putonghua, with an uneasy compromise emerging in the form of a 'trilingual and biliterate' policy. Similar debates related to language maintenance and language revitalization issues occupy the minds of language-policy decision makers in other parts of China as well.

Code switching

A common phenomenon related to bilingual communities that has been extensively studied is *code switching*, generally defined as the use of two or more different language systems within a single speech exchange. In Chinese communities where English is widely spoken, e.g. Singapore, Malaysia, Hong Kong, Taiwan, and even mainland China, particularly among university students and professionals, many speakers often produce Chinese sentences interspersed with English words, phrases, and clauses. Depending on various factors—including topic, setting, interlocutors, purpose, and especially interlocutor fluency or proficiency—one language often dominates in the conversation. The more dominant language is often referred to in the literature as *the matrix language*, or base or host language, while the less dominant language is referred to as *the embedded language*, or donor or guest language (Myers-Scotton, 1993).

Code switching is often grouped into three major types: tag switching, inter-sentential switching, and intra-sentential switching (Poplack, 1980). Tag switching involves the insertion of a parenthetical expression, such as a discourse marker or sentence adverbial, from a donor language (say, the English *you know*) into an otherwise fully independent clause in the host language, say Cantonese. These parenthetical or 'tag' expressions typically express speaker mood or stance, as in the sentence *keoi5 m4 hai6 hou2 helpful gaa3, you know* (S/he's not very helpful, you know). Worth noting in this example is that the Cantonese sentence-final particle *gaa3* expresses a similar speaker mood value as the English tag expression, *you know*, which supports observations in the literature that code switching often serves to repeat the same idea or message in both languages, sometimes for clarification or emphasis (Gumperz, 1982), and sometimes to signal a shift to a new significant part of an ongoing narrative (Tsitsipis, 1988).

In terms of syntactic position, tag switching can sometimes occur in more than one position. For example, in addition to the sentence-final position discussed above, *you know* could also appear in sentence-initial position: *You know, keoi5 m4 hai6 hou2 helpful gaa3* (You know, s/he's not very helpful, I tell you).

Unlike tag switching, inter-sentential switching is syntactically more restricted. Switches between clauses occur at clausal or sentential boundaries, or utterance boundaries in spoken discourse, with clauses from each language faithfully conforming to the rules of their respective languages. For example, in the Cantonese/English expression *keoi5 cam4jat6 ceng2 ngo5, but I didn't feel like going* (S/he invited me yesterday, but I didn't feel like going), the first clause conforms fully to the grammar of Cantonese, while the second clause conforms fully to the grammar of English.

Code mixing

Intra-sentential switching, also referred to as *code mixing*, involves the insertion of smaller morphosyntactic constituents, such as words or phrases, from one language (the donor or embedded language) into another (the host or matrix language). Studies on code mixing have identified *lexical items*, such as nouns, verbs (including phrasal verbs), adjectives, adverbs, and even idiomatic expressions as code-mixable items, whereas *grammatical items* such as modal verbs, auxiliary verbs, pronouns, possessives, and quantifiers are generally non-code-mixable items. It is worth noting here that, whereas Joshi (1985) classifies prepositions as non-code-mixable 'closed class items', in other words, equivalent to our use of the term *grammatical items*, prepositions are often found to be code switchable among Cantonese/English bilinguals (Chan, 1998).

In this regard, it is also interesting to note some recent developments in which grammatical markers, such as the English progressive aspectual suffix, *–ing* have crept into the weblog writings of some university students in Hong Kong (example from Lee, Tse, & Yu, 2008, p. 10), as seen in (15) below.

(15) *jan1wai6 keoi5 tung4 ngo5 deoi3mong6* ***–ing***
because s/he with I look.at.each.other-PROG
Because s/he and I were look**ing** at each other.

This is an interesting development, since it is more common for Cantonese bilinguals to either borrow entire verb phrases, such as *were staring at each other*, from English, as shown in (16), or partially borrow from the English verb phrase while retaining, or adding, the Cantonese progressive aspect marker *gan2*, as in (17). Worth noting is that the use of aspectual suffix *–ing* is not generally accepted in spoken discourse, indicating that the constraints on grammatical items, such as aspectual affixes, are still strongly in place, despite emerging evidence of morphosyntactic flexibility in more informal weblog discourse.

(16) *jan1wai6 keoi5 tung4 ngo5* **were staring at each other**
because s/he with I
Because s/he and I were staring at each other.
jan1wai6 keoi5 tung4 ngo5 ***stare**-gan2* ***at each other***
because s/he with I-PROG
Because s/he and I were *staring* at each other. (emphatic effect)

Linguistic analysis of code-switching sites has also revealed 'a frequency hierarchy of switchable constituents' (Romaine, 1995, p. 124). Lexical items, particularly nouns, were found to be 'the single most often switched constituent' in studies on Hebrew/Spanish code switching (Berk-Seligson, 1986, pp. 325–326; see also Scotton, 1988, for Swahili/English). Frequency studies are lacking in research on code mixing involving Chinese as the matrix language. However, the code switching of nouns is well attested. Indeed, the distinction between lexical borrowing and phonologically nativized loanwords is generally seen as a continuum, influenced to a great extent by frequency of use.

The frequency hierarchy

In terms of syntactic constituents, Poplack (1980) found that full clauses are the most frequently switched categories (inter-sentential switching); next come switches within topic-comment structures (often ambiguous between inter-sentential and intra-sentential switching); then come switches within major constituents, such as noun phrases or verb phrases, i.e. intra-sentential switching. These findings strongly point to a frequency hierarchy in which 'the higher the level of the syntactic constituent, the more likely it is to serve as the potential site for a switch' (Romaine, 1995, p. 124). From a psycholinguistic perspective, Clyne (1987, p. 278) also makes the interesting observation that in perception studies, 'Correct recall of actual words (rather than meanings) was very significantly better when the switch occurred at the clause boundary than when it came elsewhere'.

Poplack's frequency findings were based on a study of Spanish/English code switching. With respect to Cantonese/English code switching, we earlier saw an example of inter-sentential switching: *keoi5 cam4jat6 ceng2 ngo5, but I didn't feel like going* (S/he invited me yesterday, but I didn't feel like going). An example of intra-sentential switching (or code mixing) within the noun phrase is [*go2go3* ***little boy***] ([that **little boy**]), while an example within the verb phrase is *bong1 ngo5* [*maai5* ***ten tickets***] *hou2 maa3* (Help me [buy ten tickets], will you?). In cases such as *bong1 ngo5* [*maai5* ***tickets***] *hou2 maa3*, absence of the English indefinite article leaves open the question of whether *ticket* constitutes a switched constituent to be understood as a whole noun phrase, i.e. *a ticket*, or a nativized loanword, in which case the speaker may intend *maai5 ticket* to be understood as a VN-type activity that could involve the purchase of more than one ticket, i.e. Help me **buy tickets**, will you?

Language-specific factors between Cantonese and English, such as absence vs. presence of a count/mass distinction (at least at the noun level) not only give rise to structural ambiguity, but can also provide evidence of language dominance. In this particular example, whether we construe the embedded word *ticket* to mean 'a ticket' (lacking an indefinite article) or 'tickets' (lacking the plural marker –s), the constituent can be interpreted as conforming more to Cantonese grammar than to English grammar.

One possibility for the asymmetry in the frequency hierarchy, perhaps applicable only to balanced or fluent bilinguals, is that there is less risk of violation to the rules of either the matrix language or the embedded language when the switches involve clausal constituents. The risk, however, increases as code switching occurs intra-sententially, particularly at switch sites where the matrix and embedded languages follow different rules, as seen in our discussion of differences in count/mass noun distinction in the example of Cantonese/English code switching discussed above.

Models of code switching

The frequency hierarchy also has important implications for our understanding of the interaction between syntax and the lexicon. In particular, identification of switch sites and types and sizes of code-switchable constituents carries important implications for our understanding of how language is represented and processed. Within sociolinguistic research, several models related to constraints on code switching have been proposed. These models do not directly address the cognitive questions being asked at the level of representation and processing, but they are useful in helping us examine what type and size of constituents are switchable, what relations hold between the code-switched constituents, and what factors contribute to degree of integration/independence between the switched constituents. Below we briefly review some of these models, summarizing their claims and noting some of their shortcomings in light of counterexamples from code-switching data involving Cantonese/English.

We begin with Sankoff and Poplack's (1980) context-free grammar model, which relies on notions such as linear order and adjacency. This model came with two major constraints. The first constraint, known as the 'free morpheme constraint', predicts that no switch can occur between a bound morpheme and a lexical morpheme unless the lexical morpheme has been phonologically integrated into the language of the bound morpheme. In such a scenario, the lexical morpheme necessarily comes from the embedded or guest language, but is phonologically nativized in accordance with the rules of the matrix language.

This process is illustrated by the Cantonese/English utterance *keoi5* ***send*** *zo2 fung1 seon3 mei6 aa3* (Has s/he sent off the letter yet?), where the lexical morpheme is actually pronounced as Cantonese/ sen1/ instead of English /s nd/. This constraint, however, fails to account for cases such as the newly emerging pattern in (15) above, where it is the bound morpheme (in this case, progressive aspectual suffix *–ing*) that needs to be phonologically integrated into the matrix language. That is, when found in spoken discourse, this bound morpheme needs to be expressed using the Cantonese high tone 1 rather than the English sentence-final falling tone for declarative mood. A revision to the free morpheme constraint may need to take into consideration the possibility that either a lexical morpheme or a bound morpheme can come from the embedded language.

Additional constraints, such as a hierarchy favoring lexical items over grammatical items as more code switchable, may also need to apply. In the preface to a reprint of Poplack (1980/2000), it was pointed out that the free morpheme constraint has since been updated and relabeled as the 'nonce-borrowing hypothesis', in recognition of the fact that this constraint makes a clear distinction between nonce borrowings or loanwords and single-word switches, the former showing phonological and morphosyntactic nativization to the matrix language, the latter retaining characteristics of the embedded or lexifier language.

The second constraint in Sankoff and Poplack's (1980) model was the 'equivalence constraint'. According to this constraint, code switching cannot include constituents that violate the syntactic rules of either the embedded language or the matrix language. However, Cantonese/ English code switching makes productive use of A-not-A constructions as well as reduplicated adjectives, both of which violate English morphosyntax. Examples from Chan (1998, p. 195) are given below:

(18) *nei5 ting1jat6* ***free-m-free*** *a3*
you tomorrow free-not-free INT
Are you free tomorrow?

(19) *nei5 gam1jat6 hou2ci5* ***high high dei2*** *gam2*
you today seem high (REDUP) a bit (ASP) PRT
You seem a bit high-spirited today.

Apparent violations to the equivalence constraint, such as (18) and (19) above, can be resolved when we take into account the reformulated nonce-borrowing hypothesis and treat the A-not-A construction as a type of nonce borrowing. That is, instead of viewing *free-m-free* and *high high dei2* as expressions violating English morphosyntax, we could instead view them as phonologically and morphosyntactically nativized loan expressions, or 'lone other-language lexical items' in the words of Poplack (2000). Evidence that such is the case can be seen in the use of Cantonese high-level tone 1 for the morpheme *free*. Moreover, the morpheme *free-m-free* can often be heard as *fee-m-fee* when uttered by a native speaker of Cantonese with lower proficiency in English. Similarly, the reduplicated morpheme *high high* is pronounced with Cantonese high-level tone 1, and must appear with diminutive *dei2* in conformity with adjective reduplication rules in Cantonese. As noted in the preface to Poplack (2000), refinement of the free morpheme constraint (reformulated as the nonce-borrowing hypothesis) makes it possible for us to reanalyze some apparent counterexamples to the equivalence constraint.

A hierarchical model was proposed by Woolford (1983), based on Chomsky's (1981) government and binding theory. This generative model relies on dominance, precedence (linear order), and dependency relations between constituents. For example, in prepositional phrases, such as *in the kitchen*, the preposition, *in*, is viewed as the head, and it governs (or dominates) its complementary noun phrase, *the kitchen*. According to Woolford's model, switching cannot occur between the two constituents, because they are bound to a common phrase structure, in this case, the preposition phrase *in the kitchen*, and one of the constituents (*in*) dominates the other (*the kitchen*). However, counterexamples are often found in Cantonese/English code switching, as shown in (20) from Chan (1998, p. 196):

(20) *gaau3juk6 hok6jyun2 hai6* [***under*** *gaau3juk6 si1cyu5*]
Education college COP under Education Department
The Education colleges are under the Education Department.

Romaine (1986) entertains several possibilities why the government model does not always work. One possibility is 'that the government relations haven't been articulated correctly in the first place' (Romaine, 1995, p. 157). Conceptual shifts within the generative domain in recent years have given rise to minimalist structures, with recursive specifier/head+complement configurations, with no reference now being made to the notion of 'government'. A code-switching model based on more recent generative frameworks is still lacking, and further investigation will be needed to examine whether the minimalist framework can provide a proper hierarchy of code-switching constraints.

Given counterexamples such as (18) and (19) above, i.e. A-not-A constructions and reduplicated adjective expressions respectively, it may be necessary to formulate a hierarchy of constraints that allow for more numerous switch sites, but which at the same time may favor certain switch sites over others. It may also be necessary to consider developing an optimality ranking for various constraints, thus making the model more responsive to other contributing factors, including non-morphosyntactic considerations, such as phonological weight and frequency of use. The latter would align the model with the nonce-borrowing hypothesis by taking into account differences between borrowings and switches. Interface research could also make a generative model more responsive to other language usage factors, such as type and degree of bilingual proficiency.

Another possibility considered by Romaine (1986) to account for the shortcomings of the government model is that code-switching sites are not properties of deep (or hierarchical) structure, but rather of surface structure. Given that the latter is not base generated, code-switching sites cannot therefore be determined by a government and binding theory. Clyne (1987) supports this alternative possibility based on evidence from Dutch/English and German/English code switching. According to Clyne (1987), bilinguals process meaning via non-language-specific processing, then map meaning into one or the other language. Code switching, in this view, is thus a surface-structure phenomenon, not subject to government and binding principles. The constraint of linear order equivalence, which he also refers to as the structural integrity constraint, can then apply as a surface-structure constraint.

A more recent model, proposed by Myers-Scotton (1993), is the 'matrix language frame model'. This model makes use of the notion of 'islands' and identifies the language that is more frequently activated as the matrix language. Essentially, within the islands of the matrix language (ML), constituents follow the word order of the matrix language, and within the islands of the embedded language (EL), constituents follow the word order of the embedded language. In addition, there are also combination ML+EL islands, with constituents coming from both the matrix and embedded languages, M and E, respectively. These constituents follow the morpheme order of the matrix language in accordance with the morpheme-order principle, and their system morphemes—equivalent to functional heads in generative syntax—come from the matrix language as well in accordance with the system morpheme principle. We illustrate with example (21) below, taken from Chan (1998, p. 203):

(21) *Essex go2dou6 bei2 zo2 [* ***go3*** *conditional offer*]NP *ngo5*
Essex CL place give PERF CL conditional offer me
Essex (The University of Essex) gave me a conditional offer.

The ML island in (21) above exhibits the word order for a double object construction in Cantonese. That is, NP–V–DO–IO, where NP is the noun phrase *City U*, V is the verb phrase *bei2* (give), DO is the direct object *go3 conditional offer* (a conditional offer), and IO is the indirect object *ngo5* (me). Within this ML island, the direct object (DO) is expressed by a combination ML+EL island. It comprises a Cantonese classifier, *go3*, and an English adjective, *conditional*, as well as English noun, *offer*. Crucially, these mixed Cantonese and English constituents follow the word order of the matrix language (M), in this case Cantonese: classifier + adjective + N. Additionally, the system morpheme is Cantonese classifier *go3*, indicating that a grammatical morpheme from the matrix language (M) is in place.

Note that the government model discussed earlier cannot handle code-switched utterances such as (21), since it predicts that switches cannot occur between constituents that are in a government relation, in this case, classifier, *go3*, is a functional head that governs the complement noun phrase, *conditional offer*. In this case, the matrix language frame model accounts for a wider range of code-switched utterances. However, Chan (1998, p. 208) reports that Cantonese provides some evidence that the system morpheme principle is sometimes violated, as shown in (22):

(22) *I'm speaking of [* ***go3*** *cost* $]_{NP}$ *m4hai6 functionality.*
CL cost NEG.COP functionality
I'm speaking of the cost, not the functionality.

In (22), if we assume that the matrix language (M) is English, we encounter a problem for the matrix language frame model because it predicts that the system morpheme within the ML+EL island, *go3* cost, 'the cost', ought to be an English functional morpheme. However, we find instead a system morpheme from Cantonese, namely, classifier *go3*. Essentially, the model is not sufficiently powerful, since it cannot accommodate ML+EL islands with system morphemes from either the matrix language *or* the embedded language. A possible way out of this problem is to view each speech exchange from a larger discourse perspective, in which case it may turn out that the overall morpho-syntactic frame for the code-switched utterances, in other words the matrix language, is Cantonese rather than English. Discourse-based studies will be needed to resolve such issues.

In the words of Romaine, 'Future research on code switching must try to bring together the linguistic and pragmatic perspectives' (1995, p. 177). This micro-level and macro-level approach will help ensure that we move closer toward constructing a more comprehensive model of constraints on code switching, and do a better understanding of cognitive representation and processing. Fortunately, to date we have a number of studies that have looked at the discourse functions of code switching in Chinese, e.g. Bond & Lai, 1986; Chan, 1998, 2003; Fu, 1975; Gibbons, 1987; Kawangamalu & Lee, 1991; Lee, Tse, & Yu, 2008; Li, 1994, 1998; Li, Milroy, & Pong, 1992; Luke, 1998. More such studies are needed, in particular the highly challenging interface studies that add socio-pragmatic considerations into code-switching models.

Overall conclusion and future directions

Bilingualism is by no means a simple phenomenon. When it involves Chinese it is complicated further because of the huge geographical spread of Chinese communities around the globe, and thus we are confronted with a very large variety of second, or sometimes first, languages as well as learning situations. The above discussion makes it clear that both the processing and results of bilingualism depend critically on how the languages in question are learned, and also the detailed characteristics of the two languages, the similarity of which impacts on possible transfer between them. Therefore bilingualism is better seen as a multi-parameter, socio-political-linguistic phenomenon, the processing and final results of which may not, and should not, be directly compared to those of the 'standards' produced by native speakers. Future research may pay more attention to the exact contexts under which bilingualism develops, and make use of working hypotheses derived not from traditional models of monolingual processing but from the uniqueness of bilingualism as a pervasive phenomenon in its own right.

Chapter notes

1 Cantonese examples are represented here using the *Jyut6ping3* romanization system developed by Tang et al. (2002).
2 Age is indicated by figures separated by semi-colons, referring respectively to year, month, and day.

References

Aaronson, D. & Ferres, S. (1986). Sentence processing in Chinese-American bilinguals. *Journal of Memory and Language, 25*, 136–162.

Annamalai, E. (1978). The anglicized Indian languages: a case of code-mixing. *International Journal of Dravidian Linguistics*, 7, 239–247.

Baker, C. (2001). *Foundations of bilingual education and bilingualism*, 3rd edn. London: Clevedon.

Basnight-Brown, D. M., Chen, L., Hua. S., Kostic. A., & Feldman, L. B. (2007). Monolingual and bilingual recognition of regular and irregular English verbs: Sensitivity to form similarity varies with first language experience. *Journal of Memory and Language, 57*, 65–80.

Berk-Seligson, S. (1986). Linguistic constraints on intrasentential code-switching: a study of Spanish/Hebrew bilingualism. *Language in Society, 15*, 313–348.

Bialystok, E. (2001). *Bilingualism in development: Language, literacy and cognition.* Cambridge: Cambridge University Press.

Bond, M. H. & Lai, T. M. (1986). Embarrassment and code-switching. *Journal of Social Psychology, 126*, 179–186.

Bosch, L. & Sebastián-Gallés, N. (2001). Early language differentiation in bilingual infants. In Cenoz, J. & F. Genesee, (eds) *Trends in bilingual acquisition* (pp. 71–93). Amsterdam, The Netherlands: John Benjamins.

Chan, A. W. S. (in press). The development of *bei* double object constructions in bilingual and monolingual children. *International Journal of Bilingualism.*

Chan, B. H.-S. (1998). How does Cantonese-English code-switching work? In M. C. Pennington (ed.), *Language in Hong Kong at century's end* (pp. 191–216). Hong Kong: Hong Kong University Press.

Chan, B. H.-S. (2003). *Aspects of the syntax, the pragmatics, and the production of code-switching: Cantonese and English.* New York: Peter Lang.

Chee, M. W. L., Soon, C. S., & Lee, H. L. (2003). Common and segregated neuronal networks for different languages revealed using functional magnetic resonance adaptation. *Journal of Cognitive Neuroscience, 15*, 85–97.

Chen, E.-S. (2003). Language convergence and bilingual acquisition: The case of conditional constructions. *Annual Review of Language Acquisition, 3*, 89–137.

Chen, H. C., Cheung, H., & Lau, S. (1997). Development of Stroop interference in Chinese-English bilinguals. *Psychological Research, 60*, 270 –283.

Cheung, H., Chan, M. M. N., and Chong, K. K.-Y. (2007). Use of orthographic knowledge in reading by Chinese-English bi-scriptal children. *Language Learning, 57*, 469–505.

Cheung, H. & Chen, H. C. (1998). Lexical and conceptual processing in Chinese-English bilinguals: Further evidence for asymmetry. *Memory and Cognition, 26*, 1002–1013.

Cheung, H., Chen, H.-C., Lai, C. Y., Wong, O. C., & Hills, M. (2001). The development of phonological awareness: Effects of spoken language experience and orthography. *Cognition, 81*, 227–241.

Cheung, H. & Lin, A. M. Y. (2005). Differentiating between automatic and strategic control processes: Toward a model of cognitive mobilization in bilingual reading. *Psychologia: An International Journal of Psychology in the Orient, 48*, 39–53.

Cheung, M. C., Chan, A. S., Chan, Y. L., & Lam, J. M. K. (2006). Language lateralization of Chinese-English bilingual patients with temporal lobe epilepsy: A functional MRI study. *Neuropsychology, 20*, 589–597.

Chomsky, N. (1981). Lectures on government and binding. Dordrecht: Foris.

Chu, P. C. K. (2008). *Tonal development of Cantonese in Cantonese-English bilingual children.* Unpublished MPhil thesis, Chinese University of Hong Kong.

Ciocca, V. & Lui, J. Y. K. (2003). The development of the perception of Cantonese lexical tones. *Journal of Multilingual Communication Disorders, 1*, 141–147.

Clyne, M. (1987). Constraints on code-switching: how universal are they? *Linguistics*, 25, 739–764.

De Houwer, A. (1990).*The acquisition of two languages from birth: A case study.* Cambridge, England: Cambridge University Press.

Ding, G., Perry, C., Peng, D., Ma, L., Li, D., Xu, S., Luo, Q., Xu, D., & Yang, J. (2003). Neural mechanisms underlying semantic and orthographic processing in Chinese-English bilinguals. *Neuroreport: For Rapid Communication of Neuroscience Research, 14*, 1557–1562.

Döpke, S. (ed.) (2000). *Cross-linguistic structures in simultaneous bilingualism.* Amsterdam, The Netherlands: John Benjamins.

Francis, A. L., Ciocca, V., & Ng, B. K. C. (2003). On the (non) categorical perception of lexical tones. *Perception and Psychophysics, 65*, 1029–1044.

Fu, G. S. (1975). *A Hong Kong perspective: English-language learning and the Hong Kong student.* Unpublished doctoral dissertation, University of Michigan.

Gandour, J., Dzemidzic, M., Wong, D., Lowe, M., Tong, Y., Hsieh, L., Satthamnuwong, N. & Lurito, J. (2003) *Temporal integration of speech prosody is shaped by language experience: An fMRI study. Brain and Language 84*, 318–336.

Gandour, J., Tong, Y., Talavage, T., Wong, D., Dzemidzic, M,, Xu, Y., Li, X., & Lowe, M. (2006). Neural basis of first and second language processing of sentence-level linguistic prosody. *Human Brain Mapping, 28*, 94–108.

Genesee, F., Nicoladis, E., & Paradis, J. (1995). Language differentiation in early bilingual development. *Journal of Child Language, 22*, 611–631.

Gibbons, J. (1987). *Code-mixing and code choice: A Hong Kong case study.* Clevedon, England: Multilingual Matters.

Goetz, P. J. (2003). The effects of bilingualism on theory of mind development. *Bilingualism: Language and Cognition*, 6, 1–15.

Goffman, E. (1974). *Frame analysis.* New York: Harper & Row.

Gu, C. J. C. (in press). The acquisition of dative constructions in Cantonese-English bilingual children. *International Journal of Bilingualism.*

Guo, T. & Peng, D. (2006). Event-related potential evidence for parallel activation of two languages in bilingual speech production. *Neuroreport: An International Journal for the Rapid Communication of Research in Neuroscience, 17*, 1757–1760.

Gumperz, J. J. (1982). *Discourse strategies.* Cambridge, England: Cambridge University Press.

Gupta, A. F. (1994). *The Step-tongue: Children's English in Singapore.* Clevedon, England: Multilingual Matters.

Ho, D. Y. F. (1987). Bilingual effects on language and cognitive development: With special reference to Chinese-English bilinguals. *Bulletin of the Hong Kong Psychological Society, 18*, 61–69.

Hsieh, S. L. & Tori, C. D. (1993). Neuropsychological and cognitive effects of Chinese language instruction. *Perceptual and Motor Skills, 77*, 1071–1081.

Jackson, N. E., Lu, W. H., and Ju, D. S. (1994). Reading Chinese and reading English: similarities, differences, and second language reading. In V. W. Berninger (ed.), *The varieties of orthographic knowledge I: Theoretical and developmental issues.* (pp. 73–109). New York: Kluwer Academic Publishers.

Jia, G. (2006). Second language acquisition by native Chinese speakers. In P. Li, L. H. Tan, E. Bates, & O. Tzeng (eds), *The handbook of East Asian psycholinguistics* (pp. 61–69). Cambridge, England: Cambridge University Press.

Jia, G. & Aaronson, D. (2003). A longitudinal study of Chinese children and adolescents learning English in the US. *Applied Psycholinguistics, 24*, 131–161.

Jiang, N. (1999). Testing processing explanations for the asymmetry in masked cross-language priming. *Bilingualism: Language and Cognition, 2*, 59–75.

Joshi, A. K. (1985). Processing of sentences with intra-sentential code-switching. In D. R. Dowty, L. Kartnnen, & A. M. Zwicky (eds), *Natural language parsing* (pp. 190–205). Cambridge, UK: Cambridge University Press.

Kamwangamalu, N. M. & Lee, C. L. (1991). Chinese-English code-mixing: A case of matrix language assignment. *World Englishes, 10*, 247–261.

Kroll, J. F. & Stewart, E. (1994). Category interference in translation and picture naming: Evidence for asymmetric connection between bilingual memory representations. *Journal of Memory and Language, 33*, 149–174.

Kuhl, P. K. (1993). Innate predispositions and the effects of experience in speech perception: The native language magnet theory. In B. deBoysson-Bardies, S. de Schonen, P. Jusczyk, P. McNeilage, & J. Morton (eds), *Developmental neurocognition: Speech and face processing in the first year of life* (pp. 259–274). Dordrecht, The Netherlands: Kluwer Academic Publishers.

Kwan-Terry, A. (1986). The acquisition of word order in English and Cantonese interrogative sentences: A Singapore case study. *RELC Journal, 17*, 14–39.

Kwan-Terry, A. (1989). The specification of stage by a child learning English and Cantonese simultaneously: A study of acquisition processes. In H. W. Dechert & M. Raupach (eds), *Interlingual processes* (pp. 33–48). Tübingen: Gunter Narr Verlag.

Kwan-Terry, A. (1991). Through the looking glass: A child's use of particles in Chinese and English and its implications on language transfer. In A. Kwan-Terry (ed.), *Child language development in Singapore and Malaysia* (pp. 161–183). Singapore: Singapore University Press.

Kwan-Terry, A. (1992). Code-switching and code-mixing: The case of a child learning English and Chinese simultaneously. *Journal of Multilingual and Multicultural Development, 13*, 243–259.

Lanvers, U. (1999). Lexical growth patterns in a bilingual infant: The occurrence and significance of equivalents in the bilingual lexicon. *International Journal of Bilingual Education and Bilingualism, 2*, 30–52.

Lanza, E. 1997. *Language mixing in infant bilingualism: A sociolinguistic perspective.* Oxford, England: Clarendon.

Lee, K. Y. S., Chiu, S. N., & van Hasselt, C. A. (2002). Tone perception ability of Cantonese-speaking children. *Language and Speech, 45*, 387–406.

Lee, W. L., Tse, H. Y., & Yu, C. S. (2008). *The study of code-mixing in blogs among undergraduate students in Hong Kong.* Unpublished manuscript, Department of Linguistics and Modern Languages, Chinese University of Hong Kong.

Li, D. C.-S. (1994). *Why do HongKongers code-mix? A linguistic perspective.* Research Report No.40. Department of English, City University of Hong Kong.

Li, P. (1996). Spoken word recognition of code-switched words by Chinese-English bilinguals. *Journal of Memory and Language, 35*, 757–774.

Li, R., Peng, D., Guo, T., Wei, J., & Wang, C. (2004). The similarity and difference of N400 elicited by Chinese and English. *Chinese Journal of Psychology, 46*, 91–111. (in Chinese)

Li, W. (1998). The 'why' and 'how' questions in the analysis of conversational code-switching. In P. Auer (ed.), *Code-switching in conversation: Language, interaction and identity* (pp. 156–176). London: Routledge.

Li, W. & Lee. S. (2002). L1 Development in an L2 environment: The use of Cantonese classifiers and quantifiers by young British-born Chinese in Tyneside. *International Journal of Bilingual Education and Bilingualism, 4*, 359–382.

Li, W., Milroy, L., & Pong, S. C. (1992). A two-step sociolinguistic analysis of code-switching and language choice. *International Journal of Applied Linguistics*, 2, 63–86.

Light, T. (1977). Clairetalk: A Cantonese-speaking child's confrontation with bilingualism. *Journal of Chinese Linguistics, 5*, 261–275.

Linguistic Society of Hong Kong (2002). *Guide to LSHK Cantonese Romanization of Chinese Characters* (2nd edn). Linguistic Society of Hong Kong, Hong Kong.

Liu, H., Bates, E., & Li, P. (1992). Sentence interpretation in bilingual speakers of English and Chinese. *Applied Psycholinguistics, 13*, 451–484.

Liu, Y. & Perfetti, C. A. (2003). The time course of brain activity in reading English and Chinese: An ERP study of Chinese bilinguals. *Human Brain Mapping, 18*, 167–175.

Lleó, C. & Kehoe, M. (2002). On the interaction of phonological systems in child bilingual acquisition. *International Journal of Bilingualism, 6*, 233–237.

Luke, K. K. (1998). Why two languages might be better than one: Motivations of language mixing in Hong Kong. In M. C. Pennington (ed.), *Language in Hong Kong at century's end* (pp. 145–160). Hong Kong: Hong Kong University Press.

MacWhinney, B. (2000). *The CHILDES Project: Tools for Analyzing Talk.* (3rd edn) Manwah, N J: Erlbaum.

Matthews, S. & Yip, V. (2002). Relative clauses in early bilingual development: transfer and universals. In A. Giacalone (ed.), *Typology and second language acquisition* (pp. 39–81). Berlin: Mouton de Gruyter.

Mattock, K. & Burnham, D. (2006). Chinese and English infants' tone perception: Evidence for perceptual reorganization. *Infancy, 10*, 241–265.

McBride-Chang, C., Cho, J.-R., Liu, H., Wagner, R. K., Shu, H., Zhou, A., Cheuk, C. S.-M., & Muse, A. (2005). Changing models across cultures: Associations of phonological and morphological awareness to reading in Beijing, Hong Kong, Korea, and America. *Journal of Experimental Child Psychology, 92*, 140–160.

McBride-Chang, C., Shu, H., Zhou, A., Wat, C.-P., & Wagner, R. K. (2003). Morphological awareness uniquely predicts young children's Chinese character recognition. *Journal of Educational Psychology, 95*, 743–751.

Meisel, J. (2001). The simultaneous acquisition of two first languages: Early differentiation and subsequent development of grammars. In J. Cenoz & F. Genesee, (eds) *Trends in bilingual acquisition* (pp. 11–41). Amsterdam, The Netherlands: John Benjamins.

Müller, N. (1998). Transfer in bilingual first language acquisition. *Bilingualism: Language and Cognition, 1*, 151–71.

Müller, N. (ed.) (2003). *(In)vulnerable domains in multilingualism.* Amsterdam, The Netherlands: John Benjamins.

Myers-Scotton, C. (1993). *Dueling languages. Grammatical structure in code-switching.* Oxford, England: Oxford University Press.

Nicoladis, E. & Grabois, H. (2002). Learning English and losing Chinese: A case study of a child adopted from China. *The International Journal of Bilingualism, 6*, 441–454.

Odlin, T. (1989). *Language transfer: Cross-linguistic influence in language learning.* Cambridge, England: Cambridge University Press.

Paradis, J., Nicoladis, E., & Genesee, F. (2000). Early emergence of structural constraints on code-mixing: Evidence from French-English bilingual children. *Bilingualism: Language and Cognition, 3*, 245–261.

Pearson, B., Fernandez, S. C., & Oller, D. K. (1995). Cross-language synonyms in the lexicons of bilingual infants: One language or two? *Journal of Child Language, 22*, 345–368.

Perfetti, C. A. & Liu. Y. (2005). Orthography to phonology and meaning: Comparisons across and within writing systems. *Reading and Writing, 18*, 193 –210.

Pollock, K., Price, J., & Fulmer, K. C. (2003). Speech-language acquisition in children adopted from China: A longitudinal investigation of two children. *Journal of Multilingual Communication Disorders, 1*, 184–193.

Poplack, S. (1980). Sometimes I'll start a sentence in English y terminó en español: Towards a typology of code-switching. *Linguistics*, 18, 581–516. Reprinted with a preface in *The Bilingualism Reader*, edited by W. Li (2000), London: Routledge.

Poulin-Dubois, D. & Goodz, N. (2001). Language differentiation in bilingual infants: Evidence from babbling. In J. Cenoz & F. Genesee, (eds) *Trends in bilingual acquisition*, (pp. 95–106). Amsterdam, The Netherlands: John Benjamins.

Rayner, K., Li, X., Williams, C. C., Cave, K. R., & Well A. D. (2007). Eye movements during information processing tasks: Individual differences and cultural effects. *Vision Research, 47*, 2714–2726.

Roberts, J., Pollock, K., Krakow, R., Price, J., & Wang, P. (2005). Language development in preschool-age children adopted from China. *Journal of Speech, Language and Hearing Research, 48*, 93–107.

Romaine, S. (1986). The notion of government as a constraint on language mixing: Some evidence from the code-mixed compound verb in Panjabi. In D. Tannen (ed.), *Linguistics and linguistics in context: The independence of theory, data and application* (pp. 35–50). Washington, DC: Georgetown University Press.

Romaine, S. (1995). *Bilingualism*, 2nd edn. Oxford, England: Basil Blackwell.

Ruan, J. (2004). Bilingual Chinese/English first-graders developing metacognition about writing. *Literacy, 38*, 106–112.

Rusted, J. (1988). Orthographic effects for Chinese-English bilinguals in a picture–word interference task. *Current Psychology: Research and Reviews, 7*, 207–220.

Scotton, C. M. (1988). Code-switching and types of multilingual communities. In P. H. Lowenberg, (ed.), *Language spread and language policy: Issues, implications, and case studies*, (pp. 61–82). Washington, DC: Georgetown University Press.

Sankoff, D. & Poplack, S. (1981). A formal grammar for code-switching. *Papers in Linguistics*, 14, 3–46.

Smith, M. E. (1931). A study of five bilingual children from the same family. *Child Development, 2*, 184–7.

Smith, M. E. (1935). A study of the speech of eight bilingual children of the same family. *Child Development, 6*, 19–25.

Tan, L. H., Spinks, J. A., Feng, C. M., Siok, W. T., Perfetti, C. A., Xiong, J., Fox, P. T., & Gao, J. H. (2003). Neural systems of second language reading are shaped by native language. *Human Brain Mapping, 18*, 158–166.

Tang, S.-W., Fan, K., Lee, T. H.-T., Lun, C., Luke, K.-K., Tung, P., & Cheung. K.-H. (eds) (2002). *Guide to LSHK Cantonese romanization of Chinese characters*, 2nd edn. Hong Kong: Linguistic Society of Hong Kong.

Tsitsipis, L. (1988). Language shift and narrative performance: on the structure and function of Arvanítika narratives. *Language in Society*, 17, 61–88.

Volterra, V. & Taeschner, T. (1978). The acquisition of and development of language by bilingual children. *Journal of Child Language, 5*, 311–326.

Weekes, B. S., Su, I. F., Yin, W., & Zhang, X. (2007). Oral reading in bilingual aphasia: Evidence from Mongolian and Chinese. *Bilingualism: Language and Cognition, 10*, 201–210.

Wong, P., Schwartz, R. G., & Jenkins, J. J. (2005). Perception and production of lexical tones by 3-year old, Mandarin-speaking children. *Journal of Speech, Language, and Hearing Research, 48*, 1065–1079.

Woolford, E. (1983). Bilingual code-switching and syntactic theory. *Linguistic Inquiry, 14*, 520–536.

Yip, V. (1995). *Interlanguage and learnability: From Chinese to English.* Amsterdam, The Netherlands: John Benjamins.

Yip, V. & Matthews, S. (2000). Syntactic transfer in a Cantonese-English bilingual child. *Bilingualism: Language and Cognition, 3*, 193–208.

Yip, V. & Matthews, S. (2003). *Phonological hyper-differentiation in Cantonese-English bilingual children.* Paper presented at the Child Phonology Conference at the University of British Columbia, Vancouver, Canada, July.

Yip, V. & Matthews, S. (2007a). *The bilingual child: Language Contact and early bilingual development.* Cambridge, England: Cambridge University Press.

Yip, V. & Matthews, S. (2007b). Relative clauses in Cantonese-English bilingual children: Typological challenges and processing motivations. *Studies in Second Language Acquisition, 29*, 277–300.

Yip, V. & Matthews, S. (2008). *First words in Cantonese-English bilingual infants.* Poster presented at the 16th International Conference on Infant Studies, Vancouver, Canada.

Yuan, B. (1997). Asymmetry of null subjects and null objects in Chinese speakers' L2 English. *Studies in Second Language Acquisition, 19*, 467–497.

CHAPTER 10

Chinese children learning mathematics: from home to school

Yu-Jing Ni, Ming Ming Chiu, and Zi-Juan Cheng

Chinese students have excelled in many international assessments of mathematics achievement (e.g. Programme for International Student Assessment [PISA] and the Third International Mathematics and Science Study [TIMSS]), thereby drawing great interest from researchers, educators, and policy makers inside and outside the Chinese community. This chapter draws upon three strands of research (developmental, instructional, and social-psychological) cutting across three different levels (societal/cultural [macro, nation], institutional [meso/micro, family, classroom], and individual [nano]) to examine the ingredients that have shaped the mathematics achievements of Chinese students.

The chapter starts by tracing the early numerical development of Chinese children before considering learning and instruction in Chinese mathematics classrooms. Next, it explores the broader sociocultural contexts in which the Chinese way of learning and teaching mathematics is rooted and supported. Finally, we depict a profile of Chinese students' achievements in mathematics against these backgrounds. These layers of description help paint a richer understanding of Chinese students' mathematics achievement and its contexts.

Before we turn to the specific discussions, it is important to indicate upfront that the Chinese students referenced here are urban students from the mainland China, HKSAR, and Taiwan, as most of the referenced studies in the chapter involved students from Hong Kong, Taipei and several cities of mainland China (e.g. Beijing, Shanghai, Changchun, Guiyan, etc.).

Numerical development of Chinese children in their early years

Studies suggest that Chinese children and children of other countries show differences in mathematics achievement before they receive any formal school education (Ginsburg et al., 2006; Stevenson et al., 1990; Stigler, Lee, & Stevenson, 1987; Starkey & Klein, 2008). Chinese preschoolers outperformed their English-speaking counterparts from the United States on generating cardinal and ordinal number names (Miller, Major, Shu, & Zhang, 2000). They showed better understanding of the base-ten system and fractions, and using tens-complement strategy for early addition (Fuson & Kwon, 1991). Among kindergarteners to third graders solving simple addition problems, Chinese children used verbal counting strategies more often than did US children, who counted on their fingers more often. Decompositions were the primary backup strategy for the Chinese children. In contrast, the American children used finger counting as the backup strategy (Geary, Bow-Thomas, Liu, & Siegler, 1993, 1996).

The better performance by Chinese children in numerical literacy has been attributed to linguistic (Miura et al., 1994) and sociocultural factors (Ho & Fuson, 1998; Miller, Smith, Zhu, & Zhang, 1995; Saxton & Towse, 1998; Towse & Saxton, 1997). There is much greater regularity in Chinese number naming between 11 and 20 and also between 10 and 100. For example, numbers between 11 and 20 are formed by compounding the 'tens word' with the 'unit word'. Thus, the numbers 11 and 12 are spoken as 'ten-one' and 'ten-two', while 20 is spoken as 'two-tens' and 62 is spoken as 'six-tens-two'. In contrast, English-speaking children have to memorize the relatively awkward numerical names between 1 and 19 as well as all the decade names, 'twenty', 'thirty', etc. (Miura et al., 1994). The numerical names in English are in a decade structure (twenty, thirty, forty, etc.), instead of the clearer and simpler representations of two-tens, three-tens, four-tens, five-tens. The consistency of the Chinese number naming system with a base-ten system has been hypothesized to assist children in doing well on tasks relevant to base-10 values, such as counting skills and place-value competence.

However, showing that number naming in the Chinese language aided Chinese children's better performance in mathematics has been difficult, because none of these studies controlled for culture or family processes (e.g. parental expectation, parental assistance, and preschool education) as confounding variables that could also influence children's mathematics development (Saxton & Towse, 1998; Towse & Saxton, 1997; Wang & Lin, 2005). Saxton and Towse (1998) addressed this issue by comparing the numerical performance of English-speaking and Japanese-speaking children. (The Japanese and Chinese number-naming systems have the same structure.)

In their study, children were shown the relationship between the ones and tens cubes. Then, under the *prompt condition*, children were shown how to make 2 (from two units) and 13 (from one ten and three units). Under the *no-prompt condition*, children were shown how to make 2 and 5 (from unit cubes only). In the testing phase, children were asked if they could show how to make some numbers, including two-digit numbers. The results showed that under the no-prompt condition, Japanese children of six and seven years old were more likely than English-speaking children of the same age to give canonical base-10 count responses to represent two-digit numbers, which contain the maximum possible number of ten cubes plus the appropriate numbers of unit cubes. However, under the prompt condition, the two groups of children performed at a comparable level to give the base-10 responses (Saxton & Towse, 1998).

Fuson, Smith, and Lo Cicero (1997) and Othman (2004) also showed that giving explicit instructions to English-speaking and Arabic-speaking children about the base-10 structure of numbers could improve their arithmetic performance (both the English and the Arabic number-naming systems are irregular and incongruent with the base-10 system). These studies showed the importance of adult instruction in children's learning of mathematics, as such instruction could mediate the role of the linguistic feature of a number naming system.

While US mothers value literacy skills more than mathematics skills in early childhood education, Chinese mothers believe that their children should master both skills before first grade in order to support academic success (Hatano, 1990; Stevenson & Lee, 1990). Kelly (2003) showed that American mothers mostly emphasized reading preparations before their children started school, while Chinese mothers focused on both reading and mathematics for such preparation. In addition, Chinese parents believe that children's trajectories in mathematics achievement are already established early in preschool and tend to persist in elementary school; thus, they think that preschool children who lag behind their peers in mathematics performance tend to fall further behind in elementary school. Hence, Asian parents, particularly Chinese parents, put early pressure on their children to learn, and on preschools to teach, the mathematics curricula.

Chinese parents' expectations affect preschool curriculum and instruction. To meet parental demands, preschool mathematics curricula have absorbed formal mathematics curricula from elementary schools in Hong Kong and in mainland China (Starkey & Klein, 2008; Cheng & Chan, 2005). The mathematics curricula for four- to six-year-old children in many cities, e.g. Hong Kong, Shanghai, Beijing, are similar to those for first- and second-grade students. Many Chinese children, even as young as two to three years old, begin to learn counting, digit recognition, and writing.

At five years old, they are asked to do arithmetic exercises, including addition and subtraction with and without carry-over. Adults, preschool teachers, parents and grandparents help coach children to solve mathematics problems (Cheng, Chan, Li, Ng, & Woo, 2001). (As Chinese have a collectivist culture, grandparents often live near their grandchildren and attend to their care and early education much more than do their Western counterparts [Georgas et al., 2001].) For example, the adults at home and at preschools often teach children to recite 1 to 100 repeatedly. Also, adults generally teach children to do addition and subtraction by counting their fingers. For instance, adults can ask children to compute '7 + 5 =' with the *counting-on* strategy by putting 7 in their mind, opening five fingers and counting up 'eight, nine, ten, eleven, twelve!' (Cheng & Chan, 2005). Urban Chinese children who attended regular preschool and kindergarten education usually can count, add, and subtract 0–20 proficiently before entering first grade (Zhang, Li, & Tang, 2004).

While some preschools believe that early childhood education should not include mathematics, others prepare students for primary-school mathematics (Clements, 2001). Chinese society as a whole adopts the latter view, and uses an adult-centered instructional approach to teach children numerical facts and skills. Supporting this approach, emerging evidence from infant research shows that preschool children can naturally acquire and use whole numbers, just as they acquire and use spoken language (Gallistel & Gelman, 1992; Geary, 1994; Ni & Zhou, 2005; Starkey & Klein, 2008).

The *operational mathematics curriculum* is one early childhood curriculum used in China since the 1900s to introduce mathematics to preschoolers in an accessible manner and to prepare them for primary-school mathematics (Cheng, 2007, 2008). Like Montessori schools, the operational learning curriculum concretizes mathematics (e.g. by using a 10 x 10 grid), but also connects them to their respective mathematics concepts (e.g. cardinal and ordinal numbers, place values, arithmetic operations) and organizes them to highlight their systematic structure (e.g. addition, subtraction, and part–whole structures in a base-10 system). As a result, students can create an image of the logico-mathematical system of concepts and operations, thereby aiding their learning of abstract logico-mathematics in Chinese elementary schools (Cheng, 2007; 2008).

Consider the following example: children are shown four faces and asked to identify attributes that may be used to classify the faces into different groups. These four faces feature three attributes: one face has a hat and three do not; two happy faces and two angry faces; and three circular faces and one square face. Preschool teachers ask their students to observe and analyze the attributes and relationships of the four faces. Then, they guide the students' use of beads to model the relationships as they solve addition and subtraction problems within this universe of 4 (e.g. 1 + 3 = 4, 2 + 2 = 4, 3 + 1 = 4; 4 – 1 = 3, 4 – 2 = 2, 4 – 3 = 1). Next, the students develop their understanding of part–whole relations for the numbers 2, 3, and 5 to 10 by doing classification tasks with these numbers on a 10 x 10 grid.

The grid and these part–whole relationships can help preschoolers use composition and decomposition strategies to solve addition and subtraction problems involving larger numbers. For example, consider solving 8 + 7 with the decomposition to 10 strategy (8 + 7 = 8 + [2 + 5] = [8 + 2] + 5 = 10 + 5 = 15). First, teachers guide children to focus on the first addend (8 dots) and decide how many extra dots are needed to make up a row of 10 on the grid (in this case, 2 + 8 = 10). Second, teachers ask students to split 7 into 2 dots and a remaining portion of 5 dots (7 = 2 + 5). Third, teachers guide students to add 8 and 2 to create a row of 10 on the grid (8 + 2 = 10). In the fourth step, students add the remaining 5 to the row of 10, yielding 15 (10 + 5 = 15). Then children work independently on addition problems yielding sums greater than 10 (e.g. 5 + 9). This operational approach helps students acquire the skill components necessary for mathematics competence (Cheng, 2008).

As indicated in the above discussions, Chinese preschoolers benefit from higher parental expectations and assistance, linguistic advantages, and supportive preschool mathematics compared to their Western counterparts. As a result, Chinese preschoolers outperform Western preschoolers in many areas of mathematics (Miller, Kelly, & Zhou, 2005; Miller, Major, Shu, & Zhang, 2000), creating an advantage that can continue through their later years of schooling.

Instruction in Chinese mathematics classrooms

The importance of classroom instruction is highlighted by findings of similar IQ-test scores by American and Chinese children, similar numeracy skills of Chinese and American adults, but Chinese children's *higher* numeracy test scores compared to US children (Geary et al., 1996; Stevenson et al., 1985). These observations along with Chinese students' superior performance on international assessments point to the capacity of mathematics curriculum and instruction to increase the mathematics achievement of Chinese children (Stigler & Hiebert, 1999).

The Chinese mathematics curriculum in the mainland emphasizes *two-basics* (basic mathematics concepts and basic mathematics skills), and Chinese classroom instruction focuses on *refined lectures* and *repeated practice* (Zhang et al., 2004). The two-basics view emphasizes foundational knowledge content and skills over creative thinking process (Leung, 2001; Li & Ni, 2007). Chinese educators argue that repeated practice aids memorization and that greater exposure can help students think about the underlying concepts more deeply (Dhlin & Watkins, 2000; for detailed socio-historical analyses of the origins of these Chinese beliefs, see Wong, 2004; Zhang et al., 2004). Hence, Chinese mathematics curricula have four student goals: 1) fast, accurate manipulation and computation of arithmetic, fractions, polynomials, and algebra; 2) accurate recall of memorized mathematics definitions, formulas, rules, and procedures; 3) understanding of logical categorizations and mathematics propositions; and 4) facile matching of solution patterns to types of problems via transfer (Zhang et al., 2004).

To implement these curricula, teachers present well-prepared lessons that include strong teacher control, coherent instruction, and abstract mathematics (*refined lectures*; Zhang et al., 2004). To deliver such refined instruction, teachers in Beijing and Taipei spend over six hours each day examining students' work and preparing lessons with colleagues, far more than do their US counterparts (Stevenson & Stigler, 1992).

Teachers often maintain control by direct teaching to the whole class. Direct teaching helps teachers control the lesson flow to maintain class discipline (especially with forty to sixty students per class in China), while engaging students in the learning activities (Huang & Leung, 2004). As Confucian culture assigns content expertise to teachers, traditional Chinese students are also more receptive to the teacher's dominant role. Stevenson and Stigler (1992) reported that Chinese teachers led their classes 90 per cent of the time, whereas US teachers did so 47 per cent of the time.

Secondly, the refined lecture should unite teaching content and classroom discourse through coherent connections that guide students toward their learning goal for each lesson (Wang & Murphy, 2004). Chinese teachers' lesson plans also enhance instructional coherence by emphasizing the relationships among mathematics concepts. For example, some studies, that involved teachers and students from Illinois of the USA and those from Guiyang of mainland China, showed that Chinese teachers helped their students specify the similarities and differences between ratios and fractions to clarify their relationship, whereas American teachers did not (Cai, 2005; Cai & Wong, 2006).

Also, when students make mistakes, Chinese teachers often view them as learning opportunities and have the mathematics mastery to ask leading questions that guide students to correct answers (Stevenson & Stigler, 1992). By so doing, Chinese teachers encourage students who have erred to persevere, understand their mistake, and correct it. In contrast, American mathematics teachers typically have less mathematics knowledge than their Chinese counterparts, often feel uncomfortable with student mistakes, and try to avoid them (Ma, 1999; Stevenson & Stigler, 1992; Wang & Murphy, 2004).

Schleppenbach, Perry, Miller, Sims, and Fang (2007) also compared the coherence of mathematics lessons in seventeen Chinese and fourteen American elementary classrooms by examining the frequency and content of extended discourses. Extended discourses are relatively sustained exchanges that occur when a student gives a correct answer to a question (by another student or by the teacher) and the teacher asks a follow-up question, instead of simply evaluating the student's answer. Here is an example of extended discourse (Schleppenbach et al., 2007):

Teacher : Is this equation, $2xy = 5$, an instance of a linear equation with two unknowns?
Student A: No.
Teacher : Why not?

Student A: The power of each unknown should be one for a linear equation in two unknowns. But for this equation, 2xy is one unit and its power is two.
Teacher : The power of this single unit is two; therefore it does not belong to the type of linear equations in two unknowns. Do you agree or disagree?
Student B: Agree.
Teacher : Could you give an example of linear equation in two unknowns?
Student B: $3x + 2y = 25$

Schleppenbach et al. (2007) found that extended discourse episodes were longer and occurred more often in Chinese lessons than in American lessons.

Chinese teachers also plan more coherent sequences of lessons, as shown in these four lessons from a Shanghai teacher of the highest ranking (*first class*) who had taught secondary-school mathematics for twenty years (Lopez-Real, Leung, & Marton, 2004). The step-by-step tasks and activities found in these four lessons help students learn linear equations with two unknowns in a logically progressive way.

In the first lesson, the teacher introduced coordinates and identified a point in the coordinate plane uniquely with an ordered pair (x, y). To emphasize precise notation and procedure, the teacher gave examples, asked students to express the ordered pairs of points on the plane and to compare them (e.g. [2, 5] and [5, 2]).

In the second lesson, the teacher briefly reviewed the ideas of the first lesson, then asked students to develop the complementary skill of identifying the locations of ordered pairs on the coordinate plane (e.g. [1, 2]). Then he drew a square on a coordinate plane and shifted the square in the different directions. To review, evaluate, and consolidate their understandings through extended discourse, he asked the students to find the new coordinates of each vertex as the square changed its positions.

In the third lesson, the teacher asked how many combinations of \$1 stamps and \$2 stamps a person can buy with \$10. Through trial and error, the students discovered many answers (e.g. four \$1 stamps and three \$2 stamps; \$10 = [4 x \$1] + [3 x \$2]). The teacher then helped the students represent and solve the problem using an equation with two unknowns (e.g. x[1] + y[2] = 10). Next, he asked them to analyze the situation and summarized their answers; the linear equation must contain two unknowns and the power of each unknown is one. Afterwards, the teacher asked what values of x and y would satisfy $x + 2y = 10$, ignoring the stamp context and focusing only on the equation itself. After trying many examples, the students figured out that there are infinite solutions to the equation. The teacher then generalized the rule that any linear equation with two unknowns has an infinite number of solutions.

By opening the fourth lesson as follows, the teacher highlighted general relationships and abstractions to further the students' learning:

> In the previous lessons we've learned about the ... concepts of linear equations in two unknowns and ... the coordinate plane. We know that after setting up a coordinate plane, the points in the plane can be represented by pairs of ordered numbers ... So is there any connection between the two concepts? Let's use the equation $2x - y = 3$ as an example for investigation'
>
> (Lopez-Real et al., 2004, p. 404).

These well-designed and coherent mathematics lessons reduced ambiguity and confusion, aiding students as they progressed toward their challenging learning goals of memorization and understanding of mathematics concepts and skills (Dhlin & Watkins, 2000; Wong, 2004).

Related to instructional coherence, Chinese teachers value and use more abstraction to generalize mathematics relationships in their instruction compared to American teachers who value concrete representations more (Correa, Perry, Sims, Miller, & Fang, 2008). Specifically, Chinese and American middle-school teachers differed in their use of concrete representations, predictions of student strategies, and assessments of student strategies (Cai, 2005; Cai & Lester, 2005). Chinese teachers exclusively used concrete representations to mediate students' understanding of the main mathematics concept in the lesson (e.g. diagram of four cups with different amounts of water to help students compute and understand the concept of arithmetic mean). In contrast, American teachers used concrete representations to generate data (e.g. students' heights and arm lengths as data to find their mean height and arm lengths). Furthermore, Chinese teachers were more likely to predict algebraic strategies for their students while American teachers were more likely to predict drawing or guess-and-check strategies for their students. When students used drawing strategies or estimates that yielded correct answers, American teachers scored them higher than Chinese teachers did, as the latter viewed these strategies as less generalizable.

Thus, the approach of the two-basics curriculum and the refined lecture with repeated practice may contribute to more effective Chinese mathematics instruction. The two-basics curriculum might focus students on the key mathematics concepts, skills, categorizations, and flexible applications to problems. Meanwhile, the refined lecture with repeated practice instruction, serving the two-basics curriculum well, might facilitate teachers' classroom management, increase lesson coherence, and help students generalize mathematics relationships in a step-by-step way. Together, these factors might help Chinese students learn more mathematics than their non-Chinese counterparts.

Cultural contexts of Chinese students' mathematics achievement

As shown in the previous discussion, teaching and learning are always a cultural act. The Chinese way of teaching and learning mathematics is rooted in and supported by its cultural-social contexts (see also McBride-Chang, Lin, Fong, & Shu; Kember & Watkins; Hau & Ho, this volume). Researchers have observed that Chinese Americans have outperformed other Asian-Americans and Caucasian-American students in mathematics (Huntsinger, Jose, Larson, Balsink, & Shalingram, 2000), even when these Chinese-Americans were not exposed to formal Chinese schooling. Asian-Europeans also outperformed the native Europeans (Sirin, 2005). These results show that school factors alone do not fully explain achievement differences between Chinese and non-Chinese students. So we next consider more general, social-cultural factors.

Grounded in government exams, collectivist beliefs, and economic rewards, Chinese people (especially parents, schools, and teachers) have traditionally supported students' high academic achievement. The *Keju* civil service exam system from 606 to 1905 not only selected China's government officials but also gave proportional financial rewards, prestige, power, and fame to their extended family, thereby powering collectivist beliefs, values and norms (Suen & Yu, 2006). Unlike Europeans, Chinese people believe that education drives economic success, not negotiation of higher salaries via stronger labor unions (Addison & Schnabel, 2003; Reitz & Verman, 2004). In Hong Kong's education-rewarding wage system, a high-school teacher earns a manual worker's lifetime wages in fifteen years while a professor earns it within five years (McLelland, 1991). As a result, Chinese parents, schools, and teachers strongly support students' academic achievement, especially in mathematics, which opens a door to many professions (Wise, Lauress, Steel, & MacDonald, 1979).

Chinese parents support their children's mathematics learning through high expectations, educational resources, and homework assistance. Unlike American parents, Chinese parents view effort as more important than ability for learning mathematics (Stigler, Lee, & Stevenson, 1990). Thus, Chinese parents encourage their children to study diligently and expect them to excel (Hau & Salili, 1996). Chinese parents further enhance their children's academic motivation by wielding their collectivist beliefs, for example, by reminding them that their success or failure affects their entire family's reputation (Chiu & Ho, 2006). As a result, Chinese parents showed higher expectations for their children, expressed less satisfaction, and were more likely to recognize their children's learning problems compared to American mothers (Stevenson et al., 1990).

Chinese parents also invest heavily in their children's education (e.g. buying books, tutoring children themselves, etc.) to motivate them and raise their academic achievement (Lam, Ho, & Wong, 2002). Within a given family budget, buying proportionately more educational resources reinforces family commitment to children's learning, implicitly suggesting further social rewards and incentives for higher achievement (Chiu & Ho, 2006). Extra educational resources also give children more learning opportunities on which they can capitalize to improve their academic achievement (Chiu, 2007). Chinese-American parents also spent more time with their children and used more formal teaching methods than European-American parents (Huntsinger et al., 2000). Chinese parents were also more likely than American counterparts to monitor their children's homework or help them directly (Stevenson et al., 1990). As greater parental homework assistance does not necessarily yield higher student mathematics achievement, however, the benefit is likely more motivational than instructional (Chiu & Ho, 2006).

Prodded by parents' and society's high expectations, schools in Chinese societies use challenging curricula, require certified teachers, support group teaching preparation, and share the knowledge of expert teachers. Schools in collectivist Chinese societies implement these high expectations through a national mathematics curriculum and standardized textbooks, whose difficulty typically exceeds that of their American counterparts' diverse curricula and textbooks (Geary et al., 1996; Leung, 1995; Mayer, 1986; Stigler et al., 1987). To teach these challenging curricula, most teachers in Chinese schools are certified, like those in most East-Asian countries (Akiba, LeTendre, & Scribner, 2007; Chiu & Khoo, 2005; OECD, 2003).

Furthermore, teachers often work together and share their knowledge. Group teaching preparation is common in urban schools of mainland China (Ni & Li, 2009). Teachers work together to help individual teachers understand the teacher manuals, the student textbooks, the curriculum standards, and teaching methods that are believed to be effective. The Ministry of Education officially approves student textbooks and teacher manuals (schools can use only approved textbooks), endorsing them as effective mathematics teaching (J.-H. Li, 2004). In addition, education administrative agencies direct good teachers (e.g. first-class teachers) to demonstrate their classroom teaching to their colleagues inside and outside their school districts for other teachers to learn and improve their teaching.

As a result, Chinese teachers' lesson plans for a given teaching unit resembled one another's (including similar learning goals, worked-out examples, homework problems, and presentation structures). In contrast, the lesson plans of American teachers varied substantially, even for teachers in the same school (Cai, 2005; Cai & Wong, 2006). A highly centralized educational system within a collectivist culture (as in mainland China and Hong Kong) aids organizational and administrative efficiency by quickly disseminating socially and culturally favored teaching methods. As Stevenson and Stigler (1992, p. 198) put it:

> The techniques used by Chinese and Japanese teachers are not new to the teaching profession nor are they foreign or exotic. In fact, they are ones often recommended by American educators. What the Chinese and Japanese examples demonstrated so compellingly is when widely and consistently implemented, such practice can produce extraordinary outcomes.

Taken together, family, school, and teachers' high expectations and support of students tend to raise students' standards, increase their motivation, enhance their learning behaviors, and raise their mathematics achievement (Geary et al., 1996). The combination of collective family expectations, challenging mathematics curriculum, and complex lesson activities helps students appreciate the difficult mathematics they must master to perform well on national, university entrance exams (Davey, Lian, & Higgins, 2007; Wong, 1993). Combined with their collective belief that their academic success or failure affects their family, Chinese students are motivated to study diligently while lacking confidence and fearing failure (Lam et al., 2002; Whang & Hancock, 1994).

Western educators generally believe that intrinsic motivations (e.g. getting students interested in mathematics) would benefit students to learn, while extrinsic motivations would only cause anxiety in students and hinder learning. In contrast, Chinese students believe that extrinsic motivations aid learning, in addition to intrinsic motivation. These extrinsic motivators (e.g. examinations, expectations, and social status) are deeply rooted in the Chinese culture (J. Li, 2003). Driven by these intrinsic and extrinsic motivations, Chinese students are both more likely to do their homework and both spend more time doing homework than either American or Japanese students (Chen & Stevenson,

1989; 1995; Stigler et al., 1990). Their greater motivation and efforts typically yield higher mathematics performance (Beaton et al., 1996; Chiu & Zeng, 2008).

A portrait of Chinese students' mathematics achievements

Taught in a curriculum emphasizing the two-basics and classroom instruction using a highly directive approach, Chinese students' mathematics performance showed certain characteristics (Cai & Cifarelli, 2004): Chinese students had strong computation skills and solved routine mathematics problems well but had more difficulties with non-routine problems. An example of a routine question is: 'The actual distance between Maple County and Orange County is 54 km. On the map, the distance between the two counties is 3 cm. The distance between Orange County and Lake County is 12 cm. What is the actual distance between Lake County and Orange County? Show how you found your answer.' An example of a non-routine problem with multiple answers is: 'Ming and Fang, high-school students, take part-time jobs. Ming earns 15 RMB per day and Fang earns 10 RMB per day. How many days do Ming and Fang have to work respectively so that they will earn the same amount of money? Show how you found your answer.'

Chinese students performed better than American students on the routine problems but not on the non-routine problems (Cai, 2000). Results of the international comparative studies also suggested that Chinese students' performance on practical, non-routine mathematics problems weaker than their performance on routine, math test items (Fan & Zhu, 2004).

Chinese students demonstrated high levels of accuracy and efficiency in dealing with word problems in mathematics. In particular, they were more likely than American students to use abstract and generalized strategies to solve the problems. Both American and Chinese students were more likely to solve mathematics problems correctly when they used symbolic representations (Cai & Hwang, 2002; Cai & Lester, 2005; Fan, & Zhu, 2004), suggesting that the preference for abstract strategies helped Chinese students to solve the problem. As noted earlier, Chinese teachers urge their students to express mathematics ideas formally and precisely (Lopez-Real et al., 2004). In contrast, American teachers let their students express mathematics ideas informally (e.g. in their own words: see Cai, 2005; Schleppenbach et al., 2007).

Chinese students also used more conventional strategies than did American students to solve mathematics problems, resulting in highly accurate solutions (Cai, 2000; Wang & Lin, 2005). When asked if each girl or each boy gets more pizza when 7 girls share 2 pizzas equally and 3 boys share 1 pizza equally, the Chinese and American sixth-grade students used eight different strategies to solve the problem. For those who used appropriate strategies, over 90 per cent of the Chinese students used the conventional strategy of comparing the fractions 1/3 with 2/7. However, only about 20 per cent of the US students used this strategy. The majority of the American students used less precise, non-conventional strategies (e.g. 3 girls share a pizza and the other 4 girls share a pizza; each of the latter 4 girls gets less pizza than do each of the 3 boys).

Chinese students were able to generate more solutions than did American students, suggesting the effectiveness of the two-basics curriculum and coherent classroom instruction. When American seventh and eighth graders and Chinese sixth graders were asked to generate three different solutions to the above pizza problem, about 40 per cent of the Chinese students generated more than one solution, but only about 20 per cent of the American students did so. Again, Chinese students preferred abstract representations such as: 7/2 = 3.5 and 3/1 = 3; therefore 3.5 girls share 1 pizza and 3 boys share 1 pizza; so fewer boys share the same-size pizza and each one gets more pizza (Cai & Lester, 2005).

Chinese students appeared less willing to take risks to solve mathematics problems. Given a problem that they did not know how to solve, Chinese students were more likely to leave it blank, but American students often wrote down something anyway (Cai & Cifarelli, 2004). It is unclear why Chinese students did not want to guess an answer to the problem to which they did not have a solution. One speculation might be related to the beliefs of teachers about the nature of mathematics. Wong and his associates (N.-Y. Wong, Lam, K. Wong., Ma, & Han, 2002) reported that Chinese teachers tended to view mathematics as a fixed set of rules and algorithms discovered by great mathematicians. They believed that to learn mathematics is to master the rules and algorithms and to match them to types of problems to be solved. The conceptions of mathematics might lead to an oversight by the teachers on the aspects of mathematics thinking as induction, imagination and hypothesis testing in their mathematics teaching (Wong, 2002; Wong et al., 2002). This in turn might affect students' views about mathematics (e.g. getting right answers is the most important thing in learning mathematics) and consequently their approaches to learning the subject (e.g. less willing to take risks and to be creative).

It is an empirical question whether or not the conceptions of mathematics would make Chinese teachers more likely to discourage guessing at answers than are non-Chinese teachers, e.g. American teachers in classroom teaching and assessment. An additional reason might be that Chinese students were instructed by their teachers that it is dishonest for one to pretend to know when one does not know, which is a Confucian doctrine and also an aspect of moral education in schools of mainland China. In connection to this, the teachers might deduct marks for wrong answers to deter students from guessing in testing.

Despite the small samples involved, these observations suggest some limitations to Chinese students' mathematics achievement. One question is whether this is a trade-off for Chinese students' high performance on basic mathematics concepts and computations (especially with directive teachers and high student–teacher ratios). While directive teaching and coherent instruction in Chinese mathematics classrooms probably reduced ambiguity for students, it might also have constrained students from taking risks or being creative. The observations also serve as a caution for the importance of carefully interpreting Chinese and non-Chinese students' mathematics achievement in international studies.

The new mathematics curriculum of mainland China, which was implemented in 2006 (Ministry of Education, 2002), has taken note of the limitations to Chinese students' achievement in mathematics. The new curriculum will have a more balanced curricular and instructional treatment to nurture in Chinese students the skills of mathematical computations, the skills of carrying out mathematical explanations and communications, and interest in and disposition towards mathematics (Ni, Li, Cai, & Hau, 2008).

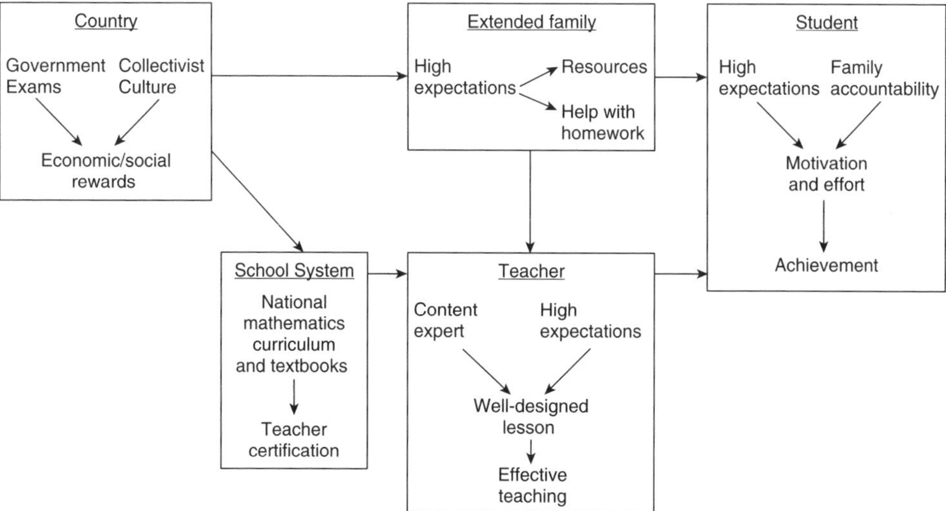

Fig. 10.1 Constituents of Chinese students' mathematics achievement.

In 2008, Professor Shing-Tung Yau of Harvard University, a Fields Medalist for mathematics, established the Yau Shing-Tung mathematics scholarship for secondary-school students in mainland China. In an interview, he was asked why he set up the scholarship since Chinese students have done so well in international assessments and mathematics Olympiads. Professor Yau explained that the scholarship can encourage Chinese students to pose meaningful mathematics questions and to work independently on a posed problem for a substantial period of time (such as a few months, rather than the few hours which is required by the Olympiads). Professor Yau's vision for Chinese mathematics education points to new horizons for Chinese students.

In sum, the Chinese students' mathematics achievement, for its strengths and weaknesses, is a result of the developmental, instructional, and social/cultural contexts that they experience (summarized in Figure 10.1). Moreover, the relationship of the contributing factors is viewed to be adaptive rather than additive (Stigler & Hiebert, 1999), as the factors function as parts of an ecological system. After all, Chinese students' mathematics achievement is a product of their enculturation.

References

Addison, J. T. & Schnabel, C. (2003). *International handbook of trade unions.* Northampton, MA: Edward Elgar.

Akiba, M., LeTendre, G. K., & Scribner, J. P. (2007). Teacher quality, opportunity gap, and national achievement in 46 countries. *Educational Researcher, 36*, 369–387.

Beaton, A. E., Mullis, I. V. S., Martin, M. O., Gonzalez, E. J., Kelly, D. L., & Smith, T. A. (1996). *Mathematics achievement in the middle school years: IEA's Third International Mathematics and Science Study (TIMSS).* Chestnut Hill, MA: Boston College.

Cai, J. (2000). Mathematical thinking involved in US and Chinese students' solving process-constrained and process-open problems. *Mathematical Thinking and Learning: An International Journal, 2*, 309–340.

Cai, J. (2005). US and Chinese teachers' constructing, knowing, and evaluating representations to teach mathematics. *Mathematical Thinking and Learning: An International Journal, 7*, 135–169.

Cai, J. & Cifarelli, V. (2004). Thinking mathematically by Chinese learners. In L. Fan, N.-Y. Wong, J. Cai, & S. Li (eds), *How Chinese learn mathematics: Perspectives from insiders* (pp. 71–106). River Edge, NJ: World Scientific.

Cai, J. & Hwang, S. (2002). Generalized and generative thinking in US and Chinese students' mathematical problem solving and problem posing. *Journal of Mathematical Behavior, 21*, 401–421.

Cai, J. & Lester J. (2005). Solution representations and pedagogical representations in Chinese and U.S. classrooms. *Journal of Mathematical Behavior, 24*, 221–237.

Cai, J. & Wong, T. (2006). US and Chinese teachers' conceptions and constructions of representations: A case of teaching ratio concept. *International Journal of Science and Mathematics Education, 4*, 145–186.

Chen, C. & Stevenson, H. W. (1989). Homework: A cross-cultural examination. *Child Development, 60*, 551–561.

Chen, C. & Stevenson, H. W. (1995). Motivation and mathematics achievement: A comparative study of Asian-American, Caucasian-American, and East-Asian high school students. *Child Development, 66*, 1215–1234.

Cheng, Z. J. (2007). <操作材料對兒童理解加減法關係和選擇計算策略的影響>.《教育學報》第35卷 頁 93–111. [The effects of teaching materials on children's understanding and choice of computational strategies in addition and subtraction. *Education Journal, 35*, 93–111.] (in Chinese)

Cheng, Z. J. (2008). <學前數學操作式和多元化:幼兒學習評估>. [*Operational Mathematics in Preschool: Children Learning Evaluation.*] Hong Kong: Layout Tuning Limited. (in Chinese)

Cheng, Z. J. & Chan, L. K. S. (2005). Chinese number-naming advantages? Analyses of Chinese preschoolers' computational strategies and errors. *The International Journal of Early Years Education, 13*, 179–192.

Cheng, Z. J., Chan, L. K. S., Li, Y. L, Ng, S. N., & Woo, Y. S. (2001). <香港入學前兒童真實的計算能力>.《教育學報》第29卷 頁 121–135. [Real computational skills of preschool children in Hong Kong. *Education Journal, 29*, 121–135.] (in Chinese)

Chiu, M. M. (2007). Families, economies, cultures and science achievement in 41 countries: Country, school, and student level analyses. *Journal of Family Psychology, 21*, 510–519.

Chiu, M. M. & Ho, S. C. (2006). Family effects on student achievement in Hong Kong. *Asian Pacific Journal of Education, 26*, 21–35.

Chiu, M. M. & Khoo, L. (2005). Effects of resources, inequality, and privilege bias on achievement: Country, school, and student level analyses *American Educational Research Journal, 42*, 575–603.

Chiu, M. M. & Zeng, X. (2008). Family and motivation effects on mathematics achievement. *Learning and Instruction, 18*, 321–336.

Clements, D. H. (2001). Mathematics in the preschool. *Teaching Children Mathematics, 7*, 270–276.

Correa, C. A., Perry, M., Sims, L. M., Miller, K. F., & Fang, G. (2008). Connected and culturally embedded beliefs: Chinese and US teachers talk about how their students best learn mathematics. *Teaching and Teacher Education, 24*, 140–153.

Davey, G., Lian, C. D., & Higgins, L. (2007). The university entrance examination system in China. *Journal of Further and Higher Education, 31*, 385–396.

Dhlin, B. & Watkins, D. A. (2000). The role of repetition in the processes of memorizing and understanding: A comparison of the views of Western and Chinese school students in Hong Kong. *British Journal of Educational Psychology, 70*, 65–84.

Fan, L. & Zhu, Y. (2004). How have Chinese students performed in mathematics? A perspective from large-scale international mathematics comparisons. In L. Fan, N.-Y. Wong, J. Cai, & S. Li (eds), *How Chinese learn mathematics: Perspectives from insiders* (pp. 3–26). River Edge, NJ: World Scientific.

Fuson, K. C. & Kwon, Y. (1991). Chinese-based regular and European irregular systems of number words: The disadvantages for English-speaking children. In K. Durkin & B. Shire (eds), *Language in mathematical education* (pp. 211–226). Philadelphia, PN: Open University Press.

Fuson, K. C., Smith, S. T., & Lo Cicero, A. M. (1997). Supporting Latino first graders' ten-structured thinking in urban classrooms. *Journal for Research in Mathematics Education, 28*, 738–766.

Gallistel, C. R. & Gelman, R. (1992). Preverbal and verbal counting and computation. *Cognition, 44*, 43–74.

Geary, D. C. (1994). *Children's mathematical development.* Washington, DC: American Psychological Association.

Geary, D. C., Bow-Thomas, C. C., Liu, F., & Siegler, R. S. (1993). Even before formal instruction, Chinese children outperform American children in mental addition. *Cognitive Development, 8*, 517–529.

Geary, D. C., Bow-Thomas, C. C., Liu, F., & Siegler, R. S. (1996). Development of arithmetical competencies in Chinese and American children: Influences of age, language, and schooling. *Child Development, 67*, 2022–2044.

Georgas, J., Mylonas, K., Bafiti, T., Poortinga, Y. H., Christakopoulou, S., Kağıtçıbaşı, Ç. et al. (2001). Functional relationships in the nuclear and extended family: A 16-culture study. *International Journal of Psychology, 36*, 289–300.

Ginsburg, H. P., Kaplan, R. G., Cannon, J., Cordero, M. I., Eisenband, J. G., Galanter, M., & Morgenlander, M. (2006). Helping early childhood educators to teach mathematics. In Z. Martha & I. Martinez-Beck, (eds), *Critical issues in early childhood professional development* (pp. 171–202). Baltimore, MD: Paul H. Brookes Publishing Co.

Hatano, G.. (1990). Toward the cultural psychology of mathematical cognition. Comment on Stevenson, H. W., & Lee, S.-Y. (1990). *Context of achievement: a study of American, Chinese, and Japanese children. Monographs of the Society for Research in Child Development, 55* (1–2, Serial No. 221), 108–115.

Hau, K. T., & Salili, F. (1996). Achievement goals and causal attributions of Chinese students. In S. Lau (ed.), *Growing up the Chinese way* (pp. 121–145). Hong Kong: The Chinese University Press.

Ho, C. S-H. & Fuson, K. C. (1998). Children's knowledge of teen quantities as tens and ones: Comparisons of Chinese, British, and American kindergartners. *Journal of Educational Psychology, 90*, 1536–1544.

Huang, R. & Leung, K. S. F. (2004). Cracking the paradox of Chinese learners: Looking into the mathematics classrooms in Hong Kong and Shanghai. In L. Fan, N. Y. Wong, J. Cai, & S. Li (eds) *How Chinese learn mathematics: Perspectives from insiders* (pp. 348–381). River Edge, NJ: World Scientific.

Huntsinger, C. S., Jose, P. E., Larson, S. L., Balsink, K. D., & Shalingram, C. (2000). Mathematics, vocabulary, and reading development in Chinese American and European American children over the primary school years. *Journal of Educational Psychology, 92*, 745–760.

Kelly, M. K. (2003). Getting ready for school: A cross-cultural comparisons for entry into first grade in China and the United States. *Dissertation Abstracts International, 63*(11-B), p. 5550.

Lam, C. C., Ho, E. S. C., & Wong, N. Y. (2002). Parents' beliefs and practices in education in Confucian heritage cultures: The Hong Kong Case. *Journal of Southeast Asian Education, 3*, 99–114.

Leung, F. K. S. (1995). The mathematics classroom in Beijing, Hong Kong, and London. *Educational Studies in Mathematics, 29*, 297–325.

Leung, F. K. S. (2001). In Search of an East Asian Identity in Mathematics Education. *Educational Studies in Mathematics, 47*, 35–51.

Li, J. (2003). US and Chinese cultural beliefs about learning. *Journal of Educational Psychology, 95*, 258–267.

Li, J.-H. (2004). Thorough understanding of the textbook—A significant feature of Chinese teacher manuals. In L. Fan, N.-Y. Wong, J. Cai, & S. Li (eds), *How Chinese learn mathematics:Perspectives from insiders* (pp. 262–279). River Edge, NJ: World Scientific.

Li, Q. & Ni. Y. J. (2007). <中國大陸新一輪基礎教育數學課程改革及其爭議>.《台灣數學教師期刊》第11卷 頁1–11. [Debates on the new mathematics curriculum for the compulsory education in Mainland China. *Taiwan Journal of Mathematics Teacher, 11*, 1–11.] (in Chinese)

Lopez-Real, R., Mok, A. C., Leung, K. S., & Marton, F. (2004). Identifying a pattern of teaching: An analysis of a Shanghai teacher's lessons. In L. Fan, N.-Y. Wong, J. Cai, & S. Li (eds), *How Chinese learn mathematics: Perspectives from insiders* (pp. 282–412). River Edge, NJ: World Scientific Publishing.

Ma, L. (1999). *Knowing and teaching elementary mathematics: Teachers' understanding of fundamental mathematics in China and the United States.* Mahwah, NJ: Erlbaum.

Mayer, R. (1986). Mathematics. In R. F. Dillon & R. J. Sternberg (eds), *Cognition and instruction* (pp. 127–154). San Diego, CA: Academic Press.

McLelland, G. (1991). Attainment targets and related targets in schools. In N. B. Crawford & E. K. P. Hui (eds), *The curriculum and behavior problems in Hong Kong: A response to the Education Commission Report No. 4* (Education Papers No. 11). Hong Kong: The University of Hong Kong, Faculty of Education.

Miller, K. F., Kelly, M., & Zhou, X. (2005). Learning mathematics in China and the United States: Cross-cultural insights into the nature and course of preschool mathematical development. In J. I. D. Campbell (ed.), *Handbook of mathematical cognition.* (pp. 163–177). New York: Psychology Press.

Miller, K. F., Major, S. M., Shu, H., & Zhang, H. (2000). Ordinal knowledge: Number names and number concepts in Chinese and English. *Canadian Journal of Experimental Psychology, 54*, 129–139.

Miller, K. F., Smith, C. M., Zhu, J., & Zhang, H. (1995). Preschool origins of cross-national differences in mathematical competence: The role of number-naming systems. *Psychological Science, 6*, 56–60.

Ministry of Education (2002). <九年義務教育數學科課程標准 >. [Curriculum Standards for Mathematics Curriculum of Nine-Year Compulsory Education. Beijing: Ministry of Education.] (in Chinese)

Miura, I. T., Okamoto, Y., Kim, C. C., Chang, C.-M., Steere, M., & Fayol, M. (1994). Comparisons of children's cognitive representation of number: China, France, Japan, Korea, Sweden, and the United States. *International Journal of Behavioral Development, 17*, 401–411.

Ni, Y. J. & Li, Q. (2009). *Effects of curriculum reform: Looking for evidence of change in classroom practice.* Paper presented at the Chinese-European Conference on Curriculum Development, The Hague, The Netherlands, March.

Ni, Y. J., Li, Q., Cai, J., & Hau, K. T. (2008). *Effects of a reformed curriculum on student learning outcomes in primary mathematics.* Paper present at the Annual Meeting of American Educational Research Association, New York, March.

Ni, Y. J. & Zhou, Y. (2005). Teaching and learning fraction and rational numbers: The origin and implications of whole number bias. *Educational Psychologist, 40*, 27–52.

Organization for Economic Cooperation and Development (OECD) (2003). *Literacy skills for the world of tomorrow.* Paris: Author.

Othman, N. A. (2004). Language influence on Children's Cognitive Number Representation. *School Science and Mathematics, 104*, 105–111.

Reitz, J. G. & Verma, A. (2004). Immigration, race, and labor. *Industrial Relations, 43*, 835–854.

Saxton, S. & Towse, J. N. (1998). Linguistic relativity: The case of place value in multi-digit numbers. *Journal of Experimental Child Psychology, 69*, 66–79.

Schleppenbach, Perry, Miller, Sims & Fang (2007). Answer is only the beginning: extended discourse in Chinese and US Mathematics classrooms. *Journal of Educational Psychology, 99*, 380–396.

Sirin, S. R. (2005). Socioeconomic status and academic achievement: A meta-analytic review of literature. *Review of Educational Research, 75*, 417–453.

Starkey, P. & Klein, A. (2008). Sociocultural influences on young children's mathematical knowledge. In O. N. Saracho & B. Spodek (eds), *Contemporary perspectives on mathematics in early childhood education* (pp. 45–66). Baltimore. MD: IAP, INC.

Stevenson, H. W., Lee, S. Y., Chen, C., Lummis, M., Stigler, J. W., Liu, F., & Fang, G. (1990). Mathematics achievement of children in China and the United States. *Child Development, 61*, 1055–1066.

Stevenson, H. W. & Stigler, J. W. (1992). *The learning gap.* New York: Simon & Schuster.

Stevenson, H. W., Stigler, J. W., Lee, S.-Y., Lucker, G. W., Kitamura, S., & Hsu, C. C. (1985). Cognitive performance and academic achievement of Japanese, Chinese, and American children. *Child Development, 56*, 718–734.

Stigler, J. W. & Hiebert, J. (1999). *The teaching gap.* New York: Free Press.

Stigler, J. W., Lee, S. Y., & Stevenson, H. W. (1990). *Mathematical knowledge of Japanese, Chinese, and American elementary school children.* Reston, VA: National Council of Teachers of Mathematics.

Stigler, J. W., Lee, S., & Stevenson, H. W. (1987). Mathematics classrooms in Japan, Taiwan, and the United States. *Child Development, 58*, 1272–1285.

Suen, H. K. & Yu, L. (2006). Chronic consequences of high-stakes testing? Lessons from the Chinese civil service exam. *Comparative Education Review, 50*, 46–65.

Towse, J. N. & Saxton, M. (1997). Linguistic influences on children's number concepts: methodological and theoretical considerations. *Journal of Experimental Child Psychology, 66*, 362–375.

Wang, J. & Lin, E. (2005). Comparative studies on US and Chinese mathematical learning and the implications for standards-based mathematics teaching reform. *Educational Researcher, 34*, 3–13.

Wang, T. & Murphy, J. (2004). An examination of coherence in a Chinese mathematics classroom. In L. Fan, N. Y. Wong, J. Cai, & S. Li (eds), *How Chinese learn mathematics Perspectives from insiders* (pp. 107–123). River Edge, NJ: World Scientific.

Whang, P. A. & Hancock, G. R. (1994). Motivation and mathematics achievement: Comparisons between Asian-American and non-Asian students. *Contemporary Educational Psychology, 19*, 302–322.

Wise, Lauress L., Steel, L., & MacDonald, C. (1979). *Origins and career consequences of sex differences in high school mathematics achievement.* Palo Alto, CA: American Institute for Research.

Wong, N.-Y. (2004). The CHC learner's phenomenon: Its implications for mathematics education. In L. Fan, N.-Y. Wong, J. Cai, & S. Li (eds), *How Chinese learn mathematics: Perspectives from insiders* (pp. 503–534). River Edge, NJ: World Scientific.

Wong, N.-Y. (1993). Mathematics education in Hong Kong: Development in the last decade. In G. Bell (ed.), *Asian perspectives on mathematics education* (pp. 56–69). Lismore, Australia: Northern Rivers Mathematical Association.

Wong, N.-Y. (2002). <數學觀研究綜述>.《數學教育學報》第11卷 第1期, 頁1–7. [State of the art in conception of mathematics research. *Journal of Mathematics Education, 11*, 1–7.] (in Chinese)

Wong, N.-Y., Lam, C. C., Wong, K. M., Ma, Y. P., & Han, J. W. (2002). <中國內地中學教師的數學觀>.《課程、教材、教法》第1期, 頁 68–73. [Conceptions of mathematics by middle school teachers in mainland China. *Curriculum, Teaching Materials and Methods, 1*, 68–73.] (in Chinese)

Zhang, D., Li, S., & Tang, R. (2004). The 'two basics:' Mathematics teaching and learning in Mainland China. In L. Fan, N.-Y. Wong, J. Cai, & S. Li (eds), *How Chinese learn mathematics Perspectives from insiders* (pp. 189–207). River Edge, NJ: World Scientific.

CHAPTER 11

The thinking styles of Chinese people

Li-Jun Ji, Albert Lee, and Tieyuan Guo

For centuries, ancient China has been known to the West as the largest exporter of tea, porcelain, and silk. The Four Great Inventions of China—the compass, gunpowder, paper, and printing—are also celebrated by Westerners as the jewels of Chinese wisdom that have exerted a tremendous impact on the technological growth of civilizations all over the world. However, Chinese thought processes have been difficult to comprehend—'inscrutable' is the term most often favored by the Western world to describe this puzzlement. Thus, especially since the turn of the twentieth century, Westerners have expressed serious curiosity about and appreciation of the philosophical endeavours of the Chinese and the cognitive strategies they use for everyday functioning.

In this chapter, we will discuss the many important differences in the thinking styles between Chinese and European North Americans. 'Thinking styles' here is a generic term. To be precise, it represents the ontological frameworks that people use intuitively to make sense of their social world. In other words, these frameworks can be seen as the 'building blocks' for the construction and perception of reality (Jones & Nisbett, 1972). In this chapter, the term 'European North Americans' primarily refers to Americans and Canadians of European descent. We sometimes use 'Americans' or 'North Americans' as the short form. In the next section, we will describe how Chinese favor a more holistic framework (i.e., attending to the entire field, accepting contradiction and non-linear change) in processing information, whereas European North Americans rely on a more analytical framework that emphasizes the use of formal logic and one-to-one relationships. We will then discuss a concept central to understanding Chinese thinking: *zhong yong*, or the doctrine of the mean, which encapsulates the virtues of pursuing the middle ground. We will also examine another hallmark of Chinese thinking: the belief that things can change from one extreme to another. Finally, we will end the chapter with brief summaries of the major schools of Chinese philosophies (e.g. Confucianism, Taoism, and Buddhism) and their roles in shaping modern Chinese thinking.

Holistic versus analytic thinking

Perhaps one of the biggest surprises for contemporary psychologists is the discovery that people do not necessarily perceive and respond to their social world in the same manner. Up to this point, researchers have conceptualized two frameworks that are qualitatively distinct from one another, and it is assumed that whichever framework becomes the default largely depends on the specific cultural environment in which people are submerged. A large body of cross-cultural research has shown that Westerners have a proclivity to meet their daily challenges in an analytic fashion, whereas traditional Chinese tend to take a holistic approach in response to their everyday demands (see Nisbett, 2003; Nisbett, Peng, Choi, & Norenzayan, 2001 for a review). One characteristic of analytic thinking is the tendency to extract the underlying properties of an object or phenomenon from its context. Allegedly influenced by Platonic philosophy, analytic thinkers believe that social information should be defined and organized on the basis of their inherent qualities. Peripheral details are regarded as 'shadows of the real world' which we derive from the material world, which makes them unreliable sources in the understanding of true forms (Plato, 360 BC/1956). Decontextualization is also a foundation in the study of argumentation. It concerns the abstract, universal representation of ideas and statements. Thus, in analytical thinking, the truthfulness (i.e. validity and soundness) of an argument requires a logical evaluation of its pure structure and not of its context.

Holistic thinking lies in stark contrast to analytic thinking. In this framework, nothing exists in isolation; things are interconnected with each other, be this directly or indirectly. Thus, contemplation of the entire field is the hallmark of this mode of thinking. Objects are defined mainly in terms of their connections with their contexts, whereas knowledge tends to be organized in a thematic and relational fashion (see also Ji, Zhang, & Nisbett, 2004; Morris & Peng, 1994; Peng & Nisbett, 1999). In short, it is the dynamics among the elements, rather than the elements themselves, that serve as the primary units of analysis in the eyes of holistic thinkers.

Perception

Ji, Peng, and Nisbett (2000) offered empirical support to the idea that the tendency towards holistic thinking differs across cultures. Specifically, they asked East Asians (mainly Chinese) and European-American students in the United States to complete the *rod-and-frame test.* In this task, a rod is positioned inside a frame. Both the frame and rod can be rotated independently of one another. The task for participants is to determine when the rod is at a vertical position, regardless of the orientation of the frame surrounding it. European-Americans made significantly fewer errors than East Asians. Moreover, such cultural discrepancy in performance was not due to a speed–accuracy trade-off, as the reaction time of both cultural groups was comparable. This set of results suggests that the East-Asian sample had greater difficulty dissociating an object from its context, indicating that they were more field-dependent than their American counterparts.

Although our focus is on research pertaining to Chinese thinking, the cross-cultural literature does contain work showing that East Asians, in general, are more holistic and Americans are more analytic. For instance, Masuda and Nisbett (2001) presented European-American and Japanese participants with eight animated vignettes of underwater scenes, each containing a focal object (e.g. a fish) surrounded by other marine elements (e.g. seaweed, rocks, or other inconspicuous creatures). After viewing these vignettes, participants were given a surprise recall test on what they had seen. Results showed that Japanese remembered significantly more background information (e.g. bubbles) and inert objects (e.g. plants and seashells) than did the Americans. However, no cultural difference emerged in their ability to recall the focal fish or other living creatures (e.g. other fish, frogs). Additionally, an examination of the first item in their recall list revealed that Americans tended to start off by mentioning the more salient objects in the vignettes, whereas Japanese were more likely to begin with inert and background objects. These results led to the conclusion that, not only do ontological frameworks influence perception, but they also influence memory.

Categorization

Another cognitive task on which Chinese and European-Americans have shown systematic differences is categorization (Chiu, 1972; Ji, Zhang, & Nisbett, 2004). This is perhaps not so surprising, considering that Chinese tend to navigate their thoughts by contextual and relational details, whereas Westerners are more inclined to interpret the world based on the underlying properties of the object. Early evidence came from a study conducted by Chiu (1972), in which the researcher asked fourth and fifth graders in China and the United States to classify pictures of different objects. It was found that American children showed a strong preference for categorizing objects on the basis of physical similarities (e.g. grouping human figures together 'because they are both holding a gun'). In contrast, Chinese children tended to make their categorization decisions in terms of how the objects were thematically related to each other (e.g. grouping human figures together 'because the mother takes care of the baby').

Ji, Zhang, and Nisbett (2004) replicated Chiu's (1972) study with a more demographically diverse sample, which included European American university students in the United States, and Chinese university students recruited from the United States, mainland China, Taiwan, Hong Kong, and Singapore. Chinese students were tested either in English or Chinese, whereas Americans were tested only in English. All participants were presented with sets of three words (e.g. monkey, panda, and banana), and asked to select the word pair that were most closely related. Each triad of words was designed such that there were two meaningful ways of grouping. For example, if monkey and banana were selected, that would be a decision based on thematic relationships. If, however, monkey and panda were selected, then the outcome would constitute a grouping based on taxonomic categories.

Ji et al. (2004) found that, regardless of the testing location and testing language, Chinese students showed a greater preference for relational (thematic) groupings than did European Americans, who preferred categorical (taxonomic) groupings more than relational groupings. The European Americans' tendency to group categorically can be taken as a reflection of their cultural penchant for formal logic rules, whereas the Chinese tendency to group relationally speaks to the holistic nature of their thinking style.

In a series of experiments, Norenzayan, Smith, Kim, and Nisbett (2002) showed that, when asked to categorize pictorial objects, the physical resemblance among these objects (i.e., examplar-based categorization) exerted more influence on East Asians than on European Americans, who tended to make rule-based categorization. In each trial, European Americans and East Asians (Chinese and Koreans) were to pair up an imaginary animal with one of two other animals: one from Venus and the other from Saturn. Participants in the rule-based condition were given complex rules to determine the membership of the target animal. When physical resemblance pointed to one answer but the rules suggested a different one, East Asians, compared to European Americans, were more willing to set aside the rules in favor of the physical resemblance, resulting in slower responses and more errors.

In a subsequent study, Norenzayan and colleagues (2002) asked participants to categorize a target into one of two sets of artificially created objects. The stimuli were constructed in such a way that selecting one category suggested the use of a rule-based categorization style, while selecting the other category suggested a categorization style based on overall physical resemblance. Results indicated that European Americans were more likely to solve the problems by searching for a defining characteristic that was shared by the target object and the stimuli objects, whereas East Asians were more likely to evaluate the overall physical resemblance between the target object and the two stimuli groups. These findings provided support for the prediction that the tendency for exemplar-based categorization is stronger in East Asians, whereas the preference for rule-based categorization is stronger in European Americans. Such cultural difference is especially pronounced when the two systems of categorizations are interfering with one another.

Attribution styles

The cultural divergence in thinking styles between Chinese and European North Americans also manifests itself in their respective ways of making causal attributions. The discovery of the fundamental attribution error among European Americans was a demonstration of an interesting bias in social settings. Essentially, the fundamental attribution error occurs when we over-attribute someone's behavior to personal dispositions and underestimate the role of the situation in bringing about the behavior. Given the tendency of Chinese to conceptualize objects in relation to the context, they would be expected to show a weaker level of the fundamental attribution error than European Americans.

This phenomenon was indeed demonstrated by Morris and Peng (1994), who found that, in comparison with European Americans, Chinese participants made fewer internal attributions and more external attributions, but this was true only for social events (e.g. the swimming pattern of a school of fish) but not physical events (e.g. the trajectory of balls). In subsequent studies, the researchers also found that, when reporting on the same story, Chinese-language newspaper reporters made fewer dispositional attributions for a crime than their English-language counterparts. Interestingly, American reporters were found to show the 'ultimate attribution error', whereas Chinese reporters did not. This ultimate attribution error involved Americans making more dispositional attributions for a Chinese murderer than for an American murderer, thus showing in-group bias. In a similar study, they asked both Chinese and European American graduate students to 'weight' the importance of the causes offered by various media sources for a particular murder. Chinese weighted situational factors more heavily while European Americans assigned greater weight to accounts related to personal dispositions. Chinese participants also believed that the murders would have been much less likely to occur had the situational factors been different.

In a study examining the attribution styles contained in sports articles and editorials found in American and Chinese (Hong Kong) newspapers, Lee, Hallahan, and Herzog (1996) found that attributions made in American articles were generally more dispositional than those in the Chinese articles. In addition, American sports articles contained significantly more dispositional attributions than American editorials. In contrast, Hong Kong sports articles were higher in situational attribution than were Hong Kong editorials. Overall, American sports articles were highest in making dispositional attribution, followed by American editorials, Hong Kong editorials, and finally, Hong Kong sports articles.

These findings not only support the previous finding that Americans are more dispositional and Chinese more situational in their attributions, but they also extend the research to show that these differences are attenuated when cognitive effort is applied. Lee and colleagues (1996) suggested that, contrary to sports articles, editorials deal with more complex subject matter that are more ambiguous and open to multiple interpretations. Also, editorials are more often subject to greater accountability and public scrutiny. For these reasons, editorial writers tend to expend more cognitive energy in editorial writing than do sports writers. As a result, American editorials are less dispositional and Chinese editorials are less situational than are their sports counterparts.

Chinese *zhong yong* (midway) thinking

Zhong yong, or the doctrine of the mean, advocates moderation and modesty in the interest of achieving and maintaining interpersonal harmony. Similar to holism, the *zhong yong* mode of thinking emphasizes looking at the whole picture. However, the *zhong yong* principle focuses more on social morals and aims at providing guidelines for people's behavior and attitudes. According to the *zhong yong* principle, people should consider things carefully from different perspectives, avoid going to extremes, behave in situationally appropriate ways, and maintain interpersonal harmony. The concept is central to understanding the ways Chinese people navigate themselves in interpersonal relationships (Wu & Lin, 2005; Yang & Chiu, 1997; See also Kwan, Hui, & McGee, this volume).

The *zhong yong* approach in resolving conflicts

When social conflicts arise, *zhong yong* suggests that one should examine the situation carefully and inspect the opinions and interests of other people from various perspectives. Actions should be taken only after such contemplation. Such an approach is believed to facilitate a reasonable resolution, usually by taking 'the middle way' through cooperative and compromise strategies in resolving interpersonal conflicts.

It is considered more important to maintain harmony with family members and friends than with those who are not in the immediate social network (see also Hwang & Han; Leung & Au, this volume). Thus, the endorsement of *zhong yong* thinking should associate with more resolutions between people who are close than those who are not. Consistent with this reasoning, Wang and colleagues (2008) found that Chinese university students were more likely to adopt behaviors that were consistent with *zhong yong* ideals when solving conflicts with people to whom they were close than not.

Because of the influence of the *zhong yong* principle, Chinese are expected to adopt a compromising approach in solving interpersonal conflicts more than Americans. To test this prediction, Peng and Nisbett (1999) presented Chinese and American participants with a mother–daughter conflict scenario, as shown below, and asked them to describe how such a conflict happened and what the mother and daughter should do:

> Mary, Phoebe, and Julie all have daughters. Each mother has held a set of values which has guided her efforts to raise her daughter. Now the daughters have grown up, and each of them is rejecting many of her mother's values.

Peng and Nisbett found that Chinese students tended to blame both the mother and the daughter for causing the conflict and proposed a compromise approach to solve the problem. In contrast, Americans tended to blame only one individual, either the mother or the daughter, and believed that the person at fault should change, reflecting a non-compromise approach to solving the interpersonal conflict.

Zhong yong thinking affects not only how people deal with interpersonal conflicts, but also the approaches people adopt to solve conflicts in other domains. In the study discussed above, Peng and Nisbett (1999) also presented European-American and Chinese participants with an intrapsychic conflict between having fun and doing schoolwork. Again, they found that Chinese students were more likely to use compromise solutions than were American students.

Furthermore, in a study of consumer decision-making behavior, Briley, Morris, and Simonson (2000) presented Americans and Hong Kong Chinese with a series of consumer product categories, such as computers and portable CD players, and asked them to choose a product from each category. Within each category, participants were presented with two extreme options (i.e. options that 'are best on one dimension and worst on the other', e.g. a computer with a large RAM and a small hard drive, and another computer with a small RAM and a large hard drive) and a compromise option (i.e. a compromise between the two dimensions, e.g. a computer with a RAM of moderate size and a hard drive of moderate size). In one condition, before making the choice, participants were asked to write down the key reasons to justify their choices. The justification manipulation aimed at highlighting the cultural ideals on how to make a choice when having contradictions. The researchers found that in the justification condition, Hong Kong Chinese chose the compromise options more than Americans did, even though the two groups did not differ in the control condition when no justification was required before choice.

Emotion regulation

The *zhong yong* principle discourages the experience and expression of extreme emotions, as they are believed to disrupt psychological well-being and social harmony. Instead, people are encouraged to hold and express peaceful or moderate emotions (see also Yik, this volume).

Consistent with the *zhong yong* principle, empirical research has shown that the desirable or ideal affective state for Chinese people in Hong Kong is low-arousal positive states, such as calm, relaxed, and peaceful. In contrast, the ideal affective for European Americans is high-arousal positive states, such as enthusiastic, excited, and elated (Tsai, 2007). For example, when reporting their ideal affects, European Americans valued high-arousal positive affects more and low-arousal positive affects less than Hong Kong Chinese. Chinese Americans were positioned in between, due to their bicultural background (Tsai, Knutson, & Fung, 2006). The same pattern of results was also found with European American children (aged between three and five years old) and their Chinese counterparts in Taiwan (Tsai, Louie, Chen, & Uchida, 2007).

Ethnographic studies suggest that Chinese culture places a greater emphasis on emotion moderation and control than does North American culture (Potter, 1988). In Chinese culture, emotion moderation and control are believed to be beneficial to both the individual and the society (Bond, 1993). Chinese children, for instance, are socialized to control impulse at a young age (Ho, 1994).

Tsai and Levenson (1997) provided empirical evidence that Chinese-American dating couples showed more emotion moderation in their conversation than their European-American counterparts. Similarly, Soto, Levenson, and Ebling (2005) found that Chinese Americans reported experiencing significantly less extreme negative and positive emotions than did Mexican Americans.

Subjective well-being

As discussed above, people influenced by *zhong yong* thinking tend to examine daily situations from different perspectives. Thus, they tend to have good interpersonal skills which may lead to a more successful social life in a Chinese cultural environment. As a result, *zhong yong* thinkers may have higher levels of overall life satisfaction. Wu (2006) investigated the relationship between *zhong yong* thinking and overall life satisfaction among university students in Taiwan. To assess a person's level of *zhong yong* thinking, he administrated the *zhong yong* thinking style scale developed by Wu and Lin (2005) to university students. As expected, Wu found a positive effect of *zhong yong* thinking on overall life satisfaction, which was sequentially mediated by social competence and the quality of the respondent's social life.

One may need to be cautious when generalizing such a finding, however (see also Lu, this volume). The positive relationship between *zhong yong* thinking and life satisfaction may not necessarily hold in Western contexts. Wu's (2006) study was conducted in a Chinese context, where *zhong yong* thinking is both pervasive and prized. However, in a Western context, *zhong yong* thinking and associated enactments are not mainstream, and may not fit as well into the Western social cultural context. For example, a person trying to compromise in conflicts may be perceived as weak, indecisive, and incompetent. Such a reputation might lead to negative consequences in social life, and one's subsequent self-assessment and subjective well-being.

Chinese belief in change

People develop lay (or implicit) theories to make sense of how events develop over time (see also Leung, this volume). Such lay theories of change affect people's predictions, decisions, and subsequent behaviors. Ji and colleagues (Ji et al., 2001; Ji, 2005) have argued that Americans and Chinese have different predominant lay theories of change. The Chinese lay theory of change is nonlinear, even cyclical. To most Chinese, events are changing all the time and they change in a cyclical fashion. In addition, many events are believed to be associated with one another. In contrast, European North Americans tend to hold a relatively linear theory of change, that is, a belief in either no change or change only in a linear fashion (e.g. things at rest tend to stay at rest; things in motion tend to stay in motion).

In a series of studies, Ji, Nisbett, & Su (2001) found that Chinese were more likely than Americans to predict changes in event development, changes in the directions of change, and changes in the rates of change. For example, when asked to predict the probability that two children who are fighting in kindergarten will become lovers one day, Chinese reported higher probabilities than did Americans. In addition, people who anticipated change to occur were perceived to be wiser by Chinese than by Americans. Thus, it appears that, in comparison with European North Americans, Chinese make fewer linear predictions but more non-linear or cyclical predictions. Different lay theories of change across cultures have implications for reasoning, information processing, judgment and decision making, and optimism, to name a few.

Implications for stock market decisions

One implication of these culture-specific ways of viewing change is that people may behave differently when investing in the stock market. In comparison with North Americans, Chinese would make more non-linear predictions for stock prices, (i.e. expecting the price of a falling stock to go up and expecting the price of a rising stock to go down). As a result, Chinese participants would be more likely than Americans to keep or buy falling stocks and sell rising stocks. Such a tendency for investors to hold on to their losing stocks longer than the winning ones is called the *disposition effect* in behavioral finance (Odean, 1998; Shefrin & Statman, 1985).

Research conducted in the laboratory and online has found that Chinese show a greater disposition effect than North Americans (Ji, Zhang, & Guo, 2008). When presented with simple stock market trends, compared with Canadians, Chinese were less willing to sell and more willing to buy falling stock. But when the stock price was rising, the opposite occurred: Chinese were less willing to buy and more willing to sell. When presented with complex stock price trends, Canadians were strongly influenced by the most recent price trends: they tended to predict that recent trends would persist and made selling decisions without considering the rest of the trend patterns. In contrast, Chinese made reversed predictions for the dominant trends, and made decisions that took both recent and early trends into consideration. The results were replicated with experienced individual investors. The findings in these studies are consistent with Ji et al. (2001), in which American participants, more often than Chinese participants, relied on immediate temporal information to form predictions and generally predicted a continuation of the immediate trends.

Implications for appreciating regression toward the mean

Another implication of these different lay theories of change in different cultures lies in cultural differences in appreciation for regression toward the mean. Past research has demonstrated that people often fail to understand the phenomenon of regression toward the mean, a fact that those with extreme scores on any measure at one point in time will, for purely statistical reasons, probably have less extreme scores (or scores closer to the mean) the next time they are tested. When people encounter a regression, they tend to invent spurious explanations to account for it. Given that North Americans expect linear change, it is not surprising that there is evidence that they fail to anticipate regression toward the mean. Whether they are given an extreme measure at one point in time, a succession of extreme measures, or a trend that is progressing towards an extreme point, North Americans tend to predict a similar or more extreme value for a subsequent measure. In contrast, Chinese are more likely to expect non-linear change over time: if given a trend that is progressing toward an extreme point, they tend to predict a less extreme result on a subsequent measure. Similarly, if given an extreme outcome at one point in time or a succession of extreme outcomes, Chinese tend to predict a subsequently less extreme outcome.

Thus, Chinese are expected to be more likely than North Americans to anticipate regression toward the mean. Ji, Spina, Ross, Zhang, and Li (in press) conducted a few studies to investigate culture differences in predicting and understanding regression toward the mean. They found, with tasks in such domains as athletic competition, health, and weather, that Chinese were more likely than Canadians to make predictions consistent with regression toward the mean. They also demonstrated that Chinese were more likely than Canadians to choose a regression-consistent explanation to account for regression toward the mean (e.g. believing that an extremely positive performance by an individual is not typical of that individual's abilities and indeed is a chance performance). This result suggests that not only did Chinese participants think more in line with regression toward the mean, but they also understood the rationale behind the phenomenon better than Canadian participants did.

It is important to examine cultural differences in understanding regression toward the mean, as different predispositions could have significant practical implications. When regression-consistent phenomena take place, members of an international team may have different explanations for them (see Thomas & Liao, this volume). For example, a new intervention program may appear to be effective, whereas in fact the improvement or success is entirely due to chance or random factors. A Canadian team member may choose to invest more resources in the program whereas a Chinese team member may insist otherwise. Likewise, a Canadian may suggest canceling a program that seems to have failed due to regression toward the mean, whereas a Chinese may disagree. Depending on the intragroup dynamics of conflict resolution at play, these differences may lead to unnecessary conflict among members and result in poorly executed decisions (see Leung &Au, this volume).

Implications for optimism

The predominant Chinese lay theory of change may allow individuals to predict more change when life is moving in a positive direction, or when life seems to be getting worse. Thus, Chinese people may remain hopeful when suffering hardship, and remain watchful and cautious when experiencing good fortune. In contrast, the predominant linear theory of change held by most European North Americans may lead them to predict that things will simply continue as they are. We therefore expect that Chinese people would be more optimistic than North Americans when faced with a negative situation and more pessimistic than North Americans in a positive situation. Two pieces of evidence support these predictions.

Ji and colleagues (Ji, Zhang, Usborne, & Guan, 2004) conducted a survey to investigate optimism across cultures in the context of the SARS (severe acute respiratory syndrome) outbreaks in Canada and China. They measured unrealistic optimism among Chinese students in Beijing and European Canadians in Toronto in the context of SARS. Participants were first asked to estimate their own chance of being infected relative to an average person of similar gender and age, on a scale ranging from 1 (much less likely than an average person) to 5 (much more likely than an average person). Although both groups demonstrated unrealistic optimism (i.e., reporting that they themselves were less likely than an average person to become infected with SARS), such optimistic bias was stronger among Chinese than among Canadians.

Then participants were asked to estimate their own chance of being infected. Compared to the actual infection rates in Beijing (.018 per cent) and Toronto (.005 per cent), both Chinese (1.79 per cent) and Canadian (10.28 per cent) participants overestimated their own chances of being infected, indicating that they were being pessimistic. Indeed, Canadians were more pessimistic than Chinese by over-estimating their own chance of getting infected to a much greater degree. In addition, even though Chinese reported more inconvenience to themselves brought about by SARS than did Canadians, they also reported more positive changes, reflecting the Chinese dialectical views of events.

Ji and colleagues (see Ji, Zhang, & Usborne, under review) also conducted three laboratory studies to investigate cross-cultural differences in optimistic responses in positive and negative contexts. When asked to list all kinds of outcome events following a target-positive or target-negative event, Canadians were more likely than Chinese to anticipate positive outcomes following positive events and negative outcomes following negative events. The researchers also found that cultural differences in optimism were somewhat dependent on lay theories of change, contributing to our understanding of the mechanism underlying cultural differences in optimism.

Developmental origins of beliefs in change

Previous research has provided convincing evidence that Chinese and North Americans have different lay theories of change: implicit beliefs about how the world develops and changes over time (see also Leung, this volume). To further investigate the relationships between culture and lay theories of change, it is essential to examine the issue from a developmental perspective. Specifically, how do children in different cultures develop these lay theories, and when do cultural differences in predictions start to emerge?

Ji (2008) compared Chinese and Canadian children in order to examine cultural and developmental differences in lay theories of change. Chinese and Canadian children (aged seven, nine, and eleven years) made predictions about hypothetical people's future performance, relationships, happiness, and parental incomes based on a series of scenarios. Change was measured by the absolute difference between a state given in the scenario and children's predicted state. Overall, Chinese children predicted greater change than did Canadian children, indicating that they believed more in change than did the Canadians. Moreover, cultural differences increased significantly with age. In comparison with their Canadian counterparts, Chinese children made no more change predictions at age seven, made slightly more change predictions at age nine, and made significantly more change predictions at age eleven. This was true for questions starting with an extremely positive or negative state and those starting with a neutral state.

The results are attributable to different socialization processes for Chinese and North American children (see Wang & Chang, this volume). In particular, Chinese socialization focuses on the idea of transformation between failure and success, the importance of effort and self-improvement, and harmonizing negative emotional experience. In contrast, North American socialization emphasizes children's success and good feelings about themselves (especially about their abilities), and values self-expression and self-understanding. These cultural differences in socialization may, in turn, have led to differences in reasoning among Chinese and North American children. Together with Miller's study (1984) in which she found that cultural differences in person descriptions between Americans and Indians became divergent with age, this study by Ji (2008) suggests that cultural influences on reasoning processes follow certain developmental trajectories, and that a period may exist at which the acculturation process starts to exert significant influence.

Malleability of the belief in change

Cultural psychologists are expected not only to describe cultural differences, but also to explain them. One way of unpackaging culture is to search for the corresponding psychological constructs that are responsible for cultural differences (Bond & van de Vijver, 2009). In terms of understanding cultural differences in lay theories of change, one may ask: are there any contextual factors contributing to cultural differences in change predictions; if so, can we make people think differently by changing or highlighting such contextual factors?

One candidate that can account for the cultural divergence in lay theories of change is the differential tendency to attend to the past. Specifically, Ji and colleagues (Ji, Guo, Zhang, & Messervey 2009) found that Chinese attended to a greater range of past information than did Canadians. In two studies, Canadian and Chinese participants read a description of a theft that had taken place. They were then presented with a list of behaviors exhibited by various people who were associated with the theft. The behaviors occurred in either the past or the present. The task was to rate how relevant each behavioral item was in helping to solve the theft case. Chinese participants rated behaviors that had taken place in the past as more relevant to solving the case than did Canadians, indicating that Chinese considered the past to be more important for solving the case. Also in a recall task, Chinese participants recalled more past behavioral items than did Canadians. Another study in which participants recalled the first day of class two weeks after it had taken place showed that Chinese participants recalled more details about past events than did Canadians. Overall, Chinese attended to a greater range of past information than did Canadians, a finding that has significant theoretical and practical implications.

After establishing cultural differences in attending to the past, the next question is whether such cultural differences would lead to different beliefs about change. Guo and Ji (2008) conducted a couple of studies to show that, after recalling their past, or after looking at words and pictures associated with the past, both Chinese and Canadian participants were more likely to predict reversals in trend developments rather than continuation, indicating that attending to the past may have allowed participants to be more aware of non-linear changes and therefore make more non-linear predictions. This research thus has successfully unpackaged culture by examining the mediating factor, attending to the past.

While empirical works on the existing differences between Chinese and North Americans are abundant, theories that speculate the historical origins of such differences remain limited. It is widely believed that the systematic discrepancies between the mindsets of Chinese and North American people are fostered and reinforced by their very unique philosophical traditions. We will end the chapter by a brief discussion of the major Chinese intellectual traditions while contrasting them with Greek philosophies.

Chinese philosophies

From the beginning, Chinese and Greek philosophies have followed very different routes. These intellectual traditions are markedly dissimilar in a number of ways: topics of concern, general objectives, approaches to problems, and even the basic principles they assume (i.e. axioms). This differentiation is by no means a coincidence. The cultural success of a novel philosophical idea depends on its compatibility with numerous factors, such as cultural propensities,[1] ecological conditions, and socioeconomic structures (for a detailed review, see Berry, 1976; Diamond, 1997; Mu, 1997; Nisbett, 2003). It is not surprising, then, for Chinese and Greek philosophical traditions to proceed in different directions. China has historically been an agrarian culture that demanded high levels of cooperation and mutual support (Yang, 1986). As a result, intellectual discussions have focused on the ways to restrict personal desires in exchange for a harmonious and orderly society. In fact, the three major schools of thoughts in traditional China—Confucianism, Buddhism, and Taoism—all revolve around issues on two levels of harmony: the harmony between individuals and the harmony between humanity and the capricious Great Nature.

Confucianism

Confucianism provides relatively lucid interpretations of the law of nature and a set of rather unambiguous moral guidelines (Berger, 2008; Fung, 1983; Hansen, 2000; Mu, 1997). Central to this tradition is the awareness that one's existence is defined by the countless interpersonal connections in one's social matrix. Thus, every individual is attached with different social roles ascribed by the society, and is expected to carry out the particular duties associated with each role in a socially appropriate fashion (Mu, 1997; Munro, 1985; Zhai, 2006).

The doctrine of the mean and the law of the excluded middle. As discussed, an important concept that formed the backbone of the Confucian framework is the doctrine of the mean (*zhong yong*), or the notion that attitudes or behaviors must never go to excess. Instead, they should be kept moderate (*zhong*) and indistinguishabe from those of others in a group (*yong*). This principle is widely considered as the highest ideal in Confucianism (e.g. Ivanhoe, 2000; Liang, 2001; Nivison, 1997). Accordingly, Chinese are encouraged to argue for both sides in a debate (i.e. both arguments are correct), or to assign equal responsibilities in a dispute (i.e. no party is at complete fault). This presents an interesting contrast with the law of the excluded middle in Western philosophies, according to which one ought to eliminate ambiguity or inconsistency by selecting one and only one of the conflicting ideas. Unlike the Chinese tradition, it assumes no merit in the middle ground.

Buddhism

Originating from India, Buddhism has absorbed numerous cultural and intellectual elements indigenous to China and eventually flourished into a philosophical tradition that is representative of the Chinese civilization.

Impermanence and the law of non-contradiction. In general, Buddhism embraces the fundamental concept of impermanence (*wu chang*), in which the universe is regarded as being in a state of constant flux and within it all phenomena are continuously changing their forms and properties (Fung, 1983; Nisbett, 2003; Wei, 1983). In other words, every entity in the universe acts as both a source of influence and a recipient of external influences from every direction. This suggests that phenomena arise and cease without necessarily following any consistent, predictable path (Mote, 1971).

According to Buddhist teachings, understanding the harmony between mankind and the Great Nature requires one to accept the transitory character of reality. The world we perceive is merely a snapshot of the ever-changing universe. The present, illusory and deceiving, should thus be disregarded in the pursuit of reality. Instead, one is encouraged to assume a broad focus and speculate both the distant past and future. An extension of the temporal purview also implies that two seemingly incompatible phenomena (e.g. 'There is a river' versus 'There isn't a river') can both be true at the same time. The tolerance of multiple truths or paradoxical propositions is in stark contrast with the law of non-contradiction in Western philosophy. In Aristotelian logic, if two competing propositions are inconsistent with one another, then at least one of them must be false.

Taoism

Similar to Buddhism, Taoism also subscribes to the notion that objects, ideas, or phenomena are amorphous in their forms and properties. However, Taoism emphasizes the complex interaction of forces and the balanced exchange of these forces.

Yin–yang and the law of identity. The *yin-yang* symbol is perhaps the most perceptible signifier of Taoism. It represents the two forces that purportedly form the universe, *yin* and *yang*. These two ostensibly opposing but complementary forces are each in pursuit of the other's tail in a cyclical fashion, suggesting that a phenomenon will start regressing in the opposite direction once it reaches the extreme (Fung, 1983; Hansen, 2000; Tan, 1992). The two dots in each of the two twirls symbolize the idea that things exist only in relation to the opposite form (Nisbett, 2003; Yang, 1986; Yin, 2005). This conceptualization is in sharp contrast to Greek philosophies, in which the inherent attributes of an entity or construct are thought to be definitive and unchanging (i.e. essence). As a result, whereas the great minds in ancient China emphasized the role of relationships in discovering the *truth* the brilliant thinkers in ancient Greece believed that the *truth* can only be understood when the problem is analyzed step by step in isolation of its context (for a review, see Korzybyski, 1994; Nisbett, 2003).

Epilogue

Imagine there is a shadow on a curtain. Whereas philosophers are concerned with the true object behind the curtain, cultural psychologists are more interested in how this shadow is interpreted by people. As discussed, Chinese and Westerners have acquired different perceptual and cognitive strategies from their respective cultural and social environments, which allow them to draw different interpretations out of the same shadow. Although exploring cultural differences is important and interesting in its own right, future research can direct more attention to apply our knowledge of culture in more practical settings such as international negotiations, clinical interventions, and education systems, to name a few. More effort can also be devoted to uncovering the cultural and demographic correlates (e.g. religions, traditional values, geographical features) that constitute the differences, in order to better understand the intertwining relationship between culture and cognition.

Chapter notes

1 'Cultural propensities' here is a general term that captures the psychological and sociocultural features of a given cultural group. Examples are the group's moral priorities, predilections, linguistic properties, or modes of communications.

References

Berger, D. (2008). Relational and intrinsic moral roots: A brief contrast of Confucian and Hindu concepts of duty. *Dao, 7*, 157–163.

Berry, J. W. (1976). *Human ecology and cognitive style: Comparative studies in cultural and psychological adaptation.* Beverly Hills, CA: Sage.

Bond, M. H. (1993). Emotions and their expression in Chinese culture. *Journal of Nonverbal Behavior, 17*, 245–262.

Bond, M. H. & van de Vijver, F. (2009, forthcoming). Making scientific sense of cultural differences in psychological outcomes: Unpackaging the *magnum mysterium*. In D. Matsumoto & F. van de Vijver (eds), *Cross-cultural research methods.* New York: Oxford University Press.

Briley, D. A., Morris, M. W., & Simonson, I. (2000). Reasons as carriers of culture: Dynamic versus dispositional models of cultural influence on decision making. *Journal of Consumer Research, 27*, 157–178.

Chiu, L. (1972). A cross-cultural comparison of cognitive styles in Chinese and American children. *International Journal of Psychology, 7*, 235–242.

Diamond, J. (1997). Guns, germs and steel: The fates of human societies. W.W. Norton & Company.

Fung, Y.L.冯友兰 (1983). A history of Chinese philosophy (translated by Derk Bodde), Princeton, NJ: Princeton University Press.

Guo, T. & Ji, L. J. (under review). *What do I expect in the future? Ask me about the past: Cultural differences in temporal information focus and trend predictions.* Unpublished manuscript, Queen's University, Canada.

Hansen, C. (2000). *A Daoist theory of Chinese thought: A philosophical interpretation.* New York: Oxford University Press.

Ivanhoe, P. J. (2000). *Confucian moral self cultivation.* Indianapolis, IN: Hackett Publishing Company Inc.

Ji, L. J. (2008). The leopard cannot change his spots, or can he: Culture and the development of lay theories of change. *Personality and Social Psychology Bulletin, 34*, 613–622.

Ji, L. J. (2005). Culture and lay theories of change. In R. M. Sorrentino, D. Cohen, J. Olson, & M. Zanna (eds), *Culture and social behaviour: The tenth Ontario symposium* (pp. 117–135). Hillsdale, NJ: Erlbaum,.

Ji, L. J., Guo, T., Zhang, Z., & Messervey, D. (2009). Looking into the past: Cultural differences in perception and representation of past information. *Journal of Personality and Social Psychology, 96*, 761–769.

Ji, L. J., Nisbett, R. E., & Su, Y. (2001) Culture, change, and prediction. *Psychological Science, 12*, 450–456.

Ji, L. J., Peng, K., & Nisbett, R. E. (2000). Culture, control and perception of relationships in the environment. *Journal of Personality and Social Psychology, 78*, 943–955.

Ji, L. J., Spina, R., Ross, M., Li, Y., & Zhang, Z. (in press) Why best can't last: Cultural differences in anticipating regression toward the mean. *Asian Journal of Social Psychology.*

Ji, L. J., Zhang, Z., & Guo, T. (2008). To buy or to sell: Cultural differences in stock market decisions based on stock price trends. *Journal of Behavioral Decision Making, 21*, 399–413.

Ji, L. J., Zhang, Z., & Nisbett, R. E. (2004). It is culture, or is it language? Examination of language effects in cross-cultural research on categorization. *Journal of Personality and Social Psychology, 87*, 57–65.

Ji, L. J., Zhang, Z., Usborne, E., & Guan, Y. (2004). Optimism across cultures: In response to the SARS outbreak. *Asian Journal of Social Psychology, 7*, 25–34

Ji, L. J., Zhang, Z., & Usborne, E. (under review) *Culture and optimism in context.* Unpublished manuscript, Queen's University.

Jones, E. E. & Nisbett, R. E. (1972). The actor and the observer: Divergent perceptions of the causes of the behavior. In E. E. Jones, D. E. Kanouse, H. H. Kelley, R. E. Nisbett, S. Valins and B. Weiner (eds), *Attribution: Perceiving the Causes of Behavior* (pp. 79–94). Morristown, NJ: General Learning Press.

Korzybyski, A. (1994). *Science and sanity: An introduction to non-Aristotelian systems and general semantics.* Englewood Cliffs, NJ: Institute of General Semantics. (Original work published 1933).

Lee, F., Hallahan, M., & Herzog, T. (1996). Explaining real-life events: How culture and domain shape attributions. *Personality and Social Psychology Bulletin, 22*, 732–741.

Liang, H. 梁海明 (2001). 大学;中庸. 太原:书海出版社.

Masuda, T. & Nisbett, R. E. (2001) Attending holistically versus analytically: Comparing the context sensitivity of Japanese and Americans. *Journal of Personality and Social Psychology, 81*, 992–934.

Miller, J. G. (1984). Culture and the development of everyday social explanation. *Journal of Personality & Social Psychology, 46*(5), 961–978.

Morris, M. W. & Peng, K. (1994). Culture and cause: American and Chinese attributions for social and physical events. *Journal of Personality and Social Psychology, 67*, 949–971.

Mote, F. W. (1971). *The intellectual foundations of China.* New York: Knopf.

Mu, Z. 牟宗三 (1997). 中国哲学的特质. 上海瑞金二路:上海古籍出版社.

Munro, D. J. (1985). Individualism and holism: Studies in Confucian and Taoist values. Ann Arbor, MI: Center for Chinese Studies, University of Michigan.

Nisbett, R. E. (2003). *The geography of thought: How Asians and Westerners think differently … and why.* New York: The Free Press.

Nisbett, R. E., Peng, K., Choi, I., & Norenzayan, A. (2001). Culture and systems of thought: holistic versus analytic cognition. *Psychological review, 108*(2), 291–310.

Nivison, D. S. (1997). *The ways of Confucianism: Investigations in Chinese philosophy.* Chicago, IL: Open Court Publishing Company.

Norenzayan, A., Smith, E. E., Kim, B. J., & Nisbett, R. E. (2002). Cultural preferences for formal versus intuitive reasoning. *Cognitive Science: A Multidisciplinary Journal, 26*, 653–684.

Odean, T. (1998). Are investors reluctant to realize their losses? *Journal of Finance, 53*, 1775–1798.

Peng, K. & Nisbett, R. (1999). Culture, dialectics, and reasoning about contradiction. *American Psychologist, 54*, 741–754.

Plato (360 BC/1956). The republic. In E. H. Warmington & P. G. Rouse (eds), *Great dialogues of Plato* (pp. 125–422). New York: Mentor.

Potter, S. H. (1988). The cultural construction of emotion in rural Chinese social life. *Ethos, 16*, 181–208.

Shefrin, H. & Statman, M. (1985). The disposition to sell winners too early and ride losers too long: Theory and evidence. *Journal of Finance, 40(3)*, 777–790.

Soto, J.A., Levenson, R.W., & Ebling, R. (2005). Cultures of moderation and expression: emotional experience, behavior, and physiology in Chinese Americans and Mexican Americans. *Emotion, 5*, 154–165.

Tan, Y. 谭宇权 (1992). 老子哲学评论. 台北: 文津出版社有限公司.

Tsai, J. L. (2007). Ideal affect: Cultural causes and behavioral consequences. *Perspectives on Psychological Science*, 2, 242–260.

Tsai, J. L., Knutson, B. K., & Fung, H. H. (2006). Cultural variation in affect valuation. *Journal of Personality and Social Psychology, 90*, 288–307.

Tsai, J., & Levenson, R. W. (1997). Cultural influences on emotional responding: Chinese American and European American dating couples during interpersonal conflict. *Journal of Cross-Cultural Psychology, 28*, 600–625.

Tsai, J. L., Louie, J., Chen, E., & Uchida, Y. (2007). Learning what feelings to desire: Socialization of ideal affect through children's storybooks. *Personality and Social Psychology Bulletin, 33*, 17–30.

Wang, F., Wu, Q., Liang, K., Chen, J., & Li, H. 王飞雪,伍秋萍,梁凯怡,陈俊,李华香 (2006). 中庸思维与冲突情境应对策略选择关系的研究, 《科学研究月刊》, 第16期, 114–117.

Wei, Z. 韦志林 (1983). 佛学文物馆: 典籍篇. 台北县板桥市: 长圆图书出版社.

Wu, J. (2006). *Zhongyong* makes my life better: The effect of *Zhongyong* thinking on life satisfaction. *Journal of Psychology in Chinese Societies. Special Issue: Psychology in Health Services and Health Promotion, 7*, 163–176.

Wu, J. & Lin, Y. 吴佳辉、林以正(2005). 中庸思维量表的编制。《本土心理学研究》, 24期, 247–300.

Yang, K. S. (1986). Chinese personality and its change. In M. H. Bond (ed.). *The psychology of the Chinese people* (pp. 106–170). Hong Kong: Oxford University Press.

Yang, Z. & Chiu, C.Y. 杨中芳、赵志裕(1997). 中庸概念初探. 第四届中国人的 心理及行为科际研讨会, 台北

Yin, C. 殷昆 (2005). 老子为道. 兰州: 甘肃文化出版社.

CHAPTER 12

Approaches to learning and teaching by the Chinese

David Kember and David Watkins

There is a common perception that Chinese students have a tendency towards rote learning. Rote learning has been associated with a surface approach to learning, which is normally envisaged as less desirable than a deep approach, particularly in higher education. Abundant research into approaches to learning has shown that such an approach to learning should lead to poor learning outcomes (for reviews and overviews see Dart & Boulton-Lewis, 1998; Marton, Hounsell & Entwistle, 1984; Prosser & Trigwell, 1999; Richardson, 1994, 2000).

Biggs (1987) developed the 3P (Presage, Process, Product) model to explain how students approach their learning. Presage variables are of two types; background variables such as prior knowledge and ability, and situational or contextual variables such as teaching method and curriculum design. These are seen as influencing the motive and strategy components of approaches to learning, which occupy an intermediate position in the model. Approaches to learning, as the process part of the model, in turn influence the final products of the model, which include learning outcomes and assessment results.

In spite of the negative perceptions of rote learning, there is now much evidence that Chinese students in a number of countries outperform their Western counterparts in international comparisons of educational achievement, as reported in the next chapter of this handbook by Hau and Ho. The apparent discrepancy between anecdotal observations of Chinese students seemingly employing approaches to learning associated with poor outcomes in Western research, while actually performing well, gives rise to the so-called 'paradox of the Chinese learner'. The paradox has been much discussed in the literature (Watkins & Biggs, 1996), as it is a case of research on Chinese psychology investigating a construct discovered and characterized in the West and finding additional dimensions, which have led to a re-appraisal of the nature of approaches to learning.

Deep and surface approaches to learning

The original characterization of approaches to learning for a specific task was essentially dichotomous. Marton and Säljö (1976) claimed that, when students were asked to read an academic text, they adopted either a deep approach, by trying to understand the underlying meaning intended by the author, or a surface approach in which superficial features are committed to memory. Fuller characterizations of deep and surface approaches (e.g. Biggs, 1987, p. 15; Entwistle, 1998, p. 74) are consistent with their portrayals by Kember with McNaught (2007, p. 25).

Deep approach:

- A deep approach is adopted when the student is interested in the topic or the academic task.
- As a result there is an attempt to understand key concepts or the underlying meaning of an article.
- An attempt is made to relate the concepts together to make a coherent whole. A piece of writing will be logically related with an introduction and conclusion.
- New knowledge will be related to previous knowledge and to personal experiences.

Surface approach:

- An activity or assignment is undertaken because it is a set task and the course cannot be passed unless the assignment is completed. The task does not arouse the learner's interest.
- As a result the minimum possible time and effort are devoted to the task.
- There is no attempt to reach understanding of key concepts; instead reliance is often placed upon memorization of model answers or key facts perceived as likely to appear in tests or examinations.
- Coherence of the topic is not sought; so material is seen as a set of unrelated facts.
- Concepts are not related to personal experience; so remain abstract theory. As a result, what has been memorized is normally quickly forgotten.

A large volume of research into approaches to learning followed from the initial study, with the bulk of the work in the seventies, eighties and early nineties taking place in the West (for overviews of Western research into approaches to learning, see Marton, Hounsell, & Entwistle, 1984; Prosser & Trigwell, 1999; Richardson, 2000). The corpus of studies largely served to reinforce the accepted position that students adopted either deep or surface approaches to learning, depending on their perception of the learning task and the prevailing teaching and learning environment. Most students use a combination of approaches as their strategies will differ between tasks and courses. For overall or predominant approach, as measured by questionnaires, deep and surface approaches are then orthogonal in relationship.

Intermediate approaches

The 'paradox of the Chinese learner' stimulated research into approaches to learning in Hong Kong and to a lesser extent in mainland China. The anecdotal accounts of widespread rote learning were confounded by large surveys of approaches to learning that accessed students in Hong Kong. Initial results, from a substantial sample at one university in Hong Kong, showed deep approach scores on the Study Process Questionnaire (SPQ: Biggs, 1987) higher than those from a comparable Australian sample (Kember & Gow, 1991). The results were consistent with surveys conducted in other educational institutions, reviewed in Biggs (1992).

The surprising survey results provided further stimulus to researchers in the field to seek solutions to the paradox of the Chinese learner. The investigations began to provide evidence of approaches to learning inconsistent with the original Western formulations of deep and surface approaches. A combination of approaches comparing factor structures of questionnaire data with those from elsewhere, and interviews with students about their approaches to tackling specific academic tasks suggested that memorization might be occurring in conjunction with attempts to reach an understanding of the material (Kember & Gow, 1989, 1990). Students utilizing the approach worked systematically through material section by section, attempting to understand each new concept and then committing it to memory before proceeding to the next. The following interview quotation illustrates the 'narrow intermediate approach':

> I read in detail section by section. If I find any difficulties, I try my best to solve the problem before I go on to the next section ... If you don't memorize important ideas when you come across them, then you will be stuck when you go on. You must memorize and then go on—understand, memorize, and then go on—understand, memorize, and then go on. That is my way of studying.
>
> Kember & Gow, 1990, p. 361

Other intermediate approaches have subsequently been identified. Tang (1991) observed students initially employing a deep approach by trying to understand concepts, but then committing the material to memory to satisfy assessment requirements. This intermediate approach was used by students who had a preference for seeking understanding, but recognized that their examinations normally required them to reproduce material. They, therefore, tried to understand the concepts, and then made sure the material was memorized so they could get a good grade in the examination.

Tang (1993) found variants on a surface approach by which Hong Kong school students made limited attempts to order or understand material to reduce the memorization load. The approach was called an elaborated surface approach. The students initially intended to memorize material, but found the memory load became such that some selection became necessary as they progressed through the years at school.

Watkins (1996) interpreted interviews with Hong Kong secondary school students as showing that students developed through a sequence of three or four stages. Initially their intention was to achieve through reproduction, by rote learning everything. The students then passed to the next stage of rote learning things perceived as more important. In the subsequent developmental stage, the students started to see the benefit of trying to understand material before committing it to memory. The existence of the stages could be interpreted as a developmental sequence in which students progressively refine their learning approaches by seeking heightened levels of understanding, while still clinging to predominantly reproductive conceptions of learning.

Marton, Dall'Alba, and Kun (1996) distinguished mechanical memorization and memorization linked with understanding. They reported two combinations of the latter, distinguished by whether the attempt to understand came before or after the memorization. When understanding came first, the process involved making conscious efforts to remember that which had been understood. The approach with understanding preceding memorization is similar to the narrow approach described by Kember and Gow (1989, 1990). It is also related to the approach identified by Tang (1991) by which students first tried to understand material and then memorized it for assessment purposes. When memorization came first, it could be used as an attempt to reach understanding. Dahlin and Watkins (2000) found that 90 per cent of a sample of Hong Kong Chinese students could remember reciting texts at primary or junior secondary school. There were several mechanisms by which repetition could go beyond mechanical memorization towards reaching an understanding of the text. The most common among the Hong Kong Chinese students was that repetition plus attentive effort led to new meanings. This approach to learning may be a legacy of learning a character-based language, which is traditionally mastered through repetition of the characters.

The tendency for repetition to be accompanied by attentive effort suggested that Chinese students tend to see understanding itself as a long process requiring much effort, rather than as a rapid, insightful process which Western students are more likely to believe (Dahlin & Watkins, 2000). This was consistent with the work of Elliot and Chan (1998), who found that describing the epistemological beliefs of Hong Kong Chinese students needed a dimension called 'belief that learning requires significant effort' (p. 8).

The discovery of the intermediate approaches provided one of two contributing explanations for the paradox. Approaches to learning were originally portrayed in the West as competing deep and surface approaches. At least some Chinese students observed as apparently memorizing material could also have been trying to understand. Those noting symptoms of students appearing to be memorizing material may have interpreted their observations as suggesting that the students were rote learning or employing a surface approach consistent with the original Western formulation. However, the students may well have been employing one of the intermediate approaches, thereby reaching some level of understanding as well as committing material to memory. Observations of apparent memorization may, therefore, not have precluded seeking understanding, judged as the superior approach. If understanding were combined with being able to remember what had been understood, there would be a chance of good performance in examinations, as assessment often rewards those able to remember material. This intermediate or combined approach could be contributing to the good international record of Chinese students noted in the following chapter.

A synthesis of Chinese and Western research

Integration of Western and Chinese research has been attempted by proposing that approaches to learning be envisaged as a spectrum between deep and surface poles. Kember (1996, 2000a) suggested that the various forms of combining memorization and understanding meant that approaches to learning might be better characterized as a continuum. The positions upon the continuum are characterized by the intention and the strategy employed (see Table 12.1).

It has yet to be established whether all positions on the spectrum are found universally or whether some are specific to Asia or Confucian-heritage countries. Besides Hong Kong, evidence of the intention to both understand and memorize has also been found in mainland China (Marton et al., 1996) and Japan (Hess & Azuma, 1992), so it may be quite widespread among Asian students. This has led to some interpretations that Chinese or Asian learners have distinct approaches to learning from those characterized in the West. There is, though, no clear evidence for this position. It is possible that the central approaches combining understanding and memorization (Kember & Gow, 1990; Marton et al., 1996) may be more common in Asia: Kember (1996) has speculated that influences on their adoption may come from learning a character-based language, learning in a second language or being brought up in a traditionally orderly society.

Other intermediate positions on the spectrum, though, seem more likely to be adopted as responses to prevailing contexts of learning and assessment. There is some evidence from the work of Entwistle and Entwistle (2003) that the intermediate positions close to the deep and surface poles of the continuum may occur in the West. They identified a range of interpretations of understanding in Western students revising for examinations. Some of these showed signs of both memorizing and understanding. Case and Marshall (2004) identified intermediate procedural approaches to learning in engineering students in South Africa and the UK. The focus of the approaches was on problem solving. In some cases there was an intention to understand, at some point, through application or learning problem-solving procedures. Other cases were classified as surface procedural as the students mechanically solved problems by using algorithms.

The revised Study Process Questionnaire (R-SPQ-2F: Biggs, Kember, & Leung, 2001) was completed by large samples of university students in Australia and Hong Kong (Leung, Ginns, & Kember, 2008). Multiple-group analyses using structural equation modelling showed configural invariance, implying that students from the two countries were employing the same conceptual frame of reference when responding to the R-SPQ-2F. This finding suggests that the continuum characterization of approaches to learning is likely to be applicable for Western as well as Chinese subjects. The correlations between

Table 12.1 Approaches to learning as a continuum between deep and surface poles

APPROACH	INTENTION	STRATEGY
surface	memorizing without understanding	rote learning
intermediate 1	primarily memorizing	strategic attempt to reach limited understanding as an aid to memorization
understanding and memorizing	understanding and memorizing	repetition and memorizing to reach understanding seeking comprehension then committing to memory
intermediate 2	primarily understanding	strategic memorization for examination or task after understanding reached
deep	understanding	seeking comprehension

deep and surface approaches for universities in both Hong Kong and Sydney were negative (Hong Kong = –0.39, Sydney = –0.63). These substantial negative correlations are consistent with the continuum model of approaches to learning, as they imply that the deep and surface approaches can be envisaged as opposite ends of a spectrum.

Comparison of mean scores showed the Hong Kong sample to be higher on both deep *and* surface approaches, with the difference on surface approach being substantially larger than for deep approach ($d = 0.75$ versus $d = 0.24$, respectively). The difference in mean scores suggested that the Hong Kong sample seemed to have a greater propensity to employ combinations of approaches or what we have termed 'intermediate' approaches.

Influence of context upon approaches to learning

When Chinese students do use a superficial approach, it is commonly, as with students everywhere, a response to the perceived context (Marton, Hounsell, & Entwistle, 1984; Prosser & Trigwell, 1999). Students often have a preferred or predominant approach to studying, but it is well established that approaches are influenced by students' perceptions of the nature of an assigned learning task, or item of assessment, or the prevailing teaching and learning environment.

The effect of context was noted in the surveys with the SPQ of university students in Hong Kong referred to above. Comparison of overall deep approach scores by year of study showed a consistent fall from the point students entered their program to the time they graduated (Gow & Kember, 1990; Kember & Gow, 1991). These data are best interpreted as implying that students' perceptions of curriculum design and the prevailing teaching and learning environment are such that their use of a deep approach declines as they proceed through their degree. This interpretation poses an unflattering portrayal of the nature of teaching and learning within the university in which the data were collected. However, similar results have been found in other large surveys of approaches to learning across multiple disciplines in several other universities in Hong Kong (Biggs, 1992) as well as in other countries (Biggs, 1987; Watkins & Hattie, 1985).

Such apparently negative effects of curriculum design and learning environments are by no means confined to universities. Indeed, the pressures on school children in East Asian countries are such that it must be hard to resist the compulsion to resort to approaches most likely to produce better examination results. Unfortunately, the assessment systems all too often reward strategies like remembering model answers. These strategies are hardly consistent with supposedly enlightened Western models of good learning!

Part of the pressure on students comes from the fact that many Asian countries still have elite educational systems. At the time of writing, the Hong Kong school system, for example, is highly selective and competitive, as only about one-third of the age cohort is able to obtain a place in Form 6 for the final two years of secondary schooling (Education and Manpower Bureau, 2003). In Hong Kong, there are currently seven universities funded by the University Grants Council of Hong Kong. Only about 17 per cent of the age cohort currently gain entry into one of these universities (University Grants Committee of Hong Kong, 2006). So the UGC scheme can be considered an elitist higher education system. The percentages obtaining places in the more prestigious universities are obviously lower still, thus placing even more pressure on the many students who aim for the most prestigious programs in the top universities.

These pressures on both teachers and students are exacerbated by large class sizes. Cortazzi and Jin (2001) report that primary and middle-school classes in China commonly have fifty to sixty pupils. Class sizes in Hong Kong are often over forty (Biggs & Watkins, 1996), and the government has not bowed to pressure to significantly reduce numbers.

Having to learn in a second language can be an additional complicating factor. Most education in the mainland is conducted in the mother tongue. In Hong Kong, the majority of schools use Cantonese, but English is the official language for the majority of university lectures, and required readings are often in English. Johnson and Ngor (1996) argued that this language consideration means that weaker students resort to survival strategies. Questions can be answered by copying sections of text containing the key words in the question. Memorization is another very common survival strategy, and quite substantial sections of text, such as model answers, may be memorized. Observations of students using this survival strategy would create the impression of rote learning, but the reason for its use is clearly different to the reason Western students use a surface approach. It could also be the case that the students have understood the underlying concept through listening to an explanation in their mother tongue, but then remembered an answer in English if that is the language of the examination.

There are also pressures which arise from the traditional respect shown to education in Confucian-heritage societies. Lee (1996) reviews the writing of Confucius on the topic of education. Lee believes that the term *learning* pervades the *Analects* to the extent that it might be interpreted as a book of learning. The philosophy became enshrined in a tradition of cultivation of the self and of scholarship to provide a preparation for government office.

In addition, pressures result from the family and societal nature of achievement motivation in Chinese societies, resulting in parental pressures for academic success. In Western society, achievement motivation is normally characterized as having an individual orientation. However, Yang and Yu (1988) and Yu (1996) believe that in Chinese society achievement motivation has more social orientation (SOAM) (see Hau & Ho, this volume). The pressures resulting from SOAM are reinforced by the strong tradition of filial piety (Chen, this volume; Ho, 1996). There is, therefore, an expectation that students will strive hard to meet the expectations of family members and close social contacts.

These SOAM-related pressures are often reinforced by expectations of social advancement through education. It is common for one generation of an extended family to make financial sacrifices to enable the next generation to receive a better education than they did. This creates a burden both to do well in studying to take full advantage of the opportunity provided and also to ensure that results are good enough to obtain a prestigious well-paid position which will enhance the status of the family and result in a financial dividend for the sacrifice.

The overall effect of the contextual, cultural and systemic pressures on approaches to learning constitutes the second contribution to the paradox of the Chinese learner. If Chinese students are genuinely observed to be rote learning or employing surface approaches to learning, this is not a manifestation of a cultural predisposition or an inherent characteristic of Chinese learners. It is, rather, a response to perceptions of contextual factors in the teaching and learning environment and the influence of cultural and societal expectations.

Western students experience these contextual influences also. However, it may be that the pressures are less intense. Few Western educational systems still retain elite structures, with most attaining mass or even universal higher education (Trow, 2006). Pressures tend to be less from families as societies are less collective and more individualistic in nature (Hofstede, 2001; Kulich, this volume; Kwan & Hui, this volume). Achievement motivation has been defined in the West as an individual competitive drive (Biggs, 1987), thus lacking the collective or social element in traditional Chinese forms (Yang & Yu, 1988; Yu, 1996; Hau & Ho, this volume). Respect shown to education varies between cultural groups, but few societies place as much importance on education as the Chinese (Ho, 1996; Stevenson & Lee, 1996).

Students' beliefs about teaching, learning, and knowledge

Experiences during schooling influence students' conceptions of teaching and learning and also their epistemological beliefs. Kember (2001) analysed interviews with fifty-three part-time students in Hong Kong. Thirty-five of the students were novices, in the early stages of taking a part-time first degree, having failed to obtain a place for full-time undergraduate study. The remaining sixteen students were taking part-time higher degrees, having earlier completed their undergraduate degree through a full-time university program.

Analysis of the interview transcripts revealed insights into the students' beliefs about teaching, learning, and knowledge. These beliefs were normally related in a logically consistent manner to the extent that they were best envisaged as an inter-connected trilogy of beliefs. Most students held beliefs consistent with contrasting naïve and sophisticated sets, with few intermediate cases, perhaps a function of the sampling.

The large majority of the novice students held a trio of beliefs labelled 'didactic/reproductive'. They believed that the role of the teacher was to transmit or teach a body of knowledge. Their role as students was to absorb the knowledge decided as appropriate by the teacher or the examination authority. The outcome of the process of teaching and learning was judged by whether the students were able to reproduce the body of knowledge for the examinations and other forms of assessment. They believed that knowledge is defined by an authority, and so is either right or wrong. Where multiple opinions exist, an authority will eventually decide which is correct.

Holding the naïve trio of beliefs could easily result from pressures to do well in the examinations which are all-important for success in the elite educational systems common in East Asia. The examinations are so important to future prospects that it is highly tempting for both students and teachers to concentrate narrowly upon material in the examination syllabus. This inevitably leads to teachers coaching for the examinations and students learning model answers to questions likely to feature in the exams.

There are no reliable data on the relative preponderance of the contrasting trios of beliefs in different cultures. It might be thought that the naïve beliefs would be more prevalent in elite educational systems. However, King and Kitchener (1994) examined the epistemological beliefs of US college students using a seven-stage classification scheme. First-year students had mean scores of around 3.5 and senior students 4.0 on the seven-point scale. This implies that the average US college student is still at a quasi-reflective stage, so many hold beliefs similar to the naïve trio.

The more experienced and sophisticated students usually held a different trio of beliefs called 'facilitative/transformative'. Their epistemological beliefs were more complex, so learning became a more constructive process. To help them with this form of learning, the teacher needed to adopt a facilitative stance. Several could remember making the transition from the more naïve set of beliefs during their undergraduate degrees. The two belief sets are contrasted in Table 12.2.

This classification of the beliefs is broadly consistent with Western research into students' conceptions of learning (Marton, Dall'Alba, & Beaty, 1993) and teaching (Kember, 1997). For these conceptions, fine-grained analysis found multiple conceptions, but in each case it was reasonable to group the conceptions under two higher-order orientations similar to the beliefs in Table 12.2. This is also consistent with the results of a study of conceptions of learning of Hong Kong high-school students (Marton, Watkins, & Tang, 1997). These researchers classified conceptions into four categories: committing to memory (words), committing to memory (meaning), understanding (meaning), understanding (phenomenon). It would again be reasonable to see the first two categories as being distinct from the latter two.

Table 12.2 Contrasting beliefs of novice and sophisticated students

	Didactic/reproductive	Facilitative/transformative
Teaching	A didactic process of transmitting knowledge	Teaching is a process of facilitating learning
	The teacher is responsible for ensuring that learning takes place	The student is responsible for learning independently with guidance from the teacher
Learning	The role of the students is to absorb the material defined by the teacher	The role of the students is to reach an understanding of relevant concepts
	Outcomes are judged by the students' ability to reproduce material	The outcome is the student transforming knowledge for own purposes and context
Knowledge	Defined by an authority	Transformed or constructed by the individual
	Knowledge and theories are right or wrong	Judgements have to be made about alternative theories based upon evidence and analysis

Good teaching

An interesting and highly significant consequence of the contrasting belief sets is that they resulted in very different conceptions of what constitutes good teaching (Kember, Jenkins, & Ng, 2003). Those holding the naïve belief set preferred teacher-centered forms of teaching. They wanted a lecture in which knowledge was transmitted; so they preferred didactic teaching. By contrast, those with the facilitative/transformative set of beliefs wanted the teacher to act as a facilitator to assist them in their learning. The outcome is that the conceptions of good and poor teaching are diametrically opposite (see Figure 12.1).

The teaching paradox

There then arises a second paradox: school learning environments in most Chinese societies, which have an overemphasis on assessment and teacher-centered instruction together with their typically large class sizes, do not conform to Western models of good practice; nevertheless, many Chinese students achieve outstanding results. How is this possible? We argue that there are cultural differences in emphases related to the very nature of teaching which lead to misperceptions of the worth derived from typical teaching practices in Chinese classrooms.

What is teaching?

In every culture it seems clear that the main role of a teacher is to teach. But does 'teaching' mean the same thing in every culture? The work of Stigler and Hiebert (1999) suggests that there may well be little such agreement. In their well-known book, *The teaching gap*, these authors were able to describe the nature of the pedagogical flow of educational systems in Germany, Japan, and the United States. After analyzing videotapes of secondary-school classrooms in these countries, they were 'amazed at how much teaching varied across cultures, and how little it varied within cultures' (p. 10). It seemed that each culture had developed its own script for teaching, and Stigler and Hiebert concluded that

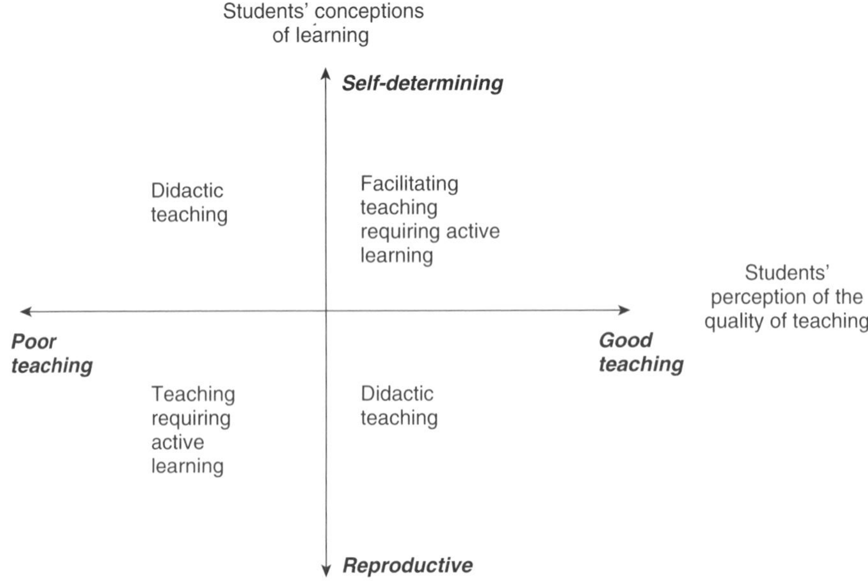

Fig. 12.1 Contrasting conceptions of good teaching.

superior learning outcomes in Japan were due to a better script rather than a better actor delivering it. They concluded that the Japanese teaching script was both more student centered and more focused on higher-quality learning outcomes than was the American or German.

Follow-up observational studies compared typical mathematics classes in Hong Kong, Austria, Czechoslovakia, the Netherlands, Sweden, and America (Leung, 2003). According to the judgement of an expert panel, the Hong Kong Chinese teachers, while they talked far more, also covered topics in much greater depth and with far greater coherence, and were much more likely to engage their students in understanding the topics covered than were their counterparts in all the other countries. Leung (2005) concluded that the observed teacher-centered Hong Kong classrooms involved a much higher quality of teaching and learning than the much more student-centered classes in at least four of the other countries (see Fan, Wong, Cai, & Li, 2004, for further evidence of how Chinese mathematics teachers enhance student learning in ways rather different from Western approaches).

Chinese views of teaching

More than two thousand five hundred years ago, Confucius stated that education is an important way for people to acquire knowledge, ability, and virtues, and thus it plays a substantial role in personal transformation and enhancement. He maintained that every man can receive education regardless of his social status or class (*You Jiao Wu Lei*). 'Confucius himself set an example by never refusing to teach whosoever came with a nominal ceremonial tutorial fee' (*Analects*, VII.7, cited in Lee, 1996, p. 28). Many of today's Hong Kong teachers seem to share such views, judging by the following quotes volunteered by such teachers in the second author's ongoing research:

> 'The mission of teachers is to teach students how to be a good person. I pay attention to the conduct of students, as in a Confucian society, moral values are important.'
>
> 'Teachers can bring about changes in students, and those changes may last for their whole life. My teacher affected me in my attitudes towards life and I have learnt from him the Confucian philosophy.'
>
> 'I myself trust in the Confucian ideologies … I act as a role model for them. I also use personal stories of some famous athletes to teach them the philosophy of life.'

In Hong Kong, Chinese schoolteachers typically see their role as extending far beyond the classroom (I. Ho, 2001). What consistently comes through the research in this area is that teachers in China and Hong Kong believe that they have the role of *cultivating* not only their students' cognitive development but also promoting positive attitudes to society and responsible moral behavior.

Based on the analysis of in-depth interviews and classroom observation of eighteen secondary-school teachers of physics in Guangzhou, China, Gao and Watkins (2001) developed a model of the teaching conceptions held by these teachers. This model was later supported in a quantitative study of over 700 such teachers. The model developed involved two higher orientations of Moulding (with sub-areas of Knowledge Delivery and Exam Preparation) and Cultivating (with sub-areas of Ability Development, Attitude Promotion, and Conduct Guidance). These two orientations have some elements in common with the teacher-centered/content-oriented and student-centered/learning-oriented views identified in Kember's (1997) review of research on university teaching, but extend the latter to affective and moral areas. The emphasis on cultivating attitudes and good citizenship is consistent with the Chinese cultural value of '*jiao shu yu ren*' (teaching involves developing a good person).

However, it is important to realize that the teaching of such values, a goal supported by all 700 Chinese teachers in the research of Gao and Watkins (2001), is primarily conveyed implicitly in the teacher's performance and modeled during teacher–student interactions. The Chinese teacher is expected not only to have competent instructional skills, but also to be a good moral role model in all areas of life, a mandate expressed in Chinese as '*wei ren shi biao*'.

It might be argued that this view of teaching would also be commonly held by Western schoolteachers rather than the university teachers who were the focus of the research reviewed by Kember (1997). However, in a comparison of Australian and Hong Kong secondary-school teachers, Ho (2001) found that the former felt their responsibilities ended in teaching the curriculum inside the classroom. The Australians typically did not feel responsible for their students' personal or family problems or even for their unfinished homework. The Hong Kong teachers saw things very differently, and like their Guangzhou counterparts described above, voiced a pastoral as well as an instructional view of teaching. Such a pastoral view of teaching is also rarely mentioned in recent US discussions of effective teaching (cf. Berliner, 2005).

The research of Cortazzi and Jin (2001) depicts a similar view of Chinese teachers. They refer to education as 'books and society', and the teacher as 'friend and parent'. They too argue that this viewpoint reflects the holistic Chinese view of teaching, where teaching refers not only to the cognitive but also the affective and moral, including teaching children their place in society (see Hwang & Han, this volume, on learning one's place). Such views were not found in their survey of the views of British teachers. So it seems that Chinese and Western educators differ in terms of the very meanings they take to teaching.

However, the Chinese cultural value of revering one's teacher can also lead to a too-ready acceptance of the teachers' and textbooks' views, and current educational reforms in a number of Chinese societies are designed to encourage greater creativity and critical thinking. This will not be an easy process, however, as curriculum reform will need to deal with the entrenched attitudes of students, teachers, and parents.

Beliefs of university teachers

Kelly and Watkins (2002) reported a Hong Kong study of effective university teachers. The research involved four components: (1) a survey using open-ended questions of twenty-seven Western and fifty-four Hong Kong Chinese lecturers from four Hong Kong universities; (2) focus-group interviews with twenty-four lecturers from three Hong Kong universities; (3) a survey of 405 second- and third-year Chinese undergraduates from seven departments of the same universities as in (1) above, and (4) focus-group discussions with eleven Chinese students from nine departments in three universities.

Both the Chinese and Western lecturers consistently reported that the focus of their teaching was to develop their students' independent problem solving and their critical and analytical thinking. However, when the ways the lecturers reported trying to achieve these goals were examined, clear differences emerged. The Western lecturers typically emphasized what the researchers termed a *professional model* of effective teaching. They showed how they cared for their students by their careful preparation of lectures and the use of good instructional methods. The following quotes illustrate this view:

> 'The critical thing is to have a professional approach to the relationship in the learning environment.' *(expatriate lecturer—interview response)*
>
> 'So I'm caring in the classroom, like I give them lecture notes, OK. I write lecture notes and these are very special, showing I'm interested in this unit ... so that's how caring I can be. Anyway so that's how caring I am, and besides that I am pretty cool. I wouldn't have a party with them. When they ask me to take a picture with me I will say "Are you sure?" So that's this anonymity thing, I put that on a similar level. I don't want to know their names.' *(expatriate lecture— interview response)*
>
> 'My attitude towards whether I think that I care for students is whether I believe that I have what I would call a professional approach ... that means they know what is expected of them, they know that I will deliver to them, and they know that what I do in terms of assessment is going to be fair. In terms of my business of caring for them, if I do that properly, then I believe that I'm caring for them.' *(expatriate lecturer–interview response)*

Responses of the Chinese lecturers showed that most wanted to develop a more personal relationship with the students. Typically they reported that they cared for their students not just by using good instructional methods, but especially by the relationships they developed with them:

> 'They [the students] need caring teachers. I think that's partly what one can do in a small group or one-to-one basis ... you have different people giving different lectures, they need that one (person) for personal care.' *(Chinese lecturer—interview response)*

The students also consistently commented on how student–teacher relationships enhanced effective teaching:

> 'He established a close relationship with students so, during lessons, students pay more attention to the lecture and dare to ask questions.' *(survey response—student)*
>
> 'He is concerned about students' feelings. During tutorial classes he listened to students attentively and gave feedback. In addition he sometimes makes an appointment to talk to students after class.' *(survey response—student)*

Such good relationships were much more common with Chinese lecturers, however:

> 'The Chinese way of teaching is ... not just restricted to knowledge ... but also the students, students' life, students' future. They are concerned about these things. But Western teachers are only concerned about students' knowledge in the field of study. They focus on the subject discipline.' *(interview response—student)*
>
> 'It depends on whether they have the heart to understand Hong Kong students ... but if some lecturers can chat with students after talking about the assignments, they can understand more about their students. Some Western lecturers only know that we are young adults. If they put in more effort, I think they can understand more about Hong Kong students.' *(interview response - student)*

Constructivism: a Western theory that works in Asia?

Current educational reforms in Hong Kong have advocated more student-centered, constructivist teaching methods (Education Commission of Hong Kong, 2000). Constructivist approaches emphasize the need for the students to be active in developing their own understanding of what is being studied if high-quality learning outcomes are to be achieved. But there have been claims that constructivist teaching approaches are not appropriate for Hong Kong classrooms, as Chinese culture has emphasized more teacher-centered transmission methods, with the teacher regarded as an authority not to be questioned. Indeed, research in Hong Kong has shown that classrooms described by students as 'teacher led' were more likely to encourage deeper-level approaches to learning (Ma, 1994; Chan & Watkins, 1994).

However, Biggs (1996) argued forcefully that, while cultural differences are evident at specific levels of abstraction, the principles of good teaching are universal at more general levels. In particular, Biggs points to the underlying constructivist nature of effective teaching in both Chinese and Western classrooms. Thus, in both contexts the focus of good teaching is appropriate individual and social learning activities, as advocated by both *cognitive* and/or *social constructivism.*

A number of examples of successful teaching innovations based on such constructivist principles are reported by Watkins and Biggs (1996, 2001). These include problem-based learning (Stokes, 2001); conceptual-change interventions (Chan, 2001; A. Ho, 2001); computer-supported collaborative learning (Chan, 2001); and teacher education based on 'reflective practitioner' principles (So, 2001; Tang, 2001). Ching (2001) also showed that changing to a cognitive constructivist teaching approach led to higher-order cognitive strategies and learning outcomes in an experimental class compared to a control class of Form 3 Hong Kong Chinese secondary-school students studying history. So teaching and learning based on traditional cognitive and social constructivist principles seem to be appropriate for Hong Kong classrooms.

There is also a substantial body of evidence from the university sector of students adapting well to constructivist and student-centered forms of learning. For over five years, Kember (2000b) ran an inter-institutional initiative known as the Action Learning Project which supported ninety action-research projects within eight universities and colleges in Hong Kong. In these projects teachers introduced a wide variety of innovative forms of teaching and learning into their courses—almost anything other than didactic lecturing. The Action Learning Project was evaluated with a multiple-method, multiple-voice approach. The substantial majority of the respondents believed that their projects had resulted in:

- improved teacher–student relationships
- improvements in students' attitude
- improvements in students' learning approaches
- improvements in students' performance.

Each of the projects was extensively evaluated, so these responses would have been informed by evaluation data. This study would seem to provide evidence that Chinese students can adapt to constructivist learning approaches, can come to see their advantages, and can benefit academically from their application.

Recent research even suggests that Hong Kong students may prefer a *critical constructivist* learning environment, with an emphasis on open discussion, and where the students and teachers have an almost equal say in the running of the classroom. Moreover, it would seem that a closer fit to such an environment may lead to better cognitive and affective learning outcomes (Wong, Watkins, & Wong, 2006). Fok and Watkins (2007) showed how such a critical constructivist approach could be successfully implemented in a Hong Kong economics classroom with a resulting increase in the use of deeper level learning strategies.

Helping students to change beliefs and approaches

In an earlier section on students' beliefs about teaching and learning, it was suggested that those holding a naïve trio of beliefs about learning, teaching, and knowledge can be reluctant to engage in class discussion and forms of learning which involve student activity. The preceding section, though, presented evidence of students' being able to overcome an initial unfamiliarity with active involvement in class and to eventually participate willingly in such learning activities. For this process to happen, it seems as though there must have been some shift in their beliefs about teaching and learning. Any active engagement in learning activities is seen as poor teaching to those holding naïve beliefs. So some shift in beliefs seems to be either a precondition or an accompanying transitional element in the change process, if students are to willingly contribute and participate in class.

Evidence of changes in beliefs about learning came from interviews with experienced part-time students who were asked to compare their learning experiences as full-time undergraduate students with current practices as part-time students enrolled for higher degrees (Kember, 2001). These parts of the interviews provided rich evidence of a shift in beliefs about learning and were analyzed in detail. A typical quotation is given below:

> 'I think my learning method changed after my second year of university.'
>
> Q: 'From what to what?'
>
> 'Because [I am] from Hong Kong schools, I was trained to memorize, revise, not to think that much. And I tried the same method in the first two years of university. My grade points weren't high enough, because the exams are not oriented towards memorizing everything. For example, the lecturer will give you a take-home exam.

> You know, you take your final exam home and you ... and to give you one week to do your final exam. So, when I had it first outside yes, very easy. You know ... but it was very hard. It was harder than writing an exam because there are no right answers. They make you think. And because I really thought it would be easy. But in fact, you would realize that there were no right answers. There will be no right answer at all. You have to think and analyze and how you present your thoughts ... And in my third and fourth year of my undergraduate course, I learnt to think and present my thoughts. And I wasn't memorizing any more. I understood what was happening. Memorizing did not help.'
>
> Kember, 2001, pp. 213–214

This student made this conceptual change through exposure to a type of assessment incompatible with existing beliefs about learning, though earlier experiences had clearly raised doubts. There was also evidence of other experienced postgraduate students in the sample holding sophisticated beliefs and having made the change to these from the more naïve set. As a result of pressure from examinations and parental expectations, it is common for students to enter university envisaging learning as remembering model answers for examinations. Such beliefs are clearly incompatible with university study, and so need to be challenged. University teachers recognize this expectation from previous schooling as a problem which needs to be dealt with:

> 'Unfortunately, in Hong Kong education, they [the students] are not trained to discuss and debate at primary and secondary levels. It's difficult for them to put down the old mode of learning and pick up discovery ... Students who grow up in Hong Kong, however, are generally frightened, as they are so used to have model answers given to them in their secondary school training. "You just give me the model answers, tell me all about the author, and I will memorize so that I can regurgitate during exams." There were times when students were really frightened and dissatisfied with the fact that I had not given them the absolute model answers. So it takes rather a long time to convince the students that the teacher is not there to tell me everything or hand down knowledge. It is I myself who need to think independently, analyze, discover and eventually understand.'
>
> Lo Wai Luen, Chinese University of Hong Kong, lecturer in Chinese Literature, quoted in Kember with McNaught, 2007, p. 40

This quotation makes it clear that changing deep-seated beliefs is never an easy process, especially when the beliefs in question are central to a person's role, as beliefs about teaching and learning are to students. The naïve trio of beliefs about teaching, learning and knowledge is clearly not suited to the ideals of university education, yet is hard, and even traumatic, to change as it becomes entrenched through the years of schooling. Changing beliefs needs a challenge to one or more of the components of the trio through exposure to practices consistent with more sophisticated beliefs.

However, the exposure needs to be progressive and support should be provided. When students enter a program believing that all questions have answers which are either right or wrong, activities and assessments might be planned so as to progress from relatively straightforward tasks at the outset to more open-ended ones as the program progresses:

> 'So, my teaching will move from a more structured approach at the beginning to a more open-ended one towards the end; the teacher will move away from readily providing answers to giving no concrete answers eventually. This is exactly what the real world is: no definite answers for questions. At the start, they will gain confidence from "getting the answers right". This confidence is important to enable them to gradually discover that there are no absolute concrete answers but [rather] a logic or framework of thinking base upon which they can formulate their viewpoints, judgments, and predictions. Learning is about developing their own thinking rather than finding model answers.'
>
> Andrew Chan, Chinese University of Hong Kong, lecturer in Marketing, quoted in Kember with McNaught, 2007, p. 64

Kember (2007) synthesized five key principles extracted from the adult education literature on developing self-direction in learning for aiding students to change the trio of beliefs:

1. The change needs to be progressive or gradual, rather than abrupt.
2. Change should be from the familiar or known territory to the unknown.
3. There needs to be a challenge to existing beliefs through exposure to contrary positions, which in this case means exposure to types of teaching and learning inconsistent with existing beliefs.
4. Exposure to contrary positions needs to leave students dissatisfied with their existing beliefs, in this case by showing that the alternative forms of teaching and learning lead to better learning outcomes.
5. Social and intellectual support needs to be provided for what can be a difficult, and even traumatic, process.

A Hong Kong example of putting the principles into practice comes from Kember et al (2001, Chapter 10 in particular). This book reports on courses which challenged learners' beliefs about the reproduction of academic material by focusing towards the development of reflective practitioners. This posited the students' experience as a significant source of knowledge for the course. The courses were initially quite discomfiting for the majority of the students. With support from the teachers and fellow students, though, most adapted to and eventually came to prefer reflective to reproductive learning. In the process they also became more self-directing.

Conclusion

It has appeared to Western observers working from their Western psychological frameworks that Chinese practices with respect to teaching and learning are unenlightened and retrogressive. Yet, as is shown by Hau and Ho (this volume), Chinese students and those from East Asian countries consistently outperform their Western counterparts in international comparisons and other comparative studies. More fine-grained analysis of teaching and learning in Chinese contexts has uncovered explanations for the paradoxes which have occasioned a reconsideration of Western interpretations of how the Chinese approach learning and teaching.

Research into approaches to learning by students from Confucian-heritage countries has revealed approaches which combine memorizing and understanding in various ways. Adopting such approaches is consistent with high achievement, as the approaches incorporate the superior intellectual outcome of a deep approach with the ability to perform well in tests and examinations, which all too often reward recall. The discovery of these intermediate approaches in East Asia has led to a reconsideration of the nature of approaches to learning in the West, demonstrating real intellectual synergy through this exchange.

Teachers in Hong Kong and mainland China face large classes and intense pressure to help their students perform well in the all-important public examinations. Their teaching may, therefore, appear less student-centered according to Western frameworks. However, the teachers appear to have developed a style which adapts to the context by providing explanations which are coherent and in-depth, permitting their students to reach an understanding of a topic. There is also evidence of Chinese teachers showing a high level of pastoral care for their students, particularly outside the classroom. The international comparison studies have raised concerns in Western countries and forced them to re-examine models of good teaching practice.

A current and future concern for mainland China and Hong Kong is retaining the benefits of existing approaches to teaching and learning, while at the same time blending in elements of student-centered or constructivist teaching. Current approaches to teaching serve well for the acquisition and application of knowledge, which is what tends to be measured in international comparisons. It is not easy to construct valid measures which test intellectual capabilities such as critical thinking or the ability to deal with ill-defined cases, which can be incorporated into tests to be administered to large samples in many countries in standard conditions (King & Kitchener, 1994). However, knowledge-based economies need creative and critical thinkers, qualities which need to be practiced in the classroom to enhance their development. Constructivist forms of teaching and learning promote this development, as they require students to be engaged in critical dialogue with teachers and peers. Because Chinese students are so achievement oriented, constructivism will only be successful if the school and university assessment is aligned with high-quality learning outcomes (see Biggs & Tang, 2007).

References

Berliner, D.C. (2005). The near impossibility of testing for teaching quality. *Journal of Teacher Education, 56*, 205–213.

Biggs, J. & Tang, C. (2007). *Teaching for quality learning at university*, 3rd edn. Buckingham, UK: Society for Research in Higher Education and The Open University Press.

Biggs, J. & Watkins, D. (1996). The Chinese learner in retrospect. In D. Watkins & J. B. Biggs (eds), *The Chinese learner: Cultural, psychological and contextual influences* (pp. 269–285). Melbourne and Hong Kong: Australian Council for Educational Research and the Comparative Education Research Centre, University of Hong Kong.

Biggs, J. (1987). *Student approaches to learning and studying.* Melbourne: Australian Council for Educational Research.

Biggs, J. (1992). *Why and how do Hong Kong students learn? Using the Learning and Study Process Questionnaires.* Hong Kong: Hong Kong University.

Biggs, J., Kember, D. & Leung, D. Y. P. (2001). The revised two-factor Study Process Questionnaire: R-SPQ-2F. *British Journal of Educational Psychology, 71*, 133–149.

Biggs, J. B. (1996). Stages of expatriate involvement in educational development. *Educational Research Journal, 11*(2), 157–164.

Case, J. & Marshall, D. (2004). Between deep and surface: Procedural approaches to learning in engineering education contexts. *Studies in Higher Education, 29*, 605–615.

Chan, C. K. K. (2001). Promoting learning and understanding through constructivist approaches for Chinese learners. In D. A. Watkins & J. B. Biggs (eds), *Teaching the Chinese learner: Psychological and pedagogical perspectives* (pp. 181–204). Hong Kong/Melbourne: Comparative Education Research Centre/Australian Council for Educational Research.

Chan, Y. Y. G. & Watkins, D. (1994). Classroom environment and approaches to learning: An investigation of the actual and preferred perceptions of Hong Kong secondary school students. *Instructional Science, 22*, 233–246.

Ching, C. S. (2001). *The effects of constructivist teaching on students' learning in history.* Unpublished Master of Education thesis, University of Hong Kong.

Cortazzi, M. & Jin, L. (2001). Large classes in China: 'Good' teachers and interaction. In D. A. Watkins & J. B. Biggs (eds), *Teaching the Chinese learner: Psychological and instructional perspectives* (pp. 113–132). Hong Kong/Melbourne: Comparative Education Research Centre/Australian Council for Educational Research.

Dahlin, B. & Watkins, D. (2000). The role of repetition in the process of memorising and understanding: A comparison of the views of German and Chinese secondary school students in Hong Kong. *British Journal of Educational Psychology, 70*, 65–84.

Dart, B. & Boulton-Lewis, G. (eds) (1998). *Teaching and learning in higher education.* Melbourne: Australian Council for Educational Research.

Education and Manpower Bureau (2003). *Education statistics.* Hong Kong: Education and Manpower Bureau.

Education Commission of Hong Kong (2000). *Excel and grow: Education blueprint for the 21st century.* Hong Kong: Hong Kong Government Printer.

Elliot, B. & Chan, K. W. (1998, September). *Epistemological beliefs in learning to teach: Resolving conceptual and empirical issues.* Paper presented at the European Conference on Educational Research in Ljubljana, Slovenia.

Entwistle, N. & Entwistle, D. (2003). Preparing for examinations: The interplay of memorising and understanding, and the development of knowledge objects. *Higher Education Research and Development, 22*, 19– 41.

Entwistle, N. (1998). Approaches to learning and forms of understanding. In B. Dart & G. Boulton-Lewis (eds). *Teaching and learning in higher education* (pp. 72–101). Melbourne, Australia: Australian Council for Educational Research.

Fan, L., Wong, N. Y., Cai, J., & Li, S. (2004). *How Chinese learn mathematics: Perspectives from insiders.* Singapore: World Scientific.

Fok, A. & Watkins, D. (2006). Does a critical constructivist learning environment encourage a deeper approach to learning? *Asian Pacific Education Researcher, 16*, 1–10.

Gao, L. & Watkins, D. A. (2001). Identifying and assessing the conceptions of teaching of secondary school physics teachers in China. *British Journal of Educational Psychology, 71*, 443–469.

Gow, L. & Kember, D. (1990). Does higher education promote independent learning? *Higher Education, 19*, 307–322.

Hess, R. D. & Azuma, M. (1991). Cultural support for schooling: Contrasts between Japan and the United States. *Educational Researcher, 20*, 2–8.

Ho, A. S. P. (2001). A conceptual change approach to university staff development. In D. A. Watkins & J. B. Biggs (eds), *Teaching the Chinese learner: Psychological and instructional perspectives* (pp. 237–252). Hong Kong/Melbourne, Australia: Comparative Education Research Centre/Australian Council for Educational Research.

Ho, D. Y. F. (1996). Filial piety and its psychological consequences. In M. H. Bond (ed.), *The handbook of Chinese psychology* (pp. 155–165). Hong Kong: Oxford University Press.

Ho, I. T. (2001). Are Chinese teachers authoritarian? In D. A. Watkins & J. B. Biggs (eds), *Teaching the Chinese learner: psychological and instructional perspectives* (pp. 97–112). Hong Kong/Melbourne, australia: Comparative Education Research Centre/Australian Council for Educational Research.

Hofstede, G. H. (2001). *Culture's consequences: Comparing values, behaviors, institutions, and organisations across nations.* Thousand Oaks, CA: Sage.

Johnson, R. K. & Ngor, A. Y. S. (1996). Coping with second language texts: the development of lexically-based reading strategies. In D. Watkins & J. B. Biggs (eds). *The Chinese learner: Cultural, psychological and contextual influences* (pp. 123–140). Melbourne, Australia and Hong Kong: Australian Council for Educational Research and the Comparative Education Research Centre, University of Hong Kong.

Kelly, E. & Watkins, D. A. (2002, April). *A comparison of the goals and approaches to teaching of Expatriate and Chinese lecturers at universities in Hong Kong.* Paper presented to Hong Kong branch of the Higher Education Research and Development Society of Australasia, City University of Hong Kong.

Kember, D. (1996). The intention to both memorise and understand: Another approach to learning? *Higher Education, 31,* 341–351.

Kember, D. (1997). A reconcepualisation of the research into university academics' conceptions of teaching. *Learning and Instruction, 7,* 255–275.

Kember, D. (2000a). Misconceptions about the learning approaches, motivation and study practices of Asian students. *Higher Education, 40,* 99–121.

Kember, D. (2000b). *Action learning and action research: Improving the quality of teaching and learning.* London: Kogan Page.

Kember, D. (2001). Beliefs about knowledge and the process of teaching and learning as a factor in adjusting to study in higher education. *Studies in Higher Education, 26,* 205–221.

Kember, D. (2007). *Reconsidering open and distance learning in the developing world: Meeting students' learning needs.* Abingdon, Oxfordshire: Routledge.

Kember, D. et al (2001). *Reflective teaching and learning in the health professions.* Oxford, England: Blackwell Science.

Kember, D. & Gow, L. (1989). *Cultural specificity of approaches to study.* Paper presented at the 6th Annual Conference of the Hong Kong Educational Research Association, Hong Kong.

Kember, D. & Gow, L. (1990). Cultural specificity of approaches to study. *British Journal of Educational Psychology, 60,* 356–363.

Kember, D. & Gow, L. (1991). A challenge to the anecdotal stereotype of the Asian student. *Studies in Higher Education, 16,* 117–128.

Kember, D. & McNaught, C. (2007). *Enhancing university teaching: Lessons from research into award winning teachers.* Abingdon, England: Routledge.

Kember, D., Jenkins, W., and Ng, K. C. (2003). Adult students' perceptions of good teaching as a function of their conceptions of learning – Part 1. Influencing the development of self-determination. *Studies in Continuing Education, 25,* 240–251.

King, P. M. & Kitchener, K. S. (1994). *Developing reflective judgement: Understanding and promoting intellectual growth and critical thinking in adolescents and adults.* San Francisco, CA: Jossey-Bass.

Lee, W. O. (1996). The cultural context for Chinese learners: Conceptions of learning in the Confucian tradition. In D. Watkins & J. B. Biggs (eds). *The Chinese learner: Cultural, psychological and contextual influences* (pp. 25–41). Melbourne, Australia and Hong Kong: Australian Council for Educational Research and the Comparative Education Research Centre, University of Hong Kong.

Leung, D. Y. P., Ginns, P., & Kember, D. (2008). Examining the cultural specificity of approaches to learning in universities in Hong Kong and Sydney. *Journal of Cross-Cultural Psychology, 39*(3), 251–266.

Leung, F. K. S. (2005). Some characteristics of East Asian mathematics classrooms based on data from the TIMSS 1999 Video Study. *Educational Studies in Mathematics, 60,* 199–215.

Ma, K. H. (1994). *The relationship between achievement and attitude towards science, approaches to learning and classroom environment.* Unpublished Master of Education dissertation, University of Hong Kong.

Marton, F. & Säljö, R. (1976). On qualitative differences in learning, outcome and process I. *British Journal of Educational Psychology, 46,* 4–11.

Marton, F., Dall'Alba, G., & Beaty, E. (1993). Conceptions of learning. *International Journal of Educational Research, 19,* 277–300.

Marton, F., Dall'Alba, G., & Kun, T. L. (1996). Memorising and understanding: the keys to the paradox? In D. Watkins & J. B. Biggs (eds), *The Chinese learner: Cultural, psychological and contextual influences* (pp. 69–84). Melbourne, Australia and Hong Kong: Australian Council for Educational Research and the Comparative Education Research Centre, University of Hong Kong.

Marton, F., Hounsell, D., & Entwistle, N. (1984). *The experience of learning.* Edinburgh, Scotland: Scottish Academic Press.

Marton, F., Watkins, D., & Tang, C. (1997). Discontinuities and continuities in the experience of learning: an interview study of high-school students in Hong Kong. *Learning and Instruction, 7,* 21–48.

Prosser, M. & Trigwell, K. (1999). *Understanding learning and teaching: The experience in higher education.* Buckingham, England: Society for Research into Higher Education and Open University Press.

Richardson, J. T. E. (2000). *Researching student learning: Approaches to studying in campus-based and distance education.* Buckingham, England: Society for Research into Higher Education and Open University Press.

Richardson, J. T. E. (1994). Cultural specificity of approaches to studying in higher education: A literature survey. *Higher Education, 27,* 449–468.

So, W. M. (2003). *Perceptions of competition in Hong Kong schools.* Unpublished BEd Honours dissertation, University of Hong Kong.

Stevenson, H. W. & Lee, S. Y. (1996). The academic achievement of Chinese people. In M. H. Bond (ed.), *The handbook of Chinese psychology* (pp. 124–142). Hong Kong: Oxford University Press.

Stigler, J. & Hiebert, J. (1999). *The teaching gap.* New York: The Free Press.

Stokes, S. (2001). Problem-Based Learning in a Chinese context: faculty perceptions. In D. A. Watkins, & J. B. Biggs (eds), *Teaching the Chinese learner: Psychological and pedagogical perspectives* (pp. 203–216). Hong Kong/Melbourne, Australia: Comparative Education Research Centre/Australian Council for Educational Research.

Tang, K. C. C. (1991). *Effects of different assessment methods on tertiary students' approaches to studying.* Unpublished Ph. D. Dissertation, University of Hong Kong.

Tang, T. (1993). Inside the classroom: The students' view. In J. B. Biggs & D. A. Watkins (eds), *Learning and teaching in Hong Kong: What is and what might be.* Hong Kong: Faculty of Education, Hong Kong.

Tang, T. K. W. (2001). The influence of teacher education on conceptions of teaching and learning. In D. A. Watkins & J. B. Biggs (eds), *Teaching the Chinese learner: Psychological and pedagogical perspectives* (pp. 219–236). Hong Kong/ Melbourne, Australia: Comparative Education Research Centre/Australian Council for Educational Research.

Trow, M. (2006). Reflections on the transition from elite to mass to universal access: Forms and phases of higher education in modern societies since WWII. In J. J. F. Forest & P. G. Altbach (eds), *International handbook of higher education* (pp. 243–280). Amsterdam, The Netherlands: Springer.

University Grants Committee of Hong Kong. (2006). *Facts and figures 2005.* Hong Kong: University Grants Committee Secretariat. Retrieved August 16, 2006, from http://www.ugc.edu.hk/english/documents/figures/

Watkins, D. & Biggs, J. B. (1996) (eds). *The Chinese learner: Cultural, psychological and contextual influences.* Melbourne, Australia and Hong Kong: Australian Council for Educational Research and the Comparative Education Research Centre, University of Hong Kong.

Watkins, D. & Hattie, J. (1985). A longitudinal study of the approaches to learning of Australian tertiary students. *Human Learning, 4,* 127–141.

Watkins, D. (1996). Hong Kong secondary school learners: a developmental perspective. In D. Watkins & J. B. Biggs (eds), *The Chinese learner: Cultural, psychological and contextual influences* (pp. 107–119). Melbourne, Australia and Hong Kong: Australian Council for Educational Research and the Comparative Education Research Centre, University of Hong Kong.

Wong, W. L., Watkins, D., & Wong, N. Y. (2006). Cognitive and affective outcomes of person-environment fit to a critical constructivist learning environment: A Hong Kong investigation. *Constructivist Foundations, 1,* 49–55.

Yang, K. S. & Yu, A. B. (1988). *Social- and individual-oriented achievement motivation: Conceptualization and measurement.* Paper presented at the symposium on Chinese personality and social psychology, 24th International Congress of Psychology, Sydney, Australia.

Yu, A. B. (1996). Ultimate life concerns, self, and Chinese achievement motivation. In M. H. Bond (ed.), *The handbook of Chinese psychology* (pp. 227–246). Hong Kong: Oxford University Press.

CHAPTER 13

Chinese students' motivation and achievement

Kit-Tai Hau and Irene T. Ho

The study of students' achievement and related motivational characteristics in different cultural groups has been of great interest to researchers in the past two decades. The discovery of similarities and differences in the application of existing motivational theories in different cultures provides the chance to revise, accommodate, and expand those theories, so that they could become more accurate and more comprehensive (Pintrich, 2003). We believe that the complexity of achievement motivation cannot be fully understood without its being examined in different contexts and cultural settings.

Among the various cultural groups being studied, Chinese and other Asian students from the Confucian cultural heritage have drawn special attention because of their outstanding performance in international comparisons of achievement (e.g. Beaton et al., 1996; Lapointe, Askew, & Mead, 1992; Lapointe, Mead, & Askew, 1992; Leung, 2002; Mullis et al., 1997; OECD, 2003; Stevenson & Lee, 1996; Sue & Okazaki, 1990). While academic success could be attributed to a large number of educational factors at both individual and contextual levels, an important focus of research has been on students' motivational characteristics engendered from their specific cultural and educational environments.

In this chapter, we will first review recent evidences about Chinese students' outstanding academic performance, followed by a discussion of major themes and issues arising from the study of their motivational characteristics (see also Kember & Watkins, this volume).

Academic performance

International comparisons

Stevenson and his colleagues (Chen & Stevenson, 1995; Stevenson & Lee, 1996) were among the first to provide evidence for the superior performance of Chinese and other Asian students through systematic examinations of their achievement from kindergarten to high school. In a curriculum-based mathematics test, Chinese and Japanese students were found to outperform Asian-American students, who in turn outperformed Caucasian-American students (Chen & Stevenson, 1995).

It is important to note that comparing students' academic achievement across countries and cultural contexts has never been easy, as diverse curricula, language systems, and educational settings would make the interpretation of observed differences in performance difficult. As a result, mathematics and science are often the targets of international comparisons, since they are core subjects in basic education which are relatively more language free, each with its own 'symbols' of communication. Examples include the studies by the International Association for the Evaluation of Educational Achievement (IEA) [the First and Second International Mathematics Studies, the Second International Science Study, and the Third International Mathematics and Science Study (TIMSS)] (Beaton et al., 1996; Lapointe, Askew et al., 1992; Lapointe, Mead et al., 1992; Leung, 2002; Mullis et al., 1997). More recently, despite knowing the serious limitations and potential caveats in interpretation, educational researchers have stretched their limits by assessing and comparing students' verbal competence across different countries and languages in the Programme for International Student Assessment (PISA) conducted by the Organisation for Economic Co-operation and Development (OECD, 2003). The study included, for example, comparisons of comprehension abilities among Chinese students reading in Chinese, US students reading in English, Japanese students reading in Japanese, and French students reading in French.

Despite the difficulties involved, findings from these large-scale international studies largely provide converging evidence for the outstanding performance of Chinese and other Asian students. For example, in the Second IEA study (Lapointe, Askew et al., 1992; Lapointe, Mead et al., 1992), thirteen-year-olds from mainland China and Taiwan were among the top in achievement, and Chinese migrants also consistently outperformed other ethnic groups within Western countries. Similarly, in the TIMSS (Beaton et al., 1996; Mullis et al., 1997), Grade 4 and Grade 8 students in Hong Kong, Japan, South Korea, and Singapore outperformed their counterparts from other countries (twenty-six countries in Grade 4, forty-one in Grade 8). These Chinese and other Asian countries/cities all share the Confucian cultural heritage.

Similar results were obtained in the PISA study (OECD, 2003), a more recent large-scale international comparison research project. Hong Kong and South Korea were among the three top countries/cities (the other being Finland) with more than half of their students performing at the top three levels in the seven-level scale. In terms of country mean score rankings, among the forty participating countries/cities in the PISA study, students from Hong Kong (1st, 10th, and 3rd in mathematics, reading, and science, respectively), South Korea (3rd, 2nd, 4th), Japan (6th, 14th, 2nd), and Macau (9th, 15th, 7th) also performed outstandingly.

Thus, across different studies, there has been consistent evidence for the outstanding academic achievement of Chinese students and other Asian students sharing the same cultural heritage. While it is true that educational success denotes more than high test scores in a few academic subjects, these scores are by and large useful and important indicators of such success. On the one hand, test performances provide a more objective basis for comparison. On the other hand, they also significantly determine and limit students' future educational and career opportunities. Observations of these outstanding academic achievements of Chinese and other Asian students have prompted researchers to seek explanations.

Inadequacy of economic explanations

As economic advantage often contributes to better educational opportunities with more resources for learning, we will first look for explanations from this perspective. The evidence available does not suggest this to be a significant determining factor, because Chinese and other Asian societies do not rank higher than Western countries on the world GDP list. Based on the data in 2007, Japan, South Korea, Macau, and Singapore ranked 18, 30, 29, and 17, respectively, among the list of 179 countries in the world (International Monetary Fund, 2007). Even for Hong Kong, which ranked sixth on the GDP list, the public expenditure on education relative to the size of its economy was lowest among the high-performing countries (Leung, 2002).

Furthermore, in terms of educational environment, schools in Chinese and other Asian societies do not fare better than their Western counterparts. Take class size, which is often considered an important indicator of quality education, as an example: the unique feature shared by schools in the four best-performing Chinese and Asian countries in TIMSS was that they all had large class sizes, in contrast to the much smaller classes in Western countries.

Another observation to note is that while it is generally recognized that high parental socioeconomic status (SES) is conducive to students' academic performance, this effect was found to be much smaller among Chinese and Asian students than among their Western counterparts in the PISA study (OECD, 2003). As a standard of reference, averaging over all OECD countries, SES explained 11.7 per cent of the variance in students' mathematics performance and one standard deviation (16.4 units) of SES improvement raised 33.7 units of mathematics score (standard error = 0.40). For Chinese and other Asian students, SES explained a much smaller percentage of variance and benefited less: for Hong Kong, it explained 3.6 per cent of variance, 22.6 units of mathematics score for one standard deviation increase of SES; for Japan, 4.4 per cent and 23.0 units; for South Korea, 5.5 per cent and 26.4 units; and for Macau, 1.0 per cent and 11.7 units. These findings suggest that Chinese and Asian students from low-SES families are educationally much less disadvantaged as compared to Western students from low-SES families. In other words, SES is not as significant a correlate of academic achievement for Chinese students as it is for Western students

In summary, at the country level, the relatively low GDP of Chinese and other Asian societies suggests that the economic situation and government investment in education do not explain why Chinese and other Asian students are doing so well academically. At the family level, high SES has a smaller positive effect on these students' achievement than on that of their Western counterparts.

If economic situations both at the country level and the family level do not point to better educational provisions or opportunities, alternative explanations for Chinese or other Asian students' high achievement need to be found. Some discussions have also explored the possibilities of differences in intelligence or everyday experiences, but these do not seem to have provided convincing explanations (see reviews by Chen & Stevenson, 1995; Stevenson & Lee, 1996; Sue & Okazaki, 1990). As neither hereditary nor economic factors provide convincing explanations, researchers have turned their search to sociocultural and motivational factors. Here we will summarize some important findings with a focus on Chinese students.

Sociocultural and motivational explanations

Research on Chinese students' motivation has been highly varied in terms of the participant groups, the psychological constructs or processes examined, and the methodology employed. Some researchers focus on an in-depth analysis of a particular motivational construct, while others examine the relationships among multiple variables. Most empirical studies have been conducted based on social-cognitive models and constructs. Often the focus is on understanding how Chinese students' patterns and levels of motivation differ or relate to achievement in comparison with other cultural groups, and discussions have centered around the influences of the Confucian-collectivistic tradition, in contrast to Socratic-individualistic influences in Western societies (e.g. Tweed & Lehman, 2002).

In a review of what motivates students in the classroom, Pintrich (2003) presents five general principles from a Western and social-cognitive perspective: 1) adaptive self-efficacy and competence beliefs motivate students; 2) adaptive attributions and control beliefs motivate students; 3) higher levels of interest and intrinsic motivation motivate students; 4) higher levels of achievement value motivate students; and 5) achievement goals motivate and direct students. As most empirical studies on the motivation of Chinese students have examined similar and related constructs, the following review will be organized around these themes. We will begin by examining the role of values and source of motivation, followed by a description of findings about competence beliefs, attributions, and goal orientations.

The value of academic achievement

Any examination of Chinese students' motivation would very likely make reference to the high regard for academic achievement in the Confucian tradition, a regard which underlies their strong engagement in academic activities, such as attending school, participating in after-school classes, and studying in general (Fuligni & Stevenson, 1995; Salili, 1994, 1996; Stevenson & Lee, 1996). Closely related is a cluster of valued attitudes, such as striving to enhance the family's status, providing the best learning environment for children, emphasizing effort and practice, belief in persistence to obtain success, and upholding high standards of excellence, all of which provide the background for Asian students' outstanding academic performance (Eaton & Dembo, 1997; Li, 2002, 2004, 2005; Stevenson & Lee, 1996).

In the Western scenario, learning-task value is usually defined in terms of interest, utility, importance, or cost from an individualistic point of view, meaning whether students find value in such tasks is a highly individualized matter arising from different developmental trajectories (Eccles & Wigfield, 1995; Wigfield & Eccles, 1992, 2002). In contrast, related discussions about Chinese students talk about the value of school achievement as a central tenet in the Confucian culture (Li, 2002, 2004, 2005), a tenet to which all members of the culture generally subscribe.

Educational achievement is often emphasized as a social obligation, especially obligation to parents and the family (Hostede, 1983; Li, 2002, 2004, 2005; Tseng, 2004; Wang & Li, 2003). Indeed, parental influences have often been found to be an important aspect of Chinese children's achievement motivation (see Liu, Yue, & Li, this volume, for historical rationale). For example, Chow and Chu (2007) found filial piety, especially 'self-sacrificing obedience', and parental value of education to be significant contributors to Hong Kong Chinese students' achievement motivation. Moreover, the influence of parenting style on Chinese students' learning goal orientations as well as these students' stronger emphasis on achieving for the sake of authority figures have been reported (Cheng, 2005; Yeung, 2005). In a study by Fuligni and Zhang (2004) of 700 urban and rural high-school students in China, consistent links were found between academic motivation and a sense of obligation to support, assist, and respect the family. Very often this sense of obligation remains even after migration to Western individualistic societies (e.g. Fulgni, Tseng, & Lam, 1999).

Other than the fulfilment of social obligations, learning as a means for self-cultivation and self-perfection has also been underscored in the Chinese culture. In fact, it has been suggested that in contrast to other social achievement domains, learning is a unique domain in which Chinese students show a greater and more developed individualistic and independent self-construal. Li (2006) asked Chinese adolescents aged twelve to nineteen to respond to open-ended probes about their goals (desired future outcomes) in learning and found that students expressed significantly more individual than social goals. Goals of aspiration, cognitive development, social contribution, socioeconomic advancement and moral development were most salient and frequently mentioned by students. In another study (Li, 2002), Chinese college students reported both benefits to oneself (e.g. fulfilment of oneself) and benefits to others (e.g. contribute to society) in their stated purposes of learning.

Li and colleagues (Li, 2006; Wang & Li, 2003) argue that the stronger sense of self-reliance displayed by Chinese students in learning is a manifestation of the autonomous and competitive self rather than the relational and interdependent self, and self-development is definitely an important academic goal. It should be noted, however, that in contrast to Western children's notion of self-development through learning as a process of ability enhancement and task attempting, Chinese children see learning as a process of self-perfection with an emphasis on exerting diligence and persistence (Li, 2004). Li (2005) differentiates such relative emphases in terms of Western students adopting a *mind* orientation to learning and Chinese students adopting a *virtue* approach to learning. Thus, there is a dual emphasis in how Chinese students perceive the value of learning. On the one hand, students are propelled by a sense of obligation to their parents, the family, and society. On the other hand, they also clearly see the importance of education as a means for personal cultivation and perfection.

How Chinese students in modern times navigate their learning path while harboring both collectivistic and individualistic tendencies requires closer examination. Nevertheless, the strong moral undertone associated with the importance of being a good student has been consistent, embodying duties of self-cultivation as well as duties to the family and society (Li, 2002, 2004, 2005, 2006). No matter where the importance of academic achievement lies, Chinese teachers could rely on their students having an inherent identification with the value of academic pursuits more than Western teachers could, who often need to put in extra effort to make learning activities useful, meaningful, and relevant in order to engage their students (Brophy, 1999).

Intrinsic or extrinsic motivation

It is generally accepted among Western educators that higher levels of intrinsic motivation would result in more cognitive engagement and higher levels of achievement by students, and intrinsic motivation is often equated with interest (Eccles, Wigfield, & Schiefele, 1998; Pintrich & Schunk, 2002; Schiefele, Krapp & Winteler, 1992). What is of concern to Western researchers is not demonstrating that interest matters, but rather trying to understand how interest affects learning or how it could be developed (Pintrich, 2003).

The relationship between interest and academic performance among Chinese students does not appear to be as straightforward. Although higher interest is generally associated with better performance when analyzing motivation at the level of the individual student, country-level analyses have shown a different pattern of results. In the large-scale international TIMSS, it was found that Chinese students in Hong Kong and Singapore, together with Japanese and Korean students who also share the Confucian culture, outperformed their Western counterparts in mathematics, yet they displayed relatively negative attitudes towards the subject (Leung, 2002). While interest does not seem to contribute to high achievement, consistently higher than average correlations between sense of belonging to school and examination performance were found among Chinese and other Asian students in the PISA study (OECD, 2003). These suggest the more prominent role of internalized values and beliefs related to schooling than personal interest in accounting for academic success in collectivistic cultures.

Further evidence of this kind was generated in a study by d'Ailly (2004): Anglo-Canadian children, especially boys, put in more effort when they thought they were good at or interested in the task, whereas Chinese children spent equal effort on all tasks irrespective of their interest or self-efficacy. In another study (d'Ailly, 2003), it was also found that for Taiwan Chinese children, intrinsic interest and fun might not be as strong a motivator for hard work as external rules and values. All these seem to suggest that extrinsic motivation could work equally well with Chinese students, and intrinsic motivation is not as important as in the Western context in promoting student engagement.

Recent research from self-determination theory has expanded the traditional distinction between intrinsic and extrinsic motivation into a more differentiated structure of extrinsic motivation, comprising 1) external control or constraints imposed by others, such as reward and punishment; 2) introjection, reflecting the beginning of internalization of values, or seeking approval from others, which is still largely externally controlled; 3) identification characterized by self-endorsement of values and goals, with more internal control; and 4) integration, signifying congruence between the self and values or goals, with high internal control (Ryan & Deci, 2000). The theory postulates that more internalized styles of motivation would result in better performance as well as greater psychological well-being. The implication is that even though the original source of motivation may be extrinsic, the process of internalizing related values and goals could result in a high degree of self-direction and motivation.

This extension of the concept of extrinsic motivation beyond that representing total external control would explain motivation in the Chinese context much better than the simple intrinsic–extrinsic dichotomy. Although personal interest may not appear to be a strong motivating force for Chinese students' learning, they could still be adaptively motivated through internalizing the related values for learning. In other words, the distinction between intrinsic and extrinsic motivation could become blurred, as originally external forces could be transformed into internal drives. Indeed, it has been found that among the Chinese, extrinsic motivation and intrinsic motivation tend to co-occur rather than be antithetical (Salili, Chiu, & Lai, 2001), whereas Western students striving for external goals, such as high marks or pleasing others, often report less intrinsic motivation for learning.

A related line of research has been conducted to investigate whether greater self-determination, which supposedly fosters intrinsic motivation in learning, would have the same effects on Chinese students.

Iyengar and Lepper (1999) demonstrated in two studies that, while Anglo-American children showed less intrinsic interest when choices were made for them, the contrary was true for Asian-American children, who preferred choices being made for them by trusted authority figures or peers.

In an attempt to test this phenomenon among Chinese children in Taiwan, d'Ailly (2003) found that, with other variables being held constant, children perceiving themselves as having more autonomy actually tended to have lower achievement in school. Perceived autonomy also did not have a direct impact on effort expenditure. It was suggested that while directives from authority figures may be perceived as controlling and thus decreasing a sense of autonomy in Western children, these may be perceived as caring or helping by Chinese students in the Confucian learning context (see also Ho, 2001). In fact, a corresponding finding from this study was that in contrast to Western findings (Deci, Schwartz, Sheinman, & Ryan, 1981), whether teachers adopted a more autonomy-supporting motivating style seemed to have little relationship with any measure of their students' motivation.

A recent study by Vansteenkiste, Zhou, Lens, and Soenens (2005) provided further insights in relation to the role of autonomy. They demonstrated that experiences of relative autonomy were in fact conducive to optimal learning among Chinese students. When the total measure of autonomy was broken down into components of positive autonomy and negative control, it was found that the former was related positively to adaptive learning and performance, while the latter had opposite effects. Findings such as these suggest the need to take a closer look at the nature of constructs such as autonomy and independence or control and conformity in different cultural contexts when examining their effects on students.

To sum up, research findings strongly suggest that behind Chinese students' high academic performance is their willingness to exert effort on tasks of even low interest or under external pressure, a focus that has been attributed to their greater sense of responsibility and value attached to learning. Nevertheless, it is not accurate to conclude that Chinese students put in effort only because of their compliance with authority or external social pressure. Probably the positive effects of intrinsic motivation and self-determination on learning are quite universal, yet what constitutes or contributes to intrinsic motivation may vary in different cultural contexts. A clear implication is that there is the need to move beyond examinations of learning motivation in terms of a simple intrinsic versus extrinsic perspective to a more precise understanding of the cultural meaning of related constructs as well as their interactions.

Self-efficacy and competence beliefs

It has been a major finding in Western research that if students believe they are able to do well, they are more likely to be motivated, put in effort, persist, and perform better (Pintrich & Schunk, 2002). Competence beliefs and their effects on achievement behavior have been studied in terms of a variety of expectancy constructs (Bandura, 1997; Eccles et al., 1998; Pintrich & Schunk, 2002; Weiner, 1986), among which the construct of self-efficacy is a major one. According to this theory (Bandura, 1997), an important source of self-efficacy is mastery or success experience, and adaptive self-efficacy beliefs should be marked by accurate calibrations of one' capability to perform certain tasks. Overly pessimistic perceptions of efficacy would lower expectancy for success and thus motivation, whereas an overestimation of one's capability might deter students from changing their behavior in the face of feedback (Pintrich, 2000a; Pintrich & Zusho, 2002).

Despite Chinese students' high academic achievement, research has shown that they actually display a generally lower sense of efficacy than their Western counterparts. For example, Salili and colleagues (Salili, Lai, & Leung, 2004) found that the academic self-efficacy of Hong Kong Chinese students was significantly lower than that of Canadian-Chinese or European-Canadian students. Similar results were found in studies comparing students from the United Kingdom and China (Rogers, 1998), or Asian and non-Asian students in America (Eaton & Dembo, 1997). Moreover, Hong Kong and Singaporean students, most of whom are Chinese, outperformed many Western students in the TIMSS mathematics tests, but showed a striking lack of confidence in the subject (Leung, 2002).

Similar trends of results were found in research on students' self-concept across many countries. Although at the individual level, students with higher academic achievement generally demonstrate higher self-concept (Marsh, Martin, & Hau, 2006), analyses at the country level have shown that students in Asian countries with better academic achievement do not have particularly high self-concept. For example, Hong Kong Chinese students have been found to rank among the lowest in a list of countries in this respect (Leung, 2002).

Different explanations have been put forward for this lower average sense of efficacy among Chinese students despite their outstanding achievement. In the first place, the highly competitive examination systems characterizing Chinese schooling would produce a lot of failure experiences for the general student population. This, together with high expectations for all students to achieve in school, is naturally not conducive to the development of a high sense of efficacy. Moreover, this lower reported sense of efficacy has also been attributed to the valued virtue of humility and modesty, to the extent that students may be self-effacing when asked about their competence (Eaton & Dembo, 1997; Leung, 2002; Salili et al., 2004). In other words, Western students nurtured in an individualistic culture experience pride upon success and low self-worth upon failure, when their emphasis in learning is on personal achievement. Therefore higher achievement leads to higher self-efficacy and vice versa. In contrast, Chinese students remain humble upon success and feel guilt and shame upon failure, which is a result of their emphasis on learning as a duty to self (self-perfecting) and duty to the family and society (Li, 2005). Thus reported self-efficacy tends to be lower regardless of achievement (see also the low ratings on the competence facet of NEO-PIR conscientiousness: McCrae, Costa, & Yik, 1996). A related finding is that while higher self-efficacy would motivate Western children to put more effort into the task, Chinese children would spend equal effort on all tasks irrespective of their sense of efficacy (d'Ailly, 2004). The implication is that even low-performing students would keep on trying despite experiences of failure.

To sum up, research has shown that there are at least two ways in which Chinese students differ from their Western counterparts in relation to competence beliefs. Firstly, with academic success being emphasized as a fulfilment of one's duty and achieved through effort, these success experiences may not be as significant a source of self-efficacy as in the Western context. Secondly, the importance of self-efficacy may not be as prominent in producing achievement behavior as in the West, since there is no demonstrated relationship between their sense of efficacy and effort expenditure. Therefore, while Western researchers are concerned about calibrating efficacy beliefs (i.e. not overly optimistic or pessimistic) in order to optimize their motivating effects on students (Stone, 2000), this does not seem to be as important an issue in the Chinese context. Chinese students are not prone to having overly high perceptions of their competence, and low competence beliefs may actually foster rather than reduce striving for achievement, when they are determined to succeed.

Attributions and control beliefs

In learning situations students inevitably encounter successes and failures, and their beliefs about the causes of success and failure would affect their subsequent achievement strivings. For example, according to Weiner's attribution theory of motivation (Weiner, 1986, 2004), attributing success to stable and controllable causes would enhance future achievement behavior, whereas attributing failure to stable and uncontrollable causes would have opposite motivational consequences. Among the various causes relevant to academic achievement, ability and effort have received most attention.

Research on Western students has generally shown that they value ability and prefer to be seen as achieving by ability. This is closely related to the desire to enhance self-worth in an individualistic culture (Covington, 1992; Crocker & Wolfe, 2001; Weiner, 1986). Correspondingly, Western students tend to attribute academic success to inherent ability or having a good teacher (Stevenson, Chen, & Lee, 1993; Stevenson & Stigler, 1992), which are less controllable factors. In contrast, studies of Chinese students' attributions have consistently found high levels of internal rather than external attributions for both success and failure, and there is clear evidence for the predominance of effort attribution (Hau & Salili, 1991, 1996; Ho, Salili, Biggs, & Hau, 1999; Lau & Chan, 2001). These differential patterns of attribution suggest a highly adaptive attributional style on the part of Chinese students, as higher internal locus of causality, especially an attribution to the more controllable cause of effort, would contribute to their continued striving even in the face of failure.

Further evidence of Chinese students' adaptive control beliefs comes from studies on their conceptions about ability. While ability is considered a relatively stable and uncontrollable trait in the Western context (Weiner, 1986), Chinese students generally consider ability to be malleable through hard work (Hau & Salili, 1991, 1996). This belief in the incremental nature of ability enhances perceptions about opportunities for improvement through practice and learning, thus resulting in greater achievement striving (Dweck, 1999; Dweck & Elliot, 1983). In other words, with this belief, ability to the Chinese people becomes controllable and unstable. Therefore, while attributing failure to ability would produce debilitating effects on Western students' motivation and self-esteem, the same effects may not be as significant among Chinese students.

Besides studies from the attribution and ability theory perspectives, other investigations of Chinese students' general conceptions about learning have also pointed to converging evidence about the perceived importance of effort in learning. In Li's (2006) study of Chinese adolescents, the participants expressed a strong sense of personal agency in learning, emphasizing diligence, endurance of hardship, perseverance, concentration, self-discipline, and taking initiative—termed 'learning virtues' (p. 485) and synonymous to effort.

Achievement goal orientation

A great deal of evidence shows that the goals students bring into specific achievement situations direct their achievement behavior. In Western research, the basic framework for examining achievement goals is the mastery versus performance dichotomy, although recently there has been an addition of the approach-avoidance dimension to this theorizing (see reviews by Meece, Anderman, & Anderman, 2006; Pintrich, 2003). Mastery goals (focusing on task mastery and skill development) are generally considered more desirable than performance goals (emphasizing the demonstration of ability and outperforming others), as the former would be more associated with positive affect, interest, and engagement in learning (Ames, 1992; Kaplan & Middleton, 2002; Midgley, Kaplan, & Middleton, 2001). The effects of performance goals after a setback are particularly debilitating, as they are linked to ability evaluations and are ego involved. Therefore students adopting these goals are more likely to withdraw in the face of failure or difficulties, so as to preserve self-worth (Grant & Dweck, 2003).

Studies of Chinese students' achievement goals have generated important insights on cross-cultural differences. In the first place, there has been consistent evidence showing moderate to high positive correlations between mastery and performance goals among Chinese students, and both produce positive effects on achievement (Chan, Lai, Leung, & Moore, 2005; Ee & Moore, 2004; Ho & Hau, 2008; Ho, Hau, & Salili, 2007; Salili & Lai, 2003). These observations do not match with the normative goal theory in the West, where the two goals are more dichotomous in nature with the negative effects of performance goals being emphasized.

A longitudinal study of 1,807 junior high-school students in Hong Kong over three years (Salili & Lai, 2003) provided compelling evidence that Chinese students adopted performance goals more than mastery goals, irrespective of gender, school type, or ability. This suggests a highly competitive orientation in their learning, which may not characterize or be well regarded in the Western context, but nonetheless underlies the high achievement of these students.

Furthermore, the adequacy of the mastery/performance dimensions in capturing Chinese students' learning goals has been queried, as these dimensions have been formulated in terms of the individual-oriented motivation model. Recent studies have shown that in the collectivistic Chinese context, socially oriented learning goals (striving to satisfy affiliation or recognition needs) constitute an important dimension that has not been well articulated in Western goal theory. For instance, Hong Kong Chinese students have been found to emphasize social purposes of academic achievement

(Tao & Hong, 2000), and a study of Singaporean Chinese students revealed that socially oriented goals were positively related to both mastery and performance goals (Chang & Wong, 2008).

Thus, in the Western-individualistic context, students approach academic tasks with the intention of enhancing their ability (mastery) or of demonstrating competence (performance), and educators try to foster a focus on mastery, as this orientation has fewer implications for self-worth, and therefore is more adaptive especially in the face of setbacks. Although the more recent multiple-goals perspective suggests that the role of performance-approach goals may not be as maladaptive as previously assumed (Harackiewicz, Baron, Pintrich, Elliot, & Thrash, 2002; Pintrich, 2000b), this suggestion has not been widely accepted (Kaplan & Middleton, 2002; Midgley et al., 2001). In contrast, the multiple goals phenomenon appears to have always existed at the background of Chinese students' high achievement (e.g. the importance of social goals discussed by Yu, 1996). They attempt to master the materials and outperform peers at the same time in a competitive learning environment, while also striving to gain recognition from significant others.

There are two possible explanations for the apparent lack of adverse effects produced by the predominance of performance goals in the Chinese context. Firstly, performance goals may in fact be quite adaptive when one has to achieve in a competitive learning environment. Secondly, Chinese students' strong effort attribution for achievement outcomes would significantly weaken the link between performance and ability evaluations. When achievement is considered a moral obligation and with the belief that you can do it if you try hard enough, the main issue becomes whether one has put in adequate effort rather than the demonstration of ability. Failing to perform would result in guilt and shame which may in fact serve as a driving force for the person to work even harder.

Integrated analysis

Individual studies often focus on only one or a few aspects that are considered important. Yet in reality, all related variables operate together to produce effects. The social-cognitive variables examined in the above review could be summarized under three major components of achievement motivation, namely value perceptions, expectancy beliefs, and goal orientations (Eccles & Wigfield, 2002). Values provide the reason for investing effort, whereas expectancy for success keeps one going. Together they determine the kind of goals and approaches that students adopt in their learning.

In this section we will summarize the insights generated from diverse studies on culturally Western and culturally Chinese students' motivation in terms of these value, expectancy, and goal aspects. Discussions of differences in the motivational characteristics of Western and Chinese students have usually been carried out in terms of broad individualistic–collectivistic (Hofstede, 1983), Socratic–Confucian (Tweed & Lehman, 2003), or mind–virtue (Li, 2005) dichotomies. Although the labels differ, detailed analyses of what they represent actually converge onto particular features in values and beliefs, social relationships, and behavioral manifestations that differentially characterize these two cultural groups. As the above review shows, these cultural features are clearly exhibited in Chinese and Western students' engagement in educational activities. There are major differences in the meaning attached to such activities (value), in their beliefs about how to go about these activities (expectancy), and in their achievement orientations (goals).

The Western scenario

In the Western Socratic-individualistic context, the *independent self* is the focus of motivational analysis. Whether academic pursuit is of any value is a highly individualized matter, and achievement is largely conceptualized in terms of the gain to the individual, such as *self-actualization*. Motives for achievement are largely linked to *self-worth* or *self-enhancement*. Tasks that are worth learning should be of *personal interest or relevance*, and a sense of *self-efficacy* and *self-determination* are important to keep one going. Furthermore, attributions for outcomes tend to focus more on the *personal attribute* of ability. It is against this background of values and beliefs, which are largely self-referent, that Western schools operate.

As individual differences are highly respected in the individualistic culture, students bring with them to school varied aspirations, values and interests, which are not necessarily in tune with the nature and requirements of formal schooling where some degree of externally imposed aims, rules, and activities is inevitable. Yet in a culture where the major energizing sources rest with the self, intrinsic motivation is desirable for any individual to invest consistent effort into any endeavor. Relying on compliance to bring about achievement is often not as effective, and may generate reactance. These are realities of individualistic societies that have to be reconciled in instructional planning. The implication is that teachers need to spend a lot of effort negotiating individual student needs and group requirements. From the point of view of how to enhance the perceived value of learning, teachers need to make the learning meaningful and relevant in order to enhance its utility value for students. They also need to provide choices and make tasks novel or interesting to enhance their interest value (Brophy, 1999; Morrone & Pintrich, 2006; Pintrich, 2003). Otherwise, students may see very little reason for engaging in learning.

Even when schools are successful in promoting students' identification with the value of academic achievement, there is still the issue of how to maintain motivation, especially in the face of obstacles and setbacks. Promoting expectancies for success thus becomes important. In individualistic cultures, success is generally attributed to personal factors, and self-directed initiatives characterize the process. Therefore, a sense of efficacy and a sense of control over the process are important for positive expectancies about the outcome. Among the motivational strategies advocated in the West, most have to do with enhancing such positive expectancies (e.g. Morrone & Pintrich, 2006). Examples include calibrating tasks to the ability of individual students so that they are challenging and yet not too difficult, minimizing competition that would have negative implications on one's ability in the face of failure, and emphasizing lack of effort or ineffective strategies as causes of failure so as to preserve self-worth. These are intended to reduce the possibility of developing negative self-concepts or a low sense of competence. Moreover, it is desirable to provide students with opportunities to participate in instructional decisions, i.e. providing opportunities for greater self-determination, in order to increase sense of control and intrinsic motivation.

Finally, with ability being an important indicator of personal worth, which is considered largely inherent and therefore relatively uncontrollable and stable, it is important to emphasize mastery rather than performance goals in the Western classroom. Performance goals with their associated competitive environments and a focus on comparing with others would have significant negative implications for one's ability when there is negative feedback or challenges.

The Chinese scenario

In the Confucian-collectivistic culture, analyses of motivational dynamics would involve the *interdependent self* to a much greater extent than in the Western context. Achieving academic excellence is more than a personal matter and the motives to achieve involve *fulfilling obligations* to oneself as well as to the family and society. This strong moral undertone makes educational achievement a *virtuous pursuit*, thus undermining the importance of personal interest or self-efficacy as necessary conditions for students to work hard (see also Yu, 1996). Moreover, with *hierarchical social relationships* being an ingrained feature of society, *teacher-directed learning* has always been accepted in the Confucian tradition, and the lack of self-determination on the students' part is much less an issue in the Chinese classroom. Furthermore, the dominant *effort attribution* for achievement outcomes, together with the belief that effort can change ability, makes low ability an unconvincing reason for not achieving.

Thus, Chinese schools operate in a context with more uniform values and aspirations for academic achievement, and there is less need to convince students of the value of learning. With the importance and utility of achievement being firmly established by the cultural code, interest and cost are no longer of major concern. In other words, even if the task appears uninteresting, the student will more readily accept the need to accomplish it, as it is their duty to do so. Li (2002) calls this the 'heart and mind for wanting to learn'. With this contextual support, it is not always necessary to have intrinsic motivation backing achievement striving, and externally imposed aims and requirements are often sufficient to propel students. In fact, Chinese teachers tend not to spend as much energy catering for individual differences in aspiration and interest. Rather, they focus on making the best use of the tuned-in initiatives and efforts that students bring with them to school to promote higher achievement.

Just like their Western counterparts, Chinese students inevitably encounter setbacks and challenges in their learning. In fact, failure experiences probably occur more frequently in Chinese schools, where learning is often competitive and where instructional designs do not necessarily take into account variations in student abilities. This failure is often more publicly obvious. According to Western theory, these features of the learning environment should produce significant negative effects on students' sense of competence and expectancy for success.

Nevertheless, although research findings do suggest a generally lower sense of efficacy or self-concept among Chinese students, these do not seem to have deterred them from doing well. Other than the strong will to succeed, effort attributions and beliefs about the malleability of ability would also counteract the negative effects of low self-efficacy, fueling continuous striving and persistence even in the face of failure. Similarly, this effort-focused conception of learning would probably contribute to the necessary sense of control in learning, as effort is relatively controllable. Therefore Chinese students might still feel self-directed in their learning even if there is little room for self-determination or choice. Actually students often prefer to be told what to do by those in authority, as this would indicate care and nurture rather than negative control from those authority figures (Ho, 2001).

The simultaneous adoption of performance, mastery, and social goals reflects the multiple sources of influence on Chinese achievement motivation. A competitive learning environment, which is often a built-in feature of Chinese schooling, naturally fosters a strong emphasis on performance goals. Yet, it should be noted that performance motives may actually foster effort rather than deter participation, when the students' minds are set on achieving. Then there are influences of collectivistic values, resulting in social goals being an inevitable part of the motivational structure. The notion that educational success is a collective business entails not just dutiful participation on the students' part but also strong support from families and teachers, and this is an added advantage that helps Chinese students persevere against all odds. Lastly, it goes without saying that mastery goals would foster the building of academic skills; thus incorporating this aspect of motivation into their goal structure would also help Chinese students' enhance their performance.

To conclude, school systems and the related activities may appear quite similar in culturally Western and culturally Chinese societies in the modern world. Yet differences in the values and beliefs underlying schooling, leading to different levels of effort and persistence, could produce very different outcomes. At the individual student level, it is without argument that higher intrinsic motivation, task value, sense of efficacy, sense of control, and mastery orientation predict better achievement outcomes. This is universally applicable. However, Chinese students as a group do seem to enjoy cultural advantages that enable them to cope better with the realities of modern schooling, namely that academic subjects are often not intrinsically interesting or of immediate value, that challenges and setbacks with negative implications for one's ability are inevitable, and that some level of competition is unavoidable.

In the face of these realities, Confucian-collectivistic values and beliefs seem to make a significant difference. Two features of this culture are of particular salience in making Chinese students adaptive learners against all odds. Firstly, the high value accorded to educational achievement serves as a strong driving force: where there is a will, there is a way. Then there is the phenomenal belief in effort: you will get there if you put in enough effort.

Further research

We started with a review of recent evidence documenting the outstanding academic achievement of Chinese students, among other Asian groups who also share the Confucian cultural heritage.

Then we attempted to understand from research the sociocultural and motivational factors that have contributed to such achievement. Research findings clearly suggest that beliefs and psychological processes do reflect potent influences of culture. Also, related studies have come a long way in the past decade in terms of the variety of national groups and psychological constructs being examined as well as the diversity in their methodology (see Hau & Ho, 2008). We will conclude the present chapter by highlighting a few current trends in research, which are likely to continue and contribute to our understanding of the effects of culture on learning as well as to the development of more universally applicable motivation theories.

Constructs with greater specificity

Research has shown that supposedly antithetical motivational processes often operate simultaneously in the Chinese context. It appears that in different cultural contexts, psychological constructs may carry different meanings and connotations, or the same process may generate different effects. For example, the intrinsic/extrinsic nature of motives is conceptualized as a continuum in the Western context (cf. self-determination theory, Ryan & Deci, 2000), and enhancement of motivation involves moving from the more extrinsic end towards the most intrinsic end (i.e. greater self-determination), as intrinsic motivation is associated with higher achievement. However, findings about Chinese students clearly indicate the lesser role of intrinsic motivation as marked by interest, or self-determination as reflected in the notion of autonomy in the Western sense, in achievement situations. Probably in collectivistic, Confucian cultures, where internalization of external values and norms is rife, the differentiation between what is intrinsic and what is extrinsic, or what is internal and what is external, is less clearly differentiated or important.

Another example is the distinction between mastery goals and performance goals. Western researchers and educators often pit one against the other, and mastery orientations in learning are definitely favored as precursors to high achievement. However, research has clearly shown that the joint forces of performance and mastery goals would be most adaptive in the Chinese learning environment.

A further example has to do with conceptions about effort and ability. In the Western context, the two constructs are quite clearly differentiated, with ability being stable and uncontrollable and effort being unstable and controllable. In contrast, there is clear evidence that Chinese people consider effort and ability to be coinciding, as greater effort would lead to higher ability. Therefore, both are quite unstable and controllable.

In view of this mounting evidence, attempts at developing motivational theories that are more universally applicable should move beyond relying on simple dichotomized constructs (e.g. intrinsic versus extrinsic, mastery versus performance, control versus autonomy) to derivations of more refined dimensions of constructs with greater specificity in meaning. Some recent studies have already been moving in this direction. For example, in an investigation of the role of autonomy in collectivistic cultures, Rudy and colleagues (Rudy, Sheldon, Awong, & Tan, 2007) demonstrated the need to distinguish between 'inclusive autonomy', in which 'my family and I' are the subject of motivation, and 'individual relative autonomy', in which 'I' is the subject. Their results showed that the former was positively related to the well-being of collectivistic Chinese Canadians and Singaporeans, but not European Canadians.

Another example relates to the need for more differentiated conceptualizations of achievement goals. Among the findings in a series of studies by Grant and Dweck (2003), it was discovered that ability-linked performance goals (with outcomes being perceived as measures of ability) predicted withdrawal and poor performance in the face of challenges, whereas normative performance goals (wanting to outperform others) would not. The latter was in fact found to be associated with higher levels of perceived ability. Such findings provide good explanations for the apparent differences in performance goal effects between Western and Chinese students discussed earlier, as different types of performance goals could be in operation in the two cultural contexts. More refined elaborations of dimensions or components of motivation constructs like these would enable researchers to make more accurate comparisons across cultural groups. At the same time, they would help us see more clearly why certain broad constructs seem to have divergent effects in different cultural contexts.

Of special importance are clearer delineations of the meaning and measure of 'self'-related constructs in cross-cultural examinations. It has become clear from research in the past decades that the construct of self is central in motivational processes, as in self-efficacy, self-determination, self-regulation, etc. While 'self' in the individualistic context refers largely to the independent self, the same construct would incorporate more of the component of the interdependent self in collectivistic settings. The present review has provided examples concerning how the self construal may explain differential effects of motivational processes in different cultural contexts.

Recent insights from research further suggest that the self-construal may be different across domains, even among people of the same cultural group (see also Kwan, Hui, & McGee, this volume). Wang and Li (2003) cited various studies to argue that learning may be a unique domain in which Chinese students demonstrate a greater and more refined individualistic or independent sense of self, emphasizing self-reliance and individual responsibility. This individualistic orientation is in contrast to the collectivistic orientations that Chinese people usually display in social and familial relationships. Allegedly domain-specific motivational attitudes stem from students' reaction to the characteristics of particular domains as well as to sociocultural, developmental and environmental factors. These observations point to the dynamic and situated nature of motivational processes in response to a variety of contextual factors, a complexity of influences that should be taken into consideration when conducting related studies.

Broader perspectives

The interest in studying Chinese and other Asian students' motivation has in part arisen from their outstanding achievement, so research that helps to identify specific motivational profiles that have strong links to actual learning outcomes would be of considerable value. Many previous studies have focused on only limited motivational constructs, or on the relationships between a few constructs without relating them to actual achievement outcomes. While these are useful in helping us understand the nature of specific processes, more direct examinations of motivation-achievement relationships would be desirable. In view of the fact that there is a myriad of motivation processes interacting to produce effects on achievement, systematic investigations including a wider range of motivational constructs and outcome measures would help to generate a clearer and more convincing big picture about motivation-achievement relationships, and how they differ in different cultural contexts. The examination of the relationships between a wide range of motivation-related variables and a number of achievement outcomes in the PISA study across a large number of countries is a recent example of this type of investigation (see more details in Marsh, Hau, Artelt, Baumert, & Peschar, 2006).

It is worth noting that the index for educational outcome in previous examinations has largely been restricted to test scores. In the discussion of Chinese students' learning motivation, researchers have suggested that these students' high achievement has been attained at a cost, as they are constantly being urged to achieve in competitive learning environments (see Stevenson & Lee, 1996). Their display of low interest, low self-concept, or lack of confidence despite high achievement in certain academic subjects probably indicates that high performance has come about at the expense of other aspects of development (Leung, 2002; Salili et al., 2004). If we are to gain a more comprehensive understanding of the role and nature of motivational processes in education, research incorporating a wider range of treasured educational outcomes other than test scores would be of value.

Other methodological issues

Designing studies and instruments that enable valid comparisons between cultural groups has always been a challenge. A few issues in this regard are worth mentioning. Many studies comparing motivational constructs between Chinese and other students have involved direct comparisons of means based on attitudinal instruments. However, there are inherent problems associated with this procedure, as differences between cultural groups could be artificially created due to the choice of wordings and anchor descriptors for items in the translation process. It is almost impossible to guarantee that a '4' in a five-point scale, for example, carries identical meaning to the '4' in another culture (see also Schwarz & Oyserman, 2001, on biases resulting from questionnaire construction).

One solution is to rely less on the direct comparison of means, but to rely more on the examination of cultural differences based on comparisons of patterns of relationships (e.g. correlations) among variables, which would not be affected by any artificial shifting in means across cultural groups. An example would be to examine the differential correlations between autonomy and interest across Chinese and non-Chinese students rather than comparing their respective means for these variables (see also Bond's suggestion for doing Newtonian, cross-cultural research, in press). Other suggestions for more refined studies include the use of experimental and longitudinal designs to better delineate causal relationships, gathering parent reports in addition to self-reports by students, and cross-validations of observations for related constructs.

Finding comparable samples in the cultures under study and choosing measures that are psychometrically equivalent, valid, and reliable are also issues of concern. As with research in other psychological domains, some researchers have emphasized the importance of developing ecologically valid, emic motivational instruments which more fully reflect culture-specific characteristics (see Smith, this volume). While this view is legitimate and such instruments are sometimes necessary, etic tools that are psychometrically sound and are usable across a wide range of cultural and educational settings are still highly desirable so that more direct comparisons across cultural groups could be made.

The SAL (Student Approaches to Learning) instrument used in the PISA study (OECD, 2003) is one such tool that has been administered to possibly the largest number of students and countries (over 100,000 students from thirty-two countries in the year 2000 assessment). It consists of a wide range of motivation and strategy constructs (fifty-two items, fourteen scales) including instrumental motivation, control/memorization/elaboration strategies, effort and perseverance, self-efficacy, control expectation, interest in reading/mathematics, cooperative/competitive learning, and reading/mathematics/academic self-concept. Marsh et al (2006) evaluated the applicability of the SAL scales across cultural groups and concluded that, 'based on appropriately designed materials, appropriate samples, and carefully standardized administration procedures, there is strong support for cross-cultural generalizability [of the instrument]' (p. 353). As such, the SAL becomes a valuable tool providing a rich database enabling interrelationships among constructs to be explored across cultural groups.

Another recent example was a study conducted by McInerney and Ali (2006). They reported on an examination of the factorial structure of a multidimensional achievement goal instrument in large samples of American, African, Australian (Anglo, migrant, and Aboriginal groups), Hong Kong, and Navajo high-school students. Results showed an invariant pattern in the multidimensional and hierarchical relations among the scale constructs, and supported a strong theoretical structure necessary for conducting research in these diverse cultural groups. Thus, research investigating the cross-cultural applicability of measures of motivation in terms of factor structure equivalence and psychometric properties are of particular value, as too much emphasis on the development of emic instruments would frustrate cross-cultural comparisons.

Concluding remarks

The proliferation of research on students' achievement motivation since the 1990s is a consequence of two major forces. On the one hand, educators in many parts of the modern world actively seek solutions to educational problems, among which poor school engagement and declining achievement have caused great concern. Observations of Chinese and other Asian students' outstanding achievement despite apparently less favorable learning conditions has spurred interest in examining the so-called 'paradox of the Chinese learner' (Watkins & Biggs, 1996), and related findings do provide important insights. On the other hand, psychological studies have increasingly emphasized person–environment interactions as determinants of human behavior. Cultural factors, being an important aspect of environmental influences, have therefore received greater attention in research, resulting in an increased interest in cross-cultural studies. Studies of this kind would generate insights into how theories originated in Western contexts apply in other cultures, therefore contributing to the development of more precise theories.

Finally, it is worth noting that with modernization and the development of the global village, inter-culture influences are increasing, and rapid economic and social changes have been taking place in many Chinese societies. The extent to which traditional collectivistic-Confucian tenets will continue to exert influences on schooling in these societies in the same way they have been is still to be seen.

Authors' note

Please address all correspondence to Professor Kit-Tai Hau, Faculty of Education, The Chinese University of Hong Kong, Shatin, N.T., Hong Kong (Email: kthau@cuhk.edu.hk).

References

Ames, C. (1992). Classrooms: Goals, structures, and student motivation. *Journal of Educational Psychology, 84*, 261–271.

Bandura, A. (1997). *Self-efficacy: The exercise of control.* New York: Freeman.

Beaton, A. E., Mullis, I. V. S., Martin, M. O., Gonzalez, E. J., Kelly, D. L., & Smith, T. A. (1996). *Mathematics achievement in the middle school years: IEA' s Third International Mathematics and Science Study (TIMSS).* Chestnut Hill, MA: TIMSS International Study Center, Boston College.

Bond, M. H. (in press). Circumnavigating the psychological globe: From yin and yang to starry, starry night ... In A. Aksu-Koc & S. Beckman (eds), *Perspectives on human development, family and culture.* Cambridge, England: Cambridge University Press.

Brophy, J. (1999). Toward a model of the value aspects of motivation in education: Developing appreciation for particular learning domains and activities. *Educational Psychologist, 34*, 75–85.

Chan, K. W., Lai, P. Y., Leung, M. T., & Moore, P. J. (2005). Students' goal orientations, study strategies and achievement: A closer look in Hong Kong Chinese cultural context. *The Asia-Pacific Education Researcher, 14*, 1–26.

Chang, W. C. & Wong, K. (2008). Socially oriented achievement goals of Chinese university students in Singapore: Structure and relationships with achievement motives, goals and affective outcomes. *International Journal of Psychology, 43*, 880–885.

Chen, C. & Stevenson, H. W. (1995). Motivation and mathematics achievement: A comparative study of Asian-American, Caucasian-American, and East Asian high school students. *Child Development, 66*, 1215–1234.

Cheng, R.W. (2007). Effects of social goals on student achievement motivation: The role of self-construal (Doctoral dissertation, The University of Hong Kong, 2005), *Dissertation Abstract International Section A: Humanities and Social Sciences, 67*(8-A), 2876.

Chow, S. S. & Chu, M. H. (2007). The impact of filial piety and parental involvement on academic achievement motivation in Chinese secondary school students. *Asian Journal of Counselling, 14*, 91–124.

Covington, M. V. (1992). *Making the grade: A self-worth perspective on motivation and school reform.* New York: Cambridge University Press.

Crocker, J. & Wolfe, C. (2001). Contingencies of self-worth. *Psychological Review, 108*, 593–623.

d'Ailly, H. (2003). Children's autonomy and perceived control in learning: A model of motivation and achievement in Taiwan. *Journal of Educational Psychology, 95*, 84–96.

d'Ailly, H. (2004). The role of choice in children's learning: A distinctive cultural and gender difference in efficacy, interest, and effort. *Canadian Journal of Behavioural Science, 36*, 17–29.

Deci, E. L., Schwartz, A. J., Sheinman, L., & Ryan, R. M. (1981). An instrument to assess adults' orientations toward control versus autonomy with children: Reflections on intrinsic motivation and perceived competence. *Journal of Educational Psychology, 73*, 642–650.

Dweck, C. S. (1999). *Self-theories: Their role in motivation, personality, and development.* New York: Psychology Press.

Dweck, C. S. & Elliot, E. S. (1983). Achievement motivation. In P. Mussen & E.M. Hetherington (eds), *Handbook of child psychology* (pp. 643–691). New York: Wiley.

Eaton, M. J. & Dembo, M. H. (1997). Differences in the motivational beliefs of Asian American and non-Asian students. *Journal of Educational Psychology, 89*, 433–440.

Eccles, J. & Wigfield, A. (1995). In the mind of the actor: The structure of adolescents' achievement task values and expectancy-related beliefs. *Personality and Social Psychology Bulletin, 21*, 215–225.

Eccles, J. S. & Wigfield, A. (2002). Motivational beliefs, values, and goals. *Annual Review of Psychology, 53*, 109–132.

Eccles, J., Wigfield, A., & Schiefele, U. (1998). Motivation to succeed. In W. Damon (series ed.) & N. Eisenberg (vol. ed.), *Handbook of child psychology: Vol. 3. Social, emotional, and personality development* (5th edn, pp. 1017–1095). New York: Wiley.

Ee, J. & Moore, P. J. (2004). Motivation, strategies and achievement: A comparison of teachers and students in high, average and low achieving classes. In J. Ee, A. S. C. Chang, & O. S. Tan (eds), *Thinking about thinking (pp. 142–160).* Singapore: McGraw-Hill Education.

Fuligni, A. J. & Stevenson, H. W. (1995). Time use and mathematics achievement among American, Chinese, and Japanese high school students. *Child Development, 66*, 830–842.

Fuligni, A. J., Tseng, V., & Lam, M. (1999). Attitudes toward family obligations among American adolescents with Asian, Latin American, and European backgrounds. *Child Development, 70*, 1030–1044.

Fuligni, A. J. & Zhang, W. (2004). Attitudes toward family obligation among adolescents in contemporary urban and rural China. *Child Development, 74*, 180–192.

Grant, H. & Dweck, C. S. (2003). Clarifying achievement goals and their impact. *Journal of Personality and Social Psychology, 85*, 541–553.

Harackiewicz, J., Barron, K., Pintrich, P. R., Elliot, A., & Thrash, T. (2002). Revision of achievement goal theory: Necessary and illuminating. *Journal of Educational Psychology, 94*, 638–645.

Hau, K. T. & Ho, I. T. (2008). Editorial: Insights from research on Asian students' achievement motivation. *International Journal of Psychology, 43*, 865–869.

Hau, K. T. & Salili, F. (1991). Structure and semantic differential placement of specific causes: Academic causal attributions by Chinese students in Hong Kong. *International Journal of Psychology, 26*, 175–193.

Hau, K. T. & Salili, F. (1996). Prediction of academic performance among Chinese students: Effort can compensate for lack of ability. *Organizational Behavior and Human Decision Processes, 65*, 83–94.

Ho, I. T. (2001). Are Chinese teachers authoritarian? In D. A. Watkins & J. B. Biggs (eds), *Teaching the Chinese Learner: Psychological and pedagogical perspectives* (99–114). Hong Kong, China: CERC/Melbourne, Australia: ACER.

Ho, I. T. & Hau, K. T. (2008). Academic achievement in the Chinese context: The role of goals, strategies, and effort. *International Journal of Psychology, 43*, 892–897.

Ho, I. T., Hau, K. T., & Salili, F. (2007). Expectancy and value as predictors of Chinese students' achievement goal orientation. In F. Salili & R. Hoosain (eds), *Culture, learning, and motivation: A multicultural perspective* (pp. 69–90). Charlotte, NC: Information Age.

Ho, I. T., Salili, F., Biggs, J. B., & Hau, K. T. (1999). The relationship among causal attributions, learning strategies and level of achievement: A Hong Kong Chinese study. *Asia Pacific Journal of Education, 19*, 44–58.

Hofstede, G. (1983). Dimensions of national cultures in fifty countries and three regions. In J. B. Deregowski, S. Dziurawiec, & R. C. Annis (eds), *Expiscations in cross-cultural psychology* (pp. 335–355). Lisse, The Netherlands: Swets & Zeitlanger.

International Monetary Fund. (2007). *World economic outlook database.* Washington, DC: The author. (List of countries by GDP (PPP) per capita retrieved June 3, 2007-06-03 from Wikipedia; http://en.wikipedia.org/wiki/List_of_countries_by_GDP_(PPP)_per_capita)

Iyengar, S. S., & Lepper, M. R. (1999). Rethinking the value of choice: A cultural perspective on intrinsic motivation. *Journal of Personality and Social Psychology, 76*, 349–366.

Kaplan, A. & Middleton, M. (2002). Should childhood be a journey or a race? A reply to Harackiewicz et al. *Journal of Educational Psychology, 94*, 646–648.

Lapointe, A. E., Askew, J. M., & Mead, N. A. (1992). *Learning science.* Princeton, NJ: Educational Testing Service.

Lapointe, A. E., Mead, N. A., & Askew, J. M. (1992). *Learning mathematics.* Princeton, NJ: Educational Testing Service.

Lau, K. L. & Chan, D. W. (2001). Motivational characteristics of under-achievers in Hong Kong. *Educational Psychology, 22*, 417–430.

Leung, F. K. S. (2002). Behind the high achievement of East Asian students. *Educational Research and Evaluation, 8*, 87–108.

Li, J. (2002). A cultural model of learning: Chinese 'heart and mind for wanting to learn'. *Journal of Cross-Cultural Psychology, 33*, 248–269.

Li, J. (2004). Learning as a task or a virtue: U.S. and the Chinese preschoolers explain learning. *Developmental Psychology, 40*, 595–605.

Li, J. (2005). Mind or virtue: Western and Chinese beliefs about learning. *New Directions in Psychological Science, 14*, 190–194.

Li, J. (2006). Self in learning: Chinese adolescents' goals and sense of agency. *Child Development, 77*, 482– 501.

Marsh, H. W., Martin, A. J., & Hau, K. T. (2006). A Multiple Method Perspective on Self-concept Research in Educational Psychology: A Construct Validity Approach. In M. Eid & E. Diener (eds), *Handbook of multimethod measurement in psychology* (pp. 441–456). Washington, DC: American Psychological Association.

Marsh, H. W., Hau, K. T., Artelt, C., Baumert, J., & Peschar, J. L. (2006). OECD's brief self-report measure of educational psychology's most useful affective constructs: Cross-cultural, psychometric comparisons across 25 countries. *International Journal of Testing, 6, 311–360.*

McCrae, R. R., Costa, P. T. Jr, & Yik, M. S. M. (1996). Universal aspects of Chinese personality structure. In M. H. Bond (ed.). *The handbook of Chinese psychology* (pp. 189–207). Hong Kong: Oxford.

McInerney, D. M. & Ali, J. (2006). Multidimensional and hierarchical assessment of school motivation: Cross-cultural validation. *Educational Psychology: An International Journal of Experimental Educational Psychology, 26*, 595–612.

Meece, J. L., Anderman, E. M., & Anderman, L. H. (2006). Classroom goal structure, student motivation, and academic achievement. *Annual Review of Psychology, 57*, 487–503.

Midgley, C., Kaplan, A., & Middleton, M. (2001). Performance-approach goals: Good for what, for whom, under what circumstances, and at what cost? *Journal of Educational Psychology, 93*, 77–86.

Morrone, A. S. & Pintrich, P. R. (2006). Achievement motivation. In G. G. Bear & K. M. Minke (eds), *Children's needs III: Development, prevention, and intervention* (pp. 431–442). Bethesda, MD: National Association of School Psychologists.

Mullis, I. V. S., Martin, M. O., Beaton, A. E., Gonzalez, E. J., Kelly, D. L., & Smith, T. A. (1997). *Mathematics achievement in the primary school years: IEA's Third International Mathematics and Science Study (TIMSS).* Chestnut Hill, MA: Boston College.

Organisation for Economic Co-operation and Development (OECD). (2003). *Literacy skills for the world of tomorrow—further results from PISA 2000.* Paris: Author.

Pintrich, P. R. (2000a). The role of goal orientation in self-regulated learning. In M. Boekaerts, P. R. Pintrich, & M. Zeidner (eds), *Handbook of self-regulation* (pp. 451–502). San Diego, CA: Academic Press.

Pintrich, P. R. (2000b). Multiple goals, multiple pathways: The role of goal orientation in learning and achievement. *Journal of Educational Psychology, 92*, 544–555.

Pintrich, P. (2003). A motivational science perspective on the role of student motivation in learning and teaching context. *Journal of Educational Psychology, 95*, 667–686.

Pintrich, P. R. & Schunk, D. H. (2002). *Motivation in education: Theory, research, and applications* (2nd edn). Upper Saddle River, NJ: Prentice Hall.

Pintrich, P. R. & Zusho, A. (2002). The development of academic self-regulation: The role of cognitive and motivational factors. In A. Wigfield & J. Eccles (eds), *Development of achievement motivation* (pp. 249–284). San Diego, CA: Academic Press

Rogers, C. (1998). Motivational indicators in the United Kingdom and the People's Republic of China. *Educational Psychology, 18*, 275–291.

Rudy, D., Sheldon, K. M., Awong, T., & Tan, H. H. (2007). Autonomy, culture, and well-being: The benefits of inclusive autonomy. *Journal of Research in Personality, 41*, 983–1007.

Ryan, R. M. & Deci, E. L. (2000). Self-determination theory and the facilitation of intrinsic motivation, social development, and well-being. *American Psychologist, 55*, 68–78.

Salili, F. (1994). Age, sex, and cultural differences in the meaning and dimensions of achievement. *Personality and Social Psychology Bulletin, 20*, 635–648.

Salili, F. (1996). Achievement motivation: A cross-cultural comparison of British and Chinese students. *Educational Psychology, 16*, 271–279.

Salili, F., Chiu, C. Y., & Lai, S. (2001). The influence of culture and context on students' motivational orientation and performance. In F. Salili, C. Y. Chiu, & Y.Y. Hong (eds), *Student motivation: The culture and context of learning* (pp. 221–247). New York: Kluwer Academic/Plenum Publishers.

Saili, F. & Lai, M. K. (2003). Learning and motivation of Chinese students in Hong Kong: A longitudinal study of contextual influences on students' achievement orientation and performance. *Psychology in the Schools, 40*, 51–70.

Salili, F., Lai, M. K., & Leung, S. S. K. (2004). The consequences of pressure on adolescent students to perform well in school. *Hong Kong Journal of Paediatrics, 9*, 329–336.

Schiefele, U., Krapp, A., & Winteler, A. (1992). Interest as a predictor of academic achievement: A meta-analysis of research. In K. A. Renninger, S. Hidi, & A. Krapp (eds), *The role of interest in learning and development* (pp. 183–212). Hillsdale, NJ: Erlbaum.

Schwarz, N. & Oyserman, D. (2001). Asking questions about behavior: Cognition, communication and questionnaire construction. *American Journal of Evaluation, 22*, 127–160.

Stevenson, H. W., Chen, C., & Lee, S.-Y. (1993). Mathematics achievement of Chinese, Japanese, and American children: Ten years later. *Science, 259*, 53–58.

Stevenson, H. W., & Lee, S.-Y. (1996). The academic achievement of Chinese students. In M. Bond (ed.), *The handbook of Chinese psychology* (pp. 124–142). Hong Kong: Oxford University Press.

Stevenson, H. W., & Stigler, J. W. (1992). *The learning gap: Why our schools are failing and what we can learn from Japanese and Chinese education.* New York: Simon & Schuster.

Stone, N. (2000). Exploring the relationship between calibration and selfregulated learning. *Educational Psychology Review, 12*, 437–475.

Sue, S. & Okazaki, S. (1990). Asian-American educational achievements: A phenomenon in search of an explanation. *American Psychologist, 45*, 913–920.

Tao, V. & Hong, Y. Y. (2000). A meaning system approach to Chinese students' achievement goals. *Journal of Psychology in Chinese Societies, 1*, 13–38.

Tseng, V. (2004). Family interdependence and academic adjustment in college: Youth from immigrant and U.S.-born families. *Child Development, 75*, 966–983.

Tweed, R. G. & Lehman, D. R. (2002). Learning considered within a cultural context: Confucian and Socratic approaches. *American Psychologist, 57*, 89–99.

Vansteenkiste, M., Zhou, M., & Soenens, B. (2005). Experiences of autonomy and control among Chinese learners: Vitalizing or immobilizing. *Journal of Educational Psychology, 97*, 468–483.

Wang, Q. & Li, J. (2003). Chinese children's self-concepts in the domains of learning and social relations. *Psychology in the Schools, 40*, 85–101.

Watkins, D.A. & Biggs, J. B. (1996). *The Chinese learner: Cultural, psychological, and contextual influences.* Hong Kong, China: CERC/Melbourne, Australia: ACER.

Weiner, B. (1986). *An attributional theory of motivation and emotion.* New York: Springer-Verlag.

Weiner, B. (2004). Attribution theory revisited: Transforming cultural plurality into theoretical unity. In D. M. McInerney & S. V. Etten (eds), *Research on sociocultural influences on motivation and learning: Big theories revisited* (Vol. 4, pp. 13–29). Greenwich, CT: Information Age.

Wigfield, A. & Eccles, J. (1992). The development of achievement task values: A theoretical analysis. *Developmental Review, 12*, 265–310.

Wigfield, A. & Eccles, J. (2002). *Development of achievement motivation.* San Diego, CA: Academic Press.

Yeung, W. M. L. (2008). Relationships between parenting styles, goal orientations and academic achievement in the Chinese cultural context (Doctoral dissertation, University of Southern California, 2005), *Dissertation Abstract International Section A: Humanities and Social Sciences, 68*(90-A), 3736.

Yu, A.-B. (1996). Ultimate life concerns, self, and Chinese achievement motivation. In M. Bond (ed.), *The handbook of Chinese psychology* (pp. 227–246). Hong Kong: Oxford University Press.

CHAPTER 14

How unique is Chinese emotion?

Michelle Yik

In 1996, James Russell and I published a comprehensive review of the literature on Chinese emotion in the first edition of *The Oxford handbook of Chinese psychology* (Russell & Yik, 1996). The amount of evidence collected and the breadth of discussion of the topic to that point was discouragingly small. We raised questions and suggested topics for further study. More than ten years have passed. In this chapter, I review theoretical and empirical advances achieved during the last decade, with an overriding purpose of addressing the question: What is universal and what is unique about Chinese emotion?

Several research themes have been pursued in the past decade, and I focus on four of those themes in this chapter. First, I seek to explore questions on how emotion is described and structured among the Chinese. Related to that interest, I discuss how the study of emotion can benefit from the use of a circumplex model; second, I review research on self-conscious emotions, including shame, guilt, and pride in Chinese subjects; third, I summarize research on emotional responding, including facial expressions and physiology; last, I examine the socialization of emotions.

Structure of emotion

Analysis of the Chinese emotion lexicon can help to reveal the concepts available to Chinese people through which they categorize the experience they witness. In parallel fashion, analysis of the structure implicit in the emotion lexicon can help to reveal aspects underlying the affective experience.

All human groups have a vocabulary for describing people (Dixon, 1977) and the Chinese group is no exception. Ethnographic research has argued that the Chinese culture encourages emotional restraint (Bond, 1993), although empirical research has shown that emotion terms are abundant in the Chinese language. Difficulties encountered in delimiting the domains of emotion terms are consistent with prototype theory that suggests emotion is prototypically organized, and that the boundary between emotion and non-emotion is fuzzy (Russell, 1991). Regardless of the disputes on delimiting emotion terms, a fundamental but under-studied question is how to describe the set of relations among the various emotional concepts. In doing so, different writers have begun with different sets of emotion terms on the basis of different theoretical assumptions.

To import a concept from one culture into another has been labeled as the 'imposed-etic' approach to doing cross-cultural research (Berry, 1969). For instance, a researcher translates a happiness scale from English into Chinese, administers the scale to a group of Chinese subjects, and then makes inferences about the happiness level of the Chinese people. This procedure presupposes the universality of the construct of happiness. In this section, I examine the usefulness of the happiness scale and other emotion scales in mapping out the affective experience of Chinese people. More generally,

I seek to explore the everyday conception of emotional experience among the Chinese and aspects, if any, underlying the covariations of these everyday feelings.

Imported approach

Wang, Li, Liu, and Du (2007) translated the Positive and Negative Affect Scale (PANAS; Watson, Clark, & Tellegen, 1988) and administered it to 1,163 college students in the People's Republic of China (PRC). Subjects were asked to provide the frequency of experiencing each emotion in the last few weeks, the results of which provided overwhelming support for the structural validity of the PANAS in both exploratory and confirmatory factor analyses. The Positive Affect (PA) and Negative Affect (NA) scales were found to be unrelated. When Yik and Russell (2003) followed Green, Goldman, and Salovey's (1993) multi-response formats procedure and tested the PA–NA relation on momentary affect, they found that PA and NA were correlated at –.61 and –.56 on two large samples of Hong Kong Chinese (see also Yik, Russell, Ahn, Fernández Dols, & Suzuki, 2002 for similar results on other language groups). The NA feeling was counteracted by the PA feeling among Hong Kong Chinese. These findings are in stark contrast to those reported by Bagozzi, Wong, and Yi (1999).

In a trilingual study, Bagozzi et al. (1999) offered correlational evidence from American, PRC Chinese, and Korean respondents in support of the interaction effect between gender and culture on the relation between PA and NA. A strong positive correlation between PA and NA was found among Chinese subjects; the correlation was stronger among females than among males. The writers marshaled the cultural hypothesis that, because the Chinese are more tolerant of contradictions and hence of polar opposite feelings, there was a strong positive correlation between the opposites, PA and NA. (A strong negative correlation was found among their American subjects.) Further, since females are more knowledgeable about emotional feelings, the positive correlation was stronger among females than among males.

Stimulated by the cultural hypothesis of Bagozzi et al. (1999), researchers examined the relation between PA and NA in the PRC and Hong Kong (e.g. Schimmack, Oishi, & Diener, 2002; Scollon, Diener, Oishi, & Biswas-Diener, 2005). Surprisingly, results from different Chinese samples diverged, although these studies found a null gender effect. To further unravel the role played by culture on the emotional experience, intracultural studies are needed to initiate a careful analysis of the relation between PA and NA.

As argued elegantly by Russell and Carroll (1999), a strict test of the relation between PA and NA demands the consideration of several factors simultaneously, among which the time frame of the assessment is of extreme importance. Emotion ratings based on reports over an extended time frame, including intensity 'in general' and 'frequency in the past month' (e.g. Wang et al., 2007), do not rule out the possibility of feeling positive at one time and negative at another over an extended period of time. An emotional person, for instance, may experience plenty of ups and downs throughout a month, and hence may report high levels of PA and high levels of NA, leading to a substantial positive correlation between PA and NA.

However, when emotion ratings are based on one thin slice in time, a substantial negative correlation will be found (see Yik, 2007, 2009a). When one is happy at one specific time, one is not sad. (Just as, when one feels hot at one specific time, one does not feel cold.) When the language of an instrument is the same and the subject pools are similar, then I suspect that the discrepancies in results, for instance, such as those between Wang et al. (2007) and Yik and Russell (2003), can be partly explained by the time frame of assessment, among other factors (see Yik, 2009b). Further studies are needed to explore the role played by different factors in determining the phenomenological reports of emotion.

Indigenous approach

The data examined so far suggest that emotions identified in English populations could be measured in Chinese samples via translation and that similar structures surfaced. In that sense, PA and NA can summarize the variety of affects experienced by Chinese people, suggesting a universal structure of affect. However, the fact that the structure of PA and NA can be recovered in Chinese samples is not equivalent to saying that that structure represents the most natural way of describing or structuring emotional experiences among the Chinese.

This argument is related to the proposal forwarded by cross-cultural psychologists who point out that to provide a comprehensive descriptive map of affect for the Chinese, researchers should take a distinctly Chinese approach (viz. an emic approach), such that they should look for indigenous Chinese terms to describe emotion. Hamid and Cheng (1996) took the lead in indigenizing the descriptive map for emotional experience by developing the Chinese Affect Scale (CAS). They began with 124 terms culled from a free-listing task conducted among Hong Kong Chinese. Multivariate analyses resulted in the final form of CAS consisting of ten positive and ten negative affects, which were found to be useful in describing both trait and state affects. The positive affects cover pleasant feelings with varying degrees of arousal; the negative affects cover unpleasant feelings with varying degrees of arousal. The indigenously derived scales were found to demonstrate convergent and discriminant validities, and were sensitive to mood induction procedures as well as episodic mood changes over a day.

Guided by the lexical hypothesis (Goldberg, 1981), Zhong and Qian (2005) began their search for emotion terms using two Chinese dictionaries. With the help of expert judgments and prototypicality ratings, they reduced their pool from 786 to 100 terms. Over 1,000 PRC Chinese students described their 'general' feelings using these 100 terms on a five-point Likert scale. Factor analyses showed that four factors, namely agitated, happy and excited, painful and sad, and angry and hateful, represented a comprehensive descriptive map of Chinese emotion. The authors argued for the superiority of the four orthogonal factors to a circumplex model in capturing Chinese emotion, even though the correlations between the three unpleasant factors were as high as .70.

A combined approach

The research efforts presented so far focused on a bottom-up approach, such that emotion terms were either translated from English into Chinese or culled from written materials in Chinese; exploratory factor analyses were performed on the emotion ratings; factors, with varying numbers from two to four, were reported.

Yet another group of researchers have used a top-down approach to elucidate the structure underlying affective experiences among the Chinese. Russell (1983) began with the least-adequate pool of twenty-eight emotion-related words (simply through translation of English terms). Subjects were Chinese-speaking residents of Canada, and they provided an indirect measure of similarity through a sorting procedure. Multidimensional scaling resulted in a circumplex model in which emotion-related words fell roughly in a circle with its axes interpretable as pleasure-displeasure and arousal-sleepiness. Despite its humble beginning, this circumplex model has turned out to be robust across changes in method. For example, a similar result was obtained from Hong Kong Chinese subjects in a study in which emotion words were bypassed altogether by using facial expressions shown in photographs (Russell, Lewicka, & Niit, 1989; see also Chan, 1985).

In the past decades, various dimensional models have been proposed to characterize the covariations of self-reported affective feelings in English. Major models include Russell's (1980) circumplex, Thayer's (1996) energetic and tense arousal, Larsen and Diener's (1992) eight combinations of pleasantness and activation, and Watson and Tellegen's (1985) positive and negative affect. As the names of the principal dimensions of these models suggest, they all seem to capture similar phenomena and are therefore ripe for integration. One proposal is that all dimensions fit within the same two-dimensional space with 45° between major dimensions (Larsen & Diener, 1992; Russell, 1979; Yik, Russell, & Barrett, 1999; Watson & Tellegen, 1985). Yik and Russell (2003) tested the integration hypothesis in two independent samples of Hong Kong Chinese people by *importing* the affect dimensions via translation. The four dimensional models were mappable onto one another within the integrated space (see Yik, Russell, Ahn, Fernández Dols, & Suzuki, 2002 for the generalizability of the space to other language groups).

To produce a finer-grained measurement space, Yik (2009c) attempted to carve out and cross-validate a twelve-segment circumplex model, namely the Chinese Circumplex Model of Affect, with three large samples of Hong Kong Chinese. In addition to the affect items imported via translation, she added indigenous terms obtained in a free-listing task to cover some possible 'holes' in the circumplex space. The twelve-segment space received strong support in different samples across different recall methods. It provided a level of precision that allowed for better estimates of affect, and hence provided a stronger platform on which to extend the nomological net of affect (e.g. Yik, 2009d; Zeng & Yik, 2009). Although affect was tapped by twelve segments, the model remained parsimonious because, in the circumplex, the twelve segments were reducible to two dimensions (pleasure and arousal).

Figure 14.1 presents the Chinese Circumplex Model of Affect (CCMA), with sample affect terms in English translation. On the right-hand side are the pleasure states; on the left-hand side are the displeasure states. The upper half shows the activated states; the lower half shows the deactivated states. Any specific affective state is composed of different blends of pleasure and arousal. The affect dimensions fall in a circular ordering along the perimeter. The circumplex structure of affective states has received strong empirical support (Remington, Fabrigar, & Visser, 2000; Yik, Russell, & Barrett, 1999).

In summary, when dimensions of self-reported feelings are sought, Chinese yield at least two dimensions very similar to those obtained in other languages, a result consistent with the general pattern seen across languages and cultures (Russell, 1991). Extrapolating from the general trend observed so far, Chinese carve their affective space into broad dimensions of pleasure-displeasure and activation-deactivation, a structure that appears to be pan-cultural. Nevertheless, none of these results should be regarded as confirming that the Chinese emotional experience can be captured *only* by these two dimensions. I would argue that these two dimensions are necessary but not sufficient to describe the structure of affect among the Chinese. Lacking are research efforts in drawing comparisons between indigenous and imported models of affect in describing the emotional experience of the Chinese. Further studies are needed to provide joint factor analyses of these models to map out their relations and possibly compare their usefulness in predicting criterion variables, be these variables behaviors or motivations or beliefs.

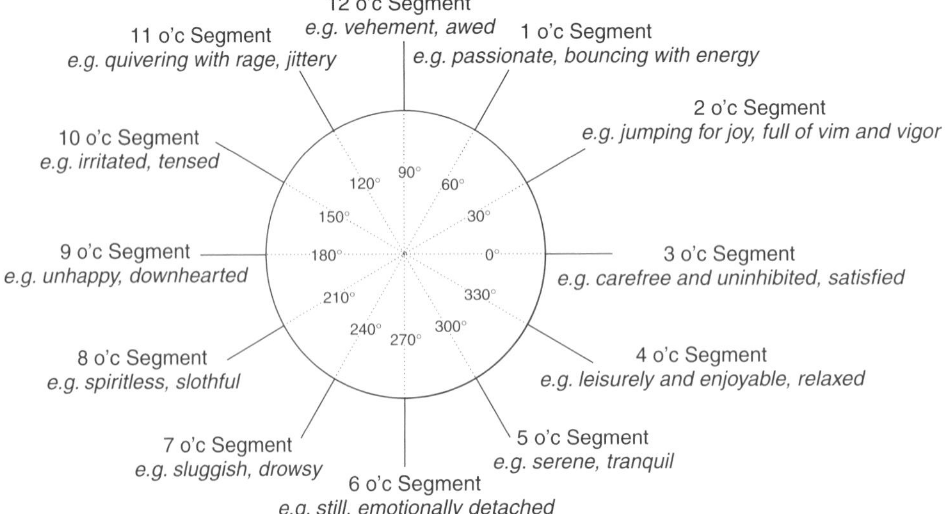

Fig. 14.1 The Chinese Circumplex Model of Affect (CCMA). This figure shows a schematic diagram of the hypothetical locations of the 12 segments.

Application of a circumplex model to studying ideal affect

The role of culture continues to fascinate emotion researchers. Recently, Tsai and her colleagues argued that cultural differences are evident in the types of ideal affect, or the pleasant feelings, that individuals value (Tsai, Knutson, & Fung, 2006). Individuals coming from an interdependent culture, such as the Hong Kong Chinese culture, desire to experience deactivated affect (calmness), whereas those from an independent culture, such as the American culture, desire to experience activated affect (*excitement*). The writers relied on their eight Affect Valuation Index (AVI) scales, whose items were selected to characterize eight octants of the circumplex model (Tsai et al., 2006). Unfortunately, the dimensional structure of these scales was never explicitly tested, and analyses were mostly restricted to high-arousal positive (HAP) and low-arousal positive (LAP) only (approximately 45° and 325° in Figure 14.1).

The research program on ideal affect will greatly benefit from testing for rather than from assuming the circumplex structure of the ideal affect scales. To test this idea, Jiang and Yik (2009) began with a small-scale study on testing the viability of the CCMA in capturing the structure of ideal affect. Results provided overwhelming support for the CCMA, which integrates the AVI scales, in a sample of 203 Hong Kong Chinese. In contrast to Tsai et al.'s (2006) finding that Hong Kong Chinese sought the feeling of *calm* (pleasant feelings with low arousal), Jiang and Yik found that their Chinese subjects sought the feelings of *energetic* and *peppy* (pleasant feelings with medium arousal). To address the question of the ideal affect pursued by "an average person" in the sample, researchers can rely on the 12 segment scores, each averaged across the sample of participants. These 12 scores can then be used to estimate an angle on the CCMA to indicate the feelings that average person desires to experience. The principle is that the magnitude of the 12 segment scores rises and falls in a cosine wave pattern as we move around the circumference (see Wiggins, 1979; Yik, Russell, & Steiger, 2010). For instance, seeking a certain segment in the affective space implies avoiding the affect segment 180° away on the circle. That is, seeking *calmness* implies avoiding feeling *tense*; seeking *excitement* implies avoiding feeling *gloomy*. There is a clear need for future research on advancing our understanding of the nature of ideal affect.

Self-conscious emotions

Self-conscious emotions refer to a category of emotions that involves reflection on the individual's own actions (Tangney & Fischer, 1995), among which shame, guilt, and pride represent the prototypes. They are generated in situations in which people compare a personal attribute or an outcome of a behavior to a standard (Stipek, 1998). When the comparison is favorable, *pride* will be generated. When the comparison is unfavorable, *shame* or *guilt* will be generated. Guilt is associated with transgression of social rules and comes from the internal voice of the conscience; shame is associated with failure to meet a standard, and comes from one's fear of social exclusion (see Fung, 1999; Ho, Fu, & Ng, 2004).

Hypercognition of shame

Although shame has been found to exist in all human cultures (Casimir & Schnegg, 2003), large cross-cultural differences have been documented in its situational antecedents, subjective experiences, and action tendencies. For instance, shame was found to be more prevalent among East Asian people than among North American counterparts (Benedict, 1946; Chu, 1972; Kitayama, Markus, & Matsumoto, 1995). In studies of emotion concepts, Levy (1973) argues that one language provides a large set of concepts for a particular type of emotion (hypercognition) and a small set of concepts for other types of emotion (hypocognition). The terms related to shame appear to be hypercognized in the Chinese language relative to English. The abundance of shame-related words is evident in Shaver, Wu, and Schwartz's (1992) list of 110 prototypical Chinese emotion terms, not to mention Li, Wang, and Fischer's (2004) list of 113 prototypical Chinese shame terms. With the extensive number of shame-related terms, how is the concept of shame organized in Chinese people's minds?

Shaver and his colleagues (Shaver et al., 1992; Shaver, Murdaya, & Fraley, 2001) took the lead in examining the organization of emotion terms in Chinese, Indonesian, English, and Italian using prototype approach. On the basis of the similarity ratings in a sorting task, respondents in all four languages categorized emotion terms similarly. Positive and negative emotions occupied the superordinate level; joy, anger, sadness, fear, and love occupied the basic level. Among all but the Chinese subjects, self-conscious emotions were grouped under other emotion categories. Chinese subjects produced the additional basic category of shame, including shame-related terms such as *xiukui, cankui, xiuchi.* These Chinese words represent different kinds of shameful experiences that are difficult to translate into different English equivalents. Standard Chinese–English dictionaries translate all these terms as shame or as a combination of 'shame' with other emotions.

Inspired by Shaver's pioneering work on Chinese emotion lexicon, Li et al. (2004) adopted a similar approach in examining the organization of shame concepts among PRC Chinese living in North America. They began with 144 terms resulting from their dictionary search and interviews with native speakers of Mandarin Chinese. Of these terms, 113 were rated as important shame concepts. A hierarchical cluster analysis of the similarity ratings among the 113 terms resulted in two superordinate categories. The first one was 'shame state', which describes various experiences actually felt by the subjects themselves at the time of a shame episode (see also Kam & Bond, 2008). Guilt, defined by thirteen terms, was represented as a basic category under the 'shame state' superordinate category. The second superordinate category was 'reactions to shame', which describes reactions to shameful acts committed by others (see Singelis, Bond, Sharkey, & Lai's [1999] 'other-induced embarrassment'). This category appears to be odd because the reactions to shame do not directly pertain to a shame episode per se. Nonetheless, the subjects preserved 43 per cent of the word list for this second superordinate category, implying that at least in the Chinese language, the reactions to shameful acts occupy an important representation in the Chinese mind. Is this 'reactions' category specific to PRC Chinese subjects? This is certainly an area for fruitful research in intra-cultural studies as well as cross-cultural studies.

Chinese culture, along with other Asian cultures, has long been labeled as a 'shame culture' and the United States as a 'guilt culture' (Benedict, 1946; Chu, 1972; Leighton & Kluckhohn, 1947; Schneider, 1977; Schoenhals, 1993). How does this shame-versus-guilt dichotomy survive in the recent literature? What is the relation between shame and guilt? In the studies reported so far, the results are inconsistent with this dichotomous characterization but consistent with recent empirical findings on the close relation between guilt and shame. When Li (2002) studied the role played by shame and guilt among Chinese students facing failure in learning, she found no difference between the two emotions. When Tangney, Miller, Flicker, and Barlow (1996) examined the differences between shame and guilt among undergraduates in the USA, they concluded that no differences could be found in the degree of the moral stand, sense of responsibility and motivation to make amends. Hence, although Ho, Fu, and Ng (2004) offered a theoretical perspective for distinguishing shame from guilt (see also Bedford, 2004), my review of empirical studies gives little support for the shame-guilt dichotomy.

Socially appropriate emotions in different cultures

Frijda and Mesquita (1995) suggest that the effect of culture on emotional experience depends upon the significance an emotion has for an individual and upon how valuable that emotion is in a culture. Foods found delightful in one culture (e.g. chickens' feet or cottage cheese) might be considered disgusting in another. In parallel fashion, an emotion such as pride may be perceived to be appropriate in one culture but inappropriate in another. Emotions differ in perceived appropriateness and desirability across cultures.

People from different cultural traditions think about and therefore experience emotions differently (Markus & Kitayama, 1991). In particular, people from the Aristotelian cultural tradition ('the West') tend to endorse an independent self-construal consisting of inner attributes that make an individual distinct from others. The mission is to become independent from others and to pursue personal goals. People from the Confucian cultural tradition ('the East') tend to endorse interdependent self-construal, which is characterized by the belief that the self cannot be separated from the social context. The self is embedded in layers of relationships and people regulate their emotions and thoughts to fit the agendas of others. The ideal is to maintain harmony with others and to fulfill one's social duties (see Kwan, Hui, & McGee, this volume; Leung & Au, this volume).

Close connections were hypothesized between self-construal and regulatory focus (approach vs. avoidance), and these connections have significant implications on the norms for experiencing different kinds of emotions. Lee, Aaker, and Gardner (2000) suggested that people with interdependent self-construals are prevention focused, and they focus on information that prevents them from disturbing harmony and interpersonal relationships. They value negative information (see also Sommers, 1984). Emotions that signal that social norms have been violated or that social obligations have not been fulfilled, such as guilt, are therefore important to interdependent cultures. In contrast, people with independent self-construals are promotion focused, and they focus on information that is relevant to the accomplishment of their own aspirations and the expression of their own attributes. They value positive information. Emotions that signal the successful achievement of personal goals, such as pride, are therefore important to independent cultures (see also Wyer & Hong, this volume).

In a large-scale cross-cultural study, Eid and Diener (2001) examined the norms for experiencing eight different emotions in collectivist countries (e.g. PRC) and individualist countries (e.g. USA) using latent class models, with norms being defined as emotions that are *appropriate and desirable* to experience. They found that the collectivistic and individualistic cultures differed most in the norms for experiencing guilt and pride. Whereas guilt was highly valued by PRC Chinese, pride was highly valued by Americans. On the other hand, when Stipek (1998) studied antecedents to feeling pride in American and PRC students, she found that feeling pride was from achievements that benefited others than from those due to personal achievement among the Chinese subjects (see also Sommers, 1984). Chinese extended this self-conscious emotion to their close relatives, which may reflect the malleable boundaries between self and others as dictated by the dominant cultural tradition (Bond, 1993; see also Lu, this volume).

Interestingly enough, research on ideal affect, which is a set of emotions that one *ideally wants to experience*, has found that both Hong Kong Chinese and Asian-Americans desire to experience calmness (low-arousal positive affect) more than do European-Americans (Tsai et al., 2006). European-Americans and Asian-Americans desire to experience excitement (high-arousal positive affect).

In comparing these two accounts, we must recognize that they cannot be pitted against each other on a level playing field. The norms study defined its criterion variables as eight discrete emotions (four pleasant and four unpleasant); the ideal affect study relied on eight different scales that were hypothesized to underline the circumplex model shown in Figure 14.1. The norms study measured emotions that are perceived to be *appropriate and desirable*; the ideal affect study considered emotions that people *ideally want to experience*. Do these two sets of measures tap into the same psychological space? Do people in a culture *want* to experience the emotions that are considered to be *appropriate* in that culture? (In their first footnote, Eid and Diener [2001] reported a correlation of .77 between the 'appropriateness' and 'desirability' ratings.) Lastly, the two studies relied on two different groups of Chinese, namely those from the PRC and those from Hong Kong. Clearly, much research remains to document the complex relations between the norms for experiencing emotions and the ideal feelings one seeks to feel under cultural influences (e.g. Jiang & Yik, 2009).

Emotional responding

From a lay person's perspective, it is relatively straightforward to label someone's emotion. However, scientific analysis as of today suggests that understanding someone's emotion remains one of the vexing issues of this century (Mauss & Robinson, 2009). Emotion theorists have developed various measures to tap a person's emotional responses including subjective experience, physiology, and behaviors. In this section, I review the latest research on Chinese facial expressions and physiology.

Development of indigenous facial stimulus materials

Some writers have emphasized the pan-cultural facial expressions of basic emotions that are universally recognized (Ekman et al., 1987; Izard, 1977), whereas others have argued in favor of a culture-specific hypothesis, suggesting that people in a culture have unique ways of expressing and hence recognizing emotions (Klineberg, 1938). The enthusiasm for research on emotion recognition has continued to grow in the last decade (Markham & Wang, 1996; Yik, Meng, & Russell, 1998; Yik & Russell, 1999). Of particular interest is that researchers working with Chinese subjects have invested considerable effort in developing indigenous stimulus materials, such as prototypical facial expressions (see Bai, Ma, & Huang, 2005; Wang & Markham, 1999).

The International Affective Picture System (IAPS; Lang, Bradely, & Cuthbert, 2001) consists of 823 pictures covering nine different domains. It has been widely used in cross-cultural research. To test the cross-cultural compatibility of the pictures in Chinese, Hu, Wei, and Guo (2005) conducted a large-scale normative study in which PRC subjects rated each picture for pleasure and arousal. The resulting ratings were found to be very similar to the American norms and it was concluded that the IAPS could be comfortably used in research on Chinese subjects.

Taking the IAPS as their model, Bai et al. (2005) developed the Chinese Affective Picture System (CAPS), an indigenous system consisting of 852 pictures of Chinese faces, scenes, and animals (e.g. Panda bears). Affective ratings of the pictures for pleasure, arousal, and dominance were obtained; internal validities were established. This system provided indigenous materials for research on emotion recognition among Chinese subjects.

While the above studies based the development of facial expressions on themes, another group of studies started with basic emotions (Ekman et al., 1987). Wang and his colleagues spearheaded a program of research on developing facial expressions to define happiness, anger, sadness, fear, surprise, and disgust. Wang and Markham (1999; see also Wang, Hoosain, Lee, Meng, Fu, & Yang, 2006) created a set of Chinese faces expressing these six basic emotions, resulting in 400 pictures, among which sixty-two were found to reliably express one of the six emotions.

Emotion recognition

To what extent is the recognition of emotion in faces universal or specific to a particular culture? This question has been as fascinating as it has been vexing to emotion psychologists since the time of Charles Darwin, as has the role of culture in emotion recognition. The consensus is that, first, emotions are recognizable at above-chance levels across cultures, although cultural variation is consistent across cultures; and, second, people of different cultures differ in their ability to recognize emotions in facial expressions.

The cultural variations in emotion recognition have inspired a line of research studying the effect of in-group advantage, in which higher recognition accuracy rates are evident in cases when both the encoder (the subject in the picture) and the decoder (the subject looking at the picture) belong to the same cultural group (Elfenbein & Ambady, 2002). This finding is also consistent with Klineberg's (1938) proposition that 'photographs illustrating these [Chinese-specific] literary expressions are judged more easily by Chinese than by American subjects' (p. 520). When Caucasian facial stimuli (e.g. IAPS) were used, recognition rates were always higher in North American samples than in Asian samples (see Yik & Russell, 1999). The question 'If Chinese facial stimuli are used, will Chinese subjects perform better than their American counterparts?' remains unanswered.

Yik et al. (1998) conducted a trilingual study on emotion recognition using Meng, Yan, and Meng's (1985) thirteen spontaneously posed pictures of PRC Chinese babies under different mood inductions. Contrary to the predictions based on in-group advantage, their Hong Kong Chinese subjects performed worse than their Canadian counterparts; their Japanese subjects fell between the prior groups. Chinese were less accurate than Americans in recognizing emotions in facial expressions. When the indigenous pictures, along with Ekman's pictures, were administered to PRC Chinese and Australian children who were four, six, and eight years old, the emotions on the Chinese faces were better recognized by both cultural groups than were the emotions on the Caucasian faces (Markham &

Wang, 1996). This finding contradicts the findings reported by Elfenbein and Ambady (2003), who found that emotions on Chinese faces were more difficult for participants to recognize than were emotions on Caucasian faces, regardless of their culture.

Taken together, these results appear to suggest that the in-group advantage was at work when facial stimuli in pictures of PRC Chinese were shown to PRC Chinese subjects, but not to Hong Kong Chinese subjects. The results, although tentative, are fascinating and consistent with Elfenbein and Ambady's (2003) cultural familiarity hypothesis. When the authors compared recognition abilities among PRC Chinese, Chinese living in the United States, Chinese-Americans, and Americans of non-Asian ancestry, they found that the accuracy and speed of emotion recognition were greater when the subjects had greater exposure to the posers' cultural group. It was thus a 'familiarity breeds accuracy' effect, rather than an in-group effect that accounted for superior performance in emotion recognition (see Matsumoto, 1992, for a different view). Perhaps by being exposed to the PRC Chinese posers, the PRC Chinese subjects gained an advantage in recognizing the emotions in the pictures.

To summarize, the past decade has witnessed a growth of research on developing indigenous Chinese facial stimuli to provide inputs for conducting intra-cultural studies. Studies of facial expressions of emotions were primarily restricted to recognition research and to providing support for the universality hypothesis, but there are some indicators of cultural differences. Unfortunately, how extensive the differences are and why there are differences remain to be explored. In-group advantage, or the cultural familiarity hypothesis, certainly provides a head start in understanding cultural variations in emotion recognition.

Currently, these hypotheses have been tested by comparing responses from Chinese living in different parts of the world with responses from European-Americans. Future studies can be directed at testing them using Chinese living in different provinces in the PRC, thereby controlling for ethnic background (see Beaupré & Hess, 2005). Last but not least, the studies reviewed here concern the capacity to attribute an emotion label to an expression inside the laboratory. Results do not indicate how emotions are expressed and recognized in everyday life (see Yik & Russell, 1999).

Physiological and behavioral responses

James (1884) was among the first psychologists to propose that different emotional states are associated with specific patterns of autonomic nervous system changes. His speculations are central to many theories such that there is a notion that any Autonomic Nervous System (ANS) pattern is a straightforward reflection of the emotional state of the individual (Mauss & Robinson, 2009). In studying the emotional responses elicited during a conversation about a conflict, Tsai and her colleagues (Tsai & Levenson, 1997; Tsai, Levenson, & McCoy, 2006) measured physiological changes and behaviors in addition to subjective self-reports of emotions. The team found that physiological measures were least susceptible to cultural influences as compared with self-reports and behaviors.

Soto, Levenson, and Ebling (2005) examined reactions to aversive acoustic startle stimuli in Chinese-Americans and Mexican-Americans. Consistent with the ethnographic account that Chinese are emotionally restrained (Bond, 1993; Kleinberg, 1938; Potter, 1988), the Chinese subjects reported fewer emotions than did the Mexican subjects. Nonetheless, neither emotional behaviors (facial and upper body movements) nor physiological measures (e.g. finger temperature, skin conductance level, blood pressure, finger pulse) revealed significant differences between the two criterion groups.

In summary, the notion obtained from ethnographic studies that culture influences the experience of emotion received mixed support in the studies reviewed here. In line with the findings reporting null findings for the effect of culture on emotional responses to a startle stimulus (Lee & Levenson, 1992) and to emotion-induction films (Tsai, Levenson, & Carstensen, 2000), no cultural difference was found in the physiological measures. Perhaps ANS activity simply indexes the arousal level of an emotional state rather than its distinct emotional nature (Cannon, 1931; Duffy, 1957; Schachter & Singer, 1962). Perhaps finer-grained ANS measures will lead to emotion-specific patterns in the future, but more studies are certainly needed before firm conclusions can be drawn.

Somatization

In Chinese societies, emotions are thought to be associated with physiological events. Somatization refers to the experience of bodily or somatic symptoms in place of an emotion and this has been said to be common among the Chinese in their reactions to emotional states. Some writers argued that the phenomenon reflects the lack of a working vocabulary on emotion in Chinese, although Russell and Yik (1996) have demonstrated otherwise. Still other writers have suggested that somatization implies the lack of psychologization (Kleinman & Kleinman, 1985; Tseng, 1975). Wu (1982) suggested that culture-specific expression of an emotion in Chinese is dependent upon the situation. As Ots (1990) argued, 'Chinese are culturally trained to "listen" within their body' (p. 26).

Tsai, Simeonova, and Watanabe (2004) tested the culture-specific hypothesis by comparing the words used in expressing emotional experiences between Chinese-American and European-American subjects (with English used for all participants). Their results showed that the Chinese group deployed more somatic (e.g. dizzy) and social (e.g. friends) words when they talked about their emotions. Using a representative community sample of over 1,700 Chinese Americans living in Los Angeles, Mak and Zane (2004) found that reports of somatic symptoms (e.g. dizzy, hot/cold spells) were not related to the length of their stay in the USA; rather, they were related to negative emotions reported, such as anxiety and depression.

These two studies employed Chinese subjects with different levels of exposure to American culture and yielded different results. One relied on in-depth interviews and qualitative analysis of the conversational scripts; the exposure to American culture was restricted to two levels. The other study relied on a quantitative survey approach in which the level of exposure or acculturation to American culture was treated as a continuous variable in testing for the effect of culture. The divergence in their conclusions clearly provides an avenue for future intra-cultural research, be the research quantitative or qualitative, to compare the interplay between the level of acculturation to Chinese values, beliefs, and norms and the level of somatization within the geographical map of the PRC.

Socialization of emotions

One early socialization task for children is to learn to 'express and regulate their emotions in socially desirable and valued ways' (Eisenberg, Cumberland, & Spinrad, 1998, p. 242). Most children have acquired basic understanding of emotions by the age of three to four, which also marks their earliest recollections of childhood in their memories (Wang, 2008). Research has shown that mother-child relations during childhood shape the emotional experiences of children as they grow up. These experiences have direct influence on autobiographical memory and emotional expressivity (Camras, Chen, Bakeman, Norris, & Cain, 2006; Wang, 2008). Although a significant number of studies have examined parental socialization of emotion, little research has looked into the mechanisms through which children learn emotions (Tsai, Louie, Chen, & Uchida, 2007). In this section, I examine two possible pathways to socialization of emotions, namely mother-child interactions and storybooks.

Mother-child interactions

Autobiographical memory, the recollection of childhood events, refers to specific, long-lasting memories of significant personal experiences in an individual's life. It encompasses memories of personally significant episodes (Nelson & Fivush, 2004), and is critical to the formation of self-identity and psychological well-being (Fivush, 1998). Research has found that the autobiographical memory is characterized by heightened emotional arousal (McGaugh, 2003). What are the antecedents to autobiographical memory? Writers have spearheaded a pioneering line of studies on examining one such antecedent, namely emotion knowledge, among US and PRC children.

Emotion knowledge facilitates the understanding and organization of significant event information and contributes to building autobiographical memory. Wang (2008) conducted the first longitudinal study to test the contribution of emotion knowledge to autobiographical memory in children who were European-American, Chinese immigrants to the USA, and PRC Chinese. Children were visited three times at ages three, three and a half, and four. In each visit, they described two events that had happened in the past two months. Their autobiographical recollections were coded for specificity and emotion language. Their emotion knowledge was tapped by the number of situations they could provide for provoking happy, sad, fearful, and angry emotions. European-American children showed an overall better understanding of emotion situations than did their Chinese peers; they recalled events by giving more specific details and using more emotion terms. All three groups demonstrated improvement in memory specificity over time. Emotion knowledge contributed uniquely to the ability to report quality autobiographical memories and this effect was robust across the three cultural groups and age groups.

Similarly, Wang (2001a) found that American adults' reports were lengthy, detailed, and emotionally elaborated; their earliest memory could be dated back to age three and a half. The Chinese adults' reports were relatively brief and centered on collective activities and emotionally neutral events; their earliest memory could be dated back to age four.

Wang's (2008) study provides compelling evidence for the close connections between emotion knowledge and autobiographical memory. Still, what can possibly account for the cultural variations in both children's and adults' recollections? Childhood narratives provide one possibility. Fivush and Wang (2005) studied the mother-child dialogues about their past events and found that Chinese dyads used more negative emotion words than did the American dyads. Perhaps the discussion of negative emotion serves the purpose of educating children in the culturally appropriate way to display emotion. In Wang's (2001b) discursive analysis, Chinese mothers were found to demonstrate an emotionally critical style that focused on proper behavior in children and gave few explanations for the experienced emotions. In stark contrast, American mothers adopted an emotionally explanatory style that emphasized an understanding of, and explained the antecedents to, emotions. Such dialogues seem to serve the culture-specific mission of transmitting to children knowledge about emotions. In studies comparing PRC Chinese with American children of ages three to six in their ability to identify the emotions expressed in twenty short stories, Americans demonstrated greater understanding of emotion (Wang, 2003).

To summarize, studies of autobiographical memory have provided apparent support for the importance of emotion knowledge and mother-child interactions in the cultural learning process. The strength of the relation between emotion knowledge and autobiographical memory varied across cultures, although the children's performance improved with age. No gender difference was noted. Interestingly enough, all previous studies have focused upon the mothers' role in the socialization process. A much broader spectrum of cultural agents, such as fathers and teachers, should be consulted in future research, and mediating variables explored to account for the cultural differences found (Bond & Van de Vijver, in press). It is not enough to merely document differences; it is time to explain their underpinnings (Bond, 2009).

Storybooks

So far, studies seem to suggest that culture exercises its influence on emotional experience via mother-child or family narratives. Parents or mothers certainly play an important role in the socialization of emotion. Camras and her colleagues have found that, compared with PRC Chinese, European-American mothers reported more positive emotional expressions (Camras, Kolmodin, & Chen, 2008); their children smiled more in a mood induction study (Camras et al., 2006). In addition, parents might expose their children to other cultural practices or media. Children were read books that were selected by parents or teachers (Miller, Wiley, Fung, & Liang 1997) through which they learned, for instance, what feelings are desired or valued in their culture.

Tsai, Louie, Chen, and Uchida (2007) tested this alternative pathway through books to socialize children's ideal affects. They found that European-American preschoolers preferred exciting activities more and perceived an excited smile as happier than did their Taiwanese peers. When they compared the contents of the best-selling storybooks in the USA and Taiwan, American bestsellers were found to portray more excited expressions, wider smiles, and stronger arousing activities than did Taiwanese storybooks.

Inspired by the cultural variation in the ideal affect sought by people of different cultures (Tsai et al., 2006), Tsai et al. (2007) examined children's exposure to storybooks as a pathway to socialization of ideal affect, and found that cultural variations generalized to the American and Taiwanese preschoolers. Culture comprises socially transmitted ideas that are supported by practices, products, and institutions extant in the cultural context (see Kroeber & Kluckhohn, 1952; Markus, Uchida, Omoregie, Townsend, & Kitayama, 2006). Future studies should explore other socialization practices such as interactions between parents and children, and teachers and children.

Conclusion

Chinese are in certain respects

a. like all other people

b. like some other people

c. like no other people.[1]

Those seeking to understand the universal aspects of emotion have often turned to China for their research. Those seeking to understand culture-specific aspects of emotion have also turned to China for their research. In the last decade, Chinese emotion research has immensely benefited from researchers coming from different perspectives and taking important steps in the clarification of Chinese emotion. They have taken the step from studying Chinese undergraduate students in their own countries to studying Chinese groups differing in age and country of residence. The field has witnessed the expansion of comparison groups to Chinese (PRC, Hong Kong, Taiwan), Chinese living in the USA, Caucasians of Asian ancestry, and Caucasians of non-Asian ancestry. To me, this enlargement is already a quantum leap towards a paradigmatic shift, a shift that will be further accelerated by including a broader spectrum of samples and age groups.

Here, I have tried to summarize the evidence so far offered in the debate between the universality thesis and the culture-specific thesis of emotion. Given the four areas that were reviewed in this chapter, it may be tempting to conclude that the evidence seems to suggest that the similarities between Chinese and other people outweigh the differences. I argue that this conclusion is premature on the following grounds. First, the general trend observed seems to suggest that at the general level, Chinese are similar to people from other cultures. However, it seems that the more fine-grained the analysis, the greater the number of differences that tend to be uncovered. Second, my conclusions on such areas are only as good as the evidence collected. Cultural variations were usually supported in studies in which groups were presumably exposed to different levels of Chinese culture (e.g. European-Americans, PRC Chinese, Chinese immigrants). Culture was, however, assumed rather than measured. Culture seems to be a very encompassing concept and was hypothesized to influence many different emotions, from calm, happy, and excited, to shame and guilt. The nature of the cultural influence exercised needs to be identified and theoretically linked in future research (see Bond & Van de Vijver, in press) to further inform us of what is universal and what is unique about Chinese emotion. These are not tangential questions; their answers represent a fundamental but under-studied issue that illuminates the ultimate concerns informing the psychology of emotion.

Author's note

Preparation of this chapter was facilitated by the RGC General Research Fund (Project No. 644508). I thank Stephen Choy, Jessica Jiang, Bobo Lau, Sky Ng, Virginia Unkefer, and Kevin Zeng for their help in preparing this chapter. I also wish to thank Steven, Stephanie and Christopher So, who go to sleep just early enough to allow me to pursue my many projects on Chinese emotion; they also taught me a working vocabulary for everyday feelings. Finally, I would like to dedicate this chapter to Jim Russell, whose decade of assiduous mentoring has made my work possible.

Correspondence concerning this chapter should be addressed to Michelle Yik, Hong Kong University of Science and Technology, Division of Social Science, Clear Water Bay, Kowloon, Hong Kong S.A.R., China. Email: Michelle.Yik@ust.hk.

Chapter note

1 I am indebted to Kluckhohn and Murray (1953), whose original observation I have applied here to the Chinese people.

References

Bagozzi, R. P., Wong, N., & Yi, Y. (1999). The role of culture and gender in the relationship between positive and negative affect. *Cognition and Emotion, 13*, 641–672.

Bai, L., Ma, H., & Huang, Y. (2005). The development of Native Chinese Affective Picture System – A pretest in 46 college students. *Chinese Mental Health Journal, 19*, 719–722. (in Chinese)

Beaupré, M. G. & Hess, U. (2005). Cross-cultural emotion recognition among Canadian ethnic groups. *Journal of Cross-Cultural Psychology, 36*, 355–370.

Bedford, O. A. (2004). The individual experience of guilt and shame in Chinese culture. *Culture & Psychology, 10*, 29–52.

Benedict, R. (1946). *The chrysanthemum and the sword.* Boston, MA: Houghton-Mifflin.

Berry, J. W. (1969). On cross-cultural comparability. *International Journal of Psychology, 4*, 119–128.

Bond, M. H. (1993). Emotion and their expression in Chinese culture. *Journal of Nonverbal Behavior, 17*, 245–262.

Bond, M. H. (2009). Circumnavigating the psychological globe: From yin and yang to starry, starry night. In S. Bekman & A. Aksu-Koç (eds), *Perspectives on human development, family, and culture* (pp. 31–49). Cambridge, UK: Cambridge University Press.

Bond, M. H. & Van de Vijver, F. J. R. (in press). Making scientific sense of cultural differences in psychological outcomes: Unpackaging the *Magnum Mysterium.* In D. Matsumoto & F. J. R. Van de Vijver (eds), *Cross-cultural research methods.* New York: Oxford University Press.

Camras, L. A., Chen, Y., Bakeman, R., Norris, K., & Cain, T. R. (2006). Culture, ethnicity, and children's facial expressions: A study of European American, Mainland Chinese, Chinese American, and adopted Chinese girls. *Emotion, 6*, 103–114.

Camras, L. A., Kolmodin, K., & Chen, Y. (2008). Mothers' self-reported emotional expression in Mainland Chinese, Chinese American and European American families. *International Journal of Behavioral Development, 32*, 459–463.

Cannon, W. B. (1927). The James–Lange theory of emotions: A critical examination and an alternative theory. *The American Journal of Psychology, 39*, 106–124.

Casimir, M. J. & Schnegg, M. (2003). Shame across cultures: The evolution, ontogeny, and function of a 'moral emotion'. In H. Keller, Y. H. Poortinga, & A. Scholmerich (eds), *Between culture and biology: Perspectives on ontogenic development* (pp. 270–300). Cambridge, UK: Cambridge University Press.

Chan, D. W. (1985). Perception and judgment of facial expressions among the Chinese. *International Journal of Psychology, 20*, 681–692.

Chu, C. L. (1972). On the shame orientation of the Chinese from the interrelationship among society, individual, and culture. In I. Y. Lee & K. S. Yang (eds), *Symposium on the character of the Chinese: An interdisciplinary approach* (pp. 85–125). Taipei, Taiwan: Institute of Ethnology, Academia Sinica. (in Chinese)

Dixon, R. M. W. (1977). Where have all the adjectives gone? *Studies in Language, 1*, 19–80.

Duffy, E. (1957). The psychological significance of the concept of arousal or activation. *Psychological Review, 64*, 265–275.

Eid, M. & Diener, E. (2001). Norms for experiencing emotions in different cultures: Inter- and intranational differences. *Journal of Personality and Social Psychology, 81*, 869–885.

Eisenberg, N., Cumberland, A., & Spinrad, T. L. (1998). Parental socialization of emotion. *Psychological Inquiry, 9*, 241–273.

Ekman, P., Friesen, W. V., O'Sullivan, M., Chan, A., Diacoyanni-Tarlatzis, I., Heider, K., Krause, R., Le Compte, W. A., Pitcairn, T., Ricci Bitti, P. E., Scherer, K., Tomita, M., & Tzavaras, A. (1987). Universals and cultural differences in the judgments of facial expressions of emotion. *Journal of Personality and Social Psychology, 53*, 712–717.

Elfenbein, H. A. & Ambady, N. (2002). Is there an in-group advantage in emotion recognition? *Psychological Bulletin, 128*, 243–249.

Elfenbein, H. A. & Ambady, N. (2003). When familiarity breeds accuracy: Cultural exposure and facial emotion recognition. *Journal of Personality and Social Psychology, 85*, 276–290.

Fivush, R. (1998). Children's recollections of traumatic and nontraumatic events. *Development and Psychopathology, 10*, 699–716.

Fivush, R. & Wang, Q. (2005). Emotion talk in mother–child conversations of the shared past: The effects of culture, gender, and event valence. *Journal of Cognition and Development, 6*, 489–506.

Frijda, N. H. & Mesquita, B. (1995). The social roles and functions of emotions. In S. Kitayama & H. R. Markus (eds), *Emotion and culture: Empirical studies of mutual influence* (pp. 51–87). Washington, DC: American Psychological Association.

Fung, H. (1999). Becoming a moral child: The socialization of shame among young Chinese children. *Ethos, 27*, 180–209.

Goldberg, L. (1981). Language and individual differences: The search for universal in personality lexicons. *Review of Personality and Social Psychology, 2*, 141–165.

Green, D. P., Goldman, S. L., Salovey, P. (1993). Measurement error masks bipolarity in affect ratings. *Journal of Personality and Social Psychology, 64*, 1029–1041.

Hamid, P. N. & Cheng, S. T. (1996). The development and validation of an index of emotional disposition and mood state: The Chinese Affect Scale. *Educational and Psychological Measurement, 56*, 995–1014.

Ho, D. Y. F., Fu, W., & Ng, S. M. (2004). Guilt, shame, and embarrassment: Revelations of face and self. *Culture and Psychology, 10*, 64–84.

Hu, S., Wei, N., & Guo, W. (2005). Cross-cultural study of affective reactions of Chinese and American healthy adults. *Chinese Journal of Clinical Psychology, 13*, 265–276. (in Chinese)

Izard, C. E. (1977). *Human emotions.* New York: Plenum Press.

James, W. (1884). What is an emotion? *Mind, 9*, 188–205.

Jiang, D. & Yik, M. (2009, May). *What affective feelings do Chinese want to feel?* Poster session presented at the 2009 APS Annual Convention, San Francisco, CA.

Kam, C. C. S. & Bond, M. H. (2008). The role of emotions and behavioral responses in mediating the impact of face loss on relationship deterioration: Are Chinese more face-sensitive than Americans? *Asian Journal of Social Psychology, 11*, 175–184.

Kitayama, S., Markus, H. R., & Matsumoto, H. (1995). Culture, self, and emotion: A cultural perspective on 'self-conscious' emotions. In J. Tangley & K. W. Fischer (eds), *Self-conscious emotions: The psychology of shame, guilt, embarrassment, and pride* (pp. 439–464). New York: Guilford.

Kleinman, A. & Kleinman, J. (1985). Somatization: The interconnections in Chinese society among culture, depressive experiences, and the meanings of pain. In A. Kleinman & B. Good (eds), *Culture and depression: Studies in the anthropology and cross-cultural psychiatry of affect and disorder* (pp. 429–490). Berkeley, CA: University of California Press.

Klineberg, O. (1938). Emotional expression in Chinese literature. *Journal of Abnormal and Social Psychology, 33*, 517–520.

Kluckhohn, C. & Murray, H. A. (1953). *Personality in nature, society and culture.* New York: Alfred A. Knopf.

Kroeber, A. L. & Kluckhohn, C. (1952). *Culture: A critical review of concepts and definitions.* Cambridge, MA: Peabody Museum of Archaeology & Ethnology.

Lang, P. J., Bradeley, M. M., & Cuthbert, B. N. (2001). *International Affective Picture System (IAPS): Instruction Manual and Affective Ratings. Technical report A-5.* Gainesville, FL: The Center for Research in Psychophysiology, University of Florida.

Larsen, R. J. & Diener, E. (1992). Promises and problems with the circumplex model of emotion. In M. S. Clark (ed.), *Review of Personality and Social Psychology: Emotion* (Volume 13, pp. 25–59). Newbury Park, CA: Sage.

Lee, A. Y., Aaker, J. L., & Gardner, W. L. (2000). The pleasures and pains of distinct self-construals: The role of interdependence in regulatory focus. *Journal of Personality and Social Psychology, 78*, 1122–1134.

Lee, K. J. & Levenson, R. W. (1992, October). *Ethnic differences in emotional reactivity to an unanticipated startle.* Paper presented at the meeting of the Society for Psychophysiological Research, San Diego, CA.

Leighton, D. & Kluckhohn, C. (1947). *Children of the people: The Navaho individual and his development.* Cambridge, MA: Harvard University Press.

Levy, R. I. (1973). *Tahitians: Mind and experience in the Society Islands.* Chicago, IL: University of Chicago Press.

Li, J. (2002). A cultural model of learning: Chinese 'heart and mind for wanting to learn'. *Journal of Cross-Cultural Psychology, 33*, 248–269.

Li, J., Wang, L., & Fischer, K. W. (2004). The organization of Chinese shame concepts. *Cognition and Emotion, 18*, 767–797.

Mak, W. W. S. & Zane, N. W. S. (2004). The phenomenon of somatization among community Chinese Americans. *Social Psychiatry and Psychiatric Epidemiology, 39*, 967–974.

Markham, R. & Wang L. (1996). Recognition of emotion by Chinese and Australian children. *Journal of Cross-Cultural Psychology, 27*, 616–643.

Markus, H. R. & Kitayama, S. (1991). Culture and the self: Implications for cognition, emotion, and motivation. *Psychological Review, 98*, 224–253.

Markus, H. R., Uchida, Y., Omoregie, H., Townsend, S., & Kitayama, S. (2006). Going for the gold: Models of agency in Japanese and American contexts. *Psychological Science, 17*, 103–112.

Matsumoto, D. (1992). American-Japanese cultural differences in the recognition of universal facial expressions. *Journal of Cross-Cultural Psychology, 23*, 72–84.

Mauss, I. B. & Robinson, M. D. (2009). Measures of emotion: A review. *Cognition and Emotion, 23*, 209–237.

McGaugh, J. L. (2003). *Memory and emotion: The making of lasting memories.* New York: Columbia University Press.

Meng, Z., Yan, J., & Meng, X. (1985). A preliminary study on facial expression patterns of infants. *Acta Psychologica Sinica, 1*, 55–61. (in Chinese)

Miller, P. J., Wiley, A. R., Fung, H., & Liang, C. H. (1997). Personal storytelling as a medium of socialization in Chinese and American families. *Child Development, 68*, 557–568.
Nelson, K. & Fivush, R. (2004). The emergence of autobiographical memory: A social cultural developmental theory. *Psychological Review, 111*, 486–511.
Ots, T. (1990). The angry liver, the anxious heart, and the melancholy spleen: The phenomenology of perceptions in Chinese culture. *Culture, Medicine, and Psychiatry, 14*, 21–58.
Potter, S. H. (1988). The cultural construction of emotion in rural Chinese social life. *Ethos, 16*, 181–208.
Remington, N. A., Fabrigar, L. R., & Visser, P. S. (2000). Re-examining the circumplex model of affect. *Journal of Personality and Social Psychology, 79*, 286–300.
Russell, J. A. (1979). Affective space is bipolar. *Journal of Personality and Social Psychology, 37*, 345–356.
Russell, J. A. (1980). A circumplex model of affect. *Journal of Personality and Social Psychology, 39*, 1161–1178.
Russell, J. A. (1983). Pancultural aspects of the human concept organization of emotions. *Journal of Personality and Social Psychology, 45*, 1281–1288.
Russell, J. A. (1991). Culture and the categorization of emotions. *Psychological Bulletin, 110*, 426–450.
Russell, J. A. & Carroll, J. M. (1999). On the bipolarity of positive and negative affect. *Psychological Bulletin, 125*, 3–30.
Russell, J. A., Lewicka, M., & Niit, T. (1989). A cross-cultural study of a circumplex model of affect. *Journal of Personality and Social Psychology, 57*, 848–856.
Russell, J. A. & Yik, M. (1996). Emotion among the Chinese. In M. H. Bond (ed.), *The handbook of Chinese psychology* (pp. 166–188). Hong Kong: Oxford University Press.
Schachter, S. & Singer, J. E. (1962). Cognitive, social, and physiological determinants of emotional state. *Psychological Review, 69*, 379–399.
Schimmack, U., Oishi, S., & Diener, E. (2002). Cultural influences on the relation between pleasant emotions and unpleasant emotions: Asian dialectic philosophies or individualism-collectivism? *Cognition and Emotion, 16*, 705–719.
Schneider, C. D. (1977). *Shame, exposure, and privacy.* Boston, MA: Beacon.
Schoenhals, M. (1993). *The paradox of power in a People's Republic of China middle school.* Armonk, NY: Sharpe.
Scollon, C. N., Diener, E., Oishi, S., & Biswas-Diener, R. (2005). An experience sampling and cross-cultural investigation of the relation between pleasant and unpleasant affect. *Cognition and Emotion, 19*, 27–52.
Shaver, P. R., Murdaya, U., & Fraley, R. C. (2001). Structure of the Indonesian emotion lexicon. *Asian Journal of Social Psychology, 4*, 201–224.
Shaver, P. R., Wu, S., & Schwartz, J. C. (1992). Cross-cultural similarities and differences in emotion and its representation: A prototype approach. In M. S. Clark (ed.), *Review of Personality and Social Psychology* (Vol. 13, Emotion, pp. 175–212). Newbury Park, CA: Sage.
Singelis, T. M., Bond, M. H., Sharkey, W. F., & Lai, C. S. Y. (1999). Unpacking culture's influence on self-esteem and embarrassability: The role of self-construals. *Journal of Cross-Cultural Psychology, 30*, 315–341.
Soto, J. A., Levenson, R. W., & Ebling, R. (2005). Cultures of moderation and expression: Emotional experience, behavior, and physiology in Chinese Americans and Mexican Americans. *Emotion, 5*, 154–165.
Sommers, S. (1984). Adults evaluating their emotions: A cross-cultural perspective. In C. Z. Malatesta & C. Izard (eds), *Emotion in adult development* (pp. 319–338). Beverly Hills, CA: Sage.
Stipek, D. (1998). Differences between Americans and Chinese in the circumstances evoking pride, shame, and guilt. *Journal of Cross-Cultural Psychology, 29*, 616–629.
Tangney, J. P. & Fischer, K. W. (1995). *Self-conscious emotions: The psychology of shame, guilt, embarrassment, and pride.* New York: Guilford.
Tangney, J. P., Miller, R., Flicker, L., & Barlow, D. H. (1996). Are shame, guilt, and embarrassment distinct emotions? *Journal of Personality and Social Psychology, 70*, 1256–1269.
Thayer, R. E. (1996). *The origin of everyday moods: Managing energy, tension, and stress.* New York: Oxford University Press.
Tsai, J. L., Knutson, B., & Fung, H. H. (2006). Cultural variation in affect valuation. *Journal of Personality and Social Psychology, 90*, 288–307.
Tsai, J. L. & Levenson, R. W. (1997). Cultural influences on emotional responding: Chinese American and European American dating couples during interpersonal conflict. *Journal of Cross-Cultural Psychology, 28*, 600–625.
Tsai, J. L., Levenson, R. W., & Carstensen, L. L. (2000). Autonomic, subjective, and expressive responses to emotional films in older and younger Chinese Americans and European Americans. *Psychology and Ageing, 15*, 684–693.
Tsai, J. L., Levenson, R. W., & McCoy, K. (2006). Cultural and temperamental variation in emotional response. *Emotion, 6*, 484–497.
Tsai, J. L., Louie, J. Y., Chen, E. E., & Uchida, Y. (2007). Learning what feelings to desire: Socialization of ideal affect through children's storybooks. *Personality and Social Psychology Bulletin, 33*, 17–30.
Tsai, J. L., Simeonova, D. I., & Watanabe, J. T. (2004). Somatic and social: Chinese Americans talk about emotion. *Personality and Social Psychology Bulletin, 30*, 1226–1238.
Tseng, W. S. (1975). The nature of somatic complaints among psychiatric patients: The Chinese case. *Comprehensive Psychiatry, 16*, 237–245.
Wang, K., Hoosain, R., Lee, T. M. C., Meng, Y., Fu, J., & Yang, R. (2006). Perception of six basic emotional facial expressions by the Chinese. *Journal of Cross-Cultural Psychology, 37*, 623–629.

Wang, L., Li, Z., Liu, H., & Du, W. (2007). Factor structure of general dimension scales of PANAS-X in Chinese people. *Chinese Journal of Clinical Psychology, 15*, 565–568. (in Chinese)

Wang, L. & Markham, R. (1999). The development of a series of photographs of Chinese facial expressions of emotion. *Journal of Cross-Cultural Psychology, 30*, 397–410.

Wang, Q. (2001a). Culture effects on adults' earliest childhood recollection and self-description: Implications for the relation between memory and the self. *Journal of Personality and Social Psychology, 81*, 220–233.

Wang, Q. (2001b). 'Did you have fun?': American and Chinese mother–child conversations about shared emotional experiences. *Cognitive Development, 16*, 693–715.

Wang, Q. (2003). Emotion situation knowledge in American and Chinese preschool children and adults. *Cognition and Emotion, 17*, 725–746.

Wang, Q. (2008). Emotion knowledge and autobiographical memory across the preschool years: A cross-cultural longitudinal investigation. *Cognition, 108*, 117–135.

Watson, D., Clark, L. A., & Tellegen, A. (1988). Development and validation of brief measures of positive and negative affect: The PANAS Scale. *Journal of Personality and Social Psychology, 54*, 1063–1070.

Watson, D. & Tellegen, A. (1985). Toward a consensual structure of mood. *Psychological Bulletin, 98*, 219–235.

Wiggins, J. S. (1979). A psychological taxonomy of trait-descriptive terms: The interpersonal domain. *Journal of Personality and Social Psychology, 37*, 395–412.

Wu, D. Y. H. (1982). Psychotherapy and emotion in traditional Chinese medicine. In A. J. Marsella & G. M. White (eds), *Cultural conceptions of mental health and therapy* (pp. 285–301). Dordrecht, Holland: D. Reidel.

Yik, M. (2007). Culture, gender, and the bipolarity of momentary affect. *Cognition and Emotion, 21*, 664–680.

Yik, M. (2009a). The bipolarity of momentary affect: Reply to Schimmack. *Cognition and Emotion, 23*, 605–610.

Yik, M. (2009b). *The structure of affect in a stressful moment.* Poster session presented at the 2009 APS Annual Convention, San Francisco, CA.

Yik, M. (2009c). Studying affect among the Chinese: The circular way. *Journal of Personality Assessment, 91*, 416–428.

Yik, M. (2009d). *What's interpersonal about the Chinese circumplex model of affect?* Poster session presented at the Association for Research in Personality, Evanston, IL.

Yik, M., Meng, Z., & Russell, J. A. (1998). Adults' freely produced emotion labels for babies' spontaneous facial expressions. *Cognition and Emotion, 12*, 723–730.

Yik, M. & Russell, J. A. (1999). Interpretation of faces: A cross-cultural study of a prediction from Fridlund's theory. *Cognition and Emotion, 13*, 93–104.

Yik, M. & Russell, J. A. (2003). Chinese Affect Circumplex: I. Structure of recalled momentary affect. *Asian Journal of Social Psychology, 6*, 185–200.

Yik, M., Russell, J. A., Ahn, C. K., Fernández Dols, J. M., & Suzuki, N. (2002). Relating the Five-Factor Model of personality to a circumplex model of affect: A five language study. In R. R. McCrae & J. Allik (eds), *The Five-Factor Model of personality across cultures* (pp. 79–104). New York: Kluwer Academic/Plenum.

Yik, M., Russell, J. A., & Barrett, L. F. (1999). Structure of self-reported current affect: Integration and beyond. *Journal of Personality and Social Psychology, 77*, 600–619.

Yik, M., Russell, J. A., & Steiger, J. H. (2010). *A 12-point circumplex model of core affect.* Manuscript submitted for publication.

Zeng, K. J. & Yik, M. (2009). *Testing relativity in the perception of emotion within the circumplex model.* Poster session presented at the 2009 APS Annual Convention, San Francisco, CA.

Zhong, J. & Qian, M. (2005). A study of development and validation of Chinese Mood Adjective Check List. *Chinese Journal of Clinical Psychology, 13*, 8–13. (in Chinese)

CHAPTER 15

Beliefs in Chinese culture

Kwok Leung

In the previous edition of *The Oxford handbook of Chinese psychology*, I presented a review of the literature on beliefs among the Chinese people. The study of beliefs is important because in addition to values, norms, and personality, beliefs are a major antecedent of social behaviors (Bond, 2009). This chapter provides an update of the earlier chapter by integrating research that has emerged thereafter. The two major objectives of the current review are to consolidate what we know about beliefs in Chinese culture, and to identify fruitful directions for future research on this important topic. As in the earlier review, I exclude personality traits, because they typically contain some beliefs mixed together with other constructs. Readers interested in this topic are referred to the relevant chapter in the present handbook by Cheung, Zhang, and Cheung, as well as elsewhere (McCrae, Costa, & Yik, 1996; Yang, 1986).

A typology of beliefs

Following Katz (1960) and Bar-Tal (1990), beliefs are concerned with propositions about an object or a relation between objects or concepts. The proposition can be causal or correlational, and may involve any content. A belief can be judged with regard to its likelihood of being true or correct. We note that beliefs are different from values, because values typically refer to the importance or desirability of a construct (e.g. peace is important or good). Beliefs are different from norms because norms refer to a preferred mode of behavior or action (e.g. you should work hard). An example of a belief is: 'Working hard leads to success.' Note that the importance or desirability of 'hard work' represents a value, and the statement 'you should work hard' refers to a norm; a belief is conceptually different.

Schwartz (1992) has argued that values function to help individuals meet three universal requirements of human existence: needs of the individual, needs for coordinated social interaction, and needs for the survival and well-being of the group. Leung and Bond (1992) proposed that this functional framework is applicable to beliefs, in that beliefs also function to help individuals meet these three requirements of human existence. Following this functionalist framework, beliefs can be classified into three major types based on their functional domain. Psychological beliefs are concerned with the characteristics of individuals; social beliefs are concerned with the beliefs about social interactions and social groups; and environmental beliefs are concerned with the beliefs about the physical world or supernatural context. These beliefs are assumed to help individuals interact effectively with other people and thrive in their physical and social environment across the lifespan. In the following review, salient beliefs in Chinese societies are organized by these three major types of belief.

Chinese traditional beliefs

Chinese culture is rich in the variety and quantity of traditional beliefs because of its long history, but few of these rich belief constellations have been explored by psychologists. For the sake of comprehensiveness, a few major traditional beliefs deemed important for future psychological research are briefly reviewed in the following.

Psychological beliefs

The assumption in Confucianism that individuals are basically benevolent (Chien, 1979) has exercised a major impact on the social practices and structures of Chinese societies. For instance, the Confucian emphasis on education regardless of social class and background reflects the basic belief that all individuals have the potential to be developed. The emphasis on effort by Chinese, which will be discussed in a subsequent section, is related to the Confucian belief of self-cultivation and self-perfection. The Taoist belief of following the way of nature as ideal may be related to optimism and coping behaviors (see Cheng, Lo, & Chio, this volume).

The Buddhist belief that desires are root causes of unhappiness may be related to self-management and anti-materialism, which may have important implications for psychotherapy (Wallace & Shapiro, 2006; see also Liu & Leung, this volume). Interestingly, Tsai, Knutson, and Fung (2006) found that Chinese valued low-arousal affect (e.g. calm) more than Americans, and this difference may be linked to Buddhist beliefs (Tsai, Miao, & Seppala, 2007). There is not much psychological research on Chinese traditional belief systems, and more work is needed to probe how they are related to the social behaviors of Chinese people.

Social beliefs

In Confucian thought, individuals are believed to have the ability to cultivate their morality and self-control. The social and political organization of traditional Chinese societies is primarily based on this belief, which emphasizes individual morality and diminishes the role of legal regulations (Pye, 1984). This belief in individual morality is often invoked to account for the lack of a systematic, objective legal system in traditional Chinese societies (Ju, 1947). In fact, Chinese traditionally resist rigid rules and prefer flexibility in their social life. For instance, Pugh and Redding (1985) found that firms in Hong Kong were less likely to use rules and procedures to regulate work behavior than British firms. Jiang, Lambert, and Wang (2007) found that Chinese university students who endorsed a Confucian belief concerning law and punishment with its emphasis on individual exercise of self-control, were favorable towards informal means for social and crime control. The belief in the capacity for individual morality may also explain why Chinese authority figures tend to resist objective systems for monitoring their own behavior and performance (Bond & Hwang, 1986). Such monitoring is often seen as an affront to their moral face and trustworthiness.

The Taoist belief of following the way of nature has implications for social interaction as well. One interesting consequence of this philosophical orientation is that rules and the notion of morality are de-emphasized (Sun, 1991), which in fact contradicts Confucianism. In Taoist thought, the most effective government governs through *wu wei* (non-action) (Pye, 1984). A better understanding of this belief may shed light on political and managerial behaviors in Chinese societies. Chinese people are jointly influenced by Taoism and Confucianism, and we do not know much about how the interplay of these two traditional thoughts influences work and political behaviors of Chinese people.

Environmental beliefs

Feng shui, which refers to the influence on people exercised by the relative position of buildings and furniture in relation to each other and in relation to the physical environment, is a complex of supernatural beliefs widely shared by traditional as well as modern Chinese (Pye, 1984). To avoid bad luck and to enhance good luck, some people hire *feng shui* masters to advise them on decorating homes, shops, factories, and offices. Some research has been conducted on this centuries-old Chinese belief. Masuda and Nisbett (2001) have argued that the holistic thinking style of East Asians as opposed to the analytical thinking style of Westerners is related to the popularity of *feng shui* beliefs in East Asia, a belief system which emphasizes the importance of the context. Tsang (2004) found that paying attention to *feng shui* helps Chinese business people to cope with the anxiety associated with uncertainty. *Feng shui* masters actually offer more than *feng shui* advice to their clients, and may also play the roles of consultant and counsellor.

However, *feng shui* beliefs may be fading among young Chinese, as Lee and Bishop (2001) found that Chinese Singaporeans endorsed *feng shui* beliefs only to a limited extent in terms of etiology and treatment of psychological problems. Lee and Bishop (2001) attributed their findings to the dominance of English-language education in Singapore. Studies of the modernization process may help illuminate the distribution of these beliefs across time and demographics in Chinese societies (see e.g. Yang, 1996). The beliefs reviewed above have not received much attention from psychologists, but they probably have important implications for the behavior of Chinese and should definitely be explored in future research. In the following, beliefs that have received more empirical attention are reviewed.

Psychological beliefs

Locus of control

Locus of control is a widely researched belief complex in Chinese societies. Internal control refers to the belief that reinforcements are under the control of the individuals, whereas external control refers to the belief that reinforcements are under the control of external forces, such as fate, luck, or chance (Rotter, 1966). Because of the collectivistic orientation and the Confucianist/Buddhist/Taoist traditions of Chinese people, it is widely accepted that Chinese possess a stronger belief in external control than do Westerners (e.g. Bond, 1986). However a careful review of the literature suggests that this conclusion is an over-simplification.

Several studies support the widespread belief that Chinese are more external than Westerners. Based on Rotter's Internal–External Control of Reinforcement Scale (I–E scale), Hsieh, Shybut, and Lotsof (1969) found that Hong Kong Chinese were more external than American-born Chinese, who in turn were more external than Anglo-Americans. Hamid (1994) found that university students in Hong Kong were more external than their counterparts in New Zealand. Spector et al. (2002) found that Chinese from Hong Kong, mainland China, and Taiwan scored in a more external direction on the Work Locus of Control Scale than samples from North America and Europe. Chia, Moore, Lam, Chuang, and Cheng (1995) found that American university students reported higher internal locus of control than their counterparts in Taiwan. However, the results of a study that is often cited to support the externality of Chinese are ambiguous. Using Rotter's I–E scale, M. S. Tseng (1972) reported that Asians in the United States were more external than Caucasian-Americans. However, it is unclear whether Chinese were included in Tseng's sample and it is not sure whether the results are relevant.

On the other hand, a few studies have cast doubt on the stereotype that Chinese are more external. Tsui (1978) found that, based on Rotter's I–E scale, Hong Kong Chinese undergraduates were actually more internal than American-born Chinese undergraduates in the United States. Hung (1974) reported that, based on Rotter's I–E scale, undergraduates in Taiwan did not differ from American undergraduates in internality, as had been reported by Parsons and Schneider (1974). Liu and Yussen (2005) compared mainland Chinese and American primary students with regard to control beliefs measured by the Revised Control, Agency, and Means–End Interview, and found no systematic evidence for the externality of Chinese students. Smith, Trompenaars, and Dugan (1995) reported data collected from employees of business organizations from forty-five countries using Rotter's I–E scale. Their use of a large, multi-cultural sample gives greater credence to their findings that the internality of Chinese respondents from mainland China and Hong Kong was similar to that of respondents from quite a few Western nations (e.g. Netherlands, Belgium, Austria), and was actually higher than that of persons from several other Western countries (e.g. UK, Sweden). Smith et al. (1995) did not perform statistical tests on the national differences observed, but it is clear from their results that Chinese are not necessarily more external than all Westerners.

Studies employing a more complex conceptualization of control points to the possibility that the externality of Chinese is context-specific. Levenson (1974) proposed that locus of control consists of three facets. General internality refers to the belief that reinforcements are controlled by personal factors; powerful others refer to the belief that reinforcements are controlled by various powerful others; and chance refers to the belief that reinforcements are controlled by chance factors. In a comparison of undergraduates in Taiwan and the USA, Lao (1977) found that Chinese females were more external than American females with regard to general internality, but that Chinese of both sexes were more internal with regard to powerful others than were Americans. There was no difference between the two groups with regard to the chance dimension. In contrast, Chia et al. (1995) found that American university students were higher in internality and lower in chance than were Chinese students in Taiwan, but there was no difference in powerful others. Leung (2001) reported that Chinese overseas students and migrants in Australia showed higher external locus of control with regard to chance and powerful others than did Anglo-Australians, but there was no difference in internal locus of control between these two groups. In sum, no consistent pattern has been established across studies.

Chan (1989) administered Rotter's (1966) I–E scale to undergraduates in Hong Kong and compared the results reported by Parsons and Schneider's (1974) in eight countries. Parsons and Schneider (1974) have classified the I–E items into five content areas: luck–fate, respect, academics, leadership–success, and politics. It turned out that the Hong Kong Chinese were actually more internal in respect, academics, and leadership–success than were respondents from several Western nations (USA, West Germany, France, and Italy). They were more external than respondents from these Western nations only in luck–fate. Chen (1989) further observed that, after comparing the I–E scores of Americans reported in studies in the sixties and the seventies, Americans seem to be getting more external over time.

Spector, Sanchez, Siu, Salgado, and Ma (2004) argued that one reason why Chinese are found to be more external than Westerners is because Western instruments may omit practices used by Chinese to control their environment. To address this potential bias, they created a scale to measure *socioinstrumental control*, which refers to the use of social means to influence the environment for goal attainment. A sample item of this scale is: 'You can get your own way at work if you learn how to get along with other people.' As expected, Chinese from Hong Kong and mainland China scored higher than Americans in socioinstrumental control, but lower in work locus of control. Interestingly, higher socioinstrumental control was related to positive job attitudes for both Chinese and Americans. Consistent with the notion of socioinstrumental control, Chia, Cheng, and Chuang (1998) found that, based on the Shapiro Control Inventory, Americans reported higher overall control and control from the self, but Chinese from Taiwan reported higher control from others, family, and government, all of which are forms of indirect control through other people.

In summary, the general conclusion that Chinese are more external than Westerners has not been consistently demonstrated and probably represents an oversimplification of the control concept. The externality of Chinese is likely to be context-specific, and a few well-researched contexts are reviewed below.

Externality and performance outcome

Because of the influence of Confucianism, modesty is a salient norm in Chinese societies (e.g. W. S. Tseng, 1972). Consistent with a modesty norm, Farh, Dobbins, and Cheng (1991) found that Chinese employees in Taiwan evaluated their performance less positively than did their supervisors, a pattern opposite to that commonly observed in the USA. The modesty norm is in conflict with externality beliefs with regard to negative outcomes. In fact, consistent with the modesty norm, Chinese are likely to take responsibility for negative outcomes. McCormick and Shi (1999) found that compared to mainland Chinese teachers, Australian teachers were more likely to attribute their occupational stress to causes distal to self, such as the Department of Education, and less likely to attribute it to more proximal causes, such as self and superiors.

Anderson (1999) found that compared to American students, mainland Chinese students accepted more responsibility for interpersonal and non-interpersonal failures, and took less credit for interpersonal success. Rogers (1998) found that, compared to their UK counterparts, mainland Chinese secondary students were less likely to attribute success to ability, and more likely to attribute failure to effort. Chiu (1986) administered the Intellectual Achievement Responsibility (IAR) questionnaire to children in sixth to eighth grades in Taiwan and in the USA. The IAR questionnaire consists of thirty-four forced-choice items describing either a positive or a negative achievement experience and two explanations for each experience, with one explanation attributing the event to internal factors, and the other to external factors. American children selected a larger number of internal explanations for successful than for failure situations, whereas Chinese children selected more internal explanations for failures than for successful situations.

Crittenden (1991) administered the Attributional Style Questionnaire (ASQ) to undergraduates in Taiwan and the USA. The ASQ asks respondents to make causal interpretations for six affiliative events involving interpersonal relationships and six achievement events, as if the events had actually happened to them. Results showed that compared with American undergraduates, Taiwan undergraduates were more external in their attributions for achievement events, and were more self-effacing in their attributional pattern. In other words, Taiwanese students were more likely to make external attributions for successes, and internal attributions for failures. With regard to affiliative events, there was no difference in externality between these two groups, but the Taiwanese women were more self-effacing than were their American counterparts.

Lee and Seligman (1997) administered the ASQ to three groups of undergraduates: Americans, Chinese-Americans, and Chinese in mainland China. Their results showed that compared to the two American groups, mainland Chinese were more inclined to make external attributions for both negative as well as positive events. To compare their results with those of Crittenden (1991), their data were transformed to obtain a score to reflect overall internality and another score to reflect self-effacement. Although no statistical tests can be performed on these transformed scores, it was found that, consistent with Crittenden's (1991) results, Chinese were more external in their attributions and more self-effacing than the other two American groups.

In line with the link between the modesty norm and the tendency for Chinese to make external attributions for successes and internal attributions for failures, Bond, Leung, and Wan (1982) found that Hong Kong Chinese who followed the modesty norm in explaining their success or failure were in fact better liked by other Chinese observers. Consistent with the impression management interpretation, Wan and Bond (1982) showed that Hong Kong Chinese made self-effacing attributions for their performance in public, but self-enhancing attributions in private, at least for the attribution category of luck. Kemp (1994) also found that secondary-school children in Hong Kong reported a higher level of self-concept in an anonymous situation than in an identifiable situation.

It seems clear that the internality beliefs of Chinese are qualified by the nature of the outcome, and Chinese do not show across-the-board externality beliefs. Two interesting issues are noteworthy in my review of this literature. First, while Chinese are less likely to make self-serving attributions, there is evidence to show that Chinese make group-serving attributions in that they attribute high group performance to internal attributes and low group performance to external attributes (Ma, 2003). Ng and Zhu (2001) also found that New Zealanders made more internal attributions for social behaviors than Hong Kong and Beijing Chinese but only in individual-acting conditions, not in group-acting conditions.

Second, it is interesting to consider the psychological consequences of self-effacing attribution. While it seems able to generate liking from others in the Chinese cultural context, and elicit striving and effort exertion for task accomplishment, it may incur some psychological cost. Anderson (1999) has presented some evidence that the self-effacing attributional style of Chinese is related to their higher levels of loneliness and depression than Americans. Rogers (1998) found that ability attribution for success and effort attribution for failure are correlated positively with self-esteem in British secondary students, and these correlations are in a similar, but somewhat weakened, direction for mainland Chinese secondary students. Man and Hamid (1998) found that for student-teachers in

Hong Kong, participants with high self-esteem were more likely to make external attributions for failures in classroom management than were low self-esteem participants. These findings suggest that self-effacing attributions may lower the self-esteem of Chinese, and their net effect on the overall well-being and performance of Chinese is a very interesting topic for future research.

Effort and ability attributions in academic settings

Stevenson and his collaborators have consistently found that compared with Americans, Chinese believe that academic achievement is more strongly related to effort. For instance, Stevenson, Lee, Chen, Stigler, Hsu, and Kitamura (1990) found that Chinese parents of primary students in Taiwan stressed the importance of hard work more, and the importance of innate ability less, than did American parents in explaining their children's academic performance. Watkins and Cheng (1995) found that when university students in Hong Kong were asked to explain their academic performance, over 80 per cent chose effort as the explanation. The importance of effort was confirmed with students at various levels as well as teachers in Hong Kong (Hau & Salili, 1996). Hess, Chang, and McDevitt (1987) compared mothers' attributions for their children's performance in mathematics in three groups: Caucasian-Americans, Chinese-Americans, and Chinese from China. As expected, in explaining why their children did not do better than they did, Caucasians attributed to ability most, followed by Chinese-Americans, and then by Chinese. In a similar vein, Chinese mothers attributed to lack of effort most, followed by Chinese-Americans, and then by Caucasian-Americans. This pattern of attributions was also found when children were asked to explain their poor performance. Kinlaw, Kurtz-Costes, and Goldman-Fraser (2001) found that, compared to European-Americans, Chinese-Americans rated effort more highly, and ability less highly, as causes for academic success. The importance of effort is beyond academic achievement. Ho (2004) found that Chinese teachers in Hong Kong were less likely than Australian teachers to make ability attribution, but more family attribution, for the misbehavior of students.

Chen and Uttal (1988) have suggested that the emphasis on effort is rooted in the belief of human malleability endorsed and advocated in Chinese philosophy, especially Confucianism. This philosophical perspective has been ingrained in the minds of Chinese, as reflected in the common adage, 'Genius comes from hard work and knowledge depends on accumulation' (Tong, Zhao, & Yang, 1985). Bond (1991) has referred to this emphasis on effort in Chinese societies as the 'cult of effort'. Chen and Uttal (1988) concluded that 'according to the Chinese perspective, innate ability may determine the rate at which one acquires knowledge, but the ultimate level is attained through effort' (p. 354).

The emphasis on effort by Chinese is supported by a global study on social axioms which refer to general beliefs about the material, social, and spiritual world (Leung et al., 2002; Leung & Bond, 2004). A five-dimensional structure was initially identified at the individual level, and subsequently confirmed in forty cultural groups around the world. *Reward for application* is one of the five dimensions identified, which refers to the belief that the investment of effort, knowledge, careful planning, and other resources will lead to positive outcomes. In general, Chinese from Hong Kong, Taiwan and mainland China showed higher endorsement of reward for application than did people from Western nations, especially Chinese from mainland China and Taiwan. As effort is an internal attribute, Chinese are therefore not more external than Westerners in domains where the role of effort is salient. In fact, Munro (1977) concluded that 'it is accurate to describe the Chinese position as a belief that inner causes (correct thoughts, wishes) can have important effects in changing the material world' (p. 18). In the academic setting, Chinese are in fact more internal than Westerners in failure situations and in their association of effort with academic achievements.

Control, psychological adjustment, and social behavior

Many studies have shown that, similar to US results, externality in locus of control is related to poor adjustment and psychological health among Chinese. For instance, Kuo, Gray, and Lin (1979) found that Chinese-Americans who were more external as measured by the Personal Efficacy Scale showed a higher level of psychiatric impairment and depression, and manifested more problems such as low esteem, apprehension, insomnia, headaches, and other psychophysiological symptoms. Chien (1984) found that primary students in Taiwan who were internal as measured by the Nowicki-Strickland Locus of Control Scale were better adjusted personally and socially. Van Haaften, Yu, and Van de Vijver (2004) reported that external locus of control as measured by the Spheres of Control Scale was related to lower resilience (depression, stress, and marginalization) in China. Hwang (1979) reported that primary-school pupils in Taiwan who were high in internality as measured by the Nowicki-Strickland Locus of Control Scale scored higher in self-acceptance and emotional maturity. Chan (1989) showed that Chinese undergraduates in Hong Kong who were external as measured by Rotter's I–E scale had a higher level of adjustment problems as measured by the General Health Questionnaire. Leung, Salili, and Baber (1986) found that Chinese adolescents in Hong Kong who were external as measured by the Nowicki-Strickland Locus of Control Scale reported more adjustment and health problems. Lau and Leung (1992b) also found that Chinese adolescents who were external as measured by the Nowicki-Strickland Locus of Control Scale reported a lower self-concept, more delinquent behaviors, and poorer relationships with school and parents. Liu, Tein, Zhao, and Sandler (2005) found that external locus of control as measured by the Nowicki-Strickland Locus of Control Scale was related to suicidal ideation among rural youths in China. Gan, Shang, and Zhang (2007) reported that external locus of control as measured by Rotter's I–E scale was predictive of burnout among university students in China. Using the Back Pain Locus of Control Scale, Cheng and Leung (2000) found that in Hong Kong, while internal locus of control did not predict pain intensity, it was negatively related to perceived disability. In summary, the negative impact of externality on psychological adjustment and health seems to be generalizable across Chinese societies and the USA.

In contrast, the relationship between control beliefs and social behavior seems to show some cultural variation. Hamid (1994) found that for university students in both Hong Kong and New Zealand, the relationship between control and number of social interactions was similar. Externals reported a larger number of social interactions than internals when their level of self-monitoring was high, but the pattern was the opposite when their level of self-monitoring was low. However, when the level of self-disclosure of these interactions was analyzed, cross-cultural differences emerged. Internals reported a higher level of self-disclosure than externals for New Zealanders, whereas the opposite was true for Chinese.

Aryee, Lo, and Kang (1999) found that in contrast to Western findings, internal work locus of control on the part of protégé in the work setting was not related to protégé-initiated mentoring relationships and mentoring received in Hong Kong. Hamid and Cheng (1995) found that in contrast to Western findings, locus of control was not related to the intention to sign an anti-pollution petition in Hong Kong. Spector et al. (2004) found that external work locus of control was correlated negatively to interpersonal conflict for Chinese, but this relationship was positive in the USA.

In summary, locus of control seems to be related to social behavior in a complex way among Chinese people, and internals do not necessarily fare better in terms of exhibiting more positive social behavior than externals. Future work is obviously needed to explore the relationship between control beliefs and different types of social behavior among Chinese people.

Other control constructs

Locus of control is a construct initially identified and operationalized in America, so there is always the possibility that it may not capture all the important control-related beliefs held by Chinese (see Lu, this volume, for a similar concern about the concept of happiness). In fact, there is some evidence that under some circumstances, the internal–external distinction is not applicable to Chinese. Luk and Bond (1992) found that when the causes of illnesses provided by university students in Hong Kong were factor analyzed, external and internal items loaded in the same factor. As suggested by Luk and Bond (1992), Chinese may endorse an interactionist perspective in their attribution style, at least with regard to the causes of illnesses.

This notion is supported by the global project on social axioms mentioned before (Leung et al., 2002; Leung & Bond, 2004). *Fate control* is one of the five axiom dimensions identified, which asserts that life events are predetermined by external forces, but that there are ways for people to foretell and influence the negative impact of these forces. Thus, the distinction of internality and externality is fuzzy in the notion of fate control, because the fatalistic part is obviously external in nature, but the belief that fate can be improved by active intervention involves an internality belief.

This conflation of internality and externality is not unique to Chinese, as its construct validity is supported in many cultural contexts, including the West. It is possible that the distinction of internality and externality is more salient for researchers than for people in their social environment. When asked to do so, people can respond to questions that are based on a sharp contrast of internality and externality, but this distinction is often fuzzy when people assess their social world naturally and without a structure provided by researchers. Consistent with the interactionist notion suggested by Luk and Bond (1992), Chinese from mainland China, Taiwan, and Hong Kong are relatively high in fate control when compared with Western groups, especially Chinese from mainland China and Taiwan. We do not know much about the consequences of fate control, a topic which represents an intriguing and novel line of research that may complement the research guided by the internality–externality distinction.

Self-concept

Chinese culture is described as group-oriented, and individuals often believe that the group rather than the individual is the basic unit in society (e.g. Hsu, 1981). Based on an analysis of traditional thoughts and the Chinese culture, Hsu (1971b) has proposed that social relationships and roles constitute the core of the self in Chinese culture. In line with this reasoning, Yang (1991) has criticized the use of Western instruments to measure self-concepts in Chinese societies because these instruments fail to capture the social components of the self in Chinese societies. This argument has high face validity, but the empirical evidence in its favor is equivocal (see also Kwan, Hui, & McGee, this volume).

Triandis, McCusker, and Hui (1990) found that the collective self was more salient for participants from mainland China than for Americans. Specifically, when participants were asked to complete twenty statements that began with 'I am …', the number of responses made by mainland Chinese in the collective category (e.g. I am a member of a specific group) was almost three times as many as that of the Americans. The problem is that Chinese from Hong Kong responded at a level similar to Americans, making it difficult to conclude whether the difference between American and mainland Chinese was due to cultural or political and economic differences. However, using a procedure similar to that used by Triandis et al. (1990), Ip and Bond (1995) provided results that support the social nature of the self-concept of Chinese. Self-descriptions and social roles were used more frequently by university students in Hong Kong than by American undergraduates.

There are at least two studies that cast some doubt on the conclusion that the self in the Chinese culture is more social in nature. Using a similar procedure to that of Triandis et al. (1990), Bond and Cheung (1983) found that Hong Kong Chinese undergraduates actually reported *fewer* statements that fell into the collective category than did American undergraduates. Yu, Chang, and Wu (1993) adopted the same procedure as Triandis et al. (1990) with college students in Taiwan and found that over 90 per cent of the attributes used for self-description were individual attributes, and social attributes were mentioned at a very low frequency. Yu et al. (1993) concluded that there seems to be no evidence in support of the position of Yang (1991). Note that both Bond and Cheung (1983) and Yu et al. (1993) used an open-ended format to obtain self-descriptions from participants and the results are not biased by instruments that are individual-oriented. To sum up, the proposal that the conception of the self entails more collective elements among Chinese appears to be an oversimplification. Ip and Bond (1995) have suggested that the nature of the coding scheme may affect the results obtained. This complex issue has not been resolved and should be examined systematically in future work.

There is a different line of research in the educational setting that argues for the multidimensional structure of self-concept, consisting of such facets as physical abilities, physical appearance, academic ability, relations with peers, relations with parents, and relations with school (e.g. Marsh, Relich, & Smith, 1983). This complex view of the self-structure seems to be applicable to Chinese, and has been confirmed with secondary children from Hong Kong (Kemp, 1994; Leung & Lau, 1989) and Beijing (Watkins & Dong, 1994). However, it is possible that the self of the Chinese may entail components that are not observed in the West. For instance, Yeung and Wong (2004) found that verbal self-concept can be broken down into different components for teachers in Hong Kong, who are typically multilingual, which is not found among monolinguals, who are common in the West. This topic has not received much attention and provides a fertile ground for future research.

Beliefs about the self-concept

A number of studies have shown that Chinese hold a less positive view about the self than do Americans (see also Kwan, Hui, & McGee, this volume). Bond and Cheung (1983) analyzed the spontaneous statements about the self provided by Hong Kong Chinese and American undergraduates, and found that Chinese reported a less positive ratio of statements about the self than did Americans. Similar results were obtained by Ip and Bond (1995). Stigler, Smith, and Mao (1985) administered the Perceived Competence Scale for Children (PCSC) to primary students in Taiwan and the USA. The PCSC taps three distinct domains of perceived competence: cognitive (or academic), social, and physical, as well children's general self-esteem. Stigler et al. (1985) found that the factor structure of these four subscales was highly similar across the two cultural groups, and that Chinese children scored lower in three subscales: cognitive, physical, and general self-esteem. Turner and Mo (1984) reported that Chinese primary students in Taiwan scored lower on self-image than American primary-school students. White and Chan (1983) found that Chinese-American graduate students and professionals regarded themselves as less active, attractive, sharp, and beautiful than did Caucasian-Americans. Paschal and Kuo (1973) found that Chinese undergraduates from Taiwan reported a lower level of self-esteem than did American undergraduates. Huang (1971) found that Chinese undergraduates in the USA reported a lower self-esteem than did American undergraduates.

Studies involving other Western groups show similar cultural differences. Kemp (1994) found that Chinese secondary students in Hong Kong reported a lower level of self-concept than their Australian counterparts across all the facets of self-concept measured by the Self Description Questionnaire developed by Marsh et al. (1983). Chen, Willy, and Franz (1997) found that, based on the Self Description Questionnaire, mainland Chinese children generally reported lower self-concept than did Dutch children. Watkins and Dong (1994) reported that secondary-school children in Beijing reported a lower general self-concept than their Australian counterparts. Interestingly, the Chinese children also scored higher than the Australian children in some facets of self-concept, including physical appearance and mathematics. Unexpectedly, Wang and Ren (2004) found that with a Chinese self-concept scale, Chinese children from Beijing reported higher self-concept than did American children. In sum, despite some contradictory findings, we may conclude that Chinese tend to report a lower level of self-concept than do their counterparts in the West.

The reason for the lower self-concept of Chinese as compared to their Western counterparts is not entirely clear. Bond and Hwang (1986) attributed this pattern to the humility norm emphasized in Chinese societies, and suggested that 'in the absence of further research, one cannot assume that low self-esteem in the Chinese has the same implications for social functioning as the same level in respondents from some other cultures' (p. 236). Given the emphasis on effort by Chinese, an alternative explanation is plausible, one which asserts that Chinese *actually* have a less positive self-concept than Westerners. Research has shown that compared with Americans, Chinese are more likely to attribute failure to a lack of effort rather than to some external factors. Research in the USA and Australia has shown that effort attributions for failures are related to a lower self-concept (for reviews, see Marsh, 1984; Marsh, Cairns, Relich, Barnes, & Debus, 1984). Huang, Hwang, and Ko (1983) also found that Chinese undergraduates in Taiwan reported a higher level of depression when they made internal attribution for failures. In a similar vein, Chung and Hwang (1981) found that in Taiwan, the attribution of failures to stable and internal factors was related to poorer self-esteem and a lower level of well-being. These empirical findings suggest that the lower self-concept of the Chinese may be attributed to their greater tendency to attribute negative outcomes to internal factors. Unfortunately, this possibility has not been directly tested.

A third plausible explanation is based on the indigenous Chinese concept of *yuan*, which refers to the belief that interpersonal outcomes are determined by fate or supernatural forces. Yang (1982) argued that because *yuan* is an external explanation for interpersonal outcomes, the use of *yuan* attributions by those who enjoy a positive interpersonal relationship will protect the face of others who enjoy less favorable interpersonal outcomes. It should be noted that this argument contrasts sharply with the empirical results obtained in the USA, which typically document a pattern of ego-defensive attributions—external causes are more likely to be attributed to failures than to successes (Zuckerman, 1979). For negative interpersonal outcomes, Yang (1982) and Lee (1982) argued that *yuan* attributions function as a defense mechanism, shielding an individual from the negative emotions associated with negative interpersonal outcomes, such as divorce. In fact, the process of attributing *yuan* to negative interpersonal outcomes is equivalent to ego-defensive attributions frequently observed in the West. *Yuan* is similar to the notion of bad luck in the West in terms of their ego-enhancing function in the face of negative outcomes.

To evaluate the ego-defensive function of *yuan* attributions, Huang et al. (1983) divided their undergraduate participants in Taiwan into high- and low-depression groups, and found that the high-depression group indeed was less likely to make *yuan* attributions for negative interpersonal outcomes. In support of the face-saving function of *yuan* for other people, Huang et al. (1983) also found that both groups made more *yuan* attributions for positive than for negative interpersonal outcomes.

These empirical results suggest that the belief in *yuan* may lead Chinese to attribute positive interpersonal outcomes to an external cause, thus weakening their self-esteem. In fact, Huang et al. (1983) reported that Chinese who made external attributions for positive interpersonal outcomes indeed showed a higher level of depression. Thus, the belief in *yuan* may be a two-edged sword. It serves as a defense against negative outcomes, but in the case of positive outcomes, its face-saving function may come at the expense of one's self-esteem. *Yuan* thus functions as a moderating personal force, of crucial importance to the Chinese search for moderation in all things. This intriguing possibility should be explored in future research.

Correlates of self-esteem

The relationships between self-concept and a wide array of variables in Chinese societies are similar to those identified in the USA. The general pattern is that a positive self-concept is related to better psychological adjustment. For instance, among Chinese adolescents in Hong Kong, positive self-esteem is related to a lower level of anxiety, social dysfunction, and depression (Chan & Lee, 1993), a higher level of psychological well-being (Leung & Leung, 1992; Yang, 2002), fewer delinquent behaviors (Leung & Lau, 1989), and better relations with parents and school (Cheung & Lau, 1985; Lau & Leung, 1992a). Chang (1982) found that, in Taiwan, a positive self-concept is related to more satisfactory interpersonal relationships.

However, some evidence shows that some antecedents of self-esteem may vary across cultures. Marsh, Hau, Sung, and Yu (2007) found that for Chinese children, in contrast to Western results, body fat was not related to global self-esteem, and was positively related to health self-concept. In a similar vein, Lau, Lee, Ransdell, Yu, and Sung (2004) reported that actual–ideal body-size discrepancy was not predictive of global self-concept and global self-esteem among Chinese children in Hong Kong. In other words, the self-concept of Chinese children seems less affected by obesity and body image than that of Western children. This line of work has not received much attention and may yield results that lead to major revision of Western theories of self-esteem.

Social beliefs

Collectivist beliefs

Chinese culture is characterized as collectivistic (e.g. Bond & Hwang, 1986; Hofstede, 1980; Hsu, 1981). There is some research on the belief system of Chinese that is related to collectivism, and a number of conclusions can be drawn. First, the basic belief underlying Chinese collectivism is that individuals from the same in-group are interrelated and their well-being depends upon their collective effort. If each person follows the norms of the group and acts in the interest of the group, that group will be harmonious and prosperous. This reasoning has been supported by empirical findings. For instance, Leung and Bond (1984) found that Chinese from Hong Kong allocated a larger share of a group reward to in-group members than did Americans. Earley (1989) found that Chinese displayed less social loafing, the tendency to reduce one's input on a group task, than did Americans.

Second, the collectivism of Chinese leads them to believe that an effective way to get things done is often through one's *guanxi*, or interpersonal connections (e.g. King, 1991; Hwang, 1987, 2000). For instance, *guanxi* has been shown to affect a member's effectiveness in a team in Taiwan (Chou, Cheng, Huang, & Cheng, 2006). Hu, Hsu, and Cheng (2004) found that people allocated a larger reward to others who had good *guanxi* with them in Taiwan. *Guanxi* seems to engender trust in a target person, which results in positive behaviors toward the target person, and these behaviors are reciprocated (Chou et al., 2006; Peng, 2001).

Third, Chinese tend to believe that out-group members are less dependable and trustworthy. For instance, Leung (1988) found that Chinese from Hong Kong were more likely to sue a stranger than were Americans. Li (1992) found that, compared to Americans, Chinese in Taiwan regarded strangers as less likable, less likely to be from the same group, and less fair. However, Zhang and Bond (1993) found that there was no difference among American, Hong Kong Chinese, and mainland Chinese university students with regard to their trust level towards relatives. But mainland Chinese students showed a higher level of trust towards both friends and strangers than both American and Hong Kong Chinese students. Perhaps the tendency for Chinese to harbor negative beliefs about out-group members may not be straightforward, and this issue should be explored in future work.

Fourth, Triandis et al. (1990) found that mainland Chinese perceived Chinese as more homogeneous than other national groups, whereas no comparable results were obtained with Americans. Triandis et al. (1990) interpreted this finding as supporting the argument that the collectivistic Chinese believed that the group is the basic unit of analysis, and thus perceived more homogeneity in their in-group than in out-groups. In a study of Chinese minority youth in the Netherlands, Verkuyten and Kwa (1996) also found that the in-group homogeneity effect was stronger than the out-group homogeneity effect. In contrast, Lee and Ottati (1993) found that both American and mainland Chinese perceived the other national groups as more homogeneous than their own group. In the study of Triandis et al. (1990), homogeneity refers to behavioral standards and norms, whereas in Lee and Ottati (1993), the measure of homogeneity was broader and included such elements as clothing and physical appearance. Thus, it is not certain why these studies yielded divergent results, and further work is needed to examine the beliefs concerning in-group homogeneity endorsed by Chinese people.

Finally, Triandis et al. (1990) found that contrary to common stereotype, Chinese from Hong Kong and mainland China regarded the group as less effective than did Americans. However, Triandis et al. (1993) reported that, based on an independence factor which included items comparing the effectiveness of the group and the individual, Americans clearly endorsed independence more strongly than did Chinese from Hong Kong and mainland China. Because the independence factor identified by Triandis et al. (1993) contained items concerning friends as well, this result must be interpreted with caution. Again, more research is needed to shed light on the beliefs of Chinese about the effectiveness of the group versus the individual.

Beliefs related to power distance

The social structure in Chinese societies is characterized as hierarchical (e.g. Bond & Hwang, 1986; Hsu, 1981; King & Bond, 1985) and exhibits a large power distance (Bond, 1996; Hofstede, 1980). According to King and Bond (1985), the basic belief underlying this orientation is that the ideal way to organize a collective is through a well-defined hierarchy, with clear responsibilities for each role in the hierarchy. So the typical leadership pattern in Chinese societies tends to be paternalistic (Cheng, Chou, Wu, Huang, & Farh, 2004), ideally benevolent. Not much is known about this important belief complex, which awaits exploration in future research (see Chen & Farh, this volume).

Environmental beliefs

Primary and secondary control

Rothbaum, Weisz, and Snyder (1982) pointed out that in the West, a major way to attain one's goals and wishes is to attempt to bring about objective changes in the environment, and this type of control is called 'primary control'. Weisz, Rothbaum, and Blackburn (1984) further argued that a different type of control, secondary control, is prevalent in the East. Because of the emphasis on interdependence and harmony in groups, East Asians show a stronger tendency to adjust themselves to fit the environment. Peng and Lachman (1993) administered primary and secondary control scales to American and Chinese-American adults, and, as expected, American respondents scored higher on primary control and lower on secondary control than did Chinese-American respondents. It is interesting to note that primary control was related to positive psychological adjustment for both groups. However, Spector et al. (2004) found that in the work context, mainland Chinese and Americans showed similar levels of secondary control and higher secondary control than Hong Kong Chinese. Nonetheless, secondary control was related to a number of variables in a similar fashion for both Hong Kong Chinese and Americans. Despite the fact that the notions of primary and secondary control have been around for quite some time, the findings in this area are inconclusive and more research is needed.

Beliefs about uncertain events

Wright and his associates (1978) have examined the cultural differences in probabilistic thinking between British and three groups of South-east Asians, including Hong Kong Chinese. Their major finding is that British participants tended to adopt a probabilistic view of uncertainty, and were more accurate in their assessment of the likelihood of occurrence of uncertain events. In contrast, the South-east Asians, including the Hong Kong Chinese, tended to view the world in terms of total certainty or uncertainty, and were less inclined to make a probabilistic judgement of uncertain events. Their conclusion echoes the impression of a team of American decision analysts from the University of Michigan who worked with a Chinese team to control the water pollution of the Huangpu River in mainland China (Pollock & Chen, 1986). They noted that their Chinese counterparts showed a lack of concern for uncertainty, assumed complete certainty for all important information relevant to the decision tasks, and found the necessity of assigning probabilities to events strange and unnatural. This dramatic difference in the dynamics of decision making has sobering implications for the management of intercultural teams.

In the absence of relevant data, however, it is not clear how a less differentiated view towards uncertainty affects the social behavior of the Chinese. This non-probabilistic world view may be related to Confucianism, Taoism, and Buddhism, resulting in the extensive use of intuition in Chinese culture (Chou, 1981). The reliance on intuition is in fact common among Chinese business people, especially among entrepreneurs (Redding, 1978). Another possibility is that a probabilistic view of the world is conducive to a rational approach in decision making, and to the use of facts and figures, which supports the social logic of low power distance. In contrast, a non-probabilistic world view would diminish the importance of objective facts and figures, thus making the role of intuition important and arbitrary authority acceptable. Unfortunately, this area of research has not received much attention in the past decade, and awaits future research to unravel the dynamics involved.

Religiosity beliefs

A dimension of religiosity is identified in the social axioms project orchestrated by Leung and Bond (2004). This constellation refers to the belief in a supreme being and in the positive consequences on people and societies of religion, its institutions and practices. Data from many societies around the world are available, and Chinese are moderate in their religiosity belief. Leung et al. (2007) found that religiosity is moderately related to values in a coherent way. For instance, it is related to tradition, benevolence, and conformity values positively, and hedonism, achievement, and power values negatively. These correlations suggest that the religiosity beliefs of Chinese may have important implications for some social behaviors (e.g. Bond, Leung, Au, Tong, & Chemonges-Nielson, 2004), a topic that needs to be explored in future research.

Indigenous beliefs in Chinese culture

With the exception of *yuan*, the studies reviewed above focus primarily on universal belief constellations that can be found in Chinese as well as Western societies. In this section, a few indigenous beliefs are reviewed.

Psychological beliefs: beliefs about death

Hui, Chan, and Chan (1989) administered a set of thirty statements about death to Chinese adolescents in Hong Kong and extracted five factors. The first factor, Buddhist and Taoist belief, is an indigenous belief constellation and pertains to beliefs about reincarnation. The second factor is just-world belief, which emphasizes the different destinations of the virtuous and the evil-doers. The third factor was labeled naturalistic belief, which suggests that life ends with death. The fourth factor was labeled immortal-soul belief, which asserts that the soul will persist after death. Finally, the fifth factor, Protestant belief, is a Western belief, which suggests that Christians will go to paradise and non-believers will be punished. Hui et al. (1989) also reported that this factor pattern was replicated in a different sample of Chinese adolescents in Hong Kong.

It is interesting that an indigenous belief, the Buddhist/Taoist belief, and a Western belief, the Christian belief, coexist, which leads Hui et al. (1989) to conclude that Chinese in Hong Kong are under the influence of both traditional and Western belief systems simultaneously. However, this line of research has not been followed up in the past decade, and we do not know if the death beliefs of Chinese have changed as they continue to modernize (see Shek, this volume).

Health beliefs

The health model states that beliefs about the seriousness of a disease are related to the perceived susceptibility to the disease (e.g. Rosenstock, Strecher, & Becker, 1988). This model has been confirmed among Chinese (e.g. Wang, Borland, & Whelan, 2005; Wong & Tang, 2005). However, a number of uniquely Chinese health beliefs can also be identified. The most researched belief in this area is probably the tendency to somaticize by some Chinese who suffer from psychopathological problems. Chinese in Taiwan and Hong Kong display a tendency to associate several types of psychosomatic problems with physical causes (for a review, see Cheung, 1986; Parker, Gladstone, & Kwan, 2001). The belief underlying such a somatization tendency is that some psychosomatic problems are viewed as caused by physical factors only (e.g. Luk & Bond, 1992), which may be regarded as an immature defense against psychological investigation (Chan, 1997). More recent research has suggested that the somatization tendency of Chinese may be related to externally oriented thinking, itself related to a tendency not to focus on one's emotional state (Ryder et al., 2008). Interestingly, Parker, Chan, Tully, and Eisenbruch (2005) found that Chinese in Sydney reported a lower tendency to somatize if they are acculturated to the Australian culture. However, Mak and Zane (2004) found that acculturation was not related to the somatization tendency among Chinese Americans. It remains to be confirmed whether exposure to a Western culture may reduce the tendency of the Chinese to somatize.

In some ancient Chinese writings, the semen of men is regarded as a source of strength and energy, and thus frequent intercourse and ejaculation are believed to be associated with a loss of physical strength (Van Gulik, 1961). Menstruation is also regarded as unclean. In a survey of medical students in Hong Kong, Chan (1986) reported that these two traditional beliefs were strongly endorsed. Despite their training in modern medicine, over 90 per cent of the respondents believed that the following statements are to some extent true: (1) frequent ejaculation leads to a loss of physical strength; (2) frequent masturbation is injurious to heath; (3) frequent intercourse is injurious to health; and (4) the healthy vagina is essentially unclean and not bacteria-free.

More recent research has supported the continued influence of these traditional beliefs. Yeung, Tang, and Lee (2005) found that pre-menarcheal teenage girls harbored mostly negative expectations about menarche, and their anticipated emotional responses were more negative than the experiences of post-menarcheal girls (Tang, Yeung, & Lee, 2004). Cain et al. (2003) found that Chinese-American women regarded sex as less important than did Caucasian and African-American women. Luo, Gao, Ye, and Chen (2002) found that secondary-school students who masturbated reported more negative emotions, and Hong, Fan, Ng, and Lee (1994) reported generally negative attitudes toward masturbation among university students in Shanghai. To sum up, traditional sex-related beliefs seem to persist despite the proliferation of modern medical knowledge. It remains to be demonstrated what role they play in the overall belief system, sexual and social behavior of modern Chinese.

Social beliefs: beliefs about reciprocity and retribution

Under the influence of Confucianism and Buddhism, Chinese have developed an indigenous concept of retribution, *bao* (e.g. Hsu, 1971a; Hwang, 1987; Yang, 1957). *Bao* covers both positive and negative events, and thus includes both reciprocity and retribution. With regard to positive outcomes, *bao* requires individuals not to owe others any favors, either tangible or intangible, and to make an effort to repay them. The belief underlying *bao* is that if individuals do not repay the favors of others, then their relationship will become difficult and social harmony hard to sustain (Hsu, 1971a). Consistent with this argument, Cheung and Gui (2006) found that Shanghainese who made job referrals for others are driven by the expectation of reciprocity from the beneficiaries. In Hong Kong, elderly women who had to care for their husbands and daughters who had to care for their elderly parents were also driven by a sense of obligation arising from their sense of *bao* (Holroyd, 2001; 2005).

With regard to negative outcomes, Chinese often believe that retribution towards a harm-doer may not necessarily be delivered by the victim, and that supernatural forces may punish harm-doers to restore a state of justice. For instance, Chiu (1991) analyzed popular Chinese sayings about inequity and classified them into seven types. One type is obviously indigenous, and suggests that retribution may occur to the perpetrator's descendants. It is possible that bad deeds will bring disasters to the descendants of perpetrators or result in their having unfilial descendants. Yeo et al. (2005) reported that Chinese in Australia mentioned *bao* as a cause of cancer, an illness seen as a form of retribution for misdeeds of the patient or his/her ancestors. Likewise, Chinese in Australia with children who faced the risk of cancer mentioned retribution as a cause of the occurrence of faulty genes that may cause cancer (Eisenbruch et al., 2004). These interesting findings suggest that the impact of the *bao* constellation of beliefs, values, and norms on the social behavior of Chinese should be further explored.

Belief about morality and social influence

In Confucian thought, morality (*de*) is believed to be able to elicit deference from others and to confer greater authority (Pye, 1984; Yang & Tseng, 1988). This belief, which may be termed the morality power belief, has not been empirically verified, but some indirect evidence hints at its prominence in contemporary Chinese societies. In a study of leadership behavior in mainland China, Ling and his associates (Ling, Chen, & Wang, 1987; Ling, Chia, & Fang, 2000) found that in addition to the two traditional leadership dimensions, namely, performance and maintenance, a third and separate dimension was identified. This new dimension, labeled the morality dimension, includes behaviors manifesting such virtues as honesty, integrity, and commitment. This morality dimension is subsequently found to be a core component of a model of paternalistic leadership for Chinese (Cheng et al., 2004), which is able to elicit a variety of positive reactions from subordinates (Cheng, Li, & Farh, 2000). Thus, research on paternalistic leadership supports the notion that high perceived morality is indeed associated with positive social influence and group performance.

Conclusion

There is a gap of over ten years between the first edition of this chapter (Leung, 1996) and the current version. In the previous edition of the handbook, I concluded that there was a dearth of theorizing and data on the belief systems of Chinese. While there is notable progress in a few areas, my current review shows that there are still many gaps in our knowledge about beliefs among Chinese and how they function to influence social behaviors. The tripartite classification of beliefs used to organize the current chapter continues to be a useful scheme for organizing the diverse findings in this area, however. Finally, I have identified a number of directions for future research, which I hope will stimulate more empirical work to address the major gaps in this important topic area for psychologists.

References

Anderson, C. A. (1999). Attributional style, depression, and loneliness: A cross-cultural comparison of American and Chinese students. *Personality and Social Psychology Bulletin, 25*, 482–499.

Aryee, S., Lo, S., & Kang, I. L. (1999). Antecedents of early career stage mentoring among Chinese employees. *Journal of Organizational Behavior, 20*, 563–576.

Bal-Tal, D. (1990). *Group beliefs: A conception for analyzing group structure, processes, and behavior.* New York: Springer-Verlag.

Bond, M. H. (ed.) (1986). *The psychology of the Chinese people.* Hong Kong: Oxford University Press.

Bond, M. H. (1991). Cultural influences on modes of impression management: Implications for the culturally diverse organization. In R. A. Giacalone & P. Rosenfield (eds), *Applied impression management: How image-making affects managerial decisions* (pp. 195–218). Newbury Park, California: Sage.

Bond, M. H. (1996). Chinese values. In M. H. Bond (ed.), *The handbook of Chinese psychology* (pp. 208–226). Hong Kong: Oxford University Press.

Bond, M. H. (2009). Believing in beliefs: A scientific but personal quest. In K. Leung & M. H. Bond (eds), *Psychological aspects of social axioms: Understanding global belief systems* (pp. 319–341). New York: Springer SBM.

Bond, M. H. & Cheung, T. S. (1983). College students' spontaneous self-concept: The effect of culture among respondents from Hong Kong, Japan, and the United States. *Journal of Cross-Cultural Psychology, 14*, 153–171.

Bond, M. H. & Hwang, K. K. (1986). The social psychology of Chinese people. In M. H. Bond (ed.), *The psychology of the Chinese people* (pp. 213–266). Hong Kong: Oxford University Press.

Bond, M. H., Leung, K., Au. A., Tong, K. K., & Chemonges-Nielson, Z. (2004). Combining social axioms with values in predicting social behaviors. *European Journal of Personality, 18*, 177–191.

Bond, M. H., Leung, K., & Wan, K. C. (1982). The social impact of self-effacing attributions: The Chinese case. *Journal of Social Psychology, 13*, 186–200.

Cain, V. S., Johannes, C. B., Avis, N. E., Mohr, B., Schocken, M., Skurnick, J., et al. (2003). Sexual functioning and practices in a multi-ethnic study of midlife women: Baseline results from SWAN. *Journal of Sex Research, 40*, 266–276.

Chan, D. W. (1986). Sex misinformation and misconceptions among Chinese medical students in Hong Kong. *Medical Education, 20*, 390–398.

Chan, D. W. (1989). Dimensionality and adjustment: Correlates of locus of control among Hong Kong Chinese. *Journal of Personality Assessment, 53*, 145–160.

Chan, D. W. & Lee, B. H. C. (1993). Dimensions of self-esteem and psychological symptoms among Chinese adolescents in Hong Kong. *Journal of Youth and Adolescence, 22*, 425–440.
Chan, D. W. (1997). Defensive styles and psychological symptoms among Chinese adolescents in Hong Kong. *Social Psychiatry and Psychiatric Epidemiology, 32*, 269–276.
Chang, C. F. (1982). Interpersonal relations and self concept, attribution traits in college freshmen. *Journal of Education and Psychology, 5*, 1–46. (in Chinese)
Chen, C. S. & Uttal, D. H. (1988). Cultural values, parents' beliefs, and children's achievement in the United States and China. *Human Development, 31*, 351–358.
Chen, G., Willy, P., & Franz, M. (1997). A comparative study on self-concept of Chinese and Dutch children with high or average IQ. *Psychological Science (China), 20*, 19–22. (in Chinese)
Cheng, B. S., Chou, L. F., Wu, T. Y., Huang, M. P., & Farh, J. L. (2004). Paternalistic leadership and subordinate responses: Establishing a leadership model in Chinese organizations. *Asian Journal of Social Psychology, 7*, 89–117.
Cheng, B. S., Li, L. F., & Farh, J. L. (2000). A triad model of paternalistic leadership: The constructs and measurement. *Indigenous Psychological Research in Chinese Societies, 14*, 3–64. (in Chinese)
Cheng, S. K. & Leung, F. (2000). Catastrophizing, locus of control, pain, and disability in Chinese chronic low back pain patients. *Psychology and Health, 15*, 721–730.
Cheung, C. & Gui, Y. (2006). Job referral in China: The advantages of strong ties. *Human Relations*, 59, 847–872.
Cheung, F. M. C. (1986). Psychopathology among Chinese people. In M. H. Bond (ed.), *The psychology of the Chinese people* (pp. 171–212). Hong Kong: Oxford University Press.
Cheung, P. C. & Lau, S. (1985). Self-esteem: Its relationship to the family and school environments among Chinese adolescents. *Youth and Society, 16*, 438–456.
Chia, R. C., Moore, J. L., Lam, K. N., Chuang, C. J., & Cheng, B. (1995). Locus of control and gender roles: A comparison of Taiwanese and American students. *Journal of Social Behavior and Personality, 10*, 379–393.
Chia, R. C., Cheng, B. S., & Chuang, C. J. (1998). Differentiation in the source of internal control for Chinese. *Journal of Social Behavior and Personality, 13*, 565–578.
Chien, M. (1979). *Chinese national character and Chinese culture from the viewpoint of Chinese history.* Hong Kong: Chinese University of Hong Kong Press. (in Chinese)
Chien, M. F. (1984). The effect of teacher leadership style on adjustment of elementary school children. *Bulletin of Educational Psychology, 17*, 99–120. (in Chinese)
Chiu, C. Y. (1991). Responses to injustice in popular Chinese sayings and among Hong Kong Chinese students. *Journal of Social Psychology, 131*, 655–665.
Chiu, L. H. (1986). Locus of control in intellectual situations in American and Chinese school children. *International Journal of Psychology, 21*, 167–176.
Chou, L. F., Cheng, B. S., Huang, M. P., & Cheng, H. Y. (2006). *Guanxi* networks and members' effectiveness in Chinese work teams: Mediating effects of trust networks. *Asian Journal of Social Psychology, 9*, 79–95.
Chou, Y. S. (1981). *Crisis and outlook of the Chinese culture.* Taipei: Shih Bao Publishing Company. (in Chinese)
Chung, Y. C. & Hwang, K. K. (1981). Attribution of performance and characteristics of learned helplessness in junior high school students. *Acta Psychologica Taiwanica, 23*, 155–164. (in Chinese)
Crittenden, K. (1991). Asian self-effacement or feminine modesty? Attributional patterns of women university students in Taiwan. *Gender and Society, 5*, 98–117.
Earley, P. C. (1989). Social loafing and collectivism: A comparison of the United States and the People's Republic of China. *Administrative Science Quarterly, 34*, 565–581.
Eisenbruch, M., Yeo, S. S., Meiser, B., Goldstein, D., Tucker, K., & Barlow-Stewart, K. (2004). Optimising clinical practice in cancer genetics with cultural competence: Lessions to be learned from ethnographic research with Chinese-Australians. *Social Science and Medicine, 59*, 235–248.
Farh, J. L., Dobbins, G. H., & Cheng, B. S. (1991). Cultural relativity in action: A comparison of self-ratings made by Chinese and U.S. workers. *Personnel Psychology, 44*, 129–147.
Gan, Y., Shang, J., & Zhang, Y. (2007). Coping flexibility and locus of control as predictors of burnout among Chinese college students. *Social Behavior and Personality, 35*, 1087–1098.
Hamid, P. N. (1994). Self-monitoring, locus of control, and social encounters of Chinese and New Zealand students. *Journal of Cross-Cultural Psychology, 25*, 353–368.
Hamid, P. N. & Cheng, S. T. (1995). Predicting antipollution behavior: The role of molar behavioral intentions, past behavior, and locus of control. *Environment and Behavior, 27*, 679–698.
Hau, K. T. & Salili, F. (1996). Motivational effects of teachers' ability versus effort feedback on Chinese students' learning. *Social Psychology of Education, 1*, 69–85.
Hess, R. D., Chang, C. M., & McDevitt, T. M. (1987). Cultural variations in family beliefs about children's performance in mathematics: Comparisons among People's Republic of China, Chinese-American, and Caucasian-American families. *Journal of Educational Psychology, 79*, 179–188.
Ho, I. T. (2004). A comparison of Australian and Chinese teachers' attributions for student problem behaviors. *Educational Psychology, 24*, 375–391.
Hofstede, G. (1980). *Culture's consequences.* Beverly Hills, CA: Sage.

Holroyd, E. (2001). Hong Kong Chinese daughters' intergenerational caregiving obligations: A cultural model approach. *Social Science and Medicine, 53*, 1125–1134.
Holroyd, E. (2005). Developing a cultural model of caregiving obligations for elderly Chinese wives. *Western Journal of Nursing Research, 27*, 437–456.
Hong, J. H., Fan, M. S., Ng, M. L., & Lee, L. K. C. (1994). Sexual attitudes and behavior of Chinese university students in Shanghai. *Journal of Sex Education and Therapy, 20*, 277–286.
Hsieh, Y. W., Shybut, J., & Lotsof, E. (1969). Internal versus external control and ethnic group membership. *Journal of Consulting and Clinical Psychology, 33*, 122–124.
Hsu, F. L. K. (1971a). Eros, affect and *pao*. In F. L. K. Hsu (ed.), *Kinship and culture* (pp. 439–475). Chicago, IL: Aldine.
Hsu, F. L. K. (1971b). Psychological homeostasis and *jen*: Conceptual tools for advancing psychological anthropology. *American Anthropologist, 73*, 23–44.
Hsu, F. L. K. (1981). *Americans and Chinese: Passage to differences.* Honolulu, HI: University of Hawaii Press.
Hu, H. H., Hsu, W. L., & Cheng, B. S. (2004). Reward allocation decisions of Chinese managers: Influence of employee categorization and allocation context. *Asian Journal of Social Psychology, 7*, 221–232.
Huang, H. C., Hwang, K. K., & Ko, Y. H. (1983). Life stress, attribution style, social support and depression among university students. *Acta Psychologica Taiwanica, 25*, 31–47. (in Chinese)
Huang, L. J. (1971). Sex role stereotypes and self-concepts among American and Chinese students. *Journal of Comparative Family Studies, 2*, 215–234.
Hui, C. H., Chan, I. S. Y., & Chan, J. (1989). Death cognition among Chinese teenagers: Beliefs about consequences of death. *Journal of Research in Personality, 23*, 99–117.
Hung, Y. Y. (1974). Socio-cultural environment and locus of control. *Acta Psychologica Taiwanica, 16*, 187–198. (in Chinese)
Hwang, C. H. (1979). A study of the internal–external control of Chinese school pupils. *Bulletin of Educational Psychology, 12*, 1–14. (in Chinese)
Hwang, K. K. (1987). Face and favor: The Chinese power game. *American Journal of Sociology, 92*, 944–974.
Hwang, K. K. (2000). Chinese relationalism: Theoretical construction and methodological considerations. *Journal for the Theory of Social Behaviour, 30*, 155–178.
Ip, G. W. M. & Bond, M. H. (1995). Culture, values, and the spontaneous self-concept. *Asian Journal of Psychology, 1*, 30–36
Jiang, S., Lambert, E. G., & Wang, J. (2007). Capital punishment views in China and the United States: A preliminary study among college students. *International Journal of Offender Therapy and Comparative Criminology, 51*, 84–97.
Ju, T. Z. (1947). *Chinese law and Chinese society.* Beijing, China: Min Mian Publishing Company. (in Chinese)
Katz, D. (1960). The functional approach to the study of attitudes. *Public Opinion Quarterly, 24*, 163–204.
Kemp, S. (1994). *An investigation into the self-concept of junior secondary students in Hong Kong.* Unpublished master's thesis, University of Hong Kong.
King, A. Y. C. & Bond, M. H. (1985). The Confucian paradigm of man: A sociological view. In W. S. Tseng & D. Y. H. Wu (eds), *Chinese culture and mental health* (pp. 29–45). New York: Academic Press.
King, A. Y. C. (1991). *Kuan-hsi* and network building: A sociological interpretation. *Daedalus, 120*, 63–84.
Kinlaw, C. R., Kurtz-Costes, B., & Goldman-Fraser, J. (2001). Mothers' achievement beliefs and behaviors and their children's school readiness: A cultural comparison. *Journal of Applied Development Psychology, 22*, 493–506.
Kuo, W. H., Gray, R., & Lin, N. (1979). Locus of control and symptoms of psychological distress among Chinese Americans. *International Journal of Social Psychiatry, 25*, 176–187.
Lao, R. C. (1977). Levenson's IPC (internal–external control) scale: A comparison of Chinese and American students. *Journal of Cross-Cultural Psychology, 9*, 113–124.
Lau, P. W. C., Lee, A., Ransdell, L., Yu, C. W., & Sung, R. Y. T. (2004). The association between global self-esteem, physical self-concept and actual vs ideal body size rating in Chinese primary school children. *International Journal of Obesity, 28*, 314–319.
Lau, S. & Leung, K. (1992a). Relations with parents and school and Chinese adolescents' self-concept, delinquency, and academic performance. *British Journal of Educational Psychology, 62*, 193–202.
Lau, S. & Leung, K. (1992b). Self-concept, delinquency, relations with parents and school and Chinese adolescents' perception of personal control. *Personality and Individual Differences, 13*, 615–622.
Lee, B. O. & Bishop, G. D. (2001). Chinese clients' belief systems about psychological problems in Singapore. *Counselling Psychology Quarterly, 14*, 219–240.
Lee, R. P. L. (1982). Social science and indigenous concepts: With 'Yuen' in medical care as an example. In K. S. Yang & C. I. Wen (eds), *The Sinicization of social and behavioral science research in China* (pp. 361–380). Taipei, Taiwan: Institute of Ethnology, Academia Sinica. (in Chinese)
Lee, Y. T. & Ottati, V. (1993). Determinants of in-group and out-group perceptions of heterogeneity: An investigation of Sino–American stereotypes. *Journal of Cross-Cultural Psychology, 24*, 298–318.
Lee, Y. T. & Seligman, M. E. P. (1997). Are Americans more optimistic than Mainland Chinese? *Personality and Social Psychology Bulletin, 23*, 32–40.

Leung, C. (2001). The psychological adaptation of overseas and migrant students in Australia. *International Journal of Psychology, 36*, 251–259.
Leung, J. P. & Leung, K. (1992). Life satisfaction, self-concept, and relationship with parents in adolescence. *Journal of Youth and Adolescence, 21*, 653–665.
Leung, K. (1988). Some determinants of conflict avoidance. *Journal of Cross-Cultural Psychology, 19*, 125–136.
Leung, K., Au, A., Huang, X., Kurman, J., Niit, T., & Niit, K. K. (2007). Social axioms and values: A cross-cultural examination. *European Journal of Personality, 21*, 91–111.
Leung, K. & Bond, M. H. (1984). The impact of cultural collectivism on reward allocation. *Journal of Personality and Social Psychology, 47*, 793–804.
Leung K. & Bond, M. H. (1992). *A psychological study of social axioms.* Research grant proposal, Chinese University of Hong Kong.
Leung, K. & Bond, M. H. (2004). Social axioms: A model for social beliefs in multicultural perspective. In M. P. Zanna (ed.), *Advances in experimental social psychology* (Vol. 36, pp. 119–197). San Diego, CA: Elsevier Academic Press.
Leung, K., Bond, M. H., de Carrasquel, S. R., Muñoz, C., Hernández, M., Murakami, F., et al. (2002). Social axioms: The search for universal dimensions of general beliefs about how the world functions. *Journal of Cross-Cultural Psychology, 33*, 286–302.
Leung, K. & Lau, S. (1989). Effects of self-concept and perceived disapproval on delinquent behavior in school children. *Journal of Youth and Adolescence, 18*, 345–359.
Leung, P. W., Salili, F., & Baber, F. M. (1986). Common adolescent problems in Hong Kong: Their relationship with self-esteem, locus of control, intelligence and family environment. *Psychologia, 29*, 91–101.
Levenson, H. (1974). Activism and powerful others: distinction within the concept of internal–external control. *Journal of Personality Assessment, 38*, 377–383.
Li, M. C. (1992). Cultural difference and in-group favoritism: A comparison of Chinese and American college students. *Bulletin of the Institute of Ethnology, Academia Sinica, 73*, 153–190. (in Chinese)
Ling, W., Chen, L., & Wang, D. (1987). The construction of the CPM scale for leadership assessment. *Acta Psychologica Sinica. 19*, 199–207. (in Chinese)
Ling, W., Chia, R., & Fang, L. (2000). Chinese implicit leadership theory. *Journal of Social Psychology, 140*, 729–739.
Liu, X., Tein, J. Y., Zhao, Z., & Sandler, I. N. (2005). Suicidality and correlates among rural adolescents of China. *Journal of Adolescent Health, 37*, 443–451.
Liu, Y. & Yussen, S. R. (2005). A comparison of perceived control beliefs between Chinese and American students. *International Journal of Behavioral Development, 29*, 14–23.
Luk, C. L. & Bond, M. H. (1992). Chinese lay beliefs about the causes and cures of psychological problems. *Journal of Social and Clinical Psychology, 11*, 140–157.
Luo, B., Gao, Y., Ye, L., & Chen J. (2002). Sex development of teenagers in East China. *Chinese Mental Health Journal, 16*, 124–126. (in Chinese)
Ma, W. (2003). Self-serving versus group-serving tendencies in causal attributions of Chinese people. *Japanese Journal of Social Psychology, 19*, 135–143.
Man, K. & Hamid, P. N. (1998). The relationship between attachment prototypes, self-esteem, loneliness and causal attributions in Chinese trainee teachers. *Personality and Individual Differences, 24*, 357–371.
Mak, W. W. S., & Zane, N. W. S. (2004). The phenomenon of somatization among community Chinese Americans. *Social Psychiatry and Psychiatric Epidemiology, 39*, 967–974.
Marsh, H. W., Relich, J. D., & Smith, I. D. (1983). Multidimensional self-concepts: The construct validity of interpretations based upon the SDQ. *Journal of Personality and Social Psychology, 45*, 173–187.
Marsh, H. W. (1984). Relations among dimensions of self-attribution, dimensions of self-concept, and academic achievements. *Journal of Educational Psychology, 76*, 1291–1308.
Marsh, H. W., Cairns, L., Relich, J., Barnes, J., & Debus, R. L. (1984). The relationship between dimensions of self-attribution and dimensions of self-concept. *Journal of Educational Psychology, 76*, 3–32.
Marsh, H. W., Hau, K. T., Sung, R. Y. T., & Yu, C. W. (2007). Childhood obesity, gender, actual–ideal body image discrepancies, and physical self-concept in Hong Kong children: Cultural differences in the value of moderation. *Developmental Psychology, 43*, 647–662.
Masuda, T. & Nisbett, R. E. (2001). Attending holistically versus analytically: Comparing the context sensitivity of Japanese and Americans. *Journal of Personality and Social Psychology, 81*, 922–934.
McCormick, J. & Shi, G. (1999). Teachers' attributions of responsibility for their occupational stress in the People's Republic of China and Australia. *British Journal of Educational Psychology, 69*, 393–407.
McCrae, R. R., Costa, P. T. Jr., & Yik, M. S. M. (1996). Universal aspects of Chinese personality structure. In M.H. Bond (ed.), *The handbook of Chinese psychology* (pp, 189–207). Hong Kong: Oxford University Press.
Munro, D. J. (1977). *The concept of man in contemporary China.* Ann Arbor, MI: University of Michigan Press.
Ng, S. H. & Zhu, Y. (2001). Attributing causality and remembering events in individual- and group-acting situations: A Beijing, Hong Kong, and Wellington comparison. *Asian Journal of Social Psychology, 4*, 39–52.
Parker, G., Gladstone, G., & Kuan, T. C. (2001). Depression in the planet's largest ethnic group: The Chinese. *American Journal of Psychiatry, 158*, 857–864.

Parker, G., Chan, B., Tully, L., & Eisenbruch, M. (2005). Depression in the Chinese: The impact of acculturation. *Psychological Medicine, 35*, 1475–1483.

Parsons, O. A. & Schneider, J. M. (1974). Locus of control in university students from Eastern and Western societies. *Journal of Consulting and Clinical Psychology, 42*, 456–461.

Paschal, B. J. & Kuo, Y. Y. (1973). Anxiety and self-concept among American and Chinese college students. *College Student Journal, 7*, 7–13.

Peng, S. (2001). *Guanzi*-management and legal approaches to establish and enhance interpersonal trust. *Journal of Psychology in Chinese Societies, 2*, 51–76.

Peng, Y. & Lachman, M. E. (1993, August). *Primary and secondary control: Age and cultural differences.* Paper presented at the 101st Annual Convention of the American Psychological Association, Toronto, Canada.

Pollock, S. M. & Chen, K. (1986). Strive to conquer the Black Stink: Decision analysis in the People's Republic of China. *Interface, 16*, 31–37.

Pugh, D. S. & Redding, S. G. (1985, January). *A comparative study of the structure and context of Chinese businesses in Hong Kong.* Paper presented at the Association of Teachers of Management Research Conference, Ashridge, England.

Pye, L. (1984). *China: An introduction* (3rd ed.). Boston, MA: Little, Brown and Company.

Redding, S. G. (1978). Bridging the culture gap. *Asian Business and Investment, 4*, 45–52.

Rogers, C. (1998). Motivational indicators in the United Kingdom and the People's Republic of China. *Educational Psychology, 18*, 275–291.

Rosenstock, I. M., Strecher, V. J., & Becker, M. H. (1988). Social learning theory and the Health Belief Model. *Health Education Quarterly, 15*, 175–183.

Rothbaum, F., Weisz, J. R., & Snyder, S. S. (1982). Changing the world and changing the self: A two-process model of perceived control. *Journal of Personality and Social Psychology, 42*, 5–37.

Rotter, J. (1966). Generalized expectancies for internal versus external control of reinforcement. *Psychological Monographs, 80*, 1–28.

Ryder, A. G., Yang, J., Zhu, X., Yao, S., Yi, J., Heine, S. J., et al. (2008). The cultural shaping of depression: Somatic symptoms in China, psychological symptoms in North America? *Journal of Abnormal Psychology, 117*, 300–313.

Schwartz, S. H. (1992). Universals in the content and structure of values: Theoretical advances and empirical tests in 20 countries. In M. Zanna (ed.), *Advances in experimental social psychology* (Vol. 25, pp. 1–65). New York: Academic Press.

Smith, P. B., Trompenaars, F., & Dugan, S. (1995). The Rotter locus of control scale in 43 countries: A test of cultural relativity. *International Journal of Psychology, 30*, 377–400.

Spector, P. E., Cooper, C. L., Sanchez, J. I., O'Driscoll, M., Sparks, K., Bernin, P. et al. (2002). Locus of control and well-being at work: How generalizable are Western findings? *Academy of Management Journal, 45*, 453–466.

Spector, P. E., Sanchez, J. I., Siu, O. L., Salgado, J., & Ma, J. (2004). Eastern versus Western control beliefs at work: An investigation of secondary control, socioinstrumental control, and work locus of control in China and the US. *Applied Psychology: An International Review, 53*, 38–60.

Stevenson, H. W., Lee, S. Y., Chen, C. S., Stigler, J. W., Hsu, C. C., & Kitamura, S. (1990). Contexts of achievement. *Monographs of the Society for Research in Child Development, 55*, 1–120.

Stigler, J. W., Smith, S., & Mao, L. W. (1985). The self-perception of competence by Chinese children. *Child Development, 56*, 1259–1270.

Sun, L. K. (1991). Contemporary Chinese culture: Structure and emotionality. *The Australian Journal of Chinese Affairs, 26*, 1–41.

Tang, C. S., Yeung, D. Y. L., & Lee, A. M. (2004). A comparison of premenarcheal expectations and postmenarcheal experiences in Chinese early adolescents. *Journal of Early Adolescence, 24*, 180–195.

Tong, N., Zhao, R., & Yang, X. (1985). An investigation into the current ideology of middle school students. *Chinese Education, 17*, 6–21.

Triandis, H. C., McCusker, C., & Hui, C. H. (1990). Multimethod probes of individualism and collectivism. *Journal of Personality and Social Psychology, 59*, 1006–1020.

Triandis, H. C., McCusker, C., Betancourt, H., Iwao, S., Leung, K., Salazar, J. M., et al. (1993). An etic–emic analysis of individualism and collectivism. *Journal of Cross-Cultural Psychology, 24*, 366–383.

Tsai, J. L., Knuston, B., & Fung, H. H. (2006). Cultural variation in affect valuation. *Journal of Personality and Social Psychology, 90*, 288–307.

Tsai, J. L., Miao, F. F., & Seppala, E. (2007). Good feelings in Christianity and Buddhism: Religious differences in ideal affect. *Personality and Social Psychology Bulletin, 33*, 409–421.

Tsang, E. W. K. (2004). Toward a scientific inquiry into superstitious business decision-making. *Organization Studies, 25*, 923–946.

Tseng, M. S. (1972). Attitudes towards the disabled: A cross-cultural study. *Journal of Social Psychology, 87*, 311–312.

Tseng, W. S. (1972). On Chinese national character from the viewpoint of personality development. In Y. Y. Li & K. S. Yang (eds), *The character of the Chinese: An interdisciplinary approach* (pp. 227–250). Taipei, Taiwan: Institute of Ethnology, Academic Sinica. (in Chinese)

Tsui, C. L. C. (1978). Culture and control orientation: A study of internal–external locus of control in Chinese and American-Chinese women (Doctoral dissertation, University of California, Berkeley, 1977). *Dissertation Abstracts International, 39*, 770A.

Turner, S. M. & Mo, L. (1984). Chinese adolescents' self-concept as measured by the Offer Self-Image Questionnaire. *Journal of Youth and Adolescence, 13*, 131–143.

Van Gulik, R. H. (1961). *Sexual life in ancient China.* E. J. Leiden: Brill.

Van Haaften, E. H., Yu, Z., & Van de Vijver, F. J. R. (2004). Human resilience in a degrading environment: A case study in China. *Asian Journal of Social Psychology, 7*, 205–219.

Verkuyten, M. & Kwa, G. A. (1996). Ethnic self-identification, ethic involvement, and group differentiation among Chinese youth in the Netherlands. *Journal of Social Psychology, 126*, 35–48.

Wallace, B. A. & Shapiro, S. L. (2006). Mental balance and well-being: Building bridges between Buddhism and Western psychology. *American Psychologist, 61*, 690–701.

Wan, K. C. & Bond, M. H. (1982). Chinese attributions for success and failure under public and anonymous conditions of rating. *Acta Psychologica Taiwanica, 24*, 23–31. (in Chinese)

Wang, A. & Ren, G. (2004). A comparative study of self-concept in Chinese and American children. *Chinese Mental health Journal, 18*, 294–299. (in Chinese)

Wang, S. H. Q., Borland, R., & Whelan, A. (2005). Determinants of intention to quit: Confirmation and extension of Western theories in male Chinese smokers. *Psychology and Health, 20*, 35–51.

Watkins, D. & Cheng, C. (1995). The revised causal dimension scale: A confirmatory factor analysis with Hong Kong subjects. *British Journal of Educational Psychology, 65*, 249–252.

Watkins, D. & Dong, Q. (1994). Assessing the self-esteem of Chinese school children. *Educational Psychology, 14*, 129–137.

Weisz, J. R., Rothbaum, F. M., & Blackburn, T. C. (1984). Standing out and standing in: The psychology of control in America and Japan. *American Psychologist, 39*, 955–969.

White, W. G. & Chan, E. (1983). A comparison of self-concept of Chinese and White graduate students and professionals. *Journal of Non-White Concerns in Personnel and Guidance, 11*, 138–141.

Wong, C. Y. & Tang, C. S. K. (2005). Practice of habitual and volitional health behaviors to prevent severe acute respiratory syndrome among Chinese adolescents in Hong Kong. *Journal of Adolescent Health, 36*, 193–200.

Wright, G. N., Phillips, L. D., Whalley, P. C., Choo, G. T., Ng, K. O., Tan, I. et al. (1978). Cultural variation in probabilistic thinking. *International Journal of Psychology, 15*, 239–257.

Yang, C. F. (1991). A review of studies on self in Hong Kong and Taiwan: Reflections and future prospects. In C. F. Yang & H. S. R. Kao (eds), *Chinese and Chinese heart* (pp. 15–92). Taipei, Taiwan: Yuan Liu Publishing Company. (in Chinese)

Yang, H. (2002). Subjective well-being and self-concept of elementary school teachers. *Chinese Mental Health Journal, 16*, 322–330. (in Chinese)

Yang, K. S. (1982). Yuen and its functions in modern Chinese life. In *Proceedings of the Conference on Traditional Culture and Modern Life* (pp. 103–128). Taipei, Taiwan: Committee on the Renaissance of Chinese Culture. (in Chinese)

Yang, K. S. (1986). Chinese personality and its change. In M. H. Bond (ed.), *The psychology of the Chinese people* (pp. 106–170). Hong Kong: Oxford University Press.

Yang, K. S. (1996). Psychological transformation of the Chinese people as a result of societal modernization. In M. H. Bond (ed.), *The handbook of Chinese psychology* (pp. 479–498). Hong Kong: Oxford University Press.

Yang, K. S. & Tseng, S. C. (1988). *Management theories of the Chinese people.* Taipei, Taiwan: Guei Guen Publishing Company. (in Chinese)

Yang, L. S. (1957). The concept of *pao* as a basis for social relations in China. In J. K. Fairbank (ed.), *Chinese thought and institutions* (pp. 291–309). Chicago, IL: University of Chicago Press.

Yeo, S. S., Meiser, B., Barlow-Stewart, K., Goldstein, D., Tucker, K., & Eisenbruch, M. (2005). Understanding community beliefs of Chinese-Australians about cancer: Initial insights using an ethnographic approach. *Psycho-Oncology, 14*, 174–186.

Yeung, A. S. & Wong, E. K. P. (2004). Domain specificity of trilingual teachers' verbal self-concepts. *Journal of Educational Psychology, 96*, 360–368.

Yeung, D. Y. L., Tang, C. S. & Lee, A. M. (2005). Psychosocial and cultural factors influencing expectations of menarche: A study on Chinese premenarcheal teenage girls. *Journal of Adolescent Research, 20*, 118–135.

Yu, A. B., Chang, Y. J., & Wu, C. W. (1993). The content and categorization of the self-concept of college students in Taiwan: A cognitive viewpoint. In Y. K. Huang (ed.), *Humanhood, meaning, and societies* (pp. 261–304). Taipei, Taiwan: Institute of Ethnology, Academia Sinica. (in Chinese)

Zhang, J. X. & Bond, M. H. (1993). Target-based interpersonal trust: Cross-cultural comparison and its cognitive model. *Acta Psychologica Sinica, 2*, 164–172. (in Chinese)

Zuckerman, M. (1979). Attribution of success and failure revisited, or the motivational bias is alive and well in attribution theory. *Journal of Personality, 47*, 245–287.

CHAPTER 16

The multiple frames of 'Chinese' values: from tradition to modernity and beyond

Steve J. Kulich and Rui Zhang

Introduction: the context of Chinese cultural comparisons

Fascination with noting the uniqueness of 'the Chinese' and their culture has been an enduring pursuit of many throughout recent history, observations well documented, for example, by Mackarras (1991, 1999) and Spence (1998). Some of these differences have been attributed to 'Chinese values'. Western observers early took note of and tried to describe these 'Chinese characteristics' (Russell, 1922; Smith, 1890/1984), and were joined by generations of internationally educated Chinese seeking to contrast and clarify the richness of their own civilization (e.g. Ku Hong-ming's *The spirit of the Chinese*, 1915, Hu Shi's *The Chinese renaissance*, 1934, and Lin Yu-tang's *My country and my people*, 1935/2000). The insights and significance of each of those cultural 'sightings' (Spence, 1998, p. xi–xiii) still arouse the interest of both modern 'China watchers' and modernizing Chinese citizens, as evidenced by multiple recent reprints of each of those early works (having similar status as Benedict's 1946 ever-read study on the Japanese, *The chrysanthemum and the sword*). But, as Spence noted, 'Assessments of China and the Chinese people were often coarse-grained or inaccurate; they drew on imagination and stereotype as much as on any kind of informed application of intellect' (1998, p. xvii). Social psychologists have been equally intrigued with and have committed research energy toward scientifically clarifying the unique or comparable domains of Chinese cultural values.

The psychological study of Chinese values has a long history, from Chinese being included in small-set multi-nation comparative studies (e.g. Morris, 1956; Hofstede, 2001), to deeper considerations of 'the Chinese' from indigenous and emic perspectives (K. S. Yang, 1982, 2006; Chinese Culture Connection, 1987), to seeking to integrate Chinese values into universal etic frameworks (Ho, 1998a; and Chinese samples included in Schwartz, 1992, 1994a, 2005). The earlier history of this endeavor has been well documented by K. S. Yang (1986; 1996) and Bond (1996), so that the focus of this essay will be the ongoing quest of indigenous and multicultural studies that seek to duly differentiate, inclusively consider, or universally incorporate variations of Chinese values.

With the development of social science, the quality of values studies continues to improve, a trend Bond (1996) noted and predicted, where increasingly 'samples are more comparable, instruments are more comprehensive, analyses are more sophisticated, and studies are more pancultural' (p. 208). This essay will depart slightly from Bond's (ibid.) previous edition, as we now believe that some emic descriptive work can be linked and incorporated into what he terms 'more syncretic, theoretically ambitious work' for a better emic-in-etic understanding (cf. Kulich, 2009a, in line with Enriquez's cross-indigenous approach, 1979, or Leung's 'synergistic' approach, 2009) toward a more universal psychology (e.g. Berry & Kim, 1993; K. S. Yang, 2000). The aim of this chapter is therefore to position this study of 'Chinese values' in the context of the ongoing waves of global values studies and assess its contribution. Chaohua Wang has noted that 'the development of modern Chinese culture still remains only dimly visible in foreign mirrors' (2005, p. 10), so a further aim is to bring into print an extensive summary of the vast new developments in values research on the Chinese mainland that has been inaccessible or overlooked in previous reviews.

We begin with a brief review of the academic history of values studies, where the definitions, levels and frames of values are explained. Then we will analyze the approaches of more recent values research considering the varied assumptions about 'Chinese values' in their international context. Three approaches will be discussed that we think correspond to the varied contexts in which a topic as inclusive as Chinese values has been engendered: 1) the Chinese indigenous psychology of the Greater China region; 2) communication research among the Chinese diaspora; and 3) the growing contribution from the Chinese mainland in its response to unparalleled changes. We will conclude by highlighting some of the challenging domains facing ongoing work on 'Chinese values', especially as it relates to stability versus change against the face of globalization.

Values as a cornerstone for international comparisons

The analysis of cross-cultural contact suggests that whenever people of one intact social-cultural system (usually based on intuitively agreed-upon degrees of sameness) encounter one that is observably different, with perceptible degrees of 'otherness', the search for sorting out 'our values versus their values' often begins (Kulich, 2009b, and echoed by Bond in his introduction to this volume). Thus, in the humanities or social science, one finds early work seeking to clarify, categorize, or compare 'cultural values' (Kulich, 2009c).

Systematic observations of human differences were probably first made by those who are now known as the classic sociologists. Falling into the category of Weberian 'ideal types', examples include Durkheim's (1887/1933) organic vs. mechanical solidarity and Tönnies's (1957) *Gemeinschaft* vs. *Gesellschaft* relationships. While these pioneering distinctions about values were confined largely to the time when Western European societies embarked upon their own pathways of industrialization, they inspired sustained interest in more wide-ranging cultural differences. This was evident in the cultural anthropological work of Franz Boas (1928/2004) and protégés like Margaret Mead, Ruth Benedict (1946), Clyde Kluckhohn (1951, 1956), and Florence Rockwood Kluckhohn (Kluckhohn & Strodbeck, 1961), and from the American structuralist sociology of Talcott Parsons and Edward Shils (1951) with Robert Bales (1953) occurring in parallel. This corpus of work first contributed the notion of 'values orientations' (Spates, 1983, p. 31).

We detect similar assumptions operating in the work of those early Chinese literary scholars (Ku, Hu, Lin) listed above, as well as in the move toward indigenous and comparative studies from Chinese who studied abroad, noting Malinowski's (1944) influence on Xiaotong Fei (1939, 1948/1992; Fei & Chang, 1945), Kardiner and Linton's (1939; Linton, 1945) influence on Francis L. K. Hsu (1948, 1953, 1961, 1968, 1970, 1981), and Schramm's (1953, 1964) influence on Godwin Chu (1978; Chu & Hsu, 1979, 1983; Chu & Ju, 1993; Chaffee et al., 1994; Chu et al., 1995). Conceptions of society and cultures as personality writ large ('national character') guided early studies and are still evident in the much-cited work of Lianxiang Sha (1992, 2000).

The Western tradition of seeking to statistically measure values in psychology was also influenced initially by personality studies and began to take shape with the Allport-Vernon Study of Values (SOV) (1931) which was upgraded by the addition of Lindzey (1951, 1960). Morris's more philosophical Ways to Live Survey (1956) was the first to include a Chinese cultural sample. Methodological advancements came with the Value Orientations Model (VOM) put forward by Kluckhohn and Strodtbeck (1961), and the Rokeach Values Survey (RVS, 1973). Extensive cross-cultural samples first appeared with Hofstede's (1980) Values Studies Module (VSM-82, VSM-94 and now his new VSM-08), the World Values Survey (Inglehart, 1977a, 1990; his team having now run five waves, 1981–82, 1990–91, 1995–98, 1999–2000, 2005–6; cf. Inglehart & Welzel, 2005), Kahle and associates' List of Values (LOV, Kahle, 1983, Beatty et al., 1985) or their related Values and Life Style (VALS, Kahle, Beatty & Homer, 1986) identifying consumer values, and the more integrated universal values structure of the Schwartz Values Survey (SVS, Schwartz, 1992) along with his parallel instrument for less-educated or less-individualistic societies, the Portrait Values Questionnaire (PVQ, Schwartz et al. 2001; the PVQ40 in Schwartz, 2005b). These research ventures are mentioned because each of them has also been used, with varying degrees of rigor, in some studies with the Chinese, though the results, observations and implications have not yet been adequately summarized or integrated.

This list of studies is also mentioned because with the uneven opening of the Chinese mainland, current scholars still at times use older instruments, perhaps due to limited exposure to new developments in the field (e.g. Xie's, 1987, and B. Xu & Yang's, 1999, use of Morris's Ways to Live Survey; Y. Xu & Wang's, 2001, comparative study of Hong Kong and Beijing students and Y. Xu et al., 2004, using Allport et al's 1960 SOV to analyze value shifts as a result of the SARS outbreak). Updated international instruments seldom appear in the mainland values literature and, if ever they do (notable exceptions are Bond & Chi, 1997, and Jin & Xin, 2003), assume an increasingly indigenous form (see 'Work from within the mainland', below). Regardless of which scholar's work is the point of reference, values studies are alive and well in Chinese societies, for reasons we will suggest below.

Western conceptions applied toward understanding cultural values

Definitions of values

Though recent years have witnessed extensive theoretical and methodological debate over diverse conceptualizations of culture (cf. Borofsky, Barth, Shweder, Rodseth, & Stolzenberg, 2001; Heine, Lehman, Peng, & Greenholtz, 2002; Kitayama, 2002), a core body of research on the values construct (Hitlin & Piliavin, 2004; Oyserman, Coon, & Kemmelmeier, 2002) has emerged. Several influential definitions continue to guide most values studies (even in China, e.g. Jin & Xin, 2003):

> A value is a conception, explicit or implicit, distinctive of an individual or characteristic of a group, of the desirable which influences the selection from available modes, means and ends of action.
>
> Kluckhohn, 1951, p. 395

> A value is an enduring belief that a specific mode of conduct or end state of existence is personally or socially preferable to an opposite or converse mode of conduct or end state of existence.
>
> Rokeach, 1973, p. 5

> [V]alues are (a) concepts or beliefs, (b) about desirable end states or behaviors, (c) that transcend specific situations, (d) guide selection or evaluation of behavior and events, and (e) are ordered by relative importance.
>
> Schwartz & Bilsky, 1987, p. 551

> I define values as desirable transsituational goals, varying in importance, that serve as guiding principles in the life of a person or other social entity.
>
> Schwartz, 1994, p. 21

These formulations span the latter half of the twentieth century and have been extensively drawn on to evaluate diverse bodies of research, incorporate broad multinational comparative samples (e.g. Hofstede, 1980, 2001), and develop more integrated theories (Schwartz, 1992). Though interest in values may have waned in some branches of the social sciences, Hitlin & Pivilian's extensive review (2004), interestingly titled 'Values: Reviving a dormant concept', has sparked renewed interest by highlighting Schwartz's universal values model. Though Hofstede's 5-D model can boast wide application to many areas where fairly broad distinctions about cultural difference can be applied (with now well over 6,000 citations), social psychologists are increasingly adopting the *a priori* work of Schwartz as a theoretical underpinning (e.g. Davidov, Schmidt, & Schwartz, 2008, 'Bringing values back in'), encouraged by the first volume dedicated specifically to psychological studies of value (Seligman, Olson, & Zanna, 1996), and highlighted by Bond (1996) in the previous edition of this handbook.

What is important to note in these definitions is not only what values are, but what they are not. The historical and current challenge of values studies is the difficult issue that we are attempting to clarify. Kluckhohn (1951, p. 390) cautions:

> Reading the voluminous, and often vague and diffuse, literature on the subject of the various fields of learning, one finds values considered as attitudes, motivations, objects, measurable quantities, substantive areas of behavior, affect-laden customs or traditions, and relationships such as those between individuals, groups, objects, events.

M. Brewster Smith (1969, p. 98) also lamented the 'proliferation of concepts akin to values' which might be labeled as core attitudes, sentiments, preferences, cathexes, and valences. Rohan (2000, cleverly titled 'A rose by any name?') notes, 'The status of values theory and research suffers because the word, "values", is open to abuse and overuse by nonpsychologists and psychologists alike' (p. 255). Historically and operationally then, this is a very difficult academic terrain to manage.

However, in light of the definitions above that tend to see values as individual cognitive structures reflecting group functioning and represented in distinctive motivational goals, some of the constructs that have been conflated with values are less controversial than others. First, personal values are the active internalization and individualized construction of a culture, and so are not equivalent or reducible to modal personalities (Inkeles & Levinson, 1954/1969), cultural norms, or collectively cherished practices (Hsu, 1961, 1981). Second, values are pitched at a level that is higher in abstraction than attitudes attached to a specific issue or social object, though the latter can be value expressive (e.g. Maio & Olson, 2000). Third, values differ from value orientations (Kluckhohn & Strodtbeck, 1961) and generalized beliefs (e.g. social axioms, Leung et al., 2002; Leung & Bond, 2004) in that values are evaluative and not restricted to a statement of how two entities are related.

Challenges facing values researchers

In the development of scientific approaches to values research, a number of authors have also cautioned against a list of epistemological pitfalls and design dangers (e.g. Hitlin & Piliavin, 2004, pp. 360–362; Kahle & Xie, 2008, p. 576; Spates, 1983; Stewart, 1995, p. 1). Here we restate and extend some of these main concerns as a cautionary checklist for values researchers:

- entativity and essentializing: over-generalizing cultural stereotypes of groups to construe 'them' as a coherent entity or exhibiting some inherent, essential characteristics (Jussim, in press). Researchers are not necessarily impervious to this view of 'naïve scientists as unwittingly biased' that has been documented in cognitive psychology (e.g. 'out-group homogeneity'). However, the goal of values studies is not to view all groups in non-essentialist terms, but rather to convey 'an understanding of the role of situation, historical and cultural factors in creating groups and group differences' (ibid. p. 18) and to determine when attributing characterizations are appropriate.
- ethnocentrizing or promoting the 'normative': subconsciously advancing cultural superiority, placing or preaching 'our' values over 'yours', and using values as a pretext for cultural justification (e.g. the 'value justification hypothesis': Kristiansen & Hotte, 1996; the 'backlash hypothesis': Faludi, 1991), the xenophobic defense (Biernat et al., 1996), or other forms of 'moral exploitation' (Kristiansen & Hotte, 1996, p. 83).

- oversimplifying or polarizing: delimiting complex data along binary dimensions and reductionist/minimalist framing (which comparative culture scholars from Parsons and Shils, 1951, E. T. Hall, 1976, Inkeles and Levinson, 1954/1969, to Hofstede, 1980, 2001 have been repeatedly accused of doing). How can values be viewed across more realistic ranges of options (e.g. Kluckhohn & Strodtbeck, 1961, Condon & Yousef, 1975) or in an integrated field (e.g. Schwartz, 1992, 1994) circumplex?
- over-differenting: presumably as a result of essentializing, maximizing intergroup differences, stigmatizing out-groups, breeding prejudices (Biernat et al., 1996; Rokeach, 1968), or mystifying 'exotic others' (e.g. Orientalizing).
- projecting similarity: assuming commonality, homogeneity (often a feature of diplomacy or political campaigns); projecting Western ideologies or global uniformity ('They want the same things we want,' Ball-Rokeach, 1985).
- idealizing: imbuing values with positivity (Kahle & Xie, 2008. p. 579; Seligman & Katz, 1996, p. 73) without realistically looking at deficits or 'negative' value influences (Fung et al., 2003); elevating cultural unity and continuity (e.g. promoting educational programs that socialize 'good', 'harmonious' values); overemphasizing the positive benefits of shared ideologies, whether it be a vision of the 'world at peace' guided by neo-Confucianist ideals or global free trade.
- linealizing or framing: a linear developmental view that traditionality is either preserved or progresses into modernity; not realizing that, in societies undergoing rapid change, value priorities might be not be sorted out yet (Kluckhohn & Strodtbeck, 1961) or even merged in a blended matrix of traditionality in modernity and individuality in collectivity (Tu, 2000; K. S. Yang, 1998).
- conflating: 'pinning it all on values' due to not carefully defining broad psychological constructs as noted above (Hitlin & Piliavin, 2004) or not carefully noting problems associated with levels of analysis ('ecological fallacy': Hofstede, 2001, p. 16).
- reifying: a conceptualizing of values as derived from a monolithic view of culture without a dynamic or temporal dimension; isolating values over other constructs, ignoring complex linkages of related factors.
- objectifiying: avoiding the complexity of values research due to a bias against subjectivity (Hechter, 2000); excluding potentially abstract elements due to narrower theorizing; failing to account for interpretive content meaning and contextual diversity in core culture domains (McGuire, 1983).
- paradigmatic prioritizing: moving on from past buzzwords to more currently enticing, ideologically opportune, or politically correct conceptions; progressive debunking or devaluing of values research as a relic of the past (Hechter, 1993, p. ix) rather than affirming it as necessary in increasingly plural and global contexts.

Integrating etic and emic perspectives in values research

In this chapter we are attempting to take a limited 'both–and' approach (e.g. Leung, 2009). Attempts to completely empiricise and standardize values run the risk of stripping them of some of their potentially deeper and dynamic meaning in specific contexts (cf. Seligman & Katz, 1996). To seek to descriptively, discursively, or qualitatively elicit perceived values runs the risk of highlighting potentially rich content that cannot be cross-culturally compared.

The definitions of values that have guided this chapter are those that include comparable etic domains or dimensions and yet allow for regional variance and 'thick' cultural description. Some value items that Chinese claim as central in their 'cultural core' may not be as unique to one cultural system as is sometimes supposed (as Bond has pointed out, 2007, pp. 242, 243; 2009). But, Chinese themselves, from street level to scholar, will continue to suggest that Westerners do not fully understand the imbued meaning or latent operation of their values. Some of these are intrinsic to how most Chinese define themselves as a cultural entity, and so must be considered.

We in fact find that many Chinese scholars, whether those trained in social psychology, those more specifically advancing indigenous psychology, or those in communication disciplines, tend to devote a significant amount of their energy trying to define, describe, measure, map, compare, and link these 'Chinese values' (see Hwang & Han; Lu; Shi-xu & Feng-bing, all this volume). We therefore proceed with a keen eye on how this Chineseness is represented within a more inclusive values framework while noting conceptual and measurement inconsistencies and, finally, research challenges posed by the reality of increasingly fluid and modernized Chinese populations.

Approaches to studying 'the Chinese'

Perspectives on enduring unity and distinctiveness of Chinese culture

Increasingly, scholars have been discussing the probability that globalized diversity in Chinese communities may have broken down the monolith of what was once clearly considered 'Chineseness' (e.g. Bond, 2007). Nonetheless, there persists a general assumption that 'the Chinese' can be somehow identified as being a distinct entity for cross-cultural measurement in contrast to other cultural groups.

We note the increasing interdisciplinary fusion of Chinese values studies with fields like China studies, intercultural communication, and cultural or cross-cultural psychology (cf. Kulich, 2007a, 2007b). These studies are demonstrating what Kroeber and Kluckhohn (1952, p. 174) suggested in their early, influential manuscript:

> Comparisons of cultures must not be simplistic in terms of an arbitrary or preconceived universal value system, but must be multiple, with each culture first understood in terms of its own particular value system and therefore its own idiosyncratic structure. After that, comparison can with gradually increasing reliability reveal to what degree values, significances, and qualities are common to the compared cultures, and to what degree distinctive.

This is indeed what the study of Chinese values seems to be contributing to cross-cultural values research. To illustrate, the work of scholars outside the Chinese mainland will first be presented concisely, since most of this literature is available to the English reading public. More extensive treatment will be given to what has been developing within the mainland over the last decade, which instead has been published almost exclusively in Chinese.

Work in non-mainland Chinese societies

Indigenous work from within Chinese societies. One could argue that the mainstream of psychological studies on Chinese values originated and continues in 'offshore' Chinese communities. While some studies continue to use Western-derived instruments (as Yang also did initially, 1972), much Chinese scholarship on their own culture has moved toward a more contextualized approach. Since those early years, the indigenous Chinese psychology movement primarily led by Kuo-shu Yang and Kwang-Kuo Hwang has published scores of monographs, hundreds of journal articles and several encyclopedic volumes, many of them related to specific values-related domains of Chinese culture. Though many of these studies originated in Chinese (e.g. two volumes specifically entitled 'Chinese values' edited by Wen, 1989; K. S. Yang, 1994), Yang (1986, 1996) and Bond (1996) have documented this work in English. While Taiwanese researchers spearheaded the indigenization movement, its repercussions have rippled to both the Hong Kong SAR and mainland with different degrees of intensity and reaction (Yang, 2004, pp. 11–24). Interested readers are directed to the work of influential mainland researchers (e.g. Sha, 1992, 2000; Zhai, 1999, 2005; Zhai & Qu, 2001) and others who have benefited from such educational and scholarly cross-fertilization (see also Peng, 2001; Zhang & Yang, 1998).

Wang (2005) provides the most up-do-date summary of overall values research among this group, suggesting that indigenous scholars must always position their work between the fundamental issues of specific situational and trans-situational values. Two important implications for studying Chinese values are highlighted here. The first is to investigate the subjective meanings of those values that may be central to the functioning of Chinese culture and yet overlooked in the objective approach. The second concerns the continuity and change of values confronting individuals living in the societies that are striving to join the ranks of the developed world. In what follows, we will review the Chinese emic concepts that have been most extensively studied and the revised modernity hypothesis.

From an emic perspective, key concepts in the indigenous study of Chinese values by this community of scholars are shown in Table 16.1, with representative psychological research cited in the second column.

Table 16.1 Significant research literature on specific, core Chinese values

Chinese core cultural value orientation	Studies from social/indigenous psychology	Studies from overseas Chinese communication studies
集体 *jiti* (collectivism & the interdependent self)	Ho, Chan, Peng, & Ng, 2001; Ho & Chiu, 1994; K. S. Yang, 2006; C. F. Yang, 2006	individualism vs. collectivism, Cai, 2005; X. Lu, 1998
面子 *mianzi*, 脸 *lian* (face, face-saving, face-giving)	Ho, 1976, 1994; K. K. Hwang, 1987, 2005; see also Hwang & Han, this volume	Chang & Holt, 1994b; G. Chen, 2004b; Jia, 1997–8, 2001, 2003, 2006b; see note on link with *guanxi* below
孝 *xiao* (filial piety)	K. S. Yang, 1988a, 1988b; Ho, 1994, 1996, 1998; Ho & Peng, 1999; K. K. Hwang, 1999; Yeh, 2003; Yeh & Bedford, 2003, 2004	Huang, 1988, 1999; Q. Xiao, 2002
关系 *guanxi* (social networking, mutual obligations, interrelationships)	Ho & Peng, 1998; Ho, 1998; Ho, Chan, & Zhang, 2001; Hwang, 1997–8; see also Chen & Farh; Hwang & Han, this volume	Chang & Holt, 1991a; Jia, 2006a; Ma, 2004; see note on link with *mianzi* below
儒家教育观 (Confucian educational value orientation)	Ho, 2002; Ho, Peng, & Chan, 2001a, 2001b; Ho, Ng, Peng, & Chan, 2002; Lin, 2003; see also Hau & Ho; Ni, Chiu, & Cheng, this volume	Chen & Chung, 1994
成就 *chengjiu* (achievement)	Yu, 1996, 2005; Yang & Lu, 2005	
道德 *daode* (morality)	authoritarian moralism, Ho, 1994; Hoshmand & Ho, 1995; Fung, 2006; see also Hwang & Han, this volume	
人情 *renqing* (interpersonal sentiment)	Ho, 1999; C. F. Yang, 1999; C. F. Yang & Peng, 2005; see also Chan, Ng, & Hui, this volume	Jia, 2006a, 2006b
仁 *ren* (human-heartedness)	In Hwang's model (2007)	Xiao, 1996
礼 *li* (rites or decorum)	see also Hwang & Han, this volume	X. Xiao, 2002
客气 *keqi* (politeness)	see also Shi & Feng, this volume	Feng, 2004;
和谐 *hexie* (harmony)	L. L. Huang, 2005; see also Leung & Au, this volume	H. Chang, 2001a; G. Chen, 2001, 2002; S. Huang, 2000, Edmondson & Chen, 2008 (special issue), including Chen, 2008b; Jia, 2008

Table 16.1 (continued) Significant research literature on specific, core Chinese values

Chinese core cultural value orientation	Studies from social/indigenous psychology	Studies from overseas Chinese communication studies
缘 *yuan* (fatalism, predestined relations, destiny)	K. S. Yang & Ho, 1988; K. S. Yang, 2005; see also Leung, this volume	H. Chang, 2002; Chang & Holt, 1991b; Chang, Holt, & Lin, 2004; L. Chen, 2002a
家(族主义) *jia* (*zu zhu yi*) (family, clan, familism, parenting)	Ho, Peng, & Lai, 2001; Fung, Lieber, & Leung, 2003, Yang & Yeh, 2005; see also Wang & Chang, this volume	See note that extends '*mianzi-guanxi*' below
羞 *xiu* (shame and embarrassment)	Bedford, 2004; Ho, Fu, & Ng, 2004; Fung, Lieber, & Leung, 2003, Fung, 2006; see also Yik, this volume	
忍 *ren* (endurance)	Li & Yang, 2005	
报 *bao* (reciprocity or retribution/reward of good and evil)	Z. X. Zhang, 2006; Zhang & Yang, 1998	Chang & Holt, 1994a; Holt & Chang, 2004
气 *qi* (inner power, energy)		Chung, 2004; Liu, 2008; Chung, 2008; Yao, 2008; Starosta, 2008
中 *zhong* (centrality)		Xiao, 2003
矛盾 *maodun* (paradoxical contradictions)	see also Ji, Lee, & Guo, this volume	Yu, 1997–8, Chen, Ryan, & Chen, 2000
上司 *shangsi* (hierarchical relations, defer to superiors)	see also Chen & Farh, this volume	Chen & Chung, 2002; Chung, 1997
风水 *feng shui* (the art of spatial arrangement)	see also Leung, this volume	G. Chen, 2004a
占卜 *zhanbu* (divination)		Chuang, 2004

Compiled from multiple sources, but of special usefulness for psychology was Bond (1996) and for communication studies, G. M. Chen (2007, pp. 306–308).

The significance of these psychological studies is that they empirically test, challenge, or expand value orientations that have been posited in the West with non-Western populations, namely the Chinese. For example, Ho and Chiu (1994) expanded the individualism and collectivism framework, and developed two basic schemes of classification based upon the three guidelines proposed by Kağıtçıbaşı and Berry (1989) and echoed by Schwartz (1992): that two contrasting items are multidimensional, not bipolar opposites, each with different implications for social organizations. Ho and Chiu's first scheme, CIC (Components of Individualism and Collectivism) has eighteen elements that can be further combined into five major categories, viz. values, autonomy/conformity, responsibility, achievement, and self-reliance/interdependence. The second scheme, the CSO (Components of Social Organization), comprises eight components and is used to divide social organizations into two major categories: the integrative and non-integrative. These two schemes could provide a comprehensive classification standard for the value elements in any society or culture and serve as a scale for categorizing a culture into either a more individualistic or collectivistic system.

Because every Chinese society has been undergoing rapid development and transitions, an emphasis has been both to clarify the emic domains that specify Chineseness, as well as to analyze how traditional Chinese values are changing with modernity. While the interest in 'the modernization of man' waned with the decline of classical modernization theory in the 1980s, indigenous psychologist K. S. Yang and his colleagues in Taiwan have continued with the research on Chinese individual traditionality/modernity (T/M). This decades-long devotion has resulted in the construction and validation of T/M instruments (MS-CIT and MS-CIM), laudable empirical evidence documenting personality changes (Yang, 1986, 1996) and, perhaps more importantly, a revival of interest in this topic in Asia (i.e. a special issue devoted to individual T/M in *Asian Journal of Social Psychology* in 2003; for data on Chinese Singaporeans, see Chang, Wong, & Koh, 2003).

Two important contributions from this body of work are noteworthy (though the theoretical grounding is critiqued in Hwang, 2003a, 2003b). The empirical coexistence of traditionality and modernity as measured by the MS-CIT and MS-CIM supports what Yang (1988) termed a limited convergence hypothesis. It postulates that the modern psychological characteristics in all contemporary societies will only partially converge, and the traditional psychological characteristics will only partially diverge, consistent with the thinking of modernity theorists (Eisenstadt, 2001; Tu, 2000). This line of research also holds great promise as a reference and integration point with the psychology of globalization and acculturation (as proposed at the end of this chapter). For example, the statistical independence of individual T from M is paralleled by what has been observed in various measures of individualism/collectivism; the model of the traditional-modern bicultural self (Lu & Yang, 2006) echoes the recent attempts in psychology to conceptualize the self in the global era as the dynamic confluence of multiple cultures (Arnett, 2002; Hermans & Kempen, 1998; Hong, Morris, Chiu, & Benet-Martínez, 2000).

As one would expect when dealing with traditionality, Confucian explanations figure prominently in the grounding of these value studies, especially in the work of Hwang (e.g. 2007). Though certainly more influential in some Chinese societies than others (note that the mainland once sought to wipe out such 'feudal influences'), Confucianism is but one facet of the multifarious Chinese culture. While it can be argued that most people of Chinese descent share a deep sense of traditional and core 'Chinese values', the varied contexts in which Chinese live suggest that different perceptions may exist of how such a set of Chinese values should be arranged or prioritized. Of interest is the emic collection of value-laden proverbs from young adults in the mid-90s in Shanghai, where not one of the twenty-two values arising from Confucianism in the Chinese Culture Connection's (1987) Chinese Value Survey appeared in the multiple-frequency self-generated sample of sayings (Kulich, 1997).

Indigenization has also been taken on by communication scholars, mostly 'residing abroad'. The point of interest is: Which set of 'distinctive Chinese values' have they selected as they sought to challenge and expand Western perceptions or theories?

From the outside—studies by members of the Chinese diaspora. Naturally, classic values dimensions like individualism and collectivism have been evaluated with new sensibilities and insights (e.g. Cai, 2005; X. Lu, 1998). Xia (2006) provided a general introduction to the link between Chinese values and communication style, but G. M. Chen (2007) has given a definitive summary of this work so far and extensively documented these types of studies. Noted above are those (Table 16.1, the right column, with some additions) which he entitled, 'the study of Chinese culture-bound concepts' (ibid, pp. 306–308).

Obviously, whenever two or more cultural systems come into interaction, certain indigenous terms may be so culture-rich and meaning-laden, that translation into other linguistic terminology inevitably weakens or loses some of the inherent meaning. In the table above, we sought to provide the best approximation of each Chinese term, and list significant research related to that concept.

Summary and comparison of key indigenous value themes. For indigenous psychologists, the 'top five' focus seems to have been primarily testing conceptions of collectivism, face, filial piety (and its influence on indigenous authoritarian hierarchies), *guanxi*, and the influence of Confucian values and morality (like benevolence *ren*, righteousness *yi*, decorum *li*). Specifically included are those embedded in valuing face/*guanxi* relations (cf. Hwang, 2007; Huang & Han in this volume) or valuing success/achievement (see Hau & Ho in this volume). For communication scholars the order and focus are somewhat different, as the 'big five' have been studies on aspects of face, *guanxi*, harmony, *yuan*, and values related to conflict management or avoidance, as would be expected given the more communicative orientation to value-behavior relations.

As Chen notes (2007, p. 307), '*guanxi* and *mianzi* are the two most commonly studied' Chinese cultural influences (see also Hwang, 1997–8; 2007), and a wide range of literature further explores comparative aspects and Chinese expectations in:

1. interpersonal relationships or friendships (Anderson, Martin, & Zhong, 1998; Chang & Holt, 1996, 1996b; Chen, 1998a; X. Lu, 1998; Ma, 1992; Ma & Chuang, 2002; Myers & Zhong, 2004; Myers, Zhong, & Guan, 1998; Myers, Zhong, & Mitchell, 1995; M. Wang, 2004; see also Chan, Ng, & Hui, this volume);
2. the dynamics of family communication (G. Chen, 1992; Huang, 1999, 2000; Huang & Jia, 2000; Sandel, 2002, 2004; Sandel, Cho, Miller, & Wang, 2006; Sandel, Liang, & Chao, 2006; Zhong, 2005; Zhong, Myers, & Buerkel, 2004; see also Wang & Chang, this volume); and those in
3. corporate communication (Chen & Chung, 1994; G. Chen, 2006; Liu & Chen, 2002; Liu, Chen, & Liu, 2006; X. A. Lu, 2005; Wang & Chang, 1999; Yu, 2000, 2002; see also Shi-xu & Feng-bing, as well as Chen & Farh, this volume).

But Chen (2001, 2007, p. 308) suggests that, underlying the Chinese values of face and an emphasis on social networking, is perhaps the most important value animating Chinese culture: harmony (*he xie*). This value is currently being promoted in the Chinese mainland as the key traditional virtue for integrating society and moderating the impact of modernization. Chen considers harmony as 'the axis of the wheel of Chinese behaviors, which is supported by two spokes, i.e. *guanxi* and *mianzi*' (ibid).

Both Hwang (1987, 1997–8, 2007, pp. 262, 265–9) and Chen (2001, 2007) have argued that the traditional Confucian influences of *jen* (benevolence, humanism), *yi* (righteousness), and *li* (propriety, rites) form the core of social relations, face and favor negotiations, and conflict management. Hwang (ibid.) also argues that showing *renqing* ('the affection rule', human-heartedness) is an essential mechanism enabling all social ties (Hwang, 1987, 2007, p. 263). But each admits that the employment of power (Chen, 2001, p. 58; Hwang, 1987) is also a very important, albeit latent, motif in the delicate, sometimes seemingly contradictory, world of Chinese interpersonal 'games'.

Cultural values are, however, operative at multiple levels. Kluver suggests that scholars should expand the list, to include not just interpersonal values but also traditional Chinese values played out in larger social contexts. Values are externalized in cultural products such as political culture, nationalism, social conflict sensibility and resolution, media preference, privacy in Chinese Internet usage, organizational structures, honoring of intellectuals or valuing elite-based discourse (cf. Kluver, 1997, 1999, 2001, 2004). Some of the communication studies listed above have addressed these issues, and other related studies can be found in published bibliographies (cf. Chen, 2008; Miike, 2009; Miike & Chen, 2006; Powers, 2000).

Though Table 16.1 shows some of the different focal points for psychologists and communication scholars, in recent years the range of areas has been increasingly merged and broadened through mutual stimulation. In the 1990s it seemed that more of the traditional value or culture-laden terms had been studied by transplanted Chinese scholars, possibly because first-hand experience of cultural differences and communication barriers evoked a yearning to rediscover and reclaim cultural roots. Such studies provide important observations about historical, philosophical, and religious heritage which explicate some of the deeper meanings that sustain the identity, cultural continuity, and collective ties for those of Chinese descent in any society. They also make us more aware of how to interpret and extrapolate the situated meaning of etic dimensions in cross-cultural studies. And of interest for psychologists might be the way these studies descriptively link emic values to specific communicative behaviors or expectations, addressing a weakness that is often noted concerning values studies (e.g. Bond, 2009; Hechter, 2000; Kristiansen & Hotte, 1996, p. 79).

What has been little analyzed is whether there are variations in themes and style of coverage of these emic topics depending on one's point of origin and how the variations interact with differences in academic standards, group status or intergroup relations in a given society. For example, some cross-cultural psychologists relying on a more etic approach tend to subsume Confucian concepts (e.g. filial piety: Chen, Bond & Tang, 2007; Confucian values: Fu & Chiu, 2007; Lam, Lau, Chiu, Hong, & Peng, 1999) under the universalist framework, thus making it hard to put their work in an unequivocal category. Meta-studies of 'cultural imprinting' might help explain some variation of approach, content, and philosophical orientation. Mainland readers of such studies comment that though some aspects clearly reflect what they construe to be Chinese, some explanations of those values are not presented in ways that they can readily identify with in their situated history and context.

Work from within the mainland

Re-launching social science and studies on values. How does one study a Chinese society that spent decades trying to cut off and debunk its 'feudal' cultural roots? K. S. Yang (1996, p. 107) has noted some of the factors that brought about several decades of 'no empirical research'. The ideological and historical realities of the Chinese mainland cause us to pause and rethink many of our social-psychological assumptions about 'Chinese values', which for understandable reasons until recent years have been under-studied. Some, including the author (Kulich, 2004), have perhaps overemphasized that the majority of work on Chinese values (and there was precious little earlier) was descriptive, partly due to its being mostly written in Chinese (cf. Yang, 1996, p. 107); and its being distributed across a wide range of journals, monographs, or books.

Another factor has been the slow but steady availability of library resources in the mainland. Only in recent years has extensive sourcing become more possible, since the Chinese National Knowledge Infrastructure, CKNI, was first established in 1996. Further, in an academic context seeped in a more holistic, philosophical, and ideological approach to general knowledge (the Confucian legacy overlaid with Marxist orthodoxy) where academic scholarship purports erudite language, broad postulations, and integration of ideas, a greater tolerance for ambiguity has affected social science research and writing. In consequence, many articles have eloquently proposed ideas with limited citation or empirical support (only recently is a system of tiered or refereed journals emerging).

In part, these conditions reflect the general pace of post-Cultural Revolution, Open Door and Reform and now WTO modernizations, where social science has just in the last few years begun adopting international standards of literature citation (to comply with intellectual property rights), theoretical review, hypothesis testing, and rigorous statistical design. So, on almost every topic of CNKI literature reviews conducted for this chapter, we note a marked increase in the number of accessible articles since 2000.

Similarly, until recently, psychological research in China has generally aimed at descriptive or analytical overviews rather than empirical research. Many studies either report on or seek to adapt the Western literature on values (e.g. Ning, 1996a) or grapple with cultural interpretations about the nature of values and definitions, classification and characteristics of specific value items (e.g. Liu & Zhong, 1997; Shen, 2005; Wei, 2006). Some consider the relations of values to other related and salient psychological constructs, like cognitive choices or decision making, subject constraints in a social system, or the needs of subjects (Ma, 1999; Shen, 2005; Y. Y. Yang, 1998b).

Some types of publications serve social purposes, even some quantitative or comparative ones, and seek to advance political agendas (e.g. Meng, 2002), or focus on 'values education' to maintain essentialized Chinese qualities (e.g. Zhang & Lv, 2004; Zhao & Bi, 2004). Others seek to analyze, balance, and apply pluralistic values assumptions, discuss values clarification approaches, and value shifts over time periods by contrasting China's history with (and seeking to learn from) Western developments (e.g. S. G. Yang, 2004). A number of studies suggest that values clarification is closely linked with mental health (e.g. the student samples of Shi, 1997, using the INDCOL with the SCL-90, N = 200; Zeng, 2004); their findings with university students suggested that collectively-oriented students were more psychologically healthy (Shi, 1997) in the Chinese context of that time. A number of writers note that while most values are positive and optimistic, there are some selfish and negative values (Yao & He, 2007) and suggest promoting pro-social values (though not always documenting which ones specifically) toward enhancing students' positive life outlook for this period of social transformation (Huang & Zhang, 1998; see also Bond & Chi, 1997).

Developing empirical values studies in the mainland—starting with reviews. Nonetheless, a more empirical field of values research has been developing. It assumes both an introspective (look inside) and comparative (look afield) form. Chuanxiang Lai (1994) was perhaps the first to consider changes in Chinese values, focusing his analysis on how modernization was bringing about shifts in economic, political, and cultural values. Xiting Huang and his protégé Jinfu Zhang at Southwestern China Normal University published their first work on values in 1989 and 1994. Yongfang Liu and Yinping Zhong (1997) then provided the first review, though the sparse literature cited was mostly Chinese and philosophical.

Yiyin Yang (1998a) greatly expanded previous reviews, especially bringing in the Western cultural and cross-cultural psychology along with Chinese indigenous psychology traditions. She provided mainland Chinese scholars with the first broad review of the values-studies tradition of Parsons, Kluckhohn, Morris, Rokeach, Robinson, Traindis, Gudykunst, Bond, Schwartz, and the work of overseas Chinese scholars like C. F. Yang, K. K. Hwang, Francis L. K. Hsu, Godwin Chu, and compared domestic scholars Yinhe Li and Xiting Huang, also putting forward a wide range of value applications for further study.

More reviews followed like Junfeng Ma's domestic approach (1999) and Xuewei Zhai's historical, chronological classification to emphasize emic values (centered on *renqing*, *mianzi*, and *guanxi*; 1999, pp. 118–126). Zhai and Yong Qu's (2001) later review and application studied eight demographic variables, showing age and occupation to be the main predictors of difference in emic values. Maotang Dai and Yang Jiang (2001) then produced a descriptive volume about traditional Chinese values and their changes in contemporary times. Xinhan Chen (2002) offered a review of Chinese values studies in this transitional period, and another general review was done by Xiaoming Ouyang (2002), more from a sociological and social-psychological perspective. Kulich and Zhu (2004) sought to bring a 'China studies' perspective to English teaching programs, integrating cross-cultural psychology and intercultural communication toward improving 'own culture' awareness, and began emic studies on Chinese values, reporting their initial results (Kulich, Zhang & Zhu, 2006), which showed a similar values hierarchy as that for identity (Zhang & Kulich, 2008).

From reviews to new empirical surveys. Though initiated from outside the mainland, one of the first, rigorous empirical studies done cooperatively and under a Chinese agency was that of Bond and Chi (1997), supported by the CIER (Central Institute for Educational Research, Beijing). Using an emically extended version of the Schwartz SVS (adding four items deemed important in China: achievement, patriotism, competitiveness, and interest in politics) and a Moral Education Survey (measuring pro-social and antisocial behaviors), data were collected from representative middle and high schools (ages eleven to seventeen years) in eleven locations across China (N = 1,841). Responses were factor analyzed and the data best fit a seven-factor solution (Social Harmony, Pro-social, Power, Stimulation, Achievement, Happiness, and Detachment).

Using Smallest Space Analysis (cf. Schwarz & Bilsky, 1987) results were re-analyzed along theoretically meaningful regions and the seven resulting factors could be labeled in accord with Schwartz's ten domains, though with some merging (e.g. Security, Hedonism, Power, Stimulation–Achievement, Self-Direction, Universalism–Benevolence–Conformity, Tradition). 'Such a merging has not been found with previous adult samples from China (Schwartz, 1992). So, its identification here probably arises from the lack of differentiation across such prosocial value domains in young adolescents' (Bond & Chi, 1997, p. 261). Though values accounted for only a portion of the variance in moral behaviors measured in that study (ibid., p. 263), linking values to social behavior, analyzing the meaning of shifts, and considering trends has become an increasing focus in the mainland as new theoretically grounded quantitative work has emerged.

In an initial effort to test emic content, Jinfu Zhang & Zhaoyuan Zhang (2001) pre-selected seventy proverbs and common sayings and had 700 students from thirteen colleges in different parts of China rate them on a standard Likert scale. Similar to Kulich's (1997) findings was the less positive response to the more traditional values, and twenty-one of the proverbs were distinctly rejected. Shuiyuan Xiao and Desen Yang (2002) sought to establish a theory and measure of traditional Chinese values for applications to psychotherapy. After a review of some of the Western literature and Chinese philosophical concepts, they postulated four traditional-to-modern dimensions (non-action vs. action, loyalty vs. benefit/profit, reason (*dao*) vs. desire, and altruism vs. egoism), but it appears that these scales have not yet been tested.

The first comprehensive solidly etic and carefully emic Chinese review was Shenghua Jin and Zhiyong Xin's (2003), the most referenced paper in ongoing values work in the mainland. Because they covered both qualitative theoretical studies and quantitative empirical research, they were able to apply it in a series of well-designed studies through their Questionnaire of Value Orientations for Chinese (QVOC), launching a new period of Chinese values research. This forty-item, eight-dimension survey (money and power, justice and truth, study and job, public services, law and regulations, family, love, and public interests) was generated *a priori* in a way similar to Schwartz's (1992), though some conflation of values with attitudes, opinions and behaviors exist, as operational definitions are not clear.

Awarded national funding, it has been used to analyze a wide range of samples from different provinces, ethnicity, gender, ages, marital status, occupations, and educational backgrounds (young professionals in Jin & Li, 2003; middle-school students in Jin, Sun, Ng, & Shi, 2003; peasants in Jin, Wang et al., 2003; workers and peasants in Jin & Li, 2004; workers in Jin & Liu, 2005; and adolescents in Jin & Li, 2007), in each case examining the effect of reforms and social changes on sub-populations. The peasant-based studies were conducted in the diverse geographic regions of Jiangsu, Fujian, Shandong, Liaoning, Inner Mongolia, and Shanxi provinces along the variables of age, education, and marital status. Some provincial differences were identified, and even though peasants and workers reported generally similar values, there were statistical differences in the value domains of justice–doctrine, marriage–family, and public interests.

Constructing value scales with Chinese characteristics. By 2005, Jin and Liu were able to report on their series of studies (through twenty-five interviews, sixty open questionnaires, then 813 survey responses) on college students' work values using separate exploratory and confirmatory factor analyses to develop a four-factor SEM for intentional work values (family protection 家庭维护, status pursuit 地位追求, achievement realization 成就实现, and social promotion 社会促进), and a six-factor instrumental work value model (ease and stability 轻松稳定, interest and personality 兴趣性格, norms and morals 规范道德, payment and reputation 薪酬声望, career and development 职业发展, and welfare and treatment 福利待遇). Xin and Jin (2005) then updated the model (with a value system incorporating individual, social and super-ordinate objectives, their means and rules/regulations), and used laboratory experiments to study college students in ten diverse locations. This study noted some inconsistencies between belief and behavior (Xin & Jin, 2005, pp. 22–27). They also furthered this project through interviews, sentence completion and computer-based implicit association tests (Xin & Jin, 2006, pp. 85–92). These techniques helped them graphically map a values hierarchy on how their participants conceived of values, both at conceptual and personal levels (consistent with their 2005 study).

What is interesting from this research is how it extends the theoretical conceptions of Rokeach using emic data, suggesting that in the Chinese context, there are not just the classic two types of instrumental and terminal values, but actually three: a more pragmatic terminal set (goal-oriented values), instrumental (functional-means values: how those goals can be realized) and the new dimension, regulatory (evaluative) values (as Zhang, 1998 also postulated). Might this self-regulatory dimension have arisen due to the more interdependent, group-oriented context in a socialist or Confucian-heritage culture?

In terms of the priorities given to the individual values items generated, these are listed according to the following hierarchy (with the most-rated items at the top):

A Under goal-oriented values there are three types (of relatively equal importance):

1 Personal motives (individual objectives):
self-accomplishment
professional achievement
fame and social position
money and materials.

2 Social motives (relational objectives):
being a qualified citizen
having friendship and love
marriage and family.

3 Transcendent motives (super-ordinate objectives):
returning to nature (Taoist ideals)
contributing to the state (Confucian/communist ideals)
the happiness of human beings.

B Functional-means values (the more instrumental type):
hard study for building knowledge
character and personality
intelligence and opportunity.

C Regulatory values (evaluative):
morality and conscience
laws
public opinion.

Both the list and the order provide interesting insights (for example that the terminal values generated are not nearly as universalistic as Schwartz's, e.g. no measure tapping world at peace, world of beauty, etc.) in the current orientation of Chinese university students. Jin's team continues to test his theory at varied social and economic levels.

However, the QVOC survey is as yet proprietary, and appears to have not yet been made available to other researchers for use, comparison, or critique. But their (and Zhang's, 1998) theoretical proposal of there being value goals, value means, and value regulation has been widely adopted (e.g. Wang & Zhang's, 2006, study applying this to knowledge values). Further advances could be made if Jin's emic concepts could be correlated with Schwartz's or other universal theories.

More literature reviews and research ideas have followed. Huang and Zheng (2005) proposed ten types/domains of values they consider salient to China's youth, while Zhu and Chen (2006) focused on work values of employers and managers from China and abroad; funded national key projects have also continued. Another set of these studies used the Questionnaire on Chinese Citizen's Human Qualities (QCCHC) (Chen, 2006a, 2006b; Deng, 2006; Li, 2006; Xu & Ding, 2006), but this instrument follows the Allport legacy in locating values in six preferred behavioral categories: moral qualities, legal awareness, civic awareness, economic interest, aesthetic attributes, and environmental awareness (which under an atheist ideology replaces the religious with 'one with the cosmos'). Chinese studies seem just as prone to conflate 'values' with other psychological concepts (e.g. interest in marriage and love: Deng, 2006; affective attitudes toward beauty: Li, 2006; attitudes toward science and use of leisure time: Xu & Ding, 2006; Xu & Zhou, 2006). Furthermore, most of this work reports only basic, descriptive statistics.

Songqing Ye (2006) conducted a 'Project on Adolescent Values' with a large sample of middle-school students in eight cites and rural areas of Anhui Province supported by another national grant. Again, items in the survey conflate values with attitudes and morality issues, and mix and match the terms values, ideologies, moralities, attitudes toward life, study, love (e.g. Ye, 2007a; 2007b), though for one section it does use a translation of the Rokeach Values Survey. However, translation problems have been noted ('pleasure' as 'hedonism', Zhao et al., 2007), again illustrating the important issue of etic to emic equivalence of meaning. Dealing with these 'thick culture' qualities (Geertz, 1973) continues to be a problematic area in Chinese value studies.

Though earlier than Jin and Xin's work above, Jinfu Zhang has similarly postulated three domains of values and developed three forty-item scales to measure what he calls 'life value goals', 'life value means', and 'life value evaluations' (J. Zhang, 1998). Some items on the scales are drawn from overseas work, yet he has added emic contents based on his own rationale. In their present state, these scales appear to have limited usefulness for cross-cultural comparisons, an insular trend in many studies in the mainland, where Zhang's mentor, Xiting Huang, advocates 'Chinanization' of personality and psychological studies (Huang, 2007; a term he seems to prefer to K. S. Yang's 'Sinicization,' 1982).

This emphasis follows the spirit of the historical-political calls for developing socialism, economics, and modernization 'with Chinese characteristics'. The historian Fitzgerald (1999) provides an explanation for the continuing tendency (especially in the mainland) to assert that there are special 'Chinese characteristics' or a unique 'Chinese context'. 'These claims are founded on the old dictum that universal principles and historical processes always assume indigenous forms' (p. 29). Huang (2007) argues that this focus is not just a nationalistic fad, but reveals an inherent difference from mainstream psychology's focus on individuality. Chinese culture philosophically espouses the 'person and nature as a unity', harmony in interpersonal relations, and harmony between persons and nature. An increasing number of mainland scholars seek to build an empirical basis for these arguments as they relate to values. It seems evident that their joint efforts, by applying careful and standard methods to construct scales capturing values with Chinese characteristics, will not be short-lived, but will continue to thrive.

Some of these new scales have very good internal consistency (all three with alphas over .89), and the findings (Zhang's 1998 study using the 'life value goals scale') appear to correspond with those using Schwartz's approach in other research (e.g. Kulich, Zhang, & Zhu, 2006). The data show that among China's college students more individually directed goals are on the increase (career success, pure love, good health, knowledge, good mood, sincere friendship), with fewer socially embedded goals (national prosperity, harmonious family, happy marriage, and world peace, as in Zhang, 1998).

Use of appropriate methodologies is an increasing concern, and some mainland researchers are addressing this shortfall. Noteworthy is Huang Xiting's team (e.g. Dou & Huang 2006), whose adaptation of the Rokeach Values Survey and its ranking method was used with a large sample (N = 3,796). With factor analysis and non-metric multidimensional scaling, they extracted six factors: a comfortable life, excitement, happiness, ambition, honesty, and self-respect. Concerned with the limitations of statistical methods developed for interval data, they then re-analyzed this same data set (Huang, Dou, & Zheng, 2008) using rank-ordered logit model estimation based on discrete choice methods, and found that the most important terminal values of college students were family security, happiness, pleasure, freedom, and self-respect; the most important instrumental value item preferences were honesty, ability, responsibility, and broad-mindedness. These results suggest the return of traditional culture characteristics.

Enriching the abstract meaning of universal values. To deal with the complexities of an ancient civilization confronting a technologically sophisticated and increasingly interdependent world, Chinese mainland scholars may be finding ways to conceptually expand some of the universal items in Schwartz (1992) that in certain cultures may seem too 'thin' or impoverished. For example, one universal item that Schwartz has termed 'family security', is enlarged by Jinfu Zhang (1998) to multiple items, like 'family harmony (家庭和睦)', 'satisfying marriage (美满婚姻)', 'advancing family prosperity (发家致富)', 'having blessed children and grandchildren (造福子孙)', and 'well-behaved and high-achieving children (子女有为)'. These family-related idioms thus go beyond the value of security and serve potentially different motivational goals. This approach shows that such universal frameworks as that of Schwartz, rather than restricting situated research, can provide an open frame for comparing basic values (selected specifically to reflect distinctive goals) with meaning-rich indigenous values to clarify the possibly multiple motivational underpinnings embedded in the latter (for one example, linking big-five personality and values, see Roccas, Sagiv, Schwartz, & Knafo, 2002; see also Bond & Chi, 1997).

Expanding 'core culture' conceptions was also advocated in the initial emic-to-etic work by Kulich et al. (2006). Some researchers suggest that there is likely an individualistic bias in the items generated in Western research frameworks (cf. Huang, 2004) and that indigenous studies from collective cultures might help to culturally counterbalance values work, especially if the translation and correlation work can be done to more clearly link them to inclusive frameworks. Bond and Chi (1997) found that the addition of four 'values of indigenous concern joined with other values to form constructs that had been identified in previous research' (p. 261). For a large and diverse country, the 'patriotism' measured in Bond and Chi would be considered important for binding citizens in a national identity, so their added patriotism item grouped with the Social Harmony factor and fell into the large Universal–Benevolence–Conformity domain. The other indigenous inputs likewise merged with existing constructs, confirming that the Schwartz instrument appears to provide a comprehensive measure of the value universe, and can be enhanced by emic integration.

Comparative approaches. Increasingly, a few mainland articles seek to compare value orientations cross-culturally (e.g. generally in Wan, 1994; specifically regarding Chinese and American values on success in Hu, 2006; on learning in Li & Cole, 2005, and economic values, Zhou et al., 2005) or extend these ideas to inter-ethnic research (e.g. Hou & Zhang, 2006; Li & Jiang, 2007), though most still tend to be of analytical, descriptive nature and not of empirical design (a noteworthy exception through international cooperation is Bond & Mak, 1996). Use of collectivism–individualism (particularly Hofstede's version of this dimension, 1980, 2001) as the main explanatory factor is common (cf. Wan, 1994; Wu, 2003; Tang & Chen, 2007, and related to self-construal, Yang, 1998b). As in the West, college students continue to be the most studied social group (cf. Ma, He, & Guo, 2008).

Jinfu Zhang and Yongping Zhao (2006) conducted a study on generational differences between parents and their children in Chongqing, and found that values differed according to ages and grades in school. Specifically there are parent–child gaps in values on self, family, independence, privacy, equality, knowledge, and responsibility (Zhang & Zhao, 2006, p. 1225, a trend also seen in the work of Xiting Huang, Shenghua Jin and others). Han, Wang, and Liu (1998) sought to examine some rural value changes during the period of social transition. They surveyed 141 peasants in Shanxi (1998, pp. 70–77) using twenty-four questions on six different value orientations that they created (feudal ethic beliefs, traditional Chinese social moral values, communist moral ideals, early socialist moral values, contemporary Western individualistic values, and individualistic self-pursuit). Though such categories seem to bear ideological overtones, their findings showed differences in gender, age, educational background as well as careers, and the results seem to reflect some of the unique economic, political, and historical context of Shanxi province, the wartime revolutionary base of Mao's communist army.

As with the work abroad, new studies are moving into applied areas. Ling, Fang, and Bai (1999) and Yu et al. (2004) examined vocational values, which they argue guide vocational behavior and work results. Jinfu Zhang's team has examined fertility values (Zhang, Tong, & Bi, 2005). Based on open-ended interviews, overviews of former studies, counsel from experts and a small-sample test, they developed a theoretical hypothesis about fertility values and constructed an *a priori* questionnaire. Using structural equation modeling (N = 692, roughly half male and half female), they showed that fertility values are a multi-level and multidimensional construct (nine factors, again under three general categories). For readers in the mainland, their careful empirical methodologies are as instructive as their findings.

Values research expanded through complex modernization. Newer versions of modernization theory (Inglehart, 1997b; Inglehart & Baker, 2000; Yang, 2003) argue that 'modernization is not linear' (Inglehart, 1997b, p. 5), and that traditionality and modernity may in fact be 'two separate, independent multidimensional psychological syndromes' (Yang, 2003, p. 266). As such, they can coexist as 'concurrent psychological traits appearing and functioning together in … time and space' (ibid., p. 236) specific to a person's life domains (see also R. Zhang, 2006, J. Shen, 2007). We suggest that Kluckhohn's fifth assumption (Kluckhohn & Strodtbeck, 1961, p. 10; Kulich, 2009a) about value priorities being unclear in rapidly changing societies is manifested in a coexisting duality of value domains (a yin/yang type of values matrix). Individuals, or even cultural institutions, on the one hand are seeking to ride the modern/postmodern wave, but at the same time feel uncertain and insecure, producing the counteracting need to fall back on familiar culture-as-we-have-known-it values for comfort or maintaining a preferred cultural stability.

Can the Chinese mainland be taken as a viable example of this dynamic in the sociology of knowledge creation? Historically speaking, China has been put into precisely such a position since the launch of the Open Door policy by Deng after 1978. Analysts would concur that the changes since the mid-1990s have been most noticeable and almost exponential. China has almost consistently maintained double-digit economic growth, massive rural and urban restructuring, along with increasing levels of social openness, specifically through the exposure that the Internet revolution has brought about. It thus seems evident that mainland China is a fertile territory to carry forward the T/M research initiated by the indigenous psychologists in Taiwan.

In fact, partly encouraged by a review paper published in the mainland (Y. Y. Yang, 2001), such research has already begun to take shape (e.g. Zhang, Zheng, & Wang, 2003). For example, Guo (2001) sought to examine moral value shifts among urban residents, assuming there are contradictory attitudes toward traditional Chinese values. He found that those holding less traditional values were less dissatisfied with contemporary reality (with age, income, and educational level also being influential).

Values research revived through 'societies in change'. A related phenomenon is the 'need for values clarification in confrontation or change' hypothesis (Kulich, 2009b), where the more that cultural participants are made aware of or are confronted by 'Other', the more they initially need to re-evaluate what their enduring cultural values and roots are (S. Yang, 2004) in order to begin embracing some levels of change from a more secure position. While the checks and balances of defensiveness versus growth seem to be a universal theme (Pyszczynski, Greenberg, & Goldenberg, 2003), it becomes an important matter of social interest whenever a nation or people are thrust into a period of rapid change. The 'values clarification in change' hypothesis we put forward suggests that environments of rapid social change will likely bring about corresponding levels of discussion on the erosion or needed revival of traditional cultural values and mores.

Based on a citation analysis conducted on the topic of traditional Chinese values, we find this emerging discourse to be taking place (Wang, Yan, & Yu, 2008). Of ninety-four articles located in the Chinese mainland's CNKI citation database, all were expressly related to aspects of Chinese culture, traditions, or traditional values. Many of these are polemical discussions on what aspects of China's great cultural heritage are worth maintaining, must be maintained, or will complementarily benefit modern realities. The trend of publications also corresponds to the proposed hypothesis, with only six such articles being published before 1994, fourteen from 1994–1999, fifty-three from 2000–2004, and another twenty-three just in the last three years. Maintaining tradition versus adopting western values (e.g. Wang, 2006), and co-opting traditionality in modernity (e.g. Tu & Huang, 2005) have become hot scholarly topics, maintaining a long tradition of academic concern (Bond & King, 1985).

This pattern of course mirrors government and educational policies designed to revive a new form of Confucianism and 'Chineseness' (Tu, 1995) to bring content to the value vacuum of an increasingly materialistic society. Zhai and Qu (2004) conducted one of the few empirically designed psychological studies examining tradition and modernization ($N = 694$), and indeed found that, though there are (1) many new values perspectives, (2) the traditional core has not disappeared (e.g. Confucian ethics such as face, *guanxi*) and is still viewed positively; but (3) value orientations are currently obscure: many respondents have no clear idea about their value choices. Education and region were found to be not as influential to value development as age and professional identifications. As Li and Zhang (2001) suggest, there is increasing evidence of value conflicts: cultural convergence is *not* happening; instead, multiple modernities are appearing (Tu, 2000; R. Zhang, 2006).

Domain-specific 'emic' values being studied in the mainland. Besides general studies on the broader Chinese value system, specific domains continue to draw much attention: happiness (see Lu, this volume), filial piety (see Hwang & Han, this volume), work values (see Chen & Farh, this volume), education values (see Kember & Watkins, this volume), and gender values (see Tang, this volume). In line with the highly cited tome by German sinologist Wolfgang Bauer on 'China and the search for happiness' (1971/1976,) more than sixty studies have appeared in Chinese mainland publications regarding this concept, most since 2000 (the year China 'arrived' internationally by entering the WTO, being granted their first-ever Olympics, launching the *Shenzhou* 1 rocket, getting their first men's football team into the World Cup, and maintaining their economic boom). We submit that happiness, as a broad emotional state, should be considered the consequence of pursuing or achieving important values rather than a value per se (since it can be attained through the successful pursuit of many different values, cf. Schwartz, 1992, Footnote 2, p. 60). Yet there are good reasons to include it (noting it appeared as a factor in the Bond & Chi, 1997, study), as there seems to be such a surge of interest granting it value status in the mainland. The quality and focus of these 'studies' are varied, some summarizing traditional Chinese views of happiness (four identified), general comparisons of happiness in the West compared to China (seven), some outlining happiness in today's society (five) some discussing the happiness of specific groups; the majority deal specifically with college students' views of happiness (eighteen), some suggesting appropriate model views of happiness (seven).

The study of values related to subjective well-being (SWB) is also an area of interest. Research like Li and Peng's (2000), linking happiness to initiative, self-confidence and contentment, Li and Zhang's (2001) analyzing seven factors influencing the happiness of college students, Li, Yang, and You's (2002), comparing females and males, or Zhang and You's (2000), comparing happiness levels between urban and rural students, are breaking new ground. Weng's (2008) SVS-related extension of Kulich's (1997) analysis of values appearing in self-generated sayings suggests that such a conception might also be termed 'optimism' (cf. Weng & Kulich, 2009).

Since filial piety was included in the forty values of the Chinese Value Survey (Chinese Culture Connection, 1987), it has continued to be investigated as an indicator of traditional Chineseness, and is also controversial as it influenced less-desired cultural expressions (the subservience of women, sons subject to fathers) as well as still-lingering aspects such as respect/subservience for elders (see Ho, 1996; also Hwang & Han, this volume). A recent citation review conduced by Yuan and Qian (2008) identified thirty-six articles specifically on this topic in mainland journals. The trend is from descriptive studies to more data-based ones, and with increased modernization, also an exponential growth in interest in the topic. This trend is seen for many traditional value topics, where the discussion focuses on how much is being lost to modernizing, global influences, and how much should be retained.

Conversely, the analysis of work values is promoting the rapid development of more international mindsets. Leading Western research by Super (1957, 1970), Herzberg (1966), Hofstede (1980), Ros, Schwartz, and Sukis (1999) have been applied as early as the work of Huang, Zhang, and Li (1994), Ning (1996b), and in recent seminal reviews by Zheng and Yan (2005), and Z.Q. Jin and Z.S. Li (2007).

Indigenous theory building. Several scholars are working on projects aimed at developing context-sensitive theories (cf. Ling et al., 1999; Meng, 2007; Xu, 2005; Yu et al., 2004). In an earlier emic study, Ling, Fang, and Bai (1999) sought to develop their own twenty-two-item 'localized Holland' (1985) scale which led to their isolating three vocational factors of value, namely, health care, fame/power, and development (408 college students). Using a massive database, Xu (2002, N = 3,183) built on that research and, carefully comparing rural and urban, coastal and inland Chinese mainland residents over the age of eighteen, noted shifts in the rating of occupational prestige, job preferences, and acceptance of mobility. This study primarily found that: (1) differentiation of elite stratification sets in motion changes in Chinese social relations and the reorganization of social structure; (2) these changes accelerate social mobility which, in turn, leads to increasingly stronger market orientation (more respondents come to consider entrepreneurship as an indicator of success); and (3) all these factors bring about changes in Chinese cultural values (from a national character perspective. This study reinforces the notion again that China has moved from a period with limited or specific areas of economic activity into a period of immense social change, bringing psychological change in its wake. Related research on work values is also expanding exponentially, tracking this change (see Xin, 2006 below).

Yu et al. (2004) further tested Ling et al's (1999) work with a twenty-three-item scale of vocational values (referring also to Super, Holland and other international researchers), administered to postgraduate students (N = 103). Emergent factors were again healthcare and fame/power (two of the three 1999 factors), but found two new factors in this test group: 1) interpersonal relationships in the workplace, and 2) self-actualization, which had the highest rating, though males also rated fame/power high (Yu et al., 2004, p. 40). The authors concluded that this factor structure was more in line with Maslow's hierarchy of human needs.

Meng (2006) also extended Ling et al's (1999) localized 'Career Interest Inventory' to test the structure of work values with Chinese youth. His resulting forty-three-item survey yielded eight factors:

- Soft work environment and individual development and achievement (工作软环境与个人发展成就);
- Social prestige and status (社会声望与地位);
- Solid work environment and security (工作硬环境与职业安全);
- Internal value of work (工作内在价值);
- Promotion opportunity and contribution (成长机会与贡献);
- Position and power (有职有权);
- Welfare and insurance (福利与保障); and
- Freedom and economic rewards (自由与经济报酬).

These factors appear to have some correspondence to both Schwartz's ten individual-level domains (2006) and seven cultural-level domains (2007). If the degree of overlap is analyzed with etic value surveys in the next step, such indigenous work may eventually provide some useful theoretical enhancements, paralleling that provided by the Chinese Culture Connection's (1987) identification of Confucian work dynamism which was later incorporated in the Hofstede (2001) model as the long-term orientation (though this addition has had its detractors; cf. Fang, 2003). Leung (2009), addressing cross-cultural management research specifically, expresses the similar idea that the integrative roads, though still less traveled by indigenous researchers, are necessary for generating 'innovative and culture-general theories' (p. 4).

In related theoretical work, Xin (2006) sought to generate a six-dimension structure of Chinese work values and conducted a careful, open-ended survey of college students for questionnaire development, analyzed survey results by exploratory factor analyses of college students and workers, and then checked external validation with different samples. His work isolated:

- Self-development;
- Safeguards and material benefits;
- Family-orientation;
- Sense of contribution and collectivism;
- Esteem and reputation;
- Social relationships.

These show trends that would be typically reported in various analyses of values shifts, and concur with findings of other reports. Faure and Fang (2008) analyze eight pairs of paradoxical values in business and social contexts:

- *Guanxi* vs. professionalism;
- Importance of face vs. self-expression and directness;
- Thrift vs. materialism and ostentatious consumption;
- Family and group orientation vs. individuation;
- Aversion to law vs. respect for legal practices;
- Respect for etiquette, age and hierarchy vs. respect for simplicity, creativity and competence;
- Long-term vs. short-term orientation;
- Traditional creeds vs. modern approaches.

They conclude, as we have above, that the cultural changes contemporary China has undergone are not linear, but include the contradictory management of paradoxes and remain anchored in a classical *yin–yang* approach. More applications of models that can show this 'field' or 'matrix' approach across Chinese populations could significantly advance contextual extensions of universal theories (i.e. adaptations of Schwartz might map out concentration areas or highlight 'thick value' clusters).

Chinese in a universal framework: integrating etic and emic domains. The general trends emerging both in studies in the mainland or in other Chinese communities reflect attempts to carefully consider emic data in its respective context and on its own terms. But the weakness of these studies is also their localized, often student-based, focus, their inaccessibility to international readership (most studies in the mainland are written in Chinese), conceptual isolation (some exclusively with emic domains) and tangential universal theory linkages. So where exactly do the Chinese fit in a universal framework of values before an initial attempt at a more global integrating theory is warranted? We choose to focus on Schwartz's comprehensive framework for some clues. As Bond (1996, p. 218) suggested:

> [I]t appears that Schwartz's value survey [SVS] will become the standard measure against which other value instruments will be examined ... [toward providing] a value map for the world's cultures, a map which will empirically anchor discussions of value similarities and differences. This is an important development for a cross-cultural social science.

This claim is particularly true as Schwartz and his collaborators have been careful to include representative samples from each of the Chinese regions discussed in this chapter. SVS data from Hong Kong has been analyzed in separate samples of teachers in 1988 and 1996 and of students in 1988, 1996, and 2001 (these data sets are incorporated in each of Schwartz's theoretical papers that include Hong Kong as an entity, e.g. Schwartz, 1992, 1994, 2005a). The Taiwan samples were from Taipei, teachers in 1988 and 1993 and students in 1994 (all combined in later papers). Chinese samples from Singapore included teachers in 1991 and students in 1991 and 1997. The mainland samples included teachers from Shanghai (1988), from Guangzhou (1989), from Hebei (1989) (combined in most papers), and students from Shanghai (1988 and 1995). Each of these studies constitutes an important part of the data pool that has substantiated Schwartz's circumplex theory with ten individual-level value types (1992, 1994, 2005a).

Further, based on rigorous procedures by which originally only the forty-five values (in recent analyses, now forty-six of the potential pool of fifty-seven) shown statistically to have cross-cultural equivalence of meaning were reanalyzed at the culture level, his currently seven-domain culture level model along three theoretical dimensions was substantiated (e.g. Schwartz, 1994, 1996, 2004, 2005b). This culture-level work comes close to Bond's hope for a world values map, and goes beyond the foundations that Hofstede (1980, 2001) laid by empirically documenting the necessary distinction between the individual and culture levels of values (see also Bond, 1988), with specific data analysis procedures and theoretical models for each.

In addition, Schwartz and his collaborators have noted that in some cultural contexts values terminology can be too abstract or distant from people's daily realities. To meet this need, he and his collaborators developed the more descriptive Portrait Values Questionnaire (PVQ) (Schwartz et al., 2001; Schwartz, 2005b). This independent measure of values has substantiated his theoretical models at both the individual and cultural levels. A useful measure for less mature or less educated participants in rural areas, it is also valid for older and educated samples around the world. As many as six Chinese versions of the PVQ have been prepared, but no published research using the complete PVQ has yet been located for Chinese populations in any region (for partial applied use see Chan et al. 2004; Lam et al., 2004).

The Schwartz SVS research samples, together with its empirical findings reviewed elsewhere (e.g. Schwartz, 1994), do show variations among Chinese communities, requiring us to pause and ponder what we mean before speaking about 'Chinese values'. Bond (1996) noted that the 'four Chinese societies present very different profiles' (p. 217). The Chinese are not as homogeneous as one may think. Yet Schwartz (1992; personal correspondence) maintains that in the larger world picture of comparisons among seventy-seven countries (Schwartz, 2008), all of these Chinese samples share a strong emphasis on cultural hierarchy and mastery and a weak emphasis on cultural egalitarianism and autonomy, though he also notes there are variations among samples.

It should be pointed out that almost all the studies reviewed above examine values at the individual level, which should be distinguished from the cultural level of analysis (Smith, 2002). In making emic and etic comparisons on Chinese values to provide food for thought, there is a risk of committing the 'ecological fallacy' (cf. Smith, Bond, Kağıtçıbaşı, 2006, Chapter 3). Hofstede (2001) and Schwartz suggest that cultures are relatively resistant to change, but one can expect to see more variable value profiles at the individual level. One fruitful solution, demonstrated by Schwartz and Bardi (2001), is to interpret sample profiles against a pancultural normative baseline.

It is hoped more research will be done specifically on the accumulated Schwartz data sets both toward mapping the differences among the specific Chinese contexts (like the work in progress by Littrell & Montgomery), as well as toward charting the trajectories of change that each has taken in both cross-sectional and time-series samples. Furthermore, emic and etic research are not necessarily antagonistic to each other (Leung, 2008b). These types of research approaches and theoretical developments show promise for a psychology that builds on robustly tested etics and seeks to apply them sensitively in situated emics. More of this reciprocal etic-to-emic and emic-to-etic data gathering and theoretical enrichment is needed.

Conclusions and future issues in research on Chinese values

Considering limitations of approach and scope

What contribution has the social scientific undertaking of values research made towards deciphering the centuries-old mystery of the Chinese people? By focusing on the reaction of Chinese intellectual communities to the values research that derived largely from cross-cultural psychology, our review summarizes their various attempts to make sense of 'Chinese values' and distinguishes three situated contexts in which such investigation or introspection has been carried out and distinguished from or (inter)related with universal values frameworks. Generally accepted definitions of the values construct were first laid out, cautions raised, mainstream research reviewed, and emic content put forward to consider whether it can be integrated with etically inclusive frameworks.

We believe that the advantages of contextualizing Chinese values and encouraging local conceptualizations outweigh the disadvantages of possible inconsistency and confusion. Substantial space was devoted to the assessment of the growing number of values studies on the Chinese mainland, a valuable resource that has not been systematically reviewed before. The overall conclusion seems to be that, despite diffuse interests and fragmented findings, integration of Chinese values is forming on both theoretical and empirical fronts. Expanding research horizons and increased collaboration will undoubtedly move such fledging integration toward one more solidly linked with and feeding back into the current frameworks.

A review topic as broad as Chinese values necessarily requires that we fill some gaps we deem important and leave others for future investigation. We have selectively focused on studies that highlight broad concepts of values over domain-specific ones, which are currently beyond our analytical capacity. We have also eschewed discussions regarding the levels of measurement or analysis (see Smith et al., 2006, Chapter 3), since these are less relevant to the more monoculturally-oriented emic studies we have reviewed.

There has also been limited coverage of organizational studies, since such data is usually analyzed at different levels (e.g. Kirkman, Lowe, & Gibson, 2006). A similar extensive review on studies influenced by or applying Hofstede's dimensions in China is recommended (Min, Deng, Zhang, & Wang, 2008) and more attention can be given in future reviews to the application of values to Chinese business (see Chen & Farh, this volume) and consumer contexts (see Wyer & Hong, this volume). A number of recent studies have also applied Schwartz's model to Chinese business contexts, whether it be on leadership, ethics, facilitating the adaptation of Chinese employees to international corporations, or other cross-cultural management applications (cf. Hughes, 2007; Littrell, 2002; Montgomery, 2006). A whole body of research on consumer values is being undertaken (see Wu, 2005).

With the increasing influence on value shifts, many studies are focusing on changes of family values (Yan et al., 2004; Zhu, 1998), marriage values (e.g. Fan & Hu, 1997; Luo, 2004), gender values (e.g. female students: Gong & Xing, 1994; or educated women: Zhu, 1995), consumption values (e.g. Zhou & Peng, 2003; and see Deng, Tang, & Zhang's, 2008, review), or the positive and negative impact of media or the Internet in bringing in new or replacing more traditional values (see Wang, Chen, & Zhang's, 2008, extensive review of more than thirty studies in the mainland since starting in 2001). More work is needed to document and develop each of these areas.

Areas for extending future research

To build on what has been covered, however, it is also important to provide some suggestions for future research that will best consider Chinese values in this increasingly global world. For this initiative, we draw on different strands of kindred research and our own persuasions. Our main objective is to inspire more research on cultural complexity, diversity, and globalized differentiation across Chinese contexts.

First, we hope this review sufficiently illustrates the complexity of studying 'Chinese values' among diffusely scattered populations, and the intricate connections with the varied socio-historical and geopolitical situations out of which they arise. In each social context, though studies have often moved first from local applications of Western measures toward increasing levels of indigenization, this process started earlier in the communities outside the mainland. Finding ways to meta-analyze the studies conducted and the factors derived in Hong Kong or Taiwan that K. S. Yang reported (1996, pp. 481–485) with those highlighted above from the mainland could shed important light both on commonalities and contextual or temporal variance (e.g. comparing Hwang's 1995 factor structure and loadings to Zhang's, 1998; or Xin & Jin's, 2005, 2006). The appropriation or reinterpretation of some 'Chinese values' from this large cultural repository among the differently situated Chinese populations has propelled the need, in this global milieu, to seek a consensus on what 'the core' Chinese values really are. From a psychological perspective, this perception of Chinese 'entativity' may indeed be reinforced rather than weakened, at the levels of both researchers and lay people, by the globalization processes.

Globalization extends and transforms the way the imagined worlds or groups are constructed (Appadurai, 1996), possibly beyond the geographical or political boundaries previously delineated by the 'imagined communities' of nationalism (Anderson, 1983). It can also intensify the extent to which intergroup comparisons or even competitions are engaged, a process considered in the tradition of social identity theory to maximize intergroup differences (against the tacit background of the Western world). The same can even be said of the popularity of the East Asia–North America comparisons that tend to direct the attention away from the differences that exist within each social context. It remains to be further understood where this strained relation between the discourse on cultural Chineseness and its actual manifestations across regions will lead.

Given the mounting evidence reviewed above suggesting the coexistence of traditional and modern values, the second question will be the specific forms this blending takes. This calls for a need to integrate values studies with decades of research on acculturation and intercultural communication that has entertained the possibility of a bicultural/multicultural self (e.g. Hermans & Kempen, 1998; Hong et al., 2000). For example, given the diffusion of cultural influences across bounded regions, acculturation does not have to entail a physical relocation. Also, not to fall prey to the old fallacy of misconstruing acculturation as unidirectional influence, this emerging form of blending is not restricted only to the non-Western world or a culturally bound phenomenon. The psychology of globalization (Arnett, 2002; Chiu & Cheng, 2007; Jensen, 2003) should be studied in conjunction with the psychology of acculturation in order to examine 'globalizing acculturation' processes (Chen, Benet-Martínez, & Bond, 2008) on local values and identity hybridization.

Third, the specific form of blending may depend on the extent to which global forces penetrate the local cultural system and its reaction to them. There are two types of global influences that can be described in broad strokes: direct and indirect. The changes of the local socio-economic landscapes brought by global processes are considered to be direct, because they exert influences or selective forces (in the evolutionary sense) on the local meaning system. Compared to the direct influences, the indirect influences are channeled mainly through productions of global media. These two influences can combine or act interactively to affect one's value system. One reasonable hypothesis on value changes is that they should be most readily observed when both forces are in place. Indeed, some of the mainland studies reviewed above seem to make such an implicit assumption in terms of cultural change, as they report one of the most conspicuous changes to be in the economy-related domains, where globalization forces are most at work. On the other hand, the media-based experience alone provides the opportunity to test the role of possible selves (Markus & Nurius, 1986) in facilitating local identification with 'imagined communities' beyond a national boundary.

From a statistical point of view, values can be compared across groups both in terms of their means and their variances. From a theoretical point of view, it is also meaningful to move from a means analysis to a variability analysis that looks at the degree of consensus in values. If it is assumed that globalization can weaken the capacity of local culture to regulate or monitor the behaviors of its members, globalization should be associated with not only more importance but also more diversity of certain values (Schwartz & Sagie, 2000). The domain on which there may be less consensus is likely to be traditional values, and this outcome seems to be occurring on the Chinese mainland now. Studies on generational or regional differences can benefit from incorporating measures of value consensus. Q-methodologies (e.g. Green, Deschamps, & Páez, 2005) or the Hayashi method (Chu, Hayish, Akuto, 1995, p. 3) could be utilized to seek to identify clusters of shared value grouping within increasingly diverse Chinese contexts.

The value and behavior linkage may still be the most important controversial issue (e.g. Bardi & Schwartz, 2003). The controversy derives from a basic question: if values are conceptualized to be the guiding principles to one's life, why do they sometimes fail to predict the behaviors those values are supposed to underlie? It presumably motivated some researchers to explore other individual-difference variables such as social axioms (e.g. Bond, Leung, Au, Tong, & Chemonges-Nielson, 2004) to better predict social behaviors. On the grander scale of cross-cultural research, the use of (self-report) values as a paradigmatic explanation of culture has yielded relatively moderate to small cross-cultural differences compared to that of behavioral measures (Kitayama, 2002; Oyserman, Coon, & Kemmelmeier, 2002; cf. Rozin, 2003). One contestant for the explication of the value–behavior discrepancy, which we suggest here, is perceived norms (Shteynberg, Gelfand & Kim, 2009; Wan, Chiu, Peng & Tam, 2007), which can attenuate certain value–behavior associations (Bardi & Schwartz, 2003). The knowledge of what most people do (or shared reality) (Shteynberg, Gelfand, & Kim, 2009) can override one's personal values in directing one's behavior, especially when there is perceived normative pressure.

With respect to this review, what are the implications of the value–behavior issue for societies with modernization currently in full swing? The paucity of research on this topic, even though relatively ignored in indigenous psychology, does not lend itself to a straightforward answer. In light of the broad distinction identified above between direct and indirect influences, however, we note some testable hypotheses for future research. For example, it has been shown that culture-referenced values are more correlated with norm-governed behaviors, while personal values are more correlated with behaviors that are not governed by norms (Fischer, 2006). Translated into the context of transitional change, this suggests two likely scenarios: first, personal values newly acquired merely through mass media (i.e. indirect influence) can be influential in the domain of behavior less monitored by cultural norms than other domains. This hypothesis can be tested in consumer or marketing research for relatively noticeable individualist tendencies. In contrast, cultural values may still retain their power in driving people even with different sets of personal values toward normative behaviors, unless globalization processes penetrate to the point at which the mechanism put in order to monitor such behaviors begins to be restructured (cf. Leung, 2008a). In the latter case, the new values may replace the old as normative at the cultural level (e.g. 'Making money is glorious'). The strong entrepreneurial orientation exhibited by the mainland and the high endorsement of the mastery value in Schwartz's cultural value mapping accords with this view.

Given the converging interest in happiness in the mainland (see above) and indigenous psychology (Lu, this volume), another future direction is to explicate the types of values endorsed in a transitional society that are conducive or maladaptive to one's sense of well-being. The 'cultural fit' hypothesis, for example, postulates that individuals function better psychologically when their personal values are in line with cultural values (Li & Bond, in press; Sagiv & Schwartz, 2000). When the societal system of reward shifts swiftly to externally oriented values such as material and wealth, the pursuit of which are generally known to undermine well-being (Kasser & Ryan, 1993; Li & Bond, in press; Vansteenkiste, Duriez, Simons, & Soenens, 2006), are people better off if they align their values with those aspirations? Alternatively, do people actively maintain some traditional values for psychological equanimity (the content side of happiness) in order to cope with the vicissitudes of external realities? Might this explain why modern adherents in youth or early career stages seem to move back toward the affirmation of more traditional values in their later life? Value shifts across the lifespan are as yet under-studied. These are important questions to address at this interaction of values studies and the psychology of development and globalization.

Related to this is the challenge sometimes noted in the value domain of hedonism in the SVS. Ratings in some samples may reflect negative connotations (especially of the 'self-indulgence' SVS value item), translation problems, or social undesirabilty. In Chinese samples, the value items, enjoying life and pleasure (but not self-indulgence), are normally located close to each other in the domain of hedonism (occasionally in a mixed power and hedonism region). The pancultural hierarchical order of the ten individual-level values in Schwartz and Bardi (2001) places hedonism in the lower middle range of preference, ahead of power, tradition, and stimulation. Future research can clarify how Chinese value enjoyment, entertainment and pleasure, and how positive and negative connotations of indulgence influence the rank order of hedonism compared with the pancultural baseline (cf. Littrell & Montgomery). Perhaps the mainland research trend noted above focusing on emically derived conceptions of happiness hints at an eventual coordination with the Schwartz hedonism items.

Finally, we note that a weakness of Chinese (and possibly all) values studies is to generally emphasize positive values and overlook those that may be viewed negatively, but actually function as significant underlying motivators of choices, responses, and action (Fung, Lieber, & Leung, 2003). From an organismic perspective which postulates humans are active, growth-oriented organisms that integrate new information into the existing self-concept (Deci & Ryan, 2000), the valence of values swings from positivity to negativity depending on the extent to which they are internalized.

In other words, some values may be experienced negatively if individuals do not feel autonomous but experience external or introjected pressures in endorsing them (Chirkov, Ryan, Kim, & Kaplan, 2003). According to this view, most values can take on negative connotations, if they are not well integrated. To facilitate internalization and optimal psychological integrity, Kağıtçıbaşı (2005) proposed a model of the autonomous-related self, which fits quite nicely with the recent findings on the evolving parenting styles in Chinese child-rearing that are characterized by both order setting and warmth or autonomy support (e.g. Zhou, 2008).

In a similar vein, we suggest that the embeddedness dimension in Schwartz's framework of cultural values may not have been fully explicated in Chinese (or other Asian or Confucian) contexts. R. Zhang (2006) noted two indigenous ways of dealing with interpersonal conflict: (1) a 'respect' (*zunzun*) rule that applies where social distance exists and (2) an 'affection' (*qinqin*) rule within close and intimate relationships (see also Hwang & Han, this volume). Might such a duality structurally complete the theory that already notes the twin domains of intellectual and affective autonomy? Such duality in embeddedness makes sense from a perspective that considers differential degrees of internalization and has found that horizontal values are more readily internalized (Chirkov et al., 2003). It seems this proposed split might help differentiate values items that locate on the hierarchy/embeddedness border regions in SVS, and also fits with the characterization by other researchers that social embeddedness has two forms, relational and group embeddedness (Brewer & Chen, 2007). Research designs need to be developed to test this and note which value items cluster with social group/role/face-guided embeddedness (out-group social relations) and which with personal/affective/familial embeddedness (close or in-group/commitment relations). Extensive Chinese region studies might be just the testing grounds for clarifying such hypotheses.

Further research will hopefully continue to provide deeper insights into 'Chinese values' and how those concepts and domains relate to similar constructs in their situated and global context. As C. H. Wang (2005, p. 10) notes:

> Such an understanding is not a mere concern for 'area studies'. In the past decade, debates among Chinese intellectuals have acquired an ever-stronger global color; they can be seen as attempts to think not just about their own country's problems, but about issues that confront the world as a whole. So, a record of their contributions is also a way to provide and participate in an intellectual engagement across frontiers.

Such stimulus from the intellectual cross-fertilization on issues regarding what scholars consider to be 'Chinese values' and how to study them has been an aim of this review. New and enhanced understandings will be needed to help us continue to explicate, compare, and integrate variations of 'Chinese' values into contextual, critical, and universal schemes.

Author's note

Sourcing, translation and writing for this chapter were carried out under a five-year SISU Key Disciplinary Development Research Project grant (No. KX161010, 2007–2012) to the SISU Intercultural Institute (SII) and grants to the first author by Resource Exchange International, Inc. (REI#CHN-Kul-2-96: the 'Shanghai Chinese Values Project [SCVP]', and REI#CHN-Kul-5-08/5: 'New Methods of Identifying Chinese Values Changes in Transition'). Special thanks are extended to SII research assistants Chi Ruobing, He Jia, and Ma Sang.

References

Allport, G. W. & Vernon, P. E. (1931). *Study of values: A scale for measuring the dominant interests in personality.* Boston, MA: Houghton Mifflin.

Allport, G. S., Vernon. P. E., & Lindzey, G. (1951). *A study of values.* Boston, MA: Houghton, Mifflin.

Allport, G. S., Vernon. P. E., & Lindzey, G. (1960). Study of values [SOV]. *A scale for measuring the dominant interests in personality* (3rd edn) (manual). Boston, MA: Houghton, Mifflin.

Anderson, B. (1983). *Imagined communities: Reflections on the origin and spread of nationalism.* London: Verso.

Anderson, C. M., Martin, M. M., & Zhong, M. (1998). Motives for communicating with family and friends: A Chinese study. *Howard Journal of Communications, 9,* 109–123.

Appadurai, A. (1996). *Modernity at large: Cultural dimensions of globalization.* Minneapolis, MN: University of Minnesota Press.

Arnett, J. J. (2002). The psychology of globalization. *American Psychologist, 57,* 774–783.

Ball-Rokeach, S. J. (1985). The origins of individual media system dependency: A sociological framework. *Communication Research, 12,* 485–510.

Bardi, A. & Schwartz, S. H. (2003). Value and behaviour: Strength and structure of relations. *Personality and Social Psychology Bulletin, 29,* 1207–1220.

Bauer, W. L. (1976). *China and the search for happiness: Recurring themes in four thousand years of Chinese cultural history* (Michael Shaw, Trans. of *China und die Hoffnung auf Glueck: Paradiese, Utopien, Idealvorstellungen*). New York: Seabury Press. (Original work published 1971 in German)

Beatty, S. E., Kahle, L. R., Homer, P. M., & Misra, S. (1985). Alternative measurement approaches to consumer values: The list of values and the Rokeach value survey. *Psychology and Marketing, 2,* 181–200.

Bedford, O. A. (2004). The individual experience of guilt and shame in Chinese culture. *Culture & Psychology, 10,* 29–52.

Benedict, R. (1946). *The chrysanthemum and the sword: Patterns of Japanese culture.* Boston, MA: Houghton Mifflin.

Berry, J. W. & Kim, U. (1993). The way ahead: From indigenous psychologies to a universal psychology. In U. Kim & J. W. Berry (eds), *Indigenous psychologies: Research and experience in cultural context* (pp. 277–280). Newbury Park, CA: Sage.

Biernat, M., Vescio, T. K., Theno, S. A., & Crandall, C. S. (1996). Values and prejudice: Toward understanding the impact of American values on outgroup attitudes. In C. Seligman, J. M. Olson, & M. P. Zanna (eds), *The psychology of values: The Ontario symposium* (Vol. 8, pp. 153–189). Mahwah, NJ: Lawrence Erlbaum Associates.

Boas, F. (2004). *Anthropology and modern life.* New York: Norton. (Original work published 1928)

Bond, M. H. (1988). Finding universal dimensions of individual variation in multi-cultural studies of value. *Journal of Personality and Social Psychology, 55,* 1009–1015.

Bond, M. H. (1996). Chinese values. In M. H. Bond (ed.), *The handbook of Chinese psychology* (pp. 208–226). Hong Kong: Oxford University Press.

Bond, M. H. (2007). Fashioning a new psychology of the Chinese people: Insights from developments in cross-cultural psychology. In S. J. Kulich & M. H. Prosser (eds). *Intercultural perspectives on Chinese communication, Intercultural research, Vol. 1* (pp. 233–251). Shanghai: Shanghai Foreign Language Education Press.

Bond, M. H. (2009). Going beyond Chinese Values: An insider's retrospections. In S. J. Kulich & M. H. Prosser (eds), *Values frameworks at the theoretical crossroads of culture, Intercultural research, Vol. 2* (in press). Shanghai, China: Shanghai Foreign Language Education Press.

Bond, M. H. & Chi, V. M. Y. (1997). Values and moral behavior in Mainland China. *Psychologia, 40*, 251–264.

Bond, M. H. & King, A. Y. C. (1985). Coping with the threat of Westernization in Hong Kong. *International Journal of Intercultural Relations, 9*, 351–364.

Bond, M. H., Leung, K., Au, A., Tong, K.-K., & Chemonges-Nielson, Z. (2004). Combining social axioms with values in predicting social behaviours. *European Journal of Personality, 18*, 177–191.

Bond, M. H. & Mak, A. L. P. (1996). Deriving an inter-group topography from perceived values: Forging an identity in Hong Kong out of Chinese tradition and contemporary examples. In *Proceedings of the conference on mind, machine and the environment: Facing the challenges of the 21st century* (pp. 255–266). Seoul, Korea: Korean Psychological Association.

Borofsky, R., Barth, F., Shweder, R. A., Rodseth, L., & Stolzenberg, N. M. (2001). When: A conversation about culture. *American Anthropologist, 103*, 432–446.

Brewer, M. B. & Chen, Y. (2007). Where (who) are collectives in collectivism? Toward conceptual clarification of individualism and collectivism. *Psychological Review, 114*, 133–151.

Cai, B. (2005). Are Chinese collectivists twenty years later: A second look at the individualism and collectivism construct? *Aurco, 11*, 67–80.

Chaffee, S. H., Chu, G. C., Ju, Y. A., Pan, Z. D. (1994). *To see ourselves: Comparing traditional Chinese and American values.* Boulder, CO: Westview.

Chan, S. K.-C, Bond, M. H., Spencer-Oatey, H., & Rojo-Laurilla, M. (2004). Culture and rapport promotion in service encounters: Protecting the ties that bind. *Journal of Asian Pacific Communication, 14*, 245–260.

Chang, H.-C. (2001a). Harmony as performance: The turbulence under Chinese interpersonal communication. *Discourse Studies, 3*, 155–179.

Chang, H.-C. (2001b). Learning speaking skills from our ancient philosophers: Transformation of Taiwanese culture as observed from popular books. *Journal of Asian Pacific Communication, 11*, 109–133.

Chang, H.-C. (2002). The concept of *yuan* and Chinese conflict resolution. In G. M. Chen & R. Ma (eds), *Chinese conflict management and resolution* (pp. 19–38). Westport, CT: Greenwood.

Chang, H.-C. & Holt, G. R. (1991a). More than relationship: Chinese interaction and the principle of *Guan-hsi. Communication Quarterly, 39*, 251–271.

Chang, H.-C. & Holt, G. R. (1991b). The concept of *yuan* and Chinese interpersonal relationships. In S. Ting-Toomey & F. Korzenny (eds), *Cross-cultural interpersonal communication* (pp. 28–57). Newbury Park, CA: Sage.

Chang, H.-C. & Holt, G. R. (1994a). Debt-repaying mechanism in Chinese relationships: An exploration of the folk concepts of *pao* and human emotional debt. *Research on Language and Social Interaction, 27*, 351–387.

Chang, H.-C. & Holt, G. R. (1994b). A Chinese perspective on face as inter-relational concern. In S. Ting-Toomey & D. Cushman (eds), *The challenge of facework* (pp. 95–132). Albany, NY: State University of New York Press.

Chang, H.-C. & Holt, G. R. (1996a). An exploration of interpersonal relationship in two Taiwanese computer firms. *Human Relations, 49*, 1489–1517.

Chang, H.-C. & Holt, G. R. (1996b). The changing Chinese interpersonal world: Popular themes in interpersonal communication books in modern Taiwan. *Communication Quarterly, 44*, 85–106.

Chang, H.-C., Holt, G. R., & Lin, H. D. (2004). *Yuan* and Chinese communication behaviors. In G. M. Chen (ed.), *Theories and principles of Chinese communication* (pp. 451–481). Taipei, Taiwan: WuNan.

Chang, W. C., Wong, W. K., & Koh, J. B. K. (2003). Chinese values in Singapore: Traditional and modern. *Asian Journal of Social Psychology, 6*, 5–29.

Chen, G. M. (1992). Change of Chinese family value orientations in the United States. *Journal of Overseas Chinese Studies, 2*, 111–121.

Chen, G. M. (1998). A Chinese model of human relationship development. In B. L. Hoffer & H. H. Koo (eds), *Cross-cultural communication East and West in the 90's* (pp. 45–53). San Antonio, TX: Institute for Cross-Cultural Research.

Chen, G. M. (2001). Toward transcultural understanding: A harmony theory of Chinese communication. In V. H. Milhouse, M. K. Asante, & P. O. Nwosu (eds), *Transcultural realities: Interdisciplinary perspectives on cross-cultural relations* (pp. 55–70). Thousand Oaks, CA: Sage.

Chen, G. M. (2002). The impact of harmony on Chinese conflict management. In G. M. Chen & R. Ma (eds), *Chinese conflict management and resolution* (pp. 3–19). Westport, CT: Ablex.

Chen, G. M. (2004a). *Feng shui* and Chinese communication behaviors. In G. M. Chen (ed.), *Theories and principles of Chinese communication* (pp. 483–502). Taipei, Taiwan: WuNan.

Chen, G. M. (2004b). The two faces of Chinese communication. *Human Communication: A Journal of the Pacific and Asian Communication Association, 7*, 25–36.

Chen, G. M. (2006). Asian communication studies: What and where to now. *Review of Communication, 6*, 295–311.

Chen, G. M. (2007). Intercultural communication studies by ACCS scholars on the Chinese. In S. J. Kulich & M. H. Prosser (eds), *Intercultural perspectives on Chinese communication. Intercultural Research Vol. 1* (pp. 302–337). Shanghai, China: Shanghai Foreign Language Education Press.

Chen, G. M. (2008a). Intercultural communication studies by ACCS scholars on the Chinese: An updated bibliography. *China Media Research, 4*(2), 102–113.

Chen, G. M. (2008b). Towards transcultural understanding: A harmony theory of Chinese communication. *China Media Research 4*(4), 1–13.

Chen, G. M. & Chung, J. (1994). The impact of Confucianism on organizational communication. *Communication Quarterly, 42*, 93–105.

Chen, G. M. & Chung, J. (1997). The five Asian dragons: Management behaviors and organizational communication. In L. A. Samovar & R. E. Porter (eds), *Intercultural communication: A reader* (pp. 317–328). Belmont, CA: Wadsworth.

Chen, G. M. & Chung, J. (2002). Superiority and seniority: A case analysis of decision making in a Taiwanese religious group. *Intercultural Communication Studies, 11*, 41–56.

Chen, G. M., Ryan, K., & Chen, C. (2000). The determinants of conflict management among Chinese and Americans. *Intercultural Communication Studies, 9*, 163–175.

Chen, L. (2002). *Romantic relationship and the concept of 'yuan': A study of Chinese in Hong Kong*. Paper presented at International Communication Association Annual Conference, Seoul, Korea, July.

Chen, L. (2006). Western theory and nonwestern practice: Friendship/ dialectics for Chinese in Hong Kong. *China Media Research, 2*(1), 21–31.

Chen, S. X., Benet-Martínez, V., & Bond, M. H. (2008). Bicultural identity, bilingualism, and psychological adjustment in multicultural societies: Immigration-based and globalization-based acculturation. *Journal of Personality, 76*, 803–838.

Chen, S. X., Bond, M. H., & Tang, D. (2007). Decomposing filial piety into filial attitudes and filial enactments. *Asian Journal of Social Psychology, 10*, 213–223.

Chen, X. H (2002). On the Chinese value study in the transitional period. *Tendency of Psychology, 7*, 16–20. (in Chinese)

Chen, X. R. (2006a). A survey on high school students' moral value orientations and life experience. *Shanghai Education Research, 8*, 4–7. (in Chinese)

Chen, X. R. (2006b). An investigation of current status on moral values among Chinese teachers and students. *Chinese Journal of Moral Education, 1*(3), 50–56. (in Chinese)

Chinese Culture Connection (1987). Chinese values and the search for culture-free dimensions of culture. *Journal of Cross-Cultural Psychology, 18*, 143–164.

Chirkov, V., Ryan, R. M., Kim, Y., & Kaplan, U. (2003). Differentiating autonomy from individualism and independence: A self-determination theory perspective on internalization of cultural orientations and wellbeing. *Journal of Personality and Social Psychology, 84*, 97–110.

Chiu, C.-Y. & Cheng, S. Y. Y. (2007). Toward a social psychology of culture and globalization: Some social cognitive consequences of activating two cultures simultaneously. *Social and Personality Psychology Compass 1*, 84–100.

Chu, G. C. (ed.). (1978). *Popular media in China: Shaping new cultural patterns*. Honolulu. HI: University Press of Hawaii.

Chu, G. C. & Hsu, F. L. K. (eds) (1979). *Moving a mountain: Cultural change in China*. Honolulu, HI: University Press of Hawaii.

Chu, G. C. & Hsu, F. L. K. (eds) (1983). *China's new social fabric*. New York: Kegan Paul International.

Chu, G. C. & Ju, Y. N. (1993). *The great wall in ruins: Communication and cultural change in China*. Albany, NY: State University of New York Press.

Chu, G. C., Hayashi, C., & Akuto, H. (1995). Comparative analysis of Chinese and Japanese cultural values. *Behaviormetrika, 22*, 1–35.

Chuang, R. (2004). *Zhan bui* and Chinese communication behaviors. In G. M. Chen (ed.), *Theories and principles of Chinese communication* (pp. 503–515). Taipei, Taiwan: WuNan.

Chung, J. (1997). Cultural impacts on non-assertiveness of East Asian subordinates. *Management Development Forum, 2*, 53–72.

Chung, J. (2004). The *qi* communication theory and language strategy. In G. M. Chen (ed.), *Theories and principles of Chinese communication* (pp. 517–539). Taipei, Taiwan: WuNan.

Chung, J. (2008). The *chi/qi/ki* of organizational communication: The process of generating energy flow with dialectics. *China Media Research, 4*(3), 92–100.

Condon, J. C. & Yousef, F. (1975). *An introduction to intercultural communication*. Indianapolis, IN: Bobbs-Merrill.

Dai, M. T. & Jiang, Y. (2001). *Traditional values and contemporary China*. Wuhan: Hubei People's Press. (in Chinese)

Davidov, E., Schmidt, P., & Schwartz, S. H. (2008). Bringing values back in: The adequacy of the European Social Survey to measure values in 20 countries. *Public Opinion Quarterly 72*, 420–445.

Deci, E. L. & Ryan, R. M. (2000). The 'what' and the 'why' of goal pursuits: Human needs and the self-determination of behaviour. *Psychological Inquiry, 11*, 227–268.

Deng, D. Y., Tang, L. F., & Zhang, L. (2008). *University student's consuming values*. Unpublished manuscript, SISU Intercultural Institute, Shanghai International Studies University.

Deng, Q. (2006). Research on marriage and love value orientations of present Chinese young people. *Inner Mongolia Social Sciences, 27*(4), 99–102. (in Chinese)

Dou, G. & Huang, X. T. (2006).The latent structure of ipsative data of contemporary Chinese college students' value. *Psychological Science, 29*, 1331–1335. (in Chinese)

Durkheim, E. (1933). *The division of labor in society*. New York: Macmillan (Original work published 1887).

Edmundson, J. J. Z. & Chen, G. M. (eds) (2008). Construction of harmonious society: A communication perspective [Special issue]. *China Media Research, 4*(4)

Enriquez, V. G. (1979). Towards cross-cultural knowledge through cross-indigenous methods and perspectives. In J. L. M. Binnie-Dawson, G. H. Blowers, & R. Hoosain (eds), *Perspectives in Asian cross-cultural psychology* (pp. 29–41). Lisse: Swets & Zeitlinger, BV.

Eisenstadt, S. N. (2001). The civilizational dimension of modernity: Modernity as a distinct civilization. *International Sociology, 16*, 320–340.

Faludi, S. (1991). *Backlash: The undeclared war against American women*. New York: Anchor.

Fan, H. & Hu, Y. (1997). The changes of Chinese women's marriage values since the Opening-up Policy. *Journal of Women's University of China, 4*, 39–42. (in Chinese)

Faure, G. O. & Fang, T. (2008). Changing Chinese values: Keeping up with paradoxes. *International Business Review, 17*, 194–207.

Fei, X. T. (1939). *Peasant life in China: A field study of country life in the Yangtze Valley*. Preface by Bronislaw Malinowski. London: G. Routledge and New York: Dutton.

Fei, X. T. (1992) *From the soil: The foundations of Chinese society*. (Gary G. Hamilton & Wang Zheng Trans. of *Xiangtu Zhongguo* [Rural China]. Shanghai: Guancha). Berkeley, CA: University of California Press. (Original work published 1948)

Fei, X. T. & Chang Chih-yi [Zhang Ziyi] (1945). *Earthbound China: A study of rural economy in Yunnan*. Chicago, IL: University of Chicago Press.

Feng, H. R. (2004). *Keqi* and Chinese communication behaviors. In G. M. Chen (ed.), *Theories and principles of Chinese communication* (pp. 435–450). Taipei, Taiwan: WuNan.

Feng, T. (2003). A critique of Hofstede's fifth national cultural dimension. *International Journal of Cross-Cultural Management, 3*, 347–368.

Fischer, R. (2006). Congruence and functions of personal and cultural values: Do my values reflect my culture's values? *Personality and Social Psychology Bulletin, 32*, 1419–1431.

Fitzgerald, F. (1999). The unfinished history of China's future. *Thesis Eleven, 57*, 17–31.

Fu, J. H.-Y., & Chiu, C.-Y. (2007). Local culture's responses to globalization: Exemplary persons and their attendant values. *Journal of Cross-Cultural Psychology, 38*, 636–653.

Fung, H. (2006). Affect and early moral socialization: Some insights and contributions from indigenous psychological studies in Taiwan. In U. Kim, K. S. Yang, & K. K. Hwang (eds), *Indigenous and cultural psychology:Understanding people in context* (pp. 175–196). New York: Springer Science+Business Media, LLC.

Fung, H., Lieber, E., & Leung, P. W. L. (2003). Parental beliefs about shame and moral socialization in Taiwan, Hong Kong, and the United States. In K. S. Yang, K. K. Hwang, P. B. Pedersen, & I. Daibo (eds), *Progress in Asian social psychology: Conceptual and empirical contributions* (pp. 83–109). Westport, CT: Praeger Publishers.

Geertz, C. (1973). *The interpretation of cultures: Selected essays*. New York: Basic Books.

Garrott, J. R. (1995). Chinese cultural values: New angles, added insights. *International Journal of Intercultural Relations, 19*, 211–225.

Gong, H. X. & Xing, (1994). Research on value orientations towards life of female students in teaching colleges. *Journal of Zhejiang Normal University (Social science Edition), 3*, 113–118. (in Chinese)

Gorer, J. (1948). *The American people: A study in national character*. New York: W. W. Norton.

Green, E. G. T., Deschamps, J.-C., & Páez, D. (2005). Variation of individualism and collectivism within and between 20 countries: A typological analysis. *Journal of Cross-Cultural Psychology, 36*, 321–339.

Guo, X. H. (2001).The change of moral values in Chinese urban residents. *Jianghai Journal for Study, 3*, 32–38. (in Chinese)

Hall, E. T. (1976). *Beyond culture*. Garden City, NY: Anchor.

Han, X. M., Wang, F. L., & Liu, R. M. (1998). A research on moral value orientation of peasants in Shanxi in the social transitional period. *Journal of Shanxi University. 3*, 70–77. (in Chinese)

Hechter, M. (1993). Acknowledgements. In M. Hechter, L. Nadel, & R. E. Michod (eds). *The origin of values* (pp. 31–46). New York: Aldine/Walter de Gruyter.

Hechter, M. (2000). Agenda for sociology at the start of the twenty-first century. *Annual Review of Sociology, 26*, 697–698.

Heine, S. J., Lehman, D. R., Peng, K., & Greenholtz, J. (2002). What's wrong with cross-cultural comparison of subjective Likert scales? The reference-group effect. *Journal of Personality and Social Psychology, 82*, 903–918.

Hermans, H. J. M. & Kempen, H. J. G. (1998). Moving cultures: The perilous problems of cultural dichotomies in a globalizing society. *American Psychologist, 53*, 1111–1120.

Herzberg, F (1966). *Work and the nature of man*. New York: Thomas Y. Crowell.

Hitlin, S. & Piliavin, J. A. (2004). Values: Reviving a dormant concept. *Annual Review of Sociology, 30*, 359–393.

Ho, D. Y. F. (1976). On the concept of face. *American Journal of Sociology, 81*, 867–884.

Ho, D. Y. F. (1994a). Face dynamics: From conceptualization to measurement. In S. Ting-Toomey (ed.), *The challenge of facework: Cross-cultural and interpersonal issues* (pp. 269–286). Albany, NY: State University of New York Press.

Ho, D. Y. F. (1994b). Filial piety, authoritarian moralism, and cognitive conservatism. *Genetic, Social, and General Psychology Monographs, 120*, 347–365.
Ho, D. Y. F. (1996). Filial piety and its psychological consequences. In M. H. Bond (ed.), The handbook of Chinese psychology (pp. 155–165). Hong Kong: Oxford University Press.
Ho, D. Y. F. (1998a). Filial piety and filicide in Chinese family relationships: The legend of Shun and other stories. In U. P. Gielen & A. L. Comunian (eds), *The family and family therapy in international perspective* (pp. 134–149). Trieste, Italy: Edizioni LINT.
Ho, D. Y. F. (1998b). Indigenous perspectives. *Journal of Cross-Cultural Psychology, 29*, 88–103.
Ho, D. Y. F. (1999). Interpersonal feelings and *jen ching*. *Indigenous psychological research in Chinese societies, 12*, 181–187. (in Chinese)
Ho, D. Y. F. (2002). Myths and realities in Confucian-heritage education. In D. W. K. Chan & W. Y. Wu (eds), *Thinking qualities initiative conference proceedings 2000 and 2001* (pp. 3–19). Hong Kong: Centre for Educational Development, Hong Kong Baptist University; Hong Kong Society for the Advancement of Learning and Teaching of Thinking.
Ho, D. Y. F. & Peng, S. (1998). Methodological relationalism and its applications in Eastern and Western cultures. *Sociological Research, 4*, 34–43. (in Chinese)
Ho, D. Y. F. & Peng, S. (1999). Filial piety and filicide. *WAY, 90*, 34–36. (in Chinese)
Ho, D. Y. F., Chan, S. F., Peng, S. Q., & Ng, A. K. (2001). The dialogic self: Converging East–West constructions. *Culture & Psychology, 7*, 393–408.
Ho, D. Y. F., Chan, S. F., & Zhang, Z. X. (2001). Metarelational analysis: An answer to 'What's Asian about Asian social psychology?' *Journal of Psychology in Chinese Societies, 2*, 7–26.
Ho, D. Y. F. & Chiu, C.-Y. (1994). Component ideas of individualism, collectivism, and social organization: An application in the study of Chinese culture. In U. Kim, H. C. Triandis, Ç. Kağıtçıbaşı, S. C. Choi, & G. Goon (eds), *Individualism and collectivism: Theory, method, and applications* (pp. 137–156). Thousand Oaks, CA: Sage.
Ho, D. Y. F., Peng, S. Q., & Lai, A. C. (2001). Parenting in Mainland China: Culture, ideology, and policy. *International Society for the Study of Behavioral Development Newsletter, 38*, 7–9.
Ho, D. Y. F., Peng, S. Q., & Chan, S. F. (2001a). Authority and learning in Confucian-heritage education: A relational methodological analysis. In F. Salili, C.-Y. Chiu, & Y.-Y. Hong (eds), *Multiple competencies and self-regulated learning: Implications for multicultural education* (pp. 29–47). Greenwich, CT: Information Age Publishing.
Ho, D. Y. F., Peng, S. Q., & Chan, S. F. (2001b). An investigative research in teaching and learning. In F. Salili, C.-Y. Chiu, & Y.-Y. Hong (eds), *Multiple competencies and self-regulated learning: Implications for multicultural education* (pp. 215–244). Greenwich, CT: Information Age Publishing.
Ho, D. Y. F., Ng, A. K., Peng, S. Q., & Chan, S. F. (2002). *Authority relations in Confucian-heritage education: Knowledge is a dangerous thing.* Unpublished manuscript, University of Hong Kong.
Ho, D. Y. F., Fu, W., & Ng, S. M. (2004). Guilt, shame, and embarrassment: Revelations of face and self. *Culture & Psychology, 10*, 159–178.
Hofstede, G. (1980). *Culture's consequences: International differences in work-related values.* Newbury Park, CA: Sage.
Hofstede, G. (2001). *Culture's consequences: Comparing values, behaviors, institutions, and organizations across nations* (2nd ed.). Thousand Oaks, CA: Sage.
Holland, J. L. (1985). *A theory of vocational personalities and work environments.* Englewood Cliffs, NJ: Prentice-Hall.
Holt, R. & Chang, H.-C. (2004). *Bao* and Chinese interpersonal communication. In G. M. Chen (ed.), *Theories and principles of Chinese communication* (pp. 409–434). Taipei, Taiwan: WuNan.
Hong, Y.-Y., Morris, M. W., Chiu, C.-Y., & Benet-Martínez, V. (2000). Multicultural minds: A dynamic constructivist approach to culture and cognition. *American Psychologist, 55*, 709–720.
Hoshmand, L. T. & Ho, D. Y. F. (1995). Moral dimensions of selfhood: Chinese traditions and cultural change. *World Psychology, 1*, 47–69.
Hou, A. B. & Zhang, J. F. (2006). A psychological perspective on ethnic values. *Journal of the Central University for Nationalities (Philosophical and Social Science Edition), 33*, 37–42.
Hsu, F. L. K. (1948). *Under the ancestor's shadow: Chinese culture and personality.* New York: Columbia University Press.
Hsu, F. L. K. (1953). *Americans and Chinese: Two ways of life.* New York: H. Schuman.
Hsu, F. L. K. (1961). *Psychological anthropology: Approaches to culture and personality.* Homewood, IL: Dorsey Press.
Hsu, F. L. K. (1968). *Clan, caste and club.* New York: Van Nostrand, Reinhold Co.
Hsu, F. L. K. (1970). *Americans and Chinese: Purpose and fulfillment in great civilizations.* Garden City, NY: Natural History Press.
Hsu, F. L. K. (1981). *Americans and Chinese: Passages to differences.* Honolulu, HI: The University of Hawaii Press.
Hu, C. (2006). A comparative study of Chinese and American success value. *Journal of Ningbo University (Liberal Arts Edition), 3*, 112–117.
Hu, S. (1934). *The Chinese renaissance: the Haskell lectures, 1933.* Chicago, IL: University of Chicago Press.
Huang, J. H. (1988). The practice of filial piety in contemporary society. In K. S. Yang (ed.), *Chinese Psychology* (pp. 25–38). Taipei: Laurel Publishing Inc. (in Chinese)
Huang, L. L. (2005). Interpersonal harmony and interpersonal conflict. In K. S. Yang, K. K. Hwang, & C. F. Yang (eds), *Chinese indigenous psychology* (pp. 521–566). Hong Kong: Yuan Liou. (in Chinese)

Huang, S. (1999). Filial piety is the root of all virtues: Cross-cultural conflicts and intercultural acceptance in Lee's two movies. *Popular Culture Review, 10*, 53–67.

Huang, S. (2000). Ten thousand businesses would thrive in a harmonious family: Chinese conflict resolution styles in cross-cultural families. *Intercultural Communication Studies, 9*, 129–144.

Huang, S. & Jia, W. (2000). The cultural connotation and communicative function of China's kinship terms. *American Communication Journal, 3*, 43–61.

Huang, X. T. (2004). Reflections on Chinanization of personality studies. *Journal of Southwest China Normal University, 30*(6), 5–9. (in Chinese)

Huang, X. T. (2007). Chinanized psychology research and the construction of harmonious society. *Advances in Psychological Science, 2*, 193–195. (in Chinese)

Huang, X. T., Dou, G., & Zheng, Y. (2008). Discrete choice methods estimation of contemporary Chinese college students' values. *Psychological Science, 31*, 675–680. (in Chinese)

Huang, X. T., & Yang, X. (1998). Constructing a scale of self-worth for young students. *Psychological Science, 21*, 289–293. (in Chinese)

Huang, X. T., & Zheng, Y. (2005). *Research on contemporary values of Chinese youth.* Beijing, China: People's Education Press (in Chinese).

Huang, X. T., Zhang, J. F., & Li, H. (1994). *Values and education of contemporary Chinese youth.* Chengdu, China: Sichuan Education Press. (in Chinese)

Huang, X. T., Zhang, J. F., & Zhang, S. L. (1989). A survey on young students' values in five cities. *Psychological Journal, 22*, 274–283. (In Chinese).

Hughes, N. (2007). *Changing faces: Highly skilled Chinese workers and the cultural adaptation required to work at a foreign multinational corporation.* Unpublished doctoral dissertation, the Fielding Graduate University, Santa Barbara, California.

Hwang, K. K. (1987). Face and favor: The Chinese power game. *American Journal of Sociology, 92*, 944–974.

Hwang, K. K. (1995). The modern transformation of Confucian values: Theoretical analyses and empirical research. *Indigenous Psychological Research in Chinese Societies, 3*, 276–338. (in Chinese)

Hwang, K. K. (1997–8). *Guanxi* and *mientze*: Conflict resolution in Chinese society. *Intercultural Communication Studies, 7*, 17–37.

Hwang, K. K. (1999). Filial piety and loyalty: Two types of social identification in Confucianism. *Asian Journal of Social Psychology, 2*, 163–183.

Hwang, K. K. (2003a). Critique of the methodology of empirical research on individual modernity in Taiwan. *Asian Journal of Social Psychology, 6*, 241–262.

Hwang, K. K. (2003b). In search of a new paradigm for cultural psychology. *Asian Journal of Social Psychology, 6*, 287–291.

Hwang, K. K. (2005). Face in Chinese society. In K. S. Yang, K. K. Hwang, & C. F. Yang (eds), *Chinese indigenous psychology* (pp. 365–405). Hong Kong: Yuan Liou. (in Chinese)

Hwang, K. K. (2007). The development of indigenous social psychology in Confucian society. In S. J. Kulich & M. H. Prosser (eds), *Intercultural perspectives on Chinese communication: Intercultural Research Vol. 1.* Shanghai, China: Shanghai Foreign Language Education Press.

Inglehart, R. (1977a). *Modernization and postmodernization: Cultural, economic, and political change in 43 societies.* Princeton, NJ: Princeton University Press.

Inglehart, R. (1977b). *The silent revolution: Changing values and political styles in advanced industrial society.* Princeton, NJ: Princeton University Press.

Inglehart, R. et al. (1990). *World values survey, 1981–1983. Computer file and codebook (2nd edn).* Ann Arbor, MI: University of Michigan, Inter-University Consortium for Political and Social Research.

Inglehart, R. & Baker, W. E. (2000). Modernization, cultural change and the persistence of traditional values. *American Sociological Review, 6*, 19–51.

Inglehart, R. & Welzel, C. (2005), *Modernization, cultural change and democracy.* Cambridge, England: Cambridge University Press.

Inkeles, A. & Levinson, D. J. (1969). National character: The study of modal personality and socio-cultural systems. In G. Lindzey & E. Aronson (eds), *Handbook of social psychology* (Vol. 4, pp. 418–506). New York, NY: McGraw-Hill. (original work published in 1954)

Jensen, L. A. (2003). Coming of age in a multicultural world: Globalization and adolescent cultural identity formation. *Applied Developmental Science, 7*, 189–196.

Jia. W. (1997–8). Facework as a Chinese conflict-preventive mechanism: A cultural/ discourse analysis. *Intercultural Communication Studies, 7*, 43–61.

Jia, W. (2001). *The remaking of the Chinese character and identity in the 21st century: The Chinese face practices.* Westport, CT: Ablex.

Jia, W. (2003). Chinese conceptualizations of face: Personhood, communication and emotions. In L. A. Samovar & R. E. Porter (eds), *Intercultural communication: A reader* (*10th edn*) (pp. 53–61). Belmont, CA: Wadsworth.

Jia, W. (2006a). The *wei* (positioning)–*ming* (naming)–*lianmian* (face)–*guanxi* (relationship)–*renqing* (humanized feelings) complex in contemporary Chinese culture. In. P. D. Hershock & R. T. Ames (eds), *Confucian cultures of authority* (pp. 49–64). Albany, NY: SUNY Press.

Jia, W. (2006b). The *wei* (positioning)–*ming* (naming)–*lianmian* (face) continuum in contemporary Chinese culture. In L. A. Samovar, R. E. Porter, & E. R. McDaniel (eds), *Intercultural communication: A reader* (*11th ed.*, pp. 114–122). Belmont, CA: Wadsworth.
Jia, W. (2008). Chinese perspective on harmony: An evaluation of the harmony and peace paradigm. *China Media Research, 4*(4), 25–30.
Jin, S. H. & Li, H. (2003). Value orientation of present Chinese professionals. *Studies of Psychology and Behavior, 1*(2), 100–104. (in Chinese)
Jin, S. H. & Li, X. (2004). Comparison of value orientation between contemporary peasant/farmers and workers. *Chinese Journal of Applied Psychology, 10*(3), 28–32. (in Chinese)
Jin, Z. Q. & Li, Z. S. (2007). A summary of adolescent work values study. *Journal of Career Education, 6*, 41–47 (in Chinese).
Jin, S. H. & Liu, B. (2005). The value orientation of contemporary Chinese workers: Status and characteristics. *Psychological Science, 28*, 244–247. (in Chinese)
Jin, S. H. & Xin, Z. Y. (2003). The status quo of Chinese values study and its trends. *Journal of Beijing Normal University, 177*(3), 56–64. (in Chinese)
Jin, S. H., Sun, N., Shi, Q. M., & Tian, L. L. (2003). Research on the characteristics of contemporary middle school students' values. *Psychological Exploration, 2*, 30–34. (in Chinese)
Jin, S. H., Wang, H. T., Tian, L. L., Shi, Q. M., Liu, B., Li, H., & Sun, N. (2003). A study of value orientation of contemporary peasants/farmers. *Chinese Journal of Applied Psychology, 9*, 20–25. (in Chinese)
Jussim, L. (in press). Stereotypes. In D. Matsumoto (ed.), *Cambridge dictionary of psychology*. New York: Cambridge University Press.
Kağıtçıbaşı, Ç., & Berry, J. W. (1989). Cross-cultural psychology: Current research and trends. *Annual Review of Psychology, 40*, 493–531.
Kağıtçıbaşı, Ç. (2005). Autonomy and relatedness in cultural context: Implications for self and family. *Journal of Cross-Cultural Psychology, 36*, 403–422.
Kahle, L. R. (ed.)(1983). *Social values and social change: Adaptation to life in America.* New York: Praeger.
Kahle, L. R., Beatty, S. E., & Homer, P. (1986). Alternative measurement approaches to consumer values: The List of Values (LOV) and Value and Life Style (VALS). *Journal of Consumer Research, 13*, 405–409.
Kahle, L. R. & Xie, G. X. (2008). Social values and consumer behavior: Research from the list of values. In C. P. Haugtvedt, P. M. Herr, & F. R. Kardes (eds), *Handbook of consumer psychology* (pp. 573–588). Mahwah, NJ: Psychology Press.
Kardiner, A. & Linton. R. (1939). *The individual and his society.* New York: Columbia University Press.
Kasser, T. & Ryan, R. M. (1993). A dark side of the American dream: Correlates of financial success as a central life aspiration. *Journal of Personality and Social Psychology, 65*, 410–422.
Kitayama, S. (2002). Culture and basic psychological processes: Toward a system view of culture: Comment on Oyserman et al. (2002). *Psychological Bulletin, 128*, 89–96.
Kirkman, B. L., Lowe, K. B., & Gibson, C. B. (2006). A quarter century of *Culture's Consequences*: A review of empirical research incorporating Hofstede's cultural values framework. *Journal of International Business Studies, 37*, 285–320.
Kluckhohn, C. K. M. (1951). Values and value orientations in the theory of action. In T. Parsons & E. Shils (eds), *Toward a general theory of action* (pp. 388–433). Cambridge, MA. Harvard University Press.
Kluckhohn, C. K. M. (1956). Universal values and education. In R. Kluckhohn (ed.), *Culture and behavior: The collected essays of Clyde Kluckhohn.* Glencoe, IL: The Free Press.
Kluckhohn, F. R., & Strodtbeck, F. (1961). *Variations in value orientations.* Evanston, IL: Row, Peterson & Co.
Kluver, R. (2001). Political culture and political conflict in China. In G. Chen & R. Ma (eds), *Chinese conflict management and resolution* (pp. 223–240). Westport, CT: Greenwood Publishing.
Kluver, R. (1999). Elite based discourse in Chinese civil society. In R. Kluver & J. Powers (eds), *Civic discourse, civil society, and the Chinese world.* Stamford, CT: Ablex.
Kluver, R. (1997). Political identity and national myth: Toward an intercultural understanding of political legitimacy. In A. Gonzales & D. Tanno (eds), *Politics, culture, and communication: International and intercultural communication annual, 20* (pp. 48–75). Newbury Park, CA: Sage Publications.
Kluver, R. (2004). The internet in China: A symposium. In *The International Institute of Asian Studies Newsletter, 33.* Retrieved March 12, 2009, from http://www.iias.nl/iiasn/33/index.html
Kristiansen, C. M. & Hotte, A. M. (1996). Morality and the self: Implications for the when and how of value–attitude–behavior relations. In C. Seligman, J. M. Olson, & M. P. Zanna (eds), *The psychology of values: The Ontario symposium* (Vol. 8, pp. 77–105). Mahwah, NJ: Erlbaum.
Kroeber, A. L. & Kluckholn, C. K. M (1952). *Culture: A critical review of concepts and definitions.* Cambridge, MA: Harvard University Press.
Ku, H. M. (2006). *The spirit of the Chinese people.* Beijing: Foreign Language Teaching & Research Press. (Original work published 1915, Peking: Peking Daily News)
Kulich, S. J. (1997). *Apt aphorisms: The search for Chinese values in Self-selected sayings.* Paper presented at the 3rd annual conference on East–West Communication: Challenges for the New Century, the David C. Lam Institute for East–West Studies, HKBU, Hong Kong, November.
Kulich, S. J. (2007a). Introduction: Linking intercultural communication with China studies – Language and relationship perspectives. In S. J. Kulich & M. H. Prosser (eds), *Intercultural perspectives on Chinese communication, Intercultural research, Vol. 1* (pp. 3–21). Shanghai, China: Shanghai Foreign Language Education Press.

Kulich, S. J. (2007b). Expanding the Chinese intercultural paradigm with social science research: Toward a multi-level model of cultural analysis. In S. J. Kulich & M. H. Prosser (eds), *Intercultural perspectives on Chinese communication, Intercultural research, Vol. 1* (pp. 203–251). Shanghai, China: Shanghai Foreign Language Education Press.

Kulich, S. J. (2008). Getting the big picture on Chinese values: Developing approaches to study the shifting core of Chinese culture. *Intercultural Communication Studies, XVII*(2), 15–30.

Kulich, S. J. (2009a). *Applying cross-cultural values research to 'the Chinese': A critical integration of etic and emic approaches.* Unpublished doctoral dissertation, Humboldt University of Berlin, Germany.

Kulich, S. J. (2009b in press). Values studies: The origins and development of cross-cultural comparisons. In S. J. Kulich & M. H. Prosser (eds). *Values frameworks at the theoretical crossroads of culture, Intercultural research, Vol. 2).* Shanghai, China: Shanghai Foreign Language Education Press.

Kulich, S. J. (2009c in press). Values studies: History and concepts. In S. W. Littlejohn & K. A. Foss (eds), *The encyclopedia of communication theory.* Newbury Park, CA: Sage Publications.

Kulich, S. J. & Zhu, M. (2004). Getting to the core of culture – Introducing the Shanghai Chinese Values Project (SCVP). In Y. F. Wu & Q. H. Feng (eds), *Foreign language and culture studies, Vol. 4,* (pp. 805–832). Shanghai, China: Shanghai Foreign Language Education Press.

Kulich, S. J., Zhang S. T., & Zhu, M. (2006). Global impacts on Chinese education, identity and values – Implications for intercultural training. *International Management Review, 2,* 41–59.

Lai, C. X. (1994).The modern shift of traditional Chinese values. *Jianhan Luntan, 7,* 36. (in Chinese)

Lam, S.-F., Lau, I. Y., Chiu, C.-Y., Hong, Y.-Y., & Peng, S. Q. (1999). Differential emphases on modernity and Confucian values in social categorization: The case of Hong Kong adolescents in political transition. *International Journal of Intercultural Relations, 23,* 237–256.

Lam, T. H., Stewart, S. M., Yip, P. S. F., Leuna, G. M., Ho, L. M., Ho, S. Y., & Lee, P. W. H. (2004). Suicidality and cultural values among Hong Kong adolescents. *Social Science & Medicine, 58,* 487–498.

Leung, K. (2008a). Chinese culture, modernization, and international business. *International Business Review, 17,* 184–187.

Leung, K. (2008b). Never the twain shall meet? Integrating Chinese and Western management research. *Management and Organization Review, 5,* 121–129.

Leung, K. & Bond, M. H. (2004). Social axioms: A model for social beliefs in multicultural perspective. In M. P. Zanna (ed.), *Advances in Experimental Social Psychology, Vol. 36* (pp. 119–197). New York: Academic Press.

Leung, K., Bond, M. H., Carrasquel, S. R., Munoz, C., Hernández, M., Murakami, F., Yamaguchi, S., Bierbrauer, G., & Singelis, T. M. (2002). Social axioms: The search for universal dimensions of general beliefs about how the world functions. *Journal of Cross-Cultural Psychology, 33,* 286–302.

Li, J. (2006). A survey on aesthetic value of performance artists in West China. *Arts Exploration, Journal of Guangxi Arts College, 20*(6), 124–126. (in Chinese)

Li, B. M. & Cole, G. (2003). A comparison of different learning ideas of Chinese and American college students. *Comparative Education Review, 7,* 37–45. (in Chinese)

Li, L. & Jiang, Y. N. (2007). The cross-culture study of value orientation between the Han, the Miao and the Dong college students. *Journal of Kaili University, 25,* 86–88. (in Chinese)

Li, M. L. & Yang, K. S. (2005). The psychology and behavior of *ren* (endurance). In K. S. Yang, K. K. Hwang, & C. F. Yang (eds), *Chinese indigenous psychology* (pp. 599–629). Hong Kong: Yuan Liou. (in Chinese)

Li, W. M. & Bond, M. H. (in press). Does individual secularism promote happiness? The moderating role of societal secularism. *Journal of Cross-Cultural Psychology.*

Li, Z. & Zhang, X. D. (2001). Investigation on the view of happiness of urban only-child college students. *Journal of Chongqing University, 2,* 82–85. (in Chinese)

Li, Z., Yang, Z. W., & You, B. (2002). Research on the features of nowadays female college students' view of happiness and education strategy. *Journal of Chongqing University of Posts and Telecommunications, 9,* 85–88. (in Chinese)

Li, Z. & Peng, X. L. (2000). Comparative research on the college students' happiness ideas of initiative type and contentment type. *Journal of Chongqing University, 3,* 106–109. (in Chinese)

Lin, W. Y. (2003). The role of social and personal factors in the Chinese view of education. In K. S. Yang, K. K. Hwang, P. B. Pedersen, & I. Daibo (eds), *Progress in Asian social psychology: Conceptual and empirical contributions* (pp. 111–132). Westport, CT: Praeger.

Lin. Y. T. (2000). *My country and my people.* Beijing: Foreign Language Teaching & Research Press. (Original work published 1935, New York: John Day Company)

Ling, W. Q., Fang, L. L., & Bai, L. G. (1999). A study on the vocational values of Chinese college students. *Acta Psychologica Sinica, 31,* 342–348. (in Chinese)

Linton, R. (1945). *The cultural background of personality.* New York: Appleton-Century-Crofts.

Littrell, R. F. (2002). Desirable leadership behaviours of multi-cultural managers in China. *Journal of Management Development, 21,* 5–74.

Littrell, R. F., & Montgomery, E. (in progress). *Psychometric properties of the SVS in Mainland China—An analysis and cross-cultural comparison.* Unpublished study underway, Centre for Cross-Cultural Comparisons, Auckland, New Zealand.

Liu, S. & Chen, G. M. (2002). Collaboration over avoidance: Conflict management strategies in state-owned enterprises in China. In G. M. Chen & R. Ma (eds), *Chinese conflict management and resolution* (pp. 163–182). Westport, CT: Ablex.

Liu, S., Chen, G. M., & Liu, Q. (2006). Through the lenses of organizational culture: A comparison of state-owned enterprises and joint ventures in China. *China Media Research, 2*(2), 15–24.

Liu, Y. F. & Zhong, Y. P. (1997). The psychological conception of values and analysis of its psychological activities. *Journal of Xiangtan Normal University, 5*, 84–87. (in Chinese)

Liu, Y. M. (2008). Naturalistic *chi(qi)*–based philosophy as a foundation of *chi(qi)* theory of communication. *China Media Research, 4*(3), 83–91.

Lu, L. & Yang, K. S. (2006). Emergence and composition of the traditional–modern bicultural self of people in contemporary Taiwanese societies. *Asian Journal of Social Psychology, 9*, 167–175.

Lu, X. (1998). An interface between individualistic and collectivistic orientations in Chinese cultural values and social relations. *The Howard Journal of Communications, 9*, 91–107.

Lu, X. A. (2005). Business decision-making in the public and private sectors. *China today: An encyclopedia of life in the People's Republic* (pp. 57–60). Westport, CT: Greenwood.

Luo, S. H. (2004). Statistical research on the transformation of marriage values. *Sociology Study, 2*, 37–47. (in Chinese)

Ma, J. F. (1999). Chinese value study: Features and problems. *Journal of Literature, History and Philosophy, 5*, 12–15. (in Chinese)

Ma, R. (1992). The role of unofficial intermediaries in interpersonal conflicts in the Chinese culture. *Communication Quarterly, 40*, 269–278.

Ma, R. (2004). *Guanxi* and Chinese communication behaviors. In G. M. Chen (ed.), *Theories and principles of Chinese communication* (pp. 363–377). Taipei, Taiwan: WuNan.

Ma. R. & Chuang, R. (2002). Karaoke as a form of communication in the public and interpersonal contexts of Taiwan. In X. Lu, W. Jia., & D. R. Heisey (eds), *Chinese communication studies: Contexts and comparisons.* Westport, CT: Ablex.

Ma, S., He, J., & Guo, Y. F. (2008). *Literature review on contemporary Chinese college student's values.* Unpublished manuscript, SISU Intercultural Institute, Shanghai International Studies University.

Mackerras, C. P. (1991/1999) *Western images of China (2nd ed.).* Hong Kong: Oxford University Press.

Maio, G. R. & Olson, J. M. (2000). What is a 'value-expressive' attitude? In G. R. Maio and J. M. Olson (eds), *Why we evaluate: Functions of attitudes* (pp. 97–131). Mahwah, NJ: Lawrence Erlbaum.

Malinowski, B. (1944). *A scientific theory of culture.* New York: Galaxy Books.

Markus, H. & Nurius, P. (1986). Possible selves. *American Psychologist, 41*, 954–969.

McGuire, W. J. (1983). A contextualist theory of knowledge: Is implications for innovation and reform in psychological research. In L. Berkowitz (ed.), *Advances in experimental social psychology, Vol. 16* (pp. 2–47). San Deigo, CA: Academic Press.

Meng, D. F. (2002). On the political value orientation of graduate students. *Journal of Hebei Youth Administration Cadres College, 56*, 21–23. (in Chinese)

Meng, X. D. (2006) The Investigation on work values of the college graduating students in Beijing. *Population and Economy, 1*, 41–47. (in Chinese)

Miike, Y. (2009). 'Cherishing the old to know the new': A bibliography of Asian communication studies. *China Media Research, 5*(1), 95–103.

Miike, Y. & Chen, G. M. (2006). Perspectives on Asian cultures and communication: An updated bibliography. *China Media Research, 2*(1), 98–106.

Min, T. X., Deng, D. Y., Zhang, L., & Wang, X. M. (2008). Hofstede's influence and applications in China. In S. J. Kulich (ed.), *Intercultural values and core culture studies: A student sourcebook: Volume 2 (Chinese studies)* (pp. 111–156). Shanghai, China: The SISU Intercultural Institute.

Montgomery, E. (2006). *Fire on the lake: Chinese urban micro-business owner-managers: Values and perspectives on international development ethics.* Unpublished doctoral dissertation, Fielding Graduate University, Santa Barbara, California.

Morris, C. W. (1956). *Varieties of human value.* Chicago, IL: University of Chicago Press.

Muenchmeier, R. (2007). Studying youth in Germany: The 13th Shell youth study. In Hegasy, S. & Kaschl, E. (eds), *Changing values among youth: Examples from the Arab World and Germany. ZMO-Studien 22*, (pp. 153–154). Berlin: Klaus Schwarz Verlag.

Myers, S. A. & Zhong, M. (2004). Perceived Chinese instructor use of affinity-seeking strategies and Chinese college student motivation. *Journal of Intercultural Communication Research, 33*, 119–130.

Myers, S. A., Zhong, M., & Guan, S. (1998). Instructor immediacy in the Chinese college classroom. *Communication Studies, 49*, 240–254.

Myers, S. A., Zhong, M., & Mitchell, W. (1995). The use of interpersonal communication motives in conflict resolution among romantic partners. *Ohio Speech Journal, 33*, 1–20.

Ning, W. W. (1996a). Values: new perspectives in psychology. *Journal of Southwest China Normal University, 2*, 70–76. (in Chinese)

Ning, W. W. (1996b). Study on urban Chinese youth's work values. *Journal of Chengdu University, 4*, 10–12. (in Chinese)

Oyserman, D., Coon, H. M., & Kemmelmier, M. (2002). Rethinking individualism and collectivism: Evaluation of theoretical assumptions and meta-analysis. *Psychological Bulletin, 128*, 3–72.

Ouyang, X. M. (2002). A review and comment on the studies about the Chinese social behavior orientation, *Journal of Jiujiang Teacher's College (Philosophy and Social Science Edition), 2*, 48–51. (in Chinese)

Parsons, T. & Shils, E. (eds) (1951). *Toward a general theory of action.* Cambridge, MA: Harvard University Press.

Parsons, T., Bales, R. F., & Shils, E. (1953). *Working papers in the theory of action.* Glencoe, IL: Free Press.

Peng, S. Q. (2001). *Guanxi*-management and legal approaches to establish and enhance interpersonal trust, *Journal of Psychology in Chinese Societies, 2*, 51–76.

Powers, J. (2000). Bibliography on Chinese communication theory and research. Retrieved on March 12, 2009, from http://www.hkbu.edu.hk/~jpowers/ references.html

Pyszczynski, T., Greenberg, J., & Goldenberg, J. L. (2003). Freedom versus fear: On the defence, growth, and expansion of the self. In M. R. Leary & J. P. Tangney (eds), *Handbook of self and identity* (pp. 314–343). New York: Guilford Press.

Roccas, S., Sagiv, L., Schwartz, S. H., & Knafo, A. (2002). The big five personality factors and personal values. *Personality and Social Psychology Bulletin, 28*, 789–801.

Rohan, M. J. (2000). A rose by any name? The values construct. *Personality and Social Psychology Review, 4*, 255–277.

Rozin, P. (2003). Five potential principles for understanding cultural differences in relation to individual differences. *Journal of Research in Personality, 37*, 273–283.

Rokeach, M. (1968). *Beliefs, attitudes and values.* San Francisco, CA: Jossey-Bass.

Rokeach, M. (1973). *The nature of human values.* New York: Free Press.

Rokeach, M., Smith, P. W., & Evans, R. I. (1960). Two kinds of prejudice or one? In M. Rokeach (ed.), *The open and closed mind* (pp. 132–168). New York: Basic Books.

Rokeach, M. & Rothman, G. (1965). The principle of belief congruence and the congruity principle as models of cognitive interaction. *Psychological Review, 72*, 128–142.

Rokeach, M. & Mezei, L. (1966). Race and shared belief as factors in social choice, *Science, 151*, 167–172.

Ros, M., Schwartz, S. H., & Surkis, S. (1999). Basic individual values, work values, and the meaning of work. *Applied Psychology: An International Review, 48*, 49–71.

Russell, B. A. W. (1922). *The problem of China.* London: George Allen & Unwin.

Sagiv, L. & Schwartz, S. H. (2000). Value priorities and subjective well-being: Direct relations and congruity effects. European *Journal of Social Psychology, 30*, 177–198.

Sandel, T. L. (2002). Kinship address: Socializing young children in Taiwan. *Western Journal of Communication, 66*, 257–280.

Sandel, T. L. (2004). Narrated relationships: Mothers-in-law and daughters-in-law justifying conflicts in Taiwan's Chhan-chng. *Research on Language and Social Interaction, 37*, 365–398.

Sandel, T., L., Cho, G.. E., Miller. P. J., & Wang, S. H. (2006). What it means to be a grandmother: A cross-cultural study of Taiwanese and Euro-American grandmothers' beliefs. *Journal of Family Communication, 6*, 255–278.

Sandel, T. L., Liang, C. H., & Chao, W. Y. (2006). Language shift and language accommodation across family generations in Taiwan. *Journal of Multilingual and Multicultural Development 27*, 126–147.

Schramm, W. (ed.) (1953). *The process and effects of mass communication.* Urbana, IL: University of Illinois Press.

Schramm, W. (1964). *Mass media and national development.* Stanford, CA: Stanford University Press.

Schwartz, S. H. (1992). Universals in the content and structure of values: Theoretical advances and empirical tests in 20 countries. *Advances in experimental social psychology, Vol. 25*, (pp. 1–65). New York: Academic Press.

Schwartz, S. H. (1994a). Are there universals in the content and structure of values? *Journal of Social Issues, 50*, 19–45.

Schwartz, S. H. (1994b). Beyond individualism/collectivism: New cultural dimensions of values. In U. Kim, H. C. Triandis, Ç. Kağıtçıbaşı, S.-C. Choi, & G. Yoon (eds), *Individualism and collectivism: Theory, method, and applications* (pp. 85–119). Thousand Oaks, CA: Sage.

Schwartz, S. H. (1996). Value priorities and behavior: Applying a theory of integrated value systems. In C. Seligman, J. M. Olson, & M. P. Zanna (eds), *The psychology of values: The Ontario symposium, Vol. 8* (pp. 1–24). Hillsdale, NJ: Erlbaum.

Schwartz, S. H. (1999). A theory of culture values and some implications for work. *Applied Psychology: An International Review, 48*, 23– 47.

Schwartz, S. H. (2005a). Basic human values: Their content and structure across cultures. In A. Tamayo & J. B. Porto (eds), *Valores e comportamento nas organizationes [Values and behavior in organizations]* (pp. 21–55). Petropolis, Brazil: Vozes. (in Portuguese)

Schwartz, S. H. (2005b). Robustness and fruitfulness of a theory of universals in individual human values. In A. Tamayo & J. B. Porto (eds), Valores e comportamento nas organizationes [Values and behavior in organizations] (pp. 56–95). Petropolis, Brazil: Vozes. (in Portuguese)

Schwartz, S. H. (2006a). A theory of cultural value orientations: Explication and applications. *Comparative Sociology, 5*, 137–182.

Schwartz, S. H. (2006b). Value orientations: Measurement, antecedents and consequences across nations. In R. Jowell, C. Roberts, R. Fitzgerald, & G. Eva (eds), *Measuring attitudes cross-nationally—Lessons from the European Social Survey.* London: Sage.

Schwartz, S. H. (2008). *Cultural value orientations: Nature and implications of national differences.* Moscow: Moscow State University Higher School of Economics Press.

Schwartz, S. H. & Bardi, A. (2001). Values hierarchies across cultures: Taking a similarities perspective. *Journal of Cross-Cultural Psychology, 32*, 268–290.

Schwartz, S. H. & Bilsky, W. (1987). Toward a universal psychological structure of human values. *Journal of Personality and Social Psychology, 53*, 550–562.

Schwartz, S. H. & Sagie, G. (2000). Value consensus and importance: A cross-national study. *Journal of Cross-Cultural Psychology, 31*, 465–497.

Schwartz, S. H. & Sagiv, L. (1995). Identifying culture specifics in the content and structure of values. *Journal of Cross-Cultural Psychology, 26*, 92–116.

Schwartz, S. H., Melech, G., Lehmann, A., Burgess, S., & Harris, M. (2001). Extending the cross-cultural validity of the theory of basic human values with a different method of measurement. *Journal of Cross-Cultural Psychology, 32*, 519–542.

Seligman, C. & Katz, A. N. (1996). The dynamics of value systems. In C. Seligman, J. M. Olson, & M. P. Zanna (eds), *The Ontario symposium: The psychology of values* (Vol. 8, pp. 53–75). Mahwah, NJ: Lawrence Erlbaum Associates, Inc.

Seligman, C., Olson, J. M., & Zanna, M. P. (eds) (1996). *The Ontario symposium: The psychology of values (Vol. 8)*. Mahwah, NJ: Lawrence Erlbaum Associates, Inc.

Sha, L. X. (ed.) (1992). *National character of China*. Beijing: Renmin University Press. (Overseas edition 2000, Hong Kong: Joint Publishing House).

Sha, L. X. (ed.) (2000). *One hundred years of the Chinese: Person and personality*. Beijing: Xinhua Press. (Overseas edition 2003, Hong Kong: Joint Publishing House)

Shen, J. J. (2005). On the psychological meaning of values and its nature. *Journal of Xinyu College, 1*, 99–102. (in Chinese)

Shen, J. (2007). *Ranges of traditionality and modernity: A study on Chinese values of Shanghai college students in the global context*. Unpublished master's thesis, Shanghai International Studies University, Shanghai, China.

Shi, C. H. (1997). Research on university students' value orientation and psychological health. *China Psychology Health, 5*, 291. (in Chinese)

Shi, X. (2005). *A cultural approach to discourse. Houndsmills, UK: Palgrave Press—Macmillan.*

Shteynberg, G., Gelfand, M. J., & Kim, K. (2009). Peering into the 'magnum mysterium' of culture: The explanatory power of descriptive norms. *Journal of Cross-Cultural Psychology, 40*, 46–69.

Smith, A. H. (1984). *Chinese characteristics*. New York: Revell. (*Original work published 1890, Shanghai: North China Herald*)

Smith, M. B. (1969). *Social psychology and human values: Selected essays*. Chicago, IL: Aldine.

Smith, P. B. (2002). Levels of analysis in cross-cultural psychology. In W. J. Lonner, D. L. Dinnel, S. A. Hayes, & D. N. Sattler (eds), *Online readings in psychology and culture* (Unit 2, Chapter 7), (http://www.wwu.edu/~culture), Center for Cross-Cultural Research, Western Washington University, Bellingham, Washington USA

Smith, P. B., Bond, M. H., & Kağıtçıbaşı, Ç. (2006). *Understanding social psychology across cultures: Living and working in a changing world*. London: Sage.

Spates, J. L. (1983). The sociology of values. *Annual Review of Sociology, 9*, 27–49.

Spence, J. D. (1998). *The Chan's great continent: China in western minds*. New York: W. W. Norton.

Starosta, W. (2008). Thoughts on *qi*. *China Media Research, 4*(3), 107–109.

Stewart, S. (1995). The ethics of values and the value of ethics: Should we be studying business values in Hong Kong? In Stewart, S. & Donleavy, G. (eds), *Whose business values? Some Asian and cross-cultural perspective* (pp. 1–18). Hong Kong: Hong Kong University Press.

Super, D. E. (1949). *Appraising vocational fitness*. New York: Harper.

Super, D. E. (1957). *The psychology of careers: An introduction to vocational development*. New York: Harper & Row.

Super, D. E. (1970). *Manual for the work values inventory*. Boston, MA: Houghton Mifflin.

Tang, P. & Chen, Z. L. (2007). A statistical study on Chinese undergraduates' values of individualism /collectivism. *Journal of Sichuan College of Education, 5*, 11–15. (in Chinese)

Tönnies, F. (1957). *Community and association* (C. P. Loomis, Trans.). New York: Harper Torchbooks (Original work published 1887).

Tu, W. M. (ed.). (1995). *The living tree: The changing meaning of being Chinese today*. Palo Alto, CA: Stanford University Press.

Tu, W. M. (2000). Multiple modernities: A preliminary inquiry into the implications of East Asian modernity. In L. E. Harrison & S. P. Huntington (eds), *Culture matters: How values shape human process*, (pp. 256–267). New York: Basic Books.

Tu, W. M. & Huang, W. S. (2005). The modern meaning of traditional Chinese values: A dialogue between Du Weiming and Huang Wansheng (excerpt). *Seeking Truth, 32*(4), 28–34. (in Chinese)

Vansteenkiste, M., Duriez, B., Simons, J., & Soenens, B. (2006). Materialistic values and well-being among business students: Further evidence of their detrimental effect. *Journal of Applied Social Psychology, 36*, 2892–2908.

Wan, C., Chiu, C.-Y., Tam, K.-P., Lee, S.-L., Lau, I. Y.-M., & Peng, S. (2007). Perceived cultural importance and actual self-importance of values in cultural identification. *Journal of Personality and Social Psychology, 92*, 337–354.

Wan, M. G. (1994). Values and intercultural studies. *Social Sciences Abroad, 7*, 7–10.

Wang, C. H. (2005). Introduction: Minds of the nineties. In C. H. Wang (ed.), *One China, many paths* (pp. 9–16). London: Verso.

Wang, C. K. (2005). Chinese values research. In K. S. Yang, K. K. Hwang, & C. F. Yang (eds), *Chinese indigenous psychology* (pp. 633–664). Hong Kong: Yuan Liou. (in Chinese)

Wang, K., Yan, Q., & Yu, W. (2008). *Literature review of traditional Chinese values*. Unpublished manuscript, SISU Intercultural Institute, Shanghai International Studies University.

Wang, P. & Zhang, K. Y. (2006). An experimental study of college students' knowledge values. *Psychological Exploration, 99*, 58–64. (in Chinese)

Wang, X. M., Chen, J., & Zhang, L. (2008). Internet-related value studies in China: Zooming in on the impact of the internet on the value orientation of college students. Unpublished manuscript, SISU Intercultural Institute, Shanghai International Studies University.

Wang, M. (2004). An ethnographic study of friendship in China: Do old values still hold true? Paper presented at National Communication Association annual convention, Chicago, IL, November.

Wang, S. H.-Y. & Chang, H.-C. (1999). Chinese professionals' perceptions of interpersonal communication in corporate America: A multidimensional scaling analysis. *Howard Journal of Communication, 10*, 297–315.

Wei, Y. (2006). Definitions, features and structural character of value judgment. *Chinese Journal of Clinical Rehabilitation, 18*, 161–163. (in Chinese)

Wen, Q. Y. (1989). *Chinese People's Values.* Taiwan, Taipei: Dongda Publishing Co.

Weng, L. P. (2008). Revisiting Chinese values through self-generated proverbs and sayings. *Intercultural Communication Studies, 17*, 107–121.

Weng, L. P. & Kulich, S. J. (2009). Toward developing a master list of value-laden Chinese proverbs and sayings. *China Media Research, 5*(1), 68–80.

Wu, L. H. (2003). On individualism and collectivism in cross-cultural psychology. *Journal of Hunan First Teacher's College, 1*, 73–75. (in Chinese)

Wu. Y. (2005). The research toward modal [social stratification of Chinese consumers] of China-Vals. *Nankai Business Review, 8*, 9–15. (in Chinese)

Xia, Y. (2006). Cultural values, communication styles, and the use of mobile communication in China. *China Media Research, 2*(2), 64–73.

Xiao, Q. Z. (2002). *Filial piety in Chinese culture.* Taipei, Taiwan: Wunan Book Inc. (in Chinese)

Xiao, S. Y. & Yang, D. S. (2002). Chinese traditional value and its measurement: Theoretical assumptions. *Chinese Journal of Behavioral Medical Science, 11*, 347–349.

Xiao, X. (1996). From the hierarchical *ren* to egalitarianism: A case study of cross-cultural rhetorical mediation. *Quarterly Journal of Speech, 82*, 38–54.

Xiao, X. (2002). *Li*: A dynamic cultural mechanism of social interaction and conflict management. In G. M. Chen & R. Ma (eds), *Chinese conflict management and resolution* (pp. 39–49). Westport, CT: Ablex.

Xiao, X. (2003). *Zhong* (centrality): an everlasting subject of Chinese discourse. *Intercultural Communication Studies, 12*, 127–149.

Xie, H. L. (1987). Chinese university student's evaluation of ways to live. *Beijing Normal University Journal* (Social Science Edition), *2*, 89–96. (in Chinese)

Xin, Z. Y. & Jin, S. H. (2005). College students' value orientation and values education in the new era. *Educational Research, 10*, 22–27. (in Chinese)

Xin, Z. Y. & Jin, S. H. (2006). College students' concept and structure of values. *Journal of Higher Education, 27*, 85–92. (in Chinese)

Xu, X. X. (2005). Society, market and values: Signs of the whole change – Second research on changes in Chinese social structure as seen from occupational prestige and job preferences. *Sociological Research, 23*, 82–119. (In Chinese).

Xu, Y. & Wang, L. S. (2001). Comparative study on values of college students in Beijing and Hong Kong. *Psychological Exploration, 21*, 40–45. (in Chinese)

Xu, Y., Liu, J., Jiang, J., Wang, F., Zheng, Y. Z., & Fu, T. (2004). Influences of SARS outbreak on values of college students. *Psychological Exploration, 24*, 35–39. (in Chinese)

Xu, B. & Yang, Y. Y. (1999). A glance at life values of college students. Retrieved March 6, 2008, from http://www.sociology.cass.cn/shxw/shxlx/p02004 0413583455783534.pdf (in Chinese)

Xu, Z. & Ding, Y. H. (2006).The comparative analysis of aesthetic value and leisure value of Chinese primary and middle school teachers. *Modern Primary and Middle School Education, 9*, 7–10. (in Chinese)

Xu, Z. & Zhou, M. M. (2006). The comparative analysis of aesthetic value and leisure value of Chinese university teachers. *Journal of Changchun University of Technology, 27*, 36–39. (in Chinese)

Yan, J. W., Luo, W., Jin, Y. B., & Xu, Y. (2004). The transformation of family values and its effects on population and society based on a survey conducted in Ningbo. *Journal of Ningbo Institute of Education, 1*, 60–63. (in Chinese)

Yang, C. F. (1999). The conceptualization of interpersonal relationship and sentiment. *Indigenous Psychological Research in Chinese Societies, 12*, 105–179. (in Chinese)

Yang, C. F. (2006). The Chinese conception of the self: Toward a person-making perspective. In U. Kim, K. S. Yang, & K. K. Hwang (eds), *Indigenous and cultural psychology: Understanding people in context* (pp. 327–356). New York: Springer Science+Business Media, LLC.

Yang, C. F. & Peng, S. Q. (2005). *Renqing* and *guanxi* in interpersonal interaction. In K. S. Yang, K. K. Hwang, & C. F. Yang (eds), *Chinese indigenous psychology* (pp. 483–519). Hong Kong: Yuan Liou. (in Chinese)

Yang, K. S. (1972). Expressed values of Chinese college students. In Y. Y. Li & K. S. Yang (eds), *Symposium on the character of the Chinese: An interdisciplinary approach* (pp. 257–312). Taipei, Taiwan: Institute of Ethnology, Academia Sinica. (in Chinese)

Yang, K. S. (1982). The Sinicization of psychological research in Chinese society: Directions and issues. In K. S. Yang & C. I. Wen (eds), *The Sinicization of social and behavioral science research in Chinese societies* (pp. 153–187). Taipei, Taiwan: Institute of Ethnology, Academia Sinica. (in Chinese)

Yang, K. S. (1986). Chinese personality and its change. In M. H. Bond (ed.), *The psychology of the Chinese people* (pp. 106–170). Hong Kong: Oxford University Press.
Yang, K. S. (1988a). Chinese filial piety: A conceptual analysis. In K. S. Yang (ed.), *The metamorphosis of the Chinese people* (pp. 31–64). Taipei, Taiwan. Laureate Publishing Co.
Yang, K. S. (1988b). The concept of Chinese filial piety. In K. S. Yang (ed.), *Chinese Psychology* (pp. 39–73). Taipei, Taiwan: Laurel Publishing Inc. (in Chinese)
Yang, K. S. (1988c). Will societal modernization eventually eliminate cross-cultural psychological differences? In M. H. Bond (ed.), *The cross-cultural challenge to social psychology* (pp. 67–85). Beverly Hills, CA: Sage.
Yang, K. S. (ed.) (1994). *The values of Chinese people: Social science perspectives.* Taipei, Taiwan: Laurel Publishing Co. (in Chinese)
Yang, K. S. (1996). Psychological transformation of the Chinese people as a result of societal modernization. In M. H. Bond (ed.). *The handbook of Chinese psychology* (pp. 479–498). Hong Kong: Oxford University Press.
Yang, K. S. (1998). Chinese responses to modernization: A psychological analysis. *Asian Journal of Social Psychology, 1*, 75–97.
Yang, K. S. (2000). Monocultural and cross-cultural indigenous approaches: The royal road to the development of a balanced global human psychology. *Asian Journal of Social Psychology, 3*, 241–264.
Yang, K. S. (2003). Methodological and theoretical issues on psychological traditionality and modernity research in an Asian society: In response to Kwang-Kuo Hwang and beyond. *Asian Journal of Social Psychology, 6*, 263–285.
Yang, K. S. (2004). *The psychology and behavior of the Chinese people: Indigenous research.* Beijing, China: Chinese People's University Press. (in Chinese)
Yang, K. S. (2005). *Yuan* in interpersonal relationships. In K. S. Yang, K. K. Hwang, & C. F. Yang (eds), *Chinese indigenous psychology* (pp. 567–597). Hong Kong: Yuan Liou. (in Chinese)
Yang, K. S. (2006). Indigenous personality research: The Chinese case. In U. Kim, K. S. Yang, & K. K. Hwang (eds), *Indigenous and cultural psychology: Understanding people in context* (pp. 285–314). New York: Springer Science+Business Media, LLC.
Yang, K. S. & Ho, D. Y. F. (1988). The role of *yuan* in Chinese social life: A conceptual and empirical analysis. In A. C. Parangpe, D. Y. F. Ho, & R. W. Rieber (eds), *Asian contributions to psychology* (pp. 263–81). New York: Praeger.
Yang, K. S. & Lu, L. (2005). Social- and individual-oriented self-actualizers: Conceptual analysis and empirical assessment of their psychological characteristics. *Indigenous Psychological Research in Chinese Societies, 23*, 71–143. (in Chinese)
Yang, K. S. & Ye, M. H. (2005). Familism and pan-familism. In K. S. Yang, K. K. Hwang, & C. F. Yang (eds), *Chinese indigenous psychology* (pp. 249–292). Hong Kong: Yuan Liou. (in Chinese)
Yang, S. G. (2004). From moral relativism to core values: Psychological considerations about the reorientation of school moral education. *Educational Research, 1*, 32–37. (in Chinese)
Yang, Y. Y. (1998a). Values in social psychology. *Social Sciences in China, 2*, 82–93. (in Chinese)
Yang, Y. Y. (1998b). Self and other conceptions: A culture value orientation perspective. *Social Sciences Abroad, 6*, 24–28. (in Chinese)
Yang, Y. Y. (2001). Social change and psychological change: A review of Kuo-Shu Yang's research on Chinese individual modernity. *Journal of Social Psychology, 3*, 36–49. (in Chinese)
Yao, B. X. & He, Y. Q. (2007). On the present situation, problems and tendency in the study of university students' outlook on life. *Journal Liaoning Normal University, 1*, 56–60. (in Chinese)
Yao, G. J. & Huang, X. T. (2006). The nature of cross-cultural psychology. *Journal of Western China Normal University, 1*, 104–108. (in Chinese)
Yao, T. I. (2008). The dialectic relations among *Li* (noumenon), *Chi* (energy) and *Shih* (position) in organizational communication. *China Media Research, 4*(3), 101–106.
Ye, S. Q. (2006). Contemporary adolescent value shifts: Characteristics and influential factors. *Youth Studies, 2006, 12*, 1–9. (in Chinese)
Ye, S. Q. (2007a). Values of female middle school students: Status quo and characteristics. *Journal of Guangxi Youth Leaders College, 1*, 11–14. (in Chinese)
Ye, S. Q. (2007b). Adolescents' outlook on morality in today: Investigation and possible countermeasures. *Journal of Shandong Youth Administrative Cadres College, 5*, 20–25. (in Chinese)
Yeh, K. H. (2003). The beneficial and harmful effects of filial piety: An integrative analysis. In K. S. Yang, K. K. Hwang, P. B. Pedersen, & I. Daibo (eds), *Progress in Asian social psychology: Conceptual and empirical contributions* (pp. 67–82). Westport, CT: Praeger Publishers.
Yeh, K. H. & Bedford, O. (2003). A test of the dual filial piety model. *Asian Journal of Social Psychology, 6*, 215–228.
Yeh, K. H. & Bedford, O. (2004). Filial belief and parent–child conflict. *International Journal of Psychology, 29*, 132–144.
Yu, A. B. (1996). Ultimate life concerns, self, and Chinese achievement motivation. In M. H. Bond (ed.), *The handbook of Chinese psychology* (pp. 227–246). Hong Kong: Oxford University Press.
Yu, A. B. (2005). Achievement motivation and the concept of achievement: A Chinese cultural psychological investigation. In K. S. Yang, K. K. Hwang, & C. F. Yang (eds), *Chinese indigenous psychology* (pp. 663–711). Hong Kong: Yuan Liou. (in Chinese)
Yu, X. (1997–8). The Chinese native perspective on *Mao-dun* (conflict) and *Mao-dun* (resolution) strategies: A qualitative investigation. *Intercultural Communication Studies, 7*, 63–82.

Yu. X. (2000). Examining the impact of cultural values and cultural assumptions on motivational factors in the Chinese organizational context: A cross-cultural perspective. In D. R. Heisey (ed.), *Chinese perspectives in rhetoric and communication* (pp. 119–138). Stamford, CT: Ablex.

Yu, X. (2002). Conflict resolution strategies in state-owned enterprises in China. In G. M. Chen & R. Ma (eds), *Chinese conflict management and resolution* (pp. 183–201). Westport, CT: Ablex.

Yu, Z. H., Teng, H. C., Dai, H. Q., & Hu, Z. J. (2004). A study on the vocational values of Chinese postgraduate students. *Chinese Journal of Applied Psychology, 10*(3), 37–40. (in Chinese)

Yuan, A. & Qian, P. (2008). *Current values studies from the perspective of 'filial piety' in Mainland China.* Unpublished manuscript. SISU Intercultural Institute, Shanghai International Studies University.

Zeng, Y. D. (2004). On the impact of values conflict on psychological health. *Journal of Western Chongqing University, 4,* 91–92. (in Chinese)

Zhai, X. W. (1999). The value orientations of Chinese: Types, shifts and other issues. *Journal of Nanjing University (Philosophy, Humanities and Social Sciences), 4,* 118–126. (in Chinese)

Zhai, X. W. (2005). *Renqing, mianzi, and the reproduction of power.* Beijing, China: Beijing University Press. (in Chinese)

Zhai, X. W. & Qu, Y. (2001). The Chinese values: consistency and conflict between tradition and modernity. *Jiangsu Sociological Study, 4,* 136–142. (in Chinese)

Zhang, P. Y. & Lv, C. Z. (2004). Psychological thoughts about value education. *Truth Seeking, 2,* 82–85. (in Chinese)

Zhang, J. F. (1998). An investigation of characteristics of life values of college students in China. *Psychological Development and Education, 2,* 26–31. (in Chinese)

Zhang, J. F. & Zhang, Z. Y. (2001). A study on the traditional life values in Chinese college students. *Journal of Southwest China Normal University (Philosophy & Social Sciences Edition), 27,* 44–49. (in Chinese)

Zhang, J. F. & Zhao, Y. P. (2006). A study on the difference of values between middle school students and their parents in Chongqing. *Psychological Science, 29,* 1222–1225. (in Chinese)

Zhang, R. (2006). *Multiple modernities: A comparative study on styles of managing interpersonal conflicts between American and Chinese university students.* Unpublished master's thesis, Shanghai International Studies University, Shanghai, People's Republic of China.

Zhang, S. T. & Kulich, S. J. (2008). Analyzing Chinese identity today: New insights into identity rankings of young adults in urban China. In D. Y. F. Wu (ed.), *Discourses of cultural China in the globalizing age,* (pp. 205–232). Hong Kong: Hong Kong University Press.

Zhang, X., Zheng, X., & Wang, L. (2003). Comparative research on individual modernity of adolescents between town and countryside in China. *Asian Journal of Social Psychology, 6,* 61–73.

Zhang, X. F. & You M. H. (2000). Exploring the college students' view of happiness. *Journal of Chongqing Post College (Social Science), 1,* 54–59. (in Chinese)

Zhang, Z. X. (2006). Chinese conceptions of justice and reward allocation. In U. Kim, K. S. Yang, & K. K. Hwang (eds), *Indigenous and cultural psychology: Understanding people in context* (pp. 403–420). New York: Springer Science+Business Media, LLC.

Zhang, Z. X. & Yang, C. F. (1998). Beyond distributive justice: The reasonableness norm in Chinese reward allocation, *Asian Journal of Social Psychology,* 1, 253–269.

Zhao, J., Rong, M., Ye, R. G., & Li, X. (2007). Idealization existing with popularization, inheritance existing with transformation: A survey on the contemporary adolescent values in Anhui Province. *Journal of Shanxi College for Youth Administrators, 2,* 26–29. (in Chinese)

Zhao, Y. F. & Bi, Z. Z. (2004). On psychological study of education values. *Journal of Southwest China Normal University, 2,* 44–47. (in Chinese)

Zheng, J. & Yan, L. (2005). A summary of work values study. *Human Resource Development of China, 11,* 11–16. (in Chinese)

Zhong, M. (2005). The only-child declaration: A content analysis of published stories by China's only-children. *Intercultural Communication Studies, 14,* 9–27.

Zhong, M., Myers, S., & Buerkel, R. (2004). Communication and intergenerational differences between Chinese fathers and sons. *Journal of Intercultural Communication Research, 33,* 15–27.

Zhou, C. X. & Peng, G. M. (2003). The analysis of the media impacts on consumption values of contemporary undergraduates. *Statistics & Decision, 6,* 62–64. (in Chinese)

Zhou, H., Zeng, X. Y., & Zhao, H. P. (2005). Research comparatively on the economic value of the western and the eastern college students in contemporary China. *Journal of Hebei Institute of Architectural Science and Technology (Social Science Edition), 22,* 127–129. (in Chinese)

Zhou, Z. R. (2008). *The relationship between parenting and individual depression – Social withdrawal as a mediator.* Unpublished master's thesis, Shanghai International Studies University, Shanghai, People's Republic of China.

Zhu, L. Y. (1995) Sociological Analysis on values of present day high educated women: Research and analysis of a sample of high educated women. *Journal of Huazhong University of Science and Technology (Edition of Social Sciences), 1,* 107–110. (in Chinese)

Zhu, Q. S. & Chen, W. Z. (2006).A survey of the concept of value among Chinese employees and managers in the economic transformation. *Journal of Sichuan University (Social Science Edition), 142,* 19–23. (in Chinese)

Zhu, X. Y. (1998). A comparison of the marriage and family values between Chinese and American women. *Collection of Women's Studies, 2,* 32–35. (in Chinese)

CHAPTER 17

What do we know about the Chinese self? Illustrations with self-esteem, self-efficacy, and self-enhancement

Virginia S. Y. Kwan, Chin-Ming Hui, and James A. McGee

The ancient Greek aphorism, 'Know thyself,' represents one of the most fundamental quests for humanity. Scholars of fields as diverse as biology, psychology, philosophy, anthropology, and theology have sought to achieve a greater understanding of the nature of the self. Since its first appearance in psychology, the self has become the most studied topic in Western research on psychology.

However, the subject has been slower to develop a research tradition in the East. For example, the first edition of *The Oxford handbook of Chinese psychology* (Bond, 1996) did not include a chapter on the subject of the Chinese self. This is not entirely surprising, as it underscores the relative paucity of studies on the self in Asian culture. There are many reasons for this state of affairs. One likely reason is the differing conception of the self in Asian (typically collectivistic) cultures. This alternate conception may affect research on the self not only in the way the subject matter is addressed, but also in the relative emphasis placed on self-related psychological research.

Therefore, a central issue we aim to address in this chapter is, 'What do we know about the Chinese self?' First, to address this issue, we take a bottom-up approach to review the literature relevant to the self within a Chinese context. Second, we identify the recurring themes among the topics on the self by assessing the frequency of their appearance in the literature. There are many topics relevant to the study of self-processes. In this chapter, we can focus on only a few. We discuss three widely explored and central self-processes: self-esteem, self-efficacy, and self-enhancement. Finally, we identify emerging topics and discuss future directions for research on the self. Our goal is to generate continued interest and enthusiasm for research on the value of self-processes among Chinese.

Self-esteem

Self-esteem, the degree to which we feel good about ourselves, is the most frequently studied psychological construct in the West (see Baumeister, Campbell, Krueger, & Vohs, 2003; Kwan & Mandisodza, 2007). As many Chinese psychologists have received their training in the West, it is not surprising that self-esteem is also the most frequently studied self-process in Chinese culture. Given the popularity of self-esteem in the literature and the breadth of the relevant research questions, we are going to discuss self-esteem by addressing three major questions: (a) do the Chinese have high or low self-esteem? (b) what are the conditions that foster self-esteem for Chinese individuals? (c) what is the importance of self-esteem in Chinese culture?

To address these three questions, we have reviewed the relevant articles that we could find published in peer-reviewed journals before August, 2007. To be included in this review, an article had to have the key word 'self-esteem' coupled with any of the following key words, 'China', 'Chinese', 'Hong Kong', 'Taiwan', 'Taiwanese', 'Singapore', or 'Singaporean,' as listed in the PsycInfo database.[1] Additionally, we focused on articles about self-esteem that examined non-clinical populations. We could not locate 15 of the 134 articles, leaving 119 articles for subsequent analysis. Below we summarize what we have learned from these articles.

Do the Chinese have high self-esteem?

Twenty studies involve cross-cultural comparisons between Chinese and at least one other cultural group. Thirteen of the 20 studies compared the self-esteem level between Chinese and individuals in the West. The majority of these studies (nine out of 13) showed that Chinese report lower global self-esteem (e.g. Chung & Mallery, 1999; Singelis, Bond, Sharkey, & Lai, 1999), and lower self-esteem in the domains of decision making (e.g. Mann et al., 1998), verbal skills, parent relations, honesty, and general self-esteem at school (Rogers, 1998) than their Western counterparts. These studies suggest that Chinese have low self-esteem compared to Westerners.[2]

There are two exceptions to the general findings that Chinese have low self-esteem. The first exception is that Chinese report higher academic self-esteem in mathematics than do their Western counterparts (Rogers, 1998; Watkins, Akande, Cheng, & Regmi, 1996). One possible explanation for this finding is that Chinese students derive their academic self-esteem from their school performance. Indeed, Chinese students tend to perform well in academics compared to students in the West (Stevenson & Lee, 1996). Another possibility is that Chinese culture places heavy importance on academic performance (Sue & Okazaki, 1990), and this cultural imperative may lead to the reported high levels of academic self-esteem (see also Hau, this volume).

The second exception is that Chinese have higher levels of self-liking than their Western counterparts. Self-liking is the affective dimension of self-esteem, stemming from our interpretations of the evaluative reactions of others in social exchanges (Tafarodi & Swann, 1996). While it is not entirely founded upon the perceptions of others, it is a socially-mediated aspect of self-esteem (Tafarodi & Swann, 2001). The social nature of self-liking may be of particular importance for collectivistic Chinese culture, and may constitute a fruitful direction for future research (Schmitt & Allik, 2005).

Next, we reviewed comparisons of the self-esteem levels between Chinese immigrants or sojourners and Western hosts. There is evidence showing that Chinese-Americans have lower self-esteem than do European-Americans (e.g. Huntsinger & Jose, 2006). However, most studies that we found show Chinese immigrants to report a comparable level of self-esteem to individuals in the host country, such as Russians (Galchenko & van de Vijver, 2007), White British (Chan, 2000), and Mexican-Americans (Kiang, Yip, Gonzales-Backen, Witkow, & Fuligni, 2006). These findings are in line with previous research showing that an individual's self-esteem changes in the direction of that which characterizes members of the host culture. For example, Japanese exchange students staying in Canada demonstrated an increase in self-esteem, whereas Canadian exchange students traveling to Japan showed a decrease in self-esteem (Heine & Lehman, 2004). The changes in self-concepts for sojourners and immigrants may be explained by acculturation or self-selection effects, or both (see Kitayama, Ishii, Ishii, Imada, Takemura, & Ramaswamy, 2006).

Do Chinese have higher self-esteem than other Asian groups? Two of the five studies on this topic found that Chinese report a higher level of global self-esteem than Vietnamese (Nesdale, 2002) and Japanese (Bond & Cheung, 1983). The other studies show comparable levels of global self-esteem between exchange students from PRC and from Korea in Russia (Galchenko & van de Vijver, 2007) and among PRC Chinese, Koreans, and Asian-Americans (Kang, Shaver, Sue, Min, & Jing, 2003), and also show similar levels of self-esteem in making personal decisions in the comparison among Hong Kong Chinese, Taiwanese, and Japanese (Mann et al., 1998). These studies suggest that Chinese have at least the same or higher levels of self-esteem as other Asians.

What are the conditions that foster self-esteem for Chinese individuals?

Based on our review of the literature, we identified two broad categories of factors that show a strong relationship with degree of self-esteem: personality characteristics, and parenting and attachment styles. It is important to note that our review of these factors is based on the conclusions of the authors of the original articles. Nearly all studies of self-esteem in Chinese rely on self-report measures and use correlational designs. Thus, we should be cautious when assessing claims of causality between antecedents and consequences.

Personality. What kind of personality characteristics do Chinese individuals with high self-esteem tend to possess? In terms of the Five-Factor Model of personality, high self-esteem is correlated positively with extraversion and negatively with neuroticism (Zhang, C. M., Zou, & Xiang, 2006; Galchenko & van de Vijver, 2007; Huntsinger & Jose, 2006; Luk & Bond, 1992; Luk & Yuen, 1997). Additionally, self-esteem is moderately correlated with conscientiousness and related qualities, such as application (being hard-working) and intellect (Luk & Bond, 1992; Luk & Yuen, 1997; Yik & Bond, 1993). Some studies also show that self-esteem is weakly and positively associated with openness to experiences (C. M. Zhang et al., 2006). These connections between self-esteem and the Five-Factor Model of personality among Chinese are consistent with findings using Western samples (Aluja, Rolland, Garcia, & Rossier, 2007).

Parenting and attachment styles. More than 20 studies have established links for self-esteem with early parental influences, such as parental warmth (Bush, Peterson, Cobas, & Supple, 2002; Peterson, Cobas, Bush, Supple, & Wilson, 2005), the absence of authoritarian parenting style (Bush et al., 2002; Peterson et al., 2005; Shek, Lee, Lee, & Chow, 2006), and low levels of parent–child conflict (Shek, 1997, 1998b). Secure attachment style also predicts high self-esteem (Man & Hamid, 1998), as does parental warmth (Stewart, Bond, Kennard, Ho, & Zaman, 2002).

What is the importance of self-esteem in Chinese culture?

To address this question, we reviewed the external correlates of self-esteem with three types of adjustment: intrapsychic adjustment, interpersonal adjustment, and productivity.

Intrapsychic adjustment. Consistent findings emerged from more than 50 studies on this topic, suggesting that self-esteem is indicative of positive intrapsychic adjustment. High self-esteem is correlated positively with positive affect (Hamid & Cheng, 1996), positive body image (Davis & Katzman, 1997), quality of life (B. W. C. Leung, Moneta, & McBride-Chang, 2005), life satisfaction (Kwan, Bond, & Singelis, 1997; Stewart et al., 2002), and job satisfaction (Aryee & Luk, 1996).

On the flip side, lack of self-esteem relates to psychological problems, including depression and dysphoria (S. K. Cheng, & Lam, 1997; L. Lu, & Wu, 1998), hopelessness (C. K. Cheung & Kwok, 1996), and suicidal ideation (Jin & Zhang, 1998). The links between self-esteem and intrapsychic adjustment are similarly found across age groups (L. Zhang, 2005), and patient groups, such as those in nursing houses (L. Y. K. Lee, Lee, & Woo, 2005), and postpartum mothers (Wang, Chen, Chin, & Lee, 2005). Given its positive links with intrapsychic adjustment, researchers often use self-esteem as a predictive criterion for mental health (see Shek, 1998a, 1998b).

Interpersonal adjustment. Twenty-eight studies have examined the relations between interpersonal experiences and self-esteem. These studies suggest that individuals with high self-esteem value and enjoy interpersonal relationships more than do individuals with low self-esteem. Relationships of high self-esteem individuals are characterized by many positive attributes. We summarize these attributes as follows: (a) individuals with high self-esteem value and commit to interpersonal and romantic relationships (Cho & Cross, 1995; Chou, 2000; Lin & Rusbult, 1995); (b) they also perceive more positive communications in their relationships (Cai, Giles, & Noels, 1998); (c) individuals higher in self-esteem also enjoy friendship and romantic relationships more (Lin & Rusbult, 1995); and (d) more importantly, high self-esteem individuals have the capacity to form intimate and mature relationships (Lai, Chan, Cheung, & Law, 2001).

Productivity. Two of the most frequently studied indicators of productivity in the literature are academic and career achievement. Self-esteem has beneficial effects on both. First, high self-esteem is associated with high levels of academic achievement (e.g. Shek, 1997; C. C. W. Yu, Chan, Cheng, Sung, & Hau, 2006). Second, self-esteem is related to career satisfaction, commitment, and performance (Aryee & Debrah, 1993; Z. X. Chen, Aryee, & Lee, 2005).

What have we learned about self-esteem in the Chinese?

The first study of Chinese self-esteem was published in 1970 (Chu, 1970). Over the last three decades, research on Chinese self-esteem has gained in popularity, as demonstrated by our review. A few consistent findings have emerged: Chinese were found to have lower self-esteem than Westerners, but similar levels of self-esteem to that of other Asians; as it is currently defined in the literature, self-esteem seems to be beneficial for mental health and productivity.

Although the findings we reviewed thus far have been published in English-language journals, similar patterns of results regarding the value of self-esteem have been found by indigenous researchers. Future research should take into account these indigenous studies of self-esteem. Q. Cai, Wu, and Brown (in press) conducted a meta-analysis including all 69 studies measuring self-esteem in Chinese samples that were published in Chinese journals between 1990 and 2007 ($N = 77{,}362$). The results of this meta-analysis showed that self-esteem is positively associated with subjective well-being and negatively associated with depression and anxiety. These findings suggest that Chinese self-esteem is indicative of positive adjustment, as is the case with Western samples.

However, the question remains: what is self-esteem to the Chinese anyway? In the Chinese language, there is no equivalent term for self-esteem. From the lexical approach, whatever concepts (such as personality and values) are important for a culture will be present in the language (e.g. John, Angleitner, & Ostendorf, 1988; Renner, 2003). Not surprisingly, therefore, self-esteem has been measured using imported measures of a construct that is more salient elsewhere.

Seventy-eight of the 119 studies measured self-esteem using the Rosenberg Self-esteem Scale (RSES; Rosenberg, 1965). The second most popular self-esteem scale is the Adult Sources of Self-Esteem Inventory (Fleming & Elovson, 1988), which has been utilized in just six studies. The third most commonly used scale is the Coopersmith Self-esteem Inventory (Coopersmith, 1967), which was used in five studies. All of these measures of self-esteem were designed to assess global self-esteem across a broad range of domains and dimensions.

This pervasive use of the RSES parallels its use in the West (Kwan & Mandisodza, 2007). However, the Rosenberg Self-esteem Scale is not without problems when used for the study of Chinese populations. For example, one of the ten items on the RSES, viz. 'I wish I could have more respect for myself,' is ambiguous in Chinese studies, because it invites multiple interpretations for Chinese participants (see S. T. Cheng & Hamid, 1995; Hamid & Cheng, 1995). Some interpret it as a question concerning lack of self-respect, while others interpret it as desire for more self-worth. Indeed, it is occasionally discarded from the scale when researchers discover its weak or even negative item–whole correlation.

Another potential problem with the use of the RSES in Chinese populations is that the positively and negatively worded items may carry different meanings for Chinese than for Westerners. Conventionally, researchers form an overall score of self-esteem by averaging scores of five positively worded items and five reverse-scored, negatively worded items. The scoring method rests upon the assumption that positive and negative items represent opposite ends of a continuum. However, this may be a problem for dialectical thinkers like Chinese respondents, who are more able to endorse both sides of an issue (Peng & Nisbett, 1999). For example, non-dialectical thinkers who endorse a positive statement such as 'On the whole, I am satisfied with myself,' would not be likely to also endorse the negative statement 'I certainly feel useless at times.' Dialectical thinkers, on the other hand, may endorse both. Indeed, recent research (Kim, Peng, & Chiu, 2008; Schmitt & Allik, 2005; Spencer-Rodgers, Peng, Wang, & Hou, 2004) has shown that Chinese tend to endorse both positively and negatively worded items of the RSES. This raises an interesting question of how dialectical thinking style interacts with the Chinese self-concept and in turn impacts on assessments of their mental health.

Most of the studies of Chinese self-esteem used explicit measures of self-esteem, such as the Rosenberg Self-esteem Scale. However, implicit self-esteem is another facet of self-regard that commands attention. Self-esteem, in part, arises from peoples' gut feelings and intuitions, and may defy reason or logic (Brown, 1998). Some of these feelings may be so deep-seated that they are inaccessible during conscious introspection, and self-reported measures fail to identify them. Recently, researchers have developed measures to capture implicit attitudes toward the self. One of the most commonly used measures is the Implicit Association Test (IAT: Greenwald & Farnham, 2000), which measures response times to word associations between self- and other-related constructs and either good or bad words. Another commonly used implicit measure is the name letter test (Nuttin, 1987), which relies on the idea that people with high self-esteem will hold positive attitudes toward the letters in their own names. Implicit measures have been greeted with fanfare by Western psychologists, but the validity of these measures remains under debate.

The literature shows a disassociation between implicit and explicit measures of self-esteem; these two types of self-esteem only weakly relate to each other (see Bosson, Swann, & Pennebaker, 2000; Hetts, Sakuma, & Pelham, 1999). So these findings suggest that some people may have high self-esteem as indicated by implicit measures, but low self-esteem as indicated by explicit measures, or vice versa. Recent work has also shown this disassociation in Asian samples. Japanese and mainland Chinese show comparable levels of implicit self-esteem to Americans, despite having different levels of explicit self-esteem (Yamaguchi et al., 2007). Together, these recent findings call for future research to examine the exact nature of these two types of self-esteem.

Another important direction for future research is to examine the indigenous aspects of self-esteem in Chinese culture. According to Social Identity Theory (Tajfel & Turner, 1979; Turner, 1982), people derive their self-esteem from personal achievement, interpersonal relationships, and collective membership. The interpersonal and collective aspects may play particularly important roles in the Chinese context (L. Lu & Gilmour, 2004, 2007; Yang, 1986). Some evidence supports the idea that collective self-esteem has an influential role in predicting Chinese well-being, while personal self-esteem is less predictive of well-being in China than in America (Kang et al., 2003; Kwan et al., 1997; L. Zhang, 2005). Future research should put the interpersonal and collective aspects back into the study of self-esteem in Chinese, differentiating these components from the personal.

Self-efficacy

While researchers have studied self-esteem as a stable individual difference, those who are interested in the malleability of the Chinese self-concept focus on self-efficacy. To find out what has been done on this topic, we conducted a similar literature search for self-efficacy as we did for self-esteem. Below we summarize the common findings of the 96 articles resulting from our search.

Bandura (1977, 1993) defined self-efficacy as people's beliefs about their capabilities to control both their own level of functioning and the events that affect their lives. Compared to Westerners (e.g. Australian, Americans, Canadians, and Germans), Chinese and Chinese immigrants tend to have lower general self-efficacy (S. X. Chen, Chan, Bond, & Stewart, 2006; C. Leung, 2001; Moore & C. Leung, 2001; Schwarzer, Bassler, Kwiatek, Schroder, & J. X. Zhang, 1997; Stewart et al., 2005). Similar findings emerge when Chinese in Hong Kong were compared to Americans (S. X. Chen et al., 2006).

Although self-efficacy is a relatively recent topic of study within Chinese populations, the benefits of self-efficacy for individuals are quickly becoming apparent from recent research. They have been found in relation to both general self-efficacy and domain-specific self-efficacy, which we will discuss in turn.

General self-efficacy has been studied in relation to three main topics, agency, achievement, and well-being. General self-efficacy is indicative of agentic control over situations, such as internal health locus of control (Wu, Tang, & Kwok, 2004) and lower susceptibility to superstitious beliefs (Sachs, 2004b). Further, a general sense of self-efficacy appears to be strongly and positively related to personal accomplishment (J. S. Y. Lee & Akhtar, 2007; Yan & Tang, 2003). That success may, in turn, foster more general self-efficacy. There is some evidence that measures of financial success and security, as measured by socioeconomic status (SES), are strongly and positively associated with self-efficacy in young Chinese (Tong & Song, 2004).

General self-efficacy also fosters psychological well-being and life satisfaction. Associated indicators of psychological well-being include self-esteem (Mak & Nesdale, 2001), mental and physical health (Schaubroeck, Lam, & Xie, 2000; Siu, Lu, & Spector, 2007), and quality of life (Hampton, 2000). In addition, general self-efficacy negatively relates to indicators of maladjustment, including psychological distress (Wu et al., 2004), anxiety and depression (S. X. Chen et al., 2006; S. K. Cheung & Sun, 1999), and suicidal ideation (Lam et al., 2005). Moreover, general self-efficacy is negatively associated with burnout (J. S. Y. Lee & Akhtar, 2007; Tam, 2000; Tang, Au, Schwarzer, & Schmitz, 2001), perhaps by acting to buffer the detrimental impact of job distress on well-being (Siu, Spector, Cooper, & Lu, 2005; Siu et al., 2007).

It is important to note, however, that a sense of general self-efficacy may have a less significant association with well-being for Chinese than for Westerners. S. X. Chen et al. (2006) found that relation between self-efficacy and depressed mood was significantly stronger for Americans than for Chinese. More cross-cultural research is needed to demonstrate the moderating effects of culture on the links between self-efficacy and aspects of personal and social adjustment.

There may also be domain-specific effects of self-efficacy. The effects of domain-specific self-efficacy appear to be positive for task performance. For example, previous studies found that domain-specific self-efficacy predicts performance in that domain, such as academic outcomes (Sachs, 2004a), memory (Suen, Morris, & McDougall, 2004), and job performance (S. S. K. Lam, Chen, & Schaubroeck, 2002). Low levels of performance self-efficacy and social self-efficacy are both linked to psychological distress (Moore & Leung, 2001; Qian, Wang, & Chen, 2002). The confidence that arises from feeling efficacious buffers the detrimental effects of distress, and may in turn enhance performance (Chou & Chi, 2001; C. Q. Lu, Siu, & Cooper, 2005; Wong, Lam, & Kwok, 2003).

One of the most popular topics in the area of self-efficacy research is the relationship between self-efficacy and health-related behaviors. Self-efficacy promotes healthy and preventative behaviors, such as exercising (Chou, Macfarlane, Chi, & Cheng, 2006), self-examination for cancer (Su, Ma, Seals, Tan, & Hausman, 2006), and adherence to medical advice (Molassiotis et al., 2002). Moreover, self-efficacy is linked to a reduction in health-compromising behaviors, such as smoking (Fang et al., 2006), consumption of fat-rich diets (Liou & Contento, 2001), and risky sexual behaviors (Li et al., 2004). Self-efficacy in refusing also reduces peer-influenced smoking (Chang et al., 2006), drinking (Yeh, Chiang, & Huang, 2006), and drug abuse (R. L. Yu & Ko, 2006). Self-efficacy may influence many of these behaviors, in part by enabling individuals to exercise control against engaging in risky behaviors. This is illustrated by the fact that health-related efficacy is negatively related to fear of contracting transmissible diseases (e.g. Ho, Kwong-Lo, Mak, & Wong, 2005).

These effects of self-efficacy have practical importance, potentially guiding policy interventions to address a broad range of health and social issues. An interesting new direction for research on self-efficacy is to incorporate its measurement across time. Several recent studies have begun to evaluate the change of self-efficacy when a behavior is planned, performed, maintained, and stopped across a period of time (e.g. Ling & Horwath, 1999; Tung, Gillett, & Pattillo, 2005). The implications of such changes across different stages are of great theoretical importance, and may help us better understand about the basic functions of self-efficacy in shaping behaviors.

When comparing self-efficacy levels in Chinese immigrants and travelers to the level present in their host culture, our review revealed mixed findings. Some studies have shown that Chinese score lower than their hosts. For example, Chinese overseas or immigrant students tend to have lower social self-efficacy than Australian students and Southern European migrant students (C. Leung,

2001; Moore & C. Leung, 2001). In addition, Hong Kong immigrants tend to score a lower level of general self-efficacy than the majority of New Zealanders (Nesdale, 2002).

Yet other research suggests that Chinese may have about the same level or higher levels of self-efficacy. For example, Chinese immigrants did not differ from Canadians in terms of self-efficacy for lottery playing (Walker, Courney, & Deng, 2006), or from Malays in terms of general self-efficacy (Awang, O'Neil, & Hocevar, 2003). Finally, one study on health behavior self-efficacy showed that Chinese have lower self-efficacy than Greeks, but higher self-efficacy than Italians and Vietnamese (Swerissen et al., 2006).

The disparate findings of these studies may reflect the different domains of self-efficacy studied. However, these mixed findings are reminiscent of the results of comparisons of self-esteem between Chinese and persons of other cultures. Perhaps conclusions drawn from studies of both self-esteem and self-efficacy are being confounded by yet another form of self-process, viz. self-enhancement. If Chinese individuals have a tendency to self-enhance, or do the opposite and self-efface, then their self-reports of self-esteem and self-efficacy may reflect this bias and be positively or negatively skewed (see Farh & Dobbins, 1989). Furthermore, the self-enhancement or effacement may be domain-specific, further complicating our ability to assess the construct.

Self-enhancement bias

There has been a recent debate over whether there is a universal drive for positive self-regard. Some researchers question whether this drive exists among collectivistic East Asians (see Heine, Kitayama, & Hamamura, 2007; Sedkikides, Gaertner, & Vevea, 2007). People from individualistic and collectivistic cultural systems may strive for positive regard in different senses. If so, then, the question is not just whether the Chinese self-enhance or not. Rather, we should examine when the Chinese self-enhance and in which domains. Therefore, we conducted a literature search for self-enhancement similar to the searches we did for self-esteem and self-efficacy. Twenty-one articles were found.

The fact that the earliest article was published in 1991 suggests that self-enhancement is a new subject of research with respect to Chinese samples and has yet to receive significant attention. What limited work has been done on this topic is varied and has addressed the degree to which Chinese self-enhance both generally and in some specific domains.

Do the Chinese self-enhance?

There is evidence demonstrating self-enhancement in different populations of Chinese. For example, Taiwanese workers rated themselves more highly compared to supervisors' ratings of their job performance (Farh, Dobbins, & Cheng, 1991). There is also evidence of self-enhancement in Chinese college students and schoolchildren. Chinese university students indicate that they did more desirable and fewer undesirable things than others in responding to the Marlowe-Crowne Social Desirability Scale (Liu, Xiao, & Yang, 2003). Hong Kong elementary schoolchildren show a greater tendency toward enhancement of own competence than that of their peers in several domains (M. C. Leung, 1996). For elementary-school students, conventional values (e.g. cooperativeness, politeness, hard work) and academic achievement are the enhanced domains. Older, secondary-school students self-enhanced in the above domains as well as in physical appearance, aggression, and popularity. Similar findings were found in boys and girls.

Nevertheless, there is also evidence showing that Chinese self-efface. In contrast to Taiwanese workers, mainland Chinese workers rated themselves less positively than did their supervisors, as found by Farh et al. (1991). Together, these findings suggest that Chinese do not uniformly self-enhance or self-efface.

Do the Chinese self-enhance more or less than other cultural groups? Chinese self-enhance less than do non-East Asian groups. For example, Israelis self-enhance on academic performance more than Singaporeans (Kurman, 2001; Kurman & Sriram, 1997). Despite this difference, the authors found evidence of self-enhancement in both samples.

Compared to North Americans, such as Canadians, Hong Kong Chinese self-enhance significantly less across domains of personality perception (Yik, Bond, & Paulhus, 1998). On average, 43 per cent of Hong Kong Chinese self-enhanced, whereas 56 per cent of Canadians self-enhanced, suggesting that there are substantial individual differences in self-enhancement among both Chinese and Westerners. The personality facet of modesty (Costa & McCrae, 1992) may well be implicated in this process (S. X. Chen, Bond, Chan, Tang, & Buchtel, in press).

What characterizes self-enhancement among the Chinese?

The Chinese seem to enhance the collective aspects of their self-concepts in that they show more group-serving bias than self-serving bias. For example, M. C. Leung (1996) found evidence of group-oriented self-enhancement in Chinese schoolchildren in grades four and seven at two Hong Kong elementary schools. Compared with teacher ratings of competence, children reported biased ratings of their own social groups by not acknowledging the presence of lower-ranking peers. Similarly, Weijun (2003) found that Chinese adults tend to self-enhance in a group-serving rather than a self-serving manner, although self-serving tendencies were also found.

Chinese show more self-enhancement in certain trait domains. For example, Taiwanese self-enhance more for collectivist traits than for individualist traits (Gaertner, Sedikides, & Chang, 2008). This finding may be explained by the generally high levels of interdependent self-construal among Chinese. Consistent with this reasoning, Kurman (2001) showed that self-enhancement of agentic traits is associated with independent self-construals, and self-enhancement in communal traits is associated with interdependent self-construal across three cultures, China, Singapore, and Israel (Kurman, 2001).

Individualism is predictive of overly positive self-views. Xie, Roy, and Chen (2006) found that narcissism is associated with vertical individualism, the extent to which one values hierarchy and perceives separateness between selves (see also Triandis, 1995). In this study, participants rating higher in vertical individualism provided more positive self-ratings of their own cognitive ability than did participants who rated higher in collectivism, even though there were no differences in actual ability.

Nevertheless, when given the means to self-enhance easily, Chinese do not take the opportunity to do so. Kurman and Sriram (1997) examined self-enhancement at different levels of generality of self-evaluation. These authors expected that a self-reported criterion with a greater level of generality (e.g. self-reported general academic performance) would allow more self-relevant and subjective self-evaluations, and therefore may facilitate self-enhancement more than would a more specific criterion (e.g. self-reported grades). Findings show that while Israeli students followed this trend, Singaporean students did not. When asked for more subjective self-evaluations, only Isreali students displayed higher levels of self-enhancement. Singaporean students may face cultural norms of modesty in self-presentation (self-effacement) that prevent them from taking advantage of opportunities for self-enhancement. Also, they may receive more frequent and public feedback on their academic performance, making enhancement less likely (Oettingen, Little, Lindenberger, & Baltes, 1994).

Taken together, the findings of these studies, though limited in quantity, suggest that the Chinese self-enhance at times, but do so to a far lesser extent than do Westerners. However, the tendency to self-enhance in a particular domain may depend upon the relative importance of that domain in the surrounding culture. As we are writing this chapter, a paper by Gaertner, Sedikides, and Chang (2008) was published examining trait domains of self-enhancement in a Taiwanese sample. The authors found that Taiwanese self-enhance more for collectivist traits, e.g. compromising, self-sacrificing, than for individualist traits, e.g. independent, unique, suggesting that culture not only influences the overall level of self-enhancement in individuals, but also the specific domain being enhanced.

Another important question is how people perceive self-enhancers. Self-enhancement is a positive evaluation of oneself, and as such, necessitates a comparison between oneself and others. In a recent study, Bond, Kwan, and Li (2000) examined social perceptions of those with high self-regard versus those with low other-regard in a Hong Kong Chinese sample. Those high in self-regard were perceived by others as more assertive and more open, whereas those low in regard for others were seen as less likable, less helpful and less restrained.

In addition to self-regard and other-regard, one's merit is another important factor to be considered in the study of self-enhancement. Some recent studies showed that the link between self-enhancement and adjustment depends on the level of merit that one possesses (Kwan, John, Kenny, Bond, & Robins, 2004; Kwan, John, Robins, & Kuang, 2008). People may still like self-enhancers if they are talented and skilled, but self-enhancers with low merit have two counts against them (Kwan, Kuang, & Zhao, 2008). To have a complete understanding of the value of self-enhancement, we urge researchers to take into account (a) how individuals perceive themselves, (b) how individuals perceive others, and (c) how others perceive the individual, i.e. the social merit of the individual. Future researchers should examine the broad implications of dynamics interaction of these different aspects of social perception in a Chinese context.

Another dynamic that we should consider is whether the Chinese self-concept changes with the socio-cultural climate. Little research has been done to examine this issue thus far. Nevertheless, there is some indirect evidence that Chinese self-enhance more than they used to. For example, two recent studies have shown that young Chinese students are more narcissistic than their Western counterparts (Fukunishi et al., 1996; Kwan, Kuang, & Hui, in press). One possible cause of this phenomenon is that the younger generation of Chinese consists largely of only-children. To control its burgeoning population, the Chinese government has implemented a one-child-per-family policy since 1979. The policy and its predecessor, which merely encouraged smaller family size, have succeeded in lowering the total fertility rate (i.e. average number of births per woman) from about five to about 1.8 today (Bristow, 2007). The reduction probably would have been even more dramatic but not for the government-allowed exemptions from the policy for some families, such as those who live in rural areas and those from ethnic minorities. Notably, children born under this one-child policy have received lavish attention from their parents and grandparents, and some have received large inheritances as sole heirs. Higher levels of narcissism may be a result of this treatment (see also Wang & Chang, this volume).

The Chinese born under this policy are popularly known in China as the 'little emperor' generation. Lending empirical support to this popular conception, previous studies have found that individuals from single-child families in China are seen by their peers as more egocentric than their non-child counterparts (Jiao, Ji, & Jing, 1986). This higher level of egocentrism in only children is similar to that found in the West (Curtis & Cowell, 1993; Erying & Sobelman, 1996). There is also evidence to suggest increasing physical health problems in members of the 'little emperor' cohort, including the relatively high incidents of obesity and Type II diabetes (T. O. Cheng, 2005).

On the other hand, these 'little emperors' seem to benefit from egocentrism, as they display fewer symptoms of anxiety than children with siblings (e.g. Dong, Yang, & Ollendick, 1994; Hesketh, Qu, & Tomkins, 2003). Moreover, only children outperform children with siblings in their academic performance (Falbo & Poston, 1993; Poston & Falbo, 1990). Nevertheless, it remains unclear if the apparent achievement by only children is attributable to their better self-sustaining capacity, or to their privilege of fuller parental attention. There may be adaptive and maladaptive consequences of regarding oneself in a positive light even in a collectivistic Chinese culture, and further studies should examine these facets across a broader spectrum of the lifespan.

This elevated level of narcissism among the younger generation of Chinese deserves more focused attention from both parents and educators. It would be a valuable line of research to identify the factors that contribute to narcissism in China, and how narcissism impacts on social performance in collectivistic as compared to individualistic cultural systems. Additionally, longitudinal research in personality development among various cohorts may help gain insight into the extent to which socio-cultural factors shape changes in personality.

Discussion

What have we learned about the Chinese self? Three notable findings emerge in our review of the literature. First, we found significant differences between Chinese and Westerners in levels of self-esteem, self-efficacy, and self-enhancement bias. Second, differences between sojourners and Western hosts in these three self-processes are smaller than the differences between Chinese residing in East-Asian cultural settings and Westerners. This suggests that socio-cultural factors play an important role in the malleability of the Chinese self. Third, the Chinese self-concept has important implications for mental health, interpersonal relationships, and productivity.

So where is the research on the Chinese self heading? Inquiry into the Chinese self began in the 1970s, but the momentum of this line of research has increased dramatically since the 1990s. We anticipate that in the twenty-first century, research on the self will continue to flourish. Below, we outline a few promising directions.

One important direction is to compare and contrast the Chinese subcultures, e.g. PRC, Hong Kong, Taiwan, Singapore, Chinese-Americans. Such an examination could inform researchers about how differences in the socio-political environment across Chinese subcultures may influence how the self is constructed and enacted. Different subgroups of Chinese may fall across the spectrum of self-conceptions—some being more family-oriented, others more involved in community and charity events, with still others being more individualistic, capitalistic and, perhaps, hedonistic. Multicultural studies of the Chinese diaspora would be most revealing in this respect.

Our initial goal of the literature review was to address the issue of the Chinese self where the data are most available. However, we found that too few studies have included more than one Chinese subgroup. Among the few with more than one, the focus of the studies was on East–West differences. Injecting Western groups into these comparisons, differences between Chinese subgroups may seem insignificant. Researchers should bear in mind that the meanings of the differences in self-concept will vary depending on the comparison groups involved.

Another important direction for future research is to examine the effects of globalization on the Chinese self-concept. If the world is converging and becoming increasingly uniform due to the affordable costs of international travel and information exchange, cross-cultural differences may begin to dissipate. In its most extreme form, globalization may ultimately create a meta-culture. In the near future, collectivistic cultures will likely become more individualistic, although this hypothesis is a matter of some debate (e.g. Inglehart & Baker, 2000). The by-products of modernization and globalization include fewer extended family members, more specialized division of labor, and increasing demand for frequent relocation. All of these factors can change the meaning of interdependence and how people view the self in relation to others (see L. Lu & Yang, 2006).

Another challenging, yet intriguing, aspect of studying change in Chinese personality stems from the fact that China is in the midst of its own massive social and economic transformation (see e.g. recent work by Kohn, Li, Wang, & Yue, 2007). The changes taking place in Chinese society have the potential to greatly influence its members' self-concepts. At the most basic level, these changes have caused a divide between sub-populations within the country, thus making it more difficult for social scientists to generalize from one group to another. For example, rapid urbanization is a key aspect of China's recent development. Many young Chinese have left their rural roots to find work in China's expanding cities. Psychological research has largely drawn samples from urban populations, most commonly students at urban universities. But much of China's population still lives in rural communities. Self-processes and their correlates may be substantially different in different regions of China, as intra-national differences have been documented in studies of other cultures. For example, Vandello and Cohen (1999) found significant regional differences in self-construal in the United States. The deep southern region of the USA showed the strongest collectivism, while the plains region showed the strongest individualism. Also important is that these regional differences in self-construal predicted social correlates: individualism predicts affluence, collectivism predicts higher population density, and individualism predicts greater racial and gender equality (also see Kitayama et al., 2006 for a similar discussion on intra-national variation in Japan). Thus, future research should address the lack of inclusion of rural Chinese in studies of self-processes and explore the regional differences in self-processes within China, thereby enabling researchers to make comparisons across regions in China.

China has also taken significant steps toward establishing a more capitalistic economy. In the process, many Chinese industries have been growing rapidly and the disposable income of China's middle class has increased. This change, too, may impact upon the self-views of Chinese individuals. A recent study by Stephens, Markus, and Townsend (2007) examined conformity and socioeconomic status (SES). In a series of experiments, they found that working-class Americans were more likely to make choices that produce similarity to others, while middle-class Americans, i.e. those with a least one college-educated parent, made choices that differentiated them from others. If similar experiments were replicated in China today, perhaps we would find that the expanding Chinese middle class shows the same proclivity to differentiate themselves. Then again, the traditionally collectivistic nature of the Chinese self may dampen or eliminate the effects of rising socioeconomic status.

In closing, we believe that this is a particularly exciting time for psychologists to study the Chinese self, but it is also a time that requires unprecedented collaboration between psychologists and other social scientists. To explore regional differences in self-construal in the USA, Vandello and Cohen (1999) used data from an individualism index on the National Election Survey. In a similar vein, Stephens et al. (2007) used SES, a variable usually delegated to sociologists, to predict conformity-seeking behaviors in a study of choice. This use of theory and data traditionally within the scope of political scientists and sociologists can be a model for researchers interested in the Chinese self. When individuals are enveloped by rapid social and political change, it has the potential to exert such a strong influence on the self. In these environments, psychologists studying self-processes are likely to benefit from interdisciplinary collaboration and multi-cultural databases.

Chapter notes

1 Studies on self-esteem may be listed under the key word 'self-esteem' as well as 'self-regard', 'self-liking', or other synonyms. Due to the large number of studies on this topic, we limit our review to articles with the key word 'self-esteem' only. Some of the articles found with the key word 'self-esteem' also discuss self-liking or self-regard, and we have included these articles in our review. However, our search of these concepts is not comprehensive.

2 Researchers have discussed various explanations for these findings, and we will discuss the conceptual issues pertaining to these explanations in the 'self-enhancement' section of this chapter.

References

Aluja, A., Rolland, J. P., Garcia, L. F., & Rossier, J. (2007). Dimensionality of the Rosenberg self-esteem scale and its relationships with the three- and the five-factor personality models. *Journal of Personality Assessment, 88,* 246–249.

Aryee, S. & Debrah, Y. A. (1993). A cross-cultural application of a career planning model. *Journal of Organizational Behavior, 14,* 119–127.

Aryee, S. & Luk, V. (1996). Work and nonwork influences on the career satisfaction of dual earner couples. *Journal of Vocational Behavior, 49,* 38–52.

Awang, H. R., O'Neil, H. F. Jr, & Hocevar, D. (2003). Ethnicity, effort, self-efficacy, worry, and statistics achievement in Malaysia: A construct validation of the state–trait motivation model. *Educational Assessment, 8,* 341–364.

Bandura, A. (1977). Self-efficacy: Toward a unifying theory of behavioral change. *Psychological Review, 84,* 191–215.

Bandura, A. (1993). Perceived self-efficacy in cognitive development and functioning. *Educational Psychologist, 28,* 117–148.

Baumeister, R. F., Campbell, J. D., Krueger, J. I., & Vohs, K. D. (2003). Does high self-esteem cause better performance, interpersonal success, happiness, or healthier lifestyles? *Psychological Science in the Public Interest, 4,* 1–44.

Bond, M. H. (ed.), *The psychology of the Chinese people.* Hong Kong: Oxford University Press.

Bond, M. H. & Cheung, T. S. (1983). College students' spontaneous self-concept: The effect of culture among respondents in Hong Kong, Japan, and the United States. *Journal of Cross-Cultural Psychology, 14,* 153–171.

Bond, M. H., Kwan, V. S. Y., & Li, C. (2000). Decomposing a sense of superiority: The differential social impact of self-regard and regard-for-others. *Journal of Research in Personality, 34,* 537–553.

Bosson, J. K., Swann, W. B., & Pennebaker, J. W. (2000). Stalking the perfect measure of implicit self-esteem: The blind men and the elephant revisited? *Journal of Personality and Social Psychology, 79,* 631–643.

Bristow, M. (2007, September 20). Has China's one-child policy worked? *BBC News.* Retrieved May 29, 2008, from http://news.bbc.co.uk/2/hi/asia-pacific/7000931.stm

Brown, J. D. (1998). *The self.* New York: McGraw-Hill.

Bush, K. R., Peterson, G. W., Cobas, J. A., & Supple, A. J. (2002). Adolescents' perceptions of parental behaviors as predictors of adolescent self-esteem in mainland China. *Sociological Inquiry, 72,* 503–526.

Cai, D., Giles, H., & Noels, K. (1998). Elderly perceptions of communication with older and younger adults in China: Implications for mental health. *Journal of Applied Communication Research, 26,* 32–51.

Cai, H., Wu, Q., & Brown, J. (in press). Is self-esteem a universal need? Evidence from the People's Republic of China. *Asian Journal of Social Psychology.*

Chan, Y. M. (2000). Self-esteem: A cross-cultural comparison of British-Chinese, White British and Hong Kong Chinese children. *Educational Psychology, 20,* 59–74.

Chang, F. C., Lee, C. M., Lai, H. R., Chiang, J. T., Lee, P. H., & Chen, W. J. (2006). Social influences and self-efficacy as predictors of youth smoking initiation and cessation: A 3-year longitudinal study of vocational high school students in Taiwan. *Addiction, 101,* 1645–1655.

Chen, S. X., Bond, M. H., Chan, B., Tang, D., & Buchtel, E. E. (in press). Reconceptualizing modesty: Is It a trait or a self-presentation tactic? *Journal of Cross-Cultural Psychology.*

Chen, S. X., Chan, W., Bond, M. H., & Stewart, S. M. (2006). The effects of self-efficacy and relationship harmony on depression across cultures: Applying level-oriented and structure-oriented analyses. *Journal of Cross-Cultural Psychology, 37,* 643–658.

Chen, Z. X., Aryee, S., & Lee, C. (2005). Test of a mediation model of perceived organizational support. *Journal of Vocational Behavior, 66,* 457–470.

Cheng, S. K. & Lam, D. J. (1997). Relationships among life stress, problem solving, self-esteem, and dysphoria in Hong Kong adolescents: Test of a model. *Journal of Social and Clinical Psychology, 16,* 343–355.

Cheng, S. T. & Hamid, P. N. (1995). An error in the use of translated scales: The Rosenberg Self-esteem Scale for Chinese. *Perceptual and Motor Skills, 81,* 431–434.

Cheng, T. O. (2005). One-child policy and increased mechanization are additional risk factors for increased coronary artery disease in modern China. *International Journal of Cardiology, 100,* 333.

Cheung, C. K. & Kwok, S. T. (1996). Conservative orientation as a determinant of hopelessness. *Journal of Social Psychology, 136,* 333–347.

Cheung, S. K. & Sun, S. Y. K. (1999). Assessment of optimistic self-beliefs: Further validation of the Chinese version of the general self-efficacy scale. *Psychological Reports, 85,* 1221–1224.

Cho, W. & Cross, S. E. (1995). Taiwanese love styles and their association with self-esteem and relationship quality. *Genetic, Social, and General Psychology Monographs, 121,* 283–309.

Chou, K. L. (2000). Intimacy and psychosocial adjustment in Hong Kong Chinese adolescents. *Journal of Genetic Psychology, 161,* 141–151.

Chou, K. L. & Chi, I. (2001). Social comparison in Chinese older adults. *Aging and Mental Health, 5,* 242–252.

Chou, K. L., Macfarlane, D. J., Chi, I., & Cheng, Y. H. (2006). Physical exercise in Chinese older Adults: A transtheoretical model. *Journal of Applied Biobehavioral Research, 11,* 114–131.

Chu, C. P. (1970). A study of the effects of maternal employment for the preschool children in Taiwan. *Acta Psychologica Taiwanica, 12,* 80–100. (in Chinese)

Chung, T. & Mallery, P. (1999). Social comparison, individualism–collectivism, and self-esteem in China and the United States. *Current Psychology: Developmental, Learning, Personality, Social, 18,* 340–352.

Costa, P. T. & McCrae, R. R. (1992). Four ways five factors are basic. *Personality and Individual Differences, 13,* 653–665.

Coopersmith, S. (1967). *Self-esteem inventory.* Palo Alto, CA: Consulting Psychologists Press.

Curtis, J. M. & Cowell, D. R. (1993). Relation of birth order and scores on measures of pathological narcissism. *Psychological Reports, 72,* 311–315.

Davis, C. & Katzman, M. (1997). Charting new territory: Body esteem, weight satisfaction, depression, and self-esteem among Chinese males and females in Hong Kong. *Sex-Roles, 36,* 449–459.

Dong, Q., Yang, B., & Ollendick, T. H. (1994). Fear in Chinese children and adolescents and their relations to anxiety and depression. *Journal of Child Psychology and Psychiatry, 35,* 351–363.

Eyring, W. E. & Sobelman, S. (1996). Narcissism and birth order. *Psychological Reports, 78,* 403–406.

Falbo, T. & Poston, D. L., Jr. (1993). The academic, personality, and physical outcomes of only children in China. *Child Development, 64,* 18–35.

Fang, C. Y., Ma, G. X., Miller, S. M., Tan, Y., Su, X., & Shive, S. (2006). A brief smoking cessation intervention for Chinese and Korean American smokers. *Preventive Medicine: An International Journal Devoted to Practice and Theory, 43,* 321–324.

Farh, J. L. & Dobbins, G. H. (1989). Effects of self-esteem on leniency bias in self-reports of performance: A structural equation model analysis. *Personnel Psychology, 42,* 835–850.

Farh, J. L., Dobbins, G. H., & Cheng, B. S. (1991). Cultural relativity in action: A comparison of self-ratings made by Chinese and U.S. workers. *Personnel Psychology, 44,* 129–147.

Fleming, J. & Elovson, A. (1988). *The adult sources of self-esteem inventory.* Northridge, CA: State University of California at Northridge.

Fukunishi, I., Nakagawa, T., Nakamura, H., Li, K., Hua, Z. Q., & Kratz, T. S. (1996). Relationships between type A behavior, narcissism, and maternal closeness for college students in Japan, the United States of America, and the People's Republic of China. *Psychological Reports, 78*, 939–944.

Gaertner, L. Sedikides, C., & Chang, K. (2008). On pancultural self-enhancement: Well-adjusted Taiwanese self-enhance on personality-valued traits. *Journal of Cross-Cultural Psychology,39*, 463–477.

Galchenko, I. & van de Vijver, F. J. R. (2007). The role of perceived cultural distance in the acculturation of exchange students in Russia. *International Journal of Intercultural Relations, 31*, 181–197.

Greenwald, A. G. & Farnham, S. D. (2000). Using the implicit association test to measure self-esteem and self-concept. *Journal of Personality and Social Psychology, 79*, 1022–1038.

Hamid, P. N. & Cheng, S. T. (1995). To drop or not to drop an ambiguous item: A reply to Shek. *Perceptual and Motor Skills, 81*, 988–990.

Hamid, P. N. & Cheng, S. T. (1996). The development and validation of an index of emotion disposition and mood state: The Chinese affect scale. *Educational and Psychological Measurement, 56*, 995–1014.

Hampton, N. Z. (2000). Self-efficacy and quality of life in people with spinal cord injuries in China. *Rehabilitation Counseling Bulletin. 43*, 66–74.

Heine, S. J. & Lehman, D. R. (2004). Move the body, change the self: Acculturative effects on the self-concept. In M. Schaller & C. Crandall (eds), *Psychological foundations of culture* (pp. 305–331). Mahwah, NJ: Erlbaum.

Heine, S. J., Kitayama, S., & Hamamura, T. (2007). Which studies test the question of pancultural self-enhancement? A reply to Sedikides, Gaertner, & Vevea, in press. *Asian Journal of Social Psychology, 10*, 198–200.

Hesketh, T., Qu, J. D., & Tomkins, A. (2003). Health effects of family size: cross-sectional survey in Chinese adolescents. *Archives of Disease in Childhood, 88*, 467–471.

Hetts, J. J., Sakuma, M., & Pelham, B. W. (1999). Two roads to positive regard: Implicit and explicit self-evaluation and culture. *Journal of Experimental Social Psychology, 35*, 512–559.

Ho, S. M. Y., Kwong-Lo, R. S. Y., Mak, C. W. Y., & Wong, J. S. (2005). Fear of severe acute respiratory syndrome (SARS) among health care workers. *Journal of Consulting and Clinical Psychology, 73*, 344–349.

Huntsinger, C. S. & Jose, P. E. (2006). A longitudinal investigation of personality and social adjustment among Chinese American and European American adolescents. *Child Development, 77*, 1309–1324.

Inglehart, R. & Baker, W. E. (2000). Modernization, cultural change and the persistence of traditional values. *American Sociological Review, 65*, 19–51.

Jiao, S., Ji, G., & Jing, Q. (1986). Comparative study of cognitive development of Guangzhou only and non-only children. *Acta Psychologica Sinica, 24*, 12–19. (in Chinese)

Jin, S. & Zhang, J. (1998). The effects of physical and psychological well-being on suicidal ideation. *Journal of Clinical Psychology, 54*, 401–413.

John, O. P., Angleitner, A., & Ostendorf, F. (1988). The lexical approach to personality: a historical review of trait taxonomic research. *European Journal of Personality, 2*, 171–203.

Kang, S. M., Shaver, P. R., Sue, S., Min, K. H., & Jing, H. (2003). Culture-specific patterns in the prediction of life satisfaction: Roles of emotion, relationship quality, and self-esteem. *Personality and Social Psychology Bulletin, 29*, 1596–1608.

Kiang, L., Yip, T., Gonzales-Backen, M., Witkow, M., & Fuligni, A. J. (2006). Ethnic identity and the daily psychological well-being of adolescents from Mexican and Chinese backgrounds. *Child Development, 77*, 1338–1350.

Kim, Y. H., Peng, S., & Chiu, C. Y. (2008). Explaining self-esteem differences between Chinese and North Americans: Dialectical self (vs. self-consistency) or lack of positive self-regard? *Self and Identity, 7*, 113–128.

Kitayama, S., Ishii, K., Ishii, K., Imada, T., Takemura, K., & Ramaswamy, J. (2006). Voluntary settlement and the spirit of independence: Evidence from Japan's 'Northern Frontier.' *Journal of Personality and Social Psychology, 91*, 369–384.

Kohn, M. L., Li, L., Wang, W., & Yue, Y. (2007). Social structure and personality during the transformation of urban China: A preliminary report of an ongoing research project. *Comparative Sociology, 6*, 389–429.

Kwan, V. S. Y., Bond, M. H., & Singelis, T. M. (1997). Pancultural explanations for life satisfaction: Adding relationship harmony to self-esteem. *Journal of Personality and Social Psychology, 73*, 1038–1051.

Kwan, V. S. Y., John, O. P., Kenny, D. A., Bond, M. H., & Robins, R. W. (2004). Reconceptualizing individual differences in self-enhancement bias: An interpersonal approach. *Psychological Review, 111*, 94–111.

Kwan, V. S. Y., John, O. P., Robins, R. W., & Kuang, L. L. (2008). Conceptualizing and assessing self-enhancement bias: A componential approach. *Journal of Personality and Social Psychology, 94*, 1062–1077.

Kwan, V. S. Y., Kuang, L. L., & Hui, N. (in press). Identifying the sources of self-esteem: The mixed medley of benevolence, merit, and bias. *Self and Identity.*

Kwan, V. S. Y., Kuang, L. L., & Zhao, B. (2008). In search of the optimal ego: When self-enhancement bias helps and hurts adjustment. H. Wayment & J. Bauer (eds), *Quieting the ego: Psychological benefits of transcending ego* (pp. 43–52). Washington, DC: American Psychological Association.

Kwan, V. S. Y. & Mandisodza, A. N. (2007). Self-esteem: On the relation between conceptualization and measurement. In C. Sedikides & S. Spencer (eds), *Frontiers in social psychology: The self* (pp. 259–282). Philadelphia, PA: Psychology Press.

Kurman, J. (2001). Self-enhancement: Is it restricted to individualistic cultures? *Personality and Social Psychology Bulletin, 27*, 1705–1716.

Kurman, J. & Sriram, N. S. (1997). Self-enhancement, generality of self-evaluation, and affectivity in Israel and Singapore. *Journal of Cross-Cultural Psychology, 28*, 421–441.
Lai, J. C. L, Chan, J. Y. Y., Cheung, R. W. L., & Law, S. Y. W. (2001). Psychosocial development and self-esteem among traditional-aged university students in Hong Kong. *Journal of College Student Development, 42*, 68–78.
Lam, S. S. K., Chen, X. P., & Schaubroek, J. (2002). Participative decision making and employee performance in different cultures: The moderating effects of allocentrism/idiocentrism and efficacy. *Academy of Management Journal, 45*, 905–914.
Lam, W. W. T., Fielding, R., Chow, L., Chan, M., Leung, G. M., & Ho, E. Y. Y. (2005). The Chinese medical interview satisfaction scale—revised (C-MISS-R): Development and validation. *Quality of Life Research: An International Journal of Quality of Life Aspects of Treatment, Care, and Rehabilitation, 14*, 1187–1192.
Lee, J. S. Y. & Akhtar, S. (2007). Job burnout among nurses in Hong Kong: Implications for human resource practices and interventions. *Asia Pacific Journal of Human Resources, 45*, 63–84.
Lee, L. Y. K., Lee, D. T. F., & Woo, J. (2007). Effect of tai chi on state self-esteem and health-related quality of life in older Chinese residential care home residents. *Journal of Clinical Nursing, 16*, 1580–1582.
Leung, B. W. C., Moneta, G. B., & McBride-Chang, C. (2005). Think positively and feel positively: Optimism and life satisfaction in late life. *International Journal of Aging and Human Development, 61*, 335–365.
Leung, C. (2001). The psychological adaptation of overseas and migrant students in Australia. *International Journal of Psychology, 36*, 251–259.
Leung, M. C. (1996). Social networks and self enhancement in Chinese children: A comparison of self reports and peer reports of group membership. *Social Development, 5*, 146–157.
Li, X., Fang, X., Lin, D., Mao, R., Wang, J., Cottrell, L. et al. (2004). HIV/STD risk behaviors and perceptions among rural-to-urban migrants in China. *AIDS Education and Prevention, 16*, 538–556.
Lin, Y. H. W. & Rusbult, C. E. (1995). Commitment to dating relationships and cross-sex friendships in America and China. *Journal of Social and Personal Relationships, 12*, 7–26.
Ling, A. M. C. & Horwath, C. (1999). Self-efficacy and consumption of fruit and vegetables: Validation of a summated scale. *American Journal of Health Promotion, 13*, 290–298.
Liou, D. & Contento, I. R. (2001). Usefulness of psychosocial theory variables in explaining fat-related dietary behavior in Chinese Americans: Association with degree of acculturation. *Journal of Nutrition Education, 33*, 322–331.
Liu, C., Xiao, J., & Yang, Z. (2003). A compromise between self-enhancement and honesty: Chinese self-evaluations on social desirability scales. *Psychological Reports, 92*, 291–298.
Lu, C. Q., Siu, Q. L., & Cooper, C. L. (2005). Managers' occupational stress in China: The role of self-efficacy. *Personality and Individual Differences, 38*, 569–578.
Lu, L. & Gilmour, R. (2004). Culture and conceptions of happiness: Individual-oriented and social-oriented SWB. *Journal of Happiness Studies, 5*, 269–291.
Lu, L. & Gilmour, R. (2007). Developing a new measure of independent and interdependent views of the self. *Journal of Research in Personality, 41*, 249–257.
Lu, L. & Wu, H. L. (1998). Gender-role traits and depression: Self-esteem and control as mediators. *Counseling Psychology Quarterly, 11*, 95–107.
Lu, L. & Yang, K. S. (2006). Emergence and composition of the traditional–modern bicultural self of people in contemporary Taiwanese societies. *Asian Journal of Social Psychology, 9*, 167–175.
Luk, C. L. & Bond, M. H. (1992). Explaining Chinese self-esteem in terms of the self-concept. *Psychologia: An International Journal of Psychology in the Orient, 35*, 147–154.
Luk, C. L. & Yuen, J. L. C. (1997). The role of self-concepts of technical school students in their learning of a second language. *Psychologia: An International Journal of Psychology in the Orient, 40*, 227–232.
Mak, A. S. & Nesdale, D. (2001). Migrant distress: The role of perceived racial discrimination and coping resources. *Journal of Applied Social Psychology, 31*, 2632–2647.
Man, K. O. & Hamid, P. N. (1998). The relationship between attachment prototypes, self-esteem, loneliness and causal attributions in Chinese trainee teachers. *Personality and Individual Differences, 24*, 357–371.
Mann, L., Radford, M., Burnett, P., Ford, S., Bond, M. H., Leung, K. et al. (1998). Cross-cultural differences in self-reported decision-making style and confidence. *International Journal of Psychology, 33*, 325–335.
Molassiotis, A., Nahas-Lopez, V., Chung, W. Y. R., Lam, S. W. C., Li, C. K. P., & Lau, T. F. J. (2002). Factors associated with adherence to antiretroviral medication in HIV-infected patients. *International Journal of STD and AIDS, 13*, 301–310.
Moore, S. M. & Leung, C. (2001). Romantic beliefs, styles, and relationships among young people from Chinese, Southern European, and Anglo-Australian backgrounds. *Asian Journal of Social Psychology, 4*, 53–68.
Nesdale, D. (2002). Acculturation attitudes and the ethnic and host-country identification of immigrants. *Journal of Applied Social Psychology, 32*, 1488–1507.
Nuttin, J. M. (1987) Affective consequences of mere ownership: The name letter effect in twelve European languages. *European Journal of Social Psychology, 17*, 381–402.
Oettingen, G., Little, T. D., Lindenberger, U., & Baltes, P. B. (1994). Causality, agency and control beliefs in East versus West Berlin children: A natural experiment in the control of context. *Journal of Personality and Social Psychology, 66*, 579–595.

Peng, K. & Nisbett, R. E. (1999). Culture, dialectics, and reasoning about contradiction. *American Psychologist, 54*, 741–754.

Peterson, G. W., Cobas, J. A., Bush, K. R., Supple, A., & Wilson, S. M. (2005). Parent–youth relationships and the self-esteem of Chinese adolescents: Collectivism versus individualism. *Marriage and Family Review, 36*, 173–200.

Poston, D. L., Jr, & Falbo, T. (1990). Academic performance and personality traits of Chinese children. 'Onlies' versus others. *American Journal of Sociology, 96*, 433–451.

Qian, M., Wang, A., & Chen, Z. (2002). A comparison of classmate and self-evaluation of dysphoric and nondysphoric Chinese students. *Cognition and Emotion, 16*, 565–576.

Renner, W. (2003). Human values: A lexical perspective. *Personality and Individual Differences, 34*, 127–141.

Rogers, C. (1998). Motivational indicators in the United Kingdom and the People's Republic of China. *Educational Psychology, 18*, 275–291.

Rosenberg, M. (1965). *Society and the adolescent self-image.* Princeton, NJ: Princeton University Press.

Sachs, J. (2004a). Correlates of academic ability among part-time graduate students of education in Hong Kong. *Psychologia: An International Journal of Psychology in the Orient, 47*, 44–56.

Sachs, J. (2004b). Superstition and self-efficacy in Chinese postgraduate students. *Psychological Reports, 95*, 485–486.

Schaubroeck, J., Lam, S. S. K., & Xie, J. L. (2000). Collective efficacy versus self-efficacy in coping responses to stressors and control: A cross-cultural study. *Journal of Applied Psychology, 85*, 512–525.

Schmitt, D. P. & Allik, J. (2005). Simultaneous administration of the Rosenberg self-esteem scale in 53 nations: Exploring the universal and culture-specific features of global self-esteem. *Journal of Personality and Social Psychology, 89*, 623–642.

Schwarzer, R., Bassler, J., Kwiatek, P., Schroder, K., & Zhang, J. X. (1997). The assessment of optimistic self-beliefs: Comparison of German, Spanish, and Chinese versions of the general self-efficacy scale. *Applied Psychology: An International Review, 46*, 69–88.

Sedkikides, C., Gaertner, L., & Vevea, J. L. (2007). Inclusion of theory-relevant moderators yields the same conclusions as Sedikides, Gaertner, and Vevea (2005): A meta-analytical reply to Heine, Kitayama, and Hamamura (2007). *Asian Journal of Social Psychology, 10*, 59–67.

Shek, D. T. L. (1997). The relation of parent–adolescent conflict to adolescent psychological well-being, school adjustment, and problem behavior. *Social Behavior and Personality, 25*, 277–290.

Shek, D. T. L. (1998a). A longitudinal study of Hong Kong adolescents' and parents' perceptions of family functioning and well-being. *Journal of Genetic Psychology, 159*, 389–403.

Shek, D. T. L. (1998b). A longitudinal study of the relations between parent–adolescent conflict and adolescent psychological well-being. *Journal of Genetic Psychology, 159*, 53–67.

Shek, D. T. L., Lee, T. Y., Lee, B. M., & Chow, J. (2006). Perceived parental control and psychological well-being in Chinese adolescents in Hong Kong. *International Journal of Adolescent Medicine and Health, 18*, 535–545.

Singelis, T. M., Bond, M. H., Sharkey, W. F., & Lai, C. S. Y. (1999). Unpackaging culture's influence on self-esteem and embarrassability: The role of self-construals. *Journal of Cross-Cultural Psychology, 30*, 315–341.

Siu, O. L., Lu, C. Q., & Spector, P. E. (2007). Employees' well-being in greater China: The direct and moderating effects of general self-efficacy. *Applied Psychology: An International Review, 56*, 288–301.

Siu, O. L., Spector, P. E., Cooper, C. L., & Lu, C. Q. (2005). Work stress, self-efficacy, Chinese work values, and work well-being in Hong Kong and Beijing. *International Journal of Stress Management, 12*, 274–288.

Spencer-Rodgers, J., Peng, K., Wang, L., & Hou, Y. (2004). Dialectical self-esteem and East–West differences in psychological well-being. *Personality and Social Psychology Bulletin, 30*, 1416–1432.

Stephens, N. M., Markus, H. R., & Townsend, S. S. M. (2007). Choice as an act of meaning: The case of social class. *Journal of Personality and Social Psychology, 93*, 814–830.

Stevenson, H. W. & Lee, S. Y. (1996). The academic achievement of Chinese students. In M. H. Bond (ed.), *The handbook of Chinese psychology* (pp. 124–142). Hong Kong: Oxford.

Stewart, S. M., Bond, M. H., Kennard, B. D., Ho, L. M., & Zaman, R. M. (2002). Does the construct of *guan* export to the West? *International Journal of Psychology, 37*, 74–82.

Stewart, S. M., Kennard, B. D., Lee, P. W. H., Mayes, T., Hughes, C., & Emslie, G. (2005). Hopelessness and suicidal ideation among adolescents in two cultures. *Journal of Child Psychology and Psychiatry, 46*, 364–372.

Su, X., Ma, G. X., Seals, B., Tan, Y., & Hausman, A. (2006). Breast cancer early detection among Chinese women in the Philadelphia area. *Journal of Women's Health, 15*, 507–519.

Sue, S. & Okazaki, S. (1990). Asian-American educational achievements: A phenomenon in search of an explanation. *American Psychologist, 45*, 913–920.

Suen, L. J. W., Morris, D. L., & McDougall, G. J. Jr. (2004). Memory functions of Taiwanese American older adults. *Western Journal of Nursing Research, 26*, 222–241.

Swerissen, H., Belfrage, J., Weeks, A., Jordan, L., Walker, C., Furler, J. et al. (2006). A randomized control trial of a self-management program for people with a chronic illness from Vietnamese, Chinese, Italian and Greek backgrounds. *Patient Education and Counseling, 64*, 360–368.

Tafarodi, R. W. & Swann, W. B. Jr. (1996). Two-dimensional self-esteem: Theory and measurement. *Personality and Individual Differences, 31*, 653–673.

Tajfel, H. & Turner, J. C. (1979). An integrative theory of intergroup conflict. In W. G. Austin & S. Worchel (eds), *The social psychology of intergroup relations* (pp. 33–47), Monterey, CA: Brooks/Cole.

Tam, S. F. (2000). The effects of a computer skill training programme adopting social comparison and self-efficacy enhancement strategies on self-concept and skill outcome in trainees with physical disabilities. *Disability and Rehabilitation: An International, Multidisciplinary Journal, 22*, 655–664.

Tang, C. S. K., Au, W. T., Schwarzer, R., & Schmitz, G. (2001). Mental health outcomes of job stress among Chinese teachers: Role of stress resource factors and burnout. *Journal of Organizational Behavior, 22*, 887–901.

Tao, K. T. (1998). An overview of only child family mental health in China. *Psychiatry and Clinical Neuroscience, 52(*Suppl.), S206–S211.

Tong, Y. & Song, S. (2004). A study on general self-efficacy and subjective well-being of low SES college students in a Chinese university. *College Student Journal, 38*, 637–642.

Triandis, H. C. (1995). *Individualism and collectivism.* Boulder, CO: Westview.

Tung, W. C., Gillett, P. A., & Pattillo, R. E. (2005). Applying the transtheoretical model to physical activity in family caregivers in Taiwan. *Public Health Nursing, 22*, 299–310.

Turner, J. C. (1982). Towards a cognitive redefinition of social group. In H. Tajfel (ed.), *Social identity and intergroup relations* (pp. 15–40). Cambridge, UK: Cambridge University Press.

Vandello, J. A. & Cohen, C. (1999). Patterns of individualism and collectivism across the United States. *Journal of Personality and Social Psychology, 77*, 279–292.

Walker, G. J., Courneya, K. S., & Deng, J. (2006). Ethnicity, gender, and the theory of planned behavior: The case of playing the lottery. *Journal of Leisure Research, 38*, 224–248.

Wang, S. Y., Chen, C. H., Chin, C. C., & Lee, S. L. (2005). Impact of postpartum depression on the mother–infant couple. *Birth: Issues in Perinatal Care, 32*, 39–44.

Watkins, D., Akande, A., Cheng, C., & Regmi, M. (1996). Culture and gender differences in the self-esteem of college students: A four-country comparison. *Social Behavior and Personality, 24*, 321–328.

Weijun, M. (2003). Self-serving versus group-serving tendencies in causal attributions of Chinese people. *Japanese Journal of Social Psychology, 19*, 135–143.

Wong, D. F. K., Lam, D. O. B., & Kwok, S. Y. C. L. (2003). Stresses and mental health of fathers with younger children in Hong Kong: Implications for social work practices. *International Social Work, 46*, 103–119.

Wu, A. M. S., Tang, C. S. K., Kwok, T. C. Y. (2004). Self-efficacy, health locus of control, psychological distress in elderly Chinese women with chronic illnesses. *Aging and Mental Health, 8*, 21–28.

Xie, J. L., Roy, J. P. & Chen, Z. (2006). Cultural and individual differences in self-rating behavior: An extension and refinement of the cultural relativity hypothesis. *Journal of Organizational Behavior, 27*, 341–364.

Yamaguchi, Greenwald, Banaji et al., Yamaguchi, S., Greenwald, A. G., Banaji, M. R., Murakami, F., Chen, D., Shiomura, K., Kobayashi, C., Cai, H., & Krendl, A. (2007). Apparent universality of positive implicit self-esteem. *Psychological Science, 18*, 498–500.

Yan, E. C. W. & Tang, C. S. K. (2003). The role of individual, interpersonal, and organizational factors in mitigating burnout among elderly Chinese volunteers. *International Journal of Geriatric Psychiatry, 18*, 795–802.

Yang, K. S. (1986). **Chinese** personality and its change. In M. H. Bond (ed.), *The psychology of the Chinese people* (pp. 106–170). Hong Kong: Oxford University Press.

Yeh, M. Y., Chiang, I. C., & Huang, S. Y. (2006). Gender differences in predictors of drinking behavior in adolescents. *Addictive Behaviors, 31*, 1929–1938.

Yik, M. S. M. & Bond, M. H. (1993). Exploring the dimensions of Chinese person perception with indigenous and imported constructs: Creating a culturally balanced scale. *International Journal of Psychology, 28*, 75–95.

Yik, M. S., Bond, M. H., & Paulhus, D. L. (1998). Do Chinese self-enhance or self-efface? It's a matter of domain. *Personality and Social Psychology Bulletin, 24*, 399–406.

Yu, C. C. W., Chan, S., Cheng, F., Sung, R. Y. T., & Hau, K. T. (2006). Are physical activity and academic performance compatible? Academic achievement, conduct, physical activity and self-esteem of Hong Kong Chinese primary school children. *Educational Studies, 32*, 331–341.

Yu, R. L. & Ko, H. C. (2006). Cognitive determinants of MDMA use among college students in Southern Taiwan. *Addictive Behaviors, 31*, 2199–2211.

Zhang, C. M., Zou, H., & Xiang, X. P. (2006). The relationship between self-esteem and personality of high school students. *Chinese Mental Health Journal, 20*, 588–591. (in Chinese)

Zhang, L. (2005). Prediction of Chinese life satisfaction: Contribution of collective self-esteem. *International Journal of Psychology, 40*, 189–200.

CHAPTER 18

From indigenous to cross-cultural personality: the case of the Chinese Personality Assessment Inventory

Fanny M. C. Cheung, Jianxin Zhang, and Shu Fai Cheung

The development of personality assessment in Chinese societies has followed the research trend in cross-cultural psychology, beginning with the importation of Western theories and measures in the early stages. Personality assessment was initially used by the young profession of psychology and its practitioners in clinical and counseling settings to aid diagnostic and treatment decisions, and later in personnel selection and coaching in organizational settings.

Test translation and adaptation

In the 1970s, major instruments such as the Minnesota Multiphasic Personality Inventory (MMPI) and the Eysenck Personality Questionnaire (EPQ) were translated and used in Hong Kong and Taiwan. With the opening of mainland China to Western psychology after 1978, objective psychological assessment represented the acme of science. The use of scientific methods of objective assessment was perceived to enhance the status of the fledging profession (Cheung, 1996).

During the initial period after the resumption of scientific psychological research in China, the influence of Western theories and measures of personality was strong. The adoption of Western psychological tests proliferated in research as well as in applications to human resource management, health screening, clinical assessment, developmental assessment, and forensic evaluation (Zhang, 1988). With few local instruments available, most psychologists depended on the importation of well-developed Western personality tests (Cheung, 2004; Cheung, Leung et al., 1996). Generally speaking, these Western psychological instruments have demonstrated satisfactory reliability and validity when used among the Chinese people. However, cultural differences are evident in the items, scales, and interpretation of these imposed-etic instruments (Cheung, 2004).

The adult and junior versions of the EPQ were first translated in Hong Kong by Chan (Eysenck & Chan, 1982). In China, the 90-item version of the EPQ was first translated by Z. G. Chen at the Peking University with permission from Eysenck. The revised 48-item version was later adapted by

M. Y. Qian and her associates at the Peking University. Cross-cultural differences have been found in the mean score levels on the scales in different Chinese samples. For example, the mean scale score on extraversion in the Chinese sample was much lower than that in the UK sample, but the reverse was observed in the psychoticism scale (Barrett & Eysenck, 1984). In general, with the exception of a significant number of items tapping psychoticism, the generalizability of the EPQ dimensions was found to be good (Cheung, 2004).

As the MMPI is the most widely used personality test in the world, it is one of the instruments that the Institute of Psychology at the Chinese Academy of Science decided to translate when the discipline of psychology was reinstated in the late 1970s. Prof. Weizhen Song adopted the Chinese version originally translated by Fanny Cheung in Hong Kong. A program of collaborative research between the Chinese University of Hong Kong and the Institute of Psychology was set up to standardize the Chinese version.

This was the first time a large-scale representative national norm was developed for a personality test in China. Workshops were organized to train psychologists to use the MMPI in China and Hong Kong, facilitating its frequent utilization in psychiatric hospitals, outpatient clinics, and forensic settings. After the publication of the MMPI-2 in 1989, Jianxin Zhang at the Institute of Psychology continued collaborative efforts with Fanny Cheung to standardize the Chinese version and establish national norms.

With the support of the international MMPI network, high standards have been set for the translation and adaptation of the Chinese MMPI and MMPI-2. Careful research has been reported on the adaptations and clinical validation of the MMPI and MMPI-2 in China and Hong Kong (Cheung & Song, 1989; Cheung, Song, & Zhang, 1996; Cheung, Zhang, & Song, 2003; Cheung, Zhao, & Wu, 1992). A new Chinese Infrequency scale was developed empirically based on the Chinese normative sample (Cheung, Song, & Butcher, 1991). With the permission of the University of Minnesota Press, the Chinese MMPI-2 was published by the Chinese University Press in 2003 (Cheung, Zhang, & Song, 2003), with the rights for a joint publication granted to the Institute of Psychology for distribution in mainland China. This is the first copyright agreement on Western personality tests in the People's Republic of China.

Another popular Western personality measure that has been translated into Chinese for research use is the NEO PI-R (Costa & McCrae, 1992), which is based on the Five-Factor Model (FFM). An earlier version was translated by Michael Bond and Michelle Yik (McCrae, Yik, Trapnell, Bond, & Paulhus, 1998) in Hong Kong, and subsequently revised by Zhang and Xie in China (Leung, Cheung, Zhang, Song, & Xie, 1997). Another adaptation was translated by Dai, Yao, Cao, and Yang (2004). To date, there is no standardization study or Chinese norms on the NEO PI-R. Research with the NEO PI-R among Chinese participants showed overall convergence with the FFM, although the original structure of the openness factor was not fully recovered, just as proved difficult in other Asian studies (see Cheung, 2004; Cheung et al., 2008; Leung et al., 1997).

While the NEO PI-R was primarily used for research on the theoretical aspects of the FFM, a large-scale clinical study with 2,000 psychiatric patients was conducted in China (Yang, McCrae, Costa, Dai, Yao, Cai, & Gao, 1999). Corresponding personality profiles were obtained for six diagnostic subgroups of patients, including substance-induced psychotic disorder, schizophrenia, bipolar mood disorder (manic and depressed episodes), major depression, and neurosis. However, Yang, Bagby, and Ryder (2000) noted the effects of response-style bias that might affect the validity of the scales for some sub-samples of psychiatric patients on the NEO PI-R and highlighted the need for the introduction of validity scales.

While the importation of well-established Western personality tests provides Chinese psychologists with a wealth of scientific evidence to support their applications, cultural differences have been observed at the item, scale, and factor levels, differences that carry implications for interpreting test results. Questions about cultural relevance have led to attempts to develop indigenous measures to assess and study psychological constructs that are particularly relevant to the Chinese culture. These queries parallel the indigenization movement in Chinese psychology (see Hwang & Han, this volume).

The 'transport and test' function of test importation has aroused wider discussion in cross-cultural psychology (Cheung, Cheung, Wada, & Zhang, 2003). Initial concerns lay in the methodological issues of test translation and adaptation (Marsella, Dubanoski, Hamada, & Morse, 2000; van de Vijver & Leung, 1997). Recent advances in cross-cultural psychology have introduced useful methodological and statistical tools for research in this area, such as the *ITC Guidelines on Adapting Tests* (International Test Commission, www.intestcom.org; Hambleton, Merenda, & Spielberg, 2005; van de Vijver & Hambleton, 1996). Based on their experiences with the international applications of the MMPI/MMPI-2, Butcher and his associates have summarized a comprehensive system for cross-cultural adaptation of objective personality tests that is aimed at establishing cross-cultural test equivalence (Butcher, Mosch, Tsai, & Nezami, 2006). These methodological considerations were taken on board in the translation and adaptation of the Chinese MMPI and MMPI-2, which has also built up a program of validation studies (Butcher, Cheung, & Lim, 2003; Cheung, 1985; Cheung, Zhang, & Song, 2003). The Chinese MMPI-2 has thereby come to be regarded as an example of good practice in test translation and adaptation.

Despite methodological advances in adaptation of tests, a more theoretical and ideological issue has been raised in cross-cultural psychology. The predominance of the etic approach in Western psychology which emphasizes 'core similarities' in all human beings has ignored cultural relevance and the meaning of local conceptualizations of behavior patterns (Sue, 1983). The importation of Western assessment measures represents the imposed-etic approach in which Western constructs are assumed to be universally applicable and are 'imposed' upon the local culture. Ideologically, this approach is considered a form of cultural imperialism undermining national identity and consciousness. As Yik and Bond (1993) pointed out, even though the observed patterns of behaviors could be coaxed to fit the imposed model, these imposed-etic measures would 'cut the social-perceptual world' according to Western theories. Cross-cultural psychologists have questioned whether imported tests can adequately predict relevant criteria across cultures (Church, 2001). There may be other culture-specific or emic personality constructs that are important to the local cultures but are not covered in the imported measures, or are not construed in the same taxonomy that could provide a fuller understanding of personality in the local cultural context (Cheung et al., 2001, 2008).

The development of indigenous personality measures in Chinese culture

In the 1970s, Yang (1986; 1997) pioneered the indigenization movement of Chinese psychology in Taiwan, an initiative that focused in part on important personality constructs in Chinese societies, including traditionalism–modernity, face, harmony, and *yuan* (predestined relationship) (Hwang, 2000; Leung, this volume; Yang, 1997). A number of related scales were developed for research studies in social psychology, such as those on face by Hwang (this volume).

In the attempt to provide culturally relevant personality assessment tools, Chinese psychologists have begun to develop indigenous measures to study Chinese personality and its latent structure in the 1980s. These early attempts have been reviewed by Cheung and her associates (Cheung, 2004; Cheung, Cheung, Zhang, & Wada, 2003; Cheung, Cheung, & Zhang, 2004b).

Ko's Mental Health Questionnaire (KMHQ; Ko, 1977, 1981, 1997) was Taiwan's first attempt to develop a multidimensional personality test for clinical assessment in the Chinese cultural context. Ko originally adapted items from the MMPI based on his clinical experience, and added other scales to measure healthy personality traits that fit his general theoretical model of mental health. The KMHQ has undergone many revisions up until Ko's retirement, with different numbers of items and scales included in the various versions. Most of the publications on the KMHQ are in Chinese books or journals in Taiwan. Partly because Ko focused more on a model of mental health, he did not add any of the emic personality constructs that have been widely studied by other Chinese psychologists in the indigenous psychology movement in Taiwan (Cheung & Leung, 1998).

Another early attempt to develop an indigenous measure by psychologists in Hong Kong and Taiwan was the Multi-Trait Personality Inventory (MTPI; Cheung, Conger, Hau, Lew, & Lau, 1992). Lew and his team identified 122 bipolar items from a review of the literature on Chinese culture and personality and from interviews with Chinese students, and examined possible continuities in personality traits of Chinese populations from mainland China, Hong Kong, Taiwan, and the USA. The core traits shared among the different groups of Chinese included items that tapped indigenous elements of Chinese personality and reflected Confucian teaching and traditional values. Following Lew's retirement, no further research has been pursued with the MTPI.

The most comprehensive attempt to develop an indigenous personality measure is the Chinese Personality Assessment Inventory (CPAI) initiated by the team of psychologists at the Chinese University of Hong Kong and the Institute of Psychology of the Chinese Academy of Science. Building on their collaboration on the adaptation of the Chinese MMPI, the team embarked on the development of the CPAI in the late 1980s, resulting in the first standardized version in 1992 (Cheung et al., 1996), and the second edition in 2001 (Cheung, Cheung, & Zhang, 2004b; Cheung, Cheung, Zhang et al., 2008). The CPAI will be discussed more fully in the second part of this chapter.

Other recent indigenous approaches to personality assessment in Chinese societies adopted a psycho-lexical approach which examined personality descriptors from dictionaries, such as those by Chen and Wang (1984), Huang and Zhang (1992), and Wang, Fang, and Zhou (1995). One example is the Chinese Personality Scale (also named the Qingnian Zhongguo Personality Scale, QZPS: Wang & Cui, 2003) which extracted seven indigenous personality factors and 15 sub-factors based on adjectives selected primarily from dictionaries, and also from textbooks, newspapers, magazines, and novels. Items were then written to fit the factors. The shared variance explained by the factors was 30.09 per cent. The seven factors were extraversion, kindness, behavioral styles, talents, emotionality, human relations, and ways of life. In a joint factor analysis of the 180 items from the QZPS and 240 items from the NEO PI-R, a seven-factor structure was obtained after removing 166 items, and then accounted for 28.13 per cent of the variance (Wang, Cui, & Zhou, 2005). Wang and his colleagues have published widely in China on the QZPS, attempting to confirm a seven-factor structure in Chinese personality.

With more focus on theoretical research, few of these indigenous measures have followed through with a vigorous research program required for establishing its utility as an assessment tool. With the relatively narrow perspective of indigenous psychology, research on these indigenous measures tends to emphasize the uniqueness of their constructs or latent factor structure (Zhang & Zhou, 2006). Zhang and Zhou have contended that the number of factors and the culture-specific nature of the factors proposed depend on the orientation and methodology of the researchers, and this astute assessment of the situation accounts in part for the variation in personality questionnaires and their varying factor structures.

The broader issues of cross-cultural personality assessment that gave rise to the original concerns raised by cross-cultural psychologists remain to be addressed (Church, 2001). While some of these indigenous personality constructs and measures may serve the purpose of personality assessment in the specific cultural context, there is a need to consider their contribution to the fundamental understanding of human behavior and their utility or incremental validity beyond that provided by the imported measures. Church (2001) acknowledged that the best support to date for the incremental validity of indigenously derived personality measures has come from the research program generated by the creators of the Chinese Personality Assessment Inventory.

The Chinese Personality Assessment Inventory (CPAI)

The CPAI was developed as a joint effort of psychologists at the Chinese University of Hong Kong and the Chinese Academy of Sciences in the late 1980s. In response to the critique of the imposed-etic approach in cross-cultural personality assessment, the team considered it timely to develop an indigenous measure suitable for the Chinese people who constituted at least one-fourth of the world's population. The team built on their experience in the methodology of the adaptation and standardization of the Chinese MMPI to design a comprehensive indigenous instrument covering personality characteristics for normal as well as diagnostic assessment of the Chinese people.

They derived the personality constructs and the behavioral items from multiple sources using a bottom-up approach. Adopting the combined etic–emic approach in cross-cultural psychology (van de Vijver & Leung, 1997), the CPAI includes both universal and indigenous constructs. The determination of the personality constructs included in the CPAI was based on multiple inputs from a wide range of daily life experiences, including novels, media, and folk concepts of person descriptions, paying special attention to culturally relevant constructs empirically derived from preliminary surveys as well as those reported in the psychological literature. For the clinically based personality constructs, references were made to the clinical experiences of the local professionals and the previous applications of the Chinese MMPI. Validity scales were included to enhance the accuracy of assessment. The CPAI was standardized on a representative national norm of Chinese adults in mainland China and Hong Kong (see Cheung et al., 1996, for a detailed description of the development of the CPAI). Studies with large samples of college students in China, Hong Kong, and Taiwan confirmed the congruence of the factor structure across Chinese societies (Cheung et al., 2001). The original CPAI consisted of 22 normal personality scales loaded on four factors, 12 clinical scales with two factors, and three validity scales/indexes.

To examine its cross-cultural relevance, the team assessed the convergence and divergence of the CPAI with the NEO PI-R (Costa, & McCrae, 1992) measuring the Five-Factor Model, which was claimed to cover universal personality dimensions. A joint factor analysis of the CPAI and the NEO PI-R in both Chinese and Singaporean samples showed that the CPAI factor of Interpersonal Relatedness (IR) did not load on any of the Big Five factors (Cheung, Cheung, Leung, Ward, & Leong, 2003; Cheung, Leung et al., 2001), whereas none of the CPAI scales loaded on the Openness to Experience factor of the NEO PI-R.

To test whether the openness factor was relevant to the taxonomy of Chinese personality, six indigenously derived openness-related scales were added to the revised version, CPAI-2 (Cheung, Cheung, & Zhang, 2004b; Cheung et al., 2008). The revised version was restandardized in 2001, with a representative sample of 1,911 adults aged 18 to 70 from mainland China and Hong Kong. The CPAI-2 consists of 28 personality scales, 12 clinical scales and three validity scales. Despite the addition of the openness-related scales, however, a four-factor solution (social potency/expansiveness, dependability, accommodation, and interpersonal relatedness), similar to that of the original CPAI, was extracted from the 28 normal personality scales, accounting for 48.4 per cent of the shared variance using principal axis factoring analysis (55.4 per cent with EFA). Two factors were extracted from the 12 clinical scales (emotional problems and behavioral problems), accounting for 58.8 per cent (65.6 per cent with EFA) of their shared variance.

Four of the openness scales that cover self-oriented interests and intellectual aspects of openness are best interpreted when they are aligned with extraversion and leadership under the social potency factor. The alignment of the other two more socially oriented openness scales with the CPAI-2 accommodation and the interpersonal relatedness factors suggests that the construct of openness in Chinese culture includes not only the person's approach to ideas and interests as in Western studies of openness, but also social relationships with other people (Cheung et al., 2008). In a joint factor analysis of the NEO-FFI (the short version of the NEO PI-R) and the CPAI-2, a six-factor model of personality was again found (Cheung, Cheung, Zhang et al., 2008). The six-factor structure could be interpreted as a combination of the Five-Factor Model and the IR factor.

A version of the CPAI for adolescents, the CPAI-A, was developed in 2005 based on the framework of the CPAI-2 (Cheung, Fan, Cheung, & Leung, 2008). Using the same combined emic–etic approach, personality constructs relevant to Chinese adolescents were generated from the ground up using multiple sources of folk concepts and involving participants from mainland China, Hong Kong, and Taiwan. Scales that were particularly relevant to adolescents were added, while those CPAI-2 scales that were considered to be less important to this age group were deleted. The CPAI-A was standardized initially in Hong Kong with a representative sample of 2,689 adolescents aged 12 to 18. The CPAI-A included four factors for the 25 normal personality scales (social potency/expansiveness, emotional stability, interpersonal relatedness, and dependability), and two factors for the 14 clinical scales (emotional problems and behavioral problems). Gender differences and the developmental trends of these differences were reported (Fan, Cheung, Cheung, & Leung, 2008).

Zhou (2007) examined the impact of rapid social changes on personality based on the responses of the normative samples on the same items of the CPAI and CPAI-2. The patterns of changes in norms associated with China's modernization and economic development provide a framework to examine the stability of Chinese personality structure. The personality scales from the four normal personality factors that were stable across both age and time cohorts included universal traits such as logical vs. affective orientation, enterprise, responsibility, inferiority vs. self-acceptance, and optimism vs. pessimism, as well as indigenous traits including face, family orientation and Ah Q mentality. Zhou suggested that these dimensions may reflect a more core-level structure of Chinese personality.

On the other hand, normal personality scales from the CPAI-2 that were more likely to be affected by social and life changes included the universal traits of leadership, practical-mindedness, emotionality, and internal vs. external locus of control, as well as the indigenous traits of self vs. social orientation, veraciousness vs. slickness, traditionalism vs. modernity, harmony, *renqing*, discipline, and thrift vs. extravagance. These personality dimensions are more susceptible to environmental influences and may represent the more manifest level of personality structure that interacts with social changes. While the basis for explaining personality stability needs further research, Zhou's proposed model provides an interesting framework to examine the scales associated with the interpersonal relatedness factor that are more contextualized within the cultural environment.

Validation of the CPAI

The utility of an indigenous personality measure lies in the research database from which its interpretation can be based. An extensive research program on the validity of the CPAI/CPAI-2 has been undertaken by the test authors and other researchers in cross-cultural and Chinese psychology. The Chinese personality traits measured by the CPAI, CPAI-2, and CPAI-A have been found to be correlated with various external variables, which include variables related to basic psychological phenomena, mental health, and other outcomes in applied settings. Early research on the incremental validity of the CPAI indigenous factor in predicting different aspects of social relationships in Chinese culture, including filial piety, trust, interpersonal influence tactics, and communication style was reported by Cheung et al. (2001). The following review focuses on recent studies on the social correlates indigenous personality factors/scales and the clinical scales of the CPAI/CPAI-2/CPAI-A, as well as their contributions to various outcome variables.

Life satisfaction

In addition to universal traits such as optimism and self-acceptance that have been found to be correlated with subjective well-being and self-esteem, several indigenous scales have also been found to be associated with life satisfaction among the Chinese people. In the normative sample of the CPAI-2, the indigenously derived family orientation and harmony scales were found to be positively correlated with indices of life satisfaction, while face and defensiveness (Ah Q mentality) were negatively associated with life satisfaction (Cheung & Cheung, 2002, July). These four indigenous scales as well as social sensitivity were also found to be correlated with life satisfaction in a sample of Chinese college students (Chen, Cheung, Bond, & Leung, 2006). In a sample of Chinese adolescents using the CPAI-A, Ho, Cheung, and Cheung (2008) found that family orientation, harmony, social sensitivity, graciousness and *renqing* from the IR factor were positively correlated with life satisfaction. Family orientation and harmony contributed additional variance to life satisfaction beyond the universal scales of emotionality, inferiority, optimism, and extraversion from the CPAI-2.

These findings are consistent with the notion that Chinese societies are collectivistic, and that relationship plays an important role in life satisfaction. Having a close relationship with one's family, being sensitive to others' feelings and well-being, upholding harmony, and emphasizing reciprocal social relationships are related to life satisfaction among Chinese. Moreover, the findings among Chinese adolescents suggest that socialization of these traits occurs early in the psychosocial development of adolescents, as the associations between the relationship-related traits and life satisfaction were found even among junior high-school students. On the other hand, face concern and Ah Q mentality (defensiveness), other salient behavioural tendencies in social interaction in the Chinese culture, were negatively correlated with life satisfaction, as they interfere with achieving smooth and rewarding interpersonal relationships.

How do the relational personality traits affect life satisfaction and well-being? Ho et al. (2008) found that personality had both direct and indirect effects on Chinese adolescents' life satisfaction. Personality traits may predispose people to or protect them from negative life events, which in turn affect outcomes in subjective well-being. Ho (2008) further found that the personality factor of interpersonal relatedness moderated the relationship between exposure to violence and adjustment outcomes for adolescents in Hong Kong. Another possible explanation was explored in a study on the relationship between life satisfaction and forgiveness using the CPAI-2 (Fu, Watkins, & Hui, 2004). The study showed that among Chinese college students and teachers, the *renqing* and harmony scales significantly predicted forgiveness. Since the propensity to forgive is correlated with various indices of mental health, including life satisfaction, the results suggest that *renqing* and harmony may influence life satisfaction partly through one's willingness to forgive. It is possible that under the societal norms of avoiding overt conflict in Chinese societies, emphasis on *renqing* and harmony may lead to Chinese ways of conflict resolution, such as forgiveness, that are important to subjective well-being. Further studies examining the pattern of associations among forgiveness, conflict management, *renqing*, harmony, and life satisfaction would help to enrich our understanding of the contributions of these indigenous Chinese personality traits to well-being and interpersonal relationships.

Social beliefs

Chen, Bond, and Cheung (2005) identified several indigenous scales of the CPAI-2 that were associated with social axioms, or beliefs about the world. They correlated the CPAI-2 scales with the Social Axiom Survey, an inventory measuring five universal factors of social beliefs (Leung & Bond, 2004). Specifically, social cynicism was negatively correlated with social sensitivity, harmony, veraciousness, graciousness, and family orientation, and positively correlated with face and defensiveness. Social cynicism represents a negative view of human nature and a general mistrust of people. Its association with the CPAI-2 indigenous scales suggests that those Chinese characteristics that are facilitative of social relationship and interaction, such as harmony and being sensitive to others' feelings, are incompatible with this negative view. On the other hand, people high on face concern and defensiveness may adopt a negative view of human nature as a way to protect self-esteem, explaining away failures by attributing them to other people's wrongdoing, leading to their mistrust in people. Another social belief, reward for application was found to be positively associated with *renqing*, social sensitivity, harmony, family orientation, graciousness, and veraciousness. The original concept of reward for application emphasizes the reward (positive results) due to the investment of personal resources, such as knowledge, effort, and hard work. In the Chinese cultural context, maintaining good interpersonal relationships requires social skills, and may be considered as effort or even investment that could lead to positive rewards. Nevertheless, most of the bivariate correlations in this study were relatively small, suggesting that social beliefs and these indigenous personality dimensions are related but distinct. More research needs to be conducted to further examine the dynamics of the relationships between social beliefs and indigenous personality scales.

Gender identity

As in other Western personality measures, gender differences were observed in the mean scores of some of the CPAI-2 and CPAI-A scales. In addition to the universal traits on the social potency and dependability factors, females in the CPAI-2 normative samples also scored higher on the indigenous scales including face, harmony, and social sensitivity (Cheung et al., 2004b). More gender differences were observed in the indigenous personality scales of the CPAI-A, with girls scoring higher on most of the scales for the factor measuring interpersonal relatedness (Fan et al., 2008).

These gender differences may be understood in relation to gender role identity. Zhang and Feng (2005) studied the relationship between gender identity as measured by the Bem Sex Role Inventory, and personality traits as measured by the CPAI-2 among 1,000 undergraduates in China. They found that both androgynous and masculine undergraduates scored higher than feminine undergraduates on all social potency factor scales (e.g. novelty, leadership, logical orientation). On the scales of the interpersonal relatedness factor, androgynous undergraduates scored higher than masculine undergraduates on the CPAI-2 *renqing*, harmony, social sensitivity, and face scales, and were similar to feminine undergraduates on these four scales. However, both androgynous and masculine undergraduates scored lower than feminine undergraduates on graciousness. Moreover, androgynous undergraduates were more self-oriented than feminine undergraduates, but more social-oriented than masculine undergraduates. On the other hand, androgynous undergraduates scored higher than both feminine and masculine undergraduates on defensiveness. These findings suggest that in Chinese societies, people with androgynous gender identity may share the feminine orientation toward relationships, and at the same time share the masculine orientation toward instrumentality and rationality.

Applications of the CPAI scales

Utility of personality measures in applied settings depends on having a good research database. The different versions of the CPAI have built up a database from their applications in industrial-organizational, educational as well as clinical settings.

Leadership

The CPAI-2 profiles of over 400 MBA students at a university in Hong Kong were compared in terms of their job seniority (Cheung, Fan, & To, 2008). Those students who were senior-level executives scored higher on responsibility, self-acceptance, enterprise (adventurousness), and leadership. As a group, the MBA students scored higher than the CPAI-2 normative sample on family orientation and *renqing*. The authors discussed this relational orientation in the context of role expectations attached to Chinese leaders. To function well in business settings in Chinese societies, Chinese leaders need to take into account relationship norms and the emphasis on reciprocal favours. Moreover, Chinese culture values not only the work performance of the leaders, but also their exercise of responsibility towards their families, both at home and at work (Redding & Wong, 1986). Studies of work–family interface in Chinese societies have shown that work and family are viewed as interdependent domains. Ensuring financial security for the family is a strong incentive for commitment to work (Halpern & Cheung, 2008; Yang, Chen, Choi, & Zou, 2000).

In another study of mainland and Hong Kong senior executives at the directorate level (including chief executive officers and managing directors from business organizations), the CPAI-2 scales were found to be predictive of leadership behaviors based on Quinn's (1988) model of behavioral complexity (Cheung et al., 2008). Six aspects of leadership behaviours were included, namely leadership change, producing results, managing process, relating to people, moral character, and individual effectiveness. Consistent with findings from Western studies using universal personality measures, the CPAI-2 social potency factor was a significant predictor of the self-ratings on all six aspects, confirming the notion that social potency is a complex factor combining openness, extraversion, and leadership. Similar to results found for conscientiousness in Western studies, dependability was predictive of all aspects of leadership behaviours, except relating to people. In addition, the indigenous interpersonal relatedness factor was predictive of self-ratings on managing process, relating to people, moral character, and individual effectiveness. It was also a significant predictor of subordinate ratings on the leaders' skill in relating to people. Further analyses of the individual scales revealed that *renqing*, social sensitivity, and harmony were related to behavioral complexity (i.e. being high on multiple dimensions of leadership behaviours) and effectiveness, echoing the findings among the MBA students that interpersonal concerns are important to Chinese leadership. A replication of this study in a Western society would be helpful in discovering how distinctive such findings are to Chinese leadership (see Chen & Farh, this volume).

Job performance

The relationship between the CPAI and CPAI-2 scales and job performance has been examined in different applied settings. Kwong and Cheung (2003) administered the CPAI to supervisors in a hotel chain, and found that the scales measuring harmony and leadership were significantly correlated with supervisor-rated, interpersonal contextual behaviors, while veraciousness was significantly correlated with supervisor-rated personal contextual behaviors. Cheung, Chan, and Cheung (2007, July) administered the CPAI-2 to frontline service workers in a hotel chain. They found that some of the dependability factor scales (responsibility, meticulousness, emotionality) and harmony significantly predicted job performance as rated by supervisors. Chan (2005) examined the validity of the CPAI-2 in predicting teaching performance at a university. A sample of course tutors of the community university were administered the CPAI-2, and their scale scores were correlated with teaching evaluation ratings from their students. It was found that high scores on *renqing* were associated with high ratings on teaching attitude, while high scores on harmony were associated with high ratings on perceived motivation, presentation, teaching attitude, and interaction. These three studies all involved other-ratings of job performance. They converged in confirming the utility of the indigenous interpersonal relatedness factor scales in predicting job performance beyond the contributions of universal personality traits, especially when the job duties involve social interaction.

In a study of negotiation, Liu, Friedman, and Chi (2005) found that for Chinese graduate students of management, the CPAI-2 face, harmony, and *renqing* scales were predictive of negotiation behavior among Chinese MBA students, while the Big Five extraversion and agreeableness factors were predictive of negotiation behavior among American MBA students. To the extent that the job duties involve successful negotiation, these findings suggest that indigenous traits may play an important role in job performance in the Chinese cultural context. Sun and Bond (2000) also found that the CPAI face, harmony and *renqing* scales contributed additional variance beyond the NEO-FFI facets in predicting the use of gentle persuasion as a set of interpersonal influence tactics among Chinese managers.

Clinical validity

To establish its convergent validity in clinical assessment, the CPAI has been compared with the MMPI-2, one of the most widely used personality measures in clinical settings. Cheung, Cheung, and Zhang (2004a) administered both the CPAI and the Chinese MMPI-2 to a sample of Chinese university students and examined the correlational pattern between the corresponding CPAI clinical scales and the MMPI-2 scales. In general, the correlations between the two sets of scales that assess similar forms of psychopathology were higher than those measuring dissimilar or unrelated forms of psychopathology. The correspondence between the CPAI clinical scales and MMPI-2 content scales was stronger than that between CPAI clinical scales and MMPI-2 clinical scales, as the latter set of scales was derived empirically using American criterion groups and norms. Despite the overall correspondence, some differences were found, suggesting potential cultural differences in the manifestation of various clinical features.

The validity of the CPAI and CPAI-2 was also investigated in clinical samples. Cheung, Kwong, and Zhang (2003) administered the CPAI to a sample of prisoners incarcerated for serious violent crimes. Pathological dependence, antisocial behavior, somatization (negative) and sexual maladjustment (negative) significantly differentiated the prisoners from a matched normal comparison group. In addition, seven normal personality scales, namely extravagance, pessimism, slickness, *renqing*, flexibility, adventurousness, and traditionalism significantly differentiated prisoners from the normal comparison group.

In the second study reported in the same paper, the CPAI was administered to a sample of patients from two psychiatric hospitals in Beijing. Among the clinical scales, pathological dependence, distortion of reality, depression, sexual maladjustment, antisocial behavior, and somatization significantly differentiated the psychiatric patients from a matched normal comparison group. The psychiatric patients also scored lower than their normal counterparts on several indigenous normal personality scales, including *renqing*, face, and family orientation.

Cheung (2007) reported a large-scale study using the CPAI-2 to investigate the profiles of five diagnostic groups of psychiatric patients recruited from ten mainland and Hong Kong hospitals. Compared to the normative sample, patients with schizophrenic disorders were found to have higher scores on distortion of reality, paranoia, depression, antisocial behavior, and somatization. Patients with bipolar disorders in their manic episodes were found to be higher than their normal counterparts on hypomania, need for attention, pathological dependence, and anxiety. Patients with bipolar disorders in their depressive episodes, on the other hand, scored higher on depression, need for attention, inferiority, and distortion of reality. Patients suffering from neurotic disorders (including generalized anxiety disorders, obsessive-compulsive disorders, and other neurotic disorders) obtained elevated scores on anxiety, depression, and physical symptoms. Patients with severe major depression scored higher than the normative sample on depression, physical symptoms, and distortion of reality.

Based on the data set from this clinical study, Cheung, Cheung, and Leung (2008) investigated the CPAI-2's utility in differentiating male patients with substance-use disorders from a matched group of Chinese males from the normative sample and a matched group of psychiatric patients without disorders involving substance abuse. As hypothesized, the pathological dependence scale significantly differentiated the patients with substance use disorders from the two matched comparison groups. Two other scales, pessimism and depression, also significantly differentiated the patients with substance-use disorders from their normal counterparts. In addition, antisocial behavior significantly differentiated this clinical group from other psychiatric patients without this disorder. Apart from the clinical scales, the CPAI-2 profiles of these patients were characterized by poor dependability, emotional instability, social maladjustment, and difficulties in interpersonal relationship. In particular, low scores on the indigenous scales of family orientation and harmony, coupled with high scores on Ah Q mentality reflect problems in social adjustment. These CPAI-2 universal and indigenous personality scales helped to identify long-standing personality traits that might have implications for treatment.

The more culturally relevant content of the items on the clinical scales also provide useful measures for assessing emotional disturbance in the Chinese context. For example, Chang, Lansford, Schwartz, and Farver (2004) used the CPAI-2 depression scale to study the relationship between mothers' depression and their child's level of aggression among a group of elementary-school students in Hong Kong. They found that maternal depression had a direct effect on the child's aggression as well as an indirect effect on child aggression through harsh parenting. Li and Chang (2007) studied a sample of younger children (mean age 4.78) and found that, for sub-samples with self-reported father–child resemblance, paternal depression had a significant indirect effect on child aggression through harsh parenting.

These studies support the clinical utility of the CPAI/CPAI-2 scales in providing incremental validity when assessing specific clinical disorders in a Chinese cultural context. With the culturally relevance of its items and the availability of the Chinese norms, the CPAI-2 offers a useful tool for scientifically assessing psychopathology in Chinese societies.

From indigenous to cross-cultural personality

In meeting the challenge of cross-cultural psychologists on the incremental validity of indigenous personality measures, the CPAI has been compared with other imported measures and has been applied to other cultural groups using a translated English version (Cheung et al., 2001; Cheung, Cheung, Leung et al., 2003; Lin & Church, 2004). Even in these non-Chinese samples, the indigenous interpersonal relatedness scales could not be absorbed into the Five-Factor Model, and the CPAI factor structure with its distinctive dimension of interpersonal relatedness for these samples was congruent with that of the Chinese normative sample. The CPAI-2 has been translated into English, Korean, and Japanese. Factor analytic studies using these other language versions also showed that the interpersonal relatedness (IR) factor could be retrieved in other cultural groups including Asian-Americans, Koreans, Japanese, and different ethnic groups in Singapore (Cheung, 2006; Cheung, Cheung, Howard, & Lim 2006), leading to the renaming of the CPAI-2 as the Cross-cultural (Chinese) Personality Assessment Inventory.

Our original aim in developing the CPAI was to provide Chinese psychologists with a culturally relevant instrument for their applied needs. Learning from the experience of adapting imported measures and following international guidelines in test development, we produced an instrument that captured important dimensions of personality of the Chinese people. Cross-cultural research with the CPAI has provided an opportunity to explore the universal and culture-specific dimensions of Chinese personality. While we do not intend to impose the CPAI-2 factor structure upon other cultures, the relevance of the IR factor that is associated with complex instrumental relationships even in non-Chinese samples highlights a gap in Western personality theories and measures. The dominant Western theories of personality tend to focus on the intrapsychic aspects of the person, and neglect these important interpersonal domains.

Cross-cultural research on the CPAI-2 poses a challenge for psychologists to re-examine the controversy of the universality versus cultural specificity of personality structure, and the related polarity of the etic vs. emic approaches. Bond (1988) was the first to adopt a combined emic–etic approach in his development of the Chinese Value Survey (CVS), and tested its cross-cultural relevance in nine different cultures. The inclusion of both universal and indigenous dimensions provided a comprehensive and pancultural measure that enhances the cultural sensitivity and promotes cross-cultural comparisons at the same time. Van der Vijver and Leung (1997) advocated this convergent approach of combining emic and etic dimensions as a powerful way to break new theoretical ground in cross-cultural research. Combining indigenous and universal dimensions enables more dynamic exchanges in cross-cultural psychology that overcome the concern of 'intellectual imperialism of the West in cross-cultural psychology' (Cheung & Leung, 1998, p. 246).

By adopting a combined emic–etic approach in its development, the CPAI-2 provides 'a measure that is sensitive to the indigenous cultural context, allows cross-cultural comparison of the meaning of etic or imposed etic traits, and extends the interpretation of indigenous traits in a broader cultural context' (Cheung, 2006, p. 102). Publication of the CPAI research in international journals provides cross-cultural psychologists with a framework for understanding the fundamental structure of human personality across cultures.

This methodological approach is now considered one of the best practices in developing indigenous personality measures in non-Western cultures, and is cited as the reference model for the ambitious development of the South African Personality Inventory (SAPI; Meiring, van der Vijver, Rothmann, & de Bruin, 2008, July), a comprehensive set of personality questionnaires with 11 language versions to provide equitable and culturally valid measures of personality across all of the many cultural and language groups in South Africa.

Despite its practical origin, research with the CPAI has 'led us down a more theoretical path' to compare the cultural reality that is presented by this indigenous instrument with the imposed reality based on borrowed instruments and borrowed theories (Cheung, 2004). It has also demonstrated the usefulness of a combined emic-etic approach to study personality from a more inclusive cross-cultural perspective, and prompted us to reflect on the broader meaning of studying the psychology of the Chinese people.

Authors' note

The CPAI studies included in this chapter were funded partly by the Hong Kong Government Research Grants Council Earmarked Grant Projects (#CUHK4333/00H, #CUHK4326/01H,

#CUHK4333/00H, #CUHK 4259/03H, and #CUHK 4715/06H), and Direct Grants of the Chinese University of Hong Kong (#2020662, #2020745, #2020871).

References

Bond, M. H. (1988). Finding universal dimensions for individual variation in multicultural studies of values: The Rokeach and Chinese Value Surveys. *Journal of Personality and Social Psychology, 55*, 1009–1015.

Butcher, J. N., Cheung, F. M., & Lim, J. (2003). Use of the MMPI-2 with Asian populations. *Psychological Assessment, 15*, 248–256.

Butcher, J. N., Mosch, S. C., Tsai, J., & Nezami, E. (2006). Cross cultural applications of the MMPI-2. In J. N. Butcher (ed.). *MMPI-2: The practitioner's guide* (pp. 505–537). Washington, DC: American Psychological Association.

Chan, B. (2005). From West to East: The impact of culture on personality and group dynamics. *Cross-Cultural Management, 12*, 31–45.

Chang, L., Lansford, J. E., Schwartz, D., & Farver, J. M. (2004). Marital quality, maternal depressed affect, harsh parenting, and child externalising in the Hong Kong Chinese families. *International Journal of Behavioral Development, 28*, 311–318.

Chen, S. X., Bond, M. H., & Cheung, F. M. (2005). Personality correlates of social axioms: Are beliefs nested within personality? *Personality and Individual Differences, 40*, 509–519.

Chen, S. X., Cheung, F. M., & Bond, M. H. (2005). Decomposing the construct of ambivalence over emotional expression in a Chinese cultural context. *European Journal of Personality, 19*, 185–204.

Chen, S. X., Cheung, F. M., Bond, M. H., & Leung, J.-P. (2006). Going beyond self-esteem to predict life satisfaction: The Chinese case. *Asian Journal of Social Psychology, 9*, 24–35.

Chen, Z. G. & Wang, D. F. (1984). *Desirability, meaningfulness and familiarity ratings of 670 personality-trait adjectives.* Unpublished manuscript, Psychology Department, Peking University. (in Chinese)

Cheung, F. M. (1985). Cross-cultural considerations for the translation and adaptation of the Chinese MMPI in Hong Kong. In J. N. Butcher & C. D. Spielberger (eds), *Advances in personality assessment, Volume 4* (pp. 131–158). Hillsdale, NJ: Erlbaum.

Cheung, F. M. (1996). The assessment of psychopathology in Chinese societies. In M. H. Bond (ed.). *Handbook of Chinese psychology* (pp. 393–411). Hong Kong: Oxford University Press.

Cheung, F. M. (2004). Use of Western- and indigenously-developed personality tests in Asia. *Applied Psychology: An International Review, 53*, 173–191.

Cheung, F. M. (2006). A combined emic–etic approach to cross-cultural personality test development: The case of the CPAI. In W. Jing, M. R. Rosenzweig, G. d'Ydewalle, H. Zhang, H. C. Chen, & K. Zhang (eds). *Progress in psychological science around the world, Volume 2: Social and Applied Issues. Congress Proceedings: XVIII International Congress of Psychology, Beijing, 2004* (pp. 91–103). Hove, UK: Psychology Press.

Cheung, F. M. (2007). Indigenous personality correlates from the CPAI-2 profiles of Chinese psychiatric patients. *World Cultural Psychiatry Research Review, 2*, 114–117.

Cheung, F. M., Cheung, S. F., & Leung, F. (2008). Clinical validity of the Cross-Cultural (Chinese) Personality Assessment Inventory (CPAI-2) in the assessment of substance use disorders among Chinese mean. *Psychological Assessment, 20*, 103–113.

Cheung, F. M., Cheung, S. F., Leung, K., Ward, C., & Leong, F. (2003). The English version of the Chinese Personality Assessment Inventory (CPAI). *Journal of Cross-Cultural Psychology, 34*, 433–452.

Cheung, F. M., Cheung, S. F., Wada, S., & Zhang, J. X. (2003). Indigenous measures of personality assessment in Asian countries: A review. *Psychological Assessment, 15*, 280–289.

Cheung, F. M., Cheung, S. F., & Zhang, J. X. (2004a). Convergent validity of the Chinese Personality Assessment Inventory and the Minnesota Multiphasic Personality Inventory-2: Preliminary findings with a normative sample. *Journal of Personality Assessment, 82*, 92–103.

Cheung, F. M., Cheung, S. F., & Zhang, J. X. (2004b). What is 'Chinese' personality?—Subgroup differences in the Chinese Personality Assessment Inventory (CPAI-2). *Acta Psychologica Sinica., 36*, 491–499.

Cheung, F. M., Cheung, S. F., Zhang, J. X., Leung, K., Leong, F. T. L., & Yeh, K. H. (2008). Relevance of openness as a personality dimension in Chinese culture. *Journal of Cross-Cultural Psychology, 39*, 81–108.

Cheung, F. M., Fan, W. Q., Cheung, S. F., & Leung, K. (2008). Standardization of the Cross-cultural [Chinese] Personality Assessment Inventory for adolescents in Hong Kong: A combined emic–etic approach to personality assessment. *Acta Psychologica Sinica, 40*, 839–852. (in Chinese)

Cheung, F. M., Fan, W. Q., & To, C. (2008). The Chinese Personality Assessment Inventory as a culturally relevant personality measure in applied settings. *Social and Personality Psychology Compass, 2*, 74–89.

Cheung, F. M. & Leung, K. (1998). Indigenous personality measures: Chinese examples. *Journal of Cross-Cultural Psychology, 29*, 233–248.

Cheung, F. M., Leung, K., Fan, R., Song, W. Z., Zhang, J. X., & Zhang, J. P. (1996). Development of the Chinese Personality Assessment Inventory (CPAI). *Journal of Cross-cultural Psychology, 27*, 181–199.

Cheung, F. M., Leung, K., Zhang, J. X., Sun, H. F., Gan, Y. Q., Song, W. Z., & Xie, D., (2001). Indigenous Chinese personality constructs: Is the Five Factor Model complete? *Journal of Cross-Cultural Psychology, 32*, 407–433.

Cheung, F. M. & Song, W. Z. (1989). A review on the clinical applications of the Chinese MMPI. *Psychological Assessment, 1*, 230–237.

Cheung, F. M., Song, W. Z., & Butcher, J. N. (1991). An infrequency scale for the Chinese MMPI. *Psychological Assessment, 3*, 648–653.

Cheung, F. M., Song, W. Z., & Zhang, J. X. (1996). The Chinese MMPI-2: Research and applications in Hong Kong and the People's Republic of China. In J. N. Butcher (ed.), *International adaptations of the MMPI-2: A handbook of research and applications* (pp. 137–161). Minneapolis, MN: University of Minnesota Press.

Cheung, F. M., Zhang, J. X., & Song, W. Z. (2003). *Manual of the Minnesota Multiphasic Personality Inventory-2 (MMPI-2) Chinese edition.* Hong Kong: The Chinese University Press.

Cheung, F. M., Zhao, J. C., & Wu, C. Y. (1992). Chinese MMPI profiles among neurotic patients. *Psychological Assessment, 4*, 214–218.

Cheung, S. F., Chan, W., & Cheung, F. M. (2007, July). *Applying the item response theory to personality assessment in organizational setting: A case study of the CPAI-2 in the hotel industry.* Paper presented at the 7th Conference of Asian Association of Social Psychology, Kota Kinabalu, Malaysia.

Cheung, S. F. & Cheung, F. M. (2002, July). *The Chinese Personality Assessment Inventory-2 (CPAI-2), life satisfaction, and significant life events.* Paper presented at the Symposium on 'Validation of the Chinese Personality Assessment Inventory' at the 25th International Congress of Applied Psychology, Singapore.

Cheung, S. F., Cheung, F. M., Howard, R., & Lim, Y. H. (2006). Personality across ethnic divide in Singapore: Are 'Chinese traits' uniquely Chinese? *Personality and Individual Differences, 41*, 467–477.

Church, A. T. (2001). Personality measurement in cross-cultural perspective. *Journal of Personality, 69*, 979–1006.

Costa, P. T., Jr & McCrae, R. R. (1992). *Revised NEO Personality Inventory (NEO PI-R) and NEO Five-Factor Inventory (NEO-FFI) professional manual.* Odessa, FL: Psychological Assessment Resources, Inc.

Dai, X. Y., Yao, S. Q., Cai, T. S., & Yang, J. (2004). Reliability and validity of the NEO-PI-R in Mainland China, *Chinese Mental Health Journal, 18*, 171–174. (In Chinese)

Eysenck, S. G. & Chan, J. (1982). A comparative study of personality in adults and children: Hong Kong vs. England. *Personality and Individual Differences, 3*, 153–160.

Fan, W., Cheung, F. M, Cheung, S. F., & Leung, K. (2008). Gender difference of personality traits among Hong Kong secondary school students and their development analyses. *Acta Psychologica Sinica, 40*, 1002–1012. (in Chinese)

Fu, H., Watkins, D., & Hui, E., K. P. (2004). Personality correlates of the disposition towards interpersonal forgiveness: A Chinese perspective. *International Journal of Psychology, 39*, 305–316.

Halpern, D. F. & Cheung, F. M. (2008). *Women at the top: Powerful leaders tell us how to combine work and family.* Chichester, West Sussex: Wiley-Blackwell.

Hambleton, R., Merenda, P., & Spielberger, C. (eds). (2005). *Adapting educational and psychological tests for cross-cultural assessment.* Mahwah, NJ: Erlbaum.

Ho, M. Y. (2008). *Adjustment of adolescents who are exposed to violence: Factors associated with resilience.* Unpublished master's thesis, The Chinese University of Hong Kong, Hong Kong.

Ho, M. Y., Cheung, F. M., & Cheung, S. F. (2008). Personality and life events as predictors of adolescents' life satisfaction: Do life events mediate the link between personality and life satisfaction? *Social Indicators Research, 89*, 457–471.

Huang, X. T. & Zhang, S. L. (1992). Desirability, meaningfulness and familiarity ratings of 562 personality-trait adjectives, *Psychological Science, 5*, 17–22. (in Chinese)

Hwang, K. K. (2000). Chinese relationalism: Theoretical construction and methodological considerations. *Journal for the Theory of Social Behaviour, 30*, 155–178.

International Test Commission. *ITC guidelines for adapting tests.* Retrieved January 3, 2008 from http://www.intestcom.org/itc_projects.htm#ITC per cent20Guidelines per cent20on per cent20Adapting per cent20Tests

Ko, Y. H. (1977). *Ko's Mental Health Questionnaire Manual* Taipei, Taiwan: Chinese Behavioral Science Press. (In Chinese)

Ko, Y. H. (1981). *Ko's Mental Health Questionnaire: Revised Manual.* Taipei, Taiwan: Chinese Behavioral Science Press. (In Chinese)

Ko, Y. H. (1997). Ko's Mental Health Questionnaire Revised (KMHQ 1996). *Ce yan nian kan [Journal of Assessment], 44*, 3–28. Taipei, Taiwan: Chinese Behavioral Science Press. (In Chinese)

Leung, K., Cheung, F. M., Zhang, J. X., Song, W. Z., & Xie, D. (1997). The five factor model of personality in China. In K. Leung, Y. Kashima, U. Kim, & S. Yamaguchi (eds), *Progress in Asian social psychology* (Vol. 1, pp. 231–244). Singapore: Wiley.

Li, H. & Chang, L. (2007). Paternal harsh parenting in relation to paternal versus child characteristics: The moderating effect of paternal resemblance belief. *Acta Psychologica Sinica, 39*, 495–501. (In Chinese)

Lin, E. J. & Church, A. T. (2004). Are indigenous Chinese personality dimensions culture-specific? An investigation of the Chinese Personality Assessment Inventory in Chinese American and European American samples. *Journal of Cross-Cultural Psychology, 35*, 586–605.

Liu, L. A., Friedman, R. A., & Chi, S. C. (2005). '*Ren Qing*' versus the 'Big Five': The role of culturally sensitive measures of individual difference in distributive negotiations. *Management and Organizational Review, 1*, 225–247.

Marsella, A. J., Dubanoski, J., Hamada, W. C., & Morse, H. (2000). The measurement of personality across cultures: Historical, conceptual, and methodological issues and considerations. *American Behavioral Scientist, 44*, 41–62.
McCrae, R. R., Yik, M. S. M., Trapnell, P. D., Bond, M. H., & Paulhus, D. L. (1998). Interpreting personality profiles across cultures: Bilingual, acculturation, and peer rating studies of Chinese undergraduates. *Journal of Personality and Social Psychology, 74*, 1041–1055.
Meiring, D., van der Vijver, F., Rothmann, I., & de Bruin, D. (2008, July) *Uncovering the Personality Structure of the 11 Language Groups in South Africa: SAPI Project.* Paper presented at the Symposium on 'Testing and assessment in emerging and developing countries. II: Challenges and recent advances', the 29th International Congress of Psychology, Berlin, Germany.
Redding, G. & Wong, G. Y. Y. (1986). The psychology of Chinese organizational behaviour. In M. H. Bond (ed.), *The psychology of the Chinese people* (pp. 267–295). Hong Kong: Oxford University Press.
Sun, H. F. & Bond, M. H. (2000). Choice of influence tactics: Effects of the target person's behavioral patterns, status and the personality influencer. In J. T. Li, A. S. Tusk, & E. Weldon (eds*), Management and organizations in the Chinese context* (pp. 283–302). London: MacMillan.
Van de Vijver, F. & Hambleton, R. (1996). Translating tests: Some practical guidelines. *European Psychologist, 1*, 89–99.
Van de Vijver, F. & Leung, K. (1997). *Methods and data analysis for cross-cultural research.* Thousand Oaks, CA: Sage.
Wang, D. F. & Cui, H. (2003). The constructing process and the preliminary results of Chinese Personality Scale (QZPS). *Acta Psychologica Sinica, 35*, 125–136. (in Chinese)
Wang, D. F., Cui, H., & Zhou, F. (2005). Measuring the personality of Chinese: QZPS versus NEO PI-R. *Asian Journal of Social Psychology, 8*, 97–122.
Wang, D. F., Fang, L., & Zuo, Y. T. (1995). A psycho-lexical study on Chinese personality from natural language. *Acta Psychologica Sinica, 27*, 400–406. (in Chinese)
Yang, J., Bagby, R. M., & Ryder, A. G. (2000). Response style and the revised NEO Personality Inventory: Validity scales and spousal ratings in a Chinese psychiatric sample. *Assessment, 7*, 389–402.
Yang, J., McCrae, R. R., Costa, P. T. Jr., Dai, X. Y., Yao, S. Q., Cai, T. S., & Gao, B. L. (1999). Cross-cultural personality assessment in psychiatric populations: The NEO-PI-R in the People's Republic of China. *Psychological Assessment, 11*, 359–368.
Yang, K. S. (1986). Chinese personality and its change. In M. H. Bond (ed.), *The psychology of the Chinese people* (pp. 106–170). Hong Kong: Oxford University Press.
Yang, K. S. (1997). Theories and research in Chinese personality: An indigenous approach. In H. S. R. Kao & D. Sinha (eds), *Asian perspectives on psychology* (pp. 236–262). Thousand Oaks, CA: Sage.
Yik, M. S. & Bond, M. H. (1993). Exploring the dimensions of Chinese person perception with indigenous and imported constructs: Creating a culturally balanced scale. *International Journal of Psychology, 28*, 75–95.
Zhang, H. (1988). Psychological measurement in China. *International Journal of Psychology, 23*, 101–117.
Zhang, J. X. & Zhou, M. J. (2006). Searching for a personality structure of Chinese: A theoretical hypothesis of a six factor model of personality traits. *Advances in Psychological Science, 14*, 574–585. (in Chinese)
Zhang, L. & Feng, J. P. (2005). Study on the personality characteristics of androgyny undergraduate. *Chinese Journal of Clinical Psychology, 13*, 434–436. (in Chinese)
Zhou, M. J. (2007). *Social development and changes in Chinese personality.* Unpublished doctoral dissertation, Institute of Psychology, Chinese Academy of Sciences, Beijing, China.

CHAPTER 19

Psychology and aging in the land of the panda

Helene H. Fung and Sheung-Tak Cheng

Psychology and aging is a relatively large field of academic study. It describes and examines developmental changes in the second half of life in areas ranging from physiology, cognition, and emotion to personality and social relationships. This chapter presents a focused discussion on how aging in Chinese societies may be different from that in the West, viz. North American and Western European societies. In this paper, we review the literature on psychology and aging in Chinese societies, mostly Hong Kong, but also Macau, Taiwan, and mainland China. We review empirical findings on age differences in self- and other-perceptions, interpersonal relationships, and cognition, as well as culture-specific constructs such as filial piety and *renqing* (relationship orientation). We use examples to illustrate the instances (1) when aging processes in Chinese societies are largely identical to those observed in the Western, mostly American and German, societies; (2) when aging processes manifest themselves differently across cultures; (3) when the same aging processes lead to different outcomes in different cultures; and finally (4) when aging processes show different directions of development across cultures.

Background

We begin our discussion by providing background information on population aging in Asia, and China in particular. We highlight the specific opportunities and challenges that population aging presents to Chinese societies, relative to their Western counterparts. Some countries in East and South-east Asia are among the most rapidly aging societies in the world (Cheng, Chan, & Phillips, 2008). This region includes many Chinese societies or societies heavily influenced by Chinese culture, including Hong Kong, Macau, Singapore, and China.

The main driver of population aging in these countries is the rise in longevity, coupled with a sharp drop in fertility rates. Hong Kong and Macau, for example, where people are among the longest lived at 82 and 80 years, respectively, have at the same time the lowest fertility rates in the world, both being around 0.9. Singapore, with a life expectancy at birth of 79 years, also experienced a sharp drop in fertility rate in the past ten years from around 1.7 to 1.3. China, by virtue of the one-child policy applying to the Han majority has a more or less stabilized fertility rate of around 1.8 since the mid-1990s. But for a country as sizable as China to have a fertility rate below the natural replacement rate of 2.1, the consequences are far-reaching.

By 2030, China is expected to experience a population decline, due mainly to the decreasing number of younger persons. Within the 45-year period from 2005–50, the number of older persons will increase by 243 per cent for these four societies altogether, compared with the world average of 113 per cent. In Hong Kong and China, the numbers of persons aged 65+ years are expected to reach

2.9 million and 334 million respectively. Because of the sizes of many Asian populations, particularly those in Chinese societies, Asia will be the main driver of global aging in the decades to come, and China will play a major role in this global population transformation (see Cheng et al., 2008; Cheng & Heller, 2009; United Nations Population Division, n.d.). It is therefore fitting that this chapter focuses on the late-life development of people in the land of the panda.[1]

Other than this demographic transformation, the Chinese societies in the region, particularly mainland China, are also undergoing rapid social and cultural transformations. These transformations have implications for aging. The urbanization of cities and the breakdown of multi-generational households have resulted in more and more older people living with spouses but not with children (Cheng et al., 2008), as well as in more older persons living in institutions (Cheng & Chan, 2003). The one-child policy in China has led to an aging population that has little expectation of support from their children. Other societies such as Hong Kong and Taiwan have also witnessed a gradual, downward adjustment of filial expectations by older persons, and of the sense of obligation towards parents in younger persons (see Cheng & Chan, 2006).

Other changes taking place include the more financially secured and educated cohorts of older people in the near future, who do not necessarily share the same values as the current cohorts born before World War II. The multiple-wave World Values Survey (Inglehart & Baker, 2000), which has covered 65 countries and 75 per cent of the world's population, has shown that except in the least-developed countries, traditional values were less and less likely to be endorsed by successive cohorts, although value differences persist across the world along the lines of religion and deep-rooted value systems (e.g. Confucianism).

Aside from acknowledging that values could change with each successive cohort of older people, it should be pointed out that the term 'Chinese societies' is simply an umbrella term for different societies sharing similar cultural roots, yet with different economic development and political structures, both of which shape societal values (Inglehart & Baker, 2000). Thus, there are in fact quite a few Chinese 'cultures', not just across societies, but also across historical times within the same society. Against this cautionary note, we review the literature on psychology and aging, and compare the aging processes between Chinese and Western people.

Aging processes showing few differences across cultures

We first review areas in which our research has largely found cultural similarities in age-related processes. One of the dominant theories on aging, socioemotional selectivity theory (Carstensen, Isaacowitz, & Charles, 1999; Fung & Carstensen, 2004) postulates that goals are always set in temporal contexts and that the relative importance of specific goals within this goal constellation changes as a function of perceived time. When the future is perceived as open-ended, future-oriented goals, such as seeking information or expanding horizons, weigh more heavily and individuals pursue goals that optimize long-range outcomes. In contrast, when endings are perceived, goal constellations are reorganized such that emotionally meaningful goals, defined as goals related to feelings, such as balancing emotional states or sensing that one is needed by others, are prioritized to a greater extent, because such goals have more immediate payoffs. Many situations, ranging from graduations to geographical relocations, prime 'endings'. Although achieved more gradually, approaching old age is also associated with the increasing recognition that time is running out.

Because chronological age is negatively associated with perceived time left in life, the theory predicts systematic age differences in motivational orientation. Importantly, the posited mechanism that theoretically accounts for these age differences is not developmental changes in the traditional sense, but age-related shifts in time horizons. Thus, to the extent that other situations also reduce one's perceived time left in life, such experiences theoretically shift motivation in similar ways as the more gradual but nonetheless steady experience of growing older.

One way to assess goals is to present people with trade-offs in which particular options increase or decrease the likelihood of realizing a particular goal. To directly assess the influence of time perspective on social goals, an experimental paradigm has been developed. Under this paradigm, participants are asked to imagine that they have 30 minutes free and choose to spend that time with one of three prospective social partners, namely, an author of a book you just read, a recent acquaintance with whom you appear to have much in common, or a member of your immediate family (Fredrickson & Carstensen, 1990). Goals are inferred from expressed social preferences. A cognitive categorization task had earlier revealed that the author was rated high on the dimension of information gain, the acquaintance on future possibilities, and the family member on emotional potential (Carstensen & Fredrickson, 1998; Fredrickson & Carstensen, 1990). Choosing the family member, an emotionally close social partner, reveals a preference for emotionally meaningful goals, whereas choosing either of the other two options is regarded as showing a preference for knowledge or future possibility, that is, future-oriented goals. Over the years, other sets of social partner options have been developed (Fung & Carstensen, 2004), but they generally yield similar results to the original set.

Using this paradigm, we found that in both American and Chinese (Hong Kong, mainland Chinese and Taiwanese) cultures, older people showed preferences for emotionally close to peripheral social partners, whereas younger people did not (Americans: Fredrickson & Carstensen, 1990; Hong Kong Chinese: Fung, Carstensen, & Lutz, 1999; Taiwanese and mainland Chinese: Fung, Lai, & Ng, 2001). Moreover, experiments that manipulated perceived time effectively shifted age differences in social partner selection in predicted directions: when American and Hong Kong Chinese younger people perceived constraints on time, they too showed strong preferences for spending time with emotionally close social partners (Fredrickson & Carstensen, 1990; Fung et al., 1999). When American older people perceived expanded time, however, such preferences were eliminated (Fung et al., 1999). Age differences in social partner selection among Taiwanese and mainland Chinese were also effectively eliminated by statistically controlling for the individual differences in time perspective (Fung, Lai et al., 2001).

Fung and Carstensen (2004) further cross-validated the role of time perspective in social goals by examining the self-reported goals of younger and older Americans under a number of experimental conditions that systematically modified perceived time, and distinguished between constraints related to time and constraints unrelated to time, e.g. financial difficulties. Findings showed that it was constraints related to time that drove the effects. Regardless of age, people who perceived time constraints were more likely to seek social partners for their emotional significance, not merely for emotional support, than were those who either perceived a non-time-related constraint or no constraint at all.

Such findings are consistent with other studies showing that younger adults who are in naturalistic situations that theoretically prime endings also focus on emotionally meaningful goals. Carstensen and Fredrickson (1998), for example, found that young American men with the HIV virus and symptoms of AIDS weighted the affective dimension as heavily as did older adults on a categorization task of prospective social partners. Moreover, young Hong Kong Chinese who have a history of cancer have a greater number of emotionally close social partners in their networks and a greater need to attain emotional goals than do their age peers without a history of cancer (Kin & Fung, 2004). Hong Kong adolescents who are involved in gangs report a more limited time perspective and a higher percentage of emotionally close social partners, compared with age peers who are not gang members (Liu & Fung, 2005). Even social endings heighten the salience of emotional goals. American graduating seniors report greater emotional involvement with close friends than do students who are not graduating (Fredrickson, 1995).

If sufficient numbers of individuals focus on emotionally meaningful goals as they come to perceive future time as limited, it follows that groups that have shorter actuarial life expectancy may also be more likely to exhibit social patterns that reflect the prioritization of this type of goals than are groups with a longer life expectancy. In fact, Fung, Lai, and Ng (2001) found that mainland Chinese, whose actuarial life expectancy was seven years shorter than that of Taiwanese, were more likely to perceive time as limited. Moreover, compared with Taiwanese of a similar age range, mainland Chinese were more likely to show preferences for emotionally close social partners.

Importantly, such cultural differences in social preferences were no longer significant after statistically controlling for time perspective, suggesting it was indeed time perspective that accounted for the observed cultural differences. Similarly, African-Americans, who as a group have shorter actuarial life expectancy than their European-American age peers, were found to have relatively fewer peripheral but the same number of emotionally close social partners in their social networks (Fung, Carstensen, & Lang, 2001).

Although only modest attention has been paid to cultural (or macro-level) endings, there is some evidence that sociopolitical events, which mark time, influence motivation in similar ways as do individual endings. Fung, Carstensen, and Lutz (1999) examined age differences in social preferences one year before, two months before, and one year after the handover of Hong Kong from the United Kingdom to the People's Republic of China. The handover ended the over-150-year British rule in Hong Kong and was widely regarded in Hong Kong as a temporal marker beyond which life was uncertain. In the months prior to the handover, some political cartoons even depicted Hong Kong as a train headed for a blocked tunnel, or a tin can with 30 June 1997 (the day of the handover) as the expiry day (see Fung et al., 1999).

We construed the handover as a macro-level sociopolitical ending and predicted that the perceived limitations on time associated with the ending would influence social preferences, just as our previous time manipulation had done. Indeed, a year before the handover, older but not younger Hong Kong people preferred emotionally close social partners. However, two months before the handover, when the sociopolitical ending was very salient, both age groups preferred emotionally close social partners. One year after the handover when the transition had come and gone, the typical age differences in social preferences re-emerged. Younger Hong Kong people no longer preferred emotionally close social partners, presumably because they had turned a historical page and begun to focus again on the future. Older people, probably due to their limited time perspective at the individual level, continued to prefer emotionally close social partners.

In addition, Fung and Carstensen (2006) replicated these findings around two macro-level events in recent years, the 11 September 2001 attacks on the United States (Study 1) and the outbreak of SARS in Hong Kong (Study 2). Both studies were conducted in Hong Kong.

From the perspective of Hong Kong people, the 11 September attack was a crisis that occurred far away. Although the impact of the crisis was worldwide, neither they themselves nor members of their social circles experienced the crisis first-hand. In contrast, SARS was a crisis that directly affected the Hong Kong people. Should age-related social preferences shift in similar ways across the two macro-level events, we would have greater confidence in concluding that the age differences were probably generalizable across situations—as long as the situations prime the awareness of endings.

Indeed, findings from the studies revealed that before each of these events, Hong Kong Chinese showed the typical age differences in social preferences, with older people more likely to prefer emotionally close social partners, compared with younger people. During each of these events, the age differences disappeared, with the majority of people in every age group showing preferences for emotionally close social partners. After each of the events, the typical age differences in social preferences re-emerged. The striking similarity of findings across these naturalistic studies strongly suggests that the effects of aging, the 1997 handover, the 11 September attacks and SARS on social goals may all be attributable to the same cause: When there are cues in the environment to prime the finitude of life, people show preferences for the emotionally close and meaningful. This occurs across age, historical contexts, and cultures.

Such prioritization of emotionally meaningful goals in the face of temporal constraints has many implications for the process of aging. For example, it may be one reason why people tend to be more forgiving with age. Recently, Cheng and Yim (2008) randomly assigned younger and older Hong Kong Chinese adults into experimental conditions that were intended to create an expanded, a shortened, and an open-ended time perspective respectively. The participants then read hypothetical scenarios in which they were seriously offended by a friend, and rated their forgiveness of this friend. Results showed that older persons were more forgiving than were younger persons. Regardless of age, those who perceived time as shortened were also more forgiving than were those in the open-ended condition, who were in turn more forgiving than those who saw time as extended, i.e. they imagined that they would live 20 more years than they had expected. It may be the case that an increasingly limited time perspective that comes with age leads to the prioritization of emotionally meaningful goals. Because of this increased motivation to regulate emotions, older persons are more ready to offer forgiveness in order to restore well-being, and to repair the relationship that may be an important source of continued support in old age.

Age processes that show cross-cultural differences

Same processes, different manifestations

Socioemotional selectivity theory also has implications for aging in the area of social relationships. A particular pattern of age differences in social network characteristics (SNC) has been reliably reported in the Western (American and German) literatures, e.g. Ajrouch, Antonucci, and Janevic (2001); Carstensen (1992); Fung, Carstensen, and Lang (2001); Lang and Carstensen (1994; 2002): increasing age was associated with fewer peripheral social partners, yet the number of emotionally close social partners remained relatively stable across age. Socioemotional selectivity theory (Carstensen et al., 1999) explains these age differences in social network characteristics motivationally. It argues that goals for social interaction change as a function of future time perspective. Younger people perceive their future time as relatively more open-ended and as a result, they prefer interacting with social partners of greater diversity in order to fulfill their future-oriented goals. Their social networks thus comprise largely peripheral social partners.

When individuals grow older, however, they perceive their future as increasingly limited. They shift their attention from long-term future-oriented goals to short-term emotional goals. Consequently, they tend to interact with social partners who can best provide them with emotionally meaningful experiences. Their social networks thus mainly consist of emotionally close social partners, such as family members and close friends, but fewer peripheral social partners (Carstensen, Gross, & Fung, 1997; Lang & Carstensen, 1994). Yeung, Fung, and Lang (2008) argue that to the extent that what people seek under future time limitation is emotionally meaningful social relationships (Fung & Carstensen, 2004), then individual differences in what is considered to be emotionally meaningful may lead to different patterns of social relationships across adulthood.

Self-construal may be a good indicator of what one considers to be emotionally meaningful in social situations. According to the self-construal theory (Markus & Kitayama, 1991), people with an independent self-construal define the self as unique and separate from others, whereas those with an interdependent self-construal define the self as embedded in in-groups and interconnected with others (see also Kwan, Hui, and McGee, this volume). Most of the studies on age-related social network characteristics reviewed above were conducted in Western cultures, such as North America and Germany. People in these Western cultures are usually found to be more independent and less interdependent than are East Asians (Hofstede, 1980; Markus & Kitayama, 1991; Oyserman et al., 2002; Triandis, 1995). Such differences tend to intensify with age (Fung & Ng, 2006). East Asians such as Chinese who emphasize interdependence to a greater extent may show a different pattern of age-related social networks.

In particular, the cultural emphasis on interdependence among Chinese may have made them more likely than their Western counterparts to maintain interactions with social partners of a greater diversity even when they grow older. In order to fulfill their family and social obligations, Chinese are expected to take care of their family members and relatives (familism: Szkalay, Strohl, Fu, & Lao, 1994; Yang, 1988) and to maintain reciprocal relationships with their social partners, even peripheral ones (*renqing*: relationship orientation: Cheung et al., 2001; Yeung, Fung, & Lang, 2007; Zhang & Yang, 1998). As they grow older, therefore, Chinese may maintain a larger number of emotionally close social partners as well as peripheral social partners in their social networks than do their Western counterparts.

Confirming this hypothesis, Yeung, Fung, and Lang (2008) examined social network characteristics in a sample of Chinese adults (18–91 years old) in Hong Kong. Age was found to be positively associated with the number of emotionally close social partners and negatively associated with the number of peripheral social partners. More importantly, interdependent self-construal was found to moderate these age differences. The stability of the number of emotionally close social partners across age, typically found in Western studies, e.g. Fung et al. (2001); Lang and Carstensen (1994), was replicated only among Hong Kong Chinese with a low level of interdependent self-construal. In contrast, those with medium and high levels of interdependent self-construal exhibited a positive association between age and the number of emotionally close social partners.

A consistent pattern was also found for the association between age and the number of peripheral social partners. Although a negative association between age and the number of peripheral social partners was observed for the entire sample, the association was significant only among those with low and medium levels of interdependent self-construal. The association was much weaker, and in fact, no longer significant, among those with a high interdependent self-construal.

In another study, Fung, Stoeber, Yeung, and Lang (2008) found that age differences in specific social relationships could differ across cultures even when the cultures showed the same pattern of age differences in close and peripheral social partners. In this study, residents of Berlin, Germany were matched with residents of Hong Kong, China on age (ranging from 20 to 91 years), sex, family status (married or not, with or without children), and education level. Results showed that in both cultures, age was negatively associated with number of peripheral social partners, and was not associated with emotionally close social partners.

Nevertheless, cultural differences were found in specific social relationships across age. Age was positively associated with the proportion of nuclear family members, but negatively associated with the proportion of acquaintances among Hong Kong Chinese. In contrast, age was negatively associated with the proportion of nuclear family members, but positively associated with the proportion of acquaintances among Germans. Although age was positively associated with the proportion of extended family members and negatively associated with the proportion of friends in both cultures, the associations were stronger among Hong Kong Chinese than Germans. These findings were interpreted in terms of the stronger family bias (Bardis, 1959; Brewer & Chen, 2007; Szalay et al., 1994; Yeung, Fung, & Lang, 2007) among Hong Kong Chinese, relative to Germans. While both cultural groups drop peripheral social partners from their social networks with age, Chinese may do so by further focusing their social networks on their families and dropping non-family members from their social networks more so than do their German counterparts.

The aforementioned studies are concerned with the social relationships of community-dwelling, older persons. Recent studies have suggested that cultural factors are also in play in the maintenance of close ties and the formation of new/peripheral ties in nursing homes, though with surprising outcomes. In a qualitative study, Chinese older persons were given an interview one week after admission into a nursing home, followed by roughly six-monthly interviews (Lee, Woo, & Mackenzie, 2002). The participants' core concerns were not about maintaining their autonomy, as was typically found in American nursing home studies, but about how to fit into the homes' routines and to comply with the status quo. They were afraid of expressing their needs, because doing so would feel like putting one's needs above those of the collective, viz. the nursing home community. Worse, because having to move into a nursing home is considered a personal/family disgrace, many residents severed their long-term ties with relatives, friends and neighbors in order to conceal the fact that their children were not able, or not willing, to take care of them at home.

Hence, in a collectivistic society, residents tend to lead separate lives inside nursing homes, and to detach themselves emotionally from old social ties. More recently, (Cheng, 2009a) has interviewed nursing home residents and found an average network size of just 2.58 members, much smaller than those reported in the West. Only one-fifth reported any social connection in the home, mostly with one of the staff. Of those with children, many of them considered their children to be no longer important to their lives. On average, they received less than one visit per month from each of the children with whom they remained in regular contact. In fact, according to Lee et al. (2002), such visits were actively discouraged by the nursing home administration in order to motivate the residents to detach from the family and to settle into the nursing home routine. Cheng (2009a) has identified various cultural and systemic/organizational factors that act together to accentuate the distance between older persons and their family members following home placement, and to discourage social interactions within the home. These factors are beyond the scope of this review, but serve to underscore the importance of considering how cultural factors determine the motivation for social interactions in different situational contexts.

Other than influencing the lives of older adults directly, traditional Chinese values such as filial piety and generativity also interact with the modernization process to exert an impact on aging. Traditionally in Chinese societies, older persons are cared for by the young with minimal state intervention. In fact, a distinctive characteristic of filial expectations under Confucianism, as argued by Cheng and Chan (2006), is the filial *devotion* of their children regardless of the parents' needs, as compared to the need-based filial responsibility in Western societies. However, despite Chinese traditions, filial attitudes and behaviors are gradually on the decline in recent decades, and older people are dropping certain filial expectations faster than even younger people themselves (see review by Cheng & Chan, 2006).

Such changes are attributable to several factors that are transforming our societies, namely (a) extended families being replaced by nuclear households, and hence the decline in co-residence with older parents; (b) the decline of family values and the rise of individualism, even in mainland China; (c) the loss of status of older persons, reducing their capacity to command respect from younger generations; (d) the out-migration of young adults from rural to urban areas for employment, as is so common in China and even Taiwan; and (e) the financial independence of women, which not only reduces their involvement in caregiving, but also allows them to negotiate caregiving roles (Aboderin, 2004; Cheng & Chan, 2006; Cheng et al., 2008; Cheng & Heller, 2009). Thus, the traditional beliefs that younger people should obey parents' wishes totally and should continue the family line are less binding. Children generally feel less obliged to care for their parents, especially when it conflicts with job demands. The reliance on the eldest son and his wife is definitely diminishing, and many responsibilities traditionally held by daughters-in-law are now assumed by daughters. In China, the one-child policy hastens the changes in attitudes regarding the importance of sons. Although this cohort of older people may not be financially well off, they have relatively low expectations for financial contributions from children (see Cheng & Chan, 2006 for a review). Such attitude changes are more evident in urban than in rural China (Treas & Wang, 1993; see also Wang & Chang, this volume).

Against this backdrop, Cheng and Chan (2006) examined what they called *filial discrepancy* in older Hong Kong adults. By filial discrepancy, they meant the gap between their expectations and the children's filial behaviors, including daily maintenance (maintaining contact, practical assistance, and financial contribution), respect (obedience on important matters, accommodating on mundane matters, and showing respect before others), and sickness care (taking to doctor when ill, personal care, and listening to problems). Sickness care by children was reported to be the least likely by the older adults. This factor together with lack of respect were the only two factors that determined a sense of filial discrepancy. However, in a multivariate model that controlled for functional limitations, financial strain and filial discrepancy, it was only respect that consistently predicted psychological well-being. These findings were similar whether the older adults were rating their closest children or other, less close children. Moreover, supporting the notion of filial devotion and contradictory to Western findings, there was no evidence that overdoing one's filial role was detrimental to the parents' well-being among the Chinese.

These findings highlight the most important contours of filial expectations in today's society. For various reasons that are beyond the scope of this review, expectations for daily assistance, financial contributions, and absolute deference are much weakened. However, older people continue to expect their children to pay respect and to show a caring attitude when they become ill. These children's behaviors appear to define emotional and instrumental support to parents in contemporary Chinese societies.

In another line of research, Cheng and colleagues (Cheng, 2009b; Cheng, Chan, & Chan, 2008) investigated the social context for late-life generativity, i.e. care for the next generation. Generativity in Erikson's (1982) framework is a crucial life-stage resolution that leads to ego integrity, i.e. an affirmation of a well-lived life.

A sociocultural condition that many societies around the world share is the lack of productive roles for older citizens (Heller, 1993), or what Rosow (1985) called the 'roleless role'. Taking this idea further, Cheng and his colleagues argued that the subjective concern for the next generation cannot be sustained unless one's generative actions are valued by the younger generation. Such appreciations determine whether potentially generative actions would lead to enhanced well-being in older adults. In a longitudinal study (Cheng, 2009b), Chinese older adults responded, at baseline and 12 months later, to measures of generative concern, action, perceived respect, and psychological well-being. At both time points, the relationship between action and well-being was completely mediated by perceived respect, supporting the prediction. More importantly, a lack of perceived respect predicted lower generative concern a year later, even after controlling for baseline generative concern. Thus, when younger people do not welcome the older adults' contributions, the latter's concern for the former is gradually diminished.

Given that esteem needs are universal (see Steverink & Lindenberg, 2006), and that such unwelcoming attitudes toward older people's contributions are common around the world these days, a downward spiral in generativity development in later life appears to be a universal trend, sustained by declines in health that may create difficulties for performing certain generative behaviors. This study suggests that even if internalized values lead one to pursue generativity, generativity as a goal will be weakened rather than intensified, if the environment is not supportive. That is, generative goals will atrophy when they cannot be realized.

Same processes, different outcomes

A third implication of socioemotional selectivity theory for aging lies in the area of basic cognitive processes, such as attention and memory. The theory argues that older adults prioritize emotionally meaningful goals when they perceive future time as increasingly limited. As a result, they show preferential cognitive processing of positively-valenced relative to negatively-valenced and neutral stimuli (Carstensen & Mikels, 2005) in order to regulate their emotions. This age-related phenomenon is called the 'positivity effect'.

Mather and Carstensen (2003), for example, found the positivity effect among American older adults using a dot-probe paradigm. In two experiments, they presented younger and older adults with a pair of faces, one positive (happy) or negative (sad or angry) and one neutral, and then a dot probe that appeared behind one of the faces. They found that older adults responded faster to the dot probe if it was presented on the same side as a neutral face than on the same side as a negative face. Younger adults did not show this bias. Later, Isaacowitz and colleagues found the positivity effect using eye-tracking techniques (Isaacowitz, Wadlinger, Goren, & Wilson, 2006a; 2006b). They presented younger and older American adults with pairs of synthetic faces. Each pair included the same face in a non-emotional expression and in one of four emotional expressions (happiness, sadness, anger, or fear). They found that older adults displayed attentional preferences toward happy faces and away from angry faces (Isaacowitz et al., 2006a) as well as sad faces (Isaacowitz et al., 2006b). Young adults only showed an attentional preference toward fearful faces.

Similarly, in memory, the positivity effect has been found among American samples. The positivity effect in memory should be understood in contrast to the vast literature on 'negativity dominance' (Baumeister, Bratslavsky, Finkenauer, & Vohs, 2001; Rozin & Royzman, 2001). The gist of 'negativity dominance' is that negative stimuli tend to have uniquely potent effects on cognition, more so than positive or neutral stimuli. This occurs because such vigilance for negative information has been adaptive in human evolutionary history, to assist in avoiding predators and other kinds of danger. Empirical studies on age differences in memory generally replicated this negativity dominance among younger adults, but found either a lower level of such negativity dominance, i.e. a negativity reduction effect (e.g. Charles et al., 2003, Experiment 2; Knight, Maines, & Robinson, 2002), or superior processing of positively-valenced stimuli, i.e. a positivity enhancement effect, among older adults, (e.g. Charles et al., 2003, Experiment 1; Mather & Knight, 2005; Mikels, Larkin, Reuter-Lorenz, & Carstensen 2005).

Fung and her colleagues (Fung et al., 2008; Lu et al., 2007) argued that the positivity effect might not be generalizable to East Asian cultures. Cross-cultural studies have repeatedly found that the North American culture, being more independent (Markus & Kitayama, 1991; Triandis, 1989), i.e. valuing personal autonomy and uniqueness, may be particularly attuned to positive information (Frey & Stahlberg, 1986), in order to maintain and enhance optimism and self-esteem (Herzog et al., 1998). In contrast, East Asian cultures, valuing interpersonal relationships and interdependence (Markus & Kitayama, 1991; Triandis, 1989), may find negative information at least as useful as, if not more useful than, positive information, in avoiding mistakes and future social mishaps (Kitayama & Karasawa, 1995).

For example, in describing the construct 'happiness', Americans describe only the positive features whereas Japanese describe both positive and negative (e.g. social disruption) features (Uchida, 2007). In another study, Markus, Uchida, Omoregie, Townsend, and Kitayama (2006) found that while American athletes explained Olympic performance primarily in terms of positive attributes, Japanese athletes did so in terms of both positive and negative attributes. To the extent that people in East Asian cultures found negative information as useful as positive information, they might either not show the positivity effect or show it to a lesser extent with age.

To test this prediction, Fung, Isaacowitz, Lu, Wadlinger, Goren, and Wilson (2008) compared attention among younger (aged 18 to 23 years) and older (aged 60 to 84 years) Hong Kong Chinese, using eye-tracking techniques in the same way and with the same stimuli, as did Isaacowitz and colleagues (2006a, b). In contrast to the aforementioned positivity effect reliably found among Americans, older Hong Kong Chinese actually looked away from positive stimuli, in this case happy faces.

Similar cross-cultural differences were also noted in memory. In a study that compared memory for positive, negative, and neutral stimuli among younger and older Hong Kong Chinese (Fung & Tang, 2005), a negativity bias was found among older adults. In the study, the background music of a government TV announcement on health promotion was varied such that it conveyed positive, negative, or neutral affect. The only difference in recognition memory was found between the negative and neutral versions, with older adults showing better recognition memory for information presented in the negative version of the announcement than for that in the neutral version. Younger adults did not show such differences.

However, the methodology of Fung and Tang (2005) is different from that used in prior Western studies (e.g. Charles et al., 2003; Mathar & Knight, 2005), rendering results from the studies less comparable. To further test whether the positivity effect existed in memory among older Hong Kong Chinese, Lu et al. (2007) examined age differences in recall and recognition memory for positive, negative, and neutral images, with the same stimuli and methodology as those employed in a previous study that has found the strongest positivity effect among Americans (Charles et al., 2003, Experiment 1). Our findings revealed that, in terms of both recall and recognition memory, older Hong Kong Chinese showed better memory for positive images than neutral images, i.e. the positivity enhancement effect, but they showed the same level of memory for negative images as they did for neutral images, i.e. an absence of the negativity reduction effect.

Moreover, interdependent self-construal moderated memory. For both recall and recognition memory, older Hong Kong Chinese with lower levels of interdependent self-construal showed both the positivity enhancement effect and the negativity reduction effect, like their American counterparts examined in prior studies (e.g. Charles et al., 2003). Yet older Hong Kong Chinese with higher levels of interdependent self-construal showed only the positivity enhancement effect and not the negativity reduction effect. Younger Hong Kong Chinese showed a memory bias for negative images over positive and neutral images throughout the study, regardless of their levels of interdependent self-construal.

The absence of the negativity reduction effect among older Hong Kong Chinese is even clearer in a study on discrete emotions. Lu et al. (2007) examined recognition memory for the emotional (happy, sad, fearful, and angry) and neutral faces presented in the eye-tracking study described above (Fung, Isaacowitz, Lu, Wadlinger et al., 2008). Results showed that younger Hong Kong Chinese remembered happy faces better than all other kinds of faces. Middle-aged Hong Kong Chinese remembered happy faces better than neutral faces, but also fearful faces more than neutral faces. Older Hong Kong Chinese remembered happy faces better than neutral faces, but also fearful and angry faces better than neutral faces. In other words, while all three age groups showed the positivity enhancement effect, the negativity reduction effect declined, and even reversed, linearly across age groups.

This focus on the negative, though in direct contrast to the hallmark assumption of positive psychology, may actually be adaptive for older adults in Chinese societies. In a recent paper (Cheng, Fung, & Chan, 2009), using a concept called *discounting*, we argue that projecting a 'worse' future may be adaptive when declines and losses are normative, predictable, and, at times, irreversible in later life. We investigated the effects of discounting on well-being in Hong Kong Chinese adults aged 60 years or older. The participants rated their current and future selves in the physical and the social domains at two time points 12 months apart. Results showed that although future self was positively related to well-being concurrently at time 1, it predicted lower well-being at time 2, after controlling for time-2 physical symptoms and current self. In other words, given the same current self at time 2, those who had projected a worse future self 12 months ago actually enjoyed better well-being than those who made more optimistic predictions. These findings suggest that a negative representation of the future that is consistent with normative age-related declines and losses may be used to buffer against the effects of declines and losses when they actually occur.

Different directions of development across cultures

In the above sections, we have used our own research as examples to illustrate instances when the processes of aging are similar between Chinese and Western societies, as well as instances when cross-cultural differences occur, but only in their specific manifestations and outcomes. In this section, we will describe processes that develop with age in different directions across cultures. Such processes occur in the area of personality.

For a number of years, personality development has been assumed to manifest in exactly the same way across cultures. Indeed, cross-sectional patterns of age differences in personality were found to be largely the same across cultures ranging from Germany, Italy, Portugal, Croatia, South Korea (McCrae et al., 1999), the United Kingdom, Spain, the Czech Republic, Turkey (McCrae et al., 2000), Russia, Estonia, Japan (Costa et al., 2000) to the People's Republic of China (Labouvie-Vief, Diehl, Tarnowski, & Shen, 2000; Yang, McCrae, & Costa, 1998). These findings have often been taken as evidence that personality development is universal. Yet these cross-cultural findings were almost always obtained within the scope of the Five-Factor Model—neuroticism, extraversion, agreeableness, openness to experience, and conscientiousness—commonly known as the 'Big Five'. It remains possible that age differences in other aspects of personality such as those discussed by Cheung, Zhang, and Cheung (this volume) may differ across cultures.

Recent literature in cultural psychology (Cheung et al., 1996, 2001; Cheung, Cheung, Wada, & Zhang, 2003; Cheung, Kwong, & Zhang, 2003) has reliably documented that when personality was measured not just by measures imported from the West but also by indigenous measures developed in China, six factors—i.e. interpersonal relatedness in addition to the Big Five—were found among several Chinese samples. When the expanded measures were then imported back to the West, the interpersonal relatedness factor was again found among several American samples (Cheung et al., 2001; Cheung, Cheung, Leung, Ward, & Leong, 2003; Lin & Church, 2004).

Conceptually, what distinguishes interpersonal relatedness from the Big Five is that while there is little theoretical reason to suspect that the Big Five may differ in importance across cultures (but see Bond & Forgas, 1984), there is some cross-cultural evidence to suggest that interpersonal relatedness is more important among the Chinese than among North Americans. For example, Hong Kong Chinese are often found to be more interdependent, i.e. more likely to see themselves as being embedded in social groups than are North Americans (see Oyserman, Coon, & Kemmelmeier, 2002 for a meta-analytical review). Relationship harmony is relatively more important than self-esteem to the psychological well-being of Hong Kong Chinese, whereas the reverse is true for North Americans (Kwan, Bond, & Singelis, 1997). Similarly, in the aging literature, while most American studies, e.g. Bailey and McLaren (2005), revealed that physical activity enhanced self-esteem among older adults, this association was not found among Chinese older adults (Poon & Fung, 2008). Instead, physical activity, whether defined as housework, exercise, or recreational activities, was found to be positively associated with relatedness satisfaction. Moreover, the lexical approach of personality is based on the assumption that personality vocabulary found in a natural language represents personality attributes that 'people in the language community have found particularly important and useful in their daily interactions with each other' (John, 1990, p. 67). The fact that the interpersonal relatedness factor was first identified in China strongly suggests that it is more 'important and useful' in that culture.

To the extent that throughout the lifespan, individuals from each culture 'attune and elaborate' their self-perceptions (Heine et al., 1999. p. 767) according to what is 'important and useful' in their cultures, we would expect personality development to differ across cultures according to the values emphasized in that culture. Specifically, people in cultures emphasizing independence should become more autonomous and self-contained as they age, while people in cultures emphasizing interdependence should become more concerned about relational importance and social embeddedness as they age. To test this hypothesis, Fung and Ng (2006) examined age differences in the Big Five and interpersonal relatedness among younger (18–29 years old) and older (50–88 years old) Canadians and Hong Kong Chinese. Findings revealed that age differences in the Big Five did not differ across cultures. Yet age differences in some aspects of interpersonal relatedness were found only among Hong Kong Chinese and not Canadians. Specifically, older Hong Kong Chinese endorsed higher levels of *renqing* (relationship orientation) and lower levels of flexibility (going against norms and traditions) than did their younger counterparts. Canadians did not show these age differences. To the extent that cross-sectional age differences reflect developmental changes, these findings suggest that with age, Hong Kong Chinese are more likely to adhere to the rule of reciprocity in social relationships and are less likely to go against norms and traditions; Canadians do not seem to show this kind of personality development.

These findings were interpreted as suggesting that personality may change with age according to cultural values (Helson, Jones, & Kwan, 2002). To test whether older adults were indeed more likely to endorse and internalize cultural values than were younger adults, we (Ho, Fung, & Tam, 2007) examined personal and cultural values among younger (aged 18 to 23 years) and older (aged 54 to 89 years) Hong Kong Chinese. Values were measured by the Schwartz Value Questionnaire (1992), which consists of 56 values grouped under ten value types (see Kulich, this volume) To measure personal values, we asked participants to rate the importance of each value to the *self*. To measure cultural values, we adopted the inter-subjective importance approach (Wan et al., 2007) and asked participants to rate the importance of each value as would most people in their *culture*, in this case Chinese culture.

We first examined age differences in cultural values, in terms of the ten value types. Except for power and tradition, older participants reported higher levels of all types of cultural values than did younger participants, suggesting that people are more likely to endorse cultural values with age. Next, we examined whether older people internalized cultural values to a greater extent than did younger adults. We calculated the correlation coefficient between the ratings of personal and cultural values for *each participant*, across all 56 values. We found age differences in the correlation coefficients, such that older participants showed a higher congruence between personal and cultural values than did younger participants. We also computed mean differences between personal and cultural values for each participant and then compared their age differences. Smaller discrepancies between personal and cultural values were found among older than among younger participants.

To further investigate what drove this higher congruence of personal and cultural values among older relative to younger participants, we examined age differences in personal values. Older participants reported higher endorsement of all personal value types that are more communal in nature (i.e. universalism, benevolence, tradition, conformity, security) than did younger participants. They also reported lower endorsement of four out of five personal value types that are more agentic in nature (i.e. achievement, hedonism, stimulation, self-direction) than did younger participants. These findings, taken together, suggest that with age, Hong Kong Chinese move away from more agentic values to more communal values, resulting in a closer association between personal and cultural values. In other words, we have preliminary support for the theoretical postulate that people increasingly internalize cultural values with age.

To test whether value indeed sets the direction for personality development, Fung, Ho, Tam, and Tsai (2009) examined age differences in personality and value among a large sample of European-Americans and Chinese-Americans, aged 20 to 90 years. They replicated Fung and Ng's (2006) finding that age positively correlated with *renqing* (relationship orientation) among Chinese-Americans but not European-Americans. Moreover, they found that values moderated these age differences. The association between age and *renqing* became positive among European-Americans who valued tradition (seeking group acceptance) more. Conversely, the positive association between age and *renqing* was weaker among Chinese-Americans who valued hedonism (seeking individual pleasure) more. These findings suggest that people from each culture develop their own personality with age according to what they value, which in turn may be influenced by what they think their culture is valuing.

Further evidence for the role of cultural values in personality development was obtained in a study on age differences in dispositional optimism among Americans and Hong Kong Chinese (You, Fung, & Isaacowitz, in press). Prior cross-cultural research has suggested that optimism is closely associated with self-enhancing tendencies that are considered to be more desirable among European-Americans than among East Asians (Chang, 2002; Chang, Sanna, & Yang, 2003; see also Kwan, Hui, & McGee, this volume). Examining optimism across age, You et al. (in press) found that while Americans as a group were more optimistic than Hong Kong Chinese, this cultural difference was magnified with age. Older Americans were more optimistic than younger Americans; yet older Hong Kong Chinese were less optimistic than younger Hong Kong Chinese. These findings once again suggest that the direction of personality development may be determined by what is considered to be desirable and appropriate in each culture. Americans, living in a culture that regards optimism as desirable, become more optimistic with age. Conversely, Chinese who live in a culture that does not value optimism become less optimistic with age.

Summary, caveats and future directions

In summary, the empirical findings reviewed above suggest that aging in the land of the panda (i.e. Chinese societies) can be similar to or different from that in the West (i.e. American and European societies) depending on the particular level of analysis. At the theoretical level, i.e. when we are examining underlying mechanisms, socioemotional selectivity theory (Carstensen et al., 1999; Fung & Carstensen, 2004) seems to be generalizable across cultures, at least in the areas of age differences in social goals, social relationships, and cognition (attention and memory). People, regardless of age and culture, defined either as geographical regions or historical contexts, seem to prioritize goals that aim at regulating emotions and deriving emotional meaning from life when they perceive time as limited.

However, Chinese do not necessarily consider the same goals to be emotionally meaningful as do their Western counterparts. Even when individuals across cultures all prioritize emotionally meaningful goals with age, the behavioral manifestations of this prioritization can differ. For example, while both Germans and Hong Kong Chinese seek emotionally close social partners with age, Hong Kong Chinese do so by increasing the proportion of nuclear family members in their social networks, but Germans do so by decreasing the proportion of nuclear family members (Fung, Stobter et al., 2008). Similarly, both Americans and Hong Kong Chinese increasingly pay selective attention to what they find emotionally meaningful in their external environment with age. Yet older Americans do so by showing a bias *for* positive stimuli, whereas older Hong Kong Chinese do so by exhibiting a bias *away* from positive stimuli (Fung, Isaacowitz et al., 2008).

Interestingly, these cross-cultural differences in behavioral manifestations of goals seem to be adaptive for the particular cultural context. While selective attention to the negative is a common diagnostic tool for depression in the clinical literature, Cheng, Fung, and Chan (2009) surprisingly found that Chinese older adults who had projected a worse future self enjoyed better well-being 12 months later than those who had made more optimistic predictions. This suggests that focusing on the negative may be adaptive for Chinese older adults, buffering them against the effects of aging-related declines and losses when the latter actually occur (see also Stewart, Lee, & Tao, this volume).

The most marked cross-cultural differences in aging have been found in the area of personality. A positive association between age and *renqing* (relationship orientation) was found among Hong Kong Chinese and Chinese-Americans, but not among Canadians or European-Americans (Fung & Ng, 2006). Nevertheless, even these cultural differences are malleable. The association between age and *renqing* became positive among European-Americans who valued tradition (seeking group acceptance) to a greater extent. Conversely, the positive association between age and *renqing* was weaker among Chinese-Americans who valued hedonism (seeking individual pleasure) to a greater extent.

Implications for the study of aging

Taken together, studying aging in Chinese societies has given us two insights on adult development in general: First, aging is not defined by a specific set of behaviors. In other words, there is *not* a standard way to age. Many patterns of aging turn out to be malleable, depending on the self-construal and/or the values of the individual. For example, the stability in the number of emotionally close social partners across age, typically found in Western studies (e.g. Fung, Lang et al., 2001; Lang & Carstensen, 1994), was found only among Hong Kong Chinese with a low level of interdependent self-construal. Those with medium and high levels of interdependent self-construal showed a positive association between age and the number of emotionally close social partners (Yeung et al., 2008). The negative association between age and the number of peripheral social partners, arguably the most reliable finding in the mainstream literature on social gerontology (e.g. Ajrouch, Antonucci, & Janevic, 2001; Carstensen, 1992; Fung, Lang et al., 2001; Lang & Carstensen, 1994; 2002), was found only among Hong Kong Chinese with low and medium levels of interdependent self-construal, but not among those with a high interdependent self-construal (Yeung et al., 2008).

Similarly, the negative reduction effect in memory, i.e. showing poorer memory for negative information relative to neutral information (e.g. Charles et al., 2003), was found only among older Chinese with lower levels of interdependence. Older Chinese with higher levels of interdependence remembered positive and negative information equally well (Lu et al., 2007). Finally, as described above, the association between age and some aspects of personality such as *renqing* was found to differ according to personal values (Fung, Ho et al., 2009). All these findings suggest that it is probably not correct to assume that aging is a process that follows a single static and predetermined trajectory. Aging can differ according to cultural contexts as well as the wishes and desires of the individual.

In addition, studying aging in Chinese societies has revealed aspects of aging that were not formerly noticed. For example, findings on age differences in *renqing* among the Chinese (Fung & Ng, 2006) have cast doubt on the assertion that personality development is universal (McCrae et al., 1999), and suggested that we should examine personality development beyond the framework of the Five-Factor Model. Studying social relationships among residents in Chinese nursing homes (Lee et al., 2002) has alerted us to the possibility that moving into a nursing home may be considered a personal/family disgrace, forcing residents to sever long-term ties with friends and neighbors to hide the fact that they have moved into a nursing home. Last but not least, Cheng's (2009b) study on generativity among Chinese older adults has reminded us of the importance of taking the perspectives of both the giver and the receiver into account when studying support across generations. The subjective concern for the next generation among older adults is reduced when their generative actions are not valued by younger generations.

Future studies should further examine how culturally salient constructs, such as familism, *renqing*, and filial piety, may moderate the aging process. For example, Yeung and Fung (2008) observed that while emotional support from family members contributed to the life satisfaction of all older adults they examined, instrument support from family members was positively related to the life satisfaction of older adults who had higher levels of familism, not of those who had lower levels of familism. This might be the case because receiving instrumental support signals to oneself and others that one is in need, thereby threatening life satisfaction. Yet this taxing nature of instrumental support seems to be less severe among those who perceive less separation between themselves and their family. These people may see the instrumental support from family members as justly theirs by adopting a more encompassing definition of self that includes their family members, thus perceiving no threat to life satisfaction.

Furthermore, a recurring theme from the above review is that when cultural differences in aging occur, they are usually consistent with known cultural differences in values. These findings inspire us to argue that development across adulthood may be part of the lifelong socialization process: individuals in each culture learn to be more prototypical members of their culture as they grow older. Cultural differences in aging (i.e. age by culture interactions) occur when people from different cultural contexts learn different ways to become better members of their culture. This process is known as 'socialization' (Bronfenbrenner, 1979) or 'cultural learning' (Vygotsky (1934/1962) in the human development literature, and 'acculturation' in the immigration literature (Berry, 1997; Miller, 2007; Navas, Rojas, Garcia, & Pumares, 2007). This process is also consistent with the basic premise of lifespan developmental theories (e.g. Baltes & Baltes, 1990; Brandtstädter & Greve, 1994; Carstensen et al., 1999; Heckhausen & Schulz, 1995) positing that, as people age, they shape their world in ways that maximize their well-being. But we add that people do so within the confines and definitions of their respective cultures. Future research should test this theoretical model.

Finally, future research should examine exactly why and how some aging processes differ by culture, while others do not. For example, Park, Nisbett, and Hedden (1999) argue that the relationships between aging and cognition may differ across cultures in predictable ways. Cognitive abilities that are relatively more knowledge-based may show greater cultural differences with age, as individuals acquire more culture-specific knowledge with the passage of time. In contrast, cognitive abilities that rely more on basic cognitive resources may show smaller cultural differences with age. This is the case because basic cognitive resources tend to decline uniformly across cultures as people get older, reducing the possibility for cultural differences in associated functioning. Since cognitive functioning is at the root of many aging processes, this model may be generalizable to adult development in domains other than cognitive abilities. Future studies should explore this possibility.

To conclude, we acknowledge that due to the limited number of studies on the intersection between aging and culture, much of the empirical evidence we have cited is based on cross-sectional studies, conducted in only a couple of cultures, albeit key cultures in the development of psychology. Longitudinal studies on a wider range of cultures are needed to test many of the postulates we have raised above. However, despite the preliminary nature of the evidence, it does suggest a promising direction for future research. Aging differs across cultures, particularly in terms of personality, social relationships, and cognition. These cultural differences can be predicted. It may be fruitful to look for cultural differences in aging (i.e. culture by age interactions) in areas where known cultural differences in value (i.e. culture main effects) have already been shown to exist.

Authors' note

This chapter is supported by the Hong Kong Research Grants Council Earmarked Research Grants CUHK4256/03H and CUHK4652/05H to Helene Fung and CityU1217/02H to Sheung-Tak Cheng, as well as a Chinese University of Hong Kong Direct Grant to Helene Fung and a City University Strategic Grant to Sheung-Tak Cheng. Correspondence concerning the manuscript should be directed to Helene Fung, Department of Psychology, The Chinese University of Hong Kong, Room 328 Sino Building, Chung Chi College, Shatin, New Territories, Hong Kong. Electronic mail should be sent to hhlfung@psy.cuhk.edu.hk.

Chapter note

1 Incidentally, panda, a Chinese emblem, is the acronym of one of the premier journals in the field, *Psychology and Aging.*

References

Aboderin, I. (2004). Modernisation and ageing theory revisited: Current explanations of recent developing world and historical Western shifts in material family support for older people. *Ageing & Society, 24*, 29–50.

Ajrouch, K. J., Antonucci, T. C., & Janevic, M. R. (2001). Social networks among Blacks and Whites: The interaction between race and age. *Journal of Gerontology: Social Sciences, 56B.* S112–S118.

Baltes, P. B. & Baltes, M. M. (1990). Psychological perspectives on successful aging: The model of selective optimization with compensation. In P. B. Baltes & M. M. Margret (eds), *Successful aging: Perspectives from the behavioral sciences.* (pp. 1–34). New York: Cambridge University Press.

Bardis, P. D. (1959). Attitudes toward the family among college students and their parents. *Sociology & Social Research. 43*, 352–358

Baumeister, R. F., Bratslavsky, E., Finkenauer, C., & Vohs, K. D. (2001). Bad is stronger than good. *Review of General Psychology, 5*, 323–370.

Berry, J. W. (1997). Immigration, acculturation, and adaptation. *Applied Psychology: An International Review, 46*, 5–68.

Bond, M. H. & Forgas, J. (1984). Linking person perception to behavior intention across cultures: The role of cultural collectivism. *Journal of Cross-Cultural Psychology, 15*, 337–352.

Brandtstädter, J. (1999). The self in action and development: Cultural, biosocial, and ontogenetic bases of intentional self-development. In J. Brandtstädter & R. M. Lerner (eds), *Action and self-development: Theory and research through the life span* (pp. 37–66). Thousand Oaks, CA: Sage.

Brandtstädter, J. & Greve, W. (1994). The aging self: Stabilizing and protective process. *Developmental Review. 14*, 52–80

Brandtstädter, J. & Rothermund, K. (2002). The life-course dynamics of goal pursuit and goal adjustment: A two-process framework. *Developmental Review, 22*, 117–150.

Brewer, M. B. & Chen, Y. R. (2007). Where (Who) are collectives in collectivism? Toward conceptual clarification of individualism and collectivism. *Psychological Review. 114*, 133–151.

Bronfenbrenner, U. (1979). *The ecology of human development: Experiments by nature and design.* Cambridge, MA: Harvard University Press.

Carstensen, L. L. (1992). Social and emotional patterns in adulthood: Support for socioemotional selectivity theory. *Psychology and Aging, 7*, 331–338.

Carstensen, L. L. & Fredrickson, B. (1998). Influence of HIV status and age on cognitive representations of others. *Health Psychology, 17*, 494–503.

Carstensen, L. L., Gross, J. J., & Fung, H. H. (1997). The social context of emotional experience. In K. W. Schaie & M. P. Lawton (eds), *Annual Review of Gerontology and Geriatrics.* (vol. 17, pp. 325–354). New York: Springer.

Carstensen, L. L., Isaacowitz, D., & Charles, S. T. (1999). Taking time seriously: A theory of socioemotional selectivity. *American Psychologist, 54*, 165–181.

Carstensen, L. L. & Mikels, J. A. (2005). At the intersection of emotion and cognition: Aging and the positivity effect. *Current Directions in Psychological Science. 14*, 117–121.

Chang, E. C. (2002). Optimism-pessimism and stress appraisal: Testing a cognitive interactive model of psychological adjustment in adults. *Cognitive Therapy and Research, 26*, 675–690.

Chang, E. C., Sanna, L. J., & Yang, K. M. (2003). Optimism, pessimism, affectivity, and psychological adjustment in US and Korea: A test of a mediation mode. *Personality and Individual Differences, 34*, 1195–1208.

Charles, S. T., Mather, M., & Carstensen, L. L. (2003). Aging and emotional memory: The forgettable nature of negative images for older adults. *Journal of Experimental Psychology: General, 132*, 310–324.

Cheng, S.-T. (2009a). The social network of nursing home residents in Hong Kong. *Ageing & Society, 29*, 163–178.

Cheng, S.-T. (2009b). Generativity in later life: Perceived respect from younger generations as a determinant of goal disengagement and psychological well-being. *Journal of Gerontology: Psychological Sciences, 64B*, 45–54.

Cheng, S.-T. & Chan, A. C. M. (2003). Regulating quality of care in nursing homes in Hong Kong: A social-ecological analysis. *Law & Policy, 25*, 403–423.

Cheng, S.-T. & Chan, A. C. M. (2006). Filial piety and psychological well-being in well older Chinese. *Journal of Gerontology: Psychological Sciences, 61B*, P262–P269.

Cheng, S.-T., Chan, W., & Chan, A. C. M. (2008). Older people's realisation of generativity in a changing society: The case of Hong Kong. *Ageing & Society, 28*, 609–627.

Cheng, S.-T., Chan, A. C. M., & Phillips, D. R. (2009). Ageing trends in Asia and the Pacific. In United Nations Department of Economic and Social Affairs (ed.), *Regional dimensions of the ageing situation* (pp. 35–69). New York: United Nations.

Cheng, S.-T., Fung, H. H., & Chan, A. C. M. (2008). *Self-perception and psychological well-being: The benefits of foreseeing a worse future. Psychology and Aging, 24*, 623–633.

Cheng, S.-T. & Heller, K. (2009). Global aging: Challenges for community psychology. *American Journal of Community Psychology, 44*, 161–173.

Cheng, S.-T. & Yim, Y.-K. (2008). Age differences in forgiveness: The role of future time perspective. *Psychology and Aging, 23*, 676–680.

Cheung, F. M, Cheung, S. F., Wada, S., & Zhang, J. X. (2003). Indigenous measures of personality assessment in Asian countries: A review. *Psychological Assessment, 15*, 280–289.

Cheung, F. M, Cheung, S. F., Leung, K., Ward, C., & Leong, F. (2003). The English version of the Chinese Personality Assessment Inventory. *Journal of Cross Cultural Psychology, 34*, 433–452.

Cheung, F. M., Kwong, J., & Zhang, J. X. (2003). Clinical validation of the Chinese Personality Assessment Inventory (CPAI). *Psychological Assessment, 15*, 89–100.

Cheung, F. M., Leung, K., Fan, R. M., Song, W. Z., Zhang, J. P. (1996). Development of the Chinese Personality Assessment Inventory. *Journal of Cross Cultural Psychology, 27*, 181–199.

Cheung, F. M., Leung, K., Zhang, J. X., Sun, H. F., Gan, Y. Q., Song, W. Z., & Xie, D. (2001). Indigenous Chinese personality constructs: Is the five-factor model complete? *Journal of Cross-Cultural Psychology, 32*, 407–433.

Costa, P. T., McCrae, R. R., Martin, T. A., Oryol, V. E., Senin, I. G., Rukavishnikov, A. A., Shimonaka, Y., Nakazato, K., Gondo,Y., Takayama, M., Allik, J., Kallasmaa, T., & Realo, A. (2000). Personality development from adolescence through adulthood: Further cross-cultural comparisons of age differences. In V. J., Molfese & D. L. Molfese (eds), *Temperament and personality development across the life span* (pp. 235–252). Mahwah, NJ: Lawrence Erlbaum Associates.

Erikson, E. H. (1982). *The life cycle completed: A review*. New York: Norton.

Frey, D. & Stahlberg, D. (1986). Selection of information after receiving more or less reliable self-threatening information. *Personality and Social Psychology Bulletin, 12*, 431–441.

Fredrickson, B. L. & Carstensen, L. L. (1990). Choosing social partners: How age and anticipated endings make people more selective. *Psychology and Aging, 5*, 335–347.

Fredrickson, B. L. (1995). Socioemotional behavior at the end of college life. *Journal of Social and Personal Relationships, 12*, 261–276.

Fung, H. H. & Carstensen, L. L. (2004). Motivational changes in response to blocked goals and foreshortened time: Testing alternatives for socioemotional selectivity theory. *Psychology and Aging, 19*, 68–78.

Fung, H. H. & Carstensen, L. L. (2006). Goals change when life's fragility is primed: Lessons learned from older adults, the September 11th Attacks and SARS. *Social Cognition, 24*, 248–278.

Fung, H. H., Carstensen, L. L., & Lutz, M. A. (1999). Influence of time on social preferences: Implications for lifespan development. *Psychology and Aging, 14*, 595–604.

Fung, H. H., Carstensen, L. L., & Lang, F. R. (2001). Age-related patterns in social networks among European Americans and African Americans: Implications for socioemotional selectivity across the life span. *International Journal of Aging and Human Development, 52*, 185–206.

Fung, H. H., Ho, Y. W., Tam, K.-P., & Tsai, J. (2009). *Value moderates age differences in personality: The example of relationship orientation*. Manuscript under review.

Fung, H. L., Isaacowitz, D. M., Lu, A. Y., Wadlinger, H. A., Goren, D., & Wilson, H. R. (2008). Age-related positivity enhancement is not universal: Older Hong Kong Chinese look away from positive stimuli. *Psychology and Aging, 23*, 440–446.

Fung, H. H., Lai, P., & Ng, R. (2001). Age differences in social preferences among Taiwanese and Mainland Chinese: The role of perceived time. *Psychology and Aging, 16*, 351–356.

Fung, H. H., Siu, C. M. Y., Choy,W. C. W., & McBride–Chang, C. (2005). Meaning of grandparenthood: Do concerns about time and mortality matter? *Ageing International, 30*, 123–146.

Fung, H. H. & Ng, S. K. (2006). Age differences in the sixth personality factor: Age differences in interpersonal relatedness among Canadians and Hong Kong Chinese. *Psychology and Aging, 21*, 810–814.

Fung, H. H., Stobter, F. S., Yeung, D. Y. & Lang, F. R. (2008). Cultural specificity of socioemotional selectivity: Age differences in social network composition among Germans and Hong Kong Chinese. *Journal of Gerontology: Psychological Sciences, 63B*, P156–P164.

Fung, H. H. & Tang, L. Y. T. (2005). Age differences in memory for emotional messages: Do older people always remember the positive better? *Aging International, 30*, 244–261.

Glenn, V. O., Ottenbacger, K. J., & Markides, K. S. (2004). Onset of frailty in older adults and protective role of positive affect. *Psychology and Aging, 19*, 402–408.

Gruhn, D., Smith, J., & Baltes, P. B. (2005). No aging bias favoring memory for positive material: evidence from a heterogeneity–homogeneity list paradigm using emotionally toned words. *Psychology and Aging, 20*, 579–588.

Heckhausen, J. & Schulz, R. (1995). A lifespan theory of control. *Psychological Review, 102*, 284–304.

Heine, S. J., Lehman, D. R., Markus, H. R., & Kitayama, S. (1999). Is there a universal need for positive self-regard? *Psychological Review, 106*, 766–794.

Helson, R., Jones, C., & Kwan, V. S. Y. (2002). Personality change over 40 years of adulthood: Hierarchical linear modeling analyses of two longitudinal samples. *Journal of Personality and Social Psychology, 83*, 752–766.

Heller, K. (1993). Prevention activities for older adults: Social structures and personal competencies that maintain useful social roles. *Journal of Counseling & Development, 72*, 124–130.

Helson, R., Jones, C., & Kwan, V. S. Y. (2002). Personality change over 40 years of adulthood: Hierarchical linear modeling analyses of two longitudinal samples. *Journal of Personality and Social Psychology, 83*, 752–766.
Herzog, A. R., Franks, M. M., Markus, H. R., & Holmberg, D. (1998). Activities and well-being in older age: Effects of self-concept and educational attainment. *Psychology and Aging, 13*, 179–185.
Hofstede, G. (1980). *Culture consequences: International differences in work-related values.* Beverly Hills, CA: Sage.
Heckhausen, J. & Schulz, R. (1995). A lifespan theory of control. *Psychological Review 102*, 284–304.
Inglehart, R. & Baker, W. E. (2000). Modernization, cultural change, and the persistence of traditional values. *American Sociological Review, 65*, 19–51.
Issacowitz, D. M., Wadlinger, H. A., Goren, D., & Wilson, H. R. (2006a). Selective preference in visual fixation away from negative images in old age? An eye-tracking study. *Psychology and Aging, 21*, 40–48.
Issacowitz, D. M., Wadlinger, H. A., Goren, D., & Wilson, H. R. (2006b). Is there an age-related positivity effect in visual attention? A comparison of two methodologies. *Emotion, 6*, 511–516.
John, O. P. (1990). The 'Big Five' factor taxonomy: Dimensions of personality in the natural language and in questionnaires. In L. A. Pervin (ed.), *Handbook of personality: Theory and research.* (pp. 66–100). New York: Guilford Press.
Kin, A. M. Y. & Fung, H. H. (2004). Goals and social network composition among young adults with and without a history of cancer. *Journal of Psychology in Chinese Societies, 5*, 97–111.
Kitayama, S. & Karasawa, M. (1995). Self: A cultural psychological perspective. *Japanese Journal of Experimental Social Psychology, 35*, 133–163.
Knight, B. G., Maines, M. L., & Robinson, G. S. (2002). The effects of sad mood on memory in older adults: A test of the mood congruence effect. *Psychology and Aging, 17*, 653–661.
Kwan, V. S. Y., Bond, M. H., & Singelis, T. M. (1997). Pancultural explanations for life satisfaction: Adding relationship harmony to self-esteem. *Journal of Personality and Social Psychology, 73*, 1038–1051.
Labouvie-Vief, G., Diehl, M., Tarnowski, A., & Shen, J.-L. (2000). Age differences in adult personality: Findings from the United States and China. *Journal of Gerontology: Psychological Sciences, 55B*, 4–17.
Lang, F. R. (2000). Endings and continuity of social relationships: Maximizing intrinsic benefits within personal networks when feeling near to death? *Journal of Social and Personal Relationships, 17*, 157–184.
Lang, F. R. & Carstensen, L. L. (1994). Close emotional relationships in late life: Further support for proactive aging in the social domain. *Psychology and Aging, 9*, 315–324.
Lang, F. R. & Carstensen, L. L. (2002). Time counts: Future time perspective, goals, and social relationships. *Psychology and Aging, 17*, 125–139.
Lee, D. T. F., Woo, J., & Mackenzie, A. E. (2002). The cultural context of adjusting to nursing home life: Chinese elders' perspectives. *Gerontologist, 42*, 667–675.
Lin, E. J.-L. & Church, A. T. (2004). Are indigenous Chinese personality dimensions culture-specific? An investigation of the Chinese Personality Assessment Inventory in Chinese-American and European-American samples. *Journal of Cross-Cultural Psychology, 35*, 586–605.
Liu, C. K. M. & Fung, H. H. (2005). Gang members' social network composition and psychological well-being: Extending socioemotional selectivity theory to the study of gang involvement. *Journal of Psychology in Chinese Societies, 6*, 89–108.
Lu, A. Y., Wadlinger, H. A., Fung, H. H., & Isaacowitz, D. M. (2007). Testing the positivity effect among Hong Kong Chinese. In Q. Kenedy & H. H. Fung (chairs), *American-Chinese differences in socioemotional aspects of aging.* Symposium conducted at 115th convention of American Psychological Association, San Francisco, U.S.A., August.
Markus, H. R. & Kitayama, S. (1991). Culture and the self: Implications for cognition, emotion, and motivation. *Psychological Review, 98*, 224–253.
Markus, H. R., Uchida, Y., Omregie, H., Townsend, S. S. M., & Kitayama, S. (2006). Going for the gold: Models of agency in Japanese and Americans. *Psychological Science, 17*, 103–112.
Mather, M. & Carstensen, L. L. (2003). Aging and attentional biases for emotional faces. *Psychological Science. 14*, 409–415.
Mather, M. & Knight, M. (2005). Goal-directed memory: The role of cognitive control in older adults' emotional memory. *Psychology and Aging. Special Issue: Emotion–Cognition Interactions and the Aging Mind, 20*, 554–570.
McCrae, R. R., Costa, P. T. Jr., Ostendorf, F., Angleitner, A., Caprara, G.. V., Barbaranelli, C., Lima, M. P. D., Simoes, A., Marusic, I., Bratko, D., Chae, J.-H., & Piedmont, R. L. (1999). Age differences in personality across the adult life span: parallels in five cultures. *Developmental Psychology, 35*, 466–477.
McCrae, R. R., Costa, P. T. Jr., Ostendorf, F., Angleitner, A., Hrebickova, M., Avia, M. D., Sanz, J., Sanchez-Bernardos, M. L., Kusdil, M. E., Woodfield, R., Saunders, P. R., & Smith, P. B. (2000). Nature over nurture: Temperament, personality, and life span development. *Journal of Personality and Social Psychology, 78*, 173–186.
Mikels, J. A., Larkin, G. R., Reuter, L, Patricia, A., & Cartensen, L. L. (2005). Divergent trajectories in the aging mind: Changes in working memory for affective versus visual information with age. *Psychology and Aging. Special Issue: Emotion–Cognition Interactions and the Aging Mind, 20*, 542–553.
Miller, M. J. (2007). A bilinear multidimensional measurement model of Asian American acculturation and enculturation: Implications for counseling interventions. *Journal of Counseling Psychology, 54*, 118–131.
Navas, M., Rojas, A. J., Garcia, M., & Pumares, P. (2007). Acculturation strategies and attitudes according to the relative acculturation extended model (RAEM): The perspectives of natives versus immigrants. *International Journal of Intercultural Relations, 31*, 67–86.

Oyserman, D., Coon, H. M., & Kemmelmeier, M. (2002). Rethinking individualism and collectivism: Evaluation of theoretical assumptions and meta-analyses. *Psychological Bulletin, 128*, 3–72.
Poon, C. Y. M. & Fung, H. H. (2008). Physical activity and psychological well-being among Hong Kong Chinese older adults: Exploring the moderating role of self-construals. *International Journal of Aging and Human Development, 66*, 1–19.
Rosow, I. (1985). Status and role change through the life cycle. In R. Binstock & E. Shanas (eds), *Handbook of aging and the social sciences* (pp. 62–93). New York: Van Nostrand Reinhold.
Rozin, P. & Royzman, E. B. (2001). Negativity bias, negativity dominance, and contagion. *Personality and Social Psychology Review, 5*, 296–320.
Schwartz, S. H. (1992). Universals in the content and structure of values: Theoretical advances and empirical tests in 20 countries. In M. P. Zanna (ed.), *Advances in experimental social psychology* (Vol. 25, pp. 1–65). New York: Academic Press
Sedikides, C., Gaertner, L., Toguchi, Y. (2003). Pancultural self-enhancement. *Journal of Personality and Social Psychology. 84*, 60–79.
Szalay, L. B., Strohl, J. B., Fu L., & Lao, P. S. (1994). *American and Chinese perceptions and belief systems: A People's Republic of China–Taiwanese comparison.* New York: Plenum Press.
Steverink, N. & Lindenberg, S. (2006). Which social needs are important for subjective well-being? What happens to them with aging? *Psychology and Aging, 21*, 281–290.
Treas, J. & Wang, W. (1993). Of deeds and contracts: Filial piety perceived in contemporary Shanghai. In V. L. Bengtson & W. A. Achenbaum (eds), *The changing contract across generations* (pp. 87–93). New York: Aldine De Gruyter.
Triandis, H. C. (1989). The self and social behavior in differing cultural contexts. *Psychological Review, 96*, 506–520.
Triandis, H. C. (1995). *Individualism and collectivism.* Boulder, CO: Westview Press.
Uchida, Y. (2007). *Happiness in east and west: Themes and variations.* Paper presented at the meeting of Expanding horizons of cultural psychology: Advances in research and teaching, Stanford University, CA., August.
United Nations Population Division. (n.d.). *World population prospects: The 2006 revision population database.* Retrieved June 1, 2007 from http://esa.un.org/unpp/
Vygotsky, L. S. (1934/1962). *Thought and language.* Cambridge, MA: MIT Press.
Wan, C., Chiu, C, Y., Peng, S., & Tam, K. P. (2007). Measuring cultures through intersubjective cultural norms: Implications for predicting relative identification with two or more cultures. *Journal of Cross Cultural Psychology, 38*, 213–226.
Wan, C., Chiu, C. Y., Tam, K. P., Lee, S. L., Lau, I., & Peng, S. (2007). Perceived cultural importance and actual self-importance of values in cultural identification. *Journal of Personality and Social Psychology, 92*, 337–354.
Yang, C. F. (1988). Familism and development: An examination of the role of family in contemporary China mainland, Hong Kong and Taiwan. In D. Sinha & H. S. R. Kao (eds), *Social values and development: Asian perspectives* (pp. 93–123). Thousand Oaks, CA: Sage.
Yang, J., McCrae, R. R. & Costa, P. T. Jr. (1998). Adult age differences in personality traits in the United States and the People's Republic of China. *Journal of Gerontology: Psychological Sciences, 53B*, 375–383.
Yeung, D. Y., Fung, H. H., & Lang, F. R. (2007). Gender differences in social network characteristics and psychological well-being among Hong Kong Chinese: The role of future time perspective and adherence to Renqing. *Aging & Mental Health, 11*, 45–56.
Yeung, D. Y., Fung, H. H., & Lang, F. R. (2008). Self-construal moderates age differences in social network characteristics. *Psychology and Aging, 23*, 222–226.
Yeung, T. Y. & Fung, H. H. (2007). Social support and life satisfaction among Hong Kong Chinese older adults: Family first? *European Journal of Aging, 4*, 219–227.
You, J., Fung, H. H., & Isaacomitz, D. M. (in press). Age differences in dispositional optimism: A Cross-Cultural Study. *European Journal of Aging.*
Zhang, Z. & Yang, C. F. (1998). Beyond distributive justice: The reasonableness norm in Chinese reward allocation. *Asian Journal of Social Psychology, 1*, 253–269.

CHAPTER 20

Chinese well-being

Luo Lu

To most people, happiness often comes in a fleeting feeling attached to a nice pleasant experience, like enjoying a scoop of ice cream on a hot day, or listening to Mozart after a long day at work. However, people do not just want to feel happy for a short while, they want to feel positive about living a good life, and accomplishing things they believe are valuable and worthwhile. Over the centuries, philosophers and ordinary people have pondered what kind of life is worth living.

In the West, happiness has long been a central theme of philosophical deliberations and heated debates dating back to the Greek masters. For Aristotle, happiness (termed *eudainmonia*) was achieved through virtuous actions that fulfill the full spectrum of a person's human potential. This conceptualization of happiness laid the foundation for the modern humanistic (*eudainmonic*) approach to well-being, emphasizing meaning in life, self-realization, and cultivating a fully-functioning person (Ryan & Deci, 2001), typically referred to as *psychological well-being* (cf. Ryff, 1989). Another Greek philosophical tradition, *hedonism*, gave birth to the alternative approach to well-being, the hedonic approach, emphasizing the pleasure principle (Ryan & Deci, 2001). Although some early hedonists were concerned with the immediate pursuit of bodily pleasures, later refinements of hedonism emphasized the inclusion of mental and spiritual pleasures and the careful selection of pleasures to ensure long-term well-being (Christopher, 1999). Modern conceptions of well-being include elements from each of these traditions.

Thus, as noted above, well-being should be able to reflect the full range of things that make life worth living. It has in fact also been a subject of enquiry in a large number of other humanities and social sciences disciplines, and has been defined in theological, political, economic, and psychological terms (see Argyle, 2001; Diener, 1984; Veenhoven, 1984 for excellent reviews on the historical development of happiness studies). In this chapter, I will adopt the customary terminologies used by most current scholars and researchers (cf. Argyle, 2001; Diener, 1984) and use happiness interchangeably with subjective well-being (SWB). To reiterate, SWB is not merely hedonism, it consists of evaluations that life is being lived in a positive manner (Diener, 2000; Diener & Tov, in press).

Great breakthroughs have been achieved in the last few decades as science has begun to unravel the prevailing myth of happiness as a mysterious, ephemeral state of mind, revealing it as an ordinary, albeit positive, state of mind that can be studied and understood. SWB is now one of the most important fields in the emerging 'positive psychology' (Seligman & Csikszentmihaly, 2000), a topic that even has its own journal since 2000, when the *Journal of Happiness Studies* was launched. Over four decades of concerted scientific effort, a certain consensus has been formed among psychological researchers. First and foremost, one of the most important distinctive features of SWB is its positive nature. Happiness is now generally defined as a predominance of positive over negative affect, and as satisfaction with life, consisting of people's general evaluations of their life, affective and cognitive (Argyle, Martin, & Crossland, 1989; Diener, 1984).

Second, happiness is better conceptualized as a trait rather than a transient emotional state (Veenhoven, 1994). As Cummins (2000) puts it, happiness is a mood rather than an emotion. Emotions are fleeting, while moods are more stable. Tracking Australian happiness over 18 annual nationwide surveys of 2,000 randomly selected people, Cummins found that the level of happiness varied by only three percentage points. We found a similar phenomenon among our Taiwanese (cultural Chinese) informants. Using our standard measurement instrument, the Chinese Happiness Inventory, we noted that the level of happiness varied by only four percentage points between 1993 and 2007 (Lu, 2008). Even stronger evidence for happiness came from a panel study of 581 randomly invited adults in Taiwan, indicating that the stability coefficient of happiness over 2.5 years was .43 (Lu, 1999). This was comparable to what Veenhoven (1994) found in his meta-analysis of longitudinal studies on happiness, namely that happiness is quite stable for the short term but modestly stable for the long term, sensitive to fortune or adversity.

Third, SWB research has progressed from early social surveys looking for 'objective' external indicators (e.g. Andrews & Withey, 1976; Campbell, 1976) or scale development efforts (e.g. Andrews & Withey, 1976), to attempts at explaining the psychological mechanisms underpinning happiness (e.g. Cummins, 1995, 2000; Diener, Suh, Lucas, & Smith, 1999; Headey & Wearing, 1989), largely helped by the advancement in multivariate techniques for statistical analyses. Decades of research have revealed that effects of demographic variables or 'objective' external indicators are very small, though in general 'young, well-educated, and well-paid' represent the personal profile of the happy person (Diener et al., 1999). Based on the Chinese Happiness Inventory Database ($N = 24{,}601$, data collected between 1993 and 2007), we found similar results: female, youthful, being married or single (as opposed to being widowed or divorced), having higher education, and higher income are the demographic correlates of happiness for the cultural Chinese in Taiwan (Lu, 2008).

Finally, the issue of 'culture' is now moving to center stage, inspired and provoked by intriguing though puzzling findings from recent large-scale, cross-cultural comparisons (Diener, Diener, & Diener, 1995; Veenhoven, 1995). Substantial national differences on happiness have repeatedly been observed, even after controlling for the effects of income. Specifically, members of Western societies were generally happier than their counterparts in the East, and cultural individualism was the strongest correlate of happiness at the national level. In a comparative study of 44 nations in the early 1990s, Veenhoven (2000) reported the level of Chinese happiness at 2.92 (on a scale of 1–4). The highest-scoring nation was the Netherlands (3.39) and the lowest Bulgaria (2.33). This comparison ranked China thirtieth on the list of 44, though the author conceded that the Chinese report may be tainted with optimism, since the poor rural population was underrepresented in the study sample.

Despite encouraging progress, one thorny issue remains: psychological research as typically conducted tends to be Western in origin, ideas, and instrumentation. On the one hand, research based in the West may be culture-bound in significant ways. Even when studies are cross-cultural, they usually involve applying measures derived from Western cultural traditions and comparing results from different nations within *a priori* Western theoretical frameworks. There is a danger, therefore, of twisting non-Western cultures into showing psychological equivalence (Brislin, Lonner, & Thorndike, 1973).

This concern is all the more pressing for the study of SWB. Christopher (1999) took a deep look into the philosophical foundations of happiness studies, and concluded that both hedonic and eudaimonic approaches have Euro-American cultural roots. Specifically, happiness or well-being is based in an ontological and liberal 'I' as notions of the self, which are prescribed as normative prescriptions for the good/ideal person. In contrast, well-being in the Confucian tradition puts an individual's societal obligations and social embeddedness at the center.

Over the centuries, Chinese people have been urged to lead a virtuous life and have been socialized to pursue the greater good instead of selfish happiness (Ng, Ho, Wong, & Smith, 2003). Ng et al. (2003) went further, arguing that any conception of well-being is culturally embedded and depends on how the notions of 'well' and 'being' are defined and practiced in different cultural communities. The very word *happiness* (幸福) did not enter Chinese colloquial vocabulary until recently, and Chinese students were found to be less familiar with the concept of happiness than were their American counterparts (Diener, Suh, Smith, & Shao, 1995).

It is thus troublesome to note that while the psychological study of happiness is quickly gaining popularity in Chinese societies, culture awareness and culture sensitivity on the subject is yet to be raised and nurtured. I conducted a systematic search through major academic databases in Taiwan for research on happiness between 1992 and 2007. Among the 17 journal papers published and 141 degree dissertations completed, almost all adopted theoretical frameworks/constructs developed in the Western literature, and merely attempted to test Western formulated theories or replications of established relationships (see also Yang's, 1986, criticism of Taiwanese personality research some two decades ago). Very few researchers have contemplated the role of culture in happiness experiences, especially for the Chinese.

A truly balanced psychology of SWB should be informed by multiple cultural vantage points, Christian, Confucian, Buddhist, Hindu, Muslim, Baha'i and others. Our series of research in the past decade has focused on contrasting the Chinese against the Western (European-North American) cultural traditions in terms of how they construct their conception of happiness and consequently constrict its subjective experience. In the present chapter, I take the position that the *cultural conceptions* of happiness are critical aspects of subjective well-being. I argue that culture and SWB are most productively analyzed together as a dynamic of mutual constitution. Adopting a cultural psychological approach, I will draw specifically on our own indigenous Chinese research to elaborate on two evolving themes regarding SWB: (1) the Chinese conceptualization of happiness, and (2) cultural and psychological correlates of happiness. Finally, I will underline the emerging coexistence of contrasting cultural elements in the case of SWB. This chapter does not attempt a comprehensive review of the field, which has been accomplished by various seasoned scholars (e.g. Argyle, 2001; Diener, 1984; Kahneman, Diener & Schwarz, 1999; Ryan & Deci, 2001; Veenhoven, 1984); rather, I will use our own indigenous Chinese research to illuminate culture-related themes regarding SWB: the crucial concept of 'culture' will be underlined throughout.

Cultural conceptions of happiness

With their staunch commitment to the scientific method, Western psychologists have generally left the question of 'What is happiness?' to philosophers for debate, and gone on to study perceived happiness and its correlates. While most lay people regard happiness as a fleeting emotional state of positive nature, scientists, especially psychologists, now conceptualize happiness to be more like a mood state, which is rather stable. As such, a consensus to operationalize happiness in terms of (1) positive affect; (2) life satisfaction; and (3) absence of negative affect has been achieved.

However, such a working definition is at most an attempt to identify components/elements of the happiness experience, which reveals little about the nature and meanings of happiness, or about the beliefs people hold regarding happiness embedded in diverse cultural traditions. For instance, happiness seems to be a more salient concept for individualists (World Values Study Group, 1994). The percentage of people in the World Value Survey II who said they had never thought about whether they were happy or satisfied is higher in collectivist nations. Similarly, college students in individualist nations reported that happiness was significantly more important to them than did their counterparts in collectivist nations (Diener et al., 1995). Thus, the value one places on happiness differs across cultures; the collectivists may emphasize duty and obligation over personal 'happiness' (Triandis, 1995).

Some researchers have criticized the lack of theoretical sophistication and psychological depth entailed in the current mainstream research on SWB (Ryan & Deci, 2001; Ryff, 1989). Although the empirical study of happiness has won legitimacy and recognition in mainstream scientific psychology and flourished over the past four decades, the accumulation of data has failed to push up the level of theoretical sophistication. Comparing two extensive reviews 15 years apart (Diener, 1984; Diener et al., 1999), we now know more, with greater confidence, about correlates of SWB, but we are no closer to identifying the heartbeat of this ultimate human experience.

The hard question of 'What is happiness?' is unavoidable if we are to further our understandings of human happiness. Breaking this deadlock can also hopefully enable us to direct our scientific efforts more effectively. To this end, we have conducted two series of studies from somewhat different yet complementary perspectives: (1) the folk-psychological analysis of lay Chinese people's definitions of happiness, and (2) the cultural analysis of views of happiness molded in the Chinese and Western cultural traditions.

What is happiness? The folk-psychological approach

Because meanings and concepts are molded by culture (Bruner, 1990), it seems necessary to explore what people think about happiness as embedded in the world of meanings and values construed within a given cultural tradition. As mentioned earlier, the word *happiness* (幸福) did not appear in the Chinese language until recently. *Fu* or *fu qi* (福, 福氣) is perhaps the closest equivalent of happiness in ancient Chinese thought. *Fu* appeared as early as bone inscriptions from the Shang Dynasty, expressing human desires and prayers to a worshipped god (Bauer, 1976). What were these desires and prayers? The interpretation of bone inscriptions and the excavated luxurious burial gifts point to a twofold fundamental conception of happiness at the very beginning of Chinese civilization: blessings from the supernatural, and pleasures derived from human society.

Later, in the '*Shang Shu*', the word *fu* was more clearly defined in mundane existence to include 'longevity, prosperity, health, peace, virtue, and a comfortable death' (Wu, 1991). Another important ancient work, *Classic of ritual* (禮記), gave *fu* yet another amendment. *Fu* was 'fortunate, lucky, smooth, and free of obstacles'. Roughly, the Chinese people's conception of happiness can be traced back to the early days of civilization, and has kept some of its core ideas while evolving with the great culture. In folk wisdom, Chinese happiness seems to include material abundance, physical health, virtuous and peaceful life, and relief from death anxiety.

Ancient Chinese society was a two-tiered system. At the top of the societal pyramid, the social elite presided over the rest, enjoying power and prestige; its ideals were recorded and promulgated through the writings and teachings of great philosophers and scholars; the vast majority of working people at its base were ruled according to and preached to, using those ideals, which were also conveyed to them in the folklore described above. There is no denying that schools of great philosophy have profoundly shaped Chinese culture and the mentality of Chinese people for thousands of years (see Hwang & Han; Ji, Lee, & Guo; this volume). The tripartite of Confucianism, Taoism, and Buddhism form the backbone of orthodox Chinese culture, and each has distinct views on human happiness. Our systematic efforts at exploring the philosophical thinking of Confucianism, Taoism, and Buddhism regarding human happiness have already been detailed in various journal publications (Lu, 1998; 2001; 2008; Lu & Shih, 1997; Lu, Gilmour, & Kao, 2001). However, in the interest of depicting a cultural background for our later presentation of the Chinese fork psychology on happiness, I will sketch a brief summary below.

It needs to be noted initially that Chinese philosophical schools do not concern themselves too much about the nature of happiness; rather, they regard happiness as synonymous with optimal functioning and right living. In other words, happiness per se is not worthy of philosophical contemplation; *prescription* for actions to achieve happiness is, as such a discourse conveys the culturally sanctioned notion of good life.

In the Confucian tradition, such a good or virtuous life is achieved through 'knowledge, benevolence, and harmony of the group' (Wu, 1992, p. 31). Confucian philosophy stresses the collective welfare of the family or clan (further extending to society and the entire human race) more than individual welfare. Under this collectivist or social orientation, Chinese culture emphasizes sharing the fruits of individual success with the group. Contributing to society is the ultimate happiness, whereas hedonistic striving for happiness is regarded as unworthy and even shameful. In a nutshell, for Confucians, happiness is no longer a set of living conditions; it is the psychological state or spiritual world of a living individual. Happiness is not transient, shallow sensual pleasures; it is an eternal, deeply meaningful world of reason. Confucians regarded happiness as spiritual, not material; as moral, not circumstantial; as self-identified, not other-judged.

Taoism opposes the idea of happiness as a product of material satisfaction; it also opposes the Confucian idea of happiness as a constant self-cultivation to achieve moral rectitude. Happiness or fulfillment in Taoism is the personal liberation from all human desires, through following the natural force, not doing anything, accepting fate calmly, and facing life with a peaceful mind. In so doing, one may reach the ultimate happiness of merging with the universe, termed *tian ren he yi* (天人合一). Happiness in Taoism, therefore, is not an emotional feeling of joy; rather, it is a cognitive insight and a spiritual triumph of self-transcendence.

Although not an indigenous Chinese philosophy, after its initial introduction from India in the Han Dynasty (around AD 60), Buddhism incorporated many of the Chinese philosophical thoughts and cultural traditions since the Tang Dynasty (AD 618–907), blending in well with the Chinese way of living. Buddhism holds that there is no such thing as absolute, lasting happiness in life, since all existence on earth was poisoned by unhappiness from the very start, and only *nirvana* can offer salvation (Chiang, 1996). Happiness in Buddhism can only be found in the 'Paradise of the west' after nirvana, which promises eternal bliss beyond the everyday misery of this world. Physical exercises, meditation, doing charitable deeds, eliminating all human desires are all ways to lift up the soul to reach nirvana and eternal happiness. Buddhism does not acknowledge the existence of mundane, albeit fleeting, happiness.

For scholars, Confucianism, Taoism, and Buddhism are three entirely different, even contradictory, philosophical systems. For ordinary people, however, they have been ingeniously merged and utilized to serve in promoting a good life. People may act in accordance with Confucianism when they are interacting with other people, with Taoism when they are encountering nature, and with Buddhism when they are confronted with life's vicissitudes and death. This is the ultimate achievement of 'Chinese pragmatism' (Quah, 1995). It may be fair to conclude that, influenced by Confucian teachings, the Chinese conception of happiness is more of a 'harmony of the society' rather than a 'happiness of the individual', emphasizing collective welfare and de-emphasizing personal, hedonistic pursuits. In addition, influenced by Taoism and Buddhism teachings, the Chinese conception of happiness emphasizes mental cultivation and spiritual enlightenment rather than material abundance and worldly successes.

With such an understanding of the Chinese 'great traditions' including Confucianism, Taoism, and Buddhism, as well as the 'bourgeois traditions' of folklore, I proceeded with a thematic analysis of Chinese students' spontaneous accounts of happiness (Lu, 2001). Such a Chinese vantage point is in distinct contrast to the predominant Western cultural perspective infusing and informing most SWB research. This endeavor was also among the first attempts to bridge the gap between scholarly theories of SWB and ordinary people's lived experiences and deeply held beliefs about human happiness. Although exploratory in nature, the result is a clear map of the psychological space of Chinese happiness. Later, we continued this line of enquiry and analyzed conceptions of happiness as embedded in the Euro-American culture and American students' spontaneous accounts of their happiness, to be contrasted with our previously collected Chinese data (Lu & Gilmour, 2004a).

A sketch of the empirical findings is presented below for the purpose of drawing later comparisons between Chinese and American folk theories. One hundred and forty-two undergraduate Taiwanese students wrote free-format essays in response to a simple question, 'What is happiness?' Using thematic analysis, students' replies were categorized in the following ways: as (a) a mental state of satisfaction and contentment; (b) a variety of positive feelings/emotions; (c) a harmonious homeostasis, involving intrapersonal, interpersonal, and societal realms; (d) personal achievements and a positive outlook; and (e) freedom from ill-being.

Chinese students generally regarded happiness as a harmonious state of existence, emphasizing the following conditions as prerequisite for happiness: (a) the individual is satisfied or content; (b) the individual is the agent of his own happiness; (c) spiritual enrichment is more important than material satisfaction; and (d) the individual maintains a positive outlook towards the future.

Another distinct feature of the Taiwanese students' spontaneous accounts is their emphasis on the dialectical relationship between happiness and unhappiness. These two distinct entities or states are viewed as locked in a never-ending relationship of interdependence: each depends on the other for contrast and meaning. Moreover, this relationship between the two opposites is also dynamic and constantly changing; each relies on the other to strive. Echoing the ancient wisdom such as balancing between *yin-yang*, some Taiwanese students proclaimed that a balance should be maintained between happiness and unhappiness in life. Some went further to claim that happiness can emerge only from a backdrop of unhappiness, is cyclical, and cannot be sustained as a constant state.

Taiwanese students also had their preferred ways of achieving happiness, centering on nurturing and cultivating the following capacities: (a) discovery; (b) contentment and maintaining an attitude of gratitude; (c) giving to, sharing with, or serving others; and (d) self-cultivation.

Later, we invited 97 Caucasian-American students to write free-format essays in response to the same question, 'What is happiness?' Using thematic analysis, we discovered that American students defined happiness in seven aspects: as (a) a mental state of satisfaction and contentment; (b) a variety of positive feelings/emotions; (c) a result of personal achievements and exercising personal control; (d) a result of exercising self-autonomy; (e) freedom from ill-being; (f) a mental state orientated towards relating meaningfully to other people; and (g) the ultimate value in life.

Reading through Taiwanese and American students' rich and vivid accounts of happiness, we could easily spot both similarities and differences in their reports. Direct comparisons were thus made between the Chinese and American lay theories of happiness on each theme, especially subtle distinctions in terms of both the substances of, and approaches to, SWB, as mandated by cultural traditions in the East and the West. I will present only summaries below.

First, for the Chinese, happiness was prominently conceptualized as a harmonious homeostasis within the individual as well as between the individual and his/her surroundings. However, words such as 'harmony', 'balance' and 'fit' were nowhere to be found in the Americans' accounts. While the American accounts were emotionally charged, upbeat, and unmistakably positive, the Chinese accounts were solemn, reserved, and balanced. The Chinese concept of harmonious homeostasis seems to capture the core implication of happiness as a dynamic process of achieving and maintaining a good fit from within to without. One Taiwanese student's view was rather representative: 'Happiness is inner well-being and contentment, as well as the feeling of harmony with the external world. It is also trust, safety and stability.'

The Chinese concept of homeostasis has a philosophical depth, firmly rooted in the ancient *yin-yang* philosophy which stresses a state of homeostasis in the human mind and body, in the individual and his/her social, spiritual and natural environment. Harmony between heaven, earth and people is also the ultimate happiness aspired to by Taoists. In short, conceptualizing happiness as a harmonious homeostasis seems a distinctive Chinese view, deeply embedded in the cultural milieu, and sharply contrasting with a Western view of linearly pursuing positivity to reach happiness (see also Ji, Lee, & Guo, this volume).

Secondly, and perhaps related to the first point, the Chinese conception of happiness clearly emphasizes spiritual enrichment over hedonistic satisfaction, whereas the spiritual element of happiness was only mentioned by two American students, and then only in the context of religion. While the Americans generally emphasized concrete achievement, self-autonomy, and positive evaluations of the self, the Chinese generally emphasized mind work, self-cultivation, and achieving positive evaluations of the self by others.

The Chinese emphasis on spiritual enrichment underlines the view that happiness is not a mere reflection of the objective world. Striking demonstrations of mind power as a passport to eternal happiness are prevalent in both Buddhism and Taoism. Confucian philosophy, too, stresses mind work to suppress selfish desires and irrational demands in order to be virtuous and to serve the collective. All these traditional Chinese teachings place great emphasis on spiritual enrichment, and play down, even deny, the role of material gratification, physical comfort, and hedonic pleasures in the experience of happiness. One Taiwanese student expressed this solemn view of happiness: 'Only when the spirit is rich, the mind is peaceful and steady, is happiness then possible. Happiness is an inner feeling, not residing in the external material world.' Although this conceptualization of happiness as an individual, mental, spiritually focused state is not limited to the Chinese cultural tradition, it has not been stressed in the West in recent times. In the West, rather, the focus has been more on a conception of happiness in terms of striving for material gratification and personal achievements.

Thirdly, the Chinese conceptions of happiness clearly reflect a dialectical view, whereas the complementary relationship between happiness and unhappiness was only lightly touched upon by a very few American students. For the Chinese, happiness and unhappiness are ever present as the background to each other, whereas for the Americans, their relationship only comes to the fore when one is currently unhappy. As briefly discussed earlier, the *yin–yang* philosophy takes a clear dialectical view of the happiness–unhappiness relationship. The cosmological view that everything from the cosmos to human life is a never-ending, cyclic process of change, between good and bad, happiness and misery, well-being and ill-being, is best expressed in a Chinese proverb: 'Happiness is dependent on unhappiness, while unhappiness is hidden in happiness' (福兮禍之所倚, 禍兮福之所伏) (Lu, 1998). It seems that the dialectical view of happiness is a distinctive feature of Eastern conceptions of SWB, as our research on Chinese culture shows, and as can be seen elsewhere—for example, in the Japanese 'habit of hesitation' towards happiness (Minami, 1971).

Overall, our empirical evidence pertaining to both the Chinese and American lay theories of happiness supports our theoretical stance that culture molds meaning and concepts of psychological significance, such as SWB. Both similarities and differences we observed in the data provide testimony to the claim of cultural psychology, viz. 'one mind, many mentalities' (Shweder, Goodnow, Hatano, LeVine, Markus, & Miller, 1998, p. 87). In the current case of SWB, the empirical evidence generally supports our assertion that distinct characteristics of the conception of happiness as well as ways of achieving happiness are prevalent in Chinese and Western cultures. For the Chinese, lay theories of happiness emphasize meeting role obligations and achieving dialectical balance; for the Americans, lay theories of happiness emphasize personal accountability and explicit pursuit of personal goals.

It thus seems that people in different cultures understand happiness and experience happiness differently. So merely asking Chinese and Westerners the single question, 'How happy are you?' as in the World Values Survey, may be a seriously flawed approach to the topic. Different strengths of answer may simply indicate that different goals are being pursued, such as fulfillment of social responsibilities versus personal accomplishments. This implies that one does not really have a comparable outcome. We psychologists should be moving to examine the culturally different processes by which happiness is pursued, as in the work of Kwan, Bond, and Singelis (1997), as well as Kitayama and Markus (2000). Based upon the rich textual materials provided by Chinese and American lay theories of happiness, a more systematic and comprehensive theoretical analysis of cultural conceptions of SWB can now be attempted, and a generic cultural theory of SWB developed to guide and consolidate further empirical research.

Individual-oriented and social-oriented conceptions of SWB

To reiterate, we take the position that the *cultural conceptions* of happiness are critical aspects of SWB, an orientation to studying happiness that has largely been neglected thus far. Our views of culture and human behavior are consonant with the cultural psychological approach, whose goal is to examine the ways in which culture and the psyche intersect and interact (Markus & Kitayama, 1998; Shweder, 1991). The cultural perspective assumes that psychological processes—in this case the nature and experiences of SWB—are thoroughly culturally constituted. Thus, culture and SWB are most productively analyzed together as a dynamic of mutual constitution (Kitayama & Markus, 2000), since any notion of happiness or the good life is culturally embedded.

Taking the cultural psychological stance, we should not superimpose the Western conception of SWB onto other cultures; instead, indigenous conceptions of SWB bred in particular cultural contexts should be unraveled and systematically mapped out. In the Chinese case, this is exactly what we accomplished in our systematic examination of SWB-related concepts and ideas embedded in the classic tripartite of Confucianism, Taoism and Buddhism (Lu, 1998, 2001, 2008), those conveyed in folklore and practiced as social customs (Lu, 2001), as well as those reflected in people's free accounts of causes (Lu & Shih, 1997) and definitions of happiness (Lu, 2001).

Accordingly, the predominant Western conception of SWB is itself one of the indigenous cultural conceptions. Its cultural context, tacit understandings, implicit assumptions, invisible commitments, as well as its lived experiences for ordinary people need to be explored and contrasted with those extracted from other indigenous cultural conceptions, such as the Chinese. Our subsequent effort

(Lu & Gilmour, 2004a), mentioned above, revealed interesting cultural discourses manifested in American students' free accounts of definitions of happiness. As Kitayama and Markus (2000) point out, well-being is a 'collaborative project', in the sense that the very nature of what it means to be well or to experience well-being takes culture-specific forms (Shweder, 1998). Borrowing Suh's (2000, p. 63) metaphor of 'self as the hyphen between culture and subjective well-being', the construction of self through participation in social institutions and the daily lived world may hold the key to our understanding the meaning of happiness in various culture systems.

Below we will contrast two such cultural systems of SWB: Euro-American individual-oriented, and East Asian social-oriented cultural conceptions of SWB. Again as full texts can be found in published literature (Lu & Gilmour, 2006), only brief summaries are presented here. It is to be noted that our analysis was conducted at the theoretical level, taking a cultural contrast perspective, under the premise that the pursuit of well-being emanates from the self, which carries cultural mandates in a culturally mandated manner. However, empirical findings generated from the previously presented folk-psychological approach served to support, validate, enrich, and elaborate our theoretical statements. As noted earlier, happiness or SWB in its modern conception does not merely reflect hedonic tone, it encompasses indications that one's life is going well. Thus, I would maintain that Chinese and Western conceptions of well-being would differ as strongly and in similar ways as do their conceptions of happiness or SWB.

Our work on delineating components of the Chinese cultural conceptions of happiness can be generalized to a large extent to people living in other East Asian countries, such as Japan, Korea, and Singapore. People in these East Asian countries share similar collectivist cultures, and are so fundamentally influenced by the Confucian tradition, like the Chinese, to have earned the designation 'the Confucian circle' (Berger, 1988, p. 4). 'Bourgeois Confucianism', a deeply held and diligently practiced web of values and beliefs synthesizing Confucian and Taoist thoughts, characterizes the worldly mentality of these East Asians, and sets them diametrically apart from people in the Euro-American world (see Kulich, this volume; Leung, this volume). East Asian Buddhism is likely another common thread holding these people together, though this line of influence is still under-studied (see Ji, Lee, & Guo, this volume).

Western Euro-American theories of SWB are firmly based on a highly individualistic conception of the self, which views the person as a bounded, coherent, stable, autonomous, and free entity, set contrastively against the social environment. Furthermore, social customs, institutions, and the media in the West all conspire to foster an agentic way of being, emphasizing free will and individual reason (Markus & Kitayama, 1998).

Embedded in such a historical and cultural milieu, one distinct characteristic of the Euro-American cultural conceptions of SWB is *personal accountability*, which essentially claims that happiness is everyone's natural and inalienable right; furthermore, one should be responsible for achieving his or her own happiness. Being happy is seen as a personal accomplishment, and Western culture is obsessed with achieving personal happiness (Lasch, 1979).

Another distinct characteristic of the Euro-American cultural conceptions of SWB is *explicit pursuit*, which essentially claims that people should actively strive for happiness, and their pursuit of happiness should not be jeopardized, is justified, and should be accommodated in many ways by others. On the one hand, the active and explicit pursuit of happiness is one of the best ways of living out an independent personhood, which constantly strives to master and control the external environment, to identify and realize self potentials, to strive for and achieve personal goals. On the other hand, with an infrastructure of democracy and social equality, a constitution that upholds individual rights and their pursuit, social customs that encourage personal striving and reward personal achievements, the opportunities and freedom to pursue happiness in the West are abundant and socially potentiated.

In sum, a free individual unceasingly pursuing happiness with the blessings of the societal support of social institutions and social norms thus best portrays the Euro-American cultural conceptions surrounding individual-oriented SWB, composed of two distinct characteristics: *personal accountability* and *explicit pursuit*.

In sharp contrast to the Western view, the East Asian view of the self is of a connected, fluid, flexible, and committed being who is bound to others. Furthermore, social customs, institutions and the media in Asia all conspire to foster a *relational* way of being, emphasizing role instantiation, observation of status, and sustained, harmonious in-group membership (Markus & Kitayama, 1998).

Within this particular historical and cultural milieu, East Asian cultural conceptions of SWB have a distinct characteristic of *role obligations*, which state that happiness should be based upon the fulfillment of social role obligations, and accomplished through disciplined self-cultivation. In so doing, group welfare and social harmony can be ensured. Consequently, the fulfillment of role obligations in interdependent social relationships, the creation and maintenance of interpersonal harmony, the striving to promote the welfare and prosperity of the collective (e.g. the family), even at the apparent cost to one's personal welfare, are the core issues. Such a view of SWB is consonant with an obligation-based, Confucian moral discourse, in contrast to the Euro-American, rights-based discourse (Hwang, 2001).

Another defining characteristic of Asian social-oriented cultural conceptions of SWB is the component of *dialectical balance*. 'Happiness' and 'unhappiness' are viewed as two sides of the same coin. People should not pursue happiness in excess; rather they should search for deeper internal homeostasis and external fusion. This characteristic Oriental reservation may be traced back to the ancient *yin–yang* philosophy which takes the position that everything from the cosmos to human life is embedded within a never-ending cyclic process of change, between good and bad, happiness and misery, well-being and ill-being.

In sum, a self-cultivated person diligently carrying out his/her moral duties to pursue well-being, harmony, and integrity for the society with the cooperation of others thus best captures the essence of the East Asian cultural conceptions of SWB. We termed this view the social-oriented cultural conceptions of SWB, composed of two distinct characteristics: *role obligations* and *dialectical balance*.

We have so far attempted to demonstrate that happiness is constructed very differently in East Asian and Western cultures. Constructing a cross-culturally fair and balanced measurement tapping into these conceptions of SWB is now the next logical step to take. Adopting both inductive and deductive approaches, the 'Individual-oriented and Social-oriented cultural conceptions of SWB scales' (ISSWB) was thus developed and evaluated in a series of two studies involving Chinese and American participants (Lu & Gilmour, 2006). The 51-item measure showed good internal consistency, temporal reliability, along with convergent and divergent validities.

Further analysis showed that the Chinese possessed stronger social-oriented SWB than did Americans, while the Americans possessed stronger individual-oriented SWB than did the Chinese. There were also some intra-cultural differences among the Chinese people. For instance, Taiwanese scored higher on the social-oriented SWB beliefs than did mainland Chinese. However, the two Chinese groups were not different on their endorsement of individual-oriented SWB.

Overall, evidence was supportive for the utility of ISSWB scales in future monocultural and cross-cultural studies. Most importantly, our ability to measure individual-oriented and social-oriented cultural conceptions of SWB as dimensions of culture at the psychological level thus provides a basis to launch a concerted research effort looking at the intricate relation between psychology and culture. The 51 items used in the ISSWB scales can be found in the appendix to this chapter.

The central thesis of our generic cultural theory of SWB is as follows. Culture can be a major force constructing the conception of happiness, and consequently in shaping subjective experiences of its members. In particular, persons socialized into different cultural systems may hold diverse views of happiness, covering its definition, nature, meaning and ways to strive for SWB. Culture also constrains preferences for different conceptions of SWB, i.e. individual-oriented vs. social-oriented, and thus prescribes different sources and conditions of SWB for its members (Chiasson, Dube, & Blondin, 1996; Furnham & Cheng, 2000; Lu & Shih, 1997).

Culture also influences SWB in the way it gives shape and form to the self (see Kwan, Hui, & McGee, this volume). Different self-views (e.g. independent self vs. interdependent self) function as regulatory mechanisms when the individual attempts to judge his or her well-being. These self-regulatory mechanisms guide the individual to attend to and process information pertaining to certain aspects of the environment emphasized by the culture (Diener & Diener, 1995; Kwan et al., 1997; Lu & Gilmour, 2004b). Such mechanisms also determine how people think, feel and behave in their pursuit of SWB (Suh, 2000).

Below we will summarize our empirical findings pertaining to psychological mechanisms or pathways to achieve happiness, adopting an individual differences approach. Informed by the above theory, our recent studies have a clear focus on cultural influences, in contrast to the prevailing focus on personality and cognitive correlates in mainstream Western research on SWB.

Cultural correlates of happiness

One approach guided by our cultural theory of SWB is to look at various ways of achieving SWB for people living in individualistic and in collectivist societies. The rationale goes like this: at first, culture selects, activates, elaborates, maintains, and strengthens one distinct view of self over another; the independent and interdependent self then represent culture at the individual level; they shape and direct the individual's behaviors to reflect the core underlying cultural concerns.

In the interpersonal realm, people with a stronger independent self tend to believe more in active, primary control, whereas people with a stronger interdependent self are more inclined to emphasize secondary control and relationship harmony. Extending Weisz, Rothbaum, and Blackburn's (1984) conceptualization of primary vs. secondary control, people with primary control beliefs will typically strive to enhance their rewards by influencing existing *social* realities, by, for example, increasing effort in relationship work, whereas people with secondary control beliefs will typically seek to enhance their rewards by accommodating to existing *social* realities, such as downgrading the importance of a failed relationship. These self-regulatory mechanisms then guide people's everyday social behaviors, and the resultant feelings about these interactions will contribute to their overall SWB.

This pan-cultural, multiple-pathway model for SWB was then tested and generally supported in two cross-cultural studies involving Chinese and British respondents (Lu et al., 2001; Lu & Gilmour, 2004b). In both studies, we found that an independent self was a strong determinant of primary (active) control beliefs, whereas an interdependent self was a strong determinant of secondary control and harmony beliefs. Furthermore, beliefs about social interactions did impact on experiences of social interactions, in that secondary control beliefs had a generally negative effect while both primary control and harmony beliefs had positive effects. Finally, experiences of social interactions contributed to SWB, whether indexed by general happiness or a more cognitively based judgment of life satisfaction.

Thus, it was shown that these various ways of achieving SWB were independent and pervasive across the two markedly contrasting cultural groups. The two self views were co-determinants of SWB, acting through the mediating variables of belief systems and social relationships. In other words, culturally embedded self views and relationship beliefs are important mediators between culture and SWB. Corroborative evidence was also found in an earlier study indicating that both relationship harmony and self-esteem were mediators between culture and life satisfaction (Kwan et al., 1997). The value of exploring multiple mediators within both individualist (e.g. independent self, self-esteem) and collectivist (e.g. interdependent self, harmony) cultural traditions to understand people's subjective experiences of well-being is highlighted in these research efforts.

Another bicultural, individual-level analysis also showed that values closely related to the core of cultural collectivism, such as 'social integration' and 'human-heartedness', led to greater happiness for the Chinese but not for the British (Lu et al., 2001). A recent study with Taiwanese female schoolteachers found a similar self-regulatory effect: only domain satisfaction with consonant self-views (independent vs. interdependent self) was predictive of more positive affect and less negative affect (Han, 2003). All the evidence thus suggests that culture impacts on SWB through multiple mediators and complex mechanisms.

At the individual level, one's general beliefs about the world (i.e. social axioms, Leung & Bond, 2004) have also been found to predict life satisfaction for Chinese undergraduates in Hong Kong.

Specifically, Lai, Bond, and Hui (2006) argued that higher levels of social cynicism would predict lower satisfaction with life because people holding cynical beliefs about the social world set in motion a self-fulfilling prophecy of unrewarding interpersonal outcomes. The negative social feedback thus engendered results in lower levels of self-esteem, which further mediates the effect of socially cynical beliefs on life satisfaction. This chain of events was confirmed in the longitudinal study. For the relation-oriented, interdependent Chinese (Hwang, 2001; Kitayama & Markus, 2000), failing in social relationships is likely to have a more devastating effect on subjective well-being compared to Westerners. We need to better consider the role of beliefs about the world upon additional mediators of life satisfaction in different cultural settings. Another study with working Hong Kong adults revealed that personal strivings for intimacy and affiliation account for the greatest unique variance in SWB, as much as 14 per cent (McAuley, Bond, & Ng, 2004). Again, primacy of relationships on Chinese SWB is underlined here.

More recently, we have noticed that the degree of congruence between people's individual psychological culture and the larger cultural environment within which they live is also crucial for SWB, a hypothesis termed the 'cultural fit' proposition (Lu, 2006). In line with Kitayama and Markus's (2000) notion of well-being as a culturally 'collaborative project', I reasoned that if the larger cultural tradition is individualistic, people with consonant independent self and active control beliefs may find it easier to achieve SWB; if, in contrast, the larger cultural tradition is collectivistic, people with consonant interdependent self and harmony beliefs may find it easier to achieve SWB.

This proposition was tested with three diverse Chinese samples from Taiwan and mainland China (total $N = 581$). I again found that independent and interdependent self, active control, and harmony beliefs as measures of individual-level culture were consistently related to SWB. Specifically, independent self, active control, and harmony beliefs were consistently related to higher happiness for both mainland Chinese and Taiwanese. Furthermore, I found that differently cultured persons within collectivist cultural systems still fared differently. Specifically, people who were more in accord with the collectivist culture were generally better off with respect to SWB than those who were less in accord.

'Getting ahead' was more advantageous than 'lagging behind'. I argued that what constitutes 'getting ahead' or 'lagging behind' and their differential effects on SWB need to be understood in the context of social change characterizing contemporary Chinese societies. Numerous lines of evidence have suggested that the Chinese people are leveling with or even surpassing their Western counterparts in individualistic values and attitudes, such as independent self-construal and active control beliefs (Lu, 2003; Lu & Gilmour, 2004b; Lu, Kao, Chang, Wu, & Zhang, 2008; Lu & Yang, 2006; Yang, 1988, 1996). This 'psychological modernizing' trend is particularly salient for the young, educated, and urban residents (Lu & Kao, 2002; Lu et al., 2008). It thus seems that the current social milieu of cultural fusion and societal modernization may have provided the Chinese people with a stronger impetus to develop more assertive self-expression and active control over the surrounding environment (see Chen, this volume; Wang & Chang, this volume).

It is reasonable to infer that moving with rather than against this historical and societal tide of modernity would promote personal well-being. More specifically, 'moving ahead' for the contemporary Chinese means moving towards psychological modernization as a result of incorporating Western-originating values and beliefs, while 'lagging behind' means holding on to traditional Chinese cultural values and beliefs. In our study 'moving ahead', as manifested in endorsing a higher independent self than the average person in the society, held a clear advantage over 'lagging behind', as manifested in endorsing a less independent self than the average person in the society. Thus, the 'cultural fit' proposition was tentatively supported and the assertion to take into account the larger social milieux in examining the relationship between culture and SWB was supported.

The coexistence and integration of contrasting cultural underpinnings

One thing that keeps popping up in our cultural psychological studies of SWB is that these seemingly contrasting cultural systems could actually coexist at the individual level. Starting from a cross-cultural comparison perspective, such findings were at first puzzling, upsetting, and provocative, but eventually became enlightening and groundbreaking. This turn of events was brought about by the introduction of some form of bicultural concepts (see Yang, 1996). Most recently, Lu and Yang (2006) attempted the first systematic theoretical and conceptual analysis to describe the emergence, composition, and possible changes of the traditional–modern bicultural self of the contemporary Chinese people. The cultural and social roots of such a bicultural self were explored, its constituting elements delineated and their interrelations analyzed, and the trend of its change predicted. They then selectively reviewed empirical evidence pertaining to the Chinese bicultural self, including topics on psychological traditionality and modernity, self concept, self-esteem, self-evaluation, and self-actualization. As we argued earlier that conceptions of SWB emanate directly from conceptions of the self, and the subjective experience of SWB is an ultimate product of the self process, bicultural SWB is more than likely.

In the case of the self, Lu (2003) proposed a construct of 'composite self' to characterize an evolving self-system among contemporary Chinese people. This system of 'composite self' intricately integrates the traditional Chinese construct of 'self-in-relation' (interdependence) with the Western construct of 'independent and autonomous self' (independence). For the contemporary Chinese, the neglected, even suppressed, independent self may be nurtured, developed, elaborated and even emphasized in certain domains of life, such as work. An attitude favoring the coexistence and integration of independent and interdependent self to help deal with the apparent conflicts between strong traditionality and requisite modernity might well be the most favorable outcome for people in contemporary Chinese societies, and possibly other Asian societies (see a parallel argument by Kağıtçıbaşı, 2005).

Such a composite self with varying convictions about independence and interdependence can then be seen as a way of expressing two basic human needs: uniqueness and relatedness, similar to Bakan's (1966) notion of agency and communion. Most recent evidence has come from a nationwide survey of a representative sample in Taiwan, showing that independence and interdependence were equally strongly valued in socializing the society's young (Lu, 2009). Furthermore, this form of biculturalism in self-views has also been documented among mainland Chinese as well as Taiwanese (Lu et al., 2008). Thus, the individual-level foundation for biculturalism in a contemporary Chinese society seems to have been laid.

The idea of the coexistence of independence and interdependence as notions of the self parallels Marar's (2004) theoretical analysis of the 'happiness paradox'. Marar posited that individuals in modern societies are exposed to two sets of competing values. One set is related to the individual-oriented self, which emphasizes self-expression, achievement, and fulfillment of one's goals. Fulfillment of these needs requires individuals to turn away from people, be oneself, and break inherited rules. The other set is related to external standards, which emphasize responsibility and accountability. Fulfillment of these social-oriented needs requires individuals to turn towards people, seek others' approval, and adhere to social norms. Hence, individuals are faced with the dilemma of self-actualization versus others' approval, which he termed the 'happiness paradox'.

In the case of SWB, we have not only consistently found a significant role for both the independent and interdependent self in cross-cultural analyses (Lu et al., 2001; Lu & Gilmour, 2004b), but also noticed that independent self rather than the interdependent self sometimes better predicted happiness (Lu et al., 2001; Lu & Gilmour, 2004b). For both the Chinese people and American students, the individual-oriented and social-oriented cultural conceptions of SWB also coexisted (Lu & Gilmour, 2004b). Cross-cultural analysis still revealed a main effect of culture, with the Chinese avowing stronger social-oriented SWB than the Americans, while the Americans avowed stronger individual-oriented SWB than the Chinese. Monocultural analysis showed that the Chinese had actually endorsed equally strong convictions about individual-oriented and social-oriented conceptions for SWB.

This hybrid 'bicultural SWB' very likely emanates from the Chinese composite or bicultural self as mentioned above. Nonetheless, more systematic and fine-grained analysis is needed to look at the exact process and dynamism of such cultural integration as well as its functional values. In view of social change and psychological transformation, as the Chinese people are becoming increasingly individual-oriented in general (Lu & Yang, 2006; Lu et al., 2008), we may expect that individual-oriented cultural conceptions of SWB will assume an increasingly stronger hold on the Chinese mind, and individual-oriented ways to achieve happiness will more evidently manifest themselves in the Chinese experiences of subjective well-being.

As a final note, we are convinced that both the cultural psychological approach and the social change perspective are called for if we are to better understand the mentality and behavior of contemporary Chinese people. The cultural psychological viewpoint helps to highlight the cultural roots of the Chinese conception of happiness and their habitual ways of pursuing happiness in life; the social change perspective injects momentum into a static system to highlight the complex dynamism of any human encounter with the social environment. Specific hypotheses can be derived incorporating these two theoretical perspectives and tested scientifically. As Chinese psychologists, we firmly believe that we have a moral obligation as well as academic interest in understanding how contemporary Chinese people strive to coordinate, regulate, compromise, synthesize, and integrate the contrasting cultural rudiments, in the pursuit of a more balanced, effective, and happy life.

Items in the ISSWB scales

Individual-oriented SWB—personal accountability (ISWB—PA)

1 Happiness is a born right
2 Everyone has the right to pursue happiness
3 To pursue happiness is everyone's right
4 Happiness is the most important meaning of life
5 Happiness is the supreme goal in life
6 There's nothing better in the world than to have happiness
7 Happiness is personal successes
8 Happiness is personal victories
9 Happiness is a reward for hard work
10 Everyone has to be responsible for one's own happiness and unhappiness
11 One has to work to be happy, it doesn't just happen
12 Unhappy people are those who don't work hard enough
13 No one should be responsible for your unhappiness
14 One makes one's own unhappiness
15 One's happiness or unhappiness depends on oneself rather than others

Individual-oriented SWB—explicit pursuit (ISWB—EP)

1 One needn't be shy about pursuing happiness
2 Happiness is having goals and working toward them
3 One should be brave to pursue happiness
4 One should pursue one's happiness even in the face of great difficulties
5 Even if there are costs in pursuing happiness, one should not back off
6 The pursuit of happiness should be encouraged by society
7 Society should provide equal opportunities for individuals to pursue happiness
8 Society should provide ample opportunities for individuals to pursue happiness
9 School should teach young children the value of pursuing personal happiness
10 Society should tolerate the pursuit of personal happiness

Social-oriented SWB—role obligations (SSWB—RO)

1 Happiness is the well-being of one's family
2 Happiness of the family is a prerequisite of personal happiness
3 The happiness of my family is my happiness
4 Happiness is sharing with friends
5 Happiness is to make friends happy
6 True happiness is something friends and family share
7 Happiness is putting the welfare of society as the highest concern
8 Happiness is to sacrifice personal welfare in pursuit of societal welfare
9 Knowing that I made someone else happy makes me the happiest person
10 Happiness is the consequence of self-cultivation
11 Happiness is fulfilling one's social duties
12 Happiness is achieved through controlling one's desires
13 Being content is the rule of happiness
14 To be happy is to see through things in life

Social-oriented SWB—dialectical balance (SSWB—DB)

1 There is only a thin line between happiness and unhappiness
2 Happiness and unhappiness are two sides of the same coin
3 I believe that happiness and unhappiness coexist
4 Disasters often follow good fortune
5 Sadness often follows happiness, and good fortune may overtake ill-fortune
6 Disaster is the neighbor of good fortune
7 Happiness is a state of physical, psychological, and spiritual balance
8 Happiness is to be content with life
9 Being happy is to be at ease with oneself
10 Happiness is the harmony of interpersonal relationships
11 Happiness is finding a place in society
12 Happiness is the harmony between human-kind and nature

Author's note

Our own series of studies reported in this chapter are supported by various grants from the Taiwanese Ministry of Education (89-H-FA01-2-4-2) and the National Science Council (NSC93-2752-H-030-001-PAE,NSC94-2752-H-008-002-PAE,NSC95-2752-H-008-002-PAE, NSC96-2752-H-002-019-PAE) in Taiwan.

References

Andrews, F. M. & Withey, S. B. (1976). *Social indicators of well-being.* New York: Plenum.

Argyle, M. (2001). *The psychology of happiness* (2nd edn). London: Routledge.

Argyle, M., Martin, M., & Crossland, J. (1989). Happiness as a function of personality and social encounters. In J. P. Forgas & J. M. Innes (eds), *Recent advances in social psychology: An international perspective* (pp. 189–203). North Holland, The Netherlands: Elsevier.

Bakan, D. (1966). *The duality of human existence.* Boston, MA: Beacon Press.

Bauer, W. (1976). *China and the search for happiness: Recurring themes in four thousand years of Chinese cultural history.* New York: The Seabury Press.

Berger, P. L. (1988). An East Asian development model? In P. L. Berger & H.-H. M. Hsiao (eds), *In search of an East Asian development model* (pp. 3–11). New Brunswick, NJ: Transaction Inc.

Brislin, R. W., Lonner, W. J., & Thorndike, R. M. (1973). *Cross-cultural research methods.* New York: John Wiley.

Bruner, J. (1990). *Acts of meaning.* Cambridge, MA: Harvard University Press.

Campbell, A. (1976). Subjective measures of well-being. *American Psychologist, 31*, 117–124.

Chiang, C. M. (1996). *The philosophy of happiness: A history of Chinese life philosophy.* In Taipei: Hong Yie Publication Co. (in Chinese)

Chiasson, N., Dube, L., & Blondin, J. (1996). Happiness: A look into the folk psychology of four cultural groups. *Journal of Cross-Cultural Psychology, 27*, 673–691.

Christopher, J. C. (1999). Situating psychological well-being: Exploring the cultural roots of its theory and research. *Journal of Counseling and Development, 77*, 141–152.

Cummins, R. A. (1995). On the trail of the gold standard for subjective well-being. *Social Indicators Research, 35*, 179–200.

Cummins, R. A. (2000). Objective and subjective quality of life: An interactive model. *Social Indicators Research, 52*, 55–72.

Diener, E. (1984). Subjective well-being. *Psychological Bulletin, 95*, 542–575.

Diener, E. (2000). Subjective well-being: The science of happiness and a proposal for a national index. *American Psychologist, 55*, 34–43.

Diener, E. & Diener, M. (1995). Cross-cultural correlates of life satisfaction and self-esteem. *Journal of Personality and Social Psychology, 68*, 653–663.

Diener, E., Diener, M., & Diener, C. (1995). Factors predicting subjective well-being of nations. *Journal of Personality and Social Psychology, 69*, 851–864.

Diener, E., Suh, E. M., Lucas, R. E., & Smith, H. L. (1999). Subjective well-being: Three decades of progress. *Psychological Bulletin, 125*, 276–302.

Diener, E., Suh, M., Smith, H., & Shao, L. (1995). National and cultural differences in reported subjective well-being: Why do they occur? *Social Indicators Research, 31*, 103–157.

Diener, E. & Tov, W. (in press). National accounts of well-being. In K. Land (ed.), *Encyclopedia of social indicators and quality of life studies.* New York: Springer.

Furnham, A. & Cheng, H. (2000). Lay theories of happiness. *Journal of Happiness Studies, 1*, 227–246.

Han, K. H. (2003). The affective consequences of different self-construals and satisfaction with different life domains: A study of Taiwanese female teachers in kindergarten. *The Formosa Journal of Mental Health, 16*, 1–22.

Headey, B. & Wearing, A. (1989). Personality, life events, and subjective well-being: Toward a dynamic equilibrium model. *Journal of Personality and Social Psychology, 57*, 731–739.

Hwang, K. K. (2001). Morality: East and West. In N. J. Smelser & P. B. Baltes (eds), *International encyclopedia of the social and behavioral sciences* (pp. 10039–10043). Oxford, UK: Pergamon.

Kağıtçıbaşı, Ç. (2005). Autonomy and relatedness in cultural context: Implications for self and family. *Journal of Cross-Cultural Psychology, 36*, 403–422.

Kahneman, D., Diener, E., & Schwarz, N. (eds) (1999). *Well-being: The foundations of hedonic psychology.* New York: Russell Sage Foundation.

Kitayama, S. & Markus, H. R. (2000). The pursuit of happiness and the realization of sympathy: Cultural patterns of self, social relations, and well-being. In E. Diener & E. M. Sul (eds), *Culture and subjective well-being* (pp. 113–162). Cambridge, MA: The MIT Press.

Kwan, V. S. Y., Bond, M. H., & Singelis, T. M. (1997). Pancultural explanations for life satisfaction: Adding relationship harmony to self-esteem. *Journal of Personality and Social Psychology, 73*, 1038–1051.

Lai, J. H.-W., Bond, M. H., & Hui, N. H.-H. (2006). The role of social axioms in predicting life satisfaction: A longitudinal study in Hong Kong. *Journal of Happiness Studies, 8*, 517–535.

Lasch, C. (1979). *The culture of narcissism: American life in an age of diminishing expectations.* New York: Norton.

Leung, K. & Bond, M. H. (2004). Social axioms: A model for social beliefs in multicultural perspective. *Advanced Experimental Social Psychology, 36*, 119–197.

Lu, L. (1998). The meaning, measure, and correlates of happiness among Chinese people. *Proceedings of the National Science Council: Part C, 8*, 115–137.

Lu, L. (1999). Personal and environmental causes of happiness: A longitudinal analysis. *Journal of Social Psychology, 139*, 79– 90.

Lu, L. (2001). Understanding happiness: A look into the Chinese folk psychology. *Journal of Happiness Studies, 2*, 407–432.

Lu, L. (2003). Defining the self-other relation: The emergence of a composite self. *Indigenous Psychological Research in Chinese Societies, 20*, 139–207.

Lu, L. (2006). Cultural fit: Individual and societal discrepancies in values, beliefs and SWB. *Journal of Social Psychology, 146*, 203–221.

Lu, L. (2008). The Chinese conception and experiences of subjective well-being. *Discovery of Applied Psychology, 1*, 19–30.

Lu, L. (2009). 'I or we': Family socialization values in a national probability sample in Taiwan. *Asian Journal of Social Psychology, 12*, 145–150.

Lu, L. & Gilmour, R. (2004a). Culture and conceptions of happiness: Individual oriented and social oriented SWB. *Journal of Happiness Studies, 5*, 269–291.
Lu, L. & Gilmour, R. (2004b). Culture, self and ways to achieve SWB: A cross-cultural analysis. *Journal of Psychology in Chinese Societies, 5*, 51–79.
Lu, L. & Gilmour, R. (2006). Individual-oriented and socially-oriented cultural conceptions of subjective well-being: Conceptual analysis and scale development. *Asian Journal of Social Psychology. 9*, 36–49.
Lu, L., Gilmour, R., & Kao, S. F. (2001). Culture values and happiness: An East–West dialogue. *Journal of Social Psychology, 141*, 477–493.
Lu, L., Gilmour, R., Kao, S. F., Wong, T. H., Hu, C. H., Chern, J. G., Huang, S. W., & Shih, J. B. (2001). Two ways to achieve happiness: When the East meets the West. *Personality and Individual Differences, 30*, 1161–1174.
Lu, L. & Kao, S. F. (2002). Traditional and modern characteristics across the generations: Similarities and discrepancies. *Journal of Social Psychology, 142*, 45–59.
Lu, L., Kao, S. F., Chang, T. T., Wu, H. P., & Zhang, J. (2008). The individual- and social-oriented Chinese bicultural self: A sub-cultural analysis contrasting mainland Chinese and Taiwanese. *Social Behavior and Personality, 36*, 337–346.
Lu, L. & Shih, J. B. (1997). Sources of happiness: A qualitative approach. *Journal of Social Psychology, 137*, 181–187.
Lu, L. & Yang, K. S. (2006). The emergence and composition of the traditional–modern bicultural self of people in contemporary Taiwanese societies. *Asian Journal of Social Psychology, 9*, 167–175.
Marar, Z. (2004). *The happiness paradox*. London, England: Reaktion.
Markus, H. R. & Kitayama, S. (1998). The cultural psychology of personality. *Journal of Cross-Cultural Psychology, 29*, 63–87.
McAuley, P. C., Bond, M. H., & Ng, I. W. C. (2004). Antecedents of subjective well-being in working Hong Kong adults. *Journal of Psychology in Chinese Societies, 5*, 25–49.
Minami, H. (1971). *Psychology of the Japanese people*. Toronto, Canada: University of Toronto Press.
Ng, A. K., Ho, D. Y. F., Wong, S. S., & Smith, I. (2003). In search of the good life: A cultural odyssey in the East and West. *Genetic, Social, and General Psychology Monographs, 129*, 317–363.
Quah, S. H. (1995). Socio-culture factors and productivity: The case of Singapore. In K. K. Hwang (ed.), *Easternization: Socio-culture impact on productivity* (pp. 266–333). Tokyo: Asian Productivity Organization.
Ryan, R. M. & Deci, E. L. (2001). On happiness and human potentials: A review of research on hedonic and eudaimonic well-being. *Annual Review of Psychology, 52*, 141–166.
Ryff, C. D. (1989). Happiness is everything, or is it? Exploration on the meaning of psychological well-being. *Journal of Personality and Social Psychology, 57*, 1069–1081.
Seligman, M. & Csikszentmihaly, M. (2000). Positive psychology: An introduction. *American Psychologist, 55*, 5–14.
Shweder, R. A. (1991). *Thinking through cultures: Expeditions in cultural psychology*. Cambridge, MA: Harvard University Press.
Shweder, R. A. (1998). *Welcome to middle age! (and other cultural fictions)*. Chicago, IL: University of Chicago Press.
Shweder, R. A., Goodnow, J., Hatano, G., LeVine, R., Markus, H., & Miller, P. (1998). The cultural psychology of development: One mind, many mentalities. In W. Damon (ed.), *Handbook of child psychology: Theoretical models of human development* (vol. 1, pp. 865–937). New York: Wiley.
Suh, E. M. (2000). Self, the hyphen between culture and subjective well-being. In E. Diener & E. M. Sul (eds), *Culture and subjective well-being* (pp. 63–86). Cambridge, MA: The MIT Press.
Triandis, H. C. (1995). *Individualism and collectivism*. Boulder, CO: Westview.
Veenhoven, R. (1984). *Conditions of happiness*. Dordrecht, The Netherlands: D. Reidel.
Veenhoven, R. (1994). Is happiness a trait? Tests of the theory that a better society does not make people any happier. *Social Indicators Research, 32*, 101–160.
Veenhoven, R. (1995). The cross-national pattern of happiness: Test of predictions implied in three theories of happiness. *Social Indicators Research, 34*, 33–68.
Veenhoven, R. (2000). Freedom and happiness: A comparative study in forty-four nations in the early 1990s. In E. Diener & E. M. Sul (eds), *Culture and subjective well-being* (pp. 257–288). Cambridge, MA: The MIT Press.
Weisz, J. R., Rothbaum, F. M., & Blackburn, T. C. (1984). Standing out and standing in: The psychology of control in America and Japan. *American Psychologist, 39*, 955–969.
World Value Study Group (1994). *World Values Survey, 1981–1984 and 1990–1993*. Inter-University Consortium for Political and Social Research (ICPSR) version (computer file). Ann Arbor: Institute for Social Research, University of Michigan.
Wu, J. H. (1992). *Sources of inner happiness*. Taipei, Taiwan: Tong Da Books. (in Chinese)
Wu, Y. (1991). *The new transcription of 'shang shu'*. Taipei, Taiwan: Shan Min Books. (in Chinese)
Yang, K. S. (1986). Chinese personality and its change. In M. H. Bond (ed.), *The psychology of the Chinese people* (pp. 106–170). Hong Kong: Oxford University Press.
Yang, K. S. (1988). Will society modernization eventually eliminate cross-cultural psychological differences? In M. H. Bond (ed.), *The cross-culture challenge to social psychology* (pp. 67–85). Newbury Park, CA: Sage.
Yang, K. S. (1996). Psychological transformation of the Chinese people as a result of societal modernization. In M. H. Bond (ed.), *The handbook of Chinese psychology* (pp. 479–498). Hong Kong: Oxford University Press.

CHAPTER 21

The spirituality of the Chinese people: a critical review

Daniel T. L. Shek

A survey of the literature shows that various definitions of spirituality have been put forward by different researchers. Based on content analyses of 31 definitions of religiousness and 40 definitions of spirituality, Scott (1997) reported that the conceptions were distributed over nine content areas, with no definition containing most of the conceptions in different domains. These content areas include: 1) experiences related to connectedness or relationship; 2) processes contributing to a higher level of connectedness; 3) reactions to sacred and secular things; 4) beliefs or thoughts; 5) traditional institutional structures; 6) pleasurable existence; 7) beliefs in a sacred or higher being; 8) personal transcendence; and 9) existential issues and concerns.

There are also broad versus narrow definitions of spirituality in the literature. An example of a broad definition is from Myers, Sweeney, and Witmer (2000) who defined spirituality as '... personal and private beliefs that transcend the material aspects of life and give a deep sense of wholeness, connectedness, and openness to the infinite' (p. 265). Arising from this conception, spirituality includes: a) belief in a power beyond oneself; b) behavior in relation to the infinite, such as praying; c) meaning and purpose of life; d) hope and optimism; e) love and compassion; f) moral and ethical guidelines; and g) transcendental experience. Another broad definition can be seen in Lewis (2001) who conceived of spirituality as the life affirmed in a relationship with God, self, community, and environment which leads to the nurturing and celebration of wholeness. Within this context, spiritual needs include meaning, purpose and hope, transcendence, integrity and worthiness, religious participation, loving and serving others, cultivating thankfulness, forgiving and being forgiven, and preparation for death and dying. On the other hand, an example of a narrow definition can be seen in Ho and Ho (2007) who argued that there are three attributes of ecumenical spirituality, including the quest for answers to existential or transcendental questions, cardinal values embracing all aspects of life, and self-reflective behavior.

This chapter attempts to give a descriptive as well as a critical picture of studies examining the spirituality of Chinese people. As such, a comprehensive and broad conception of spirituality is adopted. An integration of the literature shows that several elements are commonly employed in a broad definition of spirituality. These include: meaning and purpose of life (Govier, 2000; Ho & Ho, 2007; Narayanasamy, 1999); meaning of and reactions to the limitations of life, such as pain, death, and dying (Ho & Ho, 2007); search for the sacred or infinite, including religiosity (Myers et al., 2000; Pargament, 1999); hope and hopelessness (Anandarajah & Hight, 2001; Highfield & Cason, 1983; Thompson, 2002); forgiveness (Myers et al., 2000); and restoration of health (Govier, 2000). As Chinese beliefs and values are covered in other chapters of this handbook, they are not specifically covered in this chapter.

Several issues are systematically examined in discussing each of the above-mentioned aspects of spirituality where appropriate. First, methods of assessing spirituality in Chinese people are described. Second, profiles about spirituality and their related socio-demographic correlates are outlined. Third, research findings on the relationship between spirituality and developmental outcomes are outlined, particularly in Chinese adolescents. Fourth, existing studies pertinent to the relationship between family processes and Chinese spirituality are reviewed. In the final section of the chapter, the conceptual, methodological, and practical limitations of the existing studies pertinent to spirituality of Chinese people are discussed. In this review, relevant research studies based on Chinese people living in China (including PRC, Taiwan, and Hong Kong) and overseas will be examined.

Meaning of life and purpose in life

Assessment methods and related issues

Two main approaches have been used to assess meaning of life and purpose in the lives of Chinese people. The first approach is to assess meaning of life by items or questions included in questionnaires. In the study of young people's outlook on life (The Hong Kong Federation of Youth Groups, 1997, 2000), three questions asking about the life aspirations of young people were included, e.g. respondents' ranking of the importance of six things in life, including wealth, family, health, friends, social status, and peace of mind. In the Indicators of Social Development Project (e.g. Lau, Lee, Wan, & Wong, 2005), one question was used to assess the respondents' perception of the most important ingredient for a happy life, including health, peace of mind, money, having filial children, freedom, love, marriage and family, career, material enjoyment, serving society, and others.

The second approach is to use psychological scales to assess the construct of meaning of life or purpose in life. The most commonly used measure is the Chinese version of the Purpose in Life Questionnaire which assesses levels of purpose in life (CPIL: Shek, 1986, 1988). Several cross-sectional and longitudinal studies have shown that the CPIL is valid and reliable with a stable factor structure in both Chinese adolescent and adult samples (Shek, 1986, 1988, 1992, 1994, 1999a, b & c). Another general measure of meaning in life is the Chinese version of the Existential Well-Being Scale (EXIST). The Existential Well-Being Scale, which formed a part of the Spiritual Well-Being Scale, was constructed by Paloutzian and Ellison (1982) to assess life direction and satisfaction. There have been both cross-sectional and longitudinal research findings supporting the reliability and validity of the measure in Chinese adolescents (Shek, 1993, 2003a, 2003c, 2005a; Shek et al., 2001).

Besides the above general measures of meaning of life in adolescents, subscales assessing purpose in life are also included in some of the generic measures of adolescent development. In the Chinese Positive Youth Development Scale developed by Shek, Siu, and Lee (2007), there are subscales assessing 15 positive youth development constructs. In the subscale measuring spirituality, seven items modeled after the items in the CPIL are included. In the Outlook on Life Scale (Lau & Lau, 1996), four items were used to form the subscale assessing how the respondent viewed their lifestyles, including whether 1) life is meaningless, 2) life is worth living, 3) life is full of fun and joy, and 4) one lives a positive life. In the Person–Social Development Self-Efficacy Inventory (PSD-SEI) developed by Yuen et al. (2006), there is an Interest and Life Goals Subscale that assesses the existence of life goals and related plans for their attainment in Chinese adolescents. Chan (1995) developed the Reasons for Living Inventory to assess adolescents' reasons for living and found that five dimensions (positive values and self-efficacy, optimism, family concerns, concerns for social disapproval, and suicidal fear) constituted the scale.

Finally, the Chinese Beliefs about Adversity Scale (CBA) was developed to assess how Chinese people make sense of their lives when facing adversity (Shek, 2004). There are nine items in this scale (e.g. *chi de ku zhong ku, fang wei ren shang ren*: hardship increases stature). There are research findings showing that the scale possesses acceptable psychometric properties (Shek, 2005a, Shek et al., 2001).

Profiles and socio-demographic correlates of meaning of life

Two social surveys conducted by the Hong Kong Federation of Youth Groups (1997, 2000) showed that family and health were the two most important goals of life for Chinese adolescents. In the study of youth trends in Hong Kong, the Hong Kong Federation of Youth Groups (2008) concluded that the life outlook of young people in Hong Kong was generally positive in nature, based on their responses to an item embedded within a longer questionnaire. Chan (1995) examined reasons for living among Chinese adolescents in Hong Kong. He found that the most strongly rated reasons for living were related to coping beliefs and family concerns (e.g. wanting to grow up with friends and not being fair to parents if they abandon them). On the other hand, there is research showing that Chinese adolescents' scores on the Purpose in Life Questionnaire were comparatively lower than those reported by adolescents in the United States (Shek, 1986, 1993; Shek, Hong & Cheung, 1987). In the study of Shek and Mak (1987), results showed that a significant proportion of respondents displayed signs indicating a lack of purpose in life.

Research findings on the socio-demographic correlates of meaning in life in Chinese adolescents were generally equivocal and the effect sizes small (e.g. Chou, 2000; Shek & Mak, 1987). Regarding gender differences in meaning of life among Chinese adolescents, although Shek (1986, 1989b) reported that adolescent boys displayed a higher level of CPIL scores than did Chinese girls, gender differences have not been found in other studies (Shek, 1993, 1999b). Concerning age differences in purpose in life, while Shek (1986) showed that age was positively related to purpose in life among secondary school students, Shek (1993) found that there was no relationship between age and CPIL scores. In the area of economic disadvantage, although Shek et al. (2001) showed that existential well-being in adolescents receiving welfare was not different from that based on adolescents not receiving welfare, Shek (2003b) showed that higher levels of economic stress based on ratings obtained from parents and adolescents were generally related to lower levels of adolescent existential well-being in families receiving welfare. In short, the picture concerning the socio-demographic correlates of meaning of life in Chinese adolescents is not obvious.

Purpose in life and developmental outcomes

There are research findings showing that a lower level of purpose in life is concurrently and longitudinally associated with a higher level of psychological symptoms in adolescents (Shek, 1992, 1993, 1995a, 1998d, 1999c) and people at midlife (Shek, 1994). There are also findings showing that meaning in life is negatively associated with problem behavior, including substance abuse (Narcotics Division, 1994), delinquency (Shek, 1997a; Shek, Ma, & Cheung, 1994), and behavioral intentions for engaging in high-risk behavior (Shek, Siu, & Lee, 2007). Based on the Schwartz Value Survey, Bond and Chi (1997) showed that the social harmony factor and universalism–benevolence–conformity factor (with meaning in life as part of the construct) were positively related to pro-social behavior but negatively related to antisocial behavior.

On the other hand, a higher level of meaning in life has been shown to be positively related to self-reported positive mental health measures, including ego strength and self-image (Shek, 1992), self-esteem (Shek, 1993), life satisfaction (1999c), existential well-being (Shek, 2001a, 2003b, 2004, 2005a), pro-social behavior (Shek, Ma, & Cheung, 1994), and positive youth development (Shek et al., 2007) in Chinese adolescents. Purpose in life was positively related to life satisfaction in Chinese midlife parents in Hong Kong (Shek, 1994). Adolescent life meaning was also positively related to resilience (Shek, 2001b; Shek, Lam, Lam, & Tang, 2004; Shek et al., 2003a & b).

Family processes and purpose in life

There are several cross-sectional studies showing that the quality of parenting is positively related to adolescent meaning of life indexed by the CPIL (Shek, 1989a, 1993, 1995b, 1997a; Shek, Chan, & Lee, 1997) and the Existential Well-Being Scale (Shek, 2002c, 2002e, Shek et al., 2001). There are also longitudinal research findings showing that perceived parenting characteristics are positively related to adolescent's meaning in life (Shek, 1999c, 2003a). Based on the responses of parents recruited in a community survey, Shek (1999a) further showed that the association between perceived parenting behavior and adolescent psychological well-being was stronger in adolescents with a lower sense of purpose in life than in those with a higher level of purpose, thus suggesting that a higher sense of purpose in life provides a buffer against the impact of negative parenting behavior on adolescent well-being.

Besides assessing parenting, studies have shown that parent–adolescent conflict is negatively related to meaning in life in Chinese adolescents (Shek, 1997c, 2002c; Shek et al., 1997). Similarly, longitudinal findings (Shek, 1998b) have indicated that parent–adolescent conflict based on ratings obtained from parents and adolescent children is concurrently and longitudinally related to purpose in life. The findings suggest that the relations between parent–adolescent conflict and adolescent psychological well-being are bidirectional in nature, that is, lower well-being drives conflict and conflict drives lower well-being.

Based on several quantitative and qualitative measures of paternal and maternal parenting, including adolescents' perceptions of and satisfaction with parenting styles, perceived parent–adolescent conflict, perceived frequency of parent–adolescent communication and related feelings, and perceived parent–adolescent relational quality, Shek (1999b) showed that paternal and maternal parenting characteristics generally had significant positive concurrent and longitudinal correlations with adolescent purpose in life. By using a rarely used longitudinal design, he was able to show that paternal parenthood qualities at Time 1 predicted changes in adolescent purpose in life at Time 2, whereas maternal parenthood qualities at Time 1 did not. Adolescent purpose in life at Time 1 was found to predict changes in qualities of maternal parenthood, but not qualities of paternal parenthood at Time 2. Relative to qualities of maternal parenthood, qualities of paternal parenthood were generally found to exert a stronger impact on adolescent purpose in life.

Based on a study of economically disadvantaged Chinese adolescents in Hong Kong, Shek (2005c) reported that perceived qualities of parenthood (indexed by perceived parenting styles, support and help from parents, and conflict and relationship quality with the parents) were positively related to adolescent existential well-being. Longitudinal correlation analyses showed that, while qualities of paternal parenthood at Time 1 predicted adolescent existential well-being at Time 2, qualities of maternal parenthood at Time 1 predicted adolescent substance abuse and delinquency at Time 2. In contrast, adolescent adjustment did not predict any changes in perceived qualities of parenthood over time.

Finally, there are research findings showing that marital quality (Shek, 2000) and family functioning were concurrently related to their adolescent's meaning in life (Shek, 1997b; 1998c; 2002a, b & d; 2003c). There are also studies showing that meaning in life was associated with family functioning over time (Shek, 1998a, 1998d, 2005b).

Attitudes and responses to death and dying in Chinese people

Assessment methods and related issues

Instruments translated into Chinese have mainly been used to examine attitudes toward life and death among Chinese people. The Chinese version of Templer's Death Anxiety Scale has commonly been used in the past studies (Cheung & Ho, 2004; Wu, Tang, & Kwok, 2002). Wong (2004) examined attitudes toward life and death among Chinese adolescents utilizing the Chinese version of the Multi-Attitude Suicide Tendency Scale. Although results supported the reliability and convergent validity of the scale, confirmatory factor analysis disconfirmed the original four-factor structure. Cheung and Ho (2004) used the 18-item Revised Death Fantasy Scale (positive metaphor and negative metaphor factors) to assess death metaphors among Chinese people. Both positive and negative metaphors were shown to be significantly correlated with Templer's Death Anxiety Scale. Lin (2003) used both English and Chinese versions of Springfield Religiosity Schedule, Emotional Support Index, Existential Well-Being Scale, and Death Attitudes Profile Revised for Americans and Chinese participants living in Taipei. She found that the five dimensions of death attitudes were reliable in both groups of participants.

Many qualitative methods have also been used to examine Chinese attitudes and responses to death, including open-ended questions (Yang & Chen, 2006), as well as drawing techniques and analysis of verbal commentary (Yang & Chen, 2002). Qualitative studies examining perspectives on end-of-life decisions among Chinese seniors using survey (Bowman & Singer, 2001) and case-study methodology (Kagawa-Singer & Blackhall, 2001) have also been used.

Profiles and socio-demographic correlates of attitudes and responses to death and dying

There are Chinese writings on how Chinese people deal with issues related to life and death. For example, Loewe (1982) examined the rituals and meaning of life and death during the Han period; Kutcher (1999) examined mourning in late Imperial China. Nevertheless, such reviews were basically historical research with no data collected from living informants.

Research studies in this area based on responses from children have also been conducted. Utilizing the concepts and methodology of personal construct psychology, Yang and Chen (2006) identified 26 categories of responses to death in children, showing that six categories were most frequently experienced (internal causality, negative emotion state, external causality, nonexistence, negative bodily state, and existence). Compared with previous findings based on American samples, Chinese children were more likely to view death as happening without personal choice and less likely to associate death with moral, psychological or natural meaning. They also found differences in death concepts in participants with different religious beliefs. In a study examining the meanings of death in children, Yang and Chen (2002) reported that both metaphysical and biological deaths were prominent themes, and that concepts of psychological death were presented least. Although there were age differences (biological death concepts were more common in younger children, whereas metaphysical death concepts were more prominent in older children), there were no significant differences in groups defined by gender, health status, religious beliefs, funeral attendance, prior death of relatives or pets. The authors concluded that the findings provided 'a unique window on death concepts among Chinese children' (p. 143).

Research studies based on adolescents have been conducted in this topic area. Based on the responses of Chinese college students, Tang, Wu, and Yan (2002) reported that age was negatively related to death anxiety, and that women reported more death anxiety than did men. Florian and Snowden (1989) examined differences among college students of six ethnic groups in their fear of personal death and regard for life. Although relationship between fear of personal death and positive life regard was found for White/Caucasian students, it was not found for Chinese students. Shih, Gau, Yaw, Pong, and Lin (2006) used open-ended, self-report questionnaires to examine the views of nursing students on their fears about physical death, afterlife destinations, and perceived help from nurses. A majority of them reported fears related to physical and psychological pain, and 82 per cent believed that people have a soul. The respondents expected nurses to help dying patients cultivate a peaceful mind.

Based on their responses to the Death Anxiety Scale, Wu, Tang, and Kwok (2002) concluded that Chinese old people in Hong Kong reported a low level of anxiety towards death. While death anxiety was negatively related to age, it was not related to gender, personal income, marital and employment status, or religious affiliation. Craine (1996) reported that Chinese people did not have higher anxiety than did other non-Chinese subjects, and that Chinese people viewed death as normal.

In the context of terminal illness, Woo (1999) commented that 'Little is known about how Chinese patients and their families perceive death and dying' (p. 72). Based on the responses of Chinese hospice patients with terminal illness, Mak (2002) examined the features of a 'good' death. In the study, seven elements contributing to good death were identified, including being aware of dying (death awareness), maintaining hope (hope), being free from pain and suffering (comfort), experiencing personal control (control), developing and maintaining social relationships (connectedness), preparing to depart (preparations), and accepting the timing of one's death (completion).

In addition, results showed that four circumstances facilitated patients' acceptance of the timing of their deaths. These included completion of social roles and family obligations, perception that death was good and natural, having religious faith, and experiences of having led a meaningful life. In another related paper, Mak (2001) noted that although roughly one-third of the respondents talked about death and cancer with openness, another one-third of these patients did not mention the word 'death', and the last third did not even mention that they had cancer. She concluded that death was still a social taboo in Hong Kong. Leung, Wu, Lue, and Tang (2004) attempted to understand components of quality of life (QOL) for elderly Chinese in Taiwan. Based on focus group interviews, the findings generated 15 QOL domains where religion and death were two related domains (see also Lu, this volume).

Some cross-cultural studies in this area have also been conducted. Based on the responses of key informants and focus group discussions, Braun and Nichols (1997) examined cultural variations in response to the process of dying and grieving among four Asian-American populations, including issues surrounding traditional philosophy, burial, memorial services and bereavement traditions, suicide, euthanasia, advanced directives, organ donation, changes over time, and advice for health workers. Based on the analyses, they identified Confucianism, Taoism, and Buddhism as the ideologies underlying the philosophy for Chinese-Americans.

Based on three focus groups involving social work graduates, pastors, religious leaders and service providers working with Chinese-Americans, Yick and Gupta (2002) reviewed the traditional Chinese cultural values and norms and examined the types of rituals and practices (including funeral practices, pre-burial rituals, post-burial rituals, mourning restrictions) and their associated meanings as related to Chinese cultural dimensions of death, dying and bereavement. They found that there were several reasons stated for performing death and bereavement rituals: saving face; filial piety; to get luck, blessings, and fortune from the ancestors; to appease the spirits; and to maintain the Chinese identity. Compared with Anglo-Australians, Chinese were less likely to favor euthanasia, documentation of medical directives, and truth telling about terminal illness to self and loved ones (Waddell & McNamara, 1997).

Psychosocial correlates of death attitudes and beliefs

Wu et al. (2002) showed that while death anxiety was related to psychological distress and recent stressors, it was unrelated to physical disorders. Tang, Wu, and Yan (2002) reported that while low levels of self-efficacy and external health locus of control were associated with higher levels of death anxiety, there was only a weak association between internal health locus of control and fear of death.

Lin (2003) examined the relationships between three personal factors (spirituality, emotional support, and religiosity) as independent variables and five dimensions of attitude toward death (fear of death, death avoidance, neutral acceptance of death, approach acceptance of death, and escape acceptance of death) as dependent variables. She showed that spirituality influenced fear and avoidance of death attitudes, whereas spirituality and religiosity affected approach acceptance and escape acceptance in Americans. On the other hand, spirituality affected fear of death attitudes and religiosity affected approach acceptance of death attitudes in Chinese. Despite these cultural differences, it was concluded that, while spirituality influenced negative dimensions of death attitudes (fear of death and avoidance of death), religiosity influenced the positive dimension of acceptance of death.

Hui, Bond, and Ng (2006–7) proposed that general beliefs about the world were useful defense mechanisms against death anxiety. Based on a sample of 133 Chinese university students, analyses utilizing structural equation modeling showed that while death ideation was positively related to fate control and death anxiety, it was negatively related to social cynicism and reward for application. Although death anxiety was positively related to fate control, it was negatively related to religiosity. Results also showed that belief in fate control partially mediated the relationship between death ideation and death anxiety.

Religiosity, religious beliefs and religious practice

Assessment methods and issues

In the literature, religious involvement has been commonly assessed in terms of a single item or a few items. Mui and Kang (2006) used one item to assess religiosity which was conceived as the perceived importance of religion in one's life. Hui, Watkins, Wong, and Sun (2006) assessed religious involvement by two items, including one item on religious affiliation and another item on the frequency of attending religious activities. Zhang and Jin (1996) used two common items (perceived closeness to God or other deity, frequency of attending religious activities) and two different items (saying prayers before meals and contribution to religion in American students; how important religion is to one's life and belief in afterlife in Chinese students) to assess religiosity in American and Chinese people. Zhang and Thomas (1994) used six items to assess religiosity. In addition, interviews were also used to examine religious preference and motives for ancestor worship (Smith, 1989). Finally, English questionnaires (McClenon, 1988) were used to examine anomalous experiences in Chinese people. It is noteworthy that psychometric properties of the measures of religiosity were seldom examined in these studies, so it is unclear whether the constructs as measured are coherent in Chinese cultural settings.

Leung et al. (2002) conducted two studies examining pancultural dimensions of general beliefs about the world or social axioms using a literature review, interviews of Hong Kong Chinese, and content analyses to identify the social axioms. Exploratory factor analyses showed that there were five dimensions of the scale: social cynicism, social complexity, reward for application, spirituality, and fate control. With the exception of fate control, the different dimensions could be replicated in Venezuela, Japan, USA and Germany. For the measure of spirituality (supernatural forces and the function of religious beliefs), the following items were included: 1) religious belief helps one understand the meaning of life; 2) religious belief makes people good citizens; 3) religious faith facilitates good mental health; 4) there is a supreme being controlling the universe; 5) religious people are more likely to maintain moral standards; 6) religion creates escapism; 7) ghosts or spirits are people's fantasy (reversed); and 8) religious beliefs lead to unscientific thinking (reversed). The spirituality factor was relabeled as religiosity, and found to be a coherent construct in over 40 cultural groups (Leung & Bond, 2004).

Profiles and socio-demographic correlates of religious beliefs and practices

In a study of young people's perception of superstition and destiny in Hong Kong, several phenomena were observed (The Hong Kong Federation of Youth Groups, 1993). First, although fortune-telling activities were common among young people in Hong Kong, few of them followed the related instructions. Second, young people were rarely engaged in activities involving the supernatural. Third, a majority of them believed in predestination. Fourth, religious beliefs were related to control of life and meaning in life. However, the above findings should be viewed with caution, because it is not clear whether statistical tests of significance were carried out.

In the study of youth trends in Hong Kong, several questions were used by the Hong Kong Federation of Youth Groups (2008) to understand the life outlook of Chinese adolescents in Hong Kong. Regarding the item, 'Religion is important to my life,' 36.1 per cent agreed, 62.1 per cent disagreed and 1.9 per cent of the respondents were undecided. In addition, among the respondents, 16.0 per cent agreed, 83.6 per cent of the respondents disagreed, and 0.4 per cent were undecided that their life outlook was negative.

Smith (1989) examined ancestor practices in contemporary Hong Kong. He reported significant relationships between religious preference and domestic ancestor worship and practices, and concluded that ancestor worship was more social than religious in nature. Concerning religious beliefs of people in Taiwan, Harrell (1977) interviewed Taiwanese village residents and identified four types of believers, including intellectual believers, true believers, practical believers, and non-believers, although the relative frequencies of these ideal types were not clearly stated.

In a sample of Chinese university students, Nelson, Badger, and Wu (2004) found that roughly 40 per cent of the respondents regarded religion as unimportant and 37 per cent were uncertain about their religious/spiritual beliefs. Based on a study of spiritual beliefs held by university students (N = 1,100), Song and Jin (2004) found that social beliefs (such as political beliefs) were ranked first, followed by pragmatic beliefs (such as worship of family) and supernatural beliefs (such as religious beliefs).

Yao (2007) examined changes in religious beliefs and practices in urban China from 1995 to 2005. Based on the responses of Chinese from different cities, he found that 5.3 per cent had taken part in religious activities, but 51.8 per cent regarded themselves as non-religious, and 32.9 per cent regarded themselves as firm atheists. He also reported changes in religious belief and practice across this decade: a) belief in spirits or ghosts increased from 1.5 per cent to 8.9 per cent; b) belief in Jesus increased from 2.2 per cent to 5.8 per cent; c) belief in the power of Heaven increased from 3.8 per cent to 26.7 per cent; d) belief in ancestor blessing increased from 4.6 per cent to 23.8 per cent; and e) belief in fate increased from 26.2 per cent to 45.2 per cent. McClenon (1988) examined anomalous (déjà vu, communication with the dead, etc.) Chinese experiences based on the responses of Chinese students. He found that Chinese students reported anomalous experiences at an equivalent or higher level than those found in Western populations. He argued that because students had no religious practices, such experiences were universal in nature.

Based on the data collected from 40 cultural groups, Leung and Bond (2004) showed that the composition of religiosity and fate control factors of the Social Axioms Survey were similar across cultures. Although the mean religiosity score in Chinese people was not particularly high, mean fate control score in Chinese people was on the higher side.

Zhang and Thomas (1994) examined adolescent conformity to significant others in mainland China, Taiwan, and the USA. Their findings did not support the predictions guided by modernization theory that conformity to religious figures was strongest in mainland China. While American youths scored highest on conformity to religious figures, Chinese youths scored lowest on conformity to religious figures. There were also lower religious participation and religiosity levels for Chinese people compared with Americans.

Tsang (2004) used questionnaire methodology to survey the use of services provided by *feng shui* masters and conducted semi-structured interviews with *feng shui* masters and businessmen. They found that superstition played an important role in business decision making in Chinese societies. Business people tended to justify the value of *feng shui*, although they also believed that they should not base their business decisions on superstition.

Based on the qualitative data collected from Chinese-Canadians, Molzahn, Starzomski, McDonald, and O'Loughlin (2005) found that there was a mixture of beliefs influencing organ donation, but that the participants were unable to describe the origin of their belief systems.

Psychosocial correlates of religious beliefs and practices

Religious beliefs and practices have been related to stress, coping, work behavior, and suicidal ideation. Mui and Kang (2006) showed that religiosity was negatively associated with acculturation stress. Song and Yue (2006) found that primary and secondary factors related to supernatural beliefs positively predicted coping styles indexed by remorse, recourse, fantasy, and rationalization. Chou and Chen (2005) reported that different types of faith (verticals, integrated faith, horizontals, and undeveloped faith) were associated with personality, psychosocial development and pro-social behavior, with the integrated-faith type showing more positive personality traits (indexed by higher scores on extraversion, openness, agreeableness, and conscientiousness, but lower scores on neuroticism), external behavior (indexed by higher levels of fiscal responsibility, compassion, and volunteerism) and psychosocial development (indexed by measure of psychosocial development derived from Erikson's theory of personality) than did other faith types.

Kao and Ng (1988) argued that religious and quasi-religious teachings in grass-roots traditions and folklore influenced Chinese work behavior, such as de-emphasizing the importance of self and emphasizing the importance of social harmony in the work setting. Zhang and Jin (1996) reported that, while there was a negative relationship between religiosity and suicidal ideation in American students, a positive relationship between religiosity and suicidal ideation was found for Chinese students.

Bond et al. (2004) showed that religiosity as a dimension of social axioms was related to the self-enhancement, conservation, and self-transcendence dimensions of Schwartz's (1992) model. In addition, religiosity was negatively related to conventional vocational interest, but positively related to social vocational interest and accommodation as styles of conflict resolution (Bond, Leung, Au, Tong, & Chemonges-Nielson, 2004). Lai, Bond, and Hui (2007) showed that while lower social cynicism predicted life satisfaction, religiosity did not. Based on the Schwartz Value Survey, Bond and Chi (1997) showed that the universalism–benevolence–conformity factor (including unity with nature as part of the construct) was positively related to pro-social behavior but negatively related to antisocial behavior.

Forgiveness as a spiritual quality

There are two reasons why forgiveness is included as a dimension of spirituality in this review. First, forgiveness is a value that has deep roots in different religions (McCullough & Worthington, 1999). In Christianity, for example, forgiveness is clearly reflected in the Lord's Prayer: 'Forgive us our sins, as we forgive those who sin against us' (Luke 11: 4–5). In different Chinese philosophies including Confucianism, Buddhism, and Taoism, forgiveness is also a central element in their related teachings (Fu, Watkins, & Hui, 2004). Second, forgiveness as offering mercy, compassion and love to the offender has been regarded by counselors, psychotherapists, and spiritual directors as factors leading to personal maladjustment and outcome indicator of intervention (West, 2001).

Assessment methods and related issues

Measures of forgiveness translated into Chinese, such as the Conceptual Forgiveness Questions (Hui & Ho, 2004), Enright Forgiveness Inventory (Hui & Ho, 2004), Mullet Forgiveness Scale (Fu et al., 2004; Hui et al., 2006), Vengeance Scale (Siu & Shek, 2005), Wade Forgiveness Scale (Chen, Zhu & Liu, 2006), Tendency to Forgive Scale (Hu, Zhang, Ja, & Zhong, 2005), and Objective Scale of Forgiveness (Huang, 1997), have been used with Chinese populations. In addition, Hui et al. (2006) have developed an indigenous 23-item Chinese Concepts of Forgiveness Scale.

Research findings on the dimensionality of existing measures of forgiveness have been reported: Hui et al. (2006) found that there were six factors of the Chinese Concepts of Forgiveness Scale; Hui et al. (2006) reported two factors underlying a translated 30-item measure of attitudes towards forgiveness; Fu et al. (2004) reported that there was only one interpretable factor (revenge versus forgiveness) underlying the responses of college students and teachers to the Chinese Mullet Questionnaire, an observation which was not consistent with the findings in the previous literature that there were two factors underlying the scale, a revenge factor and a forgiveness factor.

Profiles and socio-demographic correlates of forgiveness

While Hui et al. (2006) showed that lower-grade students with religious beliefs were more likely to forgive, and that female students and female teachers having religious beliefs were more likely to perceive forgiveness as compassion, Fu et al. (2004) showed that there were no gender or teacher group (university teachers versus other teachers) differences. Overall, however, research findings on the socio-demographic correlates of forgiveness are sparse.

Psychosocial correlates of forgiveness

Regarding psychological correlates of forgiveness, Hui et al. (2006) showed that, while religious affiliation predicted concepts of forgiveness, religious practice predicted one's attitude towards and practice of forgiveness. Fu et al. (2004) found that forgiveness was more related to interpersonal orientations (harmony and relationship orientation) than individual attributes (self-esteem and anxiety).

Hu, Zhang, Ja, and Zhong (2005) reported that, while revenge motivations, rumination and empathy were negative predictors of forgiveness, hurtfulness and revenge motivations were positively related to taking revenge. Siu and Shek (2005) showed that a higher level of vengeance taking was related to social problem solving and family well-being.

Based on the responses of students recruited in Hong Kong and the United States, Hui and Bond (in press) found that face loss positively predicted motivation to retaliate against a harmdoer in both samples. In addition, while face loss was negatively related to forgiveness, motivation to maintain the relationship was positively related to forgiveness in both samples. On the other hand, while motivation to retaliate was negatively related to forgiveness and face loss was negatively related to motivation to maintain relationship in Chinese students, these significant relationships were not found in US students. These findings suggest there are culture-general as well as culture-specific factors involved in forgiving 'those who trespass against us'.

Other relevant studies

There are three other studies on forgiveness in Chinese people that deserve attention. First, Fu et al. (2004) conducted in-depth interviews to explore the Chinese conceptions of forgiveness. Results showed that the informants could give personal and cultural examples to support the claim that the concept was relevant to Chinese societies. Perseveration of group harmony was given as the main reason to forgive; personality or religious influences were not regarded as important sources of forgiveness. Second, based on the responses of many community mediators, Wall and Blum (1991) found that there were 27 mediation techniques, including obtaining forgiveness, which ranked eleventh among the mediation tactics. Finally, Hui and Ho (2004) evaluated a forgiveness training program via quantitative and qualitative methods. Although there was no significant improvement in self-esteem and hope among the participants based on the pre-test and post-test scores, participants showed better conception of forgiveness and a positive attitude to using forgiveness. They concluded that it was 'viable to promote forgiveness as a classroom guidance program.' (p. 477)

Hope and hopelessness

Although there are different views on the concept of spirituality and different ingredients have been proposed to define the concept, a sense of hope is commonly regarded as an important component of spirituality. Highfield and Cason (1983) proposed that there are four types of spiritual needs, including need for meaning and purpose in life, need to receive love, need to give love, and need for hope and creativity. Thompson (2002) outlined five types of spiritual distress, including spiritual pain, spiritual alienation, spiritual guilt, spiritual loss and spiritual despair (loss of hope). In their proposed framework on spiritual assessment, Anandarajah and Hight (2001) suggested that hope and its sources should be assessed.

Assessment methods and related issues

Besides scales translated into Chinese, such as the Hopelessness Scale (Chou, 2006; Shek, 1993; Shek & Lee, 2005), Children's Hope Scale (Hui & Ho, 2004) and Herth Hope Index (Hsu, Lu, Tsou & Lin, 2003), indigenously developed measures of hope (beliefs about the future) have been developed (e.g. Shek, Siu, & Lee, 2007). Utilizing a modified Beck Hopelessness Scale, Shek (1993) showed that the Chinese Hopelessness Scale was valid, reliable, and factorially stable, yielding three meaningful factors: hopelessness, uncertainty about the future, and future expectations. Stewart et al. (2006) used confirmatory factor analysis to examine the structure of the Hopelessness scale for children in American and Hong Kong students, and reported that factor structures were similar in these different students. Shek et al. (2007) showed that scores on the belief in the future subscale of the Chinese

Positive Youth Development Scale were able to discriminate adolescents with and without emotional and behavioral problems.

Profiles and socio-demographic correlates of hope and hopelessness

Based on the responses of a large sample of secondary school students to the Chinese Hopelessness Scale in Hong Kong, Shek and Lee (2005) concluded that roughly one-fifth of Chinese adolescents displayed signs of hopelessness. In a recent comparative study of the psychological well-being of adolescents in Hong Kong and Shanghai, Shek, Han, and Lee (2006) concluded that adolescents in Hong Kong had higher hopelessness scores than did adolescents in Shanghai.

There are also findings showing that hopelessness was related to socio-demographic attributes. As far as age is concerned, adolescent age was positively related to adolescent hopelessness (Shek & Lee, 2005). Regarding gender differences, adolescent boys scored higher than adolescent girls on hopelessness, both cross-sectionally (Shek, 2005a; Shek & Lee, 2005) and longitudinally (Shek, in press). There are also research findings showing that the level of parental education was negatively related to hopelessness in their adolescent children (Shek, 2005a). Finally, there are findings showing that hopelessness was higher in adolescents growing up in non-intact families as compared to intact families (Shek, 2007; Shek & Lee, 2007; Shek, in press). This set of results indicates that a sense of hopelessness is partly related to one's position in the social structure, though the reasons offered for these differential impacts vary across researchers.

Psychological correlates of hope and hopelessness

There are research findings showing that hopelessness is related to pathological symptoms (e.g. Shek, 1993, 1999a). Hopelessness has been identified as an important predictor of suicidal ideation: Stewart et al. (2006) showed that compared to suicide attempts in Hong Kong, hopelessness was less associated with suicide attempts in the US; Ran et al. (2007) showed that hopelessness assessed by clinical interviews was an important predictor of suicide attempts; Chou (2006) showed that the relationship between depression and suicidal ideation was mediated by hopelessness, loneliness, and self-rated health status. On the other hand, hopelessness was negatively related to positive mental health measures, including purpose in life, self-esteem, life satisfaction, and existential well-being (Shek, 1993, 1999a; Shek et al., 2007).

Family processes and hope/hopelessness

There is a wealth of research showing that different family processes are related to adolescent hopelessness in Chinese culture. As far as parenting is concerned, Shek and Lee (2005) showed that although parental behavioral control was negatively related to adolescent hopelessness, parental psychological control was positively associated with adolescent hopelessness. Shek (2007) further showed that relative to those conditions in which one or none of the adolescents' parents was perceived to display high parental psychological control at Time 1, adolescent hopelessness at Time 2 was greater when both parents were perceived to display high levels of parental psychological control at Time 1. Besides, utilizing longitudinal data, Shek (1999b, 1999c) showed that there were bidirectional influences between perceived parenting qualities and adolescent hopelessness. Evidently, parents responded to their adolescent's manifestations of hopelessness with poorer parenting which might intensify the sense of hopelessness in their children.

Both cross-sectional and longitudinal research findings also revealed that better perceived parent–child relationships indexed by different measures, including level of parent–adolescent conflict (Shek, 1998a, 1998b, 1998c, 1999b, 1999c), mutual trust between the parents and adolescent children, readiness to communicate with the parent, and satisfaction with parental control (Shek, 2005d, 2006c), were related to adolescent hopelessness. Research findings also indicated that there is a bidirectional relationship between negative family functioning assessed by translated and indigenously developed measures and adolescent hopelessness (Shek, 1999a, 1999b, 1999c, 2000, 2001a, 2001b).

Other relevant work

Based on the responses of 142 Taiwan undergraduate students to the question 'What is happiness?' Lu (2001) found that a positive outlook (i.e. sense of hope) and spiritual enrichment were essential ingredients of happiness (see also Lu, this volume). In an attempt to examine Chinese belief in the future and its relevance to positive youth development programs in different Chinese contexts, Sun and Lau (2006) outlined the conceptual bases of beliefs in the future as a construct indicating positive youth development and proposed consequent implications for curriculum development. They noted that while most of the existing studies were geared towards hopelessness, there were relatively fewer studies based on the concept of hope.

Spirituality and restoration/promotion of health in Chinese people

Assessment methods and issues

As spiritual functioning is regarded as an important aspect of quality of life in health and rehabilitation contexts, attempts have been made to assess spirituality in Chinese clients and patients of social service agencies. Based on the holistic health concept of the World Health Organization, researchers developed the questionnaire version (Leung, Tay, Cheng, & Lin, 1997) and interview version (Leung, Wong, Tay, Chu, & Ng, 2005) of the World Health Organization Quality of Life Scale—Hong Kong Chinese version (WHOQOL-BREF-HK). This scale assesses four domains of quality of life (QOL) (physical health and level of independence, psychological well-being, social relationships, and quality of the environment), with an item assessing the meaning of life (spirituality) in the scale. Research findings support the reliability and validity of this scale (Leung et al., 2005; Molassiotis, Callaghan, Twinn, & Lam, 2001).

Based on the body–mind–spirit model, Ng, Yau, Chan, and Ho (2005) developed a 56-item Body–Mind–Spirit Well-Being Inventory (BMSWBI), with a 13-item spirituality subscale. Factor analyses of these 13 items showed three factors, including tranquility (contentedness, letting go, calmness, and harmony), disorientation (loss of direction in life, not understanding one's predicament in life), and resilience (gratitude, deriving strength from predicament). Findings supporting the reliability and validity of the related measures were reported.

Based on the concept of health in traditional Chinese medicine (TCM), Leung et al. (2005) proposed a model based on the equilibrium of *yin* and *yang*, involving the harmonizing of physical form and spirit, the harmonizing of man and nature, the harmonizing of man and society, and the seven emotions. Based on a series of steps including expert reviews and factor analyses, the 50-item Chinese Quality of Life Instrument (ChQOL) was found to possess acceptable psychometric properties and construct validity, including a positive correlation with the spirituality domain of the WHOQOL-100 instrument.

Models of spirituality and heath restoration/promotion in Chinese culture

Besides descriptive studies documenting religious belief systems in China (Davis, 1996; Fan, 2003; Snyder, 2006; Zhuo, 2003), researchers have attempted to examine how health is understood in different Chinese religious systems. For example, Yip (2004) examined Taoism and its impact on the mental health of Chinese communities. He described the Taoist conception of mental health in terms of several concepts, including transcendence of self and secularity, dynamic 'revertism', i.e. reversion, to nature (*Tao*), integration with the law of nature (*Tao*), and a high level of transformation as well as transcendence. He also highlighted several differences between Western and Taoist conceptions of mental health, including Western self-development vs. Taoist self-transcendence, Western self-attainment vs. Taoist integration with the law of nature, Western progressive self-endeavor vs. Taoist inaction, and Western personal interpretation vs. the Taoist infinite frame of reference.

Chan, Ho, and Chow (2001) proposed a body–mind–spirit model in which health was conceived in a holistic manner and sickness was regarded as disequilibrium between *yin* and *yang*. They further argued that techniques, such as *qi gong*, forgiveness, letting go, gaining and growing through pain, were ways to restore health and presented research findings showing that these Eastern therapeutic elements were important. Sinnott (2001) discussed the role of Chinese medicine and Buddhist meditation as complementary healing systems which 'might add to standard Western systems of healing body and mind' (p. 241). Barnes (1998) described how traditional Chinese healing practices underwent acculturation in the USA by a transformation of the religious language and indigenous practices into psychological language that is more easily understood.

There are views suggesting that Western models of health and treatment are not entirely appropriate for Chinese people. With reference to terminal illness and end-of-life decision making in Chinese people, Tse, Chong, and Fok (2003) argued that the standard palliative care approach of breaking bad news could be adopted for Chinese people, but that modifications are needed. Payne, Chapman, Holloway, Seymour, and Chau (2005) similarly argued for a culturally sensitive practice with Chinese. Tang (2000) examined meanings of dying at home for Chinese patients in Taiwan with terminal illness. Results showed that Chinese people in Taiwan preferred dying at home, and suggested the implications of this preference for practice with Chinese people.

Based on two cases (one Chinese-American family), Kagawa-Singer and Blackhall (2001) highlighted cultural differences related to issues at the end of life, and discussed the possible consequences of ignoring the techniques and strategies that could be used to address the issue. Based on their analysis, the authors proposed an ABCDE model (attitudes of patients and families, beliefs, context, decision-making styles, and environment) which could guide practitioners to ascertain the appropriate levels of cultural influence to apply.

Bowman and Singer (2001) examined perspectives on end-of-life decisions among Chinese seniors based on an analysis of qualitative survey results. They found that end-of-life decisions were based on hope, suffering and burden, the future, emotional harmony, the life cycle, respect for doctors, and the family, noting that the respondents rejected directives. Based on these findings, they suggested that attitudes toward end-of-life decisions should be understood through the Confucian, Buddhist, and Taoist traditions.

Intervention involving spiritual elements in health restoration/promotion

Utilizing a grounded theory approach to examine Chinese cultural influences on Chinese-Australian cancer patients, Chui, Donoghue, and Chenoweth (2005) showed that five culturally specific strategies were used, including traditional Chinese medicine, traditional Chinese beliefs regarding food therapy, *qi gong*, *feng shui*, and worship of ancestors, all of which could be subsumed under the philosophy of harmony involving *yin*, *yang* and *qi gong*. Xu, Towers, Li, and Collet (2006) conducted a qualitative study examining the experiences of Chinese cancer patients and TCM professionals, finding that the participants perceived TCM cancer therapy as optimal and safe. Utilizing mediation methods based on traditional Chinese medicine and mindfulness training, Tang et al. (2007) examined the effectiveness of intensive and systematic mediation training with Chinese undergraduate students. Compared with the control group, students of the experimental group showed less anxiety and fatigue, better mood, and a significant decrease in stress-related cortisol and an increase in immunoreactivity. However, Smith (2006) examined the relationship between birth year proposed by Chinese astrology and traditional Chinese medicine. In contrast to the previous findings, they did not show that Chinese-Americans were more vulnerable to diseases believed to be associated with their birth years proposed by Chinese astrology and traditional Chinese medicine.

There are also research findings showing that traditional religious beliefs can influence health outcomes. Based on the findings of Chinese residents in extended care facilities, Chan and

Kayser-Jones (2005) reported that communication barriers, dislike of Western food, and cultural beliefs and customs (including religious beliefs) were factors influencing the successful maintenance of Chinese residents. Kwok and Sullivan (2006) showed that Chinese-Australian women were heavily influenced by traditional Chinese philosophies, including fatalism. Mok, Martinson, and Wong (2004) reported that religious beliefs gave strength for the patients to cope with suffering, and that cultural worldviews helped to create meaning. Mok, Lai, and Zhang (2003) also found that meaning of life was an important motivator in the coping process for patients with renal failure, helping the patients to identify the personal significance of the illness.

There are some treatment programs incorporating Christian elements into the treatment process in a Chinese cultural context. Luk and Shek (2006a) studied the changes and related factors in ex-mental patients attending a psychiatric rehabilitation program in Hong Kong that adopted a self-help group (SHG) approach guided by Christian principles. A quasi-experimental design involving an experimental group was adopted with the participants responding to measures assessing their functioning in the physical, psychological, social, and spiritual domains. Results showed that those who joined the SHG with holistic care elements reported more friends and more social satisfaction than did the control subjects. Duration of attendance, religious involvement, and group involvement were three key factors related to these outcomes for the program participants. Based on the findings generated by the repertory grid technique, Luk and Shek (2006b) further showed that participants perceived positive changes in physical, psychological, social, and spiritual dimensions after joining the program. Finally, qualitative findings based on 20 participants of a psychiatric rehabilitation program adopting a Christian fellowship model showed that the participants perceived positive changes in their personal, social, and spiritual domains, and felt that spiritual beliefs had helped them to face the challenges of life (Luk & Shek, 2008).

Ng and Shek (2001) examined the psychology of heroin-addicted Chinese men at different stages of a Christian drug rehabilitation program, including the pre-conversion stage ($N = 26$), post-conversion stage ($N = 20$), halfway-house stage ($N = 19$), and peer-leaders stage ($N = 21$). Results showed that there was a decrease in symptoms of depression and hopelessness, but an increase in declared purpose in life through the different stages of the rehabilitation program. Analyses also showed that there was a significant enhancement in the mental health of the participants who made a religious conversion.

Conceptual, methodological and practical issues arising

At this point, it should be noted that there are few scientific studies on spirituality of the Chinese people. A computer search of the PsycINFO in March 2009 using 'spirituality' and 'Chinese' as search terms for the subtracts showed only 41 citations. An examination of the major handbooks on Chinese psychology (Bond, 1986, 1996) also showed that except in the areas of values, ultimate life concerns and beliefs, there was little work done in the area of Chinese spirituality. This observation is consistent with the conclusion of Shek, Chan, and Lee (2005) that very few studies have examined the more holistic qualities of life (including spirituality) in Chinese people (see also Lu, this volume). Furthermore, the current review shows that the related research in this area is rather unsystematic and disconnected from previous albeit related work.

Conceptual problems and issues

Varying conceptions of spirituality and Chinese spirituality. The foremost limitation in the existing literature is that spirituality and Chinese spirituality have been defined in different ways. As mentioned, a wide range of definitions is present, and most of the existing studies are based on Western conceptions of spirituality, such as concepts of the meaning of life, religiosity, and death anxiety. Obviously, how spirituality is conceived basically determines the direction of research for Chinese spirituality.

With reference to Pargament's (1999) ideas that religion is 'the search for significance in ways related to the sacred', whereas spirituality is 'the search for the sacred' (pp. 11–12), it is noteworthy the 'sacred' is conceived differently in different Chinese religions. While the *tao* (logos) is emphasized in Taoism, achieving Buddhahood is the focus in Buddhism, and different deities (such as *Wong Tai Sin, Che Kung, Tam Kung*) and supernatural forces (e.g. *fung shui, qi*) are basic to various forms of popular religions. Furthermore, it is noteworthy that meaning of life is approached differently in different Chinese philosophies. In Confucian thought, a life is meaningful if one can dedicate oneself to promote the well-being of the collective by following right practice. In Buddhist thought, the meaning of life can only be achieved if one transcends the illusions of the material world. In Taoist thought, the meaning of life can only be understood in terms of one's harmonizing with the universe. Unfortunately few psychological studies have addressed these issues and concepts in testable form.

There are also some recent research findings showing that there has been a change in the religious landscape of mainland China (Zhuo, 2003), such as the changing social background of Christians (Chen & Huang, 2004), a rapid revival of folk religions in Southern China (Law, 2005), a resurgence in local religious practices (Liu, 2003), and a wide spread of religiosity among Chinese youth (Ji, 2006). Research in response to these emerging trends is needed.

Inadequate coverage of the convergence and non-convergence between Western and Chinese concepts of spirituality. A survey of the literature shows that similarities and differences between Western concepts of spirituality (e.g. life meaning, death anxiety, life review) and Chinese concepts of spirituality, such as fate (*yuan*) in Buddhist thought (Yang & Ho, 1988), harmony (*he sei*) in Taoist thought, predestination (*meng*) in popular religions, are inadequately covered in the literature. Assuming that we can find a common platform for comparison, one should further ask whether the spirituality of Chinese people is similar to that of Western people. Although there are studies showing that different aspects of spirituality, such as forgiveness (Fu et al., 2004), anomalous experience (McClenon, 1988), and religiosity (Leung et al., 2002) are similar in Chinese and Western people, there are studies showing that conceptions of spirituality as a broader construct are not the same in Western and Chinese cultures (e.g. Yip, 2004), and that factor structures of measures of spirituality are sometimes inconsistent across cultures (e.g. Fu et al., 2004; Wong, 2004). Furthermore, some studies have shown that spirituality is differently related to behavior (i.e. functionally divergent) in Chinese and Western cultures (e.g. Zhang & Jin, 1996).

Paucity of scientific models for Chinese spirituality. This review has shown that there is a paucity of scientific models on the antecedents, concomitants, and consequences of Chinese spirituality. Such models are indispensable in guiding empirical research on Chinese spirituality. Although Western theories such as Frankl's theory on the meaning of life (Frankl, 1967) have been used as conceptual models to understand Chinese spirituality, there are several conceptual gaps (Shek, in press).

In the first place, the bidirectional influences between spirituality and developmental outcomes, e.g. between purpose in life and mental health, are rarely examined in the literature. Logically speaking, it is possible that there are mutual influences in these components of spirituality and other psychological domains. Second, further studies should be conducted adopting an ecological approach (Shek, Chan, & Lee, 2005) to examine how individual factors (e.g. economic disadvantage), family factors (e.g. family beliefs, behavioral control versus psychological control), and social factors (e.g. endorsement of Chinese superstitious beliefs) are related to Chinese spirituality.

Methodological limitations and related issues

Predominance of quantitative studies. The first limitation of the literature is that most of the measures of Chinese spirituality, including the meaning of life (Shek, 1988), attitudes toward death (Cheung & Ho, 2004), religiosity (Zhang & Thomas, 1994), hopelessness (Shek & Lee, 2005), and forgiveness (Hui & Ho, 2004), are quantitative in nature, usually relying on questionnaires imported from the West. While a positivistic approach represents the dominant research paradigm in social science research, views have been expressed pointing out its weaknesses and arguing for the greater use of qualitative methods (e.g. Ho & Ho, 2007). In fact, there are qualitative studies employing techniques, such as drawing, open-ended questions, and interviews to assess spirituality (e.g. Mak, 2001; Yang & Chen, 2002, 2006). As such, researchers should consider supplementing work on Chinese spirituality by using qualitative approaches.

Poor quality of qualitative studies. According to Patton (1990), there are several unique features of qualitative research. These include naturalistic inquiry, inductive analysis, holistic perspective, qualitative data, personal contact and insight, dynamic systems, unique case orientation, empathetic neutrality, and design flexibility. Although it is conceptually appealing to use qualitative methods to assess Chinese spirituality, there are two drawbacks in the literature on Chinese spirituality. First, although some researchers (e.g. Ho & Ho, 2007) argued for qualitative research of Chinese spirituality, they failed to specify the research paradigm they identified with. Obviously, qualitative research under post-positivism (which maintains critical realism) is essentially different from that based on constructionism and post-modernism (which maintain relativism). In the former case, it is proposed that rational criteria can be used to judge the quality of qualitative studies. In the latter case, it is argued that no rational criteria are present to judge the quality of qualitative research.

The second drawback is that it is not a common practice for qualitative researchers to assess the rigor of related studies on Chinese spirituality. Shek, Tang, and Han (2005) argued that 12 criteria should be used by qualitative researchers to assess the rigor of their studies. These include explicit statements on the philosophical base of the study, justifications for the number and nature of the participants in the study, detailed description of procedures used for data collection, discussion of biases and ideological preoccupation of the researchers, description of the steps taken to guard against biases or arguments that biases should and/or could not be eliminated, measures to assess the consistency of findings, triangulation of research approaches, peer and member checking of the findings, performing audit trails, critical evaluation of alternative explanations, accounting for negative evidence, and considering limitations to the study. It is suggested that future qualitative studies on Chinese spirituality should be evaluated in terms of these 12 criteria to enhance their scientific usefulness and integrity.

Predominance of imported measures. With the exception of a few attempts (e.g. the Chinese Beliefs about Adversity Scale: Shek, 2004), instruments assessing Chinese spirituality are mostly translated Western measures. While it is not uncommon for social scientists to use 'imported' Western conceptualizations and their attendant measures to study Chinese behavior and phenomena, it is important to reflect on whether such imported concepts can fully capture phenomena related to Chinese spirituality.

Essentially, the issue that should be addressed is whether an 'emic' (insider) or 'etic' (outsider) approach should be used to examine Chinese spirituality (see also Hong, Yang, & Chiu; Hwang; Smith; & Yang, this volume). Following the above argument on the need to examine indigenous Chinese concepts about Chinese spirituality, it would be helpful if indigenous Chinese measures on Chinese spirituality could be devised. Unfortunately, as pointed out by Shek et al. (2005), the Chinese literature on psychosocial assessment tools is thin and in need of strengthening. Of course, we should be conscious of the argument that the need for developing indigenous Chinese assessment measures may not be that strong. In the area of personality assessment, for example, Yik and Bond (1993) reported that the findings based on imported and indigenous lexical measures of personality perception for Hong Kong Chinese did not differ much, and they concluded that 'imported measures may cut the phenomenal world differently from the imported measures, but still enable scientists to predict behavior just as effectively ... the present results would challenge the investment required to develop local instrumentation on scientific grounds' (p. 75).

This conclusion can, however, only be drawn after the appropriate indigenous and imported measures have been compared. In the rare cases of such enterprising research, distinctiveness may well be found (see Bond, 1988; Cheung, Zhang, & Cheung, this volume).

Problems with the validation studies. Irrespective of whether the Chinese measure of spirituality is imported or indigenously developed, one important requirement is that the measures should be validated. Unfortunately, not all researchers are conscious of this requirement, e.g. The Hong Kong Federation of Youth Groups (2008).

Amongst the studies that have attempted to validate the Chinese spirituality measures surveyed above, there are several limitations. In the first place, test–retest reliability in quantitative measures and intra- and inter-rater reliability in qualitative assessment of Chinese spirituality have not been commonly carried out. In addition, convergent and discriminant validities are seldom established in a single validation study. Furthermore, although factor analyses have been commonly used to examine the construct validity of the translated or indigenously developed measures, this procedure has several limitations. First, although it is easy for factor-analytic findings to capitalize on chance, factorial stability has not been commonly assessed (e.g. Fu et al., 2004). Second, exploratory rather than confirmatory factor analyses have commonly been used. Although exploratory factor analyses can give an exploratory view of the dimensions underlying the items, the related findings are not definitive because goodness of fit indicators are not commonly available; they should be supplemented where possible with confirmatory factor analyses.

Finally, analysis and interpretation problems are not uncommon in the existing studies. For example, although result of a scree test suggested two factors for the Chinese Mullet Forgiveness Questionnaire (Fu et al., 2004), the second factor was dropped without further explanation because it made 'no conceptual sense' to the researchers (p. 310). In the study by Ng et al. (2005), because separate factor analyses for items in each subscale were performed (e.g. factor analysis of 13 items in the spirituality dimension), the findings cannot provide support for the four-dimensional structure (physical distress, daily functioning, affect and spirituality) of the 56-item Body–Mind–Spirit Well-being Inventory, as claimed by the researchers.

A lack of longitudinal studies. The present review shows that most of the existing studies on Chinese spirituality are cross-sectional. Although cross-sectional studies, such as surveys of psychosocial correlates of religiosity and qualitative studies based on drawings and narratives, are useful to understand Chinese spirituality at a single time point, such designs are inadequate if the researchers wish to investigate the antecedents and consequences of Chinese spirituality. For example, Lin (2003) examined the effects of spirituality in death attitudes utilizing a cross-sectional design. The limitation of the findings is that death attitudes might also influence spirituality and religiosity, rather than vice versa. Longitudinal studies using cross-lagged panel analysis can help to clarify the more probable direction of influence. Similarly, Zhang and Jin (1996) studied the influence of religiosity on suicidal ideation. However, the cross-sectional findings of the relationship between religiosity and suicidal ideation could be alternatively interpreted as the effect of suicidal ideation (as an indicator of poor mental health) on spirituality. Obviously, although cross-sectional studies can help to identify the correlates of meaning in life, causal relationships involved cannot be clearly established. As such, longitudinal research designs represent a more sensitive approach in examining the causal relationships between spirituality and other factors.

Generalizability of research findings on Chinese spirituality. The present review shows that there are few comparative studies in the field of Chinese spirituality. If a research study is to claim universal validity, it must be generalizable to different participants at different times and in different places. Generally speaking, there are two levels at which comparative studies on Chinese spirituality should be carried out. First, findings based on Chinese people may be compared to findings obtained from non-Chinese people. Such cross-cultural studies are important because they can give some ideas about the degree of universality versus relativism of relationships involving Chinese spirituality. Second, because China is a big country and there are regional differences involving different ethnic groups including the 56 designated minority communities, studies involving Chinese people from different parts of China are also important, i.e. comparative studies within the various Chinese contexts. Such research is at present non-existent.

Common methodological shortcomings. There are several common methodological shortcomings in the scientific study of Chinese spirituality. First, consistent with other areas of quantitative psychology, it is rare for researchers to collect data based on random samples. This practice obviously undermines the generalizability of the related findings. Second, in those studies utilizing statistical tests of significance, it is not common practice for researchers to report the related effect size of the significant findings, a practice increasingly required in major journals. Third, for studies where multiple tests of correlation or differences are reported, the issue of inflated Type 1 errors is not commonly addressed. Finally, in studies where multivariate analyses are performed, it is rare for researchers to examine the stability of the multivariate statistical analyses.

Practical limitations and issues

As shown in this review, techniques related to Chinese spirituality, such as *qi gong*, *tai chi*, and traditional Chinese medicine, have been applied to the treatment of bereavement and diseases, such as cancers. Nevertheless, there are two major drawbacks of such applications. First, standardized procedures are seldom specified for such techniques, with the exception of traditional Chinese medicine such as acupuncture. Obviously, without a clear specification of procedures, it would be difficult, if not impossible, for helping professionals to replicate the findings of such studies. Second, there is no systematic evaluation of treatments incorporating elements of Chinese spirituality. Without rigorous evaluation, the use of Chinese spiritual elements to treat people in need may bring more damage than benefit.

Besides attempts to use elements of Chinese spirituality in treatment contexts, one should be sensitive about how Chinese spirituality could possibly be enhanced, such as by the promotion of purpose in life and a reduction in death-related anxiety. Actually, Koenig (2006) regarded religion as a useful coping resource. Unfortunately, few systematic attempts have been made in this area in Chinese psychology. One exemplary exception is the attempt made by Hui and Ho (2004) who found that the participants had a better conception of forgiveness and a more positive attitude towards using forgiveness after joining a program promoting forgiveness.

Another example is the project entitled Positive Adolescent Training through Holistic Social Programs (Project P.A.T.H.S.) developed by academics from five universities in Hong Kong (Shek, 2006a; Shek & Ma, 2006). In the project, training units that attempt to promote spirituality in Chinese adolescents, including the search for life meaning and attitudes toward life and death, were developed. Some initial evaluation findings via different assessment strategies, including objective outcome evaluation, subjective outcome evaluation, and qualitative evaluation, showed that the program can facilitate the search for life meaning among Chinese adolescents in Hong Kong (e.g. Shek, 2006b, 2008; Shek & Sun, 2007a, 2007b, in press; Shek, Lee, Siu, & Ma, 2007).

Conclusions and future directions

Several conclusions can be highlighted from the present review. First, compared with the Western studies, the literature on Chinese spirituality is thin. With specific reference to purpose in life, except for some studies in Hong Kong which were mainly conducted by the present author, published studies in China and Taiwan are almost non-existent. Second, although some measures on Chinese spirituality are available, most are imported from the West; indigenously developed measures are few. Third, although some studies have generated profiles on different aspects of Chinese spirituality, the related findings are inconclusive. In particular, the use of a single item or question embedded in social surveys on some of the measures, such as life meaning and religiosity, casts serious doubt on the validity of the findings. Fourth, although a few socio-demographic, psychological and family correlates of Chinese spirituality have been identified, the findings are inconclusive. Finally, conceptual, methodological, and practical limitations and issues in the existing studies have been discussed. With reference to these limitations, several future research directions are proposed. First, research should be carried out to examine the convergence and non-convergence of Western and Chinese concepts of spirituality. Second, theoretical models on Chinese spirituality should be constructed. Third, more rigorous qualitative studies and construction of validated indigenous measures of Chinese spirituality should be carried out. Fourth, the quest for longitudinal studies of Chinese spirituality is in order. Finally, conducting research on Chinese spirituality with practical implications should be attempted.

Author's note

The preparation for this work was financially supported by the Wofoo Foundation Limited. The author wishes to thank Britta Lee for her assistance in the literature review process.

Address all correspondence to Daniel T. L. Shek, Department of Applied Social Sciences, The Hong Kong Polytechnic University, Hung Hom, Kowloon, Hong Kong, PRC (email address: daniel.shek@polyu.edu.hk).

References

Anandarajah, G. & Hight, E. (2001). Spirituality and medical practice: Using the HOPE questions as a practical tool for spiritual assessment. *American Family Physician, 63*, 81–88.

Barnes, L. (1998). The psychologizing of Chinese healing practices in the United States. *Culture, Medicine and Psychiatry, 22*, 413–443.

Bond, M. H. (1986). *The psychology of the Chinese people.* New York: Oxford University Press.

Bond, M. H. (1996). The handbook of Chinese psychology. New York: Oxford University Press.

Bond, M. H. (1988). Finding universal dimensions of individual variation in multi-cultural studies of values: the Rokeach and Chinese value surveys. *Journal of Personality and Social Psychology, 55*, 1009–1015.

Bond, M. H. & Chi, V. M. Y. (1997). Values and moral behavior in mainland China. *Psychologia, 40*, 251–264.

Bond, M. H., Leung, K., Au, A., Tong, K. K., & Chemonges-Nielson, Z. (2004). Combining social axioms with values in predicting social behaviors. *European Journal of Personality, 18*, 177–191.

Bowman, K. W. & Singer, P. A. (2001). Chinese seniors' perspectives on end-of-life decisions. *Social Science and Medicine, 53*, 455–464.

Braun, K. L. & Nichols, R. (1997). Death and dying in four Asian American cultures: A descriptive study. *Death Studies, 21*, 327–359.

Chan, C., Ho, P. S. Y., & Chow, E. (2001). A body–mind–spirit model in health: An Eastern approach. *Social Work in Health Care, 34*, 261–282.

Chan, D. W. (1995). Reasons for living among Chinese adolescents in Hong Kong. *Suicide and Life-threatening Behavior, 25*, 347–357.

Chan, J. & Kayser-Jones, J. (2005). The experience of dying for Chinese nursing home residents: Cultural considerations. *Journal of Gerontological Nursing, 31*, 26–32.

Chen, C. F. & Huang, T. H. (2004). The emergence of a new type of Christians in China today. *Review of Religious Research, 46*, 183–200.

Chen, X. H. S., Cheung, F. M., Bond, M. H., & Leung, J. P. (2006). Going beyond self-esteem to predict life satisfaction: The Chinese case. *Asian Journal of Social Psychology, 9*, 24–35.

Chen, Z. Y., Zhu, N. N., & Liu, H. Y. (2006). Psychometric features of the Wade Forgiveness Scale and Transgression-Related Interpersonal Motivation Scale-12-Item Form in Chinese college students. *Chinese Mental Health Journal, 20*, 617–620.

Cheung, W. S. & Ho, S. M. Y. (2004). The use of death metaphors to understand personal meaning of death among Hong Kong Chinese undergraduates. *Death Studies, 28*, 47–62.

Chou, K. L. (2000). Intimacy and psychosocial adjustment in Hong Kong Chinese adolescents. *Journal of Genetic Psychology, 161*, 141–151.

Chou, K. L. (2006). Reciprocal relationship between suicidal ideation and depression in Hong Kong elderly Chinese. *International Journal of Geriatric Psychiatry, 21*, 594–596.

Chou, T. S. & Chen, M. C. (2005). An exploratory investigation of differences in personality traits and faith maturity among major religions in Taiwan. *Chinese Journal of Psychology, 47*, 311–327.

Chui, Y. Y., Donoghue, J., & Chenoweth, L. (2005). Responses to advanced cancer: Chinese-Australians. *Journal of Advanced Nursing, 52*, 498–507.

Craine, M. A. (1996). A cross-cultural study of beliefs, attitudes and values in Chinese-born American and non-Chinese frail homebound elderly. *Journal of Long Term Home Health Care, 15*, 9–18.

Davis, S. (1996). The cosmobiological balance of the emotional and spiritual worlds: Phenomenological structuralism in traditional Chinese medical thought. *Culture, Medicine and Psychiatry, 20*, 83–123.

Fan, L. Z. (2003). Popular religion in contemporary China. *Social Compass, 50*, 449–457.

Florian, V. & Snowden, L. R. (1989). Fear of personal death and positive life regard: A study of different ethnic and religious-affiliated American college students. *Journal of Cross-Cultural Psychology, 20*, 64–79.

Frankl, V. E. (1967). *Psychotherapy and existentialism: Selected papers on logotherapy.* New York: Simons and Schuster.

Fu, H., Watkins, D., & Hui, E. K. P. (2004). Personality correlates of the disposition towards interpersonal forgiveness: A Chinese perspective. *International Journal of Psychology, 39*, 305–316.

Govier, I. (2000). Spiritual care in nursing: A systematic approach. *Nursing Standard, 14*, 32–36.

Harrell, S. (1977). Modes of belief in Chinese folk religion. *Journal for the Scientific Study of Religion, 16*, 55–65.

Highfield, M. F. & Cason, C. (1983). Spiritual needs of patients: Are they recognized? *Cancer Nursing, 6*, 187–192.

Ho, D. Y. F. & Ho, R. T. H. (2007). Measuring spirituality and spiritual emptiness: Toward ecumenicity and transcultural applicability. *Review of General Psychology, 11*, 62–74.

Hsu, T. H., Lu, M. S., Tsou, T. S., & Lin, C. C. (2003). The relationship between pain, uncertainty, and hope in Taiwanese lung cancer patients. *Journal of Pain and Symptoms Management, 26*, 835–842.

Hu, S. M., Zhang, A. Q., Ja, Y. J., & Zhong, H. (2005). A study on interpersonal forgiveness and revenge of undergraduates. *Chinese Journal of Clinical Psychology, 13*, 55–57.

Huang, S. T. T. (1997). Social convention understanding and restitutional forgiveness. *Chinese Journal of Psychology, 39*, 119–136.

Hui, E. K. P. & Ho, D. K. Y. (2004). Forgiveness in the context of developmental guidance: Implementation and evaluation. *British Journal of Guidance and Counselling, 32*, 477–492.

Hui, E. K. P., Watkins, D., Wong, T. N. Y., & Sun, R. C. F. (2006). Religion and forgiveness from a Hong Kong Chinese perspective. *Pastoral Psychology, 55*, 183–195.

Hui, V. K. Y. & Bond, M. H. (in press). Forgiving a harm doer as a function of the target's face loss and motivations: How does Chinese culture make a difference? *Journal of Social and Personal Relationships.*

Hui, V. K. Y., Bond, M. H., & Ng, T. S. W. (2006–7). General beliefs about the world as defensive mechanisms against death anxiety. *Omega, 54*, 199–214.

Ji, Z. (2006). Non-institutional religious re-composition among Chinese youth. *Social Compass, 53*, 535–549.

Kagawa-Singer, M. & Blackhall, L. J. (2001). Negotiating cross-cultural issues at the end of life: 'You got to go where he lives'. *Journal of the American Medical Association, 286*, 2993–3001.

Kao, H. S. R. & Ng, S. H. (1988). Minimal 'self' and Chinese work behaviour: Psychology of the grass roots. In D. Sinha & H. S. R. Kao (eds.), *Social values and development: Asian perspectives* (pp. 254–272). New Delhi: Sage.

Koenig, H. G. (2006). Religion, spirituality and aging. *Aging and Mental Health, 10*, 1–3.

Kutcher, N. (1999). *Mourning in late imperial China.* Cambridge: Cambridge University Press.

Kwok, C. & Sullivan, G. (2006). Influence of traditional Chinese beliefs on cancer screening behavior among Chinese-Australian women. *Journal of Advanced Nursing, 54*, 691–699.

Lai, J. H. W., Bond, M. H., & Hui, N. H. H. (2007). The role of social axioms in predicting life satisfaction: A longitudinal study in Hong Kong. *Journal of Happiness Studies, 8*, 517–535.

Lau, S. & Lau, W. (1996). Outlook on life: How adolescents and children view the lifestyle of parents, adults and self. *Journal of Adolescence, 19*, 293–296.

Lau, S. K., Lee, M. K., Wan, P. S., & Wong, S. L. (2005). *Indicators of social development: Hong Kong 2004.* Hong Kong: Hong Kong Institute of Asia-Pacific Studies, The Chinese University of Hong Kong.

Law, P. L. (2005). The revival of folk religion and gender relationships in rural China: A preliminary observation. *Asian Folk Studies, 64*, 89–109.

Leung, K. & Bond, M. H. (2004). Social axioms: A model for social beliefs in multicultural perspective. In M. P. Zanna (ed.), *Advances in experimental social psychology* (vol. 36, pp. 119–197). San Diego, CA: Elsevier Academic Press.

Leung, K., Bond, M. H., de Carrasquel, S. R., Muñoz, C., Hernández, M., Murakami, F., Yamaguchi, S., Bierbrauer, G., & Singelis, T. M. (2002). Social axioms: The search for universal dimensions of general beliefs about how the world functions. *Journal of Cross-Cultural Psychology, 33*, 286–302.

Leung, K. F., Tay, M., Cheng, S., & Lin, F. (1997). *Hong Kong Chinese version of the World Health Organization Quality of Life – Abbreviated version.* Hong Kong: Hong Kong Hospital Authority.

Leung, K. F., Wong, W. W., Tay, M. S. M., Chu, M. M. L., & Ng, S. S. W. (2005). Development and validation of the interview version of the Hong Kong Chinese WHOQOL-BREF. *Quality of Life Research, 14*, 1413–1419.

Leung, K. K., Wu, E. C., Lue, B. H., & Tang, L. Y. (2004). The use of focus groups in evaluating quality of life components among elderly Chinese people. *Quality of Life Research, 13*, 179–190.

Lewis, M. M. (2001). Spirituality, counseling, and elderly: An introduction to the spiritual life review. *Journal of Adult Development, 8*, 231–240.

Lin, A. H. M. H. (2003). Factors related to attitudes toward death among American and Chinese older adults. *Omega—Journal of Death and Dying, 47*, 3–23.

Liu, T. S. (2003). A nameless but active religion: An anthropologist's view of local religion in Hong Kong and Macau. *The China Quarterly, 174*, 373–394.

Loewe, M. (1982). *Chinese ideas of life and death.* London: Allen and Unwin.

Lu, L. (2001). Understanding happiness: A look into the Chinese folk psychology. *Journal of Happiness Studies, 2*, 407–432.

Luk, A. L. & Shek, D. T. L. (2006a). Changes in Chinese discharged chronic mental patients attending a psychiatric rehabilitation program with holistic care elements: A quasi-experimental study. *TSW Holistic Health & Medicine, 1*, 71–83.

Luk, A. L. & Shek, D. T. L. (2006b). Perceived personal changes in Chinese ex-mental patients attending a holistic psychiatric rehabilitation program. *Social Behavior and Personality, 34*, 939–954.

Luk, A. L. & Shek, D. T. L. (2008). The experiences and perceived changes of Chinese ex-mental patients attending a holistic psychiatric rehabilitation program: A qualitative study. *Journal of Psychiatric and Mental Health Nursing*, 15, 447–457.

Mak, M. H. J. (2001). Awareness of dying: An experience of Chinese patients with terminal cancer. *Omega, 43*, 259–279.

Mak, M. H. J. (2002). Accepting the timing of one's death: An experience of Chinese hospice patients. *Omega, 45*, 245–260.

McClenon, J. (1988). A survey of Chinese anomalous experiences and comparison with Western representative national samples. *Journal for the Scientific Study of Religion, 27*, 421–426.

McCullough, M. E. & Worthington, E. L. (1999). Religion and the forgiving personality. *Journal of Personality, 67*, 1141–1164.

Mok, E., Lai, C., & Zhang, Z. X. (2003). Coping with chronic renal failure in Hong Kong. *International Journal of Nursing Studies, 41*, 205–213.

Mok, E., Martinson, I., & Wong, T. K. S. (2004). Individual empowerment among Chinese cancer patients in Hong Kong. *Western Journal of Nursing Research, 26*, 59–75.

Molassiotis, A., Callaghan, P., Twinn, S. F., & Lam, S. W. (2001). Correlates of quality of life in symptomatic HIV patients living in Hong Kong. *AIDS Care, 13*, 319–334.

Molzahn, A. E., Starzomski, R., McDonald, M., & O'Loughlin, C. (2005). Chinese Canadian beliefs toward organ donation. *Qualitative Health Research, 15*, 82–98.

Mui, A. C. & Kang, S. Y. (2006). Acculturation stress and depression among Asian immigrant elders. *Social Work, 51*, 243–255.

Myers, J. E., Sweeney T. J., & Witmer, J. M. (2000). The wheel of wellness counseling for wellness: A holistic model for treatment planning. *Journal of Counseling and Development, 78*, 251–266.

Narayanasamy, A. (1999). A review of spirituality as applied to nursing. *International Journal of Nursing Studies, 36*, 117–125.

Narcotics Division. (1994). *Report on survey of young drug abusers.* Hong Kong: Narcotics Division, Government Secretariat, Hong Kong Government.

Nelson, L. J., Badger, S., & Wu, B. (2004). The influence of culture in emerging adulthood: Perspectives of Chinese college students. *International Journal of Behavioral Development, 28*, 26–36.

Ng, H. Y. & Shek, D. T. L. (2001). Religion and therapy: Religious conversion and the mental health of chronic heroin-addicted persons. *Journal of Religion and Health, 40*, 399–410.

Ng, S. M., Yau, J. K. Y., Chan, C. L. W., Chan, C. H. Y., & Ho, D. Y. F. (2005). The measurement of body–mind–spirit well-being: Toward multidimensionality and transcultural applicability. *Social Work in Health Care, 41*, 33–52.

Paloutzian, R. F. & Ellison, C. W. (1982). Loneliness, spiritual well-being and the quality of life. In L. A. Peplau & D. Perlman (eds.), *Loneliness: A sourcebook of current theory, research and therapy* (pp. 224–237). New York: Wiley.

Pargament, K. I. (1999). The psychology of religion and spirituality? Yes and no. *The International Journal for the Psychology of Religion, 9*, 3–16.

Patton, M. Q. (1990). *Qualitative evaluation and research methods.* Newbury Park, CA: Sage.

Payne, S., Chapman, A., Holloway, M., Seymour, J. E., & Chau, R. (2005). Chinese community views: Promoting cultural competence in palliative care. *Journal of Palliative Care, 21*, 111–116.

Ran, M. S., Xiang, M. Z., Li, J., Huang, J., Chen, E. Y. H., Chan, C. L. W., & Conwell, Y. (2007). Correlates of lifetime suicide attempts among individuals with affective disorders in a Chinese rural community. *Archives of Suicide Research, 11*, 119–127.

Schwartz, S. H. (1992). The universal content and structure of values: Theoretical advances and empirical tests in 20 countries. In M. Zanna (eds.), *Advances in experimental social psychology* (vol. 25, pp. 1–65). New York: Academic Press.

Scott, A. B. (1997). *Categorizing definitions of religion and spirituality in the psychological literature: A content analytic approach.* Unpublished manuscript. Cited in Hill, P. C., Pargamnet, K. I., Hood, R. W., Jr., McCullough, M. E., Swyers, J. P., Larson, D. B., & Zinnbauer, B. J. (2000). Conceptualizing religion and spirituality: Points of commonality, points of departure. *Journal for the Theory of Social Behavior, 30*, 51–77.

Shek, D. T. L. (1986). The Purpose in Life questionnaire in a Chinese context: Some psychometric and normative data. *Chinese Journal of Psychology, 28*, 51–60.

Shek, D. T. L. (1988). Reliability and factorial structure of the Chinese version of the Purpose in Life Questionnaire. *Journal of Clinical Psychology, 44*, 384–392.

Shek, D. T. L. (1989a). Perceptions of parental treatment styles and psychological well-being in Chinese adolescents. *Journal of Genetic Psychology, 150*, 403–415.

Shek, D. T. L. (1989b). Sex differences in the psychological well-being of Chinese adolescents. *Journal of Psychology, 123*, 405–412.

Shek, D. T. L. (1992). Meaning in life and psychological well-being: An empirical study using the Chinese version of the Purpose in Life Questionnaire. *Journal of Genetic Psychology, 153*, 185–200.

Shek, D. T. L. (1993). Meaning in life and psychological well-being in Chinese college students. *The International Forum for Logotherapy, 16*, 35–42.

Shek, D. T. L. (1994). Meaning in life and adjustment amongst midlife parents in Hong Kong. *The International Forum for Logotherapy, 17*, 102–107.

Shek, D. T. L. (1995a). Mental health of Chinese adolescents in different Chinese societies. *International Journal of Adolescent Medicine and Health, 8*, 117–155.

Shek, D. T. L. (1995b). The relation of family environments to adolescent psychological well-being, school adjustment and problem behavior: What can we learn from the Chinese culture? *International Journal of Adolescent Medicine and Health, 8*, 199–218.

Shek, D. T. L. (1997a). Family environment and adolescent psychological well-being, school adjustment, and problem behavior: A pioneer study in a Chinese context. *Journal of Genetic Psychology, 158*, 113–128.

Shek, D. T. L. (1997b). The relation of family functioning to adolescent psychological well-being, school adjustment, and problem behavior. *Journal of Genetic Psychology, 158*, 467–479.

Shek, D. T. L. (1997c). The relation of parent–adolescent conflict to adolescent psychological well-being, school adjustment, and problem behavior. *Social Behavior and Personality, 25*, 277–290.

Shek, D. T. L. (1998a). A longitudinal study of Hong Kong adolescents' and parents' perceptions of family functioning and well-being. *Journal of Genetic Psychology, 159*, 389–403.

Shek, D. T. L. (1998b). A longitudinal study of the relations between parent–adolescent conflict and adolescent psychological well-being. *Journal of Genetic Psychology, 159*, 53–67.

Shek, D. T. L. (1998c). A longitudinal study of the relations of family functioning to adolescent psychological well-being. *Journal of Youth Studies, 1*, 195–209.

Shek, D. T. L. (1998d). Adolescent positive mental health and psychological symptoms: A longitudinal study in a Chinese context. *Psychologia, 41*, 217–225.

Shek, D. T. L. (1999a). Meaning in life and adjustment amongst early adolescents in Hong Kong. *International Forum for Logotherapy, 22*, 36–43.

Shek, D. T. L. (1999b). Paternal and maternal influences on the psychological well-being of Chinese adolescents. *Genetic, Social and General Psychology Monographs, 125*, 269–296.

Shek, D. T. L. (1999c). Parenting characteristics and adolescent psychological well-being: A longitudinal study in a Chinese context. *Genetic, Social and General Psychology Monographs, 125*, 27–44.

Shek, D. T. L. (2000). Parental marital quality and well-being, parent–child relational quality, and Chinese adolescent adjustment. *American Journal of Family Therapy, 28*, 147–162.

Shek, D. T. L. (2001a). Meaning in life and sense of mastery in Chinese adolescents with economic disadvantage. *Psychological Reports, 88*, 711–712.

Shek, D. T. L. (2001b). Resilience in adolescence: Western models and local findings. In Chinese YMCA (ed.), *Centennial Conference on counseling in China, Taiwan and Hong Kong* (pp. 3–21). Hong Kong: The Chinese YMCA of Hong Kong.

Shek, D. T. L. (2002a). Assessment of family functioning in Chinese adolescents: The Chinese Family Assessment Instrument. In N. N. Singh, T. H. Ollendick, & A. N. Singh (eds.), *International perspectives on child and adolescent mental health* (vol. 2, pp. 297–316). Amsterdam, The Netherlands: Elsevier.

Shek, D. T. L. (2002b). Family functioning and psychological well-being, school adjustment, and problem behavior in Chinese adolescents with and without economic disadvantage. *Journal of Genetic Psychology, 163*, 497–502.

Shek, D. T. L. (2002c). Interpersonal support and conflict and adjustment of Chinese adolescents with and without economic disadvantage. In S. P. Shohov (ed.), *Advances in psychology research* (vol. 18, pp. 63–82). New York: Nova Science Publishers.

Shek, D. T. L. (2002d). Psychometric properties of the Chinese version of the Family Awareness Scale. *Journal of Social Psychology, 142*, 61–72.

Shek, D. T. L. (2002e). The relation of parental qualities to psychological well-being, school adjustment, and problem behavior in Chinese adolescents with economic disadvantage. *American Journal of Family Therapy, 30*, 215–230.

Shek, D. T. L. (2003a). A longitudinal study of parenting and adolescent adjustment in Chinese adolescents with economic disadvantage. *International Journal of Adolescent Medicine and Health, 15*, 39–49.

Shek, D. T. L. (2003b). Economic stress, psychological well-being and problem behavior in Chinese adolescents with economic disadvantage. *Journal of Youth and Adolescence, 32*, 259–266.

Shek, D. T. L. (2003c). Family functioning and psychological well-being, school adjustment, and substance abuse in Chinese adolescents: Are findings based on multiple studies consistent? In S. P. Shohov (ed.), *Advances in psychology research* (vol. 20, pp. 163–184). New York: Nova Science Publishers.

Shek, D. T. L. (2004). Chinese cultural beliefs about adversity: Its relationship to psychological well-being, school adjustment and problem behavior in Hong Kong adolescents with and without economic disadvantage. *Childhood, 11*, 63–80.

Shek, D. T. L. (2005a). A longitudinal study of Chinese cultural beliefs about adversity, psychological well-being, delinquency and substance abuse in Chinese adolescents with economic disadvantage. *Social Indicators Research, 71*, 385–409.

Shek, D. T. L. (2005b). A longitudinal study of perceived family functioning and adolescent adjustment in Chinese adolescents with economic disadvantage. *Journal of Family Issues, 26*, 518–543.

Shek, D. T. L. (2005c). Paternal and maternal influences on the psychological well-being, substance abuse, and delinquency of Chinese adolescents experiencing economic disadvantage. *Journal of Clinical Psychology, 61*, 219–234.

Shek, D. T. L. (2005d). Perceived parental control processes, parent–child relational qualities, and psychological well-being in Chinese adolescents with and without economic disadvantage. *Journal of Genetic Psychology, 166*, 171–188.

Shek, D. T. L. (2006a). Construction of a positive youth development project in Hong Kong. *International Journal of Adolescent Medicine and Health, 18*, 299–302.

Shek, D. T. L. (2006b). Effectiveness of the Tier 1 Program of the Project P.A.T.H.S.: Preliminary objective and subjective outcome evaluation findings. *The Scientific World JOURNAL, 6*, 1466–1474.

Shek, D. T. L. (2006c). Perceived parent–child relational qualities and parental behavioral and psychological control in Chinese adolescents in Hong Kong. *Adolescence, 41*, 563–581.

Shek, D. T. L. (2007). A longitudinal study of perceived parental psychological control and psychological well-being in Chinese adolescents in Hong Kong. *Journal of Clinical Psychology, 63*, 1–22.

Shek, D. T. L. (ed.). (2008). Special issue: Evaluation of Project P.A.T.H.S. in Hong Kong. *TheScientificWorldJOURNAL:TSW Holistic Health & Medicine, 8*, 1–94

Shek, D. T. L. (in press). Life meaning and purpose in life among Chinese adolescents: What can we learn from Chinese studies in Hong Kong? In P. Wong (ed.), *Human quest for meaning*. Hillsdale, NJ: Erlbaum.

Shek, D. T. L., Chan, L. K., & Lee, T. Y. (1997). Parenting styles, parent–adolescent conflict and psychological well-being of adolescents with low academic achievement in Hong Kong. *International Journal of Adolescent Medicine and Health, 9*, 233–247.

Shek, D. T. L., Chan, Y. K., & Lee, P. (eds.)(2005). *Social Indicators Research Series (vol. 25): Quality of life research in Chinese, Western and global contexts*. Amsterdam, The Netherlands: Springer.

Shek, D. T. L., Han, X. Y., & Lee, B. M. (2006). Perceived parenting patterns and parent–child relational qualities in adolescents in Hong Kong and Shanghai. *Chinese Journal of Sociology, 26*, 137–157.

Shek, D. T. L., Hong, E. W., & Cheung, M. Y. P. (1987). The Purpose in Life Questionnaire in a Chinese context. *Journal of Psychology, 121*, 77–83.

Shek, D. T. L., Lam, M. C., Lam, C. M., & Tang, V. (2004). Perceptions of present, ideal, and future lives among Chinese adolescents experiencing economic disadvantage. *Adolescence, 39*, 779–792.

Shek, D. T. L., Lam, M. C., Lam, C. M., Tang, V., Tsoi, K. W., & Tsang, S. (2003). Meaning of life and adjustment among Chinese adolescents with and without economic disadvantage. In T. A. Prester (ed.), *Psychology of adolescents* (pp. 167–183). New York: Nova Science Publishers.

Shek, D. T. L. & Lee, T. Y. (2005). Hopelessness in Chinese adolescents in Hong Kong: Demographic and family correlates. *International Journal of Adolescent Medicine and Health, 17*, 279–290.

Shek, D. T. L. & Lee, T. Y. (2007). Perceived parental control processes, parent–child relational qualities and psychological well-being of Chinese adolescents in intact and non-intact families in Hong Kong. *International Journal of Adolescent Medicine and Health, 19*, 167–175.

Shek, D. T. L., Lee, T. Y., Siu, A. M. H., & Ma, H. K. (2007). Convergence of subjective outcome and objective outcome evaluation findings: Insights based on the Project P.A.T.H.S. *The Scientific World Journal, 7*, 258–267.

Shek, D. T. L. & Ma, H. K. (2006). Design of a positive youth development program in Hong Kong. *International Journal of Adolescent Medicine and Health, 18*, 315–327.

Shek, D. T. L., Ma, H. K., & Cheung, P. C. (1994). Meaning in life and adolescent antisocial and pro-social behavior in a Chinese context. *Psychologia, 37*, 211–218.

Shek, D. T. L. & Mak, J. W. K. (1987). *Psychological well-being of working parents in Hong Kong: Mental health, stress and coping responses*. Hong Kong: Hong Kong Christian Service.

Shek, D. T. L., Siu, A., & Lee, T. Y. (2007). The Chinese Positive Youth Development Scale: A validation study. *Research on Social Work Practice, 17*, 380–391.

Shek, D. T. L. & Sun, R. C. F. (2007). Subjective outcome evaluation of the Project PATHS: Qualitative findings based on the experiences of program implementers. *TheScientificWorldJOURNAL, 7*, 1024–1035.

Shek, D. T. L. & Sun, R. C. F. (in press). Development, implementation and evaluation of a holistic positive youth development program: Project P.A.T.H.S. in Hong Kong. *International Journal of Disability and Human Development.*

Shek, D. T. L., Tang, V. M. Y., & Han, X. Y. (2005). Evaluation of evaluation studies using qualitative research methods in the social work literature (1990–2003): Evidence that constitutes a wake-up call. *Research on Social Work Practice, 15*, 180–194.

Shek, D. T. L., Tang, V., Lam, C. M., Lam, M. C., Tsoi, K. W., & Tsang, K. M. (2003). The relationship between Chinese cultural beliefs about adversity and psychological adjustment in Chinese families with economic disadvantage. *American Journal of Family Therapy, 31*, 427–443.

Shek, D. T. L., Tsoi, K. W., Lau, P. S. Y., Tsang, S. K. M., Lam, M. C., & Lam, C. M. (2001). Psychological well-being, school adjustment and problem behavior in Chinese adolescents: Do parental qualities matter? *International Journal of Adolescent Medicine and Health, 13*, 231–243.

Shih, F. J., Gau, M. L., Lin, Y. S., Pong, S. J., & Lin, H. R. (2006). *Nursing Ethics, 13*, 360–375.

Sinnott, J. D. (2001). 'A time for the condor and the eagle to fly together': Relations between spirit and adult development in healing techniques in several cultures. *Journal of Adult Development, 8*, 241–247.

Siu, A. M. H. & Shek, D. T. L. (2005). Relations between social problem solving and indicators of interpersonal and family well-being among Chinese adolescents in Hong Kong. *Social Indicators Research, 71*, 517–539.

Smith, G. (2006). The five elements and Chinese-American mortality. *Health Psychology, 25*, 124–129.

Smith, H. N. (1989). Ancestor practices in contemporary Hong Kong: Religious ritual or social custom? *The Asia Journal of Theology, 3*, 31–45.

Snyder, S. (2006). Chinese traditions and ecology: Survey article. *Worldviews, 10*, 100–134.

Song, X. C. & Jin, S. H. (2004). A research on the present situation of spiritual belief of university students. *Psychological Science, 27*, 1010–1012.

Song, X. C. & Yue, G. A. (2006). A research of 861 university students on the correlation between spiritual belief and coping style. *Chinese Mental Health Journal, 20*, 104–106.

Stewart, S. M., Felice, E., Claassen, C., Kennard, B. D., Lee, P. W. H., & Emslie, G. J. (2006). Adolescent suicide attempters in Hong Kong and the United States. *Social Science and Medicine, 63*, 296–306.

Sun, R. C. F. & Lau, P. S. Y. (2006). Beliefs in the future as a positive youth development construct: Conceptual bases and implications for curriculum development. *International Journal of Adolescent Medicine and Health, 18*, 409–416.

Tang, Y. Y., Ma, Y. H., Wang, J. H., Fan, Y. X., Feng, S. G., Lu Q. L. et al. (2007). Short-term meditation training improves attention and self-regulation. *PNAS Proceedings of the National Academy of Sciences of the United States of America, 104*, 17152–17156.

Tang, S. T. (2000). Meanings of dying at home for Chinese patients in Taiwan with terminal illness: A literature review. *Cancer Nursing, 23*, 367–370.

Tang, C. S. K., Wu, A. M. S., & Yan, E. C. W. (2002). Psychosocial correlates of death anxiety among Chinese college students. *Death Studies, 26*, 491–499.

The Hong Kong Federation of Youth Groups. (1993). *Young people's perception of superstition and destiny.* Hong Kong: The Hong Kong Federation of Youth Groups.

The Hong Kong Federation of Youth Groups. (1997). *Young people's outlook on life.* Hong Kong: The Hong Kong Federation of Youth Groups.

The Hong Kong Federation of Youth Groups. (2000). *Young people's outlook on life (II).* Hong Kong: The Hong Kong Federation of Youth Groups.

The Hong Kong Federation of Youth Groups. (2008). *Youth trends in Hong Kong 2004–2006.* Hong Kong: The Hong Kong Federation of Youth Groups.

Thompson, I. (2002). Mental health and spiritual care. *Nursing Standard, 17*, 33–38.

Tsang, E. W. K. (2004). Toward a scientific inquiry into superstitious business decision making. *Organization Studies, 25*, 923–946.

Tse, C. Y., Chong, A., & Fok, S. Y. (2003). Breaking bad news: A Chinese perspective. *Palliative Medicine, 17*, 339–343.

Waddell, C. & McNamara, B. (1997). The stereotypical fallacy: A comparison of Anglo and Chinese Australians' thoughts about facing death. *Mortality, 2*, 149–161.

Wall, J. A., Jr & Blum, M. (1991). Community mediation in the People's Republic of China. *Journal of Conflict Resolution, 35*, 3–20.

West, W. (2001). Issues relating to the use of forgiveness in counseling and psychotherapy. *British Journal of Guidance and Counseling, 29*, 415–423.

Wong, W. S. (2004). Attitudes toward life and death among Chinese adolescents: The Chinese version of the Multi-Attitude Suicide Tendency Scale. *Death Studies, 28*, 91–110.

Woo, K. Y. (1999). Care for Chinese palliative patients. *Journal of Palliative Care, 15*, 70–74.

Wu, A. M. S., Tang, C. S. K., & Kwok, T. C. Y. (2002). Death anxiety among Chinese elderly people in Hong Kong. *Journal of Aging and Health, 14*, 42–56.

Yang, K. S. & Ho, D. Y. F. (1988). The role of *yuan* in Chinese social life: A conceptual and empirical analysis. In R. W. Rieber, A. C. Paranjpe, & D. Y. F. Ho (eds.), *Asian contributions to psychology* (pp. 263–281). New York: Praeger.

Xu, W., Towers, A. D., Li, P., & Collet, J. P. (2006). Traditional Chinese medicine in cancer care: Perspectives and experiences of patients and professionals in China. *European Journal of Cancer Care, 15*, 397–403.

Yang, S. C. & Chen, S. F. (2002). A phenomenographic approach to the meaning of death: A Chinese perspective. *Death Studies, 26*, 143–175.

Yang, S. C. & Chen, S. F. (2006). Content analysis of free-response narratives to personal meanings of death among Chinese children and adolescents. *Death Studies, 30*, 217–241.

Yao, X. Z. (2007). Religious belief and practice in urban China 1995–2005. *Journal of Contemporary Religion, 22*, 169–185.

Yick, A. G. & Gupta, R. (2002). Chinese cultural dimensions of death, dying and bereavement: Focus group findings. *Journal of Cultural Diversity, 9*, 32–42.

Yik, M. S. M. & Bond, M. H. (1993). Exploring the dimensions of Chinese person perception with indigenous and imported constructs: Creating a culturally balanced scale. *International Journal of Psychology, 28*, 75–95.

Yip K. S. (2004). Taoism and its impact on mental health of the Chinese communities. *International Journal of Social Psychiatry, 50*, 25–42.

Yuen, M., Hui, E. K. P., Lau, P. S. Y., Gysbers, N. C., Leung, T. K. M., Chan, R. M. C., & Shea, P. M. K. (2006). Assessing the personal-social development of Hong Kong Chinese adolescents. *International Journal for the Advancement of Counseling, 28*, 317–330.

Zhang, J. & Jin, S. H. (1996). Determinants of suicide ideation: A comparative of Chinese and American college students. *Adolescence, 31*, 451–467.

Zhang, J. & Thomas, D. L. (1994). Modernization theory revisited: A cross-cultural study of adolescent conformity to significant others in mainland China, Taiwan and the USA. *Adolescence, 29*, 885–903.

Zhuo, X. P. (2003). Research on religions in the People's Republic of China. *Social Compass, 50*, 441–448.

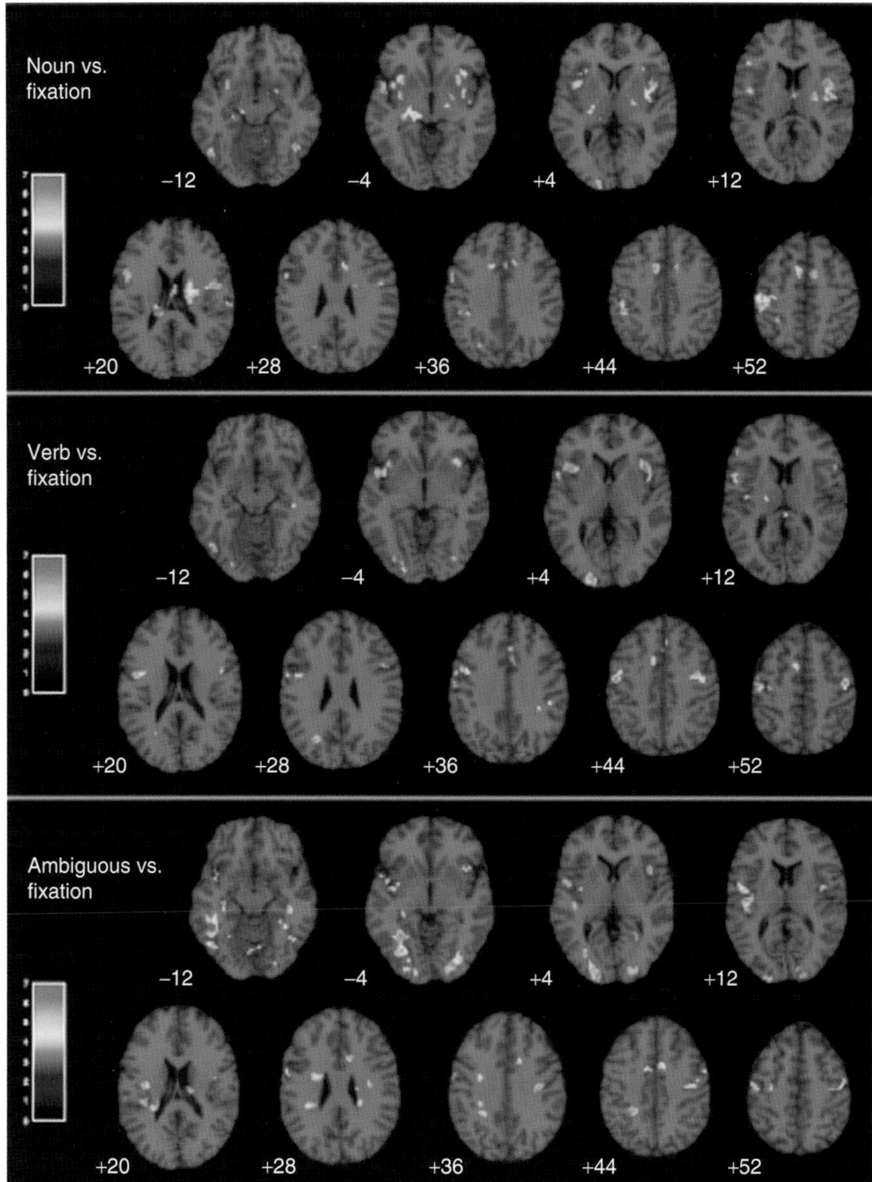

Fig. 6.7 Averaged brain activations for nouns versus fixations, verbs versus fixations, and class-ambiguous words versus fixations. No significant differences were found between nouns, verbs, and ambiguous words.

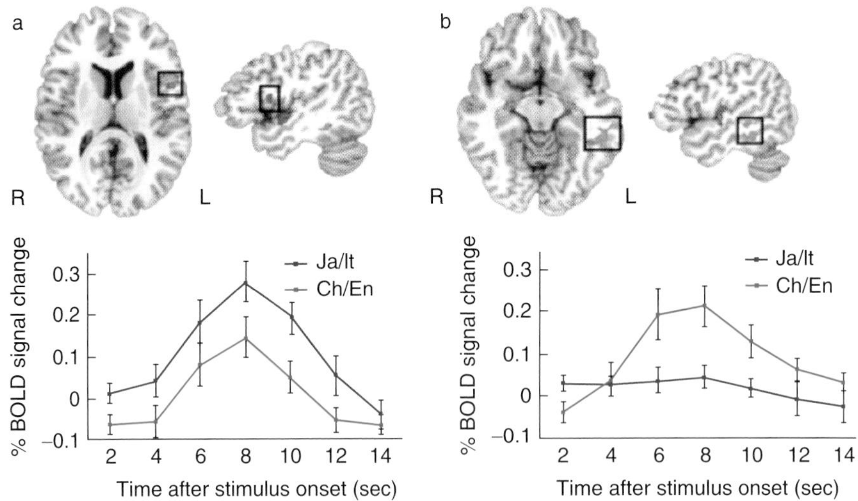

Fig. 6.8 Selected brain regions showing significant activation differences between familiar (Chinese/English) and unfamiliar (Italian/Japanese) stimulus conditions in the language discrimination task. Activation maps and time-course results indicate that (a) unfamiliar languages elicited stronger activations than familiar languages in the left inferior frontal gyrus (IFG), while (b) familiar languages elicited stronger activations than unfamiliar languages in the left inferior temporal gyrus (ITG). Error bars indicate standard errors of the mean (see Zhao et al, 2008).

CHAPTER 22

Psychiatric disorders in the Chinese

Sunita Mahtani Stewart, Peter W. H. Lee, and Rongrong Tao

Summarizing the recent advances in Chinese psychiatry in a single chapter is a daunting task. There has been an explosion of increasingly sophisticated studies in the last fifteen years. The authors of this chapter have selected a few areas to cover that are particularly relevant to the student of cross-cultural psychology, but we are keen to acknowledge that many worthy subjects have not been considered adequately, or even at all. We have hoped not just to describe some of the key findings, but also to consider and discuss these findings within the broader frameworks of understanding the changes that are currently taking place in Chinese societies. This chapter begins with a discussion of the diagnostic frameworks developed and employed in China with a focus on the conceptual similarities to and differences from both the DSM-IV and the ICD-10. This analysis is followed by a review of mental disorders in China with specific discussions on several disorders/phenomena with culture-specific manifestations, including depression, eating disorders, and suicide. Next, a review of treatment and outcomes is presented, and then our chapter concludes with a discussion of stigma of mental illness and help-seeking in China.

Diagnostic frameworks

The Chinese Classification of Mental Disorders (CMCD), a nosological system which captures locally recognized psychiatric disorders, is now in its third revision (Chinese Psychiatric Society, 2001). Few such systems exist outside the West. This revision incorporates the structure of widely used diagnostic systems such as the DSM-IV and ICD-10, and attempts to converge with their diagnoses as far as possible, thereby making it maximally accessible to international practitioners and researchers. However, it has also been developed to describe presentations that may not have parallels outside China, and to exclude diagnostic categories that are considered irrelevant in China (Y. F. Chen, 2002). The system has been guided by an etiological focus and an interest in clear description of the symptoms that form the syndromes described (S. Lee, 2001a).

In the description of the third revision (Y. F. Chen, 2002), the interest in brevity, practicality, and a structure that allows comparisons to international systems but also 'meets the needs of Chinese society' has been made explicit. A respect for Chinese norms, avoidance of stigma, and avoidance of over-medicalization of life choices has also guided this system (Charland, 2007; S. Lee, 2001a). The revision is based on systematic observation of over 1,500 adults and 750 adolescents with mental illness in mainland China, and draws on the work of 114 psychiatrists in 41 in- and outpatient settings (Y. F. Chen, 2002). For discussion of some specific differences in classification criteria between the CMCD-3 and the DSM-IV/ICD-10, see S. Lee (2001).

Personality disorders have been excluded from the CMCD-3, because many aspects of these disorders are seen as social behaviors that are either very common given the cultural dynamics of Chinese society, or are seen as 'moral choices'. For example, pathological gambling is not included because it is considered a poor life choice rather than a medical condition (S. Lee, 2001a).

Furthermore, borderline personality disorder (BPD) does not appear in the CMCD-3 because efforts to avoid abandonment would be very common in Chinese culture and medicalization of such behaviors as well as impulsivity would result in stigmatization of common patterns (Charland, 2007). However, there is some disagreement with this decision. F. Leung and collaborators (Zhong & Leung, 2007; S. Leung & Leung, in press) have argued that BPD is present in the Chinese population and that impulsive personality disorder, a personality disorder included in the CCMD-3, overlaps with BPD as described in the DSM diagnostic system. They further argued that the resistance among Chinese clinicians towards including a BPD diagnostic category is based on clinical opinion rather than empirical evidence (Zhong & Leung 2007). Although research on BPD is scarce among the Chinese population, emerging empirical evidence found that measurement derived from the BPD criteria of the DSM-IV has a similar factor structure in the Chinese population as in Western samples (S. Leung & Leung in press; J. Yang, McCrae, Costa et al., 2000; J. Yang, Bagby, Costa et al., 2002). It is recommended that a future edition of the CCMD include BPD as one of the diagnostic categories of personality disorders (Zhong & Leung, 2007).

Also of interest for the student of cross-cultural psychiatry are the writings of Sing Lee. He has traced the relationships among some of the diagnoses and current and past sociocultural influences that provide insight to the development of syndromatic expression of distress and of classification systems. S. Lee (1998) and his colleagues point out that classification schemes for psychiatric diagnoses are particularly vulnerable to sociocultural influences, and as such may serve 'diverse purposes for different parties' (S. Lee & Kleinman, 2007, p. 846). S. Lee (2002) has also pointed out the challenges that face classification systems that seek to claim universal relevance. In addition to the value of a system that incorporates both worldwide categories and those that are salient in local contexts, these systems need to be useful to meet the growing public health needs created by high rates of mental illness in areas where psychiatrists are few and far between. S. Lee points out that diagnosis influences how people think about their illness experience, and the excessive complexity of the nosology and promotion of stigma by the terminology may serve as barriers to treatment.

Several symptom categories in the CMCD-3, including neurasthenia, mental disorder due to *qi gong*, koro, and traveling psychosis are specific to Chinese or Asian culture. Neurasthenia or *shenjing shuairuo* is perhaps the best known Chinese psychiatric disorder variant. This diagnosis, first described as 'neurasthenia' in the United States in the 1800s has disappeared in the DSM-IV and is considered as a 'culture-bound syndrome', but is maintained in the ICD-10. In the most recent version of the CMCD, the CMCD-3, neurasthenia is classified under Neurotic Disorders, and requires three of the following groups of persistent symptoms: physical or mental fatigue or weakness, irritability or worry, excitability, 'nervous pain', and sleep disturbance. It also requires the exclusion of mood and anxiety disorders, a recent accommodation to strive towards convergence with other international classification systems.

Mental disorder due to *qi gong* or *zhou huo ru mo* is an indigenous symptom category included in the CMCD-3. *Qi gong* is a therapeutic practice involving movement and regulated breathing. It is designed to manage the energy field that is proposed to be connected to and maintained by respiration. It is purported to be beneficial at multiple levels, from exercise and relaxation-related stress management to spiritual and moral development. *Qi gong* appears to be widely practiced as a medical technique in traditional Chinese medicine settings. However, it has also been noted to include symptoms of mental disorder, such as somatic discomfort, motor activity, apprehension, tearfulness, irritability, delusions, identity disturbance, hallucinations, mania, depression, and bizarre, violent, and suicidal behaviors (S. Lee, 2001a). S. Lee reports that those symptoms in most cases are short-lasting and require minimal medical attention, and frequently resolve upon discontinuation of the practice. Occasionally, patients are prescribed short courses of tranquilizers.

Koro or *suo yang* is another indigenous symptom category included in the CMCD-3. Affected males believe that their penis is shrinking or retracting and even disappearing and that this phenomenon may result in death because it is the reflection of a dangerous disturbance of the *yin–yang* equilibrium of the organism (Mattelaer & Jilek, 2007). Koro epidemics have been reported in various Chinese (and other Asian) communities, although typically, koro attacks are reported to be acute, brief, and one-time events and most common in young men under 24 years of age (Cheng, 1997).

Traveling psychosis or *lutu jingshenbing* first appeared in the CCMD2-R, an earlier version of the current CMCD-3. It is characterized by transient psychotic symptoms which appear during or shortly after long-distance travel. The symptoms are preceded by mental and physical stress related to the travel, and, with rest, remit within a week after the end of the travel. The symptoms cause serious social-function impairment and frequently threaten social order. It is not diagnosed concurrent with other major psychiatric or medical disorders or substance abuse.

Actuarial approaches to psychopathology overlap only to some extent with psychiatric diagnosis, and so will not be covered in any detail here. However, of note, the instruments developed by Achenbach (the Child Behavior Checklist, the Youth Self-Report Form, and the Teachers' Report Form) have been widely validated in many cultures including with Chinese samples (e.g. Ivanova, Achenbach, Dumenci et al., 2007; Ivanova, Achenbach, Rescorla et al., 2007; P. W. L. Leung et al., 2006; Rescorla et al., 2007). These scales offer a standardized option for recording children's behaviors that obtain comparable information not only from the youths themselves but also from observers.

Prevalence of mental disorders in China

The early epidemiological studies in China in the late 1980s through 1990s (e.g. C. N. Chen et al., 1993; Hwu, Yeh, & Chang, 1989; W. X. Zhang, Shen, & Li, 1998) reported very low levels of psychopathology in Chinese groups compared to those in the West. Two recent large-scale diagnostic surveys of mental illness in the Chinese population using the WHO Composite International Diagnostic Interview or the DSM-IV structured interview (S. Lee, Tsang, Zhang et al., 2007; Shi et al., 2005) have been done since 1996. The Chinese World Mental Health Survey Initiative (S. Lee, Tsang, Zhang et al., 2007) was carried out in conjunction with the WHO World Mental Health Survey Initiative (Demyttenaere et al., 2004), using the WHO Composite International Diagnostic Interview (Kessler & Ustun, 2004). Multi-stage sampling of over 5,000 adults was conducted in Beijing and Shanghai. Lifetime prevalence of any disorder was 13.2 percent, with alcohol abuse (4.7 percent), major depression (3.5 percent) and specific phobia (2.6 percent) being the most common. Projected lifetime risk of any disorder was 18 percent. Rates remained below those reported in the United States, where projected lifetime risk is estimated to be about 46 percent (Kessler, Bergland, Demler, Jin, & Walters, 2005). Age of onset of mood, anxiety, impulse control and substance use was older than for the US population. Nevertheless, these numbers represent an increase over rates previously reported, a higher rate by a factor of four to seven in younger (ages 18–34 years) compared to older participants. Mood disorders in particular were associated with a lifetime risk 20.8 times greater in those born after 1967 than in those born prior to 1967.

Similar prevalence rates were found in another recent epidemiological survey of over 15,000 people in Zhejiang province (Shi et al., 2005) using the Structured Clinical Interview for DSM-IV (First, Spitzer, Gibbon, & Williams, 1996). Lifetime prevalence of any specific disorder was 13.4 percent, with somewhat higher rates in rural than in urban samples. Major depressive disorder (4.3 percent) and alcohol abuse (2.9 percent) were the most common disorders recorded, with a higher prevalence of both in rural than in urban areas.

The explanation for lower rates of psychiatric disorders in past surveys has included 'protective' effects of Chinese culture, such as family cohesiveness, extended adolescence, and low levels of substance use (C. N. Chen et al., 1993; Shen et al., 2006). Chan, Hung, and Yip (2001) have similarly suggested that the Chinese values for conformity, discipline and self-control have led to a lower prevalence of conduct disorders in Chinese communities. S. Lee and colleagues (S. Lee, Lee, Chiu, & Kleinman, 2005) discussed several reasons for the increase in mental disorders noted in the mainland in recent surveys. They speculated that the improved methodology of the recent studies may have reflected the true prevalence rates which were misrepresented in previous surveys. It is also possible that the younger generation may be more open-minded and less affected by stigma, thus more likely to report mental illness than older generations in previous surveys. Furthermore, it is possible that globalization and the significant social and economic changes in China have resulted in an increase in mental disorders in the last decade (Chan et al., 2001; S. Lee et al., 2005, S. Lee, Tsang, Zhang et al., 2007). Development has brought new stresses, evidenced by disorders like 'traveling psychosis', suffered by rural peasants from the interior traveling thousands of miles on overcrowded trains to reach economic opportunities (Chan et al., 2001). It seems likely that the higher rate of mental disorder in China found in recent surveys could be a reflection of both improved methodology and actual increases in the occurrence of mental disorders. This increase may be caused by increased psychological stress, an inevitable consequence of the modernization of China.

Diagnostic groupings and phenomena with culture-specific manifestations

Depression

Relatively low rates of depression in Chinese compared to Western groups have been of interest to international psychiatric epidemiologists. A proposed reason for this discrepancy is that Chinese patients may express their depression in forms that are different than those that characterize depression in the West (see Ryder, Yang, & Heini, 2002 for a thorough discussion). Specifically, it has been proposed that somatic symptoms are emphasized in Chinese groups (e.g. Parker, Gladstone, & Chee, 2001), in contrast to 'psychological' symptoms such as feelings of guilt, self-deprecation, suicidal ideation and depressed mood, which are common in Western groups (Marsella, Sartorius, Jablensky, & Fenton, 1985). Kleinman (1982) observed that Chinese patients rarely presented with complaints of depressed mood. However, neurasthenia, characterized by exhaustion, sleep problems, and concentration difficulties, was a common diagnosis. Although these patients did not spontaneously report mood symptoms, they did acknowledge them if specifically asked, and many improved with antidepressant medication.

There have been various definitions of 'somatization' in depression, and different models to explain the phenomenon (Kirmayer, 2001; Ryder et al., 2002). Somatic symptoms may be reported when patients experience somatic and report and recognize no psychological symptoms (the 'repression' hypothesis), experience and report both somatic and psychological symptoms consistent with health and illness models (the 'dualistic versus holistic' model), or experience both symptoms and recognize the predominance of psychological symptoms but choose to emphasize somatic symptoms as socially acceptable when seeking help (the 'stigma avoidance' model).

In fact, there have been few empirical investigations of somatic symptoms that included both Chinese and Western samples. Reports of the Chinese tendency to express symptoms somatically have not typically been based on any variation from a comparison group. Somatic concerns and presentation are actually quite common over the world (Kirmayer, 2001), with rates varying according to culture but also depending on the definition of somatization (Simon, von Korff, Piccinelli, Fullerton, & Ormel, 1999). A recent investigation by Ryder et al. (2008) included not only cross-cultural clinical samples (from Changsha in mainland China, and Euro-Canadians in Toronto, Canada) but also three different methods of symptom assessment. Patients reported their symptoms spontaneously, in structured clinical interviews, and on a self-completed symptom questionnaire. They also reported a) their experience with stigma, and b) their tendency to clearly experience and articulate emotional states, and their tendency to focus on these states. These additional measures allowed the investigators to potentially 'unpackage' culture, i.e. explore hypotheses regarding the mediators for variation across cultures in reports of levels of somatic symptoms.

The investigators found that Chinese patients reported more somatic symptoms on spontaneous reports and in interviews, and Euro-Canadians reported more psychological symptoms on all three methods. Furthermore, the difference between cultures in expression of somatic symptoms was mediated by 'externally-oriented thinking', or the tendency of patients to not focus on internal states.

The authors proposed that these differences should not be pathologized, because they do not reflect a capacity to experience and articulate emotional states, but rather a lack of value for these states. They also emphasized that now it is becoming evident that somatic symptoms are common, the world over, rather than somaticization being unique to Chinese samples. So it would be more appropriate to designate psychologization as a cultural phenomenon specific to the West.

Taking an experiential approach to the symptoms of depression, S. Lee and Kleinman (2007) presented the results of ethnographic interviews with 40 depressed outpatients from a clinic in Guangzhou in mainland China. The investigators coded six additional experiences and expressions. These were:

1. Local expressions that captured the symptoms that are part of the nosological system, e.g. *menmenbule* or 'bored and unhappy' for anhedonia and *sixiang hunluan* or 'brain confused' for concentration problems.
2. Embodied emotional experiences which combined affective symptoms with bodily experiences, typically those involving the heart, such as *xinfan* ('heart vexed') or *xintong* ('heart pain').
3. Social disharmony, or terms that indicated stress in personal relationships, such as *fanzao*, which means 'vexed and shaken'. These terms are usually not recognized as being indicative of depressive syndromes, but given the core importance of relationships in Chinese culture, it is not surprising that they emerge as an important part of the depressive experience.
4. Pre-verbal pain: many patients found it difficult to articulate their pain, calling it indescribable, or using related terms such as *xinku* or 'hardship'.
5. Implicit communication of deep sadness. For many patients, the term 'sadness' was not spontaneously used. As a matter of fact, when they were specifically asked if they felt sad, they expressed surprise that it had not been understood.
6. Centrality of sleeplessness. Even though many patients described their insomnia as following environmental stressors, they conceptualized their problems as being caused by insomnia rather than insomnia being a symptom of their difficulties.

S. Lee and Kleinman's (2007) study makes a significant practical and theoretical contribution to the literature on depression. It gives a glimpse to the non-Chinese clinician as to the experience of the depressed Chinese patient. It offers information for training Chinese practitioners seeking to improve their ability to recognize depressed patients. It has implications for epidemiologists, because it illustrates the difficulties of capturing diagnoses by using standardized instruments developed in the West and administered by trained non-clinicians.

The relationship between depression and *shenjing shuairuo* (neurasthenia) has received some attention. Patients who present with medically unexplained chronic fatigue in Hong Kong (S. Lee, Tsang, & Kwok, 2000) and the mainland (Chan, Yip, Au, & Lee, 2005), and also show symptoms of mood disorders, tend to show more functional impairment than those who meet the criteria for *shenjing shuairuo*. This suggests that *shenjing shuairuo* represents a mixture of sub-threshold symptoms. *Shenjing shuairuo* was the Chinese translation for neurasthenia, itself identified in the West in 1869, and was introduced into China in 1902, quickly becoming one of the most commonly diagnosed psychiatric disorders in China by the 1980s. More recently, many patients who present with symptoms that would have qualified for the diagnosis of *shenjing shuairuo* no longer meet criteria, because of the required exclusion of mood and anxiety disorders by CMCD-3 to make the manual consistent with the DSM-IV and ICD-10. It has been proposed that a number of indigenous disorders have now been captured under the umbrella of 'depression' (S. Lee, 2002).

S. Lee and Kleinman (2007) provide an interesting analysis of sociocultural changes that parallel the 'transformation' of *shenjing shuairuo* to depression. Chang et al. (2005) have proposed that despite nosological changes in the diagnosis, many patients who present with mood and mild somatic complaints in rural areas seek help in neurology departments, because of semantic connections between the disorder and the term for neurology, *shenjing ke*. Treatment-seeking in departments of neurology on the part of patients for *shenjing shuairuo* or 'weakness of nerves' is less stigmatizing than for a psychiatric diagnosis of mood disorders. Reclassification of these presentations as psychiatric disorders may have a negative effect on treatment-seeking.

Eating disorders

Eating disorders were once considered a 'culture-bound' phenomenon. In the early 1990s, Sing Lee began to report on the presence of anorexia nervosa or *yan shi zheng* in Chinese women. By 2001, he reported that his clinic received referrals at the rate of about one per week by 2000, a substantial increase from two a year a decade prior (S. Lee, 2001b). In his early papers he noted that these disorders had not been documented before, and they reflected either increased prevalence or greater awareness of the diagnosis among Western-trained psychiatrists in Hong Kong. He also noted that there were several differences in characteristics between Chinese and Western anorexic patients. Specifically, most Chinese patients were from a lower socio-economic class. Furthermore many patients described their rationale for food avoidance as gastric distress ('bloating') rather than a desire to lose weight. Finally, most of these patients did not express dissatisfaction with their bodies. S. Lee and Hsu (1993) went on to explore changes in the presentation of anorexia in Western accounts, noting that the presentation of 'fat phobia', now a required symptom for the diagnosis of anorexia nervosa, only appeared more recently. They highlighted the potential opportunity to examine the culture-general and culture-specific manifestations of this psychiatric disorder by examining these symptoms. More recently, S. Lee (2001b) has proposed that fat phobia, rather than being a core symptom in anorexia nervosa, may be a culture-specific, Western manifestation of the disturbance.

The presence of body dissatisfaction is higher in communities exposed to Western media and values than in more traditional communities, as shown in studies in three Chinese communities (S. Lee & Lee, 2000), illustrating that preoccupation with the body is influenced by cultural change. Katzman and Lee (1997) further proposed that fear of loss of control rather than fear of fat is the critical underlying factor in disordered eating. In this view, eating disturbances are a manifestation of need for control, and excessive self-control, as a result of feelings of powerlessness (S. Lee, 2001b).

The methodology of most epidemiological studies of eating disorders outside the West typically presupposes that the DSM-IV has captured universal core symptoms of psychopathology. As a result, in cultures where fat phobia is not a usual manifestation, errors are likely to be made in estimates of prevalence. Thus, S. Lee's observations of Chinese patients have also raised awareness of the pitfalls in current diagnostic systems developed out of one cultural tradition.

Suicide

There are certain unique characteristics of suicide patterns in China, specifically a particularly high suicide rate, higher relative deaths among women compared to men than anywhere else, use of particularly lethal means, and higher rural than urban ratios for completed suicide (Ji, Kleinman, & Becker, 2001; Qin & Mortensen, 2001). There has been some speculation regarding whether individuals who commit suicide in China suffer as frequently from mental disorders as has been indicated in Western studies. The national psychological autopsy study has provided considerable new information regarding the characteristics of 1,608 randomly selected individuals whose deaths were recorded as occurring as a result of suicide, injury, or mental illness over a three-to-five-year period in 23 geographically representative sites in China (Phillips et al., 2002, 2007; Conner et al., 2005, G.H. Yang et al., 2005, J. Zhang, Conwell, Zhou, & Jiang, 2004).

Suicide is the fifth leading cause of death in China, and the leading cause of death for individuals between age 15 and 34 years (Centers for Disease Control and Prevention, 2004; World Health Organization, 2003). In some parts of China, for example Hong Kong, there was a 50 percent increase in completed suicides between 1997 and 2003 (C. N. Chen et al., 2006). This increase appears to be related to specific stressors, i.e. those related to the economic downturn following the handover in 1997.

Several theories have been proposed to explain the high rate of suicides in the Chinese population. There are no strong moral taboos against suicide in China (Miller, 2006). Choice of lethal means such as pesticides and jumping from heights means that impulsive attempts, which may not otherwise have resulted in death, have fatal consequences (Conner et al., 2005; Eddleston & Gunnell, 2006). Widespread media publicity about charcoal burning, a method that was used first in 1998, has been proposed as responsible for a 20 percent increase in suicide rates in Hong Kong and Taiwan between 1997 and 2002 (K. Y. Liu et al., 2007).

Even though elderly suicide rates are high the world over, rates of elderly suicide are dramatically higher in rural China (93.2 per 100,000) compared to English-speaking countries where the highest rate is in Australia (7.6 per 100,000) (Pritchard & Baldwin, 2002). This finding presents a contrast to the traditional Chinese value of reverence for the elderly. A case-controlled autopsy study in Hong Kong revealed that 86 percent of elderly patients who had completed suicide, but only nine percent of matched controls, had psychiatric disorders (Chiu et al., 2004). Higher completed suicide rates in rural areas are distinctive to mainland China (Ji et al., 2001). In the case of both elderly (Chiu et al., 2004) and rural suicide (Jianlin, 2000), the lack of mental health services has been proposed as responsible for the elevated rate.

The paradox that depressive disorders are less frequent in China but suicide rates are higher has received some attention. Phillips et al. (2007) investigated whether limitations of Western categorization instruments contribute to the perception of a larger gap between psychiatric diagnosis and completed suicide in autopsy studies. They found that wording adaptations increased the number of autopsy-based diagnoses of individuals who had committed suicide from 26 percent to 40 percent. They retained the core structure of the instrument and the actual symptoms necessary, adding primarily wording revisions and culturally sensitive probes.

A contrasting point of view offers that psychiatric disorders are in fact less common in China among individuals who complete suicide than in the West. G. H. Yang and colleagues (2005) reported that based on their psychological autopsy study of 893 suicide victims, a substantial portion (37 percent) did not suffer from diagnosed mental illness.

Phillips et al. (2007) propose that the 'paradox' may be related to the categorical method of determining the presence of disorders. Categorical diagnoses have been used in epidemiological studies, and individuals with significant sub-threshold pathology are not counted as having psychiatric disturbance. However, in Chinese groups as in the West (Stewart et al., 2002), high levels of sub-threshold symptoms reflect equivalent degrees of dysfunction as does diagnosed disorder. Phillips et al. (2007) similarly found that among suicide completers who did not meet criteria for depression, many had shown enough distress at sub-threshold levels that they would have merited treatment. When dimensional measures rather than categorical diagnoses were used, several investigators have reported that high depressive symptoms in the time before death distinguished between individuals who attempted or committed suicide and controls (Li, Phillips, Zhang, Xu, & Yang, 2008; X. Liu, Sun & Yang, 2008; Phillips et al., 2002). These findings highlight the value of using dimensional measures of depression rather than categorical diagnosis, when considering populations designated for preventive efforts.

The sex ratio in China's rural suicide rate has attracted some interest, as there are few areas in the world where women complete suicide more frequently than do men. The low status of women has been suggested as responsible for this sex ratio being different from elsewhere (J. Zhang, Jia, Jiang, & Sun, 2006). Young women in rural areas had the highest rate of ingestion of pesticides, the highest acute stress prior to the event, and low prevalence of mental illness compared to their counterparts in urban areas and to rural and urban males who completed suicide (G. H. Yang et al., 2005).

Pearson, Phillips, He, and Ji (2002) examining suicide attempters also found high rates of impulsivity and low rates of diagnosable mental illness. The relationship between mental illness and suicide death in adults (G. H. Yang et al., 2005) as well as adolescents (Li et al., 2008) was moderated by gender, such that males who committed suicide were more likely to have a psychiatric disorder. Of interest as well have been the data indicating that impulsivity plays a major role in suicide attempts, particularly in women (Conner et al., 2005), and the availability of lethal methods may be responsible for the unusual sex ratio (Pearson et al., 2002). In examination of suicides and attempted suicides between 1990 and 2002, the Centers for Disease Control and Prevention (2004) reported that more than half of deaths in China were caused by ingesting pesticide, and 45 percent of suicide attempts were impulsive acts performed after considering suicide for less than ten minutes. Most deaths resulted from unsuccessful medical resuscitation (G. H. Yang et al., 2005).

In summary therefore, high intent to die appears to play an important role in lethal deaths. Several investigators have noted that high acute stress appears to be an alternative path than psychopathology to a fatal attempt, and women who make attempts frequently suffer severe acute stress and select lethal methods to end their lives in areas with poor medical resources for resuscitation.

Treatment and outcomes

Psychiatric treatment in Chinese cultures has been developed closely in tandem with the prevailing beliefs about psychopathology and mental illnesses. For example, given the previous association of mental disorders with incorrect political thinking (Bond, 1991), the social stigma of mental disorders was accentuated. Treatments were put forth in the form of rectification and correction of faulty thinking and conducted in a highly authoritarian manner. The therapeutic focus seemed to be geared towards retraining rather than care and support. Psycho-education, applied in a much stricter and regimented manner, is readily accepted and practiced in Chinese culture as a form of intervention, e.g. in treating drug addiction. The intense stigma attached to mental illnesses may play a role in the preference for the Chinese to present psychological and mental distresses in the form of physical symptoms (Chang, Myers et al., 2005). F. Cheung (2004) noted in her study that, expectedly, patients who used only somatic concepts were least likely to use mental health resources for their mental problems. Yet, in a study on elderly Chinese living in Macau, Da-Canhota and Piterman (2001) cautioned that 'awareness of somatic presentation of psychological illness is crucial in detecting depression in this and possibly other Chinese populations'.

However, with growing integration of China with the rest of the world, greater experimentation and acceptance of Western ideas, including those on mental illnesses, are becoming more evident. In China, psychological disorders have become more widely accepted as witnessed through popular television and radio shows on psychotherapy and alleviation of various 'problems in living', as Szasz (2007) termed them. A growing portion of individuals afflicted with various mental ailments are coming out to talk about their experiences and openly seeking professional help from local experts who are increasingly acquainted with and sometimes trained in Western traditions.

As described earlier in the chapter, the local psychiatric nosological system has been developed to be closely compatible with Western systems of diagnosis. In the recent WHO-coordinated study on the long-term course and outcome of schizophrenia, Beijing participated actively as one of the collaborative research centers (C. Chen & Shen, 2007), and had no difficulties recruiting and successfully following up on schizophrenic patients to trace their long-term course and outcome. Indeed, with standardized diagnostic and inclusion criteria aligned with those of Western psychiatry, these researchers were able to show that the outcomes of Chinese schizophrenic patients are not qualitatively different from those of the West.

Using a highly descriptive title to their paper—'Letting a thousand flowers bloom: Counseling and psychotherapy in the People's Republic of China'—Chang, Tong, Shi, and Zeng (2005) noted with a degree of optimism that Western modules of psychological intervention among the Chinese are of good potential. This is particularly so, since with growing liberalization, global media saturation, and commercialism affecting China, the form and contents of psychiatric disorders are getting more in synchrony with those of the West. The rates of depression, anxiety, suicide, violence, and substance abuse have risen correspondingly against the background of weakening of community and social supports, and great competition in the workplace. While retaining their unique Chinese flavor, psychiatric problems and themes have thus become more similar to those in the West.

Despite much Western influence, the family–community–social focus is still a prevalent form of socialization in Chinese families. A prime expectation for children is that they will serve as a safeguard for the parents' old age. There is also the expectation that regardless of the children's eminence and success, parents, in particular the father, are still the dominant people who should 'call the shots' with regard to family matters. Guilt and shame may thus be particularly pertinent in manifestations of mental disorders among the Chinese. Guilt is felt when the person feels that they have violated the family's moral order and are responsible for an undesired outcome or 'loss of face' (DeRivera, 1984). A strong commitment to personal duties is expected.

Guilt, therefore, would emerge when the family's 'child' fails to fulfill his or her duty and obligations towards first the family and second the social order. Shame, on the other hand, relates to the deliberate exposure of the failure, as the person is made to feel the loss of their social standing due to their failings (Creighton, 1988). The Confucian notion of appropriate behaviors and obligations to one's social networks, consisting of king and officials, father and son, husband and wife, brothers/sisters, and friends still constitutes a pervasive form of socialization in the Chinese. Fulfilling such obligations is said to be righteous. Non-fulfillment is shunned and shamed (see Hwang & Han, this volume). The pressure and strain of social expectation and judgment on the Chinese cannot be underestimated in any effective form of mental health interventions. At the same time, this emphasis also informs intervention. Although both interpersonal and personal factors contribute to depressive symptoms, more variance in mood is explained by the quality of relationships than by individual variables, such as self-efficacy, in adolescents from Hong Kong (Stewart et al., 2003).

Given the strict traditional notion of order and obligations as background, Western capitalistic influences and values, firstly on Chinese in Hong Kong and Taiwan, and more recently over the previous decade on the mainland Chinese, are likely to create chaos and conflicts. The contact of cultures is like a meeting of sea and lake water, where each is bound to influence the other, and is influenced in turn. A fine balance between old and new values must be achieved in order to maintain fulfillment and mental well-being. The craving for personal success and advancement has to be balanced with interpersonal harmony and 'proper' righteous behaviors. Hsiao, Klimidis, Minas, and Tan (2006) in documenting the 'cultural attribution of mental health suffering' in Chinese societies emphasized that Chinese people's well-being 'is significantly determined by a harmonious relationship with others in social and cultural context', and cautioned that 'psychotherapy emphasizing an individual's growth and autonomy may ignore the importance of maintaining interpersonal harmony in Chinese culture' (see also Lu, this volume).

Spirituality and the interdependence of human beings with the universe have always played a major role in influencing Chinese values and thoughts (see also Cheng, Lo, & Chio, this volume; Shek, this volume). The prevalent Buddhist notion of 'If you want to know what your previous life is like, look at your current life, and if you want to know what your future life will be like, consider your current deeds and behaviors' has a deep influence on presentations and conceptualizations of mental problems in the Chinese. Mental problems are at times likened to the evil spirits attaching to the individual and requiring some form of penance and spiritual cleansing to regain mental wellbeing.

A case in point was that of a businessman being treated for panic disorder, with typical symptoms of palpitations, dizziness, breathlessness, and abrupt sense of imminent death. Typical cognitive behavioral therapy (CBT) was provided. At the end of the fourth session, he was making good progress, although residual symptoms remained. The patient had by then become comfortable with the cognitive model of panic, but was nevertheless convinced that there was something more to his physical symptoms. Finally, the patient volunteered a history of some 18 years previously, when he and his wife had limited financial means to support themselves His wife became accidentally pregnant. Based on the patient's insistence, the pregnancy was terminated. Now, years later, the patient had become convinced that his deceased 'daughter' had come back to haunt him for taking her life. The remedy for such problems goes beyond typical Western psychotherapy. This patient was finally helped with a combination of CBT in addition to engagement in good deeds, to become a 'better' and 'more loving' person to humankind. His mental health appeared to be linked to repentance and reparation of wrong deeds committed. It is also notable that such traditional Chinese 'cause–effect' conceptions of mental ill health can be readily integrated with the more recent emphasis of positive psychology research (Lyubomirsky, 2008). The basic notion of doing good to redress one's sins is compatible with the happiness literature which emphasizes defocusing on oneself while striving to further the well-being of others as a means to attain happiness (see also Lu, this volume).

While psychiatric treatments developed in the West have generally been used and applied with the Chinese, there are few controlled treatment trials on their efficacy. This is particularly so with psychotherapy where, apart from actual reduction in symptoms, the 'soft' impact, e.g. on quality of life, general sense of well-being, sense of fulfillment and happiness, may be more difficult to quantify (see Lu, this volume). Nonetheless, it is not difficult in locate in the current literature successful claims of applications of Western psychotherapeutic interventions with the Chinese. Wong, Chau, Kwok, and Kwan (2007) reported successful adaptations of CBT groups with patients suffering from chronic physical illness in Hong Kong. However, the group sessions emphasized greater structure, less ambiguity, more directive leadership, and a focus on skills learning. Luk and colleagues (1991) demonstrated that CBT group therapy can be beneficially applied with positive results on individuals with depressive, neurotic, adjustment and personality problems.

Lin (2002) advocated that the CBT approach is suitable for use with the Chinese, given their expectations of counselors to be 'directive, paternalistic, nurturing, and emphatic leaders'. Cognitive behavior therapies fit well into the expected role in that they tend to focus more on offering information and advice (psycho-education), as well as solving problems and suggesting solutions (e.g. use of behavioral experiments, learning of skills) than do therapies guided by psychodynamic models. Cognitions that underlie mood appear to be common to Chinese groups (Stewart et al., 2004, 2005), providing a theoretical rationale for cognitive interventions. G. Cheung and Chan (2002) quite rightly pointed out that Chinese are less emotionally focused, and may benefit from a more structured approach in therapy to channel their emotions. The cultural exposures comprising concrete, well-structured, and hierarchical situations with well-defined roles are thus compatible with the processes of CBT. The CBT approach may also be useful in that those Chinese patients who tend to adhere too rigidly to social norms may benefit from a gentle challenge to their extreme ('irrational') assumptions (see Ellis & Bernard, 1985), thereby achieving a softening or restructuring of their cognitions to make allowance for both themselves as well as the greater society in which they reside. Hsiao, Lin, Liao, and Lai (2004) successfully used a 'focused, structured therapy group' with their Chinese patients, emphasing initially the establishment of a 'pseudo-kin' or 'own people' relationship amongst group members and then therapeutically focusing on interpersonal relationships and interpersonal problems.

In an interesting paper entitled, 'Would Confucius benefit from psychotherapy?' Hodges and Oei (2007) noted a number of instances of conceptual relationship and compatibility of the Chinese culture with CBT, including aspects such as individualism–hierarchy, individualism–assertion, discipline–assertion, and orderly autonomy. These features are generally consistent with CBT therapeutic processes which emphasize structure and direction, teaching of skills, emphasis on homework, focus on present/future experiences, information provision, and cognitive processes relating to work on irrational beliefs and thoughts. During therapy, various modifications may be required. For example, the therapist would need to assert him or herself as the expert in therapy, yet in order not to undermine the patient's own sense of importance, the patient would be framed as being the expert in their own life. A longer period of time in treatment is also anticipated to manage the delicate balance between maintaining the central role of parents and the dominant social order, but allowing a cognitive construction that also allows questioning of the absolute authority of others to determine the individual's choices, directions, and behaviors.

Stigma: the acceptability of psychological disturbance and help-seeking

Stigma attached to psychological disorders in the Chinese is driven by a number of different factors (see Mak & Chen, this volume). In the following analyses, we wish to point out that apart from stigma, other potent factors may affect the ultimate course and acceptability of help-seeking in general and psychological interventions of patients suffering from mental and psychological difficulties.

Amongst such factors is the nature of the disturbance itself. For example, while psychotic disorders, due to their more florid and unusual presentations, may still be shunned with fear and rejection, individuals with milder forms of emotional disorders are increasingly embracing help. On the other hand, low mental-health literacy and low perceived need may partly explain under-utilization of treatment resources in some cases. However, economic factors may also exert a pivotal influence on help-seeking. As healthcare costs escalate, coupled with the absence by and large of medical insurance coverage in mainland China, individuals most in need may simply be barred from receiving appropriate help, regardless of their willingness to do so.

Although discrimination against and rejection of individuals (and their family members) with severe mental disorders remains prevalent, there has been a shift in terms of acceptance of psychological treatment. The second author was impressed during his teaching tours in different parts of mainland China that quite unexpectedly, patients as well as doctors and therapists were eager to espouse and accept the need for help for emotional disorders. Pharmaceutical interventions for emotional disorders are well accepted and practiced in parallel with use of traditional Chinese medicine. Indeed, mainland China has become a major developing market for leading pharmaceutical industries, resulting in conspicuous representations throughout the mainland. Yet psychological interventions are also eagerly sought, as the limitations of a drug-only treatment for emotional and mental disorders are increasingly acknowledged.

This phenomenon is further illustrated in the findings of a survey on prevalence and needs for treatment of mental disorders conducted in Beijing and Shanghai (Shen et al., 2006), indicating that people with high incomes had a high treatment rate for sub-threshold symptoms or even no symptoms. The same study also noted a significant proportion of individuals with under- or no treatment for moderate and severe disorders over the previous 12 months. The reasons for the discrepancy are likely due to several factors: first, there has been an increase in healthcare costs, and medical insurance coverage is virtually non-existent, barring some individuals from receiving the required treatments; second, milder sub-threshold symptoms are less stigmatizing because they only minimally disrupt society's expected roles, thereby making it more likely that the individual will more openly seek help.

The stigma involved in having an emotional or psychiatric disorder thus seems not entirely dependent on whether the disorder is present, but rather whether the disorder renders one incapable of living up to the standard expected roles and responsibilities assigned by society. Stigma would thus be expected to operate more acutely in disorders which are perceived as adversely affecting one's ability to meet these perceived expectations and/or duties.

A case in point was a young woman who complained of depressed mood and a deep sense of inferiority. On further exploration, in front of an audience of about 100 clinicians and hospital nurses in a Guangzhou hospital setting, the young woman was highly apologetic for her 'disorder', yet was at pains to seek treatment for relief. She worked as a sales girl and thus in her daily work had to interact with people. She noted, however, that on meeting with male clients, she inevitably began to feel that her face as turning red and then noted intense blushing as a result. The more conscious she became of her condition, the more anxious she became, resulting in further and more sustained blushing not only on her face but visibly on her neck as well. The 'curse' for the young woman was the interpretation that by blushing in front of males, she was clearly seen as a 'bad' character in the eyes of others, in that blushing signifies unharnessed sexual desire for any male who comes her way.

Her problem and presentation illustrate two observations: firstly, stigma is intensely attached when symptoms are perceived as leading to violation of a person's ability to live up to society's expectations. In this case, the symptom of blushing was seen as being in direct violation of the woman's Confucian upbringing which placed strong value on personal propriety. Hence the deep sense of guilt and inferiority which explained her need to repeatedly apologize for her symptoms which were not under her control, even in the treatment setting of the hospital. Stigma and self-stigmatization were clearly operational here. Secondly, despite the strong stigma attached to the symptom because of its cultural meaning, the openness to and acceptance of psychological treatment was also very much evident.

Stigma has been noted to be more strongly attached to psychotic disorders in the Chinese. Goffman (1963) first cautioned that stigma 'is deeply discrediting', and the stigmatized person may be reduced 'from a whole and usual person to a tainted, discounted one' (p. 3). Link, Yang, Phelan, and Collins (2004) further noted that labeling, stereotyping, cognitive separation, emotional reactions, status loss, and discrimination may all be involved. In the Chinese, while few studies have been conducted to compare with the West, stigma towards the mentally ill was clearly evident. For example, Chong and colleagues (2007) noted that among Chinese in Singapore, 38 percent of respondents believed that people with mental problems were dangerous and 50 percent felt that the public should be protected from them. P. W. H. Lee et al. (2005) cautioned that stigma against the mentally ill comes not only from society, but that more than 40 percent of patients with schizophrenia perceived stigma and rejection from family members, partners and friends. Clearly, an important reason for stigma to be more strongly attached to psychotic disorders relates to the obvious breakdown in the patient's ability to live up to society's standards and imposed responsibilities.

In the second author's unpublished studies on the long-term course and outcome of schizophrenia, two cohorts of subjects and their parents were recruited at different time periods. The first cohort of subjects had their onset of schizophrenia in 1977/1978, and their long-term course and outcome were traced. The second cohort of schizophrenic subjects was recruited more recently in 2000, and was included in a treatment trial of CBT. In both cohorts studied over a ten-year period there was no difference in the patients' dependence on their families: three-quarters of the patients were reported to be heavily dependent on the support of their families. For both groups, help from neighbors was reported to be nil. Help from other extended family members was also limited, with 6 percent of the older group of schizophrenic patients reporting aid compared to 17 percent in the more recent cohort studied. Fifty-seven percent of the older group and 42 percent of the more recently recruited group of parents felt grief and depression for having a schizophrenic offspring.

The grief and depression, amongst other reasons, originated from the sense of non-fulfillment of one's obligations to have a good son or daughter for the family line. Interestingly, more parents of the older group of schizophrenic patients (23 percent versus 11 percent in those recruited more recently) blamed themselves and believed it was their fault that they had a schizophrenic child. This difference may be attributed to the fact that the older group of parents was much less educated. Fifty-five percent of the older group versus 26 percent of the more recent group reported not knowing any reason for their child's illness. The fact that no reason was known thus mitigated the parents' sense of responsibility and guilt, particularly for the older group. Eight percent of the older group versus 51 percent of the recent group noted that heredity was the cause of the schizophrenic illness. When heredity was regarded as an underlying cause, the stigma perceived by the parents for having a schizophrenic child escalated in parallel, as the parents began to have a reason to blame themselves for their own bad genes, not only for their child's inability to fulfill their societal obligations, but also for the parents' own failure to bring a healthy and contributing member to society.

Conclusion

The cultural, personal, and historical backgrounds of Chinese people are relevant to developments in the nosology of disorders, symptom presentation, treatment formulation, provisions, and planning. The permeating Chinese 'flavor' may be summarized as a family–community–social focus, a balance between social obligations and personal advancement, and the influence of deep-rooted beliefs about life, death, and the circular influence of causation, behaviors, and consequences. Recent exemplary studies and commentaries have advanced knowledge about psychopathology and treatment in Chinese groups using language and concepts understandable to Western scientists. At the same time, these works have also captured that which is unique in Chinese culture. More broadly, they serve as examples of work that capture both the emic and the etic in a culture.

In the same way that Chinese might by influenced by Western values, likewise Western psychological concepts and treatments, both in form and content, may also be profitably influenced by traditional Chinese values and thinking. The growing awareness that relationships are at the core of a fulfilled life, the increasing interest in alternative and traditional medicine, the incorporation of Buddhist meditation techniques such as mindfulness practice into even mainstream therapies, the appearance in intervention techniques of Chinese concepts such as peaceful acceptance of one's situation, building a better life through compassion and care of the greater world of humans and nature about us, respect of authority, tradition and history, might reflect that rapprochement and integration are bidirectional processes.

References

Bond, M. H. (1991). *Beyond the Chinese face: Insights from psychology*. Hong Kong: Oxford University Press.

Centers for Disease Control and Prevention (2004). Suicide and attempted suicide: China, 1990–2002. *Morbidity and Mortality Weekly Report, 53*, 481–484.

Chan, K. P., Hung, S. F., & Yip, P. S. (2001). Suicide in response to changing societies. *Child and Adolescent Psychiatric Clinics of North America, 10*, 777–795.

Chan, K. P., Yip, P. S., Au, J., & Lee, D. T. (2005). Charcoal-burning suicide in post-transition Hong Kong. *British Journal of Psychiatry, 186*, 67–73.

Chang, D. F., Myers, H. F., Yeung, A., Zhang, Y., Zhao, J., & Yu, S. (2005). *Shenjing shuairuo* and the DSM-IV: Diagnosis, distress and disability in a Chinese primary care setting. *Transcultural Psychiatry, 42*, 204–218.

Chang, D. F., Tong, H., Shi, Q., & Zeng, Q. (2005). Letting a thousand flowers bloom: Counseling and psychotherapy in the People's Republic of China. *Journal of Mental Health Counseling, 27*, 104–117.

Charland, L. (2007). Does borderline personality disorder exist? *Canadian Psychiatry Aujourd'hui, 3*. Retrieved March 15, 2008, from http://publications.cpa-apc.org/browse/documents/285

Chen, C. & Shen, Y. (2007). Beijing/China. In K. Hopper, G. Harrison, A. Janca, & N. Sartorius (eds), *Recovery from schizophrenia: An international perspective* (pp. 243–244). Oxford, UK: Oxford University Press.

Chen, C. N., Wong, J., Lee, N., Chan-Ho, M. W., Lau, J. T. F., & Fung, M. (1993). The Shatin community mental health survey in Hong Kong: II. Major Findings. *Archives of General Psychiatry, 50*, 125–133.

Chen, E. Y., Chan, W. S., Wong, P. W., Chan, S. S., Chan, C. L., Law, Y. W., Beh, P. S. et al. (2006). Suicide in Hong Kong: A case-control psychological autopsy study. *Psychological Medicine, 36*, 815–825.

Chen, Y. F. (2002). Chinese classification of mental disorders (CCMD-3): Towards integration in international classification. *Psychopathology, 35*, 171–175.

Cheng, S. T. (1997). Epidemic genital retraction syndrome: Environmental and personal risk factors in southern China. *Journal of Psychology and Human Sexuality, 9*, 57–70.

Cheung, F. (2004). Conceptualization of psychiatric illness and help-seeking behavior among Chinese. *Culture, Medicine and Psychiatry, 11*, 97–106.

Cheung, G. & Chan, C. (2002). The Satir Model and cultural sensitivity: A Hong Kong reflection. *Contemporary Family Therapy, 24*, 199–215.

Chinese Psychiatric Society (2001). *The Chinese classification of mental disorders* (3rd edn). Shandong, China: Shandong Publishing House of Science and Technology. (in Chinese)

Chiu, H. F., Yip, P. S., Chi, I., Chan, S., Tsoh, J., Kwan, C. W. et al. (2004). Elderly suicide in Hong Kong: A case-controlled psychological autopsy study. *Acta Psychiatrica Scandinavica, 109*, 299–305.

Chong, S. A., Verma, S., Gaingankar, J. A., Chan, Y., Wong, L. Y., & Heng, B. H. (2007). Perception of the public towards the mentally ill in developed Asian country. *Social Psychiatry and Psychiatric Epidemiology, 42*, 734–739.

Conner, K. R., Phillips, M. R., Meldrum, S., Knox, K. L., Zhang, Y., & Yang, G. (2005). Low planned suicides in China. *Psychological Medicine, 35*, 1197–1204.

Creighton, M. (1988). Revisiting shame and guilt culture: A forty-year pilgrimage. *Ethos, 18*, 279–307.

Da-Canhota, C. M., & Piterman, L. (2001). Depressive disorders in elderly Chinese patients in Macau: A comparison of general practitioners' consultations with a depression screening scale. *Australian and New Zealand Journal of Psychiatry, 35*, 336–44.

Demyttenaere, K., Bruffaerts, R., Posada-Villa, J., Gasquet, I., Kovess, V., Lepine, J. P. et al. (2004). Prevalence, severity and unmet need for treatment of mental disorders in the World Health Organization World Mental Health Surveys. *Journal of the American Medical Association, 291*, 2581–2590.

DeRivera, J. (1984). The structure of emotional relationships. *Review of Personality and Social Psychology, 5*, 116–144.

Eddleston, M. & Gunnell, D. (2006). Why suicide rates are high in China. *Science, 311*, 1711–1713.

Ellis, A. & Bernard, M. E. (eds) (1985). *Clinical applications of rational–emotive therapy*. New York: Plenum.

First, M. B., Spitzer, R. L., Gibbon, M., & Williams, J. B. (1996). *Structured clinical interview for DSM-IV axis I disorders*. Washington, DC: American Psychiatric Press.

Goffman, E. (1963). *Stigma: Notes on the management of spoiled identity*. New York: Simon & Schuster Inc.

Hodges, J. & Oei, T. P. S. (2007). Would Confucius benefit from psychotherapy: The compatibility of cognitive behaviour therapy and Chinese values. *Behaviour Research and Therapy, 45*, 901–914.

Hsiao, F. H., Klimidis, S., Minas, H., & Tan, E. S. (2006). Cultural attribution of mental health suffering in Chinese societies: the views of Chinese patients with mental illness and their caregivers. *Journal of Clinical Nursing, 15*, 998–1006.

Hsiao, F. H., Lin S. M., Liao, H. Y., & Lai, M. C. (2004). Chinese inpatients' subjective experiences of the helping process as viewed through examination of a nurses' focused, structured therapy group. *Journal of Clinical Nursing, 13*, 886–894.

Hwu, H. G., Yeh, E. K., & Chang, L. Y. (1989). Prevalence of psychiatric disorders in Taiwan defined by the Chinese Diagnostic Interview Schedule. *Acta Psychiatrica Scandinavica, 79*, 136–147.

Ivanova, M. Y., Achenbach, T. M., Dumenci, L., Rescorla, L. A., Almqvist, F., Bilenberg, N. et al. (2007). Testing the 8-syndrome structure of the Child Behavior Checklist in 30 societies. *Journal of Clinical Child and Adolescent Psychology, 36*, 405–417.

Ivanova, M. Y., Achenbach, T. M., Rescorla, L. A., Dumenci, L., Almqvist, F., Bilenberg, N., et al. (2007). The generalizability of the Youth Self-Report syndrome structure in 23 societies. *Journal of Consulting and Clinical Psychology, 75*, 729–738.

Ji, J., Kleinman, A., & Becker, A. E. (2001). Suicide in contemporary China: A review of China's distinctive suicide demographics in their sociocultural context. *Harvard Review of Psychiatry, 9*, 1–12.

Jianlin, J. (2000). Suicide rates and mental health services in modern China. *Crisis, 21*, 118–121.

Katzman, M. & Lee, S. (1997). Beyond body image: The integration of feminist and transcultural theories in the understanding of self starvation. *International Journal of Eating Disorders, 22*, 385–94.

Kessler, R. C., Bergland, P., Demler, O., Jin, R., & Walters, E. (2005). Lifetime prevalence and age-of-onset distributions of DSM-IV disorders in the National Comorbidity Survey replication. *Archives of General Psychiatry, 62*, 593–602.

Kessler, R. & Ustun, T. B. (2004). The World Mental Health (WMH) Survey Initiative version of the World Mental Health Organization (WHO) Composite International Diagnostic Interview (CIDI). *International Journal of Methods in Psychiatric Research, 13*, 93–121.

Kirmayer, L. J. (2001). Cultural variations in the clinical presentation of depression and anxiety: Implications for diagnosis and treatment. *Journal of Clinical Psychiatry, 62*, 22–28.

Kleinman, A. (1982). Neurasthenia and depression: A study of somatization and culture in China. *Culture, Medicine, and Psychiatry, 6*, 117–189.

Lee, P. W. H., Lieh-Mak, F., Fung, A. S. M., Wong, M. C., & Lam, J. (2007). Hong Kong. In K. Hopper, G. Harrison, A. Janca, & N. Sartorius (eds), *Recovery from schizophrenia: An international perspective* (pp. 255–265). Oxford, UK: Oxford University Press.

Lee, S. (1998). Higher earnings, bursting trains and exhausted bodies: The creation of travelling psychosis in post-reform China. *Social Science and Medicine, 47*, 1247–1261.

Lee, S. (1999). Diagnosis postponed: *Shenjing shuairuo* and the transformation of psychiatry in post-Mao China. *Culture, Medicine and Psychiatry, 23*, 349–380.

Lee, S. (2001a). From diversity to unity: The classification of mental disorders in 21st-century China. *Psychiatric Clinics of North America, 24*, 421–31.

Lee, S. (2001b). Fat phobia in anorexia nervosa: Whose obsession is it? In M. Nasser, M. Katzamn, & R. Gordon (eds), *Eating disorders and cultures in transition* (pp. 40–65). New York: Taylor & Francis.

Lee, S. (2002). Socio-cultural and global health perspectives for the development of future diagnostic systems. *Psychopathology, 35*, 152–157.

Lee, S. & Hsu, L. K. (1993). Is weight phobia always necessary for a diagnosis of anorexia nervosa? *American Journal of Psychiatry, 150*, 1466–71.

Lee, S. & Kleinman, A. (2007). Are somatoform disorders changing with time: The case of neurasthenia in China. *Psychosomatic Medicine, 69*, 846–849.

Lee, S., Lee, M. T. Y., Chiu, M. Y. L., & Kleinman, A. (2005). Experience of social stigma by people with schizophrenia in Hong Kong. *British Journal of Psychiatry, 186*, 153–157.

Lee, S. & Lee, A. M. (2000). Disordered eating in three communities of China: A comparative study of female high school students in Hong Kong, Shenzhen, and rural Hunan. *International Journal of Eating Disorders, 27*, 317–27.

Lee, S., Tsang, A., & Kwok, K. (2007). Twelve-month prevalence, correlates, and treatment preference of adults with DSM-IV major depressive episode in Hong Kong. *Journal of Affective Disorders, 98*, 129–136.

Lee, S., Tsang, A., Zhang, M.-Y., Huang, Y. Q., He, Y. L., Liu, Z. R. et al. (2007). Lifetime prevalence and inter-cohort variation in DSM-IV disorders in metropolitan China. *Psychological Medicine, 37*, 61–73.

Leung, P. W. L., Kwong, S. L., Tang, C. P., Ho, T. P., Hung, S. F., Lee, C. C. et al. (2006). Test–retest reliability and criterion validity of the Chinese version of CBCL, TRF, and YSR. *Journal of Child Psychology and Psychiatry, 47*, 970–973.

Leung, S. & Leung, F. (in press). Construct validity and prevalence rate of borderline personality disorder among Chinese adolescents. *Journal of Personality Disorders.*

Li, X. Y., Phillips, M. R., Zhang, Y. P., Xu, D., & Yang, G. H. (2008). Risk factors for suicide in China's youth: A case-control study. *Psychological Medicine, 38*, 397–406.

Lin, Y. N. (2002). The application of cognitive-behavioral therapy to counseling Chinese. *American Journal of Psychotherapy, 56*, 46–58.

Link, B. G., Yang, L. H., Phelan, J. C. & Collins, P. Y. (2004). Measuring mental illness stigma. *Schizophrenia Bulletin, 30*, 511–541.

Liu, K. Y., Beautrais, A., Caine, E., Chan, K., Chao, A., et al. (2007). Charcoal burning suicides in Hong Kong and urban Taiwan: An illustration of the impact of a novel suicide method on overall regional rates. *Journal of Epidemiology and Community Health, 61*, 248–253.

Liu, X., Sun, Z., & Yang, Y. (2008). Parent-reported suicidal behavior and correlates among adolescents in China. *Journal of Affective Disorders, 105*, 73–80.

Luk, S. L., Kwan, C. S. F., Hui, J. M. C., Bacon-Shone, J., Tsang, A. K. T., Leung, A. C. et al. (1991). Cognitive-behavioral group therapy for Hong Kong Chinese adults with mental health problems. *Australian and New Zealand Journal of Psychiatry, 25*, 524–534.

Lyubomirsky, S. (2008). *The how of happiness.* New York: Penguin.

Marsella, A. J., Sartorius, N., Jablensky, A., & Fenton, F. (1985). Cross-cultural studies of depressive disorders: An overview. In A. Kleinman & B. Good (eds), *Culture and depression* (pp. 299–324). Berkeley, CA: University of California Press.

Mattelaer, J. J. & Jilek, W. (2007). *Koro*: The psychological disappearance of the penis. *Journal of Sex and Medicine, 4*, 1509–15.

Miller, G. (2006). China: Healing the metaphorical heart. *Science, 311*, 462–463.

Parker, G., Gladstone, G., & Chee, KT. (2001). Depression in the planet's largest ethnic group: The Chinese. *American Journal of Psychiatry, 158*, 857–864

Pearson, V., Phillips, M. R., He, F., & Ji, H. (2002). Attempted suicide among young rural women in the People's Republic of China: Possibilities for prevention. *Suicide and Life Threatening Behavior, 32*, 359–369.

Phillips, M. R., Shen, Q., Liu, X., Pritzker, S., Streiner, D., Conner, K. et al. (2007). Assessing depressive symptoms in persons who die of suicide in mainland China. *Journal of Affective Disorders, 98*, 73–82.

Phillips, M. R., Yang, G., Zhang, Y., Wang, L., Ji, H., & Zhou, M. (2002). Risk factors for suicide in China: A national case-control psychological autopsy study. *Lancet, 360*, 1728–1736.

Pritchard, C. & Baldwin, D. S. (2002). Elderly suicide rates in Asian and English-speaking countries. *Acta Psychiatrica Scandinavica, 105*, 271–275.

Qin, P. & Mortensen, P. B. (2001). Specific characteristics of suicide in China. *Acta Psychiatrica Scandinavica, 103*, 117–121. Retrieved from http://en.wikipedia.org/wiki/Chinese_Classification_of_Mental_Disorders

Rescorla, L., Achenbach, T. M., Ginzburg, S., Ivanova, M., Dumenci, L., Almqvist, F. et al. (2007). Consistency of teacher-reported problems for students in 21 countries. *School Psychology Review, 36*, 91–110.

Ryder, A. G., Yang, J., & Heini, S. (2002). Somatization vs. psychologization of emotional distress: A paradigmatic example for cultural psychopathology. In W. J. Lonner, D. L. Dinnel, S. A. Hayes, & D. N. Sattler (eds), *Online readings in psychology and culture.* Retrived from http://www.wwu.edu/~culture

Ryder, A. G., Yang, J., Zhu, X., Yao, S., Yi, J., Heini, S. et al. (2008). The cultural shaping of depression: Somatic symptoms in China, psychological symptoms in North America? *Journal of Abnormal Psychology, 117*, 300–313.

Shen, Y. C., Zhang, M. Y., Huang, Y. Q., He, Y. L., Lin, Z. R., Cheng, H. et al. (2006). Twelve month prevalence, severity, and unmet need for treatment of mental disorders in metropolitan China. *Psychological Medicine, 26*, 257–267.

Shi, Q. C., Zhang, J. M., Xu, F. Z., Phillips, M. R., Xu, Y., Fu, Y. L. et al. (2005). Epidemiological survey of mental illnesses in the people aged 15 and older in Zhejiang Province, China. *Zhonghua Yu Fang Yi Xue Za Zhi. 39*, 229–36.

Simon, G. E., vonKorff, M., Piccinelli, M., Fullerton, C., & Ormel, J. (1999). An international study of the relations between somatic symptoms and depression. *New England Journal of Medicine, 341*, 1329–1335.

Stewart, S. M., Lewinsohn, P., Lee, P. W. H., Ho, L. M., Kennard, B. D., Hughes, C. W. et al. (2002). Symptom patterns in depression and 'subthreshold' depression among adolescents in Hong Kong and the United States. *Journal of Cross-Cultural Psychology, 33*, 559–576.

Stewart, S. M., Byrne, B. M., Lee, P. W. H., Ho, L. M., Kennard, B. D., Hughes, C. et al. (2003). Personal versus interpersonal contributions to depressive symptoms among Hong Kong adolescents. *International Journal of Psychology, 38*, 160–169.

Stewart, S. M., Kennard, B. D., Lee, P. W. H., Hughes, C. W., Mayes, T., Emslie, G. et al. (2004). A cross-cultural investigation of cognitions and depressive symptoms in adolescents. *Journal of Abnormal Psychology, 113*, 248–257.

Stewart, S. M., Kennard, B. D., Lee, P. W. H., Mayes, T., Hughes, C. W., & Emslie, G. (2005). Hopelessness and suicidal ideation among adolescents in two cultures. *Journal of Child Psychology, Psychiatry and Allied Disciplines, 46*, 364–372.

Szasz, T. S. (2007). *The medicalization of everyday life: Selected essays.* Syracuse, NY: Syracuse University Press.

Wong, D. F. K., Chau, P., Kwok, A., & Kwan, J. (2007). Cognitive-behavioral treatment groups for people with chronic physical illness in Hong Kong: Reflections on a culturally attuned model. *International Journal of Group Psychotherapy, 57*, 367–385.

World Health Organization (2003). Suicide rates (per 100,000), by country, year, and gender. Retrieved March 25, 2008, from http://www.who.int/mental_health/ prevention/suicide/suiciderates/en/ print.html

Yang, G. H., Phillips, M. R., Zhou, M. G., Wang, L. J., Zhang, Y. P., & Xu, D. (2005). Understanding the unique characteristics of suicide in China: National psychological autopsy study. *Biomedical and Environmental Sciences, 18*, 379–389.

Yang, J., Bagby, R. M., Costa, P. T. Jr, Ryder, A. G., & Herbst, J. H. (2002). Assessing the DSM-IV structure of personality disorder with a sample of Chinese psychiatric patients. *Journal of Personality Disorders, 6*, 317–31.

Yang, J., McCrae, R. R., Costa, P. T. Jr, Yao, S., Dai, X., Cai, T. et al. (2000). The cross-cultural generalizability of Axis-II constructs: An evaluation of two personality disorder assessment instruments in the People's Republic of China. *Journal of Personality Disorders, 14*, 249–63

Zhang, J., Conwell, Y., Zhou, L., & Jiang, C. (2004). Culture, risk factors and suicide in rural China: A psychological autopsy case control study. *Acta Psychiatrica Scandinavica, 110*, 430–437.

Zhang, J., Jia, S., Jiang, C., & Sun, J. (2006). Characteristics of Chinese suicide attempters: An emergency room study. *Death Studies, 30*, 259–268.

Zhang, W. X., Shen, Y. C., & Li, S. R. (1998). Epidemiological investigation of mental disorders in 7 areas of China. *Chinese Journal of Psychiatry, 31*, 69–71.

Zhong, J. & Leung, F. (2007). Should borderline personality disorder be included in the fourth edition of the Chinese classification of mental disorders? *Chinese Medical Journal, 120*, 77–82.

CHAPTER 23

Clinical neuropsychology in China

Agnes S. Chan, Winnie W. Leung, and Mei-Chun Cheung

This chapter outlines the history of clinical neuropsychology in China and reviews its latest developments, with specific reference to the three major Chinese populations of Hong Kong, Taiwan, and mainland China. The chapter traces the introduction of neuropsychology from the United States into China, and reviews its current developments, focusing on the areas of clinical training, certification, assessment, and instrumentation, highlighting some interesting research findings on Chinese patient populations. The review is based not only on the international literature, but also on research published locally in mainland China, Taiwan, and Hong Kong.

Neuropsychology was first brought into China by young Chinese scholar-researchers trained in North America, who returned to their homeland in the mid-1990s. This group of young, Western-trained neuropsychologists is still the main driving force in the development of the field today, and has been very active in advancing clinical research and practice, as well as promoting the professionalization of clinical neuropsychology in China. With their efforts, professional neuropsychological associations sprang up and the Hong Kong Neuropsychological Association was established in 1997, as a first step towards a professional development of neuropsychology in China. Clinical training is offered by local universities as well as through the different neuropsychological associations and the Board.

In addition to the formalization of clinical training, the past ten or so years have also seen the development of many neuropsychological assessment instruments, either developed indigenously or adapted from the West, that are ecologically validated with normative data for Chinese populations in the three Chinese societies. In the area of clinical research, due to the unique linguistic and cultural background of Chinese relative to that of Westerners, new windows on brain functioning have been opened in such areas as language and memory, and brain pathologies such as learning disorders, autism, brain injury, and dementia. A new program of research on the traditional Chinese medical approach to clinical neuropsychology has also been embarked upon.

Although clinical neuropsychology has enjoyed a brief history in China, this chapter shows that the impressive growth of the field during this short period of a little more than tenyears has been truly remarkable.

Clinical neuropsychology is a relatively young field in China with a short history of about 20 years. While China is regarded as one nation with the largest population in the world, now estimated at over 1.3 billion, the development of clinical neuropsychology in China has not been one homogeneous picture. This is due largely to the unique historical developments of Taiwan and Hong Kong that has made them politically independent from the mainland for the past 50 and 150 years respectively, leading to economic, scientific, cultural, and linguistic differences from the mainland. Hong Kong, in particular, has been open to heavy Western influence and has adopted much of the Western, evidence-based perspective into its practice of science and medicine. In addition, a significant number of its younger generation, especially those pursuing higher and professional education, has been educated in the West. This, as we will see, has contributed to the differential development of clinical neuropsychology in the mainland, Hong Kong, and Taiwan, the latter two being the largest Chinese societies outside the mainland.

The profession of clinical neuropsychology, like many other areas in psychology, is very responsive to ethnic, linguistic, political, and cultural differences (see Blowers, this volume). As there are significant differences in these social characteristics across the three largest Chinese societies of the mainland, Hong Kong, and Taiwan contributing to differences in clinical neuropsychological research and practices, separate reference will be made to the three regions where appropriate in the remainder of this chapter.

Overview of the history of clinical neuropsychology in China

Mainland China

Clinical neuropsychology was first introduced into mainland China during the 1980s, comparatively the earliest among the three Chinese societies. The first national conference on neuropsychology was held on the mainland in 1987, an event that is generally acknowledged to signify the establishment of neuropsychology as a field of its own in mainland China. The Association hosts biennial national neuropsychology conferences, with about 80 participants and 50 presentations at each meeting.

During the early years, the development of the field in mainland China was primarily focused on the description of syndromes and impairments resulting from brain disorders (see Gao, 2003), among which aphasia and dementia were the targets of attention. Studies were done to examine the characteristics, develop diagnostic criteria, define sub-types, develop assessment instruments, and measure cognitive deficits in relation to these two disorders, producing some knowledge as well as clinical tools for understanding these two disorders (see Gao, 2003; Wang & Wang, 2005). Considerable efforts have also been made to adapt Western tests and instruments for local use, for example, the Wechsler Adult Intelligence Scales, Wechsler Memory Tests, and the Halstead-Reitan Neuropsychological Battery (see Yuan, 2000). Apart from research on aphasia and dementia, studies were also done on childhood disorders which included mental retardation, developmental dyslexia (see Wang & Li, 2006), learning disorders, and attention deficit/hyperactivity disorder (see Hu & Yu, 1999). However, these topics were often regarded as developmental pediatrics or educational issues, and have been largely omitted from the literature in clinical neuropsychology.

Development of the field was stepped up during the 2000s through the efforts of clinical neuropsychologists from Hong Kong, as will be outlined in the following section. This has led to an expansion in research on clinical practice. Studies on dementia have shifted focus to mild cognitive impairments (MCI), and this research has also led to improved knowledge of the symptoms of the disorder and enhanced ecological validity of the diagnostic criteria, as well as spurring neuroimaging studies and development of laboratory tests, all aimed at enabling early identification and intervention of dementia (see Gao, 2003). Clinical neuropsychological research has also been conducted on amnesia, neglect, agnosia, and apraxia (Wang & Wang, 2005).

Clinical neuropsychologists, like scientists and practitioners in other fields in mainland China, are relatively secluded from the West, partly because of the relatively lower level of information flow in and out of the nation, and partly because of the language barrier, since most of the literature was published locally in Chinese. The major journals that publish studies on neuropsychology include the *Chinese Mental Health Journal*, *Chinese Journal of Clinical Psychology*, *Chinese Behavioral Medicine* (Hong, 2003), and the *Chinese Journal of Neurology*. These journals are mostly published in Chinese with local circulation, and thus were not readily accessible by neuropsychologists in the West. Due to technological advances and wider information circulation in the mainland, however, electronic databases of these locally published studies are beginning to become available. Even so, most of the full texts are still in Chinese although a small proportion has English abstracts. Hence, development in the field remains confined within the country, and has been rather isolated from the rest of the world.

Hong Kong

During the time when clinical neuropsychology was gradually developing in the mainland during the 1980s and 1990s, it took on new developments in Hong Kong, the small city at the southern part of the nation. The development of the field there was independent from that of the mainland, and was brought about by young scholars, mostly trained in the United States and North America, who returned there to work in the 1990s and brought with them the scientific research methods and evidence-based practice characteristic of the field in the West. Although it has an even shorter history compared with that of mainland China, its development has been much more rapid.

Because of their international background, this small group of clinical neuropsychologists in Hong Kong has the advantage of good networking and information flow with the rest of the world, particularly the United States, the leading country in the field. With their easy access to the most up-to-date knowledge, research skills, and technologies, a few neuropsychologists in Hong Kong have made important contributions in promoting the development of the field. With the establishment of the Hong Kong Neuropsychological Association in 1998, the field was firmly established as one specialty in the larger field of clinical psychology in Hong Kong.

During the subsequent ten years, developments in both research and clinical practice have flourished. In research, up-to-date technologies on par with the West, such as magnetic resonance imaging (MRI), functional MRI (fMRI), and quantitative electroencephalography (qEEG) have been deployed to study brain–behavior relationships in normal children and adults, as well as in patients with different brain disorders, such as autism spectrum disorders, dyslexia, temporal lobe damage due to epilepsy, mild cognitive impairments in the elderly, and Alzheimer's disease, focusing on neuropsychological functions, including attention, language, memory, and executive functioning. In clinical practice, much effort has been put into developing neuropsychological assessment instruments, either through adapting Western instruments or developing indigenous assessment tools that are ecologically valid for the local population.

Taiwan

Neuropsychology is an even newer field in Taiwan, with only a few neuropsychologists engaged in research, teaching, and clinical practice. While some clinical neuropsychologists in Taiwan are psychologically trained clinical psychologists like their counterparts in Hong Kong, some are behavioral neurologists, as in mainland China. Unlike the mainland and Hong Kong, Taiwan does not yet have its own neuropsychological association. There are, instead, two academic societies connected with clinical neuropsychology, namely the Taiwan Association of Clinical Psychology, and the Taiwan Neurological Society (Hua & Lu, 2003). The field has not yet established its own professional identity in Taiwan, and development of the field is relatively less rapid compared with that of the mainland and even less so than Hong Kong. In terms of research, the focus is less on the clinical aspects of neuropsychology than on studies on cognitive functioning of normal individuals, using brain-imaging methods and cognitive experimental paradigms.

Pan-Chinese integration

Clinical neuropsychology has been developing rapidly in Hong Kong due to the group of young, Western-trained clinical neuropsychologists who have nurtured strong networks and access to the scientific knowledge base of research and practice in the West. Among this group of young scholar-cum-practitioners, a few have had the intention to take the field further forward in the mainland, and have striven to forge collaborations with mainland researchers, clinical practitioners and institutions, with the aim of bringing up-to-date knowledge and technologies of the field to the mainland.

Teaching and research collaborations have been started since the late 1990s, and an international conference was organized in Hong Kong in 2003, to bring together practitioners from Asia, North America, and Europe, encouraging the exchange of ideas and establishing ties between the West and the mainland. In the following year, led by an enthusiastic clinical neuropsychologist in Hong Kong and supported by fellow Chinese neuropsychologists in the mainland, Taiwan, Hong Kong, Australia, and the United States, the Chinese Board of Neuropsychology was founded in 2004 with the aim of contributing to the professionalization and formalization of the field in China. One of the Board's major objectives was to promote training, and to develop a registration system for Chinese neuropsychologists, both in research and clinical practice. Continuous efforts are being made to organize training programs and courses in the mainland for the professional development of neuropsychologists in that nation.

Clinical training and certification

Training in clinical neuropsychology has not been systematic across the nation. In mainland China, training is mostly offered by medical schools as masters' and doctoral programs. Those involved in clinical practice are mostly neurologists and mid-level medical professionals who do not necessarily have a very solid foundation in neuropsychology. Neuropsychological assessments and batteries are often administered by personnel without any background in neuropsychology, and thus may pose significant problems for the validity of the assessment. More work is needed to train both clinical practitioners and research neuropsychologists in a more systematic and regulated manner (Yuan, 2000).

The situation in Hong Kong is slightly different. Training is basically offered by the departments of psychology at two local universities as part of their master's program in Clinical Psychology. Neuropsychological training is also offered by the Hong Kong Neuropsychological Association periodically. In general, neuropsychological assessment and intervention are conducted by clinical psychologists in hospital settings (Chan, 2003), and research is done by neuropsychologists working in the faculties of local universities. Since clinical neuropsychologists in Hong Kong have energetically networked with colleagues in the West and enjoy freedom of information flow and publication access to international journals, the quality of their research is guaranteed to conform with international standards. Knowledge is constantly updated on assessment of and intervention with brain disorders, thereby contributing to the high standard of clinical service delivery.

In Taiwan, clinical neuropsychologists who are clinical psychologists belong to the Taiwan Association of Clinical Psychology, and those who are behavioral neurologists belong to the Taiwan Neurological Society (Hua & Lu, 2003).

In contrast to the United States, where neuropsychology is a board-certified specialization, neuropsychologists in China do not need either certification or registration to practice. In fact, prior to the establishment of the Chinese Board of Neuropsychology in 2004, there was no system of registration for clinical neuropsychologists in any of the three Chinese societies of mainland China, Hong Kong, and Taiwan. To redress this situation, the Board introduced a registration system for neuropsychologists of Chinese ethnicity, and opened for voluntary registration. The system comprises two divisions: the Research Division and the Clinical Division. Registration as a research or a clinical neuropsychologist is approved upon fulfillment of training and practical neuropsychological work experience. At present, the registration system is not mandatory, and registration is not required to engage in clinical practice. However, it is one of the ultimate goals of the Board to implement a board certification system like the one in the United States. This would be an important step in the professionalization of the field and in guaranteeing the quality of research and clinical service delivery in China.

Assessment instrumentation

Neuropsychology is a field with a heavy emphasis on cognitive functioning that includes attention, memory, language, motor and executive functioning. Since many of the tests and assessment instruments are verbally administered, the impact of language, and to a lesser extent, of cultural difference, becomes very important in the field. As mentioned, due to unique historical developments, there exist significant linguistic, cultural, and lifestyle differences among mainland China, Hong Kong and Taiwan. The most notable difference is in language, in that Cantonese is the native tongue in Hong Kong, whereas both mainland China and Taiwan use Mandarin; while the writing system is the same in Hong Kong and Taiwan, the mainland has adopted the simplified character system. In addition, different vocabularies are sometimes used for the same concepts in the three societies, while some concepts in daily living are unique to only one society.

Since some tests are culture-sensitive, direct translation of such tests may negatively impact on the validity of the test results (Tamayo, 1987). Neuropsychological assessment belongs to this group of culture-sensitive tests, and is very sensitive to language and cultural differences not only between the West and the East, but also among mainland China, Hong Kong, and Taiwan. Thus, tests in one population are not readily usable in the other two. As a result, practitioners in the three societies have to develop their own instruments. A clear example is the adaptation of the Wechsler Intelligence Tests for adults and children. While mainland China has developed its own Chinese version of the adult scale (WAIS-R; Dai, Gong, & Zhong, 1990; Gong, 1989), Hong Kong (WAIS-R-HK; Hong Kong Psychological Society, 1989), and Taiwan (WAIS-III; Chen & Chen, 2002) also have their own adapted versions of the tests.

With the development of neuropsychology in the three Chinese societies, there was a corresponding need for neuropsychological assessment tools to use with the Chinese populations. The development of neuropsychological assessment tools in China followed the common three-stage model of direct translation, then adaptation, of Western instruments, and finally the construction of indigenous tests. During the early stages of test development, instruments in all three Chinese societies were mainly translated and adapted from Western tests (see Chan, Shum, & Cheung, 2003). Given that Chinese and Western populations have significant cultural differences, neuropsychologists saw the need to develop their own indigenous tests which can provide better ecological validity. As a result, new indigenous tests have been published with local norms (see Chan, Shum, & Cheung, 2003).

Chan et al. (2003) searched out and reviewed studies on neuropsychological assessment tools in Asia over the past 20 years, and found that the number of adapted tests to indigenously developed tests was 30:6, with a higher percentage of tests for older adults (95 per cent) compared with other age groups. The greatest number of assessment tools was for dementia screening, followed by tests of memory, learning, language, and executive functions. A summary of their findings on mainland China, Hong Kong, and Taiwan is shown in Table 23.1.

Chan and colleagues used the following five criteria to evaluate the clinical validity of the instruments for application to the local population:

1. proper documentation of the procedures for test development;
2. test validation had been conducted;
3. normative data with a reasonable sample size were available;
4. translation and back-translation had been carried out; and
5. cross-cultural comparison had been conducted.

Only eight out of the total 36 instruments met these criteria to qualify as valid assessment instruments. Three of them were indigenous tests developed locally, and five were adaptations from Western tests. Two of the eight tests were developed in mainland China and three in Hong Kong. The remaining 28 tests partially met the five criteria. For example, a number of Chinese-adapted tests fulfilled all except the cross-cultural comparison criterion, viz. the Chinese version of the Alzheimer's Disease Behavioral Pathology Rating Scale from Hong Kong (Lam, Tang, Leung, & Chiu, 2001), and the Chinese revisions of the Halstead-Reitan Neuropsychological Test Battery for adults from mainland China (Gong, 1986). A few other tests recruited too small or non-representative samples of the local populations, viz. the Cantonese version of the Western Aphasia Battery from Hong Kong (Yiu, 1992),

Table 23.1 Neuropsychological assessment tools adapted or developed in mainland China, Hong Kong, and Taiwan in the past 20 years (adapted from Chan, Shum, & Cheung, 2003, p. 261)

Mainland China		Hong Kong
Alzheimer's disease	Hiscock's forced-choice digit	Blessed-Roth dementia scale
Assessment scale (Chinese	memory test	Cantonese aphasia test
version)	Halstead-Reitan	battery
Aphasia test	neuropsychological test battery	Category fluency test (Chinese
Auditory verbal memory test	(HRNB) Chinese revision	version)
Bender visual motor gestalt test	Language ability test	Chinese anomalous
Benton line orientation test	Luria-Bebraska	sentence test
Blessed-Roth's Alzheimer's	neuropsychological battery	Chinese version of Alzheimer's
disease scale	Mini mental status examination	disease behavioral pathology
Benton visual retention test	Chinese MMSE	rating scale
Chinese neurobehavioral	Revised Chinese edition of the	Chinese version of Mattis
evaluation 2	HRNB for younger children	dementia rating scale
Chinese standard aphasia scale	Senile cognitive function scale	Clock drawing test
Chinese version expansive scale	Sorting test	Color trails test
of dementia	Trail-making test	Hong Kong list learning test
Clinical memory test	Verbal and visuospatial speed of	Neuropsychiatric inventory
Cognitive abilities screening	processing and working memory	(Chinese version)
instrument 2.0	Visual space test	Olfactory identification test
Cognitive abilities screening	Wechsler adult intelligence scale-	Trail-making test
instrument (for cross-cultural	revised (WAIS-R)	
studies)	Wisconsin card-sorting test	
Computer neurobehavioral test	(WCST)	
system	Western aphasia battery	
Digit symbol	Wechsler memory scale (WMS)	
Finger-tapping test		
Grooved pegboard		
Handed test		

the Olfactory Identification Test from Hong Kong (Chan, Tam, Murphy, Chiu, & Lam, 2002), and the Computerized Neurobehavioral Test System from China (Li et al., 2000).

Tests adapted from the West

Chinese version of the Category Fluency Test (Chan & Poon, 1999). This test is a sensitive clinical measure for dementia and schizophrenia in Hong Kong. The authors used the categories of animals and transportation, and normative data were presented based on 316 Hong Kong Chinese, aged 7 to 95. Psychometric properties of the test were consistent with those of the original test as reported in Western studies. Another set of normative data restricted to older adults in Hong Kong is provided by Chiu et al. (1997; see Chan, Shum, & Cheung, 2003).

Chinese version of the Mattis Dementia Rating Scale (CDRS) (Chan et al., 2003, Chan, Poon, Choi, & Cheung, 2001). This test for assessing dementia in Hong Kong was adapted from the original Mattis Dementia Rating Scale (Mattis, 1988). In addition to a direct translation of the original items, cultural modification was made on four items. Normative data were presented based on 83 healthy older adults and 40 adults with Alzheimer's disease. A cut-off score of 112 yielded a sensitivity of 80.0 per cent and specificity of 91.6 per cent. Comparison of older adults in Hong Kong and the United States showed that those from Hong Kong demonstrated a lower mean DRS score (see Chan, Shum, & Cheung, 2003). This might be due to another characteristic of the Chinese populations in that, due to historical reasons (war in general), elderly cohorts have relatively lower levels of education compared with elderly Western cohorts, and this is especially pronounced for females. When interpreting cognitive and neuropsychological assessment results, therefore, the educational-level factor should be considered.

Chinese Mini Mental State (CMMS) Examination (Katzman, Zhang, Qu, Want, Liu, Yu et al., 1988). This test was adapted from the Mini Mental State Examination (MMSE: Folstein, Folstein, & McHugh, 1975) in mainland China, through translation of the original items. It has demonstrated a diagnostic sensitivity and specificity of 69.5 per cent and 90.2 per cent, respectively, for dementia in a group of Shanghai adults, and was found to be one of the best tests for predicting dementia in China. A cross-cultural comparison with a group of adults from Finland and the United States showed that the scores were comparable when education level was adjusted for (see Chan, Shum, & Cheung, 2003). A Cantonese version of the MMSE was also developed in Hong Kong by Chiu, Lee, Chung, & Kwong (1994), with a recommended cut-off score of 19/20 as an indicator to do further evaluation for dementia.

Indigenous tests

Hong Kong List Learning Test (HKLLT) (Chan, 2006). This test is a verbal learning test developed in Hong Kong for assessing memory functions. Normative data were presented based on 394 Hong Kong Chinese aged 6 to 95. The test has been tested on a number of clinical populations with psychiatric and neurologic disorders, including schizophrenia (Chan, Kwok, Chiu, Lam, Pang, & Chow, 2000), temporal lobe necrosis (Cheung, Chan, Law, Chan, & Tse, 2000, 2003; Cheung & Chan, 2003) or temporal lobe epilepsy (Cheung, Chan, Chan, & Lam, 2006a, 2006b), and Alzheimer's disease (Au, Chan, & Chiu, 2003). Results show that the test was able to differentiate between acute and chronic schizophrenia, between nasopharyngeal carcinoma (NPC) patients with and without temporal lobe necrosis, and between normal adults and those with mild and moderate Alzheimer's disease (AD) (see Chan, Shum, & Cheung, 2003).

The authors made one improvement in the HKLLT, compared with some common Western list learning tests such as the California Verbal Learning Test (CVLT; Delis, Kramer, Kaplan, & Ober, 1987) and the Rey Auditory Verbal Learning Test (RAVLT; Rey, 1964; see Lezak, Howeison, & Loring, 2000). The test has incorporated recent experimental paradigms on amnesia to increase its sensitivity in differentiating between pathologies such as frontal and temporal lobe amnesia, and different etiologies such as schizophrenia and depression (see test manual, Chan, 2006). The random and the blocked lists emphasize the evaluation of organization strategies, which is sensitive to different profiles of frontal lobe pathology. In addition, comparison of an individual's performance on the random and blocked lists can provide significant clinical information for evaluating the effectiveness of memory intervention (Chan, 2006).

Clinical Memory Test (Xu & Wu, 1986). This test was developed for assessing memory in mainland China. The test was shown to be sensitive to left- and right-brain-damaged patients, but no further details could be found about the test.

Recent research findings

Due to the supportive environment for research in Hong Kong, much has been done and published in the field. A few programs of research have been conducted on specific patient populations, including children (with autism spectrum disorders), adults (with temporal lobe damage), and the elderly (with Alzheimer's disease). Some research findings from the authors' group are briefly reviewed in the remainder of this section.

Autism spectrum disorders (ASD) in children

ASD is a group of lifelong and pervasive developmental disorders characterized by poor social interaction with others, language delay or impairment, and repetitive and stereotyped behavior. Diagnosis is made before the age of three, and many of the children with the disorders are incapable of independent living, even in adulthood. Evidence shows that there seems to be an increase in ASD worldwide during recent years (Baird et al., 2000; Bertrand et al., 2001), partly due to increased recognition of the syndrome (Charman, 2002) and partly due to changes in diagnostic criteria (Baird, Cass, & Slonims, 2003; Wing & Potter, 2002). Recent statistics from the National Autism Association (2007) in the USA even reported a prevalence rate for ASD of 1 in 150 children. Figures for ASD in the three Chinese societies appear to be lower. A recent study in mainland China reported a prevalence rate of 1.10 cases per 1,000 for children aged 2 to 6 (Zhang & Ji, 2005). While no prevalence figure is available for Hong Kong (Wong & Hui, 2007), statistics at the Child Assessment Centers of the territory reported an increasing trend whereby the incidence of cases has risen from 198 in 1995 to 658 in 2004 (Mak, Lam, Ho, & Wong, 2006). A search of the literature did not turn up any information on the prevalence of ASD in Taiwan.

Traditionally, Hong Kong adopts the ICD-10 (World Health Organization, 1990) or the DSM-IV (American Psychiatric Association, 2000) criteria in diagnosing ASD (Mak et al., 2006), supplemented by the use of common observational scales translated from the West, including the Childhood Autism Rating Scale (CARS: Scholper, Reichler, & Renner, 1986), Autism Diagnostic Observation Schedule (ADOS: Lord, Rutter, Goode, Heemsbergen, Jordan, Mawhood et al., 1989), and the Autism Diagnostic Interview-Revised (ADI-R: Le Couteur, Rutter, Lord, Rios, Roberston, Holdgrafer et al., 1989).

Recent efforts have been made by the present authors and colleagues (Chan & Leung, 2005; Chan, Sze, & Cheung, 2007) to develop some objective measures of ASD in Hong Kong. They have examined the applicability of quantitative electroencephalography (qEEG) measures to differentiate ASD from normality in children, and our results have suggested that children with ASD have qEEG profiles significantly different from those of normal children, particularly in the alpha and delta bands (Chan, Sze, & Cheung, 2007). Research on using qEEG to objectively measure executive functioning is currently being conducted by the group (Chan, Cheung, Han, Sze, Leung, Man, et al., in press). Another of their studies on language deficits of ASD children has suggested that tests of expressive language are more sensitive than are those of comprehension in differentiating children with ASD from normal, age-matched children (Chan, Cheung, Leung, Cheung, & Cheung, 2005). In addition, Chen and colleagues have conducted a pilot study with two children with ASD (Chen, Liu, & Wong, 2008), and found that a short and intensive course of electroacupuncture was able to improve some core features in these children, including sensory and stereotypy features.

Temporal lobe damage in adults

Due to their dietary habits, Chinese living in the southern parts of China are found to have a significantly higher prevalence of nasopharyngeal carcinoma (NPC) than people elsewhere. NPC is often treated by radiotherapy, and the radiation often causes unintentional damage to the temporal lobes. The temporal lobe is well understood as playing an important role in mediating higher human cognitive functions, including memory and language. Thus, the unique situation in southern China has provided a window to study the language and memory functioning of patients with temporal lobe damage as a result of radionecrosis from NPC treatment.

In Hong Kong, there is a considerable number of patients with temporal lobe damage as a result of radiotherapy for NPC, which causes cognitive dysfunctions in the patients (Cheung et al., 2000, 2003). The memory profile of this group of patients is consistent with that of patients suffering from temporal lobe amnesia, and the severity of memory impairment is further found to be associated with lesion volume. The temporal lobe damage of some NPC patients is unique in that damage is mainly on the lateral temporal lobes sparing the hippocampus, a profile seldom seen in the West. The authors' group has examined this issue (Chan et al., 2003; Cheung & Chan, 2003), and their data suggest that bilateral damage of the lateral temporal lobes is also associated with both verbal and visual memory dysfunctions, and that the memory impairment is comparable to that of patients having lesions involving the hippocampus. Apart from NPC patients, the memory processing of temporal lobe epilepsy (TLE) patients has also been investigated using functional MRI (Cheung et al., 2006b). The results suggest that temporal lobe epilepsy seems to affect memory functioning progressively, i.e. the longer the duration of the illness, the lower the levels of brain activation and memory performance. In addition, the effect is not limited to the side of the seizure, but also includes the contralateral hemisphere.

Hong Kong has a distinctive linguistic environment that has provided yet another window in studying human language functioning. Hong Kong was subjected to British rule for over 150 years before its reunification with China in 1997. This created a Chinese-English, bilingual environment in Hong Kong, in which almost all individuals in the territory have learnt to speak English as a second language from the young age of about six (see Cheung, this volume). This has provided the opportunity to compare and contrast human language processing between the logographic Chinese system and the alphabetic English system.

In this area, the authors' group has done a series of studies on the language lateralization of Chinese patients with temporal lobe damage as a result of temporal lobe epilepsy (TLE) (Cheung et al., 2006a; Cheung, Cheung, & Chan, 2004). While it is well established from Western studies that language is mediated by the left hemisphere, studies from the group have provided some evidence to suggest that the neural basis of language processing in Chinese is different from that of English (Cheung et al., 2006a). Using functional MRI, Chinese-English, bilingual patients with TLE in Hong Kong were found to show the usual left-hemispheric dominance for processing English, just as English speakers do, and the results with these patients were consistent with the findings from Western studies.

The group further found that left-TLE patients were more likely than right-TLE patients to demonstrate bilateral activation in *English* word reading. This outcome is likely to be a result of neural plasticity where the right hemisphere has taken up some of the English-language mediation function of the left hemisphere. In a covert Chinese character reading task, however, both left- and right-TLE patients were found to show bilateral activation of the frontal and temporal regions. Because processing Chinese tends to involve both hemispheres, as found in normal participants, the solely right-shift pattern was not observed in Chinese reading with the TLE patients. The group further demonstrated in another study (Cheung, Cheung, & Chan, 2004) that Chinese patients with temporal lobe damage in the left and right hemispheres showed similar levels of naming impairment. This finding is in contrast with findings in the West, where damage in the left but not the right temporal lobe is associated with impaired language functioning. This series of studies on temporal lobe-damaged patients has provided important information for clinicians when assessing the language functions of Chinese patients.

Dementia in the elderly

Studies have reported lower prevalence rates of dementia in China compared with the West. A recent study in the United States (Plassman et al., 2007) reported a prevalence of 13.9 per cent among individuals aged 71 and older, a noticeably higher figure than those reported in Hong Kong, mainland China, and Taiwan, in descending prevalence. For mainland China, Zhou, Xu, Qi, Fan, Sun, Como et al. (2006) reported prevalence rates of 0.33 per cent for the age group 50–54, 0.89 per cent for 55–64, 3.43 per cent for 65–74, and 8.19 per cent for 75 and above; in Hong Kong, Chiu, Lam, Leung, Li, Law, Chung et al. (1998) reported prevalence rates of 1.7 for the age group 70–74, 4.7 per cent for 75–79, 10.7 per cent for 80–84, 18.8 per cent for 85–89, and 25.8 per cent for individuals over age 90; and in Taiwan, Liu, Lin, Teng, Wang, Fuh, Guo et al. (1995) reported prevalence rates of 0.21 per cent for the age group 60–69, 2.67 per cent for age 70–79, and 5.98 per cent for age 80–88. Alzheimer's disease (AD) is the most common cause of dementia in the West, and studies in mainland China and Taiwan have reported similar findings (Liu et al., 1995; Zhou et al., 2006). Lam (2004) also reported that AD accounts for as much as 80 per cent of all dementia cases in Hong Kong. As reported, these prevalence rates for AD are lower in Chinese societies than the West (Chiu et al., 1998; Liu et al., 1995; Zhou et al., 2006). In fact, AD appears to be receiving increasing attention in mainland China in recent years, with papers published reviewing its mechanisms, pharmacological interventions

(Jia, Yang, & Wang, 2008), epidemiology (Yang, 2008), and Chinese medical treatment (Zhu, 2008) for AD.

Diagnosis of dementia in the three Chinese societies is usually based on the translation and adaptation of Western instruments, such as the Mini Mental State Examination (MMSE; Folstein, Folstein, & McHugh, 1975), Clock Drawing Test (Critchley, 1953), Dementia Rating Scale (DRS; Mattis, 1988), and the Blessed Dementia Scale (Blessed, Tomlinson, & Roth, 1968). As previously mentioned, some of these tests have validated Chinese versions, such as the Chinese Blessed-Roth Dementia Scale (Lam, Chiu, Li, Chan, Chan, Wong, et al., 1997) and clock-face drawing test (Lam, Chiu, Ng, & Chan, 1998); some also have established local norms, such as the CDS (Lam et al., 1997), Chinese MMSE (Chiu et al., 1994; Katzman et al., 1988) and Chinese DRS (Chan et al., 2003).

In a clinical research study conducted by the authors' group in validating the Chinese DRS (Chan, Choi, & Salmon, 2001), the performance of Hong Kong Chinese elderly was compared with that of elderly in the United States. Results show that, while elderly Chinese and Americans performed comparably in terms of their total scores, they showed significantly different sub-test performance. Hong Kong Chinese elderly scored significantly higher than their American counterparts on the construction subscale, while American elderly scored higher on the initiation/perseveration and memory subscales. This study has highlighted an important issue, viz., that (Chinese) DRS subscales are sensitive to cultural difference and underscores the importance of cultural adaptation in using Western tests to assess Chinese populations.

The same study also highlighted another issue important in cross-cultural application of clinical neuropsychological assessment tools: study results showed that education has a greater effect on the DRS score for Hong Kong elderly compared with their American counterparts. As previously mentioned, this finding is likely due to the lower educational level of elderly Chinese in the three Chinese societies. In this connection, clinicians should also be aware of the large number of illiterate individuals, especially those in older age groups, and living in rural areas in mainland China. This might seriously threaten the validity of some verbal tests. In fact, lack of formal education and rural residence were found to be risk factors for dementia (see Liu et al., 1995), so these demographic variables need to be considered when assessing Chinese individuals.

The Chinese medical approach to clinical neuropsychology and brain dysfunctions

Apart from studies on the more mainstream areas in the field of clinical neuropsychology, there has also been interest in exploring the Chinese medical approach to clinical neuropsychological intervention and treatment for brain dysfunctions. The present authors are one of the pioneer research groups who have actively explored the effect of different Chinese medical treatments on the cognitive functioning of Chinese normal and patient populations in Hong Kong.

Cutaneous stimulation. Cutaneous stimulation is a traditional method in Chinese medicine to heal the body. This stimulation is done using blunt needles, and is different from acupuncture. In an eight-month intervention using this method to treat a chronic patient with cerebellar damage (Chan, He, Cheung, Bai, Poon, Sun et al., 2003) who presented with severe ataxia, fait imbalance and limb spasticity, the results were extremely encouraging. The patient's function has improved by 40 per cent, and his ataxia and hypotonia have also improved, as shown by his regaining of the abilities to grasp objects, sit upright, control his equilibrium and monitor an electric wheelchair. In a functional MRI study (Chan, Cheung, Chan, Yeung, & Lam, 2003) on cutaneous stimulation on the Dan Tian (also known as Elixir Field), the group found bilateral activation of brain regions not only in the motor cortex, but also cortical regions that mediate planning, attention and memory, suggesting that cutaneous stimulation may have an effect on neuropsychological functioning. In a third study using cutaneous stimulation on a group of children with ASD (Chan, Cheung, Sze, & Leung, 2009), results showed that a six-week intervention was found to be associated with significant improvement in the linguistic and social interaction of the children. These results all suggest that the Chinese method of cutaneous stimulation is an effective intervention for enhancing neuropsychological functioning of normal and patient groups in Hong Kong. Besides, Wong and colleagues have examined the use of tongue and body acupuncture to treat children with cortical visual impairments (Wong et al., 2006), cerebral palsy (Wong, Sun, & Yeung, 2006), and electroacupunture on children with autism spectrum disorder (Chen, Liu, & Wong 2008). Their results suggested that these Chinese medical approaches were effective in improving brain functioning in some respects.

Chinese mind–body practices. Mind–body exercises such as *tai chi* have long been practiced by Chinese for health-promoting purposes. Apart from *tai chi*, there are other kinds of Chinese mind–body practices that have been found to promote cognitive functioning in adults and children. The first author has developed a set of easy-to-practice, mind–body exercises for children, based on traditional Chinese *wushu* (a form of martial art), and has conducted a study using this exercise in a 40-session intervention for primary school children with behavioral problems (Chan, Cheung, & Sze, 2008). Results indicate that, compared with controls who underwent remedial classes, children in the intervention group showed a significant reduction in withdrawn and attention problems. They also showed improvements in cognitive functioning, including memory and cognitive flexibility.

In another study (Chan, Han, & Cheung, 2008), the authors' group examined brain activities as measured by EEG when normal healthy young adults practiced a traditional Chinese mindfulness exercise, the Triarchic Body Pathway Relaxation Technique. Results indicated increased left-sided brain activation and frontal midline power, suggesting that the mindfulness exercise gives rise to positive emotional experience and focused internalized attention.

In a third study comparing Chinese mind–body exercise and cardiovascular exercises in older adults (Chan, Ho, Cheung, Albert, Chiu, & Lam, 2005), the group found that those who practiced traditional Chinese mind–body exercise or cardiovascular exercise had significantly better memory functioning than those who did not practice any exercise; the two exercises appeared to have a synergistic effect in helping to preserve memory in older adults. This outcome has important clinical applications, since traditional Chinese mind–body exercises may be considered as an alternative to physical training for those who cannot practice strenuous physical exercise. Their use is also more compatible with Chinese cultural tradition.

Dejian mind–body intervention. A recent direction of research for the authors' group is the Dejian mind–body intervention, which is a simplified practice program developed by Master Dejian from the Shaolin Monastery. The intervention is based on over one thousand years of the Shaolin *Chan Wu Yi* culture (Zen, *wushu*, and medical practice), and Master Dejian's more than 20 years of clinical experience in practicing *Chan Wu Yi*, and helping patients (Shi & Chan, 2008). This intervention comprises four components, which include changing one's thought according to the Chan principles, herbal supplementation, internal-enhancing exercise, and a vegetarian diet.

Preliminary studies, using the Western brain science approach to enquiry, have been done on the internal-enhancing exercise and herbal supplementation components of this intervention. Outcome assessment included an fMRI experiment and an EEG experiment to examine patterns of brain activation during *Dan Tian* breathing. Results showed that *Dan Tian* breathing was associated with activation of the frontal cortex including the anterior cingulate cortex, a region that controls higher cognitive functions, while no such activation was found during usual breathing. Since *Dan Tian* breathing was shown in preliminary results to enhance brain activity level, it may be associated with the cognitive functions mediated by that region. In the EEG study on *Dan Tian* breathing by Master Dejian, the group found that, compared with normal controls who did not practice this breathing method, Master Dejian's *Dan Tian* breathing was associated with significantly enhanced frontal lobe activity (Shi & Chan, 2008). These preliminary results suggest that as a long-term practice this breathing technique might enhance functioning of the frontal lobe, which is the control center for human planning, creativity, and inhibition.

These pilot studies have provided initial evidence to suggest that at least two components of the Dejian mind–body intervention, namely Chinese herbal medicine and *Dan Tian* breathing as a form of health-promotion practice, have a beneficial effect on brain activity and functioning (Shi & Chan, 2008). The group is planning further studies to scientifically examine other components of the Dejian mind–body intervention and its effects on human brain functioning.

Chinese herbal supplementation. It is a common Chinese practice to take herbal supplements that have been developed over thousands of years in Chinese medical tradition for health-promoting purposes. In a series of pilot studies, the authors' group examined the effect of Chinese herbal medicine, prepared as nasal drops administered through the nostrils. The results suggest that this herbal preparation, compared with a control powder, was able to improve the cognitive functioning of healthy Chinese adults.

In addition, the first author has collaborated with medical professionals trained in the Western tradition to investigate the effect of some common Chinese herbal supplements on cognitive functioning. In the study on *Pureraria lobata* (Woo, Lau, Ho, Cheng, Chan, Chan, Haines et al., 2003), a common Chinese herbal preparation commercially available and commonly taken by Chinese women, results showed that *Pureraria lobata* was able to improve menopausal women's scores on the Mini Mental State Examination and their level of flexible thinking. A study on soy isoflavone extract, another common herbal supplement for Chinese women, however, found no effects on the cognitive functioning of post-menopausal women (Ho, Chan, Ho, So, Sham, Zee et al., 2007). Further studies are warranted to examine other Chinese herbal supplements for their possible beneficial effects on cognitive functioning.

In this short chapter that outlines the history of clinical neuropsychology in China, we have seen an impressive growth of the field during this short period of a little more than ten years, and the development of the field has been truly remarkable. In the coming years, we anticipate an expansion in the scope of clinical neuropsychological research, one promising direction of which is the application of Western scientific methods to explore the traditional Chinese medical approach to clinical neuropsychological intervention.

Authors' note

Authors' contact details: Agnes S. Chan, PhD, Department of Psychology, The Chinese University of Hong Kong, Shatin, NT, Hong Kong SAR, China. Tel: (852) 2609–6654; fax: (852) 2603–5019; email: aschan@psy.cuhk.edu.hk. Winnie W. Leung, MPhil, Neuropsychology Laboratory, Department of Psychology, The Chinese University of Hong Kong, Shatin, NT, Hong Kong SAR, China. Email: winnieleung@cuhk.edu.hk. Mei-Chun Cheung, PhD, Institute of Textiles and Clothing, The Hong Kong Polytechnic University, Hung Hom, Kowloon, Hong Kong SAR, China. Tel: (852)2766-6536; fax: (852)2773-1432; email: tccmchun@inet.polyu.edu.hk.

References

American Psychiatric Association. (2000). *Diagnostic and statistical manual of mental disorders* (4th edn text rev.) Washington DC: author.

Au, A., Chan, A. S., & Chiu, H. (2003). Verbal memory in Alzheimer's disease. *Journal of the International Neuropsychological Society, 9*, 363–375.

Baird, G., Cass, H., & Slonims, V. (2003). Diagnosis of autism. *British Medical Journal, 327*, 488–493.

Bertrand, J., Mars, A., Boyle, C., Bove, F., Yeargin-Allsopp, M., & Decoufle, P. (2001). Prevalence of autism in a United States population: the Brick Township, New Jersey, investigation. *Pediatrics,108*, 1155–1161.

Blessed, G., Tomlinson, B. E., & Roth, M. (1968). The association between quantitative measures of dementia and of senile change in the cerebral grey matter of elderly subjects. *British Journal of Psychiatry, 114*, 797–811.

Chan, A. (2003). *Recent development of neuropsychology in Hong Kong.* Paper presented at the International Conference on Neuropsychology, Hong Kong, December, 9–12.

Chan, A. S. (2006). *Hong Kong List Learning Test* (2nd edn). Hong Kong: Department of Psychology and Clinical Psychology Centre, The Chinese University of Hong Kong.

Chan, A. S. & Poon, M. W. (1999). Performance of 7- to 95-year-old individuals in a Chinese version of the category fluency test. *Journal of the International Neuropsychological Society, 5*, 525–533.

Chan, A. S. and Leung, W. W. M. (2006). Differentiating autistic children with quantitative encephalography: A three-month longitudinal study. *Journal of Child Neurology, 21*, 391–399.

Chan, A. S., Cheung, J., Leung, W. W. M., Cheung, R., and Cheung, M. (2005). Verbal expression and comprehension deficits in young children with autism. *Focus on Autism and Developmental Disorders, 20*, 117–124.

Chan, A. S., Cheung, M. C., Chan, Y. L., Yeung, D. K. W., & Lam, W. (2003). Bilateral frontal activation associated with cutaneous stimulation of Elixir field: An fMRI study. *American Journal of Chinese Medicine, 34*, 207–216.

Chan, A. S., Cheung, M. C., & Sze, S. L. (2008). Effect of mind–body training on children with behavioral and learning problems: A randomized controlled study. In B. N. DeLuca (ed.), *Mind–body and relaxation research focus*, pp. 165–193 Hauppauge, NY: Nova Science.

Chan, A. S., Cheung, M. C., Sze, S. L., & Leung, W. W. (2009). *Seven-star needle stimulation improves language and social interaction of children with autism spectrum disorder. American Journal of Chinese Medicine, 37*, 495–504.

Chan, A. S., Choi, M., & Salmon, D. P. (2001). The effects of age, education, and gender on the Matis Dementia Rating Scale performance of elderly Chinese and American individuals. *Journal of Gerontology, 56B*, 356–363.

Chan, A. S., Han, Y. M. Y., & Cheung, M. C. (2008). Electroencephalographic (EEG) measurements of mindfulness-based Triarchic Body-Pathway Relaxation Technique: A pilot study. *Applied Psychophysiology and Biofeedback, 33*, 39–47.

Chan, A. S., Cheung, M. C., Han, Y. M. Y., Sze, S. L., Leung, W. W, Man, H. S., & To, C. Y. (2009). Executive function deficits and neural discordance in children with Autism Spectrum Disorders. *Clinical Neurophysiology, 120*, 1107–1115.

Chan, A. S., He, W. J., Cheung, M. C., Bai, Z. K., Poon, W. S., Sun, D., Zhu, X. L., & Chan, Y. L. (2003). Cutaneous stimulation improves function of a chronic patient with cerebellar damage. *European Journal of Neurology, 10*, 265–269.

Chan, A. S., Ho, Y. C., Cheung, M. C., Albert, M. S., Chiu, H. F. K., & Lam, L. C. (2005). Association between mind–body and cardiovascular exercises and memory in older adults. *Journal of the American Geriatrics Society, 53*, 1754–1760.

Chan, A. S., Kwok, I. C., Chiu, H., Lam, L., Pang, A., & Chow, L. (2000). Memory and organizational strategies in chronic and acute schizophrenic patients, *Schizophrenia Research, 41*, 431–445.

Chan, A. S., Poon, M. W., Choi, A., & Cheung, M. C. (2001). *Dementia Rating Scale.* Hong Kong: The Chinese University of Hong Kong. (in Chinese)

Chan, A. S., Shum, D., & Cheung, R. W. Y. (2003). Recent development of cognitive and neuropsychological assessment in Asian countries. *Psychological Assessment, 15*, 257–267.

Chan, A. S., Sze, S. L., & Cheung, M. (2007). Quantitative electroencephalographic profiles for children with autistic spectrum disorder. *Neuropsychology, 21*, 74–81.

Chan, A. S., Tam, J., Murphy, C., Chiu, H., & Lam, L. (2002). Utility of Olfactory Identification Test for diagnosing Chinese patients with Alzheimer's disease. *Journal of Clinical and Experimental Neuropsychology, 24*, 251–259.

Chan, A., Choi, A., Chiu, H., & Lam, L. (2003). Clinical validity of the Chinese version of Mattis Dementia Rating Scale in differentiating dementia of Alzheimer's type in Hong Kong. *Journal of the International Neuropsychological Society, 9*, 45–55.

Chen, W., Liu W., Wong, V. C. N. (2008). Electroacupuncture for children with autism spectrum disorder: Pilot study of 2 cases. *Journal of Alternative and Complementary Medicine, 14*, 1057–1065.

Chen, Y. H. & Chen, X. Y. (2002). *Wechsler Adult Intelligence Scale-III (Chinese).* Taiwan: Chinese Behavioral Science Corporation. (in Chinese)

Cheung, M. C. & Chan, A. S. (2003). Memory impairment in humans after bilateral damage to lateral temporal neocortex. *NeuroReport, 14*, 371–374.

Cheung, M. C., Chan, A. S., Law, S. C., Chan, J. H., & Tse, V. K. (2003). Impact of radionecrosis on cognitive dysfunction in patients after radiotherapy for nasopharyngeal carcinoma. *Cancer, 97*, 2019–2026.

Cheung, M. C., Chan, A. S., Chan, Y. L., & Lam, J. M. K. (2006a). Language lateralization of Chinese-English bilingual patients with temporal lobe epilepsy: A functional MRI study. *Neuropsychology, 20*, 589–597.

Cheung, M. C., Chan, A. S., Chan, Y. L., Lam, J. M. K., & Lam, W. (2006b). Effects of illness duration on memory processing of patients with temporal lobe epilepsy. *Epilepsia, 47*, 1320–1328.

Cheung, M. C., Chan, A. S., Law, S. C., Chan, J. H., & Tse, V. K. (2000). Cognitive functions of patients with nasopharyngeal carcinoma with and without temporal lobe radionecrosis. *Archives of Neurology, 57*, 1347–1352.

Cheung, R. W., Cheung, M. C., & Chan, A. S. (2004). Confrontation naming in Chinese patients with left, right or bilateral brain damage. *Journal of the International Neuropsychological Society, 10*, 46–53.

Chiu, H. F. K., Lam, L. C. W., Chi, I., Leung, T., Li, S. W., Law, W. T., Chung, D. W. S., Fung, H. H. L.,, Kan, P. S., Lum, C. M., Ng, J., & Lau, J. (1998). Prevalence of dementia in Chinese elderly in Hong Kong. *Neurology, 50*, 1002–1009.

Chiu, H. F. K., Lee, H. C., Chung, W. S., & Kwong, P. K. (1994). Reliability and validity of the Cantonese version of Mini Mental State Examination—A preliminary study. *Journal of Hong Kong College of Psychiatrists, 4, (Suppl 2)*, 25–28.

Chiu, W. T., Yeh, K. H., Li, Y. C., Gan, Y. H., Chen, H. Y., & Hung, C. C. (1997). Traumatic brain injury registry in Taiwan. *Neurology Research, 19*, 261–264.

Critchley, M. (1953). *The parietal lobes.* New York: Hafner.

Dai, X. Y., Gong, Y. X., & Zhong, L. P. (1990). Factor analysis of the Mainland Chinese version of the Wechsler Adult Intelligence Scale. *Psychological Assessment, 2*, 31–34.

Delis, D. C., Kramer, J. H., Kaplan, E., & Ober, B. A. (1987). *California Verbal Learning Test.* New York: Psychological Corporation.

Folstein, M. F., Folstein, S. E., & McHugh, P. R. (1975). Mini Mental State: A practical method for grading the cognitive state of patients for the clinician. *Journal of Psychiatric Research, 12*, 189–198.

Gao, X. (2003). Review of neuropsychology in China. *Journal of Postgraduates of Medicine*, 26, 1–3. (in Chinese)

Gong, Y. X. (1986). The Chinese revision of the Halstead-Reitan Neuropsychological Test Battery for adults. *Acta Psychologica Sinica, 18*, 433–442. (in Chinese)

Gong, Y. X. (1989). *Manual for the Wechsler Adult Intelligence Scale: Revised in China.* Changsha, Hunan, China: Hunan Medical University. (in Chinese)

Ho, S. C., Chan, A. S. Y., Ho, Y. P., So, E. K. F., Sham, A., Zee, B., & Woo, J. L. F. (2007). Effects of soy isoflavone supplementation on cognitive function in Chinese menopausal women: A double-blind, randomized, controlled trial. *Menopause, 14*, 489–499.

Hong Kong Psychological Society (1989). *Wechsler Adult Intelligence Scales* (rev. edn)—Hong Kong. Hong Kong: author.

Hong, Z. (2003). *Brief history of Chinese neuropsychology.* Paper presented at the International Conference on Neuropsychology, Hong Kong, Dec. 9–12.

Hu, Y. & Yu, J. (1999). Research on children with attention deficit/hyperactivity disorder. *International Social Medicine, 16*, 62–66. (in Chinese)

Hua, M. S. & Lu, L. H. J. (2003). *Neuropsychology in Taiwan: The present and the future.* Paper presented at the International Conference on Neuropsychology, Hong Kong, December, 9–12.

Jia, X., Yang, L., & Wang, G. (2008). The pathological mechanism of dementia of the Alzheimer's type and advances in pharmacological intervention. *Xinjian Chinese Medicine, 26*, 62–64.

Katzman, R., Zhang, M. Y., Qu, O. Y., Want, Z. Y., Liu W. T., Yu, E. et al. (1988). A Chinese version of the Mini Mental State Examination: Impact of illiteracy in a Shanghai dementia survey. *Journal of Clinical Epidemiology, 10*, 971–978.

Lam, L. C. W., Chiu, H. F. K., Li, S. W., Chan, W. F., Chan, C. K. Y., Wong, M., & Ng, K. O. (1997). Screening for dementia—a preliminary study on the validity of the Chinese version of the Blessed-Roth Dementia Scale. *International Psychogeriatrics, 9*, 39–46.

Lam, L. C. W., Chiu, H. F. K., Ng, K. O., & Chan, C. (1998). Clock-face drawing, reading and setting tests in the screening of Dementia in Chinese elderly adults. *Journal of Gerontology: Psychological Sciences, 53B*, 353–357.

Lam, L. C. W., Tang, W. K., Leung, V., & Chiu, H. F. K. (2001). Behavioral profile of Alzheimers disease in Chinese elderly: A validation study of the Chinese version of the Alzheimer's Disease Behavioral Pathology Rating Scale. *International Journal of Geriatric Psychology, 16*, 368–373.

Lam, T. C. P. (2004). Update on dementia. *HKMA CME Bulletin, 2004 June*, 1–5.

Le Couteur, A., Rutter, M., Lord, C., Rios, P., Robertson, S., Holdgrafer, M. et al. (1989). Autism Diagnostic Interview: A standardized investigator-based instrument. *Journal of Autism and Developmental Disorders, 19*, 363–387.

Lezak, M. D., Howieson, D. B., & Loring, D. W. (2004). *Neuropsychological asessment* (3rd edn). New York: Oxford University Press.

Li, X., Wu, X., Han, L., Wang, J., Want, T., Zhuang, Y., et al. (2000). A computerized neurobehavioral test system. *Chinese Mental Health Journal, 14*, 309–311. (in Chinese)

Liu, H., Lin, K., Teng. E. L., Wang, S., Fuh, J., Guo, N., Chou, P., Hu, H., Chiang, B. N. (1995). Prevalence and subtypes of dementia in Taiwan: A community survey of 5297 individuals. *Journal of the American Geriatrics Society, 43*, 144–149.

Lord, C., Rutter, M., Goode, S., Heemsbergen, J., Jordan, H., Mawhood, L. et al. (1989). Autism Diagnostic Observation Schedule: A standardized observation of communicative and social behavior. *Journal of Autism and Developmental Disorders, 19*, 182–212.

Mak, R. H. L., Lam, C. C. C., Ho, C. C. Y., & Wong, M. M. Y. (2006). *A primer in common developmental disabilities: Experience a Child Assessment Service, Hong Kong.* Hong Kong: Child Assessment Service, Department of Health.

Mattis, S. (1988). *Dementia Rating Scale professional manual.* Odessa, FL: Psychological Assessment Resources.

National Autism Association. (2007). Downloaded from the NAA website on October 31, 2007 (http://www.nationalautismassociation.org/definitions.php).

Plassman, B. L., Langa, K. M., Fisher, G. G., Heeringa, S. G., Weir, D. R., Ofstedal, M. B. et al. (2007). Prevalence of dementia in the United States: The aging, demographics, and memory study. *Neuroepidemiology, 29*, 125–132.

Rey, A. (1964). *L'examen clinique en psychologie.* Paris: Presses Universitaires de France.

Schopler, E., Reichler, R. J., & Renner, B. R. (1986). *The Childhood Autism Rating Scale (CARS).* New York: Irvington.

Shi, D. & Chan, A. S. (2008). *Dejian Mind–body Intervention.* Hong Kong: *Chan Wu Yi* Culture. (in Chinese)

Tamayo, J. M. (1987). Frequency of use as a measure of word difficulty in bilingual vocabulary test construction and translation. *Educational and Psychological Measurement, 47*, 893–902.

Wang, H. & Li, X. (2006). Reason and essence of developmental dyslexia. *Chinese Journal of Clinical Rehabilitation, 10*, 138–140. (in Chinese)

Wang, S. & Wang, Y. (2005). Retrospect and prospect of neuropsychology in China. *The Chinese Journal of Neurology, 38*, 151–153. (in Chinese)

Wing, L. & Potter, D. (2002). The epidemiology of autism spectrum disorders: Is the prevalence rising? *Mental Retardation and Developmental Disabilities Research Review, 8*, 151–161.

Wong, V. C. N. & Hui, S. L. H. (2007). Brief report: Emerging services for children with autism spectrum disorders in Hong Kong (1960–2004). *Journal of Autism and Developmental Disorders*, published online, June 29, 2007.

Wong, V. C. N., Sun J., & Yeung, D. W. C. (2006). Pilot study of efficacy of tongue and body acupuncture in children with visual impairment. *Journal of Child Neurology, 21*, 462–473.

Wong, V. C. N., Sun J., & Yeung, D. W. C. (2006). Pilot study of Positron Emission Tomography (PET) brain glucose metabolism to assess the efficacy of tongue and body acupuncture in cerebral palsy. *Journal of Child Neurology, 21*, 455–462.

World Health Organization. (1990). *International classification of diseases* (10th edn). Geneva: author.

Woo, J., Lau, E., Ho, S. C., Cheng, F., Chan, C., Chan, A. S. Y., Haines, C. J., Chan, T. Y. K., Li, M. & Sham, A. (2003). Comparison of *pueraria lobata* with hormone replacement therapy in treating the adverse health consequences of menopause. *Menopause, 10*, 352–361.

Xu, S. & Wu, Z. (1986). The construction of 'The Clinical Memory Test'. *Acta Psychologica Sinica, 18*, 100–108. (in Chinese)

Yang, X. (2008). Epidemiological features of senile dementia and its prevention. *Occupation and Health, 24*, 1317–1318.

Yiu, E. M. L. (1992). Linguistic assessment of Chinese-speaking aphasics: Development of a Cantonese aphasia battery. *Journal of Neurolinguistics, 7*, 379–424.

Yuan, G. (2000). Improving the development of neuropsychology in China. *The Chinese Journal of Neurology, 33*, 133–134. (in Chinese)

Zhang, X. & Ji, C. (2005). Autism and mental retardation of young children in China. *Biomedical & Environemntal Sciences, 18*, 334–340.

Zhou, D. F., Xu, C. S., Qi, H., Fan, J. H., Sun, X. D., Como, P., Qiao, Y. L., Zhang, L., & Kieburtz, K. (2006). Prevalence of dementia in rural China: Impact of age, gender and education. *Acta Neurology of Scandinavia, 114*, 273–280.

Zhu, R. (2008). Approach of a pathogenesis and therapy of Alzheimer Disease in TCM. *Shanxi Journal of Traditional Chinese Medicine, 24*, 1–3.

CHAPTER 24

The *Tao* (way) of Chinese coping

Cecilia Cheng, Barbara C. Y. Lo, and Jasmine H. M. Chio

In a multiple-country survey on perceived stress[1] among entrepreneurs (Grant Thornton International, 2005), Taiwan entrepreneurs were ranked top of the list. Over 60 per cent of the Taiwan participants reported that they have experienced an increased amount of stress over the past year. Entrepreneurs from Hong Kong came second. More than half of the Hong Kong participants reported higher levels of stress. It is worth noting that only two Chinese regions were sampled in this multinational survey, but both were in the top two. By contrast, entrepreneurs from Canada, the Netherlands, and Sweden had the lowest rankings. Only about a quarter or less of the participants in these countries reported experiencing an increase in stress levels during the past year.

Although both Taiwanese and Hong Kong business entrepreneurs are on top of the stress rankings, this does not necessarily mean that the Chinese are in danger of psychological problems. As the Chinese are instructed to perceive 'opportunities amidst dangerous circumstances' (危中有機, *wei zhong you ji*), stressful experience can be transformed into opportunities for personal growth and challenge if they are handled well.

The present chapter seeks to explore the unique Chinese ways of coping with stressors. As we will point out in the following sections, an extensive review of the literature revealed that the Chinese are characterized by (a) a greater tendency to use avoidant or emotion-focused coping, (b) greater flexibility in strategy deployment across stressful situations, and (c) a propensity to seek and utilize less social support. Each of these coping characteristics is discussed in the light of traditional cultural beliefs and contemporary cultural theories of psychology.

The *Tao* of 'passive' coping

Cross-cultural studies (e.g. Maxwell, Sukhodolsky, Chow, & Wong, 2005; Selmer, 2002) have revealed that the Chinese show a greater proclivity for using avoidant or emotion-focused coping, both of which are generally labeled as 'passive' coping in the Western literature (e.g. Majer, Jason, Ferrari, Olson, & North, 2003; Neria, 2001). The Chinese way of 'passive' coping may be related to their distinct perception of personal control, which may stem from the traditional cultural values of Chinese society.

Perceived control and traditional Chinese beliefs

Distinct from those of the Western cultural heritage, Eastern philosophical teachings and cultural beliefs emphasize the importance of managing stress and emotional distress by changing one's inner thoughts and desires instead of making overt changes in the environment. For instance, the virtue of forbearance (忍, *ren*) is valued in the Confucian school of thought. As stated in the Confucian doctrines, individuals should endure stress or suffering because these 'negative' experiences can be beneficial to individuals through strengthening their will, resilience, and inadequacies:

> 「天將降大任於斯人也，必先苦其心志，勞其筋骨，餓其體膚，空乏其身行，行拂亂其所為，所以動心忍性，曾益其所不能。」《孟子·告子下》
>
> When Heaven is about to confer a great office on any man, it first exercises his mind with suffering, and his sinews and bones with toil. It exposes his body to hunger, and subjects him to extreme poverty. It confounds his undertakings. By all these methods it stimulates his mind, hardens his nature, and supplies his incompetencies.
>
> *Gaozi II* by Mencius

Instead of interpreting stressful experiences as negative, such that active changes should be undertaken to eliminate them, the Confucian doctrines advocate that individuals appreciate the meaningful aspects and consequences brought about by negative encounters. As such, negative occurrences can foster personal growth and hardiness, so both acceptance and endurance of suffering are deemed appropriate responses for the Chinese. In particular, forbearance in this sense is framed as a virtue linking with moral obligations and responsibility to others in relation to preserving social harmony and group cohesion.

In a similar vein, Buddhist doctrines state that the essential causes of stress and suffering come from imbalances generated by the individual's mind, such as desires and pleasure seeking (vs. pain aversion). The best way to mitigate stress-related distress is to encourage individuals to be mindful of their psychological states and to transform desires into constructive thoughts. Such mindful practice and transformation can potentially lead to psychological serenity (Y. Chen, 2006a). As the causes and meanings of things in life tend to change all the time, individuals should accept and embrace life as a whole, not just the positive but also its negative aspects. They should also adopt a non-judgmental perspective when observing their own minds and emotional reactivity, such that liberation from their suffering can ultimately be achieved by means of reprocessing their inner thoughts and desires.

The Taoist school of thought also emphasizes the importance of acceptance and contentment. A core concept of the Taoist philosophy is *wu-wei* (無為), which means non-intervention or doing nothing but to follow whatever is given in life. It is important to note that the Taoist concept of *wu-wei* does not encourage the Chinese to stay passive and to refrain from gaining achievement or realizing goals. Ironically, the ultimate aim of *wu-wei* is to do and achieve many things:

> 「道常無為而無不為。侯王若能守之，萬物將自化。」《道德經》
>
> The *Tao* in its regular course does nothing (for the sake of doing it), and so there is nothing which it does not do. If princes and kings were able to maintain it, all things would of themselves be transformed by them.
>
> *Tao te ching*

In order to proactively handle stressors and adversities, Taoism encourages individuals to realize and understand the way nature changes and to transform their thinking, so that it becomes in harmony with the vicissitudes of the environment (Y. Chen, 2006b). For example, the Taoist doctrines state that all things in life are only relative in nature. No things are absolutely good or bad. Opposites such as 'good' and 'bad' represent only transient assessments that operate in cyclic patterns: When the negative aspect is vanished, the positive aspect will emerge, and vice versa. Hence, the Taoist school of thought advocates that there is no need to feel worried or upset about a negative encounter or to take drastic actions to eliminate it, because nature will take its re-balancing course in its own right.

Taken together, the Eastern philosophical traditions of Confucianism, Buddhism, and Taoism similarly advocate coping with adversity through changing one's mental or goal structure. A sense of control does not come from mastering the environment, but should derive from insights gained through pondering about why and how environmental changes emerge. It is important to reiterate that these philosophical teachings do not simply instruct individuals to ignore or avoid their problems by making no responses at all. Rather, the emphasis lies on the philosophical notion that individuals have to face and re-assess the sources of their psychological stress by means of attitudinal change and personal transformation. It is reasonable to infer that the use of cognitive coping strategies and secondary control coping for emotional regulation (e.g. appreciation, letting go) may be valued in these philosophical traditions.

Perceived control and contemporary cultural theories

Traditional cultural values not only represent the thoughts and behaviors of people from many centuries ago, but are still influencing people in particular cultures at the present time (Triandis, 1995). Individuals from Western, individualistic cultures and those from Asian, collectivistic cultures differ in many ways, especially in the way they construe themselves in relation to others (Markus & Kitayama, 1991; Singelis, 1994). Markus and Kitayama put forward two models—independent and interdependent—to account for cultural variations in self-construals. According to their cultural theory, individuals from individualistic cultures have a greater orientation toward independent self-construal. These individuals tend to view themselves as being autonomous, unique, and abstracted from the environment. By contrast, individuals from collectivistic cultures have a greater orientation toward interdependent self-construal. They tend to identify themselves as an integral part of their social network, thus regarding their behaviors as being influenced by the thoughts, feelings, and behaviors of others. In other words, individuals from collectivistic cultures tend to view their 'self' as relational in nature and influenced by their interpersonal relations (see Hwang, this volume: Kwan, Hui, & McGee, this volume).

Cultural self-construals are proposed to play an influential role in the cognitive processes of causal attribution and perception of personal control. The Chinese, who tend to view themselves as inseparable from others, are proposed to consider the larger group and the environment as having a powerful impact on their and others' thoughts, feelings, and behaviors. Compared to their Western counterparts who tend to view themselves as separate from others, the Chinese are more likely to adopt an external attributional style, which refers to a proclivity for adopting external or situational factors for explaining the cause of events or behaviors (see e.g. Buchanan & Seligman, 1995). Such a notion is consistent with the results from the study by Peng and Knowles (2003). In this study, Chinese and European-American participants were shown a series of events and were instructed to explain why such events took place. Results indicated that the Chinese tend to take account of situational cues, and explain the cause of events in terms of contextual factors. European Americans tend to take account of the actor's inner attributes, and explain the cause of events in terms of dispositional factors.

As the Chinese tend to focus more on situational factors in making attributions, they may be less susceptible to the fundamental attribution error, which refers to the tendency to overestimate the influence of dispositional factors on behaviors despite the presence of environmental constraints (see Ross, 1977). Norenzayan, Choi, and Nisbett (1999) found that both Asians and European-Americans are similar in thinking in a dispositional manner when no situational information is provided. When situational cues are presented, however, Asians are more likely to consider these cues when making their attributions, whereas European-Americans tend not to consider those cues, even if they are obvious.

Apart from having an external attributional style, the Chinese are also proposed to be characterized by a weaker sense of personal control than their Western counterparts. Specifically, the Chinese may be less likely to perceive autonomy in pursuing their own goals and determining outcomes of their lives. These postulations received support from some cross-cultural studies. Sastry and Ross (1998) analyzed the data derived from the 1990 World Values Survey and compared the perception of personal control between individuals from Asian, collectivistic countries and those from Western, individualistic countries. They found that Asians generally perceive having less personal control than do those from Western countries. These results were further replicated in O'Connor and Shimizu's (2002) study, which indicates that Japanese tend to perceive a lower level of personal control over their environment than do their British counterparts (see also Bond & Tornatsky, 1973). Moreover, Chinese managers generally perceive a greater extent of external control over their actions than do their British counterparts (Lu, Kao, Cooper, & Spector, 2000).

Cultural differences can be found in not only general perception of control over one's environment, but also in the specific context of health maintenance and enhancement. The study by Wrightson and Wardle (1997) compared perceived health locus of control among Asians, Europeans, and Africans in England. Participants in this study were asked to describe how their health was influenced by internal factors over which they could exert control, i.e. under the control of their own behaviors, or external factors over which they did not have much control, i.e. under the control of powerful others or chance. Compared to their European and African counterparts, Asians were more likely to perceive their health as subject to the control from both powerful others and chance. However, there were no differences in self-evaluations of health status among the ethnic groups. One's self-reported health was not a consequence of how health outcomes were explained.

To conclude, this body of cross-cultural studies consistently reveals that, compared to individuals from individualistic countries, those from collectivistic cultures are more likely to attribute the cause of behaviors and events to external factors. Individuals from collectivistic cultures also generally perceive themselves to exercise less personal control over the environment and their own health.

Perceived control and the *Tao* of 'passive' coping

Because perceived control has been found to influence the use of coping strategies (e.g. Anderson, 1977; Birkimer, Johnston, & Dearmond, 1993; Endler, Speer, Johnson, & Flett, 2000; Osowiecki & Compas, 1999), the relatively lower levels of perceived personal control among individuals from collectivistic cultures may explain in part why they tend to use more avoidant or emotion-focused coping than do their Western counterparts. Examining cultural values and beliefs (see Leung & Li, this volume) may provide further insights onto the use of these types of coping strategy. In collectivistic cultures, social cohesion and in-group harmony are highly valued (see Triandis, Bontempo, Villareal, Asai, & Lucca, 1988). Individuals from these cultures are motivated to avoid conflicts in interpersonal relations. So, to minimize the risk of direct confrontations with others, the Chinese may prefer altering their own thoughts and behaviors than attempting to change others or the environment. They may also expect social resistance and rejection for doing so.

Benefits of emotion-focused coping for Chinese. In Western literature (e.g. Farone, Fitzpatrick, & Bushfield, 2007; Martin, Thomas, Charles, Epitropaki, & McNamara, 2005), having a strong sense of perceived control is related to positive psychological outcomes, whereas perception of an external locus of control is related to negative psychological outcomes. Although the Chinese generally perceive themselves to exercise less personal control than do their counterparts from individualistic countries, the Chinese may not necessarily experience greater maladjustment. This is probably because autonomy is less valued in Chinese society than in individualistic countries. Consistent with this notion, some cross-cultural studies have failed to reveal a reliable link between personal control and psychological well-being. The study by Sastry and Ross (1998) revealed a strong inverse relationship between perceived control and psychological well-being for individuals from individualistic countries. However, such a relationship was much weaker for Asians. Similarly, O'Connor and Shimizu (2002) showed that perceived control buffered stress-related distress among British participants but not among Japanese participants.

Ironically, having a sense of external control may be associated with adaptive outcomes for the Chinese. Jose and Huntsinger (2005) found that the effects of stress on adjustment outcomes are moderated by the specific type of coping strategies adopted by Chinese-American adolescents but not by European-American adolescents. In contrast to the Western findings that consistently revealed a link between problem-focused coping and adaptive outcomes (e.g. Elfering et al., 2005; Stoneman & Gavidia-Payne, 2006), their results indicate that problem-focused coping is related to greater psychological maladjustment at moderate to high levels of stress for Chinese-American adolescents. Avoidant coping has been found to be most effective in mitigating stress-related distress under high stress levels among Chinese-American adolescents. Such findings imply that the same type of coping strategies can have different effects on stress-related outcomes when being used by individuals from different cultures. No single type of coping strategy is equally effective across cultures.

Cultural differences in the effectiveness of avoidant or emotion-focused coping may be attributed to its specific meaning that varies across cultures. For the Chinese, deployment of avoidant or emotion-focused coping may not necessarily reflect passivity, as suggested in Western literature. It is possible that by adopting a 'passive' coping style, the Chinese can actively gain control through indirect means. This idea is consistent with the notion proposed by Rothbaum, Weisz, and Snyder (1982), who proposed that individuals can seek control via two processes, namely primary and secondary control. Primary control refers to effort made in an attempt to change external or environmental factors to fit one's needs and expectations. By contrast, secondary control refers to attempts to change one's thoughts or behaviors to fit the environment. Applying these constructs to the Chinese context, these control-seeking methods may constitute part of the passive coping style commonly observed among the Chinese. As such, adoption of avoidant or emotion-focused coping may actually be beneficial to the Chinese by increasing their sense of control.

In line with this notion, Spector and colleagues (2004) contended that changing oneself to fit the environment may be seen as an active, effective means to reserve and mobilize social resources to handle stressors, especially among individuals from collectivistic cultures. They maintained that being sensitive to others and adopting passive coping strategies functioned to cultivate what they referred to as 'socio-instrumental control', which refers to the power of changing the external environment via social means. To test their propositions, the researchers examined work stress among university students and working adults in China, Hong Kong, and the United States. Results indicate that socio-instrumental control can account for variance in work stress and strains over and above that explained by locus of control, but this pattern of results was found among Hong Kong Chinese only. Although mixed findings have emerged, such findings are still intriguing in suggesting that the use of avoidant or emotion-focused coping does not necessarily denote passivity. Instead, this type of coping strategy can reflect alternative avenues, such as social resources, for handling stressors among the Chinese.

Individual differences in emotion-focused coping. Although the Chinese collectivistic culture seems to promote greater use of avoidant or emotion-focused coping, it is important to note that intragroup differences also exist among the Chinese. For instance, variations in the use of coping strategies have been found among Chinese adolescents from different family backgrounds. Hamid, Yue, and Leung (2003) examined the possible influence of family environment on the coping style of Chinese adolescents. Their findings indicate that family environment moderates the extent to which traditional Chinese values are translated into the use of emotion-focused strategies for Chinese adolescents. To elaborate, Chinese adolescents whose families are warm, supportive, and recreation-oriented have a greater tendency to adopt 'the philosophy of doing nothing' (*wu-wei*) than do their counterparts whose families are controlling and conflict-ridden. These findings imply that the use of emotion-focused coping may vary among Chinese adolescents, and such individual differences may be explained in part by their family background.

Apart from family influences, gender is another possible factor related to individual differences in the use of emotion-focused coping. Liu, Tein, and Zhao (2004) found reliable differences in the use of emotion-focused coping between Chinese boys and girls. Results indicate that Chinese girls tend to use more emotion-focused coping strategies (e.g. 'cry by myself', 'get upset') than boys. Gender differences were also found among Chinese adults. The studies by Shek (1992) and D. W. Chan (1994) indicate that male Chinese adults are more prone to adopt personal coping, whereas Chinese female adults are more prone to seek external help for handling stressors. Such results are consistent with the traditional Chinese beliefs that place heavy emphasis on gender-role stereotypes. Specifically, Chinese men are expected to be strong and tough, whereas Chinese women are expected to be tender and caring (see e.g. X. Chen, 2000; Lii & Wong, 1982). Nevertheless, it is worth noting that other

Chinese studies (D. W. Chan, 1995; Gerdes & Ping, 1994; Wang & Chen, 2001) revealed no gender differences in the type of coping strategies used, thus leaving the role of gender on strategy deployment inconclusive. Other important, but unmeasured variables, like social axioms (see Leung & Li, this volume) for example, may be confounding the outcomes.

Balanced use of problem- and emotion-focused coping. The discussions so far suggest that the use of emotion-focused coping is common among the Chinese, but this does not necessarily mean that the use of problem-focused coping is uncommon. Such a notion is consistent with studies that examined both problem-focused and emotion-focused coping among Chinese samples. Liu, Tein, and Zhao (2004) scrutinized the coping behaviors of Chinese adolescents. Results indicate that Chinese adolescents do not confine themselves to the use of a single type of coping strategies. Instead, they tend to use a variety of coping strategies, including both problem-focused coping (e.g. 'Try to improve the situation') and emotion-focused coping (e.g. 'Take it out of my mind'). Another study by Wang and Chen (2001) explored how Chinese high school students cope with academic stressors. Chinese students were also found to deploy both problem-focused coping (i.e. problem solving and social-support seeking) and emotion-focused coping (i.e. avoidance, distancing, positive reappraisal, and self-control).

Similar findings emerge from coping studies conducted with samples of Chinese adults. Hwang and colleagues (2002) examined the coping strategies used by health-care workers and teachers from China, Taiwan, and the United States. Similar to their European-American counterparts, the Chinese from the two regions also tend to use both problem-focused coping (i.e. planful problem solving) and emotion-focused coping (i.e. distancing and positive reappraisal). The study by Cheng, Wang, and Golden (in press) indicates that, although Chinese university students generally use less problem-focused coping and more emotion-focused coping than their European-American counterparts, the Chinese do use both types of coping strategies to handle stressors. All these findings suggest that the Chinese tend to have a balanced coping profile comprising both problem- and emotion-focused coping rather than a predominant use of emotion-focused coping only. It may be that their sequencing in the use of coping strategies is worth exploring in future studies.

In conclusion, several issues regarding the use of avoidant or emotion-focused coping among the Chinese are worth noting: First, although Western studies consistently reveal a reliable link between emotion-focused coping and maladaptive outcomes, such a link is much weaker among the Chinese. Second, cross-cultural comparisons reveal that the Chinese tend to use more emotion-focused coping than do their Western counterparts. However, individual differences in the use of emotion-focused coping among Chinese can also be found and should be expected. Third, Gerdes and Ping (1994) suggested that most individuals adopt *both* problem-focused and emotion-focused coping strategies to handle stressors, but the relative weighting may vary. Some studies provide support for this notion by revealing that the Chinese do use both problem-focused coping and emotion-focused coping. This balanced coping profile may equip them with a variety of strategies to cope flexibly with an ever-changing environment.

The *Tao* of flexible coping

As mentioned in the previous section, the Chinese tend to use more avoidant or emotion-focused coping than their Western counterparts. It is noteworthy that these cross-cultural studies have adopted global measures of coping. A close examination of the studies revealed that for Western participants, the mean scores of this coping type generally fall within the 'low' range, indicating infrequent use of avoidant or emotion-focused coping strategies in most stressful situations. Although Chinese participants give lower scores than their Western counterparts, their scores generally fall within the 'moderate' rather than the 'high' range. Such moderate levels of strategy deployment imply that the Chinese may use avoidant or emotion-focused coping in certain stressful situations, but not in all.

Consistent with this notion, Cheng, Wang, and Golden (in press) adopted a situation-based measure of coping and found that Chinese participants tend to display a greater extent of coping flexibility across situations. Their proneness to vary the use of 'opposing' (i.e. approach vs. avoidant, problem-focused vs. emotion-focused, active vs. passive) coping strategies may reflect a higher capacity for dialectical thinking, which is characterized by a unique perspective on change, contradiction, and meaning of events (see e.g. Hou & Zhu, 2002; Peng & Nisbett, 1999). In view of change, dialectical thinkers tend to perceive that the world and all the events embedded in it are always changing. In view of contradiction, these individuals tend to accept that seemingly contradicting propositions can coexist in a balanced and harmonious manner. In view of meaning, they tend to regard that the meaning of an event can be reflected by its opposite predication or other relevant alternatives. The specific meaning of any event is framed by its context.

Dialectical thinking and Chinese traditional beliefs

Dialectical thinking has its roots in ancient Chinese philosophy (see Cheng, Lee, & Chiu, 1999). This mode of thinking, commonly adopted by Chinese scholars and thinkers, is best represented in Chinese classic scriptures, such as *I Ching* or *Book of Changes* (易經, *Yi Jing*), *Tao Ta Ching* (道德經, *Dao De Jing*), the *Doctrine of the Mean* (中庸, *Zhong Rong*), and the *Lu's Annals* (呂氏春秋, *Lu Shi Chun Qiu*). These classic scriptures describe dialectical views on cosmology and ways of living at the heart of Chinese traditional beliefs.

The fundamental doctrines of the Taoist *Book of Changes* (易經, *Yi Jing*) reflect ancient Chinese dialectical views of the universe, which revolve around three metaphysical themes: (a) the eternity of change in the universe, (b) accepting the inevitability of changes, and (c) the dynamism of balance between opposites. According to this classic scripture, all entities in the universe are interrelated and exist in a persistent state of flux and change. Yet order and regularity can be maintained in the midst of constant changes. A relative stability can be achieved if there is a harmonious balance of two seemingly contrasting but related natural forces of *yin* and *yang*. These two fundamental opposite forces do not simply reflect dualism. Rather, they are viewed to be constantly interacting with one another to produce changes:

> 「日往則月來，月往則日來，日月相推而明生焉。寒往則暑來，暑往則寒來，寒暑相推而歲成焉。往者屈也，來者信也，屈信相感而利生焉。」《易經·繫辭下》
>
> The sun goes and the moon comes; the moon goes and the sun comes; the sun and moon thus take the place each of the other, and their shining is the result. The cold goes and the heat comes; the heat goes and the cold comes; it is by this mutual succession of the cold and heat that the year is completed. That which goes becomes less and less, and that which comes waxes more and more; it is by the influence on each other of this contraction and expansion that the advantages (of the different conditions) are produced.
>
> *I Ching—Xi Ci II*

Dialecticism can be traced not only in ancient Taoist cosmology, but also in the Confucian canon, the *Doctrine of the Mean*. Referring to this scripture, the 'mean' or *zhongrong* (中庸) comprises the fundamental concepts of moderation, balance, and appropriateness. Practically, the doctrine of the mean and harmony can be applied to principles governing the Chinese way of living. Specifically, all behaviors contain two extremes, each having its own strengths and weaknesses. Focusing on either of the extremes is deemed inadequate, and both extremes should be considered. To act appropriately in the ever-changing environment, individuals need to avoid adhering to extremes and to place themselves in the 'middle way' (中道, *zhong dao*). If they can follow the ebb and flow of nature, they can apply one extreme in a certain situation and the other extreme when the situation changes. In this way, the two extremes are complementary to each other and a state of harmony can be attained.

In summary, dialecticism is fundamental to both the Taoist and the Confucian schools of thought (see e.g. Pang, 1984; Qian, 2001 for a discussion). The Chinese dialectical views emphasize a flexible way of handing complex matters in response to environmental changes. The Chinese saying of 'using methods appropriate to the current situation' (因時制宜, *yin shi zhi yi*) is a good reflection of the dialectical views on adaptation to the ever-changing environment.

Dialectical thinking and contemporary cultural theories

Although dialecticism has its roots in ancient times, it has been found to influence the Chinese thinking style in the present. Peng and associates (Peng & Nisbett, 1999; Peng, Spencer-Rodgers, & Nian, 2006) formulated a theory of naïve dialecticism to account for cultural differences in thinking modes (see also Ji, Lam, & Guo, this volume). Specifically, North Americans are proposed to be characterized by a synthetic mode of thinking, but East Asians are proposed to be characterized by a dialectical mode of thinking.

Peng and Nisbett (1999) conducted a content analysis on Chinese and American proverbs. They found that a greater number of Chinese proverbs contain seeming contradictions such as 'Things will develop in the opposite direction when they become extreme' (物極必反, *wu ji bi fan*) and 'Too far is as bad as not enough' (過猶不及, *guo you bu ji*). However, nondialectical American proverbs such as 'One against all is certain to fall' and 'For example is no proof' are more common. When asked to indicate their preferences, Chinese university students generally express greater liking for dialectical proverbs, whereas European-American university students generally express greater liking for nondialectical ones (Peng & Nisbett, 1999, Studies 1 and 2). These patterns of result have been replicated in the resolution of daily-life contradictions (Peng & Nisbett, 1999, Study 3) and the perception of formal arguments (Peng & Nisbett, 1999, Studies 4 and 5).

Cultural differences in naïve dialecticism can also be found in self-evaluations. Some studies (Bond & Cheung, 1983; Kanagawa, Cross, & Markus, 2001; Spencer-Rodgers, Peng, Wang, & Hou, 2004) explored the self-appraisal processes among Chinese and European-American university students. Results indicate that compared to their European American counterparts, Chinese university students tend to display greater contradictions in their self-views. Specifically, Chinese university students are more likely to endorse a relatively balanced self-view, as reflected by a proclivity of endorsing both positive and negative statements when evaluating themselves. By contrast, European American university students tend to endorse a relatively more extreme self-view, as reflected by a greater tendency to endorse positive self-statements (Ip & Bond, 1995).

Dialectical thinking and the *Tao* of flexible coping

As reviewed previously, different types of coping strategies have been identified in the literature, each having their distinct characteristics and functions. To cope with the ever-changing environment, individuals cannot adhere to a specific type of coping strategy. Rather, they may need to flexibly deploy a variety of coping strategies to meet the demands arising from a vast array of stressful situations (Cheng, 2003; Chiu, Hong, Mischel, & Shoda, 1995). Coping flexibility is thus conceptualized as '(a) variability in cognitive appraisal and coping patterns across stressful situations, and (b) a good fit between the nature of coping strategies and situational demands' (Cheng, 2001, p. 816).

Cheng and Cheung (2005a) scrutinized the cognitive mechanisms that underlie coping flexibility and identified two stress-appraisal processes: differentiation and integration. Differentiation refers to a mental ability that fosters the recognition of multiple dimensions embedded in a perceived domain, and adopting different perspectives when considering the domain (see e.g. Stephan, 1977; Tramer & Schludermann, 1974). Integration refers to a mental ability that fosters the perception of trade-offs among alternatives in combination or interaction (see e.g. Stewin, 1976; Suedfeld & Coren, 1992). Results indicate that Chinese individuals who cope more flexibly tend to differentiate among stressful events using various perceptual dimensions, and deploy an integrated strategy to handle stressors with different degrees of controllability. This integrated strategy involves greater use of problem-focused strategies in controllable situations, but lesser use of such strategies in uncontrollable situations.

Coping flexibility is proposed to be especially relevant to Chinese ways of coping because this construct is linked to dialectical thinking. A recent study by Cheng (2009) documented that Chinese individuals who display a more flexible coping pattern are characterized by a more dialectical mode of thinking. These individuals hold a unique view and tend to perceive the environment as ever-changing and the meaning of events is framed by the specific situation in which it is embedded.

They tend to recognize that a particular type of coping strategy may not always be useful to handle all stressors. Rather, the effectiveness of any type of coping strategy varies as the nature of stressors change. They also tend to acknowledge differences among the characteristics and functions of different coping strategies, and thus are ready to vary their deployment of coping strategies to handle stressors with distinct nature.

Although this body of studies reveal that the Chinese are more likely to adopt a dialectical mode of thinking than are European-Americans, this does not necessarily mean that all Chinese people are characterized by a dialectical mode of thinking and a flexible coping style. Rather, studies on coping flexibility (e.g. Cheng, 2005; Chow, Au, & Chiu, 2008; Gan, Shang, & Zhang, 2007; Lam & McBride-Chang, 2007) consistently indicate that the Chinese differ considerably in their propensity of strategy deployment to cope with stressors. Three major styles of coping flexibility have been identified, with each characterized by a unique pattern of coping across stressful situations. First, some Chinese individuals are characterized by a flexible coping style. They tend to deploy more problem-focused coping in controllable stressful situations, but more emotion-focused coping in uncontrollable stressful situations. Second, some Chinese individuals are characterized by an active-inflexible coping style. They tend to predominantly use more problem-focused coping regardless of the characteristics of stressful situations. Third, some Chinese individuals are characterized by a passive-inflexible coping style. They tend to use more emotion-focused coping regardless of the characteristics of stressful situations.

Flexible coping style. Coping flexibility delineates the process that underlies how individuals vary their strategy deployment as the characteristics of stressors change, thus emphasizing the stable, meaningful aspects of variable coping pattern associated with psychological adjustment. Consistent with this notion, Chinese studies revealed that coping flexibility was related to a number of salutary psychological outcomes, such as lower levels of anxiety and dysphoria (Cheng, 2001, 2003, 2009; Cheng, Chiu, Hong, & Cheung, 2001; Chow et al., 2008; Lam & McBride-Chang, 2007), fewer stress-related symptoms such as proneness to worry and exhaustion (Cheng, 2003, Study 3; Gan et al., 2007), more adaptive interpersonal functioning (Cheng et al., 2001; Chow et al., 2008; Lam & McBride-Chang, 2007), and a better overall quality of life (Cheng, 2003).

The relationship between coping flexibility and adaptive psychological outcomes was more robustly tested in studies that employed a longitudinal design. Studies (Cheng, 2001, Study 3; Cheng, 2003, Study 3) examined coping flexibility at baseline and its association with coping outcomes over time. Results revealed that coping flexibility predicted a reduction in anxiety and depression, palliation of symptom severity, and elevation in overall quality of life over time for the Chinese. Findings from longitudinal studies thus provide some stronger evidence for causation between coping flexibility and salutary psychological outcomes for the Chinese.

Active-inflexible coping style. Apart from including healthy individuals as participants, some Chinese studies compared the extent of coping flexibility among patients with functional gastrointestinal illnesses, whose symptoms cannot be explained by organic or biochemical causes (see e.g. Wong, Cheng, Hui, & Lam, 2003; Wong, Cheng, Hui, & Wong, 2003; Wong, Cheng, Wong, & Hui, 2003 for details). The influential role of psychological factors on functional gastrointestinal illnesses has been well documented (e.g. Drossman, 1993; Haug, Svebak, Wilhelmsen, Berstad, & Ursin, 1994; Kane, Strohlein, & Harper, 1993; Morris, 1991).

The program of studies by Cheng and colleagues (A. O. Chan et al., 2005; Cheng, Chan, Hui, & Lam, 2003; Cheng, Hui, & Lam, 1999, 2000, 2002, 2004; Cheng, Hui, Lai, & Lam, 1998; Cheng, Wong et al., 2003; Cheng, Yang, Jun, & Hutton, 2007) found that Chinese patients with functional gastrointestinal illnesses are characterized by an active-inflexible coping style. Specifically, these Chinese patients tend to display a nondiscriminating, action-oriented coping pattern across stressful situations, that is, problem-focused coping is adopted uniformly regardless of the fluctuations of events. These patients tend to perceive most stressful situations as subject to their control, experience heightened levels of anxiety, and have more stress-induced symptoms.

The coping behaviors of Chinese patients with functional gastrointestinal illnesses have also been scrutinized in a real-life, stressful encounter. Cheng and colleagues (2002) adopted an observational design to examine the coping behaviors of Chinese patients with functional gastrointestinal illnesses when they received endoscopy for the first time. Their coping behaviors were compared with those of Chinese patients having duodenal ulcer, a structural gastrointestinal disorder. Results from the observation revealed that compared with Chinese patients with duodenal ulcer, Chinese patients with functional gastrointestinal illnesses displayed more problem-focused strategies and less emotion-focused strategies. Chinese patients with functional gastrointestinal illnesses also reported greater anxiety levels before and after the endoscopy, more pain and discomfort during the endoscopy, and great dissatisfaction with the medical procedures.

Passive-inflexible coping style. In contrast to individuals with an active-inflexible coping style who predominantly use problem-focused coping, Chinese individuals with a passive-inflexible coping style are characterized by predominant use of emotion-focused coping regardless of situational characteristics. Adopting a situational analysis, Cheng (2001) found that individuals with a passive-inflexible coping style are characterized by an inflexible cognitive pattern of perceived uncontrollability. Specifically, they tend to perceive the outcome of most stressful events as beyond their control. This inflexible perceptual style is akin to the dysfunctional depressive attribution that emphasizes: (a) internality, which implies that things are generally unchangeable by oneself; (b) stability, which implies inconsistency over time; and (c) globality, which implies inconsistency across situations. Consistent with the propositions of the cognitive theories of depression (Abramson, Alloy, & Metalsky, 1986; Abramson, Metalsky, & Alloy, 1986; Beck, 1976, 1983), Cheng's findings further revealed that individuals with a passive-inflexible coping style experienced higher levels of depressive mood than those who prefer other coping styles.

Gan and colleagues (2006) expanded Cheng's work by examining the coping style of Chinese patients with neurasthenia and unipolar depression. Compared with Chinese individuals without psychological problems, Chinese patients tend to use less problem-focused coping and more emotion-focused coping. Chinese patients with unipolar depression tend to perceive most situations as uncontrollable, and are less flexible in coping than patients with neurasthenia, who in turn are less flexible in coping than Chinese individuals without psychological problems. These results thus revealed a link between the passive-inflexible coping style and depressive symptoms.

Situational influences on coping flexibility. Studies on coping flexibility reviewed so far suggest that coping flexibility is an individual difference factor. However, not many individual differences in coping flexibility have been found in studies conducted during the SARS outbreak in hard hit regions of Beijing and Hong Kong (Cheng & Cheung, 2005b; Gan, Liu, & Zhang, 2004). These studies were conducted at the beginning of the outbreak when there was still not much understanding about SARS or about treatment to cure the virus, thus leaving people scared, nervous, or even depressed (see Cheng & Ng, 2006; Cheng & Tang, 2004; Cheng, Wong, & Tsang, 2006; Tsang et al., 2003). During this period, most Chinese participants were found to be characterized by a passive-inflexible coping style, indicating a predominant adoption of avoidant or emotion-focused coping to handle the health crisis. Specifically, they avoided going out dining and shopping, shaking hands with people, as well as meeting people who coughed, sneezed, or had just returned from a SARS-infected region (Cheng & Cheung, 2005b).

These findings indicate that although individual differences in coping flexibility have been found, not many variances are found under some 'strong' stressful situations such as the SARS outbreak. 'Strong' situations are characterized by the presence of powerful social norms and behavioral controls that guide individuals what to behave (see e.g. Mischel, 1977; Snyder & Ickes, 1985). In these situations, the impact of situational characteristics can become so powerful that they may override personality characteristics in influencing individuals' behaviors. As individuals from collectivistic cultures have strong motivations to comply with social norms, it is not surprising to find individual differences in coping flexibility to have faded, at least temporarily, among the Chinese during the SARS outbreak. Hence, their coping responses were more influenced by the particular societal norms than by their own style of coping flexibility.

In summary, flexible coping has been found to be associated with dialectical thinking among the Chinese. Although the Chinese are generally characterized by a dialectical mode of thinking, individual differences exist. Some prefer to adopt a flexible coping style, whereas others prefer an inflexible coping style. Despite such individual differences, most of the Chinese have been found to behave inflexibly when coping with a 'strong' stressful context, namely the SARS outbreak.

The *Tao* of social-support seeking

When encountering stress, individuals may not always cope by themselves, but also seek support from their social network (see e.g. Cobb, 1995; Shinn, Lehmann, & Wong, 1984). As the Chinese are characterized by interdependent self-construals, they should be more motivated to seek support from others when experiencing stress than would European-Americans who are characterized by independent self-construals. Contrary to expectations, cross-cultural studies (Pines, Zaidman, Wang, Chengbing, & Ping, 2003; S. E. Taylor et al., 2004) consistently document that Asians are less likely to seek social support than their Western counterparts. Although the Chinese tend to seek social support less frequently, Chinese participants were found to place a greater value on social support than were their Jewish counterparts (Pines et al., 2003). This finding suggests that the Chinese may utilize social support in a unique manner that differs from the social-support seeking typically conceptualized in Western literature. To analyze the cultural meaning of social-support seeking among the Chinese, the characteristics of social network in traditional Chinese societies will be explored.

Collectivism in traditional Chinese societies

A significant feature of traditional Chinese societies is collectivism, which values a close-knit social structure in which group goals are placed on top of personal needs (Hofstede & Bond, 1988). Confucian philosophy has exerted a great impact on how the Chinese relate to their families or family clans, social networks, and the society at large. In the Confucian conception of society, the classic paradigm of *wu lun* (五倫) or five cardinal relations, summarizes the fundamental social dyads in the society: ruler–minister, father–son, elder brother–younger brother, husband–wife, and friend–friend. The first four dyads refer to hierarchical relations, whereas the fifth refers to social relations with an equal status. According to this paradigm, every individual is connected with others in the society in certain ways, at least at the most basic level of friend–to–friend relations. Dynamic relations among individuals are emphasized in the Confucian society. Individuals are not seen only as passive beings conforming to their specific roles in the social network, but also making active contributions to other parties and the society.

It is worth noting that *wu lun* does not simply refer to connections among individuals. Relations are 'ordered by status' (尊卑有序, *zun bei you xu*) in hierarchical relationships, and observing such order is important in Confucian society. Specifically, each party is prescribed with a specific social role and a spectrum of proper behaviors, which are referred to as *li* (禮) or propriety. All parties have to fulfill their own role and ritual propriety in social relations in order to maintain harmony in their relations and in society.

The principle of reciprocity operates in social relations. Specifically, the party with less social empowerment (i.e. ministers, sons, younger brothers, and wives) should respect and obey the other party with greater social empowerment (i.e. rulers, fathers, elder brothers, and husbands). In return, the party with less social empowerment will obtain benevolence and support from the other party. For instance, in father–son relations, the son is obliged to obey his father. The father is obliged to be just and kind to his son. Propriety represents the ideal standard of social conduct that guides appropriate responses to interpersonal relations. If any party fails to follow this ideal standard, relational harmony and social order are thought to be disrupted (see also Hwang & Han, this volume).

The Confucian doctrine of propriety provides the structure for social interactions in Chinese society. Another important doctrine, benevolence (仁, *jen*), constitutes the foundation of all social relations. The core of benevolence is to 'love all men' (*The Analects* by Yan Yuan). Benevolence also refers to a broad set of moral values such as deference, kindness, loyalty, and forgiveness. In Confucian teachings, the best way to cultivate benevolence is to empathize with others and then treat others accordingly. As Confucius remarked;

> 「己所不欲，勿施於人」《論語·衛靈公》
> Do not do to others what you would not like them to do to you.
>
> Wei Ling Gong, in *The Analects*

In Confucian thought, the superior man should live by the doctrines of propriety and benevolence. They should display virtuous behaviors in accordance with propriety when exercising multiple roles. For instance, as a minister, a person should be loyal and faithful to his ruler. As a husband, he should display justice and righteousness towards his wife. These Confucian doctrines, founded in several centuries ago, have become the rituals and standards of conduct for Chinese society over time.

Collectivism and contemporary cultural theories

The Confucian doctrines of propriety and benevolence still influence people at the present time. Specifically, the Confucian doctrine of benevolence emphasizes a concern for others in order to maintain harmonious interpersonal relations (see Yum, 1988). For the Chinese, awareness of one's relations with others constitutes an important element of *zuo ren* (做人) or 'conducting oneself'. Moreover, the Confucian doctrine of propriety denotes a system of proper conduct and decorum in interpersonal relations. For the Chinese, inappropriate behavior in the presence of others is referred to as a loss of *li* (失禮, *shi li*) or a loss of face (丟臉, *diu lian*). The Chinese are still concerned about face saving and thus tend to avoid losing face or losing *li* in social relations.

The concept of face is fundamentally important for understanding social interactions in Chinese society (see e.g. Gao, 1998; D. Y. F. Ho, 1976). For the Chinese, the influence of face is so salient that it 'exerts a mutually restrictive, even coercive, power upon each member of the social network' (D. Y. F. Ho, 1976, p. 873). There are two conceptualizations of face in Chinese culture: *lian* (臉) and *mianzi* (面子). According to Hu (1944), *lian* is related to personal integrity and moral character, and a loss of *lian* 'makes it impossible for him [or her] to function properly within the community' (p. 45). *Mianzi* is related to public self-image achieved through success, and revealing one's weaknesses or problems to others will result in a loss of *mianzi*. Losing face does not only result in a loss of one's own social standing but also brings embarrassment to one's family, and thus losing face is a highly undesirable interpersonal event for the Chinese (D. Y. F. Ho, 1994). These proposals suggest that the Chinese tend to have an overwhelming concern about others' appraisal of themselves. Such relational concerns lead to a tendency to worry about other's opinions, avoid direct communication, and meet others' expectations in order to obtain social acceptance, maintain relational harmony, preserve face, and avoid social sanctions (see Hwang & Han, this volume; Yang, 1981).

The study by Kim, Sharkey, and Singelis (1994) provided some empirical evidence on the association between interdependent self-construals and relational concerns. Compared with individuals characterized by an independent self-construal, those characterized by an interdependent self-construal were found to show greater concerns for others' feelings, such as avoid hurting others' feelings. The study by Singelis and colleagues (1999) also revealed that compared to North American participants, Chinese and Asian-American participants reported greater embarrassability, which was associated with interdependent self-construal.

Other researchers examined relational concerns and their implications for communication behaviors. Individuals in an attempt to save face tend to filter out or hide information that may cause embarrassment or evoke shame. Hence, face saving is closely related to strategies for self-disclosure. The study by Ow and Katz (1999) examined willingness to disclose problems in Chinese families with a chronically ill child. Results indicate some disclosure of family problems among the Chinese, but such disclosure is highly selective. Specifically, Chinese are most unwilling to disclose their family problems to people who are not their family members, except if they perceive such disclosure can lead to pragmatic outcomes beneficial for their family. These results are consistent with the Chinese proverb of 'do not let out an embarrassing secret of the family' (家醜不出外傳).

Apart from family problems, face concern was also found to be relevant to considerations of disclosing other types of problems and help seeking. Studies on Chinese (e.g. L. L. Chen, 1987; F. M. Cheung, 1984) and Asian-Americans (e.g. F. K. Cheung, 1980; Sue, Wagner, Ja, Margullis, & Lew, 1976) consistently revealed that when having psychological problems, Asians prefer tackling problems by themselves rather than seeking help from others. Even if they seek help from others, they prefer to approach their family members and friends rather than mental health professionals. Moreover, the study by Chiang and Pepper (2006) examined perceived barriers of reporting errors related to medication administration in a sample of Chinese nurses. Face concern is an important barrier that reduces the likelihood of reporting error in this case. These studies indicate that face concern plays a role in influencing the tendency of disclosure and help seeking for a variety of problems among individuals from collectivistic cultures.

In addition to face concerns, preference for an indirect mode of communication is also a common social behavior among the Chinese (Yum, 1988). Making obscure or ambiguous statements and talking to a third party instead of the target party are examples of indirect communication (Yum, 1988). In collectivistic cultures, individuals are prescribed not to assert themselves as well as not to demand, reject, or criticize others (Okabe, 1987). Compared to their Western counterparts, individuals from collectivistic societies tend to adopt a more indirect mode of communication to comply with these norms. More importantly, because the Chinese have a salient concern for face saving, they have stronger motives to adopt an indirect communication style. This is because indirectedness in communication can avoid hurting others and prevent embarrassment that stems from rejection or disagreement from others, thus resulting in face preservation for both parties and relational harmony (Ting-Toomey, 1988; Yum, 1988).

The *Tao* of social-support seeking in Chinese collectivistic society

Relational concerns and the reluctance to seek support. In Western literature, the beneficial role of social support in mitigating stress-related distress has been well documented (see e.g. Cobb, 1995; Cohen, 1992 for a review). As face concerns and feelings of embarrassment are major obstacles of help-seeking among the Chinese (D. Y. F. Ho, 1994), they may tend to avoid revealing their problems to others. Consistent with this notion, the study by Pine and colleagues (2003) indicates that the Chinese are more reluctant to bring up a personal problem to others than their Jewish counterparts. This reluctance about revealing problems to others may explain in part why the Chinese are less likely to seek and utilize social support than are their Western counterparts.

These results indicate that instead of benefiting from social support in mitigating stress-related distress, the Chinese may feel embarrassed and uncomfortable about receiving support. This is probably because seeking support may require raising one's personal problems and weaknesses to others' attention, which implies a loss of face. In this respect, the Chinese may perceive face preservation as more important than utilizing social support as a means to handle their own problems. This proposal received some support from the study by Taylor and colleagues (2004). In this study, European-American and Asian-American participants were asked to give reasons for their seeking of social support. Compared to their European-American counterparts, Asian participants showed greater concerns for five issues: harmony maintenance, belief that voicing out their problems will make things worse, worry of receiving criticism after making their problems known to others, face saving, and self-reliance. All these reasons given by Asian-Americans relate to concerns with face preservation and maintenance of harmonious social relations rather than concerns with handling their own problems.

The study by Lau and Wong (2008) provided some empirical support for a link between face concerns and a willingness to seek social support among Chinese mothers who have recently given birth. As predicted, results indicate an inverse relationship between face concerns and willingness to seek support from others. Specifically, Chinese mothers who have greater face concerns were more sensitive to face-losing situations and strongly motivated to avoid such situations that will arouse embarrassment. As a result, these individuals are more reluctant to disclose their problems to others, and more likely to isolate themselves from others. Such results imply that willingness to disclose one's problems and seek support from others among the Chinese may involve an estimation of perceived benefits and costs from the process. If seeking support is expected to incur costs related to face-losing, social-support seeking will be considered an undesirable behavior. The Chinese are thus less inclined to seek support from others if they perceive that it will become a threat to their face.

This body of findings implies that relational concerns may be an influential factor that accounts for the social-support seeking tendency among the Chinese. This proposal was tested in the cross-cultural study by Kim and colleagues (2006). Their study adopted an experimental design in which participants of each experimental group were instructed to write the five most important goals of one of the following targets: themselves, their in-group, or their out-group. Asian-American participants were less willing to seek social support when they were prompted to think about the important goals of their in-group, but were more willing to seek social support when they were prompted to think about the important goals for themselves. European-American participants, however, did not differ in proclivity of seeking social support across the different experimental conditions. This experimental study provides further support that an emphasis on in-group goals can lead to seeking less support from others.

Situational differences in social-support seeking. Apart from relational concerns that may undermine the effectiveness of social support, it is also possible that social support may still be beneficial for the Chinese but they seek it only when needed. In the current literature, two models, viz. the main effect model and the buffering effect model, have been formulated to address the issue on situational effects of social support (see Cohen & Wills, 1985). The main effect model hypothesizes a direct inverse relationship between social support and stress-related distress. In other words, social support functions to reduce stress-related distress under all circumstances, even when the levels of stress are low. The buffering effect model proposes an interaction between social support and stress levels such that social support may moderate stress-related distress only when the levels of stress are high.

These two models of social support were tested among the Chinese in Cheng's (1997) study. Findings provided support for the buffering effect model, thus indicating that social support serves as a 'buffer' of stress for the Chinese only when they experience a great amount of stress. The Chinese may seek social support in highly stressful situations rather than in all situations because their needs for support are perceived as relatively stronger when they experience a great amount of stress. When the stress levels are low, the Chinese may perceive that they can handle the stressors by themselves without bothering others. In this respect, their lower frequency of social-support utilization may reflect situational differences in social-support seeking among the Chinese, that is, they tend to seek social support only in times of need rather than at all times.

Such a notion receives some support from Boey's (1999) study on social-support seeking among Chinese university students. Results indicate that Chinese university students generally prefer tackling problems on their own rather than seeking support from others. It is worth noting that when the problems are recognized to be so severe that help is required, the Chinese students are willing to ask for support from their family members and friends. However, they generally do not prefer seeking support from professionals. Such findings imply that the Chinese tend to value social support but they are willing to seek it only when they cannot handle the problems by themselves. Also, they tend to be selective in choosing the target of support seeking, and prefer to approach only those whom they have closer relations with than those with more distant or even no relations (see also Leung & Liu, this volume). A recent study by M. Y. Ho and colleagues (2008) revealed that greater social support from partners was associated with a lesser extent of avoidance in romantic relations, and such a link is stronger for the Chinese than for their American counterparts. Such findings provide some support for the tendency of the Chinese to seek support from close others, and for the greater impact of such support for desirable interpersonal outcomes.

Differences in type and function of social support. The aforementioned discussions focus on social-support seeking that involves open disclosure or sharing of stressful experiences and problems with others. Taylor and colleagues (2007) labeled this type of social support as 'explicit' social support, which refers to transactions of assistance rendered by one party to another. They posited that explicit social support should be distinguished from implicit social support, which refers to 'the emotional comfort one can obtain from social networks without disclosing or discussing one's problems' (Taylor et al., 2007, p. 832). Implicit social support is proposed to be more culturally applicable to individuals from collectivistic cultures because it does not involve any open discussion of a person's problem.

To test their proposals, Taylor and colleagues (2007) compared the effects of explicit and implicit social support between European Americans and Asian Americans using an experimental design. For each cultural group, participants were randomly assigned to the explicit social-support, implicit social-support, or control experimental conditions. In the explicit social-support condition, participants were instructed to write a letter to their significant others seeking their advice or help to solve a challenging task. In the implicit social-support condition, participants were instructed to write a letter about how their significant others were important to them. Their findings documented that, compared to their counterparts assigned to the other two conditions, Asian participants assigned to the explicit social-support condition displayed greater cortisol reactivity and experienced more distress. By contrast, European-American participants assigned to the implicit social-support condition had higher levels of cortisol reactivity than did their counterparts assigned to the other two conditions. Such results provide some support to the notion that implicit social support may be more beneficial for Asians, whereas explicit social support may be more beneficial for European-Americans.

Although explicit social support and implicit social support are deemed conceptually distinct, these two types of social support belong to the same type of enacted social support (S. E. Taylor et al., 2007). According to Barrera (1986), social support refers to a multidimensional construct that encompasses three relatively independent facets. First, network support refers to the quantity and identity of individuals in one's social network. Second, enacted support refers to actual supportive behaviors rendered by members of one's social network. Third, perceived support refers to appraisals that one's social environment is supportive or helpful. Because social support 'is likely to be effective only to the extent it is perceived' (House, 1981, p. 27), an individual should appraise social support to be available before its effectiveness in buffering stress can be realized. The mere perception of the availability of social support is shown to be effective in alleviating stress-related distress (e.g. Swickert, Rosentreter, Hittner, & Mushrush, 2002; Thoits, 1995).

The potential benefits of these three types of social support for the Chinese were examined by Cheng (1998). A distinction was found among perceived social support, enacted social support, and network support. Results further showed that perceived social support was a better predictor of stress reduction than were the two other types of social support. These studies imply that the mere appraisal that one is being cared for and that one will receive social support in times of need is beneficial for the Chinese. Because perception of available support can bolster a sense of control and coping efficacy (e.g. Thoits, 1985; Wethington & Kessler, 1986), the Chinese may deal with stressors by themselves without risking harmonious relations with others. Hence, the salutary effects of social support can still be present, even when no overt helping behaviors are requested or exhibited.

In short, while Chinese may tend to seek and utilize social support less frequently, this does not necessarily reflect that support rendered by social others are unimportant to them. It is possible that the Chinese may be reluctant to ask for support from others due to their concerns about losing face or jeopardizing their harmonious relations with others. It is also possible that the Chinese selectively seek social support only when they urgently need it rather than at all times. A third possibility is that the Chinese may be benefited from social support sought via subtle, indirect means, which marks the difference in support-seeking processes between the Chinese and their Western counterparts.

What's next? The future of the *Tao* of coping

Chinese studies reviewed in this chapter have largely focused on describing their multiple ways of handling life vicissitudes in the ever-changing environment. Future studies may move beyond the existing ideological realm to further examine the mediating mechanisms that may underlie the Chinese unique ways of coping. In a recent insightful review, Taylor and Stanton (2007) advocated that in a new era of coping research, the biological underpinnings of coping processes should be unveiled. Possible biological mechanisms to be explored include (a) genetic and neurological mechanisms (e.g. dopaminergic and serotonergic systems, behavioral activation and inhibition systems) that underlie one's coping preferences, and (b) their interactions with environmental constraints in early developmental years.

Given that the Chinese tend to perceive themselves as an integral part of their social network and social milieu at large, it will be interesting to investigate whether both environment and genetic factors play a part such that family environment and parenting style may moderate the effects of genetic or temperamental vulnerabilities in early years on the coping style of the Chinese. We thus encourage Chinese coping researchers to address these unexplored but important issues. For instance, future studies may examine whether the Chinese are characterized by a unique genetic and biological predisposition in emotion-regulation processes which differs from that of their Western counterparts. It is also worthwhile to explore whether the genetic and biological predisposition may generate a greater preference for secondary control in coping by the Chinese.

The meta-analysis performed by Connor-Smith and Flachsbart (2007) further indicate that ethnicity diversity and individuals' country of origin may moderate the relationship between their personality and coping style. Specifically, their extensive review of the literature revealed that the link between neuroticism and disengagement coping is considerably weaker among Western European and Australian samples than Eastern-European and North American samples. Although these analyses focused only on diverse Western (i.e. North American, European, and Australian) samples, they shed light on a new perspective that encourages the study of sub-cultural differences in coping style among the Chinese. Future studies may explore possible differences in the link between personality and coping style among Chinese participants from diverse geographical regions, such as mainland Chinese, Hong Kong Chinese, Singaporean Chinese, and American-Chinese. Because these countries differ remarkably in socio-cultural background, such findings may provide valuable information on the socio-historical development of coping style for the Chinese.

Apart from exploring new research areas, it is also essential for Chinese researchers to scrutinize new categories of coping. Folkman and Moskowitz (2004) posited that the dimensionality of coping nomenclature could be much more complex than psychologists could imagine when this construct was proposed in the 1960s. They conjectured that new constructs, such as future-oriented proactive coping and religious coping, could be added to the existing pool of coping strategies. As the Chinese are more social-oriented than their Western counterparts, greater effort may be expended on refining aspects within the interpersonal dimension of coping. For instance, different types of social-related coping, such as social-support seeking and communal coping, may be distinguished and explored more extensively in future Chinese studies. To examine these dimensions relevant to Chinese context, Chinese researchers may conceptualize these new types of coping in light of Chinese cultural values and the unique ways of coping among the Chinese. Based on such conceptualizations, indigenous measures for assessing the proposed constructs among the Chinese can be constructed. By far, however, the majority of studies on Chinese coping rely heavily on Western translated measures. The development of indigenous coping measures tailored to the Chinese has been relatively limited, but some effort is now under way (e.g. Maxwell & Siu, 2008; Siu, Spector, & Cooper, 2006).

Epilogue

As we pointed out in this chapter, the same coping strategy may be adaptive in some stressful situations but others. Readers are left to wonder: Which coping strategy should the Chinese use to handle stressors effectively? This broad question cannot be addressed simply by naming any type of coping strategy. According to Taoism:

> 「道可道，非常道。名可名，非常名。」《道德經》
> The *Tao* that can be trodden is not the enduring and unchanging *Tao*. The name that can be named is not the enduring and unchanging name.
>
> *Tao te ching*

In this ever-changing world, perhaps the best way of coping with a stressor is to observe the stressor first. After one has come to understand the characteristics of the stressful situation and the cultural context at large, the appropriate way of coping will not be hard to find.

Author's note

Preparation of this chapter was supported by Research Grants Council's Competitive Earmarked Research Grant HKU7418/07H and Seed Funding Programme 200711159093.

Correspondence concerning this article should be addressed to Cecilia Cheng, Department of Psychology, The University of Hong Kong, Pokfulam Road, Hong Kong; email: ceci-cheng@hku.hk.

Chapter note

1 The construct of stress can refer to (a) the objective aspect of stressful life events or stressors that induce feelings of discomfort and tension, and (b) the subjective aspect of stressful feelings. To distinguish the objective aspect of stress from its subjective aspect, the former is referred to as 'stressor', whereas the latter is referred to as 'stress' in this chapter.

References

Abramson, L. Y., Alloy, L. B., & Metalsky, G. I. (1986). *The cognitive diathesis–stress theories of depression: Toward an adequate evaluation of the theories' validities.* New York: Guilford Press.

Abramson, L. Y., Metalsky, G. I., & Alloy, L. B. (1986). *The hopelessness theory of depression: Does the research test the theory?* New York: Guilford Press.

Anderson, C. R. (1977). Locus of control, coping behaviors and performance in a stress setting: A longitudinal study. *Journal of Applied Psychology, 62*, 446–451.

Barrera, M., Jr (1986). Distinctions between social support concepts, measures, and models. *American Journal of Community Psychology, 14*, 413–445.

Beck, A. T. (1976). *Cognitive therapy and the emotional disorders.* New York: International Universities Press.

Beck, A. T. (1983). Cognitive therapy of depression: New perspectives. In I. P. Clayton & J. Barrett (eds), *Treatment of depression: Old controversies and new approaches* (pp. 265–290). New York: Raven Press.

Birkimer, J. C., Johnston, P. L., & Dearmond, R. (1993). Health locus of control and ways of coping can predict health behavior. *Journal of Social Behavior & Personality, 8*, 111–122.

Boey, K. W. (1999). Help-seeking preference of college students in urban China after the implementation of the 'open-door' policy. *International Journal of Social Psychiatry, 45*, 104–116.

Bond, M. H. & Cheung, T. (1983). College students' spontaneous self-concept: The effect of culture among respondents in Hong Kong, Japan, and the United States. *Journal of Cross-Cultural Psychology, 14*, 153–171.

Bond, M. H. & Tornatsky, L. C. (1973). Locus of control in students from Japan and the United States: Dimensions and levels of response. *Psychologia, 16*, 209–213.

Buchanan, G. M. & Seligman, M. E. P. (1995). *Explanatory style.* Hillsdale, NJ: Lawrence Erlbaum Associates.

Chan, A. O., Cheng, C., Hui, W. M., Hu, W. H. C., Wong, N. Y. H., Lam, K. F., et al. (2005). Differing coping mechanisms, stress level and anorectal physiology in patients with functional constipation. *World Journal of Gastroenterology, 11*, 5362–5366.

Chan, D. W. (1994). The Chinese Ways of Coping Questionnaire: Assessing coping in secondary school teachers and students in Hong Kong. *Psychological Assessment, 6*, 108–116.

Chan, D. W. (1995). Depressive symptoms and coping strategies among Chinese adolescents in Hong Kong. *Journal of Youth and Adolescence, 24*, 267–279.

Chen, L. L. (1987). A study of the process of psychological help-seeking among college students in Taiwan. *Chinese Journal of Mental Health, 3*, 125–138. (In Chinese).

Chen, X. (2000). Growing up in a collectivist culture: Socialization and socioemotional development in Chinese children. In A. L. Comunian & G. Gielen (eds), *International perspectives on human development* (pp. 331–353). Lengerich, Germany: Pabst Science.

Chen, Y. (2006a). Coping with suffering: The Buddhist perspective. In P. T. P. Wong & L. C. J. Wong (eds), *Handbook of multicultural perspectives on stress and coping* (pp. 73–89). New York: Springer.

Chen, Y. (2006b). The way of nature as a healing power. In P. T. P. Wong & L. C. J. Wong (eds), *Handbook of multicultural perspectives on stress and coping* (pp. 91–103). New York: Springer.

Cheng, C. (1997). Role of perceived social support on depression of Chinese adolescents: A prospective study examining the buffering model. *Journal of Applied Social Psychology, 27*, 800–820.

Cheng, C. (1998). Getting the right kind of support: Functional differences in the types of social support on depression for Chinese adolescents. *Journal of Clinical Psychology, 54*, 845–849.

Cheng, C. (2001). Assessing coping flexibility in real-life and laboratory settings: A multimethod approach. *Journal of Personality and Social Psychology, 80*, 814–833.

Cheng, C. (2003). Cognitive and motivational processes underlying coping flexibility: A dual-process model. *Journal of Personality and Social Psychology, 84*, 425–438.

Cheng, C. (2005). Processes underlying gender-role flexibility: Do androgynous individuals know more or know how to cope? *Journal of Personality, 73*, 645–673.

Cheng, C. (2009). Dialectical thinking and coping flexibility: A multimethod approach. *Journal of Personality, 77*, 471–493.

Cheng, C., Chan, A. O. O., Hui, W. M., & Lam, S. K. (2003). Coping strategies, illness perception, anxiety and depression of patients with idiopathic constipation: A population-based study. *Alimentary Pharmacology & Therapeutics, 18*, 319–326.

Cheng, C. & Cheung, M. W. (2005a). Cognitive processes underlying coping flexibility: Differentiation and integration. *Journal of Personality, 73*, 859–886.

Cheng, C. & Cheung, M. W. (2005b). Psychological responses to outbreak of severe acute respiratory syndrome: A prospective, multiple time-point study. *Journal of Personality, 73*, 261–285.

Cheng, C., Chiu, C., Hong, Y., & Cheung, J. S. (2001). Discriminative facility and its role in the perceived quality of interactional experiences. *Journal of Personality, 69*, 765–786.

Cheng, C., Hui, W., & Lam, S. (1999). Coping style of individuals with functional dyspepsia. *Psychosomatic Medicine, 61*, 789–795.

Cheng, C., Hui, W., & Lam, S. (2000). Perceptual style and behavioral pattern of individuals with functional gastrointestinal disorders. *Health Psychology, 19*, 146–154.

Cheng, C., Hui, W., & Lam, S. (2002). Coping with first-time endoscopy for a select sample of Chinese patients with functional dyspepsia and duodenal ulcer: An observation study. *Psychosomatic Medicine, 64*, 867–873.

Cheng, C., Hui, W., & Lam, S. (2004). Psychosocial factors and perceived severity of functional dyspeptic symptoms: A psychosocial interactionist model. *Psychosomatic Medicine, 66*, 85–91.

Cheng, C., Hui, W. M., Lai, K. C., & Lam, S. K. (1998). Coping behavior as a risk factor of functional dyspepsia. *Gastroenterology, 114*, A90.

Cheng, C., Lee, S., & Chiu, C. (1999). Dialectic thinking in daily life. *Hong Kong Journal of Social Sciences, 15*, 1–25.

Cheng, C. & Ng, A. (2006). Psychosocial factors predicting SARS-preventive behaviors in four major SARS-affected regions. *Journal of Applied Social Psychology, 36*, 222–247.

Cheng, C. & Tang, C. S. (2004). The psychology behind the masks: Psychological responses to the severe acute respiratory syndrome outbreak in different regions. *Asian Journal of Social Psychology, 7*, 3–7.

Cheng, C., Wang, F., & Golden, D. L. (in press). Unpackaging cultural differences in interpersonal flexibility: Role of culture-related personality and situational factors. *Journal of Cross-Cultural Psychology.*

Cheng, C., Wong, W., Lai, K., Wong, B. C., Hu, W. H. C., Hui, W., et al. (2003). Psychosocial factors in patients with noncardiac chest pain. *Psychosomatic Medicine, 65*, 443–449.

Cheng, C., Wong, W., & Tsang, K. W. (2006). Perception of benefits and costs during SARS outbreak: An 18-month prospective study. *Journal of Consulting and Clinical Psychology, 74*, 870–879.

Cheng, C., Yang, F., Jun, S., & Hutton, J. M. (2007). Flexible coping psychotherapy for functional dyspeptic patients: A randomized controlled trial. *Psychosomatic Medicine, 69*, 81–88.

Cheung, F. K. (1980). The mental health status of Asian Americans. *Clinical Psychologist, 34*, 23–24.

Cheung, F. M. (1984). Preferences in help-seeking among Chinese students. *Culture, Medicine and Psychiatry, 8*, 371–380.

Chiang, H. & Pepper, G. A. (2006). Barriers to nurses' reporting of medication administration errors in Taiwan. *Journal of Nursing Scholarship, 38*, 392–399.

Chiu, C., Hong, Y., Mischel, W., & Shoda, Y. (1995). Discriminative facility in social competence: Conditional versus dispositional encoding and monitoring-blunting of information. *Social Cognition, 13*, 49–70.

Chow, D. S., Au, E. W. M., & Chiu, C. (2008). Predicting the psychological health of older adults: Interaction of age-based rejection sensitivity and discriminative facility. *Journal of Research in Personality, 42*, 169–182.

Cobb, S. (1995). Social support as a moderator of life stress. In A. M. Eward & J. E. Dimsdale (eds), *Toward an integrated medicine: Classics from Psychosomatic Medicine, 1959–1979* (pp. 377–397). Washington, DC: American Psychiatric Press.

Cohen, S. (1992). Stress, social support, and disorder. In H. O. Y. Veiel & U. Baumann (eds), *The meaning and measurement of social support* (pp. 109–124). New York: Hemisphere.

Cohen, S. & Wills, T. A. (1985). Stress, social support, and the buffering hypothesis. *Psychological Bulletin, 98*, 310–357.

Connor-Smith, J. K., & Flachsbart, C. (2007). Relations between personality and coping: A meta-analysis. *Journal of Personality and Social Psychology, 93*, 1080–1107.

Drossman, D. A. (1993). *Psychosocial factors in chronic functional abdominal pain.* New York: Elsevier.

Elfering, A., Grebner, S., Semmer, N. K., Kaiser-Freiburghaus, D., Ponte, S. L.-D., & Witschi, I. (2005). Chronic job stressors and job control: Effects on event-related coping success and well-being. *Journal of Occupational and Organizational Psychology, 78*, 237–252.

Endler, N. S., Speer, R. L., Johnson, J. M., & Flett, G. L. (2000). Controllability, coping, efficacy, and distress. *European Journal of Personality, 14*, 245–264.

Farone, D. W., Fitzpatrick, T. R., & Bushfield, S. Y. (2007). Hope, locus of control, and quality of health among elder Latina cancer survivors. *Social Work in Health Care, 46*, 51–70.

Folkman, S. & Moskowitz, J. T. (2004). Coping: Pitfalls and promise. *Annual Review of Psychology, 55*, 745–774.

Gan, Y., Liu, Y., & Zhang, Y. (2004). Flexible coping responses to severe acute respiratory syndrome-related and daily life stressful events. *Asian Journal of Social Psychology, 7*, 55–66.

Gan, Y., Shang, J., & Zhang, Y. (2007). Coping flexibility and locus of control as predictors of burnout among Chinese college students. *Social Behavior and Personality, 35*, 1087–1098.

Gan, Y., Zhang, Y., Wang, X., Wang, S., & Shen, X. (2006). The coping flexibility of neurasthenia and depressive patients. *Personality and Individual Differences, 40*, 859–871.

Gao, G. (1998). An initial analysis of the effects of face and concern for 'other' in Chinese interpersonal communication. *International Journal of Intercultural Relations, 22*, 467–482.

Gerdes, E. P. & Ping, G. (1994). Coping differences between college women and men in China and the United States. *Genetic, Social, and General Psychology Monographs, 120*, 169–198.

Grant Thornton International (2005). *International Business Owners Survey.* London, England: Grant Thornton International.

Hamid, P. N., Yue, X. D., & Leung, C. M. (2003). Adolescent coping in different Chinese family environments. *Adolescence, 38*, 111–130.

Haug, T. T., Svebak, S., Wilhelmsen, I., Berstad, A., & Ursin, H. (1994). Psychological factors and somatic symptoms in functional dyspepsia: A comparison with duodenal ulcer and healthy controls. *Journal of Psychosomatic Research, 38*, 281–291.

Ho, D. Y. F. (1976). On the concept of face. *American Journal of Sociology, 81*, 867–884.

Ho, D. Y. F. (1994). Face dynamics: From conceptualization to measurement. In S. Ting-Toomey (ed.), *The challenge of facework* (pp. 269–286). New York: State University of New York.

Ho, M. Y., Zhang, H., Lin, D., Lu, A., Bond, M. H., Chan, C., et al. (2008). Saving graces: The impact of current partner support and current maternal attachment on partner attachments in an individualistic and a collectivist cultural context. *Unpublished manuscript.*

Hofstede, G. H. & Bond, M. H. (1988). The Confucian connection: From cultural roots to economic growth. *Organizational Dynamics, 16*, 4–21.

Hou, Y. & Zhu, Y. (2002). The effect of culture on the thinking style of Chinese people. *Acta Psychologica Sinica, 34*, 106–111. (In Chinese).

House, J. S. (1981). *Work stress and social support.* Reading, MA: Addison-Wesley.

Hu, H. C. (1944). The Chinese concepts of 'face'. *American Anthropologist, 46*, 45–64.

Hwang, C., Scherer, R. F., Wu, Y., Hwang, C.-H., & Li, J. (2002). A comparison of coping factors in Western and non-Western cultures. *Psychological Reports, 90*, 466–476.

Ip, G. W. M. & Bond, M. H. (1995). Culture, values, and the spontaneous self-concept. *Asian Journal of Psychology, 1*, 29–35.

Jose, P. E. & Huntsinger, C. S. (2005). Moderation and mediation effects of coping by Chinese American and European American adolescents. *The Journal of Genetic Psychology, 166*, 16–43.

Kanagawa, C., Cross, S. E., & Markus, H. R. (2001). 'Who am I?' The cultural psychology of the conceptual self. *Personality & Social Psychology Bulletin, 27*, 90–103.

Kane, F. J., Jr, Strohlein, J., & Harper, R. G. (1993). Nonulcer dyspepsia associated with psychiatric disorder. *Southern Medical Journal, 86*, 641–646.

Kim, H. S., Sherman, D. K., Ko, D., & Taylor, S. E. (2006). Pursuit of comfort and pursuit of harmony: Culture, relationships, and social support seeking. *Personality and Social Psychology Bulletin, 32*, 1595–1607.

Kim, M., Sharkey, W. F., & Singelis, T. M. (1994). The relationship between individuals' self-construals and perceived importance of interactive constraints. *International Journal of Intercultural Relations, 18*, 117–140.

Lam, C. B. & McBride-Chang, C. A. (2007). Resilience in young adulthood: The moderating influences of gender-related personality traits and coping flexibility. *Sex Roles, 56*, 159–172.

Lau, Y. & Wong, D. F. K. (2008). Are concern for face and willingness to seek help correlated to early postnatal depressive symptoms among Hong Kong Chinese women? A cross-sectional questionnaire survey. *International Journal of Nursing Studies, 45*, 51–64.

Lii, S. & Wong, S. (1982). A cross-cultural study on sex-role stereotypes and social desirability. *Sex Roles, 8*, 481–491.

Liu, X., Tein, J.-Y., & Zhao, Z. (2004). Coping strategies and behavioral/emotional problems among Chinese adolescents. *Psychiatry Research, 126*, 275–285.

Lu, L., Kao, S., Cooper, C. L., & Spector, P. E. (2000). Managerial stress, locus of control, and job strain in Taiwan and UK: A comparative study. *International Journal of Stress Management, 7*, 209–226.

Majer, J. M., Jason, L. A., Ferrari, J. R., Olson, B. D., & North, C. S. (2003). Is self-mastery always a helpful resource? Coping with paradoxical findings in relation to optimism and abstinence self-efficacy. *American Journal of Drug and Alcohol Abuse, 29*, 385–399.

Markus, H. R. & Kitayama, S. (1991). Culture and the self: Implications for cognition, emotion, and motivation. *Psychological Review, 98*, 224–253.

Martin, R., Thomas, G., Charles, K., Epitropaki, O., & McNamara, R. (2005). The role of leader-member exchanges in mediating the relationship between locus of control and work reactions. *Journal of Occupational and Organizational Psychology, 78*, 141–147.

Maxwell, J. P. & Siu, O. L. (2008). The Chinese coping strategies scale: Relationships with aggression, anger, and rumination in a diverse sample of Hong Kong Chinese adults. *Personality and Individual Differences, 44*, 1049–1059.

Maxwell, J. P., Sukhodolsky, D. G., Chow, C. C. F., & Wong, C. F. C. (2005). Anger rumination in Hong Kong and Great Britain: Validation of the scale and a cross-cultural comparison. *Personality and Individual Differences, 39*, 1147–1157.

Mischel, W. (1977). *The interaction of person and situation.* Hillsdale, NJ: Erlbaum.

Morris, C. (1991). Non-ulcer dyspepsia. *Journal of Psychosomatic Research, 35*, 129–140.

Neria, Y. (2001). Coping with tangible and intangible traumatic losses in prisoners of war. *Israel Journal of Psychiatry and Related Sciences, 38*, 216–225.

Norenzayan, A., Choi, I., & Nisbett, R. E. (1999). Eastern and Western perceptions of causality for social behavior: Lay theories about personalities and situations. In D. A. Prentice & D. T. Miller (eds), *Cultural divides: Understanding and overcoming group conflict* (pp. 239–272). New York: Russell Sage Foundation.

O'Connor, D. B. & Shimizu, M. (2002). Sense of personal control, stress and coping style: A cross-cultural study. *Stress and Health, 18*, 173–183.

Okabe, K. (1987). Indirect speech acts of the Japanese. In D. L. Kincaid (ed.), *Communication theory: Eastern and Western perspectives* (pp. 127–136). New York: Academic.

Osowiecki, D. M. & Compas, B. E. (1999). A prospective study of coping, perceived control, and psychological adaptation to breast cancer. *Cognitive Therapy and Research, 23*, 169–180.

Ow, R. & Katz, D. (1999). Family secrets and the disclosure of distressful information in Chinese families. *Families in Society, 80*, 620–628.

Pang, P. (1984). *Ru jia bian zheng fa yan jiu.* Beijing, China: Zhonghua. (In Chinese).

Peng, K. & Knowles, E. D. (2003). Culture, education, and the attribution of physical causality. *Personality & Social Psychology Bulletin, 29*, 1272–1284.

Peng, K. & Nisbett, R. E. (1999). Culture, dialectics, and reasoning about contradiction. *American Psychologist, 54*, 741–754.

Peng, K., Spencer-Rodgers, J., & Nian, Z. (2006). Naive dialecticism and the Tao of Chinese thought. In U. Kim, K. S. Yang & K. K. Hwang (eds), *Indigenous and cultural psychology: Understanding people in context* (pp. 247–262). New York: Springer Science & Business Media.

Pines, A. M., Zaidman, N., Wang, Y., Chengbing, H., & Ping, L. (2003). The influence of cultural background on students' feelings about and use of social support. *School Psychology International, 24*, 33–53.

Qian, M. (2001). *Zhonghua wen hua shi er jiang.* Taipei, Taiwan, ROC: Lan Tai. (In Chinese).

Ross, L. (1977). The intuitive psychologist and his shortcomings. *Advances in Experimental Social Psychology, 10*, 173–220.

Sastry, J. & Ross, C. E. (1998). Asian ethnicity and the sense of personal control. *Social Psychology Quarterly, 61*, 101–120.

Selmer, J. (2002). Coping strategies applied by Western vs overseas Chinese business expatriates in China. *International Journal of Human Resource Management, 13*, 19–34.

Shek, D. T. L. (1992). Reliance on self or seeking help from others: Gender differences in the locus of coping in Chinese working parents. *The Journal of Psychology, 126*, 671–678.

Shinn, M., Lehmann, S., & Wong, N. W. (1984). Social interaction and social support. *Journal of Social Issues, 40*, 55–76.

Singelis, T. M. (1994). The measurement of independent and interdependent self-construals. *Personality & Social Psychology Bulletin, 20*, 580–591.

Singelis, T. M., Bond, M. H., Sharkey, W. F., & Lai, C. S. Y. (1999). Unpackaging culture's influence on self-esteem and embarrassability: The role of self-construals. *Journal of Cross-Cultural Psychology, 30*, 315–341.

Siu, O., Spector, P. E., & Cooper, C. L. (2006). A three-phase study to develop and validate a Chinese coping strategies scales in Greater China. *Personality and Individual Differences, 41*, 537–548.

Snyder, M. & Ickes, W. (1985). Personality and social behavior. In G. Lindzey & E. Aronson (eds), *Handbook of social psychology* (pp. 883–947). New York: Guilford Press.

Spector, P. E., Sanchez, J. I., Siu, O. L., Salgado, J., & Jianhong, M. (2004). Eastern versus Western control beliefs at work: An investigation of secondary control, socioinstrumental control, and work locus of control in China and the US. *Applied Psychology: An International Review, 53*, 38–60.

Spencer-Rodgers, J., Peng, K., Wang, L., & Hou, Y. (2004). Dialectical self-esteem and East–West differences in psychological well-being. *Personality and Social Psychology Bulletin, 30*, 1416–1432.

Stephan, W. G. (1977). Cognitive differentiation in intergroup perception. *Sociometry, 40*, 50–58.

Stewin, L. L. (1976). Integrative complexity: Structure and correlates. *Alberta Journal of Educational Research, 22*, 226–236.

Stoneman, Z. & Gavidia-Payne, S. (2006). Marital adjustment in families of young children with disabilities: Associations with daily hassles and problem-focused coping. *American Journal on Mental Retardation, 111*, 1–14.

Sue, S., Wagner, N., Ja, D., Margullis, C., & Lew, L. (1976). Conceptions of mental illness among Asian and Caucasian-American students. *Psychological Reports, 38*, 703–708.

Suedfeld, P. & Coren, S. (1992). Cognitive correlates of conceptual complexity. *Personality and Individual Differences, 13*, 1193–1199.

Swickert, R. J., Rosentreter, C. J., Hittner, J. B., & Mushrush, J. E. (2002). Extraversion, social support processes, and stress. *Personality and Individual Differences, 32*, 877–891.

Taylor, S. E., Sherman, D. K., Kim, H. S., Jarcho, J., Takagi, K., & Dunagan, M. S. (2004). Culture and social support: Who seeks it and why? *Journal of Personality and Social Psychology, 87*, 354–362.

Taylor, S. E. & Stanton, A. L. (2007). Coping resources, coping processes, and mental health. *Annual Review of Clinical Psychology, 3*, 377–401.
Taylor, S. E., Welch, W. T., Kim, H. S., & Sherman, D. K. (2007). Cultural differences in the impact of social support on psychological and biological stress responses. *Psychological Science, 18*, 831–837.
Thoits, P. A. (1985). Social support and psychological well-being: Theoretical possibilities. In I. G. Sarason & B. R. Sarason (eds), *Social support: Theory, research, and applications* (pp. 51–72). The Hague, The Netherlands: Martinus Nijhoff.
Thoits, P. A. (1995). Stress, coping, and social support processes: Where are we? What next? *Journal of Health and Social Behavior, 35*, 53–79.
Ting-Toomey, S. (1988). Intercultural conflict styles: A face negotiation theory. In Y. Y. Kim & W. B. Gudykunst (eds), *Theories in intercultural communication* (pp. 213–238). Newbury Park, CA: Sage.
Tramer, R. R. & Schludermann, E. H. (1974). Cognitive differentiation in a geriatric population. *Perceptual and Motor Skills, 39*, 1071–1075.
Triandis, H. C. (1995). *Individualism and collectivism.* Boulder, CO: Westview.
Triandis, H. C., Bontempo, R., Villareal, M. J., Asai, M., & Lucca, N. (1988). Individualism and collectivism: Cross-cultural perspectives on self-ingroup relationships. *Journal of Personality and Social Psychology, 54*, 323–338.
Tsang, K. W., Ho, P. L., Ooi, G. C., Yee, W. K., Wang, T., Chan-Yeung, M., et al. (2003). A cluster of cases of severe acute respiratory syndrome in Hong Kong. *New England Journal of Medicine, 348*, 1977–1985.
Wang, G. & Chen, H. (2001). Coping style of adolescents under academic stress: Their locus of control, self-esteem and mental health. *Chinese Mental Health Journal, 15*, 431–434.
Wethington, E. & Kessler, R. C. (1986). Perceived support, received support and adjustment to stressful life events. *Journal of Health and Social Behavior, 27*, 78–89.
Wong, W., Cheng, C., Hui, W., & Lam, S. (2003). Invited review: Non-cardiac chest pain. *Medical Progress, 30*, 15–21.
Wong, W., Cheng, C., Hui, W., & Wong, B. C. (2003). Invited review: Irritable bowel syndrome. *Medical Progress, 30*, 50–56.
Wong, W., Cheng, C., Wong, B. C., & Hui, W. (2003). Invited review: Functional dyspepsia. *Medical Progress, 30*, 112–119.
Wrightson, K. J. & Wardle, J. (1997). Cultural variation in health locus of control. *Ethnicity & Health, 2*, 13–20.
Yang, K. S. (1981). Social orientation and individual modernity among Chinese students in Taiwan. *Journal of Social Psychology, 113*, 159–170.
Yum, J. O. (1988). The impact of Confucianism on interpersonal relationships and communication patterns in East Asia. *Communication Monographs, 55*, 374–388.

CHAPTER 25

Illness behaviors among the Chinese

Winnie W. S. Mak and Sylvia Xiaohua Chen

This chapter focuses on how culture may influence the illness behaviors of Chinese, specifically with respect to mental illness. In this chapter, illness is defined as an individual's subjective meaning and interpretation of the disease in his or her social context, whereas disease is referred to as the biological pathology or malfunctioning that requires medical or professional attention (Chun, Enomoto, & Sue, 1996; Tseng, 1997). Illness behavior includes the way people experience, interpret, and cope with the disease. People experience their physical and emotional states based on their sociocultural background and familial socialization. Cultural experiences also structure and shape people's value orientations, affective and cognitive experiences, and behavioral styles (Fabrega, 1989). As such, people vary in how they perceive and define illness, the way they present the distress, and the interventions they consider and seek out based on their cultural milieux (Mechanic, 1986). Such a culture-specific view of socio-psychological experiences needs to be incorporated in understanding illness behaviors among Chinese.

Researchers studying illness behaviors have proposed conceptual models to understand the process of distress experience (Angel & Thoits, 1987; Mechanic, 1986; Young & Zane, 1994). During the process of illness labeling and evaluation, individuals first experience an internal distress. Their distress can be provoked and exacerbated by stressors that may be developed from a discrepancy between their culturally maintained beliefs and the environmental constraints on behaviors (Angel & Thoits, 1987). People may experience their distress in the forms of physiological signs, changes in their mood and perceptions, and other emotional or behavioral responses.

They generally manifest the underlying psychopathology or neurobiological changes, however, according to cultural norms. Following the manifestation of symptoms, individuals identify and interpret the symptoms based on their past learning experiences and the cultural conception of health (Mechanic, 1986). The construction and evaluation of their illness also interact with the expectations and reactions from their reference groups (i.e. individuals with whom they identify). Thus, the phenomenological experience of illness is influenced by social and cultural sanctions. Not only are individuals likely to manifest symptoms in ways that are less unacceptable in their cultures, they are also more prone to develop distress when they fall short of their personal expectations or cultural norms.

Levels of psychological distress among the Chinese

China is the most populous country in the world. Moreover, as a result of the Chinese diaspora, people of Chinese descent can be found in almost every region of the world. For instance, Chinese constitute almost 75 per cent of the population in Singapore, making it the largest ethnic group in the country (Department of Statistics, Ministry of Trade & Industry, Republic of Singapore, 2008), In the United States, 26 per cent of the foreign-born population were from Asia, of which China was the leading country of birth (US Census, 2002). To better understand the mechanisms of their distress and to provide them with culturally competent services, the distress experience of these Chinese around the world must be understood from their cultural perspective. The present chapter examines issues related to illness behaviors of these Chinese. Focus is placed on empirical studies conducted in East Asia, Southeast Asia, and North America, where most of the studies have been done, with reference to research conducted in other parts of the world wherever available.

In East Asia and Southeast Asia, Chinese have reported a high level of self-reported distress. Among adolescents and young adults in Hong Kong, Shek (1991) reported that over half of 2,150 Chinese secondary-school students reported some degrees of depressive symptoms as measured by the Beck Depression Inventory. Over 20 per cent of these students reported moderate to severe levels of depression, as indicated by sadness, pessimism, feeling of failure, self-disgust, and crying. Females reported significantly more distress and somatic symptoms than did their male counterparts (Shek, 1989). The findings were replicated in other samples of Hong Kong Chinese adolescents, which found a range of 24 per cent (as measured by the Children's Depression Inventory) to 64 per cent (as measured by the Beck Depression Inventory) of respondents falling in the depressed range (Chan, 1995, 1997). At the other end of the age continuum, in a study of 9,923 older adults in the United States, Japan, Taiwan, and the People's Republic of China, Chinese older adults from the People's Republic of China reported greater alcohol use, and Chinese older adults who were divorced or separated reported greater depressive symptoms, than their counterparts elsewhere (Krause, Dowler, Liang, Gu, Yatomi, & Chuang, 1995).

In North America, research studies have found that Chinese experienced levels of psychological distress and maladjustment that were comparable to, if not greater than, those experienced by other ethnic groups (Uba, 1994). Immigrants to the host country reported the highest level of distress in both college and community samples (Abe & Zane, 1990; Aldwin & Greenberger, 1987; Okazaki, 1997; Ying, 1988). According to past research findings, Chinese differ from European Americans in the level of psychological distress they experience and in the way they express their distress. Among college samples, Chinese and Chinese American students have reported higher levels of emotional distress than European American students. In a self-report study (Abe & Zane, 1990), Chinese American students reported significantly more interpersonal and intrapersonal distress than their European American counterparts, even after their culturally derived response tendencies (i.e. social desirability) and personality styles (i.e. self-consciousness and self-monitoring) were controlled. This difference was particularly pronounced among foreign-born Chinese students (Abe & Zane, 1990).

Chinese American students also reported greater levels of depression, anxiety, social avoidance, loneliness, and psychotic tendencies and lower self-esteem in studies that utilized various self-report measures (Aldwin & Greenberger, 1987; Cheng, Leong, & Geist, 1993; Hsu, Hailey, & Range, 1987; Okazaki, 1997; D. Sue, Ino, D. M. Sue, 1983). Chinese American adolescents reported higher levels of depression, social stress (Zhou, Peverly, Xin, Huang, & Wang, 2003), social anxiety (Austin & Chorpita, 2004), loneliness (Xie, 1997), and social adjustment difficulties (Abe & Zane, 1990) than American adolescents. Other studies found similarly high levels of depression among predominantly foreign-born samples of Chinese Americans in San Francisco (Ying, 1988) and Chinese immigrant women in Canada (Franks & Faux, 1990). In addition to depression, other community studies consistently found high levels of emotional tension, anxiety, loneliness, and physiological impairment among Chinese and Chinese Americans (Chung & Singer, 1995; Loo, 1982; Loo, Tong, & True, 1989; Sastry & Ross, 1998).

Although Chinese, particularly immigrants, have reported many symptoms of psychological distress, they generally show lower prevalence rates of psychiatric disorders under the Western diagnostic system. In the 1980s, three community studies were conducted among Chinese using the Diagnostic Interview Schedule (DIS) that was based on the DSM III. From the Shanghai Psychiatric Epidemiological Study, a rate of 0.2 per cent in major depressive disorder was found in a sample of 3,098 Chinese respondents in Xuhui, a metropolitan district in Shanghai, China (Wang et al., 1992).

Similarly, the Taiwan Psychiatric Epidemiological Project estimated a major depressive disorder rate of 0.9 per cent among 5,005 respondents in Taipei (Hwu, Yeh, & Chang, 1989); and the Shatin Community Mental Health Survey estimated a rate of 1.9 per cent among a sample of residents in Hong Kong (Chen et al., 1993).

More recently in this new millenium, higher rates have been observed, but they have remained lower than those reported in other ethnic groups. In a telephone study based on a survey instrument constructed according to the DSM-IV, the 12-month prevalence of major depressive episodes was found to be 8.4 per cent among a random sample of 5,004 Chinese in Hong Kong (Lee, Tsang, & Kwok, 2007) and the six-month prevalence of generalized anxiety disorder was 4.1 per cent in a sample of 3,304 Chinese randomly drawn from the general population (Lee, Tsang, Chui, Kwok, & Cheung, 2007). Under the World Health Organization World Mental Health (WMH) Survey Initiative, the prevalence rates for any DSM-IV anxiety disorder were found to be 2.7 per cent (12-month) and 4.8 per cent (lifetime), and the prevalence rates for any DSM-IV mood disorder were 2.2 per cent (12-month) and 3.6 per cent (lifetime) among 5,201 Chinese residents (2,633 in Beijing and 2,568 in Shanghai) using the Composite International Diagnostic Interview (CIDI) (12-month rates: Shen et al., 2006; lifetime rates: Lee et al., 2007).

Lower rates were also found among Chinese Americans. Based on a sample of 1,742 Chinese American residents in the Los Angeles County, the Chinese American Epidemiological Study (CAPES) found a lifetime DSM-III-R major depressive episode rate of 6.9 per cent (Takeuchi, Chung, Lin, Shen, Kurasaki, Chun, & Sue, 1998). This study used the same assessment instrument, the University of Michigan version of the Composite International Diagnostic Interview (UM-CIDI) as the National Comorbidity Survey (NCS). A lifetime DSM-III major depressive episode prevalence of 17.1 per cent was found for 8,098 respondents (75.1 per cent European Americans, 12.5 per cent African-Americans, 9.1 per cent Latino Americans, and 3.3 per cent Other) across the United States (Kessler et al., 1994). In the NCS Replication, which was based on the DSM-III-R diagnostic criteria as the CAPES, a lifetime prevalence of 20.8 per cent for any mood disorders (16.6 per cent for major depressive disorder) and 28.8 per cent for any anxiety disorder was reported in 9,282 respondents (72.1 per cent European Americans, 13.3 per cent African-Americans, 9.5 per cent Latino Americans, 5.1 per cent Other) (Kessler, Berglund, Demler, Jin, Merikangas, & Walters, 2005). Overall, the epidemiological studies conducted in various parts of East Asia and North America suggest that Chinese generally have low rates of depression and anxiety (see also Stewart, Lee, & Tao, this volume).

The findings based on the diagnostic criteria were not consistent with those based on self-report measures. While epidemiological studies showed a lower prevalence of psychiatric disorders among Chinese or Chinese Americans than among European Americans, Chinese or Chinese Americans tend to endorse a higher number of depressive and anxiety-related symptoms and to report a greater amount of distress than do European Americans on self-report measures. This discrepancy may be explained by cultural bias inherent in the diagnostic systems. The DSM, which was created in the West, may not accurately capture the type and range of symptoms and the extent of distress that Chinese are experiencing. Moreover, Chinese may be reporting their distress experience differently depending on whether they are self-reporting on a symptom scale or they are disclosing to an interviewer or a therapist over the telephone or during a face-to-face interview (Hwang, Myers, Abe-Kim, & Ting, 2008; Stewart et al., this volume).

Cultural expression of distress

Psychologists and other social scientists have discussed the influence of culture on mental health symptomatology. They claim that individuals have varying tendencies to somatize their psychological conditions based on the cultural values under which they were socialized. Somatization is defined as, 'the substitution of somatic preoccupation for dysphoric affect in the form of complaints of physical symptoms and even illness' (Kleinman, 1980, p. 149). The phenomenon of somatization occurs in both nonclinical and clinical settings, and its frequency and intensity vary across ethnic groups

(Mumford, 1993). Among different ethnocultural groups, Asians, particularly Chinese, are reported to have a greater likelihood to present their psychological problems as physical complaints (Chen, 1995; Hong, Lee, & Lorenzo, 1995; Parker, Gladstone, & Chee, 2001; Tabora & Flaskerud, 1994; see also Stewart et al., this volume). In a cross-cultural study conducted by Parker, Cheah, and Roy (2001), Malaysian-Chinese were more likely to express somatic symptoms, whereas Australian-Caucasians were more likely to complain of depressed mood, cognitive and anxiety symptoms.

Some researchers have tried to explain this phenomenon of somatization among Chinese in terms of their cultural values, language/semantic structure, and their conception of health. For instance, some may argue that Chinese tend to suppress their negative emotions in order to preserve harmony in social interactions. However, when directly asked, Chinese can readily express their distress in psychological terms (Cheung, 1982a; Cheung & Lau, 1982). Other researchers have theorized that Chinese lack the vocabulary to express their emotions in psychological terms; therefore, they rely on physical metaphors to describe their affect (Kleinman, 1980; Kleinman & Kleinman, 1986). Lastly, some believe that Chinese somatize their affective states because they espouse the holistic conception of the mind and the body and do not differentiate the functions between these two systems (Chaplin, 1997; Kuo & Kavanagh, 1994).

Despite researchers' assertion of such cross-cultural differences in somatization, empirical evidence is still insufficient and inconclusive. Although studies have found that Chinese and Asian Americans reported more somatic symptoms in clinical settings (Kleinman, 1980; Lin, 1982), other studies have found either no difference in the reports of somatic symptoms among all ethnic groups seen in general practice, or that reporting of somatic symptoms was very common among nonclinical populations (Escobar, 1987; Kellner, 1990; Simon, VonKorff, Piccinelli, Fullerton, & Ormel, 1999). In a community sample of Chinese in Hong Kong, the respondents reported more psychological symptoms than both psychophysiological and physiological symptoms (Cheung, 1982b). In another study, Chinese psychiatric patients were found to be able to acknowledge their affective states when they were directly asked (Cheung, Lau, & Waldmann, 1980–1). They were also found to report different symptoms according to the settings in which they sought help (Cheung, 1982a). Therefore, it was argued that instead of replacing their psychological distress with somatic symptoms, Chinese are reporting different types of symptoms depending on the reporting situation and their routes of help seeking.

In addition to the alternative hypotheses that were proposed to account for their reporting of somatic symptoms, somatization was found to be strongly related to both depression and anxiety disorders (Escobar, 1987; Kellner, 1990; Lieb, Meinlschmidt, & Araya, 2007; Simon & VonKorff, 1991). In the CAPES, using the SCL-90R somatization score, 12.9 per cent of the 1,747 Chinese Americans meet the Somatic Symptom Index (SSI) 5/5 criterion for somatization. Among them, 29.5 per cent and 19.6 per cent of them met the DSM criteria for depression and anxiety disorders, respectively (Mak & Zane, 2004). A study on depressive symptom manifestation among 1,039 Taiwanese indicated that Chinese generally expressed more somatic complaints than cognitive-affective complaints; yet those who expressed depressive symptoms emphasized somatic symptoms less than did non-depressed respondents (Chang, 2007).

Furthermore, the somatization tendencies of Chinese may be in lieu of, rather than in place of, other psychiatric disorders. Rather than somatizing their depressive symptoms, recent clinical and epidemiological studies indicate that Chinese may be experiencing a distinct form of distress, referred to as neurasthenia or *shenjing shuairuo*, independent from other Western diagnostic categories. In the CAPES study, a prevalence of neurasthenia, as defined by the ICD-10, was found to be 6.4 per cent among a random sample of Chinese Americans living in Los Angeles (Zheng, Lin, Takeuchi, Kurasaki, Wang, & Cheung, 1997). Among them, 43.7 per cent also met the diagnoses of DSM-defined mood and anxiety disorders. In other words, the majority (56.3 per cent) of individuals did not meet any current or lifetime DSM diagnoses.

In another clinical study of 139 patients at the Second Affiliated Xianga Hospital of Central South University in the Hunan Province, 35.3 per cent met the Chinese Classification System of Mental Disorders (CCMD-2-R) diagnosis of *shenjing shuairuo* (Chang, Myers, Yeung, Zhang, Zhao, & Yu, 2005). Among the diagnosed, 19.4 per cent were also diagnosed as having ICD-10 neurasthenia,

65.1 per cent with DSM-IV diagnosis, including 30.6 per cent with undifferentiated somatoform disorder, 22.4 per cent with somatoform pain disorder, 4.1 per cent with somatization disorder, and 2 per cent with hypochondriasis. Thus, 44.9 per cent of those with *shenjing shuairuo* did not meet the criteria defining any DSM diagnoses. Findings from these studies indicate that the reporting of somatic symptoms, as assessed by somatization, neurasthenia, or *shenjing shuairuo* by clinical and community samples might reflect their severe state of psychological distress that is comorbid with other psychiatric conditions. Moreover, these studies also showed that neurasthenia and *shenjing shuairuo* are distinct clinical conditions experienced by Chinese that do not necessarily overlap with any Western diagnoses.

Somatization tendencies were also related to help-seeking patterns, stress experiences, and the availability of social resources (Hoover, 1999). This issue is particularly salient among immigrant populations, whose experiences are often compounded by their lesser access to health care, their level of stress and social support they experienced and received in the host society. Chinese Americans who met the SSI 5/5 criterion were more likely to seek help from both Western and traditional Chinese doctors and to use both Western and traditional Chinese medicine than those who did not show signs of somatization. They were also more likely to seek help from psychiatrists, other medical doctors, and mental health specialists for their mental health problems than were non-somatizers (Mak & Zane, 2004). Chinese Americans with somatoform disorders were also more likely to seek professional help than were those with depressive and anxiety disorders (Kung & Lu, 2008). Finally, somatizers tended to report experiencing much more stress (daily hassles and financial strain) and less support from their family and friends than non-somatizers (Mak & Zane, 2004). All in all, the experience of somatization might be a result of severe psychological distress, excessive life strain, and a lack of social support in coping with stress among Chinese. Thus, the argument that Chinese translate their psychological distress into somatic symptoms appears to be oversimplifying the phenomenon of somatization as experienced by Chinese persons.

Cultural values and distress

In addition to understanding how culture may affect the manifestation of distress experiences among Chinese, researchers have also attempted to understand cultural influences on the experience of the distress experience itself. In other words, why do Chinese report higher level of distress compared to other ethnic groups? To account for these consistent reports of heightened distress, researchers have used various measures of acculturation and cultural value orientation to try and understand the role of culture in mental health. However, given the use of global measures and diverse Asian American samples, previous research may lack the required precision for identifying specific cultural variables that may be salient in the development of distress.

To study the effects of acculturation on distress, researchers have examined cultural influences on distress using global measures of acculturation (e.g. the Suinn-Lew Asian Self-Identity Acculturation Scale; Suinn, Rickard-Figueroa, Lew, & Vigil, 1987), global cultural value endorsement (i.e. Asian Values Scale; Kim, Atkinson, & Yang, 1999), or reports of ethnicity or nationality as proxies for cultural values. Depending on the populations observed and measurements used, acculturation to mainstream American culture has found to either enhance well-being (e.g. Organista, Organista, & Kurasaki, 2003) or to intensify distress among immigrants (e.g. Mak, Chen, Wong, & Zane, 2005). These mixed findings signify a need to examine more specific cultural concepts and identified the dynamics that come into play to shape individuals' distress experience. Constructs that have substantial bearing in a particular culture can influence the way individuals interpret their daily experiences and express their distress. Thus, the direct examination of these variables can facilitate our understanding of mental health among culturally diverse groups. Among many cultural variables, face concern may be particularly salient in understanding individuals' distress in the Chinese context (see also Cheng, Lo, & Chio, this volume).

Face concern has been identified as a key interpersonal dynamic in East Asian cultures (Bond, 1991; Ho, 1976; Hu, 1944; Ting-Toomey, 1994; Yang, 1945; see also Hwang & Han, this volume).

As social beings, people are invested in presenting to others, either implicitly or explicitly, certain claims about their character in terms of traits, attitudes, and values. Others come to recognize and accept the person's 'face' or 'line' that the person claims. This set of claims constitutes that person's face claimed (Ho, 1991). Face given refers to social image and social worth that is garnered based on one's performance in interpersonal and social contexts (Choi & Lee, 2002; Hwang, 1997–8). It represents a person's social position or prestige gained by performing one or more specific social roles that are well recognized by others (Hu, 1944). It goes beyond meeting moral and ethical standards set forth by one's social network and shame that one experiences when he/she falls short of meeting the moral demands (Ho, 1976; Hwang, 1997–8). According to the face negotiation theory, 'face is tied to the emotional significance and estimated calculations that we attach to our own social self-worth and the social self-worth of others' (Ting-Toomey, 2005, p. 73). Thus, the esteem implications of an individual's face extend beyond the individual to his or her interpersonal relationships and group positions. Given the socio-contextual nature of face, face concern can be a powerful construct that affects the distress experience of Chinese.

Compared to its social significance in individualistic societies such as the United States, face may be more salient in East Asian social relations (Kam & Bond, 2008; Oetzel et al., 2001). Face functions as an important mechanism that maintains group harmony and protects the integrity of the in-group. Concern over loss of face can potentially affect the relationship between stressful experiences and psychological distress and intensify the distress experience of individuals (see Liao & Bond, in press). Individuals who are concerned about their own face may forsake their emotional well-being to reduce conflict and maintain social order, since the avoidance of face loss is crucial to their own social image and that of their groups (Ho, 1991; Ting-Toomey & Kurogi, 1998).

The heightened vigilance in avoiding potentially face-losing situations can be psychologically taxing to the individuals and lead to distress. In a recent study, Mak and Chen (2006) have found that face was related positively to psychological distress among a community sample of 1,503 Chinese Americans, even when preexisting distress, various face-related stressors (e.g. daily hassles, financial strain), instrumental and emotional support from family and friends were taken into account. Thus, people with greater face concern are more likely to experience higher levels of distress than their counterparts with lower levels of face concern.

Rather than being a unitary construct, face concern is more complex in Chinese culture than in other cultures. Mak, Chen, Lam, and Yiu (2009) examined the role of face concern in psychological distress through a series of studies in both college students and community samples in Mainland China, Hong Kong, and the United States. Across all samples, face concern was significantly and positively related to distress above and beyond the impact of age, gender, and ethnicity. Moreover, the single-factor structure of face concern, as proposed by Zane and Yeh (2002), was confirmed among Chinese Americans and European Americans. However, face concern was decomposed into a two-factor structure, an outcome supported among both Hong Kong Chinese and Mainland Chinese university students and community samples (Mak et al., 2009). Of the two factors, self-face was found to be positively associated with distress, whereas the effect of other-face was not significant. While self-face represents the motivations for individuals to maintain their own face, other-face relates to the focus of the individuals to preserve other people's face (see also Singelis, Bond, Sharkey, & Lai, 1999, on self- and other-embarrassability). Thus, only self-face has significant bearing on individuals' psychlogical distress. This fine-tuning of the face construct may reflect the extent to which face concern is embedded in the daily interpersonal interactions among Chinese people (Bond, 1981; Bond & Hwang, 1986; Gao, Ting-Toomey, & Gudykunst, 1996; see also Hwang & Han, this volume). These findings highlight the importance of attending to specific cultural dynamics in counseling services.

Not only does face concern affect the distress experience of Chinese and Chinese Americans, it has been found to influence preferences for mental health treatment and consequent behaviors. In an experiment with Asian-American and European American students, those with high face concern regarded their counselor to be more credible in the directive counseling approach than in the non-directive counseling approach (Park, 1999). This finding may be understood in that counseling creates an environment and a therapeutic relationship that is novel to individuals entering treatment.

When expectations for social roles are ambiguous and individuals are unclear on how to behave properly, the risk for face loss becomes high. Thus, individuals with greater face concern are likely to prefer a directive counseling approach because such approach minimizes the ambiguity in the therapeutic relationship and threats to face loss (Zane & Mak, 2003). Directive therapists should be aware, however, that in another experimental study with Asian American college students, face concern was negatively related to self-disclosure, in that students with high face concern were less inclined to disclose aspects about their personality, negative aspects about themselves, and aspects about their intimate relationships (Zane, Umemoto, & Park, 1998).

Other variables characteristic of the Chinese culture, such as a strong preference for interpersonal harmony, also predict psychological distress. Individuals who endorsed a greater interdependent self-construal had a greater tendency to develop a sociotropic cognitive vulnerability that disposed them to depression and anxiety (Mak, Law, & Teng, in press). In studies among Hong Kong Chinese, relationship harmony has been found to associate negatively with depressive symptoms, and family dysfunction is even predictive of suicidal ideation (Chen, Chan, Bond, & Stewart, 2006; Chen, Wu, & Bond, 2009). This outcome is consistent with the cultural attribution of distress in Chinese populations. Due to the influence of Confucian ideals, Chinese consider interpersonal harmony to be the key element of maintaining mental health. As indicated by a narrative analysis of interviews with Chinese patients in Australia, feelings of shame and guilt arising from failure to fulfill interpersonal, especially family, obligations induced their mental illness (Hsiao, Klimids, Minas, & Tan, 2006).

Cultural influences on help seeking

The understanding of help-seeking behaviors for mental health problems has been emphasized increasingly due to its effect on long-term prognosis. Early treatment in the course of mental health problems can reduce the suffering of the affected individuals and prevent the escalation of psychological problems into chronic mental illnesses (Birchwood, McGorry, & Jackson, 1997; Linszen, Lenior, De Haan, Dingemans, & Gersons, 1998). Consequently, understanding delay in help seeking could reduce the long-term costs incurred by psychiatric interventions and the protracted rehabilitation process.

Despite the benefits of early intervention, research has consistently found disparities between the need for mental health services and their actual utilization among Chinese across various Asian regions, including Hong Kong (Chiu, 2002, 2004; Rudowicz & Au, 2001), Taiwan (Lin, 2002), Mainland China (Boey, 1999; Boey, Mei, Sui, & Zeng, 1998; Chang, Tong, Shi & Zeng, 2005; Jiang & Wang, 2003), and Singapore (Ow & Katz, 1999; Quah & Bishop, 1996). In spite of their reportedly high levels of psychological distress, Chinese and Chinese Americans underutilize professional services for their mental health problems (Leong, 1994; Mak et al., 2005; Matsuoka, Breaux, & Ryujin, 1997; Snowden & Cheung, 1990; Sue, Zane, & Young, 1994; Ying & Hu, 1994). Hong Kong and Mainland Chinese were found less likely to seek help than Chinese Americans and European Americans (Chen & Mak, 2008).

Studies on the utilization of mental health services in Hong Kong have consistently shown unfavorable attitudes towards seeking treatment and low patterns of service utilization (Chiu, 2002, 2004; Rudowicz & Au, 2001; Shek, 1998). According to the Hong Kong Health and Welfare Bureau (2001), an estimated 95,000 individuals with mental health problems required rehabilitation services in 2001. However, fewer than 18,000 psychiatric cases were reported in the same year (Hong Kong Government Information Centre, 2001). The low help-seeking rate concurs with evidence documenting the underutilization of mental health services among Chinese Americans, even though they experience stress and psychological disturbances as much as do other ethnic groups (Kung, 2003, 2004; Leong, 1994; Nguyen & Anderson, 2005; Ying & Hu, 1994).

Data from the CAPES found that only 17 per cent of Chinese Americans who experienced emotional, anxiety, drugs, alcohol or mental health problems have sought for help in the previous six months, among whom less than 6 per cent saw a mental health professional (Matsuoka, Breaux, & Ryujin, 1997). In the National Latino and Asian American Study (NLAAS), out of the 600 Chinese sampled nationally in the United States, 7.34 per cent have sought help from any services, 4.03 per cent from specialty mental health services, and 2.85 per cent from general medical services in the past year (Abe-Kim et al., 2007). Among those with a DSM-IV psychiatric disorder, only 31.02 per cent have sought help from mental health services in the past year (Abe-Kim et al., 2007). In Mainland China, the Chinese World Mental Health Survey Initiative has showed that failure to receive treatment and delay in initial contact for mental disorders is serious and pervasive, with only one in seven people with mental disorder ever received professional treatment in metropolitan areas (Lee et al., 2007b). In their study, a multi-stage interview of 5,201 adults in Beijing and Shanghai revealed that 44.7 per cent of people with anxiety, 25.7 per cent of those with substance disorder, and 7.9 per cent of those with mood disorder made treatment contact. The delay in treatment for people with anxiety and substance disorders could be as long as 17–21 years.

Cultures differ in the norms applied to the act of asking for help (Atkinson, Lowe, & Matthews, 1995; Gim, Atkinson, & Whitely, 1990; Ying & Miller, 1992). Sue (1999) has suggested that cultural factors affect underutilization of mental health services by Chinese despite their greater reporting of psychological distress (see Cheng et al., this volume). Acculturation has been found to link with favorable attitudes toward mental health services among Asian Americans (Atkinson & Gim, 1989; Tata & Leong, 1994; Zhang & Dixon, 2003). Conversely, Asian Americans who endorse more traditional Asian values have less favorable attitudes toward seeking professional help, and are less willing to see a counselor (Kim & Omizo, 2003).

In addition to accounting for their level of acculturation to the American culture (for immigrants and Chinese Americans) and the endorsement of general Asian values, it is important to explore specific cultural factors that are related to help seeking and the challenges encountered in the process. One possible explanation for the low utilization pattern is the incompatibility between Chinese cultural values and those inherent in mental health treatment. Help seeking carries many negative connotations in the Chinese culture. It may be considered as a lack of self-control in solving one's own problems (Leong, 1986), implying a weakness in character, bad thoughts, or a lack of will power (Chan & Parker, 2004). In the traditional Chinese culture where self-restraint is valued, individuals are expected to control and suppress their emotional problems, or attach little importance or concern to them (Tracey, Leong, & Gidden, 1986). Intense stigma attached to mental illness and concern about shame and face loss also hinder Chinese from seeking mental health services (Kung, 2004; Pearson, 1993).

With strong influences from the Buddhist, Taoist, and Confucian philosophies, Chinese tend to conceive themselves as part of the integral whole with other people and the environment (Cheng et al., this volume). Furthermore, the high population density and tight ecology of China dispose individuals to form close-knit ecosystems and relationships that impact on individuals' sense of self (Ekblad, 1996; Yang, 1986). Under these cultural and social conditions, face concern as an important interpersonal dynamic among Chinese may predispose individuals to further stigmatize mental illness and to avoid any behaviors that may put them at risk for disclosure of their mental health condition, such as by actively seeking help for themselves.

The pathway to help seeking postulates a series of links between the initial recognition of a problem and the eventual use of mental health services (Rogler & Cortes, 1993). Throughout the process, practical concerns may be influential in shaping service use. Lack of knowledge about available mental health treatment, cost and complexity of treatment, and time involved are all important practical barriers to accessing mental health service (Kung, 2004). Studies of Chinese Americans have demonstrated that participants rated practical barriers as more important concerns to mental health treatment compared to cultural barriers (Kung, 2004; Tabora & Flaskerud, 1996); these practical barriers were the only significant factors in reducing service use among Chinese Americans (Kung, 2004).

Cultural lay beliefs and help seeking

Among attitudinal factors, the issue of how lay beliefs about mental illness and its treatment affect help-seeking patterns is worthy of attention. Lay beliefs are those beliefs held by ordinary people in a society that have been developed for explaining certain events and social behaviors. Having examined ten universal and culture-bound psychological and social problems in Chinese culture, Luk and Bond (1992) categorized lay beliefs about causes of mental illness into two factors, namely environmental/hereditary and social-personal causes. The environmental/hereditary factor encompasses both physical and somatic sources conducive to psychological problems, such as genetic predisposition, the brain/nervous system, the working environment, and a person's state of health, whereas the social-personal factor was related to social and psychological sources, such as life quality, past experience, formal education, and religious beliefs.

Chen and Mak (2008) examined how cultural beliefs about the etiology of mental illness contributed to seeking help from mental health professionals among four cultural groups, viz. Mainland Chinese, Hong Kong Chinese, Chinese Americans, and European Americans. Lay beliefs about causes of mental illness and prior help-seeking history significantly predicted the likelihood of help seeking. They suggested that the social-personal factor resembles the etiology beliefs characterizing collectivist mental health worldviews, which regard psychological problems as personal failure, and that the environmental/hereditary factor parallels the etiology beliefs held by Western-based counselors who tend to emphasize the influence of the environment. As individuals with etiology beliefs similar to those of their counselors are more likely to perceive psychological treatments as effective, environmental/hereditary causes were found to relate positively to help-seeking likelihood; conversely, social-personal causes were found to relate negatively to help-seeking likelihood. These findings demonstrate the importance of understanding help-seeking patterns within Chinese cultural contexts and the effects of Western worldviews in shaping help-seeking propensities.

Other lay beliefs about mental illness in Chinese societies may be traced to traditional Chinese medicine, which regards health as harmony between *yin* (coldness and darkness) and *yang* (warmth and light), and illness as imbalance between bodily functions and emotions. As the good spirits (*shen*) influence the *yang* and the bad spirits (*kwei*) influence the *yin*, a considerable percentage (11–31 per cent) of psychiatric patients in Singapore believed that their illness were caused by spirit possession (Kua, Chew, & Ko, 1993). To treat the illness, the patients or their relatives consulted with a healer or medium to diagnose or identify the offending spirit and drive out the *kwei*. They then sought help from general practitioners or mental health professionals if the traditional healers failed to cure the symptoms (Kua, Chew, & Ko, 1993).

Likewise, Taiwanese hold less positive attitudes towards formal help seeking (Hong, 2000; Hsiao, 1992; Lin, 1998; Nu, 1987; Pan, 1996). Using the approach of folk psychology, Lin (2002) has identified some fundamental themes in seeking and receiving help in Taiwan. Help-seeking is considered as a sign of weakness and shame. Thus, informal help is preferred to formal help, which is thought to be a last resort for serious conditions. Regardless of the type of problems, Chinese in Taiwan tend to cope with stress in the context of social relations, by turning to friends and family members as common sources of help, instead of utilizing professional assistance (Chang, 2008).

In addition to identifying specific cultural factors and lay beliefs that may influence Chinese help-seeking, it is also important to examine the applicability of existing theory-based models in the understanding of help-seeking behavior among the Chinese. Among all health models, the theory of planned behavior (TPB; Ajzen, 1985, 1991) has been the most widely investigated. TPB suggests that a person's attitudes, subjective norms, and perceived behavioral control affect his or her intention to engage in a behavior, which is a proximal determinant of the behavior itself. Whereas individual-based variables (attitudes and perceived behavioral control) have been found to be related strongly to individuals' intention, subjective norms may be particularly relevant and important to Chinese people's decision to seek help. Whereas personal independence is particularly valued in the Western culture, Chinese culture values interpersonal relatedness, which encompasses harmony with others, adherence to reciprocal interactions, concern for losing other's face, and consideration of the self in terms of family and community relationships (Cheung, Leung, Zhang, Sun, Gan, Song, & Xie, 2001; Oyserman, Kemmelmeier, & Coon, 2002; Triandis, 1995; Triandis et al., 1986). The significance of the personal self is often downplayed in favor of group consideration, and the self-concept of Chinese individuals often evolves around significant persons integral to one's conception of self (see Kwan, Hui, & McGee, this volume).

A recent study showed that attitude, subjective norm, perceived behavioral control, and perceived barriers to seeking help significantly predicted help-seeking intention in a community sample of Chinese in Hong Kong (Mo & Mak, 2009). More importantly, in addition to having a direct relationship with help-seeking intention, subjective norm is also strongly related to people's attitudes to help seeking and their perceived behavioral control. Thus, among Chinese, the norms of their significant others is an important determinant of their own help-seeking intentions.

Stigma surrounding Chinese illness behaviors

As previously mentioned, illness behavior includes the way individuals experience, interpret, and cope with a disease. Individuals can vary in how they perceive and define illness, the way they present the distress, and the interventions they consider and seek out within a given cultural milieu and based on its cultural logic and priorities (Mechanic, 1986). As such, stigma as well as cultural values can influence the way individuals view psychological distress, help-seeking attitudes, and help-seeking behaviors. The stigma surrounding mental illness is recognized as a primary social barrier to receiving adequate care and to achieving appropriate life opportunities for individuals experiencing psychological disorders (U.S. Department of Health and Human Services, 1999). Its impact is particularly profound among collectivist Chinese, who tend to delay treatment and use fewer mental health services (U.S. Department of Health and Human Services, 2001; Zhang, Snowden, & Sue, 1998). In Australia, stigma is found to be a factor that limits access to mental health care and the quality of care received among Chinese migrants (Blignault, Ponzio, Rong, & Eisenbruch, 2008). Among Hong Kong Chinese, the use of secrecy about mental illness was found to be the most frequently endorsed way of coping with stigma (Chung & Wong, 2004).

Similar to the stigma attached to mental illness observed in other parts of the world (World Health Organization, 2008), substantial stigma has been evident in the Hong Kong general public. Despite public education efforts in the 1980s (e.g. Cheung, 1990), 40 per cent of the respondents in three large-scale telephone surveys conducted in the 1990s did not want to be neighbors of people with mental illness (Chou & Mak, 1998, Lau & Cheung, 1999; Tsang, Tam, Chan, & Cheung, 2003). Over 90 per cent of the 7,685 respondents objected to the proposal of establishing rehabilitation facilities in their community (Cheung, 1988).

The main reasons for their opposition included fear of halfway house clients, perceived incurability of mental illness, and danger and risks to community members of locating halfway houses nearby. Their fear may be attributed to the stereotypes that they hold about individuals with severe mental illnesses. Oftentimes, the lay public equates severe mental illness with insanity (Cheung, 1990). In categorizing mental illness, traditional Chinese medicine also emphasized the most severe forms of mental illness, such as psychotic disorders. The labels used, namely *tien* and *k'uang*, denote excessive emotions and craziness, connoting a sense of unpredictability and loss of control (Cheung, 1986). Those with mental illness are likely to be aware of such public sentiments and conceal their status lest they be discriminated against. They may internalize the social stigma in the form of self-stigma that dampens self-esteem and the willingness to seek treatment (Corrigan & Watson, 2002; Mak & Cheung, in press a). Given the highly stigmatized context of Chinese communities, it is essential to understand how such culturally based views of mental illnesses affect the individuals' help-seeking attitudes and patterns.

In addition to those individuals burdened by a mental illness, their close affiliates may also be stigmatized by the general public. Not only do the family members have to carry the responsibility of taking care of their relatives with mental illness in an unsupportive society (Wong, 2000; Wong, Tsui, Pearson, Chen, & Chiu, 2004), but they also need to face the misunderstanding and discrimination that abound in the community. Mental illness is often attributed as retribution for ancestral transgressions, thereby rendering the entire family responsible for the member's illness. Given that mental illness is regarded as hereditary and related to inheritance of ancestral misconduct, the afflicted as well as their siblings are deemed to be unfit for marriage and child-bearing (Ng, 1997), further deepening segregation. Research has showed that family members of individuals with mental illness or intellectual disability suffer from affiliate stigma (or the extent of self-stigma among associates of targeted minorities), which is related to greater level of subjective burden in relation to their caregiver roles (Mak & Cheung, 2008). Findings also indicate that family members who have a high level of face concern and are caring for people recovering from mental illness reported greater affiliate stigma, which adds to their caregiver burden and psychological distress (Mak & Cheung, in press b). Likewise, multiple in-depth interviews with Chinese families in Singapore showed that their disclosure of potentially distressful information was selective, and that they kept secrets within the immediate family so as to save face (Ow & Katz, 1999).

Thus, stigma may have particularly deleterious effects on Chinese in terms of delaying their help-seeking, receipt of mental health care, and acceptance by the society and the general public. While public stigma may create an unfavorable or even hostile environment against people with mental illness by limiting their social opportunities, self-stigma may further exacerbate individuals' suffering through diminished self-esteem and willingness to seek treatment or to continue treatment (Corrigan, 2004). Anti-stigma efforts are thus necessary to change public and sufferers' attitudes towards mental illness and to facilitate early detection and treatment of mental illness.

Structural issues shaping Chinese illness behaviors

With about a tenth of adults, roughly 450 million worldwide, affected by mental disorders at any one time, factors that impede access to care must be viewed seriously (Thornicroft & Maingay, 2002). In Hong Kong, among the resources allocated to mental health services in the past three years, medical services constitute the majority, whereas community-based rehabilitation services receive markedly less attention. In addition, in Hong Kong, the average waiting time was five weeks for adult psychiatric outpatient services (that for children's services was even longer, around six months), six months for halfway houses, and 6.3 years for long-stay care homes for the year 2004–05 (Legislative Council, 2005; Social Welfare Department, 2005). Given the inadequacies of the system, many individuals are left without treatment for long periods of time. Without access and utilization to care, even those individuals eager for assistance are deprived of the opportunity to be treated and to recover from their illnesses. These long waiting times are probably used by many as a rationale for not seeking treatment in the first place.

Despite these shortfalls, the Hong Kong government is making efforts to promote better mental health, with the focus from in-patient care to community and day-care services. The Hospital Authority has attempted to develop more comprehensive community-based treatment methods through their community psychiatric service, community psychiatric nursing service, and psychogeriatric service. Meanwhile, the government is taking preventive measures, such as public education to advocate the importance of mental health and ways of early identification and intervention. More avenues for seeking help and appropriate support, counseling, and medical services are being made available.

Hong Kong may become an example for other Chinese societies. Yet regional differences exist in the structure of mental health services which lead service accessibility to vary among Chinese groups. For example, the structure and procedures for mental health services have evolved from a medical model of treatment in Mainland China (Hou & Zhang, 2007). As counseling and psychotherapy in China are heavily influenced by medical science, most professionals who provide mental health services work in health-care settings such as hospitals, and were trained as physicians such as psychiatrists, neurologists, and general practitioners, and are thus identified as 'psychological doctors' (Zhang, Li, & Yuan, 2001). Moreover, Chinese clients prefer short-term and problem-focused treatment sessions with direct advice, psychoeducation, supportive listening, and medication prescription (Chang et al., 2005).

Owing to their traditional conceptions and lay beliefs about mental illness, Chinese also seek help from non-psychiatric facilities and indigenous healing methods. For instance, more than half of Mainland Chinese patients with schizophrenia attempted traditional Chinese medicine, acupuncture, *qi gong* (breathing exercise), and other folk healing methods (Tang, Sevigny, Mao, Jiang, & Cai, 2007). The common reasons for seeking alternative services include shameful feelings, stigma surrounding psychiatric hospitals, inaccessibility to professional services, and fear of being incarcerated and receiving electric shock treatment. Among these reasons, unavailability of mental health services constitutes a major structural issue in China. Thus, training among traditional healers in the identification of mental health problems, training and education of formal mental health professionals, public education about mental health and destigmatization of mental illness, and establishment of better and more accessible mental health services may be necessary to facilitate early detection and intervention. Not only in Chinese societies do structural issues exist, they also appear in other health care systems. Chinese immigrants in Canada reported unsatisfactory prior experience with clinicians, as patients felt that the social context of their lives and the nature of their problems were not fully understood. Financial constraints also prevented them from treatment methods of their own choice; therefore, they relied mostly on self-help (Lee, Rodin, Devins, & Weiss, 2001).

Changing the structure by which mental health services are delivered can probably reduce the resistance of individuals towards seeking help from mental health professionals. One of the ways to do so is to integrate mental health services with primary care. By integrating mental health services with other health care services, the stigma of seeking help for mental health services and the threat of face loss can be minimized. Such an arrangement is consonant with the Chinese holistic way of viewing physical and mental health. This kind of integrated services have been in place in Chinese American communities in New York and Boston with demonstrated effectiveness (Fang & Chen, 2004; Yeung, Kung, Chung, Rubenstein, Roffi, Mischoulon, & Fava, 2004). Similar models can be applied in other community and university-based health clinics in Chinese regions around the world (see also Chan, this volume). In addition to having integrated health services as a possible strategy to increase access and help-seeking, mental health services can also be incorporated into other services in the university (e.g. academic advising, programs for international students) and social services in Chinese communities (Constantine, Chen, & Ceesay, 1997). To effectively meet the needs of Chinese who may not be familiar with the traditional counseling and psychotherapy, mental health professionals must reach out to the communities through innovative and culturally sensitive approaches.

In understanding the underlying mechanisms that lead to inadequate care, researchers and practitioners can better design culturally relevant and effective community programs that enhance the public's willingness to reach out when they experience psychological distress. The sooner individuals seek help for their psychological distress, the greater the chances of recovery and the lesser the cost to society in terms of lost productivity, community disintegration, and health care costs. With mental illness being ranked second (after cardiovascular conditions) as a global burden of disease (Murray & Lopez, 1996), understanding the underlying mechanisms that deter individuals from seeking help can better prepare professionals in providing effective care to individuals suffering from mental illness.

Future directions

It should be noted that significant differences exist within Chinese groups. Indeed, 'Chinese' is an umbrella term which encompasses heterogeneous groups with various cultural backgrounds and social norms. Though regarded as collectivist cultures (Hofstede, 1980), Mainland China, Hong Kong, Taiwan, and Singapore constitute different political systems and socio-economic environments. Our reviews on illness behavior and help-seeking patterns suggest that within-group differences should be taken into account when we examine the mental health of Chinese people.

Related to heterogeneity within Chinese societies, the issue of language use might play a role in the mixed findings of illness behaviors from self-reports and clinician/interviewer assessments. Research on social cognition shows that bilingual Chinese shifted their self concept, values, and attributions toward the norms of the culture primed by the language being used, and accommodated their responses toward the normative patterns of that culture (e.g. Hong, Morris, Chiu, & Benet-Martínez, 2000; Oyserman & Lee; 2008; Ross, Xun, and Wilson, 2002). When bilingual Chinese express their psychological symptoms in a second language or in a different culture, such as Chinese in Western countries, recent Mainland Chinese immigrants in Hong Kong, and Chinese ethnic minorities (other than Han) in Mainland China, would they align their reports with the perceived norms of that culture? Are there differences in the manifestations of distress experience and illness behavior when they interact with mental health professionals in a second language? These questions await further empirical studies to answer.

It is of scientific interest and an ethical responsibility for researchers and practitioners to understand and serve the Chinese populations better. Being the largest population in the world, Chinese have a huge impact in many respects on this global community. With regard to illness behaviors, more basic research is necessary in understanding the nosology of psychiatric diagnoses for Chinese, so that the psychiatric classification systems can better match with their real problems. Multiple strategies must be in place to identify their symptoms and functioning so that methodological bias can be prevented. Rather than relying on self-report measures or diagnostic interviews, neurobiological measures may be taken to more objectively capture physiological and psychological changes that are going on within the individuals. Multiple informants should be involved to understand the social functioning of the individuals, as it may be manifested variably across different social contexts.

To facilitate early identification and intervention, systematic research in understanding what constitutes stigma of mental illness and what Chinese values may feed into the perpetuation of stigma needs to be in place for the development of culturally relevant and effective anti-stigma campaigns. Stigma towards mental illness may be removed through public education of mental health as part of holistic health. Myths and stereotypes of mental illness need to be changed and attributions of illness need to be changed not only at the individual level, but also at the societal level in order to facilitate help-seeking. At the system level, applied research is necessary to understand the current strengths and weaknesses of the mental health service systems for better access to care and more effective treatment modes. Without ongoing and culturally specific research in the study of Chinese illness behaviors, practitioners cannot better meet their needs and better serve them.

References

Abe, J. S. & Zane, N. W. S. (1990). Psychological maladjustment among Asian and White American college students: Controlling for confounds. *Journal of Counseling Psychology, 37*, 437–444.

Abe-Kim, J., Takeuchi, D. T., Hong, S., Zane, N., Sue, S., Spencer, M. S., Appel, H., Nicdao, E. & Alegría, M. (2007). Use of mental health-related services among immigrant and US-born Asian Americans: Results from the National Latino and Asian American Study. *American Journal of Public Health, 97*, 91–98.

Ajzen, I. (1985). From intentions to actions: A theory of planned behavior. In J. Kuhl & J. Beckman (eds), *Action control: From cognition to behavior* (pp. 11–39). New York: Springer-Verlag.

Ajzen, I. (1991). The theory of planned behavior. *Organizational Behavior and Human Decision Processes, 50*, 179–211.

Aldwin, C. & Greenberger, E. (1987). Cultural differences in the predictors of depression. *American Journal of Community Psychology, 15*, 789–813.

Angel, R. & Thoits, P. (1987). The impact of culture on the cognitive structure of illness. *Culture, Medicine & Psychiatry, 11*, 465–494.

Atkinson, D. R. & Gim, R. H. (1989). Asian-American cultural identity and attitudes toward mental health services. *Journal of Counseling Psychology, 36*, 209–212.

Atkinson, D. R., Lowe, S., & Matthews, L. (1995). Asian-American acculturation, gender, and willingness to seek counseling. *Journal of Multicultural Counseling and Development, 23*, 130–138.

Austin, A. A. & Chorpita, B. F. (2004). Temperament, anxiety, and depression: Comparisons across five ethnic groups of children. *Journal of Clinical Child & Adolescent Psychology, 33*, 216–226.

Birchwood, M., McGorry, P., & Jackson, H. (1997). Early intervention in schizophrenia. *British Journal of Psychiatry 170*, 2–5.

Blignault, I., Ponzio, V., Rong, Y., & Eisenbruch, M. (2008). A qualitative study of barriers to mental health services utilization among migrants from Mainland China in South-East Sydney. *International Journal of Social Psychiatry, 54*, 180–190.

Boey, K. W. (1999). Help-seeking preference of college students in urban China after the implementation of the 'open-door' policy. *International Journal of Social Psychiatry, 45*, 104–116.

Boey, K. W., Mei, J., Sui, Y., & Zeng, J. (1998). Help-seeking tendency of undergraduate students. *Chinese Journal of Clinical Psychology, 6*, 210–215.

Bond, M. H. & Lee, P. W. H. (1981). Face-saving in Chinese culture: A discussion and experimental study of Hong Kong students. In A. King & R. Lee (eds), *Social life and development in Hong Kong* (pp. 288–305). Hong Kong: Chinese University Press.

Bond, M. H. (1991). *Beyond the Chinese face: Insights from psychology.* Hong Kong: Oxford University Press.

Bond, M. H. & Hwang, K. K. (1986). The social psychology of Chinese people. In M. H. Bond (ed.), *The psychology of the Chinese people* (pp. 213–266). New York: Oxford University Press.

Chan, B. & Parker, G. (2004). Some recommendations to assess depression in Chinese people in Australasia. *Australian and New Zealand Journal of Psychiatry, 38,* 141–147.

Chan, D. W. (1995). Depressive symptoms and coping strategies among Chinese adolescents in Hong Kong. *Journal of Youth and Adolescence, 24,* 267–279.

Chan, D. W. (1997). Depressive symptoms and perceived competence among Chinese secondary school students in Hong Kong. *Journal of Youth and Adolescence, 26,* 303–319.

Chang, D. F., Myers, H. F., Yeung, A., Zhang, Y., Zhao, J., & Su, S. (2005). *Shenjing shuairuo* and the DSM-IV: Diagnosis, distress, and disability in a Chinese primary care setting, *Transcultural Psychiatry, 42,* 204–218.

Chang, D. F., Tong, H., Shi, Q., Zeng, Q. (2005). Letting a hundred flowers bloom: Counseling and psychotherapy in the People's Republic of China. *Journal of Mental Health Counseling, 27,* 104–116.

Chang, H. (2007). Depressive symptom manifestation and help-seeking among Chinese college students in Taiwan. *International Journal of Psychology, 42,* 200–206.

Chang, H. (2008). Help-seeking for stressful events among Chinese college students in Taiwan: Roles of gender, prior history of counseling, and help-seeking attitudes. *Journal of College Student Development, 49,* 41–51.

Chaplin, S. L. (1997). Somatization. In W. S. Tseng & J. Streltzer (eds), *Culture and psychopathology: A guide to clinical assessment,* (pp. 67–86). New York: Brunner/Mazel.

Chen, C. N., Wong, J., Lee, N., Chan-Ho, M. W., Lau, J. T. F., & Fung, M. (1993). The Shatin community mental health survey in Hong Kong II. Major findings. *Archives of General Psychiatry, 50,* 125–133.

Chen, D. (1995). Cultural and psychological influences on mental health issues for Chinese Americans. In L. L. Adler & B. R. Mukherji (eds), *Spirit versus scalpel: Traditional healing and modern psychotherapy,* (pp. 185–196). Westport, CN: Bergin & Garvey.

Chen, S. X., Chan, W., Bond, M. H., & Stewart, S. M. (2006). The effects of self-efficacy and relationship harmony on depression across cultures: Applying level-oriented and structure-oriented analyses. *Journal of Cross-Cultural Psychology, 37,* 643–658.

Chen, S. X. & Mak, W. W. S. (2008). Seeking professional help: Etiology beliefs about mental illness across cultures. *Journal of Counseling Psychology, 55,* 442–450.

Chen, S. X., Wu, W. C. H., & Bond, M. H. (2009). Linking family dysfunction to suicidal ideation: The mediating roles of self-views and world-views. *Asian Journal of Social Psychology, 12,* 133–144.

Cheng, D., Leong, F. T. L., & Geist, R. (1993). Cultural differences in psychological distress between Asian and Caucasian American college students. *Journal of Multicultural Counseling and Development, 21,* 182–190.

Cheung, F. (1982a). Somatization among Chinese: A critique. *Bulletin of the Hong Kong Psychological Society, 8,* 27–35.

Cheung, F. M. (1982b). Psychological symptoms among Chinese in urban Hong Kong. *Social Science and Medicine, 16,* 1339–1344.

Cheung, F. M. (1986). Psychopathology among Chinese people. In M. H. Bond (ed.) *The Psychology of the Chinese People,* (pp. 171–212). Hong Kong: Oxford University Press.

Cheung, F. M. (1988). Surveys of community attitudes toward mental health facilities: Reflections or provocations? *American Journal of Community Psychology, 16,* 877–882.

Cheung, F. M. (1990). People against the mentally ill: Community opposition to residential treatment facilities. *Community Mental Health Journal, 26,* 205–212.

Cheung, F. M. & Lau, B. W. K. (1982). Situational variations of help-seeking behavior among Chinese patients. *Comprehensive Psychiatry, 23,* 252–262.

Cheung, F. M., Lau, B. W. K., & Waldmann, E. (1980–1). Somatization among Chinese depressives in general practice. *International Journal of Psychiatry and Medicine, 10,* 361–374.

Cheung, F. M., Leung, K., Zhang, J. X., Sun, H. F., Gan, Y. Q., Song, W. Z. & Xie, D. (2001). Indigenous Chinese personality constructs: Is the Five-Factor model complete? *Journal of Cross-Cultural Psychology, 22,* 407–433.

Chiu, M. Y. L. (2002). Help-seeking of Chinese families in a Hong Kong new town. *Journal of Social Policy and Social Work, 6,* 221–240.

Chiu, M. Y. L. (2004). Why Chinese women do not seek help: A cultural perspective on the psychology of women. *Counselling Psychology Quarterly, 17,* 155–166.

Choi, S. C. & Lee, S. J. (2002). Two-component model of *chemyon*-oriented behaviors in Korea: Constructive and defensive *chemyon. Journal of Cross-Cultural Psychology, 33,* 332–345.

Chou, K. L. & Mak, K. Y. (1998). Attitudes to mental patients in Hong Kong Chinese: A trend study over two years. *International Journal of Social Psychiatry, 44,* 215–224.

Chun, C., Enomoto, K., & Sue, S. (1996). Health care issues among Asian Americans: Implications of somatization. In P. M. Kato & T. Mann (eds), *Handbook of diversity issues in health psychology* (pp. 347–366). New York: Plenum.

Chung, R. C. & Singer, M. K. (1995). Interpretation of symptom presentation and distress: A Southeast Asian refugee example. *The Journal of Nervous and Mental Disease, 183*, 639–648.
Chung, K. F. & Wong, M. C. (2004). Experience of stigma among Chinese mental health patients in Hong Kong. *Psychiatric Bulletin, 28*, 451–454.
Constantine, M. G., Chen, E. C., & Cessay, P. (1997). Intake concerns of racial and ethnic minority students at a university counseling center: Implications for developmental programming and outreach. *Journal of Multicultural Counseling & Development, 25*, 210–218.
Corrigan, P. (2004). How stigma interferes with mental health care. *American Psychologist, 59*, 614–625.
Corrigan, P. W. & Watson, A. C. (2002). The paradox of self-stigma and mental illness. *Clinical Psychology: Science & Practice, 9*, 35–53.
Department of Statistics, Ministry of Trade & Industry, Republic of Singapore (2008). *Monthly digest of statistics Singapore, November 2008.*
Ekblad, S. (1996). Ecological psychology in Chinese societies. In M. H. Bond (ed.), *The handbook of Chinese psychology*, (pp. 379–392). Hong Kong: Oxford University Press.
Escobar, J. I. (1987). Cross-cultural aspects of the somatization trait. *Hospital and Community Psychiatry, 38*, 174–180.
Fabrega, H. (1989). Cultural relativism and psychiatric illness. *Journal of Nervous and Mental Disease, 177*, 415–425.
Fang, L. & Chen, T. (2004). Community outreach and education to deal with cultural resistance to mental health services. In N. B. Webb (ed.), *Mass trauma and violence: Helping families and children cope* (pp. 234–255). New York: Guilford Press.
Franks, F. & Faux, S. A. (1990). Depression, stress, mastery, and social resources in four ethnocultural women's groups. *Research in Nursing and Health, 13*, 283–292.
Gao, G., Ting-Toomey, S., & Gudykunst, W. (1996). Chinese communication processes. In M. H. Bond (ed.), *The handbook of Chinese psychology* (pp. 280–293). Hong Kong: Oxford University Press.
Goldberg, D. P. & Hillier, V. F. (1979). A scaled version of the General Health Questionnaire. *Psychological Medicine, 9*, 139–145.
Ho, D. Y. F. (1976). On the concept of face. *American Journal of Sociology, 81*, 867–884.
Ho, D. Y. F. (1991). The concept of 'face' in Chinese American interaction. In W. C. Hu & C. L. Grove (eds), *Encountering the Chinese: A guide for Americans* (pp. 111–124). Yarmouth, ME: Intercultural Press.
Hong, G. K., Lee, B. S., Lorenzo, M. K. (1995). Somatization in Chinese American clients: Implications for psychotherapeutic services. *Journal of Contemporary Psychotherapy, 25*, 105–118.
Hong, L. (2000) Chinese needs and reactions within the counseling contexts. *Counseling and Guidance, 173*, 20–24.
Hong Kong Government Information Centre (2001). *Provision of psychiatric services and counseling services.* Press Release (21/11/2001). Retrieved February 16, 2009 at http://www.info.gov.hk/gia/general/200111/21/1121215.htm.
Hong Kong Health and Welfare Bureau. (2001). *Services for mentally ill persons. Towards a new rehabilitation era: Hong Kong rehabilitation programme plan (1998–99 to 2002–03).* Hong Kong: Government Secretariat.
Hoover, C. R. (1999). Somatization disorders. In E. J. Kramer, S. L. Ivey, & Y. W. Ying (eds), *Immigrant women's health: Problems and solutions* (pp. 233–241). San Francisco, CA: Jossey-Bass.
Hofstede, G. (1980). *Culture's consequences: International differences in work-related values.* Beverly Hills: Sage.
Hong, Y. Y., Morris, M. W., Chiu, C. Y., & Benet-Martínez, V. (2000). Multicultural minds: A dynamic constructivist approach to culture and cognition. *American Psychologist, 55*, 709–720.
Hou, Z. J. & Zhang, N. (2007). Counseling psychology in China. *Applied Psychology: An International Review, 56*, 33–50.
Hsiao, F.-H., Klimids, S., Minas, H., & Tan, E.-S. (2006). Cultural attribution of mental health suffering in Chinese societies: The views of Chinese patients with mental illness and their caregivers. *Journal of Clinical Nursing, 15*, 998–1006.
Hsiao, W. (1992) Chinese behavioural patterns in counseling contexts. *Newsletter of Student Guidance, 22*, 12–21.
Hsu, L. R., Hailey, B. J., & Ranger, L. M. (1987). Cultural and emotional components of loneliness and depression. *Journal of Psychology, 121*, 61–70.
Hu, H. C. (1944). The Chinese concepts of 'face'. *American Anthropologist, 46*, 45–64.
Hwang, K. K. (1997–8). *Guanxi* and *mientze*: Conflict resolution in Chinese society. *Intercultural Communication Studies, 7*, 17–42.
Hwang, W. C., Myers, H. F., Abe-Kim, J., Ting, J. Y. (2008). A conceptual paradigm for understanding culture's impact on mental health: The cultural influences on mental health (CIMH) model. *Clinical Psychology Review, 28*, 211–227.
Hwu, H. G., Yeh, E. K., & Chang, L. Y. (1989). Prevalence of psychiatric disorders in Taiwan defined by the Chinese Diagnostic Interview Schedule. *Acta Psychiatric Scandanavia, 79*, 136–147.
Jiang, G.-R. & Wang, M. (2003). A study on help-seeking propensity of Chinese undergraduates. *Chinese Journal of Clinical Psychology, 11*, 180–184.
Kam, C. C. S. & Bond, M. H. (2008). The role of emotions and behavioral responses in mediating the impact of face loss on relationship deterioration: Are Chinese more face-sensitive than Americans? *Asian Journal of Social Psychology, 11*, 175–184.
Kellner, R. (1990). Somatization: Theories and research. *Journal of Nervous and Mental Disease, 178*, 150–160.
Kessler, R. C., McGonagle, K. A., Zhao, S., Nelson, C. B., Hughes, M., Eshleman, S., Wittchen, H. U., & Kendler, K. S. (1994). Lifetime and 12-month prevalence of *DSM-III-R* psychiatric disorders in the United States: results from the National Comorbidity Survey. *Archives of General Psychiatry, 51*, 8–19.

Kessler, R. C., Berglund, P., Demler, O., Jin, R., Merikangas, K. R., & Walters, E. E. (2005). Lifetime prevalence and age-of-onset distributions of *DSM-IV* disorders in the National Comorbidity Survey Replication. *Archives of General Psychiatry, 62,* 593–602.

Kim, B. S. K., Atkinson, D. R., Yang, P. H. (1999). The Asian values scales: Development, factor analysis, validation, and reliability. *Journal of Counseling Psychology, 46,* 342–352.

Kim, B. S. K. & Omizo, M. M. (2003). Asian cultural values, attitudes toward seeking professional psychological help, and willingness to see a counselor. *The Counseling Psychologist, 31,* 343–361.

Kleinman A. (1980). The cultural construction of illness experience and behavior, 2: A model of somatization of dysphoric affects and affective disorders. In A. Kleinman (ed.), *Patients and healers in the context of culture: An exploration of the borderland between anthropology, medicine, and psychiatry,* (pp. 146–178). Berkeley, CA: University of California Press.

Kleinman, A. & Kleinman, J. (1986). Somatization: The interconnections in Chinese society among culture, depressive experiences, and the meanings of pain. In A. Kleinman (ed.), *Social origins of distress and disease: depression, neurasthenia, and pain in modern China,* (pp. 449–490). New Haven, CN: Yale University Press.

Krause, N., Dowler, D., Liang, J., Gu, S., Yatomi N., & Chuang, Y. L. (1995). Sex, marital status, and psychological distress in later life: A comparative analysis. *Archives of Gerontology and Geriatrics, 21,* 127–146.

Kua, E. H., Chew, P. H., Ko, S. M. (1993). Spirit possession and healing among Chinese psychiatric patients. *Acta Psychiatrica Scandinavica, 88,* 447–450.

Kung, W. W. & Lu, P.-C. (2008). How symptom manifestations affect help seeking for mental health problems among Chinese Americans. *The Journal of Nervous and Mental Disease, 196,* 46–54.

Kuo, C. L. & Kavanagh, K. H. (1994). Chinese perspectives on culture and mental health. *Issues in Mental Health Nursing, 15,* 551–567.

Kung, W. W. (2003). Chinese American's help seeking for emotional distress. *Social Service Review, 77,* 111–133.

Kung, W. W. (2004). Cultural and practical barriers to seeking mental health treatment for Chinese Americans. *Journal of Community Psychology, 32,* 27–43.

Lau, J. T. F. & Cheung, C. K. (1999). Discriminatory attitudes to people with intellectual disability or mental health difficulty. *International Social Work, 42,* 431–444.

Lee, R., Rodin, G., Devins, G., & Weiss, M. G. (2001). Illness experience, meaning and help-seeking among Chinese immigrants in Canada with chronic fatigue and weakness. *Anthropology & Medicine, 8,* 89–107.

Lee, S., Tsang, A., Chui, H., Kwok, K., & Cheung, E. (2007a). A Community Epidemiological Survey of Generalized Anxiety Disorder in Hong Kong. *Community Mental Health Journal, 43,* 305–319.

Lee, S., Tsang, A., & Kwok, K. (2007b). Twelve-month prevalence, correlates, and treatment preference of adults with DSM-IV major depressive episode in Hong Kong. *Journal of Affective Disorders, 98,* 129–136.

Lee, S., Tsang, A., Zhang, M. Y., Huang, Y. Q., He, Y. L., Liu, Z. R., Shen, Y. C., & Kessler, R. C. (2007). Lifetime prevalence and inter-cohort variation in DSM-IV disorders in metropolitan China. *Psychological Medicine, 37,* 61–71.

Legislative Council (2005). Agenda for May 25, 2005. Retrieved on February 16, 2009 at http://www.legco.gov.hk/yr04-05/english/counmtg/agenda/cmtg0525.htm.

Leong, F. (1986). Counseling and psychotherapy with Asian-Americans: Review of the literature. *Journal of Counseling Psychology, 33,* 196–206.

Leong, F. T. L. (1994). Asian Americans' differential patterns of utilization of inpatient and outpatient public mental health services in Hawaii. *Journal of Community Psychology, 22,* 82–96.

Liao, Y. & Bond, M. H. (in press). The dynamics of face loss following interpersonal harm for Chinese and Americans. *Journal of Cross-Cultural Psychology.*

Lieb, R., Mienlschmidt, G., & Araya, R. (2007). Epidemiology of the association between somatoform disorders and anxiety and depressive disorders: An update. *Psychosomatic Medicine, 69,* 860–863.

Lin, T. (1982). Culture and psychiatry: a Chinese perspective. *Australian and New Zealand Journal of Psychiatry, 16,* 235–245.

Lin, Y. (1998). *The effects of counselling style and stage on perceived counsellor effectiveness from Taiwanese female college freshmen.* Unpublished doctoral dissertation, University of Iowa.

Lin, Y. N. (2002). Taiwanese university students' perspectives on helping. *Counselling Psychology Quarterly, 15,* 47–58.

Linszen, D., Lenior, M., De Haan, L., Dingemans, P., & Gersons, B. (1998). Early intervention, untreated psychosis and the course of early schizophrenia. *British Journal of Psychiatry – Supplementum, 172,* 84–89.

Loo, C. (1982). Chinatown's wellness: An enclave of problems. *Journal of the Asian American Psychological Association, 7,* 13–18.

Loo, C., Tong, B., & True, R. (1989). A bitter bean: Mental health status and attitudes in Chinatown. *Journal of Community Psychology, 17,* 283–296.

Luk, C.-L. & Bond, M. H. (1992). Chinese lay beliefs about the causes and cures of psychological problems. *Journal of Social and Clinical Psychology, 11,* 140–157.

Mak, W. W. S. & Chen, S. X. (2006). Face concern: Its role on stress–distress relationships among Chinese Americans. *Personality and Individual Differences, 41,* 143–153.

Mak, W. W. S. & Cheung, R. Y. M. (2008). Affiliate stigma among caregivers of people with mental illness or intellectual disability. *Journal of Applied Research in Intellectual Disabilities, 21,* 532–545.

Mak, W. W. S. & Cheung, R. Y. M. (in press a). Self-stigma among concealable minorities in Hong Kong: Conceptualization and unified measurement. *American Jounal of Orthopsychiatry.*

Mak, W. W. S. & Cheung, R. Y. M. (in press b). Psychological distress and subjective burden of caregivers of people with mental illness: The role of affiliate stigma and face concern. *Community Mental Health Journal.*

Mak, W. W. S., Law, R. W. M., & Teng, M. Y. (in press). Cultural model of vulnerability to distress: The role of self-construal and sociotropy on anxiety and depression among Asian Americans and European Americans. *Journal of Cross-cultural Psychology.*

Mak, W. W. S., Chen, S. X., Lam, A. G., & Yiu, V. F. L. (2009). Understanding distress: The role of face concern among Chinese Americans, European Americans, Hong Kong Chinese, and Mainland Chinese. *The Counseling Psychologist, 37,* 219–248.

Mak, W. W. S., Chen, S. X., Wong, E. C., & Zane, N. W. S. (2005). A psychosocial model of stress–distress relationship among Chinese Americans. *Journal of Social and Clinical Psychology, 24,* 422–444.

Mak, W. W. S. & Zane, N. W. S. (2004). The phenomenon of somatization among community Chinese Americans. *Social Psychiatry and Psychiatric Epidemiology, 39,* 967–974.

Matsuoka, J. K., Breaux, C., & Ryujin, D. H. (1997). National utilization of mental health services by Asian Americans/ Pacific Islanders. *Journal of Community Psychology, 25,* 141–145.

Mechanic, D. (1986). The concept of illness behaviour: Culture, situation and personal disposition. *Psychological Medicine, 16,* 1–7.

Mo, P. K. H., & Mak, W. W. S (2009). Help-seeking for mental health problems among Chinese: The application and extension of the Theory of Planned Behavior. *Social Psychiatry and Psychiatric Epidemiology, 44,* 675–684.

Mumford, D. B. (1993). Somatization: A transcultural perspective. *International Review of Psychiatry, 5,* 231–242.

Murray, C. J. L. & Lopez, A. D. (1996). *The global burden of disease.* Geneva, Switzerland: World Health Organization, Harvard School of Public Health, World Bank.

Ng, C. (1997). The stigma of mental illness in Asian cultures. *Australian and New Zealand Journal of Psychiatry, 31,* 382–390.

Nu, G. (1987). Meaning and function of counselling work at university counselling centre in Taiwan. *Counselling and Guidance, 20,* 2–7.

Oetzel, J., Ting-Toomey, S., Masumoto, T., Yokochi, Y., Pan, X., Takai, J., & Wilcox, R. (2001). Face and facework in conflict: A cross-cultural comparison of China, Germany, Japan, and the United States. *Communication Monographs, 68,* 235–258.

Okazaki, S. (1997). Sources of ethnic differences between Asian American and White American college students on measures of depression and social anxiety. *Journal of Abnormal Psychology, 106,* 52–60.

Organista, P. B., Organista, K. C., & Kurasaki, K. (2003). The relationship between acculturation and ethnic minority health. In K. M. Chun, P. B. Organista, & G. Marin (eds), *Acculturation: Advances in theory, measurement, and applied research* (pp. 139–161). Washington, DC: American Psychological Association.

Ow, R. & Katz, D. (1999). Family secrets and the disclosure of distressful information in Chinese families. *Families in Society, 80,* 620–628.

Oyserman, D., Coon, H. M., & Kemmelmeier, M. (2002). Rethinking individualism and collectivism: Evaluation of theoretical assumptions and meta-analyses. *Psychological Bulletin, 128,* 3–72.

Oyserman, D. & Lee, S. W. S. (2008). Does culture influence what and how we think? Effects of priming individualism and collectivism. *Psychological Bulletin, 134,* 311–342.

Pan, T. (1996) Difficulties with and solutions of counselling at university counselling centres in Taiwan. *Guidance Quarterly, 22,* 2–9.

Park, S. S. (1999). *A test of two explanatory models of Asian-American and White students' preferences for a directive counseling style.* Unpublished doctoral dissertation, University of California, Santa Barbara.

Parker, G., Gladstone, G. & Chee, K. T. (2001). Depression in the planet's largest ethnic group: The Chinese. *American Journal of Psychiatry, 158,* 857–864.

Parker, G., Cheah, Y. C., & Roy, K. (2001). Do the Chinese somatize depression: A cross-cultural study. *Social Psychiatry and Psychiatric Epidemiology. 36,* 287–293.

Pavuluri, M. N., Luk, S. L. & McGee, R. (1996). Help-seeking for behavior problems by parents of preschool children: A community study. *Journal of the American Academy of Child and Adolescent Psychiatry, 35,* 215–222.

Pearson, V. (1993) Families in China: An undervalued resource for mental health. *Journal of Family Therapy, 15,* 163–185.

Quah, S. H. & Bishop, G. D. (1996). Seeking help for illness: The roles of cultural orientation and illness cognition. *Journal of Health Psychology, 1,* 209–222.

Rogler, L. H. & Cortes, D. E. (1993). Help-seeking pathways: A unifying concept in mental health care. *American Journal of Psychiatry, 150,* 554–561.

Ross, M., Xun, W. Q. E., & Wilson, A. E. (2002). Language and the bicultural self. *Personality and Social Psychology Bulletin, 28,* 1040–1050.

Rudowicz, E. & Au, E. (2001). Help-seeking experiences of Hong Kong social work students. *International Social Work, 44,* 75–91.

Sastry, J. & Ross, C. E. (1998). Asian ethnicity and the sense of personal control. *Social Psychology Quarterly, 61,* 101–120.

Shek, D. T. (1991). Depressive symptoms in a sample of Chinese adolescents: An experimental study using the Chinese version of the Beck Depression Inventory. *International Journal of Adolescent Medicine and Health, 5,* 1–16.

Shek, D. T. (1989). Sex differences in the psychological well-being of Chinese adolescents. *Journal of Psychology: Interdisciplinary and Applied, 123*, 405–412.

Shek, D. T. L. (1998). Help-seeking patterns of Chinese parents in Hong Kong. *Asia Pacific Journal of Social Work, 8*, 106–119.

Shen, Y. C., Zhang, M. Y., Huang, Y. Q., He, Y. L., Liu, Z. R., Cheng, H., Tsang, A., Lee S., & Kessler, R. C. (2006). Twelve-month prevalence, severity, and unmet need for treatment of mental disorders in metropolitan China, *Psychological Medicine, 36*, 257–267.

Simon, G. E. & VonKorff, M. (1991). Somatization and psychiatric disorder in the NIMH Epidemiologic Catchment Area study. *American Journal of Psychiatry, 148*, 1494–1500.

Simon, G., VonKorff, M., Piccinelli, M., Fullerton, C., & Ormel, J. (1999). An international study of the relation between somatic symptoms and depression. *New England Journal of Medicine, 341*, 1329–1335.

Singelis, T. M., Bond, M. H., Sharkey, W. F., & Lai, C. S. Y. (1999). Unpackaging culture's influence on self-esteem and embarrassability: The role of self-construals. *Journal of Cross-Cultural Psychology, 30*, 315–341.

Snowden, L. R. & Cheung, F. H. (1990). Use of inpatient mental health services by members of ethnic minority groups. *American Psychologist, 45*, 347–355.

Social Welfare Department. (2005). *Stocktaking on residential services for people with disabilities.* Hong Kong: Author. Retrieved on February 16, 2009 from http://www.legco.gov.hk/yr04-05/english/counmtg/agenda/cmtg0525.htm.

Sue, D., Ino, S., & Sue, D. M. (1983). Nonassertiveness of Asian Americans: An inaccurate assumption? *Journal of Counseling Psychology, 30*, 581–588.

Sue, D. W. & Frank, A. C. (1973). A typological approach to the psychological study of Chinese and Japanese American college males. *Journal of Social Issues, 29*, 129–148.

Sue, D. W. & Kirk, B. A. (1973). Differential characteristics of Japanese-American and Chinese American college students. *Journal of Counseling Psychology, 20*, 142–148.

Sue, S. (1999). Asian American mental health: What we know and what we don't know. In D. L. Dinnel, W. J. Lonner et al. (eds), *Merging past, present, and future in cross-cultural psychology: Selected papers from the Fourteenth International Congress of the International Association for Cross-Cultural Psychology* (pp. 82–89). Lisse, The Netherlands: Swets & Zeitlinger.

Sue, S., Zane, N., & Young, K. (1994). Research on psychotherapy with culturally diverse populations. In S. L. Garfield & A. E. Bergin (eds), *Handbook of psychotherapy and behavior change* (4th ed., pp. 783–817). Oxford, England: Wiley.

Suinn, R. M., Rickard-Figueroa, K., Lew, S., & Vigil, P. (1987). The Suinn-Lew Asian Self-Identity Acculturation Scale: An initial report. *Educational and Psychological Measurement, 47*, 401–407.

Tabora, B. & Flaskerud, J. H. (1994). Depression among Chinese Americans: A review of the literature. *Issues in Mental Health Nursing, 15*, 569–584.

Takeuchi, D. T., Chung, T. C., Lin, K., Shen, H., Kurasaki, K., Chun, C., & Sue, S. (1998). Lifetime and twelve-month prevalence rates of major depressive episodes and dysthymia among Chinese Americans in Los Angeles. *American Journal of Psychiatry, 155*, 1407–1414.

Tang, Y.-L., Sevigny, R., Mao, P.-X., Jiang, F., & Cai, Z. (2007). Help-seeking behaviors of Chinese patients with Schizophrenia admitted to a psychiatric hospital. *Administration and Policy in Mental Health and Mental Health Services Research, 34*, 101–107.

Tata, S. P. & Leong, F. T. L. (1994). Individualism–collectivism, social-network orientation, and acculturation as predictors of attitudes toward seeking professional psychological help among Chinese Americans. *Journal of Counseling Psychology, 41*, 280–287.

Thornicroft G. & Maingay, S. (2002). The global response to mental illness. *British Medical Journal, 325*, 608–609.

Ting-Toomey, S. (1994). *The challenge of facework: Cross-cultural and interpersonal issues.* Albany, NY: State University of New York Press.

Ting-Toomey, S. (2005). The matrix of face: An updated face-negotiation theory. In W. B. Gudykunst (ed.), *Theorizing about intercultural communication*, (pp. 71–92). Thousand Oaks, CA: Sage.

Ting-Toomey, S. & Kurogi, A. (1998). Facework competence in intercultural conflict: An updated face-negotiation theory. *International Journal of Intercultural Relations, 22*, 187–225.

Tracey, T. J., Leong, F. T. L., & Glidden, C. (1986). Help seeking and problem perception among Asian Americans. *Journal of Counseling Psychology, 33*, 331–336.

Triandis, H. C. (1995). *Collectivism and individualism.* Boulder, CO: Westview.

Triandis, H. C., Bontempo, R., Betancourt, H., Bond, M. H., Leung, K., Brenes, A. et al. (1986). The measurement of the etic aspects of individualism and collectivism across cultures. *Australian Journal of Psychology, 38*, 257–267.

Tsang, H. W. H., Tam, P. K. C., Chan, F., & Cheung, W. M. (2003). Stigmatizing attitudes towards individuals with mental illness in Hong Kong: Implications for their recovery. *Journal of Community Psychology, 31*, 383–396.

Tseng, W. S. (1997). Overview: Culture and psychopathology. In W. S. Tseng & J. Streltzer (eds), *Culture and psychopathology: A guide to clinical assessment* (pp. 1–27). New York: Brunner/Mazel.

Uba, L. (1994). *Asian Americans: Personality patterns, identity, and mental health.* New York: Guilford Press.

US Census Bureau. (2002). *A Profile of the Nation's Foreign-Born Population from Asia (2000 Update)* Census Brief: Current Population Survey.* Retrieved February 16, 2009 at http://www.census.gov/prod/2002pubs/cenbr01–3.pdf

US Department of Health and Human Services. (1999). *Mental health: A report of the Surgeon General.* Rockville, MD: US Department of Health and Human Services, Substance Abuse and Mental Health Services Administration, Center for Mental Health Services, National Institutes of Health, National Institute of Mental Health.

US Department of Health and Human Services. (2001). *Mental health: Culture, race, and ethnicity—A supplement to mental health: A report of the Surgeon General.* Rockville, MD: US Department of Health and Human Services, Substance Abuse and Mental Health Services Administration, Center for Mental Health Services.

Wang, C. H., Liu, W. T., Zhang, M. Y., Yu, E. S. H., Xia, Z. Y., Fernandez, M., Lung, C. T., Xu, C. L., & Qu, G. Y. (1992). Alcohol use, abuse, and dependency in Shanghai. In J. E. Helzer & G. J. Canino (eds), *Alcoholism in North America, Europe, and Asia* (pp. 264–286). New York: Oxford University Press.

Wong, D. F. K. (2000). Stress factors and mental health of careers with relatives suffering from schizophrenia in Hong Kong: Implications for culturally sensitive practices. *British Jouranl of Social Work, 30*, 365–382.

Wong, D. F. K., Tsui, H. K. P., Pearson, V., Chen, E. Y. H., & Chiu, S. N. (2004). Family burdens, Chinese health beliefs, and the mental health of Chinese caregivers in Hong Kong. *Transcultural Psychiatry, 41*, 497–513.

World Health Organization. (2008). *Policies and practices for mental health in Europe—meeting the challenges.* Copenhagen, Denmark: WHO Regional Office for Europe.

Yang, M. C. (1945). *A Chinese village: Taitou, Shatung Province.* New York: Columbia University Press.

Yang, K.-S. (1986). Chinese personality and its change. In M. H. Bond (ed.), *The psychology of the Chinese People* (pp. 106–170). Hong Kong: Oxford University Press.

Yeung, A., Kung, W. W., Chung, H., Rubenstein, G., Roffi, P., Mischoulon, D., & Fava, M. (2004). Integrating psychiatry and primary care improves acceptability to mental health services among Chinese Americans. *General Hospital Psychiatry, 26*, 256–260.

Ying, Y. (1988). Depressive symptomatology among Chinese Americans as measured by the CES-D. *Journal of Clinical Psychology, 44*, 739–746.

Ying, Y. & Hu, L. (1994). Public outpatient mental health services: Use and outcome among Asian Americans. *American Journal of Orthopsychiatry, 64*, 448–455.

Ying, Y.-W. & Miller, L. S. (1992). Help-seeking behavior and attitude of Chinese Americans regarding psychological problems. *American Journal of Community Psychology, 20*, 549–556.

Young, K. & Zane, N. (1994). Ethnocultural influences in evaluation and management. In P. Nicassio & T. W. Smith (eds), *Psychosocial adjustment to chronic illness* (pp. 163–206). Washington, DC: American Psychological Association.

Zane, N., Umemoto, D., & Park, S. (1998). *The effects of ethnic and gender match and face concerns on self-disclosure in counseling for Asian American clients.* Unpublished manuscript.

Zane, N. & Mak, W. (2003). Major approaches to the measurement of acculturation among ethnic minority populations: A content analysis and an alternative empirical strategy. In K. M. Chun, P. Balls Organista, & G. Marin (eds), *Acculturation: Advances in theory, measurement, and applied research* (pp. 39–60). Washington, DC: American Psychological Association.

Zane, N. & Yeh, M. (2002). The use of culturally based variables in assessment: Studies on loss of face. In K. Kurasaki, S. Okazaki, & S. Sue (eds), *Asian American mental health: Assessment theories and methods* (pp. 123–138). New York: Kluwer Academic/Plenum.

Zhang, N. & Dixon, D. N. (2003). Acculturation and attitudes of Asian international students toward seeking psychological help. *Journal of Multicultural Counseling and Development, 31*, 205–222.

Zhang, N., Li, J., & Yuan, Y. G. (2001). Investigation of counseling in China. *Journal of Health Psychology, 9*, 389–391.

Zhang, A. Y., Snowden, L. R., & Sue, S. (1998). Differences between Asian- and White-Americans' help-seeking and utilization patterns in the Los Angeles area. *Journal of Community Psychology, 26*, 317–326.

Zheng, Y. P., Lin, K. M., Takeuchi, D., Kurasaki, K., Wang, Y., & Cheung, F. (1997). An epidemiological study of neurasthenia in Chinese Americans in Los Angeles. *Comprehensive Psychiatry, 38*, 249–59.

Zhou, Z., Peverly, S., Xin, T., Huang, A. S., & Wang, W. (2003). School adjustment of first-generation Chinese American adolescents. *Psychology in the Schools, 40*, 71–84.

CHAPTER 26

Community psychology in Chinese societies

Charles C. Chan

At the very core of community psychology is the essentiality of seeing people within a particular social context and their respective temporal contexts of livelihood. Community psychology takes an ecological perspective. As such, it does not stop at the immediate family, friendship or work environment, but includes the intermediate- (or messo) level and macro-level contexts. In this sense, community psychology is demonstrably different from the rest of psychology both in conceptualization and methodology (Orford, 2008).

It is of interest to note that the first *Handbook of community psychology* began with a chapter not on the definition of community psychology but rather on conceptual and methodological issues in the evolution of the science and practice of prevention (Rappaport & Seidman, 2000). This orientation to the field signifies a closer allegiance of community psychology with public health[1] than perhaps with other sub-disciplines of psychology in its attempt to solve social problems of policy significance, taking equal attention to social settings and aiming at social change. The chapter in that handbook by Felner, Felner, and Silverman (2000) did not provide a single definition for community psychology, but instead made a case for a developmental and ecological model that sees people as learning to adapt to their actual environments, emphasizing repeatedly the importance of social context as necessary to understanding both developmental trajectories and behaviors.

Being different from other sub-disciplines of psychology is a large claim to make and not entirely a comfortable position to hold for long. If anything, it demands that one make clear differentiations of how business is conducted in one's zone of operation. In this regard, I am deliberately introducing community psychology and its central values and principles in general before moving into community psychology in Chinese societies.

In an attempt to search for literature, one has to face the fact that we do not have a history of development in community psychology, let alone a coherent body of literature in community psychology in Chinese societies. But what we do have can be taken as evidence for the existence of a certain character and strength of the development of the field. The case of community psychology in Hong Kong, particularly in the last decade since reunification with the mainland, will be used as an illustration of what may prove to be one of the preferred models for the development of community psychology in Chinese societies.

Defining community psychology

In one of the first textbooks of the field of community psychology, Rappaport (1977) alluded to the difficulty of defining a field that was based on a new paradigm, perspective, and thinking, with constantly emerging contours of development. In 1990, in *Researching community psychology: Issues of theory and methods*, Tolan, Key, Chertok, & Jason (1990) gave a two-decade update on the achievements of the field some twenty years from the 1965 Swampscott Conference held in Boston and commonly accepted as the beginning of the community psychology movement.

Instead of beginning with a definition of the field, the book started by describing a series of excellence criteria in community research. Forty years have passed and in a more recent volume titled *International community psychology*, Reich and her colleagues still found it difficult to come to an agreement on a definition of community psychology, its core principles and values (Reich, Riemer, Prilleltensky, & Montero, 2007). Agreement issue apart, why was it so difficult to define community psychology?

Dalton, Elias, & Wandersman (2007, p. 15) have given a descriptive definition of community psychology:

> [It] concerns the relationships of the individual with communities and societies. By integrating research with action, it seeks to understand and enhance quality of life for individuals, communities, and societies. Community psychology is guided by its core values of individual and family wellness, sense of community, respect for human diversity, social justice, citizen participation, collaboration and community strengths, and empirical grounding.

In this sense, communities are social systems that serve to meet human needs. Therefore, community psychology (CP) can be defined as understanding the needs of people and the resources available to meet those needs.

Understanding a community helps CP to focus on formulating interventions that provide optimum development of its people, because a lack of resources (individual, organizational, and community level) can have negative impacts on their mental health. For example, writing on community psychology in India, Bhatia & Sethi emphasized that 'social conditions of poverty, alienation, isolation, and, in general, a lack of social resources are clearly seen to contribute to mental health problems, yet another major domain of CP' (2007, p. 181).

Thus, one should recognize the difficulties involved in defining CP. As early as the 1930s, Kurt Lewin (1935) and Henry Murray and colleagues (1938) considered person–environment interactions in their equation of human behaviors, $B = f(P, E)$. Unfortunately, from there onwards, a psychological explanation for a human behavior has been more about the person (P), and the environment (E) has been treated as a moderator or a confusion of confounding variables to be adjusted in mainstream empirical work published by journals in psychology. The equal importance of identifying the critical 'environment' which is affecting the behaviors and thoughts of people is often neglected, if not totally absent (Seeman, 1997).

In writing the historical and theoretical orientation of community psychology in Japan, Sasao and Yasuda refer to a renaissance in psychology such that researchers are starting to realize that 'human behaviors and problems are embedded within social contexts and environments' (2007, p. 167), and that these are diverse and specific. It is as if CP uses the environment key, opening doors to other disciplines which are rich in their understanding and knowledge about the social environment, namely political science, sociology, economics, culture studies, and so forth (Angelique & Culley, 2007). Furthermore, theories and studies focusing on the environment in psychology, such as ecological systems theory (Bronfenbrenner, 1979), link individual change to environmental contexts and describe how individuals and their environments are related in 'transactional' ways. Such 'environmental' psychology is concerned with the physical or designed aspects of the world which may exercise both direct and indirect causal influences upon human behavior, health and well-being, and hence afford the possibility of designing or redesigning environments to mitigate or prevent human problems.

We can now begin to see the complexity involved and the precision needed to differentiate community psychology from its close relatives, such as environmental psychology (Bell, 2001), ecological psychology (Barker, 1968), public health psychology (Hepworth, 2004), social psychology, and applied social psychology (Schneider, Gruman, & Coutts, 2005), but also those allies in sociology, public health, community medicine, politics, and economics. One has to give proper recognition and credit to many of these fields which share the same epistemological view of human behavior as understood within its social and cultural context, similar multi-level approaches in research and with whom community psychologists are partnering in taking on critical moves toward means to solving problems that are structural, gendered, cultural, social, economic, political, and environmental in nature. Given the complexity of this interface, a more precise definition of community psychology can only come about in time.

Central values and principles

A common feature of CP is its reference to sets of central values and principles in conducting research and preventing human problems. These values, which include power and empowerment, respect for human diversity and participation, social justice and social change, caring and compassion, and health and well-being, have served both to critique mainstream psychology, which upholds the societal status quo in the name of value neutrality, and to anchor theory, research, and action in CP (Angelique & Culley, 2007; Dalton et al., 2007; Prilleltensky & Nelson, 1997). For example, Prilleltensky, Peirson, Gould, and Nelson (1997) used these values in their consultation with a children's mental health agency undergoing an organizational renewal process. Similarly, Nelson, Lavoie, and Mitchell (2007) wrote about Canadian community psychologists' use of a number of theoretical concepts based on values of empowerment, community integration, and social justice to guide their work. Of course, Nelson and colleagues are not the only group; community psychologists—and politicians—quickly grasped the enormous potential of turning to governmental and community resources available in the environment to solve societal problems, such as poor health and escalating healthcare costs in developed countries. Several government policy documents have emphasized the importance of social networks, health promotion, and community resources in the achievement of health for all (Epp, 1986; Paquet et al., 1985; Trainor, Pomeroy, & Pape, 1999), and are good examples of how these values and principles were central to the work of community psychologists positively impacting on governmental policy.

British veteran community psychologist, Orford (2008), criticizes mainstream psychology for focusing too much on the individualistic values of agency, mastery, control, and status, resulting in popular views that equate psychology with 'stress management' or enhancing 'coping skills' and pay insufficient attention to evidence relating power and social class to mental distress (e.g. Sampson, 1981). So failure to master one's distress among 'disempowered' groups feeds a sense of shame, and those affected blame themselves for a state of affairs that is really not their fault nor can be changed at the individual or micro levels of interaction. Higher levels of analysis including prevailing norms that govern family and gender relationships in society and the social and material constraints on resources and opportunities for the individual are necessary to address these problems of human suffering. A process of empowerment is often seen as a valued entry point for many in community psychology.

Power and empowerment

Generally speaking, people, organizations, and communities gain a better sense of mastery over issues of concern to them through a process of empowerment (Rappaport, 1987). Empowerment is a mechanism through which people gain greater control over their lives, raise their awareness of democratic participation in communities as well as the sociopolitical environment (Perkins & Zimmerman, 1995). Prilleltensky, Nelson, and Peirson (2001) further note that empowerment is 'a state of affairs in which people have enough power to satisfy their needs and work in concert with others to advance collective goals' (p. 36). Orford (2008, p. 38) argues that promoting people's 'power to modify' their disadvantageous circumstances transforms them into proactive agents.

Many, however, have pointed out the downside of empowerment. Zimmerman (1995) differentiates psychological empowerment from gaining actual power. Riger (1993) points to people's tendency to conflate actual power with a sense of empowerment. Smail (1994, 1995) talked about this inflated sense of power and the danger of psychologizing power as an internal personal attribute. When power is said to reside in the hands of individuals, it may result in shifting the responsibility to the individuals when, in fact, power is in the hands of some groups and directly related to the disempowerment of other groups. Empowerment is therefore not a psychological event, but a social event. It requires participation, especially in the decision-making process of the individual and the group concerned to learn or equip to make their own decisions and to not allow others make the decision for them.

Nevertheless, empowerment is still seen as superior on a number of levels: firstly, it involves collaboration over expert control; secondly, it requires the examination and expansion of existing strengths and competencies; and thirdly, it urges naturalistic, multi-level analysis versus a sterile, 'expert-controlled' program (Rappaport, 1981). Francescato and Tomai (2001) posit that there exists a European tradition of political concern to promote social capital. It is based on the belief that 'each person is born in a social environment embedded in an historically created hierarchical context ... [that] a disempowered person rarely can empower herself solely by her own efforts, and that the recorded history of mankind shows that individual empowerment has occurred through collective struggles for civil, human and social rights' (p. 373). Community psychology offers a framework for working with those marginalized by the social systems focusing on value-based, participatory work and the forging of alliances (Burton, Boyle, Psy, & Kagan, 2007).

Diversity and participation

In a similar vein, Orford (2008) argues that CP should promote respect for group diversity and difference, and support the equalization of power between groups. The line between 'expert' and 'ordinary' folk would be blurred by the concept of empowerment, because participants are the real experts about their problems and situation. Mentors, family members, and others are agents of change in human development, not psychologists and other social scientists alone (Angelique & Culley, 2007).

To some, embracing this principle as a central value will mean de-professionalization. Focusing on providing education and training to the public, respecting the public's expertise regarding their own problems, and empowering them to solve their problems may be seen as an inevitable outcome of 'giving psychology away'[2] (Miller, 1969). Respecting diversity and promoting participation means that one must begin with people where they are, rather than assuming that we as experts know where they should be. We must diagnose and solve the problems people think that they have, not the problems we as experts judge them to have. More importantly, CP promotes change in the social, economic, and environmental arrangements that give rise to such problems, leaving room for people to develop and solve their problems in their own ways. Equally, governmental resources should be the focus for 'articulat[ing] the relationship between socio-psychological processes and particular kinds of social systems, preferably taking into account social change' (Bhatia & Sethi, 2007, p. 185) through enhanced participation.

Collaboration

At the heart of the exhortation to 'give psychology away' is the use of participatory methods and the forging of alliances to encourage the development of social, organizational, and economic networks, with the long-term goal of increasing social cohesion and social capital (Orford, 2008), especially among the marginalized and the disempowered. Community psychologists will inevitably find themselves called to work with others from education, social welfare, and the health sectors through community groups in a more overtly political way.

Assuming the role of a leader, popular educator, change facilitator, consultant, evaluator, systems organizer in such collaboration will be a matter of personal choice (Bennett et al., 1966). However, the role of community psychologist as researcher will always be present, and that is to identify relevant explanatory constructs and social influence for particular human behavioral changes. A broader role of community psychologist in changing the structures and practices of organizations and institutions and engaging with public policy, which might include advocating for changes in the law as a social activist, may be a potential outcome from fostering long-term collaboration in the community (Albee & Gullotta, 1997; Blair, 1992; Levine, 1998).

Justice

Being a scientific subject does not disqualify CP from embracing social justice as a core value and principle. Just as poverty, globalization, and migration are legitimate subjects of study by disciplines such as economics, public health, and medicine, so too should community psychology place itself as a discipline within the broader society; it should not only aspire to be a legitimate science conducted within the walls of a laboratory.

Embracing these core values and principles requires new understanding of how to promote social change. CP targets social systems rather than individuals; work will depend on appreciation of variations by context, including time, culture, and power structures. It becomes important to use frameworks that pay careful attention to values, language, and systems as well as stakeholders who generate dialogue and ask for whom and in which context a process might be adaptive. Finally, promoting positive processes rather than aiming at particular end states or outcome indicators will be seen as additional, or even as more appropriate, goals in evaluation studies conducted by community psychologists (Tseng et al., 2002).

Example

The earthquake of May 2008 in Sichuan, China provides an illustration that the above core values and principles adopted by CP not only set it apart from other sub-disciplines of psychology, but also contribute to better human well-being. Sichuan experienced a major earthquake, measuring 8.0 on the Richter scale. It left more than 90,000 persons dead and missing, and over 5 million people homeless. The response from other Chinese societies and the world was immediate. Care for the survivors' psychological needs was repeatedly mentioned not just by people in psychology but by all the contemporary media as well as the leaders of the Chinese communist party and the central government right from the beginning and through the ensuing weeks.

Almost all of the responses to the provision of psychological counseling by authorities in psychology focused on the survivors' diagnosis (whether post-traumatic stress disorder was evident or not), and how people may be helped to express the emotions of shock, grief, and guilt. When the interest was on building resilience in the survivors, the emphasis was still likely to be placed with the individual. For example, how stressful events were faced and personally appraised before the quake was taken as prognostic of whether the person could learn to use the extra-familial resources available in the immediate environment.

Community psychologists, however, would look beyond the individual to the available, non-family support networks, including government officials, the police, the army, volunteers[3] and social service organizations. They would focus on humane practice in the temporary settlements (power and empowerment), the provision of daily activities (diversity and participation), government policies announced addressing the alleged sub-standard school building (justice), the attitude of the civil ministry and other non-governmental organizations in disseminating welfare and compensational packages as the main avenues for understanding the survivors of the earthquake (caring and compassion; collaboration).

Heeding a detailed ecological analysis from community psychology not only could have restored respect for the individuals' behavior of guarding their own 'houseland', but could also have led directly to the preferred civil practice of land registration, preventing worsening of individual anxiety and often mass distrust or even conflict and physical violence. Stories with vivid images of extraordinary recovery by the worst prognostic cases were abundant, defying many of the traditional clinical and research models of predictions about human calamity. Clearly in this case, the contribution derived from the perspective of community psychology would have a contribution equal to if not greater than one relying only on a narrow clinical perspective with its focus on the individual.

Community psychology in Chinese societies

Taking on these added perspectives, how does community psychology distinguish itself from social intervention and social development in general or even plain humanitarian work? It is worth acknowledging here that much of the work done in community psychology but not known as such happens in societies other than Chinese. Shadish, Matt, Navarro, & Phillips (2000) observed that some community researchers are themselves ambivalent about the extent to which the concept of community ought to be the dominant metaphor for the field. He pointed out that the very first *Annual review of psychology* chapter on the topic, and all chapters since then, were not titled 'Community psychology', but were more broadly titled 'Social and community interventions' (Cowen, 1973). In fact, to this date, it is still a matter of debate which vision of the field is best: a broader label addressing social problems or a specific label based on the notion of community that gives people a sense of unique identity. In short, there are obvious and significant overlaps between the two positions.

A systematic review of literature on community psychology in Chinese societies will have to face squarely the reality that it will be an extremely scattered body of knowledge, more often than not published in seemingly unrelated journals or hidden away in unpublished reports of one kind or another. In the last two decades, two review papers on community psychology in Hong Kong (Cheng & Mak, 2007; Lam & Ho, 1989) and one in the Chinese mainland (Yu & Yang, 2008) have contributed greatly to this exercise. To my knowledge, no similar published paper is available from other Chinese societies, including Taiwan and Singapore.

Community psychology in Hong Kong

Lam and Ho (1989) described the movement in community mental health from the 1960s in terms of significant increase in mental health service in hospitals and clinics as the major impetus for the development of CP in Hong Kong. To them, service delivery by an increasing number of psychological practitioners working in community-based service settings represented the main thrust of CP. It is worth noting that there was no reference to any empirical studies in applied research in their review article. In the areas of consultation for community organization, they noted the training of non-professionals in counseling, again without providing any references for further detail. Very limited studies were cited on public attitudes towards the mentally ill as support for CP to conduct public education. They moved on to discuss six assumptions of CP from the mainstream literature[4] and their applicability in Hong Kong, positively affirming the generalizability of these core concepts to the Chinese cultural context of Hong Kong.

Almost two decades after the Lam and Ho review, Cheng and Mak (2007) opined that, rather than being an organized field, community psychology is practiced in an idiosyncratic manner by a few psychologists who are trained with a community orientation in Hong Kong. They looked at the sense of community from a historical perspective constructed mainly from the local literature of socio-political analysis, portraying an image of Hong Kong as 'Little changed after 1997, and the Government's main duty is to maintain order and stability while creating an economic environment for sustainable prosperity' (p. 204). They highlighted only individual and isolated achievements in the arena of social welfare, community mental health, self-help groups, prevention, and policy development. This picture of development, limited by international standards, is attributed to a lack of infrastructure and funding resources. They concluded that, 'Community psychology has a long way to go in contributing to community and social development in Hong Kong' (p. 200).

One way to understand this somewhat unenthusiastic assessment of the development of CP in Hong Kong may be to interprete Cheng and Mak (2007) as having adopted the Western model of CP development and used it as a template for scrutinizing what was happening in Hong Kong. This approach, while inevitable in conducting comparative analysis, runs the risk of missing out on the evidence of positive development generated from a society's own unique but often transient socio-political context. An obvious omission arising from using their chosen template was to have missed all the initiatives supported by the government of the Hong Kong Special Administration Region (HKSAR) in a number of major policy reforms post-1997 via the setting up of a multitude of designated funds specifically targeting large-scale community programs. In consequence, large numbers of academics from universities have offered their respective expertise in conducting and subsequently promoting social experimentation among the designated populations in the community.

In this connection, two important questions must be addressed. First of all, is this type of Western model of development a viable pathway for the growth and development of CP in a Chinese society? Secondly, do we have any evidence that CP can develop following another form, in particular one that reflects 'a culturally sensitive way to imprint a lasting effect on the changing society' (Cheng and Mak, 2007, p. 200), These two questions are important in that a positive answer to the first question will help steer future efforts at promoting CP in Chinese societies. If the answer were to be negative, future reviews and evaluations of CP in Chinese societies will have to avoid using the Western model of development as a reference for comparison. I intend to address the first question here by drawing on a review paper on the topic published in the Chinese mainland. In answering the second question, I shall use the example of how a government-led initiative in addressing identified social problems proved to be a valuable source of evidence for building culturally sensitive models of community psychology development in a Chinese society.

Research on community psychology in the Chinese mainland

Yu and Yang (2008) conducted a review of community psychology research in China based on some 30 empirical studies published in the Chinese mainland dating back to 2001. The authors did not provide information about the scope and method of their search, which means that readers cannot judge either the coverage or representativeness of these studies. They emphasized the target of study as the person-in-environment, and, apart from treating community psychology as a sub-discipline of psychology, these authors presented it as a helping profession. From a similar literature search conducted in late 2008 very similar results[5] to their review were found. Thus, the small number of studies covered in Yu and Yang's review may reflect the use of a set of carefully drafted and stringent selection criteria according to a precise understanding of community psychology.

Yu and Yang (2008) highlighted five principles of community psychology: prevention should be weighted more heavily than treatment; an ecological perspective on interactive role of the person and the environment should be taken; coordinated effort on changing environment and helping individuals to adapt to the environment should be valued; diversity should be respected, thus giving attention to minority and marginalized groups in the society; and individuals should be empowered towards active control of their lives. Given clearly identified goals, they categorized their selection of published studies into youth, elderly, and other groups of people in the community, including women in poor health, people in rehabilitation, and domestic migrants.

Unfortunately, there is evidence that the majority of the studies used survey methods, relying instead on self-reports from small samples yielding correlational data. The few intervention studies tended to be isolated efforts of expert-led educational and therapy programs. There is a clear absence of large-scale, published studies of community-wide prevention efforts among targeted populations. None of the studies met the criteria of being delivered in and by the community.

Given such limitations, Yu and Yang (2008) made recommendations for future research, reflecting priorities arising from some unique features and needs of the mainland at this point in time.

They encouraged more attention to social justice issues particularly among migrant populations in major cities. They issued a call for a macro-perspective in forming geographic communities by forging an alignment between available resources and the needs of urban, suburban, and rural communities. On methods and approaches of conducting community psychology research, they recommended breaking with tradition by looking more at the interrelations of social problems identified instead of holding to a single problem focus, and by introducing group and community variables, such as community capacities and the formation of community support coalitions for promotion and evaluation of harmonious society.

Readers familiar with the writing conventions characteristic of mainland academic journal articles will recognize the effort made by Yu and Yang (2008) to link substantive matters with government policy directives. The authors began their paper with a reference to Chinese President Hu Jintao's pledge to build a harmonious society as the impetus behind the gradual attention paid by psychologists to community psychology. Such linkage strengthens this paper's impact by allying it with publicly stated government policy, an essential tactic in protecting community practitioners in a hierarchical social system.

It is clear from Yu & Yang's review that a serious and persistent investment by psychologists in applying the aims, methods, and approaches of CP to future studies will be needed for such research to grow in prominence and quality, thereby contributing towards building a more harmonious society. It is equally clear that they never lose sight of the role of central government in prioritizing what constitutes a good cause in a given context of policy and politics. From this perspective, theirs may be taken as a good representation of the current status of research on community psychology in the Chinese mainland.

Government-led initiatives: community psychology, Hong Kong style

Still focusing on the role of government, I note that since the mid-1990s the Hong Kong government has successfully established a number of designated funds in the areas of health services and research on the promotion of health, social services, and education, to signal the government's commitment to its prioritized policy reforms. Despite a lack of published formal evaluation on the impact of these funds on Hong Kong society in general and the government's policy agenda in particular, the degree to which these funds have been instrumental in the development of community psychology will be evident in the following discussion.

Large-scale government-designated funds. In 1993 and 1995, the government created two dedicated avenues to support local academic research in health services and community health promotion, using public funding for the first time (Collins et al., 2008). These sources were open to all professionals from academic institutions, public and private health and social care sectors in Hong Kong. Up to December 2007, between the Health Service Research Fund (known as Health and Health Service Research Fund, HHSRF after 2002) and the Health Care and Promotion Fund (HCPF), 224 projects out of 975 applications were approved for funding,[6] an investment worth HK$87.24 million (HK$7.8=US$1) (Collins et al., 2008). Applications are subjected to a stringent peer review by both international and local experts, processed under the Research Office of the then Health and Welfare Bureau of the HKSAR government. Since 2002, a total of 150 non-research health promotion projects with a total grant value of HK$41.50 million has been supported by the HCPF to finance activities related to health promotion and preventive care in the community. The majority of the principal applicants (90.6 per cent) of approved research applications were based at tertiary academic institutions, while about three-quarters of the non-research health promotion projects went to professionals working in the non-governmental organizations (NGOs).[7] The Hong Kong Medical Journal Supplement has so far published research reports of the completed projects up to series nine as of June 2008.

In the area of social services, a HK$300 million Community Investment and Inclusion Fund (CIIF) was set up in 2001 with the explicit object of promoting the effectiveness of a tripartite model, viz.

partnership between the government, corporations, and the community. What evidence is there for the impact of these tripartite efforts? What do we know about how to make effective public health and welfare programs last? Apart from institutionalization, do we know whether social structures of sustainability (Pluye, Potvin, & Denis, 2004) and multiple sources of financing are being created successfully?

According to a number of evaluative reports commissioned by the CIIF and conducted by university academics that are publicly available,[8] five observations may be drawn, in order of their significance of impact in terms of empirical evidence: first, the majority of the funded programs are popular, i.e. well attended and well received by the public and in many cases, the targeted population; second, cooperation between the government and the program providers, mainly non-profit NGOs, has improved over the course of program delivery in the community; third, informal coalitions have been formed for the purpose of smoothing out delivery efforts; fourth, little was mentioned about the sustainability of the partnerships, which were specified as essential to the delivery of the intervention programs proposed in the first place; fifth, more often than not, and in many well-identified cases, there was complete silence on how the well-received programs, subsequent to the end of the funding cycle, were being delivered by which qualified staff and community partners supported by what kind of mechanisms of program delivery, so as to demonstrate proper implementation of the program in its original form.

In the area of education reform, the government established a HK$5 billion Quality Education Fund (QEF) in 1998 with the objective of promoting community initiatives in quality education in Hong Kong.[9] The fund is relevant to our discussion here in that, in its ten years of operation, 6,357 QEF projects have been underwritten with a total funding of HK$3.35 billion. The majority (81 per cent) of projects were undertaken by pre-primary, primary, and secondary schools, involving 1,373 schools in 5,670 QEF projects, or about four projects per school, to a total amount of HK$1.6 billion. These projects have focused on five areas, i.e. effective learning, all-round education, school-based management, education research, and information technology. Large sums of money went to academics (not limited to faculties of education) at the seven universities in Hong Kong. In short, over two-thirds of all local schools were grantees, and participation by the university sector was substantial.

Another major reason why the QEF is relevant here is that, after its first decade of operation, it has set an explicit objective to encourage collaboration amongst schools, government, NGOs, and the private sector to further quality education. Additionally, the QEF has established professional networks called Quality Thematic Networks (QTNs) centered on certain project themes/categories for the sustainable development and capacity building of the schools concerned. Here is another clear endorsement of the tripartite model promoted by the CIIF which is occurring in the education sector, sustained by a huge, long-term financial commitment from the HKSAR government. So far, only the QEF has commissioned a large-scale study aimed at assessing the fund's impact in enhancing a school culture of quality education in Hong Kong. Thus, the synergistic effect of these large-scale, government-led initiatives[10] cannot and should not be neglected in any discussion on the development of community psychology.

The animating spirit of community psychology values collaboration between stakeholders from diverse backgrounds who can participate on issues of social concern and justice, resulting in the empowerment of the people and groups in the community to assert their power of self-determination in the improvement of human well-being. In terms of participation, hundreds of experts and lay stakeholders are routinely invited to serve on these funds in the form of membership in high-level government committees set up to steer the direction of operation, to assess the quality of the project applications, as well as to promote and disseminate products and outcomes of these time-limited 'social experimentations'. In terms of settings, these funded projects typically take place in schools, hospitals, old peoples' homes, social service agencies of various kinds, and the local communities. This state of affairs is augmented by the fact that public discourse on these 'bottom-up' projects happens not only behind closed doors of these committee meetings but also in person and on 'road shows' in the community. Series after series of video programs are now routinely commissioned by the government and the project 'grantees' to be televised on free-to-air television stations, some of them aired during prime time television.

These government-led initiatives may have laid the groundwork necessary for the development of community psychology in Hong Kong. Proponents of the community psychology movement have been joined by the public in endorsing these social experiments as necessary precursors to institutionalization of certain 'good practices' from within the respective sectors, as long as they fall within the ambit of the government's policy reform agenda, sometimes known as 'research thematic priorities'.

Synergy between government funds: the example of the Child Development Fund. In 2005, the HKSAR Government set up a high-level Commission on Poverty (CoP) chaired by the then Finance Secretary, Mr. Henry Tang, now the Chief Secretary of the HKSAR government. Pressing agenda items included a coordinated effort toward locating a comprehensive local review of effective measures to alleviate poverty among the elderly population, the potential of a widening gap between the rich and the poor, the propensity of inter-generational poverty among new arrivals and children and adolescents growing up in disadvantaged families, and building partnerships between the community, the third sector, the private sector, and across the government.

About a year after its establishment, the CoP hosted a widely publicized symposium keynoting international experts who introduced to Hong Kong society a few well-known large-scale social experiments, including some from the USA, Taiwan, and the UK, using development funds and trust funds for children and adolescents.[11] The Commission also held multiple public consultations which were all well attended by local stakeholders as well as many concerned public bodies. A local TV station was commissioned to televise multiple episodes of how the issue of intergenerational poverty was being addressed in the world and how it might be addressed in Hong Kong.[12]

At this juncture, a QEF-funded, locally designed and evaluated project known as the Intensive Community Mentoring (ICM) program[13] led by a multidisciplinary team including community and clinical psychologists, sociologists, school principals, and teachers and social workers (Chan, 2004; Chan & Ho, 2006, 2008) caught the attention of the CoP. After extensive consultations, the mentoring approach was formally adopted as one of the three components of what is now known as the Child Development Fund (CDF) pioneer projects (the other two are the target savings plan[14] and the personal development plan) granted to six NGOs in seven districts in a HK-wide experiment beginning in late 2008 for a three-year period.

This detour into the process of how the HK$ 300 million CDF[15] came about serves as one of the most recent examples of how the HKSAR government has chosen to work, and how the current system allows initiatives from the community and the academics and professionals a reasonable share of influence on the government's steering efforts in shaping community programs of policy priority, in this case an inter-generational poverty prevention program. This can also serve as a clear example of how programs of proven efficacy (in this case, youth mentoring programs) that are well documented in the Western world (DuBois, Holloway, Valentine, & Cooper, 2002; Herrera et al., 2007; Tierney, Grossman, & Besch, 1995) are being piloted in territory-wide efforts before their formal adoption (or institutionalization).

Synergy in government funds is happening on other levels as members of these high-level committees engage in 'continuous self-improvement' by selecting their fund objectives and outcome indicators through refinement of their funding criteria and dissemination of quality programs. For example, the HCPF announced in 2007 yet another scheme called the Seed Fund, in addition to its regular, annual calls for applications. The criteria for the Seed Fund has two additional items on top of that of the regular calls, viz. the potential to build a long-term platform for health promotion in the target community, thereby building capacities of the community, and extending the sustainability and effectiveness of the proposed program. The QEF, on the other hand, announced in 2006 the setting up of Quality Thematic Networks (QTNs) by inviting applications from previous grantees who had successfully completed well-implemented and well-received programs to provide support and training to other schools interested in adopting similar programs.[16]

Taking these changes at face value, the funds have become explicitly concerned that the approval and accountability processes should be more 'evidence-based' and that programs proven to be efficacious are being deployed by the grantees for well-identified targets of populations.

Reading further into these gradual but definite changes in the rules of the game, so to speak, indicates on the part of the government, the funds or people representing the interests of the funds, a certain measure of maturity and readiness to demonstrate commitment to properly adopt the program through networking for training and implementation partnerships within the community. This I believe speaks volumes about the level of maturity of the community of Hong Kong in the core values and principles of community psychology that we have identified in the first part of this chapter.

Proponents of community psychology will readily note how these developments and the philosophy and rationale behind the continuous operation of the funds coincides with models of multi-level community-based public health interventions (Green & Mercer, 2001; Mercer, DeVinney, Fine, Green, & Dougherty, 2007; Naylor, Wharf-Higgins, Blair, Green, & O'Connor, 2002). One well-known model is a theoretically driven framework designed to be compatible with a social ecological approach for use in the evaluation of effectiveness of community programs known by the acronym RE-AIM (Glasgow, Bull, Gillette, Klesges, & Dzewaltowski, 2002; Glasgow, Klesges, Dzewaltowski, Estabrooks, & Vogt, 2006; Glasgow, McKay, Piette, & Reynolds, 2001; Glasgow, Vogt, & Boles, 1999). The acronym stands for reach, efficacy, adoption, implementation, and maintenance, the very components that I have just summarized in the previous paragraph for the development of the funds, albeit from an insider's perspective.[17]

Re-aligning the development of community psychology in Chinese societies

Glasgow and his colleagues have repeatedly demonstrated the importance of using the RE-AIM model in the identification and evaluation of the factors critical for the success of community projects. There are precise definitions and coding schemes built around the five domains. It is not the intention of this chapter to go into the what and the how of that model—there already exists a good example of the model's application in the evaluation of community health programs in Hong Kong (Chan & Chan, 2006). Instead, I focus on the potential of this model for realigning the research direction and methodology of community psychology in Chinese societies, especially when all core components of that model have now been identified in the various large-scale government funds, as evidenced in the previous discussion.

Positive factors for the development of CP in Hong Kong may not be entirely appropriate for what should take place in other Chinese societies, but will certainly be of value as reference. A more important question is whether other Chinese societies, in particular the Chinese mainland, should be encouraged to take similar steps in its own development stages. James Kelly (2006, p. 140) has listed seven criteria for conducting community-based prevention research in contrast with traditional psychological inquiry. They are used here as a springboard providing a unified set of goals and methods for the development of community psychology in Chinese societies:

1. select variables that illustrate developmental processes for individuals, groups and organizations;
2. assess social settings and persons simultaneously;
3. develop methods to assess reciprocal effects between persons and social settings;
4. assess the direct, indirect, and side effects of interventions;
5. create social settings for participants to contribute to and benefit from the research;
6. establish social settings to appraise the ethics of interventions;
7. create new organizational forms for doing prevention research.

These criteria point to directions and skills of multi-level action planning and require cross-disciplinary expertise in order to complete a good study in community psychology. Psychologists should claim no monopoly of the methods and expertise associated with these criteria. Psychologists cannot achieve a positive influence on government policy reforms in isolation. The Cheng and Mak (2007) review gave a report card of limited achievement by community psychologists in Hong Kong, precisely for this reason.

The impetus for the development of community psychology needs to come not only from within the circle of psychologists. I have demonstrated how in the last decade or so the HKSAR government, in promoting its policy reform agenda, has unknowingly been 'fueling' the development of good-quality community psychology. For places like Hong Kong, where government polices and funding schemes have already indicated the inclination and official requirements for demonstrated evidence, the above criteria can be used as a point-by-point guide to the design, implementation, data analysis and organization building necessary for doing value-for-investment prevention research.[18]

The merits of a top-down approach to CP development, as in the case of Hong Kong, the fruits from good-quality social experiments aiming for large-scale studies with the potential of formulating empirically supported models of sustainable community efforts will, in time, prove to be equally important to other Chinese societies. In the Chinese mainland, for example, a history of development for the designated funds targeting sustainable community programs has not been at the same level as that in Hong Kong. Nonetheless, it is important for community psychologists to discover the ways by which similar social problems may be addressed at the community level. The importance of utilizing Kelly's seven criteria in conducting community programs and research solely based on community or neighborhood funds cannot be overestimated.

Conclusion

Cronbach, who is known to have contributed to the internal validity of psychological measurement, made the following comments on the importance of improving external validity, at a 1983 conference on the potentialities for knowledge in social science:

> The style and procedures preferred for one inquiry can be ill-suited for another topic or at another stage in the evolution of knowledge or for an investigator in different circumstances. With that caveat, I recapitulate a few preferences I have suggested: for more exploratory work, for less emphasis on the magnitude and statistical significance of 'effect size', for more effort to record concomitant and intermediate events that help explain local variation, for more discussion of research plans and interpretations with peers having disparate backgrounds. Each piece of research should be an effort to give an unimpeachable and reasonably full account of events in a time, place, and context. Multiple interpretations of information already in hand will often be more instructive, at less cost, than additional data gathering. I have encouraged critical analysis of research methods and their further development, along with substantive criticism of extrapolations. To advocate pluralistic tolerance of alternative accounts is in no way to advocate tender-mindedness.
>
> Kelly, 2006, pp. 178–179

The question remains: Will as many community psychologists as clinical psychologists be appearing on the TV screens or in newspaper headlines and providing consultation to large-scale government efforts of rescue when the earth quivers again— heaven forbid—in China? I remain a cautious optimist. But, if we were to change the question to whether psychologists' views will focus more on the community rather than staying at the individual level, I am confident that the answer will be in the affirmative. The balance between the person and the social ecosystems that we live in is in the hands of community psychologists who work and contribute to the welfare of persons in Chinese societies.

Chapter notes

1 In Rappaport and Seidman's introduction in this chapter, they actually highlighted that the approach Felner et al. took was to make 'an explicit break with the traditional public health framework that has served as a bridge from clinical to community models in the field of mental health. The traditional (blended) view of treatment and prevention (in which degrees of prevention—primary, secondary, tertiary—are acknowledged) is eschewed in favor of a more explicit distinction

between individual clinical work and mass-oriented or population-focused prevention, which aims to modify processes and mediating conditions that create a risk for problems in living' (Rappaport & Seidman, 2000, p. 2). It is not therefore at variance with my use of the term public health here.

2 According to George Miller (1969), a Past President of the American Psychological Association, the real impact of psychology will be felt not through the technological products it places in the hands of powerful men but through its effects on the public at large, through a new and different public conception of what is humanly possible and what is humanly desirable. (p. 1074)

He also feels that psychology must be practiced by non-psychologists. Facts should be passed out freely to all who need and can use them. Scientific results must be 'instilled in the public consciousness in a practical and usable form' (pp. 1070–1071). 'The practice of valid psychology by non-psychologists will inevitably change people's conception of themselves and what they can do' (p. 16). Miller further asserted that one does not need authority over a social organization in order to reform it. It is more important to understand the system than to control the system. Valid conception of system can allow one to introduce small changes with extensive consequences. Other Past Presidents, such as Philip Zimbardo, Robert Sternberg and Ronald Levant, have continued this emphasis and made it their presidential theme.

3 The Yazhou Zhoukan (21 December 2008) issue front-paged that the number of registered volunteers in Sichuan from all over China had reached 1.18 million on the sixth day of the quake, as reported by the provincial Chinese Communist Youth League.

4 The six assumptions, not unlike the core values and principles discussed in this chapter, are: 1. An intervention is most effective if it is conducted in a setting familiar to the target individual; 2. Mental disorder, and indeed all problems in living, are influenced by social-environmental factors in addition to psychological or biological ones; 3. Social factors are legitimate targets of intervention; 4. The community psychologist must be adept at performing different functions; 5. The focus of community intervention is the at-risk group or the population at large; and 6. Community members should be active participants rather than passive recipients (Lam & Ho, 1989).

5 The search was conducted at the Network for Health and Welfare Studies, Department of Applied Social Sciences, Hong Kong Polytechnic University, using the China Academic Journals Full-text Database (CAJ). CAJ is the largest searchable full-text and full-image interdisciplinary Chinese Journals database in the world, covering over 8,460 journals since 1994 (5,058 science and technology journals and 3,402 social sciences and humanities journals) by the end of 2007 with over 25 million article counts. The title search, using 'community+psychology+intervention' yielded 46 items, 31 of them including empirical research. Five articles have 'community intervention' in their title; two of them reported empirical research. Adding subject search of the word 'policy' to the title search 'community+psychology' yielded six items, three of which included empirical research, one on migrant workers, and two were related to chronic disease patients. As far as we can determine, most of the studies were conducted by medical researchers rather than psychologists.

6 The success rate for application was 23 per cent, compared to the UK Medical Research Council's 24 per cent (2006–7) and the US National Institute for Health's 31.5 per cent (1997–2001).

7 Websites: http://www.fhb.gov.hk/grants/english/funds/funds_hcpf/funds_hcpf_abt/funds_hcpf_abt.html and http://fhbgrants.netsoft.net/english/funded_list/funded_list.php

8 Website: http://www.ciif.gov.hk/en/evaluation/index_e.html

9 Website: http://qef.org.hk/eng/index.htm

10 We did not include funds open for public applications and operated by statutory bodies in the government bureau, such as the Occupational Health and Safety Council or other smaller-scale funds operated under government departmental level.

11 Website: http://www.info.gov.hk/gia/general/200611/10/P200611100314.htm

12 Website: http://www.hkatv.com/infoprogram/06/careforchildren/

13 This project was supported by a grant from the Quality Education Fund (Project EMB/QEF/2003/0727), Education Bureau, Hong Kong SAR Government to the author.

14 The participating children and the families are expected to save up a predetermined sum of money within a two-year period by which a community or private donation will provide at least on a one-to-one matching fund. When such a 'matured' case is presented to the CDF, the HKSAR government will award a lump sum of HK$3,000 to the child's family for the sole purpose of materializing the personal development plan of the participating children and adolescents. (http://www.cdf.gov.hk/english/aboutcdf/aboutcdf_int.html)

15 Website: http://www.cdf.gov.hk/english/aboutcdf/aboutcdf_int.html

16 Website: http://qef.org.hk/eng/user/function_display.php?id=118

17 It is appropriate to declare my interest in this matter here. In my capacity as a university academic and a professionally qualified clinical psychologist, I was appointed by the HKSAR government to be a member of a number of these high-level committees associated with the Quality Education Fund, Health Care and Promotion Fund, Health and Health Services Research Fund, etc. I am therefore in a well-informed position on the funds' development and have access to the planning papers of the funds. I have however adhered strictly to the code of practice both as a professional psychologist as well as a member of these committees that the entirety of the information and views expressed in this chapter involved only those attainable from publically accessible websites and did not include, to my knowledge, any privy information of restrictive nature to the committees concerned.

18 In Hong Kong, a couple of 'new organization forms' for doing prevention research have been developed (http://www.apss.polyu.edu.hk/nhws/, http://www.childinjury.org.hk/ and http://www.hkcnp.org.hk/, etc.) in the areas of child injury prevention and adolescent positive development which meet the above criteria, or to be exact, are inspired by and follow the criteria diligently. The major lesson is that there exist universal principles governing the reciprocal effects of person and social settings development but the design and analyses of prevention research have to be local.

References

Albee, G. W. & Gullotta, T. P. (1997). Primary prevention's evolution. In G. W. Albee & T. P. Gullotta (eds), *Primary prevention works* (pp. 3–22). Thousand Oaks, CA: Sage.

Angelique, H. & Culley, M. (2007). History and theory of community psychology: an international perspective of community psychology in the United States: returning to political, critical and ecological roots. In S. M. Reich, M. Riemer, I. Prilleltensky, & M. Montero (eds), *International community psychology: History and theories* (pp. 37–62). New York: Springer.

Barker, R. G. (1968). *Ecological psychology.* Palo Alto, CA: Stanford University Press.

Bell, P. A. (2001). *Environmental psychology* (5th ed.). Fort Worth, TX: Harcourt College Publishers.

Bennett, C. C., Luleen, A., Saul, C., Leonard, H., C., K. D., & Gershen, R. (1966). *Community psychology: A report of the Boston conference on the education of psychologists for community mental health.* Boston, MA: Boston University Press.

Bhatia, S. & Sethi, N. (2007). History and theory of community psychology in India: An international perspective. In S. M. Reich, M. Riemer, I. Prilleltensky, & M. Montero (eds), *International community psychology: History and theories* (pp. 180–199). New York: Springer.

Blair, A. (1992). The role of primary prevention in mental health services: A review and critique. *Journal of Community and Applied Social Psychology, 2,* 77–94.

Bronfenbrenner, U. (1979). *The ecology of human development experiments by nature and design.* Cambridge, MA: Harvard University Press.

Burton, M., Boyle, S., Psy, C., & Kagan, C. (2007). Community psychology in Britain. In S. M. Reich, M. Riemer, I. Prilleltensky, & M. Montero (eds), *International community psychology: History and theories* (pp. 219–237). New York: Springer.

Chan, C. C. (2004). *Intensive community mentoring—An international initiative and a Hong Kong response.* Hong Kong: Network for Health and Welfare Studies, Department of Applied Social Sciences, The Hong Kong Polytechnic University.

Chan, C. C. & Chan, K. (2006). Programs effectiveness, process outcomes, and sustainability of health promotion interventions in Hong Kong: Applying the RE-AIM framework. *Journal of Psychology in Chinese Societies, 7,* 5–28.

Chan, C. C. & Ho, W. C. (2006). The Intensive Community Mentoring Scheme in Hong Kong: Nurturing police–youth intergenerational relationships. *Journal of Intergenerational Relationships: Programs, Policy, and Research, 4,* 101–106.

Chan, C. C. & Ho, W. C. (2008). An ecological framework for evaluating relationship-functional aspects of youth mentoring. *Journal of Applied Social Psychology, 38*, 837–867.
Cheng, S.-T. & Mak, W. (2007). Community psychology in a borrowed place with borrowed time: The case of Hong Kong. In S. M. Reich, M. Riemer, I. Prilleltensky, & M. Montero (eds), *International community psychology: History and theories* (pp. 200–216). New York: Springer.
Collins, R. A., Johnston, J. M., Tang, A. M. Y., Chan, W. C., Tsang, C. S. H., & Lo, S. V. (2008). Summary of research projects supported by the Health Services Research Fund (HSRF) and the Health Care and Promotion Fund (HCPF). *Hong Kong Medical Journal, 14*(3 (S3)), S4–S8.
Cowen, E. L. (1973). Social and community interventions—Introduction—Scope of the field. *Annual Review of Psychology, 24*, 423–472.
Dalton, J., Elias, M., & Wandersman, A. (2007). *Community psychology linking individuals and communities* (2nd ed.). Belmont, CA: Thomson Higher Education.
DuBois, D. L., Holloway, B. E., Valentine, J. C., & Cooper, H. (2002). Effectiveness of mentoring programs for youth: A meta-analytic review. *American Journal of Community Psychology, 30*, 157–197.
Epp, J. (1986). Achieving health for all: A framework for health promotion. *Health Promotion International, 1*, 419–428.
Felner, R. D., Felner, T. Y., & Silverman, M. M. (2000). Prevention in mental health and social intervention: Conceptual and methodological issues in the evolution of the science and practice of prevention. In J. Rappaport & E. Seidman (eds), *Handbook of community psychology* (pp. 9–42). New York: Kluwer Academic/Plenum Publishers.
Francescato, D. & Tomai, M. (2001). Community psychology: Should there be a European perspective? *Journal of Community and Applied Social Psychology, 11*, 371–380.
Glasgow, R. E., Bull, S. S., Gillette, C., Klesges, L. M., & Dzewaltowski, D. A. (2002). Behavior change intervention research in healthcare settings—A review of recent reports with emphasis on external validity. *American Journal of Preventive Medicine, 23*, 62–69.
Glasgow, R. E., Klesges, L. M., Dzewaltowski, D. A., Estabrooks, P. A., & Vogt, T. M. (2006). Evaluating the impact of health promotion programs: Using the RE-AIM framework to form summary measures for decision making involving complex issues. *Health Education Research, 21*, 688–694.
Glasgow, R. E., McKay, H. G., Piette, J. D., & Reynolds, K. D. (2001). The RE-AIM framework for evaluating interventions: What can it tell us about approaches to chronic illness management? *Patient Education and Counseling, 44*, 119–127.
Glasgow, R. E., Vogt, T. M., & Boles, S. M. (1999). Evaluating the public health impact of health promotion interventions: The RE-AIM framework. *American Journal of Public Health, 89*, 1322–1327.
Green, L. W. & Mercer, S. L. (2001). Can public health researchers and agencies reconcile the push from funding bodies and the pull from communities? *American Journal of Public Health, 91*, 1926–1929.
Hepworth, J. (2004). Public health psychology: A conceptual and practical framework. *Journal of Health Psychology, 9*, 41–54.
Herrera, C., Grossman, J. B., Kauh, T. J., Feldman, A. F., McMaken, J., & Jucovy, L. Z. (2007). *Making a difference in schools: The Big Brothers Big Sisters school-based mentoring impact study.* Philadelphia, PA: Public/Private Venture.
Kelly, J. G. (2006). *Becoming ecological: An expedition into community psychology.* New York: Oxford University Press.
Lam, D. J. & Ho, D. Y. F. (1989). Community psychology in Hong Kong—Past, present, and future. *American Journal of Community Psychology, 17*, 83–97.
Levine, M. (1998). Prevention and community. *American Journal of Community Psychology, 26*, 189–206.
Lewin, K. (1935). *A dynamic theory of personality.* New York: McGraw-Hill.
Mercer, S. L., DeVinney, B. J., Fine, L. J., Green, L. W., & Dougherty, D. (2007). Study designs for effectiveness and translation research—Identifying trade-offs. *American Journal of Preventive Medicine, 33*, 139–154.
Miller, G. A. (1969). Psychology as a means of promoting human welfare. *American Psychologist, 24*, 1063–1075.
Murray, H. A., Barrett, W. G., Homburger, E., et al. (1938). *Explorations in personality: A clinical and experimental study of fifty men of college age.* New York: Oxford University Press.
Naylor, P. J., Wharf-Higgins, J., Blair, L., Green, L., & O'Connor, B. (2002). Evaluating the participatory process in a community-based heart health project. *Social Science & Medicine, 55*, 1173–1187.
Nelson, G., Lavoie, F., & Mitchell, T. (2007). The history and theories of community psychology in Canada. In S. M. Reich, M. Riemer, I. Prilleltensky, & M. Montero (eds), *International community psychology: History and theories* (pp. 13–36). New York: Springer.
Orford, J. (2008). *Community psychology: Challenges, controversies, and emerging consensus.* Chichester, England: Wiley.
Paquet, R., Lavoie, F., Harnois, G., Fitzgerald, M., Gourgue, C., & Fontaine, N. (1985). *La santé mentale: Rôles et place des ressources alternatives.* In *Collection: Avis du Comité de la Santé mentale du Québec.* Québec City, Canada: Gouvernement du Québec.
Perkins, D. D. & Zimmerman, M. A. (1995). Empowerment theory, research, and application. *American Journal of Community Psychology, 23*, 569–579.
Pluye, P., Potvin, L., & Denis, J.-L. (2004). Making public health programs last: Conceptualizing sustainability. *Evaluation and Program Planning, 27*, 121–133.
Prilleltensky, I., & Nelson, G. (1997). Community psychology: reclaiming social justice. In D. Fox & I. Prilleltensky (eds), *Critical psychology: an introduction* (pp. 166–184). London: Sage Publications.
Prilleltensky, I., Nelson, G., & Peirson, L. (2001). The role of power and control in children's lives: An ecological analysis of pathways toward wellness, resilience and problems. *Journal of Community and Applied Social Psychology, 11*, 143–158.

Rappaport, J. (1977). *Community psychology: Values, research, and action.* New York: Holt, Rinehart and Winston.
Rappaport, J. (1981). In praise of paradox—a social policy of empowerment over prevention. *American Journal of Community Psychology, 9*, 1–25.
Rappaport, J. (1987). Terms of empowerment/exemplars of prevention: toward a theory for community psychology. *American Journal of Community Psychology, 15*, 121–148.
Rappaport, J. & Seidman, E. (2000). *Handbook of community psychology.* New York: Kluwer Academic/Plenum Publishers.
Reich, S., Riemer, M., Prilleltensky, I., & Montero, M. (2007). An introduction to the diversity of community psychology internationally. In S. M. Reich, M. Riemer, I. Prilleltensky, & M. Montero (eds), *International community psychology: History and theories* (pp. 1–9). New York: Springer.
Riger, S. (1993). Whats wrong with empowerment. *American Journal of Community Psychology, 21*, 279–292.
Sampson, E. E. (1981). Cognitive psychology as ideology. *American Psychologist, 36*, 730–743.
Sasao, T. & Yasuda, T. (2007). Historical and theoretical orientations of community psychology practice and research in Japan. In S. M. Reich, M. Riemer, I. Prilleltensky, & M. Montero (eds), *International community psychology: History and theories* (pp. 164–179). New York: Springer.
Schneider, F. W., Gruman, J. A., & Coutts, L. M. (2005). *Applied social psychology: Understanding and addressing social and practical problems.* Thousand Oaks, CA: Sage.
Seeman, M. (1997). The neglected, elusive situation in social psychology. *Social Psychology Quarterly, 60*, 4–13.
Shadish, W. R., Matt, G. E., Navarro, A. M., & Phillips, G. (2000). The effects of psychological therapies under clinically representative conditions: A meta-analysis. *Psychological Bulletin, 126*, 512–529.
Smail, D. (1994). Community psychology and politics. *Journal of Community and Applied Social Psychology, 4*, 3–10.
Smail, D. (1995). Power and the origins of unhappiness: Working with individuals. *Journal of Community and Applied Social Psychology, 5*, 347–356.
Tierney, J. P., Grossman, J. B., & Besch, N. L. (1995). *Making a difference. An impact study of big brothers/big sisters.* Philadelphia, PA: Public/Private Ventures.
Tolan, P., Key, C., Chertok, F., & Jason, L. (1990). *Researching community psychology: Issues of theory and methods.* Washington, DC: American Psychological Association.
Trainor, J., Pomeroy, E., & Pape, B. (1999). *Building a framework for support a community development approach to mental health policy.* Toronto, Canada: Canadian Mental Health Association.
Tseng, V., Chesir-Teran, D., Becker-Klein, R., Chan, M. L., Duran, V., Roberts, A., et al. (2002). Promotion of social change: A conceptual framework. *American Journal of Community Psychology, 30*, 401–427.
Yu, H. L. & Yang, Y. (2008). Review of Community Psychology Research in China. *Journal of Shandong Institute of Commerce and Technology, 8*, 13–18.
Zimmerman, M. (1995). Psychological empowerment: Issues and illustrations. *American Journal of Community Psychology, 23*, 581–599.

CHAPTER 27

Psychotherapy with the Chinese: an update of the work in the last decade

Wai-Sum Liu and Patrick W.-L. Leung

Culture matters in psychotherapy. Culture, or, as it is called, the 'collective programming of the mind' (Hofstede, 2001, p. 9), infuses itself into different human experiences, and, with no exception, also into the experience of distress and the coping processes it initiates. It has long been recognized that every therapeutic encounter is embedded in a cultural context and that effective coping, to some extent, serves a sociocultural purpose (Draguns, 1975).

Although such viewpoints are not new in themselves, the global movement of people and the flow of scientific knowledge around the world have given fresh impetus to the research on psychotherapy in various cultural settings. Growing attention is being paid to the question of how various forms of contemporary psychotherapy, which are often regarded as Euro-American products, can be applied to clienteles of different cultural worldviews. In fact, culture-centered intervention is now regarded as a fourth force in psychotherapy, on par with psychodynamic, humanistic, and cognitive behavioral schools of thought and practice (Pederson, 1999). Furthermore, empirical support has been found for the efficacy and effectiveness of culturally sensitive mental health interventions (Griner & Smith, 2006).

This increasing awareness of culture's importance in psychological intervention is highly relevant to the Chinese. In the first edition of this handbook (Bond, 1996), P. W. L. Leung and Lee (1996) reviewed how psychotherapy with the Chinese had come a long way from using culture-bound, indigenous healing methods to the importation of Western interventions. They commented that the Chinese cultural context, owing to its huge diversity and rapid changes, could provide a 'natural laboratory' for research addressing the complex interplay between culture and psychotherapy. In the ten-year span since the publication of their review, numerous outputs have been generated from this 'natural laboratory'. Many advances have been made, related to either research (C. Xu, Wang, Miao, & Ouyang, 2002; S. Zhao, Wu, & Neng, 2003) or clinical application (Yue & Yan, 2006). Both practitioners and researchers are interested in how Western therapy is being applied and can best be applied to the Chinese, as well as the value of indigenous healing methods in the modern world.

The present chapter aims to describe this proliferating knowledge. It starts with a review of indigenous therapies and Western psychotherapy methods in the Chinese cultural context. However, we cannot fully appreciate the validity of a therapy if we do not understand the psychopathological processes associated with the disorders that it treats. Thus, this chapter also examines the psychopathological processes identified in the Chinese, and their compatibility with what are proposed in

Western theories. Finally, we look into how Eastern philosophy has recently been integrated into some variants of Western therapy to form new treatment methods.

Acknowledging that a monolithic Chinese entity is non-existent, this chapter reviews findings from a myriad of Chinese groups both between and within Chinese societies. The issues under review are intriguing and complex. By attempting to pull together all these pieces, we hope to offer a panoramic view of psychotherapy with the Chinese. We also hope that this review can shed some new light on a theme that we explored ten years ago: the perennial debate about the cultural specificity or universality of psychotherapy.

Owing to the rich literature but the brevity of our coverage in one single chapter, we cannot claim that this review is exhaustive. Nevertheless, efforts were made to ensure its thoroughness. In exploring the literature, relevant materials were searched using the Social Sciences Citation Index at Web of Science, PsycInfo, and Wengfang Data, a Chinese journal database, plus the bibliographies of the papers so identified. We mainly focused on studies published during the past ten years after the publication of our 1996 chapter in the first edition of this handbook (P. W. L. Leung & Lee, 1996), but also included some important older publications. It should be noted that this review does not mean to be a detailed account of the historical development of psychotherapy in the People's Republic of China (PRC). On this topic, interested readers are referred to other reviews (D. F. Chang, Tong, Shi, & Zeng, 2005; Qian, Smith, Chen, & Xia, 2001).

Indigenous psychotherapy

Indigenous psychotherapy refers to the healing practices that are developed within a specific culture milieu or society for its own inhabitants (D. W. Sue & Sue, 2003). It typically involves some key components of psychotherapy, namely, a healing agent, a help seeker, a healing relationship, and an objective of removing distress (P. W. L. Leung & Lee, 1996). By examining extant indigenous treatment methods, one can gain better understanding of how cultural outlook impacts on them to deal with the various problems arising from living in a particular cultural setting.

This section thus starts with a review of the philosophical ideologies underpinning Chinese culture. It then follows with an update on psychotherapy by Chinese medical practitioners and on supernaturally oriented folk therapy. We have dropped the discussion of 'communist psychotherapy' raised in our previous review (P. W. L. Leung & Lee, 1996). Although political influence still has a bearing on the practice of psychotherapy in mainland China (S. A. Leung, Guo, & Lam, 2000), this special form of 'communist psychotherapy', also called 'rapid integrated psychotherapy', has ceased to be practiced, and is regarded as a historical relic that served specific socio-political needs at a particular time in Chinese history (Tseng, Lee, & Lu, 2005).

Confucianism, Buddhism, and Taoism

Confucianism, Buddhism, and Taoism are the three major philosophical systems of the Chinese. Although they are not psychotherapy, their doctrines serve psychotherapeutic functions, given their emphasis on self-improvement and humanity (P. W. L. Leung & Lee, 1996). Confucianism espouses interpersonal harmony and hierarchical relationship. It emphasizes the virtues of humanity, benevolence, and moderation. People are expected to cultivate themselves in order to achieve moral ideals. These philosophical ideas, with a positivist outlook, can be readily incorporated into psychotherapy for the Chinese (Yan, 2005). However, Confucianism espouses a more active stance, encouraging people to live up to the ideal code of conduct and ethics (Yan, 2005; Y. Zhang et al., 2002). It is thus deemed more useful in improving the moral standard of people's lives, not during times of distress, but when everything is going smoothly.

Both Buddhism and Taoism espouse liberation from worldly desires. Buddhist teaching is premised on the idea that life is fraught with sufferings due to excessive cravings for the illusory materials of this transient world (S. C. Chang & Dong-Shick, 2005). Letting go of the attachment to excessive desires is one means of alleviating suffering. Buddhism also emphasizes the interconnectedness between one's personal and social life, past deeds and future consequences. Therefore, to be freed from suffering and to achieve tranquility, one has to bear the responsibility of leading a righteous life and relating to others with virtue and integrity.

Attempts have been made to apply the teachings of Buddhism to therapy with the Chinese. For instance, based on clinical experience, Yeung and Lee (1997) suggested that incorporating Buddhist stories into psychotherapy would be beneficial to Asians, including the Chinese. Besides, it has been noted that Morita therapy, a form of Japanese therapy which incorporates the teaching of Zen Buddhism, is quite popular in mainland China (Tseng et al., 2005). Its popularity is possibly owing to the fact that the Buddhist ideologies embedded in Morita therapy are part of the Chinese culture (Cui, cited in Tseng et al., 2005; Qian, Smith et al., 2001).

In Taoism (also called Daoism), the major philosophical tenet is the *dao* which is the fundamental principle of nature. Taoism holds that human beings are parts of the unity of the universe and that life has its own natural course. What people need to do is to be flexible, follow nature, and *wu wei* (not to intervene). Covetousness is warned against, but contentment with life is encouraged. Recognizing the influence of Taoism in the Chinese way of coping and thinking, Chinese Taoist cognitive therapy (CTCP) has been developed in mainland China to match the cultural milieu of the Chinese (Young, Tseng, & Zhou, 2005; see also Cheng, Lo, & Chio, this volume).

This innovation is essentially a form of Western cognitive therapy which incorporates Taoist values. Besides understanding stress factors, belief systems, and coping styles, the clinician also introduces Taoist philosophies in the treatment process (Y. Zhang & Yang, 1998). By advocating ideas like detachment from excessive desires and compliance with the course of nature, the therapist expects that distressed individuals can make use of these principles to handle their psychosocial stressors and difficulties in life. Some evidence has come to light which supports the beneficial effects of CTCP with the Chinese (see, for example, J. Wang & Wu, 2005; Y. Zhang et al., 2002).

The above review shows that over the past ten years, researchers and clinicians have drawn from the wealth of traditional Chinese philosophies in improving psychotherapy with the Chinese. The psychotherapeutic functions of Chinese philosophies are no longer mere academic speculation. Particularly, CTCP offers a good example of how Chinese culture can be blended into Western psychotherapy and is found to be beneficial to the Chinese.

Psychotherapy by Chinese medical practitioners

Traditional Chinese medicine (TCM) adopts a dynamic and holistic orientation to understand a person's well-being. Flaws and Lake (2001) and Y. Zhang (2007) have given lucid accounts of the relationship between TCM and psychiatric or emotion-related disorders. In essence, the human body and mind are continuously affected by two polarizing yet complementary forces in the universe, namely *yin* and *yang*. Dysregulation of and imbalance between these two forces may result in vulnerability to illness. *Qi* (or vitality) and blood provide the essence for the body's various activities. Righteous *qi* energizes the body and evil *qi* upsets bodily functions. Excessive emotions can cause damage to visceral organs and vice versa, which may then become manifest in emotional, behavioral, and somatic symptoms. In this way, the *yin–yang* balance, *qi*, and blood regulation may also be disrupted. A harmonious relationship between the mind, body, and nature as a coordinated unit is regarded as the cornerstone of physical and mental health.

This way of theorizing has implications for the clinical practice of TCM. Since emotion-related problems and visceral functions are interrelated, emotional problems are always conceptualized as physical illness, and the treatment usually targets bodily dysfunctions (Z. Li, 2006; Qian, Smith et al., 2001; Y. Zhang, 2007). Common treatment modalities include *qi gong*, acupuncture, and herbal medicine. While an extensive review of such somatic interventions is beyond the scope of this chapter, we note some studies that report the beneficial effects of these interventions for depression and schizophrenia (Edzard, Rand, & Stevinson, 1998; Rathbone et al., 2007; Tsang, Fung, Chan, Lee, & Chan, 2006).

Despite putting greater emphasis on handling physical dysfunction, 'psychology' and 'psychotherapy' are not considered as lying outside the paradigm of TCM. We suggest that the relationship between physical illness and emotional dysregulation is mentioned in ancient literature dating back two thousand years and that the concept of 'psychotherapy' does appear in classical literature (Z. Li, 2006; S. H. Xu, 1996). One important therapeutic skill identified is to counteract any excessive affect by an antagonistic emotion. One ancient case record described a man who suffered from heartache after his father died. His grief and sadness were cured by a practitioner who made him laugh with nonsense blabbering. This is an example showing how joy can overcome sadness (S. H. Xu, 1996). Many researchers also see commonalities between Chinese medical psychotherapy and Western psychotherapy in terms of their common use of behavioral and cognitive strategies to handle emotional problems (Z. Li & Chen, 2007; H. Xiang & Zuang, 2006; Q. Yang, 2006).

While many investigators have tried hard to historicize Chinese psychotherapy within the context of TCM, the intriguing medical case records unearthed, as noted above, should be treated with caution. In the modern practice of TCM, the systematic use of such therapeutic skills as described above is rare. Often the 'verbal therapy' provided is no more than giving general advice (Flaws & Lake, 2001). In ethnographic fieldwork carried out in mainland China, Y. Zhang (2007) found that although patients' emotional and social difficulties were addressed by the clinicians, the approach resembled more a conversation with close friends or family members in which culturally appropriate solutions were usually imparted.

Nevertheless, in comparison to the development of TCM ten years ago, we note that more efforts have been made to demonstrate the link between TCM and modern science. Scattered studies, unfortunately with substandard methodologies, have examined the therapeutic effects of Chinese medical psychotherapy (see, for example, Guan & Hu, 2007; Jiang, Xu, Zheng, & Zhou, 2002). Despite this improvement, more systematic efforts at organizing and empirically studying this repertoire of psychotherapeutic techniques are called for.

Supernaturally oriented folk psychotherapy

Supernaturally oriented healing methods have been used among the Chinese since time immemorial. Common healing methods include shamanism, fortune telling, divination, and *fung shui* (geomancy). These forms of therapeutic practice are deeply embedded in traditional Chinese culture. In shamanistic practice, religious rites are performed to bridge the communication between the human and the spiritual planes (B. Lee & Bishop, 2001; Tseng, 1999). Many shamans consider mental disturbances to be caused by the ancestors' spirits. Thus, the prescription of activities to restore proper family functioning, like ancestral worship, is common. Divination involves fortune telling that relies on divine instructions (Tseng, 1999). One particular form of divination is the drawing or casting of *chien* (bamboo sticks) and the interpretation of *chien wen*. *Chien wen*, which is said to contain messages from the gods, typically consists of culturally sanctioned means of coping. Furthermore, one's fortune can also be told through palm reading and astrology. These avenues can help people to find ways to adjust to their fate and live harmoniously with nature (Tseng, 1999). The practice of *fung shui* is premised on the view that disharmony between the person and the environment may cause problems. Restoring balance by modifying the environment is advised. Despite the procedural differences among these time-honored healing practices, they involve catharsis and the provision of explicit suggestions (Jilek, 1993), with the goal of restoring balance between the supernatural world, the environment, the socio-cultural system, and the person involved.

Given that Chinese people hold a pragmatic and pluralistic attitude towards healing, it is not uncommon for the Chinese and their families to seek help from traditional folk healers nowadays, (J. K. So, 2005). In a study that examined 100 Chinese psychiatric patients in Singapore, 36 per cent had consulted a traditional healer before seeking psychiatric services (Kua, Chew, & Ko, 1993). In a study conducted in Taiwan, it was found that among a sample of 41 schizophrenic patients, over 70 per cent had sought help from shamans or had worshipped deities of folk religions in order to seek relief (Wen, 1998). Among schizophrenic patients living in rural parts of mainland China, 54.5 per cent reported receiving traditional spiritual treatment (Ran, Xiang, Li et al., 2003).

Supernaturally oriented therapy has not been systematically subjected to empirical examination. Outcomes of this form of therapy are still largely unknown, leading to questions on its purported treatment effects. In an early anthropological study of shamanism in Taiwan, it was hypothesized that the shared explanatory model and worldview between therapists and clients may contribute to a powerful placebo effect (Kleinman & Sung, 1979). More systematic efforts are called for to scrutinize the possible benefits or ill effects of this form of therapy. Unfortunately, its practice may at times jeopardize the use of proper psychiatric treatment for mental disorders. For example, seeking traditional spiritual healing was found to hinder long-term psychiatric treatment of schizophrenia, because a majority of the families would resort to spiritual healing when initial psychiatric treatment was not rapidly effective (Ran, Xiang, Li et al., 2003).

Despite their lack of alignment with modern science, indigenous healing methods should not be dismissed outright (D. W. Sue & Sue, 2003). This caution is vividly echoed in a case study by Tang (2007). The author described her therapeutic encounter with a Chinese woman who suffered from traumatic bereaved grief. The woman did not benefit from standard psychotherapy. Instead, by consulting a fortune teller and worshipping an indigenous god, she was able to find some solace. The treatment impasse was resolved by the therapist's willingness to discuss traditional beliefs and fortune telling in therapy sessions, from which the client was able to find culturally relevant meaning in her traumatic experience. Tang (2007) warned that being oblivious to cultural issues would hinder treatment progress and might lead to premature termination in therapy. Although there has been no great advancement in the empirical examination of supernaturally oriented therapy since our last review ten years ago (P. W. L. Leung & Lee, 1996), occasional publications, such as the recent one by Tang (2007), keep reminding us of the importance of incorporating a culture's supernatural beliefs into the psychotherapeutic process.

Western psychotherapy with the Chinese

Applicability

The foregoing review of indigenous psychotherapy illuminates how culture permeates healing practices. Values such as harmony, collectivism, and moderation, that characterize a sociocentric culture of the Chinese, are emphasized in its indigenous therapy. They advocate accommodation to the environment, i.e. a collectivistic goal. These cultural values are fundamentally different from those seen in the West. For example, Draguns (2008) posited that Western psychotherapy was very much shaped by American values like 'optimism, individualism, egalitarianism, glorification of social mobility, and encouragement of personal change' (p. 24). These values tend to promote active changing of a client's life circumstances to meet personal goals. How would these cultural differences between the East and the West generate obstacles, or to the contrary, possibly new opportunities for the application of Western psychotherapy to the Chinese?

One measure of the applicability of Western psychotherapy to the Chinese can perhaps be shown in the rates of service utilization for Western mental health services by the Chinese. It is reasonable to conjecture that the clash in expectations for treatment, beliefs about etiology, and goals for outcome, etc., would impede Chinese entry into Western therapy. Research findings did show that Asians, including the Chinese, used Western mental health services less frequently (Leong, Chang, & Lee, 2007; Ng, Fones, & Kua, 2003; S. Sue, Fujino, Hu, Takeuchi, & Zane, 1991; P. S. Wang et al., 2007; see also Mak & Chen, this volume). Kim and his associates, using cultural values as planned variables in their studies, found that among Asian-American college students, adherence to Asian values like collectivism, emotional self-control, and avoidance of shame was associated with more negative attitudes towards help seeking (Kim & Omizo, 2003; Kim, 2007). Other Asian cultural values, for instance the belief that mental illness is brought on by internal physical factors (Leong & Lau, 2001) and the tendency to keep information within the kinship group (Ho & Chung, 1996; Leong & Lau, 2001), have also been suggested to interfere with timely service utilization.

We should also be cautious not to minimize other important non-cultural barriers, like the inaccessibility or underdevelopment of the mental health services, especially in rural areas of mainland China (Ho & Chung, 1996; Kung, 2004; P. S. Wang et al., 2007). In one study with Chinese-Americans, practical barriers were found to be more salient than cultural barriers in help seeking (Kung, 2004). With better accessibility and more exposure to Western psychotherapy, the service utilization rate is likely to increase, while the attitude towards help seeking will become more positive. In fact, one recent study found that college students in mainland China had a generally positive attitude towards seeking psychological help, and this attitude was associated with prior counseling contact and knowledge of psychology and counseling (Goh et al., 2007). In addition, in other recent treatment studies that also examined Chinese participants' attitude towards Western psychological treatment, generally positive results were noted (Shen, Alden, Sochting, & Tsang, 2006; C. Y. C. So, Leung, & Hung, 2008).

For those Chinese who are willing to enter into therapy, one potential stumbling block is the difference between clients' and therapists' perceptions of psychological problems and their solutions. The typically tacit, individualistic treatment goal of Western psychotherapy may not be readily accepted by the Chinese because they conflict with values of a collectivistic culture which emphasize relational harmony and enhancement of relationships (Draguns, 2004). Imposing an individualist goal often results in the Chinese patients' feeling alienated by the treatment model and being forced to compromise or give up their own cultural values (G. Cheung & Chan, 2002). One good example is assertiveness training which aims at helping a person to express their personal needs. This practice is noted to be difficult among the Chinese, because it may result in interpersonal disharmony and conflicts (S. W. H. Chen & Davenport, 2005; Lin, 2002).

The importance of adhering to Chinese collectivistic values of familism instead of pursuing individualistic self-liberation is illustrated in the following case study. P. W. L. Leung and Sung-Chan (2002) reported a Chinese woman who suffered from low back pain associated with sexual guilt. She was helped by the therapist's emphasis on her duty to fulfill the familial roles of a wife and mother instead of focusing on her own individualistic self-liberation. Hence, working towards a collectivistic treatment goal helps alleviate distress in a case such as this, since it is grounded in a culturally relevant conceptualization of the case.

The interaction within the client and therapist dyad is also impacted by cultural values. Chinese people emphasize deference to authority figures. High power distance is a strong value orientation in all Chinese cultural groups (Bond, 1996). Given that Chinese people often consider therapists as experts whose role is to give directions and advice, they are less likely to accept a non-directive therapy style, e.g. client-centered therapy and psychoanalysis. Besides, Chinese patients are more inclined to conform to and less disposed to disagree openly with the advice given by authority figures (S. W. H. Chen & Davenport, 2005; Lin, 2002; Qian, Smith et al., 2001). Such behaviors are counterproductive to the *modus operandi* of Western therapy, which emphasizes a collaborative relationship and more independence on the part of the client. Moreover, Chinese people are socialized to control their emotions and their expression (Bond, 1993; S. W. H. Chen & Davenport, 2005; Lin, 2002; see also Yik, this volume). Emotive exercises or abreaction may pose difficulty and create embarrassment for the client, especially in the initial stages of therapy.

It should also be noted that therapists, just like their clients, are not immune to cultural clashes. W. Zhang (1994), a school counselor from mainland China, depicted his training in the USA as characterized by recurrent conflicts between his classmates' individualistic and his collectivistic viewpoint. He had difficulties in understanding and accepting the case conceptualization and treatment strategies put forward by his American counterparts, which emphasized an individual's needs over the interests of the family, the clan, and the state. W. Y. Lee (2004), a seasoned family therapist, described a consultation session which ended with the wife being able to assert her needs in the marriage and make more demands on her depressed husband. This case scenario, however, aroused debates among an audience of Chinese psychiatrists and psychologists over the Western and Chinese values of marriage and family. What these examples seem to highlight is that therapists may also need to undergo a process of cultural training in alternative worldviews (Koltoko-Rivera, 2004) in order to recognize values affecting their psychotherapy practice.

However, in our previous review (P. W. L. Leung & Lee, 1996), we noted that both collectivistic and individualistic goals were adopted by Chinese clients. Balance, as one of the more important Chinese cultural values, if not the most important one, is probably at work to mediate between collectivistic and individualistic goals of therapy among Chinese clients (see also Ji, Lee, & Guo, this volume). Furthermore, when we review more recent literature on Chinese culture and Western psychotherapy, there is more interest in exploring cultural compatibilities than incompatibilities.

For instance, family therapy, which places the individual in the family context and approaches psychological issues in a systemic perspective, is considered suitable for the Chinese who embrace a collectivist culture (G. Cheung & Chan, 2002). Parent training is also suggested to be relevant to the Chinese because of the cultural emphasis on the parents' role in supervising the children. Promoting pro-social behaviors is also consistent with Chinese parenting practice, which focuses on filial piety and training (Wang & Chang, this volume; Ho et al., 1999; C. Y. C. So et al., 2008). Additionally, Hodges and Oei (2007) explored the conceptual compatibilities between cognitive behavioral therapy (CBT) and core Chinese values. They suggested that the high power distance of the Chinese fit the CBT therapists' active stance of defining problems, setting goals, and doing evaluation. The educational aspect of CBT was in line with the pragmatic characteristics of the Chinese who preferred practical solutions to problems. Homework assignments, an essential component of CBT, were likely to be welcomed by the Chinese who valued self-cultivation and diligence. They concluded that there was a strong degree of compatibility between CBT and Chinese culture.

This viewpoint has been shared by a number of other researchers (e.g. S. W. H. Chen & Davenport, 2005; Foo & Kazantzis, 2007; Ho et al., 1999; Hodges & Oei, 2007; Hwang, Wood, Lin, & Cheung, 2006; Lin, 2002; Stewart, Lee, & Tao, this volume). They offered suggestions, such as having the therapist presenting as an expert, educating the patients about the process of psychotherapy, providing gentler assertiveness training, refraining from discussion of intense emotions in the initial stage of treatment, etc., in order to make the therapy more acceptable to the Chinese. By and large, these strategies are recommended on the basis of clinical experience. As suggested by Leong and Lee (2006), we cannot assume that the incorporation of cultural concerns would invariably make the therapy more culturally valid. Empirical studies are needed to determine the clinical advantages of such efforts.

Outcome studies

In this section, we review outcome studies of Western psychotherapy conducted with the Chinese. This is a selective review which mainly focuses on studies using controlled trials. However, for some treatment methods with limited research findings, we also include less sophisticated studies, such as case reports and uncontrolled pre-test–post-test studies.

Cognitive behavioral therapy. In this review, CBT is a generic term that refers to a broad range of intervention strategies, including those otherwise called cognitive therapy, rational emotive therapy, behavior therapy/modification. Under this broad definition, we identify quite a number of outcome studies on CBT. Comparative studies conducted in mainland China had consistently shown that medication coupled with CBT was more successful than medication alone in treating anxiety disorders (Feng, Han, Gan, & Liu, 2003; Guo, Guo, Yang, & Zhang, 2004; Ren, 2003; H. Su, Wang, & Liu, 2005; C. Zhao, Wang, Shen, & Geng, 2003), depression (Long, Wang, Liu, & Zhang, 2005; Zheng, Li, & Liu, 2007), and comorbid anxiety with depression (H. Chen, Cui, & Wang, 2007; Niu, Xie, & Pei, 2006).

Group CBT for anxiety and depressive disorders has also been researched. It was found beneficial in treating Chinese with social anxiety (D. F. K. Wong & Sun, 2006) and anxiety/depression (T. Chen, Lu, Chang, Chu, & Chou, 2006; Dai et al., 1999; Shen et al., 2006).

CBT is also found to be beneficial in general medical settings with Chinese patients. Improvement in quality of life, coping abilities, or post-operative outcomes had been found in HIV-infected patients (I. Chan et al., 2005; Molassiotis et al., 2002), adults with epilepsy (Au et al., 2003), chronically ill patients (Wong, Chau, Kwok, & Kwan, 2007), and women with elective hysterectomy (L. Cheung, Callaghan, & Chang, 2003). However, in one study, CBT was not beneficial to cancer patients (Y. M. Chan et al., 2005).

There are a few studies with Chinese schizophrenic patients. Several randomized controlled trials confirm the therapeutic benefits of CBT as an adjunct to medication in improving social functioning, reducing symptoms, and lowering hospitalization and relapse rates (F. Li & Wang, 1994; Mak, Li, & Lee, 2007; Y. Xiang et al., 2007; Zhou & Li, 2005). Psychoeducation of patients' families, as a component of CBT, was able to enhance treatment compliance and reduce relapse rates (Z. Li & Arthur, 2005; Ran, Xiang, Chan et al., 2003; M. Zhang, He, Gittelman, Wong, & Yan, 1998).

Regarding treatment for Chinese children and adolescents, fewer studies have been conducted on emotional problems. In one study, CBT was able to reduce cognitive dysfunction, but had no effect in alleviating anxiety and depressive symptoms in adolescents (Q. Su et al., 2006). In contrast, another study found that CBT could prevent the development of depressive symptoms in a group of children in mainland China (Yu & Seligman, 2002). More studies target externalizing disorders. A randomized controlled trial (C. Leung, Sanders, Leung, Mak, & Lau, 2003) and two pre-test–post-test single-group studies (Ho et al., 1999; H. L. Huang, Chao, Tu, & Yang, 2003) showed that parent training was able to reduce disruptive behaviors of children and improve parent–child interaction. A recent randomized controlled study also showed the effectiveness of combined behavior therapy and medication with children having attention deficit/hyperactivity disorder (C. Y. C. So et al., 2008).

Some of the above-mentioned studies not only document pre–post treatment gains, but also the maintenance of benefits in a follow-up period. The therapeutic effects were found to be maintained from six weeks to as long as two years (Feng et al., 2003; Ho et al, 1999; C. Y. C. So et al, 2008; Y. Xiang et al., 2007; Zheng et al., 2007).

Chinese Taoist cognitive therapy. As pointed out earlier in this review, CTCP is a modified form of Western CBT which incorporates elements of Chinese Taoist philosophy. There is some initial evidence for its benefits. The combination of CTCP with medication has been found to be more beneficial than medication alone in the treatment of post-stroke depression (J. Wang & Xu, 2005), depression in late life (J. Yang, Zhao, & Mai, 2005), generalized anxiety disorder (Y. Zhang et al., 2002), and neuroticism among college students (X. Huang, Zhang, & Yang, 2001), with effects maintained from six months to one year. According to Y. Zhang et al. (2002), the treatment effects were better for anxiety neurosis and depression than those specific forms of anxiety like obsessive-compulsive disorder (OCD) or phobia. Although the above findings are encouraging, we know of no research on the additive value of CTCP to the conventional form of CBT.

Family therapy. A few case studies (Ma, Chow, Lee, & Lai, 2002; Ma, 2005; Mei & Meng, 2003) had shown that family therapy was beneficial in treating eating disorders. In a controlled trial, the effects of structural family therapy combined with medication were found to be better than using medication alone when treating anorexia (Y. Li, Wang, & Ma, 2006) and childhood OCD (Cai, 2007). Therapeutic effects for drug rehabilitation have also been reported (Sim, 2005).

Psychoanalysis. Although Y. Zhang and colleagues (2002) commented that psychoanalysis was almost non-existent in Chinese societies, a culturally modified, short-term psychodynamic therapy, named 'cognitive insight therapy', has been developed and practiced in mainland China (Qian, Smith et al., 2001; Y. B. Zhong, 1988). This approach to treatment posits that psychological symptoms are related to early traumas and immature coping strategies. Medication plus cognitive insight therapy has been found to be superior to medication alone in the treatment of some psychological problems, including OCD (Q. Li, Yue, & Qian, 2007) and social phobia (H. Liu & Ma, 2002). Case studies had also documented its benefits for treatment of sexual paraphilia (S. Chen & Li, 2006).

Other forms of psychotherapy. Other forms of therapy have also been practiced with the Chinese. Controlled trials or case studies have documented therapeutic effects of solution-focused therapy (F. R. Yang, Zhu, & Luo, 2005), eye-movement desensitization and reprocessing (Wu, 2002), and hypnotherapy (Poon, 2007). However, so far, little is known about the utilization and effects of dialectical behavior therapy (DBT), acceptance and commitment therapy (ACT), mindfulness cognitive behavior therapy (MCBT), and interpersonal psychotherapy among the Chinese.

Caveats of the outcome studies

First, we note that the standard of the studies conducted in the past ten years has been steadily improving. The field has moved beyond the use of single case studies and has adopted various research methodologies, including randomized controlled trials. Standardized assessment tools are more frequently used as outcome measures. Other than pre–post symptom improvement, relapse rate, maintenance of the effects, quality of life, etc., are measured in some studies. They provide more comprehensive information about treatment outcomes. However, it is sometimes difficult to assess the methodological rigor of some studies. For example, studies published in Chinese-language journals tend to be brief, making it hard to adequately assess the scientific rigor of the research design.

Many of the studies cited above examine mainly the effectiveness of psychotherapy in front-line clinical practice and are invariably conducted within the constraints usually found in real-life clinical settings. Such conditions as the scant use of treatment manuals to ensure treatment integrity (e.g. see Ren, 2003; Q. Su et al., 2006), the lack of rigorous treatment control, randomization, and blinding of researchers involved in the data collection (e.g. see Q. Su et al., 2006; C. Zhao et al., 2003), a diverse group of patients with various comorbid conditions (e.g. see Ho et al., 1999), and non-standardized therapist training (e.g. see Feng et al., 2003) threaten the internal validity of the studies and bias their reported outcomes. In a meta-analysis of Morita therapy with Chinese schizophrenics, He and Li (2007) found that the standard of their reviewed studies was of medium to poor quality, and the findings might well be biased, with 40 per cent overestimation of positive therapeutic effects.

Second, studies with various types of research design are needed. Many of the studies, especially those reported in Chinese-language journals, examine combined treatment effects of medication and psychotherapy. This probably reflects the prevailing influence of the biomedical conceptualization of mental illness, and perhaps the influence of the pharmaceutical industry (D. F. Chang & Kleinman, 2002). While such studies can enhance our understanding of the benefits of psychotherapy as an adjunct to medication, examining psychotherapy conducted alone, and comparison among different forms of psychotherapy with various disorders are also needed in order to understand what kinds of treatment are effective with what disorders (Chambless & Hollon, 1998). For instance, it was found in the West that for some anxiety disorders, psychotherapy could produce effects that are equal to or superior to medication (Lambert & Archer, 2006). It is not clear whether similar therapeutic effects can be found among the Chinese. Such information will be useful for clinicians to maximize the clinical utility of psychotherapy.

Third, while many of the studies report statistically significant results from psychotherapy, many fewer explicitly document the magnitude of the improvement or the effect size. Furthermore, few attempts have been made to use the statistical technique of meta-analysis (Rosenthal, 1984) to synthesize the large quantity of psychotherapy research with the Chinese.

Fourth, there is a paucity of information on the side effects of psychotherapy with the Chinese. Lambert and Archer (2006) examined studies done in the West and estimated that about 5 to 10 per cent of clients became worse off during treatment, while another 15 to 25 per cent showed no measurable improvement. However, it must be cautioned that not all deterioration is produced by the therapy itself. Nonetheless, examination of negative outcomes, side effects, and their correlates is crucial, because it can help to evaluate the costs and benefits of psychotherapy and provide clues for preventing harmful effects during therapy.

Finally, the majority of the studies involve Chinese from mainland China, Hong Kong, and Taiwan. There is a dearth of treatment studies involving overseas Chinese in foreign cultures, except for a few pilot studies and case vignettes (Dai et al., 1999; Hwang et al., 2006; Shen et al., 2006). More research is thus needed to understand the psychological needs of these overseas Chinese who have varying levels of acculturation with their host cultures and thus have more complex cultural identities to manage (see Ward & Lin, this volume). Will the current psychotherapy be able to help these overseas Chinese to meet such challenges? Or how should the existing psychotherapy be adapted to meet these special challenges?

Process studies

Process research attempts to identify the curative ingredients of psychotherapy and the mechanisms of change (Kopta, Lueger, Saunders, & Howard, 1999). A number of studies found that among the

Chinese, the use of a directive approach was related to client-rated helpfulness, therapist credibility, competence, and a better working alliance (Kim & Omizo, 2003; L. C. Li & Kim, 2004; Snider, cited in Draguns, 2004; Wei & Heppner, 2005). Alongside directiveness, other therapeutic factors like therapist's empathy and positive attitude were also found to be related to therapist's credibility among Chinese clients (Akutsu, Lin, & Zane, 1990; Wei & Heppner, 2005).

Another important line of research has investigated whether ethnic match between therapists and clients can enhance treatment outcomes. In a series of earlier archival studies, it was demonstrated that therapist–client match in ethnicity was associated with an increased number of therapy sessions attended and a decreased rate of premature termination among Asian-Americans (Fujino, Okazaki, & Young, 1994; S. Sue et al., 1991). However, in more recent analogue studies, there were contradictory findings about the benefit of ethnic match (Kim & Atkinson, 2002; Kim, Li, & Liang, 2002).

It has been postulated that ethnic match does not necessarily lead to a match in cultural outlook or other attributes. For instance, family therapists in Hong Kong found that their worldviews and beliefs were quite different from those of their Chinese clients from mainland China, Taiwan, and Singapore (W. Y. Lee, 2002; Ma, 2007). In this regard, Zane et al. (2005) suggested going beyond studying ethnic match, instead focusing on the cognitive match between the therapists and clients, an approach to the issue that was found to be positively related to treatment outcome and session impacts.

The foregoing review finds that process research with the Chinese is rather underdeveloped. P. H. Chen and Tsai (1998) reviewed 50 studies on psychotherapy process conducted in Taiwan and noted no conclusive findings because they were generally small-scale studies. Leong et al. (2007) also added that process research with Asian-Americans was also plagued by methodological limitations, e.g. the use of analogue research, small sample sizes, and the focus on college students. Better research is thus urgently called for.

The yield from these empirical studies

There are considerably more studies examining the effects of CBT with the Chinese (C. Xu et al., 2002; S. Zhao et al., 2003), and it is widely used (see Stewart et al., this volume). Beneficial treatment effects have been consistently found in CBT with the Chinese for various emotional disorders, antisocial/externalizing problems, and schizophrenia. These results are by and large in line with the guidelines for empirically validated therapy advocated in the West (Chambless et al., 1998). Furthermore, support for the culturally modified form of CBT, e.g. CTCP, has also come to light.

Other forms of psychotherapy, such as psychodynamic or family therapy, are much less well researched with the Chinese. Given the different volumes of accumulated research findings, it is perhaps still premature to confirm an 'equal outcome phenomenon' for psychotherapy with the Chinese, which suggests that all forms of psychotherapy are perhaps equally beneficial for the Chinese. This is so, despite our previous review (P. W. L. Leung and Lee, 1996) where we suggested the possibility of such a conclusion then considered provisional.

Furthermore, we were unable in our previous review (P. W. L. Leung and Lee, 1996) to answer the important question of, 'What treatment, by whom, is most effective for this individual with this specific problem, under this set of circumstances?' (Paul, 1967, p. 111). We are still unable to answer this question. The major reason is that the evidentiary value of those recent findings is still threatened by substandard research methodologies. In this regard, perhaps we should not overlook an even more fundamental issue: the adequacy of training for the psychotherapists who work with the Chinese. As pointed out by some researchers (S. A. Leung et al., 2000; Yue &Yan, 2006), many therapists in mainland China are practitioners with limited training and questionable professional credentials. Insufficient training inevitably confounds the effectiveness and efficacy of various forms of psychotherapy (Cheung, 2000). Thus, better-designed studies with therapy to be performed by well-trained therapists are required to answer the question put forward eloquently by Paul (1967).

Psychopathological processes

Psychotherapy should be a theory-based practice. Each therapeutic approach has its assumptions about human nature and behavior, along with associated theories of psychopathological processes which lead to disorders. They are keys to case conceptualization and intervention strategies. For this reason, if we want to examine whether a form of psychotherapy is truly applicable to a population, we cannot ignore one fundamental question, viz. how are the psychopathological processes assumed in a therapeutic approach compatible with what are actually identified in a population?

Any unique psychopathological processes found in one population can have important implications for clinical practice. They hint at ways to modify therapeutic elements of an intervention in order to make them more relevant to culturally grounded psychopathological processes. In the following, we address this question in the Chinese cultural context. Knowledge of this area constitutes the missing link between culture and the forms of psychotherapy that can accommodate to the psychopathological processes of the Chinese.

As noted above, CBT is a form of psychotherapy with empirical evidence for its benefits with the Chinese. In CBT, it is argued that cognition is a key factor that mediates between mood and external events. To what extent is this cognitive model relevant to the psychopathological processes of the Chinese? A study by Yu and Seligman (2002) on depressive symptoms among children in mainland China suggested that a pessimistic cognitive style could prospectively predict depressive symptoms through an interaction effect with negative life events. They also found that a preventive program based on the CBT approach helped redress depressive symptoms in these Chinese children. Its therapeutic effect was mediated by an improvement in the cognitive style. This series of carefully designed longitudinal and experimental studies lends support to the applicability of the cognitive theory of depression to Chinese children. It also helps us to understand why CBT, which is based upon this cognitive theory, is found to be beneficial to the Chinese in outcome studies reviewed above.

The above finding on cognitive style is similar to that of a cross-cultural study of Chinese and American college students by Anderson (1999). His study found few cultural differences in the relationships between maladaptive cognitive styles, depressive symptoms, and loneliness. This study again supports the applicability of the cognitive theory of psychopathology and its CBT to the Chinese.

In another series of studies, Stewart and colleagues (Stewart et al., 2003, 2004, 2005) examined the association between cognitive variables, depressive symptoms, and suicidal ideation. They found that self-efficacy, negative cognitive errors, and hopelessness were associated with and predictive of depressive symptoms and suicidal ideation among Chinese adolescents, similar to findings in the West. However, commonalities aside, the researchers consistently found that self-efficacy was a less salient determinant of psychopathology among the Chinese than the Americans. In one of their studies, both level and structural analyses were used to examine cultural differences in predicting depression (S. X. Chen, Chan, Bond, & Stewart, 2006).The pathway from self-efficacy to depression was found to be stronger for American students, while the pathway via interpersonal relationships was equally important to both American and Hong Kong Chinese students.

This group of researchers (S. X. Chen et al., 2006; Stewart et al., 2003, 2004, 2005) have explained that, in the collectivistic Chinese culture, individuals were less attentive to their inner states and that positive feelings stemmed relatively more strongly from positive relationships established with others. Consequently, paying attention to interpersonal relationship might be more important than having a sense of mastery (i.e. self-efficacy). Albeit a promising speculation, it remains to be tested.

P. W. L. Leung and Poon (2001) found some support for the cognitive specificity model of CBT among Chinese adolescents. Depression was found to be related to sense of loss and failure, anxiety to perception of danger and threat, while aggression to a sense of injustice, as predicted from the Western literature. Attempts have also been made to examine the cognitive theory of psychopathology via an information-processing paradigm. Using cognitive experiments like the Stroop task and dot-probe paradigm, support for attentional and cognitive bias has been found among Chinese with high anxiety (X. Liu, Qian, Zhou, & Wang, 2006; X. Liu, Qian, & Zhou, 2007; Qian, Wang, & Liu, 2006; but note different findings from X. Chen, Zhong, & Qian, 2004).

Other than CBT, attention has also been paid to family therapy. Family therapy identifies a person's problems and their curative mechanisms as arising from the family context. With regard to the treatment of eating disorder, Ma and colleagues (2002) reported that etiological factors cited in Western literature, e.g. triangulation or using food refusal as a means of control, were similarly found in research on Chinese families. On the other hand, they also identified such cultural factors as filial piety and the traditionally lower social status of females in Chinese societies as providing culturally unique meanings to self-starvation. Concerning the therapeutic processes, it was found to be equally important to help the Chinese families to play out their family drama, which is an essential component in family therapy regardless of the cultures from which the families came (W. Y. Lee, 2004).

The above findings are gleaned from an etic approach in which Western constructs are researched for their relevance in a Chinese culture. They show that both common processes (e.g. cognitive bias, triangulation, etc.) and culturally specific processes (e.g. de-emphasizing self-efficacy in favor of interpersonal relationship, filial piety, etc.) exist in the development of psychopathology among the Chinese. We can also take an emic approach to examine psychopathology from a culture-specific perspective. One area that has been gaining attention is the unique relationship between shame and psychopathology among the Chinese. Shame is a self-conscious emotion which stems from other people's opinions of the self. The person who possesses shame experiences severe self-contempt, particularly in front of others (Fung, Lieber, & Leung, 2003; Qian, Liu, & Zhu, 2001). Shame is more relevant to the Chinese sociocentric culture because of its strong emphasis on interpersonal relationship. Indeed, it has been proposed that shaming is a major dimension of child-rearing practices among the Chinese (see Wang & Chang, this volume). It serves the function of inhibiting the display of inappropriate behavior, leading to adherence to moral standards against which a person evaluates their behavior (Lieber, Fung, & Leung, 2006).

Studies conducted in mainland China found that shame proneness was related to mental ill health and social anxiety (B. Li, Qian, & Ma, 2005; B. Li, Zhong, & Qian, 2003; J. Zhong, Li, & Qian, 2002). In a more recent study among Chinese college students, the relationship between parenting style and social anxiety was found to be mediated by self-esteem, personality, and shame. The latter had the highest correlation with social anxiety (B. Li, Qian, & Zhong, 2005). Interestingly, this shame-mediated relationship was not found in American college students (J. Zhong et al., 2008; see also Lee, Kam, & Bond, 2007).

These studies on shame are illuminating, as they identify a culturally specific psychopathological process among the Chinese. At the treatment level, CBT targeting shame-related cognition and behavior was found to be superior to conventional CBT in the treatment of social anxiety with a group of Chinese (Li, Qian, & Ma, 2006). This series of research implies that attention to shame can aid case conceptualization and enhance treatment of social anxiety.

There are other culturally specific risk processes for the Chinese. For instance, learning motivation to compete for high grades and academic excellence (see Hau & Ho, this volume) was found to be particularly prominent among Chinese adolescents in their development of emotional problems (Essau, Leung, Conradt, Cheng, & Wong, 2008; Greenberger, Chen, Tally, & Dong, 2000). Besides, what is considered adaptive and maladaptive can be different across cultures. Hwang and Wood (2007) noted that the self-defeating cognition was less detrimental to the mental health of the Chinese. In fact, it could have a different meaning, serving as a self-motivating force instead of an obstacle to achieving goals (see also Kwan, Hui, & McGee, this volume).

In addition, the Chinese may have a culturally preferred way of presenting problems. One example is the somatization of psychological problems, especially depression, among the Chinese (Parker, Gladstone, & Chee, 2001; but note different findings from Yen, Robins, & Lin, 2000). The focus on physical instead of psychological symptoms is possibly related to the influence of a holistic conception of illness (see Cheng et al; Ji et al., this volume) or less stigma attached to physical problems (see Mak & Chen, this volume). Despite this preference, the focus on physical symptoms may not hold up for long upon further exploration (Parker et al., 2001; see also Stewart et al., this volume). Chinese people, similar to people from different cultural groups, also experience emotional and cognitive symptoms of depression (Hwang et al., 2006).

As Lopez and Guarnaccia (2000) eloquently pointed out, studying general and cultural-specific psychopathological processes as well as their interplay is essential in studies of mental health and its treatment. Missing either process would make the picture incomplete. The above brief review illustrates the intricate interrelationship between culture, psychopathological processes, and psychotherapy in the context of the Chinese. More research is needed to be done on the psychopathological processes of the Chinese, because the findings will inevitably inform the necessary and effective ingredients of psychotherapy with the Chinese. In the meantime, the small volume of available studies helps to explain the applicability of CBT to the Chinese in terms of the commonalities of cognitive bias in the genesis of psychopathology across cultures. At the same time, attention should be drawn to such culture-specific processes as de-emphasizing self-efficacy to interpersonal relationship, shaming, and somatization when practicing therapy with the Chinese.

A paradigm shift: East meets West

Thus far, we have focused on how Western treatment modalities are being actively transplanted to the East. But the connection between Eastern and Western mentality and therapy is not one-way traffic. In the following, we review how Eastern philosophies have impacted upon the development of Western psychotherapy. One influential Asian cultural worldview is Buddhism or Zen Buddhism. Although Buddhism is not entirely of Chinese origin, this religion or way of life has spread, grown, and blossomed since its importation to China in ancient times (Kwee & Ellis, 1998).

The compatibilities between the cognitive approach to therapy (i.e. CBT) and Buddhism have been acknowledged by originators of the former. Kwee and Ellis (1998) noted that both approaches focus on the alleviation of suffering, and that suffering is considered 'illusory', dependent on the personal point of view. Besides, the two approaches emphasize personal responsibility to liberate oneself from worldly cravings. In a similar vein, Beck (2005b) concluded that CBT aimed at achieving the Buddhist objective of alleviating mental affliction by evaluating one's own thoughts, focusing on the logical.

Although Buddhism is the philosophy most compatible with CBT, one fundamental difference between the cognitive approach and Buddhism lies in the way of dealing with cognitions (Beck, 2005c; Dowd & McCleery, 2007; Kwee & Ellis, 1998). While CBT advocates active cognitive restructuring, Buddhism focuses on the acceptance of cognitions. This apparent gulf has given impetus for further development of the cognitive approach to therapy.

In the last decade, several new variants of CBT have become prominent in the West. They are mindfulness cognitive behavioral therapy (MCBT), acceptance and commitment therapy (ACT), and dialectical behavior therapy (DBT). Interestingly, these enriched forms of CBT (Hofmann & Asmundson, 2008) have explicitly incorporated elements of Buddhism in their theoretical bases (Dowd & McCleery, 2007; Hayes, 2002; Robins, 2002). DBT, for example, is premised on a dialectical philosophy, with a particular emphasis on the dialectic between the Zen principle of acceptance and the CBT principle of changing dysfunctional cognitions and behaviors (Heard & Linehan, 1994; Robins, 2002).

Realizing that a mere focus on change may backfire, arousing a sense of loss of control and invalidation when certain external adversities cannot be changed, practitioners of DBT also advocate acceptance of what is unchangeable and inevitable. Thus, in DBT, both change-oriented and acceptance-oriented strategies are considered equally crucial. This nicely delineated and balanced framework tightly interweaves the two seemingly opposing philosophical and cultural orientations: the 'change' and 'can do' optimism of the West with the acceptance or *wu wei* and *dao* of the East. Similarly, MCBT emphasizes decentering and acceptance of problems and ACT promotes acceptance of suffering and compassion. The Chinese philosophy of acceptance as their core element is self-evident, on top of its grounding in CBT.

Dowd and McCleery (2007) recognized that these enriched forms of CBT are successful in treating problems in the West that prove difficult by conventional therapy. For example, DBT has been found to successfully treat borderline personality disorder; and MCBT, recurrent depression. Recently, Hofmann and Asmundson (2008) reviewed CBT and ACT in the broader context of the literature on emotion regulation. They postulated that CBT strategies were primarily antecedent-focused, emotion-regulation strategies, as they promote cognitive appraisal of antecedent triggers of emotion. On the other hand, ACT strategies worked against those maladaptive, response-focused strategies of emotion regulation by discouraging unproductive emotion avoidance or suppression. The respective CBT and ACT stances of changing and letting go thus seem to be two sides of the same coin: they work at the different ends of our emotional processes (i.e. CBT at the initial appraisal, ACT at the response end). Yet both strategies are useful in the adaptive regulation of human emotions.

The above brief review illustrates the cross-fertilization of Eastern philosophy and Western psychotherapy. The sweet harvest thus resulting tempts us to posit that ideas of coping, which seem to originate from one culture, are not necessarily that culture bound. Particularly, while it may seem that there are irreconcilable differences between Eastern and Western philosophies of coping, characterized respectively by acceptance and change, they may actually be complementary to each other in the management of negative emotions and distress across cultures.

Although those enriched forms of psychotherapy (i.e. DBT, MCBT and ACT), which explicitly incorporate Asian cultural philosophy, are found beneficial to Westerners (e.g. see Forman, Herbert, Morita, Yeomans, & Geller, 2007; Kabat-Zinn et al., 1992; Linehan et al., 2006; S. H. Ma & Teasdale, 2004), we have as yet not seen evidence of their efficacy and effectiveness from research done in Chinese societies. Nonetheless, their initial success in the West may perhaps be a demonstration of our shared humanity between East and the West, and our residence in a 'global village'. This is underlined by the fact that an early section of this chapter has already indicated the success of Western psychotherapy with the Chinese, while this section describes the recent trend of a reverse impact, i.e. incorporating Asian cultural elements to enhance the benefits of Western psychotherapy.

Future directions

The growth rate of the research related to psychotherapy with the Chinese has been impressive in the last decade. From this large body of literature, we recognize that indigenous psychotherapy is still practiced, and, in some instances, is being revitalized, in the Chinese cultural context. Besides, Western psychotherapy has been gradually taking root among the Chinese. Supportive empirical evidence has been found for various types of therapy, particularly CBT, a result consistent with the findings noted in the West (Beck, 2005a).

Despite the impressive increase in publications, we still have difficulty drawing more than a provisional conclusion regarding psychotherapy with the Chinese. The methodological weaknesses of many studies remain a telling concern. Here are some suggestions pertaining to possible avenues of advancement in psychotherapy research with the Chinese. The first and foremost step is to ensure better and more systematic training of researchers and therapists. A larger pool of well-trained professionals is a prerequisite for and a cornerstone to effective treatment and quality research work. Second, the identification and specification of clinical dysfunctions and samples should be more precise. Third, with regard to treatment administration, operationalized treatment manuals as well as validated and standardized assessment instruments should be adopted. This can help ensure the integrity of treatment and allow replication or cross-validation by other researchers. Fourth, more diverse and sophisticated research methods should be employed. For instance, under the context of a randomized controlled trial (RCT), we can use a dismantling or constructive treatment design which aims at analyzing the separate components of a given treatment package by either dismantling or constructing it step by step. Fifth, informative but scarcely used statistical methods, such as effect size computation or meta-analysis, should be considered.

In reviewing the literature, our attention has constantly been drawn to specific and universal therapeutic elements for the Chinese. Draguns (2008) commented that cross-cultural research tends to emphasize differences. Interestingly, however, we also find many commonalities in human maladjustment and its remedies. The successful transplantation of Western therapy (e.g. CBT) to the Chinese illustrates that the cognitive approach to psychopathology and psychotherapy is by and large generic in comprehending and treating human mind and behavior. Furthermore, the enrichment of Western therapy with Eastern philosophy shows that apparently unique cultural elements can be utilized to help people from around the world, underlining the universality of psychotherapy. All seem to suggest a degree of underlying shared humanity among people from different cultures.

Such an understanding of psychopathology and psychotherapy has important implications for the indigenization of psychotherapy, which is a controversial topic among Chinese researchers and practitioners (Hodges & Oei, 2007; see also Smith, this volume). According to Shek (1999), indigenization should be grounded on evidence showing that Western theories of psychopathology and therapy are neither valid nor suitable for the Chinese, as well as the proof that the indigenous counterparts are more valid and suitable for the Chinese. Based on our present review, we cannot find strong support for these claims. Western theories of psychopathology and psychotherapy (e.g. the cognitive model of psychopathology and its CBT) are found to be applicable to the Chinese. Thus, there seems to be no pressing need to create totally brand new forms of indigenous therapy.

On the other hand, the above does not mean that current psychotherapy will not require some fine-tuning when practiced with the Chinese. Clinicians dealing with the Chinese are encouraged to equip themselves with greater cultural competence (Tseng, 1999). For example, in the above review of psychopathological processes, we are alerted to some specific processes of the Chinese, including de-emphasizing self-efficacy relative to interpersonal relationship, shaming, and somatization, that we should attend to when practicing therapy with the Chinese.

Only with solid knowledge of both culture and psychotherapy can clinicians appreciate the link between universal, cultural, and individual factors in a therapeutic encounter. To successfully handle this complex network, it is imperative for therapists to exercise 'dynamic sizing', the essence of which is flexibility: knowing when to generalize cultural knowledge and when to individualize treatment for the particular circumstance of an individual (S. Sue, 1998; see also Hwang, 2006). This balanced approach can prevent the development of rigid overgeneralization and stereotyping of members from any ethnic group. This cautionary note is particularly important for psychotherapy with the Chinese, given the presence of a wide range of subcultures and the steady modernization of traditional values over the years (W. Y. Lee, 2002; 2004).

In their previous review, P. W. L. Leung and Lee (1996) suggested that due to the advancement of mass communication and ease in travel, all cultures will become more pluralistic, and thus a multitude of different forms of psychotherapy will be needed to address this diversity. As predicted, in the past decade, the development in psychotherapy has embraced this trend of diversification. Traditional, contemporary, Eastern, and Western forms of psychotherapy all coexist and are practiced with the Chinese. There is also a parallel trend of coalescence to form new variants of psychotherapy (e.g. CTCP, DBT, MCBT and ACT). Wisdom from diverse cultures has been distilled, blended, and drawn to solve problems of living in this 'global village' of our modern world. In a sense, with better understanding of the universality of human maladjustment and its treatment, the cultural frontiers in the landscape of psychotherapy have been blurring. In the coming decade, we look forward to vigorous scientific scrutiny on these emerging parallel trends of diversification and coalescence of psychotherapies.

It is only fitting to end this chapter by recalling the core Chinese philosophy of *yin* and *yang*, which espouses balance and integration. Drawing upon this analogy, the two apparently polar forces of coalescence and diversification in the development of psychotherapy may prompt a synergetic integration that brings together the idiosyncratic and shared characteristics of humanity and their remedy (i.e. psychotherapy) between the East and the West. The originally narrow focus of our chapter on psychotherapy with the Chinese somehow seems to be able to inform a broader picture of what psychotherapy really is.

References

Akutsu, P. D., Lin, C. H., & Zane, N. W. (1990). Predictors of utilization intent of counseling among Chinese and white students: A test of the proximal-distal model. *Journal of Counseling Psychology, 37*, 445–452.

Anderson, C. A. (1999). Attributional style, depression, and loneliness: A cross-cultural comparison of American and Chinese students. *Personality and Social Psychology Bulletin, 25*, 482–499.

Au, A., Chan, F., Li, K., Leung, P., Li, P., & Chan, J. (2003). Cognitive-behavioral group treatment program for adults with epilepsy in Hong Kong. *Epilepsy & Behavior, 4*, 441–446.

Beck, A. T. (2005a). The current state of cognitive therapy. *Archives of General Psychiatry, 62*, 953–959.

Beck, A. T. (2005b, spring). From the president: Buddhism and cognitive therapy. *Beck Institute Newsletter.* Retrieved April 14, 2008 from http://www.beckinstitute.org/Library/InfoManage/Guide.asp?FolderID=227&SessionID={7D31F2A5-4B9B-4675-8EB7-9613A9AE45E5}.

Beck, A. T. (2005c, Fall). From the president: Reflections on my public dialog with the Dalai Lama. *Beck Institute Newsletter.* Retrieved April 14, 2008 from http://www.beckinstitute.org/Library/InfoManage/Guide.asp?FolderID=238&SessionID={7D31F2A5-4B9B-4675-8EB7-9613A9AE45E5}

Bond, M. H. (1993). Emotions and their expression in Chinese culture. *Journal of Nonverbal Behavior, 17*, 245–262.

Bond, M. H. (1996). Chinese values. In M. H. Bond (ed.), *The handbook of Chinese psychology* (pp. 208–226). Hong Kong: Oxford University Press.

Cai, J. (2007). Observation of structural family therapy combined with Clomipramine in treating adolescent obsessive-compulsive disorder. *China Journal of Health Psychology, 15*, 831–833. (in Chinese)

Chambless, D. L., Barker, M. J., Baucom, D. H., Beutler, L. E., Calhoun, K. S., Crits-Christoph, P., et al. (1998). Update on empirically validated therapies, II. *The Clinical Psychologist, 51*, 3–16.

Chambless, D. L. & Hollon, S. D. (1998). Defining empirically supported therapies. *Journal of Consulting and Clinical Psychology, 66*, 7–18.

Chan, I., Kong, P., Leung, P., Au, A., Li, P., Chung, R., et al. (2005). Cognitive-behavioral group program for Chinese heterosexual HIV-infected men in Hong Kong. *Patient Education and Counseling, 56*, 78–84.

Chan, Y. M., Lee, P. W. H., Fong, D. Y. T., Fung, A. S. M., Wu, L. Y. F., Choi, A. Y. Y., et al. (2005). Effect of individual psychological intervention in Chinese women with gynecologic malignancy: A randomized controlled trial. *Journal of Clinical Oncology, 23*, 4913–4924.

Chang, S. C. & Dong-Shick, R. (2005). Buddhist teaching: Relation to healing. In W. Tseng, S. C. Chang, & M. Nishizono (eds), *Asian culture and psychotherapy: Implications for East and West.* (pp. 157–165). Honolulu, HI: University of Hawaii Press.

Chang, D. F. & Kleinman, A. (2002). Growing pains: Mental health care in a developing China. *Yale–China Health Studies Journal, 1*, 85–89.

Chang, D. F., Tong, H., Shi, Q., & Zeng, Q. (2005). Letting a hundred flowers bloom: Counseling and psychotherapy in the People's Republic of China. *Journal of Mental Health Counseling, 27*, 104–116.

Chen, H., Cui, Z., & Wang, Q. (2007). Paroxitine plus cognitive behavior therapy in treatment of depression associated with anxiety. *BMU Journal, 30*, 274–275. (in Chinese)

Chen, P. H. & Tsai, S. L. (1998). Review and vision of Taiwanese counseling process research in the past decade. In Chinese Guidance Association (ed.), *The great trends of guidance and counseling* (pp. 123–164). Taipei, Taiwan: Psychological Publishing. (in Chinese)

Chen, S. & Li, S. (2006). Cognitive and insight therapy for fetishism. *Chinese Journal of Clinical Rehabilitation, 10*, 161–163. (in Chinese)

Chen, S. W. H. & Davenport, D. S. (2005). Cognitive-behavioral therapy with Chinese American clients: Cautions and modifications. *Psychotherapy: Theory, Research, Practice, Training, 42*, 101–110.

Chen, S. X., Chan, W., Bond, M. H., & Stewart, S. M. (2006). The effects of self-efficacy and relationship harmony on depression across cultures: Applying level-oriented and structure-oriented analyses. *Journal of Cross Cultural Psychology, 37*, 643–658.

Chen, T., Lu, R., Chang, A., Chu, D., & Chou, K. (2006). The evaluation of cognitive-behavioral group therapy on patient depression and self-esteem. *Archives of Psychiatric Nursing, 20*, 3–11.

Chen, X., Zhong, J., & Qian, M. (2004). Attentional bias in social anxious individuals. *Chinese Mental Health Journal, 18*, 846–849. (in Chinese)

Cheung, G. & Chan, C. (2002). The Satir model and cultural sensitivity: A Hong Kong reflection. *Contemporary Family Therapy, 24*, 199–215.

Cheung, L., Callaghan, P., & Chang, A. M. (2003). A controlled trial of psycho-educational interventions in preparing Chinese women for elective hysterectomy. *International Journal of Nursing Studies, 40*, 207–216.

Dai, Y., Zhang, S., Yamamoto, J., Ao, M., Belin, T. R., Cheung, F., et al. (1999). Cognitive behavioral therapy of minor depressive symptoms in elderly Chinese Americans: A pilot study. *Community Mental Health Journal, 35*, 537–542.

Dowd, T. & McCleery, A. (2007). Elements of Buddhist philosophy in cognitive psychotherapy: The role of cultural specifics and universals. *Journal of Cognitive and Behavioral Psychotherapies, 7*, 67–79.

Draguns, J. G. (1975). Resocialization into culture: The complexities of taking a worldwide view of psychotherapy. In R. W. Brislin, S. Bochner, & W. J. Lonner (eds), *Cross-cultural perspectives on learning* (pp. 273–289). Beverly Hills, CA: Sage.

Draguns, J. G. (2004). From speculation through description toward investigation: A prospective glimpse at cultural research in psychotherapy. In U. P. Gielen, J. M. Fish, & J. G. Draguns (eds), *Handbook of culture, therapy, and healing* (pp. 369–387). Mahwah, NJ: Erlbaum.

Draguns, J. G. (2008). Universal and cultural threads in counseling individuals. In P. B. Pedersen, J. G. Draguns, W. J. Lonner, & J. E. Trimble (eds), *Counseling across cultures* (6th edn, pp. 21–36). Los Angeles, CA: Sage.

Edzard, E., Rand, J. I., & Stevinson, C. (1998). Complementary therapies for depression. *Archives of General Psychiatry, 55,* 1026–1032.

Essau, C. A., Leung, P. W. L., Conradt, J., Cheng, H., & Wong, T. (2008). Anxiety symptoms in Chinese and German adolescents: Their relationship with early learning experiences, perfectionism and learning motivation. *Depression and Anxiety, 25,* 801–810.

Feng, D., Han, Z., Gan, l., & Liu, J. (2003). Treatment effectiveness of Paroxetine and cognitive therapy for generalized anxiety disorder. *Guangdong Medical Journal, 24,* 407–408. (in Chinese)

Flaws, B. & Lake, J. (2001). *Chinese medical psychiatry: A textbook & clinical manual.* Boulder, CO: Blue Poppy Press.

Foo, K. H. & Kazantzis, N. (2007). Integrating homework assignments based on culture: Working with Chinese patients. *Cognitive and Behavioral Practice, 14,* 333–340.

Forman, E. M., Herbert, J. D., Morita, E., Yeomans, P. D., Geller, P. A. (2007). A randomized controlled effectiveness trial of acceptance and commitment therapy and cognitive therapy for anxiety and depression. *Behavior Modification, 31,* 772 –799.

Fujino, D. C., Okazaki, S., & Young, K. (1994). Asian-American women in the mental health system: An examination of ethnic and gender match between therapist and client. *Journal of Community Psychology, 22,* 164–176.

Fung, H., Lieber, E., & Leung, P. W. L. (2003). Parental beliefs about shame and moral socialization in Taiwan, Hong Kong, and the United States. In K. S. Yang, K. K. Hwang, P. B. Pederson, & I. Daibo (eds), *Progress in Asian social psychology: Conceptual and empirical contributions* (pp. 83–109). Westport, CT: Praeger.

Goh, M., Xie, B., Wahl, K. H., Zhong, G., Lian, F., & Romano, J. L. (2007). Chinese students' attitude towards seeking professional psychological help. *International Journal for the Advancement of Counseling, 29,* 187–202.

Greenberger, E., Chen, C., Tally, S. T., & Dong, Q. (2000). Family, peer, and individual correlates of depressive symptomatology among US and Chinese adolescents. *Journal of Consulting and Clinical Psychology, 68,* 209–219.

Griner, D. & Smith, T. B. (2006). Culturally adapted mental health interventions: A meta-analytical review. *Psychotherapy: Theory, Research, Practice, Training, 43,* 531–548.

Guan, X. & Hu, S. (2007). A comparative study of Chinese medical psychotherapy plus *Caihushugansan* and hypnotherapy for neurosis. *Beijing Journal of Traditional Chinese Medicine, 26,* 649–650. (in Chinese)

Guo, K. F., Guo, S., Yang, W., & Zhang, J. (2004). Psychotherapy and drug treatment for anxiety neurosis: A randomized control study. *Chinese Journal of Clinical Rehabilitation, 8,* 412–413. (in Chinese)

Hayes, S. C. (2002). Buddhism and acceptance and commitment therapy. *Cognitive and Behavioral Practice, 9,* 58–66.

He, Y. & Li, C. (2007). Morita therapy for schizophrenia. *Cochrane Database Systematic Reviews, 1.* doi: 10.1002/14651858.CD006346.

Heard, H. L. & Linehan, M. M. (1994). Dialectical behavior therapy: An integrative approach to the treatment of borderline personality disorder. *Journal of Psychotherapy Integration, 4,* 55–82.

Ho, T. P., Chow, V., Fung, C., Leung, K., Chiu, K. Y., Yu, G., et al. (1999). Parent management training in a Chinese population: Application and outcome. *Journal of the American Academy of Child and Adolescent Psychiatry, 38,* 1165–1172.

Ho, T. P. & Chung, S. Y. (1996). Help-seeking behaviors among child psychiatric clinic attenders in Hong Kong. *Social Psychiatry and Psychiatric Epidemiology, 31,* 292–298.

Hodges, J. & Oei, T. P. S. (2007). Would Confucius benefit from psychotherapy? The compatibility of cognitive behavior therapy and Chinese values. *Behavior Research and Therapy, 45,* 901–914.

Hofmann, S. G. & Asmundson, G. J. G. (2008). Acceptance and mindfulness-based therapy: New wave or old hat? *Clinical Psychology Review, 28,* 1–16.

Hofstede, G. H. (2001). *Culture's consequences: Comparing values, behaviors, institutions, and organizations across nations* (2nd edn). Thousand Oaks, CA: Sage.

Huang, H. L., Chao, C. C., Tu, C. C., & Yang, P. C. (2003). Behavioral parent training for Taiwanese parents of children with attention-deficit/hyperactivity disorder. *Psychiatry and Clinical Neurosciences, 57,* 275–281.

Huang, X., Zhang, Y., & Yang, D. (2001). Chinese Taoist cognitive therapy in prevention of mental health problems of college students. *Chinese Mental Health Journal, 15,* 243–246. (in Chinese)

Hwang, W. C. (2006). The psychotherapy adaptation and modification framework (PAMF): Application to Asian Americans. *American Psychologist, 61,* 702–715.

Hwang, W. C. & Wood, J. J. (2007). Being culturally sensitive is not the same as being culturally competent. *Pragmatic Case Studies in Psychotherapy, 3,* 44–50. Retrieved March 5, 2008, from http://pcsp.libraries.rutgers.edu/index.php/pcsp/article/viewArticle/906

Hwang, W. C., Wood, J. J., Lin, K. M., & Cheung, F. (2006). Cognitive-behavioral therapy with Chinese Americans: Research, theory, and clinical practice. *Cognitive and Behavioral Practice, 13,* 293–303.

Jacobson, N. S. & Christensen, A. (1996). Studying the effectiveness of psychotherapy: How well can clinical trials do the job? *American Psychologist, 51,* 1031–1039.

Jiang, L., Xu, Q., Zheng, C., & Zhou, Y. (2002). Clinical observation of Chinese medical psychotherapy for apoplexy with depression in 30 cases. *Shanghai Journal of Traditional Chinese Medicine, 8*, 17–18. (in Chinese)

Jilek, W. G. (1993). Traditional medicine relevant to psychiatry. In N. Sartorius, G. De Girolamo, G. Andrews, G. A. German, & L. Eisenberg (eds), *Treatment of mental disorders: A review of effectiveness* (pp. 341–390). Washington, DC: American Psychiatric Press.

Kabt-Zinn, J., Massion A. O., Kristeller, J., Peterson, L. G., Fletcher, K. E., Pbert, L., et al. (1992). Effectiveness of a meditation-based stress reduction program in the treatment of anxiety disorders. *American Journal of Psychiatry, 149*, 936–943.

Kim, B. S. K. (2007). Adherence to Asian and European American cultural values and attitudes toward seeking professional psychological help among Asian American college students. *Journal of Counseling Psychology, 54*, 474–480.

Kim, B. S. K. & Atkinson, D. R. (2002). Asian American client adherence to Asian cultural values, counselor expression of cultural values, counselor ethnicity, and career counseling process. *Journal of Counseling Psychology, 49*, 3–13.

Kim, B. S. K., Li, L. C., & Liang, C. T. (2002). Effects of Asian-American client adherence to asian cultural values, session goal, and counselor emphasis of client expression on career counseling process. *Journal of Counseling Psychology, 49*, 342–354.

Kim, B. S. K. & Omizo, M. M. (2003). Asian cultural values, attitudes toward seeking professional psychological help, and willingness to see a counselor. *Counseling Psychologist, 31*, 343–361.

Kleinman, A. & Sung, L. H. (1979). Why do indigenous practitioners successfully heal? *Social Science and Medicine, 13B*, 7–26.

Koltko-Rivera, M. E. (2004). The psychology of worldviews. *Review of General Psychology, 8*, 3–58.

Kopta, S. M., Lueger, R. J., Saunders, S. M., & Howard, K. I. (1999). Individual psychotherapy outcome and process research: Challenges leading to greater turmoil or a positive transition? *Annual Review of Psychology, 50*, 441–469.

Kua, E. H., Chew, P. H., & Ko, S. M. (1993). Spirit possession and healing among Chinese psychiatric patients. *Acta Psychiatrica Scandinavica, 88*, 447–450.

Kung, W. W. (2004). Cultural and practical barriers to seeking mental health treatment for Chinese Americans. *Journal of Community Psychology, 32*, 27–43.

Kwee, M. & Ellis, A. (1998). The interface between Rational Emotive Behavior Therapy (REBT) and Zen. *Journal of Rational Emotive and Cognitive Behavior Therapy, 16*, 5–43.

Lambert, M. J. & Archer, A. (2006). Research findings on the effects of psychotherapy and their implications for practice. In R. J. Sternberg, C. D. Goodheart, & A. E. Kazdin (eds), *Evidence-based psychotherapy: Where practice and research meet* (pp. 111–130). Washington, DC: American Psychological Association.

Lee, B. & Bishop, G. D. (2001). Chinese clients' belief systems about psychological problems in Singapore. *Counseling Psychology Quarterly, 14*, 219–240.

Lee, W. Y. (2002). One therapist, four cultures: Working with families in greater China. *Journal of Family Therapy, 24*, 258–275.

Lee, W. Y. (2004). Three 'depressed families' in transitional Beijing. *Journal of Family Psychotherapy, 15*, 57–71.

Lee, Y. Y., Kam, C. C. S., & Bond, M. H. (2007). Predicting emotional reactions after being harmed by another. *Asian Journal of Social Psychology, 10*, 85–92.

Leong, F. T. L., Chang, D. F., & Lee, S. (2007). Counseling and psychotherapy with Asian Americans: Process and outcomes. In A. G. Inman, L. H. Yang, F. T. L. Leong, A. Ebreo, & L. Kinoshita (eds), *Handbook of Asian American psychology* (2nd edn, pp. 429–447). Thousand Oaks, CA: Sage.

Leong, F. T. L. & Lau, A. S. L. (2001). Barriers to providing effective mental health services to Asian Americans. *Mental Health Services Research, 3*, 201–214.

Leong, F. T. L. & Lee, S. (2006). A cultural accommodation model for cross-cultural psychotherapy: Illustrated with the case of Asian Americans. *Psychotherapy: Theory, Research, Practice, Training, 43*, 410–423.

Leung, C., Sanders, M. R., Leung, S., Mak, R., & Lau, J. (2003). An outcome evaluation of the implementation of the Triple P-Positive Parenting Program in Hong Kong. *Family Process, 42*, 531–544.

Leung, P. W. L. & Lee, P. W. H. (1996). Psychotherapy with the Chinese. *The handbook of Chinese psychology* (pp. 441–456). Hong Kong: Oxford University Press.

Leung, P. W. L. & Poon, M. W. L. (2001). Dysfunctional schemas and cognitive distortions in psychopathology: A test of the specificity hypothesis. *Journal of Child Psychology and Psychiatry, 42*, 755–765.

Leung, P. W. L. & Sung-Chan, P. P. L. (2002). Cultural values and choice of strategic move in therapy: A case of low back pain in a Chinese woman. *Clinical Case Studies, 1*, 342–352.

Leung, S. A., Guo, L., & Lam, M. P. (2000). The development of counseling psychology in higher educational institutions in China: Present conditions and needs, future challenges. *Counseling Psychologist, 28*, 81–99.

Li, B., Qian, M., & Ma, C. (2005). The influential effect of undergraduates' shame proness on social anxiety: A longitudinal study. *Chinese Journal of Clinical Psychology, 13*, 156–158. (in Chinese)

Li, B., Qian, M., & Ma, C. (2006). Group therapy on social anxiety of college students. *Chinese Mental Health Journal, 20*, 348–349. (in Chinese)

Li, B., Qian, M., & Zhong, J. (2005). Undergraduates' social anxiety: A shame proneness model. *Chinese Mental Health Journal, 19*, 304–306. (in Chinese)

Li, B., Zhong, J., & Qian, M. (2003). Regression analysis on social anxiety proneness among college students. *Chinese Mental Health Journal, 17*, 109–112. (in Chinese)

Li, F. & Wang, M. (1994). A behavioral training program for chronic schizophrenic patients: A three month randomized controlled trial in Beijing. *British Journal of Psychiatry, 165*(suppl. 24), 32–37.

Li, L. C. & Kim, B. S. K. (2004). Effects of counseling style and client adherence to Asian cultural values on counseling process with Asian American college students. *Journal of Counseling Psychology, 51*, 158–167.

Li, Q., Yue, G., & Qian, L. (2007). Effects of Zhong Youbin's psychoanalytic therapy in obsessive-compulsive disorders. *China Journal of Health Psychology, 15*, 596–597. (in Chinese)

Li, Y., Wang, J., & Ma, J. (2006). A controlled clinical trial of Citalopram and Citalopram combined with family therapy in the treatment of anorexia nervosa. *Shanghai Archives of Psychiatry, 18*, 158–160. (in Chinese)

Li, Z. (2006). Research on psychotherapy in traditional Chinese medicine. *Journal of Shanghai Jiaotong University (Medical Science), 26*, 1182–1185. (in Chinese)

Li, Z. & Arthur, D. (2005). Family education for people with schizophrenia in Beijing, China: Randomized controlled trial. *British Journal of Psychiatry, 187*, 339–345.

Li, Z. & Chen, X. (2007). Exploring behavior therapy in ancient medical case records. *Shanghai Archives of Psychiatry, 19*, 118–121. (in Chinese)

Lieber, E., Fung, H., & Leung, P. W. L. (2006). Chinese child-rearing beliefs: Key dimensions and contributions to the development of culture-appropriate assessment. *Asian Journal of Social Psychology, 9*, 140–147.

Lin, Y. N. (2002). The application of cognitive-behavioral therapy to counseling Chinese. *American Journal of Psychotherapy, 56*, 46–58.

Linehan, M. M., Comtois, K. A., Murray, A. M., Brown, M. Z., Gallop, R. J., Heard, H. L., et al. (2006). Two-year randomized trial and follow-up of Dialectical Behavior Therapy vs. Therapy by experts for suicidal behaviors and borderline personality disorder. *Archives of General Psychiatry, 63*, 757–766.

Liu, H. & Ma, Z. (2002). A comparative study of cognitive insight therapy and medication on social anxiety. *Health Psychology Journal, 10*, 265–266. (in Chinese)

Liu, X., Qian, M., & Zhou, X. (2007). Patterns of attentional bias of highly anxious individuals by repeating the occasions of word stimulus. *Chinese Mental Health Journal, 21*, 769–772. (in Chinese)

Liu, X., Qian, M., Zhou, X., & Wang, A. (2006). Repeating the stimulus exposure to investigate what happens after initial selective attention to threatening pictures. *Personality and Individual Differences, 40*, 1007–1016.

Long, J., Wang, Y., Liu, X., & Zhang, h. (2005). Efficacy of Citalopram combined with cognitive therapy in treatment of the post-stroke depression patients. *Chinese Journal of Health Psychology, 13*, 302–303. (in Chinese)

Lopez, S. R. & Guarnaccia, P. J. J. (2000). Cultural psychopathology: Uncovering the social world of mental illness. *Annual Review of Psychology, 51*, 571–598.

Ma, J. L. C. (2005). Family treatment for a Chinese family with an adolescent suffering from anorexia nervosa: A case study. *The Family Journal, 13*, 19–26.

Ma, J. L. C. (2007). Journey of acculturation: Developing a therapeutic alliance with Chinese adolescents suffering from eating disorders in Shenzhen, china. *Journal of Family Therapy, 29*, 389–402.

Ma, J. L. C., Chow, M. Y. M., Lee, S., & Lai, K. (2002). Family meaning of self-starvation: Themes discerned in family treatment in Hong Kong. *Journal of Family Therapy, 24*, 57–71.

Ma, S. H. & Teasdale, J. D. (2004). Mindfulness-Based Cognitive Therapy for depression: Replication and exploration of differential relapse prevention effects. *Journal of Consulting and Clinical Psychology, 72*, 31–40.

Mak, G. K. L., Li, F. W. S., & Lee, P. W. H. (2007). A pilot study on psychological interventions with Chinese young adults with schizophrenia. *Hong Kong Journal of Psychiatry, 17*, 17–23.

Mei, Z. & Meng, F. (2003). The structural family therapy of anorexia nervosa: A case report. *Shanghai Archives of Psychiatry, 15*, 30–32. (in Chinese)

Molassiotis, A., Callaghan, P., Twinn, S. F., Lam, S. W., Chung, W. Y., & Li, C. K. (2002). A pilot study of the effects of cognitive-behavioral group therapy and peer support/counseling in decreasing psychologic distress and improving quality of life in Chinese patients with symptomatic HIV disease. *AIDS Patient Care and STDs, 16*, 83–96.

Ng, T. P., Fones, C. S. L., & Kua, E. H. (2003). Preference, need and utilization of mental health services, Singapore National Mental Health Survey. *Australian and New Zealand Journal of Psychiatry, 37*, 613–619.

Niu, H., Xie, Y., & Pei, G. (2006). Sertraline plus psychotherapy in the treatment of comorbid depression and anxiety. *Journal of Clinical Psychosomatic Disease, 12*, 250–251. (in Chinese)

Parker, G., Gladstone, G., & Chee, K. T. (2001). Depression in the planet's largest ethnic group: The Chinese. *American Journal of Psychiatry, 158*, 857–864.

Paul, G. L. (1967). Outcome research in psychotherapy. *Journal of Consulting Psychology, 31*, 109–118.

Pedersen, P. B. (ed.). (1999). *Multiculturalism as a fourth force.* Philadelphia, PA: Brunner/Mazel.

Poon, M. W. L. (2007). The value of using hypnosis in helping an adult survivor of childhood sexual abuse. *Contemporary Hypnosis, 24*, 30–37.

Qian, M., Liu, X., & Zhu, R. (2001). Phenomenological research of shame among college students. *Chinese Mental Health Journal, 15*, 73–75. (in Chinese)

Qian, M., Smith, C. W., Chen, Z., & Xia, G. (2001). Psychotherapy in China: A review of its history and contemporary directions. *International Journal of Mental Health, 30*, 49–68.

Qian, M., Wang, C., & Liu, X. (2006). The attentional bias of different threatening words among high social anxiety subjects. *Psychological Science, 29*, 1296–1299. (in Chinese)

Ran, M., Xiang, M., Chan, C. L. W., Leff, J., Simpson, P., Huang, M. S., et al. (2003). Effectiveness of psychoeducational intervention for rural Chinese families experiencing schizophrenia. A randomized controlled trial. *Social Psychiatry and Psychiatric Epidemiology, 38*, 69–75.

Ran, M., Xiang, M., Li, S., Shan, Y., Huang, M., Li, S., et al. (2003). Prevalence and course of schizophrenia in a Chinese rural area. *Australia and New Zealand Journal of Psychiatry, 37*, 452–457.

Rathbone, J., Zhang, L., Zhang, M., Xia, J., Liu, X., Yang, Y., et al. (2007). Chinese herbal medicine for schizophrenia: Cochrane systematic review of randomized trials. *British Journal of Psychiatry, 190*, 379–384.

Ren, X. (2003). Fluoxetine combined with cognitive behavior therapy in treatment of obsessive-compulsive disorder. *Journal of Clinical Psychological Medicine, 13*, 338–339. (in Chinese)

Robins, C. J. (2002). Zen principles and mindfulness practice in dialectical behavior therapy. *Cognitive and Behavioral Practice, 9*, 50–57.

Rosenthal, R. (1984). *Meta-analytic procedures for social research.* Beverly Hills, CA: Sage.

Shek, D. T. L. (1999). The development of counseling in four Asian communities: A critical review of the review papers. *Asian Journal of Counseling, 6*, 97–114.

Shen, E. K., Alden, L. E., Sochting, I., & Tsang, P. (2006). Clinical observations of a Cantonese cognitive-behavioral treatment program for Chinese immigrants. *Psychotherapy: Theory, Research, Practice, Training, 43*, 518–530.

Sim, T. (2005). Familiar yet strange: Involving family members in adolescent drug rehabilitation in a Chinese context. *Journal of Systematic Therapies, 24*, 90–103.

So, J. K. (2005). Traditional and cultural healing among the Chinese. In R. Moodley & W. West (eds), *Integrating traditional healing practices into counseling and psychotherapy* (pp. 100–111). Thousand Oaks, CA: Sage.

So, C. Y. C., Leung, P. W. L., & Hung, S. (2008). Treatment effectiveness of combined medication/behavioral treatment with Chinese ADHD children in routine practice. *Behavior Research and Therapy, 46*, 983–992.

Stewart, S. M., Byrne, B. M., Lee, P. W. H., Ho, L. M., Kennard, B. D., Hughes, C., et al. (2003). Personal versus interpersonal contributions to depressive symptoms among Hong Kong adolescents. *International Journal of Psychology, 38*, 160–169.

Stewart, S. M., Kennard, B. D., Lee, P. W. H., Hughes, C. W., Mayes, T. L., Emslie, G. J., et al. (2004). A cross-cultural investigation of cognitions and depressive symptoms in adolescents. *Journal of Abnormal Psychology, 113*, 248–257.

Stewart, S. M., Kennard, B. D., Lee, P. W. H., Mayes, T., Hughes, C., & Emslie, G. (2005). Hopelessness and suicidal ideation among adolescents in two cultures. *Journal of Child Psychology and Psychiatry, 46*, 364–372.

Su, Q., Wang, X., Su, L., Li, G., Chen, J., & Ren, G. (2006). A study on cognitive therapy for adolescent patients with first-onset major depressive disorder. *Chinese Journal of Behavioral Medical Science, 15*, 1079–1080. (in Chinese)

Su, H., Wang, J. T., & Liu, X. F. (2005). Clinical application of the cognitive exposure therapy to the acute stress disorder. *Chinese Mental Health Journal, 19*, 97–99. (in Chinese)

Sue, D. W. & Sue, D. (2003). *Counseling the culturally diverse: Theory and practice* (4th edn). New York: Wiley.

Sue, S. (1998). In search of cultural competence in psychotherapy and counseling. *American Psychologist, 53*, 440–448.

Sue, S., Fujino, D. C., Hu, L. T., Takeuchi, D. T., & Zane, N. W. S. (1991). Community mental health services for ethnic minority groups: A test of the cultural responsiveness hypothesis. *Journal of Consulting and Clinical Psychology, 59*, 533–540.

Tang, C. S. K. (2007). Culturally relevant meanings and their implications on therapy for traumatic grief: Lessons learned from a Chinese female client and her fortune-teller. In B. Drozdek & J. Wilson (eds), *Voices of trauma: Treating psychological trauma across culture* (pp. 127–149). New York: Springer.

Tsang, H. W. H., Fung, K. M. T., Chan, A. S. M., Lee, G., & Chan, F. (2006). Effect of a *qi gong* exercise programme on elderly with depression. *International Journal of Geriatric Psychiatry, 21*, 890–897.

Tseng, W. (1999). Culture and psychotherapy: Review and practical guidelines. *Transcultural Psychiatry, 36*, 131–179.

Tseng, W., Lee, S., & Lu, Q. (2005). The historical trends of psychotherapy in China: Cultural review. In W. Tseng, S. C. Chang, & M. Nishizono (eds), *Asian culture and psychotherapy: Implications for east and west* (pp. 249–279). Honolulu, HI: University of Hawaii Press.

Wang, J. & Xu, J. (2005). Effects of Taoist cognitive psychotherapy in the treatment of post-stroke depression. *Chinese Journal of Behavioral Medical Science, 14*, 490–491,521. (in Chinese)

Wang, P. S., Aguilar Gaxiola, S., Alonso, J., Angermeyer, M. C., Borges, G., Bromet, E. J., et al. (2007). Use of mental health services for anxiety, mood, and substance disorders in 17 countries in the WHO world mental health surveys. *Lancet, 370*, 841–850.

Wei, M. & Heppner, P. P. (2005). Counselor and client predictors of the initial working alliance: A replication and extension to Taiwanese client–counselor dyads. *Counseling Psychologist, 33*, 51–71.

Wen, J. (1998). Folk belief, illness behavior and mental health in Taiwan. *Chang Gung Medical Journal, 21*, 1–12.

Wong, D. F. K. & Sun, S. Y. K. (2006). A preliminary study of the efficacy of group cognitive-behavioral therapy for people with social anxiety in Hong Kong. *Hong Kong Journal of Psychiatry, 16*, 50–56.

Wong, D. F. K., Chau, P., Kwok, A., & Kwan, J. (2007). Cognitive-behavioral treatment groups for people with chronic physical illness in Hong Kong: Reflections on a culturally attuned model. *International Journal of Group Psychotherapy, 57*, 367–385.

Wu, K. K. (2002). Use of eye movement desensitization and reprocessing for treating post-traumatic stress disorder after a motor vehicle accident. *Hong Kong Journal of Psychiatry, 12*, 20–24.

Xiang, H. & Zuang, G. (2006). Review and reflection of indigenous psychotherapy in China. *Medicine and Philosophy, 27*, 64–65. (in Chinese)

Xiang, Y., Weng, Y., Li, W., Gao, l., Chen, G., Xie, L., et al. (2007). Efficacy of the community re-entry module for patients with schizophrenia in Beijing, China: Outcome at 2-year follow-up. *British Journal of Psychiatry, 190*, 49–56.

Xu, C., Wang, J., Miao, D., & Ouyang, L. (2002). Comparison of psychotherapy literature increase in China and abroad. *Journal of the Fourth Military Medical University, 25*, 1908–1912. (in Chinese)

Xu, S. H. (1996). The concept of mind and body in Chinese medicine and its implication for psychotherapy. In W. Tseng (ed.), *Chinese psychology and psychotherapy* (pp. 391–415). Taipei, Taiwan: Gui Guan Tu Shu Gu Fen You Xian Gong Si. (in Chinese)

Yan, H. (2005). Confucian thought: Implications for psychotherapy. In W. Tseng, S. C. Chang, & M. Nishizono (eds), *Asian culture and psychotherapy: Implications for East and West* (pp. 129–141). Honolulu, HI: University of Hawaii Press.

Yang, F. R., Zhu, S. L., & Luo, W. F. (2005). Comparative study of Solution-Focused Brief Therapy (SFBT) combined with Paroxetine in the treatment of obsessive-compulsive disorder. *Chinese Mental Health Journal, 19*, 288–290. (in Chinese)

Yang, J., Zhao, L., & Mai, X. (2005). A comparative study of Taoist cognitive psychotherapy from China and Mianserin in the treatment of depression in late life. *Chinese Journal of Mental and Nervous Diseases, 31*, 333–335. (in Chinese)

Yang, Q. (2006). An investigation of behavior therapy in Chinese medical psychotherapy. *Journal of Guangzhou University of Traditional Chinese Medicine, 23*, 189–192. (in Chinese)

Yen, S., Robins, C. J., & Lin, N. (2000). A cross-cultural comparison of depressive symptoms manifestation: China and the United States. *Journal of Consulting and Clinical Psychology, 68*, 993–999.

Yeung, W. H. & Lee, E. (1997). Chinese Buddhism: Its implications for counseling. In E. Lee (ed.), *Working with Asian Americans: A guide for clinicians* (pp. 452–476). New York: Guilford.

Young, D., Tseng, W., & Zhou, L. (2005). Daoist philosophy: Application in psychotherapy. In W. Tseng, S. C. Chang, & M. Nishizono (eds), *Asian culture and psychotherapy: Implications for East and West* (pp. 142–155). Honolulu, HI: University of Hawaii Press.

Yu, D. L. & Seligman, M. E. P. (2002). Preventing depressive symptoms in Chinese children. *Prevention & Treatment, 5*.

Yue, X. & Yan, F. (2006). The development of psychological counseling in China mainland: Problems and countermeasures. *International Chinese Application Psychology Journal, 3*, 193–199. (in Chinese)

Zane, N., Sue, S., Chang, J., Huang, L., Huang, J., Lowe, S., et al. (2005). Beyond ethnic match: Effects of client–therapist cognitive match in problem perception, coping orientation, and therapy goals on treatment outcomes. *Journal of Community Psychology, 33*, 569–585.

Zhang, M., He, Y., Gittelman, M., Wong, Z., & Yan, H. (1998). Group psychoeducation of relatives of schizophrenic patients: Two-year experiences. *Psychiatry and Clinical Neurosciences, 52*(Suppl.), S344–S347.

Zhang, W. (1994). American counseling in the mind of a Chinese counselor. *Journal of Multicultural Counseling and Development, 22*, 79–85.

Zhang, Y. (2007). Negotiating a path to efficacy at a clinic of traditional Chinese medicine. *Culture, Medicine and Psychiatry, 31*, 73–100.

Zhang, Y. & Yang, D. (1998). The cognitive psychotherapy according to Taoism: A technical brief introduction. *Chinese Mental Health Journal, 12*, 188–190. (in Chinese)

Zhang, Y., Young, D., Lee, S., Li, L., Zhang, H., Xiao, Z., et al. (2002). Chinese Taoist cognitive psychotherapy in the treatment of generalized anxiety disorder in contemporary China. *Transcultural Psychiatry, 39*, 115–129.

Zhao, C., Wang, Y., Shen, X., & Geng, D. (2003). Venlafaxine plus cognitive behavior therapy in treatment of panic disorder. *Shandong Archives of Psychiatry, 16*, 12. (in Chinese)

Zhao, S., Wu, H., & Neng, C. (2003). The curves of document increase in the field of psychotherapy, a comparison between Chinese and international documents. *Chinese Mental Health Journal, 17*, 794–795. (in Chinese)

Zheng, S., Li, X., & Liu, Y. (2007). A comparative study of cognitive therapy and extended release Velafaxine in the treatment of depression in old age. *Journal of Psychiatry, 20*, 287–288. (in Chinese)

Zhong, J., Li, B., & Qian, M. (2002). Esteem in the personality, shame, and mental health relation model: The direct and moderate effect. *Chinese Journal of Clinical Psychology, 10*, 241–245. (in Chinese)

Zhong, J., Wang, A., Qian, M., Zhang, L., Gao, J., Yang, J., et al. (2008). Shame, personality, and social anxiety symptoms in Chinese and American nonclinical samples: A cross-cultural study. *Depression and Anxiety, 25*, 449–460.

Zhong, Y. B. (1988). *Chinese psychoanalysis*. Shenyang, China: Liaoning People's Publishing Co.

Zhou, B. & Li, C. (2005). Influence of cognitive therapy combined with drug therapy on the social function of convalescent schizophrenic patients. *Chinese Journal of Clinical Rehabilitation, 9*, 46–47. (in Chinese)

CHAPTER 28

Face and morality in Confucian society

Kwang-Kuo Hwang and Kuei-Hsiang Han

Concepts of face in Confucian society are too complicated to understand for many Westerners in contact with Chinese people for the first time. In order to trace the cultural origins of the Chinese concepts of face, it is necessary to elaborate their relationships with Confucian ethics. Under the influence of Confucian ethics for ordinary people, all 'persons in relation' (see below) and involved in a certain event may be considered to constitute a given individual's psychosociogram in which they have to earn others' positive evaluations and protect their public image for the sake of maintaining their psychosocial equilibrium. Their sense of having or losing face can be defined as their socially contingent self-esteem in a particular situation.

The vocabularies for describing Chinese usage of face can be divided into two broad categories, namely moral face and social face. Both are related to Confucian concepts of morality. The relevant features of Confucian morality will be analyzed and discussed from three different ethical perspectives. The conceptual framework thus obtained will be used to explain the commonality in findings from two separate empirical studies on episodes of losing face conducted in Taiwan and mainland China.

In Confucian society, not only do protective face and acquisitive face constitute significant orientations of personality, but such indigenous concepts as *zuo mianzi* (making face) and *zheng mianzi* (keeping up face) may also have important psychological implications which may be measured and studied. Under the influence of Confucian relationalism, Chinese people are concerned not only about enhancing or losing the face of one's 'small self', but also about enhancing or losing the face of one's 'big self' arising from significant moral or social episodes. One's patterns of emotional reaction, including feelings of having or losing face, in response to these episodes are determined by the role relationships involved and can be explained in terms of the role obligations between the dyads involved as defined by Confucian ethics. For example, an actor's parent, teacher, and classmate may have different types of face feeling for the actor's success or failure in pursuing academic and other achievement goals. The main arguments of this chapter will be illustrated by research findings using various methods of social psychology.

The mystery of face in Confucian society

Since the early 1900s when Western contact with the East increased in frequency, many missionaries, diplomats, and travelers have attempted to describe their experiences in the Orient to the people in their home countries. Many mentioned the fact that Chinese emphasize the importance of face, and felt it to be a key concept for understanding Chinese psychology and behavior (Gilbert, 1927; Smith, 1894; Wilhelm, 1926). They advised that anyone ignorant about the dynamics of face would certainly encounter trouble in dealing with Chinese people. They also agreed that it is difficult for Westerners to understand the Chinese concept of face because it implies meanings that are much more complicated than they could narrate. Let us, however, try.

The reason why Western people think that the Chinese concept of face is so abstruse and difficult to understand is because they lack a profound understanding of the deep structure of Confucian culture. In fact, even a Chinese person might have the same feeling, if they knew little about the deep structure of Confucianism. For example, during the period of the May 4th Movement, the famous writer, Lu Xun, who had endeavored his whole life to study the national character of Chinese people and the reconstruction of Chinese culture, said, 'What is going on about "face"? It is wise not to think about it. When you think of it, you will get confused' (Lu, 1991, p. 126).

In the 1940s, the Chinese anthropologist, Hu (1944), explained the meanings of many Chinese terms and phrases related to *lian* and *mianzi* that are frequently used in daily life. Inspired by Hu's work, American sociologist Goffman (1955) studied face in interpersonal interaction. Goffman defined face as the public image created by the actor for which applause is won. In any social interaction, one of the participants may claim to possess some values praised by society, such as wealth, achievement, or ability. When others recognize and accept this claim, the person gains face; if the claim is challenged or rejected, the person loses face. According to this definition, individuals do not have a constant claim to face; an individual's face varies with the situation (Goffman, 1955).

Goffman's work (1955, 1959, 1967) resulted in a series of experimental studies. Because an individual's face depends upon social circumstances, several psychologists conducted studies in which they deliberately arranged situations that would threaten the individual's sense of self, and then recorded the individual's responses for further analysis. For instance, they asked university students to suck nipples, sing songs in public, learn about their poor performance on an ability test, and be frustrated in a negotiation process (Brown, 1968, 1970; Brown & Garland, 1971; Garland & Brown, 1972). However, careful examination of Goffman's work and the follow-up studies reveals that what was actually studied were interaction rituals in American society, which are significantly different from ideas about *mianzi* and *lian* in Chinese culture.

American anthropologists Brown and Levinson (1987) further investigated the relationship between face and the language of politeness used in daily life. In their view, maintaining face is a kind of human need. Every competent adult in every society needs it, and knows that others also need it. People learn how to use 'the language of politeness' to express concern for the other's face and to protect their own face from being threatened. Brown and Levinson differentiated face into two categories. *Positive face* referred to the need to be recognized or praised by particular others for some aspect of one's highly valued self. *Negative face* referred to the need for freedom of action and freedom from being obstructed or compelled. Although Brown and Levinson regarded face as a universal need, the concepts of face in their discourse, especially the public image of independence emphasized by negative face, carry certain cultural values that are different from the concept of face in Confucian cultures.

The cultural origin of the Chinese concept of face

The German missionary Wilhelm (1926), who lived in China for 25 years, was the first author to trace the cultural origins of the Chinese concept of face. He indicated that Confucianism and Taoism are the cultural roots of the Chinese character. Confucian emphasis on harmony traditionally caused Chinese people to strive for what they deserved within the social order of their clan. This striving could result in two types of character, namely, *face loving* (*ai mianzi*) and *having no way* (*mei fazi*).

In the 1940s, Hu (1944) used an anthropological approach to analyze situations for using various words relevant to *lian* and *mianzi* in Chinese social life. She indicated that, as shown in ancient Chinese literature, the emergence of the term *mianzi* in Chinese verbal communication was much earlier than the term *lian*. Before the fourth century BC, the term *mianzi* was symbolically used to denote the relationship between an individual and society. *Lian*, however, has been used only in relatively modern times. It was first cited in the *Kangxi* dictionary in a reference to the Yuan dynasty

(AD 1227 to 1367). The term *lian* originated in northern China. It gradually replaced the physical meaning of *mianzi* (a person's physical face) in usage, and then became endowed with symbolic significance.

In daily usage, *mianzi* represents the kind of social reputation that is highly valued by Chinese. It is the kind of fame that has been deliberately accumulated by a person through effort and achievement, with consequent pride, during the course of his or her life. In order to have this kind of face, one must rely on the social environment to secure affirmation from other people. *Lian* is the social respect offered by a group to an individual with high morality. A person with *lian* would do what is proper no matter what difficulties were encountered, and would behave honestly in every situation. *Lian* represents public trust in the individual's morality. Once lost, an individual cannot function as usual in the group. *Lian* is not only a social constraint for maintaining moral standards, but also an internalized force of self-restriction. *Mian* is more variable than *lian*. Everyone has only one *lian*, but possesses various levels of *mian* in different social situations. The relationship between *lian* and *mian* was just like the difference between *personality* and *title* as emphasized by Confucianism. In reality, an individual has only one personality, but may possess many titles.

The sociologist, King (1988), indicated that Hu's distinctions between *lian* and *mianzi* can only be applied to northern China where Mandarin is used. In areas of southern China where Cantonese and Hakka are spoken, the term *mian* denotes the meanings of both *lian* and *mianzi*. King indicated that dialects in southern China, especially Cantonese, were developed earlier than Mandarin. Absence of the word *lian* in the Southern dialects reveals that the concept of *lian* appeared later than did the concept of *mianzi*; the meanings of *mianzi* and *lian* are blended in Cantonese.

Ho (1976) published an article entitled, 'On the concept of face' where he discussed the differences between face and such concepts as status, dignity, honor, reputation, personality, and standards for behavior. He then proposed a definition of face (1976, p. 883):

> Face is the respectability and/or deference which a person can claim for himself from others, by virtue of the relative position he occupies in his social network and the degree to which he is judged to have functioned adequately in that position as well as acceptably in his general conduct; the face extended to a person by others is a function of the degree of congruence between judgments of his total condition in life, including his actions as well as those of people closely associated with him, and the social expectations that others have placed upon him. In terms of two interacting parties, face is the reciprocated compliance, respect, and/or deference that each party expects from, and extends to, the other party.

Ho (1976) indicated that his definition of face entails some essential differences between the Chinese concept of face and the Western concept (see also Chou & Ho, 1993). Chinese face is tightly linked with vertical relationships and close others. Its operation follows a compelling principle of reciprocity. In contrast, Western face emphasizes the separateness of an individual. A person is not required to assume responsibility for the behavior of relatives or family members. Social interactions abide by the principle of reciprocity, but they tend to maintain the individual's autonomy.

Ho's (1976) definition of face highlighted some significant features of Chinese culture, and aroused social scientists' interest in this issue, but it did not give a clear picture of exactly what the Chinese concept of face is. What are the specific features of the Chinese concept of face that are so hard to comprehend that they puzzle social scientists?

As a consequence of the indigenization movement in Chinese social sciences, many Chinese psychologists (Chen, 1988; Chou & Ho, 1993; Chu, 1989, 1991) researched the issue of the relationship between face and morality. Cheng (1986) pointed out that the fundamental contents of face for Chinese are the five Confucian cardinal ethical principles. Likewise, Zai (1995) and Zuo (1997) published books that have contributed much to the understanding of the Chinese concept of face. Zai pointed out that although there is a rough connection between *lian* and morality, and a rough connection between *mian* and social achievement, either *lian* or *mianzi* can involve morality in some situations, while having no connection with it in other situations. In other words, *lian* and *mianzi* cannot be fully differentiated on the basis of involvement with morality. What kinds of situations might tie *lian* and *mianzi* with morality? And in what type of situations have they no link to it? In order to answer these questions, the special features of the Chinese concept of morality must first be presented.

Confucian ethics for ordinary people

Hwang (1987) proposed a theoretical model to elaborate how people in Chinese society interact with others of various relations by different rules of exchange. Based on this theoretical model, he subsequently analyzed the inner structure of Confucian thought (Hwang, 1988, 1995, 2001). According to his analysis, the Confucian ethical system of benevolence–righteousness–propriety for ordinary people emphasizes two fundamental principles for social interaction, namely the principle of respecting the superior and the principle of favoring the intimate.

When interacting with the other party, in each of the five cardinal relations between father and son, brothers, husband and wife, friends, and sovereign and minister, an individual should recognize the role relationships within the dyad along two cognitive dimensions: the first is the superiority or inferiority of their status, while the second is the closeness or distance of their relations (see also McAuley, Bond, & Kashima, 2002). Viewed from the perspective of justice theory in Western social psychology, Confucianism suggests that, in situations of social interaction, the dyad has to decide who is the 'resource allocator' according to the 'principle of respecting the superior' and the 'principle of favoring the intimate'. Viewed from the perspective of Confucian ethics for ordinary people, a consideration of the closeness/distance relationship within the dyad should refer to the Confucian value of *jen* (benevolence); the choice of appropriate rule for social exchange refers to the Confucian value of *yi* (righteousness); the proper behavior for social interaction within the dyad emphasizes the value of *li* (propriety) (see Figure 28.1).

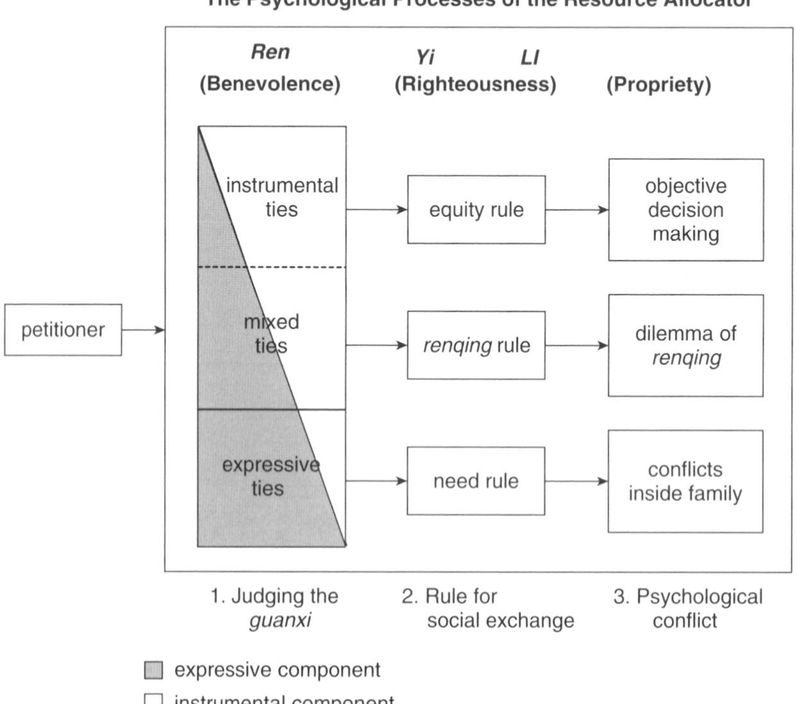

Fig. 28.1 The Confucian ethical system of benevolence–righteousness–propriety for ordinary people (adapted from Hwang, 1995, p. 233).

In this model, the rectangle of *quanxi* is separated into two parts by a diagonal line. The gray part is called the expressive component, while the blank part is called the instrumental component. This distinction indicates that the Confucian principle of *jen* advocates favoring the intimate instead of treating all men alike. The rectangle of *quanxi* is divided into three portions by a solid line and a dotted line. They are respectively called expressive ties, mixed ties, and instrumental ties in consideration of the expressive component contained in the *quanxi*. One should interact with them by different rules of social exchange; namely, the need rule, the *renqing* rule, and the equity rule. Instrumental ties and mixed ties are separated by a dotted line, indicating that a dyad of the instrumental tie may become one of the mixed tie through the interpersonal process of *la quanxi* or 'reinforcing connections'. The expressive ties within the family and the mixed ties outside the family are separated by a solid line, however, implying that Confucianism suggests an impermeable social psychological boundary between family members and outsiders.

Psychosociogram in Chinese society

According to the perspective of 'methodological relationalism' proposed by Ho (1991), 'Confucian ethics for ordinary people' describes how an individual interacts with others of various relationships in Confucian society. These 'persons in relation' constitute the psychosociogram proposed by Hsu (1971).

The idea of a 'psychosociogram' is crucial for understanding the Chinese concept of face. Viewed from the biological perspective, everybody has a face. It is the most unique feature representing individual identity. During social interaction, everyone tries to understand others by the messages revealed through their faces; they also try to create certain images about themselves in others' minds through their facial, and other, expressions.

'Face', then, is the evaluation of one's public image after an individual reflects upon the impact of their actions in a given social situation (Brown & Levinson, 1987). It is one's self-identification in a particular social situation, so it can be called one's situated identity (Alexander & Knight, 1971; Alexander & Lauderdale, 1977; Alexander & Rudd, 1981; Alexander & Wiley, 1980). An individual may judge that they are losing, maintaining, or increasing face after imagining the social evaluation of their performance in that situation. Thus, self-perceived face can also be called 'socially contingent self-esteem' (Hwang, 2006).

An individual will certainly get involved in a variety of social events in daily life. Others involved in those social events constitute their 'persons in relation' (Ho, 1991); the individual's perception of their relations with these persons forms the psychosociogram. The number of persons in relation interacting with an individual in a given event is variable, and the duration of their social interaction may be short or long. One's interaction with others of instrumental ties might be terminated at the end of that event. However, one's social interaction with others of expressive ties might result in stable and durable relationships. In this case, protecting one's face in order to maintain psychosocial equilibrium with these persons in relation becomes extremely important. When an individual perceives that their behavior might cause negative evaluations from the persons in relation, they will anticipate losing face and will take actions to restore psychosocial equilibrium by avoiding actions leading to that loss of face.

Under the influence of the Confucian cultural tradition, the most important social relations for Chinese are those with family members. How to maintain one's self-image in front of family members becomes an important consideration for maintaining one's psychosocial equilibrium. For example, Han and Li's (2008) research constructed two scenarios: the actor, Yu-chu, in one of them found that they were infected with venereal disease; the same actor in another scenario had gallstones. The information about who could offer Yu-chu help was described as:

> Yu-chu's parents had paid close attention to their children's education since they were young. All children in Yu-chu's family had a good educational background and careers. Yu-chu's older brother (older sister) happened to be a urologist (a surgeon in another scenario). Though Yu-chu did not study medicine, he

(she) had some classmates who became medical doctors, since he (she) had studied in a well-known senior high school. One of them was also a urologist.

After reading the scenario, participants in the study were asked two hypothetical questions:

1. In the event that Yu-chu has to seek treatment from a medical doctor in a given field, assuming that all the following targets can provide the same treatment for Yu-chu and the degree of convenience is also similar, whom do you think Yu-chu will choose for treatment? (single choice, please check with a ✓ in □)
   □ Yu-chu's older brother (older sister)
   □ Yu-chu's classmate in senior high school, who is a urologist
   □ the urologist whom Yu-chu doesn't know
2. Assuming you are the actor, Yu-chu, if all the following three targets are capable of helping you, and the degree of convenience is similar, whom will you seek for help? (Please check in □)
   □ your family member (older brother or sister)
   □ your friend or classmate
   □ the urologist you don't know

The results of their research showed that in the situation where Yu-chu would not lose face (having a gallstone), most participants recommended that Yu-chu seek help from a family member (92 per cent) of the expressive tie; only very few of them suggested turning to a friend (8 per cent) of the mixed tie; no one chose a stranger from the instrumental tie. In the situation where Yu-chu's face might be threatened (having a venereal disease), most participants recommended a stranger (91 per cent) of the instrumental tie. Only very few chose a friend (9 per cent) of the mixed tie, and no one chose a family member of the expressive tie.

Han and Li (2008) suggested that the main reason for Chinese to 'seek far for what lies close at hand' and look for help from strangers in a situation that might threaten their 'moral faces' was that they intended to 'save their face', hoping that the loss of face from their contracted disease would not be exposed to their acquaintances. In order to test this hypothesis, they asked participants to evaluate three major factors for consideration when an 'actor in the scenario' or 'oneself' looked for help from different targets, including 'face maintenance' ('it was better that this kind of event would not be exposed to the acquaintances', and 'I wouldn't feel a loss of face by this action'), 'better help' ('because of my relationship with him (her), I would have better assistance', and 'I could rely on his (her) professional competence) and 'indebtedness' ('I would not have a problem of owing favor to others afterwards'). After the participants chose the helper, they had to evaluate the importance of each factor in their selection of that target.

Results showed that the participants' evaluation of the importance of 'face maintenance' in the situation of 'losing face' (venereal disease) was significantly higher than that in which they 'would not' lose face (gallstones). On the other hand, their evaluation of the importance of 'better help' was significantly lower than the situation in which they 'would not' lose face. Their considerations of 'indebtedness' did not show any significant difference. In the situation when they 'would' certainly lose face (venereal disease) and there were only 'family member' and 'friend' for choice, the participants' evaluations on these three factors including 'face maintenance', 'better help' and 'indebtedness' did not show any significant differences.

These results demonstrated that when Chinese have to ask for help from others in an event that would not threaten their face and there are family members, friends and strangers available to offer the same help, they tend to seek for help from family members of the expressive tie. The sequential order of seeking help is 'from close to distant', or from 'friend' to 'stranger'. However, in the situation that might threaten one's 'face', the order of seeking for help is reversed to become 'from distant to close'; they would rather seek for help from a stranger of instrumental tie than a friend or family member. The reason that the participants adopted the strategy of asking for help 'from far to near' is because having venereal disease means that an individual has violated sexual morality and might completely lose face in front of family members (Han & Li, 2008).

This strategy may help an individual to maintain his face. However, violating sexual morality is not the only way in which Chinese can lose face. In Confucian culture, there are many other reasons for an individual to sense that he or she has lost face. What are these factors that can make an individual feel that they are losing face in Confucian society?

Morality in Confucian society

In order to explain the difference between the obligation-based ethics of Confucianism and the rights-based ethics of Western individualism, Hwang (1998) described the significant features of Confucian ethics in terms of the distinctions between perfect/imperfect and negative/positive duties as proposed by Western scholars. He indicated the inadequacy of the Western ethics of rationalism for understanding Confucian ethics, and proposed a revised system to denote the significant features of Confucian ethics constructed on the basis of interpersonal affection (Table 28.1).

According to Nunner-Winkler (1984, p. 349), the distinction between perfect and imperfect duties was first introduced by Kant (1797/1963) in his *Metaphysik der Sitten*, and later elaborated as negative and positive duties respectively by Gert (1973) in his book, *The Moral Rules*. Negative duties simply require abstention from action (e.g. do not kill, do not cheat; do not steal). They are duties of omission. So long as they are not in conflict with other duties, they can be followed strictly by anyone in any situation with regard to all other persons. In Kant's metaphysics of morality, they are termed perfect duties.

Positive duties are usually stated as maxims that guide actions (e.g. practice charity, help needy persons). They are duties of commission, but they do not specify which and how many good deeds have to be performed to the beneficiary so that the maxim can be said to have been performed. The application of any positive maxim requires the actor to take into consideration all concrete conditions and to exercise powers of judgment. Because it is impossible for an individual to practice any positive maxim all the time and with regard to everybody, positive duties are called imperfect duties in the terminology of Kantian ethics.

Viewed from the perspective of Western ethics for judging actions (Gert, 1973), the Confucian golden rule, 'Do not do to others what you do not want to be done to you,' should be classified in the category of negative duties, while the Confucian ethics for scholars with its core value of loyalty should be termed positive duties (see Table 28.1).

However, from the perspective of Kantian ethics, any demands emanating from the Confucian Way of Humanity, regardless of whether they are positive or negative duties, are all considered imperfect duties. Kant was a rationalist. He proposed that there is a single, categorical imperative applicable to all rationalists: Act so that the outcome of one's conduct is 'the universal will'. Principles derived from an individual's feelings, affections, dispositions, or preferences may not be universally applicable to others, and should be considered merely subjective principles. The fact that an individual following the golden rule must rely on personal feelings and preferences led Kant to include a

Table 28.1 Significant features of Confucian ethics from the perspectives of action, rationality, and affection

Concepts of Confucian ethics	Gert's perspective of action	Kant's perspective of rationality	Hwang's perspective of affection
Golden rule	Negative duty	Imperfect duty	Negative duty (perfect duty)
Ethics for ordinary people (filial piety)	Positive duty	Imperfect duty	Unconditional positive duty
Ethics for scholars (loyalty)	Positive duty	Imperfect duty	Positive duty (imperfect duty)

footnote in *Metaphysik der Sitten*, pointing out that this Confucian maxim cannot be a universal law, because it:

> ... contains no basis for prescribing duties to oneself or kindness to others (e.g. many people would agree that others should not help him or her if they don't expect help themselves), or clearly/demarcated duties towards others (otherwise, the criminal would be able to dispute the judge who punished him, and so on).
>
> Kant, 1797/1963, p. 97

Therefore, viewed from Kant's perspective of rationality, Confucian ethics for ordinary people, ethics for scholars, and the golden rule are all imperfect duties. Based on his meta-ethical reflection on the nature of the Western ethics of rationalism, Hwang (1998) further argued that the contents of the Confucian Way of Humanity can be classified into three categories on the basis of the moral agent's omission/commission of conduct: negative, unconditional positive, and positive duties (Table 28.1). As discussed above, the golden rule is a negative duty that serves as a principle of conduct for life (Yen Yuan in *The Analects*). So long as the injunction is not in conflict with other duties, it can and should be followed by everyone in all situations.

Mencius emphasized that 'One would not have committed one act of unrighteousness, or put to death one innocent person in order to obtain the throne' (*Kung-sun Chau* 1, chapter 2). His argument can be considered as an implementation of golden rule. Put in terms of Kant's ethics, every individual, as the subject of morality, has inborn human rights and dignity. Unless one should be punished for a breach of morality, they cannot be sacrificed or utilized as tools to accomplish certain goals, even for obtaining the throne!

Filial piety, the essential core of the Confucian ethics for ordinary people, is a positive duty. All people should act in a prescribed way towards their parents. From the Confucian perspective, an individual does not have a choice in deciding whether to be filial or not. The Confucian view of life emphasizes that one's life is an extension of one's parents' lives, so doing one's filial duty is clearly an obligation, and not behaving in accordance with filial piety is an unforgivable fault:

> Even if a parent has a fault, (the son) should, with bated breath and bland aspect and gentle voice, admonish him ... If the parent becomes angry and (more) displeased, and beats him until blood flows, he should not presume to be angry and resentful ... he should follow (his remonstrance) with loud crying and tears ... showing an increased degree of reverence, but without abandoning his purpose.
>
> Li Chi

In other words, showing filial piety to one's parents is not just a positive duty, it is an unconditional positive duty, which should be carried out in spite of any revelation about one's parents.

However, the relationship between sovereign and minister is completely different. There was a time when King Hsun of Chi asked Mencius for advice about the office of high ministers. Mencius remarked that there is a distinction between a relationship in which the high ministers are in the nobility and are relatives of the prince, and those in which they have different surnames from the prince. For those in the first category who have a blood connection with the prince, if the prince makes serious mistakes and does not respond to their respected admonitions, the minister should overthrow the prince and supersede his administration if the prince might do harm to the state.

High ministers with different surnames from the prince have no inseparable connection with him. If the prince makes mistakes and does not accept their repeated advice, they can just leave the state for another one. If the only emperor is tyrannical and does not practice benevolent government, then powerful chiefs of state should step forward and 'punish the tyrant and console the people' (*The Works of Mencius*, Chapter 1B: King Hui of Liang).

It is obvious that, although being a benevolent sovereign and being a loyal minister are defined by Confucians as positive duties for both roles, a minister should take into account all the objective conditions to determine whether the sovereign deserves loyalty. In other words, being loyal is a typical imperfect duty in the Kantian sense, and may be termed a 'conditional positive duty' or simply a 'positive duty'.

Losing face in Taiwan

An examination of the significant features of Confucian ethics enables us to understand the factors that may lead an individual to have the feeling of losing face in traditional Confucian culture. Nearly half century ago, American anthropologist Eberhard (1967) collected the fictions and publications (including books of righteousness) which had been popular in traditional Chinese society, analyzed the stories recorded, and allocated the sins in traditional Chinese society to four categories: sexual sins, social sins, sins against property, and sins against religion. These included almost all 'positive duties' and 'negative duties' suggested by Confucian ethics. The stories he collected revealed that when an individual committed these sins, he and his family would encounter disdain from others. Even if his sins were not found out, after his death he might go to hell and be punished by the King of Hell. The arguments reflect the 'ethics of divinity' (Shweder, Much, Mahapatra, & Park, 1997) constructed in traditional Chinese society and combining Confucian culture and Buddhism.

In her paper, 'The threat to face and its coping behaviors', Chu (1991) conducted a survey on face issues in Taiwan. She asked a total of 201 respondents to describe an occasion on which they felt shame or loss of face, and obtained a total of 110 situations that were likely to cause the feeling of losing face. Based on these cases, Chu developed a questionnaire and asked a total of 745 college students to assess the extent of losing face for each of these different occasions. Results were subjected to factor analysis and four factors were obtained: ability and status, morality and law, reputation and esteem, and sexual morality. Two of them, morality and law, and sexual morality are related to moral face.

Comparing these results with research findings obtained by Eberhard (1967), it is apparent that Chu and Eberhard's *sexual sins* correspond to the factor of sexual morality. The factor of morality and law corresponds to *social sins* and *sins against property*. Eberhard's *sins against religion* were not mentioned in Chu's study. One probable reason for their omission is that Chu conducted her study from the viewpoint of Chinese concepts of face, which are rooted in the Confucian ethics of community (Shweder et al., 1997). Sins against religion are emphasized by the ethics of divinity for Buddhists. The latter may lead to a feeling of guilt or sin. Evidently, none of Chu's participants reflected a Buddhist perspective in their reported episodes.

Some aspects of Chu's (1991) findings deserve closer examination. First, the mean of subjects' responses falls above the mid-point for all items in three of the four factors: morality and law, reputation and esteem, and sexual morality. But only four items from the ability and status factor have an average value well above the mid-point. These achievement-related items are 1) having good-for-nothing children, 2) being abandoned or dumped, 3) disclosure of personal secrets, and 4) being fired or laid off. These facts are serious social events that may cause a feeling of losing face, but they are irrelevant to morality. In other words, for Chu's respondents, a moral episode is more likely to cause a sense of losing face than an episode concerning one's capability or status. This finding supports the argument that for Chinese, a moral episode can cause a sense of shame far stronger than achievement-related issues (Cheng, 1986; King, 1988; Zai, 1995).

Secondly, in the factor of morality and law, the moral episodes that may result in a sense of losing face include not only a violation of negative duties such as stealing, robbing, and lying, but also an unwillingness to fulfill positive duties defined by family ethics of Confucianism, such as not educating children properly, violating female virtues, being unfilial, falsely incriminating friends, breaking promises, and abandoning one's wife. Those behaviors against sexual morals in the factor of sexual morality can also be classified under this category. Viewed from the perspective of Confucian relationalism, it is clear that all those behaviors are contradictory to the Confucian ethics for ordinary people within the family circle.

Additional episodes that may result in losing face include those that are contrary to public morality, such as defecating, spitting phlegm, throwing rubbish on the street, or talking too loudly in public. Other ways to lose face include betraying one's loyalty to a social group to which one belongs, for example, betraying one's country, accepting bribes, evading military service, spying for foreign powers, illegally making money, etc. According to Confucian relationalism, the latter categories of behavior violate Confucian ethics for scholars, which advocate extending the loyalty or commitment to one's family to wider society.

Behaviors such as not engaging in proper duties or work, fooling around, living as a bum, and leading an unproductive and pessimistic life all have profound implications in the context of Confucian tradition. Because these behaviors imply a weakness in the self-cultivation advocated by Confucianism, people who engage in them should feel a sense of shame as a result.

Losing face in mainland China

Some may speculate that Chu's (1991) study would have shown a different outcome had it been conducted in a different time and place. However, Zuo (1997) made a similar survey of 192 citizens in the Wuhan area of mainland China, and obtained similar results. Zuo asked his respondents to assess the extent of losing face in each of 30 given episodes. His respondents mainly comprised 120 college students, while the rest were political cadres, businessmen, and college teachers. Zuo used the technique of cluster analysis to analyze the data and consequently came up with four clusters defined as follows (Zuo, 1997, p. 36):

1. Behavior against morality. Any speech or behavior that violates social ethics and moral standards recognized by the public, or any criminal action that violates the national laws should result in losing face to the person involved. In contrast, if one abides by the laws and acts with good manners and integrity, one will gain face rather than losing it.
2. Incompetent behavior. If one cannot perform an important task successfully when one is believed to possess the capability of doing so, or if one's performance is obviously lagging behind that of others in some key respect, the person involved will be liable to lose face.
3. Bad habits. Bad habits and disgraceful acts in daily life, such as spitting, not being hygienic, loosening one's belt while eating, doing up the wrong buttons, being argumentative over small amounts of money, swearing, or using foul language all lead to losing face. Being neat and tidy, elegant, generous, cultured, and polite will either maintain or gain face for the person involved.
4. Private matters being disclosed. In general, one will be highly ashamed of oneself if subjected to events such as accidental exposure of the body, invasion of privacy, or when evil thoughts or plans in one's mind are guessed by others.

Zuo's (1997) and Chu's (1991) studies were not exactly the same with respect to the contents of the face episodes assessed. Further, one of the studies was conducted in Taiwan. It was separated in terms of time and space from the other, which was completed in mainland China. Nonetheless, both studies came up with similar findings despite the fact that they respectively adopted the methods of factor analysis and cluster analysis for analyzing their data.

In view of the Confucian ethical system of benevolence–righteousness–propriety, proper behavior is emphasized during interpersonal interactions, where one should express appropriate respect to other people and receive respect from others at the same time. It is very hard for an individual with a reputation for immorality to earn respect from others; likewise for a person of low social standing caused by his or her personal character. An individual showing disgraceful behaviors or poor manners to others might well be deemed 'uncultivated' and lose face in front of others. Thus, face in Confucian society is closely linked to one's status and reputation in one's interpersonal network. Any factor that may damage one's status or anything that may sway an individual's status in their interpersonal network might make them feel face loss, assuming of course that the individual is sufficiently socialized to realize that they have behaved inappropriately.

Protective and acquisitive face orientation

In order to maintain one's status in one's interpersonal network, individuals in Confucian society must passively protect their own faces from loss and also actively adopt actions to promote their social status and reputation. Yet the need felt to protect face and the motive to win face are the result of an individual's socialization history; there are considerable individual differences. In general, those who are 'thin-skinned' are more likely to feel face loss when misconduct is exposed. On the other hand, those who are 'thick-skinned' are less likely to have such a feeling. Even if they engage in immoral acts, they appear careless and carefree, as if nothing had happened. Then others may refer to them as 'having no face'.

Similarly, one with high achievement motivation and high expectation in certain social situations would act in 'face-saving' ways. If one were to succeed in social competition, one would judge that one had face; if one were to fail, one would feel a loss of face.

Since the degree of one's disposition for face-saving and one's thickness or thinness of face rely on socialization experiences, insight on face can be gained through examining one's personality. Chou (1997) adapted Arkin's (1981) style of self-presentation and classified face concern into two major orientations of face types: protective and acquisitive. Protective face orientation guards the self from losing face. People with this orientation have five key characteristics: (1) concern for not losing face, (2) avoidance of public exposure, (3) sensitivity to negative evaluation, (4) conservativeness and caution, and (5) tendency for self-protection. Acquisitive face orientation motivates improvement of a person's public image. People of this orientation also have five key characteristics: (1) pursuance of face, (2) ostentation, (3) risk taking and competitiveness, (4) desire for social acclaim, and (5) aggressive self-promotion.

Based on these concepts, Chou (1997) developed a Protective and Acquisitive Face Orientation Scale and administrated it to 300 Singaporean adults. Her studies showed that these two types of face orientation show discriminant validity, differing in their patterns of correlations with social desirability, achievement orientation, self-monitoring, social anxiety and interpersonal relationships. How these two face orientations relate to recent work on preventive and promotive orientations (Higgins, 1998) is a matter of some interest.

Making face and keeping up face

In Confucian society, individuals may feel that they 'have face' because of their distinctive achievement in certain fields and their social status. Chen (1988) developed a scale for measuring one's face demands, which included two subscales: the *Ai Mianzi* (face-loving) scale is designed to measure the significance a person attaches to honorable episodes; the *Po Lianpi* (thin-faced) scale is aimed at measuring a person's sensitivity to disgraceful episodes.

However, some people without actual accomplishment like to use symbolic decoration, action, or language to claim a special position. In Chinese culture, these tactics are designed to 'make face' or 'win face'. Face built by this way is called *Hsu Mianzi* (virtual face). Chen (1988) also developed the *Hsu Mianzi* Scale to measure a person's carefulness about face. It includes two subscales: the *Zuo Mianzi* (making face) scale and the *Chern Mianzi* (maintaining face) scale. The former is an instrument for measuring an individual's orientation towards exerting effort to obtain the attention or admiration of others. The latter is for measuring a person's disposition to cover up weaknesses by using all forms of impression management.

In the terminology of Western psychology, making face (*zuo mianzi*) and keeping up face (*zheng mianzi*) can both be seen as strategies of impression management or face work. According to impression management theory as proposed by Tedeschi and others (e.g. Tedeschi, 1981; Tedeschi, Schlenker, & Bonoma, 1971), the major objective of impression management is to maintain a consistency of self-image. But, according to Chen's (1988) conceptual analysis, the specific goal of making face or keeping up face is to gain face or to obtain appreciation which is explicitly expressed by others, rather than to maintain a consistent self-image. With 412 Taiwanese college students as subjects, Chen's research indicated that the correlation between the students' demand for face and their ratings on the *Hsu Mianzi* (virtual face) scale were as high as $r = .46$ ($p<.001$).

However, in Chinese society, being face-loving (*ai mianzi*) or wishing for face (*yao mianzi*) may not only trigger actions for all kinds of virtual face (*hsu mianzi*), but also make a person take actions to compete for face (*zheng mianzi*), or to quest for practical achievement. Chu (1989) also developed another scale on demand for face by measuring the impact of ability-related episodes that may cause a sense of having no face (*mei mianzi*) in the respondents. Out of 299 freshman students surveyed, the correlation between ratings for the demand of face and their social-oriented achievement motivation was $r = .43$ ($p<.001$). Compared with the findings of Chen's (1988) research, it is clear that in Chinese society, a person who is face-loving may strive for either real or virtual face. The former type of face means that the person can live up to the honor or title given, whereas the latter means the person does not necessarily have the competency to live up to the honor.

Big self and small self

The above-mentioned studies involve the face feeling caused by one's own personal ethics or achievement. We may call it the face of 'small self'. However, the uniqueness of Chinese face is that an individual may take action not only to achieve face for the small self but also for the 'big self'. Face for the big self is again closely connected to Confucian ethics. In comparison with Western ethics of individualism, the major feature of Confucian ethics for ordinary people is emphasizing the core value of filial piety as 'unconditional positive duty'.

The basic difference between Confucianism and Christianity can be traced back to their fundamental discrepancy in explaining the origin of life (Hwang, 1999). Christianity proposes that each person is an independent entity created by God. An individual should strive to defend the territory of self that has been drawn around the immediate surface of the physical body. In contrast, according to Confucianism, individuals' personal lives are a continuation of their parents' lives, who have in turn succeeded their ancestors. As a result, an individual's family members, especially parents or children, are more likely to be included in the territory of one's self. The relationship between parents and children is usually perceived as a single body in the eyes of Chinese people. Family members are described as intimately as one's own flesh and blood. As a result, family members are especially liable to the feelings of 'having glory or shame together under the construction of the big self.

Confucian ethics for ordinary people are constructed on the core value of benevolence (Hwang, 2001). The Confucian idea of filial duty stresses the importance of 'benevolent father, filial son': parents should treat the children kindly, and their children should make every effort to pursue vertical achievement to meet their parents' expectations. Hwang, Chen, Wang, and Fu (in press) reviewed a series of empirical studies and suggested that parents in Confucian society tend to encourage their children to pursue the 'goals of vertical distinctiveness' approved by society. When the children attain these kinds of goals, they and even their parents will feel that they have gained face. By contrast, when the children fail in pursuing goals of vertical distinctiveness, the children and parents will both feel a loss of face.

Based on such reasoning, Su and Hwang (2003) used a paired comparison technique with retirees and college students to examine the feeling of 'having face' arising from their own moral or academic (or career) performance, that of their children (or parents), or that of their friends. The results are presented in Figure 28.2. The same method was used to compare the feeling of 'losing face' experienced when their own (or their family member's or friend's) immoral conduct or academic (or career) failure was exposed in public. These results are presented in Figure 28.3. The numerical values represent the extents of having or losing face for various incidents experienced by the participants.

As indicated in Figure 28.2, the first two incidents that make retirees most feel they 'have face' are when their children are morally upright and successful in their careers. The next two incidents pertain to their own performance, and the last two relate to that of their friends. The order of the first two pairs for college students is opposite to that of retirees. Because college students hope to enter the job market soon, they most feel they 'have face' when they do well in their academic performance, followed by being morally upright. Next in importance is when their parents are morally upright and successful in their careers, and last is when their friends are morally upright and have a good academic performance.

The data reflect an important fact about Chinese face: in general, moral face is more basic and important to most people than social face earned through the achievements of oneself or one's family (Cheng, 1986). Also, their own achievement and moral performance may make college students feel that they have more face than their parents, a stance that reflects an individualistic orientation.

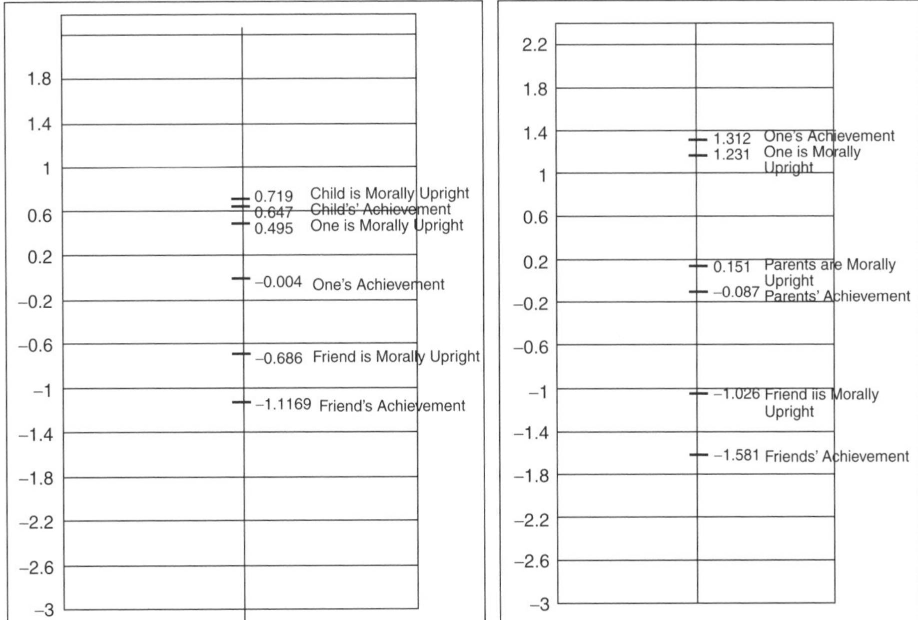

Fig. 28.2 Extent of having face caused by two types of incident for retirees and for college students.

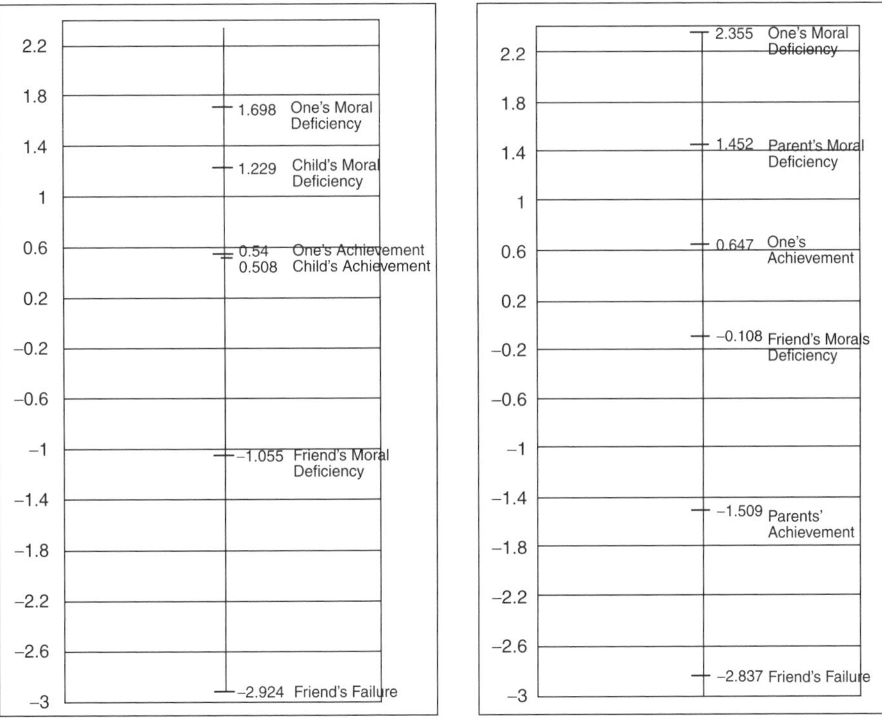

Fig. 28.3 Extent of losing face caused by two types of incident for retirees and for college students.

In contrast, retirees have more face from their children's moral performance and academic achievements than from their own, a stance that reflects a social (Yang, 1981) or relational (Ho, 1991; Hwang, 2001) orientation. Since the university students are entering the work environment, they value social face acquired by personal talent, capacity, or effort; the retirees have left the work environment, so they no longer pay attention to their own distinctiveness, but rather to the achievements of those persons with a blood relationship to them.

Social incidents of losing face

Moral face is the baseline for being an upright person, a reputation which should not be lost in any situation. Once it is lost, it is very hard for an individual to maintain a position in the community. As indicated in Figure 28.3, the incident that caused retirees the most serious feeling of losing face was personal moral deficiency. The next most serious was the moral deficiency of their son or daughter, personal career failure, and then a failure of their son or daughter. Moral deficiency or career failure of a friend ranked lowest. The whole sequence reflects the differential structure of Chinese relationalism: individuals tend to maintain psychosocial homeostasis by arranging interpersonal relationships with others from intimates to those more remote (Fei, 1948; Hsu, 1971; Hwang, 2000, 2001).

Guanxi and having/losing Face

Because university students are preparing for the pursuit of careers, academic achievement is more important than being morally upright for them to feel that they have face. In other words, with regard to the positive events resulting in their having face, social face is more important than moral face. However, moral face is the bottom line for establishing the social integrity of personality. Although an individual may not strive for it intentionally, moral face should not be lost in any situation. In other words, in terms of the negative events that result in people losing face, moral face is more important than social face. Under the influence of Confucian relationalism, however, once any person experiences success or failure in affairs of either achievement or morality, not only that person but also those related will experience a sense of either gaining or losing face, and the intensity of that feeling will vary as a function of the person's intimacy with the actor.

Similarly, as demonstrated by Liu (2002), incidents of positive achievement were generally evaluated by college students to be experienced with a more intense feeling of having face than were incidents of positive morality. Incidents of negative morality were experienced with a more intense feeling of 'having no face' than were incidents of negative achievement. In addition, for a positive incident of having face, the intensity of emotional reaction experienced by acquaintances (including good friends, classmates, and teachers) was generally lower than that of family members. The difference was not as drastic, however, as in the negative incidents of having no face.

In other words, participants believed that acquaintances and family members might experience a similar intensity of face for one's positive incidents. When an individual suffers from a negative incident of having no face, family members may also experience a feeling of having no face, but acquaintances may sever relationships and thus will not experience a similar feeling of having no face. The pattern of emotional reactions reflects the Chinese conceptualization of family as a whole body sharing the experience of having face or losing face. While one's acquaintances may share positive incidents, they do not seem to share the negative ones.

Role obligation and achievement type

Viewed from the perspective of Confucian relationalism, people of different relationships with the actor may have different expectations for the actor's performance, so they may have different face feeling for the actor's outcomes. Their expectations vary as a function of the nature of the event and their role obligations to the actor. Hwang, Chen, Wang, & Fu (in press) emphasized that there are two types of achievement goals pursued by students in Confucian society. 'Vertical distinctiveness' goals are those approved by the general public. Having achieved the goal, the actor may obtain praise from the whole society. 'Horizontal distinctiveness' goals are those pursued by the actor out of personal interest. Though the peer group may share similar interests with the actor and approve of these personal goals, significant others and the general public in the society may not do so.

In consideration of these two types of achievement, Liang, Bedford, & Hwang (2007) designed a series of scenarios and instruments for their assessment. Every scenario had an actor and two related others. The actor received different outcomes in events of vertical or horizontal achievement. Participants evaluated the face feeling for three types of related others, including parents, teacher, and classmates.

Face feelings of related others were compared in scenarios of success and failure. Compared with performance in horizontal distinctiveness goals, performance in vertical distinctiveness goals will make parents and teachers feel a higher degree of having face or having no face in the scenarios of success or failure. School fellows, however, show a reversed effect of face feelings in the scenarios of success and failure (see Figures 28.4 and 28.5).

In Chinese parenting, parents would usually encourage children to pursue socially approved 'vertical goals', hoping to receive thereby more social achievement (see Wang & Chang, this volume). However, for the 'horizontal goals' that children personally embrace, Chinese parents would not necessarily give the same support. Although Chinese have a concept of 'family as a whole', compared with vertical distinctiveness, parents feel a lesser degree of having or not having face as a result of their children's achievement or failure in horizontal goals.

There is a definite role standard for interaction between teacher and student. Students' distinctiveness in vertical events would get approval from society and is also highly related to the role obligations of teachers. In contrast, students' performance in horizontal goals has nothing to do with teachers' role obligations. Compared with horizontal distinctiveness, teachers and parents show stronger feelings of having or not having face when the actor succeeds or fails in situations involving vertical distinctiveness.

In a peer relationship, an individual has to pursue the vertical distinctiveness approved by society and, on the other hand, the recognition by the group to which an individual belongs. For pursuing

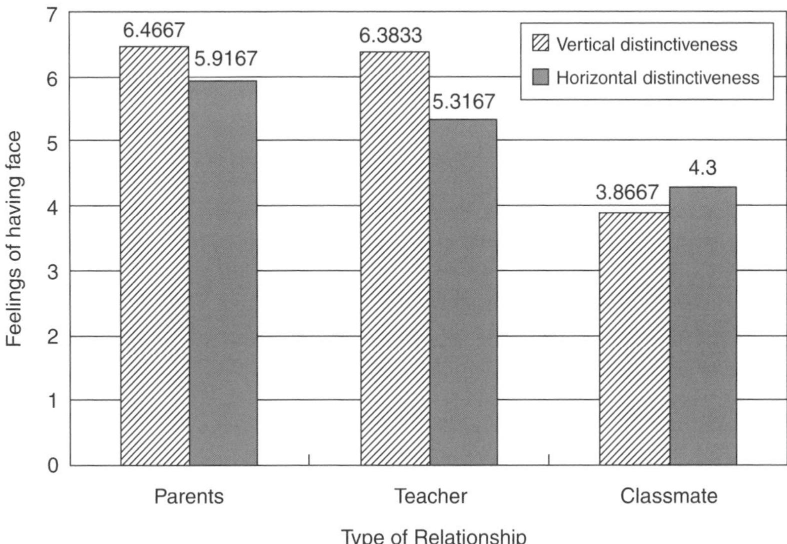

Fig. 28.4 The interaction of relation type and distinctiveness type on a related other's feeling of having face due to an actor's success.

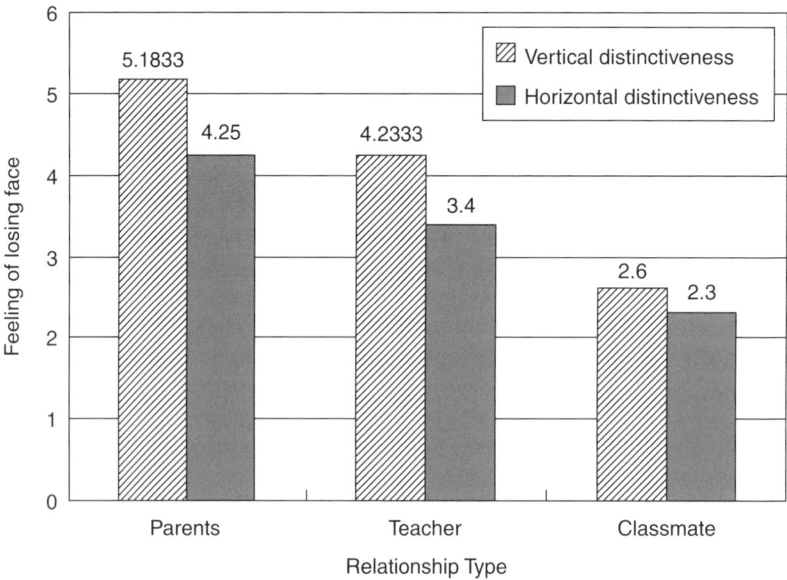

Fig. 28.5 The interaction of relation type and distinctiveness type on a related other's feeling of losing face due to an actor's failure.

vertical distinctiveness goals, the actor has to shoulder the pressure of social comparison. As a whole, it is easier to cause severe competition among peers when pursing vertical distinctiveness; it is easier to receive praise from one's peer group when pursing horizontal distinctiveness. Therefore school fellows would feel a higher degree of having face with regard to the actor's horizontal distinctiveness than to vertical distinctiveness. Yet school fellows would feel a higher degree of having no face on the failure of vertical achievement than on the failure of horizontal achievement.

Gift giving and consumer behaviors

This chapter has adopted the research strategy of indigenous psychology advocated by Hwang (2004; 2005a, b; 2006) to construct a series of theoretical models based on Confucian relationalism, and use them as guidelines for empirical research to study the connection between concepts of face and morality in Confucian society. This approach is very different from the cross-cultural approach of comparing East and West from a particular theoretical position (see Wyer & Hong, this volume).

This point can be illustrated by some research on gift giving and consumer behaviors. An empirical research by Bao, Zhou, and Su (2003) indicated that face consciousness and risk aversion are two cultural dimensions that differentiate consumers' decision-making styles in the USA and those of their counterparts in China. Wong and Ahuvia (1998) argued that the cultural factors of personal taste and family face lie behind the practices of luxury consumption in Western and Confucian societies.

Researchers of this kind typically describe the context distinguishing Confucian and Western cultures. However, what are the collectivistic values defining Confucian culture? Can we use the all-inclusive concept of collectivism to understand such Chinese personality factors as social potency, dependability, accommodation, or interpersonal relatedness (Cheung et al., 2001)? How can they influence Chinese social behaviors in general, or consumer behaviors in particular? Questions of this kind are difficult to answer through the research strategy of cross-cultural psychology. But they can be explored through the indigenous approach of psychology. For example, Qian, Razzaque, and Keng (2007) investigated the gift-giving behaviors of consumers in the city of Tianjin during the

Chinese New Year. They found that Chinese cultural values as a whole as well as most of their components investigated in this research had positive effects on the various gift-giving behaviors. However, the face component was found to affect only the importance attached to gift giving, the amount given, and the choice of brand.

Face dynamics in organizations

The concepts of *quanxi* and *mianzi* are fundamentally important in understanding social interactions in China, and can be extended to study relationships between firms and with governmental bodies. Buckley, Clegg, and Tan (2006) suggested that foreign investors in China must be aware of these key concepts, and use their knowledge to establish better institutional connections with locally owned partners and government officials. Using these concepts to build trust lies at the heart of interactions with all local stakeholders.

Kim and Nam (1998) proposed face as a key variable that can explain much of the complexity of social interactions in Asian organizations (see also Chen & Farh, this volume). They argued that scholars have to go beyond the individualistic assumption about human behavior implicit in theories of organizational behavior in the West to better understand that the richness of organizational behavior in Asia is better predicted by an individual's external attributes such as face than by internal attributes such as desires, emotions, and cognition.

Inspired by findings of research on concepts of face in Confucian culture, the organizational face theory proposed by Earley (1997) argued that face is a reflection of the individual's struggle for self-definition and understanding for the sake of positioning the self relative to others in a social setting. He presented a model of culture and face in the sense of self-presentation and social evaluation in which two general categories of face, *lian* and *mianzi*, are described in relation to the social exchange practices observed in various societies. *Lian* refers to a general attachment and enactment of social norms and morals. After their attachment is affirmed, a key aspect of face becomes that of *mianzi*, or social status (Earley, 2001). In order to understand face across cultural boundaries, these two aspects of face should be explored by using two key concepts of cultural variation, individualism–collectivism and power distance.

This is a popular way of thinking among cross-cultural psychologists in conceptualizing social behaviors in various cultures all over the world. For example, in order to study conflicts in multicultural and global contexts, Ting-Toomey (1994) proposed a face negotiation theory which differentiated various conflict approaches along the two grids of an individualism–collectivism continuum and a small–large power distance continuum: the *impartial approach* consists of a combination of an individualistic and small power distance value orientation; the *status-achievement approach* reflects a combination of an individualistic and large power distance value orientation; the *benevolent approach* consists of a combination of a collectivistic and large power distance value orientation; and the *communal approach* reflects an orientation of collectivistic and small power distance value orientation. But is this approach adequate to the realities of the phenomena to be explained?

Lee (1998) indicated that facework related to *lian* and *mianzi* is an integral part of daily activities and official functions of the Chinese people. The sensitivity to face threat is heightened with the degree of formality of the situation. In informal situations, Chinese people may not be as sensitive to face threats as in formal occasions. Formality of the situation means the occasion in which persons are requested to interact according to their role relationship and in which all parties are urged to fulfill their role obligations. Workplace, wedding, or funeral ceremonies are examples of situations with a high degree of formality. The formality of social interaction will be increased when two parties to the interaction get involved in interpersonal conflict and request the opposite party to fulfill his/her role obligation.

It is relatively unusual for Western theories of cross-cultural psychology to incorporate the idea of either role obligations or the formality of situations in Confucian culture (but see Triandis, 1977). Face negotiation theorists claim that it can be used to explain interpersonal interactions in multicultural workplace settings. However, it was constructed on the presumption of individualism without a careful consideration of the particularistic *quanxi* and its accompanying role obligations emphasized in Confucian societies. In order to study the social interaction in Chinese society, the cultural tradition of Confucian relationalism (Hwang, 2000, 2001) should be incorporated into a new theoretical model. For example, Hwang (1997–8) developed a model of conflict resolution in Chinese society. It classifies interpersonal relationship into three categories: vertical in-group, horizontal in-group, and horizontal out-group. It proposes twelve kinds of conflict resolution for three types of interpersonal relationships based on the consideration of the goal, harmony maintenance vs. personal goal attainment, coordination for attaining the goal, and dominant response of the scheme adopted.

When a subordinate conflicts with a superior in a vertical relationship, they must protect the superior's face for the sake of maintaining interpersonal harmony. In this case, the dominant response may be endurance. If one intends to pursue a personal goal, one may pretend to obey, while privately pursuing a personal goal.

The conflict-management strategies one may utilize in horizontal relationships depend on whether the other party is an in-group or out-group member. When an actor is in conflict with an in-group member, they may communicate directly. For the maintenance of harmonious relationship, they will probably 'give face' to each other and reach a compromise. When one of them insists on attaining their personal goal in spite of the other's feelings, the two may fight for a while. On the other hand, if both insist on attainment of their personal goals, they may begin to treat each other as out-group members and confront one another. Meanwhile, they may disregard interpersonal harmony and strive to protect their own face. In order to resolve the conflict situation, a third party may be invited to mediate. The dominant response after the conflict may be to sever the relationship.

When a superior insists on the attainment of a personal goal while disregarding feelings of subordinates in a vertical relationship, subordinates may also react to oppose the superior by severing the relationship.

This model can be viewed as a new product of integrating face negotiation theory and Confucian relationalism. It is best discussed under the theme of conflict resolution, so we do not go into its details here in this chapter (see Leung & Au, this volume). Comparing this model with face negotiation indicates that vertical relationship or power distance is their common concern, but the concept of collectivism has been replaced and elaborated by more differentiated theoretical construction. Previous attempts to use the construct of collectivism to study Chinese face interaction have not proved fully adequate (e.g. Singelis, Bond, Sharkey, & Lai, 1999). It can stand as inspiration to future research into Chinese social dynamics to carefully consider the powerful shaping of interpersonal relations by Confucian relationalism described in this chapter. Whether and how its influence may be integrated with extant cross-cultural models for social functioning (see Smith, Bond, & Kağıtçıbaşı, 2006) remains to be seen.

References

Alexander, C. N. & Knight, G. W. (1971). Situated identities and social psychological experimentation. *Sociometry, 34,* 65–82.

Alexander, C. N. & Lauderdale, P. (1977). Situated identities and social influence. *Sociometry, 40,* 225–233.

Alexander, C. N. & Rudd, J. (1981). Situated identities and response variables. In J. T. Tedeschi (ed.), *Impression management theory and social psychological research* (pp. 83–103). New York: Academic Press.

Alexander, C. N. & Wiley, M. C. (1980). Situated activity and identity formation. In M. Rosenberg & R. Turner (eds), *Sociological perspectives on social psychology* (pp. 269–289). New York: Basic Books.

Arkin, R. M. (1981). Self-presentation styles. In J. T. Tedeschi (ed.), *Impression management: Theory and social psychological research* (pp. 311–333). New York: Academic Press.

Bao, Y., Zhou, K. Z., & Su, C. (2003). Face consciousness and risk aversions: Do they affect consumer decision-making? *Psychology & Marketing, 20,* 733–755.

Brown, B. R. (1968). The effects of need to maintain face on interpersonal bargaining. *Journal of Experimental Social Psychology, 4,* 107–122.

Brown, B. R. (1970). Face-saving following experimental-induced embarrassment. *Journal of Experimental Social Psychology, 6,* 255–271.

Brown, B. R. & Garland, H. (1971). The effects of incompetency, audience acquaintanceship, and anticipated evaluative feedback on face-saving behavior. *Journal of Experimental Social Psychology, 7*, 490–502.
Brown, P. & Levinson, S. C. (1987). *Politeness: Some universal in language usage.* New York: Cambridge University Press.
Buckley, P. J., Clegg, J., & Tan, H. (2006). Cultural awareness in knowledge transfer to China: The role of *guanxi* and *mianzi. Journal of World Business, 41*, 275–288.
Chen, C. C. (1988). The empirical research and theoretical analysis of face in psychology. In K. S. Yang (ed.), *The psychology of Chinese people* (pp. 7–55). Taipei, Taiwan: Laureate Book Co. (in Chinese)
Cheng, C. Y. (1986). The concept of face and its Confucian roots. *Journal of Chinese Philosophy, 13*, 329–348.
Cheung, F. M., Leung, K., Zhang, J. X., Sun, H. F., Gan, Y. G., Song, W. Z. & Xie, D. (2001). Indigenous Chinese personality constructs: Is the five-factor model complete? *Journal of Cross-Cultural Psychology, 32*, 407–433.
Chou. M. L. (1997). *Protective and acquisitive face orientations: A person by situation approach to face dynamics in social interaction.* Unpublished doctoral dissertation, University of Hong Kong.
Chou, M. L. & Ho, D. Y. F. (1993). A cross-cultural perspective of face dynamics. In K. S. Yang & A. B. Yu (eds), *The psychology and behaviours of the Chinese: Conceptualization and methodology* (pp. 205–254). Taipei, Taiwan: Laureate Book Co. (in Chinese)
Chu, R. L. (1989). Face and achievement: The examination of oriented motives in Chinese society. *Chinese Journal of Psychology, 31*, 79–90.
Chu, R. L. (1991). The threat to face and coping behavior. *Proceedings of the National Science Council, Republic of China: Humanities and Social Science, 1*, 14–31.
Earley, P. C. (1997). *Face, harmony, and social structure: An analysis of organizational behavior across cultures.* New York: Oxford University Press.
Earley, P. C. (2001). Understanding social motivation from an interpersonal perspective: Organizational face theory. In M. Erez, U. Kleinbeck, & H. Thierry (eds), *Work motivation in the context of a globalizing economy* (pp. 369–379). Mahwah, NJ: Erlbaum.
Eberhard, W. (1967). *Guilt and sin in traditional China.* Berkeley, CA: University of California Press.
Fei, S. T. (1948). *Rural China.* Shanghai, China: Observer. (in Chinese)
Garland, H. & Brown, B. R. (1972). Face saving as affected by subjects' sex, audiences' sex and audience expertise. *Sociometry, 35*, 280–289.
Gert, B. (1973). *The moral rules.* New York: Harper & Row.
Gilbert, R. Y. (1927). *What's wrong with China.* London: J. Murray.
Goffman, E. (1955). On face-work: An analysis of ritual elements in social interaction. *Psychiatry, 18*, 213–231.
Goffman, E. (1959). *The presentation of self in everyday life.* New York: Doubleday, Anchor.
Goffman, E. (1967). *Interaction ritual: Essays on face-to-face behaviour.* London: Penguin.
Han, K. H. & Li, M. C. (2008). Strangers are better than the familiar ones: The effect of 'face-threatening' on Taiwanese choice of helper. *Chinese Journal of Psychology, 50*, 31–48.
Higgins, E. T. (1998). Promotion and prevention: Regulatory focus as a motivational principle. In M. P. Zanna (ed.), *Advances in experimental social psychology* (vol. 30, pp. 1–46). New York: Academic Press.
Ho, D. Y. F. (1976). On the concept of face. *American Journal of Sociology, 81*, 867–884.
Ho, D. Y. F. (1991). Relational orientation and methodological relationalism. *Bulletin of the Hong Kong Psychological Society, 26–27*, 81–95.
Hsu, F. L. K. (1971). Psychological homeostasis and *jen:* Conceptual tools for advancing psychological anthropology. *American Anthropologist, 73*, 23–44.
Hu, H. C. (1944). The Chinese concepts of 'face'. *American Anthropologist, 46*, 45–64.
Hwang, K. K. (1987). Face and favor: The Chinese power game. *American Journal of Sociology, 92*, 944–974.
Hwang, K. K. (1988). *Confucianism and East Asian Modernization.* Taipei, Taiwan: Chu-Liu Book Co. (in Chinese)
Hwang, K. K. (1995). *Knowledge and action: A social-psychological interpretation of Chinese cultural tradition.* Taipei, Taiwan: Sin-Li. (In Chinese)
Hwang, K. K. (1997–8). Guanxi and mientze: Conflict resolution in Chinese society. *Intercultural Communication Studies, 7*, 17–37.
Hwang, K. K. (1998). Two moralities: Reinterpreting the findings of empirical research on moral reasoning in Taiwan. *Asian Journal of Social Psychology, 1*, 211–238
Hwang, K. K. (1999). Filial piety and loyalty: The types of social identification in Confucianism. *Asian Journal of Social Psychology, 2*, 129–149.
Hwang, K. K. (2000). The discontinuity hypothesis of modernity and constructive realism: The philosophical basis of indigenous psychology. *Hong Kong Journal of Social Sciences, 18*, 1–32.
Hwang, K. K. (2001). Morality: East and West. In N. J. Smelser (ed.), *International encyclopedia of the social and behavioral sciences* (pp. 10039–10043). Amsterdam, The Netherlands: Pergamon.
Hwang, K. K. (2004). The epistemological goal of indigenous psychology: The perspective of constructive realism. In B. N. Setiadi, A. Supratiknya, W. J. Lonner, & Y. H. Poortinga (eds), *Ongoing themes in psychology and culture* (pp. 169–186). Amsterdam, The Netherlands: Swets and Zeitlinger.
Hwang, K. K. (2005a). From anticolonialism to postcolonialism: The emergence of Chinese indigenous psychology in Taiwan. *International Journal of Psychology, 40*, 228–238.

Hwang, K. K. (2005b). A philosophical reflection on the epistemology and methodology of indigenous psychologies. *Asian Journal of Social Psychology, 8*, 5–17.
Hwang, K. K. (2006). Moral face and social face: Contingent self-esteem in Confucian society. *International Journal of Psychology. 41*, 276–281.
Hwang, K. K., Chen, S. W., Wang, H. H., and Fu, B. J. (in press). Life goals, achievement motivation and value of effort in Confucian society. In U. Kim & Y. S. Park (eds), *Asia's educational miracle: Psychological, social and cultural perspectives.* New York: Springer.
Kant, I. (1797/1963). *Groundwork of the metaphysic of morals.* (H. J. Paton, trans. and analyzed). New York: Harper & Row.
Kim, J. Y. & Nam, S. H. (1998). The concept and dynamics of face: Implications for organizational behavior in Asia. *Organization Science, 9*, 522–534.
King, A. Y. C. (1988). Face, shame and the analysis of Chinese behaviors. K. S. Yang (ed.), *The psychology of the Chinese* (pp. 319–345). Taipei, Taiwan: Laureate Book Co. (in Chinese)
Lee, S. H. (1998). Facework in Chinese cross-cultural adaptation. *Dissertation Abstracts International Section A: Humanities and Social Sciences, 59*, 539–539.
Liang, C. J., Bedford, O., & Hwang, K. K. (2007). *Face due to the performance of a related other in a Confucian society.* Working paper for In Search of Excellence for the Chinese Indigenous Psychological Research Project, Department of Psychology, National Taiwan University.
Liu, D. W. (2002). *Relational others' emotional reactions to negative episodes of agency evaluated by college students in Taiwan.* Unpublished master's thesis, National Taiwan University.
Lu, X. (1991). On 'face'. In Editorial Office of People's Literature Publishing House (ed.), *Complete Works of Lu Xun* (Vol. 6, pp. 126–129). Beijing, China: People's Literature Publishing House.
McAuley, P., Bond, M. H., & Kashima, E. (2002). Towards defining situations objectively: A culture-level analysis of role dyads in Hong Kong and Australia. *Journal of Cross-Cultural Psychology, 33*, 363–380.
Nunner-Winkler, G. (1984). Two moralities? A critical discussion of an ethic of care and responsibility versus an ethic of rights and justice. In W. M. Kurtines & J. L. Gewintz (eds), *Morality, moral behavior, and moral development* (pp. 348–361). New York: Wiley.
Qian, W., Razzaque, M. A., & Keng, K. A. (2007). Chinese cultural values and gift-giving behavior. *Journal of Consumer Marketing, 24*, 214–228.
Shweder, R. A., Much, N., Mahapatra, M., & Park, L. (1997). The 'big three' of morality (autonomy, community, and divinity), and the 'big three' explanations of suffering, as well. In A. M. Brandt & P. Rozin (eds), *Morality and health* (pp. 119–169). New York: Routledge.
Singelis, T. M., Bond, M. H., Sharkey, W. F., & Lai, C. S. Y. (1999). Unpackaging culture's influence on self-esteem and embarrassment: The role of self-construals. *Journal of Cross-Cultural Psychology, 30*, 315–341.
Smith, A. H. (1894). *Chinese characteristics.* New York: F. H. Revell Company.
Smith, P. B., Bond, M. H., & Kağıtçıbaşı, Ç. (2006). *Understanding social psychology across cultures.* London: Sage.
Su, S. Y. & Hwang, K. K. (2003). Face and relation in different domains of life: A comparison between senior citizens and university students. *Chinese Journal of Psychology, 45*, 295–311.
Tedeschi, J. T. (ed.) (1981). *Impression management theory and social psychological research.* New York: Academic Press.
Tedeschi, J. T., Schlenker, B. R., & Bonoma, T. V. (1971). Cognitive dissonance: Private ratiocination or public spectacle? *American Psychologist, 26*, 185–695.
Ting-Toomey, S. (1994). Face and facework: An introduction. In S. Ting-Toomey (ed.), *The challenge of facework: Cross-cultural and interpersonal issues* (pp. 1–14). Albany, NY: State University of New York Press.
Triandis, H. C. (1977). *The psychology of interpersonal behavior.* Belmont, CA: Brooks-Cole.
Wilhelm, R. (1926). *Die seele Chinas.* Berlin: Reimar Hobbing. (in German)
Wong, N. Y. & Ahuvia, A. C. (1998). Personal taste and family face: Luxury consumption in Confucian and Western societies. *Psychology & Marketing, 15*, 423–441.
Yang, K. S. (1981). Social orientation and individual modernity among Chinese students in Taiwan. *Journal of Social Psychology, 113*, 159–170.
Zai, S. W. (1995). *Chinese view of lian and mian.* Taipei, Taiwan: Laureate Book Co. (in Chinese)
Zou, B. (1997). *Chinese 'lian'and 'mianzi'.* Wuhan, China: Huazhong Normal University Press. (in Chinese)

CHAPTER 29

Chinese cooperation and competition

Hildie Leung and Winton W.-T. Au

We begin this chapter with two sets of contrasting quotations from the literature on Chinese cooperation and competition.

On cooperation:

> Research has found that Chinese in the People's Republic of China and Chinese-Americans are more cooperative or equalitarian than are Caucasian Americans.
>
> Gabrenya & Hwang, 1996, p. 316

> Chinese made less cooperative decisions ... than did Australians ... Chinese tend to focus more on egoistic interest and act accordingly.
>
> X. P. Chen & Li, 2005, p. 632

On competition:

> Chinese see conflict as a zero-sum game in which there must be a loser and the relationship is terminated. Conflict is sidestepped by avoidance strategies and by compromise.
>
> Gabrenya & Hwang, 1996, p. 319

> ... conflict can have positive consequences in China as well as in the West and ... conflicts can be addressed directly, supportively, and constructively in China.
>
> Tjosvold, Hui, & Sun, 2004, p. 365

The quotations describing cooperation and competition among Chinese extracted from the first volume of *The handbook of Chinese psychology* (Bond, 1996) compared with the contrasting quotations from recent studies illustrate that much has changed in the field of cooperation–competition research over the past decade. The complexities of culture and its effects on cooperation and competition have been revealed through more recent discoveries which confront previous stereotypical perceptions of the Chinese. Many of these findings help to enrich our understanding of whether and how Chinese cooperate or compete relative to Westerners.

While most research is concerned with concepts derived from individualism and collectivism and focuses on investigating their links with cooperation and competition, we hope to take the analyses beyond this initial notion of differences in cultural values to further unpackage the variations found in cooperation and competition between the East and the West. In doing so, we will review findings on how various intra-individual and inter-individual variables underlie cultural differences in cooperative and competitive behaviors. We will look first at intra-individual variables, such as beliefs and values, risk preferences, regulatory focus, and conflict-management styles, and explain how these variables impact on competition and cooperation in different cultural contexts. We then explore the inter-individual variables related to cooperative conflicts, conversational style, power, fairness, interactional justice, and trust, and assess how these factors affect the two concepts from one nation to another. We will conclude by discussing multiple views on competition.

The Intra-individual Level

Collectivism

As mentioned in the first volume of *The handbook of Chinese psychology* (Gabrenya & Hwang, 1996), research in social psychology has continuously assessed the tendencies of individuals to cooperate or compete on interactive tasks, such as the various trust games, public goods dilemmas, and resource dilemmas. Previous research on the social loafing effect (Latané, Williams, & Harkins, 1979) that is, the tendency of individuals to exert less effort when being a member of the group, has demonstrated that social loafing occurs in individualistic groups but not in collectivistic groups. Chinese students, when asked to perform moderately intellective tasks were found to perform better as a group, while the opposite pattern was observed among American students (Gabrenya, Latané, & Wang, 1983; Karau & Williams, 1993). Similarly, Japanese students, who are considered to be highly collectivistic (Hofstede, 1991) also performed better when in groups than when alone (Matsui, Kakuyama, & Onglatco, 1987). Therefore, the apparently consistent theme at that time was that Chinese (Domino, 1992) and Chinese-Americans (e.g. Cox, Lobel, & McLeod, 1991) often behaved in a more cooperative manner than did Caucasians. The underlying idea is that increased collectivism leads to more cooperation, while increased individualism leads to more competition. Many articles have supported these findings and authors have even concluded that it is a phenomenon which no longer needs much examination (e.g. C. C. Chen, X. P. Chen, & Meindl, 1998).

However, more recent cross-societal studies contrast with the previously established paradigm (e.g. Koch & Koch, 2007; Yamagishi & Yamagishi, 1994). Yamagishi (1988) compared cooperative tendencies between members from the United States and Japan in social dilemmas and found that, in contrast to previous predictions of a positive relationship between collectivism and cooperation, Japanese participants actually cooperated less than Americans. Yamagishi (2003) proposed an institutional view of culture to explain these findings. He posited that the reason why Japanese preferred to belong to groups and to put a group's interest before their own is not because of their intrinsic tendencies but rather the existence of a system of formal and informal mutual monitoring and sanctioning. Once these sanctions are absent, such as in cases where interacting members are complete strangers, individuals' behaviors will no longer be constrained by their concerns for others, and as a result they will more likely reveal their egoistic sides and behave accordingly.

Yamagishi's (2003) institutional view of culture provides a new perspective for interpreting previous results from the cross-national social loafing studies. Specifically, a possible reason for the cooperative behaviors of participants demonstrated in previous studies could well be the presence of other participants whom they knew. They may have had interactions with them prior to the experiment or anticipated such interactions later or perceived the experimental group as an in-group; thus, informal mutual monitoring or sanctioning for social loafing may have been present as a social reality. X. P. Chen and S. Li (2005) examined Yamagishi's (2003) institutional view of culture by comparing Chinese and Australians and found supportive results demonstrating that Chinese made fewer cooperative decisions in mixed-motive business settings than did Australians. When Chinese participants were removed from a group boundary and in a situation where no formal sanctions were present, they demonstrated egoistic interests and behaved accordingly. Despite their results which showed that Chinese were less cooperative than Australians, the authors cautioned the readers not to generalize their findings to other situations uncritically. It is increasingly clear that Chinese are not always more cooperative; however, we shall not conclude that 'Chinese are less cooperative' because this phenomenon occurs under some special conditions only (for details refer to X. P. Chen & S. Li, 2005).

Indeed, the problem of using a specific Chinese sample and generalizing findings from such a sample to the country as a whole is not something unusual and has existed throughout past research. These Chinese samples were primarily gathered from more developed or economically prosperous areas such as Beijing, Shanghai, and Guangzhou. Advancements over the years have resulted in significant differences in economic development between different geographic regions of China. Koch and Koch (2007) noted the importance of examining differences between the more- and less-developed areas in China in order to better understand the link between cooperation and collectivism. They used Hofstede's individualism–collectivism scale (1980) at a group level, to examine the pre-established relationship of collectivism and cooperation as measured by an experimental method. They found that participants from more developed coastal areas were more individualistic than those from inland China, and groups with higher individualistic scores were more cooperative than those groups with higher collectivistic scores.

In essence, these findings show that the collectivism–cooperation link may not be as simple and straightforward as was previously thought. Both X. P. Chen and S. Li (2005) and Koch and Koch (2007) have argued that collectivism only increases cooperation in certain kinds of relationships and situations; particularly, they attributed their findings to the group studies being composed of out-group members. These two studies contribute significantly to the understanding of the individualism–collectivism and competition–cooperation link and reveal the complexities of the relationship.

Social axioms

In addition to Hofstede's (1980) attempt to define and measure culture with the individualism–collectivism dimension, Leung et al. (2002) have broadened the range of the conceptual tools included in cross-cultural analysis and proposed the use of *social axioms*, or people's beliefs about how the world functions, as a different type of general orientation that may augment the predictive power of values. Leung and Bond (2004) conducted quantitative research in 40 nations confirming the existence of five orthogonal dimensions of social axioms, namely social cynicism, social complexity, reward for application, religiosity, and fate control. A study conducted in Hong Kong by Bond and colleagues (2004) also demonstrated that the use of social axioms supplemented past measures of values in significantly predicting social performance across three classes of social behaviors: styles of conflict resolution, ways of coping, and vocational interests. Particularly, the study found the axiom dimensions of religiosity, social cynicism, and social complexity to be related to cooperation and competition in managing interdependencies.

Firstly, the study found an apparently 'paradoxical' relationship between religiosity and both accommodation *and* competition in conflict resolution, meaning that individuals who believe in the socially positive functioning of religious institutions will be more likely to give in to or struggle against others. They attributed this phenomenon to religious persons' reliance on or preference for third parties or institutional procedures to intervene and resolve conflicts. When facing conflict without such institutional support, on the one hand religious individuals would choose to surrender or struggle against their competitors. On the other hand, those low in religiosity possess a different mentality in resolving conflicts by taking a more proactive role and seeking out common ground and viable bargaining positions. Furthermore, social complexity was found to be positively related to collaboration and compromise when confronted with conflicts. Individuals who believe that there are multiple ways of achieving a given outcome often appreciate the interdependency of actors and institutions; in addition, their belief that human behavior is variable across situations leads them to seek out solutions where all parties involved are considered. Lastly, social cynicism was found to be negatively related to collaboration and to compromise, a finding that is not surprising: individuals who possess a pessimistic view of society and social institutions would reject collaboration and compromise in resolving conflicts, as they believe that interpersonal interdependencies will only result in domination by one party over the other.

A recent study by Kaushal and Kwantes (2006) found results which were in line with Bond and colleagues' (2004) findings on social cynicism. They used both values and social axioms to operationalize culture to examine their relationship with conflict-management strategies. They found social cynicism to predict a dominating style of conflict management, where individuals are highly concerned for their own interests and possess low concern for others.

Much research in the past concerning conflict management and social axioms has been conducted at the individual level of analysis. However, social axioms may also exist as a group-level construct, and there is evidence that conflict may arise at a group level as well as at the individual level. Group conflict, for example, can manifest itself in competition for limited resources between groups. Future research in this area can therefore investigate how generalized social beliefs or social axioms at the group level may impact on levels of inter-group conflict (Kwantes & Karam, 2008).

Risk preferences

Analyses of risk effects in social dilemmas suggest that individual risk preferences may affect cooperation in exchanges based on the notion of reciprocity (Taylor, 1987). It is generally argued that risk aversion favours cooperation or, conversely, that risk seeking undermines cooperation in repeated social dilemma interactions (Snijders & Raub, 1998; van Assen, 1998). Reciprocity in this interaction centers on the notion of the 'shadow of the future' which operates to deter rational participants from a defection because they anticipate the possible undesirable consequence of losing others' cooperation in the future. In this situation, risk aversion favours cooperation because, based on the logic of conditional cooperation, the rational actor faces the problem of having to weigh the short-term incentive to exploit partners who cooperate conditionally, against the expected long-term cost of such competitive behavior. A risk-averse actor will tend to cooperate while, conversely, a risk-seeking actor will tend to compete (Raub & Snijders, 1997).

Hsee and Weber (1999) explored cross-national differences in choice-inferred risk preferences between Americans and Chinese. Stereotypically, Americans are often portrayed to be more adventurous, aggressive, and risk seeking than Chinese. This presumption is consistent with Hsee and Weber's findings that both Americans and Chinese participants *predicted* that Americans would be more risk seeking. However, contrary to this pervasive stereotype, a robust effect was found where Chinese were *actually* more risk seeking than Americans when making financial decisions. The authors proposed a cushion hypothesis to explain what happens to Chinese compared with Americans when they encounter adverse outcomes after selecting a risk option. It was suggested that Chinese in a collectivist culture possess close family and social ties; therefore, in times of financial trouble, they can look to their larger network of close family members and friends for financial help. As a result, they tend to perceive the same risk options to be less risky than Americans would do because there is a 'cushion' to support them should they fall. Thus, they could afford to take more financial risks as opposed to Americans. Unfortunately, this conjecture was not directly tested in Hsee and Weber's study, but could easily be in future research.

In addition to the cultural differences in interpreting similar situations, differences in deeply rooted cultural values of nations, reflected and manifested in traditional cultural products, such as classical literature, proverbs, and fables, can also explain cross-national variances in risk preferences. Indeed, Weber, Hsee, and Sokolowska (1998) found that Chinese proverbs provided more risk-seeking advice than American proverbs, and American proverbs were found to be less applicable to risks in the social domain as compared with Chinese proverbs.

The above findings on cooperation, risk preferences, and their cross-national variance suggest that Chinese, being more risk seeking than Americans, would be less likely to cooperate with others. Although this seems counter-intuitive to the broad view of Chinese as being more collective and cooperative than those in individualistic cultures, results from X. P. Chen and S. Li's (2005) experiment did find Chinese participants to be less cooperative than Australian participants in a mixed-motive business context. Their intriguing findings echo the results for variations in risk preferences noted by Hsee and colleagues (1999). There appears to be a lack of research that investigates cultural differences in risk preferences and its effects on cross-national variation in the tendency toward cooperation. Future studies are called for to better determine the consequences of cross-national differences in risk preferences in light of pressures for cooperation and competition.

Regulatory focus

Based on his regulatory focus theory, Higgins (1997) proposed a framework to examine the different strategies for approaching positive outcomes and avoiding negative outcomes. His two broad frames, namely promotion focus and prevention focus, may affect individuals' inclinations towards cooperation or competition. On the one hand, promotion focus, driven by nurturance needs, is characterized by a sensitivity to the positive outcomes arising from one's behaviors. Individuals with a stronger promotion orientation regulate their behavior towards advancement, aspirations, and accomplishments. On the other hand, prevention focus, driven by security needs, leads to heightened sensitivity about negative outcomes arising from one's actions; individuals with prevention orientation regulate their behavior toward protection and safety issues (Florack & Hartmann, 2007).

Promotion and prevention orientations have been thought to result from social learning. Socialization that emphasizes duty and responsibilities nurtures an inclination towards prevention focus: a chronic concern for security, protection, and avoiding losses. Socialization that emphasizes rights and accomplishments instills a promotion focus: a chronic concern for growth, advancement, and gain. Chinese socialization practices appear to induce a prevention orientation, as individuals from a collectivistic culture tend to have strong interdependent self-construal which defines the self as a part of a network of interpersonal relationships (Markus & Kitayama, 1991). Individuals are motivated to fit in with their groups to maintain social harmony. As a result, they often focus on their responsibilities and obligations to others while trying to avoid conducting behaviors that may result in social disruptions. Those from collectivistic cultures view information about failures as more relevant to their self-esteem than information about successes (Kitayama, Markus, Matsumoto & Norasakkunkit, 1997; see also Kwan, Hui, & McGee, this volume).

The relevance of prevention frames to decision making has been found in studies such as that by Lee, Aaker, and Gardner (2000), who found that East Asians (prevention oriented) viewed tennis games that were framed as opportunities to avoid a loss as more important than did North Americans, whereas North Americans (promotion oriented) viewed the same games when framed as opportunities to secure a win as more important than did East Asians. In addition, it was found that the induction of prevention focus increased selections of loss-minimizing options in a decision-making context (Briley & Wyer, 2001).

Based on these findings, Briley, Morris, and Simonson (2005) conducted an experiment with bicultural Hong Kong Chinese, and explored compromise as an indication of prevention focus. The authors were particularly interested in investigating whether language manipulation (Cantonese versus English) would lead to shifts in the general strategy of avoiding losses rather than pursuing gains, which is more often exhibited by Chinese than Westerners. Results from their study showed that the language used to communicate to bicultural participants affected their use of decision guidelines in choosing proverbs. Particularly, it led them to choose proverbs which advocate moderation (as opposed to extremeness). In addition, when experiments were conducted in Chinese rather than in English, participants were more likely to be prevention focused, as reflected by their preferences for compromise and motivation to avoid loss or disappointment. Language in such contexts acts as a cue which influences behaviors by increasing the accessibility of particular rules or norms of the culture and also in increasing the motivation to behave in a way that is consistent with these cued rules (e.g. orienting a prevention focus among Chinese). We anticipate that this prevention orientation found among individuals socialized by Chinese practices upholding the cultural ideals of responsibility will enhance cooperation, while, simultaneously, their inclination to adopt loss-minimizing options will reduce competition.

Conflict-management style

Interpersonal conflict exists in any cultural system requiring human communication and interpersonal coordination, i.e. in all cultures. Conflict arises from the interaction between parties who perceive incompatible goals and scarce resources (Ross, 1993). Although present in any culture, how it is expressed, perceived, and handled varies across cultures. Studies have explored cross-cultural variations of conflict resolution styles in the workplace based on Rahim's (1979) conceptualization of interpersonal conflict styles: concern for self and concern for others. Concern for self is about the extent (high or low) to which an individual attempts to satisfy their own concerns; concern for others is about the extent (high or low) to which an individual attempts to satisfy the concern for others. The combination of these two dimensions results in five specific styles of handling interpersonal conflict, namely: integrating (high concern for self and others); obliging (low concern for self and high concern for others); dominating (high concern for self and low concern for others); avoiding (low concern for self and others); and compromising (intermediate in concern for self and others).

Empirical studies have demonstrated that cultural background influences conflict styles, with persons from the United States being more likely to use a dominating style of conflict resolution than those from Japan or Korea, and that members from China or Taiwan were inclined to make use of the obliging and avoiding styles more often than those from the United States (Ting-Toomey et al., 1991). The Chinese and Taiwanese tendencies toward the obliging style of conflict resolution reflect their collectivistic natures which socialize a form of selfless orientation, putting aside one's own needs to please others, and expressing harmony and cooperation (Hocker & Wilmot, 1998; see also Chen, this volume; Wang & Chang; this volume).

A recent study that further explored the relationship among culture, personality, and conflict resolution styles (Kaushal & Kwantes, 2006) found results that support culture's role in accounting for the variance in choice among strategies for conflict resolution. Particularly, the dominating style was found to be positively associated with both vertical individualism and vertical collectivism, which commonly emphasize the individual and a concern for the self. In contrast, a positive association between the obliging style and vertical collectivism is rooted in the group-based identity of collectivism. Furthermore, the avoiding style was found to be negatively associated with horizontal individualism, which places less emphasis on the individual as well as the group. Kaushal and Kwantes believe that Rahim's (1979) conceptualization of conflict-management strategies based on the concerns for the self versus others overlaps with the individualism–collectivism dimension (Singelis, Triandis, Bhawuk, & Gelfand, 1995), and they interact to determine the individual's choice of conflict resolution strategy across cultures.

The inter-individual level

Cooperative conflict

It is generally argued that, as collectivists, Chinese value interpersonal harmony and aim to avoid conflicts (e.g. Leung, 1997); conflicts have always been seen as antithetical to team functioning, so that collectivists are not trained to handle them and want to avoid their outbreak. Conflicts, however, do not universally undermine team cooperation. Whereas conflicts over relationships undermine group performance, conflicts over task issues can often help the work of the team (e.g. De Dreu, Van Vianen, Harinck, & McCusker, 1998). It is therefore more important to examine *how* a team manages conflicts.

Tjosvold and associates distinguish between two types of conflict resolution approaches based on Deutsch's (1980) conceptualization: protagonists may pursue a *cooperative goal*, believing that a win–win situation is possible, or a *competitive goal*, believing that one person's win is another person's loss. Conflicts, if resolved cooperatively, are actually an opportunity to foster confidence and to strengthen relationships among team members in the process of achieving mutual benefits.

When conflicts are approached competitively as a zero-sum game, confidence in a relationship may be undermined, and a group becomes less effective.

Tjosvold's theoretical argument and empirical findings on a universalistic aspiration of the theory of cooperation and competition show that not only Westerners but also Chinese are able to benefit from managing conflicts openly in a cooperative manner. His thesis contradicts earlier conceptualizations that Chinese avoid dealing with conflicts openly (e.g. Nibler & Harris, 2003), and that conflict avoidance is more preferred and more functional for Chinese than for Western people (e.g. Tse, Francis, & Willis, 1994).

In a study of more than 100 teams in Shanghai enterprises, Tjosvold, Poon, and Yu (2005) found converging evidence that, as in the West, cooperative conflicts in Chinese enhanced confidence in relationships and in turn improved team productivity and commitment. As long as face concerns are observed, open and direct discussion of conflicts and controversy may induce open-mindedness and receptivity, so that people asked more questions, explored opposing views, demonstrated more knowledge of opposing arguments, and were more eager to work towards integrating viewpoints (Tjosvold, Hui, & Sun, 2004).

Specifically, as opposed to the use of coercion, the use of persuasion that communicates respect provides the crucial cooperative context for conflict management (Tjosvold & Sun, 2001). An open discussion of conflicts in a cooperative manner also promotes task reflexivity, so that team members were able to reflect upon how they worked together, develop and implement plans, collect feedback and to act on this feedback, thereby improving their team dynamics and performance (Tjosvold, Hui, & Yu, 2003). When groups engage in cooperative problem solving, speakers also directly address specific targets instead of tossing out ideas to no one in particular. In cooperative groups, members also take shorter turns, show attentive listening, and invite others to participate (Chiu, 2000). Adopting a cooperative orientation in discussion facilitates conflict resolution.

Further evidence supporting the Chinese's capacity to directly deal with conflicts comes from Brew and Cairns (2004). They found that Chinese were indirect only when they were dealing with their superiors. When interacting with their peers, Chinese were no less indirect than Australians were. Chinese can indeed approach decision conflicts directly in order to reach true agreement.

In addition to their capacity to handle conflicts cooperatively, Chinese are also capable of endorsing the use of *soft* tactics when influencing others (Leong, Bond & Fu, 2006). Since Chinese societies possess a high power distance, one would expect its members to prefer the use of *hard* tactics when influencing others, especially their subordinates. Leong and colleagues studied managers from the United States, People's Republic of China, Taiwan, and Hong Kong, and found interesting results contrary to expectations. They explored the perceived effectiveness between two broad dimensions of influence: the more nurturing gentle persuasion (GP) and the more agentic contingent control (CC). Managers in all four cultures perceived GP as a much more effective influencing strategy than CC.

These findings converged with Sun and Bond's (2000) earlier study that the two salient indigenous Chinese personality characteristics of harmony and face were related to the use of GP. They found that Chinese managers who were concerned with harmony and face tend to place higher value on interpersonal relations; therefore, they preferred to use GP to gain compliance from their targets. Chinese employees' preference for GP over CC observed in the above studies illustrate, firstly, that Chinese managers are aware of the possible negative consequences of CC such as resentment, resistance or retaliation from their targets, and secondly, that the perceived effectiveness of GP over CC is probably an etic phenomenon.

Conversational style

Conversational style of argumentation may also affect cooperation during teamwork and conflicts. Yeung (2001) investigated the question of indirection in Chinese and Australian patterns of discourse during participative decision-making sessions at various banks in Hong Kong and Australia. She examined different linguistic devices used to redress the bluntness of a proposition (i.e. the more linguistic devices used, such as rhetorical questions, mention of possibilities and suggestions, the more indirect the proposition).

Results of the study seemed to contradict the persistent view that Chinese communicators prefer indirectness; Australians, rather, were found to be more indirect and hedged three times more often than Chinese. In addition, Chinese and Australians differed in the use of politeness strategies in formulating propositions. On the one hand, for Hong Kong Chinese, they tended to use Cantonese phrases such as '*hommhoyi*' (can [we] / [is it] possible) in order to ask for permission, '*juiho*' (best), to give advice or recommendation, and '*heimong*' (hope) to express a wish. On the other hand, Australians used phrases such as 'I think we should' in order to express an opinion about obligation or necessity, and 'I think we could' to convey an assessment of ability or possibility. The Chinese use of politeness strategies confirms the theory that Chinese communication is oriented towards maintaining interpersonal relationship and enlisting the others' cooperation. Furthermore, discourse analyses revealed that Chinese used rhetorical questions more than Australians did. Rhetorical questions function by strongly implying an answer, which negate the alternative point of view that exists. Rhetorical questions have the effect of involving the audience more and sometimes the unexpected effect of inviting a counter-argument. Therefore, the greater frequency with which Chinese use rhetorical questions suggests that, contrary to what is believed, Chinese can also be direct in disagreeing with others and are unafraid of confrontations (Yeung, 2001).

In addition to the differences found in conversational strategies and linguistic devices used, studies have also shown variations in features of discourse among members of different cultural groups. Stewart, Setlock, and Fussell (2004) found that as compared with Americans, Chinese tended to engage in more complex argumentation. Chinese also took a longer time in their interactions (Setlock, Fussell & Neuwirth, 2004). But more importantly, Chinese showed more agreement with their partners after discussion, whereas Americans showed more disagreements (Setlock et al., 2004). Apparently, during discussion Americans utilized proportionally more statements of convergence (i.e. agreements, acknowledgements and concessions); but there was actually less persuasion, fewer shifts in opinions, and fewer true agreements (Stewart et al., 2004).

When Chinese people interact, they may also have an edge over Westerners in maintaining a harmonious relationship. In an experimental study examining Chinese and Canadian people role playing doctor/patient conversations, Li (2001) found that when two persons interrupted each other, which is a common form of turn-taking in conversations, Chinese–Chinese dyads engaged in more cooperative interruptions, whereas Canadian–Canadian dyads had more intrusive interruptions. Chinese interruptions were not disruptive—they interrupted each other in order to assist or agree with the speaker, to help the speaker clarify or to explain previous information. These interruptions actually facilitate the ongoing conversation and, we anticipate, would also facilitate Chinese dyads in reaching cooperative agreements.

Power

People's belief regarding power affects whether they take a cooperative or competitive goal orientation. Three types of power beliefs can be distinguished (Tjosvold, Coleman, & Sun, 2003). Expandable power refers to the belief that power is expandable. As a manager empowers subordinates, both the manager and the subordinates become even more powerful and successful. A manager who believes that power is limited restricts sharing power with subordinates, because it is believed that a person who shares power will become less powerful. In a laboratory study, Tjosvold et al. (2003) showed that participants who were led to endorse an expandable-power belief were more likely to perceive a cooperative goal and were more willing to share their information power to assist others. *Guanxi* (relationships), in-group relationships, harmony-enhancement motives, benevolent and participative leadership are also conducive to adopting a cooperative goal (Tjosvold, Leung, & Johnson, 2000).

Similarly, a culture that focuses more on emotional ties between superiors and subordinates will see more collective or bottom-up decision making, indicating that superiors are releasing more power to their subordinates to make decisions (Fukada, 1982). While Chinese, relative to Americans, are less forceful and less autocratic in top-down decision making, Japanese support even more of this collective and bottom-up decision-making culture (Bi, Xi, & Wang, 2003). Compared with Japanese, Hong Kong Chinese interpersonal relationships between leader and subordinates place greater emphasis on rational commitment consistent with a formal hierarchical structure (Fukada, 1982). The tendency of Chinese towards sharing power with subordinates also differs among subgroups of Chinese (Tse, Lee, Vertinsky, & Wehrung, 1988). In this cross-cultural study comparing Hong Kong Chinese, mainland Chinese, and Canadians on an in-basket exercise that tapped participative decision making, the Hong Kong Chinese profile was similar to that of Canadians but different from that of mainland Chinese. In particular, both Hong Kong Chinese and Canadians were more inclined towards participative decision making, whereas mainland Chinese conferred more authority upon the leader. Confirming evidence showing concentration of power onto a few top leaders in mainland China is also reported in qualitative studies of several joint ventures (e.g. Eiteman, 1990; Hendryx, 1986; Redding & Wong, 1986).

As a cautionary note, these findings were published nearly 20 years ago and the prevalent Chinese norms may have changed since then. Indeed, Chinese nowadays are moving towards sharing power rather than withholding it (see Chen & Farh, this volume). A recent survey comparing adolescents in urban and rural China and in urban Canada found that adolescents in both countries favored fundamental democratic principles like representation, voice, and majority rule (Helwig, Arnold, Tan, & Boyd, 2007). Chinese nowadays seem to be endorsing an expandable view of power that facilitates establishing a cooperative goal.

Fairness

Fair treatment of both parties is essential to developing cooperation. Chinese, however, may consider fairness differently than other people depending on whether they are asked to evaluate fairness or to act on a fair principle (Bian & Kelller, 1999). When Chinese and Americans evaluated fairness in societal decisions concerning health and safety risks, both groups maintained similar fairness perceptions. Both groups perceived that an equality treatment was fairer. For example, when faced with a situation where all have a 1 per cent chance of dying and a situation where one person's sacrifice can save the lives of 99 other people, both Chinese and Americans consider that the equality (i.e. the latter) situation is fairer. However, when people were asked to choose between these two actions, Americans were more likely to choose the equality action than were the Chinese. In essence, Chinese tended to endorse the collective welfare over fairness.

Bian and Keller (1999) also found that in an interview study, Chinese government and business executives considered business and economic achievement as more important than fairness concerns. It seems that Chinese consider more of the contextual factors in decision making, whereas Americans stick to more of the equality principle in both their belief and actions. These findings supported earlier findings by Leung and Bond (1984) that in allocation decisions in a work context, Chinese relied on an equity rule more than Americans did for out-group members, but not for in-group members. Similarly, the cultural priming study of Wong & Hong (2005) also found that cultural priming affected cooperation for friends but not for strangers. Chinese cooperation behaviors are more responsive to the situation and to the people involved.

Interactional Justice

Closely related to fairness perception is interactional justice that also affects cooperative behaviors. Chinese people who received fair interpersonal treatment in negotiations, (e.g. when the opponent was willing to listen and to explain, asked open-ended questions, appreciated suggestions, etc.), arrived at fewer stalemates, reached settlements quicker, and were more likely to agree to settlements less in their favor (Leung, Tong, & Ho, 2004). A distinctive contributor to interactional justice for Chinese may perhaps be *renqing* and *guanxi*. *Renqing* is the affect or sentiment a person has towards another person (Zhang & Yang, 1998). Chinese maintain harmonious relationships with others by enacting *renqing* in the sense of showing care and concern, expressing positive emotions and giving favors. And the extent of the *renqing* expressed to others depends on the *guanxi* between the two persons. We thus reason that receiving *renqing* from the opponent will render the impression of interactional justice. As an act of reciprocation, we also expect that a person who is bestowed with *renqing* will return the favor (or *renqing*) by being more agreeable in a negotiation (see also Hwang & Han, this volume).

We can use *renqing* and *guanxi* to understand how Chinese may seem to have deviated from a fairness principle in Bian and Keller's (1999) study of health and safety risk. One of the resolutions given by Chinese participants who suggested sacrificing one person in order to save the other 99 people was to choose a criminal who deserves to die. Apparently we may envision that this criminal to be sacrificed has no existing *guanxi* with the decision maker. Another resolution was for someone to sacrifice willingly and gloriously for others he or she loved. Doing this great favor, viz. sacrificing one's life, for a loved one also exemplifies *renqing* bestowed upon a person with a very close *guanxi*. These two examples may illustrate how Chinese may adjust their fairness behaviors depending on their *guanxi* and *renqing* with different people.

As demonstrated by Zhang and Yang (1998) in a survey among partners in different relationships, Chinese people allocating rewards abide by a reasonableness norm (*heqingheli*) that emphasizes both reason and affect. Reason is like the equity and fairness principle, whereas affect concerns the interaction between *renqing* and *guanxi*. A partner with a closer *guanxi*, e.g. parents and siblings, received more allocations than did acquaintances and strangers. This distribution of allocations was found to be similar to the distribution when respondents were asked to allocate 'reasonably'. All these findings suggest that beyond equity, Chinese also consider *renqing* and *guanxi* in distributing resources with others.

Trust

Citizenship behaviors are a manifestation of cooperation in work settings, and trust in supervisors has been found to induce citizenship behaviors (Konovsky & Pugh, 1994). One antecedent of trust is perception of procedural and distributive justice, and power distance affects the linkage between justice perception and trust in supervisors. Power distance is the belief in the amount of power a supervisor should have over a subordinate. A low power distance person believes that a smaller degree of power is appropriate. Among these people low in power distance, procedural justice exerts a stronger influence on their trust in supervisors. For people high in power distance, the effect of procedural justice has a smaller effect on employee's trust. We anticipate that Chinese, who are high on power distance, at least in terms of their values (Bond, 1996), may find that procedural justice will have small effects on trust, and therefore small effects on citizenship behaviors.

There is also other evidence showing that cooperation among Chinese may be undermined by a lack of trust. Wang and Clegg (2002) studied the leader–subordinate relationship and distinguished between two types of trust: (a) trust by leader of subordinates' psychological maturity, and (b) trust by leader of subordinate's job maturity (i.e. their relevant skills and technical knowledge). They found that Chinese managers trusted their subordinates' psychological maturity less than Australian managers did. Trust of subordinates' job maturity, however, did not differ between Australian and Chinese managers. Chinese believe that their subordinates can do the task, but do not trust that they are willing to assume responsibility for the task. The authors reasoned that this cultural difference was consistent with the argument in the literature that degrees of trust in interpersonal relationships correlated with power distance (Porta et al., 1997). Chinese societies are characterized by larger power distance, such that the authority who typically exercises control does not usually trust the subordinates, who are often viewed as dependent and obedient 'children'. As subordinates look to their boss for instructions, the subordinates may seem to lack initiative, a restraint that reinforces or induces the boss to consider subordinates as unwilling to take up responsibility. Both studies tend to suggest that high power distance among Chinese undermines trust between leader and subordinates and in turn also affects cooperation.

The detrimental effect of power distance on trust among Chinese people may be offset by China's economic development. Henrich, Boyd, Bowles, Camerer, Fehr, Gintis, and McElreath (2001) found that national levels of trust were influenced by economic welfare. Societies with stronger market integration had citizens who were more trusting. The institutions of such societies are more likely to 'strain towards fairness'. Their members give higher offers in ultimatum games and have higher rejection rates (punishment) for lower offers. Intriguing results from Allik and Realo's (2004) analyses on individualism-collectivism and trust among 42 cultures found that China had nearly the highest level of interpersonal trust. This finding was consistent with that from Zhang and Bond's (1993) study where mainland Chinese gave more trust toward their acquaintances and strangers than did either Hong Kong or American participants. Therefore, perhaps, economic advancement and modernization in China have helped to lessen the impact of power distance on trust among Chinese.

Trust between partners also affects how conflicts are resolved. One conflict resolution tactic is coercion, a high-pressure tactic that pressures the other party through threats, promises, and/or legalistic pleas to compel immediate responses. In a study of architects and contractors in Hong Kong, Lui, Ngo, and Hon (2006) found that partners with stronger interpersonal trust used coercive strategies to a lesser extent. In addition, among institutional partners who were similar and enjoying a better reputation, less coercion was used; this effect was fully mediated by trust at both the interpersonal and inter-organizational levels. One might expect that with higher stakes, i.e. more assets in both time and money committed to the partnership, there would be stronger trust. On the contrary, the extent of assets committed undermined inter-organizational trust and did not affect interpersonal trust. More importantly, people used coercive tactics more often to manipulate each other as their committed assets increased. In summary, partners who are more similar to one another and present a better reputation to others enjoy strong trust at both the interpersonal and inter-organizational levels, and they use fewer coercive tactics against each other to resolve conflicts.

In another study based on the same sample of Hong Kong architects, Lui and Ngo (2004) distinguished between goodwill trust and competence trust, and examined how these two types of trusts affected inter-firm cooperation through risk perception. They found that goodwill trust affected perceptions of relational risk and competence trust affected perceived performance risk on inter-firm cooperation.

Multiple views of competition

Chinese are not only versatile in being able to confront conflicts directly through aspiring to cooperative goals; they also see that competition is not always a bad thing. Fülöp and her associates (2006) examined beliefs and attitudes towards competition at both a personal level and an economic level. Four factors were distinguished: (a) a personal-positive factor considers that competition motivates people to achieve goals, and that people need to compete in order to survive and prosper; (b) a personal-negative factor considers competition as creating stress and anxiety for people and leading to tension and conflict between individuals; (c) an economic-positive factor suggests that in a market economy, viz. one that implies free competition, everyone observes the moral rules of business and only the hardworking ones will be successful; and (d) an economic-negative factor stipulates that competition is an unfortunate part of society that contributes to war and injustice, and that people get rich at the expense of others.

In comparison with the French (as persons from a developed country) and the Hungarians (as persons from a post-socialist country), mainland Chinese adolescents (as persons from a socialist country) showed a moderately positive attitude towards competition: Chinese were not different from Hungarian and French on the personal-positive aspect, but were lower than members of both countries on the personal-negative aspect. Most interestingly, Chinese adolescents were significantly higher than Hungarians and French on both the economic-positive and economic-negative aspects. In summary, on a personal level Chinese were moderately positive towards competition and saw both the advantages and disadvantages of a market economy. The ambivalent attitudes of Chinese towards competition were also found in an earlier study comparing Chinese, Americans, and Russians (Hemesath & Pomponio, 1995). While Chinese students were like American and Russian students in desiring material gains and believing in the importance of material incentives in a market economy, these same Chinese students were more supportive of government interventions in the market. In essence, Chinese adolescents have a strong commitment towards competition in business life; they also see competition as being exploitative.

Uniform views of cooperation

While Chinese do not abhor competition, they also embrace cooperation. Chinese, compared to Hungarian pre-schoolers, were more likely to choose an equality option over an unequal option that gave themselves an advantage (Sándor, Berkics, Fülöp, & Xie, 2007). These preferences need not be nurtured through ingrained socialization; cultural values can be primed to induce cooperative behaviors. Chinese-American biculturals who were primed with Chinese icons, e.g. Chinese dragons or Chinese *kung fu*, were more cooperative towards their friends in a prisoner's dilemma game (Wong & Hong, 2005). These Chinese cultural primes may have activated the motives of trust and altruism towards in-group members that are essential to cooperation in a social-dilemma situation (Markoczy, 2004).

Directions for future research

Previous research in cross-cultural psychology has generally viewed competition as a characteristic of individualistic, particularly Western, societies, while cooperation has been viewed as a feature of collectivistic, Eastern, societies. Literature has treated competition and cooperation as mutually exclusive concepts, with cooperation regarded as more favorable. As mentioned in the present chapter, recent research has demonstrated that firstly, the common stereotypical belief of the individualism–collectivism and competition–cooperation link is no longer as direct and straightforward as previously believed.

Secondly, a new line of organizational research, coined 'coopetition', focuses on studying the joint occurrence and interplay of cooperation and competition. Although coopetive behavior has long been observed between organizations, it is only recently that the subject has gained importance academically (Walley, 2007). According to a study conducted with managers from 500 firms in metropolitan China, at an intra-firm level the authors found that the presence of cooperation allows for knowledge transfer among cross-functional groups. Simultaneously, competition facilitates this knowledge transfer, given the underlying motive and incentive of employees to understand the position of competing functions (Luo, Slotegraaf, & Pan, 2006). Intensive cooperation across competing departments not only enables the sharing of information and knowledge but also stimulates superior performance by promoting a shared understanding of customer needs, providing the grounds for collaborative and effective decision making within an organization (Ghoshal, Korine, & Szulanski, 1994). This communion of cooperation and competition has been shown to create synergies that translate into competitive advantage, nurturing productive interactions that facilitate internal efficiencies, thereby resulting in better overall performance (Luo et al., 2006). These findings provide significant implications for managers or team members who wish to enhance organizational or group performance. Therefore, future research can focus on developing paradigms for examining competition-cooperation interaction that transcend the common assumption of exclusivity, and investigating the cross-cultural variation of the two concepts within such a paradigm.

In addition to the exclusivity assumption of cooperation and competition, cooperation has consistently been assumed to be desirable and competition to be harmful. However, Fülöp and her colleagues (Fülöp, 1992, 1999a, 1999b, 2001–2002, 2002; Fülöp & Berkics, 2002; Watkins, Fülöp, Berkics, & Regmi, 2003) have surveyed young people's perceptions of competition from countries such as Canada, USA, UK, Japan, Nepal and Hungary, finding that respondents from North America and UK believe that they live in relatively competitive societies and take competition for granted but regard it as neutral. Japanese and Nepalese respondents have even been able to generate sophisticated views of competition and its positive effects on their lives and societies.

A similar study was conducted with Hong Kong Chinese adolescents, investigating their views on the role of competition in Hong Kong (Watkins, 2006). Results from the study showed that, consistent with Fülöp's findings on Japanese and Nepalese respondents, Hong Kong adolescents viewed competition as very important and as a positive force leading to the improvement of Hong Kong at both the societal and individual levels. The above findings show that perceptions of competition are not one-sided as once commonly believed, and that they vary across cultures; collectivistic societies and their members can be just as or sometimes even more competitive than individualistic societies and their members. It will be interesting for future studies to further investigate the evaluation of the role of competition across cultures, looking, for instance, into whether societal and personal values and beliefs affect evaluations of the concept.

Chinese culture, just as much as other cultures, is a dynamic entity. We are excited to see how Chinese cooperation and competition may evolve with time, and hope that our understanding can keep pace with the emerging reality.

References

Bi, P. C., Xi, Y. M., & Wang, Y. Y. (2003). Cross-cultural impact on groupthink: A comparison of China, America and Japan. *Forecasting, 6*, 1–10.

Bian, W.-Q. & Keller, L. R. (1999). Chinese and Americas agree on what is fair, but disagree on what is best in societal decisions affecting and safety risks. *Risk Analysis, 19*, 439–452.

Bond, M. H. (1996). Chinese values. In M. H. Bond (ed.), *The handbook of Chinese psychology* (pp. 208–226). Hong Kong: Oxford University Press.

Bond, M. H., Leung, K., Au, A., Tong, K. K., de Carrasquel, S. R., Murakami, F. et al. (2004). Culture-level dimensions of social axioms and their correlates across 41 cultures. *Journal of Cross-Cultural Psychology, 35*, 548–570.

Brew. F. P. & Cairns, D. R. (2004). Do culture or situational constraints determine choice of direct or indirect styles in intercultural workplace conflicts? *International Journal of Intercultural Relations, 28*, 331–352.

Briley, D. A., Morris, M. W., & Simonson, I. (2005). Cultural chameleons: Biculturals, conformity motives, and decision making. *Journal of Consumer Psychology, 15*, 351–362.

Briley, D. A. & Wyer, R. S. (2001). Transitory determinants of values and decisions: The utility (or nonutility) of individualism and collectivism in understanding cultural differences. *Social Cognition, 19*, 197–227.

Chen, C. C., Chen, X. P., & Meindl, J. R. (1998). How can co-operation be fostered? The cultural effects of individualism and collectivism. *Academy of Management Review, 23*, 285–304.

Chen, X. P. & Li, S. (2005). Cross-National differences in cooperative decision making in mixed-motive business contexts: The mediating effect of vertical and horizontal individualism. *Journal of International Business Studies, 36*, 622–636.

Chiu, M. M. (2000). Group problem-solving processes: Social interactions and individual actions. *Journal for the Theory of Social Behaviour, 30*, 27–49.

Cox, T. H., Lobel, S. A., & McLeod, P. L. (1991). Effects of ethnic group cultural differences on cooperative and competitive behavior on a group task. *Academy of Management Journal, 34*, 827–847.

De Dreu, C. K. W., Van Vianen, A. E. M., Harinck, F., & McCusker, C. (1998). *Social-emotional and task-related conflict in groups: Implications for contextual and task performance.* Paper presented at the Society for Industrial and Organizational Psychology Conference, Dallas, Texas, USA, July.

Deutsch, M. (1980). Fifty years of conflict. In L. Festinger (ed.), *Retrospections on social psychology* (pp. 46–77). New York: Oxford University Press.

Domino, G. (1992). Cooperation and competition in Chinese and American children. *Journal of Cross-Cultural Psychology, 23*, 456–67.

Eiteman, D. K. (1990). America executives' perceptions of negotiating joint ventures with the People's Republic of China: Lessons learned. *Columbia Journal of World Business, 25*, 59–67.

Florack, A. & Hartmann, J. (2007). Regulatory focus and investment decisions in small groups. *Journal of Experimental Social Psychology, 43*, 626–632.

Fukuda, K. J. (1982). Decision-making in organizations: A comparison of the Japanese and Chinese Models. *Hong Kong Journal of Public Administration, 4*, 176–183.

Fülöp, M. (1992). Cognitive concepts on competition. *International Journal of Psychology, 27*, 316.

Fülöp, M. (1999a). Students' perception of the role of competition in their respective countries: Hungary, Japan and the USA. In A. Ross (ed.), *Young citizens in Europe* (pp. 195–219). London: University of North London.

Fülöp, M. (1999b). Japanese students' perception of the role of competition in their country. *Asian and African Studies, 3*, 148–174.

Fülöp, M. (2001–2). Competition in Hungary and Britain as perceived by adolescents. *Applied Psychology in Hungary, 3–4*, 33–53.
Fülöp, M. (2002). Intergenerational differences and social transition: Teachers' and students' perception of competition in Hungary. In E. Nasman & A. Ross (eds), *Children's understanding in the new Europe* (pp. 63–89). Stoke-on-Trent, England: Trentham Books.
Fülöp, M. & Berkics, M. (2002). Economic education and attitudes towards enterprise, business and competition among adolescents in Hungary. In M. Hutchings, M. Fülöp, & A. Van Den Dries (eds), *Young people's understanding of economic issues in Europe*. Stoke-on-Trent, England: Trentham Books.
Fülöp, M., Roland-Levy, C., Ya, Y., & Berkics, M. (2006). *Chinese, French and Hungarian adolescents' perception and attitude towards competition in economic life*. Paper presented at the 18th International Congress of the International Association of Cross-Cultural Psychology, July 11–15, Spetses, Greece, July.
Gabrenya, W. K. Jr & Hwang, K. K. (1996). Chinese social interaction: Harmony and hierarchy on the good earth. In M. H. Bond (ed.), *The handbook of Chinese psychology* (pp. 309–321). Hong Kong: Oxford University Press.
Gabrenya, W. K. Jr, Latané, B., & Wang, Y.-E. (1983). Social loafing in cross-cultural perspective. *Journal of Cross-Cultural Psychology, 14*, 368–384.
Ghoshal, S., Korine, H., & Szulanski, G. (1994). Interunit communication in multinational corporations. *Management Science, 40*, 96–110.
Helwig, C. C., Arnold, M. L., Tan, D., & Boyd, D. (2007). Mainland Chinese and Canadian adolescents' judgments and reasoning about the fairness of democratic and other forms of government. *Cognitive Development, 22*, 96–109.
Hemesath, M. & Pomponio, X. (1995). Student attitudes toward markets: comparative survey data from China, the United States of America and Russia. *China Economic Review, 6*, 225–238.
Hendryx, S. R. (1986). The China trade: Making the deal work. *Harvard Business Review, 64*, 75, 81–84.
Henrich, J., Boyd, R., Bowles, S., Camerer, C., Fehr, E., Gintis, H., & McElreath, R. (2001). In search of *homoeconomicus*: behavioral experiments in 15 small-scale societies. *American Economic Review, 91*, 73–78.
Higgins, E. T. (1997). Beyond pleasure and pain. *American Psychologist, 52*, 1280–1300.
Hocker, J. L. & Wilmot, W. W. (1998). *Interpersonal conflict*. (5th edn). Madison, WI: Brown & Benchmark.
Hofstede, G. H. (1980). *Culture Consequences: International Differences in Work-related Values*. London: Sage.
Hofstede, G. H. (1991). *Cultures and organizations: Software of the mind*. London: McGraw-Hill.
Hsee, C. K., Loewenstein, G. F., Blount, S. & Bazerman, M. H. (1999). Preference reversals between joint and separate evaluations of options: A review and theoretical analysis. *Psychological Bulletin, 125*, 576–590.
Hsee, C. K. & Weber, E. U. (1999). Cross-national differences in risk preferences and lay predictions for the differences. *Journal of Behavioral Decision Making, 12*, 165–179.
Karau, S. J. & Williams, K. D. (1993). Social loafing: A meta-analytic review and theoretical integration. *Journal of Personality and Social Psychology, 6*, 681–706.
Kaushal, R. & Kwantes, C. T. (2006). The role of culture and personality in choice of conflict management strategy. *International Journal of Intercultural Relations, 30*, 579–604.
Kitayama, S., Markus, H. R., Matsumoto, H., & Norasakkunkit, V. (1997). Individual and collective processes in the construction of the self: Self-enhancement in the United States and self-criticism in Japan. *Journal of Personality and Social Psychology, 72*, 1245–1267.
Koch, B. J. & Koch, P. T. (2007). Collectivism, individualism, and outgroup cooperation in a segmented China. *Asia Pacific Journal of Management, 24*, 207–225.
Konovsky, M. A. & Pugh, S. D. (1994). Citizenship behavior and social exchange. *Academy of Management Journal, 37*, 656–669.
Kwantes, C. T. & Karam, C. M. (in press). Social axioms and organizational behavior. In K. Leung & M. H. Bond (eds), *Beliefs around the world: Advancing research on social axioms*. New York: Springer SBM.
Latané, B., Williams, K., & Harkins, S. (1979). Many hands make light the work: The causes and consequences of social loafing. *Journal of Personality and Social Psychology, 37*, 822–832.
Lee, A. Y., Aaker, J. L., & Gardner, W. L. (2000). The pleasures and pains of distinct self-construals: The role of interdependence in regulatory focus. *Journal of Personality and Social Psychology, 78*, 1122–1134.
Leung, K. (1997). Negotiations and reward allocations across cultures. In P. C. Earley & M. Erez (eds), *New perspectives on international industrial/organizational psychology* (pp. 640–675). San Francisco, CA: Jossey-Bass.
Leung, K. & Bond, M. H. (1984). The impact of cultural collectivism on reward allocation. *Journal of Personality and Social Psychology, 47*, 793–804.
Leung, K., Bond, M. H., Reimel de Carrasquel, S., Muñoz, C., Hernández, M., Murakami, F., et al. (2002). Social axioms: The search for universal dimensions of general beliefs about how the world functions. *Journal of Cross-Cultural Psychology, 33*, 286–302.
Leung, K., Tong, K.-K., & Ho, S. S.-Y. (2004). Effects of international justice on egocentric bias in resource allocation decisions. *Journal of Applied Psychology, 89*, 405–415.
Li, H. Z. (2001). Cooperative and intrusive interruptions in inter- and intracultural dyadic discourse. *Journal of Language and Social Psychology, 20*, 258–284.
Lui, S. S. & Ngo, H.-Y. (2004). The role of trust and contractual safeguards on cooperation in non-equity alliances. *Journal of Management, 30*, 471–485.

Lui, S. S., Ngo, H.-Y., & Hon, A. H.-Y. (2006). Coercive strategy in interfirm cooperation: Mediating roles of interpersonal and interorganizational trust. *Journal of Business Research, 59*, 466–474.

Luo, X., Slotegraaf, R., & Pan, X. (2006). Cross-functional coopetition: the simultaneous role of cooperation and competition within firms. *Journal of Marketing, 70*, 67–80.

Markoczy, L. (2004). Multiple motives behind single acts of co-operation. *The International Journal of Human Resource Management, 15*, 1018–1039.

Markus, H. & Kitayama, S. (1991). Culture and the self: Implications for cognition, emotion, and motivation. *Psychological Review, 98*, 224–253.

Matsui, T., Kakuyama, T., & Onglatco, M. L. U. (1987). Effects of goals and feedback on performance in groups. *Journal of Applied Psychology, 72*, 407–15.

Morris, M. W. & Peng, K. (1994). Culture and cause: American and Chinese attributions for social and physical events. *Journal of Personality and Social Psychology, 67*, 949–971.

Nibler, R. & Harris, K. L. (2003). The effects of culture and cohesiveness on intra-group conflict and effectiveness. *Journal of Social Psychology, 143*, 613–631.

Rahim, A. (1979). Managing conflict through effective organization design: An experimental study with the MAPS design technology. *Psychological Reports, 44*, 759–764

Raub, W. & Snijders, C. (1997). Gains, losses, and cooperation in social dilemmas and collective action: The effects of risk preferences. *Journal of Mathematical Sociology, 22*, 263–302.

Redding, G. & Wong, G. Y. Y. (1986). The psychology of Chinese organizational behaviour. In M. H. Bond (ed.), *The psychology of the Chinese people* (pp. 267–295). New York: Oxford University Press.

Ross, M. H. (1993). *The management of conflict: Interpretations and interests in comparative perspective.* New Haven, CN: Yale University Press.

Sándor, M., Fülöp, M., Berkics, M., Xie, X. (2007) A megosztó viselkedés kulturális és helyzeti meghatározói magyar és kínai óvodáskorú gyerekeknél. (Cultural and situational determinants of sharing behaviour among Hungarian and Chinese kindergarten children) *Pszichológia, 27*, 281–310. (in Hungarian)

Setlock, L. D., Fussell, S. R., & Neuwirth, C. M. (2004). Taking it out of context: Collaborating within and across cultures in face-to-face settings and via instant messaging. *Proceedings of the ACM Conference on Computer Supported Collaborative Work, 6*, 604–613.

Singelis, T. M., Triandis, H. C., Bhawuk, D. S., & Gelfand, M. (1995). Horizontal and vertical dimensions of individualism and collectivism: A theoretical and measurement refinement. *Cross-Cultural Research, 29*, 240–275.

Snijders, C. & Raub, W. (1998). Revolution and risk. Paradoxical consequences of risk aversion in interdependent situations. *Rationality and Society, 10*, 405–425.

Stewart, C. O., Setlock, L. D., & Fussell, S. R. (2004). Conventional argumentation in decision making: Chinese and US participants in face-to-face and instant-messaging interactions. *Discourse Processes, 44*, 113–139.

Taylor, M. (1987).*The possibility of cooperation.* Cambridge, England: Cambridge University Press.

Ting-Toomey, S., Gao, G., Trubisky, P., Yang, Z., Kim, H. S., Lin, S.-L., & Nishida, T. (1991). Culture, face maintenance, and styles of handling interpersonal conflict: A study in five cultures. *International Journal of Conflict Management, 24*, 275–296.

Tjosvold, D., Coleman, P. T., & Sun, H. F. (2003). Effects of organizational values on leaders' use of informational power to affect performance in China. *Group Dynamics: Theory, Research, and Practice, 7*, 152–167.

Tjosvold, D., Hui, C., & Sun, H. (2004). Can Chinese discuss conflicts openly? Field and experimental studies of face dynamics in China. *Group Decision and Negotiation, 13*, 351–373.

Tjosvold, D., Hui, C., & Yu, Z. (2003). Conflict management and task reflexivity for team in-role and extra-role performance in China. *International Journal of Conflict Management, 14*, 141–163.

Tjosvold, D., Leung, K., & Johnson, D. W. (2000). Cooperative and competitive conflict in China. In M. Deutsch & P. T. Coleman (eds), *The handbook of conflict resolution: Theory and practice* (pp. 475–495). San Francisco, CA: Jossey-Bass.

Tjosvold, D., Poon, M., & Yu, Z.-Y. (2005). Team effectiveness in China: Cooperative conflict for relationship building. *Human Relations, 58*, 341–367.

Tjosvold, D. & Sun, H. F. (2001). Effects of influence tactics and social contexts in conflict: An experiment on relationships in China. *International Journal of Conflict Management, 12*, 239–258.

Tse, D. K., Francis, J., & Willis, J. (1994). Cultural differences in conducting intra- and inter-cultural negotiations: A Sino–Canadian comparison. *Journal of International Business Studies, 24*, 537–555.

Tse, D. K., Lee, K.-H., Vertinsky, I., & Wehrung, D. A. (1988). Does cultural matter? A cross-cultural study of executives' choice, decisiveness, and risk adjustment in international marketing. *Journal of Marketing, 52*, 81–95.

Van Assen, M. (1998). Effects of individual decision theory assumptions on predictions of cooperation in social dilemmas. *Journal of Mathematical Sociology, 23*, 143–153.

Walley, K. E. (2007) Coopetition: An Introduction to the Subject and an Agenda for Research. *International Studies of Management and Organization, Special Issue on Coopetition, 37*, 11–31

Wang, K. Y. & Clegg, S. (2002). Trust and decision making: Are managers different in the People's Republic of China and in Australia? *Cross-Cultural Management, 9*, 30–45.

Watkins, D. (2006). The role of competition in today's Hong Kong': The views of Hong Kong Chinese adolescents in comparative perspective. *Journal of Social Sciences, 2*, 85–88.

Watkins, D., Fülöp, M., Berkics, M., & Regmi, M. (2003). *The nature of competition in Nepalese schools.* Paper presented at European Regional Conference International Association of Cross-Cultural Psychology, Budapest, July.

Weber, E. U. & Hsee, C. K. (1998). Cross-cultural differences in risk perception but cross-cultural similarities in attitudes towards risk. *Management Science, 44,* 1205–1217.

Weber, E. U., Hsee, C. K., & Sokolowska, J. (1998). What folklore tells us about risk and risk taking: Cross-cultural comparisons of American, German, and Chinese proverbs. *Organizational Behavior and Human Decision Processes, 75,* 170–186.

Wong, R. Y.-M. & Hong, Y. Y. (2005). Dynamic influences of culture on cooperation in the prisoner's Dilemma. *Psychological Science, 16,* 429–434.

Yamagishi, T. (1988). The provision of a sanctioning system in the United States and Japan. *Social Psychology Quarterly, 51,* 265–71.

Yamagishi, T. (2003). Cross-societal experimentation on trust: A comparison of the United States and Japan. In E. Ostrom & J. Walker (eds), *Trust and reciprocity* (pp. 352–370). New York: Russell Sage Foundation.

Yamagishi, T. & Yamagishi, M. (1994). Trust and commitment in the United States and Japan. *Motivation and Emotion, 18,* 129–166.

Zhang, J. X. & Bond, M. H. (1993). Target-based interpersonal trust: Cross-cultural comparison and its cognitive model. *Acta Psychologia Sinica,* 164–172. (in Chinese with English abstract)

Zhang, Z. & Yang, C.-F. (1998). Beyond distributive justice: The reasonableness norm in Chinese reward allocation. *Asian Journal of Social Psychology, 1,* 253–269.

CHAPTER 30

Interpersonal relationships in rapidly changing Chinese societies

Darius K.-S. Chan, Theresa T.-T. Ng, and Chin-Ming Hui

Since 1970, mainland China has been undergoing social and economic reforms that have brought about astonishing economic success. The continuous double-digit growth in GDP in the mainland signifies the increasing wealth that many Chinese along the two shores of the Taiwan Strait are enjoying. China's pace toward industrialization and modernization has been at full speed in the last 20 years (Chia, Allred, & Jerzak, 1997). These social and economic changes have also led to many changes in Chinese interpersonal relationships, and family structures and processes, including the transformation of marriage from institutional control towards greater degrees of personal choice (Thornton & Lin, 1994; Xu & Whyte, 1990). Importantly, such normative changes in relationships are not limited to mainland China but can also be seen in other Chinese habitats, such as Hong Kong, Singapore, and Taiwan.

In this chapter, we focus on Chinese relationship research conducted in the last decade, and examine how the rapid social and economic changes in Chinese societies have exerted an impact on the various types of interpersonal relationship. We also look at how traditional Chinese values (e.g. Confucianism and collectivism) continue to shape interpersonal relationships amidst the increasing influence of modernization and globalization.

A search of the relevant literature reveals that since the last review by Goodwin and Tang (1996) on this same topic, there has been a steady increase in the number of published empirical studies on interpersonal relationships involving Chinese. The research reviewed below comes primarily from the diverse disciplines of psychology, sociology, family studies, gerontology, and health research. While some of these studies are cross-cultural comparisons, mono-cultural studies on Chinese are growing in number, reflecting increased research attention to Chinese relationships within Chinese societies and their possible distinctive features. It is also exciting to see some studies comparing Chinese from different regions as well as relationship research published in Chinese-language journals. This chapter attempts to integrate the available empirical evidence from all these sources. In terms of interpersonal relationships, we focus on four broad domains, namely friendship, romantic relationships, marital relationships, and family relationships, providing a review of the relevant studies in each domain.

Friendship

Recent studies on friendship involving Chinese participants can be broadly classified into three groups. Findings from the first group of studies suggest that the general mechanisms of friendship development are probably more similar to than different from those found in the West. The second group of research consists of monocultural studies using indigenous measures to examine Chinese friendship. The third group of research includes studies examining two emerging topics in friendship research, namely online friendships and friendships among elderly Chinese.

Similarities to Western friendships

Whereas the cultural construct of individualism–collectivism (I–C) has often been used as a variable for explaining cultural differences between the East and West, friendship research involving Chinese participants in the last decade seems to suggest more similarities than differences across cultures. As reviewed below, results from both monocultural studies and cross-cultural comparisons indicate that, despite cultural mean differences in certain measures relevant to friendships, the general mechanisms or processes of friendship development among Chinese and its psychosocial correlates are similar to those found among Western samples.

In terms of friendship perception, Li (2002) adapted the Inclusion of Other in the Self scale (Aron, Aron, & Smollan, 1992) to examine how Canadian and mainland Chinese construed their relationship with family members and friends. Consistent with the I–C construct, Chinese were more interdependent in terms of connectedness between self and family members than were Canadians. However, no cultural effects were found when it came to friendship; Canadians felt as close to their closest friends as mainland Chinese did. Similar findings were replicated in Li, Zhang, Bhatt, and Yum (2006).

In terms of friendship quality, Lin and Rusbult (1995) used the constructs of the investment model to explain relationship commitment in cross-sex friendships and dating relationships among American and Taiwanese college students. Their findings revealed that the associations between the investment model variables, such as investment size with satisfaction level and commitment across the two types of relationship were similar for both samples. In other words, factors such as investment size and satisfaction level are important explanatory variables in predicting relationship commitment for participants from both cultures (see also Ho, Chen, Bond, Chan, & Friedman, 2008). These results thus failed to support their hypothesis that the investment model should have greater predictive power among Americans based on their hypothesis that individualistic 'calculations' such as investments and alternatives are largely Western concepts.

Monocultural studies on Chinese friendships also reveal important psychosocial correlates that have consistently been found to be predictive in Western samples. For example, Chou (2000) examined the role of intimacy among friends and demonstrated its importance for psychosocial development among Chinese adolescents in Hong Kong, a finding that is consistent with Western studies (e.g. Buhrmester, 1990; Giordano, Cernkovich, Groat, Pugh, & Swinford, 1998). Wong and Bond (1999) examined friendship development among university roommates in Hong Kong and found that among other personality characteristics, self-disclosing behavior was a significant correlate of friendship strength among their participants, a finding that is consistent with Western theories, e.g. Altman and Taylor's (1973) social penetration theory and research (see Collins & Miller, 1994 for a review) on relationship development.

One interesting aspect of friendship is its voluntary nature (see e.g. Fehr, 1996), and Chinese friendships are no exception. Across different Chinese societies, individuals are generally free to choose their friends. Among the four types of relationships reviewed in this chapter, normative influence seems to have the least impact on friendship, as discussed below. Thus, with rapid modernization and Westernization, it is not surprising to find that the general mechanisms of friendship development among Chinese are in fact similar to those in the West.

Some indigenous Chinese studies

A few studies on Chinese friendship adopted an indigenous approach. Having developed indigenous measures of personality and friendship strength, Bond and his associates conducted a series of studies on roommate friendship among Hong Kong Chinese college students in order to find out important factors contributing to a harmonious relationship among Chinese roommates.

Using an indigenously derived measure of personality, i.e. the Sino American Person Perception Scale (SAPPS; Yik & Bond, 1993), Lee and Bond (1998) examined the association of personality traits and mutual friendship ratings among college roommates. It should be noted that it is unusual in the friendship literature to look at mutuality in friendship. Their results reveal that the personality variable associated with mutual friendship was the roommate's perceived higher level on four of the eight desirable dimensions of Chinese personality, namely helpfulness, intellect, openness to experience, and extraversion. In addition to the similarity effect that has consistently been found in the interpersonal attraction literature, these authors suggested that desirable personality characteristics may be more important in predicting Chinese roommates' relationship quality. A subsequent study by Wong and Bond (1999) also reported that roommates' qualities of helpfulness and intellect contributed additional prediction to friendship ratings, beyond the effect of self-disclosure. These results highlight the importance of certain personality characteristics, i.e. helpfulness and intellect, in Chinese friendship development (see also Bond & Forgas, 1984).

Extending previous research on friendship development that has typically focused on single, psychological measures (such as dimensions of personality), Tam and Bond (2002) examined how personality characteristics and roommate behaviors were associated with friendship quality among a sample of Hong Kong Chinese college students. The two indigenous factors of interpersonal behaviors, namely, beneficence and restraint, were found to be associated with friendship strength even when the personality variables captured by SAPPS were controlled for. These two sets of behavior help explain the intricacies of friendship interactions among Chinese, beyond the influence of the typically used personality measures.

Emerging issues in friendship research

Given our limited knowledge of the ever-growing phenomenon of online friendships across the globe, Chan and his associates conducted a few studies to examine the nature and qualities of online friendships among young Chinese adults in Hong Kong. For instance, Chan and Cheng (2004) compared face-to-face and online friendships, finding that online friendships were similar to face-to-face friendships in terms of friendship qualities like patterns of disclosure, understanding, and commitment, particularly for those developed over a longer period of time. More interestingly, they also found that the qualities of cross-sex online friendships were higher than those of same-sex online friendship, implying that the influence of the structural and normative constraints surrounding gender and typically found in face-to-face interaction may be different in the online setting.

Cheng, Chan, and Tong (2006) examined the effects of gender composition on the qualities of online friendships. Consistent with the findings on face-to-face friendships, the quality of online friendships involving various gender compositions continued to improve as the relationships progressed. However, male–male online friendships were consistently rated as lower than friendships of other gender composition. While these findings are derived from Chinese samples, they expand our general understanding of online friendships that have no geographical boundary.

Interesting studies have also been conducted to examine the role that friendship plays among elderly Chinese and how various types of social support are associated with their psychological well-being. For instance, Siu and Phillips (1999) examined the associations among friendship, family support, and psychological well-being among older women (aged 60 or above) in Hong Kong. One interesting finding is that older women's perceived importance of their friendships was predictive of their positive affect, whereas perceived importance of family was not.

Consistent with findings in Western societies, these authors explained that older Chinese women may have to reply on emotional and instrumental support from friends instead of family members, because of the increasingly prevalent nuclear families in Hong Kong due to rapid industrialization and modernization. However, Boey (1999) examined the associations among family networks, friendship networks, and various indices of psychological well-being among a sample of elderly Hong Kong Chinese (mean age 77), and reported that the associations of friendship networks with the well-being measures were weaker than those of family networks. Recent studies by Lam and Boey (2005) and Yeung and Fung (2007) also revealed that family support, particularly emotional support, contributed more to the psychological well-being of Chinese elderly than did friend support. Yet Lee, Ruan, and Lai (2005) compared older adults in Hong Kong and Beijing, and found that family and friends were equally important in providing emotional support to their participants. Based on the same data set, Chan and Lee (2006) reported that elderly Chinese in both cities were happier with a larger social network and that perceived social support played a mediating role in explaining their happiness.

While it is encouraging to see some studies on the psychosocial correlates of friendship networks among elderly Chinese, the conflicting findings on the importance of friendship warrant more empirical investigation. These seemingly contradictory findings may be due to such factors as the types of support being examined, e.g. instrumental vs. emotional support, sample characteristics, e.g. socioeconomic status, and the types of well-being measures used. Moreover, few studies have focused on the structure and process of friendships among older Chinese. For instance, little is known about the effects of gender composition on older Chinese friendships. With the inevitable trend of aging across different Chinese societies, we plead for more research on friendship dynamics among elderly Chinese.

Romantic relationships

The amount of research on romantic relationships among Chinese has also been rising in the last decade. In mainland China, dating behavior has become increasingly common as arranged marriages have been gradually replaced by love matches after the new Marriage Law was passed in 1950 (Xu, 1994; Xu & Whyte, 1990). In previous centuries, parents exercised full control over the marriages of their children, so individuals had no rights to choose or date their potential marital spouses. However, in the flux of societal change, voluntary dating relationships have become a legitimate step toward marriage.

Many Chinese believe that the purpose of dating is to find a marital partner, as opposed to a social partner. According to Tang and Zuo (2000), 42 per cent of college students held such a belief. Moreover, there are two important features in Chinese dating relationships. First, dating relationships in Chinese societies seem to involve less hedonic aspiration, but a larger degree of relational obligations and mutual respect than those in Western societies. Second, Chinese prefer to be psychologically closer to or dependent on their romantic partners than do Westerners. To illustrate these two claims, we review two sets of evidence from the research on preferences of romantic partners and love styles, and interpersonal and sexual behaviors.

Preferences for love styles

In the cross-cultural literature, it has been widely agreed that preferences of romantic partners and love styles are not just biologically predisposed but also largely determined by cultural systems (e.g. Buss, 1989; Goodwin & Tang, 1991; Lucas et al., 2004). Indeed, recent empirical studies have suggested some Chinese–Western differences in relational preferences.

One major theme is the lower Chinese emphasis on personal needs but their higher valuation of shared interests between the partners. The first evidence is that, compared to Westerners, both male and female Chinese valued partners' physical attractiveness, which is typically considered as an important element of romantic love in Western research, to a lesser degree (Dion, Pak, & Dion, 1990;

Toro-Morn & Sprecher, 2003). Moreover, assessing their current romantic relationship with Sternberg's triangular theory of love scale (Sternberg, 1986), Gao (2001) showed that Chinese scored lower in passion than Westerners, while they did not differ in terms of commitment and intimacy.

In contrast to the Westerners' emphasis on self-gratification, Chinese seem to place more emphasis on the interdependent nature of a romantic relationship. For instance, Wan, Luk, and Lai (2000) measured Hong Kong college students' endorsement of the six love styles proposed by Hendrick and Hendrick (1986), and found that *agape* (selfless love) and *storge* (friendship love) were the most endorsed. A similar pattern of results was also found in a comparison between Chinese-Canadians and European-Canadians (Dion & Dion, 1993). These results reflect the potential influence of the traditional Chinese value of collectivism (over individualism or hedonism; Markus & Kitayama, 1991; Oyserman, Coon, & Kemmelmeier, 2002) in romantic relationships, and the nature of dating relationships as a step toward marriage (Tang & Zuo, 2000). While cross-cultural research on mate preferences consistently reveals men's greater valuation of partners' physical attractiveness and women's greater valuation of partners' social status, a pattern that is also found with Chinese (e.g. Shackelford, Schmitt, & Buss, 2005), the studies discussed above highlight some Chinese–Western differences in love styles.

It is worth noting that an individual's self-report about preferences for an ideal romantic partner does not directly correspond to the potential partners they actually desire (Eastwick & Finkel, 2008). Little is known about whether individuals in fact desire and select potential partners according to their introspected criteria for mate selection. For instance, it remains uncertain whether Chinese really place less emphasis on physical attractiveness of potential partners than Westerners when choosing their potential romantic partners for dating or marriage. We encourage further studies to pursue this fertile research question.

Experiences and attachment with romantic partners

Recent research suggests that Chinese tend to maintain a larger degree of closeness with their romantic partners than do Westerners. It has been widely documented that Chinese desire and experience a larger degree of closeness with in-group members than Westerners (except with friendship, as discussed above), due to a higher level of interdependence (e.g. Li, 2002; Li et al., 2006). Similarly, Moore and Leung (2001) reported that Chinese residing in Australia preferred to establish a higher level of closeness with their partners compared with Australians, as indicated by their preference of 'clingy and fickle' styles of loving. These authors explained that the fickle love style is an oscillation between approach and avoidance of mature relationships, reflecting the internal conflict of the individualistic and collectivist norms experienced by this sample of Chinese. Given their preoccupation with relational needs, Chinese have also been found to experience more loneliness than Westerners (DiTommaso, Brannen, & Burgess, 2005; Moore & Leung, 2001).

However, whether Chinese actually experience a higher level of attachment insecurity than Western counterparts remains uncertain (DiTommaso et al., 2005; Doherty, Hatfield, Thompson, & Choo, 1994; Schmidt et al., 2004). Despite the debate on the *personal* endorsement of attachment style, it has been reported that the *normative* or *ideal* attachment style of the Chinese is an anxious or preoccupied type (Schmidt et al., 2004; Wang & Mallinckrodt, 2006). Researchers argue that the anxious attachment style enables individuals to be more sensitive to relational expectations and demands. And this anxious attachment style matches the demand of the Chinese collectivistic culture.

It should also be noted that Chinese attachment styles have attracted more research attention in recent years. In general, the typology (i.e. models of self and others) and dimensionality (i.e. anxiety and avoidance) of Chinese attachment styles closely resemble those found in Western cultures (Ho et al., 2008; Schmidt et al., 2004; Wang & Mallinckrodt, 2006). It has also been shown that attachment styles are linked to relational outcomes in romantic relationships. For instance, it was found that attachment avoidance was negatively related to relational commitment (Chan, 2005), and relationship-driven self-improvement (Hui & Bond, in press). Further studies are encouraged to apply attachment theories in the study of romantic relationships among Chinese.

Interpersonal and sexual behaviors between romantic partners

Chinese dating relationships show a high degree of self-restraint, probably as a sign of respect for their romantic partners. For instance, when engaging in a conflictual conversation with romantic partners, Chinese-Americans were less emotionally irritable than European-Americans (Tsai & Levenson, 1997; Tsai, Levenson, & McCoy, 2006). Chinese have also been found to accommodate to their romantic partners to a larger extent than Westerners (Yum, 2004). Moreover, based on their partner's report and their own self-rating, Chinese men also displayed a lower frequency of initiating unwelcome sexual advances than their Western counterparts (Tang, Critelli, & Porter, 1995). The accommodating nature of Chinese may reflect their socialization of accomplishing relational or in-group interests through sacrificing their own interests (Bond, 1991; Yang, 1986).

It has been widely reported that compared to Westerners, Chinese are sexually conservative (e.g. Chan & Cheung, 1998; Higgins, Zheng, Liu, & Sun, 2002; Ng & Lau, 1990; Tang & Zuo, 2000), and premarital sexual behaviors are discouraged or even prohibited. However, possibly as a consequence of the increasing prevalence of late marriages (Wei, 1983; Wong, 2003), the occurrence of premarital sex has been rising rapidly among youth in Chinese societies (see e.g. Hong Kong Family Planning Association, 2006 for the statistics in Hong Kong; Yeh, 1998, for the statistics in Taiwan). Pan (1993) reported that 81.2 per cent of mainland Chinese marrying after 1979 had sexual intercourse before their marriages. Tang and Zuo (2000) also found that among a sample of college students in Shanghai who were dating, 62 per cent of them admitted to having had sexual intercourse. In Hong Kong, about 47 per cent of men and 39 per cent of women aged 27 or below admitted that they were sexually experienced (Hong Kong Family Planning Association, 2006). Paralleling this increase in sexual activity, researchers report that the percentage of unmarried clients obtaining abortions is increasing (Bullough & Ruan, 1994). These findings are consistent with the fact that despite their engagement in sexual activities, nearly half of the sexually active adolescents and young adults remain ignorant about condom use or other birth control measures (Hong Kong Family Planning Association, 2006; Zhao, Wang, & Guo, 2006). More institutional and educational efforts are necessary to resolve this growing societal problem.

Given that premarital sexual intercourse has become quite prevalent in Chinese societies, it is important to examine its nature (e.g. casual sex versus sex with the exclusive romantic partner). This information may unveil an evolved form of sexual conservatism in response to modernization. Generally speaking, Chinese tend to be conservative in their sexual behavior, as they may seldom have sexual involvement with someone who is not expected to be their future spouse. Yeh (2002) conducted individual interviews and suggested that one core reason for premarital sex among Taiwanese youth, both male and female, was to preserve the fantasy of romantic innocence, i.e. to sustain their sense of an exclusive romantic relationship. Moreover, in a cross-cultural comparison, around 35 per cent of mainland Chinese (versus 2.3 per cent of British) endorsed the statement that a couple who have had sexual intercourse before marriage ought to marry each other (Higgins et al., 2002). Consistent with this social logic, Pan (1993) showed that the target of premarital sex was exclusively the intended future spouse (89.2 per cent) as opposed to boyfriend/girlfriend (8.9 per cent; also see Li & Yang, 1993b for similar findings).

In sum, the pattern of results suggests that even though premarital sex is becoming more prevalent in Chinese societies, Chinese are quite conservative in terms of choosing their partners for premarital sex. Specifically, they tend to have sex primarily with intended future spouses; premarital sex is employed as a means for promoting a potentially long-lasting romantic relationship.

Cultural beliefs in Yuan and the malleability of personality

Cross-cultural studies have shown that Chinese habitually acknowledge the importance of contextual factors in human outcomes (e.g. Knowles, Morris, Chiu, & Hong, 2001; Nisbett, Peng, Choi, & Norenzayan, 2001; Peng & Nisbett, 1999) and also the changeability of personal attributes. These socialized sensitivities are presumed to influence Chinese relational orientations.

In managing romantic relationships, Chinese also tend to ascribe the relational future to the implicit forces known as *yuan* (e.g. Chang & Chan, 2007; Goodwin & Findlay, 1997; Lu, this volume). *Yuan* is a Buddhist term referring to 'the chief force that allows contextual factors to influence relationship development and processes' (Chang & Chan, 2007, p. 66). As Chinese tend to attribute the successes of the relationships more to external forces than to personal control (Chang & Chan, 2007), they would also hold less optimistic views about the romance and expect more suffering in the future, as implied in the content of popular Chinese love songs (Rothbaum & Tsang, 1998). On the other hand, the endorsement of belief in *yuan* may allow them to ascribe the causes of negative interpersonal events to external forces, resulting in relationship-protective attribution patterns (Stander, Hsiung, & MacDermind, 2001). While results from past research tend to incorporate *yuan* as a post-hoc explanation of research findings, we encourage future research to further examine its nature in romantic relationships, and how it relates to other psychological constructs, such as love styles or attachment dynamics.

In addition, cross-cultural research has shown that Chinese are more likely to hold a malleability belief of their personal attributes than are Westerners (Chiu, Hong, & Dweck, 1997; Chiu, Morris, Hong, & Menon, 2000). Malleability belief of personal attributes refers to believing whether a particular attribute is changeable or fixed over time (Dweck, 2006). This line of research suggested that individuals holding this malleability belief are more tolerant of their partners, such that the assessment of their partners is less predictive of their relational satisfaction (Ruvolo & Rotondo, 1998).

Moreover, malleability believers are more proactive in expressing their concerns in relational conflicts (Kammrath & Dweck, 2006). Applying these Western constructs in the Chinese context, Hui (2007) examined the role of malleability beliefs in shaping the value of effort from one's romantic partner. Specifically, Chinese who held malleability beliefs showed more accommodating behaviors and relational satisfaction in response to their partners' effort to improve. This pattern of findings did not hold for those who did not endorse the beliefs. Given the fact that the malleability beliefs are more prevalent among Chinese than Westerners, this may partially explain why Chinese lovers are more forgiving and accommodating to their partners (Yum, 2004).

Marital relationships

In modernizing Chinese societies, many societal changes have been instituted and are believed to work against traditional Chinese family values (Wei, 1983; Wong, 2003; but see also Kulich, this volume). For instance, since the passing of the new Marriage Law in 1950 in mainland China, the freedom to choose mates has been liberated, and love matches have quickly replaced arranged marriages among mainland Chinese (Evans, 1995). Across Chinese societies, the extended family structure has been gradually replaced by the smaller units of nuclear families. Furthermore, advocacy of equal rights between men and women has also reduced gender differences in their social status. All these changes have exerted a profound impact on the two main areas to be discussed, namely the new meaning of marriage, and the issues of late marriages and divorces.

New meanings of marriage

In response to the societal changes and the feminist movement, the decision of marriage has mostly become a matter of choice between partners rather than of social obligations (Chang & Chan, 2007; Wong, 2003). Nevertheless, it is worth noting that non-relational factors, such as parental approval or the cultural belief in *yuan*, still play equally important roles as relational factors affecting the choice of partner (Chang & Chan, 2007; Goodwin, 1999). In addition, more gender differences in Chinese attitudes toward marriage have emerged over the years.

Specifically, Chinese women seem to hold more egalitarian attitudes toward marriage than ever (Chia et al., 1986). For instance, Wong (2003) recently interviewed Hong Kong Chinese women about their meaning of marriage. The results show that, to the majority (71.3 per cent) of Hong Kong women, marriage is no longer a family obligation but a personal aspiration to share life with a loved one. Only 30 per cent of women cited 'bearing and raising children' as the reason for marriage. Moreover, fewer than 20 per cent chose 'family responsibilities' and 'financial security'. Interestingly enough, around 20 per cent of women preferred singlehood, and this pattern did not change across age cohorts. These figures suggest that Chinese women now get married to satisfy their own interests and not in order to meet the familial obligations associated with traditional Chinese values.

While Chinese men may also have been changing their attitudes toward marriage, their change was reported to be much slower than that of females (Chia et al., 1986). Consistently, recent research reported that mainland Chinese men still strongly prefer a partner who wants children and is a good housekeeper (Toro-Morn & Sprecher, 2003). Unlike their female counterparts, Chinese men tend to prefer a partner who observes the traditional gender roles. The attitudes of Chinese men towards marriage seem to have remained stable over the past few decades.

Given that Chinese men tend to hold more traditional attitudes toward marriage than women and that these attitudinal discrepancies are increasing, potential marital problems can be provoked due to the gender differences in marital expectations.

We next review studies on two related issues, namely, increase in late marriage and divorce in Chinese societies.

Increase in later marriage and divorce

In Chinese societies, the age of first marriage has been increasing rapidly along with economic growth, the introduction of nuclear families, and the popularity of post-secondary education (see e.g. Hong Kong Census and Statistics Department, 2007; Wei, 1983). With rapid economic growth, traditional extended families have been divided into smaller units of nuclear families. Along with this transition, the traditional female role as a housekeeper and a caregiver has been largely reduced in modern Chinese societies. Moreover, as indicated by the reduction in relative status between the two sexes, more than 50 per cent of Hong Kong women opted for having established a financial foundation and job security as prerequisites before entering marriage (Wong, 2003). A similar pattern has also been found in mainland China (Wei, 1983). These reasons may partially explain why late marriages have become prevalent in Chinese societies.

It is interesting to note that even though Chinese women are enjoying more freedom in recently liberated Chinese societies than ever before, no evidence suggests that women's practice of singlehood is on the rise (Wong, 2003). Perhaps one major reason is social pressure. When Chinese women remain single in middle adulthood, they will experience heavy parental and peer pressure to find a partner and get married (Liu, 2004). Parents, and sometimes peers, will constantly look out for potential partners, and display serious concern about their daughter's or friend's remaining single. Moreover, unmarried Chinese women are still the targets of prejudice and discrimination. According to Liu, the occurrence of such acts intensifies when they reach middle adulthood.

Since the establishment of new marriage policies in mainland China, the divorce rate has been constantly growing, a trend that has also been observed in other Chinese societies (see e.g. Engel, 1984; Hong Kong Census and Statistics Department, 2007; Liao & Heaton, 1992; Sullivan, 2005). For instance, the divorce rate in Hong Kong in 2006 was eight times that in 1981. This dramatic change may be attributable to the new meaning of marriage for women, viz. to live with a loved one instead of fulfilling familial obligations (Wong, 2003). Moreover, due to societal changes, normative and familial disapproval of divorce has been greatly reduced (Engel, 1984). Given these changes, staying in a marriage has become a personal and voluntary decision among Chinese.

So, what constitutes the personal decision to divorce? The major reason given by participants is 'personality mismatch' (cited in Li & Yang, 1993a). Although personality mismatch, however understood, can affect the quality of marriage (Ye, Wan, & Wang, 1999), Li and Yang (1993a) found that it was not a strong predictor of divorce. These authors speculated that individuals may quote a more socially acceptable reason instead of the true reasons, such as sexual dissatisfaction (Pan, 1993) and domestic violence (Tang & Lai, 2008). In the past, Chinese women tended to endure domestic violence without the option of getting a divorce (Liu & Chan, 1999). However, given the liberation of

Chinese societies, violence against women has received growing attention (Tang, Wong, & Cheung, 2002), and divorce has become a viable option to avoid continuing marital problems for women.

It is worth noting that research on divorce mostly relies on retrospective self-report from either the husband or the wife after the divorce. We are not sure if each partner of a couple would agree and give the same reason(s). Moreover, the retrospective self-report may suffer numerous methodological artifacts, such as vulnerability to social desirability and memory distortion. Acknowledging these limitations, more dyadic and longitudinal analyses should be conducted to trace the actual developmental trajectory of divorced (versus intact) couples in Chinese societies.

Family relationships

When reviewing studies on family relationships among the Chinese, we focus more on the familial interactions such as various types of intergenerational support, living arrangements, and their underlying constructs such as filial piety; we focus relatively less on the area of parenting styles (and the related issues such as the one-child policy in mainland China), because an entire chapter in this volume is devoted to that topic area (see Wang & Chang's chapter in this volume). Our analysis reveals that a considerable amount of family research conducted in Chinese communities in the last decade has focused on outcome variables, such as psychological well-being, with elderly parents and adolescents as the target populations.

Intergenerational support in Chinese families

Family research on elderly Chinese has mainly focused on the relationship between intergenerational support, among other factors such as health and financial status, and psychological well-being of the elderly parents. Many of these studies aimed to examine the measures that governments should adopt in response to the aging population in Hong Kong, mainland China, and Taiwan (e.g. Chen & Silverstein, 2000; Chou, Chi, & Chow, 2004; Weinstein et al., 2004). Specifically, they have looked into the various types of social support, including financial and emotional support, received by the elderly from their family or friends and how institutional support interweaves with these social supports to affect their well-being (see also Cheng, Lo, & Chio, this volume).

It has been found that in Chinese societies, such as mainland China and Hong Kong, parents often receive financial support from their children (e.g. Pei & Pillai, 1999; Silverstein, Cong & Li, 2006; Yan, Chen, & Murphy, 2005). Receiving financial support from children is not only found to be a norm, but is associated with better psychological well-being among elderly parents (Chen & Silverstein, 2000). Chou et al. (2004) reported that older adults whose major sources of income were from their adult children or children-in-law were less likely to report depressive symptoms than were those whose major source of income was not.

While parents have been found to benefit from receiving financial support from children, research reveals that parents also provide instrumental support, such as caretaking of grandchildren or housekeeping, to their children in return (Chen & Silverstein, 2000; Silverstein et al., 2006). According to Chen and Silverstein, provision of such instrumental support to children would exert a positive impact on the psychological well-being among the elderly.

Some other studies have investigated how Chinese traditional values affect the intergenerational relationship and exchanges of support. As summarized by Cheung, Kwan, and Ng (2006), in Chinese culture filial piety is a favored virtue where people take care of their elderly parents through providing care, respect, and financial support; showing obedience and regard, thereby pleasing them. The scope of filial piety thus covers more than the sole provision of instrumental and financial support to aging parents, and research reveals that filial piety is still valued in Chinese communities (e.g. Chinese Culture Connection, 1987; Yan et al., 2005; see also Hwang & Han, this volume).

Interestingly, research conducted in Western countries reveals that financial transfers predominantly happen in a downward manner, flowing from the elderly to their children or grandchildren, while time transfers generally take place in an upward direction (e.g. Attias-Donfut, Ogg, & Wolff,

2005). Some researchers may attribute such a difference to the emphasis of filial piety in traditional Confucian teachings. However, given the difference between the social security and pension system in Western countries and Chinese communities, it is difficult to determine whether the difference is a result of cultural difference or a difference emerging from the different financial status of the elderly in the East and the West.

It is also worth noting that studies in the West reveal a relation between attachment style and intergenerational support exchanged between daughters and elderly mothers (Schwarz & Trommsdorff, 2005). Attachment of middle-aged respondents to their children was found to be associated with their filial closeness to elderly parents (Perigg-Chiello & Hopflinger, 2005). While further studies are needed to provide a clearer picture of how these factors interplay with one another, these results suggest that long-lasting developmental dynamics should be taken into consideration when studying intergenerational relationships (Litwin, 2005). In addition to the traditional virtues of filial piety, future studies on Chinese intergenerational relationships could adopt a developmental perspective to examine how specific features of Chinese relationships between parents and children, such as attachment, evolve, and how these developments affect intergenerational relationships later in life.

Living arrangements

The relationship between housing arrangements and intergenerational exchange of support has also sparked much research interest. Co-residence of two or even three generations allows for more efficient sharing of monetary resources as well as exchange of services, and has traditionally been practiced in Chinese families (Yeh, 2002). However, due to modernization along with architectural, demographic, and social transformations, numerous studies reported that the prevalence of co-residence among elderly with their children has been declining (e.g. Pei & Pillai, 1999; Silverstein et al., 2006; Sun, 2002; Yeh, 2002). Findings generally suggest that sharing the same household with children is associated with better morale among parents aged 55 years or more in Chinese societies (e.g. Chen & Silverstein, 2000; Pei & Pillai, 1999; Silverstein et al., 2006). Focusing on the kinds of support exchanged between parents and children in the urban cities of mainland China, Sun (2002) reported that geographic proximity plays a crucial role in some specific forms of support: children living away from their parents were more likely to provide monetary support than to help with daily activities. Chen and Silverstein (2000) noted that the positive effect of co-residence with children on elderly parents' morale was mediated by receiving financial and emotional support from children. The effect of receiving financial and emotional support from children was in turn found to be attributable to elevated satisfaction of the parents with their children. Together, these findings seem to suggest that the positive impact of living with children could be attributed to the greater possibilities of receiving emotional support and exchanges of instrumental support among elderly Chinese.

It is interesting to note that, despite findings revealing the positive impact of co-residence on the psychological well-being of elderly parents, it has been found in several studies that co-residence is no longer the dominating preference for housing among the aging population. Stronger preferences for living independently were found more often among Hong Kong Chinese who were more educated and professionals (Lam, Chi, Piterman, Lam, & Lauder, 1998). Moreover, Lam et al. also found that elderly women preferred to live independently if they were disabled, a finding that echoes Yeh (2002) who reported that elderly parents attributed their preference for not living with their children to differences in character, values, and lifestyle. Together with the changes in most urban Chinese societies to becoming more individualistic, many elderly parents prefer to live apart from their children to avoid becoming a burden on, or having interpersonal conflicts with, their children.

Parental roles and parent–child interactions

Issues revolving around Chinese parenting continue to attract research attention. Many of these studies have explored the relationship between parenting and outcome variables, such as children's self-esteem (e.g. Bush et al., 2002; Stewart et al., 1998), academic achievement (e.g. McBride-Chang & Chang, 1998), and psychological disorders (e.g. depression and eating disorders; Cheng, 1997; Ma et al., 2002; Wang & Crane, 2001). Research efforts have also been devoted to defining Chinese parenting and comparing it to Western parenting. For instance, researchers are interested to find out to what extent Baumrind's (1971) classification of parenting styles is applicable to Chinese parenting, or how indigenous parenting concepts such as *chiao shun* (training) and *guan* (control and governance; Chao, 1994) can be understood in contemporary Chinese parenting (Stewart et al., 1998; see Wang & Chang, this volume for a thorough review of this research).

To understand Chinese parenting, efforts have been devoted to exploring how traditional Chinese views on familial relationships affect contemporary Chinese parenting. As suggested by Shek (2001), fathers in Chinese families are traditionally regarded as having a more prestigious and crucial role: *yi jia ji ju*, or the master of the family. Consistent with this traditional assertion on the role of fathers within the family, Shek's research on Hong Kong Chinese reveals that fathers' dyadic relationships with adolescent children, as well as their perceived marital quality, were found to exert a stronger influence on family functioning than were those of the mothers.

Apart from the emphasis on respect for fathers, in terms of parental role, Chinese fathers are regarded as chiefly responsible for the discipline of children, while mothers are responsible for caring for and nurturing them (Shek, 2007). These traditional parental roles of 'strict father, kind mother' seem to continue to operate in contemporary Chinese families in both intact and non-intact families. Shek (2000) reported that Hong Kong adolescents perceived fathers, as compared to mothers, to be less responsive, less demanding, to demonstrate less concern, and to be harsher. Paternal parenting was generally less liked than maternal parenting. If strictness is defined in terms of harshness, Shek's findings supported the traditional Chinese saying of 'strict father, kind mother'. However, he also noted that if strictness is defined in terms of demandingness, his data indicated that mothers were in fact stricter than fathers.

In the context of non-intact families, studies conducted both in the West and in Hong Kong found that compared to non-resident mothers, non-resident fathers are less involved in the care-giving and nurturing of their children. Notably, non-resident fathers in Hong Kong were found to be more involved in the discipline of their children, unlike their Western counterparts who tend to take a more playful role in interacting with their children (Lau, 2006). This echoes the findings on Chinese intact families that the traditional parental roles emphasize the discipline-giving role of fathers and the care-giving role of mothers, roles that continue in non-intact families.

It is worth noting that studies conducted in the West on parents of preschool children reveal that spousal reports of perceived differences in parenting styles were greater than their parenting styles measured by self-report (Winsler, Madigan, & Aquilino, 2005). According to Winsler et al., such perceived differences appeared to fall in line with the traditional stereotypes of the father being the authoritarian figure and the mother being more permissive and responsive. In addition, Simons and Conger (2007) reported that the most commonly found parenting styles in the West were those in which both parents display the same type of parenting style, implying that the perceived differences in parenting styles among parents may not reflect the true picture. As previous research on Chinese parenting mostly employed self, spousal, or children's report, it remains unclear whether the differences between paternal and maternal parenting are perceived only or exist when measured independently. Future studies in this area may consider using multiple sources of ratings to address such issues.

In addition to parental roles, some studies have been conducted to examine the issue of parent–adolescent conflict in the context of a modern Chinese society. Yau and Smetana (1996) reported that lower socioeconomic status adolescents in Hong Kong had frequent but generally mild conflicts with parents over everyday issues, despite the collectivistic nature and the emphasis on harmony among Chinese. Shek (2002) conducted a longitudinal study on Hong Kong adolescents and found that parent–adolescent conflict and perceived parenting style had negative, reciprocal effects on each other. Negative parenting styles were associated with more parent–adolescent conflict one year later, and conflict in turn affected perceived parenting styles. With more conflicts, fathers were perceived as less warm and harsher, and mothers were perceived to engage in more monitoring behavior one year later. Understanding these conflicts has important implications; Chen, Wu, and Bond's (2008) study suggests that family dysfunction can lead to depressive self-views and negative world views, which in turn lead to greater suicidal ideation among young adults in Hong Kong.

More recently, Yau and Smetana (2003) conducted in-depth interviews to compare parent–adolescent conflict among adolescents in Hong Kong and Shenzhen. Consistent with the sociocultural differences between the two cities, such as living space, emphasis on academic achievement, etc., more conflicts over chores and interpersonal relationships were found in Hong Kong than in Shenzhen, and more conflicts over schoolwork in Shenzhen than in Hong Kong. These authors also discussed that, compared to adolescents in the West, the later timetables for behavioral autonomy among Chinese adolescents and their reactions to conflicts with parents are likely to be shaped by the traditional Confucian values about the family, suggesting that traditional familial values still operate in contemporary Chinese societies.

It is also worth noting that Yau and Smetana's (2003) comparison between adolescents in Hong Kong and Shenzhen is one example of the growing number of family studies comparing different subgroups of Chinese, e.g. Pei and Pillai (1999) on elderly Chinese living in rural vs. urban mainland China; Yin, Jing, and Shi (2007) on Uygur vs. Han adolescents in mainland China; Zhang and Lin (1998) on rural vs. urban adolescents in mainland China. As noted by other researchers such as Tardif and Miao (2000), substantial differences exist across different Chinese societies, e.g. among Hong Kong, Taiwan, and big cities in mainland China such as Beijing, between urban and rural areas, and even within different Chinese ethnic groups. In order to gain a better understanding of Chinese families, future research on family relationship should continue to explore the differences across subgroups of Chinese that differ across theoretically relevant dimensions.

Conclusion

As emphasized at the beginning of the chapter, we aimed to focus our review on the empirical evidence in the domains of Chinese friendship, romantic relationships, marriage, and family relationships. Given the diverse outlets for publishing the relevant studies on each of these domains, we may have omitted some important studies. By limiting our review to these four domains, we may also have neglected relationship research on some commonly known Chinese concepts. One such example is the research on *guanxi*, as most if not all of the recent empirical studies on this concept are in the organizational/work context and are outside the scope of this chapter (see Chen & Farh, this volume). Furthermore, as we put our emphasis on reviewing empirical evidence from published studies, we may have overlooked theories and/or conceptual frameworks specifically developed for Chinese relationship research (see Lu, this volume; Smith, this volume).

Having acknowledged these potential weaknesses, we would like to conclude our review with three sets of observations, namely, on the encouraging trends in Chinese relationship research, on areas that need further improvement, and on additional research questions that span different domains of relationship.

Encouraging trends in Chinese relationships research

The foremost positive trend in Chinese relationships research is the increase in the amount of empirical research on Chinese interpersonal relationships over the last decade. While we would not characterize it as a proliferation, the amount of empirical studies in various domains has been increasing steadily. It would probably have been even more heartening if more theories or conceptualizations about Chinese relationships had been developed (see e.g. Ho, 1998) to guide and stimulate this energetic data collecting.

With the advances in psychological measures targeting Chinese, we also witness more studies on Chinese relationships using indigenous measures, e.g. Man and Bond's (2005) development and use of an indigenous measure of relationship in their friendship studies; Shek's (2007) indigenous measure of parental control in his parenting studies. Echoing to the call for more indigenous psychological research, e.g. Yang (1999), these studies offer some unique perspectives and understanding about Chinese relationships that Western research cannot accomplish unaided by indigenous inputs.

In addition to the many cross-cultural studies comparing Chinese with other cultural groups, some of the studies reviewed were monocultural in nature, designed to advance general understanding in a specific area of interpersonal relationship research. For instance, Chan and associates' (Chan & Cheng, 2004; Cheng, Chan, & Tong, 2006) research on online friendships are not intended solely for the Hong Kong context. Rather, their findings can help fill the void in our limited knowledge of the ever-growing phenomenon of online friendships across the globe. They are of value in their own right, and have obvious extensions into the cross-cultural arena.

Areas for improvement

First, most of the studies reviewed collected data from a single source. In relationship research, it is important to collect data from multiple sources, e.g. use of dyadic analysis. Second, most of the studies focus primarily on outcome variables, e.g. relationship satisfaction, psychological well-being, etc., with little emphasis on process variables, such as measures of interpersonal interaction or changes in interpersonal perception. Third, as Goodwin and Tang (1996) pointed out more than ten years ago, it is important to examine the potential differences among various ethnic groups or Chinese residing in different geographical locations. As indicated above, we were able to find a few relationship studies comparing Chinese from different regions or ethnic groups. However, such comparative studies are needed to further advance our understanding of the complexity and diversity of Chinese people.

Spanning domains of relationship

In addition to the research questions mentioned in our review of each domain, there are two more challenging research inquiries that span domains of relationship: First, it would be interesting to investigate the effect sizes of the presumed Chinese–Western differences in the different domains of interpersonal relationships. Oyserman et al's (2002) meta-analysis indicated that Chinese are indeed more collectivistic than other cultural groups. However, they did not examine how I–C relates to different domains of relationship. From our review, it is plausible to expect that in certain relationship domains such as friendship, the Chinese–Western differences may not be as large as many cross-cultural psychologists would anticipate. With more empirical studies accumulated, this question can be examined by a meta-analysis, with year of publication as a potential moderator.

Second, it would also be important to examine how Chinese at different life stages and ages would try to balance and prioritize their interpersonal relationships. Little empirical research has been conducted to examine the changes in Chinese social networks and interpersonal relationships across the life span. Chow and Ng (2004) examined the characteristics of personal ties (*guanxi*) among Hong Kong adults and found that participants shared more with close associates (friends or colleagues) than with family members, implying a weakening of the family unit in Hong Kong. Ruan et al. (1997) found that compared to a study conducted seven years earlier, Chinese in Tianjian reported having more ties to friends and to associates beyond work and family, and fewer workplace ties and far fewer family ties.

A recent study on the social network characteristics of Hong Kong Chinese also reveals some interesting age differences in their social relationships that have not been reported in the West (Yeung, Fung, & Lang, 2008). More relationship research should take a holistic, lifespan approach to examine the relative importance that Chinese would attach to different interpersonal relationships as they age and the underlying mechanisms governing these differences (see Fung & Cheng, this volume). Yeung et al. proposed that independent vs. interdependent self-construal is one underlying factor. Another possibility is the concept of face. According to Su and Hwang's (2003) study on Taiwanese, the concept of face seems to affect elderly Chinese and college students' interpersonal behaviors differently, supporting Hwang's (1987; see also Hwang & Han, this volume) conceptualization of face.

Concluding remarks

As social psychologists have learned, the best predictor of future behavior is past behavior. With the advances in Chinese relationship research that we have witnessed over the last ten years, it is our hope and belief that this trend of progress will continue and that our insights into Chinese interpersonal relationships will be further enhanced.

References

Altman, I. & Taylor, D. (1973). *Social penetration: The development of interpersonal relationships.* Rinehart & Winston: New York.

Aron A., Aron, E. N., & Smollan, D. (1992). Inclusion of others in the Self Scale and the structure of interpersonal closeness. *Journal of Personality and Social Psychology, 63,* 596–612.

Attias-Donfut, C., Ogg, J., & Wolff, F. C. (2005). European patterns of intergenerational financial and time transfers. *European Journal of Ageing, 2,* 161–173.

Baumrind, D. (1971). Current patterns of parental authority. *Developmental Psychology Monograph, 4.* (1, Pt. 2).

Boey, K. W. (1999). Social factors of subjective well-being of the elderly. *Chinese Mental Health Journal, 13,* 85–87. (in Chinese)

Boey, K. W. (2005). Life strain and psychological distress of older women and older men in Hong Kong. *Aging and Mental Health, 9,* 555–562.

Bond, M. H. (1991). *Beyond the Chinese face.* Hong Kong: Oxford.

Bond, M. H. & Forgas, J. (1984). Linking person perception to behavior intention across cultures: The role of cultural collectivism. *Journal of Cross-Cultural Psychology, 15,* 337–352.

Buhrmester, D. (1990). Intimacy of friendship, interpersonal competence, and adjustment during preadolescence and adolescence. *Child Development, 161,* 1101–1111.

Bullough, V. L., Ruan, F. F.. (1994). Marriage, divorce and sexual relations in contemporary China. *Journal of Comparative Family Studies, 25,* 383–393.

Bush, K. R., Peterson, G. W., Cobas, J. A., Supple, A. J. (2002). Adolescents' perceptions of parental behaviors as predictors of adolescent self-esteem in mainland China. *Sociological Inquiry, 72,* 503–526.

Buss, D. (1989). Sex differences in human mate preferences: Evolutionary hypotheses tested in 37 cultures. *Behavioural and Brain Sciences, 12,* 1–49.

Chan, C. (2005). *Romantic attachment in Hong Kong: Its relationship with parental attachment, relationship outcomes and psychological well-being.* Unpublished master thesis, Chinese University of Hong Kong, Hong Kong.

Chan, D. K.-S. & Cheung, S. F. (1998). An examination of premarital sexual behavior among college students in Hong Kong. *Psychology & Health, 13,* 805–821.

Chan, D. K.-S. & Cheng, H. L. (2004). A comparison of offline and online friendship qualities at different stages of relationship development. *Journal of Social and Personal Relationships, 21,* 305–320.

Chan, Y. K. & Lee, R. P. L. (2006). Network size, social support and happiness in later life: A comparative study of Beijing and Hong Kong. *Journal of Happiness Studies, 7,* 87–112.

Chang, S. C. & Chan, C. N. (2007). Perceptions of commitment change during mate selection: The case of Taiwanese newlyweds. *Journal of Social and Personal Relationships, 24,* 55–68.

Chao, R. K. (1994). Beyond parental control and authoritarian parenting style: Understanding Chinese parenting through the cultural notion of training. *Child Development, 65,* 1111–1120.

Chen, S. X., Wu, W. C. H., & Bond, M. H. (under review). *Linking family dysfunction to suicidal ideation in counseling and psychotherapy: The mediating roles of self-views and world-views.* Manuscript submitted for editorial consideration.

Chen, X. & Silverstein, M. (2000). Intergenerational social support and the psychological well-being of older parents in China. *Research on Aging, 22,* 43–65.

Cheng, C. (1997). Role of perceived social support on depression in Chinese adolescents: A prospective study examining the buffering model. *Journal of Applied Social Psychology, 27,* 800–820.

Cheng, H. L., Chan, D. K.-S., & Tong, P. Y. (2006). Qualities of online friendships with different gender compositions and durations. *CyberPsychology & Behavior, 9* (1), 14–21.

Cheung, C. K., Kwan, A. Y. H, & Ng, S. H. (2006). Impacts of filial piety on preference for kinship versus public care. *Journal of Community Psychology, 34,* 617–634.

Chia, R. C., Chong, C. J., Cheng, B. S., Castellow, W., Moore, C. H., & Hayes, M. (1986). Attitude toward marriage roles among Chinese and American college students. *Journal of Social Psychology, 126,* 31–35.

Chinese Culture Connection (1987). Chinese values and the search for culture-free dimensions of culture. *Journal of Cross-Cultural Psychology, 18*, 143–164.
Chiu, C. Y., Hong, Y. Y., & Dweck, C. S. (1997). Lay dispositionism and implicit theories of personality. *Journal of Personality and Social Psychology, 73*, 19–30.
Chiu, C. Y., Morris, M. W., Hong, Y. Y., & Menon, T. (2000). Motivated cultural cognition: The impact of implicit theories on dispositional attribution varies as a function of need for closure. *Journal of Personality and Social Psychology, 78*, 247–259.
Chou, K. L. (2000). Intimacy and psychosocial adjustment in Hong Kong Chinese adolescents. *Journal of Genetic Psychology, 161*, 141–151.
Chou, K. L., Chi, I., & Chow, N. W. S. (2004). Sources of income and depression in elderly Hong Kong Chinese: Mediating and moderating effects of social support and financial strain. *Aging & Mental Health, 8*, 212–221.
Chow, I. H. S. & Ng, I. (2004). The characteristics of Chinese personal ties (*guanxi*): Evidence from Hong Kong. *Organization Studies, 25*, 1075–1093.
Collins, N. L. & Miller, C. (1994). Self-disclosure and liking: A meta-analysis. *Psychological Bulletin, 116*, 457–475.
Dion, K. L. & Dion, K. K. (1993). Gender and ethnocultural comparisons in styles of love. *Psychology of Women Quarterly, 17*, 463–473.
Dion, K. K., Pak, A. W., & Dion, K. L. (1990). Stereotyping physical attractiveness: A sociocultural perspective. *Journal of Cross-Cultural Psychology, 21*, 158–179.
DiTommaso, E., Brannen, C., & Burgess, M. (2005). The universality of relationship characteristics: A cross-cultural comparison of different types of attachment and loneliness in Canadian and visiting Chinese students. *Social Behavior and Personality, 33*, 57–68.
Doherty, R. W., Hatfield, E., Thompson, K., & Choo, P. (1994). Cultural and ethnic influences on love and attachment. *Personal Relationships, 1*, 391–398.
Eastwick, P. W. & Finkel, E. J. (2008). Sex differences in mate preferences revisited: Do people know what they initially desire in a romantic partner? *Journal of Personality and Social Psychology, 94*, 245–264.
Engel, J. W. (1984). Divorce in the People's Republic of China: Analysis of a new law. *International Journal of Family Therapy, 6*, 192–204.
Evans, H. (1995). Defining difference: The 'scientific' construction of sexuality and gender in the People's Republic of China. *Signs, 20*, 357–394.
Fehr, B. (1996). *Friendship processes.* Thousand Oaks, CA: Sage.
Gao, G. (2001). Intimacy, passion, and commitment in Chinese and US American romantic relationships. *International Journal of Intercultural Relations, 25*, 329–342.
Giordano, P. C., Cernkovich, S. A., Groat, H. T., Pugh, M. D., & Swinford, S. P. (1998). The quality of adolescent friendships: Long term effects? *Journal of Health and Social Behavior, 39*, 55–71.
Goodwin, R. (1999). *Personal relationships across cultures.* London: Routledge.
Goodwin, R. & Findlay, C. (1997). 'We were just fated together' … Chinese love and the concept of *yuan* in England and Hong Kong. *Personal Relationships, 4*, 85–92.
Goodwin, R. & Tang, C. K. S. (1996). Chinese personal relationships. In M. H. Bond (ed.), *The handbook of Chinese psychology* (pp. 294–308). Hong Kong: Oxford University Press.
Goodwin, R. & Tang, D. (1991). Preferences for friends and close relationships partners: A cross-cultural comparison. *Journal of Social Psychology, 131*, 579–581.
Hendrick, C. & Hendrick, S. S. (1986). A theory and method of love. *Journal of Personality and Social Psychology, 50*, 392–402.
Higgins, L. T., Zheng, M., Liu, Y., & Sun, C. H. (2002). Attitudes to marriage and sexual behaviors: A survey of gender and culture differences in China and United Kingdom. *Sex Roles, 46*, 75–89.
Ho, D. Y. F. (1998). Interpersonal relationships and relationship dominance: An analysis based on methodological relationalism. *Asian Journal of Social Psychology, 1*, 1–16.
Hong Kong Census and Statistics Department (2007). Marriage and Divorce Trends in Hong Kong, 1981 to 2006. http://www.censtatd.gov.hk/products_and_services/products/publications/statistical_report/feature_articles/population/index.jsp
Hong Kong Family Planning Association. (2006) FPAHK youth sexuality study 2006. The Family Planning Association of Hong Kong. http://www.famplan.org.hk/fpahk/en/template1.asp?style=template1.asp&content=info/research.asp
Hui, C. M. (2007). *Why does(n't) partner's effort count? The role of implicit theories on relational self-regulation.* Unpublished manuscript, Chinese University of Hong Kong, Hong Kong.
Hui, C. M. & Bond, M. H. (in press). To please or neglect your partner?: Attachment avoidance and relationship-driven self-improvement. *Personal Relationships.*
Hwang, K. K. (1987). Face and favor: The Chinese power game. *American Journal of Sociology, 92*, 944–974.
Kammrath, L. K. & Dweck, C. (2006). Voicing conflict: Preferred conflict strategies among incremental and entity theorists. *Personality and Social Psychology Bulletin, 32*, 1497–1508.
Knowles, E. D., Morris, M. W., Chiu, C. Y., & Hong, Y. Y. (2001). Culture and the process of person perception: Evidence for automaticity among East Asians in correcting for situational influences on behavior. *Personality and Social Psychology Bulletin, 27*, 1344–1356.

Lam, C. W. & Boey, K. W. (2005). The psychological well-being of the Chinese elderly living in old urban areas of Hong Kong: a social perspective. *Aging Mental Health, 9*, 162–166.
Lam, T. P., Chi, I., Piterman, L., Lam, C., & Lauder, I. (1998). Community attitudes toward living arrangements between the elderly and their adult children in Hong Kong. *Journal of Cross-Cultural Gerontology 13*, 215–228.
Lau, Y. K. (2006). Nonresidential fathering and nonresidential mothering in a Chinese context. *The American Journal of Family Therapy, 34*, 373–394.
Lee, R. P. L., Ruan, D., & Lai, G. (2005). Social structure and support networks in Beijing and Hong Kong. *Social Networks, 27*, 249–274.
Lee, Y. P. & Bond, M. H. (1998). Personality and roommate friendship in Chinese culture. *Asian Journal of Social Psychology, 1*, 179–190.
Li, H. Z. (2002). Culture, gender and self–close–other(s) connectedness in Canadian and Chinese samples. *European Journal of Social Psychology, 32*, 93–104.
Li, H. Z., Zhang, Z., Bhatt, G., & Yum, Y. O. (2006). Rethinking culture and self-construal: China as a middle land. *Journal of Social Psychology, 146*, 591–610.
Li, L. & Yang, D. (1993a). A control study on the personality of 100 couples in divorce proceedings. *Chinese Mental Health Journal, 7*, 70–72. (in Chinese)
Li, L. & Yang, D. (1993b). Sexual behavior, wife abuse, and divorce proceedings, *Chinese Mental Health Journal, 7*, 131–134. (in Chinese)
Liao, C. & Heaton, T. B. (1992). Divorce trends and differentials in China. *Journal of Comparative Family Studies, 23*, 413–429.
Lin, Y. H. W. & Rusbult, C. E. (1995). Commitment to dating relationships and cross-sex friendships in America and China. *Journal of Social and Personal Relationships, 12*, 7–26.
Litwin, H. (2005). Intergenerational relations in an aging world. *European Journal of Ageing, 2*, 213–215.
Liu, J. (2004). Holding up the sky? Reflections on marriage in contemporary China. *Feminism and Psychology, 14*, 195–202.
Liu, M. & Chan, C. (1999). Enduring violence and staying in marriage: Stories of battered women in rural China. *Violence against Women, 5*, 1469–1492.
Lucas, T. W., Wendorf, C. A., Imamoglu, E. O., Shen, J., Parkhill, M. R., Weisfeld, C. C., & Weisfeld, G. E. (2004). Marital satisfaction in four cultures as a function of homogamy, male dominance and female attractiveness. *Sexualities, Evolution and Gender, 6*, 97–130.
Ma, J. L. C., Chow, M. Y. M., Lee, S., & Lai., K. (2002). Family meaning of self-starvation: themes discerned in family treatment in Hong Kong. *Journal of Family Therapy, 24*, 57–71.
Man, M. M. M. & Bond, M. H. (2005). A lexically derived measure of relationship concord in Chinese culture. *Journal of Psychology in Chinese Societies, 6*, 109–128.
Markus, H. R. & Kitayama, S. (1991). Culture and the self: Implications for cognition, emotion, and motivation. *Psychological Review, 98*, 224–253.
McBride-Chang, C. & Chang, L. (1998). Adolescent–parent relations in Hong Kong: Parenting styles, emotional autonomy, and school achievement. *The Journal of Genetic Psychology, 159*, 421–436.
Moore, S. M. & Leung, C. (2001). Romantic beliefs, styles, and relationships among young people from Chinese, southern European, and Anglo-Australian backgrounds. *Asian Journal of Social Psychology, 4*, 53–68.
Ng, M. L. & Lau, M. P. (1990). Sexual attitudes in the Chinese. *Archives of Sexual Behavior, 19*, 373–388.
Nisbett, R. E., Peng, K., Choi, I., & Norenzayan, A. (2001). Culture and systems of thought: Holistic versus analytic cognition. *Psychological Review, 108*, 291–310.
Oyserman, D., Coon, H. M., & Kemmelmeier, M. (2002). Rethinking individualism and collectivism: Evaluation of theoretical assumptions and meta-analysis. *Psychological Bulletin, 128*, 3–72.
Pan, S. M. (1993). A sex revolution in current China. *Journal of Psychology and Human Sexuality, 6*, 1–14.
Pei, X. & Pillai, V. K. (1999). Old age support in China: The role of the state and the family. *International Journal of Aging and Human Development, 49*, 197–212.
Peng, K. & Nisbett, R. E. (1999). Culture, dialectics, and reasoning about contradiction. *American Psychologist, 54*, 741–754.
Perrig-Chiello, P. & Hopflinger, F. (2005). Aging parents and their middle-aged children: demographic and psychosocial challenges. *European Journal of Ageing, 2*, 183–191.
Rothbaum, F. & Tsang, B. Y. P. (1998). Love songs in the United States and China: On the nature of romantic love. *Journal of Cross-Cultural Psychology, 29*, 306–319.
Ruan, D., Freeman, L. C., Dai, X., & Pan, Y. (1997). On the changing structure of social networks in urban China. *Social Networks, 19*, 75–89.
Ruvolo, A. P. & Rotondo, J. L. (1998). Diamonds in the rough: Implicit personality theories and views of partner and self. *Personality and Social Psychology Bulletin, 24*, 750–758.
Schmitt, D. P., Alcalay, L., Allensworth, M., Allik, J., Ault, L., Austers, I. et al. (2004). Patterns and universals of adult romantic attachment across 62 cultural regions: Are models of self and of other pancultural constructs? *Journal of Cross-Cultural Psychology, 35*, 367–402.

Schwarz, B. & Trommsdorff, G. (2005). The relation between attachment and intergenerational support. *European Journal of Ageing, 2*, 192–199.

Shackelford, T. K., Schmitt, D. P., & Buss, D. M. (2005). Universal dimensions of human mate preferences. *Personal and Individual Differences, 39*, 447–458.

Shek, D. T. L. (2000). Differences between fathers and mothers in the treatment of, and relationship with, their teenage children: Perception of Chinese adolescents. *Adolescence, 35*, 135–146.

Shek, D. T. L. (2001). Paternal and maternal influences on family functioning among Hong Kong Chinese families. *The Journal of Genetic Psychology, 162*, 56–74.

Shek, D. T. L. (2002). Parenting characteristics and parent–adolescent conflict: A longitudinal study in the Chinese culture. *Journal of Family Issues, 23*, 189–208.

Shek D. T. L. (2007). Perceived parental control based on indigenous Chinese parental control concepts in adolescents in Hong Kong. *The American Journal of Family Therapy, 35*, 123–137

Silverstein, M., Zhen, C., & Li., S. (2006). Intergenerational transfers and living arrangements of older people in rural China: Consequences for psychological well-being. *Journal of Gerontology, 61B*, 256–266.

Simons, L. G. & Conger, R. D. (2007). Linking mother–father differences in parenting to a typology of family parenting styles and adolescent outcomes. *Journal of Family Issues, 28*, 212–241.

Siu, O. L. & Phillips, D. R. (2002). A study of family support, friendship, and psychological well-being among older women in Hong Kong. *International Journal of Aging and Human Development, 55*, 299–319.

Stander, V. A., Hsiung, P. C., & MacDermind, S. (2001). The relationship of attributions to marital distress: A comparison of mainland Chinese and US couples. *Journal of Family Psychology, 15*, 124–134.

Sternberg, R. J. (1986). A triangular theory of love. *Psychological Review, 93*, 119–135.

Stewart, S. M., Rao, N., Bond, M. H., McBride-Chang, C., Fielding, R., & Kennard, B. (1998). Chinese dimensions of parenting: Broadening western predictors and outcomes. *International Journal of Psychology, 33*, 345–358.

Su, S. Y. & Hwang, K. K (2003). Face and relation in different domains of life: A comparison between senior citizens and university students. *Chinese Journal of Psychology, 45*, 295–311.

Sullivan, P. L. (2005). Culture, divorce, and family mediation in Hong Kong. *Family Court Review, 43*, 109–123.

Sun, R. (2002). Old age support in contemporary urban china from both parents' and children's perspectives. *Research on Aging, 24*, 337–359.

Tardif, T. & Miao, X. (2000). Developmental psychology in China. *International Journal of Behavioral Development, 24*, 68–72.

Tam, B. K. & Bond, M. H. (2002). Interpersonal behaviors and friendship in a Chinese culture. *Asian Journal of Social Psychology, 5*, 63–74.

Tang, C. S. K., Critelli, J. W., & Porter, J. F. (1995). Sexual aggression and victimization in dating relationships among Chinese college students. *Archives of Sexual Behavior, 24*, 47–53.

Tang, C. S. K. & Lai, B. P. Y. (2007). A review of empirical literature on the prevalence and risk markers of male-on-female intimate partner violence in contemporary China, 1987–2006. *Aggression and Violent Behavior, 13*, 10–28.

Tang, C. S. K., Wong, D., & Cheung, F. M. C. (2002). Social construction of women as legitimate victims of violence in Chinese societies. *Violence against Women, 8*, 968–996.

Tang, S. & Zuo, J. (2000). Dating attitudes and behaviors of American and Chinese college students. *Social Science Journal, 37*, 67–78.

Torn-Morn, M. & Sprecher, S. (2003). A cross-cultural comparison of mate preferences among university students: The United States vs. the People's Republic of China (PRC). *Journal of Comparative Family Studies, 34*, 151–170.

Tsai, J. L. & Levenson, R. W. (1997). Cultural influences on emotional responding: Chinese American and European American dating couples during interpersonal conflict. *Journal of Cross-Cultural Psychology, 28*, 600–625.

Tsai, J. L., Levenson, R. W., & McCoy, K. (2006). Cultural and temperamental variation in emotional response. *Emotion, 6*, 484–497.

Wan, W. W. N., Luk, C. L., & Lai, J. C. L. (2000). Personality correlates of loving styles among Chinese students in Hong Kong. *Personality and Individual Differences, 29*, 169–175.

Wang, C. C. & Mallinckrodt, B. S. (2006). Differences between Taiwanese and US cultural beliefs about ideal adult attachment. *Journal of Counseling Psychology, 53*, 192–2004.

Wang, L. & Crane, D. R. (2001). The relationship between marital satisfaction, marital stability, nuclear family triangulation, and childhood depression. *The American Journal of Family Therapy, 29*, 337–347.

Wei, Z. (1983). Chinese family problems: Research and trends. *Journal of Marriage and the Family, 45*, 943–948.

Weinstein, M., Glei, D. A., Yamazaki, A., Chang, M. C. (2004). The role of intergeneraltional relations in the association between life stressors and depressive symptoms. *Research on Aging, 26*, 511–530.

Winsler, A., Magdigan, A. L., & Aquilino, S. A. (2005). Correspondence between maternal and paternal parenting styles in early childhood. *Early Childhood Research Quarterly, 20*, 1–12.

Wong, O. H. (2003). Postponement or abandonment of marriage? Evidence from Hong Kong. *Journal of Comparative Family Studies, 34*, 531–554.

Wong, S. C. & Bond, M. H. (1999). Personality, self-disclosure and friendship between Chinese university roommates. *Asian Journal of Social Psychology, 2*, 201–214.

Xu, X. (1994). The determinants and consequences of the transformation from arranged marriages to free-choice marriages in Chengdu, the People's Republic of China. In P. L. Lin, K. W. Mei, & H. C. Peng (eds), *Marriage and the family in Chinese societies* (pp. 249–266). Indianapolis, IN: University of Indianapolis Press.

Xu, X. & Whyte, M. K. (1990). Love matches and arranged marriages: A Chinese replication. *Journal of Marriage and the Family, 52*, 709–722.

Yan, J., Chen, C., & Murphy, M. (2005). Social support for older adults in China. *Psychological Science (China), 28*, 1496–1499. (in Chinese)

Yang, K. S. (1986). Chinese personality and its change. In M. H. Bond (ed.), The *psychology of the Chinese people* (pp. 106–170). Hong Kong: Oxford.

Yang, K. S. (1999). Towards an indigenous Chinese psychology: A selected review of methodological, theoretical, and empirical accomplishments. *Chinese Journal of Psychology, 41*, 181–211.

Yau, J. & Smetana, J. (1996). Adolescent–parent conflict among Chinese adolescents in Hong Kong. *Child Development, 67*, 1262–1275.

Yau, J. & Smetana, J. (2003). Adolescent–parent conflict in Hong Kong and Shenzhen: A comparison of youth in two cultural contexts. *International Journal of Behavioral Development, 27*, 201–211.

Ye, M., Wen, S., & Wang, L. (1999). Quality of marriage and personality match of couples. *Chinese Mental Health Journal, 13*, 298–299. (in Chinese)

Yeh, C. Y. (1998). Determinants of condom use intention in the prevention of HIV/AIDS among Taiwanese junior college students. *Nursing Research, 6*, 264–278.

Yeh, C. H. (2002). Sexual risk taking among Taiwanese youth. *Public Health Nursing, 19*, 68–75.

Yeh, K. H. (2002). Is living with elderly parents still a filial obligation for Chinese people? *Journal of Psychology in Chinese Societies, 3*, 61–84.

Yeung, D. Y., Fung, H. H., & Lang, F. R. (2008). Self-construal moderates age differences in social network characteristics. *Psychology and Aging, 23*, 222–226.

Yeung, G. T. Y. & Fung, H. H. (2007). Social support and life satisfaction among Hong Kong Chinese older adults: Family first? *European Journal of Ageing, 4*, 219–227.

Yik, M. S. M. & Bond, M. H. (1993). Exploring the dimensions of Chinese person perception with indigenous and imported constructs: Creating a culturally balanced scale. *International Journal of Psychology, 25*, 333–341.

Yin, W. J., Jing, C. H. & Shi, J. N. (2007). Parenting styles of parents of Uygur and Han adolescents. *Chinese Journal of Clinical Psychology, 15*, 516–518. (in Chinese)

Yum, Y. O. (2004). Culture and self-construal as predictors of responses to accommodative dilemmas in dating relationships. *Journal of Social and Personal Relationships, 21*, 817–835.

Zhang, W. & Lin, C. (1998). The relationship of adolescent self-esteem to parenting style—Consistencies and differences in different subgroups, *Psychological Science (China), 6*, 489–493. (in Chinese)

Zhao, F., Wang, L., & Guo, S. (2006). Investigation on sexual behavior with non-spouse and condom use among reproductive age men and women. *Chinese Journal of Public Health, 22*, 1309–1310. (in Chinese)

CHAPTER 31

A gender perspective on Chinese social relationships and behavior

Catherine So-kum Tang, Zhiren Chua, and Jiaqing O

In recent decades, Chinese societies have undergone rapid social, economic, and political changes. These changes have significant impacts on the way Chinese conduct their daily lives as well as the way they view themselves and the world around them (Chan & Lee, 1995; Croll, 1995; Goodwin & Tang, 1996; Yang, 1996). In this chapter, we adopt a social constructionist approach (Gergen, 2001) to review the empirical literature on contemporary Chinese social relationships and behavior as accessed through the gender lens. We are also guided by hypotheses generated from social role theory (Eagly, Wood, & Diekman, 2000) and feminist constructionist perspectives (Bohan, 1993), in which social roles, gender stereotypes, and gender socialization processes are deemed to be important psychosocial mechanisms regulating social behavior. In the first part of this chapter, we briefly present basic approaches that explain social behavior of men and women. We then examine traditional and contemporary economic and social influences on Chinese social relationships. In particular, Chinese attitudes toward men and women in traditional and non-traditional social roles within the family and in the society are reviewed. This is followed by exploring whether Chinese men and women behave similarly as they assume similar social roles or show divergent behavioral tendencies in light of modernization. We focus the latter part of this chapter on the implications of prevailing gender attitudes and changing social roles on Chinese social relationships, with a review of the literature on gender conflict and violence within the family and in the community.

Basic approaches to understanding the social behavior of men and women

There are two basic approaches in examining social behavior through the gender lens. The essentialist approach argues that individual internal attributes contribute to gender asymmetry in social behavior. Major proponents of this approach are evolutionary psychologists (Buss, 1995; Buss & Kenrick, 1998), who reason that these essential attributes were established through early human attempts to maximize survival. For example, ancestral men had to compete with other men for sexual access to women to reproduce offspring in order to continue the family line. Men's evolved psychological dispositions thus include aggression, competition, and risk taking as well as control of women's sexuality to increase paternity certainty. The essentialist approach predicts a coherent and stable pattern of gender differences in social behavior across societies.

The social construction approach (Gergen, 2001), on the other hand, argues that social behavior is contextualized in social structures and systems. What we purport to know about social behavior depends on the language, communities, and cultural contexts that have created and sustained them. Men and women conduct themselves in accordance to societal expectations for gender-appropriate behavior. Cultural myths and practices serve to sustain this gendered expectation. In general, social constructionists incorporate cultural relativism and predict variability in social behavior across social and cultural contexts (Stein, 1996). Within the social construction approach, social role theory (Eagly et al., 2000) views men and women as behaving in accordance with their prescribed social roles. As women are typically assigned to caring roles in the family and in the community, they are thus expected to demonstrate warm, nurturant, and compassionate behavior (Williams & Best, 1990). Accordingly, the feminist constructionist perspective (Bohan, 1993) argues that behavior, traits, and abilities are reflective of the relative status and power of men and women in any given society, and this relative status will vary across time and cultures (http://www.weforum.org/pdf/gendergap/report2008.pdf).

Empirical support for contrasting predictions generated from the essentialist and the constructionist approaches has been equivocal (Eagly, 1995; Eagly & Wood, 1999; Hyde, 2005; Wood & Eagly, 2002). In a recent review of meta-analytic studies conducted from 1985 to 2003, Hyde (2005) found that gender differences were small on most social and personality attributes, with the exception of aggression. This review also noted that in studies that removed the influence of social roles, gender asymmetry in aggression also disappeared (Lightdale & Prentice, 1994). Research tracking gender differences across recent time periods in the United States has shown that women's self-reports of assertiveness, dominance, and masculinity have become more similar to men's, observations related to women's entry into male-dominated roles in recent decades (Twenge, 1997; 2001). These findings generally favor the social constructionist approach. However, in a cultural analysis of social behavior of men and women in industrial and postindustrial societies, Wood and Eagly (2002) noted a systematic, gendered patterning of division of labor in the family, with men contributing more to subsistence and women performing most childcare and domestic activities. These researchers also found an overreaching cross-cultural tendency for women to be disadvantaged relative to men in terms of power, status, and control of resources, especially in non-industrial societies (see also http://www.weforum.org/pdf/gendergap/report2008.pdf). Based on these findings, Wood and Eagly (2002) have proposed a new biosocial approach blending the essentialist and social constructionist approaches. According to this new approach, the social behavior of men and women reflects culturally shared, social expectations and self-evaluations, which are shaped by both socialization and biological processes. Men and women are biologically specialized to perform their different activities efficiently. Men can more readily perform activities that confer status and power, they are thus advantaged in a gender hierarchy.

In this chapter, we adopt the social constructionist approach (Gergen, 2001) to examine the impact of rapid social changes on social relationships and behavior of Chinese men and women. In line with the social role theory (Eagly et al., 2000) and the feminist constructionist perspectives (Bohan, 1993), we reckon that social role assignment, shared expectations, and relative power and status in the society are important psychosocial mechanisms that regulate the behavior of Chinese men and women. In this chapter, we cover major geographic regions of mainland China, Hong Kong, Taiwan, and Singapore, given their shared cultural heritage despite diversities in socioeconomic and political development. We are also cognizant of urban-rural divides as well as sub-cultural differences among ethnic and religious minorities in these societies, and will consider these issues despite the dearth of data.

Traditional and contemporary influences on Chinese social behavior

Traditional influences

For many centuries, Chinese social relationships and behavior have been heavily influenced by the highly scripted, Confucian ethical principles of *wu lu* regarding relationships between emperors and ministers, fathers and sons, husbands and wives, among brothers, and among friends (Goodwin & Tang, 1996; Gabreya & Hwang, 1996; see also Hwang & Han, this volume). Men typically had more power and status than women, given their differential role assignment in the family and in the society. Until recent decades, only men could pass on the family name and inheritance, perform ancestral worship ceremonies, pursue educational and occupational goals, and become heads of cities, provinces, and nations. Men were the *de facto* breadwinners and family heads who presided over major decision-making in the family. Within social relationships, men were expected to behave according to broad principles of *ren* (benevolence*)*, *yi* (righteousness) and *li (*justice). For women, their social behavior was governed by Confucian principles of three obedience and four virtues, *san cong sei de.* These principles emphasized obedience and subservience of women to their fathers when young, to their husbands when married, and to their sons when widowed. Women's social roles were narrowly defined within the family to reproduce offspring, to serve and care for family members, and to maintain the tidiness and orderliness of households. Women were generally assigned no other social roles beyond those of daughters, wives, and mothers, and did not work outside the home. Even when they were forced to work due to economic necessity, they still worked inside other people's households as wet nurses, maids, cooks, or in other service roles. In general, there were few disputes and open challenges about shared expectations of gender-specific social roles and their associated behaviors (Honig & Hershatter, 1988; Wolf, 1987). As such, these rigid gender norms and gendered social hierarchy have served to maintain gender harmony and protect the power of Chinese men and their status in the society.

Traditional gender roles and gender stereotypes

Gender schema theories (Bem, 1981) maintain that gender is a major component around which individuals organize information. Gender roles and stereotypes are shared or individual subjective perceptions of what men or women should be and how they should behave. Chinese societies are typically classified as collective cultures, with an emphasis on individual compliance to shared social norms, including gender role norms (Marshall, 2008). Earlier research in the 1980's on gender roles in Chinese societies confirmed gender role stereotypes found in Western studies. Young children and adolescents were found to possess stereotypical perceptions of gender roles and had distinct gender-specific expectations for men and women (Cheung, 1986; Keyes, 1983; Lai & Bond, 1997). Men were described more often than women in terms that connoted intellectual competence, whereas women were often seen as incompetent and passive although they were also portrayed positively for their warmth and expressiveness. In general, masculine characteristics were considered more desirable and preferred than feminine characteristics in both private and public domains (Francesco & Hakel, 1981; Lai & Bond, 1997). Gender roles were also valued differentially, and individuals with masculine and androgynous roles as compared to those with feminine roles typically reported higher self-esteem (Lau, 1989; Lai & Bond, 1997). Confucian gender ideals and principles persisted as the protocol for proper family life in China, Taiwan, Hong Kong, and Singapore (Chan, 2000; Chan & Lee, 1995; Wong, 1972). Division of labor within the family was determined according to gender role stereotypes, with men dominating over major decision making in the family and women being responsible for caring of children and other family members. Aggression within the family, particular parent-to-child and husband-to-wife physical discipline, was legitimized and defended as the prerogative of males within the rules of the family, *jia fa*, to ensure that members behaved within gender role expectations and cultural rules.

Contemporary economic, political, and social changes

In the past century, Chinese societies have evolved from planned economies into varying forms of market-based economies - a bottom-up social system in which the prices of goods and services are determined in a pricing system freely determined by supply and demand. The basic function of the market economy is to enable people to cooperate with one another without coercion or undue interference from the central government. In contrast to the emphasis on prescribed roles and power in traditional Chinese ethos, the ideology of the market economy focuses on individual choice and freedom, and is believed to be a necessary condition for creation and sustainability of civil and political freedoms (Friedman & Friedman, 1980).

Along with economic liberalization, political changes and legal reforms in recent decades have also impacted on the relative status of men and women in contemporary Chinese societies (Chan, 2000; Cheung & Tang, 2008), just as has generally happened elsewhere (see http://www.weforum.org/pdf/gendergap/report2008.pdf). Equal rights for women have been explicitly stipulated in local and national legislatures in mainland China, Hong Kong, Taiwan, and Singapore. Even in the private sphere, marriage and family laws have also been reviewed to codify gender equality in these regions. Important international instruments on the protection of women such as the Convention on the Elimination of All Forms of Discrimination Against Women (CEDAW) have also been endorsed.

The rapid economic and social changes in Chinese societies have brought increased opportunities for education and employment, especially for women. These changes have in turn modified traditional Chinese family structure (Chan, 2000; Cheung & Tang, 2008; Thornton & Lin, 1994). The age of first marriage of men and women and consequently age of childbirth have increased in all Chinese societies. Access to contraception for either voluntary or imposed birth control has resulted in the overall decline in fertility rate and smaller family size with an average of less than two children per couple. More and more couples choose to cohabit and live separate from their parents, and the proportion of nuclear families has increased significantly in recent years. Family members become isolated from each other and are less able to offer mutual support and assistance. There are also growing concerns about the state of marriage. At the beginning of the last century, it was almost universal marriage. Nowadays, many men and women spend a significant part of their adulthood as single persons. Marriage dissolution and divorce rates are also climbing in all Chinese societies.

In light of the above changes in contemporary Chinese societies, the first question we ask is: Have social roles of men and women changed? A related question is: Have shared expectations and individual perceptions of gender-specific role assignment and behavior changed? More importantly, do Chinese men and women behave differently as a result of modernization? Social constructionists seem to provide contrasting responses to these questions. According to social role theory (Diekman & Eagly, 2000), gender differences in social behavior will be eroded when Chinese men and women are assigned similar roles. Female gender stereotypes will be particularly subject to change, given the restrictive roles previously assigned to Chinese women and they will enjoy more latitude for expansion compared to Chinese men. However, the feminist constructionist perspectives (Bohan, 1993) argue that social roles function to uphold Chinese men's power and status and are thus impervious to change. Gender asymmetry in social behavior will persist and women will continue to be disadvantaged in the gender hierarchy relative to men. In subsequent sections, we will examine the extent to which these contrasting predictions facilitate the understanding of contemporary Chinese social relationships and behavior of men and women.

Changes in social roles and gender stereotypes

Changes in social roles

Nowadays, instead of being confined to domestic activities, about half of Chinese women are expected to participate in paid employment outside their homes at various life stages (Cheung & Tang, 2008). As in other countries, the employment status of Chinese women as compared to Chinese men is more affected by their marital status and family life-cycle stages, and is typically contingent on child-care and domestic responsibilities (Tang, Au, Chung, & Ngo, 2000; Yi & Chien, 2002). Women are more likely to hold part-time jobs and to be unemployed or underemployed, particularly during adverse economic conditions. Vertical and horizontal occupational segregation by gender remains strong in Taiwan (Bowen, 2003), Hong Kong (Tang et al., 2000), and Singapore (Chan, 2000). Relative to men, women are more likely to be concentrated in the agricultural sector of rural areas and in the clerical and service industries of urban cities. There is also inequality within women workers, especially in the service industry. Youthful, feminine, and urban women are valued, while middle-aged and rural women are simultaneously devalued (Hanser, 2005). Women constitute the minority in managerial, administrative, legislative, and government ministerial positions. The barrier facing women getting into senior positions at work is related to their family responsibilities. Although legislation is in place to protect the employment rights of women during pregnancy and those with family responsibilities, biases of employers and actual family commitments create the glass ceiling for many women aspiring for advancement (Bowen, 2003; Cheung & Tang, 2008; McKeen & Bu, 2005; Tang et al., 2000).

With women's increasing participation in the labor force, the number of dual-earner families has increased *pari passu*, with women bringing in additional financial income to the family (Tang et al., 2000). However, housework sharing is still divided according to traditional gender roles - women shoulder most of the burden of domestic work and in providing care for family members. In China, although men and women share housework, there is a significant difference in the amount of time that women and men spend on household chores (Lu, Maume, & Bellas, 2000). In Taiwan, the participation rate of women doing domestic work is over 75 per cent, while the male rate is only 31 per cent to 35 per cent (Foundation of Women's Rights Promotion and Development, 2005). In Hong Kong, a study on time use conducted in 2001 showed that employed women spent an average of 1.7 hours on household labor per day as opposed to 0.7 hours among employed men (Census & Statistics Department, 2003). Even for families who have hired domestic/household helpers, women still bear the major responsibility in caring for children, sick, and elderly family members (Choi & Lee, 1997). Contrary to Western findings that women in higher occupational positions may have more power to negotiate the division of housework with their husbands, Hu and Kama (2007) found that when wives in Taiwan made relatively more money in comparison with their husbands, they spent relatively more time on the housework especially among those with extended families. The researchers termed this phenomenon as the 'deviance neutralization effect', i.e. high-salaried employed women have to spend more time on housework in order to compensate for their unconventional role.

Shared and individual perceptions toward gender role and gender stereotypes

Sociological research on attitudes has argued that education is the most likely herald of changes in values and attitudes (Stember, 1961). This is also evident in contemporary Chinese societies. Flexible and equalitarian gender role attitudes are generally endorsed by better-educated individuals, especially female university students, in China (Chia, Allred, & Jerzak, 1997), Hong Kong (Leung & Ng, 1999), Taiwan (Zhang, 2006), and Singapore (Teo, Graham, Yeoh, & Levy, 2003). Using a national sample of individual and community-level data in mainland China, Sue (2004) found that education influenced attitudes toward women's careers, marriage rights, sexual freedom, and the importance of having sons. This study found that better-educated individuals, especially women, tended to hold more egalitarian gender attitudes. Furthermore, egalitarian gender attitudes also trickled down through education, as individuals in communities with high (urban) than low (rural) education endorsed more egalitarian attitudes. Within Chinese societies, individuals from regions with relatively higher (e.g. Hong Kong and Taiwan) than lower literacy rates (mainland China) held more liberal attitudes toward non-traditional roles of men and women (Tang, Cheung, Chen, & Sun, 2002; Tu & Liao, 2005). In an influential cross-cultural study on university students, Williams and Best (1990) found that Singapore was on similar level with the United States and Canada in the middle range of egalitarian in gender role attitudes. In a more recent study, Zhou, Dawson, Herr, and Stukas (2004) found that university students in mainland China had less gender bias about people's occupations, housework responsibilities, and hobbies as compared to American university students.

Despite a trend toward more egalitarian gender role attitudes, many traditional gender attitudes still prevail in contemporary Chinese societies. Gender stereotypes continue to be transmitted and reinforced in schools and universities in Hong Kong (Yim & Bond, 2002), Taiwan (Hong, 2004; Hong, Veach, & Lawrenz, 2003), and Singapore (Tay & Gibbons, 1998; Ward, 1990). For example, with a large sample of senior high students in Taiwan, Hong et al. (2003) found widespread gender-stereotypical thinking, such as the belief that boys were superior to girls in logical thinking, mathematics, and science, whereas girls were better at language and liberal arts. Students in this study also held that boys should be brave and strong than weak and withdrawn, whereas girls should be tender and friendly and focused on indoor activities. Boys relative to girls and low-performing relative to high-performing students showed stronger gender-stereotypical thinking. In another study on Taiwanese university students (Hong, 2004), female students who were majoring in dance, interior design, fine arts, and product design as compared to students from other majors showed the most sexist attitudes of the sort that would limit women's social, political, economic, and psychological development. Women relative to men were perceived as more thoughtful, kind, sympathetic, delicate, passive, and timid. Women were viewed as belonging to families; hence, they were expected to stay at home to care for children. In contrast, men were seen as breadwinners, courageous, pushy, making final decisions at home and sexually active (see also Lai & Bond, 1997). Teachers were found to encourage boys to take science subjects and girls to take arts subjects. Similar to the results of studies conducted in other countries (Debacker & Nelson, 2000; Eagly, 1995), these stereotypes were related to students' choice of school subjects and career as well as lower academic aspirations of female students. Traditional gender role messages in different media such as television, magazines, and popular culture in Chinese societies also reinforced gender stereotypes, with men typically portrayed in authoritative roles and women in subordinate roles (Furnham, Mak, & Tanidjojo, 2000; Tan, Ling, & Theng, 2002). In a study on the media representation of politicians in Singapore from 1984 to 1999, Chew (2002) found that women candidates were presented and portrayed differently from men candidates. Women candidates were typically packaged within the gender stereotype - as 'the weaker sex' who operated within the framework of the family as wives and mothers.

Research also indicates that gender stereotypes and conservative attitudes toward family roles are still endorsed by the general public as well as by social service professionals in Chinese societies (Tang, Pun, & Cheung, 2002; Tang, Wong, & Cheung, 2002). While Chinese have become less rigid about women's roles and status relative to men's in educational, occupational, and social domains, especially among young university students (Zhou, Dawson, Herr, & Stukas, 2004), many Chinese still believe that women's proper place should be in the family where they are primarily responsible for household chores and caring of their husbands and children. Public attitudes toward employed women who are successful in their careers are both positive and negative. On the one hand, these women are being seen as achievement-oriented, dominant, rational, decisive, and competent; on the other hand, they are also being criticized as lacking nurturance, being selfish, aggressive, and non-domestic (Lee & Hoon, 1993; Tang, Pun et al., 2002; Zou, 2003). Chinese also have a tendency to blame women when there are marital conflict and marriage problems (Tang, Wong et al., 2002). Public attitudes towards divorced women and single mothers are negative, and they are often socially isolated with a low chance of remarriage (Cheung & Liu, 1997, Tang, & Yu, 2005; Kung, Hung, & Chan, 2004).

Gender stereotypes are evident in the workplace and are often used for guiding recruitment and promotion decisions. In a study of Chinese employers in Hong Kong, Tang (2006) found that their recruitment decisions were strongly associated with their gender stereotypes. Employers with conservative gender-role attitudes were more likely to emphasize applicants' physical ability and gender, but rated applicants' sense of responsibility and interview performance as less important. These employers also adhered closely to job gender-typing in recruitment decisions, i.e. preferring men for 'masculine jobs' and women for 'feminine jobs'. Physical ability was viewed as an important selection in recruiting individuals to male-typed than to female-typed jobs; and a pleasant personality was emphasized in recruiting individuals to female-typed than to male-typed jobs. In Singapore, Lee and Hoon (1993) noted that there was little change in attitudes toward women in management throughout the years. Men as compared to women were less accepting of career women who were married with children, and both men and women preferred to have a male boss. The public typically viewed the success of a female manager as relying on a support system that consisted of a male mentor, a male supportive husband, and a mother or maid to help in household chores; whereas the success of a male manager depended entirely on himself. Zou (2003) found that masculinity was the key to success in urban China. However, if women acted like men, the public would be harsh on them, and interpret their masculine behavior as a sign of arrogance or selfishness, unless they also fulfilled feminine roles at home.

Gender role stress and multiple role involvement

Gender role stress

Research on Western samples has shown that a strong commitment to gender stereotypes will distort individuals' cognitive appraisal of situations and restrict the types of coping strategies available to them (Eisler & Blalock, 1991; Gillespie & Eisler, 1992). In a study on Chinese university students and working adults in Hong Kong, Tang and Lau (1996a) found that Chinese men felt particularly stressed when they were in situations that required them to make decisions, to express emotions, and to be subordinate to women. Chinese women, on the other hand, experienced stress when they perceived themselves as physically unattractive and not nurturant, had to behave assertively, and had to cope with experiences of potential victimization. Compared to middle-aged working adults, university students felt more stressed in meeting standards of gender role or in exhibiting behaviors that violated gender role imperatives in formal as well as in intimate social relationships. Chinese men as compared to women felt more compelled to adhere to gender stereotypes. Associations between gender role stress and negative mental health outcomes found among Western samples are also evident among Chinese. Chinese men and women working in gender-typed professions (nurses and police officers) as compared to those working in a gender-neutral profession (high school teachers) reported more psychological distress and burnout symptoms at work (Tang & Lau, 1996b). Zhou et al. (2004) also found that Chinese men as compared to women felt more uncomfortable when their spouses were superior in earnings, achievements, and social status.

Gender role conflict and multiple role involvement

With the increasing number of dual-earner families, Chinese men and women nowadays lead very full lives, combining their social roles as paid workers, spouses, and parents. Multiple social role involvement is particularly stressful for Chinese women, as the duty of balancing demands of work and family falls disproportionately on them (Choi & Lee, 1997, Hu & Kama, 2007; Lu et al., 2000). Chinese women typically evaluate their role experience and performance according to the internalized gender role message, and family roles remain the most central among their various social roles (Tang & Tang, 2001). In a recent book on top women leaders with family responsibilities, Halpern and Cheung (2008) found that women leaders in Hong Kong and China still considered children and/or family their priority. Only a few of these women leaders considered work and family demands to be in conflict. Particularly, some of the senior women leaders in China took pride in the recognition of their success in both work and family. A happy family was regarded as a measure of the success of their work. Other researchers have also argued that in contrast to American culture, social roles of the individual and family are blurred in Chinese culture, where work serves a utilitarian function for the long-term benefits of the family (Aryee, Luk, Leung, & Lo, 1999; Tang, 2009a; Yang, 2005). Thus, family-work conflict is not considered as inevitable. The support of the extended family and the contribution to the family through work may facilitate commitment and satisfaction of both family and work roles.

In line with gender role stress research, Tang and Tang (2001) found that employed Chinese women who held traditional gender role beliefs felt more negative about their role as mothers and experienced more somatic symptoms than those who endorsed liberal gender role beliefs. Tang, Lee, Tang, Cheung, and Chan (2002) noted that the quality of social roles rather than the number of roles *per se* was related to the psychological health of Chinese women. These researchers also found that not all social roles had similar mental health benefits, and that the paid worker role seemed to confer more advantages on women's mental health as compared to intra-familial roles, such as wife and mother. The expansionist theory (Barnett & Hyde, 2001) reasons that this may be related to the fact that as paid workers, women can bring in additional financial resources to the families, have more negotiating power in obtaining additional help from their spouses or hiring domestic helpers, and have increased opportunity to contact with people who can provide social support. Moreover, employment also brings women additional sources of self-esteem, control, and social support outside their families. However, for women who worked in low-reward but high-demand jobs in mainland China (Lai, 1995) and Hong Kong (Yeung & Tang, 2001), their worker role was found to adversely affect their psychological health.

Research has indicated that experiences in one social role may spill over to another social role to influence psychological health (e.g. Grzywacz & Marks, 2000). Juggling family-work roles can have either beneficial or detrimental impacts on individuals' well-being, depending on the direction and nature of the spillover. In a study on employed mothers in Hong Kong, Tang (2009a) found spillover effects of role experiences on psychological health as well as asymmetrical permeability of family and work boundaries. In particular, positive work experience was found to permeate through family boundaries into family experience to reduce psychological distress. However, positive family experience did not spill over to influence the overall quality of work experience to enhance psychological health. For Taiwanese employees, work demands were related to work-family conflict, whereas both work and family demands were related to family-work conflict (Lu, Kao, Chang, Wu, & Cooper, 2008). Aryee (1992) also reported that the inability to fulfill conflicting demands from work and family was related to mental ill-health of employed married women in Singapore. In almost all Chinese societies, spousal support (Aryee et al., 1999; Ngo & Lau, 1998; Shaffer, Harrison, Gilley, & Luk, 2001; Yang, 2005) and workplace flexibility (Lu, Kao, Chang, Wu, & Cooper, 2008; Jones et al., 2008) are consistently found to be important in influencing the work-family interface and its mental health outcomes.

Contemporary Chinese social relationships and behavior

Sexuality and sexual behavior

Among various aspects of social relationships and behavior, we focus on impacts of rapid economic and social changes on sexuality and sexual behavior, mate preference and selection, and the marital relationships of Chinese men and women. For many centuries, Chinese sexuality was heavily governed by Confucian ethics which accorded men the superior role. Relative to women, men were allowed greater sexual promiscuity and control over both sexual and reproductive decision-making. However, there is evidence of changing attitudes toward sex and sexuality in contemporary Chinese societies, including more liberal attitudes toward sexuality, pre- and extramarital sexual activities, masturbation, homosexuality, and prostitution (Chia & Lee, 2008; Pei, Ho, & Ng, 2007; Tang, 2004; Wang & Hsu, 2006; Watts, 2008). These changes are generally more noticeable for women than for men. Pei et al. (2007) critically reviewed studies on women's sexuality in China since 1980 and found that women today did not invariably see themselves as good wives and asexual beings. Instead, they could talk about their sexual experiences. Women also use sex to gain power, so that the boundary between 'good girls' and 'bad girls' has become blurred.

Nowadays, sexual activities between Chinese men and women are increasingly practiced for mutual pleasure in addition to its procreative function. In Taiwan, the prevalence of sexually active adolescent girls has increased from 1 per cent in 1983 to 6 per cent in 1995 and to 17.8 per cent in 2004 (Wang & Hsu, 2006). There has also been a concomitant increase in teenage pregnancy and induced abortion from 1980's to 2000s in Taiwan, although adolescent girls who had steady boyfriends often reported being in control of their sexual behavior (Sun, 2005). In Hong Kong, the percentages of university students reporting premarital sexual activities has also increased from 6.25 per cent for men and 3.5 per cent for women in the 1980's to about 11 per cent across genders in the mid-1990's (Tang, Lai, & Chung, 1997). University students in Singapore also endorsed liberal sexual attitudes and believed that their peers are significantly more sexually active than in previous generations (Chia & Lee, 2008). Among adult Chinese, sexual activities between men and women are no longer confined to couples who are married. Watts (2008) found that nowadays, about 70 per cent of adults in China had engaged in premarital sex prior to marriage, compared with only 16 per cent at the end of the 1980's. There was also greater acceptance of casual sexual encounters with strangers and extra-marital sexual liaisons.

Rapid economic and social changes in China have also led to significant problems associated with population migration, a growing sex industry, and concurrent increases in sexually transmitted diseases (STD) and HIV infection (Tang, 2008; Watts, 2008). As in other countries, Chinese women are found to be more vulnerable than men to HIV infection (Cutter, Lim, Ang, Lyn, & Chew, 2004; Lin, McElmurry, & Christiansen, 2007; Tang, 2008). In a study that reviewed behavioral studies on female sex workers in China from 1990 to 2006, Hong and Li (2008) found that these women were young and mobile, most of them had both commercial and non-commercial sex partners, had low rates of consistent condom use, high rates of STD and HIV infection, and some also engaged in drug use. Tang (2008) found that married women with disrupted marriages due to economic reasons were also vulnerable to these sexual health problems. In recent years, many mobile and cross-border workers are married men, who commute between their workplaces in China and their homes in Hong Kong on weekends or during long holidays. With increased freedom, surplus income, and feelings of loneliness away from home, these mobile workers frequently engage in casual/commercial sex in China (Lau & Thomas, 2001; Tucker et al., 2005). When they return home during weekends or long holidays to Hong Kong, their wives dare not enrage their husbands by asking about their sexual liaisons in China or defying their demand for unprotected sex, given that these women are often financially dependent on their husbands (Tang, 2008).

Mate selection and preference

Current literature suggests that Confucian values still prevail when Chinese select their mates and marriage partners. In a 37-country study on international preferences in selecting mates, Buss et al. (1990) found that compared to samples from other countries, Chinese in China and Taiwan were similar and placed greater value on good heredity but less emphasis on dependability, mutual attraction, sociability, a pleasing disposition, an exciting personality, appearance, and religious similarity. In a more recent study, Toro-Morn and Sprecher (2003) found robust gender differences in criteria for mate selection in Chinese societies. Women as compared to men put greater value on a sense of humor, health, material possessions, power, and athleticism, whereas men as compared to women valued a partner with good housekeeping skills. Men have also increasingly expressed a stronger preference for a much younger, physically attractive, and sexy-looking female partner.

Other research shows that different personality traits are preferred for romantic partners and husbands. Hofstede (1996) found that women in Hong Kong and Singapore viewed important qualities of husbands as 'healthy, rich, and understanding'; whereas boyfriends should have more 'personality', affection, intelligence, and sense of humor. In a more recent study on mate preference traits, mainland Chinese university students as compared to American students valued social status and filial piety more highly, but both groups also preferred steadfast support and authenticity in communication over social status and physical attractiveness (Kline, Horton, & Zhang, 2008). Traditional marriage norms for older, better-educated husbands and younger, less-educated wives are still held by many Chinese. Compared to British students, this traditional 'male-superior' norm in mate selection is preferred by more Chinese university students in China than British students, and by more female than male students (Higgins, Zhang, Liu, & Sun, 2002). Chinese working women, especially women in China, were found to prefer their husbands to hold jobs with higher pay and better prestige than their own jobs (McKeen & Bu, 2005).

Marital relationship and marriage dissolution

Current literature indicates that traditional Chinese family values have gradually moved toward Western egalitarian gender ideologies on marital roles and decision-making power. In a study in Hong Kong, Tang (1999) examined the distribution of marital power regarding family entertainment, interacting with relatives, amount of money spent on food, major financial decision-making, such as buying a house or a car, working outside the family, and having a child. She found that about half of the respondents reported sharing equal decision power with their marriage partners, 15 per cent having the final say for different decisions by themselves or by their partners, and only 28 per cent being dominated by their marriage partners. Egalitarian distribution of power in marital decision-making was more likely found among women who were professionals or those with at least a university education. However, Xu and Lai (2004) maintain that egalitarian gender ideology may not directly lead to higher or lower levels of marital quality unless it can be successfully translated into egalitarianism in marital role performance. These researchers argue that if egalitarian gender ideology can result in an equitable distribution of labor division and decision-making power in the relationship, then marital bonds, in turn, can be strengthened and the well-being of marriage can be improved.

In a series of studies, Quek and Knudson-Martin (2006; 2008) described how dual-career newlywed couples in Singapore reshaped their marital power to create equality. They found that these couples typically placed their own and partners' careers as central to the relationship, devised flexible allocation of household duties, maintained open dialogue regarding conflict, allowed equal power in decision-making, and continued to self-reflect on their marital relationship. Men also learned to change role expectations with wives' career, took on more household tasks, valued wives' housework and financial contributions, and attended to their wives emotionally. Couples would then gradually shift toward equality by creating a gender structure within the family where men retained the ultimate choice regarding power shifts and wives found ways to influence their husband's decisions.

In other Chinese societies, women would use different strategies to gain marital power. Some women take more active steps to resist their traditional marital roles to recreate their identities beyond wifehood and motherhood. Ho (2007) noted that many middle-aged women in Hong Kong rejected women's identity as centered on their maternal roles and opposed the derogatory term, *si-nai*, used exclusively for middle-aged, married women who were ignorant, overweight, and penny-wise but pound-foolish. These women learned to be 'flexible housewives' by actively expanding their life space from motherhood to diversified spheres as they entered mid-life rather than holding on to family roles of their younger days. They sought self-fulfillment and constantly assessed their lives to create alternate meanings for themselves and to gain recognition by enrolling in vocational programs, voluntary work, investment, and pursuit of pleasures through leisure activities and even extra-marital affairs.

As in other countries, marriage dissolution is becoming more frequent in Chinese societies. For example, Wang (2001) found that the number of divorces per 1,000 married population had increased from 0.82 to 1.71 from 1979 to 1997 in China, and estimated that the divorce rates would continue to rise. The increases in overall divorce rates in Chinese societies have been attributed to more liberal attitudes toward divorce, simplified marriage and divorce laws, greater economic independence among women, increased exposure to democratic ideas, and attitudes favorable to seeking personal happiness. Compared to past decades, more Chinese women are initiating divorce applications

(Cheung & Tang, 2008), a strategy also used by battered women as a way to end their husbands' abuse (Tang, 1999).

Adjusting to divorce and transitioning to single parenthood is a stressful time for both men and women. Single mothers and fathers who have been socialized with gender-specific values and beliefs may face challenges of single parenthood differently and encounter unique adjustment experiences. For divorced single fathers, rigid masculine gender role socialization may have influenced their judgments of the divorce, financial strain, and performing housework and child-caring duties in a particularly negative way. Internalization of these rigid gender stereotypes may also make them feel shameful about admitting their vulnerability and toward seeking help from others (see also Cheng, Lo, & Chio, this volume). Tang and Yu (2005) found that divorced single fathers in Hong Kong experienced great difficulty in adjusting to the 'mother' or child-carer role. Single fathers found supervision of their children at home and over school work particularly stressful. They also found it time-consuming in preparing meals for the family, taking their children to school, and picking them up after school. They were uncomfortable doing 'women's work', such as cooking, washing clothes, and buying grocery in the market. For divorced single mothers, those with rigid feminine gender ideals may view themselves as 'failed wives and mothers' who are unable to face life challenges. Tang and Yu (2005) found that divorce women in Hong Kong were typically granted custody of the children and often experienced a significant reduction in the family income. Many felt shameful about their divorce and became socially isolated from others. They were often rejected by their in-laws or social networks of their ex-husbands, although their maiden family sometimes provided emotional support to them. In Tang and Yu's (2005) study, both men and women reported poor psychological health and frequent suicidal thoughts during their first year of divorce and single parenthood.

Gender relationships and violence

Gender conflict and violence

Modernization and rapid economic development in contemporary Chinese societies have brought about changes in social role assignment of men and women as well as the pattern of gender relations within the family and in the society. Social role theory (Eagly et al., 2000) suggests that more similar social roles for Chinese men and women will lessen traditional differences in power and status between them. Gender relations will thus become more harmonious. However, the feminist constructionist perspectives (Bohan, 1993) argue that any change in power structure between Chinese men and women in the family and in the society will create a high level of gender conflict, since male prerogatives are being challenged. This may increase occurrences of gender disharmony and violence, as in battering, rape, and sexual harassment directed by men toward women. Through actual acts of violence or creating a culture of fear, men will be able to control women's behavior by keeping them out of the public sphere or by confining women's participation to domestic affairs. As such, violence against women also serves to maintain the gender inequality by preventing the full advancement of women (Brownmiller, 1975; Dobash & Dobash, 1992).

There is evidence that despite changing social roles of men and women, traditional gender ideologies and cultural myths that perpetuate men's violence against women still prevail in contemporary Chinese societies. In a recent focus-group study conducted in China, Hong Kong, and Taiwan (Tang, Wong et al., 2002), researchers have found that Chinese tended to view sexually victimized women as sex objects who trigger men's sexual impulses or provoke them to sexual violence. Women who were battered by their husbands are typically viewed as failing to fulfill their family duties, being unfaithful to their husbands by having extramarital affairs, failing to please their husbands, such as inability to produce a son, and/or refusing to have sex. Many Chinese judged that these women deserved to be physically disciplined by their husbands. Similar victim-blaming attitudes were also held by Chinese in Singapore (Choi & Edleson, 1996). In addition, women were also found to embrace traditional gender attitudes toward their marital roles (Tang, 2008; Tang, Wong, & Lee, 2001). They considered that they should be sexually available to their husbands and saw such complaisance as an intrinsic part of being 'virtuous wives', even though this would conflict with their own sexual desires and the need to protect themselves from sexually transmitted disease or HIV infection.

The above pro-violence cultural myths and victim-blaming attitudes were found to be common among Chinese who were of the male gender, older age, and lower education attainment (Tang, Pun et al., 2002; Tang, Wong et al., 2002). The representation of women as legitimate victims of violence provides a justification for men's violent behavior and undermines restraints against their behavior. Other studies also showed that Chinese men who espoused traditional attitudes toward women and victim-blaming explanations were more likely to report engaging in violent acts against their intimate partners (Chan, 2004; Tang, 1999). Wife batterers in Hong Kong were found to adhere rigidly to traditional gender role expectations for men (Chan, 2004). They believed that men could bleed but not cry, and only immature and incompetent men expressed their emotions before others. However, younger and relatively well-educated Chinese in China, Hong Kong, Taiwan reject various cultural myths about gender violence, oppose victim-blaming explanations, and challenge pro-violence beliefs (Ng & Wong, 2002; Tang, Wong et al., 2002).

More recent research in the United States has examined women who committed violence against their male intimate partners and challenged the feminists' view that these women engaged in less serious and self-defensive violence (e.g. Archer, 2000; Carney, Buttell, & Dutton, 2007). Systemic research in Chinese societies on this topic is lacking, although there are occasional media reports on women-to-men violence among dating and marital couples. In a recent qualitative study of women's aggression in dating relationships in China, Wang and Ho (2007) found that both men and women refused to label women's aggression as violence but defined it as normal, and argued that it served many functions, such as being a form of playful fighting, a means of communication, and a method of increasing affection. In the context of infidelity of their dating partners, women defined their violent behavior not as violence but as a form of justice that punished the former. In the context of mutual violence, women ignored their own aggressive behavior, attached themselves to the victim role, and redefined the mutual violence as a private matter.

Physical violence in intimate relationships

With increasing education and occupational opportunities in contemporary Chinese societies, women have begun to demand greater decision power in various family matters and become less tolerant of sexual infidelity by their husbands. Men may, however, be reluctant to give up their marital power and sexual prerogatives as prescribed by traditional Confucian principles. This could create a high level of marital conflict, and couples may use aggression against each other to resolve disputes (Chen, 1999; Tang, 1999). Given the centrality of wife and mother roles, family responsibilities also create barriers for women to continue to participate in the labor force or to attain senior positions at work. Occupational success often becomes a source of women's frustration and conflict with their husbands (Tang et al., 2002). As women become more financially independent and enjoy more opportunities outside their homes, they will be more open to end their unhappy marriages and initiate divorce (Tang & Yu, 2005). However, this option may not be available to women in rural China who are still in disadvantaged position with respect to resource control. For them, enduring the violence of their abusive husbands and staying in the marriage may be the only option (Liu & Chan, 1999). Conflict in couples also persists throughout the divorce process in relation to alimony and maintenance, child custody, and other financial and housing arrangements. Men may use violence to retaliate against the 'betrayal' of their wives, to restore power and control over her, and as a desperate attempt to force reconciliation. In fact, current literature in Western countries has indicated that male to female partner violence is common around divorce negotiation, during the divorce application, and in the post-separation period (Brownridge, 2006).

Tang and Lai (2008) have recently conducted a review of available empirical literature on intimate partner violence (IPV) in China and Hong Kong within the past 20 years in order to better understand the nature and magnitude of the problem. Information was drawn from 19 empirical studies and a total of 49,201 adult Chinese residing in these two regions. The average lifetime and year prevalence of men-to-women IPV was respectively 19.7 per cent and 16.8 per cent for any type, 42.6 per cent and 37.3 per cent for psychological violence, and 13.5 per cent and 6.7 per cent for physical violence. Higher lifetime prevalence of any type of IPV was reported by rural respondents, from studies conducted in healthcare settings, and from studies using standardized scales to assess IPV. Women were at increased risk of IPV when they and/or their partners were of lower education and socio-economic status, grew up in rural areas, and exhibited the behavioral problems of smoking, alcoholism, and illicit drug use. IPV was also related to a longer duration of marriage, poorer marital quality, more frequent marital conflicts, sexual jealousy and extra-marital affairs, status/power disparity between the partners, inadequate social support, and extended family structure. Cultural and societal risk markers included patriarchal beliefs, wife-beating myths, and political/legal sanction of violence. In another study on 1,143 aboriginal women in Taiwan (Yang, Yang, Chou, Yang, & Wei, 2006), about 15.3 per cent of the women had experienced physical violence from husbands or intimate partners, and another 7 per cent were physically abused during their recent pregnancy. This study also found that risk factors for abuse among pregnant aboriginal women were lower education, unemployment of husband, unequal power within the marriage, and husbands' alcohol, cigarette and non-prescription drug use.

Xu (1997) also examined the extent to which marriage laws and legal protection of women's rights in the society were related to the prevalence of men-to-women IPV. By comparing five marriage cohorts in China from 1933 to 1987, he found that, relative to the period before the formation of the People's Republic of China, incidents of wife abuse declined in the earlier period of the Communist regime from 1949 to 1965. He attributed this reduction to direct efforts made by the government to improve women's socio-economic status, as women's legal rights for the first time were codified in the Marriage Law in 1950. However, he found that there was an upsurge of wife abuse during the Cultural Revolution. He argued that this was a result of the approval and employment of the large-scale and pervasive violence used to reinforce ideological hegemony and social control. In the post-Mao reform period to the late 1980's, incidents of wife abuse tended to decrease or level off. Xu (1997) predicted that with economic and political reforms in the early 1990's, especially with rapid growth of the market economy and weakening of central policies, gender discrimination against women might increase and wife abuse would become more visible.

Research on the negative impacts of intimate partner violence on Chinese women is also available. Married women in Hong Kong (Tang, 1997) and Taiwan (Hou, Hsiu, & Chung, 2005) who had a history of physical or non-physical violence perpetrated by their husbands frequently reported high levels of somatic problems, insomnia, depressive moods, suicidal thoughts, and post-traumatic responses. Those who had experienced partner abuse during pregnancy also showed symptoms of postnatal depression after delivery (Leung, Kung, Lam, Leung, & Ho, 2002). Consistent with available literature on family violence, children are often the intended as well as unintended victims of parental violence. Tang (1997) found that children witnessing parental violence tended to manifest both internalized and externalized behavioral problems. Contrary to the common belief that abused wives would batter their children, men who used physically violent acts against their wives were found to use physically punitive means to discipline their children.

Sexual violence

Among various forms of violence that men use against women, rape and sexual violence is the most feared by women across countries. It is predominately perpetrated by intimate partners and frequently used as a weapon during war and armed conflict (World Health Organization, 2002). In contrast to American feminist scholars' emphasis on the violent aspect of rape (Brownmiller, 1975), the sexual aspect of rape is more salient in the context of Chinese culture (Luo, 2000). In ancient Chinese societies, rape was often employed by men to acquire sexual access to desired women as a socially acceptable precedent to marriage. Even nowadays in Taiwan, a woman who has survived acquaintance rape is still encouraged to marry her rapist in order to preserve her chastity and to avoid social disgrace to her family (Chou, 1995; Luo, 2000). The legal systems in the past also viewed rape incidents as personal problems of women that should be settled privately to protect the reputation of the family. For example, the criminal law in Taiwan until 1999 permitted the public prosecutors the option to not press charges against the assailant in deference to the wish of rape victims. Many Chinese also dispute the concept of marital rape, and view being always sexually available to husbands as an intrinsic part of the role of 'virtuous wives' (Tang et al., 2001; Tang, Wong et al., 2002).

In Chinese societies, very little is known about the prevalence of rape and sexual violence, given the immense stigma attached to sexual victimization. In Taiwan, it was estimated by criminologists that there would be 20 to 27 incidents of sexual assault per day with only a 10 per cent reporting rate (Luo, 2000). The life time and year prevalence for sexual violence committed by intimate partners or husbands in China and Hong Kong was respectively 9.8 per cent and 5.4 per cent (Tang & Lai, 2008). Studies on sexual aggression showed that 2-5 per cent of surveyed young adult women (Tang, Critelli, & Porter, 1995) and 4 per cent of surveyed teenage girls (Chiu & Ng, 2001) in Hong Kong reported being raped by their male dating partners. In the educational settings of Hong Kong, about 5 per cent of surveyed female university students reported being forced to engage in sexual intercourse by either their teachers or fellow students (Tang, 2009b). Coercive sexual activities perpetrated by classmates were also reported by 1-2 per cent of surveyed female students in high school (Tang, 2004). In the work settings of Hong Kong, 1-4 per cent of surveyed female secretaries admitted to being coerced or bribed into sexual activities either by their supervisors or co-workers (Chan, Tang, & Chan, 1999). In another large scale survey on university students in Hong Kong (Tang, 2002), the overall prevalence rate of reported childhood sexual abuse was 6 per cent, with females being twice as likely as males to be sexually victimized. In a recent large national probability study in urban China, the overall reported childhood sexual abuse by either adults or peers before age 14 was about 4 per cent (Luo, Parish, & Laumann, 2008).

In a study of 35 female rape survivors in Taiwan, Luo (2000) identified eight recurring themes experienced by these women: feeling shameful over the loss of their virginity or chastity; considering themselves as damaged and undesirable for future sexual interaction; expressing extreme fear and anxiety about possible exposure of rape incidents to their social networks; feeling guilty about bringing disgrace to their family, particularly their sexual partners; self-blaming for failing to take precautions and communicating possible cues of promiscuity; being traumatized by negative responses from their social networks, such as being ridiculed and blamed, being repeatedly raped by the same assailant, and being induced to and considering marriage proposal by their assailants.

Sexually victimized Chinese women typically indicate the presence of many aspects of the rape trauma syndrome and adverse impacts on their physical, mental, and interpersonal functioning. Cheung and Ng (2004) found that woman survivors of sexual violence in Hong Kong often reported severe psychological distress and suicidal rumination at the time of seeking crisis intervention. Almost half of them had engaged in self-mutilating behaviors and about 20 per cent had made actual suicide attempts after the sexual assault. Research in China and Hong Kong also documented that sexually victimized children manifested many emotional and behavioral symptoms of traumatic sexuality, regardless of their age at which the sexual violence had occurred; these symptoms frequently persisted even though the sexual assault had stopped (Chen, Dunne, & Han, 2006; Luo, Parish, & Laumann, 2008; Tsun, 1999). For example, Tsun (1999) found that sexually victimized children in Hong Kong typically felt ashamed, guilty, confused, and powerless. When perpetrators were their fathers or family members, they felt betrayed and yet sometimes found themselves emotionally dependent upon them. They became anxious and scared if perpetrators used threats to initiate sexual activities and worried about the disclosure of their sexual liaison. These children were also angry with themselves and other adults for failing to stop the sexual assault. In a case of older brother-younger sister incest, Tsun (1999) also noted that the surviving woman still experienced intense emotional reactions even after the sexual abuse had stopped for almost ten years, and that her childhood sexual trauma also negatively affected her current relationship with men.

Sexual harassment

Sexual harassment is widespread across countries, occurs mostly in educational and work settings, usually targets women, and refers to a wide range of behaviors. It has been identified as one of the most damaging and ubiquitous barriers to the pursuit of higher education (Paludi, 1996), career success, and job satisfaction for women (Willness, Steel, & Lee, 2007). Sexual harassment is a relatively new concept in Chinese societies, with only two decades of public discourse and a recent legal history. With a large stratified probability adult sample in mainland China, Parish, Das, and Laumann (2006) found that 12.5 per cent of all women and 15 per cent of urban women reported experiencing some form of harassment in the past year. Most cross-sex harassment was not from supervisors or supervisors, but from co-workers, strangers, and dates and boyfriends. When compared to an earlier study conducted in 1992 (Tang, Yik, Cheung, Choi, & Au, 1996), a large territory-wide survey of full-time university students in Hong Kong found that, while prevalence rates for gender harassment and unwelcome intimate bodily touch had decreased slightly, incidents of sexual coercion perpetrated by peers and teachers were on the rise (Tang, 2009b). In the work setting, a survey conducted in the early 80's showed that about half of the surveyed female employees reported personal experiences of sexual harassment at work during the previous three years (Dolescheck, 1984). Another survey on a small sample of female secretaries in Hong Kong in the late 1990's revealed that about 30 per cent of these women were subject to sexist remarks and dirty jokes at work, 22 per cent received unwanted physical touch, and 1-4 per cent were bribed or coerced to sexual activities by male employers, supervisors, or co-workers (Chan et al., 1999).

Men and women have very different perceptions of and tolerance toward sexual harassment. In a meta-analysis of 62 studies on gender difference in the perception of sexual harassment, Rotundo, Nguyen, and Sackett (2001) found that gender differences were larger for behaviors that involved hostile work environment harassment, derogatory attitudes toward women, dating pressure, or physical sexual contact than sexual propositioning or sexual coercion. Similar gender differences were found among university students in Hong Kong (Tang et al., 1996; Tang, 2009b). Compared to females, male university students were more tolerant of sexually harassing behaviors, and were also more likely to blame women for exaggerating the problem and for over-reacting to the situation. Intolerance toward gender harassment was found to associate with support for gender equality ideology and flexible gender roles. In a multi-ethnic country like Singapore, Li and Lee-wong (2005) found that culture and language affected the interpretation of sexual harassment. Their findings showed that certain cues such as personal space were judged differently by different ethnic groups in Singapore, and English as a communicating language further complicated the understanding of victims' reaction to the situation.

Chinese women who had been sexually victimized or harassed in schools, at work, or in the community typically use indirect and nonassertive coping strategies, such as wishing the assault had not occurred, ignoring the incident, avoiding the perpetrator/harasser, or leaving the situation/setting where the assault or harassment took place (Chan et al., 1999; Cheung & Ng, 2004; Tang, 2004; Tang et al., 1996). About one-third of the victimized women also reported a lowering of self-esteem as well as feelings of depression, insecurity, and a lower sense of belonging to the institution/organization subsequent to their sexual harassment victimization (Chan et al., 1999; Tang, 2009b; Tang et al., 1996). Victims of sexual harassment also received less sympathy than victims of other violent behaviors from the general public (Tang 2009b) as well as from public service professionals, such as police officers, social workers, and medical officers (Tang, Pun et al., 2002).

Conclusions

Many social scientists have argued that Chinese are now at the crossroad of modernism and traditionalism (Chan & Lee, 1995; Croll, 1995; Edwards & Roces, 2000). In our review of the available empirical literature on social relationships and behavior in contemporary Chinese societies, we note that impacts of rapid economic, social, and political changes are not gender-neutral. The lives of

Chinese women relative to Chinese men have been affected to a greater extent by these changes, especially in education, occupation, marriage, and family domains. As predicted by social role theory (Eagly et al., 2000), shared and individual perceptions toward gender roles and gender stereotypes are being challenged and modified as Chinese women continue to expand their activities outside of the family. Also, in line with predictions by the feminist constructionist perspectives (Bohan, 1993), traditional gender ideologies and gender norms still persist, even though social roles for both genders have become more similar. In general, Chinese men as compared to Chinese women are less willing to give up traditional gender beliefs. While new trends towards more egalitarian and harmonious gender relationships have emerged within the family and in the society, gender violence has also become more visible in families, education settings, and workplaces. As modernization of Chinese societies necessitates the redefinition of the relative status and power between men and women, we anticipate the nature of gender relationships will become increasingly diversified and dynamic.

In our review, we note that the current knowledge base focuses on the impacts of rapid social changes on Chinese women. Other than the discourse on gender violence, relatively little research has been conducted on Chinese men's responses to women's inroads upon traditional male social roles and the latter's challenge to male prerogatives. Available literature informs us that Chinese men tend to hold on to masculine gender stereotypes and feel stressful when they are unable to perform according to their internalized and cultural gender expectations. Men's domination over women in sexuality, marital relationship, and workplace is also increasingly contested by women. How do Chinese men handle these challenges? It is too simplistic to conclude that men turn to violence when their masculinity is being threatened. We need to learn how Chinese men embrace the new gender order and how they negotiate with women to redefine themselves within the family and in the society. Is the 'new men movement' in developed countries (Connell, 2005) also evident in contemporary Chinese societies? How are contemporary mothers and fathers socializing their offspring to accommodate emerging gender roles?

The majority of research on these topics is conducted with university students and urban dwellers. Very little is known about how modernization in Chinese societies affects gender relationships and behavior among rural men and women, and among the various ethnic minority groups in Chinese societies. Also lacking in the literature is information about how individuals with non-conventional social roles and life trajectories, such as never married or re-married men and women, single fathers and mothers, and individuals with different sexual orientations, defy traditional gender role stereotypes. In sum, we deem it necessary to continue to examine Chinese social relationships and behavior through the gender lens in order to gain a better understanding of the life experiences of Chinese persons in contemporary societies.

References

Archer, J. (2000). Sex differences in aggression between heterosexual partners: A meta-analytic review. *Psychological Bulletin, 126*, 651–680.

Aryee, S. (1992). Antecedents and outcomes of work–family conflict among married professional women: Evidence from Singapore. *Human Relations, 45*, 813–837.

Aryee, S., Luk, V., Leung A., & Lo, S. (1999). Role stressors, inter-role conflict and well-being: The moderating influence of spousal support and coping behaviors among employed parents in Hong Kong. *Journal of Vocational Behavior, 54*, 259–278.

Barnett, R. C. & Hyde, J. S. (2001). Women, man, work, and family: An expansionist theory. *American Psychologist, 56*, 781–796.

Bem, S. L. (1981). Gender schema theory: A cognitive account of sex typing. *Psychological Review, 88*, 354–364.

Bohan, J. S. (1993). Regarding gender: Essentialism, constructionism, and feminist psychology. *Psychology of Women Quarterly, 17*, 5–21.

Bowen, C. (2003). Sex discrimination in selection and compensation in Taiwan. *International Journal of Human Resource Management, 14*, 297–315.

Brownmiller, S. (1975). *Against our will: Men, women, and rape.* New York: Simon & Schuster.

Brownridge, D. (2006). Violence against women post-separation. *Aggression & Violence, 11*, 514–530.

Buss, D. M. (1995). Evolutionary psychology: A new paradigm for psychological science. *Psychological Inquiry, 6*, 1–30.

Buss, D. M. & Kenrick, D. T. (1998). Evolutionary social psychology. In D. T. Gilbert, S. T. Fiske, & G. Lindzey (eds), *The handbook of social psychology, 4th edn, 2*, (pp. 982–1026). Boston, MA: McGraw-Hill.
Bus, D. M., Max, A., Alois A., & Armen, A. et al. (1990). International preferences in selecting mates. *Journal of Cross-cultural Psychology, 21*, 5–47.
Carney, M., Buttell, F., & Dutton, D. (2007). Women who perpetrate intimate partner violence: A review of the literature with recommendations for treatment. *Aggression and Violent Behavior, 12*, 108–115.
Census and Statistics Department (2003). *Thematic household survey report no. 14: Time use pattern.* Hong Kong: Hong Kong SAR Government.
Chan, D., Tang, C., & Chan, W. (1999). Sexual harassment: A preliminary analysis of its effects on Hong Kong Chinese women in the workplace and academia. *Psychology of Women Quarterly, 23*, 661–672.
Chan, H. & Lee, R. P. L. (1995). Hong Kong families: At the crossroads of modernism and traditionalism. *Journal of Comparative Family Studies, 26*, 83–99.
Chan, J. (2000). The status of women in a patriarchal state: The case of Singapore. In L. Edwards & M. Roces (ed.), *Women in Asia: Tradition, modernity and globalization* (pp. 188–207). Melbourne, Australia: Allen & Unwin.
Chan, K. L. (2004). Correlates of wife assault in Hong Kong Chinese families. *Violence & Victims, 19*, 189–201.
Chen, J., Dunne, M. P., & Han, P. (2006). Child sexual abuse in Henan province, China: Associations with sadness, suicidality, and risk behaviors among adolescent girls. *Journal of Adolescent Health, 38*, 544–549.
Chen, R. (1999).Violence against women in Taiwan: A review. In F. M. Cheugn, M. Karlekar, A. de Dios, J. Vichit-Vadakan, & L. R. Quisumbing (eds), *Breaking the silence: Violence against women in Asia* (pp. 174–184). Hong Kong: Equal Opportunities Commission.
Cheung, C. & Liu, E. (1997). Impacts of social pressure and social support on distress among single parents in China. *Journal of Divorce and Remarriage, 26*, 65–82.
Cheung, F. M. (1986). Development of gender stereotype. *Educational Research Journal, 1*, 68–73.
Cheung, F. & Ng, W. C. (2004). *Rainlily build-in study report.* Hong Kong: The Chinese University of Hong Kong and The Association Concerning Sexual Violence Against Women.
Cheung, F. M. & Tang, C. (2008). Women's lives in contemporary Chinese societies. In U. P. Gielen & J. L. Gibbons (eds), *Women around the world: Psychosocial perspectives.* Greenwich, CT: Information Age Publishers.
Chew, P. (2002). Political women in Singapore: A socio-linguistic analysis. *Women's Studies International Forum, 24*, 727–736.
Chia, R. C., Allread, L. J., & Jerak, P. (1997). Attitudes toward women in Taiwan and China: Current Status, problems, and suggestions for future research. *Psychology of Women Quarterly, 21*, 137–150.
Chia, S. C. & Lee, W. (2008). Pluralistic ignorance about sex: The direct and the indirect effects of media consumption on college students' misperception of sex-related peer norms. *International Journal of Public Opinion Research, 20*, 52–73.
Chiu, S. & Ng, W. C. (2001). *Report on sexual violence among secondary school students in Hong Kong.* Hong Kong: The Association Concerning Sexual Violence of Women.
Choi, A. & Edleson, J. L. (1996). Social disapproval of wife assaults: A national survey of Singapore. *Journal of Comparative Family Studies, 27*, 73–88.
Choi, P. K. & Lee, C. K. (1997). The hidden abode of domestic labour: The case of Hong Kong. In F. M. Cheung (ed.). *Engendering Hong Kong society: A gender perspective of women's status* (pp. 157–200). Hong Kong: The Chinese University Press.
Chou, Y. C. (1995). *Marital violence.* Taipei, Taiwan: Gu-Lyn.
Connell, R. W. (2005). Change among the gate keepers: Men, masculinities, and gender equality in the global arena. *Signs: Journal of Women in Culture and Society, 30*, 1801–1825.
Croll, E. (1995). *Changing identities of Chinese women: Rhetoric, experience and self-perception in twentieth-century China.* Hong Kong: Hong Kong University Press.
Cutter, J., Lim, W., Ang, L., Tun, Y., James, L., & Chew, S. (2004). HIV in Singapore – Past, present, and future. *AIDS Education and Prevention, 16*, 110–118.
Debacker, T. K. & Nelson, R. M. (2000). Motivation to learn science: Differences related to gender, class type, and ability. *Journal of Educational Research, 93*, 245–254.
Diekman A. B. & Eagly, A. (2000). Stereotypes as dynamic constructs: Women and men of the past, present, and future. *Personality and Social Psychology Bulletin, 26*, 1171–1188.
Dobash, R. & Dobash, R. (1992). *Women, violence, and social change.* New York: Routledge.
Dolecheck, M. M. (1984). Sexual harassment of women in the workplace – a hush-hush topic in Hong Kong. *Hong Kong Manager, 20*, 23–27.
Eagly, A. H. (1995). The science and politics of comparing men and women. *American Psychologist, 50*, 145–158.
Eagly, A. H. & Wood, W. (1999). The origins of sex differences in human behavior. *American Psychologist, 54*, 408–423.
Eagly, A. H., Wood, W., & Diekman, A. B. (2000). Social role theory of sex differences and similarities: A current appraisal. In T. Eckes & H. M. Taunter (eds), *The developmental social psychology of gender* (pp. 123–174). Mahwah, NJ: Erlbaum.
Edwards, L. & Roces, M. (2000). *Women in Asia: Tradition, modernity and globalization.* Melbourne, Australia: Allen & Unwin.

Eisler, R. M. & Blalock, J. A. (1991). Masculine gender role stress: Implications for the assessment of men. *Clinical Psychology Review, 11*, 45–60.
Foundation of Women's Rights Promotion and Development (2005). *Images of women in Taiwan 2005.* Retrieved October 10, 2008 from http://v1010.womenwebpage.org.tw
Francesco, A. M. & Jakel, M. (1981). Gender and sex as determinants of hireability of applicants for gender-typed jobs. *Psychology of Women Quarterly, 5*, 747–757.
Friedman, M. & Friedman, R. (1980). *Free to choose: A personal statement.* New York: Harcourt Brace Jovanovich.
Furham, A., Mak, T., & Tanidjojo, l. (2000). An Asian perspective on the portrayal of men and women in television advertisements: Studies from Hong Kong and Indonesian television. *Journal of Applied Social Psychology, 30*, 2341–2364.
Gabrenya, W. & Hwang, K. K. (1996). Chinese social interaction: Harmony and hierarchy on the good earth. In M. H. Bond (ed.), *The handbook of Chinese psychology* (pp. 309–321). Hong Kong: Oxford University Press.
Gergen, M. (2001). *Feminist reconstructions in psychology: Narrative, gender, and performance.* Thousand Oaks, CA: Sage.
Gillespie, B. L. & Eisler, R. M. (1992). Development of the feminine gender role stress scale: A cognitive-behavior measure of stress, appraisal, and coping for women. *Behavior Modification, 16*, 426–438.
Goodwin, R. & Tang, C. (1996). Chinese personal relationships. In M. H. Bond (ed.), *The handbook of Chinese psychology* (pp. 294–308). Hong Kong: Oxford University Press.
Grzywacz, J. G.. & Marks, N. F. (2000). Reconceptualizing the work–family interface: An ecological perspective on the correlates of positive and negative spillover between work and family. *Journal of Occupational Health Psychology, 5*, 111–126.
Halpern, D. & Cheung, F. (2008). *Women at the top: Powerful leaders tell us how to combine work and family.* New York: Wiley.
Hanser, A. (2005). The gendered rice bowl: The sexual politics of service work in urban China. *Gender and Society, 19*, 581–600.
Higgins, L. T., Zhang, M., Liu, Y., & Sun, C. H. (2002). Attitudes to marriage and sexual behaviors: A survey of gender and culture differences in China and United Kingdom. *Sex Roles, 46*, 75–89.
Ho, P. (2007). Eternal mothers or flexible housewives? Middle-aged Chinese married women in Hong Kong. *Sex Roles, 57*, 249–265.
Hofstede, G. (1996). Gender stereotypes and partner preferences of Asian women in masculine and feminine cultures. *Journal of Cross-Cultural Psychology, 27*, 533–546.
Hong, Y. & Li, X. (2008). Behavioral studies of female sex workers in China: A literature review and recommendation for future research. *AIDS and Behavior, 12*, 623–636.
Hong, Z. (2004). An investigation of Taiwanese female college students' sexist attitudes. *Sex Roles, 51*, 455–467.
Hong, Z., Veach, P. M., & Lawrenz, F. (2003). An investigation of the gender stereotyped thinking of Taiwanese secondary school boys and girls. *Sex Roles, 48*, 495–504.
Honig, E. & Hershatter, G. (1988). *Personal voices: Chinese women in the 1980's.* Stanford, CA: Stanford University Press.
Hou, W., Wang, H., & Chung, H. (2005). Domestic violence against women in Taiwan: Their life-threatening situation, post-traumatic responses, and psycho-physiological symptoms. An interview study. *International Journal of Nursing Studies, 42*, 629–636.
Hu, C. Y. & Kama, Y. (2007). The division of household labor in Taiwan. *Journal of Comparative Family Studies, 38*, 105–124.
Hyde, J. S. (2005). The gender similarities hypothesis. *American Psychologist, 60*, 581–592.
Jones, B. L., Scoville, P.E., Hill, J., Childs, G., Leishman, J. M., & Nally, K. S. (2008). Perceived versus used workplace flexibility in Singapore: Predicting work–family fit. *Journal of Family Psychology, 22*, 774–783.
Keyes, S. (1983). Sex differences in cognitive abilities and sex-role stereotypes in Hong Kong Chinese adolescents. *Sex Roles, 9*, 853–870.
Kline, S., Horton, B., & Zhang, S. (2008). Communicating love: Comparisons between American and East Asian university students. *International Journal of Intercultural Relations, 32*, 200–214.
Kung, W. W., Hung, S., & Chan, C. L. W. (2004). How the socio-cultural context shapes women's divorce experiences in Hong Kong. *Journal of Comparative Family Studies, 35*, 33–50.
Lai, G. (1995). Work and family roles and psychological well-being in urban China. *Journal of Health & Social Behavior, 36*, 11–37.
Lai, M. & Bond, M. H. (1997). Gender stereotypes and the self-concept in Hong Kong. *Bulletin of the Hong Kong Psychological Society, 38/39*, 17 – 36.
Lau, S. (1989). Sex role orientation and domains of self-esteem. *Sex Roles, 21*, 411–418.
Lau, J. & Thomas, J. (2001). Risk behaviors of Hong Kong male residents traveling to mainland China: A potential bridge population for HIV infection. *AIDS Care, 13*, 71–81.
Lee, J. & Hoon, T. H. (1993). Rhetorical vision of men and women managers in Singapore. *Human Relations, 46*, 527–542.
Leightdale, J. R., & Prentice, D. A. (1994). Rethinking sex differences in aggression: Aggressive behavior in the absence of social roles. *Personality and Social Psychology Bulletin, 20*, 34–44.

Leung, W., Kung, F., Lam, J., Leung, T., & Ho, P. (2002). Domestic violence and postnatal depression in a Chinese community. *International Journal of Gynaecology & Obstetrics, 79*, 159–166.

Leung, A. S. & Ng, Y. C. (1999). From Confucianism to egalitarianism: Gender role attitudes of students in the People's Republic of China. *International Review of Women and Leadership, 5*, 57–67.

Li, S. & Lee-Wong, S. (2005). A study on Singaporean's perceptions of sexual harassment from a cross-cultural perspective. *Journal of Applied Social Psychology, 35*, 699–717.

Lin, K., McElmurry, B. J., & Christiansen, C. (2007). Women and HIV/AIDS in China: Gender and vulnerability. *Health Care for Women International, 28*, 680–699.

Liu, M. & Chan, C. (1999). Enduring violence and staying in marriage: Stories of battered women in rural China. *Violence Against Women, 5*, 1469–1492.

Lu, L., Kao, S., Chang, T, Wu, H., & Cooper, C. (2008). Work/family demands, work flexibility, work/family conflict, and their consequences at work: A national probability sample in Taiwan. *International Journal of Stress Management, 15*, 1–21.

Lu, Z. Z., Maume, D. J., & Bellas, M. L. (2000). Chinese husbands' participation in household labor. *Journal of Comparative Family Studies, 31*, 191–215.

Luo, T. (2000). 'Marrying my rapists?' The cultural trauma among Chinese rape survivors. *Gender & Society, 14*, 582–597.

Luo, Y., Parish, W., & Laumann, E. 92008). A population-based study of childhood sexual contact in China: Prevalence and long-term consequences. *Child Abuse & Neglect, 32*, 721–731.

Marshall, T. C. (2008). Cultural differences in intimacy: The influence of gender-role ideology and individualism collectivism. *Journal of Social and Personal Relationships, 25*, 143–168.

McKeen, C. A. & Bu, N. (2005). Gender roles: An examination of the hopes and expectations of the next generation of managers in Canada and China. *Sex Roles, 52*, 533–546.

Ng, I. & Wong, M. (2002). *Public opinion on rape and services for rape victims.* Hong Kong: The Hong Kong Polytechnic University and Association Concerning Sexual Violence Against Women.

Ngo, H. Y. & Lau, C. M. (1998). Interferences between work and family among male and female executives in Hong Kong. *Research & Practice in Human Resource Management, 6*, 17–34.

Paludi, M. A. (1996). *Sexual harassment on college campuses: Abusing the ivory tower.* Albany, NY: State University of New York Press.

Parish, W., Das, A., & Laumann, E. (2006). Sexual harassment of women in urban China. *Archives of Sexual Behavior, 35*, 411–425.

Pei, Y., Ho, P., & Ng, M. N. (2007). Studies on women's sexuality in China since 1980: A critical review. *Journal of Sex Research, 44*, 202–212.

Quek, K. & Knudson-Martin, C. (2008). Reshaping marital power: How dual-career newlywed couples create equality in Singapore. *Journal of Social and Personal Relationships, 25*, 511–432.

Quek, K. & Knudson-Martin, C. 2006). A push toward equality: Processes among dual-career newlywed couples in collectivist culture. *Journal of Marriage and Family, 68*, 56–69.

Rotundo, M., Nguyen, D., & Sackett, P. R. (2001). A meta-analytic review of gender differences in perceptions of sexual harassment. *Journal of Applied Psychology, 86*, 914–922.

Shaffer, M. A., Harrison, D. A., Gilley, K. M., & Luk, D. M. (2001). Struggling for balance amid turbulence on international assignments: work–family conflict, support and commitment. *Journal of Management, 27*, 99–121.

Stein, H. F. (1996). Cultural relativism. In D. Levinson & M. Ember (eds), *Encyclopedia of cultural anthropology, 1* (pp. 281–285). New York: Holt.

Stember, C. H. (1961). *Education and attitude change.* New York: Institute of Human Relations Press.

Su, X. (2004). Education and gender egalitarianism: The case of China. *Sociology of Education, 77*, 311–336.

Sun, T. (2005). Adolescent sexuality and reproductive health in Taiwan. *International Quarterly of Community Health Education, 23*, 139–149.

Tan, T., Ling, L., & Theng, E. (2002). Gender-role portrayals in Malaysian and Singaporean television commercials: An international advertising perspective. *Journal of Business Research, 55*, 853–861.

Tang, C. (1997). Psychological impact of wife abuse: Experiences of Chinese women and their children. *Journal of Interpersonal Violence, 12*, 466–478.

Tang, C. (1999). Marital power and aggression in a community sample of Hong Kong Chinese families. *Journal of Interpersonal Violence, 14*, 586–602.

Tang, C. (2002). Childhood experience of sexual abuse among Hong Kong Chinese college students. *Child Abuse & Neglect, 26*, 23–37.

Tang, C. (2004). *A study on adolescent sexuality and peer sexual abuse in Hong Kong.* Hong Kong: The End Child Sexual Abuse Foundation.

Tang, C. (2006). Gender stereotypes and recruitment decisions: A study of Chinese employers in Hong Kong. In J. A. Arlsdale (ed.), *Advances in social psychology research* (pp. 97–110). New York: Nova Science Publishers.

Tang, C. (2008). The influence of gender-related factors on HIV prevention among Chinese women with disrupted marital relationship. *Sex Roles, 59*, 119–126.

Tang, C. (2009a). The influence of mastery on family–work role experience and psychological health of Chinese working mothers. *Journal of psychology, in press. Paper presented to the 2nd Asian Psychological Association, Kula Lumpur, Malaysia.*

Tang, C. (2009b). *Sexual harassment in tertiary institutions in Hong Kong: Revisted after 10 years.* Manuscript in submission.
Tang, C., Au, W., Chung, Y. P., & Ngo, H. Y. (2000). Breaking the patriarchal paradigm: Chinese women in Hong Kong. In L. Edwards & M. Roces (ed.), *Women in Asia: Tradition, modernity and globalization* (pp. 188–207). Melbourne, Australia: Allen & Unwin.
Tang, C., Cheung, F., Chen, R., & Sun, X. (2002). Definition of violence against women: A comparative study in Chinese societies of Hong Kong, Taiwan, and the People's Republic of China. *Journal of Interpersonal Violence, 17,* 671–688.
Tang, C., Critelli, J., & Porter, J. (1995). Sexual aggression and victimization in dating relationships among Chinese college students. *Archives of Sexual Behavior, 24,* 47–53.
Tang, C. & Lai, B. (2008). A review of empirical literature on the prevalence and risk markers of male-on-female intimate partner violence in contemporary China, 1987–2006. *Aggression and Violent Behavior, 13,* 10–28.
Tang, C., Lai, F., & Chung, T. (1997). Assessment of sexual functioning for Chinese college students. *Archives of Sexual Behavior, 26,* 79–90.
Tang, C. & Lau, B. (1996a). The Chinese gender role stress scales: factor structure and predictive validity. *Behavior Modification, 20,* 321–337.
Tang, C. & Lau, B. (1996b). Gender role stress and burnout in Chinese human service professionals in Hong Kong. *Anxiety, Stress, and Coping, 9,* 217–227.
Tang, C., Lee, A. M., Tang, T., Cheung, F. M., & Chan, C. (2002). Role occupancy, role quality, and psychological distress in Chinese women. *Women & Health, 36,* 49–66.
Tang, C., Pun, S., & Cheung, F. (2002). Responsibility attribution for violence against women: A study of Chinese public service professionals. *Psychology of Women Quarterly, 26,* 175–185.
Tang, N. & Tang, C. (2001). Gender role internalization, multiple roles, and Chinese women's mental health. *Psychology of Women Quarterly, 25,* 181–196.
Tang, C., Wong, C., & Lee, A. (2001). Gender-related psychosocial and cultural factors associated with condom use among Chinese married women. *AIDS Education and Prevention, 13,* 329–342.
Tang, C., Wong, D., & Cheung, F. (2002). Social construction of women as legitimate victims of violence in Chinese societies. *Violence against Women, 8,* 968–996.
Tang, C., Yik, M., Cheung, F., Choi, P., & Au, K. (1996). Sexual harassment of Chinese college students. *Archives of Sexual Behavior, 25,* 201–215.
Tang, C. & Yu, J. (2005). *Challenges of single parenthood in Hong Kong.* Paper submitted to the 1st Asia-Pacific Conference on Trauma Psychology: Life Adversities and Challenges, Hong Kong.
Tay, l. & Gibbons, J. L. (1998). Attitudes toward gender roles among adolescents in Singapore. *Cross-cultural Research, 32,* 257–278.
Teo, P., Graham, E., Yeoh, B., & Levy, S. (2003). Values, change and inter-generational ties between two generations of women in Singapore. *Ageing and Society, 23,* 327–347.
Thorton, A. & Lin, H. (1994). *Social changes and the family in Taiwan.* Chicago, IL: University of Chicago Press.
Toro-Morn, M. & Sprecher, S. (2003). A cross-cultural comparison of mate preferences among university students: The United States vs The People's Republic of China. *Journal of Comparative Family Studies, 34,* 151–170.
Tsun, A. (1999). Sibling incest: A Hong Kong experience. *Child Abuse and Neglect, 23,* 71–79.
Tu, S. & Liao, P. (2005). Gender differences in gender-role attitudes: A comparative analysis of Taiwan and coastal China. *Journal of Comparative Family Studies, 36,* 545–566.
Tucker, J., Henderson, G., Wang, T., Huang, Y., Parish, W., Pan, S. et al. (2005). Surplus men, sex work, and the spread of HIV in China. *AIDS, 19,* 539–547.
Twenge, J. M. (1997). Changes in masculine and feminine traits over time: A meta-analysis. *Sex Roles, 36,* 305–325.
Twenge, J. M. (2001). Changes in women's assertiveness in response to status and roles: A cross-temporal meta-analysis, 1931–1993. *Journal of Personality and Social Psychology, 81,* 133–145.
Wang, Q. (2001). China's divorce trends in the transition toward a market economy. *Journal of Divorce and Remarriage, 35,* 173–188.
Wang, R. & Hsu, H. (2006). Correlates of sexual abstinence among adolescent virgins dating steady boyfriends in Taiwan. *Journal of Nursing Scholarship, 38,* 286–291.
Wang, X. & Ho, P. (2007). My sassy girl: A qualitative study of women's aggression in dating relationships in Beijing. *Journal of Interpersonal Violence, 22,* 623–638.
Ward, C. (1990). Gender stereotypes in Singaporean children. *International Journal of Behavioral Development, 13,* 309–315.
Watts, J. (2008). Sex, drugs, and HIV/AIDS in China. *Lancet, 37,* 103–104.
Williams, J. E. & Best, D. L. (1990). *Measuring sex stereotypes: A thirty-nation study.* Beverly Hills, CA: Sage.
Willness, C. R., Steel, P., & Lee, K. (2007). A meta-analysis of the antecedents and consequences of workplace sexual harassment. *Personnel Psychology, 60,* 127–162.
Wolf, M. (1987). *Revolution postponed: Women in contemporary China.* London, England: Metheun.
Wong, F. M. (1972). Modern ideology, industrialization, and conjugalism: The Hong Kong case. *International Journal of Sociology of the Family, 2,* 139–150.
Wood, W. & Eagly, A. (2002). A cross-cultural analysis of the behavior of women and men: Implications for the origins of sex differences. *Psychological Bulletin, 128,* 699–727.

World Health Organization. (2002). *World report on violence and health.* Geneva, Switzerland: Author.
Xu, X. (1997). The prevalence and determination of wife abuse in urban China. *Journal of Comparative Family Studies, 28,* 280–303.
Xu, X. & Lai, S. (2004). Gender ideologies, marital roles, and marital quality in Taiwan. *Journal of Family Issues, 25,* 318–355.
Yang, K. S. (1996). The psychological transformation of the Chinese people as a result of societal modernization. In M. H. Bond (ed.), *The handbook of Chinese psychology* (pp. 479–498). Hong Kong: Oxford University Press.
Yang, M., Yang, M., Chou, F., Yang, H., & Wei, S., & Lin, J. (2006). Physical abuse against aborigines in Taiwan: Prevalence and risk factors. *International Journal of Nursing Studies, 43,* 21–27.
Yang, N. (2005). Individualism–collectivism and work–family interfaces: A Sino–US comparison. In Steven A. Y. Poelmans (ed.), *Work and family—An international research perspective* (pp. 287–318). Mahwah, NJ: Erlbaum.
Yeung, D. & Tang, C. (2001). Impact of job characteristics on psychological health of Chinese single working women. *Women and Health, 33,* 85–100.
Yi, C. & Chien, W. (2002). The linkage between work and family: Female's employment patterns in three Chinese societies. *Journal of Comparative Family Studies, 33,* 451–474.
Zhang, N. (2006). Gender role egalitarian attitudes among Chinese college students. *Sex Roles, 55,* 545–553.
Zhou, L., Dawson, M., Herr, C., & Stukas, S. (2004). American and Chinese students' predictions of people's occupations, housework responsibilities, and gender influences. *Sex Roles, 50,* 547–563.
Zuo, J. (2003). From revolutionary comrades to gendered partners: Marital construction of breadwinning in post-Mao urban China. *Journal of Family Issues, 24,* 314–337.

CHAPTER 32

Chinese cultural psychology and contemporary communication

Shi-xu & Feng-bing

Chinese Cultural Psychology and Contemporary Communication

The study of the human mind has by and large continued to proceed from a universalist, but often in fact, West-centric model and philosophy (Cole, 1996; Shweder, 1990). To some extent, even cross-cultural psychology seems to have been guided by this dominant perspective. Consequently, culturally particular, locally grounded approaches have not received sufficient attention in the international arena as they deserve.

In this study we attempt to offer an initial and sketchy account of a culturally different, specifically Chinese, psychology - not from the conventional, familiar perspective, but from the vantage point of linguistic communication in contemporary China. That is, Chinese cultural psychology will not be assumed as consisting in a set of abstract mental properties, processes and strategies, but rather, as embodied in the forms of social cultural practice, particularly, as found in historically and culturally situated language activities or 'discourse'. As such, they are considered as resources, rules, values, perspectives, frames etc. with respect to which and through which people, especially linguistically, interact with one another and get things done. From another point of view, it may be said that people in their practical life (re)create, draw upon, utilize, maintain, transmit and change 'psychological' mechanisms, processes, strategies, etc., when engaged in linguistic communication (Billig, 1991; Shi-xu, 2007).

The particular sort of Chinese psychology we want to offer here may be characterized by a system of distinctive categories, traits and principles that set Chinese culture apart from other Eastern and Western cultures. For example, there are unique Chinese concepts such as *ren* 仁 (personhood), *li* 礼 (rites), *he* 和 (equilibrium), *mianzi* 面子 (face) and *yuan* 缘 (predestined favorable chance), worldviews (e.g. *tianren heyi* 天人合一 - holism), ways of reasoning (e.g. *yin-yang* 阴阳 - dialectic), moral values (*zhong yong* 中庸 - moderation) and *heqi* 和气 (being gentle), collective memory (e.g. of humiliation in modern Chinese history), attitudes toward other cultural groups (e.g. opposition to hegemony, empathy with the Third World), and feelings about one's country (e.g. *aiguo zhuyi* 爱国主义 (patriotism)).

These culture-specific traits, propensities and principles can be seen at the same time as embodied in the ways that Chinese conduct themselves in social life in general and in linguistic communication in particular. The problem is that although there is a host of cultural psychological concepts and principles that are directly linked with use of language and communication, there has hitherto been little systematic knowledge of the relationship between Chinese cultural psychology and contemporary communication.[1]

In this paper and drawing on the insights from existing Chinese psychological and linguistic scholarship, we shall attempt an initial integration (Feng-bing, 2005; Shi-xu, 2006). In particular, we shall be spelling out some of the key cultural psychological characteristics and try to link them up with the typical patterns of speaking and writing in contemporary Chinese communication. In addition, we shall suggest how this Chinese discursive-psychological framework may be used for not just making sense of texts and talk in contemporary Chinese society, but also for critically evaluating them.

Although there has been a revived interest in Chinese psychology (e.g. Bond, 1986, 1991, 1996, 2000; Wang & Zheng, 2005; Yan, 1998), there has been little attention paid to its relation with Chinese linguistic communication, which we consider to be, not peripheral, but central to the former. The study of Chinese communication, on the other hand, seems to have often been subjected to Western political-economy models, and consequently the role of Chinese psychology in the production and interpretation of contemporary Chinese communication is usually ignored. The current study is intended to put together an integrated understanding of Chinese psychology and contemporary communication.

Characteristics of Chinese psychology and communication

Chinese psychology has been analyzed in terms of a myriad dimensions, categories, and processes, for example, worldviews, values, the self-concept, categorization, beliefs, attitudes, opinions, and emotions (Chu, 1985). These properties in question may themselves be based on particular kinds of values, beliefs, and worldviews; similarly, Chinese cultural psychology as a whole may be seen as rooted in the Chinese philosophical and religious traditions of Confucianism, Daoism and Buddhism, respectively (e.g. *he* 和, *zhongyong* 中庸, *dao* 道, *tianren heyi* 天人合一). Wang and Zheng (2005, pp. 334-52) have characterized Chinese psychology in terms of eight preferred 'ways of thinking': 1) holism, 2) dialecticism, 3) moderation, 4) intuitiveness, 5) authority-worshipping, 6) pragmatism, 7) image-proneness, and 8) circular-thinking. Our account below overlaps with their version at a number of points, but differs in several other ways. First, ours refers not only to preferred 'ways of thinking' or mental strategies, as their account does, but also to other psychological categories, such as norms, beliefs or worldviews and memories. Second, we highlight new contents of Chinese culture like *dao* 道 and *jindai shi* 近代史, which are unique to contemporary Chinese culture.

Below we shall first introduce a particular mental property that is central to Chinese psychology, and then reformulate it in discursive terms. We shall use examples from contemporary Chinese linguistic communication to illustrate this approach (all are my translation and the bold type is added to indicate relevant linguistic strategies).

Dao 道

One of the most central and underlying elements in the Chinese belief system or worldview is that of *dao* 道, the core concept of Daoism founded by Laozi and Zhuangzi, two Chinese classical philosophers, or the Way as is customarily translated (see also Ji, Lam, & Guo, this volume; Lu, this volume).

[1] Chinese scholarship of language and communication, ranging from the classical *Analects* of Confucius to the modern *Xiuci Xue Fafan* 修辞学发凡 (*Development of rhetorics*) by Chen (1979), has a history of at least over two thousand years and contains rich seams to be mined about values, ideals, concepts, theories, and methods (Chen, 2004; Heisey, 2000; Shen, 1996; Shen, 2001; Xing, 2000).

According to Laozi and Zhuangzi, *dao* 道 is both the origin of all things in the universe and the basis for them. It does not have an external, independent existence, but is always embodied in concrete things or processes, though it is unalterable; we do not have direct access to *dao* 道, but instead must find or invent indirect strategies to get at it.

This accounts for the tendency for Chinese to seek continuously to transcend all appearances in order to ascertain the true nature or significance of existence. This also explains why Chinese practice the favored strategy of accomplishing order through inaction. This psychological propensity has been given a concrete form in Chinese literary scholarship. Namely, it is understood as having meaning and significance beyond symbolic expressions. Thus, *Discourse and dragon carving* 文心雕龙 by Liu Xie presents such unique notions about Chinese discourse as *yan bu jing yi* 言不尽意 (not all meaning is produced in and through language), *fenggu* 风骨 (essence) and *shensis* 神思 (infinite imagination).

As a consequence of this understanding of the relationship between *dao* 道 and action and between language and meaning, a number of discursive strategies have developed in order to confront this situation and overcome the difficulty of achieving meaning and *dao* 道: to tell much by speaking little, to achieve meaning according to the classics, to obtain meaning by using images, etc. (Cao et al., 2001).

Tianren Heyi 天人合一

One of the foundational beliefs in the Chinese worldview is *tianren heyi* 天人合一, namely, all things, from nature to man, are interrelated parts of a unified whole. The idea can be traced back to at least *Yijing* 易经 and is also one of the basic tenets of two-thousand-year-old Confucianism. This basic understanding of the universe primes Chinese people into ways of thinking that emphasize (a) the wholeness of things and (b) harmony amongst things. These may be characterized as 'holistic way of thinking'.

In verbal communication, it can be observed for example that Chinese people speak highly of *he* 和 (harmony based on diversity). For the same reason, they may pay special attention to *unity* between man and nature. Then it is not difficult to understand why *hexie* 和谐 (harmony) and *hexie shehui* 和谐社会 (harmonious society) have become common currency and a cornerstone in contemporary Chinese political and social communication:

> Hu Jingtao points out, the kind of socialist harmonious society we want to build up should be one that is characterized by democracy, law and order, justice, trust and friendship, vitality, stability and peace between man and nature. These factors are inter-related, inter-active and should be managed as a whole in the process of building a comprehensive affluent society.
>
> *Xinhua Wang* 新华网 www.ce.cn

> People's everyday life is linked with a nation's future, societal construction is inextricably linked with people's happiness. The overall structure of the characteristically Chinese socialist cause comprises economic construction, political construction, cultural construction and societal construction. Here ... the four factors are complementary to one another and not one is dispensable.
>
> *Give priority to the improvement of people's everyday life, Wenhui Bao* 文汇报, 5 November, 2007

Likewise:

> Chinese medicine takes it for granted that human health depends on the dynamics of balance between man and nature, man and society and man's internal *yin–yang*.
>
> Zhang et al., 2006, pp. 81–82

It may be noted that links, inter-relations, the whole picture, balance, etc. are stressed. It should be pointed out, however, that the belief complex of *tianren heyi* 天人合一 is a much wider concept than the English word, 'harmony', indicates; it implies diversity and balance on the basis of which harmony arises and rests. For this reason, when confronted with the US government's cultural hegemony on the issue of human rights, the Chinese public media use a variety of discursive strategies to counter-balance its strident, uncompromising position (Shi-xu & Cheng, forthcoming).

Bianzheng 辨证

A near equivalent of this propensity in English may be the dialectic way of thinking. It is a mental habit or way of reasoning that is anchored in the classical Chinese notion of *yin-yang* 阴阳, which can also be traced back to *yijing* 易经. That is, everything is composed of two interlinked, interchanging and interpenetrating parts. This view of the universe shapes Chinese to experience and see (a) *interrelations* between things *in opposition* and (b) the *dynamic* nature of things.

In discourse, the consequence is that Chinese people are inclined to avoid absolute terms and expressions, emphasize connections between things and draw attention to the opposites constituting all things:

> No society can exist without contradictions; human societies develop and make strides forward in and through the dynamics of contradictions.
>
> Xinhua News Agency, 18 October, decision of the Chinese Communist Party Central Committee on major issues in the construction of socialist harmonious society

Again:

> Chinese medicine takes it for granted that human health depends on the dynamics of balance between man and nature, man and society and man's internal *yin–yang*.
>
> Zhang et al., 2006, 38(6): pp. 81–82

> At the high-level forum on innovative economy and enterprise finance in central China, the Dean of the Research Institute of Speculative Investment, Chen Gongfeng, said, 'Financing is a double-edged sword. The current financial "crisis" is on the one side dangerous; if the bubbles of the financial crisis continue to grow, then China will sustain severe injuries. But on the other side, the 'crisis' also offers opportunities.' He believed that the current financial crisis will bring about positive effects on China's stock market. Besides, during this financial turbulence, China can try to attract some excellent overseas Chinese from Wall Street to start business in China.
>
> http://www.chinahrd.net/zhi_sk/jt_page.asp?articleid=149052

In these examples, it may be observed that, consistent with the emphasis on a holistic approach, both the oppositions between things and their unity are highlighted. In addition, and characteristic of Chinese culture, permanent change of the relationship between the oppositions is recognized.

Zhongyong 中庸

This may be characterized by the notion of a propensity for the middle way or point between diverse or even extreme choices. This way of thinking is derived from one of the core and most typical Confucian tenets on social conduct. To put it more specifically, this is a moral teaching that one should not go to extremes, one should opt for neither end of any continuum of choices but one should (literally!) use the middle, just as the expression goes. This moral code primes Chinese people to take a moderate attitude towards everything and avoid taking a prominent position in anything.

This mental tendency has obvious implications for Chinese ways of speaking in social contexts. This may be demonstrated by not only premonitions for speech communication, but also for everyday linguistic practice. Listen to what a Chinese businessman says:

> I feel an enterprise should not operate too fast but pursue stability. It should not be overfed but should not starve either. I hope to build up a stable business, a business that lasts for a hundred years.
>
> www.51Labour.com, 20 May 2006

> Do not show your superiority, do not tell others you are cleverer ... tolerance and forbearance are a great wisdom ... do not make others lose face when criticizing them ... there is no absolute justice; do not be a perfectionist ...
>
> Song, 2008, p. 2, Table of Contents

> At present, our society is on the whole in harmony. But, there exist many contradictions and problems that negatively affect social harmony.
>
> Xinhua News Agency, 18 October, decision of the Chinese Communist Party Central Committee on major issues in the construction of socialist harmonious society

Here not only is moderation advocated and defended, but balance in speech is also enjoined when negative assessments are involved.

Zhijue 直觉

This is yet another typically Chinese mental strategy in perceiving and understanding the universe. In comparison with the other forms of thinking that we saw above, this can be relatively easily translated into '(resorting to) an intuitive and/or experience-based form of thinking'. That is to say, Chinese people more often than not use intuition in making judgments or decisions and do so in a huge variety of settings, including poetic interpretation and academic tasks. This also means that they make judgments that are general, simplified, and vague, and that they do so fast.

This kind of psychological propensity may often be seen in not just everyday forms of communication, but also in literary and even scientific genres:

> Zhang Ailing: *Yuan* (缘, fate) can be understood as something in a remark like: 'Oh, you are here as well?'
>
> Zhang, 1949, p. 10

Again:

> In the last few years, I suddenly realize, the Western Indo-European languages are not the same sort of things as the Chinese of China. The Western patterns of thought are analytic, while the Eastern ones, including of course the Chinese, are synthetic.
>
> Ji, 1997/2002, p. 7

What is particularly remarkable is that such a broad and complex phenomena as Chinese languages and Indo-European languages as well as their thought patterns are characterized on the basis of 'sudden realization' and the writer is one of the most famous scholars in the contemporary Chinese scene.

Quanwei 权威

In the Chinese tradition over the past two thousand years, there is a dominant way of thinking that habitually takes anyone that is the most senior, the most knowledgeable or the most authoritative, as the arbiter of truth or moral order, or 'Quanwei' in Chinese. This kind of what might be called authority-minded way of thinking is of course linked with the traditional Chinese ethical system of social hierarchy: namely, we should give the highest respect to the head of the state, the elder(ly), the father and this kind of moral order is extended to wider society today (see Chen & Farh, this volume; Hwang & Hau, this volume).

This cultural psychological pattern accounts for the widespread phenomenon of citing, referring to, drawing upon and expressing respect or awe towards the powerful, the knowledgeable, and the elder(ly) as the arbiter or guarantor of truth, standard or moral code. The following statement may be seen as evidence of this psychology:

> Experts analyze the situation and point out that, in comparison with Tangshan earthquake, fewer people died in the Wenchuan earthquake mainly because the former occurred at night when most people were asleep, whereas the latter during the day. Besides, the former took place in the urban area, whereas the latter in the mountainous countryside where the population is not dense.
>
> http://news.xinhuanet.com/politics/2008-05/18/content_8197178.htm
> (Experts detail why the damages of Wenchuan earthquake are bigger than those of Tangshan earthquake.)

In this example, it should be noticed that experts are marshaled to present their views, but that what they say is common sense. Of course, consensus is thereby mobilized to follow 'common sense'.

The same is true of the following:

> Yesterday, many SARS experts and UN Health Organization China officials said when interviewed by the Morning Newspaper that at present they are not certain whether the retracted virus of the suspicious SARS cases of Guangzhou originates in rats, but they do not rule out the possibility.
>
> *Eastern Morning Paper*, 5 January 2004

SARS was first discovered in 2003, but in 2004 already the honorific, 'SARS experts', has been conferred. But, what they are called upon to resolve here is no more than what common knowledge would provide. Such a statement of the obvious is needed because only the presence and voice of an expert or experts, no matter whether or not they specialize on the subject, are deemed suitable for an unknown situation.

Jindaishi 近代史

One piece of the Chinese collective memory that is particularly worth noting in relation to contemporary communication is the historical experience of aggression, exploitation and domination by the Western colonial and imperialist powers since the Opium Wars in the 1840s. These collective memories are filled with humiliation, bitterness, and indignation. Arguably, it is this constellation of memories that has led to 'natural' feelings of opposition to cultural hegemony and of love of the mother country or patriotism (Shi-xu, 2006).

This position is most vociferously attested to by the well-known documentations such as *Zhongguo Keyi Shuo Bu* 中国可以说不 ('China can say no', by Song Qiang & Zhang Zangzang, 1996) and *Huhuan: Dangjin Zhongguo de Wuzhong Shengyin* 呼唤：当今中国的五种声音 ('The calls: Five voices of contemporary China', Lin Zhijun & Ma Licheng, 1999). But it is a common occurrence in contemporary Chinese public communication that opposition to foreign repression on the one hand and patriotism or love of the motherland on the other hand are adopted as the underlying reason for formulating the stance of China in international relations:

> Eighty years ago, the Chinese Communist Party was founded amidst of the revolutionary movements of the world's proletariat and the Chinese nation's struggle against imperialism and feudalism. This is the inevitable result of the deepening of the contradictions characterizing modern Chinese society and the people's struggle. After 1840, because of the invasion of the Western powers, China degenerated into a semi-colonized

> and semi-feudalist society. The Chinese people were doubly repressed by imperialism and feudalism at the same time …
>
> Jiang Zemin, speech at the commemoration of the 80th anniversary of the founding of the Chinese Communist Party, 1 July 2001

Again:

> Putting the State and the Nation's interest first and never succumbing to foreign aggression are the corner stone of our great nation's patriotism. In the 30s of the 20th century, the Japanese waged a full-scale war against China and brought it to the brink of national calamity …
>
> *Guangming Wang* 光明网, www.wuhai.gov.cn, 19 September 2005

Here is the modern Chinese history of foreign aggression and humiliation is called upon to commemorate the Chinese Communist Party in the first instance, and to promote patriotism in the second.

Conclusion

In this paper we have advocated the necessity to pay attention to local, indigenous, cultural psychology as a prerequisite for understanding human psychology, for achieving genuine, social scientific innovation, and ultimately for facilitating intercultural communication and relationships. We have also suggested the urgent need to do so because culturally particular, especially non-Western, forms of psychology are being marginalized and left to decay (see Smith, this volume).

To this larger problem of the cultural imbalance in the psychological discipline, we have canvassed a general picture of the Chinese cultural psychology. We have argued that psychological reality need not be seen as an independent entity external to social action. Instead, it is possible to understand it psychological properties and processes as embodied most explicitly in situated linguistic communication. To illustrate this social reality, we presented a variety of samples of contemporary, Chinese discourse.

We hope that the outline of the Chinese psychology provided here will promote understanding of contemporary Chinese culture in general, and present-day Chinese language and communication in particular. At the same time, it may be used as a normative criterion to judge and critique their communicative practice.

Chinese culture is itself multicultural and therefore broad, varied, complex, and dynamic. Future work on any aspect of Chinese psychology needs to be rendered much more inclusive and nuanced. In this regard, it must be noted that, because of the influences of globalization and international communication, it is also necessary to take into account processes of cultural transformation when essaying emerging processes in Chinese communication (see Yang, 1996).

References

Billig, M. (1991). *Ideology and opinions.* London: Sage.

Bond, M. H. (ed.) (1986). *The psychology of the Chinese people.* Hong Kong: Oxford University Press.

Bond, M. H. (1991). *Beyond the Chinese face: Insights from psychology.* Hong Kong: Oxford University Press.

Bond, M. H. (ed.) (1996). *The handbook of Chinese psychology.* Hong Kong: Oxford University Press.

Bond, M. H. (2000). Distant anguish and proximal brotherhood: Using psychology to move beyond the Chinese face. *Journal of Psychology in Chinese Societies, 1,* 143–148.

Cao, S. Q. (2001). *Zhongguo gudai wenlun huayu* (*Chinese classical literary-theoretical discourses*). Chengdu, China: Bashu Shushe. (in Chinese)

Chen, G.. M. (2001). Towards transcultural understanding: A harmony theory of Chinese communication. In V. H. Milhouse, M. K. Asante, & P. O. Nwosu (eds), *Transculture: Interdisciplinary perspectives on cross-cultural relations* (pp. 55–70). Thousand Oaks, CA: Sage.

Chen, W. D. (1979 . *Xiuci xue fafan* (*Development of rhetorics*). Shanghai, China: Shanghai Educational Press. (in Chinese)

Chu, G.. C. (1985). The changing concept of self in contemporary China. In A. J. Marsella, G. de Vos, & F. L. K. Hsu (eds), *Culture and self: Asian and Western perspectives* (pp. 252–77). New York: Tavistock.

Cole, M. (1996). *Cultural psychology: A once and future discipline.* Cambridge, MA: Harvard University Press.

Feng-bing (2005). *Ethnicity, children and habitus: Ethnic Chinese school children in Northern Ireland.* Frankfurt/New York: P. Lang.

Heisey, R. (ed.) (2000). *Chinese perspectives in rhetoric and communication.* Greenwood, CN: Ablex.

Ji, X. L. (1997/2002). Preface. In G. Qian, *Hanyu wenhua yuyong xue* (*Pragmatics in Chinese culture* (2nd edn). Beijing, China: Qinghua University Press. (in Chinese)

Jia, W. S., D. R. Heisey & X. Lu (eds) (2002). *Chinese communication theory and research.* Greenwood, CN: Ablex.

Shen, K. M. (1996). *Xiandai hanyu huayu yuyan xue* (*Modern Chinese text linguistics*). Beijing: The Commercial Press. (in Chinese)

Shen, X. (2001). *Hanyu yufa xue* (*Chinese grammar*). Nanjing, China: Jiangsu Educational Press.

Shi-xu (2005). *A cultural approach to discourse.* Basingstoke, England: Palgrave Macmillan.

Shi-xu (2006). Mind, self, and consciousness as discourse. *New Ideas in Psychology, 24,* 63–81.

Shi-xu & Cheng, W. (forthcoming). A discourse approach to contemporary Chinese media on human rights. *Journal of Asia Pacific Communication.*

Shweder, R. A. (1990). Cultural psychology—What is it? In J. W. Stigler, R. A. Shweder & G. Herdt (eds), *Cultural psychology: Essays on comparative human development* (pp. 1–43). Cambridge, England: Cambridge University Press.

Song T. T. (2008). *To be low-key as a person and use the middle in action.* Beijing, China: Zhaohua Chuban She. (in Chinese)

Wang, F. & Zheng H. (2005). *Zhongguo Wenhua xinlixue* (Chinese cultural psychology]. Guangzhou, China: Jinan University Press. (in Chinese)

Xing, F. (ed.) 2000. *Wenhua yuyan xue* (*Cultural linguistics*) (revised). Wuhan, China: Hubei Educational Press. (in Chinese)

Yan, G. (1998). *Zhongguo xinlixue shi* [*History of Chinese cultural psychology*]. Hangzhou, China: Zhejiang Educational Press. (in Chinese)

Yang, K. S. (1996). Psychological transformation of the Chinese people as a result of societal modernization. In M. H. Bond (ed.), *The handbook of Chinese psychology* (pp. 479–498). Hong Kong: Oxford University Press.

Zhang, J. X., Hou D. F., Sun J., & Jiang R. (2006).Thoughts on a Chinese-medicine approach to para-health. *New Chinese Medicine, 38,* 81–82.

Zhang, A. L. (1949) Love. *Monthly Magazine,* 13(1). (in Chinese)

Zhou, Q. G. (2002). *Zhongguo gudian jieshi xue daolun* [Introduction to classical Chinese hermaneutics]. Beijing, China: Zhonghua Shuju. (in Chinese)

CHAPTER 33

Chinese political psychology: political participation in Chinese societies

Isabel Ng

Western scholars define political participation as behaviors aimed at shaping governmental policy. For example, Verba, Nie, and Kim (1978) define political participation as 'those legal acts by private citizens that are more or less directly aimed at influencing the selection of governmental personnel and/or the actions that they take' (p. 1). Forms of political participation, such as electoral voting, political lobbying, and civil disobedience, have generated a large body of research in democratic societies. These behaviors, however, may not represent political participation in societies with other forms of political systems, such as the Chinese, where people may express political opinions through various forms of participation or non-participation that are different from those in a democracy (Shi, 1997).

This chapter explores the published literature on Chinese people's political participation in relation to three questions: 1) how do Chinese participate in politics? 2) why do Chinese participate in politics? and, 3) what does participation in politics do to an individual? During the past two decades, a body of literature on political participation in Chinese societies has developed, so it is useful to take inventory of what has been done, and identify new directions for the future. More importantly, it is hoped that this chapter can serve as a platform for psychologists, political scientists, and other social scientists, who are interested in developing the field of Chinese political psychology as a vibrant, open and scientifically grounded sub-discipline of psychology.

We will devote most attention to the mainland China, followed by Hong Kong, Taiwan, and Singapore. Political participation in China is especially noteworthy, since the market reform in the past three decades have radically changed many aspects of the society; a systematic look at the current literature may give us some ideas about implications of the economic reforms in China on its political system. Political participation in Hong Kong may also be of particular interest, since conventional wisdom maintains that Hong Kong people are indifferent to politics. Has there been any change in Hong Kong's political culture after the hand-over to China in 1997? Moreover, as Taiwan is the only Chinese society with democratic political institutions, its example may be informative for those who are interested in whether or how a political system may affect individual attitudes, values or ideology. Therefore, this chapter will highlight the longitudinal research that examines people's change in attitudes over time. Finally, some studies (albeit very few) concerning political participation in Singapore will also be included.

Because of the tremendous effort required to collect representative survey data on political participation, it is noteworthy that the literature on Chinese political participation is primarily contributed by a few key individuals, such as Tianjian Shi, Wenfang Tang, and Siu Kai Lau, especially in the early period of this research activity. These scholars have published books and/or journal articles on political participation which draw empirical evidence from large-scale surveys that they themselves or others collected. The Asian Barometer project is another important source of empirical data on Chinese political participation. It is an ongoing project that examines the attitudes and values towards politics, power, and citizens' political actions in seventeen Asian political systems. Because of time, resources, and chapter space constraints, our focus will be on English-language journals at this initial step. Admittedly, the sources in this review are all invariably westernized and adopt an implicitly western framework, especially *vis-a-vis* democracy. We hope more scholars from within China may be interested in the topic of political behavior and psychology in the future.

The remainder of this chapter will be organized in three sections, examining the above three review questions in turn. The first section is about the kind of channels Chinese use to express their opinions, and the effectiveness of those channels. The second section deals with the antecedents of political participation. On one hand, as a society gets modernized, people should be able to accumulate more objective resources, thereby increasing their capability of participating in politics. On the other hand, a society's political culture determines whether those who are capable to participate would choose to participate or not. No political participation will be taken if it is seen as socially undesirable or contradicting one's values. Thus, to evaluate these seemingly opposite positions, we will first examine the literature and find out how Chinese traditional values, such as Confucianism, may influence Chinese people's attitudes to politics, or political participation; then, we will also look at the evidences in the literature on whether economic development may lead to more participation. In the third and final section, we will examine the consequences of political participation. What does it do to the individual? Does it liberate? Does taking part change one's attitudes? Increase one's knowledge? Alter one's affective evaluation of other individuals, or of political institutions? For instance, with years of experience practicing democracy, do Chinese in Taiwan manifest a different set of psycho-political characteristics (such as internal/external efficacy, political trust, understanding of democracy, political ideology) as compared with their Chinese counterparts in Hong Kong and mainland China? Also, what may be the consequences of political engagement for involvement in voluntary associations in China?

Varieties and modes of political participation

Political participation in China

The literature of the 1950s and 1960s on totalitarian dictatorship dismisses the study of political participation as irrelevant to communist systems, and substitutes the notion of regime mobilization. The accumulated evidence suggests that political participation in China clearly contradicts this view of a passive (or merely mobilized) citizenry. Since the outset of post-Mao economic and political reforms in the late 1970s, more and more ordinary citizens have been reportedly participating in public affairs and politics across both urban and rural areas of China (Jennings, 1997; Manion, 1996; Shi, 1997; Tang & Parish, 2000), even though China's political system has never been democratic, at least by Western standards.

For the purpose of this chapter, political participation is broadly defined as 'actions undertaken by ordinary citizens that are intended, directly or indirectly, to influence the selection of government personnel and/or the policy decisions they make' (Bennett & Bennett, 1986, p. 160). Past studies of political participation in China have established that, despite the constraints of a Leninist party-state, Chinese citizens do engage in various activities regularly to try to influence government policies, especially during the stage of policy implementation. In his survey of political participation in Beijing, for example, Shi (1997) found that in the five years prior to the survey, 90 per cent of those surveyed had engaged in at least one form of political activity. Excluding voting (the only activity studied for which the regime actively mobilizes citizens), 73 per cent had engaged in at least one activity, and 57 per cent had engaged in two or more. Twenty per cent of those surveyed had participated in at least one act of protest, which includes slowdowns, strikes, demonstrations, and acts to incite others against leaders or elections. The implication of Shi's data is that political participation in Beijing, while different in form, is no less common than participation in many democracies.

Shi (1997) also pointed out some unique aspects of political participation in China. First, work units (*danwei*) in urban China are the center of some citizens' life. In urban China, these work units rather than functional government agencies are responsible for representing the government to provide a broad array of services to their employees. The Chinese work unit is charged with political, economic, and social functions that range from serving as a political control tool to a government propaganda machine, from distributing apartments to providing education, and from solving marital problems to maintaining social order. Shi (1997) suggested that this feature of the institutional setting determines that most political participatory acts in the PRC occur in the work units, a context that is different from most other societies. Second, political participation in China focuses mainly on the stage of policy implementation rather than the stage of policy making.

In democratic societies, elections and group-based political activities are often the two ways that people can use to exert influence on government policy. However, in China, many governmental policy outputs are assigned to the grassroots. As the locus of decision-making descends to the local level, people's strategy for pursuing their interests fundamentally changes. Shi (1997) maintains that the primary strategy of interest articulation becomes aimed at persuading the leaders of one's organization to distribute the desirable material and nonmaterial resources to oneself instead of to the group. Political acts for most issues in China are therefore highly particularistic, and individual-based instead of group-based. Individual members of subordinate social groups pursue their interests not by banding together for coordinated group action, but by cultivating ties based on the exchange of loyalty and advantage with individuals of higher status and power, an exchange which Walder (1986) called 'patron-client ties.' (see also Chen & Farh, this volume; Hwang & Han, this volume).

Shi's claims are adequately supported by his data, for the period of time concerned. Beijing residents were found to be heavily involved in making appeals and particularized contacts. Appeals involve citizen meetings with government officials at various levels or with leaders of the work unit. People in Beijing frequently engage in these acts. More than half of the respondents reported having contacted leaders of their work units. Others made complaints though outlets, such as the bureaucratic hierarchy (43 percent), trade unions (19 percent), political organizations (15 per cent), and deputies of people's congresses (9 percent). Particularized contacting involves interest articulation through managing instrumental personal ties (*gao guanxi*). While citizens in China cannot go on strikes or protests to express their opinions, the institutional arrangements in China do allow people to work at the stage of policy implementation to articulate their interests. Because lower-echelon bureaucrats in China have great discretionary power to implement government policies, some citizens manage to persuade officials to ignore policy made by the government and even to twist government policy at the implementation stage through cronyism to protect their interests. On the other hand, regime-challenging political actions, such as adversarial activities, resistance, and boycotts, are rare. Only around five per cent reported either that they had whipped up public opinion against government officials or that they had persuaded others to boycott unfair elections. Also, a majority of these activities occurred in respondents' work units, and the targets of those acts were usually work unit leaders rather than the political system itself (Shi, 1997).

Shi's study was conducted in the late 1980s. Have there been any subsequent changes in how people express their opinions? Tang (2005) compared the effectiveness of a variety of channels for voicing opinions, beginning with the more traditional, institutionally oriented channels originating in work units, and continuing through government bureaus and mass organizations, mass media appeals, personal networking, and newly emerging elections and elected representatives. Based on the findings of public opinion surveys conducted in 1987 (8 cities), 1992 (40 cities), and 1999 (6 cities), Tang (2005) noted several changes during the period between 1987 and 1999. First, although traditional channels for voicing opinions remained dominant over time, the emphasis within traditional channels shifted from the work unit to government bureaus. Contact with the government (government bureaus and mass organizations combined) increased from 1987 (37 per cent), and became the dominant mode of problem solving by 1999. Work units, once the all-encompassing universe of one's life in China, became less important in one's political world.

Second, the overall responsiveness by all channels increased over time, particularly in government bureaus and mass organizations, at the workplace, and through elected local officials. The problem-solving rate for non-work complaints doubled from 1987 to 1999. Nevertheless, similar to what Shi (1997) had found in earlier period, most of the issues about which people could voice their opinions and hope to see some resolution still involved parochial or lower-level political issues, ranging from personal welfare to public policy issues, such as inflation, the environment, and the public services. There was no evidence that the highest levels of the Chinese political system were responsive to higher level political issues and challenges.

Political participation in Hong Kong and Taiwan

Shi extended his work on political participation to include two other Chinese societies - Hong Kong and Taiwan. He found that voting participation in Hong Kong was significantly lower than that of the mainland China and Taiwan. While 91 and 75.3 per cent of people in Taiwan and mainland China voted in elections, only 29.6 per cent of people in Hong Kong reported that they did so (Shi, 2004). The high voting participation rate in Taiwan was probably due to a long history of election practice in Taiwan. It has also been documented and confirmed that institutional constraints, such as registration requirement, set hurdles to voting participation and that mobilization efforts promote it (Verba, Nie, & Kim 1978; Wolfinger & Rosenstone, 1980). Among three populations, the mainland Chinese is the most active in campaign activities, followed by the Taiwanese, and last by the Hong Kong Chinese. Nearly a quarter of the population in mainland China reported that they have engaged in campaign activities at election time, 17.5 per cent of Taiwanese people campaigned in elections for governors and members of the legislative council. Only 7.3 per cent of the population in Hong Kong reported that they had engaged in campaign activities. As for particularized contacting, people in Hong Kong and Taiwan were found to be much less likely than those in mainland China to get involved in such acts to pursue their interests. In Taiwan, people's dissatisfaction of governmental output may easily translate into demand input through periodical elections, as shown above with a higher participation rate in voting and electoral activities.

The picture is very different when it comes to unconventional, elite-challenging political acts such as resistance and adversarial protests. For adversarial protest, people in Hong Kong were substantially more active than people in mainland China and Taiwan (Shi, 2004). More than 14 per cent of people in Hong Kong reported that they engaged in protest, and 9.1 per cent of people chose adversarial activities to pursue their interests. The percentage of political actors in Hong Kong who have engaged in protest activities nearly tripled that of the protesters in mainland China and was ten times more than that in Taiwan.

Political participation in Singapore

Research on political participation in Singapore is limited, with only two published articles on political participation available. Ooi, Tan, and Koh (1999) conducted a national survey between 1997 and 1998. Their findings showed that, while large proportion of the respondents reflected a desire for greater political participation (87 per cent) and would like the government to take more time to listen to citizens (73 per cent), a much lower proportion of citizens (24 per cent) have indicated that they would participate in governance, whether at the local or national level; only 9 per cent has ever made their views known to the government on any public policy. Among the majority who had never expressed their views, 54 per cent listed their reasons for not doing so because they had no strong views. Another 15 per cent said they felt there were no channels available. A similar proportion, 16 per cent, thought that none of the channels was effective and as a result, had not expressed any views. As for those who expressed their opinions, the channels most often cited for expressing views on public policy to the government were letters to the local newspapers, and Members of Parliament's (MPs) meet-the-people sessions at their local constituencies.

Taken together, these studies indicate that political participation in Chinese societies, especially mainland China, may not be characterized as passive citizens driven by regime mobilization aimed at carrying out predetermined goals. Paradoxically, people in the mainland under the most authoritarian regime are the most active, particularly at the grassroots level. Their participation has a distinctly instrumental purpose of solving the problems of daily life through appealing to authorities and mobilizing *guanxi* or personal relations (Kuan & Lau, 2002); people in Hong Kong participate the least and when they do, protest is the most prevalent mode of action. Such protest appears more expressive than instrumental and rarely leads to physical violence or property destruction.

Antecedents of political participation

After discussing *how* people participate in politics, we would now like to know *why* they get involved. Historically, in the field of political science, two theories – modernization theory and political culture theory dominate when it comes to predicting political participation.

Economic development has generally been perceived to be associated with rising levels of political participation. The basic idea is that the process of economic development leads to a series of social changes that transform the social structure, institutions and political culture of a society, as well as shaping people's psychological orientations and preferences. For example, Inglehart (1997) argues that when there is sufficient economic development to provide for the basic material needs of the population, to create a varied economy with a strong service sector and to educate a high proportion of its population, two psychological changes particularly stand out: cognitive mobilization and a shift from materialist to postmaterialist values. Inglehart asserts that these changes in turn make the people more likely to want democracy and more skillful in getting it. Thus, to some, socio-economic modernization is the motor of change driving the values of individualism and demands for civic liberties.

Others, by contrast, tend to regard politics as a product of historical, deeply-rooted attitudes about authority that will affect citizen's acceptance of different kinds of regimes. Therefore, changing economic features of a social system is largely irrelevant. To the culturalists, Chinese culture acts as a force that pushes Chinese towards an authoritarian political system. One of the pioneers in studies of Chinese political culture, Lucian Pye (1992), identified a number of key characteristics that have been continuous through imperial and modern history in shaping and maintaining a paternalistic political order.

Modernization theory and political culture theory thus propose two diametrically opposed views of how culture relates to economic change.

In the last century, China has embarked on market-oriented reform for more than two decades. Will the rapid socio-economic transformation result in evolution of its political system, and if so, how? Modernization theory would postulate that rapid socio-economic modernization, especially in the coastal provinces, and the practicing of grassroots democracy would be conducive to the growth of popular demand for greater scope in freedom, political participation and popular accountability. On the other hand, according to political culture theory, value change in Confucian societies, such as China, has been and will continue to be rather slow and uneven, regardless of the transformative forces of modernization and globalization or the effects of democratic practice. For ordinary citizens, values that are more compatible with traditional philosophy might be relatively easy to acquire. Certain liberal values not so compatible with tradition, such as individualism, pluralism, and the rule of law, would be more difficult to infuse into the prevailing value structure. China, which has been undergoing rapid social and economic transformations for the past decades, provides a fertile ground for testing these two perspectives.

Examining the modernization claim

People participate in politics because they receive something in consequence. Political participation usually has a price because such activities put demands on people's scarce resources. Thus, the decision for individuals to participate is a product of cost-benefit calculation. Cross-national studies of political participation have found that certain sociological resources may have both direct and indirect effects on such calculations. Among these resources are income, education, urban residence, and having white-collar jobs. Economic development can increase these sociological resources in a society. In this section, I will review the literature and see whether the distribution of sociological resources in Chinese societies varies with their respective level of economic development, as suggested by modernization theorists.

Economic development and sociological resources. Voting studies in the West suggest that people of better economic standing tend to be more active in election participation. This can be understood in terms of Maslow's theory of the hierarchy of human needs, where one can afford to pursue an interest in politics and public affairs once one's basic needs are satisfied. Some also believe that people of better economic standing tend to be more involved because they have greater stakes in politics, i.e. vested economic interest (Verba & Nie, cited in Zhong & Kim, 2005). In general, this line of thought can be termed 'the resource hypothesis'. However, one may also argue that people of lower income might participate in politics more often, as they may have more problems and complaints about their poor economic conditions and hope that the government will address their concerns by participating. This is termed the 'deprivation hypothesis' (Gurr, 1970).

Empirical studies in the Chinese societies seem to suggest that both hypotheses can be true, depending on the modes of political participation. Based on his survey data with urban Chinese collected in Beijing in the late 1980s, Shi (1997) found that those most likely to engage in campaign activities, adversarial activities, cronyism, resistance, and boycotts are the more disadvantaged groups in Beijing. By contrast, the 'resource hypothesis' seems to fit better with findings regarding the relationship between resources and voting. Similarly, Tang (2005) found support for both hypotheses with the 1997 Employee Survey conducted by the All-China Federation of Trade Unions. Regarding the more spontaneous acts of labor disputes, Tang (2005) found that low-ranking, male, non-party, and rural employees working in private firms showed a higher probability of getting involved in labor disputes. In contrast, employees with higher rank and education and who had party membership and seniority working in large organizations or stock firms (part market-driven, part state-owned) were all more likely to make suggestions at work and to have their suggestions adopted than those of lower socioeconomic status. On the other hand, in another study (Shi, 2004), the relationship between income and political participation of all kinds was found to be a linear one in Taiwan.

In addition to improving incomes, modernization may also increase the number of people with better education. There are reasons for the positive relationship between education and one's level of political interest and participation. For one, education equips a person with the cognitive capability to receive and digest political information. Education also increases one's capacity to understand personal implications of political events and affairs along with one's confidence in his or her ability to influence politics, if given the opportunity.

In Taiwan and Hong Kong, education, political knowledge, and media exposure are found to be positively associated with political participation (Kuan & Lau, 2002). The effect of education on participation was also found to be strongest in Hong Kong comparing Hong Kong, Taiwan, and the mainland in Shi (2004). In rural China, Jennings (1997) found that peasants with a higher level of education were more active in public affairs. More recently, Zhong and Kim (2005) show that education was positively related to political interest in their rural Chinese sample. Moreover, older and better educated males tend to be more interested in politics and public affairs than the young, the less educated, and females (Zhong & Kim, 2005). In their study of urban Chinese in Beijing, Chen and Zhong (1999) also find that education was positively related to one's level of engagement in politics and public affairs. Taken together, the data from Taiwan, Hong Kong, and China seem to support the view that sociological resources such as income and education generally facilitate political participation.

Economic development and psychological resources. In addition to increasing sociological resources, economic development may also facilitate change in people's psychological orientation which may then play an important role in prompting people to participate in politics. Does the evidence suggest that economic development brings about changes in people's psychological orientation, in terms of psychological involvement in politics (political information and political interest), political efficacy (in terms of internal and external efficacy), and their orientation toward power and authorities?

Psychological involvement in politics (including both political information and political interests) is closely and positively associated with economic development (Shi, 2004). People in Hong Kong are highest in their political interest, followed by people in Taiwan, and then people in mainland China. The relationship between economic wealth and political interest is also independent of the effects of institution. Comparison of distribution of political interest within mainland China shows that people living in the underdeveloped areas are less interested in politics than are people in richer areas.

Economic development also exercises a strong and significant impact on people's orientation toward power and authorities. 85 per cent of the population in mainland China perceives their relationship with authority as hierarchical, while only 35 per cent of people in Hong Kong regard their relationship with the government as hierarchical. The same orientation of people in Taiwan falls between these two. More importantly, within-country analysis also reveals that the distribution of people's orientation toward power and authorities within mainland China also strongly associates negatively with their level of economic development.

By contrast, economic development is not associated with political efficacy. Economic wealth neither makes people more confident in their ability to participate in politics nor believe that their government would be responsive to their demands. People in the mid-developed Taiwan are highest in internal efficacy, followed by people in mainland China. People in Hong Kong are at least confident, in their ability both to understand political issues and to participate in politics. In addition, there is no statistically significant difference in internal efficacy among populations across different areas of development in mainland China.

A more surprising and counter-intuitive finding is that *external efficacy* is highest among people in mainland China (see Leung, this volume, on the distinction between fate control and reward for application). Despite the fact that mainland China is still under communist rule and the level of economic development is much lower than in the other two Chinese societies, more Mainlanders believe their government would be responsive to their demands than do Taiwanese and people in Hong Kong. This is not only true for the cross-society comparisons, but also true across regions of different level of economic development in mainland China. Taken together, these findings show that economic wealth is associated with certain psychological resources but not others, as suggested by the modernization claims.

Economic development and institutional setting. Shi's (2004) findings challenge the logic of modernization scholars - while the Mainlanders are the least resource-rich in terms of sociological and psychological resources among people in the three societies, they participate more than do people in the other Chinese societies. This outcome alerted Shi (2004) to the possibility that participation in places of different levels of economic development requires different strategies and resources from political actors. A direct test of this claim comes from a within-country, cross-regional comparison of mainland China, including developed coastal areas, middle developed, inland provinces, and backward, northwest regions. Such a comparison allows for a test of the relationship between economic development and political participation, while holding the regime type or political culture constant. As expected, political actors in more organizations where authorities still control social resources directly, such as state and collective enterprises in urban China, prefer to get involved in such parochial political acts as appeals and cronyism to deal with public authorities. Simultaneously, people belonging to modern sectors where the authorities have lost direct control over social resources, such as people in rural areas and private enterprises in urban China, prefer to get involved in adversarial activities and protest in their interest articulation, because these are more effective ways for them to influence policy formulation (Shi, 2004).

An important implication is that economic development not only increases resources of political actors as suggested by modernization theorists, but also transforms the function of public authority. Although such transformation may be and usually is associated with economic development, economic development may not necessarily produce such a change. For example, while economic development based on free-market enterprises transformed institutional settings in the poor areas of mainland China, development based on collective enterprises fossilized political process in mid-developed areas.

Examining the culturalist claim

In their chapter on Chinese social identity, Liu, Li, and Yue (this volume) propose that Chinese people may have different ideals from their Western counterparts about how society should be organized. They contrasted the benevolent authority model, a person-relationship centered model of authority, with contemporary Western model in which the mandate of authority rests in the law, an impartial set of rules that transcend the individuals who occupy positions circumscribed by that law. According to Western ideals, 'No one is above the law' and 'justice is blind'; whereas in the Confucian model, the person of the ruler, the benevolent authority, is at the top of the authority structure (see Figure 33.1).

At the top of Figure 33.1 are two ideals, and at the bottom is represented some of the struggle that goes into maintaining an actual system of governance: For East Asians, a strict, centralized, and

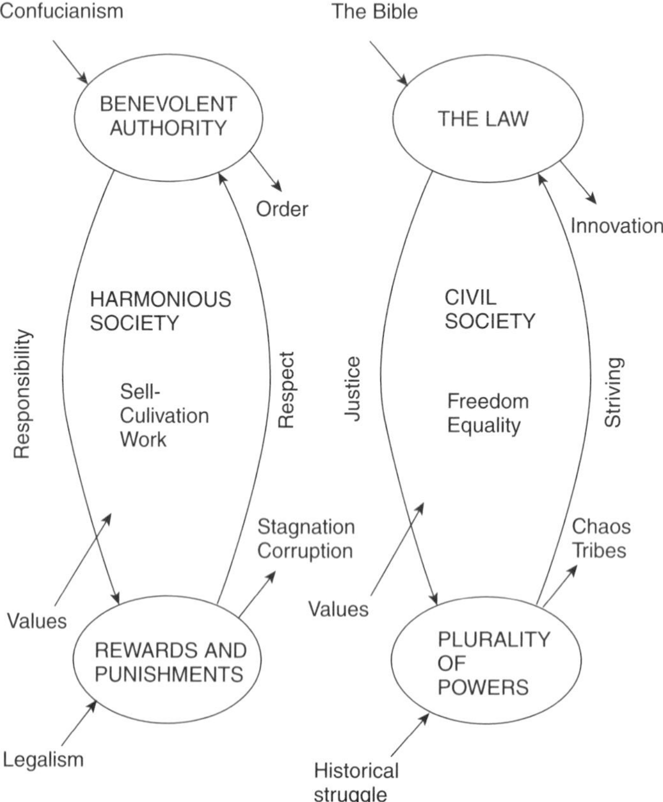

Fig. 33.1 Historical affordances for authority, adapted from Liu & Liu, 2003, p. 47.

hierarchical system of rewards and punishments; in the West, a host of competing powers and groups striving against one another to further their own interests under the rule of law and its associated institutions. The model society in the West is a civil society, competing interests strive against one another, constrained by the rule of law, which are designed to ensure justice and keep the struggle within stable boundaries. The model society in traditional East Asia, on the other hand, is harmonious: the ruler looks after the people, the people respect the ruler, and at each level an unequal but reciprocal system of exchange serves to maintain order (Liu & Liu, 2003).

In the literature, scholars have investigated how Chinese traditional values, especially the influence of Confucianism, shape Chinese political culture. Two cultural factors, namely 1) orientation towards power and authority, and 2) orientation towards conflict, are most often examined.

Orientation towards power and authority. As indicated by the model of benevolent authority, Chinese political culture is often associated with a moralistic, paternalistic and harmony-oriented leader, not a bureaucratic official as is often found in the Western prototype. In the East, emphasis is on the personality and morally upright character of the leader, instead of on the development of stabilizing institutions surrounding that leadership (Hofstede, 1991). Due to these varying preferences for styles of leadership, the expected role of political leaders can differ between the East and the West.

In his comparative study of political trust in mainland China and Taiwan, Shi (2001) operationalized this dimension of the political culture as 'hierarchical orientation index (HOI)'. He expected that those who score high in HOI will see their relationship with the state as hierarchical, rather than reciprocal, one in which the obligations of obedience and respect are contingent upon the model behavior of those with power. He found only a modest proportion of the population in mainland China (11.4 percent) and Taiwan (29.9 percent) regarded their relationship with the authorities as reciprocal, with his data gathered from these two societies in 1993. More importantly, Shi (2001) found that government responsiveness plays a different role in Taiwan than in the PRC – in Taiwan political trust is more contingent on government performance, whereas in China political trust is more related to traditional values.

Kuan and Lau (2002) captured the moral overtones associated with 'benevolent authority'. The meanings of the moral state were tapped by the following statements: 'The profusion of moral problems in society is the fault of the government', and 'When political leaders are morally upright, we can leave everything to them'. There is a strong consensus in mainland China on the precepts of 'moral government' and 'moral leaders'. However, Taiwan and Hong Kong cannot be described as having a traditional orientation in these two respects. Kuan and Lau (2002) attribute their finding that the concept of a moral state has survived the revolution in China to the strong impact of moral exhortation under communist rule. In sharp contrast, because of its colonial nature, the 'state' in Hong Kong could not, even if it wanted to, make any moral claim *vis-a`-vis* its subjects before 1997. In Taiwan, people were exposed to the moralizing rule of the Kuomingtang before the mid-1980s, yet a more instrumental view of the state in Taiwan has come into place after over a decade of democratization.

In Kuan and Lau's (2002) work, the concept of 'paternalism' is also captured by the statement, 'The leader of the government is like the head of a big family. His decisions on public affairs should be obeyed'. According to their study, paternalism registers near consensus among respondents in the mainland; in Taiwan, less than one-third of the respondents believe in paternalism. In Hong Kong only a small minority of the respondents endorses paternalism.

Orientation towards conflict/interests. Another aspect of Chinese political culture is its unique approach to handling conflict. In Confucianism, the ideal self is defined and established in terms of one's relationship to others. Because the individual is not seen as separate from other people, a Chinese agent is obliged to work through the groups to which he or she belongs. Therefore, a person's concern for his or her own needs and rights is supposed to be subordinated to his or her social responsibilities and to the welfare of the group. If the ideal of social control in Chinese political culture 'rested upon self-discipline' (Pye, 1992, p. 86) and the Chinese 'shun the adversarial logic of the West' (Bond, 1991, p. 66), we can expect people under the influence of the traditional political culture to be willing to sacrifice their own interests to preserve the harmony of society. When they find the government to be nonresponsive to their requests, they would voluntarily forfeit their private interests rather than blaming and confronting the agents of government.

Also, another enduring characteristic of Chinese political culture is the fear of chaos (*luan*), such that many people believe initiating disputes with others is an invitation to chaos. In situations where one person's interests clash in important ways with another's, the Chinese opt for non-confrontational approaches to resolving conflict and are willing to sacrifice their own interests for the harmony of society as a whole (see also Au & Leung, this volume). Experimental research reveals that Chinese tend to cooperate even when it is not in their own interest to do so (Bond, 1991, pp. 65-66). When people under the influence of such cultural priorities find that their government fails to respond to their demands, they may forfeit their private interests for the harmony of the society, rather than withdraw their support from the government. This orientation towards conflict is measured with the Conflict Avoidance Index (CAI) by Shi. According to Shi (2001), around 44.3 per cent of respondents in the PRC and 51.3 per cent in Taiwan are willing to confront others in pursuing their interests. This finding gives pause to the stereotyped notions described above about Chinese conflict avoidance, at least in civic matters.

Kuan and Lau (2002) operationalized this cultural orientation as 'statism' (e.g. 'The individual has both priority over and is more important than the state'- reversed, and 'Do not ask what your country can do for you, but ask what you can do for your country'), and 'obsession with order' (e.g. the establishment of all kinds of different associations has a bad effect on a country's stability and harmony' and 'If the scope of democracy in [the research site] broadens, stability will be affected'). There is a positive consensus among the respondents in the mainland, but no consensus exists in the other two Chinese societies. Kuan and Lau suggested that in Taiwan and Hong Kong, individualism may have left no room for a concept such as, 'the state takes precedence over the individual' and 'me for the state', and that the tension between these two ideas concerning 'statism' may be related to the fuzziness of the concept of the state in Hong Kong where the 'state' could have been Britain, China, Taiwan, or none of them (before the handover in 1997), and in Taiwan where the issue of nation-state building is highly controversial.

Concern about the harmful effects of social pluralism is more evident in all three societies. In the mainland where there is not much pluralism to begin with, about 40 per cent of respondents are against the spread of associations for fear of instability. While Hong Kong has been quite a pluralistic society for several decades, figures here suggest that its immigrants' mentality expressed as 'don't rock the boat' has survived despite decades of socio-economic progress (Kuan & Lau, 2002; Lau & Kuan, 1988). Moreover, these authors also find it rather surprising that in democratic Taiwan over 50 per cent of respondents expressed worry about expansion of social pluralism.

Impact of cultural orientation on political participation

The literature converges in finding that Chinese in the mainland have the most traditional political orientations when compared with their counterparts in Taiwan and Hong Kong (Kuan & Lau, 2002; Shi, 2001). Shi (2001) found that those with a hierarchical orientation to power and authority have a high level of trust in the government regardless of its performance, while the political trust of those with a reciprocal orientation is more contingent on the government's performance. In a subsequent study, Shi (2004) found that the hierarchically oriented citizens tend to participate in elite-directing, traditional political acts such as appeals and contacting government officials, while the reciprocally oriented citizens tend to participate in elite-challenging acts, such as adversarial and protest activities. Kuan and Lau (2002) also found that in mainland China, but not Taiwan and Hong Kong, traditional political orientations have a positive impact on conventional participation such as voting, campaign, and appeal activities, but a negative impact on adversarial and protest activities.

Consequences of political participation

What does political participation do to the individual? Does it liberate? Does it change one's attitudes? Increase one's knowledge? Alter one's affective evaluation of other individuals, or of political institutions? In this section, we try to answer this question at two levels. At a more local level, does organizational involvement in political associations cause any attitudinal change in individuals? On the national level, do Chinese in Taiwan manifest a different set of psycho-political characteristics (such as internal/external efficacy, political trust, understanding of democracy, political ideology) after years of experience in practicing democracy?

Consequences for participation in voluntary associations

In their influential study of Italian communities, Putnam, Leonardi, and Nanetti (1993) found over time and in different regions that membership in non-family-based associations led to increased social capital based on interpersonal trust, a social resource that promoted viable democratic institutions. In his book, Putnam (1995) tried to show, firstly, that social participation improves social skills that are a precondition of social capital. Social participation in voluntary associations leads the participants to experience an associational life that includes encounters with disagreement and conflict, leading to collective problem solving, and this experience in turn improves the social skills and leadership competence of engaged individuals. Putnam's second point was that social networks within associations as well as in the outside world nourish social trust. The larger the network an individual has, the more frequent the exposure to heterogeneous others, and the greater the chance to assess a wide variety of social resources. Inglehart (1999) revitalized earlier studies of civil culture and democracy (e.g. Almond & Verba, 1993) by showing the positive effect that interpersonal trust has on the successful functioning of democratic institutions. One conclusion that comes out of social capital theory, then, is that non-family associational membership, such as in civil groups, generates interpersonal trust, which promotes democratic institutions.

Does the outcome derived from social capital theory hold in China? Does organizational involvement in China promote political participation? In the Chinese context, the four kinds of formal organizations that a citizen can be involved in are the Chinese Communist Party, the Chinese Communist Youth League, the other 'mass organizations', and civic associations. 'Mass organizations' are organizations that initially functioned as bi-directional 'transmission belts' between the Communist Party and the masses, loyally implementing Party lines and policies among their members while feeding information from the masses back to the Party according to the 'mass line', and hence the name.

According to the Xinhua New Agency (2008), there are nearly 200 national mass organizations that are fully funded and staffed by the government, with All-China Federation of Trade Unions, The All-China Women's Federation, and the Chinese Communist Youth League as the three most prominent examples. The Chinese Communist Party and the Communist Youth League require formal written application to join them, followed by a long and careful process of screening and approval on the part of the local organizations. Because of the hierarchical and compartmentalized nature of the Party and mass organizations, organizational involvement per se does not significantly increase social connectedness and social cohesion beyond the confines of the work units or administrative units. Also, the Party and the mass organizations also exert strong constraint on political participation by their members, especially those involving unconventional means. Party members are required and compelled by strict Party discipline to 'maintain a high-degree alignment with the Party center in ideology and action'. As the Party's 'transmission belt' to various social sectors, the mass organizations also have the political obligation to control and contain activities of their members, especially those collective actions that are potentially disruptive or destabilizing (Chen, 2003). In contrast with the Communist Party and the 'mass organizations,' the re-emerging civic associations have more voluntary and active members. In addition to vertical connections with potential protective patrons

(Shi, 1997, p. 244), these civic associations also connect their members horizontally with other citizens who share similar interests or concerns.

Several positive significant correlations between involvement in these various formal organizations and social networking, external efficacy, and interpersonal trust were found (Guo, 2007). However, most of the measures of social networking and of external efficacy were locally oriented and do not transcend institutional boundaries. In addition, Guo (2007) hypothesized that these formal organizations will have different 'internal effects' on their members' political participation. First, he hypothesized that involvement in the Communist Party, Youth League, and mass organizations would have a positive impact on participation through official channels, unclear impact on cronyism activities (personal connections), and a negative impact on unconventional participation. In contrast, civic associations should have positive impact on all types of participation.

Based on the survey conducted by Tianjian Shi and the Social Survey Research Center (PRC) from 1993 to 1994, Guo (2007) found that as expected, civic association is the only type of formal organization that has a consistently significant and positive 'internal effect' across all three kinds of participation. Involvement in the Party or the League also results in higher official political participation. However, the hypothesized deterrence or coercive effects of Party or League involvement on unconventional political participation did not materialize. On the contrary, there was a small but significant positive effect on participation through unconventional means. Similarly, in another study comparing party intellectuals with non-party intellectuals, Tang (2005)'s results demonstrated that the party intellectuals as a group vigorously inclined toward reform. Though the government gives Party intellectual elite more ideological education and privileges, the Party intellectuals were found to be more critical of the government and of the Party itself than the non-party intellectuals when asked about morale under reform, corruption, the rule of law and legal reform, the reputation of the party, and government efficiency. These data suggested that they support rapid reform as vigorously as their non-establishment counterparts, which may probably be an unintended effect of the socialist institutions.

Consequences of experience at practicing democracy in Taiwan

Fu Hu, Yun-han Chu, Huo-yan Shyu and their colleagues have tracked the evolution of political ideology in Taiwan over more than two decades since the 1970s, covering the entire span of the island's regime transition, from the weakening of authoritarianism to the completion of the democratic transition (Shin & Shyu, 1997; Chu & Chang, 2001). According to Fu and Chu (1996), the organizing principle of a political regime consists of three basic dimensions: (1) the legitimate power relationship among members of the political community; (2) the legitimate power relationship between the authorities and citizens; and (3) the legitimate power relationship among the government authorities themselves.

The value orientation toward political equality corresponds to the first dimension. It is a set of beliefs that all member of the political community should be equal and entitled to the same citizen rights regardless of differences in race, gender, education, religion, class, social-economic background, political affiliation, and so on. In contrast, in some societies, a majority of people believe in a hierarchical and/or exclusionary order, in which it is considered legitimate for certain groups to be privileged and others to be disfranchised or discriminated against.

The second dimension can be subdivided into three sub-dimensions: (1) the value orientation toward political liberty is a set of beliefs that there is a realm of individual liberty which should be free from state intrusion and regulation; (2) the value orientation toward pluralism is a set of beliefs holding that there should be a realm of civil society in which civic organizations can freely constitute themselves and establish arrangements to express themselves and advance their interests without state interference; and (3) the value orientation toward popular accountability refers to a set of beliefs that government authority should be accountable to the people, and that there should be some effective means for popular control and consent. In contrast, in some societies people believe that individual liberty should be minimized, civil society should be subject to state guidance and control, and the assertion of popular control over authority is unacceptable and even dangerous.

The value orientation toward separation of powers corresponds to the third dimension. It is a set of beliefs that governing authority should be divided among various branches of government, and that a good polity is achieved through a design of checks-and-balances or horizontal accountability. In contrast, in some societies people believe in the necessity and the desirability of supreme executive power or the fusion of legislative, executive and judicial authority. In sum, five dimensions of regime legitimacy (or democratic vs authoritarian value orientation) are as follows: political equality, popular accountability, political liberty, political pluralism, and separation of powers (horizontal accountability).

Focusing on these five key dimensions of democratic vs. authoritarian value orientations, the acquisition of pro-democratic value orientations along the five dimensions has been found to be uneven, suggesting the lingering influence of traditional values. Support for political equality was high from the beginning, and endorsement of popular accountability rose dramatically from 1984 to 1993 (as did belief in political pluralism, even though it remained rather low) (Fu & Chu, 1996; Shin & Shyu, 1998; Chu & Chang, 2001). The data also show that by the late 1990s substantial segments of Taiwan's public still manifested the fear of disorder and preference for communal harmony over individual freedom, a preference that Pye (1992) takes to be generally characteristic of Asian attitudes toward power and authority.

In addition to examining these value orientations, researchers have also looked at how other ideological orientations, such as social dominance orientation and right-wing authoritarianism, change as a function of political power and societal change. The social dominance orientation scale (SDO; Pratto et al., 1994) assesses individual differences in belief in inequality and preference for a hierarchically structured social system, with high levels of competition and intergroup dominance. The right-wing authoritarianism scale (RWA; Altemeyer, 1981) assesses the three traits that Altemeyer has viewed as the central aspects of the authoritarianism construct: conformity to traditional moral beliefs, submission to authorities viewed as legitimate, and punitiveness toward authority-sanctioned targets such as out-group members and criminals. Both scales have generally shown considerable validity in the prediction of various attitudes toward specific social and political issues, particularly those involving prejudice or group conflict. Liu, Huang, and McFedries (2008) examined changes in SDO and RWA using cross-sectional and longitudinal analysis of three waves of survey data before and after the 2004 Presidential election in Taiwan. Supporters of the Kuomingtang (KMT), the dominant political group that has held power for over 50 years, were found to be higher in SDO and RWA than were members of their opposition, the Democratic Progressive Party (DPP), supporting the hypothesis derived from the group socialization model. Moreover, the DPP, a formerly low-powered group, increased in their members' SDO and RWA following victory, but the levels of these political attitudes in the high-powered group was unchanged. Their findings suggest that it is easier to acquire the mindset associated with power than to lose it. Longitudinal path modeling also showed that SDO became less connected to identity and political party support after an election that consolidated societal and regime change; the role of RWA shifted even more dramatically, from being connected to one political party and social identity pre-election, to an opposing one post-election.

Conclusion

This chapter has focused on three main questions relating to Chinese political participation – how Chinese participate in politics, why they participate in politics, and what are the psychological consequences of political participation for an individual. Regarding the first question, the literature suggests that, contrary to the view of a passive (or merely mobilized) citizenry, citizens in China actively express their opinions via a variety of channels, even more often than do those in Hong Kong, in terms of conventional political participation. Their participation has a distinctly instrumental purpose of solving the problems of daily life through appeal and manipulation of *guanxi* or personal relations. Those in Taiwan have the highest participation rate in voting and electoral activities, while Hong Kong Chinese participate the least, and when they do, protest is their most prevalent mode of action.

Modernization and political culture theories dominate when it comes to predicting political participation. The modernization claim was examined in light of a comparative research on economic development and political participation in Hong Kong, Taiwan, and mainland China (as well as regions within China across various levels of development). The empirical evidence suggests that economic development relates to political participation in both direct and indirect ways. On the one hand, development promotes participation through directly boosting the sociological and psychological resources of the political actors. The data from Taiwan, Hong Kong, and China support the view that sociological resources such as income and education would facilitate political participation in general, thus supporting the claim of modernization theory. Nevertheless, it has also been found that economic wealth is associated with certain psychological resources but not others, such as political efficacy, thus challenging the modernization claim.

On the other hand, economic development influences participation indirectly through transformation of a society's institutional setting, for example by transforming the function of public authority, thereby changing the strategies people employ to articulate their interests. Regarding political culture, its explanatory power is greatest when it is used to predict specific modes of political participation instead of general levels of participation. A traditional political orientation, such as a hierarchical view of relation with power and authority, has a positive impact on conventional, elite-directing mode of participation such as appeals and contacting, but a negative impact on unconventional, elite-challenging mode of action such as protests.

Finally, the chapter also addressed the consequences of political participation. Involvement in various associations in China contributes to wider social networking, higher external efficacy, and general trust. Involvement in the Communist Party was also found to be associated with unconventional political participation, though at a modest level. There is also empirical support that party intellectuals are more critical of their government and the Party than are non-Party intellectuals when asked about morale under reform, corruption, the rule of law and legal reform, the reputation of the party, and government efficiency. At the country level, Taiwanese people were found to acquire various pro-democratic value orientations in an uneven way – a value such as political equality, which is compatible with traditional Chinese orientations, is more readily accepted than belief in political pluralism, which is less compatible, despite years of experiencing democracy.

It is hoped that this chapter can stimulate interest in developing the field of Chinese political psychology further. Political psychology is an interdisciplinary academic field dedicated to the relationship between psychology and political science. 'Political psychology' as a term appeared in the late 1960s. Scholars from both psychology and political science have long been interested in exploring, for example, attitudes, socialization, social identity, and leadership. However, because of a difference in the core foci of the two disciplines – psychologists are interested in the processes driving individual human behavior, while political scientists are more concerned about the outcomes of human behavior in the aggregate – they often talk past each other (Sears, Huddy & Jervis, 2006).

Do intellectual differences between these disciplines negate the possibility of constructive dialogue? Both Sears et al. (2006) and Wituski et al. (1998) have argued forcefully how a constructive dialogue is not only possible but also worthwhile. Some possibilities for further work include: first, while macro-level variables such as modernization force and cultural values are helpful in understanding political participation, researchers are beginning to notice the importance of psychological variables in explaining political participation. Kuan and Lau (2002) made the following comment in their comparative study of political participation in three Chinese societies: 'Cognitive-psychological ones are the most important, followed by institutional and modernization forces. Traditional political orientations can claim the least influence of all factors.' (p. 311)

How may one study political attitudes or behavior from a psychological perspective? Keung and Bond (2002) set a good example for aspiring psychologists. Adopting an expectancy-value framework which asserts that values and expectancies (beliefs) have a separate impact on behavior, they examined the predictive power of social beliefs along with values in predicting an individual's two basic dimensions of political attitudes (egalitarianism and freedom from regulation) in Hong Kong. In their study, they found that social beliefs (as measured by social axioms, see Leung, this volume) contributed predictive power above and beyond what was provided by knowledge of a respondent's values. For example, values alone predicted about 16 per cent of the variance in the dimension of freedom from regulation. This percentage sharply increased to 35 per cent when social beliefs were included as predictors. Their work shows how personal values and individual beliefs about the world, viz. social axioms, can be combined to predict political attitudes or behaviors in other Chinese societies. As these two dimensions of political attitudes appear to be basic across time and culture (Ashton et al., 2005), their use hold promise for enabling considerable integration across a variety of studies.

Second, the unconventional political participation in Hong Kong may also be another fertile ground for research. For example, what could be the psychological explanation for mass protest and social movements? Lee (2005) found that collective efficacy, defined as a citizen's belief in the capabilities of the public as a collective actor to achieve social and political outcomes, rather than internal efficacy, was positively correlated with support for democracy and political participation in Hong Kong. Future research on political participation in Chinese societies may consider the role of collective efficacy, in addition to the more traditional two-dimensional concept involving internal and external efficacy.

Third, the explosive growth in social organizations in post-Mao China has so far generated much research focusing on the macro-level relationship of those organizations with the party-state, the important theoretical and empirical question of micro-level, psychological effects on their members have rarely been explored, with the notable exception of Guo's (2007) work. Such studies can be done, using many of the constructs of political psychology described in this essay.

References

Almond, G. A. & Verba, S. (1989). *The civic culture revisited.* Newbury Park, CA: Sage.

Altemeyer, B. (1981). *Right-wing authoritarianism.* Winnipeg, Canada: University of Manitoba Press.

Ashton, M. C., Danso, H. A., Maio, G., Esses, V. M., Bond, M. H., & Keung, D. (2005). Two dimensions of political attitudes and their individual difference correlates: A cross-cultural perspective. In R. M. Sorrentino, D. Cohen, J. M. Olsen, & M. P. Zanna (eds), *Culture and social behavior, Volume 10* (pp. 1–30). Manwah, NJ: Erlbaum.

Bennett, S. E. & Bennett, L. L. M. (1986). Political participation. *Annual Review of Politica Science, 1*, 157–204.

Bond, M. H. (1991) *Beyond the Chinese face: Insights from psychology.* Hong Kong: Oxford University Press.

Chen, F. (2003). Between the state and labour: The conflict of Chinese trade unions' double identity in market reform. *China Quarterly, 176*, 1006–1028.

Chen, J. & Zhong, Y. (1999). Mass political interest (or apathy) in Urban China. *Communist and Post-Communist Studies, 32*, 281–303

Chu, Y. H. & Chang, Y. T. (2001). Culture shift and regime legitimacy: Comparing Mainland China, Taiwan and Hong Kong. In S. P. Hua (ed.), *Chinese political culture* (pp. 320–347). New York: M. E. Sharpe.

Fu, H. & Chu, Y. H. (1996). Neo-authoritarianism, polarized conflict and populism in a newly democratizing regime: Taiwan's emerging mass politics. *Journal of Contemporary China, 5*, 23–41.

Guo, G. (2007). Organizational involvement and political participation in China. *Comparative Political Studies, 40*, 457–482.

Gurr, T. R. (1970). *Why men rebel.* Princeton, NJ: Princeton University Press.

Hofstede, G. (1991). *Cultures and organizations: Software of the mind.* London: McGraw-Hill.

Inglehart, R. (1997). *Modernization and post-modernization: Cultural, economic, and political change in 43 societies.* Princeton, NJ: Princeton University Press.

Inglehart, R. (1999). Trust, well-being and democracy. In M. E. Warren, *Democracy and trust* (pp. 88–120). Cambridge, England: Cambridge University Press.

Jennings, K. (1997). Political participation in the Chinese countryside. *American Political Science Review, 91*, 361–72.

Keung, D. K. Y. & Bond, M. H. (2002). Dimensions of political attitudes and their relations with beliefs and values in Hong Kong. *Journal of Psychology in Chinese Societies, 3*, 133–154.

Kuan, H. C. & Lau, S. K. (2002). Traditional orientations and political participation in three Chinese societies. *Journal of Contemporary China, 11*, 297–318.

Lau, S. K. & Kuan, H. C. (1988). *The ethos of the Hong Kong Chinese.* Hong Kong: The Chinese University of Hong Kong Press

Lee, F. L. F. (2005). Collective efficacy, support for democratization, and political participation in Hong Kong. *International Journal of Public Opinion Research, 18*, 297–317.

Liu, J. H., Huang, L. L., & McFedries, C. (2008) Cross-sectional and longitudinal differences in social dominance orientation and right wing authoritarianism as a function of political power and societal change. *Asian Journal of Social Psychology, 11*, 116–126.

Liu, J. H. & Liu, S. H. (2003). The role of the social psychologist in the 'Benevolent Authority' and 'Plurality of Powers' systems of historical affordance for authority. In K. S. Yang, K. K. Hwang, P. B. Pedersen, & I. Daibo (eds) *Progress in Asian social psychology: Conceptual and empirical contributions.* Vol. 3, pp. 43–66. Westport, CT: Praeger.
Manion, M. (1996). The electoral connection in the Chinese countryside. *American Political Science Review, 90,* 736–748.
Ooi, G. L., Tan, E. S., & Koh, G. (1999). Political participation in Singapore: Findings from a national survey. *Asian Journal of Political Science, 7,* 126–140.
Pratto, F., Sidanius, J., Stallworth, L., & Malle, B. (1994). Social dominance orientation: a personality variable predicting social and political attitudes. *Journal of Personality and Social Psychology, 67,* 741–763.
Putnam, R. D. (1995). Bowling alone: America's declining social capital. *Journal of Democracy, 6,* 65–78.
Putnam, R. D., Leonardi, R., & Nanetti, R. V. (1993). *Making democracy work: Civic tradition in modern Italy.* Princeton, NJ: Princeton University Press.
Pye, L. W. (1992). *The spirit of Chinese politics.* Cambridge: Harvard University Press.
Sears, D. O., Huddy, L., & Jervis, R. (2003). *Oxford handbook of political psychology.* New York: Oxford University Press.
Shi, T. (1997). *Political participation in Beijing.* Cambridge, MA: Harvard University Press.
Shi, T. (2001). Cultural values and political trust: A comparison of the People's Republic of China and Taiwan. *Comparative Politics, 33,* 401–419.
Shi, T. (2004) Economic development and political participation: comparison of mainland China, Taiwan, and Hong Kong. *Asian Barometer Project. Working Paper Series: No. 24.*
Shin, D. C. & Shyu, H. (1997). Political ambivalence in South Korea and Taiwan. *Journal of Democracy, 8,* 109–124.
Tang, W. (2005). *Public opinion and political change in China.* Stanford, CA: Stanford University Press.
Tang, W. & Parish, W. (2000). *Chinese urban life under reform.* New York: Cambridge University Press.
Verba, S., Nie, N. H., & Kim, J. (1978). *Participation and political equality: A seven-nation comparison.* Cambridge, UK: Cambridge University Press.*Communist neo-traditionalism: Work and authority in Chinese industry.* Berkeley and Los Angeles, CA: University of California Press.
Wituski, D. M., Clawson, R. A., Oxley, Z. M., Green, M. C., & Barr, M. K. (1998). Bridging an interdisciplinary divide: The Summer Institute in Political Psychology. *Political Science and Politics, 31,* 221–226.
Wolfinger, R. E. & Rosenstone, S. J. (1980). *Who votes?* New Haven, CN: Yale University Press.
Xinhua News Agency. (2008, September). *Mass organizations & social groups* (online). Available at http://news.xinhuanet.com/ziliao/2002-01/28/content_285782.htm
Zhong, Y. & Kim, J. (2005). Political interest in rural southern Jiangsu province in China. *Journal of Chinese Political Science, 10,* 1–19.

CHAPTER 34

Chinese social identity and inter-group relations: the influence of benevolent authority

James H. Liu, Mei-chih Li, and Xiaodong Yue

The articulation of a contemporary perspective on Chinese social identity and intergroup relations requires integration of three basic strands of knowledge: interdependent and independent selves from cross-cultural psychology; social identity and self-categorization from intergroup psychology; and historical analysis, weaving these strands of influence into the context of Chinese culture and its evolving indigenous psychology. The theories of interdependent and independent self (Markus & Kitayama, 1991) and social identity and self-categorization (Tajfel & Turner, 1979; Turner, Hogg, Oakes, Reicher, & Wetherell, 1987) have been among the most influential developments in psychology over the past two decades, whereas indigenous psychology for Chinese is among the most vibrant in the world (Yang, 1995; Hwang, 2005). Each provides ingredients necessary, but alone are insufficient to capture the dynamics of Chinese social identity and intergroup relations.

To put these abstract ideas practically into play, the theories must be integrated within a representational account (Liu & Hilton, 2005) of the socio-historical context of (1) the ancient development of Chinese civilization as a singularly successful, multilingual enterprise, and (2) the recent development of Chinese nationalism in the context of its contemporary suffering and failures. Concepts like the interdependent self are frail abstractions without the substance of indigenous Chinese concepts like *guanxi*, the art of social relationships (Yang, 1995, 2005; Hwang, 1987, 2005; Ho, 1998). Such indigenous concepts transform general description into cultural prescription, and enable an understanding of how Chinese have understood their social identities historically, through an ethically prescribed system of Confucian ethics for hierarchical social relations.

With the onslaught of Western imperialism over the last two centuries, traditional Chinese civilization collapsed, and traditional Chinese virtues came to be understood as flaws by leading Chinese intellectuals (see Levenson, 1959) and their political rulers. The Confucian vision of state as 'family and other particularistic social relations writ large' became viewed as one of the reasons why Chinese people were unable to mobilize successful resistance to European and then Japanese invasion. Generations of intellectual and political leaders sought to instill the 'virtues' of nationalism and patriotism to Chinese people as a means of mobilizing resistance to external aggression (Unger, 1996).

This was the context from which a contemporary form of Chinese social identity emerged, very much consistent with Western ideas of nationality and the group-based social comparison processes described by social identity and self-categorization theory. The impact of two centuries of brutal experience with Western modernity has been to harden what was previously a moral/ethical identity practiced within a context of particularistic social relations into a more categorical form of binary inclusions and exclusions consistent with other national identities in the global system of nation-states.

Using a representational and historically contingent approach to social identity and intergroup relations (Liu & Hilton, 2005), we will argue that the ethical and relational origins of traditional Chinese social identity enable culturally unique predictions about how Chinese people manage cultural diversity and international relations today. Foremost among these are: (1) Chinese identity is primarily defined by role-based social relations rather than clear category boundaries, so that, (2) under conditions of low threat, traditional Chinese prescriptions for *guanxi* motivate 'benevolent paternalism' rather than out-group derogation as the default script for dealings with out-group members, and (3) under conditions of high threat, a defensive reaction in the form of nationalism fueled by a narrative of great civilization versus recent historical victimization is activated. These three predictions integrate traditional conceptions of Chinese identity within the socio-political context of its recent historical traumas, and enables researchers to examine the interactions between Chinese tradition and modernity unencumbered by either Western hegemonic views of identity or a reactionary rejection of these views.

Revolution in cross-cultural psychology

In 1991, Markus and Kitayama published a revolutionary fusion of cross-cultural psychology and American social cognition. While cross-cultural psychologists have known for the better part of a quarter century that Western, and particularly American, notions of individualism are far from universal ideals and practices of personhood (Hofstede, 1980/2001), these challenges were not heard by the American mainstream. What Markus and Kitayama (1991) did was translate the primary dimension of cultural difference that had been identified by cross-cultural psychology, individualism-collectivism, into the language and findings of social cognition. In an empirical tour-de-force, they argued that virtually everything that mainstream social psychology cherished as scientific truth, from the experience of cognitive dissonance to the beneficence of primary control and the ubiquity of self-enhancement, was actually a culture-specific manifestation of a particular sense of self construal that they called the 'independent self'. The independent self is a 'bounded whole', unique and distinct from other people and the situational context; it is conceived as self-contained, autonomous entity that comprises a unique configuration of internal attributes, and behaves primarily as a consequence of those internal attributes.

They contrasted this independent self (rooted in individualistic cultures) in dichotomy and contradistinction with an interdependent self characteristic of collectivistic cultures. This all-or-nothing approach has been effective at gaining attention, but because of serious ambiguities in defining what collectivist culture is and how the interdependent sense of self is configured (Shimmack, Oishi, & Diener, 2005), there is currently considerable controversy around this formulation (see Oyserman, Koon, & Kemmelmeier, 2002).

A self-categorization perspective on self

In an entirely separate but theoretically and temporally parallel movement, Tajfel and Turner (1979) developed social identity theory as a European alternative to American individualism in inter-group psychology. In social identity theory, the self is realized in social comparison with others - sometimes individuals, sometimes groups. To the extent that significant aspects of one's self are conceived to be part of the groups to which one belongs, there is a motivation to make characteristics of these groups or social identities positively distinct in comparison with relevant out-groups, like 'I am woman (not a man)', 'I am Chinese (not Japanese)', or 'I am a member of the Liu family (not the Li family)'.

Turner, Hogg, Oakes, Reicher, & Wetherell (1987) went on to define self-categorization theory as a more fully developed model where all psychological phenomena are again contingent upon self-construal. In self-categorization theory, a person is not theorized to have a stable or singular sense of self, but rather is conceived as having a repertoire of selves at different levels of inclusiveness, from the individual (which would be just like the independent self) to the group (the critical level of analysis for this inter-group theory), but potentially ascending to an all inclusive sense of humanity. These different senses of self are activated in response to different situations, so that the same person sometimes behaves according to internal attributes (I am naughty) and sometimes according to group norms (I am a gentlemen who treats women with respect).

The key psychological process in group behavior is self-categorization, whereby, through a process of 'de-personalization', individuality is temporarily submerged within conformity to a group prototype containing idealized characteristics of the group. Hence, in self-categorization theory, it does not make sense to speak of independent and interdependent selves as culturally-inherited scripts. Rather, each person has a repertoire of scripts for appropriate behavior that are activated in different situations (see e.g. Sarbin & Allen, 1968). Sometimes the person acts as an individual, according to personal preferences or beliefs, and at other times a group-based sense of self becomes salient, at which time the person acts according to group norms. But, behavior is still dichotomized, into the product of individual and category-based group identities.

Collectivism as relational orientation, not category-based difference

Recently, Yuki and Brewer have begun to break down this dichotomous thinking and theorize the links between the inter-group literature and individualism-collectivism in cross-cultural psychology. The basic point is that groups are ubiquitous for human survival, so it makes no sense to think of individualism as precluding group-based behavior. Rather, in a seminal paper Yuki (2003) argues that East-Asian collectivism is characterized by cooperation within a group as an interpersonal network. He cites the relational orientation of Confucianism to support his claim that East-Asian collectivism is 'an intragroup rather than intergroup phenomenon' (p. 169). Reviewing the literature, he finds no evidence that people in collectivistic cultures show more in-group favoritism than people in individualistic cultures, as should be expected if collectivism were a form of group identification in the self-categorization tradition.

Following Brewer and Gardner (1996) and Kashima and Hardie (2000), he makes a distinction between the collective self, as a depersonalized self defined in terms of the prototypical properties shared among group members, and the relational self as defined by enduring connections and role relations with significant others, arguing that the relational self is more characteristic of East-Asian collectivism. Yuki (2003) found that Japanese in-group loyalty and identity were predicted by knowledge of the relational structure within the group, knowledge of individual differences within the group, and feelings of personal interconnectedness with group members, whereas American in-group loyalty and identity was correlated with perceived in-group homogeneity and group status. Yuki, Maddux, Brewer, & Takemura, (2005) furthermore reported that Japanese trusted strangers with a potential indirect relationship link more, whereas Americans trusted strangers with whom they shared an in-group membership more. Brewer and Chen (2007) advance the more general argument that collectivism should be properly thought of as a relational orientation across the domains of identity, agency beliefs, and obligations/values, not as a tendency to categorically identify with particular in-groups, as in the social identity tradition.

An indigenous Chinese psychology of identity

The above position is highly congruent with what indigenous Chinese psychologists have argued for some time. Yang (1995, 2005) has advocated for the centrality of a relationally-focused Chinese social orientation throughout much of a career that has spanned three decades. After two decades, Hwang's (1987) citation classic on Chinese face and favor remains one of the most elegant theoretical formulations of Chinese relationalism, whereas Ho (1998) has made methodological relationalism the cornerstone of his system for doing research and analyzing research findings.

There is consensus among indigenous Chinese psychologists that an ethical system of social roles and obligations is at the core of Chinese definitions of personhood. In adopting this position, many writers have noted the extensive influence of Confucian philosophy on traditional and contemporary Chinese society. They begin with the five cardinal relationships, or *wu lun*, in setting the framework for the conduct of particular human relationships. For the purposes of this chapter, we focus our attention on the fact that three of the five cardinal relationships deal with family members, and that, beyond these three, many writers have argued that the Emperor-Minister relationship mirrors that of the Father-Son. The traditional ideology of Chinese society centers around the role of the benevolent patriarch (see Liu & Liu, 2003), cast in the roles of Father, Husband, and Ruler. Four of the five cardinal relationships involve complementary and unequal role relations that in various forms exchange benevolence on the part of the higher powered person in return for loyalty from the lower powered person. None concerns relationships between strangers. In a nutshell, it is possible to argue that a Confucian theory of statecraft is family writ large. Each person is involved in a web of social obligations to particular others, but society as a whole is woven together of many networks made of the same types of role relations. In this way, Confucianism can be considered as a universal ethic for the conduct of particular social relations (see also King & Bond, 1985).

Historical practices of Chinese statecraft and identity

Confucian ethics require high standards for particular and committed social relations, not for civil society in general. It was a highly inter-connected system where the family (or clan) was the basic administrative unit of society at both the local and state levels. But, it is important to recognize that Confucianism was only the *yang*, or the articulated face of Chinese statecraft. In practice, ideals of benevolence and morality were accompanied by the *yin* of a comprehensive, well-articulated, but also draconian legal system (see Chien, 1976; Fitzgerald, 1961 for overviews of Chinese history). Ordinary people feared magistrates and the law, regarding legal institutions more as a system of last resort than a method for ordering daily social life.

The ethics of social relations were embedded within rule-based bureaucratic practices. The Chinese state was more bureaucratically competent than comparable ancient civilizations, such as medieval Europe. Chinese society was rare and distinctive among ancient civilizations in practicing bureaucratic meritocracy, with examinations that allowed ordinary people to become officials of state (thereby increasing the fortunes of their entire clan). The caveat was that only a select few were capable of passing these rigorous examinations, as Chinese writing is pictographic (see Him, this volume), so the time and effort required for literacy was beyond the means of most people in an agrarian society. Nevertheless, meritocracy made Chinese high culture esteemed, and created a cultural psychology where education was cherished as a primary marker of Chinese identity, and a route of upward mobility.

Unlike practices in ancient Rome, where citizenship, as the official marker of Roman identity, was a legal matter of heredity and wealth, there was no formal categorical demarcation between citizens and non-citizens in ancient China. Rather, there were degrees of power and practice between the high culture of the Confucian gentleman and the low culture of the peasant in the fields. The merchant who became rich trading overseas wanted his sons to be educated. It was this high culture of committed social relations and the art of learning and working with an enormously difficult script that we consider to be the driving forces behind the creation of a prototype for Chinese social identity in ancient times.

The parallel collapses of the Roman Empire and Han dynasty provide a fascinating historical thought experiment for testing such a speculative model. Contrary to popular belief, Chinese 'dialects' are technically vernacular languages in the sense that the different 'dialects' are mutually unintelligible: a Northerner speaking Mandarin is as incomprehensible to a Southerner speaking Cantonese as German is to Dutch or French is to Italian. The Qin Emperor (259-201BC) only unified the written script of Chinese for bureaucratic purposes. His subjects spoke dozens of mutually unintelligible vernaculars, and only learned the script if they had upper-class aspirations.

In both cases, a far-flung empire encompassing a wide range of peoples speaking mutually unintelligible tongues collapsed, in the case of Rome to be replaced by dozens of smaller principalities, in the case of China to be reunited after more than 360 years. How was this reunification possible? According to Anderson (1991), it should not be possible; the central tenet of his theory of the emergence of nation-states is reification of vernacular into a marker of national identity and an instrument for bureaucratizing homogeneity within the borders of the state.

One obvious answer is physical geography (Diamond, 1999): China does not have the same natural barriers preventing military unification of its central plains. More than this environmental support, however, there was an 'imagined community' (in Anderson's, 1991, terms) of China as a singular center of civilization that was more capable of regeneration than was Rome. We believe that it was a combination of three basic factors that enabled a sense of Chineseness to endure: first, Confucian philosophy contributed a universal model of particular social relations centered on the benevolent paternalism of the Father figure. The Confucian model of benevolent paternalism allows a seamless and integrated transition between the roles of father, husband, and ruler for dominant males; the basic social unit of the family/clan is ideologically connected to the administrative unit of the nation/state. Second, this Chinese relationalism downplays categorical boundaries and privileges, so that there were no formal definitions, like heredity or citizenship, around being Chinese, but rather a high investment in skill-based practices requiring literacy and moral cultivation. Third, this cultural emphasis enabled the creation of a high culture, and a semi-permeable educated class of intelligentsia whose interests were in governing bureaucratically and perpetuating their high culture rather than ruling militarily. This class of 'mandarins' could work with anyone, including foreigners, and in periods of collapse they could retreat to the administration of smaller units. The combination of these factors allowed the Tang dynasty restoration (618-907AD) to be a political as well as cultural renaissance for China.

Because of its geographical isolation relative to other great civilizations of the ancient world, China had no peers culturally. So, its model of international relations was a center-to-periphery model. Other peoples like Koreans and Japanese borrowed liberally from Chinese culture to establish their own states, but China imported little from its neighbors other than Buddhism from far over the Himalayas. Politically, it did not recognize any other state as an equal.

However, from the very beginning when the Qin Emperor built the Great Wall, China had trouble militarily against Northern horse/herder peoples. Two of the six longest dynasties in Chinese history were ruled by non-Han, herder peoples (Qing and Yuan) from beyond the Great Wall, a third by a Northern people who had settled in China's central plains during the period of disunity after the collapse of the Han dynasty (Tang), and a fourth dynasty (Sung) had to pay continual tribute to its Northern neighbors in order to survive. With its immense population and sophisticated bureaucrats willing and able to serve whoever captured the Mandate of Heaven, Chinese culture had a way of assimilating its rulers. While Manchu people ruled China from 1644-1911, their culture and language virtually disappeared in the process, whereas Chinese culture took advantage of Manchurian military prowess to extend its sovereignty to Mongolia, Xinjiang, and Tibet. Chinese people seemed content to serve a foreign ruling class if they governed well, as did the Manchu, even though in popular literature and history, non-Chinese are often referred to with disdain as barbarians. This apparently gave Chinese people a mission to civilize their rulers, or if this proved impossible, overthrow them as they did to the Mongolian Yuan dynasty.

Painful transitions to modernity

In some ways, the Manchu Qing dynasty was the apex of traditional Chinese society. They had solved the problem of invasion from the North because they were the strongest of the Northerners, able to subjugate even the Mongols. However, they could not manage either the practices or the consciousness associated with Western forms of modernity. Chinese traditions were highly assimilative to the extent that its high culture was considered morally and administratively superior to alternatives. However, the West was not only superior militarily in the nineteenth century, but increasingly came to be perceived as superior administratively (see Pye, 1996, for an account of the Treaty port of Shanghai). According to Chinese traditions, any dynasty that lost the Mandate of Heaven, as the Qing dynasty did when it was defeated in a series of conflicts with foreign powers beginning with the Opium War in 1839, should be overthrown.

But Western support for the fading Qing dynasty prevented its overthrow. Part of the price for this support was foreign concessions carved as Treaty ports into the territory of China. What was different with these new conquerors was not only their science and industry, but their administration, which was markedly superior to that of the last imperial dynasty in its fading moments. By the late nineteenth century, for the first time in history, the Chinese intelligentsia began to consider the possibility that there might be a cultural system equal to or superior to its own. In the Treaty-port concessions, all members of Chinese society, Manchu or Han, nobility or commoners, were considered as inferior by Westerners. Such a categorical system where one group identity transcends all other social positions like class, gender, and profession, was a shock for Chinese, whose traditional model of social relations is more consistent with role theory (Stets & Burke, 2000) than this type of group-based self-categorization.

One of the elements that Chinese intellectuals began to incorporate into their new identity projects was Western forms of nationalism (Levenson, 1959). In ancient times, when martial skills like the spear, sword, horse and bow required a lifetime of training, there was no point in mobilizing the masses. Peasants were useless militarily and their consciousness of identity was rooted to the local and particular social relations of classic Confucianism. This social logic changed with the improved technology of the gun and cannon. With the pull of a trigger, a lifetime of skill and training could be obliterated. The traditional strengths of Chinese culture, where the mass of Chinese people were peasants grounded in particularistic social relations of family/clan, and hierarchically administered by a small number of bureaucratic elites, became a weakness when the agenda was to unite and expel foreign invaders and overthrow the ruling class. So, from the late nineteenth century on, there were persistent if only patchily successful efforts by Chinese intellectuals to create a Chinese nationalism patterned after Western forms of what we have referred to as categorical consciousness, the group consciousness associated with not only self-categorization theory, but Western imperialism and European nationalism.

If we examine Western history, we can find strong parallels between the benevolent paternalism of Confucianism with that of Papal doctrines within the Roman Catholic Church and ideology like the Divine Right of Kings in Europe. European peasants were just as grounded in particularistic social relations and lacking in national consciousness as were Chinese peasants prior to the democratic and industrial revolutions of the late eighteenth century (Anderson, 1991; Smith, 1971). However, what accelerated national consciousness in Europe was the constant warring between neighboring principalities, because after Napoleon, these wars were increasingly waged by conscript armies of ordinary men rather than professional warriors (Tilly, 1975).

Western colonial and imperial adventures reinforced this type of categorical consciousness even more, as any class of white person in Europe could be transformed first by a social role within some imperial project, and then into a White Person categorically superior to any Natives he was destined to encounter, whether they be Chinese, African, Native American, or Arab. Our perspective on social representations of history (Liu & Hilton, 2005; Liu & László, 2007, Liu & Atsumi, 2008) locates the cross-cultural differences between East and West described by Yuki (2003) within an ecological (Berry, 2001) and representational (Moscovici, 1988) framework wherein different types of consciousness are historically contingent on conditions characteristic of different eras. In the late nineteenth and early twentieth centuries where militantly aggressive foreign imperialism threatened not just the ruling class of China, but the very existence of Chinese culture itself, a nationalistic form of categorical consciousness was required for survival (even today, among Hong Kong Chinese stories of war can be used to prime Chinese social identity, see e.g. Hong, Wong, & Liu, 2000). It can be argued that this categorical consciousness of national identity is historically contingent on institutional forms associated with modern states (see Anderson, 1991; Liu & Hilton, 2005).

Many social scientists have argued that contemporary nationalism is a product of the industrial and democratic revolutions in Europe of the eighteenth and nineteenth centuries, mediated by advances in the technology and thinking of this era. Anderson (1991) locates the 'imagined community' of nationhood in bureaucratically advanced techniques like map-making and the use of local vernacular languages in popular publishing; Tilly (1975) complements this assessment with a military perspective such that, 'war made the nation-state and the nation-state made war' (p. 42). Smith (1971) has been at the forefront of Western scholars who argue that the nationalism we know today is a product of the transition from traditional societies where politically inert peasantry is governed by elite ruling classes into a world of nation-states where the primary units of participation are the citizen and the state, the individual and the nation. The relational and networked forms of group consciousness characteristic of traditional China and pre-modern Europe were destined to be swept away by this unstoppable combination of the culture of modernity (e.g. literacy, individual rights) and the technology of modernity (the factory and conscript army).

Narrative psychology for Chinese people

The above narrative (Liu & László, 2007; Liu & Atsumi, 2008) is an account that provides a framework for understanding that is not verifiable according to the empiricist maxims of mainstream psychology. The difficulty with historical accounts is that they are inevitably influenced by present-day politics and present-day epistemologies in ways that can distort historical facts (Wertsch, 2002). Therefore, it is necessary to move beyond historical narrative to examine how traditional Chinese forms of social organization and representations thereof interact with modernity to produce cognitive, motivational, and behavioral impacts on Chinese social identity and intergroup behavior today.

Confucianism is no more a ruling ideology for China than Catholicism is for Europe today. Both continue to exert influences as implicit theories of social organization and interpersonal relationships (Hong & Chiu, 2001), and explicitly as values and beliefs driving the formulation of ideologies and discourses. For a variety of reasons, some political, some epistemological, empirical research on Chinese social identity and intergroup relations is thin, and so we present our literature review as a proactive agenda for the future as well as a review of the existing empirical literature.

Contemporary Chinese social identity and intergroup relations

We organize our review according to three major hypotheses or themes: (1) Culture changes slowly, and so Chinese identity still takes a form whereby it is defined primarily by role-based social relations rather than analytical category boundaries; (2) Under conditions of low threat, traditional Chinese prescriptions for *guanxi* motivate 'benevolent paternalism/benevolent authority' rather than out-group derogation as the default script for dealings with out-group members, a process evidenced by the preferential treatment for ethnic minorities prevalent in China today; (3) Chinese nationalism is a new invention made necessary by external threat, and so under conditions of high threat, we hypothesize that strong forms of rather reactionary nationalism (or 'blind patriotism'), fueled by a narrative of great civilization versus recent historical victimization will be used to defend China and Chinese identity.

1. Chinese identity as role-based social relations

Several major Chinese indigenous psychologists have based their entire theoretical systems around the idea that Chinese society consists fundamentally of role-based social relations (Yang, 1995, 2005; Hwang, 1987, 2005; Ho, 1998), but they have not produced as much empirical evidence for their assertions as one might like. In the area of self-categorization, their thinking fits like hand in glove with the work of American cross-cultural psychologist Nisbett and his students (Nisbett, Peng, Choi, & Norenzayan, 2001), most notably Peng, to converge on the idea that Chinese social identity is by default not categorical but relational, and by nature is primarily judged by degrees of separation rather than absolute and analytical or logical boundaries.

According to the culture-based cognition model of Nisbett et al. (2001), social organization directs attention, and what is attended to influences beliefs and epistemology about the nature of the world and causal relations that structure it. These, together with social organization/practices, in turn direct the development and application of some cognitive processes at the expense of others, including questions of causality and use of dialectical versus analytical reasoning.

We find Nisbett et al's (2001) empirical results more compelling than the broad brush strokes of their 4-5 page summary of 2500 years of history. In a nutshell, 'the authors find East Asians to be *holistic*, attending to the entire field and assigning causality to it, making relatively little use of categories and formal logic, and relying on 'dialectical' reasoning, whereas Westerners are more *analytic*, paying attention primarily to the object and the categories to which it belongs and using rules, including formal logic, to understand its behavior' (p. 291). Most pertinent to the issue of self-categorization and social identity, they cite several studies showing Chinese grouping objects according to relationships (e.g. woman and child together because the woman takes care of the baby), whereas Americans grouped the man and woman together because they belonged to the same category of adults (p. 300). Asians in their review were less likely to use formal rules for constructing categories and making inferences from them. Furthermore, Peng and Nisbett (1997) characterized Chinese thinking as dialectic in style, based on principles of change, contradiction, and holistic relationships (see also Ji, Lam, & Guo, this volume). In a variety of studies, they have showed that Chinese tended towards a 'Middle Way' style of reasoning, whereas Americans relied more on formal logic and analytical, rule-based reasoning.

All of these studies support the idea that Chinese social identity even today may be constructed more around relationships than Western national identities, but cross-cultural empirical evidence is still rare. Bresnahan, Chiu, and Levine (2004) do report that relational self-construal was higher among Taiwanese Chinese than for Americans, whereas independent and collectivist self-construals were higher for Americans.

Aside from this study and previously cited work by Yuki and colleagues, evidence is indirect. One piece of indirect evidence is that as this chapter was drafted in June 2008, a PsycInfo search combining the terms 'minimal group' and 'Chinese' in the abstract did not yield a single reference. The minimal group paradigm (see Brewer, 1979) uses a bogus classification procedure to show that self-categorization in the absence of any relationships or other factors can produce in-group favoritism; it is proof positive of the effects of self-categorization that apparently has not yet been demonstrated among Chinese populations. This is not to say that the minimal group paradigm *will not* work on Chinese[1]: among the 197 studies on the minimal group paradigm located in our literature search, there were 5 published studies using Japanese participants, who according to Nisbett et al. (2001) use similar cognitive processing styles to Chinese. Personal communication from Yamagishi, a leader in minimal group studies in Japan (see Yamagishi, Jin, & Kiyonari, 1999, for example) signaled that it took considerable effort to make the paradigm work, and that the experimenters were forced to *truly* rather than *randomly* assign participants to groups based on their preferences for Klee versus Kandinsky. This necessary amendment to the established procedure suggests less faith in abstract categories among Japanese than Westerners.

There are, however, reasons to doubt whether the label, 'East Asian', should be stretched to fully accommodate the social orientations and thinking styles of both Chinese and Japanese, not to mention Koreans (see e.g. Bond & Cheung, 1983). In a recent study on internet trading in East Asia, Takahashi, Yamagishi, Liu, Wang, Lin, and Yu (2008) found substantial differences among Chinese and Japanese in their willingness to trust and reciprocate trust in an experimental social dilemma. Cultural Chinese, both from mainland China and Taiwan, showed a significantly higher willingness to trust a stranger in a behavioral choice with real monetary consequences than did Japanese.

Noting the widespread success of the Chinese diaspora populations compared to the more stay-at-home orientation of Japanese, Takahashi et al. (2008) speculated that among Japanese, relationships take the form of a limited set of assurances, or relationships guaranteed against exploitation, whereas among Chinese, the art of relationships or *guanxi*, takes a more expansive form where a person is more willing to take the risk of being exploited in order to build up a more potentially rewarding social network. Hwang's (1987) work on face and favor hypothesizes that Chinese have a precise set of rules to govern resource allocation/exchange: close, affective ties are governed by a need rule, mixed ties by a '*renqing*' or human relations rule, and instrumental, or distant relationships are governed by a fairness rule.

Such a set of rules for resource exchange in social relations would be highly adaptive not only for maintaining committed social relationships (what you need I will give you, and what I need you will give me), but also for using a tit-for-tat type of fairness rule to govern the expansion of the social network to accommodate new members, initially by an instrumental fairness rule, and then over time to a *renqinq* or human relations rule. Indeed, Cheung and colleague's work on Chinese personality has demonstrated that beliefs about human relations form a factor of personality that cannot be folded inside the 'Big Five' (Cheung et al., 2003).

This argument suggests that in the future, combining social identity theory with an indigenous Chinese psychology of role relations or *guanxi* could fruitfully energize the as-yet underdeveloped dialogue between the psychological theory of social identity, and identity theory based on a sociology of social roles (see Stets & Burke, 2000). Li, Liu, Huang, and Chang (2007), for example, used examples from Taiwanese history to illustrate how relationships could become the basis for category-based conflict.

2. Chinese intergroup behavior characterized by benevolent authority under conditions of low threat

At the heart of the system of Chinese intergroup relations that we are proposing is a difference not of only in thinking styles, but more importantly in ideals about how society should be organized. According to Liu and Liu (2003, p. 48):

> The model society in traditional East Asia is harmonious: the ruler looks after the people, the people respect the ruler, and at each level such an unequal but reciprocal system of exchange serves to maintain order. The model society in the West is a civil society, where competing interests strive against one another under the rule of law which administers justice in a way as to keep the struggle within boundaries. The virtues of self-cultivation and work are central to the former system, just as the values of freedom and equality are central to the latter.

While this chapter is focused on empirical research, we should not be blind to the socially constructed nature of empirical results: S.H. Liu's (1993) concept of a 'height psychology' emphasizes ideals and aspirations as well as descriptions of fact for Chinese people. In the previous sections, we presented the case that benevolent paternalism was a ruling ideology that governed social relations in ancient China, and in this section, we show evidence for the influence of benevolent authority in present times. The change in terminology is not accidental. A height psychology pays heed to the past with an eye to the future: sexist terminology is not helpful to describe authority relations in the present when increasing numbers of women in Chinese society are assuming roles of power and influence (Halpern & Cheung, 2008).

In reiterating the power of the ideals and practice of benevolent authority in contemporary Chinese societies, we are treading a tightrope between reifying outmoded ideologies of the past and defending traditional values worthy of respect. While our main defense is functional and empiricist, it is worth noting Inglehart and Baker's (2000, p. 49) conclusion to their massive study of value change in 65 societies:

> A history of Protestant or Islamic or Confucian traditions gives rise to cultural zones with distinctive value systems that persist after controlling for the effects of economic development … We doubt that the forces of modernization will produce a homogenized world culture in the foreseeable future.

Cross-cultural research like that of Inglehart and Baker or Hofstede (2001) consistently places Chinese societies with 'high power distance and collectivist' or traditional/security oriented cultures (see also Bond, 1996). Hence, traditional ideals will influence Chinese attitudes and behavior whether we articulate their influence or not. In height psychology, we attempt to describe their influence in a way that can lead to better and more modern forms of human-heartedness in leadership behavior and intergroup relations (see also Chen & Farh, this volume).

The work of Cheng and of Farh has been instrumental in rediscovering a Chinese view on what is described in the literature as 'paternalistic leadership'. Farh and Cheng (2000) describe how the seminal work of Western scholars like Silin (as cited in Farh & Cheng, 2000) not only articulated the attributes typical of contemporary Chinese business leaders, but also presented disapproving judgments of what they described as authoritarian and anti-democratic styles of leadership. Rather than capitulating to Western worldviews, Cheng, Chou, Wu, Huang, & Farh (2004) have defined paternalistic leadership as 'a style that combines strong discipline and authority with fatherly benevolence and moral integrity couched in a personalistic atmosphere' (p. 91). It encompasses three separable but correlated styles of leadership: authoritarian, benevolent, and moral.

In our review of this work, we group the latter two styles together as benevolent authority, and treat the authoritarian style separately, since Cheng et al. (2004) have found that benevolent and moral leadership styles were positively correlated, and both were negatively correlated with authoritarian leadership style (p. 30). Benevolent leadership 'demonstrates individualized, holistic concern for subordinates' personal or familial well-being', whereas moral leadership demonstrates 'superior personal virtues, self-discipline, and unselfishness' (see Cheng et al., 2004, p. 91). Both of these styles align with the original idealism in Confucianism. Benevolence emphasizes reciprocal but unequal obligations in a dyad, and treating subordinates as family members in many respects by understanding and forgiving, and in case of emergency, providing help as needed. This leadership style is expected to foster gratitude and desire for reciprocation from followers. Moral leadership, on the other hand, emanates not primarily from reciprocity or exchange, but is character-based, with such indicators as not abusing authority for personal gain, and putting collective interests ahead of personal interests. According to Farh and Cheng (2000), this style of leadership fosters identification with the leader's values and imitation of the leader by subordinates. It comes closest to Confucian ideals of statecraft, whereby the leader's moral rectitude creates the atmosphere wherein much can be achieved:

> A ruler who governs his state by virtue is like the north polar star, which remains in its place while all the other stars revolve around it.
>
> Confucian Analects (Chapter 2, discourse 1)

Cheng et al. (2004) found that benevolent leadership in Taiwan had the strongest effects on subordinate gratitude and repayment to the leader, as expected. But, it also had the most powerful effects on identification and imitation, which suggests more of a relational than a moral orientation, just as specified by Confucianism. For subordinate compliance, it was moral leadership that had the greatest effect, not authoritarian leadership as might have been expected. These effects were significant even after controlling for Western measures of transformative leadership.

Empirically, the two benevolent forms of authority are negatively correlated with authoritarian leadership that 'asserts absolute authority and control over subordinates and demands unquestioning obedience' (Cheng et al., 2004, p. 91). This style is characterized by top-down communications demanding high performance, reprimanding poor performance, and providing direct guidance and instructions for improvements from subordinates. The leader acts in a dignified manner, exhibiting high self-confidence, tight control of information, and an unwillingness to delegate authority. This leadership style fosters dependence, attentiveness, and compliance from subordinates, and while often effective, inspires fear rather than gratitude from subordinates. It is especially effective when combined with benevolence (Farh & Cheng, 2000; Cheng et al., 2004), as a combination of carrot and stick. It has its historical origins in the politicized form of

Confucianism which became fused with Legalism to become the *yang* and *yin* of top-down ideological control prevalent during two thousand years of Chinese dynastic rule (Liu & Liu, 2003; King, 1996).

While undeniably effective, especially in societies where subordinates tend to internalize top-down requirements from superiors (Farh & Cheng, 2000), from the perspective of height psychology, we would like to probe deeper and encourage research into how to modify traditional authoritarian scripts in ways that make room for the rule of law, that has been so effective in governing contemporary Western societies, and for more effective forms of remonstrance from subordinates to bring new life into Confucian doctrines.

The work of Huang, an indigenous feminist psychologist, is relevant to this second issue. Huang's (1999) model of harmony and conflict centers on dynamics of relationship management. Huang and Huang (2002) used an experimental paradigm to show that Taiwanese mothers preferred to use didactic reasoning over coercion to influence their children to achieve in their academic tasks, but did resort to authority and coercion when their children strayed off-task. The unquestioning, one-way obedience required of Chinese children in tradition has been converted by Taiwanese mothers into more of a didactic, feminine style that cuts across the paternalistic styles of leadership identified by Farh and Cheng (2000).

In organizational behavior, Huang, Jone, and Peng (2007) found that Taiwanese subordinates do not adopt a single conflict resolution style to appeal to their superiors, but most typically use direct encounter/confrontation followed by compromise in dealing with their bosses. Far from avoiding conflict or immediately accommodating their supervisor, only one-third of their sample used such strategies initially. Huang et al. (2007) reported that subordinates with a good relationship to their supervisor typically used a direct encounter or direct encounter followed by compromise to resolve conflict, whereas employees with superficially harmonious relationships tended towards accommodating or conflict-avoidant styles. After being rebuffed by their bosses and retreating into accommodating or avoidant styles, subordinates' relationship with their supervisor often deteriorated into 'superficial harmony'. This is consistent with Cheng et al's (2004) review of the literature and results suggesting that 'some cultural values were preserved, but an authoritarian orientation had faded, as it may be unsuitable to modern trends' (p. 96). Taiwanese Chinese employees will adopt a traditional accommodating or submissive style if they have no recourse, but they will not appreciate their bosses for being forced to do so.

Similar results were found for Yeh and Bedford's (2004) dual filial piety model where reciprocal filial piety, defined as 'emotionally and spiritually attending to one's parents out of gratitude for their efforts in having raised one, and physical and financial care for one's parents as they age' (p. 216), was associated with enhanced intergenerational relationships among young people; authoritarian filial piety, defined as 'suppressing one's own wishes and complying with one's parents ... because of the force of role requirements' (p. 216) was linked to less affection, and more hierarchy-enhancing and submissive attitudes.

The data and theory thus show that for organizational behavior and social identification with small groups and families, benevolent authority in Chinese societies is alive and well, and changing to keep up with modernity (see Yang, 1996). Sociological evidence from Taiwan at the macro-level complements this micro-level evidence. Hu, Chu, Shyu and their colleagues have tracked the evolution of political ideology in Taiwan over more than two decades, covering the entire span of the island's political transition, from the weakening of authoritarianism to the completion of the democratic transition since the 1970s (Chu & Chang 2001; Hu, 1997; Shin & Shyu, 1997). According to these scholars, support for political equality was high from the beginning, and endorsement of popular accountability rose dramatically from 1984 to 1993 (as did belief in political pluralism, even though it remained rather low). Their data also show that by the late 1990s substantial segments of Taiwan's public still manifested fear of disorder and preference for communal harmony over individual freedom. Taiwan has been moving steadily from authoritarianism to democracy, and its political attitudes have been changing with them, melding Western and traditional Chinese ideas of the ideal society (see also Ng, this volume; Huang et al., 2004).

On the mainland, preferential treatment of ethnic minorities in the People's Republic of China (PRC) has been documented by a variety of observers, particularly by Safran (1998) and by Mackerras (2003). In accord with the theory of benevolent authority articulated here, Sautman (1998) writes that, 'preferential policies are a key legitimizing strategy of a regime which is overwhelmingly Han Chinese and claims that Han culture is more 'advanced' than minority groups' (pp. 86-7). Scholars in China Studies are in broad agreement that non-Han peoples are currently beneficiaries of significant forms of preferential treatment. The first and most important is that the 55 state-defined ethnic minorities, who made up about 8.4 per cent of the population of the PRC in 2002 have more exemptions from the one-child policy than are allowed to Han Chinese. This is the most potent indicator of preferential treatment that also extends to other areas, including lower grade requirements for university entrance, and preferences in regional taxation policies.

It is impossible to understate the extent of difference in this area of social policy between China and the West. But the best illustration is to ask readers to imagine a scenario where the United States of America passed into effect a law where African, Latino, and Asian-Americans could have up to four children, whereas Euro-Americans were entitled to have only one child, and be subject to loss of state benefits initially and forced tubal ligation subsequently for violations of this policy.

As in the West, the issue of ethnicity in preferential treatment is conflated with economic issues; ethnic minorities in China have lower incomes and tend to live in less prosperous areas far from the fast-developing coast and away from urban centers. However, policies to redistribute wealth and opportunity in favor of ethnic minorities are accepted as a basic policy platform of the Chinese Communist Party (Sautman, 1998, pp. 87-8), whereas in the West elaborate societal discourses have emerged to position affirmative action policies in favor of ethnic minorities as creating 'fresh injustices' against majority members (Sibley, Liu, & Kirkwood, 2006; van Dijk, 1993). In Western societies, there is equality in principle, and a variety of justificatory mechanisms to explain why there is not equality in fact (Sibley, Liu, Duckitt, & Khan, 2008), but in China 'the ultimate aim is equality-in-fact' (Sautman, 2008, p. 88).

Mackerras (2003, p. 27) notes that real power is being divested from Han Chinese to ethnic minorities, such that ethnic minorities are over-represented on China's highest governmental body (about 15 per cent in 1998), but under-represented in the Communist Party (6.2 per cent, pp. 39–40). While the non-democratic nature of China's institutions may be partly responsible for the relative lack of Han Chinese backlash against such preferential treatment, Sautman (1998) argues that an ideology of benevolent authority is at least partially responsible for this massive civilizational difference in outcomes. Sautman quotes an official statement to the effect that, 'great assistance of the relatively more advanced Han is extremely important in speeding up the development of minorities. Yet the Han have selflessly regarded this kind of assistance as their responsibility' (p. 88). He summarizes China's policy towards its designated minorities as follows (p. 88):

> Jiang Zemin was telling the minorities that they would get preferential policies and treatment if they opted to stay within China, with plenty of economic and other incentives and an improving standard of living. However, the government would not tolerate separatism and would immediately suppress any attempt at succession on the part of any ethnic group.

This may be a controversial solution. For Tibetans in particular, this blend of paternalistic nationalism and didacticism may be difficult to accept (see Bass, 2005), and regarded as concealing assimilative policies. But, it should be appreciated that China is providing opportunities for its ethnic minorities that the West cannot or will not provide, and that discourses of equality in principle in the West may not always better for its disadvantaged minorities than the redistribution of resources to minorities by top-down policies justified by paternalistic discourses, as in contemporary China.

Lee, Noh, Yoo, and Doh (2007) found that for Koreans in China, greater perceived discrimination was associated with reduced ethnic identification, exactly opposite to what has been found in the USA. Their findings are consistent with the idea that it is relational, not categorical acceptance that drives Korean ethnic identification - lower discrimination from the Chinese majority encourages Koreans to express themselves more as an ethnic minority, because they can have a comfortable relationship with Chinese as Koreans without being assimilated within a superordinate category. This is exactly the opposite of American data supporting a rejection-identification model (Branscombe, Schmitt, & Harvey, 1999). In the terminology of Liu and Liu (2003), the model of benevolent authority affords a different set of possibilities in dealing with issues of majority-minority relations in China compared with the West, with far-reaching repercussions that will ultimately impinge on the ethnic makeup of China itself (see Hoddie, 1998, who argues that more Manchu are self-identifying as Manchu because of this preferential treatment).

3. Authoritarianism as the dark side to benevolent authority: categorical and defensive reactions under threat

Mainstream Western research emphasizes the dark side rather than the balance between harmony *and* hierarchy-enhancing orientations towards society that characterizes indigenous Chinese research. As early as 1967, a cross-cultural study by Meade and Whittaker found that authoritarianism measured with the F-scale was higher among Hong Kong Chinese than for Americans and Brazilians, but lower than among Indians and Rhodesians. Using a more contemporary measure of support for group-based inequality, social dominance orientation (SDO), Pratto, Liu, Levin, Sidanius, Shih, & Bachrach (2000) found SDO higher among mainland Chinese than Canadians, Taiwanese, and Israelis. Finally, and most recently, Liu et al. (2008) reported that SDO was highest in Japan, followed by China and Taiwan, with the USA and New Zealand lowest. They further found that right-wing authoritarianism (RWA), a more contemporary measure of the authoritarian personality, was highest in China, Taiwan, and Japan, lower in the USA, and lowest in New Zealand. They also found that SDO and RWA were correlated with nationalistic and anti-human rights positions as regards the cross-straits relationship between China and Taiwan and the Iraq War for both mainland Chinese and for Americans.

In summary, the available evidence (all using non-representative university student populations) suggests that Chinese people are higher on authoritarianism and SDO than Westerners, particularly mainland Chinese in comparison with Americans. Liu et al's (2008) study suggests more tentatively that these orientations towards authoritarianism and SDO predict prejudicial attitudes in international relations. It should be noted that these findings are derived from Western measures that focus on the dark side of hierarchy and inequality and do not balance or see co-existence between their light and dark sides.

From a mainland Chinese perspective, Taiwanese independence is certainly viewed as a threat (Liu et al., 2008). However, in the absence of the threat of independence, mainland Chinese showed in-group favoritism only with Japanese and not Taiwanese as out-group members in an experimental social dilemma involving real money during internet trading (Takahashi et al., 2008). Historically, Taiwan is viewed as part of China. The alienation of Taiwan is seen as a vivid reminder of the terrible period from 1840 to 1949 where many foreign powers were bent on dismembering China, and Japan succeeded in taking Taiwan (Huang et al., 2004), and much else besides. Takahashi et al's (2008) experiment demonstrated that Taiwanese are to a significant extent not viewed as outgroup members by mainland Chinese, whereas by contrast Japanese are viewed as prototypical outgroup members.

Other striking results by Takahashi et al. (2008) were that while mainland Chinese showed ingroup favoritism in both trust and trustworthiness in interacting with Japanese over the internet, Japanese university students did not display any ingroup favoritism in interacting with Chinese, even though they carried negative stereotypes of mainland Chinese into the experiment and had low expectations of cooperative behavior from their opposite numbers. This may be a legacy of the great wars of the twentieth century, where young Japanese are aware that their ancestors perpetrated something horrific to Chinese, but, given restrictive Japanese policy about curriculum content, are unclear about details. In consequence, they feel they cannot afford to be acting in a discriminatory way against Chinese, whereas Chinese believe that the Japanese have never apologized for their conduct during the wars, and are therefore unrepentant and dangerous, even in situations not involving overt threat. In fact, Japanese officials have apologized (albeit in an understated manner many times. Liu and Atsumi (2008) argue that national identities are constructed out of the raw materials of the past in response to current political needs, and that for China after Mao, a national narrative involving past victimhood became salient just as economic liberalization began.

Within mainland China, there is a paucity of psychological research on intergroup relations and national identity. Fong's (2004) anthropological fieldwork on 'filial nationalism' among teenagers in Dalian provides a good qualitative basis for future research on contemporary national identity in China, however. She argues that teenagers in an urban setting idolize wealthy Western countries, and see China as backwards by comparison. They dream of going overseas, but at the same time, regard it as their filial obligation to return home to help with modernization. While often openly critical of China themselves, particularly the use of *guanxi* to get ahead, these teenagers defended China fiercely as soon as the overseas-born author tried to chime in with criticism of her own.

Fong's (2004) work is more illustrative than definitive; the closest she comes to a definition of filial nationalism is with a quote from one of her participants: 'I love China because China is my motherland, not because I think China is better than other countries. China is poorer and more backward than other countries, but my parents are also poorer and more backward than many other people's parents. I can't renounce my motherland any more than I can renounce my parents.' (p. 641). Many forms of nationalism have been proposed by theorists to understand China (see Unger, 1996), but Fong's (2004) formulation is refreshing both in its simplicity, and its rejection of official self-aggrandizing narratives that appear abstract and hollow to ordinary people. Filial nationalism returns to the starting point of this chapter, viz. that Chinese national identity is family writ large rather than a system of categorical beliefs.

However, survey data from Hong Kong and Taiwan have in recent years provided ample evidence that people of Chinese cultural origins are perfectly capable of behaving according to the tenets of social identity and self-categorization theory, even if this is not the default position. About at the time of Hong Kong's return to the sovereignty of mainland China in 1997, Lam, Lau, Chiu, Hong, and Peng (1999) found that categorical identification among adolescents as a 'Hong Konger only', 'Hong Kong-Chinese', 'Chinese-Hong Konger' and 'Chinese only' was systematically related to attitudes of pride, trust, and cultural superiority for mainland China and Hong Kong. These attitudes in turn were associated with valuing modernity and Chinese tradition. Adolescents who identified as Hong Kongers trusted Hong Kongers more, took greater pride in being a Hong Konger, and believed in the superiority of Hong Kong and Western culture and people over Chinese culture and people compared to those who identified themselves as Chinese. Self-identified Chinese had the opposite pattern of results, and the two hybrid groups occupied intermediate attitudinal positions.

These results mirrored those of Huang (2007) in Taiwan, who found that those who identified as Taiwanese only were more against reunification with China, saw Taiwanese culture as small but beautiful, and held stronger attitudes towards self-autonomy and were more against social dominance and authoritarian conservatism than those who identified as Chinese-Taiwanese, with Taiwanese-Chinese in the middle. The two societies appear headed in opposite directions over time, however. In Hong Kong, the percentage of people taking an intermediate, hybridized position of Hong Kong Chinese or Chinese-Hong Konger in representative samples increased from 47 per cent in 1996 to 53 per cent 1999, and anxiety over Chinese military and paramilitary forces decreased (Fung, 2004). This shows a general reduction in anxiety over reunification with China, and a greater acceptance of mainland Chinese rule over time. In Taiwan, Huang et al. (2004) reported, in a non-representative but large sample, 91 per cent identifying with hybrid positions compared to 70 per cent in Huang (2007); identifying as 'Taiwanese only' increased from 7 per cent to 26 per cent, whereas identifying as 'Chinese only' dropped almost to zero.

These longitudinal results show the impact of threat on self-categorization and identification processes: in Hong Kong fear of authoritarian crackdowns has decreased after 10 years of relatively uneventful and reasonable governance by mainland China, whereas in Taiwan, the fear of threat from China has increased over the same time period, with Taiwanese attitudes edging towards independence (see Li, 2003), at least prior to the results of the 2008 election.

Conclusions

The work of Hong, Chiu and colleagues on a frame-switching theory for bicultural selves has shown potential to integrate some of the tensions between modernity and tradition for Chinese people. Hong, Morris, Chiu, & Benet-Martinez (2000) primed bilingual Hong Konger's social identities as either Chinese or Westerners using iconic cultural images like Confucius and the Great Wall for China versus Superman and the American flag for Western cultures. Respondents were found to use more situational attributions when their Chinese identity was made salient versus more dispositional attributions when a Western identity was made salient. The holistic, situational style of attribution is regarded as symptomatic of the East-Asian style thinking, and the dispositional style is typical of Westerners (Nisbett et al., 2001). Lu and Yang (2006) have further hypothesized that this type of frame switching may be a means for Chinese people to manage the impact of modernity more generally. The basic idea is that Chinese people maintain a Chinese cultural identity in some situations, effortlessly and implicitly bringing to mind culture-appropriate scripts for thought and action according to situation, but shift to Western implicit theories (like dispositional inferences) in other situations.

The empirical work of Hong et al. (2000) shows that Chinese (albeit predominantly bilinguals) are perfectly capable of maintaining segmented, categorical forms of identity when the social and historical conditions make such an identity adaptive. Hong Kong was ruled for more than 150 years as an outpost of the British Empire, where administrative power and social status was in the hands of British expatriates, who ruled the society from top-down, but did not interfere with local people's private lives. Under such circumstances, a compartmentalized form of identity, facilitated by code-switching between Cantonese and English, was highly adaptive (see e.g. Yang & Bond, 1980).

Over the larger flows of history, power and agency have been located in the West for the last 200 years (see Liu et al., 2005), so that again historical conditions favor non-Western people acquiring the skill to function by frame-switching in Western-dominated environments; Lu and Yang (2006) raise the question as to whether such frame-switching may apply to Chinese people more generally as they encounter the power and apparatus of Western forms of modernity. Supporting this proposition, recent work by Chen and Bond (2007) confirmed that not only HK Chinese, but bilingual Mainlanders as well engaged in frame-switching when primed by linguistic cues. The vision of culture provided by Hong et al. (2001) basically hypothesizes that people have a cultural navigation system inside their heads that allows that allows them to act according to different implicit theories or cultural norms depending on situational cues.

What about the larger issue of the ethical values and normative beliefs that govern a society? Surely social identity as a Chinese or Westerner must be more than an implicit theory for attributing causality to the situation versus to individuals! Following an historical contingency model, Liu and Liu (2003) drew a conceptual map of Chinese society being governed by a model of social relations centered around the figure of the benevolent authority, whereas in the Western model, society is governed by an impartial code of law grounded in historical precedent to which all are subordinate.

If this is correct, then we should be able to find evidence for an implicit theory of power relations through the cultural frame switching paradigm. When Chinese identity is primed or made salient, the moral character and benevolence particularly of leaders should be the primary criterion on which they are judged, both in terms of group prototypicality and overall evaluation; it may also shape the behaviour of leaders to become more sensitive to issues of face (Choi, Kim, & Kim, 1997; Hwang, 2005). When Western identity is primed, the law-abidingness and competence of leaders should become more central criteria for evaluation. These hypotheses have not yet been tested empirically, but techniques now exist for social scientists to more fully articulate a theory of benevolent authority, which we claim is central to the operation of most high-power distance societies like China, compared to a theory of equality under the law, which we claim is central to the operation of highly individualistic, low-power distance societies.

Besides cultural frame-switching, there is also the issue of cultural fusion (see Chen, Benet-Martinez, & Bond, 2008 for an overview of a bicultural integration model applied to Hong Kong populations). China has shaken the world with Deng Xiaoping's formulation of 'socialism with Chinese characteristics'. While some critics have translated this as 'socialism with capitalist characteristics', we do not agree with this simplification. Rather than adopt free-market capitalism, China has adopted a form of capitalism that is controlled top-down to a considerable extent, through the authority of the Chinese Communist party. It has not adopted the 'plurality of powers' model (Liu & Liu, 2003) where various moneyed interests jockey for political power through democratic processes. Rather, the Communist Party portrays itself as a benevolent authority that provides the only means for governing the nation and protecting the people from outside threat (Liu & Atsumi, 2008). A similar path has been taken in Singapore, where the political party of Lee Kuan-Yew and his son Lee Hsien-Loong, the People's Action Party, has maintained power for more than 40 years, albeit using legalistic democratic procedures rather than classic authoritarianism. Taiwan also followed this path for 50 years under the Kuo Ming Tang, but in the last decade and a half has shifted to a Western-style democracy including ferocious contests between political parties that alternate leadership (Huang et al., 2004; Huang, 2007).

Given the varying cases of China, Singapore, and Taiwan, the issue that remains unanswered is the continuing viability of 'benevolent authority' as a form of governance. Liberal theorists such as Fukuyama (1992) claim that the Western liberal state constitutes the 'end of history', towards which all nations will eventually evolve. Countering this claim, the recent experience of China, Russia, and Iraq suggests instead that there may be historical contingencies that alter the benefits of adopting liberal (and capitalist) democracy. The early developing Western nations reaped the benefits of not only escaping the tyrannical rule of kings, but simultaneously using power gained from the industrial revolution to colonize the rest of the world, thus lifting social standards for their own non-elites. By contrast, the four most salient and successful instances of development following the first wave of industrialization and democratization in the West were all by authoritarian rather than liberal democratic regimes (viz. Prussian Germany, Meiji Japan, and the Communist Soviet Union, and China). According to historians like Meisner (1996), this is in part because the authoritarian regimes insulate or protect local populations and national interests from the alternative interests of global capital and Western elites. For the developing world, democracy imposed or propped up from the outside has often had disastrous consequences. Most recently, in the case of reactions to the Iraq War, a global survey of young adults found that 4 of the 6 societies that regarded both George Bush Jr. and Adolf Hitler among the 10 most important figures in world history preferred Hitler to Bush in their ratings (Liu et al., in press). Quite clearly, 'the leader of the free world' was not regarded as very benevolent, and the seeds of democracy have not sown much joy for Iraqi people.

Given the phenomena of cultural frame switching and cultural fusion, there is no reason why Chinese societies cannot adapt their hard-won cultural scripts of benevolent authority to provide alternative means of constraining power-holders that add to the repertoires of governance developed through Western forms of individualism. The cultivation of benevolence is at the heart of the height psychology proposed by Liu (1993). Contemporary neo-Confucians see their model as both a description and an ideal, and acknowledge the need to calibrate this model according to contemporary theories of rule by law. Using elements of 'facework', like appealing to human heartedness and using public opinion to instill a sense of shame for bad behavior are traditional means for Chinese people to inculcate and cultivate desirable behavior among not only common people, but also among political elites.

This art of cultivating leaders as benevolent authorities is taking on new life with the empirical work of indigenous Chinese psychologists working in the areas of paternalistic leadership, harmony and conflict, and filial piety. We have high hopes that this work will inspire Chinese leaders to show more human heartedness towards their followers, and for Chinese culture to contribute new models of moral guidance and political stewardship to a world culture in dire need of new paths forward.

Chapter note

1 However, the second author has tried several times to run minimal group studies among Taiwanese Chinese without success.

References

Anderson, B. (1991). *Imagined communities: Reflections on the origin and spread of nationalism.* London: Verso.
Bass, C. (2005). Learning to love the motherland: Educating Tibetans in China. *Journal of Moral Education, 34*, 433–449.
Berry, J. W. (2001). Contextual studies of cognitive adaptation. In J.M. Collis & S. Messick (eds), *Intelligence and personality: Bridging the gap in theory and measurement.* (pp. 319–333). Mahwah, NJ: Lawrence Erlbaum Associates.
Bond, M. H. (1996). Chinese values. In M. H. Bond (ed.), *The handbook of Chinese psychology* (pp. 208–226). Hong Kong: Oxford University Press.
Bond, M. H. & Cheung, T. S. (1983). The spontaneous self-concept of college students in Hong Kong, Japan, and the United States. *Journal of Cross-Cultural Psychology, 14*, 153–171.
Branscombe, N., Schmitt, M. T., & Harvey, R. D. (1999). Perceiving pervasive discrimination among African Americans: Implications for group identification and well-being. *Journal of Personality and Social Psychology, 77*, 135–149.
Bresnahan, M. J., Chiu, H. C., & Levine, T. R. (2004). Self-construal as a predictor of communal and exchange orientation in Taiwan and the USA. *Journal of Social Psychology, 7*, 187–202.
Brewer, M. B. (1979). In-group bias in the minimal intergroup situation: A cognitive-motivational analysis. *Psychological Bulletin, 86*, 307–324.
Brewer, M.B. & Chen, Y.R. (2007). Where (who) are collectives in collectivism? Toward conceptual clarification of individualism and collectivism. *Psychological Review, 114*, 133–151.
Brewer, M. B. & Gardner, W. (1996). Who is this 'we'? Levels of collective identity and self representations. *Journal of Personality and Social Psychology, 71*, 83–93.
Chen, S. X., Benet-Martinez, V., & Bond, M. H. (2008). Bicultural identity, bilingualism and psychological adjustment in multicultural societies: Immigration-based and globalization-based acculturation. *Journal of Personality, 76*, 803–838.
Chen, S. X. & Bond, M. H. (2007). Explaining language priming effects: Further evidence of ethnic affirmation among Chinese-English bilinguals. *Journal of Language and Social Psychology, 26*, 398–406.
Cheng, B. S, Chou, L. F., Wu, T. Y, Huang, M. P., & Farh, J. L. (2004). Paternalistic leadership and subordinate responses: Establishing a leadership model in Chinese organizations. *Asian Journal of Social Psychology, 7*, 89–117.
Cheung, F. M., Cheung, S. F., Leung, K., Ward, C., & Leong, F. (2003). The English version of the Chinese Personality Assessment Inventory. *Journal of Cross-Cultural Psychology, 34*, 433–452.
Chien, M. (1976). *The spirit of Chinese history.* Taipei, Taiwan: Tung-tu Picture Books (Eastern Ground). (in Chinese)
Choi, S. C., Kim, U., & Kim, D. I. (1997). Multifaceted analysis of *chemyon* ('social face'): An indigenous Korean perspective. In K. Leung. U. Kim, S. Yamaguchi, & Y. Kashima (eds), *Progress in Asian social psychology (Vol. 1)*, pp 3–22. New York: Wiley.
Chu, Y. H. & Chang, Y. T. (2001). Culture shift and regime legitimacy: Comparing Mainland China, Taiwan and Hong Kong.' In Shiping Hua (ed.), *Chinese political culture* (pp. 320–347). New York: M. E. Sharpe.
Diamond, J. (1999). *Guns, germs, and steel: The fates of human societies.* New York: Norton.
Farh, J. L. & Cheng, B. S. (2000). A cultural analysis of paternalistic leadership in Chinese organizations. In J. T. Li, A. S. Tsui, & E. Weldon (eds), *Management and organizations in the Chinese context* (pp. 84–130). London: Macmillan.
Fitzgerald, C. P. (1961). *China: A short cultural history* (3rd edn). New York: Praeger.
Fong, V. (2004). Filial nationalism among Chinese teenagers with global identities. *American Ethnologist, 4*, 631–648.
Fung, A. (2004). Postcolonial Hong Kong: Hybridising the local and the national. *Social Identities, 10*, 399–414.
Fukuyama, F. (1992). *The end of history and the last man.* New York: Avon Books.
Halpern, D. & Cheung, F. M. (2008). *Women at the top: Powerful leaders tell us how to combine work and family.* New York: John Wiley & Sons
Ho, D. Y. F. (1998). Interpersonal relationships and relationship dominance: An analysis based on methodological relationalism. *Asian Journal of Social Psychology, 1*, 1–16.
Hoddie, M. (1998). Ethnic identity change in the People's Republic of China: An explanation using data from the 1982 and 1990 census enumerations. In W. Safran (ed.), *Nationalism and ethnoregional identities in China,* (pp. 119–141). London: Frank Cass.
Hofstede, G. (1980/2001). *Culture's consequences.* First and Second Editions. Thousand Oaks, CA: Sage.
Hong, Y. Y., Morris, M. W., Chiu, C. Y., & Benet-Martinez, V. (2000). Multicultural minds: A dynamic constructivist approach to culture and cognition. *American Psychologist, 55*, 709–720.
Hong, Y. Y., Wong, R., Liu, J. H. (2001). History of war enhances ethnic identification. *Journal of Psychology in Chinese Societies, 2*, 77–106.
Hu, S. (1997). Confucianism and Western democracy. *Journal of Contemporary China, 6*, 347–63.
Huang, L. L. (2007). M shape versus Bell shape: The ideology of national identity and its antecedent psychological factors in Taiwan. *Chinese Journal of Psychology, 49*, 451–470. (in Chinese)

Huang, L. L. (1999). *Interpersonal harmony and conflict: Indigenous Chinese theory and research.* Taipei, Taiwan: Tu Kui Publishing House. (in Chinese)
Huang, L. L. & Huang, H. L. (2002). Prototypes of mother–child conflict in Chinese society: An indigenous dynamic approach to parenting. *Journal of Psychology in Chinese Societies, 3,* 15–36.
Huang, L. L., Jone, K. Y., & Peng, T. K. (2007). Conflict resolution patterns and relational context: An exploratory study combining etic and emic theories in Taiwan. In J. H. Liu, C. Ward, A. Bernardo, M. Karasawa, & R. Fischer (eds)(in press). *Progress in Asian social psychology: Casting the individual in societal and cultural contexts,* Vol. 6, (pp. 61–82). Seoul, South Korea: Kyoyook Kwahaksa.
Huang, L. L., Liu, J. H., & Chang, M. (2004). The 'Double Identity' of Taiwanese Chinese: A dilemma of politics and culture rooted in history. *Asian Journal of Social Psychology, 7,* 149–189.
Hwang, K. K. (2005). The theoretical structure of Chinese social relations (*guanxi*). In K. S. Yang, K. K. Hwang, & C. F. Yang (eds), *Chinese indigenized psychology* (pp. 215–248). Hong Kong: Yuan Liu University Press. (in Chinese)
Hwang, K. K. (1987). Face and favor: The Chinese power game. *American Journal of Sociology, 92,* 944–974.
Inglehart, R. & Baker, W. E. (2000). Modernization, culture change, and the persistence of traditional values. *American Sociological Review, 65,* 19–51.
Kashima, E. S. & Hardie, E. A. (2000). The development and validation of the Relational, Individual, and Collective self-aspects (RIC) scale. *Asian Journal of Social Psychology, 3,* 19–48.
Kashima, Y. (2005). Is culture a problem for social psychology? *Asian Journal of Social Psychology, 8,* 19–38.
King, A. Y. C. (1996). State Confucianism and its transformation: The restructuring of the state–society relation in Taiwan. In W. M. Tu (ed.), *Confucian traditions in East Asian modernity* (pp. 228–243). Cambridge, MA: Harvard University Press.
King, A. Y. C. & Bond, M. H. (1985). The Confucian paradigm of man. In W. S. Tseng & D. Y. H. Wu (eds), *Chinese culture and mental health: An overview* (pp. 29–45). Orlando, FL: Academic Press.
Lam, S. F., Lau, I. Y., Chiu, C. Y., Hong, Y. Y., Peng, S. Q. (1999). Differential emphasis on modernity and Confucian values in social categorization: The case of Hong Kong adolescents in political transition. *International Journal of Intercultural Relations, 2,* 237–256.
Lee, R. M., Noh, C. Y., Yoo, H. C., & Doh, H. S. (2007). The psychology of diaspora experiences: Intergroup contact, perceived discrimination, and the ethnic identity of Koreans in China, *Cultural Diversity and Ethnic Minority Psychology, 13,* 115–124.
Levenson, J. R. (1959). *Liang Ch'i-chao and the mind of modern China, 2nd edn.* Berkeley, CA: University of California Press.
Li, M. C. (2003). The basis of ethnic identification in Taiwan. *Asian Journal of Social Psychology, 6,* 229–237.
Li, M. C., Liu, J. H., Huang, L. L., & Chang, M. L. (2007). Categorization cues and the differentiation of ingroup–outgroup in Taiwan from past to present. In A. Bernardo, M. C. Gastardo-Conaco, & M. E. C. D. Liwag (eds) *Progress in Asian social psychology: The self, relationships, and subjective well-being in Asia,* Vol. 5 (pp 39–60). Seoul, South Korea: Kyoyook Kwahaksa.
Liu, J. H. & Atsumi, T. (2008). Historical conflict and resolution between Japan and China: Developing and applying a narrative theory of history and identity. In T. Sugiman, K. J. Gergen, W. Wagner, & Y. Yamada (eds), *Meaning in action: Constructions, narratives, and representations* (pp 327–344). Tokyo, Japan: Springer-Verlag.
Liu, J. H., Hanke, K., Huang, L. L., Fischer, R., Adams, G., Wang, F. X., Atsumi, T., & Lonner, W. J. (2008). *The relativity of international justice concerns: Attitudes towards the Iraq War and the Cross Straits relationship between China and Taiwan in 5 societies.* Manuscript submitted for review.
Liu, J. H. & Hilton, D. (2005). How the past weighs on the present: Social representations of history and their role in identity politics. *British Journal of Social Psychology, 44,* 537–556.
Liu, J. H. & László, J. (2007). A narrative theory of history and identity: Social identity, social representations, society and the individual. In G. Moloney & I. Walker (eds), *Social representations and identity: Content, process and power,* p 85–107. London, England: Palgrave Macmillan.
Liu, J. H. & Liu, S. H. (2003). The role of the social psychologist in the 'Benevolent Authority' and 'Plurality of Powers' systems of historical affordance for authority. In K. S. Yang, K. K. Hwang, P. B. Pedersen, & I. Daibo (eds) *Progress in Asian social psychology: Conceptual and empirical contributions.* Vol. 3 (pp. 43–66). Westport, CT: Praeger.
Liu, S. H. (1993). The psychotherapeutic function of the Confucian discipline of *Hsin* (mind–heart). In L. Y. Cheng, F. Cheung, & C. N. Chen (eds), *Psychotherapy for the Chinese* (pp. 1–17). Hong Kong: Department of Psychiatry, Chinese University of Hong Kong.
Lu, L. & Yang, K. S. (2006). Emergence and composition of the traditional–modern bicultural self of people in contemporary Taiwanese societies. *Asian Journal of Social Psychology, 9,* 167–175.
Mackerras, C. (2003). *China's ethnic minorities and globalization.* New York: Routlege Curzon.
Markus, H. & Kitayama, S. (1991). Culture and self: Implications for cognition, emotion and motivation. *Psychological Review, 98,* 224–253.
Meade, R. D. & Wittaker, J. O. (1967). A cross-cultural study of authoritarianism. *Journal of Social Psychology, 72,* 3–7.
Meisner, M. J. (1996). *The Deng Xiaoping era: An inquiry into the fate of Chinese socialism, 1978–1994.* New York: Hill and Wang.

Moscovici, S. (1988). Notes towards a description of social representations. *European Journal of Social Psychology, 18*, 211–250.

Nisbett, R. E., Peng, K., Choi, I., & Norenzayan, A. (2001). Culture and systems of thought: Holistic versus analytic cognition. *Psychological Review, 108*, 291–310.

Oyserman, D., Coon, H. M., & Kemmelmeier, M. (2002). Rethinking individualism and collectivism: Evaluation of theoretical assumptions and meta-analyses. *Psychological Bulletin, 128*, 3–72.

Peng, K. & Nisbett, R. E. (1999). Culture, dialectics, and reasoning about contradiction. *American Psychologist, 54*, 741–754.

Pratto, F, Liu, J. H., Levin, S., Sidanius, J., Shih, M., Bachrach, H. (2000). Social dominance orientation and the legitimization of inequality across cultures. *Journal of Cross-Cultural Psychology, 31*, 369–409.

Pye, L. (1996). How China's nationalism was Shanghaied. In J. Unger (ed.), *Chinese nationalism* (pp. 86–112). New York: East Gate.

Safran, W. (1998) (ed.). *Nationalism and ethnoregional identities in China.* London: Frank Cass.

Sarbin, T. R. & Allen, V. L. (1968). Role theory. In G. Lindzey & E. Aronson (eds), *Handbook of social psychology*, 2nd edn, (Vol. 1, pp. 488–567). Reading, MA: Addison-Wesley.

Sautman, B. (1998). Preferential policies for ethnic minorities in China: The case of Xinjiang. In W. Safran (ed.), *Nationalism and ethnoregional identities in China* (pp. 86–118). Frank Cass: London.

Shimmack, U., Oishi, S., & Diener, E. (2005). Individualism: A valid and important dimension of cultural differences between nations. *Personality and Social Psychology Review, 9*, 17–31.

Sibley, C. S., Liu, J. H., Duckitt, J., & Khan, S. S. (2008). Social representations of history and the legitimation of social inequality: The form and function of historical negation. *European Journal of Psychology, 38*, 542–565.

Sibley, C. G., Liu, J. H., & Kirkwood, S. (2006). Toward a social representations theory of attitude change: The effect of message framing on general and specific attitudes toward equality and entitlement. *New Zealand Journal of Psychology, 35*, 3–13.

Shin, D. C. & Shyu, H. (1997). Political ambivalence in South Korea and Taiwan. *Journal of Democracy*, 8, 109–124.

Stets, J. E. & Burke, P. J. (2000). Identity theory and social identity theory, *Social Psychology Quarterly, 63*, 224–237.

Smith, A. D. (1971). *Theories of nationalism.* New York: Harper & Row.

Tajfel, H. & Turner, J. C. (1979). The social identity theory of intergroup behaviour. In S. Worchel & W. Austin (eds) *Psychology of intergroup relations* (pp. 33–48). Chicago, IL: Nelson-Hall.

Turner, J. C., Hogg, M. A., Oakes, P. J., Reicher, S. D., & Wetherell, M. S. (1987). *Rediscovering the social group: A self-categorization theory.* New York: Basil Blackwell.

Takahashi, C., Yamagishi, T., Liu, J. H., Wang, F. X., Lin, Y. C., & Yu, S. H., (2008). The intercultural trust paradigm: Studying joint cultural interaction and social exchange in real time over the internet. *International Journal of Intercultural Relations, 32*, 215–228.

Tilly, C. (1975). *The formation of national states in Western Europe.* Princeton, NJ: Princeton University Press.

Unger, J. (1996). *Chinese nationalism.* New York: East Gate.

Van Dijk, T. (1993). *Elite discourses and racism.* London: Sage.

Wertsch, J. (2002). *Voices of collective remembering.* Cambridge, England: Cambridge University Press.

Yamagishi, T., Jin, N., & Kiyonari, T. (1999). Bounded generalized reciprocity: Ingroup boasting and ingroup favoritism. *Advances in Group Processes, 16*, 161–197.

Yang, K. S. (2005). Theoretical analysis of Chinese social orientation. In K. S. Yang, K. K. Hwang, & C. F. Yang (eds), *Chinese indigenized psychology* (pp. 173–214). Yuan Liu University Press: Hong Kong. (in Chinese)

Yang, K. S. (1995). Chinese social orientation: An integrative analysis. In T. Y. Lin, W. S. Tseng, & E. K. Yeh (eds), *Chinese societies and mental health* (pp. 19–39), Hong Kong: Oxford University Press.

Yang, K. S. (1996). The psychological transformation of the Chinese people as a result of societal modernization. In M. H. Bond (ed.), *The handbook of Chinese psychology* (pp. 479–498). Hong Kong: Oxford University Press.

Yang, K. S. & Bond, M. H. (1980). Ethnic affirmation by Chinese bilinguals. *Journal of Cross-Cultural Psychology, 11*, 411–425.

Yeh, K. H. & Bedford, O. (2003). A test of the dual filial piety model. *Asian Journal of Social Psychology, 6*, 215–228.

Yuki, M. (2003). Intergroup comparison versus intragroup comparison: A cross-cultural examination of social identity theory in North American and East Asian cultural contexts. *Social Psychology Quarterly, 66*, 166–183.

Yuki, M., Maddux, W. W., Brewer, M. B., & Takemura, K. (2005). Cross-cultural differences in relationship- and group-based trust. *Personality and Social Psychology Bulletin, 31*, 48–62.

CHAPTER 35

Developments in understanding Chinese leadership: paternalism and its elaborations, moderations, and alternatives

Chao C. Chen and Jiing-Lih Farh

China has been steadily integrating into the world economy, exerting as well as receiving influence over these last few decades. There have been abundant writings on leadership, government, and management in Chinese social, philosophical and political classics. Chinese leadership theory and empirical research has taken leaps and bounds over this same time period. Indeed there has been dramatic increase of the volume of Chinese leadership research in only the decade or so, some of which was published in premier international journals of organization and management.

A review of Chinese leadership research by Smith and Wang (1996) only a dozen years ago defined leadership broadly to include studies of organizational structure, general management beliefs and values, and challenges for China-foreign joint ventures. Furthermore the body of research reviewed in Smith and Wang seemed to be dominated by descriptive and comparative studies documenting organizational and managerial practices of Chinese managers, how they differed from Western managers in and out of China, and the challenges that Chinese managers face as they experience market-oriented economic reform and business globalization. While these studies made important contributions to the understanding of Chinese leadership, Smith and Wang (1996) pointed out conceptual and methodological limitations of the literature and called for indigenous theorization of the Chinese leadership. What was also apparent was the need for the field to generate research that systematically builds and tests theoretical models of leadership antecedents, processes, and outcomes. It appears that the field of Chinese leadership research in the following decade has made long strides in exactly this direction.

Leadership in Chinese organizations is a complex phenomenon, which includes both culturally universal (etic) and culturally specific (emic) aspects. The etic aspects may be attributed to the modern forces that bombard Chinese societies and shape Chinese organizations on a daily basis. These modern forces include market economy, global competition, the technological revolution, and individualistic ideologies (such as the press for universal human rights). However, with its 5000 years plus unbroken history, China is also deeply rooted in rich and unique cultural traditions. Major elements of this tradition include core ideologies (Confucianism, Daoism, Buddhism, Legalism – see e.g. C. C. Chen & Lee, 2008a; Li, Lam, & Guo, this volume), relational rules (*guanxi*, *renqing*, face, and respect for authority – see e.g. Hwang & Han, this volume), and social institutions (familism – see e.g. Chan, this volume), and ideographic language (see e.g. McBride. Lin, Fong, & Shu, this volume). Moreover, the last 60 years of communist rule has also left deep marks on the Chinese psyche with its inculcation of socialistic values and institutional practices (i.e. Maoism, central planning, and state-owned enterprises – see e.g. Kulich, this volume).

The complexity and changeability of the Chinese context dictates that leadership in Chinese organizations is a difficult phenomenon to grapple, one that could be understood only through both etic and emic approaches. On one hand, there are many studies that have borrowed and tested Western leadership concepts and theories in the Chinese setting and found considerable support. For example, using ISI Web of Science, an electronic search of journal articles published from January 1990 to August 2008, results in 187 leadership-related entries that involve the Chinese context. After deleting irrelevant articles, such as those about product and cost leadership in the marketing literature, we identified 66 articles on Chinese leadership. A content analysis of these articles reveals that they cover a wide range of topics with the majority (about three fourths) examining the generalizability of Western leadership theories to the Chinese context, e.g. transformational/charismatic leadership, delegation and empowerment, supportive leadership, leader-member exchange, and interactional justice.

On the other hand, we also see leadership research that focused on the emic aspects of Chinese leadership and constructed leadership concepts and models based on uniquely Chinese social and cultural traditions. Some of these studies have appeared in English journals (e.g. Cheng, Chou, Wu, Huang, & Farh, 2004); many others in edited volumes (e.g. C. C. Chen & Lee, 2008a; Li, Tsui, & Weldon, 2000; Tsui, Bian, & Cheng, 2006) and Chinese-language journals (e.g. Cheng, Chou, & Farh, 2000; Cheng, Chou, Huang, Farh, & Peng, 2003).

In this chapter we seek to take stock of the developments and progress in Chinese leadership theory and research. We approach this review from both etic and emic perspectives. A body of scientific literature can be reviewed with regards to its empirical or theoretical contributions. While an empirical contribution is concerned primarily with how a theory is supported by data, a theoretical contribution is primarily concerned with how it relates to other relevant theories. We start with some indigenous Chinese thoughts on leadership and analyze how these foundational thoughts get elaborated into theoretical models of leadership and how these models fare from the perspectives of other Chinese and Western leadership theories that have been employed to study Chinese leadership phenomena.

We borrowed from Wagner and Berger (1985) who identified a variety of ways in which a theory or a set of theories can grow. Here we adopted three of these ways, namely elaboration, competition, and integration (see also C. C. Chen & Zhang, 2008). Elaboration refers to extending extant theories by adding something new so that a new theory becomes either more comprehensive (for example adding new independent variables or dependent variables for new settings or new phenomena) or more specific (for example, adding mediating mechanisms or moderating conditions to make the theory more detailed or precise). Elaboration often involves some degree of modification of the original model but in general the basic theoretical assumptions and rationale of the theories are maintained. In contrast, competition refers to proposing new theories and perspectives that challenge the basic assumptions of existing theories and often lead to different predictions for the same phenomena. Finally, integration refers to creating theoretical models on the basis of two or more, well-established theories with the new theory adding more understanding than either of the existing individual theories.

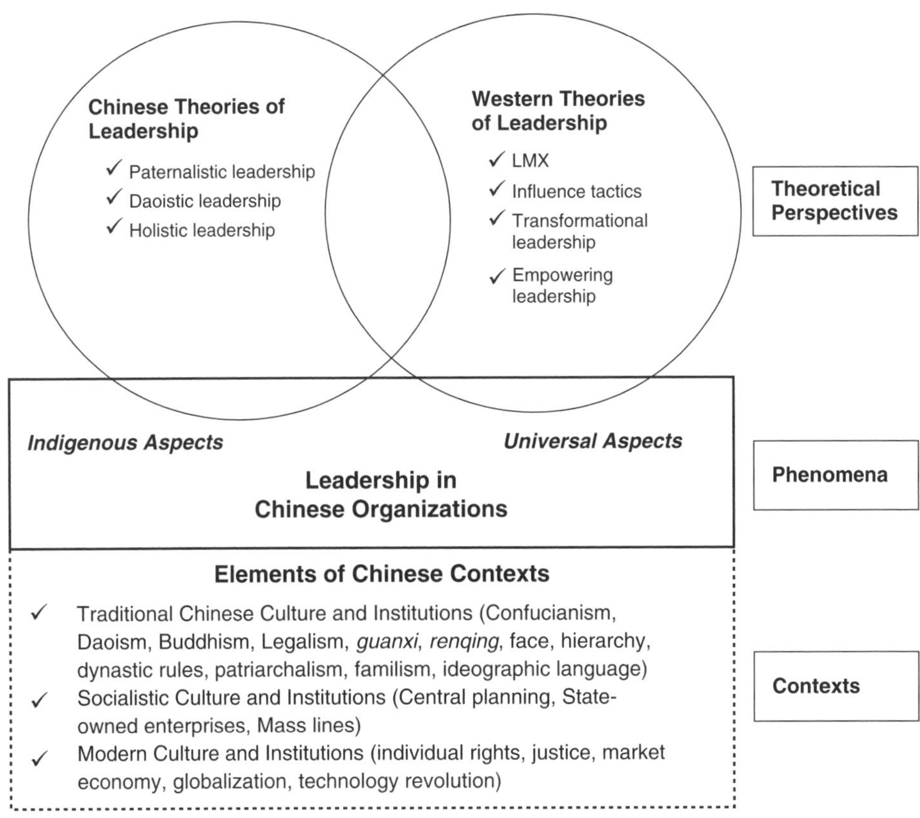

Fig. 35.1 Overall conceptual framework.

Of the Chinese leadership theories, the one that is most well developed, systematically researched, and clearly indigenous is the paternalistic leadership (PL) model (Farh & Cheng, 2000; Farh, Cheng, Chou, & Chu, 2006; Farh, Liang, Chou, & Cheng, 2008). In our review we will therefore take PL as our base and primary referent. We will first briefly introduce the origin of PL and trace its further elaborations. We then explore how the indigenous Chinese model came into contact and was joined with certain elements of Western leadership models. Thirdly, we present perspectives and theories that present challenges and alternatives to Chinese traditional leadership. Finally we propose research directions that integrate Chinese and Western perspectives on leadership.

The original model of paternalistic leadership

In the second half of last century, entrepreneurship among overseas Chinese exploded not only in Chinese-dominated communities such as Hong Kong, Singapore and Taiwan, but also in South-east Asian countries, such as Indonesia, Malaysia, Thailand, and the Philippines, where the Chinese were in the minority (Weidenbaum, 1996). Scholars who were intrigued by this phenomenon embarked on a series of ideographic studies on the practices of overseas Chinese businesses. In the late 1960s, Robert Silin went to Taiwan to study large, private enterprises controlled by single individuals. After a year-long study involving 100 hours of interviews with the chief executive officers (also referred to as the 'boss', 'leader', or 'owner/manager'), middle managers and workers, he provided a detailed account of the leadership philosophy and behavioral patterns of the owners/managers of these enterprises (Silin, 1976). Silin identified the essential characteristics of PL, although he did not label them as 'paternalistic' in his work. He found that the leadership styles of the owners/managers could be characterized by moral leadership (acting as a morally superior individual by rejecting egocentric impulse), didactic leadership (conveying to subordinates the methods by which he has achieved business success), centralized authority, maintaining social distance from subordinates, keeping intentions ill defined (hiding intentions from subordinates to maintain authority and control), and implementing control practices (e.g. adopting divide-and-rule tactics, appointing loyal subordinates to several positions concurrently, rarely expressing confidence in subordinates in public to maintain an imbalance of power).

Inspired by the phenomenal success of overseas Chinese Family Businesses in the 1970s and 1980s, Redding began an intense study of management practices in such firms in Hong Kong, Singapore, Taiwan and Indonesia in 1980s (Redding, 1990, Redding and Wong 1986).Through in-depth interviews with 72 owner managers, he identified a distinct brand of economic culture he called Chinese capitalism, in which paternalism is a key element. Building on works by Silin (1976), Deyo (1978, 1983) and Pye (1985), Redding broke down paternalism into seven themes: 1) dependence of the subordinate as a mind-set; 2) personalized loyalty, leading to subordinates' being willing to conform; 3) authoritarianism modified by sensitivity to subordinates' views; 4) authority not divisible when it has become clearly identified with a person; 5) aloofness and social distancing within the hierarchy; 6) allowance for the leader's intentions to remain loosely formulated and unarticulated; and 7) the leader as exemplar and 'teacher' (Redding, 1990, p. 130).

In the late 1980s, Cheng (1995c) began to use the case study approach to examine the leadership style of owners/managers of Taiwanese family-owned businesses. In an in-depth case study of a CEO, Cheng found that the CEO's leadership pattern shared many of the features reported by Silin (1976) and Redding (1990). According to Cheng (1995a, 1995c), paternalistic leadership in Taiwanese family businesses consists of two broad categories of behavior: *shi-en* (grant favors) and *li-wei* (inspire awe or fear). For each category of leadership behavior, Cheng further identified specific behavioral patterns as well as corresponding subordinate responses.

Taken together, the above three ideographic studies describe a distinct management/leadership style, widely practiced among the owners/managers of overseas Chinese family businesses. Apparently paternalism, which is rooted in the traditional Chinese family structure, has crossed the boundary of families and generalized to the workplace. Like the father in a Chinese family, the superior in a company is expected to lead morally by example, maintain authority and control, provide guidance, protection, and care to the subordinate; like a dutiful son, the subordinate, in return, is obligated to be loyal and deferent to the superior. Paternalism has become a salient feature that characterizes the vertical interactions within Chinese organizations.

Elaborations and modifications of paternalistic leadership

Three-dimensional model of paternalistic leadership (PL)

Based on an extensive review of this literature, Farh and Cheng (2000) proposed a Three Dimensional Model of Paternalistic Leadership (see Figure 35.2), in which PL was defined as a type of leadership that combines strong and clear authority with concern, consideration,` and elements of moral leadership. At the heart of the model are the three dimensions of PL (i.e. authoritarian leadership, moral leadership, and benevolent leadership) and their corresponding subordinate responses. Moral leadership is defined as leader behaviors that demonstrate superior moral character and integrity in leading by example and not acting selfishly. Authoritarian leadership is defined as leader behaviors asserting strong authority and control over subordinates and demanding their unquestioning obedience. Finally, benevolent leadership is defined as leader behavior that demonstrates individualized, holistic concern for subordinates' personal and familial well-being.

Each leadership dimension is further hypothesized to be matched with distinct subordinate role responses. Specifically, the leader's authoritarian behavior is expected to evoke dependence and compliance on the part of subordinates, whereas the leader's benevolence is expected to be met by the subordinate's gratitude and obligation to pay back; the leader's morality is expected to lead to the subordinate's respect for and identification with the leader. These subordinate role responses are presumed to be rooted in traditional Chinese culture, which emphasizes dependence on and submission to authority on the part of the follower in a hierarchical relationship, obligations to repay favors given by others, and the importance of accepting moral teachings.

Therefore, the phenomenon of PL is hypothesized to thrive in the context of a host of facilitative social/cultural and organizational factors. The key social/cultural factors consist of a strong emphasis on familism and the Confucian values of respect for authority, personalism/ particularism, the norm of reciprocity (*bao*), interpersonal harmony, and leadership by virtuous example. The key organizational factors comprise family ownership (which eases the transfer of a family-based model to business settings), unity of ownership and management (which confers strong authority on the manager), entrepreneurial structure (which frees managers from bureaucracy to act), and simple task environment and stable technology (which makes managers less dependent on subordinate initiatives). It is predicted that PL is more likely to be practiced (and perhaps more effective) in family-owned and -managed businesses than in non-family-owned businesses. Individuals who identify with traditional Chinese cultural values (such as respect for authority) are more likely to respond positively to PL than those who do not. PL will lead to more positive outcomes when it is practiced in small organizations with limited product lines, simple task environments, and stable technology than in large organizations with diverse product lines, complex environments, and unstable technology.

In sum, to advance theorizing and research on paternalism, Farh and Cheng (2000) proposed a three dimensional model of PL, which built on and elaborated the seminal ideas of paternalism by Silin (1976), Redding (1990) and Cheng (1995c). The model identified three key dimensions for PL, suggested corresponding subordinate role responses for each dimension, and outlined a set of facilitative cultural and organizational conditions for PL. This provides a fertile ground for subsequent research on PL.

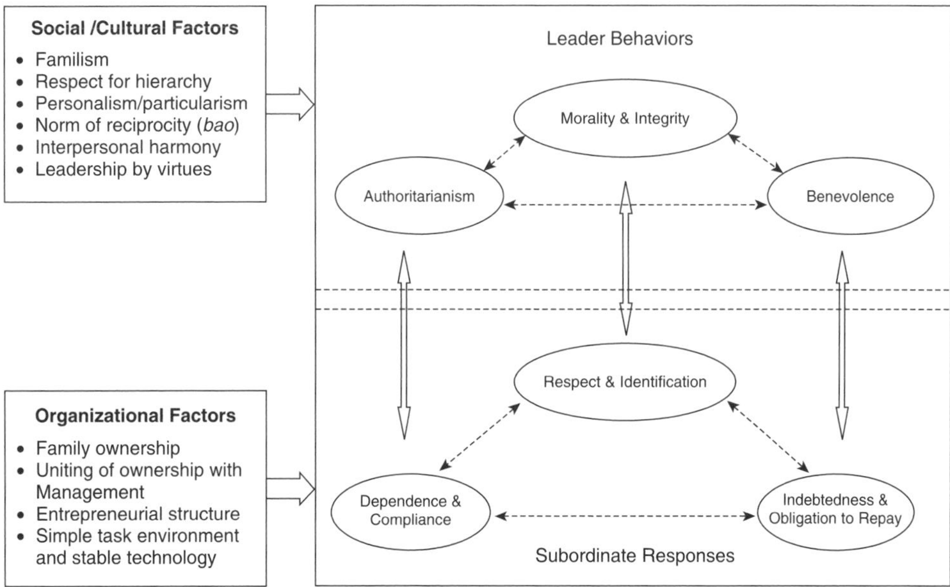

Fig. 35.2 Farh and Cheng's (2000) model of paternalistic leadership.

Empirical research on paternalistic leadership

Based on Farh and Cheng's (2000) model, a series of empirical studies was conducted to examine the model's validity. These efforts first focused on the development of a research instrument to measure the three dimensions of PL components, then examined the effects of PL dimensions on the subordinate's psychological responses (defined as compliance without dissent, gratitude and repayment, and identification and imitation), and finally explored the impact of PL dimensions on a variety of subordinate outcomes such as workplace emotion, job performance, job attitudes, and organizational citizenship behavior (see Farh, Cheng, Chou, & Chu, 2006 for a review).

Empirical research thus far has shown that Farh and Cheng's (2000) model is a viable framework to conceptualize PL in Chinese contexts. The three dimensions of PL are conceptually and empirically distinct (Cheng, Chou, & Farh, 2001). They also account for a significant amount of variance in subordinates' psychological responses and attitudinal and behavioral outcomes beyond those explained by theories of Western transformational leadership (e.g. Cheng, Chou, Wu, Huang, & Farh, 2004; Cheng, Hsieh, & Chou, 2002).

Since Farh and Cheng's (2000) model of PL is embedded in a set of social/cultural/organizational conditions, the effects of PL on subordinate outcomes are not expected to be uniform across all situations. Two situational factors have been studied in the PL literature: subordinate traditionality and subordinate dependence on the leader for resources.

Subordinate traditionality. The construct of Chinese traditionality was conceived by K. S. Yang in the 1980s and defined as 'the typical pattern of more or less related motivational, evaluative, attitudinal and temperamental traits that is (sic.) most frequently observed in people in traditional Chinese society and can still be found in people in contemporary Chinese societies, such as Taiwan, Hong Kong, and mainland China' (K. S. Yang, 2003: 265). Farh, Earley, and Lin (1997) first introduced this construct into organizational science. They selected five items to measure the degree to which an individual endorses the hierarchical role relationships specified by Chinese traditional culture. Social order in traditional Chinese societies is founded on five fundamental relationships (called '*wu-lun*' in Chinese) of Confucianism: emperor-subject, father-son, husband-wife, elder-younger and friend-friend. Four of these five cardinal relationships are hierarchical in nature. Individual loyalty and obedience to the authorities are viewed as the prerequisites of social harmony (Bond & Hwang, 1986).

Nowadays, Chinese people differ greatly in their degrees of modernization, education, wealth, and values. Unquestioned obedience to authority is no longer a 'taken for granted' value for all Chinese, especially for the younger generations with higher education (Cheng & Farh, 2001; K. S. Yang, 1996; see Kulich, this volume). Empirical studies have shown that individual differences in traditionality affect Chinese workers' attitudes and behaviors in a variety of organizational contexts (e.g. Farh et al., 1997; Farh, Hackett, & Liang, 2007; Hui, Lee, & Rousseau, 2004; Xie, Schaubroeck, & Lam, 2008).

PL theory predicts that individuals who identify with traditional Chinese cultural values (especially submission to authority) are more likely to respond positively to PL than are those who do not. Two of three studies examining this moderating role of individual traditionality found general support for this proposition. For example, Cheng et al. (2004) reported that in terms of the three psychological responses to PL (identification, compliance, and gratitude), authoritarian leadership had no effects on subordinates with low traditionality, but had positive effects on those with high traditionality. Farh et al. (2006) reported that authoritarianism had a strong negative effect on satisfaction with the leader for subordinates with a low endorsement of traditional Chinese values, but it had no such negative effect for those with a high endorsement.. Cheng, Chou, Huang, Farh, & Peng (2003), however, failed to find the moderating effect of traditionality in a sample from the Chinese mainland. In summary, there is evidence that subordinates' responses to authoritarianism are contingent on their individual values for traditionality, but the findings have not been consistent across studies.

Subordinate dependence on the leader for resources. Besides traditionality, the dependence of subordinates on their supervisors for resources may also affect subordinates' responses to PL dimensions.

Redding (1990) suggested that the strong dependence of the subordinates on their supervisor is a salient characteristic of paternalism in overseas Chinese family businesses. Therefore, it is expected that subordinates are less likely to respond to paternalistic leadership when they are resource-independent than when they are resource-dependent.

Farh et al. (2006) studied the moderating effects of the subordinate's dependence on the leader for resources on the relationship between the PL dimensions and subordinates' outcomes. Consistent with their general predictions, they found that: (i) authoritarianism is more strongly associated with fear of the leader when the subordinates' resource dependence is high than when it is low; (ii) benevolence has a stronger, positive effect on subordinates' identification, compliance, and organizational commitment when subordinates' resource dependence is high than when it is low. These findings, taken together, suggest that when subordinates depend heavily on their leaders for resources, authoritarian and benevolent leadership tend to have stronger effects on subordinates.

Interestingly, Farh et al. (2006) reported a 'reverse' moderating effect for moral leadership. That is, the leader's morality had a stronger positive effect on the subordinates' identification, compliance, and commitment when subordinates' dependence was low than when it was high. In other words, leader's morality actually had a more potent effect when subordinates did not depend on their leaders for resources. If these results can be replicated in future research, they suggest that the three dimensions of PL involve different psychological mechanisms in influencing workers' attitudes and behaviors.

Summary and discussion. The empirical research on PL shows that it works more positively or less negatively when subordinates endorse traditional values and when subordinates heavily depend on their leaders for resources. These findings provide support for the general proposition that the PL model is embedded in the Chinese context, and its effects on subordinates are conditioned by a set of situational factors. Future research should examine more systematically how situational factors, ranging from subordinates' values and personalities to the leader's characteristics to task and organizational characteristics, may amplify or neutralize the effects of PL on subordinates' and work unit outcomes. Cross-cultural replications of these research designs could also be attempted to assess their generality, and to further unpackage the processes involved.

Leader–member exchange and paternalistic leadership

Of all Western leadership theories, leader–member exchange theory (LMX) has received the most attention by scholars of Chinese leadership. While Hui and Graen (1997) identified some key distinctions between LMX and leadership-member *guanxi* (LMG), most of the research adopting LMX in China has, in our view, complemented and validated the underpinnings of Chinese traditional leadership philosophy in general and paternalistic leadership in particular. These leadership underpinnings focus on dyads as the fundamental units of leadership emphasizing personal long-term relationship-making, hierarchical and reciprocal leader-follower role obligations, and differentiation of members on the basis of personal loyalty and performance. Of the half-dozen empirical papers on LMX we reviewed, most focused on the relationship quality of LMX and found that relationship quality affects outcomes, such as organizational citizenship behavior (OCB), job satisfaction, task performance, withdrawal behavior of the subordinates (Aryee & Chen, 2006; Hackett, Farh, Song, & Lapierre, 2003; Hui, Law, & Chen, 1999; Liang, Ling, & Hsieh, 2007), and participative leadership and open discussion of opposing views between managers and their subordinates (Y. F. Chen & Tjosvold, 2006, 2007). The quality of the leader-member relationship was also found to mediate the effects of transformational leadership, negative affectivity, and cooperative goals (Hui, Law, & Chen, 1999; Wang, Law, Hackett, Wang, & Chen, 2005).

LMX research on Chinese leadership complements and enriches the traditional study of Chinese leadership in a number of ways: First, it empirically demonstrates that the dyadic leader-member relationship has positive effects that go beyond the job attitudes and performance of the subordinates or interpersonal social-psychological dynamics between the leader and the followers. These positive effects spread over attitudes and behaviors toward coworkers and the organization, such as organizational commitment, turnover, and peer-oriented or organization-oriented citizenship behavior. Second, without invoking the more specific and differentiated psychological dynamics of the subordinates posited in PL (e.g. feelings of dependence, identification, and obligation), LMX quality as perceived from the subordinates seems to have the capacity to parsimoniously capture the socio-emotional closeness of the leader-member *guanxi* (X. P. Chen & Chen, 2004). It is therefore a potentially crucial mediator between leadership behavior and follower outcomes. To some extent, LMX quality may serve as a general proxy of the various psychological mechanisms posited in the PL. Third, due to its psychological generality, LMX quality opens up opportunities for exploring antecedents that are different from but compatible with paternalistic leadership behaviors. For example, supervisor control of rewards, work group climate of trust, openness, consensus, cooperative goals between the leader and the members, and transformational leadership behaviors have been found to affect Chinese LMX quality, which in turn has positive effects on subordinates' attitudes and behaviors (Aryee & Chen, 2006; Y. F. Chen & Tjosvold, 2006, 2007; Wang et al., 2005).

That these factors enhance LMX quality by no means challenges the theoretical arguments of paternalism. The firm control of rewards and resources by the leader is inherent in the Chinese hierarchical relationship and is posited as an important antecedent of guanxi strategy (Bond & Hwang, 1986; Hwang, 1987); cooperative goals are assumed in a situation of benevolent leadership; a trustful work-group climate grows naturally from prosocial and moral leadership.

It is worth noting that LMX researchers of Chinese leadership have chosen to focus on the compatible aspects of LMX rather than their distinctions. Later, we will discuss how those distinctions may pose challenges to Chinese traditional leadership theories.

Transformational leadership and paternalistic leadership

Since transformational leadership is more contemporary than traditional transactional theories of leadership, one might expect it to differ sharply from traditional theories of Chinese leadership. Yet, transformational leadership may turn out to be most compatible with them. To start with, relative to transactional leadership, transformational leadership is more leader-centric (Meindl, 1990), in that the leader is clearly the agent of the transformation, whereas the organization and the followers are the target of the transformation. This presumption fits well with the hierarchical structuring of Chinese leadership. Secondly, the defining characteristic of transformational leadership is the ability to transcend the individual interests of the followers, uniting them behind the collective interests of the organization. This orientation fits perfectly the Confucian definition of the sagely king or the superior gentleman (X. H. Yang, Peng, & Lee, 2008). This aspect of transformational leadership is also reflected in the PL dimension of moral leadership. Third, the component of individualized consideration characterizing transformational leadership largely mirrors Confucian philosophy of benevolence, explicitly conceived as benevolent leadership in PL. Lastly, transformational leadership and its core component of charisma defines leadership in terms of followers' identification with the leader. Again, followers' social-emotional loyalty to and identification with the leader is the hallmark of effective leadership in the Chinese Confucian tradition.

Given that transformational leadership is based on charismatic leadership, which according to Weber (1968) derives authority from the superior quality of the person, whereas Confucian governance rests on the superior character and conduct of the sagely king, it is no coincidence that there is so much overlap between transformational leadership and Confucian paternalistic leadership. One striking difference, however, is in the latter's emphasis on the leader's continuous self-cultivation, an exhortation largely missing in transformational leadership (C. C. Chen & Lee, 2008b). There is evidence for the continuing importance of moral character in modern Chinese organizations as demonstrated in research in PL and other Chinese leadership studies. Ling and colleagues (1987), for example, through surveying large samples of subordinates working in Chinese factories, discovered a third dimension called character in addition to the well established two dimensions of leadership behaviors: task and people orientation in the U.S. and performance and maintenance orientation in Japan (Misumi, 1985). Character refers to the perceived moral integrity of the supervisor and was related to leadership effectiveness (see also Peterson, 1988).

Thus, one would expect that transformational leadership is appealing and generalizable to Chinese leadership situations, especially at a time when market-oriented economics and enterprise reform have afforded more power and opportunities to business executives, allowing for the emergence of transformational and charismatic business leaders. In the following we report studies that demonstrated some evidence of transformational leadership being applicable in Chinese organizations.

In a comparative study, Javidan and Carl (2005) asked Canadian and Taiwanese middle and senior managers to assess their immediate superiors on a set of role behaviors. The found a common cluster of three factors of charismatic leadership, namely, visionary, symbolizer (representing the vision), and self-sacrificer. It suggests that Chinese managers are familiar with core features of charismatic leadership as conceived in the West. In the Confucian philosophy of governance by virtue and rule of propriety (Peng, Chen, & Yang, 2008), the leader is entrusted with the supreme task of culture building. Chinese managers, especially those at the top, are expected to build organizational culture. In a study of middle level managers in mainland China, Tsui and colleagues (2004, 2006), based on focus group discussions and interviews with managers, and surveys of around 1500 middle level managers from hundreds of companies, identified six types of executive leadership behaviors: risk taking, relating and communicating, articulating vision, showing benevolence, monitoring operations, and acting authoritatively. We note that in the above studies transformational leadership behaviors such as risk taking and articulating vision coexist with the paternalistic behaviors of showing benevolence and being authoritative. In another study of mainland managers and their subordinates, Wang and colleagues (2005) found that the level of transformational leadership of the supervisor significantly affected both in-role and extra-role performance of the subordinates. More importantly, they found that the effect of transformational leadership was mediated by the level of LMX quality that measures the loyalty and respect that followers felt toward the leader. Transformational leadership and LMX quality were highly correlated ($r = .71$, $p < .001$).

To us, the study highlights the theoretical compatibility among transformational leadership, LMX quality, and traditional Chinese leadership even though the authors did not explicitly draw such a connection. Other authors have argued and found evidence that transformational leadership is more compatible with collectivistic values. For example, Walumba and colleagues (Walumbwa, Lawler, & Avolio, 2007; Walumbwa & Lawler, 2003) in their studies of Chinese, Indians, Kenyans, and Americans found that the effects of transformational leadership in increasing job satisfaction and organizational commitment and lowering turnover intentions were stronger for subordinates who score higher on individual-level measures of collectivism.

One could argue that transformational and charismatic leadership theories are not merely compatible but have enriched and elaborated certain aspects of Confucian leadership philosophy and PL. For example, the notion of visionary leadership, while seeded in Confucian value-based leadership (Fernandez, 2004; Peng, Chen, & Yang, 2008) and to some extent in PL (e.g. the didactic behavior of the leader), becomes a primary behavioral dimension of transformational leadership. Furthermore, transformational leadership draws attention to institutionally oriented leadership behaviors, elevating the level of analysis from the dyadic, interpersonal level to the organizational level of analysis. Such elevation is important and desirable as executives of modern business organizations have to display charismatic and visionary leadership not only at the interpersonal level but also at the organizational and community levels. Identifying these executive behaviors at the organizational or collective level is also a step toward understanding system level characteristics, such as organizational culture.

Increasingly, effective leadership is manifested at the organizational level. Tsui and colleagues' (2006) executive behavior dimensions, for example, are mostly targeted at the system level or at the collectivity of organizational members. Such behaviors allow the authors to theorize about the linkage of leadership and organizational culture. Tsui and colleagues found that the majority of the companies in the two samples they studied (72 per cent and 60 per cent) showed a strong correlation between the ratings of leadership behavior dimensions and ratings of cultural dimensions. In other words, as perceived by middle level managers, strong leaders create strong cultures. Lastly, the above reviewed research identified important contingencies under which transformational and charismatic leadership is more or less effective. Walumbwa and Lawler (2003) pointed to the moderating effect of subordinates' characteristics, such as their value orientation, whereas Tsui and colleagues (2006) pointed to organizational level contingencies, such as large company size, scarce company resources, and state-ownership limit executives' capacity to shape or change organizational culture.

Influence tactics and traditional Chinese leadership

Cross-cultural research on the influence tactics involving Chinese managers also revealed results that confirm some Chinese traditional leadership values. A U.S.-China comparison (Fu & Yukl, 2000) found that in making a difficult request from subordinates, peers, or superiors, American managers judged that influence tactics aimed directly at the targeted person are more effective, whereas Chinese managers viewed indirect influence tactics through third parties, such as appealing to higher authority or asking another person to help (coalition), to be more effective. These findings are consistent with the Chinese leadership values of respecting authority, face saving, and harmony. The authors also observed through interviews different sequencing of tactics by American and Chinese managers. Americans often preferred using direct tactics followed by indirect tactics, whereas the Chinese may appeal to third parties, often informally, for help before directly approaching the target person. It appeared that upward appeal and coalition are perceived and used as hard tactics of pressure in America, whereas in China the same tactics may often be used as ways of side-stepping direct confrontation so as to save face and protect relationship harmony for both parties.

Alternative perspectives and theories to traditional, authoritarian leadership

The diversity of Chinese leadership philosophies and practices

Indigenous Chinese leadership theory and research has used Chinese tradition and Confucianism as its primary foundation. Western China researchers often compare modern and contemporary Western values and norms with Chinese ones traced all the way back to ancient Confucianism. While this partly reflects the continuous and powerful impact of Confucianism on Chinese culture, it nevertheless ignores the obvious fact that contemporary China is not replica of ancient China, and that ancient China is more than Confucianism. In an edited monograph, C. C. Chen and Lee (2008a) featured the diversity and dynamism of ancient Chinese philosophies of Confucianism, Daoism, and Legalism as well as the diversity and dynamism of modern and contemporary thoughts on leadership by Mao, Deng, and Western philosophers. In particular, C. C. Chen and Lee (2008b) reviewed and analyzed similarities and differences among various ancient Chinese schools of thoughts on issues, such as: 1) human goodness and evil; 2) rule of virtue versus rule of law; 3) individualism, relationalism, and collectivism; 4) social hierarchy versus social equality; 5) individual, dyadic and institutional levels of leadership; and 6) active non-action (*wu wei*) leadership. The authors further illustrated how contemporary Chinese paternalism and socialism are influenced by ancient Chinese and modern Western thought and practices concerning leadership.

Based on content analysis of interviews, Z. X. Zhang and colleagues (2008) identified seven philosophical leadership maxims as aspired and practiced by Chinese business executives: sincerity, pursuit of excellence, social responsibility, harmony, the golden mean (acting according to the middle way), specialization, and scientific management. These business executives traced Chinese and Western sources that shaped their management and leadership philosophies. In general, the executives reflected that they drew guidance for strategic and relationship issues from Chinese sources, but for operational tasks they drew guidance from Western sources.

The diversity perspective was also emphasized by Tsui and colleagues (2004) by titling their work, 'Let a hundred flowers bloom'. The authors identified four distinctive leadership styles by identifying patterns of six executive leadership behaviors, viz. risk taking, relating and communicating, articulating vision, showing benevolence, monitoring operation, and being authoritative. The four styles were: Advanced, i.e. above average on all behaviors except for being authoritative; Authoritative, i.e. high on being authoritative, but average or low on all other behaviors; Progressive, i.e. average on all behaviors; and Invisible, i.e. below average on all behaviors. A few points are worth noting about the above styles. First, both the advanced and the progressive styles used a combination of behaviors that are not authoritative. Second, only one of the four styles is purely authoritative. Third, the invisible style can be as Chinese as the authoritative style, because the former is consistent with the Daoist tradition, whereas the latter is part of the Confucian tradition. Indeed, as we pointed out earlier one could argue that the advanced and progressive styles are combinations of the diverse modern and traditional Chinese leadership philosophies and practices.

All the above reviewed works challenge a monolithic and static view of Chinese culture and Chinese leadership. Together, they expand thinking and research on Chinese leadership from traditional to modern periods and from Confucianism to other Chinese schools of thought.

A justice perspective on leadership styles

Authoritarian leadership is one of the three main components of PL. While benevolence and moral leadership are integral, authoritarianism stands out, at least in the assessment by Western researchers, as the most prominent and most representative of the Chinese leadership tradition. Authoritarian leadership is based on the legitimacy of unequal authority and rights granted to unequal roles, with more authority and rights accorded to the superior and less to the subordinate. To be sure, Confucian authoritarianism balances greater authority and rights of the superior with greater moral, social, and economic responsibilities and obligations associated with the exercise of that authority. Theoretically, at least the Confucian conception of authoritarian leadership is tightly coupled with benevolent and moral leadership.

Confucian authoritarianism may face an increasing challenge of legitimacy for those who hold more egalitarian values. First, the theoretical balance between authority and obligation often fails in practice, as superiors may abuse formal authority without living up to their moral or social obligations (King & Bond, 1985). While the subordinate's obligation to obey authority is absolute except in extreme conditions of brutal tyranny, Confucian authoritarianism affords scant recourse and few mechanisms by which subordinates can take action to protect their own rights or to revoke the rights of the superior in case of power abuse. As a result, there is a large asymmetry of power tilted heavily toward the superior, leading to potential abusive behavior. Second, the world has changed and progressed with more people accepting the notion that all human beings have some basic rights due to their humanity, regardless of their gender, age, social status, and role positions. For instance, the superior may have the right to make a job-related decision, but the subordinate may feel entitled to be informed of the decision in a timely and respectful way, if the decision affects the job performance of the subordinate. Even if a superior has a benevolent intention and the usual moral authority, a subordinate may resent the superior's authoritarian behavior that violates the sense of respect and dignity of the subordinate.

Consistent with the above lines of reasoning, Aryee and colleagues (2007) used dyadic data from supervisors and subordinates to explore the link between authoritarian leadership and abusive supervision and their effects on subordinate attitudes and behaviors. In addition, the authors examined the effect of interactional justice as perceived by supervisors and subordinates on the above relationships. It was found that authoritarian leadership was positively related to abusive supervision, which in turn negatively related to organizational commitment and OCB. More importantly, such negative effects of abusive supervision were fully mediated by interactional justice as perceived by subordinates. Interestingly, the authors also found an interaction effect on abusive supervision between supervisors' authoritarian leadership and how these supervisors were treated by their own bosses, i.e. supervisors' perceived interactional justice. Specifically, there was a significant negative effect of supervisors' perceived interactional justice on abusive supervision for supervisors with higher levels of authoritarian leadership but not for those with lower levels (See Figure 2, Aryee et al., 2007).

Our reinterpretation of the interaction effect is that the negative effect of authoritarian leadership on abusive supervision is reduced by supervisors' perceived interactional justice. In other words, authoritarian leaders are less likely to engage in abusive supervision to the extent they themselves have been treated fairly by their own bosses. These findings, while preliminary, provide evidence for the link between authoritarian leadership and abusive supervision, and the importance of interactional justice in both explaining and moderating such a link. Personally experiencing interactional justice not only motivates positive attitudes and behaviors of subordinates toward the organization, but also inhibits some negative effects of authoritarian leadership. One wonders if interactional justice at the dyadic level can be extended to group or organizational levels, for example, a climate of interactional justice, and whether such extension would have similar positive effects.

There are other studies that showed negative impact of authoritarian leadership. Liang, Ling, and Hsieh (2007), for example, studied PL in military units, where authoritarian leadership style is most expected, and found that while benevolent and moral leadership positively affected OCB of subordinates, authoritarian leadership style negatively affected OCB. Furthermore, the authors found that the effects of benevolent and authoritarian leadership on OCB were mediated through the quality of the LMX relationship. One wonders whether the negative effect of authoritarian leadership on the LMX relationship was due to subordinates' resentment about disrespectful treatment, i.e. low perceived levels of interactional justice.

Empowering leadership

A functional critique of authoritarianism is that it is limited in achieving desired outcomes. The major purpose of authoritarian leadership is to ensure obedience and compliance of the subordinates, so as to create an orderly and stable organization or society at large. This vision of organization was more desirable than one of complete disorder, anarchy, and disunity. However, to be orderly and stable may not provide a competitive advantage in today's dynamic and competitive environment, which requires organizations to be continuously vibrant and innovative. For achieving this superior vision of organizational life and purpose, there needs to be higher level of motivation, such as affective commitment and trust rather than obedience and compliance. One limit of authoritarian leadership is that it lacks the capacity to generate higher levels of commitment and initiative from employees. The other is that the work force has changed, as more workers are being better educated, wanting more autonomy, a greater share of decision-making authority, greater opportunities to use their talents and contribute to the organization. They perceive greater levels of interactional injustice when these opportunities are not provided by their supervisors.

In response to the changing and changed needs of the organization and its employees, various leadership styles ranging from delegation and participation to coaching and development have been proposed in the West, many of which were included under the broad concept of empowering leadership (Arnold, Arad, Rhoades, & Drasgow, 2000; Konczak, Stelly, & Trusty, 2000). Recent years have witnessed research on empowering leadership in Chinese organizations. Huang and colleagues (2006) examined whether participative leadership, namely, encouraging suggestions from subordinates and incorporating them in managerial decision-making had differential effects on employees who joined state-owned enterprises before and after the year of 1997, when those firms were transformed into market-oriented enterprises. It was found that participative leadership was positively related to organizational commitment for employees who joined after the enterprise transformation, but not for those who joined before it. Furthermore, the differential effect was mediated through the feeling of competence, a dimension of psychological empowerment.

The findings supported the reasoning that participative leadership is more effective for generating commitment when employees are less enculturated to traditional hierarchical beliefs or the ideology of a command economy. Z. X. Chen and Ayee (2007) examined the effect of delegation, defined as assigning new responsibilities to subordinates and providing them with the authority to carry out these responsibilities, on employee outcomes, and explored its mediation and moderating processes in China. They found that delegation has a positive effect on employee job satisfaction, affective organizational commitment, task performance, and innovative behavior. Furthermore, the positive outcomes were fully mediated by two self-concepts, namely organizational based self-esteem and perceived organizational insider status; job satisfaction was partially mediated by these self-concepts. Finally, traditionality, in terms of individual values of respect for hierarchy, moderated the positive relationship between delegation on one hand and organizational self-esteem and perceived organizational insider status on the other, weakening these relationships.

In another study of Chinese empowering leadership, C. C. Chen, Wang, and Zhang (2008) found that power sharing and delegation had a positive impact on employee job satisfaction, task performance, and OCB, and that such effects were mediated through psychological empowerment. The authors also found that control behavior of the supervisors, defined as setting performance goals and monitoring work processes, enhanced the positive effect of greater power sharing with subordinates.

While the above studies confirmed the positive outcomes of empowering leadership on Chinese employees' attitudes and behaviors, some studies have examined the antecedents of empowering leadership. Tjosvold, Hui, and Law (1998) studied the effects of perceived cooperative goals between leaders and subordinates on the perception of leadership style. Participants of the study were asked to recall critical leadership incidents in which a participant was either a leader or a follower, including its settings, interaction dynamics, and outcomes. These were coded into key variables of research interest. It was found that cooperative goal orientation had positive effects on leader-member relationships, task performance, and perception of democratic leadership. Such positive effects were mediated through open-minded discussion of issues, a process variable called constructive controversy. Another study (Y. F. Chen & Tjosvold, 2006) explored similar issues but used a survey method with mainland Chinese who worked with Chinese and American managers. The authors distinguished leader-member *guanxi* and LMX quality, with the former defined as the extent to which subordinates build *guanxi* with supervisors outside work and the latter as the quality of supervisor-subordinate relationship at work. It was found that cooperative goals had a positive effect on leader-member *guanxi* and LMX quality, which in turn affected perceived participative leadership measured by joint decision-making and constructive controversy.

The study reported two interesting cross-cultural differences with regard to the effects of goal orientation and leader-member *guanxi*. The first is that independent goals, i.e. goals that are different but are neither cooperative nor competitive, negatively affected Chinese employees' LMX quality and leader-member *guanxi* with Chinese managers, but this was not the case with America managers. Second, leader-member *guanxi* had a positive effect on constructive controversy for Chinese employee-Chinese manager relations, but did not show a significant effect for Chinese employee-American manager relations. This suggests different dynamics in within-culture versus across-cultural relationships between leaders and members. Chinese employees and their managers seem to expect cooperative goals as necessary for relationship building and relationship quality, and *guanxi*-building outside work as essential means of establishing the trust necessary for constructive controversy. These more stringent conditions, however, were not required for participative interactions with American managers.

While the above research on leadership empowerment did not directly contrast empowering leadership with traditional authoritarian leadership, it nevertheless showed its functional superiority in: 1) cultivating more positive and intrinsic motivational processes, such as organizational self-esteem, competence, and psychological empowerment; 2) inspiring more intense positive attitudes, such as job satisfaction and organizational commitment; and 3) motivating positive discretionary behaviors, such as OCB, constructive controversy, and innovation. The research also suggested that empowering leadership, perhaps less familiar, less articulated, and less dominant in Chinese culture, is compatible with some elements of Chinese culture. For instance, one would expect that even in traditional Chinese hierarchies, there should be more empowerment of subordinates if the latter are considered by the superiors to be more closely related (e.g. kinship), more loyal, and more competent (Cheng, 1995b).

Leader–member exchange theory revisited

While we discussed compatible elements between LMX and Chinese LMG (leader-member guanxi) earlier, here we highlight some important challenges that LMX presents for traditional views of Confucian leadership. To start with, LMX does not assume or insist on a strictly hierarchical relationship between the leader and the follower, as do the Confucian prescriptions for the superior-subordinate relationship. The American L-M exchange is more open and transparent and it allows subordinates, at least theoretically, equal legitimacy and opportunities as it does leaders to initiate give-and-take in negotiations and exchanges. Such would not be permissible or practical in the Confucian cardinal relationships. The end result of LMX exchanges may largely capture the relational closeness of *guanxi*, but the process and dynamics of LMX could be quite different from those of *guanxi* building (X. P. Chen & C. C. Chen, 2004; Y. F. Chen & Tjosvold, 2006; Law, Wong, & Wong, 2000). Had researchers taken a more comparative or contrastive approach on the processes of relationship building in Chinese and Western contexts, they would have discovered more differences than are revealed by the current research on LMX in China.

Second, while both LMX and Confucianism advocate differentiating subordinates rather than treating them in the same ways, the basis of such differentiation is often different. Cheng (1995b), for example, found that Chinese executives typically categorized their subordinates into groups based on *guanxi*, personal loyalty, and competence. Hui and Graen (1997) called it loyalty versus competence. We believe that competence has always been a key criterion of Chinese organization and management in personnel selection, appraisal, and reward. The distinction is not so much that the Chinese do not value competence or performance, but that they also hold other competing criteria of differentiation as equally or even more important, be those criteria kinship, personal loyalty, or Maoist political correctness. As a result, the competence criterion in practice often becomes displaced by or secondary to relationship considerations.

Third, the boundary of ingroup-outgroup is more permeable and changeable in the West than in the Chinese context. The Chinese LMG is built on bases that are either ascribed to the individuals, such as kinship and birthplace, or predetermined by connections to common institutions, such as former schools and workplaces. These bases tend to reinforce each other, leading to what sociologist called homo-production, resulting in the stubborn exclusion of outsiders. To be sure, LMX face similar challenges in the West, as in the so-call old boy networks. However, due to anti-discrimination laws and by limiting competence- and performance-based exchanges to the work place, LMX is arguably less suspect to charges of favoritism and discrimination, and more conducive to network sharing among core members of the organization, whose competence and performance are the keys to the survival and competitive advantage of the organization.

The above major principles of differentiated leadership style from LMX could therefore be used as a critique of some of the *guanxi* practices characteristic of traditional Chinese leadership. At the dyadic level, *guanxi* practices lead to LMX quality and positive exchanges involving those within the dyadic relationships. However, for those outside the dyads, the group or organization as a whole, *guanxi* practices reduce trust in the leader and his or occasionally her organization, raising questions of procedural and interactional justice (C. C. Chen & Chen, 2009; C. C. Chen, Chen, & Xin, 2004). In summary, LMX has the potential to provide competing assumptions and practices to Chinese LMG if researchers look beyond the relational outcomes into the different premises and dynamics of relationship crafting.

Future directions of Chinese leadership research

Indigenous research

The indigenous research on paternalistic leadership exemplifies how Chinese indigenous research could contribute to world-wide management research. Scholars of Chinese paternalism have persistently and systematically conceived of and theorized about their object of study on the basis of Chinese traditional leadership philosophies, Chinese organizational contexts, and Chinese managers' practices. Furthermore, they have sought to formulate testable hypotheses, develop rigorous measures, and accumulate empirical evidence for the support or rejection of these hypotheses. Finally, they publish and disseminate their theory and research in Chinese-language journals, in chapters of edited volumes on Chinese management, and in mainstream journals of the English language. With Chinese scholars in the forefront of world-wide indigenous research on paternalism from the Asia Pacific, North America, and the Middle East, we begin to see its increasing impact on leadership research in Western cultures, such as the United States (Pellegrini & Scandura, 2008; see also Smith, this volume).

Re-conceptualizing authoritarian leadership. As PL becomes a universal rather than an indigenous Chinese construct, there are some emergent conceptual issues to be tackled in order to further research on this topic (Pellegrini & Scandura, 2008). In our view, the key challenge that the Chinese PL model faces is the conceptualization and operationalization of authoritarianism. One of the most obvious difficulties with the Chinese PL theory arises from the negative empirical correlations between authoritarianism and the other two core dimensions of PL, i.e. benevolent and moral leadership (Farh et al., 2008), which run counter to the initial tripartite model that assumes coherence and complementarity among the dimensions. Equally troubling are the findings that authoritarianism has a negative effect on subordinate attitudinal and behavioral outcomes whereas both benevolent and moral leadership have consistent positive effects (Farh et al., 2008).

These findings have led to some researchers concluding that PL is not a unified construct (Aycan, 2006) and that instead of studying the overall PL construct, researchers should study the three constituent dimensions separately (Farh et al., 2006). To address this conceptual difficulty, Aycan (2006) has suggested that PL should be distinguished into four separate, independent leadership styles based on two dimensions: a) the intent of the leader toward the subordinate (either benevolence or exploitation), and b) the behavioral occurrence of the leader in leading the subordinate (either care or control). It appears that the major distinction in this new approach would be between benevolent and exploitative paternalism.

We are reluctant to follow this new conception of PL for a few reasons: First, introducing intent into a leadership behavior theory may make the theory hard to verify or falsify empirically. Second, this new approach could result in blurring the conceptual distinctions between demonstrating authority and showing benevolence on one hand, and benevolent and moral leadership behavior on the other. Both these distinctions are important in the Chinese PL model and possibly elsewhere in the cultural world.

In our view, part of the reason for the negative correlations of authoritarianism with outcome variables and with other two dimensions of PL lies in the negative conceptions of the construct originally made by Western scholars (see e.g. Altemeyer, 1996; see also Wang & Chang, this volume). We therefore suggest that the dimension of *authoritarian leadership* be re-constructed as *authoritative leadership* from the indigenous perspectives of the Chinese, so that those negative elements are purged. We believe that this revision is consistent with the theoretical underpinnings of PL, which argues for positive alignment and coherence among the three dimensions. It is worth noting even with this revision, modern challenges to Confucian authoritative leadership that we discussed earlier (e.g. interactional justice) may still exist, and the empirical findings about the negative effects of authoritative leadership will have to be accommodated.

In the following we explain how the negative elements of authoritarianism came to be associated with the Chinese concept of authoritative leadership. According to the New Oxford English Dictionary, the word *authoritative* refers to: a) 'able to be trusted as being accurate or true; reliable'; b) 'commanding and self-confident; likely to be respected and obeyed'; and c) 'proceeding from an official source and requiring compliance or obedience'; whereas *authoritarian* refers to: a) 'favoring or enforcing strict obedience to authority, especially that of the state, at the expense of personal freedom'; and b) 'showing a lack of concern for the wishes or opinions of others; dictatorial'. Based on the above definitions, the term, 'authoritarianism', carries a negative connotation in the English language whereas 'authoritative' does not. In Western management literature, the term, 'authoritarian management style' is closely associated with the outdated Theory X, which assumes that humans inherently dislike responsibility and that an average employee wants to be directed (Pellegrini & Scandura, 2008). The authoritarian leadership style thus typically implies oppression, control and exploitation, and severe punishment of subordinates (Aycan, 2006).

In the Chinese language, the term used to describe the directive or the commanding aspect of leadership in organizations is called '*wei quan* or *quan wei* leadership', which is a more neutral phrase without those negative associations of authoritarianism. The English equivalent of the Chinese term is therefore authoritative leadership rather than authoritarian leadership, especially in the context of Chinese family businesses. Nevertheless, authoritarianism was the term used in the original ideographic studies of the management style of owners/managers of overseas Chinese family businesses by Western scholars (Silin, 1976; Redding, 1990). For two reasons, we argue that future conceptions of the PL should adopt the term of authoritative leadership instead of authoritarian leadership or authoritarianism: First, the meanings and connotations of authoritative leadership are more consistent with the indigenous perspectives of high power distance cultures including China (Hofstede, 1980). As such, Chinese of lower status are accustomed to defer or submit themselves to the authority of their superiors, especially when their superiors are perceived to have legitimate authority. Second, a close examination of the original concepts of PL suggests that authoritarianism could well be a misnomer for authoritative leadership. In both Silin's (1976) and Redding's (1990) accounts, a typical executive in Chinese family businesses not only possesses strong legitimate authority, since they are either founders/owners of the companies or their close associates, but also possesses strong technical expertise and business acumen because they are often hands-on managers. For example, Silin (1976, p. 128) reported that the Chinese family business owners and managers whom he studied were recognized by subordinates as superior individuals who lead because of an overwhelming superiority manifested in two ways: (1) through a leader's ability to translate abstract ideas about financial and commercial success into concrete reality, and (2) through a leader's ability to reject his egocentric impulses for a higher moral good. It is clear that from the perspectives of the Chinese subordinates, it is more appropriate to describe the leadership behaviors of these managers as authoritative rather than as authoritarian.

With these new considerations, we suggest future research on PL should re-construe authoritarian leadership as authoritative leadership, which may be defined as leader behaviors that rely primarily on legitimate authority and professional expertise to influence subordinates, such as making final calls on key decisions, expecting employees to comply with and follow through on directives, holding employees accountable for work rules and high performance standards. Accordingly, the current Paternalistic Leadership Scale developed by Cheng, Chou, and Farh (2000) needs revision. Negative behaviors that denote authoritarianism should be discarded, for example, 'belittling subordinate contribution,' 'reprimanding subordinates for poor performance,' and 'ignoring subordinate suggestions'. A recent chapter by Farh et al. (2008) offers specific suggestions on how to revise the domain of authoritarian leadership to purge its negative elements. We agree with their call and add that future researchers should revise their scales to measure authoritative rather than authoritarian leadership.

A multi-level approach to PL. In the past decade, empirical research on PL following Farh and Cheng (2000) has focused on the influence of leaders (typically lower-level managers) on their individual subordinates. This focus is in sharp contrast with earlier ideographical/anthropological research by Silin (1976) and Redding (1990), which typically focused on the paternalistic management style of CEOs and their influence on the entire organization. Since organizations are complex systems that involve interlocking processes operating at multiple levels, a more complete account of PL's effects in organizations calls for a multi-level approach. Farh et al. (2008, pp. 197–200) has recently outlined a multi-level model of paternalistic leadership. At the upper level of the organization, PL refers to the overall management style and practices used by the CEO and the top management team. PL manifests itself in management practices, such as a centralized organization structure, top down decision making style, and treating employees as family members, and results in a paternalistic climate in the workplace that influences unit performance as well as shapes the leadership style of lower-rank leaders. At the lower level of the organization, PL refers to paternalistic leader behaviors exhibited by middle or lower level managers toward their subordinates. PL impacts follower outcomes (in role performance, OCB, and work attitudes) through followers' cognitive-motivational states (fear, gratitude, and identification). According to this model, the upper level and lower level leadership processes interact in several interesting ways to determine individual and unit level outcomes. This proposed multi-level approach, which examines the impact of leadership behaviors from both the perspective of individual employees' idiosyncratic experiences, and the shared view of work-unit members' overall experience, is a worthwhile direction for future research on PL.

A configurational approach to PL. Another important direction for future research on PL is a configurational approach. As discussed in Farh and Cheng (2000), PL is a complex concept, existing in a specific socio-cultural context, embracing conflicting elements (e.g. domineering coupled with individualized care), and working through divergent psychological mechanisms. This complexity calls for a configurational approach to studying PL. Farh et al. (2008, pp. 184–192) have recently proposed a typology of paternalistic leaders based on the level of absolute values (High versus Low) on each of the three core dimensions of PL (Authoritarianism, Benevolence, and moral Character or moral leadership). As the three dimensions are dichotomized, it generates eight types of PL leaders. For example, one type of the PL leader is called 'Authentic PL leaders' which are characterized by high Authoritarianism, high Benevolence, and high moral Character. They are labeled as 'authentic', as they are closest to the ideal type of PL leaders as conceptualized by Farh and Cheng (2000).

Farh et al. (2008) provided some initial findings on: a) which PL type matches the ideal leadership type as perceived by Taiwanese employees in private firms; and b) the actual distribution of leaders across the eight PL types and subordinate responses to each type in two forms of organizations in Taiwan (public primary schools and a private conglomerate). One of their most interesting findings is that organizational context has a strong influence on the emergence of different types of paternalistic leadership. For example, PL leaders who are characterized by high authoritarianism are more prevalent and more acceptable to employees in private conglomerates than in public primary schools. Farh et al. speculated that the differential attitudes toward authoritarianism may be due to the different nature of authority in the two organizational contexts. Unlike private firms where authority is derived from private ownership and fully delegated to the management, the authority of the principals in public schools is sharply curtailed by the governmental regulations and the professional and autonomous status of the teachers. In such a context, authoritarianism by principals is more likely to be seen as illegitimate and resented by the teachers. These findings suggest that employees' reactions to the authoritarian dimension of PL are highly contingent on situational factors, and much more so than benevolent or moral leadership. This is clearly a new, stimulating direction for future research. Apart from continuing to do research on PL, there are other indigenous Chinese leadership perspectives that may be fertile areas of research.

Daoist leadership. Daoism is said to have great influence on the cognition of the Chinese people especially in terms of its dialectic view, e.g. the yin-yang perspective and its holistic view, i.e. attending to the complete field instead of only the actor or the object (Lee et al., 2008; Nisbett et al., 2001; see Ji, Lam, & Guo, this volume). Key related concepts include following the natural way, active non-action, and the coexistence, harmony, and manipulation of opposites. These concepts have been used to various degrees by management scholars. Davis (2004) identified various Daoist principles and used them to illustrate special leadership needs of global virtual teams. In an interview study by Z. X. Zhang and colleagues (2008), business executives reported their leadership philosophy of acting in the middle way. Tsui and colleagues (2006) found an example of business executives following the philosophy of active non-action. Sun and colleagues (2008) conducted content analysis of Sun Zi's 'The art of war' using the Daoist as well as Confucian philosophical concepts. The Daoist principle of reversal of opposites was also applied by Mao in his revolutionary movements, especially in military leadership (Lu & Lu, 2008). The above research endeavors point to the potential of Daoism for understanding Chinese leadership. While introducing basic Daoist philosophical principles to the leadership field is a start, to guide programmatic empirical research in the future, researchers must systematically develop essential Daoist constructs and theoretical models that have the capacity of being operationalized and empirically tested on leadership practices in contemporary Chinese organizations. In doing so researchers could follow the example of PL research in terms of persistence, systematicity, and rigor.

The holistic approach to leadership. In a holistic approach, actors tend to seek a comprehensive understanding of the issue at hand by looking at its many aspects and combining available perspectives. In such an approach, different leadership perspectives and styles are not viewed as incompatible or exclusive but rather complementary (C. C. Chen & Lee, 2008b). Our review of the leadership research found some evidence that the Chinese may have a tendency to be eclectic and holistic. Cheung and Chan (2005) conducted in depth dialogues with five eminent CEOs to explore ethical foundations of organization and management. The authors found that their business practices were guided not by a homogenous set of values but rather a synthesis of values derived from different schools of thoughts such as Confucianism, Daoism, Mohosm, and Legalism. Similarly, in an interview study of mainland Chinese executive managers, Z. X. Zhang and colleagues (2008) found that Chinese executives reported drawing upon and integrating Chinese and Western concepts of organization and management in their practices. When survey participants were given open-ended questions allowing them to propose different combinations of influence tactics, Fu and colleagues (2004) observed a pattern in the choice of influence tactics across different scenarios by both mainland and Taiwanese Chinese, i.e. multiple, different tactics (as many as five of the given 16 tactics) were often proposed in different configurations for influencing single act.

Integration of Chinese and non-Chinese perspectives and theories

As stated at the beginning of the chapter, social sciences in an increasingly globalized world could not be advanced through exclusively indigenous approaches. For Chinese leadership research to move forward, we must adopt both emic and etic approaches by integrating Chinese constructs and theories with those developed in the research community outside China, notably in the West. Integration in this context means simultaneously employing Chinese concepts and theories and those developed out of China, primarily by Western social scientists, in an attempt to shed more light on Chinese organization and management issues and making a contribution to universal concepts and theories. Specifically, in such integrative research, one can compare and contrast the validity and efficacy of Chinese and non-Chinese assumptions, concepts, and theories, the extent to which they converge, complement, enhance, or substitute for each other. Integration could be demonstrated through additional variance explained, mediation and moderating relationships between Chinese and non-Chinese concepts and theories. Studies of the moderation effects of high power distance and traditionality of the Chinese culture are good examples of how emic values may enhance or weaken certain universal relationships. Next, we further explore some additional possibilities.

Leader–member relationship building. Earlier, we pointed out that current research on LMX and *guanxi* focused primarily on the effect of LMX or *guanxi* quality rather than on antecedents and processes of how such quality is produced. While there are theories about Chinese *guanxi*-making and *guanxi*-use (C. C. Chen, Chen, & Xin, 2004; Hwang, 1987) and about LMX antecedents and relationship making (Graen, 2003), empirical research on either domain is lacking. There is great potential for comparative study of Chinese and Americans regarding how leaders and subordinates build relations. What are the roles of Chinese *guanxi* bases, such as kinships, common birthplaces, and former classmates as compared with American demographic backgrounds (Farh, Tsui, Xin, & Cheng, 1998)? At given point in time, how do these backgrounds correlate with relationship quality? Over time, how do they serve as bases that trigger ingroup relationship building? How do these bases interact with ability and performance to affect the evolution of relationship building between the leadership and members? How do social interactions outside work affect relationship quality?

Bringing a justice perspective into LMX and *guanxi*, we can ask the following questions: Are different relationship bases and different exchange activities perceived as more or less fair by the leader as opposed to the members, by ingroup as opposed to outgroup members, and by Chinese as opposed to Americans or those in other Western countries? How do fairness perceptions affect trust in the leader and performance of the ingroup members, the outgroup members, and the whole work unit? Lastly, one could examine the legitimacy and functionality of the ingroup-outgroup distinction in terms of perceived fairness, motivation, and performance. While the above questions focus on differences, one could examine similar questions from a contingency perspective, that is, the role of relationship-building bases and activities, their legitimacy, and functionality may depend on situational, institutional, and cultural factors.

Transformational leadership. We would add that empowering leadership, while challenging some of the basic assumptions of authoritarianism, can nevertheless also be integrated with PL and transformational leadership. First, the moral component of PL could be incorporated into future transformational leadership research to assess its discriminant validity in relation to other dimension as well as the whole model. Second, do transformational leaders come in all stripes in terms of their styles of relating to subordinates? Some may be more authoritative, others more participative or empowering, or still others alternating among these styles depending on situations. Studies of the Chinese executives seem to suggest such a possibility (Tsui et al., 2006). Third, is there a component of benevolence in transformational leadership? On one hand, does the individualized consideration dimension of transformational leadership, and perhaps, to a lesser extent, intellectual stimulation, overlap with benevolent leadership? On the other hand, benevolence or paternalism is arguably, some would say clearly, the antithesis of transformational leadership. While emphasizing the priority of individual self-interest to the collective organizational good, the Western brand of transformational leadership does not require the leader to be equally committed to caring for and protecting the followers from the downside of transformational change. It would be interesting to examine the extent to which transformational leaders are perceived by organizational members as benevolent - perhaps the expectation of benevolence from transformational leadership is culturally based. One would expect that benevolence is a salient if not essential component of Chinese transformational leaders, whereas it may not be so with American transformational leaders.

Empowering leadership. Research on empowering leadership has suffered from its being too broadly conceptualized. On the basis of psychological empowerment, which itself is a broadly defined multidimensional construct, empowering leadership behavior could be any behavior that enables, motivates, or supports subordinates. While efforts have been made to develop measures for sub-dimensions of empowering leadership, these dimensions often overlap with or duplicate existing constructs and measures. For example, Arnold and colleagues (200) identified five dimensions of empowering leadership and developed measure for them: leading by example, participative decision making, coaching, informing, and showing concern. Yet, measures of delegation and participative leadership (Kirkman & Rosen, 1999), supportive leadership (House, 1998), and developmental leadership (House, 1998), and supervisor mentoring (Scandura & Schriesheim, 1994) had already been developed. Empowering leadership therefore could be used as an overarching term for a variety of leadership behaviors that aim at deemphasizing and reducing the status and power hierarchy between supervisors and subordinates in order to develop and utilize the potential ability and motivation of the subordinates. For particular research purposes, researchers may pick and choose the above mentioned independent constructs to explore their applicability in Chinese organizations instead of using all empowering dimensions. Integration of Chinese and Western perspectives can be particularly interesting and fertile in this area, as it juxtaposes culturally different concepts (as for example demonstrated by the work on Interpersonal Relatedness as a dimension of personality described by Cheung, Zhang, & Cheung, this volume). For example, Z. X. Chen & Aryee (2007) found positive effects of delegation, a concept first developed and operationalized in the U.S.A., on subordinates' attitudes and performance in Chinese organizations. However, the mechanisms by which delegation influence subordinates in Chinese are culturally consistent concepts, i.e. relational mechanisms of organization-based self-esteem and insider status. Y. Zhang, Chen, and Wang (2008) found that benevolent leadership behaviors, such as caring for the career development of subordinates, affect their job satisfaction, OCB and task performance not only through the relational mechanism of supervisor identification, as posited by PL, but also through an individualistically oriented mechanism of self-determination. Furthermore, C. C. Chen, Wang, and Zhang (2008) found that power sharing and management control by supervisors positively interacted with each other to increase psychological empowerment of Chinese employees, which in turn increased the latter's positive attitudes and performance. Future research is needed to replicate these preliminary results and to expand into other areas in which seemingly incompatible concepts on the basis of cultural stereotypes may turn out to generate more knowledge together than separately.

Antecedents of leadership styles. Existing Chinese leadership research focuses more on consequences of leadership than on antecedents. Studying antecedents of Chinese leadership is important, however, as China and Chinese organizations have been experiencing unprecedented large scale, fast-paced, and drastic changes. Leadership must have been both the driving force and the emergent outcome of such changes. Do these changes lead to convergence or divergence of leadership philosophies and styles across different regions, institutions, communities within the Chinese society and between Chinese and non-Chinese leaders? Longitudinal field studies and archival data are needed to track such trends. Apart from situational antecedents of leadership practices, what role do personal traits, beliefs, values, and competencies play in leadership orientations? One interesting area of research is how prevalent is authoritarian leadership in Chinese organizations and what accounts for its persistence, even though there has been growing evidence that it engenders negative consequences for subordinates and the organization? To what extent can authoritarian leadership be explained by the authority structure of the organization, the personality of the leader, the leader-member relationship, or the characteristics of the subordinates? Similar questions could be asked about antecedents of various empowering leadership behaviors. Because these behaviors are relative new and less prevalent, it is important to identify their barriers and facilitators.

The follower perspective. Most leadership perspectives and theories, Chinese and Western alike, are top town from the perspectives of the leaders (Meindl, 1990; Chen, Belkin, & Kurtzberg, 2007). Yet, the perspectives of followers are gaining importance in contemporary organizations that aspire to operate within a flatter organizational structure, foster team work, and motivate initiative and innovation from employees. It is true that leadership research typically measures leadership styles and effectiveness from the perspectives of subordinates, yet the subordinates' perspectives, preferences, and feedback regarding the conception and practice of leadership has generally been neglected.

A number of interesting research questions can be asked regarding Chinese leadership from the follower perspective: How do subordinate characteristics, their self-interests, needs, and values, affect the attribution and assessment of leadership (C. C. Chen et al., 2007; Pastor, Mayo, & Shamir, in press)? What do subordinates think are the prototypical characteristics of ideal leaders? What leadership styles or combination of styles do employees prefer (Casimir & Li, 2005)? How do Chinese subordinates attempt to influence their managers, and how effective are those tactics (see e.g. Leong, Bond, & Fu, 2006)? How do the presence of feedback or its lack, and the nature of the feedback from subordinates contribute to the shaping and adoption of leadership styles by managers? This last question could, for example, be used to explore to what extent Chinese subordinates express their negative reactions or provide honest feedback to authoritarian managers when they dislike their style, and whether such expression and feedback has an impact on the continuation or revision of that disapproved style.

Summary and conclusion

Our review of the research on Chinese leadership shows that great strides have been made in the field over the last decade or so both in terms of the breadth of topics and in the quantity and quality of publications. We have documented how the indigenous concept of paternalism developed into a full-fledged theoretical model of paternalistic leadership, and was empirically tested in Chinese organizations. We further reviewed Chinese leadership research employing theories and concepts developed in the West (e.g. transformational leadership, delegation, and interactional justice), as well as other indigenous leadership perspectives (e.g. Daoism and the holistic perspective).

We highlighted the diversity of the theoretical and philosophical perspectives available in Chinese societies for studying Chinese leadership and analyzed how Western leadership concepts and theories were used, albeit implicitly, to elaborate and enrich as well as to contrast and challenge prevailing Chinese traditional leadership concepts and theories. We proposed areas in which indigenous and non-Chinese leadership theories and perspectives can be integrated to advance the understanding of Chinese leadership and leadership in the world. We believe that the field of Chinese leadership is still open and growing, and that it will present even more opportunities for scholars in China and the rest of the world to create, develop, and test a great variety of leadership theories.

Authors' note

We express our thanks to Zhijun Chen and Guohua Huang for their assistance in searching the literature and checking the references. This research was supported in part by Research Grants Council of the Hong Kong Special Adminstrative Region, China, Grants HKUST6458/Ø5H awarded to Jiing-Lih Farh and Rick Hackett.

References

Altemeyer, B. (1996). *The authoritarian specter.* Cambridge, MA: Harvard University Press.

Arnold, J. A., Arad, S., Rhoades, J. A., & Drasgow, F. (2000). The empowering leadership questionnaire: The construction and validation of a new scale for measuring leader behaviors. *Journal of Organizational Behavior, 21*, 250–260.

Aryee, S., Chen, Z. X., Sun, L. Y., & Debrah, Y. A. (2007). Antecedents and outcomes of abusive supervisor: Test of a trickle-down model. *Journal of Applied Psychology, 1*, 191–201.

Aryee, S. & Chen, Z. X. (2006). Leader–member exchange in a Chinese context: Antecedents, the mediating role of psychological empowerment and outcomes. *Journal of Business Research*, 59, 793–801.

Aycan, Z. (2006). Paternalism: Towards conceptual refinement and operstionalization. In K. S. Yang, K. K. Hwang, & U. Kim, (ed.), *Scientific advances in indigenous psychologies: Empirical, philosophical, and cultural contributions* (pp. 445–466). London: Cambridge University Press.

Bond, M. H. & Hwang, K. K. (1986). The social psychology of the Chinese people. In M. H. Bond (eds), *The psychology of the Chinese people* (pp. 213–266). New York: Oxford University Press.

Casimir, G. & Li, Z. (2005). Combinative aspects of leadership style: A comparison of Australian and Chinese followers. *Asian Business and Management, 4*, 271–291.

Chen, C. C., Belkin, L. Y., & Kurtzberg, T. R. (2007). A follower-centric contingency model of charisma attribution: The importance of follower emotion. In B. Shamir, R. Pillai, Bligh, M. & M. Uhl-Bien (eds), *Follower-centered perspectives on leadership: A tribute to the memory of James R. Meindl* (pp. 115–134). Greenwich, CT: Information Age Publishing.

Chen, C. C. & Chen, X. P. (2009). Negative externalities of close guanxi within organizations. *Asia Pacific Journal of Management, 26*, 37–53.

Chen, C. C., Chen, Y. R., & Xin, K. (2004). Guanxi practices and trust in management: A procedural justice perspective. *Organization Science, 15*, 200–209.

Chen, C. C. & Lee, Y. T. (2008a). *Leadership and management in China: Philosophies, theories, and practices.* New York: Cambridge University Press.

Chen, C. C. & Lee, Y. T. (2008b). The diversity and dynamism of Chinese philosophies on leadership. In C. C. Chen & Y. T. Lee (eds), *Leadership and management in China: Philosophies, theories, and practices* (pp. 1–27). New York: Cambridge University Press.

Chen, C. C., Wang, H., & Zhang, Y. (2008). Bounded empowerment: Main and joint effects of supervisory power sharing and management control. *Paper presented at IACMR Conference*, Guangzhou, China, August.

Chen, C. C. & Zhang, Z. X. (2008). Theory construction in management research. In X. P. Chen, A. Tsui, & J. L. Farh (eds), *Empirical methods in organization and management research* (pp. 60–81). Beijing, China: Peking University Press. (in Chinese)

Chen, X. P. & Chen, C. C. (2004). On the intricacies of the Chinese guanxi: A process model of guanxi development. *Asia Pacific Journal of Management, 21*, 305–324.

Chen, Y. F. & Tjosvold, D. (2006). Participative leadership by American and Chinese managers in China: The role of relationships. *Journal of Management Studies, 43*, 1727–1752.

Chen, Y. F. & Tjosvold, D. (2007). Guanxi and leader member relationships between American managers and Chinese employees: Open-minded dialogue as mediator. *Asian Pacific Journal of Management, 24*, 171–189.

Chen, Z. X. & Aryee, S. (2007). Delegation and employee work outcomes: An examination of the cultural context of mediation processes in China. *Academy of Management Journal, 50*, 226–238.

Cheng, B. S. (1995a). *Authoritarian values and executive leadership: The case of Taiwanese family enterprises.* Report prepared for Taiwan's National Science Council. Taiwan: National Taiwan University. (in Chinese)

Cheng, B. S. (1995b). Hierarchical structure and Chinese organizational behaviour. *Indigenous Psychological Research in Chinese Societies, 3*, 142–219. (In Chinese)

Cheng, B. S. (1995c). Paternalistic authority and leadership: A case study of a Taiwanese CEO. *Bulletin of the Institute of Ethnology Academic Sinica*, 79, 119–173. (in Chinese)

Cheng, B. S., Chou, L. F., & Farh, J. L. (2000). A triad model of paternalistic leadership: The constructs and measurement. *Indigenous Psychological Research in Chinese Societies, 14*, 3–64. (in Chinese)

Cheng, B. S., Chou, L. F., Huang, M. P., Farh, J. L., & Peng, S. (2003). A triad model of paternalistic leadership: Evidence from business organization in Mainland China. *Indigenous Psychological Research in Chinese Societies, 20*, 209–252. (in Chinese)

Cheng, B. S., Chou, L. F., Wu, T. Y., Huang, M. P., & Farh, J. L. (2004). Paternalistic leadership and subordinate response: Establishing a leadership model in Chinese organizations. *Asian Journal of Social Psychology, 7*, 89–117.

Cheng, B. S. & Farh, J. L. (2001). Social orientation in Chinese societies: A comparison of employees from Taiwan and Chinese mainland. *Chinese Journal of Psychology, 43*, 207–221. (in Chinese)

Cheng, B. S., Shieh, P. Y., & Chou, L. F. (2002). The principal's leadership, leader–member exchange quality, and the teacher's extra-role behavior: The effects of transformational and paternalistic leadership. *Indigenous Psychological Research in Chinese Societies, 17*, 105–161. (in Chinese)

Cheung, C. K. & Chan, A. C. F. (2005). Philosophical foundations of eminent Hong Kong Chinese CEO's leadership. *Journal of Business Ethics, 60*, 47–62.

Davis, D. D. (2004). The Tao of leadership in virtual teams. *Organizational Dynamics, 33*, 47–62.

Deyo, F. C. (1978). Local foremen in multinational enterprise: A comparative case study of supervisory role-tensions in Western and Chinese factories of Singapore. *Journal of Management Studies, 15*, 308–317.

Deyo, F. C. (1983). Chinese management practices and work commitment in comparative perspective. In L. A. P. Gosling & L. Y. C. Lim (eds), *The Chinese in Southeast Asia: Identity, culture and politics* (Vol. 2, pp. 214–230). Singapore: Maruzen Asian.

Farh, J. L. & Cheng, B. S. (2000). A cultural analysis of paternalistic leadership in Chinese organizations. In J. T. Li, A. S. Tsui, & E. Weldon (eds), *Management and organizations in the Chinese context* (pp. 94–127). London: Macmillan.

Farh, J. L., Cheng, B. S., Chou, L. F., & Chu, X. P. (2006). Authority and benevolence: Employees' responses to paternalistic leadership in China. In A. S. Tsui, Y. Bian, & L. Cheng (eds), *China's domestic private firms: Multidisciplinary perspectives on management and performance* (pp. 230–260). New York: M. E. Sharpe.

Farh, J. L., Earley, P. C., & Lin, S. C. (1997). Impetus for action: A cultural analysis of justice and organizational citizenship behavior in Chinese society. *Administrative Science Quarterly, 42*, 421–444.

Farh, J. L., Hackett, R., & Liang, J. (2007). Individual-level cultural values as moderators of perceived organizational support–employee outcome relationships in China: Comparing the effects of power distance and traditionality. *Academy of Management Journal, 50*, 715–729.

Farh, J. L., Liang, J., Chou, L. F., & Cheng, B. S. (2008). Paternalistic leadership in Chinese organizations: Research progress and future research directions. In C. C. Chen & Y. T. Lee (eds), *Leadership and management in China: Philosophies, theories, and practices* (pp. 171–205). London: Cambridge University Press.

Farh, J. L., Tsui, A. S., Xin, K., & Cheng, B. S. (1998). The influence of relational demography and guanxi: The Chinese case. *Organization Science, 9*, 471–488.

Fernandez, J. A. (2004). The gentleman's code of Confucius: Leadership by values. *Organizational Dynamics, 33*, 21–31.

Fu, P. P., Kennedy, J., Tata, J., Yukl, G., Bond, M. H., Peng, T. K., Srinivas, E. S., Howel, J. P., Prieto, L., Koopman, P., Boonstra, J. J., Pasa, S., Lacassagne, M. F., Higashide, H. & Cheosakul, A. (2004). The impact of societal cultural values and individual social beliefs on the perceived effectiveness of managerial influence strategies: A meso approach. *Journal of International Business Studies*, 35, 284–305.

Fu, P. P. & Yukl, G. (2000). Perceived effectiveness of influence tactics in the United States and China. *Leadership Quarterly, 11*, 251–266.

Graen, G. B. (2003). Interpersonal workplace theory at the crossroads: LMX and transformational theory as special cases of role making in work organizations. In G. B. Graen (ed.), *Dealing with diversity* (pp. 145–182). Charlotte, NC: Information Age Publishing.

Hackett, R. D., Farh, J. L., Song, L. J., & Lapierre, L. M. (2003). LMX and organizational citizenship behavior: Examining the links within and across Western and Chinese samples. In G. B. Graen (ed.), *Dealing with diversity* (pp. 219–264). Charlotte, NC: Information Age Publishing.

House, R. J. (1998). Measures and assessments for the charismatic leadership approach: Scales, latent constructs, loadings, Cronbach alphas, and interclass correlations. In E. Dansereau & F. J. Yammarino (eds), *Leadership: The multiple-level approaches contemporary and alternative* (Vol. 24, Part B, pp. 23–30.). London: JAI Press.

Huang, X., Shi, K., Zhang, Z., & Cheung, Y. L. (2006). The impact of participative leadership behavior on psychological empowerment and organizational commitment in Chinese state-owned enterprises: The moderating role of organizational tenure. *Asia Pacific Journal of Management, 23*, 345–367.

Hui, C. & Graen, G. (1997). Guanxi and professional leadership in contemporary Sino–American joint ventures in mainland China. *Leadership Quarterly, 8*, 451–465.

Hui, C., Law, K. S., & Chen, Z. X. (1999). A structural equation model of the effects of negative affectivity, leader–member exchange, and perceived job mobility on in-role and extra-role performance: A Chinese case. *Organizational Behavior and Human Decision Process, 77*, 3–21.

Hui, C., Lee, C., & Rousseau, D. M. (2004). Employment relationships in China: Do workers relate to the organization or to people? *Organization Science, 15*, 232–240.

Hwang, K. K. (1987). Face and favor: The Chinese power game. *American Journal of Sociology, 92*, 944–974.

Javidan, M. & Carl, D. E. (2005). Leadership across cultures: A study of Canadian and Taiwanese executives. *Management International Review, 45*, 23–44.eds), *Chinese culture and mental health: An overview* (pp. 29–45). Orlando, FL: Academic Press.

Kirkman, B. L. & Rosen, B. (1999). Beyond self-management: The antecedents and consequences of team empowerment. *Academy of Management Journal, 42*, 58–74.

Konczak, L. J., Stelly, D. J., & Trusty, M. L. (2000). Defining and measuring empowering leader behaviors: Development of an upward feedback instrument. *Educational and Psychological Measurement, 60*, 302–308.

Law, K. S., Wong, C. S. and Wong, L. (2000). Effect of supervisor–subordinate guanxi on supervisory decisions in China: An empirical investigation. *International Journal of Human Resource Management, 11*, 715–29.

Lee, Y., Han, A., Byron, T. K., & Fan, H. (2008). Daoist leadership: Theory and application. In C. C. Chen & Y. T. Lee (eds), *Leadership and management in China: Philosophies, theories, and practices* (pp. 83–107). New York: Cambridge University Press.

Leong, J. L. T., Bond, M. H., & Fu, P. P. (2006). Perceived effectiveness of influence strategies in the United States and three Chinese societies. *International Journal of Cross-Cultural Management, 6*, 101–120.

Liang, S. K., Ling, H. C., & Hsieh, S. Y. (2007). The mediating effects of leader–member exchange quality to influence the relationships between paternalistic leadership and organizational citizenship behaviors. *Journal of American Academy of Business, 10*, 127– 137.

Ling, W. Q., Chen, L., & Wang, D. (1987). The construction of the CPM scale for leadership behavior assessment. *Acta Psychologica Sinica, 19*, 199–207. (in Chinese)

Lu, X. & Lu, J. (2008). The leadership theories and practices of Mao Zedong and Deng Xiaoping. In C. C. Chen & Y. T. Lee (eds), *Leadership and management in China: Philosophies, theories, and practices* (pp. 206–238). New York: Cambridge University Press.

Meindl, J. R. (1990). On leadership: An alternative to the conventional wisdom. *Research in Organizational Behavior, 12*, 159–203.

Misumi, J. (1985). *The behavioral science of leadership*. Ann Arbor, MI: University of Michigan Press.

Nisbett, R. E., Peng, K., Choi, I, & Norenzayan, A. (2001). Culture and systems of thought: Holistic versus analytic cognition. *Psychological Review, 108*, 291–310.

Pastor, J. C., Mayo, M., & Shamir, B. (in press). Adding fuel to fire: The impact of followers' arousal on rations of charisma. *Journal of Applied Psychology*.

Pellegrini, E. K. & Scandura, T. A. (2008). Paternalistic leadership: A review and agenda for future research. *Journal of Management, 34*, 566–593.

Peng, Y. Q, Chen, C. C. & Yang, X. H (2008). Bridging Confucianism and legalism: Xunzi's philosophy of sage-kingship. In C. C. Chen & Y. T. Lee (eds), *Leadership and management in China: Philosophies, theories, and practices* (pp. 51–79). New York: Cambridge University Press.

Peterson, M. F. (1988). PM theory in Japan and China: What's in it for the United States? *Organizational Dynamics*, 22–38.

Pye, L. W. (1985). *Asia power and politics*. Cambridge, MA: Harvard University Press.

Redding, G. & Wong, G. Y. Y. (1986). The psychology of the Chinese organizational behavior. In M. H. Bond (eds), *The psychology of the Chinese people* (pp. 267–295). New York: Oxford University Press.

Scandura, T. A. & Schriesheim, C. A. (1994). Leader–member exchange and supervisory career mentoring as complementary constructs in leadership research. *Academy of Management Journal, 37*, 1588–1602.

Silin, R. H. (1976). *Leadership and value: The organization of large-scale Taiwan enterprises*. Cambridge, MA: Harvard University Press.

Smith, P. B. and Wang, Z. M. (1996). Chinese leadership and organizational structures. In M. H. Bond (ed.), *The handbook of Chinese psychology* (pp. 322–337). Hong Kong: Oxford University Press.

Sun, H., Chen, C. C. & Zhang, S. H (2008). Strategic leadership of Sunzi's 'The Art of War'. In C. C. Chen & Y. T. Lee (eds), *Leadership and management in China: Philosophies, theories, and practices* (pp. 143–168). New York: Cambridge University Press.

Tjosvold, D., Hui, C., & Law, K. S. (1998). Empowerment in the manager–employee relationship in Hong Kong: Interdependence and controversy. *Journal of Social Psychology, 138*, 624–636.

Tsui, A. S., Bian, Y., & Cheng, L. (2006). *China's domestic private firms: Multidisciplinary perspectives on management and performance*. New York: M. E. Sharpe.

Tsui, A. S., Wang, H., Xin, K. R., Zhang, L. H., & Fu, P. P. (2004). Let a thousand flowers bloom: Variation of leadership styles in Chinese firms. *Organization Dynamics, 3*, 5–20.

Tsui, A. S., Zhang, Z. X., Wang, H., Xin, K. R., & Wu, J. B. (2006). Unpacking the relationship between CEO leadership behavior and organizational culture. *Leadership Quarterly, 17*, 113–137.

Wagner, D. G. & Berger, J. (1985). Do sociological theories grow? *American Journal of Sociology, 90*, 697–728.

Walumbwa, F. O. & Lawler, J. J. (2003). Building effective organizations: Transformational leadership, collectivist orientation, work-related attitudes and withdrawal behaviors in three emerging economies. *International Journal of Human Resource Management, 14*, 1083–1101.

Walumbwa, F. O., Lawler, J. J., & Avolio, B. J. (2007). Leadership, individual differences, and work-related attitudes: A cross-culture investigation. *Applied Psychology: An International Review, 56*, 212–230.

Wang, H., Law, K., Hackett, R., Wang, D., & Chen, Z. X. (2005). Leader–member exchange as a mediator of the relationship between transformational leadership and followers' performance and organizational citizenship behavior. *Academy of Management Journal, 48*, 420–432.

Weber, M. (1968). *Economy and society*. Translated by G. Roth and C. Wittich. Berkeley, CA: University of California.

Weidenbaum, M. (1996). The Chinese family business enterprise. *California Management Review, 38*, 141–156.

Xie, J. L., Schaubroeck, J., & Lam, S. S. K. (2008). Theories of job stress and the role of traditional values: A longitudinal study in China. *Journal of Applied Psychology, 93*, 831–848.

Yang, K. S. (1996). Psychological transformation of the Chinese people as a result of societal modernization. In M. H. Bond (ed.), *The psychology of the Chinese people* (pp. 479–498). Hong Kong: Oxford University Press.

Yang, K. S. (2003). Methodological and theoretical issues on psychological traditionality and modernity research in an Asian society: In response to Kwang-Kuo Hwang and beyond. *Asian Journal of Social Psychology, 6*, 263–285.

Yang, X. H. Peng, Y. Q, & Lee, Y. T. (2008). The Confucian and Mencian philosophy of benevolent leadership. In C. C. Chen & Y. T. Lee (eds), *Leadership and management in China: Philosophies, theories, and practices* (pp. 31–50). New York: Cambridge University Press.

Zhang, Y. Chen, C. C., Wang, H. (2008). How does individualized consideration foster OCB? A comparison of three psychological mechanisms. Paper presented at the Academy of Management, Anaheim, CA, July.

Zhang, Z. X, Chen, C. C., Liu. L. A., & Liu, X. F. (2008). Chinese traditions and Western theories: Influences on business leaders in China. In C. C. Chen & Y. T. Lee (eds), *Leadership and management in China: Philosophies, theories, and practices* (pp. 239–271). New York: Cambridge University Press.

CHAPTER 36

Chinese consumer behavior: the effects of content, process, and language

Robert S. Wyer, Jr and Jiewen Hong

Writing a chapter on consumer behavior for a 'Handbook of Chinese Psychology' immediately presents two related problems. First, should the chapter focus on the psychology of Chinese consumer behavior, the Chinese psychology of consumer behavior, or both? We have adopted the former approach. In doing so, however, we find it difficult if not impossible to conceptualize Chinese consumer behavior independently of non-Chinese consumer behavior. Certainly, our accumulated knowledge about consumer behavior in general has implications for consumer behavior in China. In this regard, Markman, Grimm, and Kim (2009) argue that the goal of psychology is to describe the antecedents of behavior completely in terms of the situational and individual difference variables that give rise to it. Cultural research is often necessary in order to identify important determinants of behavior that might otherwise go undetected. Once these and other variables are incorporated into a general conceptualization of human functioning, however, cultural differences in behavior could presumably be explained in terms of this conceptualization (but see Hong, 2009, for an opposing view).

However, we are obviously a long way from developing such a conceptualization. It may therefore be useful to consider the situational and individual difference variables that are primarily (although not exclusively) characteristic of Chinese individuals and examine their implications for consumer judgment and decision processes. We will review factors that have been shown empirically to characterize both the knowledge that Chinese cultural representatives bring to bear on their interpretation of the information they receive and the way they use this knowledge to make judgments and decisions. Some of our discussion necessarily duplicates material presented in more detail both in other chapters of this volume and elsewhere (e.g. Kitayama & Cohen, 2007; Wyer, Chiu, & Hong, 2009). However, it provides a framework for conceptualizing much of the current research on consumer behavior, as we will see.

In this regard, cultural research can be distinguished in terms of its emphasis on *content* (i.e. the norms, beliefs, values and goals that characterize the members of different societies and the dimensions along which they vary) and *process* (the cognitive procedures and styles of thinking that individuals apply to the information they receive). In each case, the research is implicitly or explicitly based on one of two different assumptions. One relatively traditional view is largely sociological in nature and conceptualizes culture as a relatively stable body of norms and values that characterize a given society or social group. A more recent view, however, has its roots in theory and research on knowledge accessibility (Förster & Liberman, 2007; Higgins, 1996; Wyer, 2008). According to this view, the cognitive and motivational factors that characterize a given culture are dynamic in character, and their influence in any given situation depends in part on their accessibility in memory at the time (Hong, 2009; Chiu & Hong, 2007). Oyserman and Sorensen (2009), for example, postulate a number of 'cultural syndromes' that exist to some degree in many societies but vary across these societies in their relative pervasiveness and strength.

Although dynamic conceptualizations of culture differ in detail (cf., Hong, 2009; Oyserman & Sorensen, 2009), they converge on the conclusion that although certain norms, beliefs, goals and values are likely to be 'chronically' accessible to members of a given society as a result of having been frequently exposed to them in the course of daily life, transitory situational factors can also influence the accessibility of these cognitions and the likelihood of applying them. Other concepts and knowledge with implications for judgments and decisions also exist in memory, of course, and situational variables can call these cognitions to mind as well. Consequently, the effects of these latter cognitions can sometimes override the effects of culture-related concepts and knowledge. This possibility is particularly evident in biculturals, whose judgments and behavior are very likely to depend on situational factors that call attention to one cultural identity or the other (Hong, Morris, Chiu, & Benet-Martinez, 2000; Lau-Gesk, 2003).

In short, the impact of culture on judgments and behavior decisions is a function of both chronic and situation-specific factors. Furthermore, the effects of one set of factors cannot be understood without taking the other set into account as well. Individuals' reactions to the information they receive in a consumer context (e.g. advertising appeals), and the decisions they make on the basis of these reactions, are likely to depend not only on general differences in their cultural background but also on characteristics of the immediate situation that call different subsets of culture-related (or unrelated) knowledge to mind. It is important to consider this dependence when evaluating the implications of the discussion to follow.

In this discussion, we first review the 'content' of Chinese culture and its implications for consumer behavior, focusing on the norms, beliefs and values that Chinese cultural representatives are likely to hold and the conditions in which they are likely to be applied. In this context, we cite current research in consumer behavior to exemplify the implications of this discussion. We then turn to a discussion of the processes that Chinese consumers are likely to bring to bear on the interpretation of information and the judgments they make. Finally, we review a factor that influences both the content and processing of information that consumers are likely encounter, namely, the language in which information is received and communicated. Although the work we review in this chapter was largely conducted on Chinese individuals, we also draw upon data obtained from other East Asian societies that are likely to be similar in terms of the characteristics we consider.

Content effects: dimensions of cultural variation

Extensive research has been conducted to identify the fundamental dimensions along which cultural norms, beliefs and values are likely to vary (Hofstede, 1980; Inglehart & Baker, 2000; Schwartz, 2009; Triandis, 1989, 1995). Most of these dimensions directly or indirectly bear on individuals' perceptions of themselves in relation to others (Triandis, 1989). However, the focus of this research has been on the characterization of different cultural groups and not the individuals composing them. As Wan and Chiu (2009) argue, there can be important differences between (a) the norms and values that are perceived to characterize a cultural group by the individuals who compose it and (b) the norms and values that these individuals actually hold. Certain dimensions are nonetheless important to consider. In this section, we consider four dimensions: individualism vs. collectivism, independence vs. interdependence, power distance, and prevention vs. promotion motivation.

Collectivism–individualism and interdependence–independence

Collectivism vs. individualism. Cultures are most commonly distinguished in terms of the degree to which people think of themselves as unique individuals or, alternatively, as members of a group. Asians are typically assumed to be high in *collectivism* as opposed to *individualism.* For example, they are more likely than members of Western societies to describe themselves in terms of the social roles they occupy rather than in terms of personal attributes and dispositions (Ip & Bond, 1995; Rhee, Uleman, & Lee, 1996; Triandis, 1989; Wang, 2001). Their group-focused orientation is also reflected in a concern with duty and obligation rather than individual rights (Hong, Ip, Chiu, Morris, & Menon, 2001; Markus & Kitayama, 1991). There may nevertheless be boundaries on the collective in which these concerns are applied. Rhee et al. (1996) note that East Asians make fine distinctions between ingroup and outgroup members within a given culture, and their collectivism may often be restricted to members of a rather narrowly defined ingroup (e.g. family members or close friends).

Individualism–collectivism has typically been applied to societies as a whole. However, it characterizes the norms, beliefs and values to which individual members of these societies are frequently exposed and, therefore, are likely to be chronically accessible in memory. The accessibility of these norms and values does not guarantee their application, however (Wan & Chiu, 2009). Oyserman and Sorensen (2009) view individualism and collectivism as two of several 'cultural syndromes' or networks of loosely connected constructs that exist in memory as independent knowledge systems. Although a particular syndrome may be chronically accessible in memory as a result of being frequently exposed to the concepts and knowledge that compose it, situational factors can often activate other syndromes and, therefore, can override their effects.

Interdependence vs. independence. Markus and Kitayama (1991) proposed a conceptualization of individual differences in self-construal that incorporates many features of collectivism–individualism. They note that people may define themselves either in relation to others or, alternatively, independently of other persons. An interdependent self-construal, however, can be manifested in several ways. For example, it could be reflected in either feelings of responsibility to others or in feelings of dependence on others for social or material support. On the other hand, it might give rise to competitiveness and a desire not to be outdone by others.

These different social orientations were identified in a factor analysis of Triandis and Gelfand's (1998) individualism–collectivism scale by Briley and Wyer (2001). This analysis yielded five factors: individuality, emotional connectedness, self-sacrifice (i.e. the disposition to subordinate one's own interests to those of others), competitiveness and the motivation not to be outperformed (for other dimensions of collectivism–individualism, see Triandis et al., 1986). Chinese were lower than North Americans along the first dimensions but higher than North Americans in emotional connectedness, self-sacrifice and the desire not to be outperformed. Furthermore, exposing Chinese to cultural icons (e.g. pictures of the Great Wall, the dragon, etc.) increased the value they attached not only to self-sacrifice but also the desire not to be outperformed and (nonsignificantly) competitiveness. (In contrast, priming Americans with symbols of American culture *decreased* their competitiveness and motivation not to be outperformed.) Thus, Chinese persons' disposition to think of themselves in relation to others was manifested in values associated with quite different types of social behavior, depending on the context of this behavior. Note that the effect of priming on the values that Chinese reported confirms the assumption that cultural norms, beliefs and values are not always accessible in memory. That is, situational factors that call attention to these cognitions may be necessary for them to be activated.

Implications for consumer behavior. If norms and values govern the criteria that people use as a basis for their behavioral decisions, they may influence product evaluations and purchase intentions. Thus, if Chinese typically have a collectivist orientation and are disposed to think of themselves in relation to others, they are likely to be guided to a greater extent than members of other societies by others' opinions and by persuasive appeals that emphasize social relationships.

There is empirical support for this conjecture. Han and Shavitt (1994), for example, found that Korean advertisements, to a greater extent than Western advertisements, employ appeals that emphasize harmony, family interactions, and ingroup benefits. Furthermore, ads with these emphases are more persuasive, particularly when the products being promoted are typically used with other persons. Aaker and Williams (1998) found that Chinese participants were more persuaded by advertisements that employ other-focused emotions (e.g. empathy), whereas American participants found ego-focused emotional appeals (e.g. pride) more persuasive.

The implications of these findings should not be overgeneralized. Although a content analysis of more recent Chinese television commercials (Ji & McNeal, 2001;Lin, 2001) indicates an emphasis on traditional Chinese values, individualistic themes are gradually emerging in ads that are targeted at the youth. In fact, Zhang and Shavitt (2003) found that ads in China often emphasized *individualism*-related values, and that this was particularly true when the ads appeared in magazines that were targeted at young, educated, high income individuals. This tendency was more pronounced when the advertised products were likely to be purchased for personal use rather than for use in a group context. These results suggest that although Chinese cultures may be characterized by collectivist norms, beliefs and values, individualistic norms, beliefs and values are also relatively common and ads that endorse them may often be effective as well. These findings are consistent with the conjecture that the younger generation of Chinese tend to have a more accessible interdependent self-construal as a result of the one child policy (Lee & Gardner, 2005).

The effect of individualistic appeals is also evident in biculturals, although the nature of this effect can vary. In a study by Lau-Gesk (2003), bicultural Chinese read advertising appeals that endorsed either individualism alone, interpersonal relations alone, or both values in combination. Participants were equally influenced by appeals that emphasized individualism and appeals that emphasized interpersonal values when each set of values was endorsed in isolation. When an appeal endorsed *both* sets of values, however, biculturals with a disposition to integrate the two orientations were positively influenced, whereas biculturals with a tendency to compartmentalize the two opposing cultural orientations were negatively influenced.

The latter finding could have more general implications for the younger generation of Chinese consumers. To the extent that both collectivistic and individualistic norms are readily accessible to the younger generation of Chinese consumers, and these two sets of norms and values are represented independently in memory, appeals may be more effective if advertisers focus on only one subset of these values than if they emphasize both sets of norms and values in combination.

The aforementioned research suggests that situational as well as chronic differences in the accessibility of independent and interdependent self-construals can have an impact on individuals' reactions to product information. However, this research has largely been conducted under conditions in which participants were unlikely to expend much effort in trying to make an accurate evaluation. As Lee and Semin (2009) point out, chronically or situationally accessible norms and values may generally have more impact when individuals do not have the ability or motivation to think carefully about their judgments and decisions. Briley and Aaker (2006), for example, found that cultural differences in the interpretation of information were not evident when individuals were both able and motivated to draw upon a broader subset of their previously acquired knowledge. This suggests that the effects of cultural differences in norms might only be apparent when individuals are not inclined to think extensively about the judgments and decisions they make. However, a further qualification on this conclusion will be noted presently.

Reciprocity norms in the exchange of gifts. An additional consequence of the tendency to think of oneself in relation to others that has implications for consumer behavior occurs in the exchange of gifts. The receipt of a gift can elicit both positive feelings of appreciation and negative feelings of obligation or indebtedness (Fong, 2006; Watkins, Scheer, Ovnicek, & Kolts, 2006), and the willingness to reciprocate the gift may depend on the relative influence of these feelings and the norms they activate. This, in turn, may vary over cultures. Westerners, who have strong independent self-construals and focus their attention on positive decision outcomes, are likely to feel appreciative when they receive a gift. Their reciprocation may therefore be based on a desire to express this appreciation by doing something for the gift giver in return although they may not feel any obligation to do so.

In contrast, Chinese, who have interdependent self-construals and pay particular attention to negative consequences of their behavior, may believe they are expected to reciprocate a gift and may feel indebted and compelled to reciprocate Consequently, if Chinese feel unable or unmotivated to reciprocate a gift that is offered to them, they are likely to refuse the gift in order to avoid the negative feelings of indebtedness they would experience if they accepted. Westerners, on the other hand, may accept the gift without experiencing these negative feelings.

A series of studies by Shen, Wan, and Wyer (2009) confirmed this possibility. In a series of guided scenarios, Chinese reported significantly less willingness to accept a gift from a casual acquaintance than Canadian participants did. This difference was eliminated, however, when the gift-giver was a close friend and expectations to reciprocate were less pronounced (Joy, 2001). In two behavioral studies, Chinese participants who had agreed to help someone on a task that ostensibly required either a lot of time or little time were later willing to accept candies in proportion to the amount of help they agreed to provide, whereas Canadians accepted the same number of candies regardless of the help they indicated they would give.

Power distance and verticality

A second important dimension of cultural variation is *power distance* (Hofstede (1980), or the extent to which a society is organized hierarchically. A related variable is conceptualized by Triandis and Gelfand (1998; see also Shavitt, Lalwani, Zhang, & Torelli, 2006) in terms of the vertical or horizontal structure of the society or, alternatively, individuals' perceptions of themselves in relation to this structure. Variation along this dimension may differ qualitatively, however, depending on characteristics of individuals along other dimensions. For example, vertical collectivists encourage compliance with authority, whereas vertical individualists are concerned with improvement in social status and make distinctions among individuals in terms of achievement or social power. Horizontal collectivists focus on sociability and egalitarianism, whereas horizontal individualists encourage uniqueness, independence and self-reliance. In this typology, the Chinese are characterized as both vertical and collectivist.

Chinese may be concerned with status differences both within the collective to which they belong and between their ingroup and outgroups, rather than emphasizing sociability and egalitarianism (see Bond, 1996). This orientation has several implications for consumer information processing. For example, Asians may be particularly sensitive to the opinions of authority figures or individuals in positions of higher status. At the same time, they might be influenced by appeals that suggest the possibility of gaining personal status and prestige by using a product. Thus, they may be more influenced by prestigious brand names independently of the quality of the products themselves. Although Asians are clearly not unique in these respects, they may be more susceptible to the influence of such appeals than are individuals with an individualistic or egalitarian orientation.

Several manifestations of this emphasis are summarized by Shavitt, Lalwani, Zhang, and Torelli (2006). For example, Japanese (who, like Chinese, are vertical collectivists) are more likely than Westerners to evaluate products from their own country more favorably than foreign products (Gurhan-Canli & Maheswaran, 2000). Moreover, this preference appears to be based on concern with prestige and status rather than the superiority of the products in question. Other evidence that advertising appeals in vertical collectivist societies emphasize status and prestige was reported by Shavitt, Zhang, and Johnson (2006).

However, these appeals should be distinguished from those that are common in vertical individualist societies. In the latter appeals, *individual* status or prestige may be important rather than *collective* status. Consistent with this conjecture, Choi, Lee, and Kim (2005) found that in ads in the United States (a vertical individualistic culture), celebrity endorsers were identified by name and profession and their individual status was emphasized. In Korea (a vertical collectivist culture), however, endorsers were much less often identified by name. Rather, they played a role other than themselves in ads that emphasized collectivist values (family, belongingness, etc.).

The role of celebrity endorsers in Chinese and American advertisements deserves further consideration. As Kelman (1961) pointed out many years ago, the source of a communication can be influential because (a) the source represents a group that has power or control over the recipient's well being, (b) the source's opinion provides an indication of views that are socially desirable, or (c) the source is particularly knowledgeable in the domain in which the communication is relevant. The effects of different types of celebrity endorsers and when these effects occur is likely to depend on the type of product being advertised as well as the values of the recipient. However, these questions have rarely if ever been examined in consumer research in general, and their implications for the impact of advertising appeals in China and other countries in East Asia are particularly unclear. Future research should address these matters.

Prevention and promotion orientation

One manifestation of the disposition to think of oneself as part of a group may be a heightened feeling of responsibility to others (Hong et al., 2001). This feeling may be reflected in a tendency to compromise, and also to make decisions that minimize the likelihood of negative consequences for others. Furthermore, this motivation, once activated, may induce a *general* disposition to avoid negative outcomes (i.e. a *prevention focus*; Higgins, 1997) that influences behavioral decisions independently of whether these decisions have implications for others or only for oneself. This possibility is confirmed by Lee, Aaker, and Gardner (2000) and Aaker and Lee (2001),who showed that Hong Kong Chinese, like those who were stimulated to think of themselves as members of a group, paid particular attention to negative outcomes of behavior and were unwilling to risk negative consequences of behavioral decisions (see also Yates & Lee, 1996).

Chinese persons' prevention focus may be rooted in child-rearing and socialization practices (see Wang & Chang, this volume). This possibility is suggested in research by Peggy Miller and her colleagues (Miller, Fung, & Mintz, 1996; Miller, Wiley, Fung, & Liang, 1997). They observed Taiwanese and American mothers' interactions with their children in the course of discussing the child's misdeeds. Taiwanese parents tended to treat the misdeeds as a character deficiency that needed to be eliminated through effort. This contrasted with American parents, who acknowledged the seriousness of their child's misdeeds but appeared to view them as natural occurrences in the course of growing up that had no serious implications for the child's character. Furthermore, whereas Taiwanese parents set themselves up as positive role models for their child to emulate, American parents frequently acknowledged their own misdeeds when they were young, conveying the belief that to err is human. The effect of these differences in later life is suggested by Oishi, Wyer, and Colcombe's (2000) finding that Asians tend to take responsibility for negative consequences of their behavior, whereas North Americans typically attribute them to external, situational factors over which they had no control.

These differences in orientation have obvious implications for consumer judgment and decision-making. Chen, Ng, and Rao (2003), for example, found that American participants (who presumably have a promotion orientation) reported greater willingness to pay for the expedited delivery of a product if the appeal emphasized positive consequences (e.g. early enjoyment of the product). However, Singaporean participants (who presumably have a prevention focus) were more willing to pay for the service if the appeal emphasized the avoidance of negative consequences (a delay). Similarly, Aaker and Lee (2001) found that leading individuals to think of themselves as interdependent increased the influence of appeals that emphasized safety and security rather than positive features of the choice alternatives.

The focus on positive vs. negative outcomes of a decision may reflect a more general mindset that, once activated, generalizes over a variety of stimulus domains. A series of studies by Briley and his colleagues (Briley, Morris, & Simonson, 2000; 2005; Briley & Wyer, 2002) suggest this possibility. In one study, Briley and Wyer (2002) initially induced participants to believe they were participating as a group. In a later, ostensibly unrelated situation, these participants tended to make product choices that minimized the likelihood of negative consequences of these decisions without considering the positive features of the choice alternatives. Thus, for example, they chose products that appeared to have the least undesirable features even though these products had the least desirable features as well. Furthermore, calling participants' attention to their cultural identity, thus making them conscious of their membership in a culture-defined collective, had similar effects.

When Chinese individuals' cultural identity is not explicitly called to their attention, however, their prevention focus may be governed by a more general disposition that has been acquired through social learning (Miller et al., 1997). Nevertheless, this disposition may not have much effect unless situational factors increase its accessibility in memory. Briley et al. (2000) found that Chinese tended to choose products that minimized the likelihood of negative consequences only when they were asked to give a reason for their choice, apparently stimulating them to activate a culture-related basis for judgment. Thus, Chinese may have a disposition to avoid negative consequences of their decision. However, this disposition is likely to be pronounced only if situational factors stimulate them to think about culture-related norms and values that might otherwise not be immediately accessible.

The situational factors that activate the prevention orientation of Chinese can be rather subtle. In a later series of studies (Briley et al., 2005), Hong Kong bicultural Chinese were asked to make product choices similar to those made by participants in Briley et al's (2000) experiments. However, the experiment was conducted either in Chinese or in English. These participants were significantly more inclined to make choices that minimized negative consequences when the experiment was conducted in Chinese.

There are two alternative interpretations of this finding. On one hand, the language in which the study was conducted spontaneously activated culture-related norms and values that guided participants' choice behavior. On the other hand, it may have stimulated participants to think about the criteria they were *expected* to apply in the situational context at hand, and they employed these criteria deliberately in order to comply with these expectations.

To distinguish between these possibilities, Briley et al. (2005) asked participants to perform the decision task while trying to remember an 8-digit number. If the language in which participants were communicating spontaneously activated culture-related decision criteria, putting them under processing load should increase their likelihood of using these criteria and consequently would increase the effects of language differences. If, however, the language influenced the criteria that participants deliberately applied in order to comply with implicit social expectations, processing load should decrease their ability to engage in this cognitive deliberation and should decrease the influence of language. In fact, the latter was the case. A third study confirmed the conclusions drawn from this experiment, showing that participants' decisions were influenced by the nationality of the individuals who were ostensibly conducting the study independently of the language in which the study was conducted.

Briley et al's (2005) findings have implications for the comprehension of advertisements that are presented in a bicultural context. In Hong Kong, for example, television commercials and billboards can convey information in Chinese, in English, or in both. Consumers' attitudes toward the advertised products are influenced by their perceptions of the desirability of owning or using the product in a particular social context. In such conditions, the language in which the ad is conveyed could activate normative standards of social desirability that influence recipients' acceptance of the ad's implications. This suggests that an advertisement's effectiveness can depend on whether the context in which the advertised product is considered desirable is consistent with the context implied by the language in which the product is promoted.

Other implications of Briley et al's (2005) findings should be noted. The evidence that cultural differences in prevention orientation are not evident when participants are unable to think carefully about their decision is particularly noteworthy in the context of Lee and Semin's (2009) observation that these differences are also eliminated when participants deliberate *extensively* about the decisions they make (Briley & Aaker, 2006). Perhaps when Chinese are asked to make a decision in which they have little interest, they may do so with little thought and thus without considering culture-related norms, beliefs and values. When they think extensively about their decision, on the other hand, they may access decision-relevant knowledge in addition to culture-related criteria, and so the latter criteria may have little effect in these conditions as well. Thus, cultural norms may have their greatest impact on participants whose motivation to make a decision falls between these extremes.

A second qualification on the conclusion that Chinese avoid negative outcomes is suggested by research on risk taking. Hsee and Weber (1999) found that although Chinese were less likely than North Americans to make 'safe' choices in a risk-taking situation in which financial concerns were not involved, they were relatively more likely than Westerners to take financial risks (see also Yates & Lee, 1996). Although this contingency seems surprising on first consideration, it may indicate that whereas Chinese perceive themselves as responsible for others in social situations (and consequently desire to avoid negative decision outcomes), they may also perceive themselves as being able to depend *on* others (e.g. family) in financial situations and therefore feel relatively comfortable about taking a risk. (See Mandel, 2003, for evidence of similar effects of priming self-construals.)

The disproportionate emphasis that Chinese appear to place on negative consequences of their decisions is likely to be reflected in their impulsiveness. As Zhang and Shrum (in press) found, individuals with interdependent self-construals, who presumably are prevention focused, are more likely to suppress impulsive consumption than others are. To this extent, Chinese should be less inclined toward impulsive buying and consumption than representatives of other cultures. Indeed, a multi-country survey of consumers in Australia, United States, Hong Kong, Singapore, and Malaysia (Kacen & Lee, 2002) confirmed that Asian consumers engage in less impulsive buying than Caucasian consumers do.

Processing Differences

General considerations

Our discussion in the preceding section has implications for the type of culture related knowledge that individuals are likely to take into account when responding to product information and making purchase decisions. However, cultural differences may also exist in both the way that judgment-relevant information is *processed* and the inferences that result from this processing. Research on the role of procedural knowledge (Dhar, Huber, & Kahn, 2007; Shen & Wyer, 2008; Xu & Wyer, 2007, 2008) suggests that individuals often acquire general dispositions to process information in ways that generalize across content domains. Consequently, the activation of a procedure in one domain can influence the way in which information is processed and decisions are made in other, unrelated situations. It seems reasonable to suppose that these processing strategies may be chronic as well as situationally induced, and, once activated, may be applied to information independently of the person, object or event to which the information pertains.

Furthermore, processing strategies may vary over cultures. In some cases, these strategies could be byproducts of the dispositions discussed in the previous section. For example, the disposition to think of oneself as a member of a collective may be a manifestation of a more general tendency to think categorically about stimuli rather than to focus on their unique attributes. Similarly, the tendency to think about oneself in relation to others could reflect a general disposition to think about stimuli in relation to one another or to the context in which they are encountered.

Evidence of this generalizeability was obtained by Kühnen and Oyserman (2002). They found that activating an interdependent self-concept, which presumably increases the tendency to think about oneself in relation to others, can induce a more general disposition to think about stimuli in relation to one another regardless of whether they concern oneself or not. Thus, for example, it increases the tendency to remember the positions of objects on a page independently of their memory for the objects themselves.

If situationally induced processing styles generalize over stimulus domains, chronic styles are likely to do so as well. To this extent, Chinese individuals' disposition to think about themselves in relation to others may be a manifestation of a more general tendency to think relationally. Data summarized by Nisbett, Pen, Chen, and Norenzayan (2001; see also Ji, Pen, & Nisbett, 2000; Nisbett, 2003) suggest that this is the case. For example,Chinese are more likely than Westerners to group objects on the basis of their thematic relatedness rather than feature similarity (Ji, Zhang, & Nisbett, 2004). Thus, when given a man, woman and child, Chinese are inclined to group the woman with the child because the mother takes care of the child. Similarly, when considering a monkey, a banana and a panda, they typically group the monkey with the banana. Furthermore, Chinese and East Asians are relatively more sensitive to the contextual features of information. Masuda and Nisbett (2006), for example, found that although Asians and Westerners were equally adept at identifying and remembering differences between pictures when the differences pertained to the focal object, Asians were far better at identifying differences in contextual features.

In a particularly interesting experiment, Park, Nisbett, and Hedden (1999) asked Asian and American participants to read a series of words, each of which was presented on a separate card. In some conditions, only the word was presented on each card. In other conditions, the word was surrounded by pictures of people and objects that were irrelevant to the word's meaning. Later, participants were asked to recall the words they had read. One might expect the irrelevant context stimuli to be distracting and to decrease participants' attention to the words. In fact, however, Asians' recall of the words was actually *greater* when the contextual stimuli were presented. This was not true of the Americans. The Chinese disposition to attend to contextual features generalizes to social stimuli as well. For example, Chinese are more inclined to take situational factors into account in judging the motives that underlie a person's behavior (Choi, Dalal, Kim-Prieto, & Park, 2003; see also Ji, Lam, & Guo, this volume).

These studies indicate that contextual features facilitate Chinese individuals' comprehension and memory even when the contextual stimuli are irrelevant. However, this conclusion should not be overgeneralized. When contextual features are incompatible with the implications of the focal stimuli, Asians' attention to these features can be detrimental. Participants in a study by Krishna, Zhou and Zhang (2008) were asked to make judgments of physical stimuli in which the use of contextual features was likely either to facilitate or interfere with judgmental accuracy. Chinese participants, who presumably thought about the stimuli in relation to their context, were more accurate than North Americans in performing the first task but less accurate than North Americans in performing the second.

Two quite different studies provide further evidence of the detrimental effects of attention to context. First, East Asians are less able than Westerners in positioning a line in a vertical position when the frame surrounding it is tilted (Ji et al., 2000). Furthermore, Chinese are inclined to be influenced by their past experience when drawing conclusions from a set of premises and pay less attention than European Americans to the logical consistency of the information (Norenzayan, Smith, Kim, & Nisbett, 2002).

Implications for consumer behavior

Although the processing style of Chinese is well established (Nisbett, 2003: Oyserman & Sorensen, 2009), its role in consumer information processing has not been empirically examined. Nevertheless, several speculations seem reasonable. For example, Chinese individuals' sensitivity to the contextual features of a communication could have implications for the impact of peripheral features of an advertisement on its effectiveness. Television commercials and magazine advertisements often present product information in the context of stimuli that are largely irrelevant to the attributes of the product being presented. Chinese consumers may be more influenced by these contextual features than Western consumers are. Moreover, to the extent Park et al's (1999) findings generalize to the product domain, they suggest that these product-irrelevant features of an ad may actually *increase* Chinese consumers' memory for the more central product-related information (i.e. brand name and specific attributes) on which the advertisement is focused.

Similar considerations suggest that peripheral features of a product will have a disproportionate influence on Chinese consumers' evaluations relative to central features that have more direct implications for quality and utility. Aaker and Maheswaran (1997), for example, found that Chinese were often influenced by others' opinions about a product's quality to the exclusion of information about the product's attributes. They concluded that Chinese are particularly disposed to use heuristic bases for judgments. Although this disposition could be attributable to motivational factors, it might also reflect a general processing strategy that increases sensitivity to contextual information.

Chinese consumers' tendency to think relationally also has implications for their reactions to brand extensions. Because they focus more upon relationships between objects, they may be more sensitive than Western consumers to the similarity of a brand extension to the parent brand and more inclined to base their evaluation on this factor (Ahluwalia, 2008; Monga & John, 2007). The effects of celebrity endorsers, or a product's country of origin, mentioned earlier in this chapter, could also be partly attributable to the general sensitivity of Chinese to contextual information.

This prediction should be treated with caution pending empirical validation, however. The impact of country-of-origin is more complex than its use as a heuristic would suggest. A study by S.-T. Hong and Kang (2006) provides an example. In some conditions, Korean participants were unobtrusively primed with semantic concepts associated with either industriousness or hostility. Then, as part of an ostensibly different experiment, they evaluated products whose country of origin was Japan, Germany, or unstated. Country-of-origin information increased participants' evaluations of low-tech products when industriousness had been primed but decreased their evaluations of these products when hostility had been primed. Activating concepts associated with hostility apparently reminded participants of Japanese and German aggression during World War II, creating animosity that decreased attraction to the products being judged. (For other evidence of the effects of cultural animosity on Chinese individuals endorsement of Japanese products, see Klein, Ettenson, & Morris, 1998).

In contrast, participants evaluated high-tech products more favorably when their country of origin was specified *regardless* of whether industriousness or hostility was primed. Thus, when the quality of the products was particularly important, the effects of the country's reputation for manufacturing high quality products overrode the effects of cultural animosity. In any event, although Western participants were not considered in Hong and Kang's study, it seems likely that these effects are particularly strong among Asians as a result of their relatively greater attention to contextual information.

Effects of language

Although the exposure to culture-related icons is likely to activate culture-related concepts and knowledge, these cognitions can also be activated by more subtle, daily-life features of the situation in which judgments are made. One obvious factor may be the language in which information is presented and judgments are communicated. Bicultural individuals, for example, may have acquired different subsets of knowledge in different linguistic contexts, and communications in a particular language may increase the accessibility of this knowledge. Thus, as noted earlier, Briley et al. (2005) found that bicultural participants are more likely to make choices that minimize the likelihood of negative consequences when they are communicating in Chinese than when they are communicating in English.

The effects of language on these different dispositions in Briley et al's research, however, appeared to result from its impact on participants' perceptions of the cultural membership of the persons to whom they were communicating. For example, participants who communicated in Chinese expected that recipients of their message were likely to be Chinese. This expectation may have activated culture-related concepts that influenced the decision strategy they employed.

Although the effect of language on the processing of information is sometimes guided by the social norms and values with which the language is associated, its effect can also be influenced by characteristics of the language itself (Pierson & Bond, 1982). The last section of this chapter explores these effects (see also Ji et al., this volume).

Categorization and perception

Whorf (1956) argued that language can influence the labels that are used to categorize experience and that this categorization in turn can influence the comprehension of information and the inferences that are drawn from it. As Chiu and Hong (2007) note, little evidence supports Whorf's hypothesis that *global* differences in comprehension cognitive strategies are affected by language. However, more specific effects may indeed be evident.

For example, stimuli can be categorized differently, depending on the definitions that are assigned to the categories available (Ervin, 1962; Roberson, Davies & Davidoff, 2000; Sera et al., 2002). There is limited evidence that individuals who categorize objects in different language-specific ways actually perceive the object differently (Chiu & Hong, 2007). Nevertheless, research by Schmitt and his colleagues (Pan & Schmitt, 1996; Schmitt, Pan, & Tavassoli, 1994; Schmitt & Zhang, 1998) is provocative. Nouns in the Chinese language, unlike English or European languages, are preceded by 'classifiers' that convey more general characteristics of the class to which the referent belongs. For example, *zhang* is used to classify flat, extended objects (table, paper, etc.) and *ba* is used to classify objects that can be held in one hand (e.g. umbrella). These classifiers may sensitize Chinese to attributes of the object that Westerners do not think about (e.g. functionality). In a series of studies, Schmitt and Zhang (1998) found that Chinese were more likely than English speakers to identify classifier-related features of objects. Furthermore, they judged objects that were typically assigned the same classifier (e.g. paper and cartoons) to be more similar to one another than English speakers did.

The implications of these differences for consumer behavior arise from the fact that many objects can potentially be assigned more than one classifier and the implications of these classifiers can differ. 'Lipstick,' for example, could be preceded by either *zhi* (which refers to long, thin objects) or *guanr* (which refers to pipe-like, thick objects). In such cases, Schmitt and Zhang (1998) found that participants made different inferences about the attributes of a product, depending on the classifier that was applied. Thus, in the preceding example, they inferred that a lipstick was thinner and was of less quantity if *zhi* was used as the classifier than if *guanr* was used.

Note, however, that the likelihood of inferring attributes on the basis of the classifier may depend in part on the range of objects to which the classifier is applied. In this regard, the same classifier is often assigned to a broader range of objects in Cantonese than in Mandarin. Consistent with this observation, Schmitt and Zhang (1998) found that Cantonese speakers are less likely to infer attributes on the basis of a given classifier-noun combination than Mandarin speakers are.

As we have noted, these differences result from verbal descriptions of the objects and do not necessarily affect perceptions of physical objects themselves (Chiu & Hong, 2007). However, they may nevertheless have *indirect* effects. Research on knowledge accessibility (Förster & Liberman, 2007; Higgins, 1996; Wyer, 2008) indicates that if people have interpreted information about a stimulus in terms of a more general concept, their later judgments of the stimulus are often based on the implications of this concept rather than on the features that led the concept to be applied. For example, suppose people have learned that someone gave a friend an answer during an examination and has interpreted the behavior as 'kind.' They may later infer the person to be 'honest' on the basis of the evaluative implications of their first judgment without consulting the original behavior (Carlston, 1980). To this extent, language differences in the semantic category that is assigned to a stimulus object at the time the object is encountered could have an impact on memory and judgments at a later point in time after the stimulus is no longer present.

A second consideration arises. That is, when people learn a language in a social context, features of the context become associated with the stimuli to which the language is applied. Thus, although the concepts that are applied in different languages are similar in denotative meaning, their *connotative* meaning may differ. For example, 'moon' might elicit different associations in individuals who have grown up in Israel than to those who have grown up in China. To this extent, the use of similar terms in an advertisement could elicit different images in different languages and, therefore, could have different effects.

Auditory vs. visual processing

Language differences may exist in not only the content of information that is conveyed but also how it is presented. English, for example, is typically read from left to right, whereas Chinese is often read vertically as well. These reading habits could generalize to other domains, leading Chinese to be relatively more adept at scanning visually presented material than English speakers are (Freeman, 1980; Hoosain, 1986).

A more important difference in the processing of information that is conveyed in Chinese, which distinguishes it from the processing of English, results from the lack of relation between the way a word 'looks' and the way it 'sounds.' This relation is somewhat less apparent in English than in European languages (e.g. German). Nonetheless, one can often guess how a word is pronounced from seeing it. In these instances, the meaning of a word can be conveyed equally well when it is spoken and when it is written. Thus, children who learning to read in English can recognize a written word as one they have often heard spoken by 'sounding it out.' This is not the case in Chinese. One might therefore speculate that the sound of a word plays a less important role in processing written information in Chinese than it does in English or European languages, whereas visual cues have correspondingly greater influence (see also Cheung, this volume).

The impact of this difference on categorization and memory was identified by Tavassoli (1999). Chinese participants were asked to learn objects in two categories (fruits and animals). In some cases, the objects were pictured. In other cases, they were denoted by ideographs. Correspondingly, Americans were asked to learn the same objects on the basis of either pictures or English words. Participants were later asked to recall the objects. The order in which they were recalled suggested that when the objects were pictured, both Chinese and Americans organized the stimuli in memory according to the semantic category to which they belonged. This was also true of Chinese participants when the objects were denoted by ideographs. In contrast, Americans' recall of the words reflected the order in which the words were presented (or, in some cases, their phonetic similarity) and showed little organization by semantic category.

Two sets of studies confirm the difference in attention paid to visual and auditory features of a verbal communication by Chinese and Westerners. Pan and Schmitt (1996) asked Chinese and American participants to evaluate brand names of products that were either used by men (i.e. a power drill) or used by women (e.g. lipstick). In *auditory presentation* conditions, the stimuli were conveyed orally by either a male or female speaker. In these conditions, American participants evaluated brand names more favorably when the sex of the speaker matched the type of product being described, whereas Chinese participants' evaluations were unaffected by the speaker's sex. In *visual presentation* conditions, the brand names and products were written in a type face that was normatively either masculine or feminine. In this case, Chinese evaluated the brand name more favorably when the script matched the product being described whereas American's evaluations were unaffected.

Tavassoli and Lee (2003) showed that these differences in processing style were a function of the language in which information was conveyed and not of culture *per se*. Singapore bilingual participants read a passage describing features of a tennis racquet that was written either in English or Chinese. In some conditions, the passage was accompanied by loud, up-beat music and in other conditions it was accompanied by pictures that were irrelevant to the message content. When the passage was written in English, it had less impact on participants' product evaluations when the distracting stimulus was auditory than when it was visual. When the passage was written in Chinese, however, the reverse was true. Thus, bilinguals' processing strategy was largely determined by characteristics of the language in which information was conveyed.

It nevertheless seems reasonable to speculate that monolinguals who speak only their native language develop a general disposition to engage in visual information processing that they apply spontaneously to the information they receive. That is, Chinese, unlike Westerners, may be disposed to process information visually and they may spontaneously construct mental images of stimuli regardless of whether they are described in pictures or in writing.

The implications of this possibility for consumer information processing are suggested in a series of studies by Jiang and his colleagues (Jiang, Steinhart, & Wyer, 2009; Wyer, Hung, & Jiang, 2008). These researchers found that if individuals had a chronic disposition to process information visually (inferred from responses to a scale constructed by Childers, Houston, & Heckler, 1985), they evaluated products unfavorably when the visual images elicited by information about them were incompatible (e.g. if the information described different physical locations) and they could not construct a single visual representation of the product as a whole. This was also true when the product was novel, and so a previously formed visual representation of it did not exist in memory. In contrast, individuals with a disposition to process information verbally without forming visual images were not affected by these factors. Thus, if Chinese have a general disposition to process information visually, Jiang et al's findings suggest that advertisements that require the construction of incompatible or unfamiliar visual images will be difficult for them to comprehend, leading them to react more unfavorably to the products than Westerners would.

Normative principles of communication

Consumer information is implicitly or explicitly conveyed in a social context. In some cases, the information is exchanged in the course of a direct interaction between a customer and a salesperson. However, television commercials and magazine advertisements are also social communications that are often directed toward a certain subset of consumers. Reactions to these messages, like communications in general, may be guided by social conventions that influence the interpretation of both the verbal information that is exchanged and nonverbal cues that accompany its transmission. Although little research in consumer behavior has examined this possibility, some observations may nevertheless be worth noting.

Grice (1975) identified a number of implicit principles of social communication that are used by the communicator in generating a message and a recipient in interpreting it. For example, communicators are expected to convey information that the recipient does not already have, to tell the truth as they see it, and to be relevant to the topic at hand. Thus, when a communication's literal meaning appears to violate one of these principles, recipients may attempt to reinterpret it in a way that is consistent with the principle that was violated. For example, an advertising claim that 'Brand X contains no hydropropine,' which is uninformative to individuals who have no idea what hydropropine is. In attempting to make the statement conform to the informativeness principle, however, they may infer that (a) hydropropine is an undesirable attribute and (b) brands other than X are likely to contain it.

However, principles of communication that are important in one cultural context may be less so in other contexts (see Freeman & Haberman, 1996; Xu & Feng, this volume). In addition, communications that may appear informative or relevant in one culture may not be in another. These differences might have implications for the use of metaphors in advertising. Perhaps a communication's metaphorical meaning is only recognized if its literal meaning appears to be uninformative, irrelevant, or incorrect. To this extent, the use of metaphors in advertising may not generalize across cultures unless the amount of knowledge that individuals have available for interpreting its literal meaning is taken into account.

Nonverbal communication. A major source of miscommunication between representatives of different cultures is nonverbal. That is, much of individuals' nonverbal behavior is performed with little conscious deliberation. Facial expressions, eye contact, physical proximity, and gestures, may vary over cultures in the meaning that they convey (see Smith, Bond, & Ka ıtçıba ı, 2006, ch. 8).

Because feelings and emotions are inherently personal, the overt expression of them may be more often accepted in societies that encourage individuality and uniqueness. In contrast, collective societies that foster independence may discourage the public expression of feelings which might threaten interpersonal harmony and cohesiveness (Matsumoto et al., 2008). Bond (1993) also suggested that Chinese believe that a restrained emotional demeanor promotes social harmony. To this extent, facial expressions of emotion may be less common in Chinese and East-Asian cultures than in Western societies. In fact, Matsumoto et al. (2008) found that collectivism is positively associated with greater emotional restraint.

The difference in the cultural norms about the social appropriateness of expressing feelings might lead to different rules of nonverbal communication. Smiling, for example, may convey happiness but also amusement at another's comments or behavior, sympathy and understanding, and reassurance that everything is not as bad as it seems. Thus, a salesperson who smiles when a customer is complaining about a service failure may intend to convey reassurance and understanding, but the customer may interpret it as an indication that the salesperson considers the complaint to be amusing and is not taking it seriously. Expressions of dissatisfaction or disagreement are especially liable to such misunderstandings (Bond, Zegarac, & Spencer-Oatley, 2000).

Eye contact is normally a cue to the intensity of one's feelings (Ellsworth & Carlsmith, 1968). However, the level of eye contact that is considered normative may vary over cultures. If a person from a culture in which the normal level of eye contact is relatively low interacts with someone from a culture in which eye contact is typically high, the first person may interpret the second's behavior as conveying inappropriate intimacy, whereas the second person may interpret the first's behavior as indifference or aloofness. In interpersonal exchanges (e.g. interactions with a waiter at a restaurant), these factors could influence perceptions of one another's behavior and the evaluations that are based on these perceptions. The influence of proximity and cultural norms that guide interpersonal distance and touching behavior is likewise a sensitive area for misunderstandings (Smith et al., 2006, ch. 8).

A perhaps more obvious factor arises when one party to an interaction is less fluent than the other in the language that is used to communicate. Individuals who are familiar with a language are likely to use contextual expressions ('please,' 'I think,' etc.) in communicating, whereas less fluent individuals are more likely to convey requests or ideas without these contextual features. To this extent, the individual who is accustomed to the use of these expressions may interpret the other's behavior as aloof, intolerant or impolite.

The specific ways in which these factors enter into information processing and influence consumer behavior by Chinese is unclear, and we know of no research that directly bears on them. An investigation of these matters is nonetheless necessary to acquire a full understanding of consumer information processing in China.

Concluding remarks

We have focused on three general areas of research with implications for consumer behavior in China: the norms, beliefs and values that Chinese consumers are likely to bring to bear on the interpretation of consumer information, the processing strategies that are employed in interpreting and drawing inferences on the basis of this information, and the role of language and communication. Much of our discussion has been speculative. Furthermore, our review of the literature is incomplete; several important areas of consumer research that do not fall into the domains we have discussed have been cited superficially if at all. Despite these limitations, however, we hope that our discussion is sufficient to provide a general understanding of the primary themes that underlie consumer behavior in China and to provoke further research in this area.

Authors' note

This chapter was prepared with the support of grant no. GRF641308 from the Research Grants Council of the Hong Kong SAR, China. Appreciation is extended to Angela Lee and Sharon Shavitt for comments on earlier versions of the chapter.

References

Aaker, J. L. & Lee, A. Y. (2001). 'I' seek pleasures and 'we' avoid pains: The role of self-regulatory goals in information processing and persuasion. *Journal of Consumer Research, 28*, 33–49.

Aaker, J. L. & Maheswaran, D. (1997). The effect of cultural orientation on persuasion. *Journal of Consumer Research, 24*, 315–328.

Aaker, J. L. & Williams, P. (1998). Empathy vs. pride: The influence of emotional appeals across cultures. *Journal of Consumer Research, 25*, 241–261.

Ahluwalia, R. (2008). How far can a brand stretch? Understanding the role of self-construal. *Journal of Marketing Research, 45*, 337–350.

Bond, M. H. (1993). Emotions and their expression in Chinese culture. *Journal of Nonverbal Behavior, 17*, 245–262.

Bond, M. H. (1996). Chinese values. In M. H. Bond (ed.), *The handbook of Chinese psychology* (pp. 208–226). Hong Kong: Oxford University Press.

Bond, M. H., Zegarac, V., & Spencer-Oatley (2000). Culture as an explanatory variable: Problems and possibilities. In H. Spencer-Oatley (ed.), *Culturally speaking: Managing relations in talk across cultures* (pp. 47–71). London: Cassell.

Briley, D. A. & Aaker, J. L. (2006). When does culture matter? Effects of personal knowledge on the correction of culture-based judgments. *Journal of Marketing Research, 43,* 395–408.
Briley, D. A., Morris, M. W., & Simonson, I. (2000). Reasons as carriers of culture: Dynamic versus dispositional models of cultural influence on decision making. *Journal of Consumer Research, 27,* 157–178.
Briley, D. A., Morris, M. W., & Simonson, I. (2005). Cultural chameleons: Biculturals, conformity motives and decision making. *Journal of Consumer Psychology, 15,* 351–362.
Briley, D. A. & Wyer, R. S. (2001). Transitory determinants of values and decisions: The utility (or nonutility) of individualism and collectivism in understanding cultural differences. *Social Cognition, 19,* 198–229.
Briley, D. A. & Wyer, R. S. (2002). The effect of group membership salience on the avoidance of negative outcomes: Implications for social and consumer decisions. *Journal of Consumer Research, 29,* 400–416.
Carlston, D. E. (1980). Events, inferences and impression formation. In R. Hastie, T. Ostrom, E. Ebbesen, R. Wyer, D. Hamilton, & D. Carlston (eds). *Person memory: The cognitive basis of social perception* (pp. 89–119). Hillsdale, NJ: Erlbaum.
Chen, H., Ng., S., & Rao, A. R. (2005). Cultural differences in consumer impatience. *Journal of Marketing Research, 42,* 291–301.
Childers, T. L., Houston, M. J., & Heckler, S. E. (1985). Measurement of individual differences in visual versus verbal information processing. *Journal of Consumer Research, 12,* 125–134.
Chiu, C-Y. & Hong, Y-Y. (2007). *Social psychology of culture.* New York: Psychology Press.
Choi, I., Dalal, R., Kim-Pietro, C., & Park, H. (2003). Culture and judgment of causal relevance. *Journal of Personality and Social Psychology, 84,* 46–59.
Choi, I., Nisbett, R. E., & Norenzayan, A. (1999). Causal attribution across cultures: Variation and universality. *Psychological Bulletin, 125,* 47–63.
Choi, S. M., Lee, W.-N., & Kim, H.-J. (2005). Lessons from the rich and famous: A cross-cultural comparison of celebrity endorsement in advertising. *Journal of Advertising, 34,* 85–98.
Dhar,R., Huber, J. & Khan, U. (2007). The shopping momentum effect. *Journal of Marketing Research, 44,* 370–378.
Ellsworth, P. C. & Carlsmith, J. M. (1968). Intimacy in response to direct gaze. *Journal of Experimental Social Psychology, 10,* 15–20.
Ervin, S. M. (1962). The connotations of gender. *Word, 18,* 249–261.
Förster, J. & Liberman, N. (2007). Knowledge activation. In A. Kruglanski & E. T. Higgins (eds), *Social psychology: Handbook of basic principles* (2nd edn, pp. 201–231). New York: Guilford.
Fong, C. P. S. (2006). *The impact of favor-elicited feelings on reciprocity behavior across time.* Unpublished doctoral dissertation, Hong Kong University of Science and Technology.
Freeman, N. H. & Habermann, G. M. (1996). Linguistic socialization: A Chinese perspective. In M. H. Bond (ed.), The handbook of Chinese psychology (pp. 87–99). Hong Kong: Oxford University Press.
Freeman, R. D. (1980). Visual acuity is better for letters in rows than in columns. *Nature, 286,* 62–64.
Grice, H. P. (1975). Logic and conversation. In P. Cole & J. L. Morgan (eds), *Syntax and semantics: Speech acts* (pp. 41–58). New York: Academic Press.
Gürhan-Canli, Z. & Maheswaran, D. (2000). Cultural variations in country of origin effects. *Journal of Marketing Research, 37,* 309–317.
Higgins, E. T. (1996). Knowledge activation: Accessibility, applicability, and salience. In E. T. Higgins & A. Kruglanski (eds) *Social psychology: Handbook of basic principles* (pp. 133–168). New York: Guilford.
Higgins, E. T. (1997). Beyond pleasure and pain. *American Psychologist, 55,* 1217–1233.
Higgins, E. T. (1998). Promotion and prevention: Regulatory focus as a motivational principle. In M. P. Zanna (ed.), *Advances in experimental social psychology* (Vol. 30, pp. 1–46). San Diego, CA: Academic Press.
Hofstede, G. H. (1980). *Culture's consequences: International differences in work-related values.* Beverley Hills, CA: Sage.
Hofstede, G. H. (2001). *Culture's consequences: Comparing values, behaviors, institutions and organizations across nations.* Thousand Oaks, CA: Sage.
Hong, S.-T. & Kang, D. K. (2006). Country-of-origin influences on product evaluations: The impact of animosity and perceptions of industriousness and brutality on judgments of typical and atypical products. *Journal of Consumer Psychology, 16,* 232–240.
Hong, Y.-Y. (2009). A dynamic constructivist approach to culture: Moving from describing culture to explaining culture. In R. S. Wyer, C.-Y. Chiu, & Y.-Y. Hong (eds). *Understanding culture: Theory, research and application* (pp. 3–24). New York: Psychology Press.
Hong, Y.-Y., Ip, G., Chiu, C.-Y., Morris, M. W., & Menon, T. (2001). Cultural identity and dynamic construction of the self: Collective duties and individual rights in Chinese and American cultures. *Social Cognition, 19,* 251–269.
Hong, Y-Y., Morris, M. W., Chiu, C-Y., & Benet-Martinez, V. (2000). Multicultural minds: A dynamic constructivist approach to culture and cognition. *American Psychologist, 55,* 709–720.
Hoosain, R. (1986). Language, orthography and cognitive processes: Chinese perspectives for the Sapir-Whorf hypothesis. *International Journal of Behavioral Development, 9,* 507–525.
Hsee, C. K. & Weber, E. U. (1999). Cross-national differences in risk preference and lay predictions. *Journal of Behavioral Decision Making, 12,* 165–179.
Inglehart, R. & Baker, W. E. (2000). Modernization, cultural change, and the persistence of traditional values. *American Sociological Review, 65,* 19–51.

Ip, G. W.-M. & Bond, M. H. (1995). Culture, values and the spontaneous self-concept. *Asian Journal of Psychology, 1,* 29–35.

Ji, L., Peng, K., & Nisbett, R. E. (2000). Culture, control, and perception of relationships in the environment. *Journal of Personality and Social Psychology, 78,* 943–955.

Ji, L., Zhang, Z., & Nisbett, R. E. (2004). Is it culture or is it language? Examination of language effects in cross-cultural research on categorization. *Journal of Personality and Social Psychology, 87,* 57–65.

Ji, M. F. & McNeal, J. U. (2001). How Chinese children's commercials differ from those of the United States: A content analysis. *Journal of Advertising, 30,* 79–92.

Jiang,Y., Steinhart,Y., & Wyer, R. S. (2008). *The role of visual and semantic processing strategies in consumer information processing.* Unpublished manuscript, Hong Kong University of Science and Technology.

Joy, A. (2001). Gift-giving in Hong Kong and the continuum of social ties. *Journal of Consumer Research, 28,* 239–256.

Kacen, J. J. & Lee, J. A. (2002). The influence of culture on consumer impulsive buying behavior. *Journal of Consumer Psychology, 12,* 163–176.

Kelman, H. C. (1961). Processes of opinion change. *Public Opinion Quarterly, 25,* 57–78.

Kitayama, S. & Cohen, D. (eds). (2007). *Handbook of cultural psychology.* New York: Guilford.

Klein, J. G., Ettenson, R., & Morris, M. D. (1998). The animosity model of foreign product purchase: An empirical test in the People's Republic of China. *Journal of Marketing, 62,* 89–100.

Krishna, A., Zhou, R., & Zhang, S. (2008). The effect of self-construal on spatial judgments. *Journal of Consumer Research, 35,* 337–348.

Kühnen, U. & Oyserman, D. (2002). Thinking about the self influences thinking in general: Cognitive consequences of salient self-concept. *Journal of Experimental Social Psychology, 38,* 492–499.

Lau-Gesk, L. G. (2003). Activating culture through persuasion appeals: An examination of the bicultural consumer. *Journal of Consumer Psychology, 13,* 301–315.

Lee, A. Y., Aaker, J. L., & Gardner, W. L. (2000). The pleasures and pains of distinct self-construals: The role of interdependence in regulatory focus. *Journal of Personality and Social Psychology, 78,* 1122–1134.

Lee, A. Y. and Gardner, W. (2005). *Family size matters: The evolution of the self in modern China.* Unpublished manuscript, Northwestern University.

Lee, A. Y. & Semin, G. R. (2009). Culture through the lens of self-regulatory orientations. In R. S. Wyer, C.-Y. Chiu, & Y.-Y. Hong (eds). *Understanding culture: Theory, research and application* (pp. 299–310). New York: Psychology Press.

Lin, C. A. (2001). Cultural values reflected in Chinese and American television advertising. *Journal of Advertising, 30,* 83–94.

Luna, D., Ringberg, T., & Peracchio, L. A. (2008). One individual, two identities: Frame switching among biculturals. *Journal of Consumer Research, 35,* 279–293.

Mandel, N. (2003). Shifting selves and decision making: The effects of self-construal priming on consumers' risk taking. *Journal of Consumer Research, 30,* 30–40.

Markman, A. B., Grimm, L. R., & Kim, K. (2009). Culture as a vehicle for studying individual differences. In R. S. Wyer, C.-Y. Chiu, & Y.-Y. Hong (eds). *Understanding culture: Theory, research and application* (pp. 93–107). New York: Psychology Press.

Markus, H. R. & Kitayama, S. (1991). Culture and the self: Implications for cognition, emotion and motivation. *Psychological Review, 98,* 224–253.

Masuda, T. & Nisbett, R. E. (2006). Culture and change blindness. *Cognitive Science, 30,* 381–399.

Matsumoto, D., Yoo, S. H., Fontaine, J., Anguas-Wong, A. M., Ariola, M., Ataca, B. et al. (2008). Mapping expressive differences around the world: The relationship between emotion display rules and individualism versus collectivism. *Journal of Cross-Cultural Psychology, 39,* 55–74.

Miller, P. J., Fung, H., & Mintz, J. (1996). Self-construction through narrative practices: A Chinese and American comparison of early socialization. *Ethos, 24,* 237–280.

Miller, P. J., Wiley, A. R., Fung, H., & Liang, C. H. (1997). Personal storytelling as a medium of socialization in Chinese and American families. *Child Development, 68,* 557–568.

Monga, A. B. & Roedder, John, D. (2007). Cultural differences in brand extension evaluation: The influence of analytic versus holistic thinking. *Journal of Consumer Research, 33,* 529–536.

Nisbett, R. E. (2003). *The geography of thought: How Asians and westerners think differently.* New York: Free Press.

Nisbett, R. E., Peng, K., Choi, I., & Norenzayan, A. (2001). Culture and systems of thought: Holistic vs. analytic cognition. *Psychological Review, 108,* 291–310.

Norenzayan, A., Smith, E. E., Kim, B. J., & Nisbett, R. E. (2002). Cultural preferences for formal versus intuitive reasoning. *Cognitive Science, 26,* 653–684.

Oishi, S., Wyer, R. S., & Colcombe, S. (2000). Cultural variation in the use of current life satisfaction to predict the future. *Journal of Personality and Social Psychology, 78,* 434–445.

Oyserman, D. & Sorensen, N. (2009). Undertanding cultural syndrome effects on what and how we think: A situated cognition model. In R. S. Wyer, C.-Y. Chiu, & Y.-Y. Hong (eds). *Understanding culture: Theory, research and application* (pp. 25–52). New York: Psychology Press.

Pan, Y. & Schmitt, B. (1996). Language and brand attitudes: The impact of script and sound matching in Chinese and English. *Journal of Consumer Psychology, 5,* 263–278.

Park, D. C., Nisbett, R. E., & Hedden, T. (1999). Culture, cognition, and aging. *Journal of Gerontology, 54B,* 75–84.
Pierson, H. D. & Bond, M. H. (1982). How do Chinese bilinguals respond to variations of interviewer language and ethnicity? *Journal of Language and Social Psychology, 1,* 123–139.
Rhee, E., Uleman, J., & Lee, H. K. (1996). Variations in collectivism and individualism by ingroup and culture: confirmatory factor analysis. *Journal of Personality and Social Psychology, 71,* 1037–1054.
Roberson, D., Davies, I., & Davidoff, UJ. (2000). Color categories are not universal: Replications and new evidence from a stone-age culture. *Journal of Experimental Psychology: General, 129,* 369–398.
Schmitt, B. H., Pan, Y., & Tavassoli, N. T. (1994). Language and consumer memory: The impact of linguistic differences between Chinese and English. *Journal of Consumer Research, 21,* 419–431,
Schmitt, B. H. & Zhang, S. (1998). Language structure and categorization: A study of classifiers in consumer cognition, judgment and choice. *Journal of Consumer Research, 25,* 108–122.
Schwartz, S. H. (2009). Culture matters: National value cultures, sources and consequences. In R. S. Wyer, C.-Y. Chiu, & Y.-Y. Hong (eds). *Understanding culture: Theory, research and application* (pp. 127–150). New York: Psychology Press.
Sera, M. D., Elieff, C., Forbes, J., Burch, M. C., Rodriquez, W., & Dubois, D. P. (2002). When language affects cognition and when it does not: An analysis of grammatical gender and classification. *Journal of Experimental Psychology: General, 131,* 377–397.
Shavitt, S., Lalwani, A. K., Zhang, J., & Torelli, C. J. (2006). The horizontal/vertical distinction in cross-cultural consumer research. *Journal of Consumer Psychology, 16,* 325–342.
Shavitt, S., Zhang, J., & Johnson, T. P. (2006). *Horizontal and vertical cultural differences in advertising and consumer persuasion.* Unpublished data, University of Illinois.
Shen, H., Wan, F., & Wyer, R. S. (2009). *A cross-cultural study of gift acceptance in a consumption context: The mediating role of feelings of appreciation and indebtedness.* Unpublished manuscript, Hong Kong University of Science and Technology.
Shen, H. & Wyer, R. S. (2008). Procedural priming and consumer judgments: Effects on the impact of positively and negatively valenced information. *Journal of Consumer Research, 34,* 727–737.
Smith, P. B., Bond, M. H., & Ka ıtçıba ı, Ç. (2006). *Understanding social psychology across cultures.* London: Sage.
Tavassoli, N. T., (1999). Temporal and associative memory in Chinese and English. *Journal of Consumer Research, 26,* 170–181.
Tavassoli, N. T. & Lee, Y. H., (2003). The differential interaction of auditory and visual advertising elements with Chinese and English. *Journal of Marketing Research, 40,* 468–480.
Triandis, H. C. (1989). The self and social behavior in differing cultural contexts. *Psychological Review, 96,* 506–520.
Triandis, H. C. (1995). *Individualism and collectivism.* Boulder, CO: Westview.
Triandis, H. C., Bonempo, R., Betancourt, H., Bond, M. H., Leung, K., Brenes, A., Georgas, J., Hui, H. C. C., Marin, G., Setiadi, B., Sinha, J. B. P., Verma, J., Spangenberg, J., Touzard, H., & de Montomollin (1986). The measurement of the etic aspects of individualism and collectivism across cultures. *Australian Journal of Psychology, 38,* 257–267.
Triandis, H. C. & Gelfand, M. J. (1998).Converging measurement of horizontal and vertical individualism and collectivism. *Journal of Personality and Social Psychology, 74,* 118–128.
Wan, C. & Chiu, C.-Y. (2009). An intersubjective consensus approach to culture: The role of intersubjective norms versus cultural self in cultural processes. In R. S. Wyer, C.-Y. Chiu & Y.-Y. Hong (eds). *Understanding culture: Theory, research and application* (pp. 79–92). New York: Psychology Press.
Wang, Q. (2001). Culture effects on adults' earliest childhood recollections and self-description: Implications for the relation between memory and the self. *Journal of Personality and Social Psychology,* 81, 220–233.
Watkins, P., Scheer, J., Ovnicek, M., & Kolts, R. (2006). The debt of gratitude: Dissociating gratitude and indebtedness, *Cognition and Emotion, 20,* 217–241.
Whorf, B. L. (1956). *Language, thought and reality: Selected writings of Benjamin Lee Whorf.* New York: Wiley.
Wyer, R. S. (2008). The role of knowledge accessibility in cognition and behavior: Implications for consumer information processing. In C. P. Haugtvedg, P. M. Herr, & F. R. Kardes (eds), *Handbook of consumer psychology* (pp. 31–76). Mahwah, NJ: Erlbaum.
Wyer, R. S., Chiu, C.-Y., & Hong, Y.-Y (2009). *Understanding culture: Theory, research and application.* New York: Psychology Press.
Wyer, R. S., Hung, I. W., & Jiang,Y. (2008). Visual and verbal processing strategies in comprehension and judgment. *Journal of Consumer Psychology, 18,* 244–257.
Xu, A. J. & Wyer, R. S. (2007). The effect of mindsets on consumer decision strategies. *Journal of Consumer Research, 34,* 556–566.
Xu, A. J. & Wyer, R. S. (2008). The comparative mindset: From animal comparisons to increased purchase intentions. *Psychological Science, 19,* 859–864.
Zhang, J. & Shavitt, S. (2003). Cultural values in advertisements to the Chinese X-generation. *Journal of Advertising, 32,* 23–33.
Zhang, Y. & Shrum, L. J. (in press). The influence of self-construal on impulsive consumption. *Journal of Consumer Research.*

CHAPTER 37

Sport psychology research and its application in China

Gangyan Si, Hing-chu Lee, and Chris Lonsdale

From the outset, the purpose of sport psychology in China was to enhance performance in high level competitive sport. This direction was determined by both political and social considerations (Y. Z. Lu, 1996). In this chapter, we review the development of sport psychology in China over the last 30 years, using Chinese sources primarily from mainland China and to a lesser extent Hong Kong. Developments in the four important areas of talent identification, sport cognition, mental training models, and on-field psychological support are presented in chronological order to reflect this development.

From the early 1980s to the mid-1990s, the focus of research in sport psychology was primarily on talent identification. The movement behind talent identification was based on the belief that sporting abilities and potentials are innate, but the environment in which individuals are raised can also shape their future sporting success. Thus, factors such as characteristics of the central nervous system, personality, emotional stability, physical and mental toughness, and the age at which formal training starts were all considered important issues in talent identification. The outcomes of these research efforts have been encouraging, and include the development of a list of referential criteria and assessment tools for talent identification.

By the second half of the 1990s, researchers in China had begun to investigate cognitions in sport. Liang (2007) confirmed the existence of sport-specific cognitions in athletes across a wide variety of sports, including baseball, fencing, and table tennis. He went on to conclude that cognitions in competitive sports are characterized by four special features, namely, a narrowing of cognitive processing resources, the inability think logically during competition, the inability to process images, and the need for speedy decision making. This type of study has important implications for the practice of competitive sports.

In recent years a group of sport psychologists, in particular S. H. Liu (2001) and Si (2006), have proposed models of mental training for use in training and preparing for competition. S. H. Liu, using her years of experience in training shooting athletes, proposed a systematic and integrated model for psychological reconstruction, the focus of which was on building a positive self-image and thinking patterns in athletes from the base of a 'body-mind' technique. Si, on the other hand, developed a conceptual framework for successful adversity coping as the basis for promoting peak performance during competition. This framework emerged from an in-depth analysis and review of traditional mental training models and their shortcomings. The framework enables applied sport psychologists to help athletes assess and cope with various adverse situations during competition. Both S. H. Liu and Si's models have been widely applied in the quest for high performance in sport.

In recent years the efficacy of on-field psychological support has also received increasing attention in Chinese sport psychology research. This type of support represents the most direct manner in which sport psychologists provide their services during competitions. Si, Lee, Cheng, and S. H. Liu's (2006) study of Hong Kong elite athletes and coaches found positive perceptions of on-field psychological support, and listed a number of areas in which both the athletes and coaches could benefit from the service. This is, however, a preliminary study and requires further investigation in order to more fully test the effectiveness of these on-field interventions.

Talent identification in sport psychology

Talent identification in China

Sport psychology research in China started in the early 1960s, but was brought to a halt during the Cultural Revolution (1966-1976). At the end of the Cultural Revolution, sport psychology researchers and practitioners were allowed to resume their activities. Talent identification studies that started at the beginning of the 1980s are regarded as the origin of contemporary sport psychology research in China.

Talent identification in sport psychology refers to the assessment of the psychological activities of the athletes, including their perceptions, cognitions, and behavior. Various techniques were used to select qualified athletes for further training. Influenced by Russian sport psychology and the national sport policy which emphasized the importance of competitive sports, the focus of research on sport psychology in mainland China in the 1980s and 1990s was talent identification. Led by Qiu (Cox & Qiu, 1993), Chinese scholars completed a number of empirical investigations (in basketball, volley ball, athletics, swimming, gymnastics, and rowing) in an attempt to test their theories and methodologies for talent identification.

Historical background

During the 1950s and early 1960s China and Russia enjoyed a friendly relationship, and Chinese society was greatly influenced by contemporary Russian culture and science. Sport psychology was no exception. Russian sport psychologists identified individuals with sport talent by assessing the characteristics of the potential athletes' central nervous system (W. Y. Wang & Zhang, 1989) and their sport intelligence, using various tests and tools (Z. N. Lu, 1984; Qiu, 1990). Chinese sport psychologists began their research on talent identification by using similar theoretical concepts and research methods. They also developed a number of indigenous research tools, for example, the 808 Central Nervous System Activity Test by W. Y. Wang and Zhang (1989), using top Chinese athletes as participants in a series of studies. The outcomes were encouraging and the findings not only provided the coaches with much useful information (e.g. the knowledge of dispositions) about their athletes, but also gave sport psychologists in China the opportunity to conduct research to accumulate knowledge and experience in talent identification (Qiu, 1986; 1990).

By the end of the 1960s the friendship between China and Russia had deteriorated, and Chinese sport psychologists turned to the West for guidance in conducting research on sport psychology. Sport talent identification in China followed the trend then in vogue there, namely the investigation of the personality of high level athletes (Andrews, 1971; Fraternity & Epsilon, 1977). In particular, Cattell's 16 PF Personality Theory/Inventory and Eysenck's Personality Theory/Questionnaire were widely used to assess the personality characteristics of Chinese athletes. At the time, it was widely believed that mental abilities were determined by both hereditary and environmental factors (Plomin, 1986; Szopa, 1985). Researchers used a paradigm that compared the performance of expert and novice athletes in various sports, and attempted to use knowledge of elite athletes' personality traits in order to predict aspiring athletes' future achievements in their selected sports.

The rationale and methods for talent identification in China

Talent identification in sport psychology in China was built on the foundation of the methodologies developed in other specialties involved in sport science, such as morphology, biology, and physiology (X. W. Liu & Lin, 1987). Chinese scholars (e.g. Qiu, 1990) proposed that talent identification required both longitudinal and cross-sectional studies. In supporting the need for longitudinal studies, Tian (1986) argued that talent identification should be closely linked with the ultimate goal of long-term practice and training. In another words, the critical age at which an athlete is selected should be linked with the demand characteristics for the development of a specific sport for that athlete within particular age ranges. Puberty was identified as the critical time for selection (X. W. Liu & Lin, 1987; Tian, 1986; Zeng, Wang, & Xing, 1992).

On the other hand, Qiu (1986) proposed that talent identification should take into consideration the possible appearance of difficulties and frustration in performance during the development of the athletes. Thus, helping athletes reach their ultimate goal, i.e. becoming the champion or reaching peak performance, was also a goal for talent identification. Qiu (1986) proposed the need for longitudinal studies of the development of the athletes, in close collaboration with the coaches. As researchers developed ways to diagnose and evaluate the athletes' talents, the coaches could apply the same methods and monitor their progress in daily training.

As for identifying talents in cross-sectional studies, Chinese sport psychologists (Qiu, 1986; 1990; L. W. Zhang & Ren, 2000) used various indicators to assess the athletes' mental abilities, and completed the following types of studies:

Sport-related abilities. Sport-related abilities refer to the actual abilities demonstrated by the athletes during practice and competition, as well as their potential for further improvement (Qiu, 1990). Qiu, Bay, and Liu (1986) compiled a test for assessing the mental abilities of junior athletes from various sports, using a large sample to gauge the test's reliability and validity. The test included seven sub-tests for the purpose of assessing attentional stability, abstract reasoning, visual tracking, speed of wrist movement, eye-hand coordination, spatial judgment (rotation of square blocks), and spatial integration abilities. The findings showed that the test had acceptable validity, reliability and discriminatory power, and could be recommended for diagnostic purposes and talent identification (Gao & Yang, 2000; He, Shi, Guo, & Guo, 2002).

Intelligence. Pan and Liu (1990) used the Wechsler Adult Intelligence Scale (hereafter referred to as WAIS) to test the intellectual level of badminton players, and discovered that the IQ score of top level players was significantly higher than that of players at lower levels. L. W. Zhang and Tao (1994) used the same test (WAIS) on top Chinese table tennis players from the national team, but their results indicated that the players' IQ scores were about the same level as those of the general population. Using the Raven's Standard Progressive Matrices (Raven, 1938) to compare university students majoring in sports versus other subjects, S. H. Liu (1989) found that there were no significant differences between the two groups. In light of the conflicting findings from these studies, it was not possible to conclude whether or not intellect could be used as a critical factor for talent identification (L. W. Zhang & Ren, 2000).

Personality characteristics. More studies in China have been conducted on the personality characteristics of athletes than on other talent identification-related topics. H. C. Zhang (1987) used the Embedded Line Figure Test and Rod and Frame Test to compare the field independence and field dependence (person's perception is independent or dependent of his/her environment) of athletes from both individual and team sports, respectively. Their findings indicated that stronger field independence is a crucial quality for athletes engaging in competitive sports. X. K. Chen (1989) conducted tests on the central nervous system activity of 100 national team athletes to predict their temperamental categories, including choleric, sanguine, melancholic, and phlegmatic. He found that the three basic qualities of intensity (strong vs. weak), flexibility (flexible vs. inflexible) and balance (balanced vs. unbalanced) of central nervous system activity reliably predicted the temperamental categories to which the athletes belonged.

Further research by S. Y. Chen, Yang, Qiu, Bay, and Li (1983) employed a culturally-balanced Chinese version of the MMPI to assess the personality types of top level female Chinese volleyball players, and found that most of the players were extraverts. Other researchers conducted studies on shooting, basketball, and sprinting athletes, and identified particular personality patterns for the athletes of each respective sport (Qiu, 1986; Xie & Hu, 1983). W. Y. Wang and Zhang (1989) compiled the 808 Central Nervous System Activity Test in an attempt to categorize the personality types of child, junior, adolescent, and elite athletes. X. K. Chen (1989) used the Russian Анфынов rectified method (Z. N. Lu translated the test from Russian, 1984) to assess the working patterns of the central nervous system of female basketball players, and found that there were clear sport-related characteristics. Most of the players belonged to the flexible and calm categories, and many to the easily excitable category.

Qiu (1986) used a culturally-balanced Chinese version of Cattell's 16 PF Questionnaire to assess the personality of athletes from men's and women's basketball, volleyball, rowing, sprinting, diving, shooting, and men's soccer teams. He found that there were similarities among the athletes of various sports and that male athletes were more stable and more adventurous than male university students. These athletes exhibited behavior that conformed to the norms of the society, but they lacked the desire to learn new things. Meanwhile, female athletes were better able to handle problems independently than female university students, but were also more stubborn in sticking to their own opinions and lacked the desire to learn new things.

As far as the distribution of the personality factors on Cattell's 16 PF for the athletes of different sports was concerned, relatively large variations were found in comparisons of shooting and rowing athletes, shooting and basketball athletes, and rowing and basketball athletes. Since these were the first investigations of this kind to be conducted in China, the authors cautioned readers to avoid jumping to conclusions when interpreting the findings concerning inter-sport differences.

Cognitive qualities. Qualities that are thought to be important in sports performance include sensitivity and perceptual acuity, speed and accuracy of motor reaction, comprehensiveness and clarity of sport imagery, speed of operational thinking, concentration and memory (Qiu, 1990). Indicators of these qualities are simple visual and auditory reaction time, time perception and prediction pertaining to visual, auditory and kinesthetic aspects, spatial judgment, depth perception, visual memory, operational thinking, integrated reaction time, i.e. hand-leg coordination, selection reaction time, sense of muscle strength, perception of bodily position, e.g. arms and legs, coordination of both hands, perception of body position, floatation perception, and rotation orientation. Qiu et al. (1986) showed that these were useful indicators for talent identification in various sports, including volleyball, basketball, table tennis, sprinting, sailing, rowing, and swimming.

Controversial issues in talent identification. Despite the progress made so far, talent identification remains a controversial issue in contemporary sport psychology. First, what is the meaning of talent identification? There is considerable disagreement among experts on the nature of talent, and which factors can reliably be used in the process of identifying talent. Abbot and Collins (2004) proposed that the term 'talent' needs to be reconceptualized, and that talent identification and talent developmental processes should be perceived as dynamic and interrelated.

Second, whether the psychological parameters used in talent identification should be sport-specific is also controversial. Qiu and colleagues (Qiu, 1990; Qiu et al., 2003) believed that sport-specific parameters, e.g. operational thinking and speed perception, are equally if not more important in talent identification than a knowledge of the basic general parameters, such as personality and intelligence. It is noteworthy that the indicators used to identify talent in athletes are primarily related to the demand characteristics of the sport in question, its task requirements and the personality characteristics of the athletes. Sport-specific abilities appear to vary according to the type of sport in question. Relatively little progress has, however, been made so far in discovering sport-specific parameters in talent identification in China.

Summary

In general, the assessment of the efficacy of talent identification in sports in China is an on-going process and awaits further investigation to confirm the previous findings. In comparison with the identification of physical talents in areas such as morphological form, physical function or motor skill, evidence concerning psychological talent identification is relatively weak (X. W. Liu, 1991). The existing studies in China have been limited by the small number of indicators employed and the lack of clear-cut relationships among them. In addition, several researchers, e.g. Lidor, Côté, and Hackfort (2007), have noted that in general, there is a lack of tests to assess cognitive skills, such as game understanding, anticipation, decision making, and problem solving.

We are still at the stage in which researchers are trying to find sensitive and valid, sport-specific indicators in talent identification. Moreover, most studies conducted in China have been cross-sectional, using an expert-novice contrast paradigm. The major limitation of this kind of approach is that one cannot control for the effect of maturation or training on athletes. Longitudinal studies are therefore needed in order to test the predictive value of various psychological parameters, and their role at different stages of the athlete's development.

Due to these limitations, Chinese sport psychologists are unable to present a comprehensive picture of the psychological characteristics required for talent identification or to build a mathematical model for testing these characteristics (Qiu, Liu, Wang, & Ma, 2003). Despite these limitations, some progress has been made in locating some of the parameters for talent identification. These authors suggested that in identifying talents, their multidimensional nature should be emphasized, and that it is important to recognize the essential role played by psychology in enabling talented athletes to fulfill their potential. In general, these ideas are being taken seriously in China, and the role of psychology is increasingly being recognized (for instance, more sport psychology professionals have been invited to work with teams during past ten years) by the national sport policy makers, especially in view of the Beijing Olympic Games, 2008 and its consequences (e.g. for more medals).

Research on cognitive sport psychology

Research into cognitive sport psychology in the Western world began in 1970 when an information-processing approach was adapted for the study of motor skills (Lindquist, 1970). Then, C. M. Jones and Miles (1978) used video recordings to investigate tennis players' ability to predict the point at which a moving ball would land. The participants were divided into groups of expert and novice players and were shown videos of balls being served. Videos were frozen at 1/24 sec. prior to hitting the ball, and at 1/8 and 1/3 sec. after hitting. Participants were asked to predict where exactly the ball would land. The predictions of expert players were found to be significantly better than those of novice players.

Since then, cognitive sport psychology research has made great strides. Several studies have been completed, including studies on decision making (e.g. Straub & William, 1984), and the use of cognitive strategies in sport settings (e.g. Tenenbaum & Lidor, 2005). In the past decade researchers in mainland China have joined the quest for a better understanding of the thinking patterns athletes use during competitions. The following is a brief introduction to some of the concepts and studies in this important area.

Sport intelligence

What makes an athlete a champion? This is the core issue for those involved in competitive sports. Contemporary literature has identified important factors, such as fitness, techniques, tactics, and mental toughness (X. P. Chen, 2005; Tian & Wu, 1988). Studies on mental toughness, in particular in the area of sport intelligence, are however still insufficient. What is sport intelligence? Does it exist? What about sport-related thinking, the core of sport intelligence? The multiple intelligence theory of Gardner (1999) has alerted sport psychologists in mainland China to the possible existence of a separate and unique type of intelligence in sport. In particular, in high level competitive sports, cognitive ability and more specifically the ability to solve problems during competitions is considered to play a decisive role in the athletes' performance. But what exactly is the thinking ability which is thought to be decisive?

In 1965 the Russian scholar, Pecking, (Z. N. Lu, 1984) proposed the concept of 'operational thinking'. Operational thinking can be defined as the kind of thinking which involves both problem solving and task operation or engagement in a particular behavior at the same time. In sports, a classical example of operational thinking is the Russian 'Three chips' study (Z. N. Lu, 1984). A five-lattice board was presented with three chips placed in a particular set pattern. The experimenter then mixed the chips up in a different order. Participants (including professional and non-professional athletes and university students) were asked to restore the three chips to their original pattern in as few steps as possible. Researchers recorded the time taken for them to think and complete the task as well as the number of steps needed. The thinking involved in problem solving and the task operation in this experiment would indicate the typical characteristics of 'operational thinking'.

Sport psychology researchers in general have tended to see the 'Three chips' study as one which assessed sport-related, operational thinking. However, this type of research has not made much progress so far. What are the reasons for the lack of progress? Liang (1996) argued that in this experiment the amount of time taken to think the task through was not strictly controlled. The participants were given sufficient time to think about the task. When a decision was finally made, the participants would start moving the chips around. Thus, it was likely that they used logical thinking in the process, so that the experimental conditions were unable to accurately mimic the process of time-limited 'operational thinking' required in many sports.

Conditions and characteristics of sport-related thinking

While Liang (1996) has questioned the extent to which the 'Three chips' methodology genuinely tests sports-related thinking, he was reluctant to reject the existence of a separate type of sport-related thinking. He believed that the basic thinking pattern of an athlete initially develops in the same way as that of an average person, including in domains such as motion, image, and logical thinking. But, due to the experiences of prolonged training, competitions and the demand characteristics of sports, a unique sport-related thinking is also developed by athletes on top of the basic pattern.

Sport-related thinking (Qi, 2001) refers to the thinking processes of athletes when engaging in competitive sports. The content of this kind of thinking involves the following: selective attention to and the processing of external information and internal motion feedback data on the part of the athlete. More specifically, this thinking requires the presence of a certain amount of sport knowledge and experience from long-term memory, prior to choosing and executing a particular action, and the ability (of the athlete) to use the data as a foundation to construct an information network or to create new information loops for a particular problem.

When compared with general thinking patterns in everyday life, sport-related thinking, especially when athletes have to solve a problem (e.g. when defending in a basketball game) is characterized by three special qualities: first, in competitive sports, a number of problems are likely to appear within a relatively short period of time, and these problems tend to be continuous, random, and unpredictable. Second, problems need to be solved in a very short period of time and there is no room for hesitation. Third, a great majority of the problems will have to be resolved simultaneously while competing. In another words, athletes have to move and make decisions at the same time, working their hands, legs, body and mind all at once, often without the luxury of a break in the action. Thus, problem-solving in sports has to be speedy and continuous and completed while competing. This kind of thinking pattern will have to be unique, for it is not iconic, logical or action-oriented, the kinds of thinking normally used in people's daily lives. Thus, Liang and Han (2002) hypothesized the existence of a type of intuitional thinking in athletes.

From 2000 to 2006, Liang and his colleagues (e.g. Fu, 2004; C. Han & Liang, 2000; Li, 2005; Liang & Han, 2002; Qi, 2001; B. Wang, 2002), completed a series of empirical studies examining sport-related thinking for a number of sports. They concluded that the more familiar the athletes were with the movements, the smaller the demand on their cognitive resources and the better their performance. In the following paragraphs their findings on sport-related thinking in baseball, table tennis, and fencing athletes are briefly introduced.

Baseball. C. Han and Liang (2000) investigated the pattern of sport-related thinking in professional and amateur baseball players. The independent variables in this 2x3x3, multi-factorial design included the level of performance (professional vs. amateur), the pitching time (40 ms before pitching, and 40 ms and 120 ms after pitching), and the degree of stress (low, medium and high) of the participants. The dependent variables included the reaction time for judgments of good and bad hits for batters and the correctness of their judgments. Results showed that in all conditions of stress, the mean percentages of correct judgment of professional and amateur players were 44 per cent and 35 per cent, respectively. As for reaction time, the average time taken by both the professional players (830 ms) and amateur players (1238 ms) was significantly lower than the minimum processing time of 2000 ms for an average person to form the simplest logical deduction.

This finding suggested that the thinking of the participants was unlikely to reflect the existence of genuine thinking activities in the participants. In addition, this type of thinking is unlikely to be a normal kind of iconic or logical thinking, but rather a unique thinking pattern. C. Han and Liang simply coined it 'intuitional thinking' and considered it to be the core of sport-related thinking.

Table tennis. Li's (2005) study investigated the decision-making characteristics of table tennis athletes when receiving a ball served by their opponents, using time and spatial framing. Time framing refers to stopping a particular video frame when critical, time-related information appears, and spatial framing refers to stopping a video frame when crucial, motion-related information surfaces. The participants were elite, sub-elite, and average table tennis players. The participants were shown videos on the computer and were asked, under the conditions of time and spatial framings, to judge as precisely and as quickly as possible the point at which a serving ball fell. The findings of time framing suggested that the correctness in judging the spinning of the ball by top athletes was significantly higher than that of the other two groups. As for spatial framing, the findings showed that the server's bodily movement greatly affected the receiver's correctness in judgment of ball spin, but not speed.

Li (2005) concluded that, when receiving the ball, the judgment made by the table tennis players regarding where the ball would land was a continuous process, but the spinning judgment was made within the narrow time period of 800 ms prior to the ball actually touching the racket. Thus, the major thinking characteristics of top players when receiving the ball were considered to be the ability to receive and integrate relevant information to solve the 'problem' of receiving the ball, and simultaneously screen out all other interfering and irrelevant information within a very short period of time.

Fencing. Using video analysis and the reaction time method, Fu (2004) compiled a software program for analyzing fencers' performance. The software aimed at investigating the influence of the amount of information and the cognitive style of fencers on the speed, correctness, and stability of hitting decisions. The amount of information was divided into large (i.e. counting 7-26 seconds backwards from point scoring) and small (i.e. counting 3-6 seconds backwards from point scoring). The cognitive style referred to the concept developed by Driver and Mock (1975). They proposed a decision-style theory, which divided the information processing of decision into two dimensions, namely, a dimension of focus and a dimension tapping the amount of information utilized. These two dimensions form a matrix of four styles, namely, decisive, flexible, hierarchic, and integrated styles.

The participants were chosen from three different ability levels (i.e. elite, sub-elite and average). They were shown videos of 54 fencing sections on a computer. A small yellow circle appeared on the left or right side of the computer screen, indicating the position of the fencer who made a score. The participants were asked to pretend to be that fencer and to watch the opponent closely. The task was to push a button, using the dominant hand, as soon as the decision to hit was made. The picture would then disappear after the button was pushed, and then three multiple choice questions were asked of the participants. The questions were: (1) what information did you see from the opponent that cued you to hit? (2) where exactly on the opponent did you want to place your sword point? (3) what method did you use to hit? The next video section was shown once a selection was made.

The findings showed significant effects from the amount of information and the fencers' cognitive style on the speed, correctness, and stability of hitting decisions. Compared with average fencers, top foil and epee fencers were clearly superior in their speed at making correct hitting decisions. The higher the level of the foil fencers, the higher was their hit rate and the better their consistency in performance. On the other hand, too much information served only to slow down the decision making of the average foil fencers, but had no effect on top foil fencers. Overall, the cognitive style of all levels of the participants not only affected the foil fencers' correctness in their decision making, but also that of the epee fencers as well as their speed of decision making.

On the basis of the findings from these and other empirical studies (Abernethy, 1987; Tenenbaum & Bar-Eli, 1993; Tenenbaum & Lidor, 2005), Liang (2006; 2007) concluded that sport-related thinking has the following four characteristics:

Narrowing of cognitive processing resources. This occurs because an athlete may not be able to use the body and the mind simultaneously within a short period of time during practice or competition. The thinking pattern of an athlete in action would have to be simple, of short duration, and present-focused. The more the athletes are familiar with the techniques and movements, the bigger the cognitive capacity available for sport-related thinking and vice versa.

Inability to think logically during a competition. This is especially the case in the heat of an important competition, for an athlete has to process a large number of variables (e.g. him/herself, rival, and environment) at high speed. In addition, research in cognitive psychology (Huang, 2000; Libet, Wright, Feinstein, & Pearl, 1979) shows that it takes at least 400 ms for a concept to form and that the simplest form of deduction needs at least three concepts, two of which should be related. If less than two seconds are given, then even a simple deduction is impossible, let alone a complicated one. In many competitive sports, athletes do not have two seconds in which to make a decision and execute a movement. Thus, normal deductive thinking is not feasible.

Inability to process images. Along the same line of thinking, image processing is impossible in fierce competitions. It takes at least 550 ms to form the simplest image of a single letter of the alphabet in the brain, and more than 2 sec. to select the right kind of image from a combination of at least three images (Bisanz, Danner, & Resnick, 1979; Le, 1986). If an execution of a single movement takes less than 2 sec., then image processing is impossible in competitive sports.

Need for speedy decision making. In competition, athletes have to make instant decisions to win, and the faster the better. Any hesitation or delay in response is certain to result in a loss of control or the chance to win.

Summary

Research in cognitive sport psychology in mainland China started in the 1990s, and much progress has been made so far in the field of sport-related thinking, in particular in the introduction of the concept of intuitional thinking. The importance of intuitional thinking has been tested in various sports, including baseball, table tennis, and fencing. By comparing the performance in decision making of elite, sub-elite, and average athletes in the laboratory, sport psychologists have been able to achieve a more in-depth understanding of the characteristics of sport-related thinking. Since B. Wang's (2002) study on handball athletes, the focus of research in China on general sport-related thinking has gradually changed to investigating the decision-making abilities of the athletes, in an attempt to develop a mental training model for each particular skill. In other words, the direction of research in this area has started to move from investigating the meaning of sport-related thinking to investigating the issue of *in vivo* training and developing this ability in athletes.

Chinese mental training and its applications

To perform to their full potential is not only the objective of athletes in physical practice and competition, but also the goal of their mental training. The focus of Western sport psychology has so far been on the application of relevant research findings. Since the 1980s, sport psychologists in China have also provided relevant services to the top athletes of the national teams during their preparations for international competitions, especially the Olympic Games. In the past, Western sport psychological models, such as the iceberg profile of mood (Morgan, 1980), individualized zones of optimal functioning (Hanin, 1989), multidimensional anxiety theory (Materns, Vealey, & Burton, 1990), the catastrophe model (Hardy & Parfitt, 1991), and flow state theory (Jackson, 1996) have guided service provision in China; however, more recently Chinese sport psychologists have begun to develop their own models for the delivery of services. At present, there are two representative conceptual frameworks: (1) S. H. Liu's (2001) mental construction; and (2) Si's (2006) adversity coping.

Mental construction framework

On the basis of her experiences in training shooting athletes and her understanding of the demands of international competitions, S. H. Liu (2001) proposed a conceptual framework involving three-level mental construction. Mental and technical training forms its foundation, with positive thinking as its central idea, and a positive self-image weaving the other two parts together to form a holistic framework for mental construction.

S. H. Liu (2001) believed that mental training should be incorporated into both technical and tactical training as a starting point and the first level, the objective of which is to establish a habitual body (technical) – mind (mental) combined base. With prolonged practice, this body-mind base would function automatically. Given this strong base, the athletes may still have difficulties in coping with stress or negative emotions. Thus, to enhance their coping abilities, athletes would need to receive second-level training in positive and rational thinking as well as self-control, including that of emotions, attention, and behavior. On top of these two levels, a third level of positive self-image training is imposed, the objective of which is to facilitate athletes' self-understanding and their ability to educate and develop themselves. They would be likely to ask such questions as, 'Who am I? What can I do? What do I want? How can I reach my goal?' In asking and answering these questions, the athletes would become more self-directed in competitions.

In preparing a shooting athlete for the 2000 Sydney Olympic Games, S. H. Liu (2006) designed a systematic training program, following the guidelines found in her framework. The program included the basic training to enhance behavioral coping abilities, and by way of increasing mental loading during practice and competition, the athlete was expected to gradually form a habitual technical–mental combined base. This was followed by the second level of competition preparation, using positive thinking, adversity coping, and cognitive restructuring to increase the athlete's confidence and achievement motivation. In addition, by way of positive self-image training (through imagery and modeling), the athlete became more confident having developed better self-control and self-direction. The three years of training appeared to pay off, as the athlete won a gold and silver medal in shooting events at the 2000 Olympic Games.

S. H. Liu (2007) concluded that the three training levels are closely related and equally important, and that none can replace the others. All in all, this mental construction framework reflects the importance of integrating mental education, mental training and consultation. As she has remarked, 'Integration is creation'.

Adversity coping framework

Si's framework (2006a) originates not from integration of various approaches, but from creating a new path. Si discussed the difficulties encountered by sport psychologists when applying traditional mental training models to athletes. The main difficulty seems to be the emphasis on the concept of peak performance. The core idea behind peak performance is that athletes would have perfect performance when they possess an optimal psychological state. Some examples of this concept include the ideal iceberg profile of mood (Morgan, 1980), optimal level of anxiety (Materns et al., 1990), individualized zones of optimal functioning (Hanin, 1989), optimal combination of physical arousal and cognitive anxiety (Hardy & Parfitt, 1991), and flow state (Jackson, 1996).

Using these traditional models, practitioners seek to find this elusive aspect of peak performance by examining the athletes' past experiences, then, by way of a variety of mental skills training, attempt to activate and maintain this 'peak' state. Athletes participate in long periods of mental training, but still are often not sure if they will actually be able to reach this 'peak' state at the time when they want it. Additionally, the coaches are typically only minimally involved.

Problems with these mental training models are three-fold: (1) how to operationally find these subjective peak states in the athletes, as some young athletes may not have had the chance to experience such peak states in their previous competitions; (2) how to operationally activate peak states in the athletes at the time when they need them; and (3) as conditions change and adversities appear which can interfere with or destroy peak states, how to continuously maintain the peak states during competitions.

On the basis of practical experiences and applied research findings (Si & Liu, 2004), Si (2006a) proposed a new definition of peak performance, namely, successful adversity coping in competitions. According to Si, adversity in competition is normal, and athletes' success in coping with each adverse situation is closely related to their successful performance. In another words, even when athletes may not achieve a 'peak' state at the time of the competition, if they can reasonably cope with most or all adversities, effectively overcome their mistakes or compensate for their loss, their performance may still be judged as successful.

Along this line of reasoning, peak performance can be defined as a dynamic, continuously adjusted process during competition. In this way, the purpose of mental training is not primarily to discover or pursue the mechanism which explains the athletes' optimal performance during competition, but rather to explore the mechanism of adaptation when the athletes are placed under extremely stressful situations.

Based on this new definition, Si (2006a) developed a four-stage adversity coping training framework: (1) to identify and confirm typical adverse situations of the athletes; (2) to seek appropriate coping methods; (3) to conduct individualized training; and (4) to evaluate training outcomes. When compared with traditional mental training programs, Si's program replaces 'peak' states of athletes with their typical adverse situations, followed by appropriate mental training to enable the athletes to cope successfully and rationally with these situations. In general, this training model is characterized by a consistency in subjective (both athlete's and coach's) and objective evaluations (e.g. the number of times when an athlete is successful in handling adverse situations during competitions, and the outcome of competitions), with clear direction and close involvement of the coaches. Through adversity coping training, the athletes are getting closer to reaching an ideal performance state. In the past few years, Si's framework has been applied with encouraging outcomes in both Hong Kong and mainland China (L. Han, 2008; Si, 2006b; 2007a; 2007b; 2007c; Si, Lee, & Liu, 2008).

While preparing for the 2004 Athens Olympic Games, Si and colleagues (Si et al., 2008) used adversity coping to work with a Hong Kong table tennis player. Using data obtained from observation, videos of past competitions, and comments of the coaches and the player and his partner, the main problem was identified to be low frustration tolerance. The problem was usually triggered by specific adverse situations, such as making technical or tactical mistakes by self or partner during the competition. Rational emotive behavior therapy (Ellis & Dryden, 1997) and mental skills training (e.g. relaxation, imagery, positive self-talk and cognitive restructuring) were employed to help the player change his problematic behavior. Over the 10-month period of training that followed, Si worked closely with the player, his coach, and his partner. The outcome was positive in that the player demonstrated good self-control at the time of the Olympic Games and won a silver medal in the doubles event in table tennis.

Summary

In conclusion, these two representative training frameworks have been well received not only by sport psychologists in mainland China, but also by athletes and their coaches. Their usefulness and application in competitions will, however, need to be further tested over a longer period of time and across a wider range of sports.

On-field psychological support

On-field psychological support refers to the presence of sport psychologists at the site of competitions and their delivery of services to performing athletes and coaches. Whether sport psychologists should or should not provide on-field psychological support has become an interesting but controversial issue in recent years (Desharnais, 1983; Gorbunov, 1983; Hahn, 1983; Rushall, 1981). Some scholars believe that on-field support is crucial to competitive sports. For example, Rushall (1981), remarked that, 'There are clearly defined tasks that can be performed on-site better by a trained, competent psychologist rather than by a coach, who is emotionally involved with the athletes and their performance outcomes.' (p. 3) Others, however, have questioned the usefulness of this kind of service to the athletes. Desharnais (1983) said that he did not believe that a sport psychologist could best help the athletes by on-site intervention, and expressed concern about the 'crutch effect' of having psychologists at competitions.

Despite this controversy among sport scholars, in the past 20 years or so, some countries have been sending sport psychologists to provide on-field support at different international competitions. In 1987, the United States Olympic Committee assigned, for the first time, a sport psychologist to the medical team at the US Olympic Festival of that year, and in 1988 it sent two sport psychologists as official members of the US delegation to serve its teams at the Seoul Olympic Games (Murphy & Ferrante, 1989). In 1984, the Australian Olympic Committee appointed a team psychologist for the Los Angeles Olympic Games. This was just the beginning of a longstanding involvement by sport psychologists in Australian Olympic teams. A highlight was the appointment of nine, fully accredited positions for sport psychologists at the Atlanta Olympic Games in 1996 (Bond, 2002). Even earlier than 1984, Canada had begun to send sport psychologists to work with its athletes during the Summer and Winter Olympic Games (Orlick, 1989). More recently, at the 2006 Doha Asian Games, Hong Kong, Malaysia, Singapore, Thailand, Korea, Taiwan, and Philippines also offered on-field psychological support to their athletes (Si, 2007d). Thus, on-field psychological support has not only become increasingly popular, but has also become an important aspect of sport psychological service.

Research into on-field psychological support

While on-field psychological support has become increasingly popular, relatively little research has been conducted to evaluate the effectiveness of this practice. Research so far has been limited to either the service experiences and self-reflection of individual psychologists (Bond, 2001; Gipson, Mckenzie, & Lowe, 1989; Haberl & Peterson, 2006; Hardy & Parfitt, 1994; May & Brown, 1989; McCann, 2000; Murphy, 1988; Murphy & Ferrante, 1989; Orlick, 1989; Van Raalte, 2003), evaluation of services by athletes and coaches at the end of the competition (Anderson, Miles, Mahoney, & Robinson, 2002; Gould, Murphy, Tammen, & May, 1989; Orlick & Partington, 1987; Partington & Orlick, 1987), or theoretical and philosophical considerations (Pocrdowski, Sherman, & Henschen, 1998; Poczwardowski, Sherman & Ravizza, 2004; Si, 2003).

An application of on-field support was described in some detail by Giges and Petitpas (2000), and presented in the form of brief contacts. The two authors characterized their work as time-limited, action-oriented, and present-focused, and believed that these brief contacts could have a snowballing effect on the performance of the athletes. The prerequisite for this effect was the existence of an *a priori* relationship between the psychologists on the one hand and the athletes and coaches on the other. Bond (2001) has also discussed in great detail the kind of work he did during one day of on-field support, including the way in which he planned and implemented his services. Despite these studies, a systematic investigation of the effect of on-field psychological support on performance is still lacking.

To fill this gap, a small group of sport psychologists from Hong Kong (Si, Lee, Cheng, & Liu, 2006) conducted a pioneering study in this area, the objective of which was to find out what the athletes and coaches thought about on-field psychological support and how best to implement such support services. On the basis of their on-field support experiences and a review of related literature, these researchers developed guidelines for interviewing athletes and coaches. Participants included elite athletes and coaches from Hong Kong who had had at least one experience of on-field support. The semi-structured interviews lasted, on average, for 1 to 1½ hours and their content was recorded. The qualitative data were then content analyzed using on the steps suggested by Côté and Salmela (1994).

Findings reflected the current state of Hong Kong on-field psychological support in four aspects, namely, prerequisite conditions, service preparation, process of the service provision, and efficacy of service. Prerequisite conditions are based on five factors: (1) the relationship between the athletes and psychologists; (2) the relationship between the coaches and psychologists; (3) the competence of psychologists; (4) the needs and trust of athletes in the psychologists; and (5) the support of related departments.

As for service preparation, participants expect the psychologists to inform the athletes of their presence at competitions, participate in pre-competition meetings, obtain related information from the coaches, establish a trusting relationship with the athletes and coaches, assess the mental state of the athletes, and inform the athletes and coaches of the content of the service and other relevant specifics. In terms of service provision, athletes and coaches believed in the importance of the psychologists' participation in pre-and post-competition meetings. They also highlighted the importance of providing service at a variety of times and locations, using diverse avenues to communicate an idea, and taking the initiative in providing these services.

Finally, there were four aspects on which the quality of service was judged, namely, whether the psychologist could: (1) help the athletes adjust and improve their mental states at the site of the competition; (2) help the athletes adjust and improve their mental states outside the site of the competition; (3) help to improve the athletes' interpersonal relationships; and (4) offer other types of service, including counseling of personal problems, information-giving, and facilitating athletes' adjustment to the competitive environment. In addition, a number of athletes spontaneously remarked that consultation with a psychologist had not only resulted in performance enhancement, but had also enabled them to deal effectively with sudden occurrences and crisis events during their competitions.

Summary

In sum, the findings of this study provide important, first-hand data that form an empirical foundation on which a model for on-field psychological support can be constructed. They also show that psychologists should not only provide quality service to the competition task at hand, but should also consider how best to improve their service in future competitions and to train young students to become competent psychologists. Finally, the authors suggest that the focus of on-field support should not be on competition alone, but also on daily practice, for only from everyday practice can athletes really benefit from integrated training in the technical, tactical and mental aspects of sport. It is only through a successful transfer of ability from practice to competition that the ultimate goals of psychological service can be fully realized.

Future trends

In the light of the rapid progress of Chinese society with its emphasis on achievement (see Hau & Ho, this volume) and economic growth, as well as the increasing health concerns of the Chinese people (see Mak & Chen, this volume), we believe that future trends of research in Chinese sport psychology are likely to be two-fold: first, research on exercise psychology will become increasingly important. Indeed, the growing problem of obesity in an increasingly wealthy Chinese society is worrying (Y. Wang, Mi, Shan, Wang, & Ge, 2007), and therefore research interest in motivation to engage in physical activity (Lonsdale, Sabiston, Raedeke, Ha, & Sum, 2009; J. Wang & Wiese-Bjornstal, 1997) will likely continue to flourish; second, the experiences and knowledge obtained from research in competitive sport psychology will likely be used for the pursuit of excellence not only in the sports arena, but also in other applied fields as well, including business administration, the performing arts, medical training, pilot testing, and stress coping for the police. The application of insights and knowledge from sport psychology to these areas has already been seen in the Western world (Gould, 2002; Hays, 2002; G. Jones, 2002; Le Scanff, & Taugis, 2002; Martin, & Cutler, 2002; Newburg, Kimiecik, Durand-Bush, & Doell, 2002; Poczwardowski, & Conroy, 2002; Weinberg, & McDermott, 2002), and will surely be extended into Chinese thinking and psychological research.

References

Abbott, A. & Collins, D. (2004). Eliminating the dichotomy between theory and practice in talent identification and development: Considering the role of psychology. *Journal of Sports Sciences, 5*, 395–408.

Abernethy, B. & Russell, D. G. (1987). Expert–novice differences in an applied selective attention task. *Journal of Sport Psychology, 9*, 326–345.

Anderson, A. G., Miles, A., Mahoney, C., & Robinson, P. (2002). Evaluating the effectiveness of applied sport psychology practice: Making the case for a case study approach. *The Sport Psychologist, 16*, 432–453.

Andrews, J. C. (1971). Personality, sporting interest and achievements. *Educational Review, 2*, 126–134.

Bisanz, J., Danner, F., & Resnick, L. B. (1979). Changes with age in measures of processing efficiency. *Child Development, 50*, 132–141.

Bond, J. W. (2001). The provision of sport psychology services during competition tours. In G. Tenenbaum (ed.), *The practice of sport psychology* (pp. 217–230). Morgantown, PA: Fitness Information Technology.

Bond, J. W. (2002). Applied sport psychology: Philosophy, reflections, and experience. *International Journal of Sport Psychology, 33*, 19–37.

Chen, S. Y., Yang, B. M, Qiu, Y. J., Bay, E. B., & Li, J. N. (1983). Evaluation on some variables related to personality. *A collection of Chinese sport psychology research papers from 1979 to 1983*, China, 202–203. (in Chinese)

Chen, X. K. (1989). A research on the nerve pattern of Chinese first league female basketball players. In T. F. Zhong (ed.), *Sport psychology of basketball* (pp. 166–171). Beijing: Chinese Geographic University Press. (in Chinese)

Chen, X. P. (2005). *The hot topics of contemporary sports training.* Beijing, China: Beijing Sport University Press. (in Chinese)

Côté, J. & Salmela, J. H. (1994). A decision-making heuristic for the analysis of unstructured qualitative data. *Perceptual and Motor Skills, 78*, 465–466.

Cox, R. & Qiu, Y. J. (1993). Overview of sport psychology. In R. Cox (ed.), *Handbook of research on sport psychology* (pp. 3–31). New York: Macmillan.

Desharnais, R. (1983). Reaction to the paper by B. S. Rushall: On-site psychological preparations for athletes. In T. Orlick, J. T. Partington, & J. H. Salmela (eds), *Mental training for coaches and athletes* (pp. 150–151). Ottawa, Canada: Coaching Association of Canada.

Driver, M. J. & Mock, T. J. (1975). Human information processing, decision style theory and accounting information systems. *Accounting Review, 2*, 495–505.

Ellis, A. & Dryden, W. (1997). *The practice of rational emotive behavior therapy* (2nd edn). New York: Springer.

Fraternity, K. & Epsilon, P. (1977). *Sport personality assessment: Facts and perspectives.* New York: The Physical Educator.

Fu, Q. (2004). *The influence of amount of information and cognitive style on speed, accuracy and stability of fencers' decision-making.* Unpublished doctoral dissertation, Beijing Sports University, Beijing, China. (in Chinese)

Gao, J. & Yang, D. (2000). A study on psychological abilities of Chinese elite decathletes. *China Sport Science and Technology, 36*, 28–30. (in Chinese)

Gardner, H. (1999). *Intelligence reframed multiple intelligences for the 21st century.* New York: Basic Books.

Giges, B. & Petitpas, A. (2000). Brief contact interventions in sport psychology. *The Sport Psychologist, 14*, 176–187.

Gipson, M., McKenzie, T., & Lowe, S. (1989). The sport psychology program of the USA women's national volleyball team. *The Sport Psychologist, 3*, 330–339.

Gorbunov, G. (1983). Psychological training of Soviet athletes for the Olympics: Self-command teaching. In T. Orlick, J. T. Partington, & J. H. Salmela (eds), *Mental training for coaches and athletes* (pp. 153–156). Ottawa, Canada: Coaching Association of Canada.

Gould, D. (2002). Moving beyond the psychology of athletic excellence. *Journal of Applied Sport Psychology, 14*, 247–248.

Gould, D., Tammen, V., Murphy, S., & May, J. (1989). An examination of US Olympic sport psychology consultants and the services they provide. *The Sport Psychologist, 3*, 300–312.

Haberl, P. & Peterson, K. (2006). Olympic-size ethical dilemmas: Issues and challenges for sport psychology consultants on the road and at the Olympic Games. *Ethics and Behavior, 16*, 25–40.

Hahn, E. (1983). The psychological preparation of Olympic athletes: East and West. In T. Orlick, J. T. Partington, & J. H. Salmela (eds), *Mental training for coaches and athletes* (pp. 156–158). Ottawa, Canada: Coaching Association of Canada.

Han, C. (2000). *The influence of problem situation and skill level to athlete's intuition thinking: An experiment of reaction time and accuracy in baseball's pitch-bat.* Unpublished master's thesis, Beijing Sports University, Beijing, China. (in Chinese)

Han, L. (2008). Sport psychology consultant's working diary for the 2007 National Rhythmic Gymnastic Championship. *Chinese Journal of Sports Medicine, 27*, 511–517. (in Chinese)

Hanin, Y. L. (1989). Interpersonal and intragroup anxiety: Conceptual and methodological issues. In D. Hackfort & C. D. Spielberger (eds), *Anxiety in sports: An international perspective* (pp. 19–28). Washington, DC: Hemisphere Publishing Corporation.

Hardy, L. & Parfitt, G. (1991). A catastrophe model of anxiety and performance. *British Journal of Psychology, 82*, 163–178.

Hardy, L. & Parfitt, G. (1994). The development of a model for the provision of psychological support to a National Squad. *The Sport Psychologist, 8*, 126–142.

Hays, K. F. (2002). The enhancement of performance excellence among performing artists. *Journal of Applied Sport Psychology, 14*, 299–312.

He, Y., Shi, Y., Guo, R. L., & Guo, J. X. (2002). Research on talent selection indexes and criterion of China junior archers. *China Sport Science and Technology, 38*, 60–61. (in Chinese)

Huang, B. X. (2000). *The advanced function and the nervous network.* Beijing, China: Science Press. (in Chinese)

Jackson, S. A. (1996). Toward a conceptual understanding of the flow experience in elite athletes. *Research Quarterly for Exercise and Sport, 67*, 76–90.

Jones, C. M. & Miles, T. R. (1978).Use of advance cues in predicting the flight of a lawn ball. *Journal of Human Movement Studies, 4*, 231–235.

Jones, G. (2002). Performance excellence: A personal perspective on the link between sport and business. *Journal of Applied Sport Psychology, 14*, 268–281.

Le, G. A. (1986). *Comments on modern cognitive psychology.* Harbin, China: People's Press of Heilongjiang Province. (in Chinese)

Le Scanff, C. & Taugis, J. (2002). Stress management for police special forces. *Journal of Applied Sport Psychology, 14*, 330–343.

Li, J. L. (2005). *The characteristics of thinking of table-tennis players when receiving a service.* Unpublished doctoral dissertation, Beijing Sports University, Beijing, China. (in Chinese)

Liang, C. M. (1996). *The rationale of general psychology.* Beijing, China: Chinese Three Gorges Press. (in Chinese)

Liang, C. M. (2006). *Practical psychology.* Beijing, China: People's Press of Sports. (in Chinese)

Liang, C. M. (2007). Recent advance in research on cognitive sports psychology. In China Association for Science and Technology (ed.), *Report on advances in sports science* (pp. 131–144). Beijing, China: China Science and Technology Press. (in Chinese)

Liang, C. M. & Han, C. (2002). *Intuition and the empirical study of intuition in sports situation.* Paper presented at the 4th international conference of Chinese psychologists, Taipei, Taiwan. (in Chinese)

Libet, B., Wright, E. W., Feinstein, B., & Pearl, D. (1979). Subjective referral of the timing for a conscious sensory experience: A functional role for the somatosensory specific projection system in man. *Brain, 102*, 193–224.

Lidor, R., Côté, J., & Hackfort, D. (2007). To test or not to test? The use of physical skill tests in talent detection and in early phases of sport development. *International Society of Sport Psychology, 17*(Winter), 4.

Lindquist, E. L. (1970). An information processing approach to the study of a complex motor skill. *Research Quarterly, 3*, 396–401.

Liu, S. H. (1989). Exploration on intelligence level of the PE major students. *Journal of Beijing Sport Normal University, 1*, 1–5. (in Chinese)

Liu, S. H. (2001). A study on improving shooters' performance in the Olympic Games. In Chinese Psychological Society (ed.), *Contemporary Chinese psychology* (pp. 446–453). Beijing, China: People's Education Press. (in Chinese)

Liu, S. H. (2006). *Research and application of shooting psychology.* Beijing, China: Beijing Sport University Press. (in Chinese)

Liu, S. H. (2007). Psychological consultation and mental training provided to the Chinese Olympic athletes. In China Association for Science and Technology (ed.), *Report on advances in psychology* (pp. 102–111). Beijing, China: China Science and Technology Press. (in Chinese)

Liu, X. W. (1991). *Talent identification in sport.* Beijing, China: People's Press of Sports. (in Chinese)

Liu, X. W. & Lin, W. T. (1987). *General introduction on the genetics of sport talent.* Guangzhou, China: High Education Press of Guangdong Province. (in Chinese)

Lonsdale, C., Sabiston, C. M., Raedeke, T. D., Ha, S. C. A., & Sum, K. W. R. (2009). Self-determined motivation and students' physical activity in PE classes and free-choice periods. *Preventive Medicine, 48*, 69–73.

Lu, Y. Z. (1996). *Chinese sports sociology.* Beijing, China: Beijing Sports University Press. (in Chinese)

Lu, Z. N. (1984). *The psycho-diagnosis of sports ability.* Wuhan, China: Wuhan Institute of Physical Education, Sport Psychology Research Center. (in Chinese)

Martin, J. J. & Cutler, K. (2002). An exploratory study of flow and motivation in theater actors. *Journal of Applied Sport Psychology, 14*, 344–352.

Materns, R., Vealey, R. S., & Burton, D. (1990). *Competitive anxiety in sport.* Champaign, IL: Human Kinetics.

May, J. R. & Brown, L. (1989). Delivery of psychological services to the US Alpine Ski Team prior to and during the Olympics in Calgary. *The Sport Psychologist, 3*, 320–329.

McCann, S. C. (2000). Doing sport psychology at the really big show. In M. B. Andersen (ed.), *Doing sport psychology* (pp. 209–222). Champaign, IL: Human Kinetics.

Morgan, W. P. (1980). Test of champions: The iceberg profile. *Psychology Today, 14*, 92–108.
Murphy, S. M. (1988). The on-site provision of sport psychology services at the 1987 US Olympic Festival. *The Sport Psychologist, 2*, 337–350.
Murphy, S. M. & Ferrante, A. P. (1989). Provision of sport psychology services to the US team at the 1988 summer Olympic Games. *The Sport Psychologist, 3*, 374–385.
Newburg, D., Kimiecik, J., Durand-Bush, N., & Doell, K. (2002). The role of resonance in performance excellence and life engagement. *Journal of Applied Sport Psychology, 14*, 249–267.
Orlick, T., (1989). Reflections on sportpsych consulting with individual and team sport athletes at summer and winter Olympic Games. *The Sport Psychologist, 3*, 358–365.
Orlick, T. & Partington, J. (1987). The sport psychology consultant: Analysis of critical components as viewed by Canadian Olympic athletes. *The Sport Psychologist, 1*, 4–17.
Pan, Q. & Liu, Z. M. (1990). A research on relationship between intelligence and sport-related aptitude of female badminton players in Fujian province. *Chinese Sports Science and Technology, 10*, 23–26. (in Chinese)
Partington, J. & Orlick, T. (1987). The sport psychology consultant evaluation form. *The Sport Psychologist, 1*, 309–317.
Plomin, R. (1986). *Development, genetics, and psychology: Genetic change and developmental behavioral genetics.* Hillsdale, NJ: Erlbaum.
Poczwardowski, A. & Conroy, D. E. (2002). Coping responses to failure and success among elite athletes and performing artists. *Journal of Applied Sport Psychology, 14*, 313–329.
Poczwardowski, A., Sherman, C. P., & Henschen, K. P. (1998). A sport psychology service delivery heuristic: Building on theory and practice. *The Sport Psychologist, 12*, 191–207.
Poczwardowski, A., Sherman, C. P., & Ravizza, K. (2004). Professional philosophy in the sport psychology service delivery: Building on theory and practice. *The Sport Psychologist, 18*, 445–463.
Qi, C. Z. (2001). *Expert–novice differences in problem representations and characteristics of sport thinking in simulated competitive situation in badminton.* Unpublished doctoral dissertation, Beijing Sports University, Beijing, China. (in Chinese)
Qiu, Y. J. (1986). *Research on personality of elite athletes.* Wuhan, China: Wuhan Institute of Physical Education, Sport Psychology Research Center. (in Chinese)
Qiu, Y. J. (1990).*Psychological diagnosis in sports.* Beijing, China: Chinese Geographic University Press. (in Chinese)
Qiu, Y. J., Bay, E. B., & Liu, L. X. (1986). A study on psychomotor tests for young athletes. *Proceedings of the 3rd national conference of Chinese sport science*, China, 3, 134. (in Chinese)
Qiu, Y. J., Liu, X. M., Wang, B., & Ma, H. Y. (2003). A review on the research and development of sports psychology in China from 1980s to 1990s. *Journal of Shenyang Institute of Physical Education, 1*, 47–50. (in Chinese)
Raven, J. C. (1938). *Progressive matrices: A perceptual test of intelligence.* London: H. K. Lewis.
Rushall, B. S. (1981). On-site psychological preparation for athletes. *Science Periodical on Research and Technology in Sport, 1*, 1–8.
Si, G. Y. (2003). A model of immediate on-field support in sport psychology. *Sport Science, 23*, 97–101. (in Chinese)
Si, G. Y. (2006a). Pursuing 'ideal' or emphasizing 'coping': The new definition of 'peak performance' and transformation of mental training pattern. *Sport Science, 26*, 43–48. (in Chinese)
Si, G. Y. (2006b). Sport psychologist's working diary on the 48th World Team Table Tennis Championship Ⅰ. *Chinese Journal of Sports Medicine, 25*, 732–736. (in Chinese)
Si, G. Y. (2007a). Sport psychologist's working diary on the 19th Asian Tenpin Bowling Championship Ⅰ. *Chinese Journal of Sports Medicine, 26*, 360–363. (in Chinese)
Si, G. Y. (2007b). Sport psychologist's working diary on the 19th Asian Tenpin Bowling Championship Ⅱ. *Chinese Journal of Sports Medicine, 26*, 488–492. (in Chinese)
Si, G. Y. (2007c). Sport psychologist's working diary on the 48th World Team Table Tennis Championship. *Chinese Journal of Sports Medicine, 26*, 105–108. (in Chinese)
Si, G. Y. (2007d). Sport psychology consulting at the 15th Asian Games. *International Society of Sport Psychology* (Spring) *17*, 13.
Si, G. Y., Lee, H. C., Cheng, P., & Liu, J. D. (2006). *A conceptual framework of on-field psychological support to athletes in Hong Kong.* Unpublished manuscript, Hong Kong Sport Institute. (in Chinese)
Si, G. Y., Lee, H. C., & Liu, J. D. (2008). Intervention and evaluation for changing low frustration tolerance. *Acta Psychologica Sinica, 40*, 240–252. (in Chinese)
Si, G. Y., & Liu, H. (2004). Adversity coping in high level sports. *Proceedings of the 7th national sports science congress.* Beijing, China, 7, 100–101. (in Chinese)
Straub, W. F., & William, J. M. (1984). *Cognitive sport psychology.* New York: Sport Science Associates.
Szopa, J. (1985). Genetic and environmental factors of development of fundamental psychomotor traits in man: Results of population study on family resemblances. *Wychowanie-fizyczne-i-sport* (Warsaw), *29*, 19–36.
Tenenbaum, G. & Bar-Eli, M. (1993). Decision making in sport: A cognitive perspective. In R. N. Singer, M. Murphy, & L. K. Tennant (eds), *Handbook of sport psychology* (2nd edn, pp. 171–192). New York: MacMillan.
Tenenbaum, G. & Lidor, R. (2005). Research on decision-making and the use of cognitive strategies in sport settings. In D. Hackfort, J. L. Duda, & R. Lidor (eds), *Handbook of research in applied sport and exercise psychology: International perspectives* (pp. 75–91). Morgantown, PA: Fitness Information Technology.

Tian, M. J. (1986). *Sport training.* Beijing, China: High Education Press. (in Chinese)
Tian, M. J. & Wu, F. Q. (1988). *An exploration of scientific sports training.* Beijing, China: People's Press of Sports. (in Chinese)
Van Raalte, J. L. (2003). Provision of sport psychology services at an international competition: The XVI Maccabiah Games. *The Sport Psychologist, 17,* 461–470.
Wang, B. (2002). *An experiment on intuitive decision-making in handball situation and the preliminary theoretical construction on sport intuition.* Unpublished doctoral dissertation, Beijing sports University, Beijing, China. (in Chinese)
Wang, J. & Wiese-Bjornstal, D. M. (1997). The relationship of school type and gender to motives of sport participation among youth in the People's Republic of China. *International Journal of Sport Psychology, 28,* 13–24.
Wang, W. Y. & Zhang, Q. H. (1989). The patterns of central nervous system and athlete's talent identification. *Sport Science, 3,* 71–75. (in Chinese)
Wang, Y., Mi, J., Shan, X. Y., Wang, Q. J., & Ge, K. Y. (2007). Is China facing an obesity epidemic and the consequences? The trends in obesity and chronic disease in China. *International Journal of Obesity, 31,* 177–188.
Weinberg, R. & McDermott, M. (2002). A comparative analysis of sport and business organizations: Factors perceived critical for organizational success. *Journal of Applied Sport Psychology, 14,* 282–298.
Xie, S. C. & Hu, Z. (1983). Research on personality characteristics of Chinese shooting athletes. *A collection of Chinese sport psychology research papers from 1979 to 1983,* China, 76–95. (in Chinese)
Zeng, F. H., Wang, L. D., & Xing, W. H. (1992). *The science of talent identification on athletes.* Beijing, China: People's Press of Sports. (in Chinese)
Zhang, H. C. (1987). *Cognitive style: An experimental research in the dimension of personality.* Beijing, China: Beijing Normal University Press. (in Chinese)
Zhang, L. W. & Ren, W. D. (2000). *The new development of sport psychology.* Beijing, China: High Education Press. (in Chinese)
Zhang, L. W. & Tao, Z. X. (1994). A research on intelligence development of Chinese table tennis players. *Sport Science, 4,* 73. (in Chinese)
Zheng, R. C. (1984). A study on the temperaments of Chinese first league female volleyball players. *Psychological Science, 20,* 22–27. (in Chinese)

CHAPTER 38

四海為家 There are homes at the four corners of the seas: acculturation and adaptation of overseas Chinese

Colleen Ward and En-Yi Lin

The number of overseas Chinese has now reached 35 million, making them the largest migrant group in the world (Li, 2007). It is not surprising, then, that questions about how Chinese acculturate and adapt to new environments are becoming increasingly important in the global arena. The answers to these questions have implications not only for Chinese migrants and their families, but also for the members of most receiving societies, as they come to accommodate to the growing presence of Chinese in their midst. This chapter examines acculturation and adaptation in overseas Chinese. It focuses primarily on the experiences of Chinese sojourners and immigrants, but also makes some reference to those Chinese who are members of established ethnic communities in culturally diverse societies.

Acculturation refers to the changes arising from sustained first-hand intercultural contact (Berry, 1990; Redfield, Linton, & Herskovits, 1936). Although the number and types of acculturative changes that may be studied are virtually limitless, the factors that have received the most attention in psychological research relate to identity, intercultural relations, subjective well-being, and cultural competence. Identity and intercultural relations are examined in models of acculturation that assess short- and long-term cultural maintenance and participation in the wider society by migrants (Berry, 1997), while cultural competence and well-being form important components of research that examines the processes of psychological and socio-cultural adaptation in immigrants and sojourners (Ward, 1996).

Empirical evidence arising from both of these conceptual frameworks is reviewed in this chapter. However, it is also argued that the individualistic orientation of these approaches gives us only a partial picture of Chinese acculturation. To address this shortcoming, acculturation processes are also examined in the family context. The chapter then concludes with an overall evaluation of theory and research on Chinese acculturation and adaptation and recommendations for future work in the area.

Models of acculturation

Uni-dimensional models of acculturation

Cultural identity lies at the core of most models of acculturation, with heritage and host or 'mainstream' cultures being of fundamental concern. Early research relied upon relatively simplistic, uni-dimensional, and uni-directional models of identity and acculturation, portraying immigrants as relinquishing identification with their culture of origin and 'progressing' towards identification with their contact culture by adopting the attitudes, behaviors, and values of the host society (Ward, Bochner, & Furnham, 2001). An example of this approach is provided by Gordon's (1971) model of assimilation, used to inform G. Wong and Cochrane's (1989) somewhat dated research on the cultural, structural, and identificational acculturation of Chinese in Great Britain.

The uni-dimensional conceptualization of acculturation has measurement implications, as illustrated by the Suinn-Lew Asian Self-Identity Acculturation Scale (S-LASAS; Suinn, Rickard-Figueroa, Lew, & Vigil, 1987). The scale, which taps attitudes and behaviors relating to language usage and proficiency, identity, friendship networks, and cultural practices, has been used extensively with Chinese immigrants in the United States. Each of the S-LASAS's 21 items is accompanied by a 5-point response scale that can be scored on a continuum from a high Asian/low Western to a low Asian/high Western orientation. Suinn and colleagues have suggested that the measure may also be used to classify respondents as Asian-identified, Western-identified, or bicultural, depending on their mean item scores. Those approximating 1 on the 5-point scale would be categorized as Asian-identified, those approximating 5 as Western-identified and those with a mean score near 3 as bi-culturals.

Their conceptualization of the bi-cultural category is particularly problematic, as it does not necssarily reflect a strong attachment to both cultures, merely an orientation that is neither strongly Asian nor Western. The limitations of the S-LASAS as a measure of acculturation were noted by Tata and Leong (1994) in their study of attitudes toward psychological help-seeking in Chinese Americans. This approach has also been criticized more generally by Ward (1999) in her multi-national work on immigration and acculturation, including her research with ethnic Chinese immigrants in Singapore.

Bi-dimensional models of acculturation

Contemporary approaches are largely based on the assumption that identifications with heritage and host cultures are orthogonal or independent of one another, and that, in consequence, bi-dimensional models better capture the essence of the acculturation experience. Although discussion of this issue had been occurring in various forms for 30 years, due primarily to Berry's (1974, 1984) more complex model of acculturation and Ward's subsequent construction of the Acculturation Index (Ward & Kennedy, 1994; Ward & Rana-Deuba, 1999), the publication of Ryder, Alden, and Paulhus's (2000) research with first and second-generation Chinese in Canada seemed to mark a turning point in North American acculturation research. These authors concluded that although the uni-dimensional measure of acculturation could be linked to personality and adjustment in a coherent way, identifications with heritage and mainstream cultures are independent, just as the pattern of their relationships with external correlates.

Ryder et al. (2000) used the Suinn-Lew Asian Self-Identity Scale as a uni-dimensional measure of acculturation and two newly constructed scales to tap both heritage and 'mainstream' identification for the bi-dimensional measure. The researchers found that the uni-dimensional and bi-dimensional measures of acculturation demonstrated different patterns of relationships with the Big Five Personality Factors. More specifically, acculturation (i.e. low Asian/high Western orientation) predicted higher levels of Openness and Extraversion in Chinese Canadians, as did identification with mainstream culture. In contrast, identification with heritage culture predicted greater Conscientiousness and less Neuroticism. They also found a different pattern of relationships between the two measures and self-construals. Highly acculturated Chinese Canadians reported stronger independent self-construals; this was also true for those who identified strongly with the mainstream culture. However, identification with heritage culture predicted a stronger interdependent self-construal.

The independence of immigrants' heritage and contact cultural orientations is now widely acknowledged and has been replicated across a range of studies with Chinese, e.g. research with Chinese international students in the United States (Wang & Mallinckrodt, 2006) and Australia (Zheng, Sang, & Wang, 2004) and adolescent Chinese immigrants in New Zealand (Eyou, Adair & Dixon, 2000). It is also recognized, however, that the relationship between the two domains can be affected by contextual factors. For example, Ward (1999) reported a significant positive correlation between host and co-national identity (r=.32) among ethnic Chinese from Hong Kong, Taiwan, and mainland China who were resident in Singapore. As approximately 80 per cent of Singapore's population is also ethnic Chinese, and co-national and host national identification may be overlapping to some extent, this result is not surprising.

Costigan and Su (2004) demonstrated that the independence of heritage and contact cultural identities can also vary across family members in their Canadian study of first-generation Chinese parents and their children. Assessing cultural identities, orientations, and values, the researchers found clear support for the orthogonal model of acculturation in fathers and children, but modest negative correlations between Chinese and Canadian identities (-.36), orientations (-.29) and values (-.23) for mothers. Costigan and Su suggested that mothers may have greater concerns about the loss of Chinese cultural distinctiveness in their children's lives. They also noted that Chinese mothers may have less experience operating in the wider society and are consequently less likely to have developed strategies to separate their cultural orientations and thereby sustain bicultural identities.

Categorical models of acculturation

Conceptualization and measurement. Berry (1974, 1984) has argued that acculturating persons from non-dominant ethno-cultural groups confront two important questions arising from intercultural contact: 1) is it important to maintain my original cultural heritage? and 2) is it important to engage in intercultural contact with other groups, including members of the dominant culture? If the answers to these questions are dichotomized as yes-no responses, four acculturation orientations (also called attitudes, strategies, expectations, preferences, and modes) can be identified. If both cultural maintenance and contact are rated as important, an integrated orientation results; if neither is important, marginalization occurs. Assimilation arises when only contact is valued while separation results when only cultural maintenance is of concern. It should also be mentioned that the first dimension of Berry's model, cultural maintenance, has remained stable across international research, meaning that it has been consistently operationalized in accordance with Berry's theorizing. The second dimension, however, 'maintaining relations with other groups' has sometimes been defined in terms of contact with or participation in the wider national culture (e.g. Berry, Kim, Power, Young, & Bujaki, 1989), but also been examined in terms of adopting or idenitifying with the national culture (e.g. Snauwaert, Soenens, Vanbeselaere, & Boen; 2003; Ward, 1999; Ward & Rana-Deuba, 1999).

There are various measurement approaches that have been used to quantify integration, assimilation, separation, and marginalization. Berry and colleagues generally prefer to assess attitudes and behaviors in each of these domains, with distinctions sometimes made between actual and desired options (e.g. Berry et al., 1989; Berry, Phinney, Sam, & Vedder, 2006). This approach results in continuous data reflecting responses to each of the four options. Although this technique has been subjected to criticism on psychometric grounds, including the ipsative nature of the measurement scales (Rudmin, 2003), it remains a popular assessment technique. Others have examined the two dimensions of acculturation, reflecting heritage and contact cultural orientations, and then used these in combination with a median split to classify immigrants as integrated, separated, assimilated, or marginalized. The Acculturation Index by Ward and colleagues exemplifies this approach (Ward & Kennedy, 1994; Ward & Rana-Deuba, 1999).

Acculturation preferences and practices. Research by Berry and colleagues has indicated that integration is strongly preferred by short- and long-term migrants, and this finding is generally replicated with Chinese samples independently of the assessment technique adopted. Ward's research based on agree-disagree responses to attitudinal statements found that 80 per cent of Chinese youth in New Zealand supported integration and less than 20 per cent agreed with the practices of assimilation, separation, or marginalization (Ward & Lin, 2005).

Preferences, however, may not always be reflected in practices. Using the two dimensions of Chinese and New Zealand (European) identities and a scalar mid-point split to categorize 427 first generation migrants, Eyou et al. (2000) classified 44 per cent of primary and secondary students as integrated, 36 per cent as separated, 6 per cent as assimilated, and 14 per cent as marginalized. Research has also shown that preferences and practices change over time. Ho (1995) reported that separation was preferred by Hong Kong Chinese adolescents upon entry to New Zealand, but that this preference decreased and endorsement of integration grew stronger over the first four years of residence. A shift from separation and marginalization to integration or assimilation was also suggested in Chia and Costigan's (2006) study of native and overseas-born Chinese university students in Canada. In all likelihood, the preference and capacity for integration are enhanced by greater familiarity with the host culture and the increased acquisition of culture-specific skills. This contention is supported by research in Singapore that showed resident Chinese from Hong Kong, Taiwan, and mainland China were more likely to integrate than their British or American peers (Ward, 1999).

A slightly different approach to acculturation was undertaken in the International Comparative Study of Ethno-cultural Youth, which combined Berry's acculturation model with theory and research on ethnic identity and intergroup relations (Berry et al., 2006). The project, spanning 13 countries, more than 30 ethno-cultural groups and over 5000 immigrant youth, used cluster analysis to examine a range of factors in the search for basic acculturation profiles. The results pointed to the emergence of four basic profiles: Integrated, National, Ethnic, and Diffuse, broadly paralleling Berry's notions of Integration, Assimilation, Separation, and Marginalization, respectively.

The Integrated profile was characterized by strong ethnic and national identities, endorsement of integration, high national and moderate ethnic language proficiency, and forming of both ethnic and national peer contacts. National youth were high in national identity, low in ethnic identity, and endorsed assimilation; they also had proficient and frequent use of the national language and extensive national peer contacts. In contrast, Ethnic youth were strong in ethnic identity, had proficiency in their ethnic language and used it frequently, endorsed separation, had a weak national identity, and few national peer contacts. Finally, the Diffuse group presented a complex picture, being high in the use and proficiency of their ethnic language, but low in their ethnic identity. They also reported low proficiency in the national language, somewhat low levels of national identity and national peer contacts, and endorsed separation, assimilation and marginalization.

The clusters varied across countries and groups, but the pattern for Chinese Australians indicated that 41 per cent fell in the Integrated cluster (range 11-69 per cent), 29 per cent National (2-87 per cent), 4 per cent Ethnic (0-62 per cent) and 25 per cent Diffuse (0-65 per cent). Chinese youth in Australia were slightly above the median percentage for Integration across all samples, well above the median percentage for the Diffuse categorization, in the top quartile for the National classification, and in the bottom quartile for the Ethnic assignment. The results are encouraging in that Integration was established as the modal response of Chinese youth; however, concerns arise over the considerable proportion of Diffuse youth who appear to operate without strong cultural attachments to either Chinese or Australian cultures. It will be important to explore their acculturation outcomes longitudinally and over longer periods of time in the host country.

Chia and Costigan (2006) also adopted cluster analysis in their research with Chinese Canadians, incorporating not only measures of Chinese and Canadian identities, values and behaviors, but also in-group ethnic evaluations, suggested to be particularly relevant to members of collectivist cultures. Their results overlapped with, but were not identical to, those derived from Berry's model. More specifically, five clusters were uncovered for Chinese Canadian students: Integrated (21 per cent), Separated (22 per cent), Assimilated (10 per cent), Integrated without Chinese Practices (15 per cent), and Marginalized with Chinese Practices (32 per cent). The Integrated without Chinese practices group saw themselves as strongly Canadian and moderately Chinese; they evaluated the Chinese in-group very positively, but they did not generally engage in Chinese practices. Although this group was split between native and overseas-born Chinese, the latter had a relatively long period of residence in Canada. This Integrated group contrasted markedly with the Marginalized who maintained Chinese practices, despite identifying strongly with neither Chinese nor Canadians and leaning towards a relatively negative evaluation of the Chinese in-group. The authors cautioned against the over-simplification of Chinese acculturation processes and the lumping of attitudes, values, identity and behaviors into one amorphous category for assessment purposes (see also Feldman, Mont-Reynaud, & Rosenthal, 1992). They also opposed the determination of acculturation status based on background factors, such as language proficiency or place of birth.

Identity conflict and identity integration

Research has clearly shown that heritage and contact cultural identities are independent in Chinese migrants, but that contextual factors may contribute to the convergence or divergence of these identity domains. It follows, then, that cultural orientations may emerge as harmonious or in conflict during the acculturation process. Guided by Baumeister, Shapiro, and Tice's (1985) discussion of identity crises, Leong and Ward (2000) first investigated acculturation and identity conflict in a study of Chinese sojourners in Singapore. The research revealed that the strength of identity conflict was low to moderate ($M = 3.10$ on a 7-point scale) in international students from mainland China, with levels of that conflict predicted by a low tolerance of ambiguity, low attributional complexity, weak Chinese identity, greater perceived discrimination, and more frequent contact with Singaporeans. The last of these findings was surprising, and the authors speculated that more frequent interactions with Singaporeans may have lead to greater confusion and conflict in some Chinese sojourners, since they see Singaporeans both as Chinese *and* as different.

More recently, identity conflict in acculturating Chinese youth was explored by E.-Y. Lin (2008) who examined the underpinning influences of cultural and intergroup factors. Lin reported that a weaker sense of cultural continuity, perceptions of impermeable intergroup boundaries, less contact with host nationals, and greater perceived discrimination predicted increments in identity conflict for Taiwanese and mainland Chinese youth in New Zealand. The pattern was similar for Taiwanese and mainland Chinese students in Singapore, except that poor English language proficiency rather than infrequent host national contact predicted greater conflict. Lin's research also demonstrated the significance of cultural context in that Chinese youth in New Zealand experienced greater conflict than those in Singapore, suggesting the influence of cultural distance on acculturation outcomes.

Benet-Martínez and Haritatos (2005) have approached essentially the same issue from a different perspective in their work on Bicultural Identity Integration (BII) in first generation Chinese-Americans. BII incorporates two domains: Conflict (versus harmony) and Distance (versus blendedness). The former is an emotion-based response, encompassing the feeling of being 'torn' between two cultural orientations; the latter refers to the perceptions of compartmentalized versus overlapping identities. Benet-Martínez and Haritatos have shown that these identity domains are differentially predicted by personality and acculturative stressors. Using path analysis they reported that Agreeableness (-) and Neuroticism were linked to cultural conflict, with the influence of the former mediated by problematic intercultural relations and the latter having both direct and indirect paths through intercultural relations and poor language skills. In contrast, Extraversion and Openness led to lower levels of cultural distance. The former was mediated by cultural isolation while the latter exerted direct and indirect influences via language skills, bicultural competence, and separatism. Conscientiousness was unrelated to cultural conflict and distance. Their results thus overlap to some extent with those of Ryder et al. (2000).

Both the work on bicultural identity integration and identity conflict offer fresh approaches to identity and acculturation in Chinese and should be pursued in future research.

Acculturation and adaptation

There is no doubt that intercultural contact induces change. However, the issue as to whether the changes in short- and long-term immigrants are positive or negative, adaptive or maladaptive is a major concern. Many frameworks exist for evaluating these changes, but the international acculturation literature has relied primarily on the distinction of psychological and socio-cultural adaptation (Berry & Sam, 1997; Ward, 2001; Ward et al., 2001). Psychological adaptation refers to psychological and emotional well-being. It reflects an emphasis on affective responses to cultural change and is tapped by both positive measures, such as life satisfaction, and negative indicators, such as psychological symptoms. Socio-cultural adaptation refers to the capacity to 'fit in' or effectively negotiate intercultural interactions. It reflects a behavioral perspective on cross-cultural adaptation and is often assessed in terms of cultural competencies or difficulties as well as domain-specific achievements, e.g. work performance for expatriates or academic performance for international or immigrant students. The distinction of psychological and socio-cultural adaptation was first posed by Searle and Ward (1990) in their New Zealand-based research with Chinese students from Malaysia and Singapore and will be adopted throughout this chapter.

Identity, acculturation, and adaptation

One body of research has specifically examined acculturation attitudes and strategies as predictors of adaptation. For the most part the research indicates that integration, whether tapped as a preference or an adopted strategy, is associated with the most positive outcomes, and marginalization the most negative consequences. Assimilation and separation occupy an intermediate position with respect to their association with adaptive outcomes.

Ying's (1995) research examined acculturation and adaptation with 143 ethnic Chinese (aged 19-85) in the San Francisco area, classifying them as bicultural (integrated), separated, assimilated, or marginalized based on their participation in cultural activities. Overall, a bicultural orientation was linked to lower depression, more positive and less negative affect, and greater life satisfaction. In all instances biculturals fared better than the separated. The separated group experienced lower life satisfaction than the assimilated, and the marginalized group reported lower life satisfaction than both the biculturals and the assimilated. Finally, Chinese Americans who were assimilated expressed less negative affect than those who were separated or marginalized.

Similar findings have been reported in studies in Australia and New Zealand, where research has demonstrated that integrated Chinese students exhibit higher levels of self-esteem and subjective well-being than those who are assimilated, separated, or marginalized (Eyou et al., 2000; Ho, 2004; Zheng et al., 2004). Chia and Costigan's (2006) study of Chinese-Canadian university students further suggested that marginalized individuals are at particular risk. More specifically, they exhibited lower self-esteem and more depressive symptoms than their integrated and assimilated peers. The authors were careful to point out, however, that the absolute level of adjustment was intermediate rather than low in the marginalized group, while the integrated and assimilated groups scored at the positive ends of these outcome scales.

Although international investigations of acculturation and adaptation with Chinese sojourners and immigrants largely converge, research findings are not uniform, particularly when qualitative assessment techniques are used. Yip and Cross (2004) adopted an innovative methodology in their diary study of acculturation and adaptation in Chinese Americans. Based on daily diary entries pertaining to ethnic salience over a two-week period, research participants were classified as Chinese-oriented (47.5 per cent), American-oriented (31.5 per cent), or biculturals (21 per cent). When acculturation categories were appraised in relation to psychological adjustment, however, there were no significant differences in depression, fatigue, anger, somatic symptoms, or anxiety across these groups.

Some researchers have suggested that the basic components of Berry's (1990) model, that is orientations toward heritage and contact cultures, rather than the four strategies per se, are better predictors of adaptive outcomes. Research with Chinese international students in the United States found an American orientation was associated with fewer socio-cultural adaptation problems and fewer psychological symptoms (Wang & Mallinckrodt, 2006). This result is consistent with those from studies of Chinese Canadians, which found that orientation to the wider Canadian culture was linked to fewer psychological symptoms and better social and academic adjustment, even after controlling for the influence of extraversion and neuroticism (Ryder et al., 2000). However, Ward's (1999) study of identity and adaptation of Chinese migrants in Singapore found that a stronger co-national identity was associated with fewer depressive symptoms, while a stronger host national identity was linked to better socio-cultural adaptation. These results suggest that the characteristics of the heritage and host cultures and the relationship between them are key factors that influence the process of Chinese acculturation and adaptation.

Cheung-Blunden and Juang (2008) adopted a novel approach to Chinese acculturation by extending Berry's model to the colonial context in their study of Hong Kong students and their parents and examined orientations (values and behaviors) to both Chinese and Western cultures. Their results indicated that: 1) Chinese and Western orientations were independent, and both were moderately strong; 2) both orientations predicted socio-cultural adaptation - the Chinese orientation was associated with a higher grade point average, while the Western orientation was related to more misconduct; 3) neither orientation predicted psychological adaptation (i.e. depressive symptoms); and 4) in no instance did the interaction term (Chinese x Western), representing the four acculturation categories, predict adaptation outcomes.

There have also been studies that have examined identity conflict and identity integration in conjunction with adaptive outcomes. E.-Y. Lin (2006) reported that identity conflict was related to poorer psychological and socio-cultural adaptation in her research with Chinese migrant youth in New Zealand and Singapore. S. X. Chen, Benet-Martínez, and Bond (2008) investigated the impact of bicultural identity integration on psychological adjustment in mainland Chinese immigrants to Hong Kong. They found that bicultural identity accounted for additional variance in well-being above and beyond the influence of self-efficacy and neuroticism, suggesting that previous outcome studies exploring identity orientations were not just measuring maladaptive personality dispositions.

Acculturative stress, coping and adaptation

The dynamic process of stress and coping as proposed by Lazarus and Folkman (1984) underpins the major conceptual framework used in the study of acculturation and adaptation. In accordance with this perspective, both cross-cultural transition and intercultural contact are viewed as life events precipitating stress and requiring readjustment. The core process involves the life events associated with intercultural contact, the appraisal of change, stress and coping responses, and adaptive and maladaptive outcomes (Berry, 1997, 2006; Ward, 2001, 2004). The core process may be mediated or moderated by personal and situational variables with generic factors that affect stress and coping (e.g. personality, social support) as well as culture-specific issues (e.g. acculturation strategies, cultural distance) both contributing to the outcomes (Ward et al., 2001). This section summarizes stress and coping research, broadly defined, with Chinese sojourners and immigrants and focuses on two key questions: 1) which factors predict adaptation, and 2) how does adaptation vary over time?

Stress and coping. Acculturative stress refers to the stress reactions arising from life events rooted in the experiences of acculturation (Berry, 2005). Fundamentally, these life events may be viewed in two ways. First, for migrants who have made recent cross-cultural transitions, life changes may be examined with the Social Readjustment Rating Scale (SRRS), which is based on a range of normative and non-normative life events and is accompanied by indices of life change units (LCUs) that quantify the amount of readjustment each requires (Holmes & Rahe, 1967). Furnham and Bochner (1986) noted that the life change units routinely associated with migration, such as changes in living conditions, residence, and social activities, exceed 300 LCUs, a level concomitant with an 80 per cent risk factor of major illness. Accordingly, it is not surprising that research with (predominantly Chinese)

Malaysian and Singaporean students in New Zealand and with Malaysian students in Singapore reported a significant link between the magnitude of recent life changes as assessed by the SRRS and depression (Searle & Ward, 1990; Ward & Kennedy, 1993).

A second approach is to examine the more long-term stressors rooted in the experience of acculturation (Berry, 2005). Ying and Han (2006) have provided a useful framework for analysis of acculturative stressors in their longitudinal study of Taiwanese students in the United States, elaborating social stressors such as homesickness and isolation, cultural stressors such as cultural distance (particularly, differences in values), and functional stressors such as academic and environmental challenges. These stressors, assessed two months after arrival in the United States, predicted increased depression and lower functional adjustment up to one year later. Cross-sectional research by Wei et al. (2007) and S. X. Chen et al. (2008) converges with these findings. Acculturative stressors, including culture shock, perceived discrimination, communication difficulties, and homesickness, were associated with higher levels of depression in Chinese international students in the United States and poorer psychological adjustment of mainland Chinese immigrants in Hong Kong.

Berry and colleagues have argued that it is not the life changes per se but their appraisal that exerts a major influence on adaptive outcomes. Zheng and Berry (1991) explored stress appraisal in Chinese sojourners in Canada and in Chinese and non-Chinese Canadians. Their results revealed that Chinese sojourners perceived language and communication, discrimination, loneliness, and homesickness as more problematic than either Chinese or non-Chinese Canadians. A similar pattern was observed in research by Chataway and Berry (1989) where students from Hong Kong appraised communication difficulties and discrimination as more problematic than did either French- or Anglo-Canadians.

Chataway and Berry (1989) also examined the coping strategies preferred and used by Hong Kong Chinese students. Employing a modified version of the Ways of Coping questionnaire by Folkman and Lazarus (1985), they found that students who engaged in positive thinking were more satisfied, and those who employed withdrawal and wishful thinking were less satisfied with their ability to cope. However, there were only weak links between adopted coping styles and psychological distress. More specifically, detachment as a coping style was related to increased psychological and psychosomatic symptoms. While Zheng and Berry (1991) found that wishful thinking was among the most frequently used coping strategies of overseas Chinese students and Chinese Canadians, they failed to establish that coping strategies were significant predictors of physical and mental health.

Other studies have demonstrated links between 'higher-order' coping styles and adaptation in Asian (predominantly Chinese) samples of international students. Cross (1995) extracted items from the active coping and planning subscales of Carver, Scheier, and Weintraub's (1989) COPE to tap direct coping strategies in a sample of East-Asian (70 per cent Chinese) students in the United States. These strategies exerted a direct influence on decrements in perceived stress. Likewise, Kennedy (1999) found that direct coping enhanced the psychological adaptation of Singaporean students abroad, but that an avoidant coping style, e.g. disengagement and denial, was detrimental to their psychological well-being.

Kuo (2002) has argued that traditional stress and coping research, including studies of acculturation and adaptation, has not adequately captured the range of strategies employed across diverse cultural groups and contexts. He specifically suggested that Asians use collectivist coping styles that reflect group-referenced strategies, interpersonal interactions, and values-based responses, including conformity, interdependence, humility, social harmony, and respect for hierarchy. To test his ideas, Kuo constructed and validated the Cross-cultural Coping Scale with Individual-Oriented (problem focused and avoidance factors) and Collective-Oriented (group-referenced and values-based factors) components based on his work with over 500 Chinese Canadians.

His research demonstrated that Acculturative Stress led to the use of individualist coping but that acculturation status predicted the use of collectivist coping styles. More specifically, those who were less assimilated were more likely to employ group-referenced and values-based collectivist coping. Lau (2007), who took a somewhat different approach to collective coping, found that 'passive collective coping,' a combination of forbearance and fatalism, partially mediated the relationship between acculturative stressors, such as perceived discrimination, depression, and anxiety in Chinese international students.

Social support. While the importance of the interdependent self, interconnectedness, and group-embeddedness in Chinese culture is widely acknowledged (Markus & Kitayama, 1991), Taylor et al. (2004) have produced convincing evidence that East Asians and Asian Americans, including Chinese, are less likely to seek social support than are European Americans. They attributed these differences to the Asians' stronger beliefs that support-seeking disrupts group harmony, makes one's problems worse, and leads to loss of face. In short, Asians are concerned about the possible relational disruptions arising from support-seeking. Despite these concerns, there is strong evidence that social support exerts a direct and positive influence on the psychological adaptation of Chinese sojourners and immigrants.

Australian studies have shown that social support contributes directly to decrements in hopelessness, anxiety and trauma in Chinese primary and secondary students (Sondregger, Barrett, & Creed, 2004) and is associated with their better general health and academic achievement (Leung, 2001a). It has also been linked to better general adjustment in overseas Chinese students in Singapore (Tsang, 2001). In a large epidemiological study, Shen and Takeuchi (2001) found that social support exerted a direct influence on decreasing stress, which in turn, led to lower levels of depression in Chinese Americans. Conversely, Abbott et al. (2003) reported that low levels of emotional support predicted greater depression in elderly Chinese migrants in New Zealand.

Research has also shown that social support can arise from a variety of sources. Ye's (2006) study of traditional and online support networks revealed that, although newly arrived Chinese international students received greater support from online ethnic social groups, the use of both online and traditional sources of support were related to adaptation. More specifically, online and interpersonal networks in the host country were linked to fewer socio-cultural adaptation problems, and interpersonal and long distance networks from the home country were associated with less mood disturbance.

Although Chinese immigrants are more likely to rely on co-ethnic networks, social support from members of the host culture can also be effective in dealing with social and psychological stressors and contributing to adaptive outcomes. A. S. Mak and Nesdale (2001) reported that Anglo friendships exerted a positive influence on the psychological adaptation of first-generation Chinese migrants in Australia, while Ying and Han (2006) found that affiliation with Americans two months after arrival led to better functional adjustment in Taiwanese students one year later. Associations with locals additionally contributed to better interaction adjustment and work performance of Chinese academics in Singapore (Tsang, 2001).

The reliance on support networks can change over time as evidenced by D. F. K. Wong and Song's (2006) study of the settlement stages of mainland Chinese immigrant women in Hong Kong. Their longitudinal qualitative study with 15 immigrants indicated that in the earliest stages women mobilized instrumental and informational support from extended family members, particularly around practical issues such as finance, housing and childcare. The need for emotional support became more salient during the second stage of settlement, with other immigrant women primarily lending support. The research also indicated that the women were unlikely to seek assistance from formal networks and only rarely relied upon support from neighbors or co-workers. The preference for using inter-personal friendship networks for support and the reluctance to rely upon formal services have been widely observed in Chinese immigrants and international students from Asia, including those from China, Hong Kong and Taiwan (e.g. Yeh & Inose, 2002; Zhang & Dixon, 2003; see also Chan, Ng, & Hui, this volume).

The meaning and use of social support by Chinese immigrants in Japan was explored in a qualitative study by Matsudaira (2003). The study suggested that the meaning of social support is intimately tied to face issues associated wth *lian* 臉 (the recognition of character and integrity which is preserved by adherence to social norms) and *mianzi* 面子 (reputation gained through success and ostentation), and reflects culture-specific impression management strategies (see also Hwang & Han, this volume). Ambivalence towards support-seeking arises from beliefs and expectations about independence, face loss, and social debt. In the first instance, Matsudaira argues that Chinese immigrants have a strong belief that they should attain goals and solve problems without assistance. The achievement of these goals is seen to reflect the actor's *lian*.

If support is received, however, distinctions are made between in-group and out-group sources and their differing implications for the preservation of face. The family is seen as the primary in-group for rendering support to Chinese immigrants; interdependence motivates family members to be supportive and immigrants to express appreciation by attributing their successes to family assistance. Matsudaira argues that these dynamics provide an opportunity for immigrants to earn *lian* and share it with familial support-providers.

Finally, when immigrants' social support is received from an out-group member, in this instance a Japanese host, a social debt with the expectation of reciprocity is incurred. Matsudaira (2003) maintains that unanticipated support from out-group members, particularly in educational and business settings, may contribute to a loss of *mianzi* for Chinese immigrants, but with reciprocation of favors received, *lian* can be restored. She also notes, however, that Japanese and Chinese perspectives on giving and receiving social support are likely to differ as the concept of *lian* is lacking amongst the Japanese. Consequently, Chinese interpretations of, and the dynamics surrounding, benevolence, social debt, and reciprocity may not be shared by their Japanese hosts.

Personal and situational factors. Personal and situational factors affect both the process and outcomes of coping with acculturative stress. Among the former, the role of personality has received particular attention in studies involving Chinese sojourners, immigrants and members of established ethnic communities. Research has revealed that agreeableness, conscientiousness, hardiness, self-efficacy, and an internal locus of control are broadly linked to psychological well-being (Mak, Chen, Wong, & Zane, 2005; Tsang, 2001; Ward & Kennedy, 1993; Ward, Leong, & Low, 2004). In contrast, neuroticism, personal negativity (lack of control, pessimism and low tolerance of ambiguity), and maladaptive perfectionism are associated with negative psychological outcomes (Shen & Takeuchi, 2001; Wei et al., 2007).

In addition to these factors, research has revealed a strong link between extraversion and positive outcomes for ethnic Chinese sojourners in both longitudinal and cross-sectional studies (Searle & Ward, 1990; Ward et al., 2004; Ying & Han, 2006). These results, however, should be interpreted in relation to the characteristics of the receiving societies (United States, New Zealand, Australia), where extraversion scores on the NEO-PI-R and the EPQ tend to be higher than in Chinese societies (McCrae, 2002; Ward & Chang, 1997; Ward et al., 2004). The question remains as to whether extraversion per se is intrinsically conducive to better mental health in Chinese immigrants and sojourners or whether it influences adaptive and maladaptive outcomes by virtue of its match or mismatch with culture-specific norms. The examination of personality and adaptation of Chinese sojourners and immigrants in Asian contexts would be a step towards elucidating this process. Indeed, research with Chinese students and academics in Singapore found that extraversion did predict better intercultural interactions, but was unrelated to general adjustment (Tsang, 2001).

The influence of real and perceived cultural distance on the adjustment process of Chinese sojourners and immigrants has been repeatedly confirmed in international studies. Greater perceived cultural and value differences were found to lead to more adjustment problems in Taiwanese students in the United States (Ying & Liese, 1994). In comparative studies, mainland Chinese students in New Zealand were found to experience lower life satisfaction than students from North America, South America and Europe (Ward & Masgoret, 2004); Chinese exchange students in Russia perceived greater cultural distance and experienced poorer adjustment than did students from sub-Saharan Africa and the former Soviet Union (Galchenko & van de Vijver, 2007); and Chinese overseas and immigrant students in Australia reported greater loneliness, lower academic satisfaction and lower social self-efficacy than did second-generation immigrants from Southern Europe (Leung, 2001b). Conversely, Hong Kong and mainland Chinese residents in Singapore reported better socio-cultural adaptation, that is significantly fewer social difficulties, than did their British, American and New Zealand counterparts (Ward & Kennedy, 1999).

These findings suggest that Chinese migration to other Chinese societies may be relatively trouble-free by virtue of a common, shared cultural heritage. However, research with expatriate managers from Hong Kong assigned to work in China revealed that this is not always the case. Selmer (2002) compared the perceptions of cultural novelty, general, work and interaction adjustment, and subjective well-being of Western and Chinese expatriate managers. The comparisons indicated that Hong Kong Chinese managers experienced less cultural novelty, but reported poorer adjustment, particularly in the work domain, than did their Western peers. There were no significant differences in subjective well-being between the two groups. On the basis of their earlier qualitative, interview-based research, Selmer and Shui (1999) proposed that the common Chinese cultural heritage aggravated the adjustment of Hong Kong managers posted to Shanghai and Beijing. More specifically, they found that perceived similarity camouflaged the need for cultural sensitivity and change, leading to greater frustration, resentment and withdrawal by Hong Kong Chinese when difficulties arose. The researchers also noted that perceptions of cultural closeness affected the responses of PRC Chinese employees who were more likely to judge their Hong Kong than Western managers harshly when cultural transgressions occurred.

The special case of cultural competence. Although psychological adjustment has received the bulk of attention in studies of Chinese acculturation and adaptation, the development of cultural competencies, often discussed under the rubric of socio-cultural adaptation, is also important. Cultural learning theory, which views the acquisition of culture-specific skills as the key indicator of adaptation, provides the overall theoretical framework for understanding and explaining acculturative processes in this domain (Ward, 2004; Ward et al., 2001). Communication competence lies at the core of the process, facilitating interactions with host nationals who function as cultural informants about the wider socio-cultural environment. More frequent, satisfying, and effective interactions with host nationals lead to the development of greater cultural competencies and better socio-cultural adaptation. As adaptation arises from learning, it improves over time and is facilitated by cultural similarity rather than cultural distance (Masgoret & Ward, 2006).

In line with Masgoret and Ward's (2006) model of socio-cultural adaptation, research has corroborated the link between English-language proficiency and friendship with American peers in ethnic Chinese immigrant youth and international students (Tsai, 2006; Ying, 2002). Similar results emerged from Kuo and Roysircar's (2004) study of ethnic Chinese adolescents in Canada. Their findings showed that both length of residence in Canada and English reading ability predicted a stronger affiliation with the dominant white society. Furthermore, this affiliation was strongest in the early immigrant group. The authors concluded that language proficiency assists with the acquisition of cultural knowledge, facilitates cross-cultural interactions, and decreases the likelihood of intercultural conflicts and misunderstandings.

While host nationals provide valuable informational support and assistance with culture learning, forming intercultural friendships has been identified as a difficult task, not only for Chinese international students (Spencer-Oatey & Xiong, 2006; Ward & Masgoret, 2004), but also Chinese immigrant youth (Tsai, 2006). Despite the challenges they present, friendships and more frequent interactions with host national peers have been shown to lead to fewer psychological and socio-cultural adaptation problems (Searle & Ward, 1990; Ward & Kennedy, 1993; Ying & Liese, 1994). In contrast, there is evidence that more frequent interactions with Chinese co-nationals is associated with greater socio-cultural adaptation problems and lowered life satisfaction in Chinese international students (Ward & Kennedy, 1993; Ward & Masgoret, 2004).

While the acquisition of socio-cultural competencies is viewed as an adaptive outcome of acculturation from a culture learning perspective, it may also been seen as a resource that facilitates psychological well-being in sojourners and immigrants. Indeed, the model of psychological and socio-cultural adaptation that emerged from the International Comparative Study of Ethno-cultural Youth suggested that socio-cultural adaptation, defined in terms of school adjustment and behavioral problems, led directly to psychological adaptation, including life satisfaction and a low level of psychological symptoms (Sam, Vedder, Ward, & Horenczyk, 2006; Vedder, van de Vijver, & Liebkind, 2006).

Certainly, there is strong evidence to corroborate the link between socio-cultural and psychological adaptation in Chinese sojourners and immigrants. Wang and Mallinckrodt (2006) reported a moderate correlation between socio-cultural adaptation problems and psychological symptoms in their sample of Chinese international students in the United States, and Spencer-Oatey and Xiong (2006) noted a strong correlation between social difficulties and depression in Chinese students enrolled in a British university. Ward and Kennedy (1999) reported a low but significant correlation between socio-cultural adaptation problems and depression (.20) in Hong Kong and mainland Chinese residents of Singapore, and somewhat stronger relationships for their predominantly Chinese samples of Malaysian students in Singapore (.54), Singaporeans in the United States (.53), Singaporean and Malaysian students in New Zealand (.41), and Singaporean students in multinational destinations (.31). The authors suggested that the relationship between socio-cultural and psychological adaptation can be interpreted as an index of sojourners' and migrants' integration and participation in the wider society.

Adaptation over time. There have been relatively few longitudinal studies that have examined adaptation over time in Chinese immigrants and sojourners. Nevertheless, limited research has revealed differences in pre-departure and post-arrival adaptation, as well as predictable fluctuations over the first year of residence. Ying and Liese's (1991) investigation indicated that more than half of their sample of Taiwanese students experienced a drop in emotional well-being after their arrival in the United States. Zheng and Berry's (1991) research with Chinese scholars to Canada likewise revealed a three to four month post-arrival drop in psychological well-being. Ward and Kennedy (1996) examined both psychological and socio-cultural adaptation in a small sample of (predominantly Chinese) Singaporean and Malaysian students in New Zealand and found that the level of depression was significantly greater at one month and one year of residence compared to the intermediate six-month time point. With respect to socio-cultural adaptation, problems were greatest on entry, decreased sharply in the first six months and continued on a downward trend over the first year. When interviewed one month after arrival and asked to comment retrospectively on their entry, 68 per cent of the students described their experiences in exclusively negative terms compared to 5 per cent who used exclusively positive descriptors.

Overall, these findings are in accordance with both stress and coping and culture learning theories. The life changes encountered in the earliest stage of cross-cultural transition are likely to impact negatively on psychological well-being. Furthermore, the changes apparent during this period occur at a time when local social support networks are likely to be largely lacking. Consequently, stress and coping theories would predict that psychological adaptation declines between pre-departure and early post-arrival stages and that it improves over the first six months, as the sojourner or immigrant adjusts to change and establishes social support networks. With respect to socio-cultural adaptation, culture learning theory would predict that adaptation problems follow an inverted learning curve over time. More specifically, that there would be a sharp decrement in social difficulties over the first few post-arrival months, followed by a slower rate of decline and an eventual levelling off (Ward, Okura, Kennedy, & Kojima, 1998).

Individuals and families. The previous sections have introduced the main conceptual frameworks for the study of acculturation and adaptation as found in the international literature. They have also drawn on a large body of empirical research to elucidate the Chinese experience. As with most areas of psychological theory and research, however, the guiding paradigms and conceptual frameworks may be applicable to Chinese without capturing some of the essential issues that are most relevant to them (see Hong, Yang, & Chiu, this volume; Yang, this volume). Acculturation research, like many other topics of psychological inquiry, has been undertaken primarily from an individualistic scientific perspective. We are well informed about how Chinese individuals cross cultures, experience acculturation, and adapt to new and relatively unfamiliar environments. But, Chinese societies are built upon collectivist values and beliefs, so that the acculturation of Chinese immigrants should be examined in the family context. As such, the next section considers the dynamics of acculturation in Chinese families.

Chinese families and acculturation

Family harmony and filial piety

A fundamental Chinese value is the importance of the family unit (Phillips & Pearson, 1996). In contrast to the logic prevailing in most Western societies, Chinese regard the family instead of the individual as the basic social unit. Every Chinese, from an early age, learns to think of family first and strive to maintain close, harmonious and cohesive family relations (Hwang, 1999; Li, 1998; Mak & Chan, 1995). Individuals' identities are defined in terms of their roles and interpersonal relationships within the family rather than by their own sense of who they are as separate individuals (Hsu, 1971; Hwang, 1999). Since family life is the pivot of Chinese culture, Chinese families are structured in such a way that conformity, dependence, and obedience to parental figures are crucial (Mak & Chan, 1995), and adolescents who show loyalty to the family by maintaining good relationships with family members and fulfilling family responsibilities are perceived by the majority of Chinese parents as ideal children (Shek & Chan, 1999).

This commitment and loyalty to the family remain salient even among Chinese families in non-Chinese societies and maintain the distinction between Chinese and Western preferences (Feldman et al., 1992; Feldman & Rosenthal, 1991; Hwang, 1999; Stewart et al., 1999). The emotional attachment to the family and the sense of responsibility and obligation towards them may not be easily swayed by more independent cultural norms. For example, Feldman and colleagues (1992) found that even second-generation Chinese youth who displayed obvious signs of acculturation still valued the family significantly more than did their Western peers. Furthermore, these second-generation youth did not differ in their devotion to the family from the first-generation youth who otherwise maintained considerably more traditional values. In addition, Fuligni and colleagues found that Chinese American adolescents believed in the importance of supporting and assisting the family more than did their peers from European backgrounds, and these differences were consistent across the youth's generation, gender, family composition, and socio-economic background (Fuligni, Tseng, & Lam, 1999). Thus, it is apparent that such faithfulness to the family is viewed as a duty, not a choice, and is engrained in the core of Chinese identity.

The significance of family is also evidenced by Chinese parents considering filial piety, respect, and obedience to be amongst the most important Confucian principles. Interviews of 420 Hong Kong Chinese parents about their perceptions of attributes of the ideal child revealed that over 60 per cent of the parents regarded family-related attributes, such as good parent-child relations and fulfilment of family responsibilities, as characteristics of the ideal child (Shek & Chan,1999). This finding is consistent with the observation that filial piety, family solidarity, and mutual dependence are strongly emphasized in Chinese culture (Yang, 1981).

The few studies that have examined filial piety (孝 *xiao*) in overseas Chinese also found a strong acceptance of filial obligations, even in societies upon which individualistic Western values have exercised pervasive influence (Lin, 2006; Liu, Ng, Weatherall, & Loong, 2000). It seems that, although Chinese people have adjusted their life styles and value systems in order to adapt to the changing societies, certain aspects of filial piety still persist and continue to play an important role in people's lives (Hwang, 1999; Lin, 2000, 2004, 2006; Yeh, 1997, 2003; Yeh & Bedford, 2003).

As Chinese culture is firmly based around the family as the foundation of one's life and identity, it follows that autonomy will occur at a much later age for Chinese adolescents with the family remaining an important influence for a longer period. Indeed, many studies with Chinese immigrants have found that Chinese youth had later autonomy expectations compared to their Western peers (Deeds, Stewart, Bond, & Westrick, 1998; Feldman & Rosenthal, 1990, 1991; Fuligni, 1998; Greenberger & Chen, 1996), and that Chinese parents placed greater emphasis on parental control and were more protective of children than were Euro-American parents (Chiu, Feldman, & Rosenthal, 1992; Kelly & Tseng, 1992; Lee & Zhan, 1998; Lin & Fu, 1990).

Importance of family relations during cross-cultural transition

Studies have shown that these differences between Chinese and Western families may increase the Chinese adolescent immigrant's chances of successful adjustment to their host societies. For example, the cultural emphasis on family interdependence and maintaining a tight family structure may help Chinese immigrant families remain intact, providing a more stable and secure environment for their children. A study conducted by Florsheim (1997) on 113 Chinese youth in the United States suggested that Chinese adolescents who perceived their families as organized, cooperative, and less argumentative reported fewer psychological adjustment problems and lower emotional and acculturative distress. Also, E.- Y. Lin (2006) found that Chinese young adults who perceived greater emotional bonding between family members experienced significantly less identity conflict during cross-cultural transitions.

Recently, studies on 'parachute kids' and 'astronaut families' have further emphasized the importance of family and parental presence during cross-cultural transitions (Alaggia, Chau, & Tsang, 2001; Aye & Guerin, 2001; Chiang-Hom, 2004; Irving, Benjamin, & Tsang, 1999; Pe-Pua, Mitchell, Iredale, & Castles, 1996; Waters, 2003; Zhou, 1998).[1] Hom (2002) found that Chinese immigrant youth who lived in the United States without their parents, i.e. parachute kids, were more behaviorally maladjusted in terms of substance use, earlier and more frequent sexual activity, and group/gang fighting than were Chinese immigrant adolescents who lived with their parents.

A recent study by E.-Y. Lin (2006) also lends strong support to the importance of parental presence during cross-cultural transitions. Her study found that Chinese young adults who lived abroad *without* their parents experienced significantly greater identity conflict compared to those who lived with their parents. In other words, as a result of migrating solo and the absence of on-site parental guidance, international students and parachute adolescents were more likely to experience feelings of being 'torn apart,' cultural confusion, and maladaptation. In addition, Lin (2006) found that when parents were present, adolescents were less likely to experience identity conflict regardless of their satisfaction with the relationship with their parents. However, when parents were overseas, i.e. when the protective shield of parental presence was absent, the parent-child relationship exerted influence on the individual's level of identity conflict.

Intergenerational conflicts and acculturation differences

Past research has also documented intergenerational conflicts that are specific to immigrant families. Baptiste (1993) identified five intergenerational issues confronted by immigrant families. These are: (1) loosening of familial boundaries and generational hierarchies; (2) lessening of parental authority over children; (3) fear of losing the children to the host culture; (4) unpreparedness for change and conflict as part of the immigration experience; and (5) extended family enmeshment-disengagement problems. Baptiste attributed these intergenerational conflicts to the differential rates of parent – child adaptation/acculturation to the host culture, which result in increasing polarization of the family.

Indeed, there is substantial research showing that immigrant adolescents adopt new attitudes and values more rapidly than do their parents (Berry at al., 2006; Kwak, 2003; Phinney, Ong, & Madden, 2000; Portes & Rumbaut, 2001). This discrepancy in acculturation rates may increase the likelihood of parent-child conflicts as Chinese adolescents begin to resent and rebel against the high parental control, expectations, and restrictions that are absent in the lives of their Western peers. In turn, this escalating family conflict increases the likelihood of depression, problem behavior, such as antisocial behavior, cigarette smoking, alcohol use, school misconduct, and lower life satisfaction and poorer academic performance among Chinese adolescents and young adults (Chen, Greenberger, Lester, Dong, & Guo, 1998; Costigan & Dokis, 2006; Crane, Ngai, Larson, & Hafen, 2005; Greenberger, Chen, Tally, & Dong, 2000; Juang, Syed, & Takagi, 2007; Lee & Zhan, 1998; Rumbaut, 1997; Weaver & Kim, 2008).

Sung (1985) identified a number of cultural conflicts confronting Chinese adolescents in a Western society. These include: aggressiveness vs. non-violence; physical vs. mental development and achievement; social conformity vs. ethical values; demonstration of affection; sexuality; social acceptance vs. academic success; materialism vs. thrift; independence vs. dependence; respect for authority;

standards for role models; and collectivism vs. individualism. These cultural conflicts are only a few of the obstacles children of Chinese immigrants must negotiate with their parents as part of their ethnic identity development and acculturation process. Having conflicts with parents on a variety of acculturation issues, such as the issues listed above, level of family obligations, and friendship choices, may be normative for all adolescents, not just those from Chinese immigrant families. However, because Chinese culture emphasizes family harmony and respect for parents more strongly than many other cultures (Chinese Culture Connection, 1987), these conflicts are less acceptable and more disturbing to Chinese adolescents and parents. In addition, language barriers associated with acculturation differences, i.e. less proficiency in English on the part of parents and less proficiency in Chinese on the part of children, may make it more difficult for parents and children to communicate about subtle or difficult emotional issues; thus, they may come to feel more emotionally distant from each other (Tseng & Fuligni, 2000).

The differential rates in English acquisition may also lead to role reversals between parents and children. As children learn and adopt the English language at a faster rate than their parents, parents become dependent upon their children to talk for them in situations requiring English fluency and for many of their interactions with the host society. This dependency sharply contrasts with the usual pattern of relationships between Chinese parents and children and may lead to the feelings of helplessness, resentment, confusion, and depression among parents. On the other hand, by becoming the family's interpreter and spokesperson, children are inevitably exposed to information and situations that would normally be kept from them, placing an additional burden and stress on them (Baptiste, 1993).

Adaptation of elderly Chinese immigrants

Regarding the adaptation and family life of elderly Chinese in the host society, studies have indicated that depression, social isolation, and family conflict are major problems (Abbott et al., 2003; Mak & Chan, 1995; Mui, 1996; Wong, Yoo, & Stewart, 2006). The majority of elderly Chinese immigrate later in life to be reunited with their adult children who have already been in the host country for a substantial period of time. This group of elderly Chinese often arrives to take up domestic roles, such as caring for their grandchildren and assisting their adult children with housekeeping tasks. Although they may be highly respected in their countries of origin, elderly Chinese become highly dependent on their children (and grandchildren) to provide transportation, interpretation, and assistance even with simple tasks, such as shopping and visiting doctors. Furthermore, elderly Chinese frequently sacrifice personal benefits for the betterment of the family, although studies have shown that they often feel a lack of appreciation and respect from children and grandchildren for these sacrifices.

Research by S. T. Wong and colleagues (2006) found that many elderly Chinese felt that their place in the family had shifted from a central to a peripheral position. Furthermore, with the strong emphasis placed on nuclear families in the Western societies, they were no longer seen as authority figures in an intergenerational family. As a result, in an attempt to maintain harmony within the family, some elderly Chinese reported they were inclined to keep their feelings and thoughts to themselves, to develop a more tolerant and flexible attitude, to learn to be more self-reliant, and to expand their social network beyond their family members (Wong et al., 2006).

In summary, this section has described the dynamics of acculturation in Chinese families. In contrast to Chinese culture (which is collectivistic, family-oriented, and relational), most destination countries for Chinese immigrants embrace individualistic values where individual rights and needs take priority over the needs of the group and family. As a result, upon arriving in their new host countries, Chinese immigrants are faced with the complicated task of balancing loyalty to their family and Chinese culture with the need to create an individual identity and gain approval from the host society. Thus, it is not surprising that their cross-cultural transitions are associated with stress and conflict, especially when differential rates of acculturation exist within the family. However, it is also important to note that although acculturation differences certainly present challenges for immigrant families, studies have shown that most Chinese families deal with these challenges effectively and that

Chinese immigrants continue to be considered as the 'model minority' in many host societies (Costigan & Dokis, 2006; Ma, 2002).

Conclusion

As overseas Chinese form the largest migrant group on a world-wide basis, it is not surprising that there is a considerable body of empirical evidence on Chinese acculturation and adaptation. Indeed, the Chinese are amongst the most frequently researched acculturating groups. Nevertheless, an overview of this research reveals some noticeable shortcomings.

First, the context of acculturation research has been limited. To date, studies (at least those published in English and Chinese) have been primarily undertaken in Western countries, particularly in settler societies such as Canada, the United States, Australia, and New Zealand. For both theory development and practical application, the research context should be extended to cover a wider range of receiving societies. This includes Asian countries, where migrants may have very different expectations about acculturation experiences and where hosts may maintain perceptions of the 'ideal migrant' that diverge markedly from those held in North America and Australasia. Research in Hong Kong, Singapore and Japan has only begun to address issues relating into Chinese acculturation processes in Asian societies (e.g. Chen et al., 2008; Matsudiara, 2003; Ward & Kennedy, 1999), and more work needs to be done to examine the impact of variations in the enculturating context.

Second, the perspectives on Chinese acculturation and adaptation have been somewhat constrained. For the most part, acculturation has been studied as if it were a universal process, with little consideration of any culture-specific dynamics in the process. Is there anything distinctively Chinese about Chinese acculturation? Investigations such as those on Chinese coping styles during acculturation are a step in the right direction (Kuo, 2002; Lau, 2007). Similarly, new work that suggests there may be important differences in the long-term acculturation strategies of large ethnic groups such as Chinese compared to smaller groups may provide additional insight (Gezentsvey, 2008). The culture-specific dynamics of Chinese acculturation should be further explored in future research.

Third, the targets of Chinese acculturation research have been somewhat restricted. To date we know a lot about the acculturation experiences of Chinese adolescents and adults. We know considerably less about the elderly and almost nothing about children. In addition, in many cases the broader question remains as to whether the Chinese are best studied as acculturating individuals or as acculturating families who experience intercultural contact and change. From this perspective, inter-generational issues during acculturation may be of particular concern.

Finally, there have been relatively few studies of Chinese acculturation over time. This refers both to longitudinal studies of Chinese immigrants, such as the work undertaken by Ying and colleagues (Ying & Han, 2006; Ying & Liese, 1991), as well as studies of acculturative changes across generations (e.g. Feldman et al., 1992). Both of these approaches should be extended. In the end, when the context, perspectives, targets and approaches are broadened in future research, we will achieve a more comprehensive understanding of how Chinese acculturate and adapt.

Chapter note

1 Parachute kids are youth who arrive in a new country to attend schools by themselves, while their parents remain in their country of origin. Astronaut families are those who immigrate to a new country while one or both parents return(s) to live in the country of origin (usually for economic reasons), leaving 'satellite' adolescent children to pursue an education in the new country.

References

Abbott, M., Wong, S., Giles, L. C., Wong, S., Young, W., & Au, M. (2003). Depression in older Chinese migrants to Auckland. *Australian and New Zealand Journal of Psychiatry, 37*, 445–451.

Alaggia, R., Chau, S., & Tsang, K. T. (2001). Astronaut Asian families: Impact of migration on family structure from the perspective of the youth. *Journal of Social Work Research and Evaluation, 2*, 295–306.

Aye, A. M. M. T., & Guerin B. (2001). Astronaut families: A review of their characteristics, impact on families and implications for practice in New Zealand. *New Zealand Journal of Psychology, 30*, 9–15.
Baptiste, D. A. (1993). Immigrant families, adolescents and acculturation: Insights for therapists. *Marriage and Family Review, 19*, 341–363.
Baumeister, R., Shapiro, J. P., & Tice, D. M. (1985). Two kinds of identity crises. *Journal of Personality, 53*, 407–424.
Benet-Martínez, V. & Haritatos, J. (2005). Bicultural identity integration: Components and psychosocial antecedents. *Journal of Personality, 73*, 1015–1050.
Berry, J. W. (1974). Psychological aspects of cultural pluralism. *Culture Learning, 2*, 17–22.
Berry, J. W. (1984). Cultural relations in plural societies: Alternatives to segregation and their socio-psychological implications. In M. Brewer & N. Miller (eds), *Groups in contact* (pp. 11–27). New York: Academic Press.
Berry, J. W. (1990). Psychology of acculturation: Understanding individuals moving between cultures. In R. Brislin (ed.), *Applied cross-cultural psychology* (pp. 232–253). Newbury Park, CA: Sage.
Berry, J. W. (1997). Immigration, acculturation and adaptation. *Applied Psychology, 46*, 5–68.
Berry, J. W. (2005). Acculturation: Living successfully in two cultures. *International Journal of Intercultural Relations, 29*, 697–712.
Berry, J. W. (2006). Stress perspectives on acculturation. In D. L. Sam & J. W. Berry (eds), *The Cambridge handbook of acculturation psychology* (pp. 43–57). New York: Cambridge University Press.
Berry, J. W., Kim, U., Power, S., Young, M., & Bujaki, M. (1989). Acculturation attitudes in plural societies. *Applied Psychology, 38*, 185–206.
Berry, J. W., Phinney, J., Sam, D. L., & Vedder, P. (eds). (2006). *Immigrant youth in cultural transition: Acculturation, identity and adaptation across national contexts.* Mahwah, NJ: Lawrence Erlbaum.
Berry, J. W. & Sam, D. L. (1997). Acculturation and adaptation. In J. W. Berry, M. H. Segall, & Ç. Kağıtçıbaşı (eds), *Handbook of cross-cultural psychology: Vol. 3. Social behavior and applications* (pp. 291–326). Boston, MA: Allyn & Bacon.
Carver, C. S., Scheier, M. F., & Weintraub, J. K. (1989). Assessing coping strategies: A theoretically based approach. *Journal of Personality and Social Psychology, 56*, 267–283.
Chataway, C. J. & Berry, J. W. (1989). Acculturation experiences, appraisal, coping and adaptation: A comparison of Hong Kong Chinese, French and English students in Canada. *Canadian Journal of Behavioral Science, 21*, 295–301.
Chen, C., Greenberger, E., Lester, J., Dong, Q., & Guo, M.-S. (1998). A cross-cultural study of family and peer correlates of adolescent misconduct. *Developmental Psychology, 34*, 770–781.
Chen, S. X., Benet-Martínez, V., & Bond, M. H. (2008). Bicultural identity, bilingualism and psychological adjustment in multicultural societies. *Journal of Personality,76*, 803–838.
Cheung-Blunden, V. L., & Juang, L. P. (2008). Expanding acculturation theory: Are acculturation models and the adaptiveness of acculturation strategies generalizable in a colonial context? *International Journal of Behavioral Development, 32*, 21–33.
Chia, A.-L. & Costigan, C. L. (2006). Understanding the multidimensionality of acculturation among Chinese Canadians. *Canadian Journal of Behavioral Science, 38*, 311–324.
Chiang-Hom, C. (2004). Transnational cultural practices of Chinese immigrant youth and parachute kids. In J. Lee & M. Zhou (eds), *Asian American youth: Culture, identity and ethnicity* (pp. 143–158). New York: Routledge.
Chinese Culture Connection (1987). Chinese values and the search for culture-free dimensions of culture. *Journal of Cross-Cultural Psychology, 18*, 143–164.
Chiu, L. H., Feldman, S., & Rosenthal, D. (1992). The influence of immigration on parental behavior and adolescent distress in Chinese families in two western nations. *Journal of Research on Adolescence, 2*, 205–239.
Costigan, C. L. & Dokis, D. P. (2006). Relations between parent–child acculturation differences and adjustment within immigrant Chinese families. *Child Development, 77*, 1252–1267.
Costigan, C. L. & Su, T. F. (2004). Orthogonal versus linear models of acculturation among immigrant Chinese Canadians: A comparison of mothers, fathers and children. *International Journal of Behavioral Development, 28*, 518–527.
Crane, D. R., Ngai, S.-W., Larsen, J. H., & Hafen, M., Jr. (2005). The influence of family functioning and parent–adolescent acculturation on North American Chinese adolescent outcomes. *Family Relations, 54*, 400–410.
Cross, S. (1995). Self-construals, coping and stress in cross-cultural adaptation. *Journal of Cross-Cultural Psychology, 26*, 673–697.
Deeds, O., Stewart, S. M., Bond, M. H., & Westrick, J. (1998). Adolescents in between cultures: Values and autonomy expectations in an international school setting. *School Psychology International, 19*, 61–77.
Eyou, M. L., Adair, V., & Dixon, R. (2000). Cultural identity and psychological adjustment of Chinese immigrants in New Zealand. *Journal of Adolescence, 23*, 531–543.
Feldman, S. S., Mont-Reynaud, R., & Rosenthal, D. (1992). When East moves West: The acculturation of values of Chinese adolescents in the US and Australia. *Journal of Research on Adolescence, 2*, 147–173.
Feldman, S. S. & Rosenthal, D. A. (1990). The acculturation of autonomy expectations in Chinese high schoolers residing in two Western nations. *International Journal of Psychology, 25*, 259–281.
Feldman, S. S. & Rosenthal, D. A. (1991). Age expectations of behavioral autonomy in Hong Kong, Australian and American youth: The influence of family variables and adolescents' values. *International Journal of Psychology, 26*, 1–23.
Florsheim, P. (1997). Chinese adolescent immigrants: Factors related to psychosocial adjustment. *Journal of Youth and Adolescence, 26*, 143–163.

Folkman, S. & Lazarus, R. (1985). If it changes, it must be a process: Studies of emotion and coping in three stages of a college examination. *Journal of Personality and Social Psychology, 48*, 150–170.

Fuligni, A. J. (1998). Authority, autonomy, and parent–adolescent conflict and cohesion: A study of adolescents from Mexican, Chinese, Filipino, and European backgrounds. *Developmental Psychology, 34*, 782–792.

Fuligni, A., Tseng, V., & Lam, M. (1999). Attitudes towards family obligations among American adolescents with Asian, Latin American, and European backgrounds. *Child Development, 70*, 1030–1044.

Furnham, A. & Bochner, S. (1986). *Culture shock: Psychological reactions to unfamliar environments.* London: Methuen.

Galchenko, I. & van de Vijver, F. J. R. (2007). The role of perceived cultural distance in the acculturation of exchange students in Russia. *International Journal of Intercultural Research, 31*, 181–197.

Gezentsvey, M. A. (2008). *Journeys of ethno-cultural continuity: The long-term acculturation of Jews, Maori and Chinese.* Unpublished doctoral dissertation, Victoria University of Wellington, New Zealand.

Gordon, M. M. (1971). The nature of assimilation and the theory of the melting pot. In E. P. Hollander & R. G. Hunt (eds), *Current perspectives in social psychology* (3rd edn, pp. 102–114). New York: Oxford University Press.

Greenberger, E. & Chen, C. (1996). Perceived family relationships and depressed mood in early and late adolescence: A comparison of European and Asian Americans. *Developmental Psychology, 32*, 707–716.

Greenberger, E., Chen, C., Tally, S., & Dong, Q. (2000). Family, peer, and individual correlates of depressive symptomatology among US and Chinese adolescents. *Journal of Counseling and Clinical Psychology, 68*, 209–219.

Ho, E. S. (1995). Chinese or New Zealander? Differential paths of adaptation of Hong Kong Chinese adolescent immigrants in New Zealand. *New Zealand Population Review, 21*, 27–49.

Ho, E. S. (2004, November) *Acculturation and mental health among Chinese immigrant youth in New Zealand: An exploratory study.* Paper presented at The Inaugural International Asian Health Conference, Auckland.

Holmes, T. H. & Rahe, R. H. (1967). The Social Readjustment Rating Scale. *Journal of Psychosomatic Research, 11*, 213–218.

Hom, C. L. (2002). *The academic, psychological, and behavioral adjustment of Chinese parachute kids.* Unpublished doctoral thesis, University of Michigan, Ann Arbor.

Hsu, F. L. K. (1971). Psycho-social homeostasis and *ren*: Conceptual tools for advancing psychological anthropology. *American Anthropologist, 73*, 23–44.

Hwang, K. K. (1999). Filial piety and loyalty: Two types of social identification in Confucianism. *Asian Journal of Social Psychology, 2*, 163–183.

Irving, H. H., Benjamin, M., & Tsang, A. K. T. (1999). Hong Kong satellite children in Canada: An exploratory study of their experience. *Hong Kong Journal of Social Work, 33*, 1–21.

Juang, L. P., Syed, M., & Takagi, M. (2007). Intergenerational discrepancies of parental control among Chinese-American families: Links to family conflict and adolescent depressive symptoms. *Journal of Adolescence, 30*, 965–975.

Kelley, M. & Tseng, H. M. (1992). Cultural differences in child-rearing: A comparison of Chinese- and Caucasian-American mothers. *Journal of Cross-Cultural Psychology, 23*, 444–455.

Kennedy, A. (1999). *Singaporean sojourners: Meeting the demands of cross-cultural transition.* Unpublished doctoral thesis, National University of Singapore.

Kuo, B. C.-H. (2002). Correlates of coping of three Chinese adolescent cohorts in Toronto, Canada: Acculturation and acculturative stress. *Dissertation Abstracts International, 62* (8-B), 3806.

Kuo, B. C.-H. & Roysircar, G. (2004). Predictors of acculturation for Chinese adolescents in Canada: Age of arrival, length of stay, social class, and English reading ability. *Journal of Multicultural Counseling and Development, 32*, 143–154.

Kwak, K. (2003). Adolescents and their parents: A review of intergenerational family relations for immigrant and non-immigrant families. *Human Development, 46*, 115–136.

Lau, J. S.-N. (2007). Acculturative stress, collective coping and psychological well-being of Chinese international students. *Dissertation Abstracts International, 67*(12–B), 7380.

Lazarus, R. S. & Folkman, S. (1984). *Stress, coping and appraisal.* New York: Springer.

Lee, L. C. & Zhan, G. (1998). Psychosocial status of children and youth. In L. C. Lee & N. W. S. Zane (eds), *Handbook of Asian American psychology* (pp. 137–163). Thousand Oaks, CA: Sage.

Leong, C.-H. & Ward, C. (2000). Identity conflict in sojourners. *International Journal of Intercultural Relations, 24*, 763–776.

Leung, C. (2001a). The socio-cultural and psychological adaptation of Chinese migrant adolescents in Australia and Canada. *International Journal of Psychology, 36*, 8–19.

Leung, C. (2001b). The psychological adaptation of overseas and migrant students in Australia. *International Journal of Psychology, 36*, 251–259.

Li, M. C. (1998). Content and functions of Chinese family relationships: A study of university students. *Indigenous Psychological Research in Chinese Societies, 9*, 3–52. (in Chinese)

Li, X. (2007). A survey of overseas Chinese. In S. Li & Y. Wang (eds), *The yellow book of international politics: Report on global politics and security* (pp. 195–213). Beijing: Institute of World Economics and Politics, Chinese Academy of Social Sciences.

Lin, C. C. & Fu, V. R. (1990). A comparison of child-rearing practices among Chinese, immigrant Chinese, and Caucasian-American parents. *Child Development, 61*, 429–433.

Lin, E.-Y. (2000). *A comparison of Asian and Pakeha values and perceived intergenerational value change in New Zealand.* Unpublished Honours thesis, University of Auckland, Auckland, New Zealand.

Lin, E.-Y. (2004). *Intergenerational value differences and acculturation of Chinese youth in New Zealand.* Paper presented at the Third Biennial International Conference of the International Academy of Intercultural Research, Taipei, Taiwan.

Lin, E.-Y. (2006). *Developmental, social and cultural influences on identity conflict in overseas Chinese.* Unpublished doctoral thesis, Victoria University of Wellington, Wellington, New Zealand.

Lin, E.-Y. (2008). Family and social influences on identity conflict in overseas Chinese. *International Journal of Intercultural Relations, 32,* 130–141.

Liu, J. H., Ng, S. H., Weatherall, A., & Loong, C. (2000). Filial piety, acculturation and intergenerational communication among New Zealand Chinese. *Basic and Applied Social Psychology, 22,* 213–223.

Ma, X. (2002). The first ten years in Canada: A multi-level assessment of behavioral and emotional problems of immigrant children. *Canadian Public Policy, 28,* 395–418.

Mak, A. S. & Chan, H. (1995). Chinese family values in Australia. In R. Hartley (ed.), *Families and cultural diversity in Australia* (pp. 70–95). St. Leonard's, NSW: Allen & Unwin.

Mak, A. S. & Nesdale, D. (2001). Migrant distress: The role of perceived racial discrimination and coping resources. *Journal of Applied Social Psychology, 31,* 2632–2647.

Mak, W. W. S., Chen, S. X., Wong, E. C., & Zane, N. W. S. (2005). A psychological model of stress–distress relationship among Chinese Americans. *Journal of Social and Clinical Psychology, 24,* 422–424.

Markus, H. & Kitayama, S. (1991). Culture and self: Implications for cognition, emotion and motivation. *Psychological Review, 98,* 224–253.

Masgoret, A.-M. & Ward, C. (2006). Culture learning approach to acculturation. In D. L. Sam & J. W. Berry (eds), *The Cambridge handbook of acculturation psychology* (pp. 58–77). New York: Cambridge University Press.

Matsudaira, T. (2003). Cultural influences on the use of social support by Chinese immigrants in Japan: 'Face' as a key word. *Qualitative Health Research, 13,* 343–357.

McCrae, R. R. (2002). NEO-PI–R data from 36 cultures. In R. R. McCrae & J. Allik (eds), *The five factor model of personality across cultures* (pp. 105–126). New York: Kluwer Academic.

Mui, A. (1996). Depression among elderly Chinese immigrants: An exploratory study. *Social Work, 41,* 633–646.

Pe-Pua, R., Mitchell, C., Iredale, R., & Castles, S. (1996). *Astronaut families and parachute children: The cycle of migration between Hong Kong and Australia.* Canberra: Australian Government Publishing Service.

Phillips, M. R. & Pearson, V. (1996). Coping in Chinese communities: The need for a new research agenda. In M. H. Bond (ed.), *The handbook of Chinese psychology* (pp. 429–440). Hong Kong: Oxford University Press.

Phinney, J., Ong, A., & Madden, T. (2000). Cultural values and intergenerational value discrepancies in immigrant and non-immigrant families. *Child Development, 71,* 528–539.

Portes, A. & Rumbaut, R. (2001). *Legacies: The story of the second generation.* Berkeley, CA: University of California Press.

Redfield, R., Linton, R., & Herskovits, M. J. (1936). Memorandum on the study of acculturation. *American Anthropologist, 38,* 149–152.

Rudmin, F. W. (2003). Critical history of the acculturation psychology of assimilation, separation, integration and marginalization. *General Review of Psychology, 7,* 3–37.

Rumbaut, R. G. (1997). Ties that bind: Immigration and immigrant families in the United States. In A. Booth, A. D. Crouter, & N. Landale (eds), *Immigration and the family* (pp. 3–46). Mahwah, NJ: Lawrence Erlbaum.

Ryder, A. G., Alden, L. E., & Paulhus, D. L. (2000). Is acculturation uni-dimensional or bi-dimensional? A head-to-head comparison in the prediction of personality, self-identity and adjustment. *Journal of Personality and Social Psychology, 79,* 49–65.

Sam, D. L., Vedder, P., Ward, C., & Horenczyk, G. (2006). Psychological and socio-cultural adaptation. In J. W. Berry, J. Phinney, D. L. Sam, & P. Vedder (eds), *Immigrant youth in cultural transition: Acculturation, identity and adaptation across national contexts* (pp. 117–142). Hillsdale, NJ: Lawrence Erlbaum.

Searle, W. & Ward, C. (1990). The prediction of psychological and socio-cultural adjustment during cross-cultural transitions. *International Journal of Intercultural Relations, 14,* 449–464.

Selmer, J. (2002). The Chinese connection? Adjustment of Westerners vs. overseas Chinese expatriate managers in China. *Journal of Business Research, 55,* 41–50.

Selmer, J. & Shui, L. S. C. (1999). Coming home? Adjustment of Hong Kong Chinese expatriate business managers assigned to the People's Republic of China. *International Journal of Intercultural Relations, 23,* 447–465.

Shek, D. T. L. & Chan, L. K. (1999). Hong Kong Chinese parents' perceptions of the ideal child. *The Journal of Psychology, 133,* 291–302.

Shen, B.-J. & Takeuchi, D. T. (2001). A structural model of acculturation and mental health status among Chinese Americans. *American Journal of Community Psychology, 29,* 387–418.

Snauwaert, B., Soenens, B., Vanbeselaere, N., & Boen F. (2003). When integration does not necessarily imply integration: Different conceptualizations of acculturation orientations lead to different classifications. *Journal of Cross-Cultural Psychology, 34,* 231–239.

Sondregger, R., Barrett, P. M., & Creed, P. A. (2004). Models of cultural adjustment for child and adolescent migrants to Australia: Internal processes and situational factors. *Journal of Child and Family Studies, 13,* 357–371.

Spencer-Oatey, H. & Xiong, Z. (2006). Chinese students' psychological and socio-cultural adaptation to Britain: An empirical study. *Language, Culture and Curriculum, 19,* 37–53.

Stewart, S. M., Bond, M. H., Deeds, O., & Chung, S. F. (1999). Intergenerational patterns of values and autonomy expectations in cultures of relatedness and separateness. *Journal of Cross-Cultural Psychology, 30*, 575–593.
Suinn, R. M., Rickard-Figueroa, K., Lew, S., & Vigil, P. (1987). The Suinn-Lew Asian Self-identity Acculturation Scale: An initial report. *Educational and Psychological Measurement, 47*, 401–402.
Sung, B. L. (1985). Bicultural conflicts in Chinese immigrant children. *Journal of Comparative Family Studies, 16*, 255–289.
Tata, S. P. & Leong, F. T. L. (1994). Individualism–collectivism, social network orientation and acculturation as predictors of attitudes toward seeking professional psychological help among Chinese Americans. *Journal of Counseling, 41*, 280–287.
Taylor, S. E., Sherman, D. K., Kim, H. S., Jarcho, J., Takagi, K., & Dunagan, M. S. (2004). Culture and social support: Who seeks it and why? *Journal of Personality and Social Psychology, 87*, 354–362.
Tsai, J. H.-C. (2006). Xenophobia, ethnic community and immigrant youth's friendship network formation. *Adolescence, 41*, 285–298.
Tsang, E. (2001). Adjustment of Chinese academics and students to Singapore. *International Journal of Intercultural Relations, 25*, 347–372.
Tseng, V. & Fuligni, A. J. (2000). Parent–adolescent language use and relationships among immigrant families with East Asian, Filipino, and Latin American backgrounds. *Journal of Marriage and the Family, 62*, 465–476.
Vedder, P., van de Vijver, F. J. R., & Liebkind, K. (2006). Predicting immigrant youth's adaptation across countries and ethnocultural groups. In J. W. Berry, J. Phinney, D. L. Sam, & P. Vedder (eds), *Immigrant youth in cultural transition: Acculturation, identity and adaptation across national contexts* (pp. 143–166). Hillsdale, NJ: Lawrence Erlbaum.
Wang, C.-C. & Mallinckrodt, B. (2006). Acculturation, attachment, and psychosocial adjustment of Chinese/Taiwanese international students. *Journal of Counseling Psychology, 53*, 422–433.
Ward, C. (1996). Acculturation. In D. Landis & R. Bhagat (eds), *Handbook of intercultural training* (2nd edn, pp. 124–147). Thousand Oaks, CA: Sage.
Ward, C. (1999). Models and measurements of acculturation. In W. J. Lonner, D. L. Dinnel, D. K. Forgays, & S. A. Hayes (eds), *Merging past, present and future in cross-cultural psychology* (pp. 221–229). Lisse, The Netherlands: Swets & Zeitlinger.
Ward, C. (2001). The ABCs of acculturation. In D. Matsumoto (ed.), *Handbook of culture and psychology* (pp. 411–445). New York: Oxford University Press.
Ward, C. (2004). Psychological theories of culture contact and their implications for intercultural training. In D. Landis, J. Bennett, & M. Bennett (eds), *Handbook of intercultural training* (3rd edn, pp. 185–216) Thousand Oaks, CA: Sage.
Ward, C., Bochner, S., & Furnham, A. (2001). *The psychology of culture shock*. London: Routledge.
Ward, C. & Chang, W. C. (1997). Cultural fit: A new perspective on personality and sojourner adjustment. *International Journal of Intercultural Relations, 21*, 525–533.
Ward, C. & Kennedy, A. (1993). Where's the culture in cross-cultural transition? Comparative studies of sojourner adjustment. *Journal of Cross-Cultural Psychology, 24*, 221–249.
Ward, C. & Kennedy, A. (1994). Acculturation strategies, psychological adjustment and socio-cultural competence during cross-cultural transitions. *International Journal of Intercultural Relations,18*, 329–343.
Ward, C. & Kennedy, A. (1996). Crossing cultures: The relationship between psychological and socio-cultural dimensions of cross-cultural transition. In J. Pandey, D. Sinha, & D. P. S. Bhawuk (eds), *Asian contributions to cross-cultural psychology* (pp. 289–306). New Delhi: Sage.
Ward, C. & Kennedy, A. (1999). The measurement of socio-cultural adaptation. *International Journal of Intercultural Relations, 23*, 659–677.
Ward, C., Leong, C.-H., & Low, M. (2004). Personality and sojourner adjustment: An exploration of the 'Big Five' and the 'Cultural Fit' proposition. *Journal of Cross-Cultural Psychology, 35*, 137–151.
Ward, C. & Lin, E.-Y. (2005). Immigration, acculturation and national identity in New Zealand. In J. Liu, T. McCreanor, T. McIntosh, & T. Teaiwa (eds), *New Zealand identities: Departures and destinations* (pp. 155–173). Wellington: Victoria University Press.
Ward, C. & Masgoret, A.-M. (2004). *The experiences of international students in New Zealand: Report on the results of the national survey*. Wellington: Ministry of Education.
Ward, C., Okura, Y., Kennedy, A., & Kojima, T. (1998). The U-curve on trial: A longitudinal study of psychological and socio-cultural adjustment during cross-cultural transition. *International Journal of Intercultural Relations, 22*, 277–291.
Ward, C. & Rana-Deuba, A. (1999). Acculturation and adaptation revisited. *Journal of Cross-Cultural Psychology, 30*, 372–392.
Waters, J. (2003). Flexible citizens? Transnationalism and citizenship amongst economic immigrants in Vancouver. *The Canadian Geographer, 47*, 219–234.
Weaver, S. R. & Kim, S. Y. (2008). A person-centered approach to studying the linkages among parent–child differences in cultural orientation, supportive parenting, and adolescent depressive symptoms in Chinese American families. *Journal of Youth and Adolescence, 37*, 36–49.
Wei, M., Heppner, P. P., Mallen, M. J., Ku, T.-Y., Liao, Y.-H., & Wu, T.-F. (2007). Acculturative stress, perfectionism, years in the United States and depression among Chinese international students. *Journal of Counseling Psychology, 54*, 385–394.

Wong, D. F. K. & Song, H. X. (2006). Dynamics of social support: A longitudinal qualitative study on Mainland Chinese immigrant women's first year of resettlement in Hong Kong. *Social Work in Mental Health, 4*, 83–101.

Wong, G. & Cochrane, R. (1989). Generation and assimilation as predictors of psychological well-being in British-Chinese. *Social Behavior, 4*, 1–14.

Wong, S. T., Yoo, G. J., & Stewart, A. L. (2006). The changing meaning of family support among older Chinese and Korean immigrants. *Journal of Gerontology: Social Sciences, 61B*, S4–S9.

Yang, K. S. (1981). The formation and change of Chinese personality: A cultural-ecological perspective. *Acta Psychologica Taiwanica, 23*, 39–56. (in Chinese)

Ye, J. (2006). An examination of acculturative stress, interpersonal social support, and the use of online ethnic social groups among Chinese international students. *Howard Journal of Communication, 17*, 1–20.

Yeh, C. & Inose, M. (2002). Difficulties and coping strategies of Chinese, Japanese and Korean immigrant students. *Adolescence, 37*, 69–82.

Yeh, K. H. (1997). Changes in the Taiwanese people's concept of filial piety. In L. Y. Cheng, Y. H. Lu, & F. C. Wang (eds), *Taiwanese society in the 1990's* (pp. 171–214). Taipei, Taiwan: Institute of Sociology, Academia Sinica. (in Chinese)

Yeh, K. H. (2003). The beneficial and harmful effects of filial piety: An integrative analysis. In K. S. Yang, K. K. Hwang, P. B. Pederson, & I. Daibo (eds) *Asian social psychology: Conceptual and empirical contributions* (pp. 67–82). Westport, CN: Greenwood Publishing.

Yeh, K. H. & Bedford, O. (2003). A test of the dual filial piety model. *Asian Journal of Social Psychology, 6*, 215–228.

Ying, Y.-W. (1995). Cultural orientation and psychological well-being in Chinese Americans. *American Journal of Community Psychology, 23*, 893–911.

Ying, Y.-W. (2002). Formation of cross-cultural relationships of Taiwanese international students in the United States. *Journal of Community Psychology, 30*, 45–55.

Ying, Y.-W. & Han, M. (2006). The contribution of personality, acculturative stressors and social affiliation to adjustment: A longitudinal study of Taiwanese students in the United States. *International Journal of Intercultural Relations, 30*, 623–635.

Ying, Y.-W. & Liese, L. H. (1991). Emotional well-being of Taiwan students in the United States: An examination of pre- to post-arrival differential. *International Journal of Intercultural Relations, 15*, 345–366.

Ying, Y.-W. & Liese, L. H. (1994). Initial adjustment of Taiwanese students in the United States: The impact of post-arrival variables. *Journal of Cross-Cultural Psychology, 25*, 466–477.

Yip, T. & Cross, W. E. (2004). A daily dairy study of mental health and community involvement outcomes for three Chinese American social identities. *Cultural Diversity and Ethnic Minority Psychology, 10*, 394–408.

Zhang, N. & Dixon, D. N. (2003). Acculturation and attitudes of Asian international students toward seeking psychological help. *Journal of Multicultural Counseling and Development, 31*, 205–222.

Zheng X. & Berry, J. W. (1991). Psychological adaptation of Chinese sojourners in Canada. *International Journal of Psychology, 26*, 451–470.

Zheng, X., Sang, D., & Wang, L. (2004). Acculturation and subjective well-being of Chinese students in Australia. *Journal of Happiness Studies, 5*, 57–72.

Zhou, M. (1998). 'Parachute Kids' in Southern California: The educational experience of Chinese children in transnational families. *Educational Policy, 12*, 682–704.

CHAPTER 39

Inter-cultural interactions: the Chinese context

David C. Thomas and Yuan Liao

知己知彼，百战百胜

If you know yourself and know the other, you will win every battle.

The art of war by Sun Tzu (authors' translation)

Much of the written work on Chinese psychology identifies and describes culture-specific aspects of psychology as it relates to the Chinese people. This identification of cultural specifics (emics) is important, but it is only a first step towards understanding the interactions of Chinese people across cultures. This approach alone does not do justice to the influence of culture on interactions, because it fails to identify precisely how these cultural specifics affect the sequence of events involving the interaction of Chinese persons with individuals or groups that are culturally different. In this chapter we discuss a number of intermediate mechanisms or conduits through which Chinese culture influences these interactions. These mechanisms involve how Chinese people think about, evaluate, and respond to people who are culturally different.

We begin by identifying a general model of cultural influence in inter-cultural interactions (Shaw, 1990; Thomas, 2008). We describe a behavioral sequence between culturally different actors that involves a number of conduits that are influenced by specific aspects of Chinese culture, such as the salience of situational cues, culturally based scripts and expectations, selective perceptions, out-group identification and attitudes toward out-groups, and the motivational influence of the self-concept. Using this interaction sequence as a framework, we review the extant literature on those unique aspects of Chinese culture that influence inter-cultural interactions. Crucial in this regard is the Confucian ethic for social interaction (Gabrenya & Hwang, 1996), including social exchange norms (Hwang, 1987), the relative absence of clear norms for out-group interaction (Bond & Wang, 1983), the importance of face-work (Hu, 1944; Ting-Toomey, 1988), communication behaviors unique to Chinese culture (e.g. Gao, Ting-Toomey, & Gudykunst, 1996), the motivational influence of the socio-centered self (Markus, 1977; Kashima, Yamaguchi, & Kim, 1995), and the importance of context for attribution processes in Chinese culture (e.g. Kashima, 2001).

Based on this individual interaction sequence combined with the literature on group dynamics, we extend the discussion to the influence of Chinese culture on interactions in cross-cultural negotiations and in culturally diverse groups. We examine both cognitive and motivational mechanisms for the influence of Chinese culture in these social settings. In particular, we focus on the influence of Chinese norms for group (social) interaction, the influence of the perceived diversity within the group on Chinese group behavior (e.g. Spencer-Rodgers, Williams, Hamilton, Peng, & Wang, 2007), and the effect of relative cultural distance with other group members on Chinese behavior. The chapter concludes with a discussion of the implications of our review and discussion for research on Chinese psychology.

The inter-cultural interaction sequence

In order to suggest specifically how Chinese culture influences intercultural interactions, it is helpful to examine a series of actions and reactions that make up a typical inter-cultural encounter. The interaction sequence presented in Figure 39.1, while not exhaustive in terms of its constituent elements, is typical of those that occur regularly in a variety of inter-cultural contexts.

The interaction presented in Figure 39.1 assumes as a starting point some behavior of a person from another culture. Person A might behave according to some culturally based script for the situation, or because of an expectation about how that behavior will be perceived adjust his or her behavior. Situational cues will activate a preexisting behavioral sequence or script (often a culturally based script) that exists for the situation. If a script does not exist or because of the individual's cued motivation, he or she may give more thought as to how to behave and how such behavior might be perceived. Next, Person B, perceiving the behavior, interprets the meaning of these actions. This interpretation can be thought of as occurring in two stages. The first is the identification of the behavior. This identification can be influenced by culturally based selective perception. An important part of the identification of behavior is the categorization of the person as a member of another culture (out-group). This categorization can influence the extent to which the behavior exhibited matches the perceiver's expectation. Behavior that matches expectations may be processed more automatically, whereas behavior that is inconsistent with expectations may require more active cognitive processing.

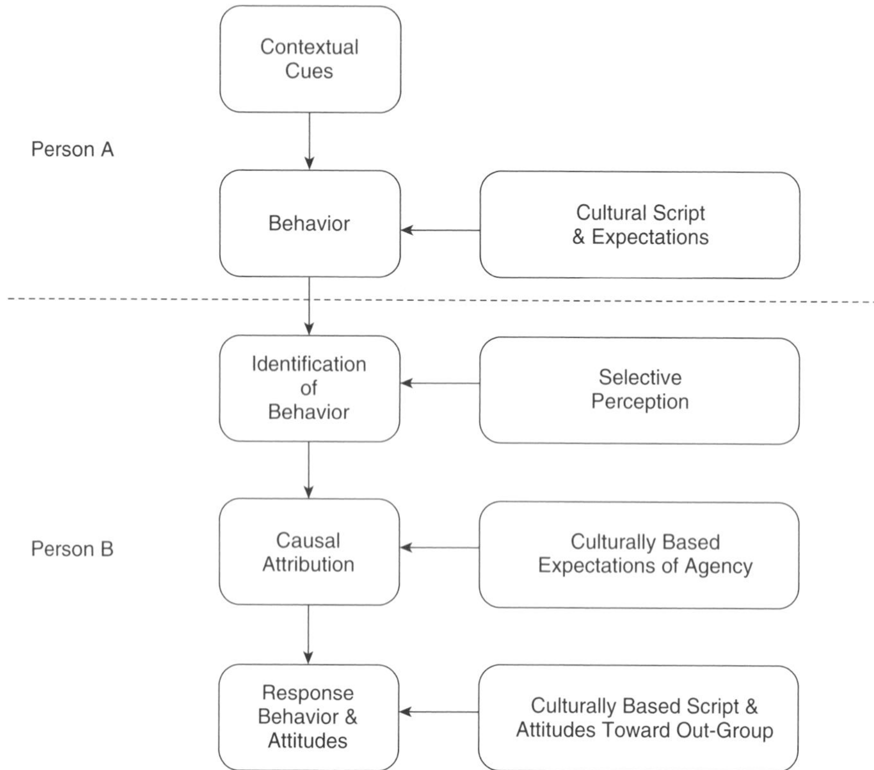

Fig. 39.1 Basic cross-cultural interaction sequence.

The second part of the process is attributing the observed behavior to a cause. This attribution is influenced by the culturally based expectation that the perceiver has for people from the other culture. The extent to which situational cues with regard to the cause of the behavior are present, as well as the relative development of the perceiver's cognitive representation of the other culture, influences this attribution. We might expect that people with well developed representations of the other culture will likely be less extreme (more accurate with regard to the possible range of behavior appropriately attributed to any individual, e.g. less stereotypic) in their assessments. In situations where behavioral cues provide limited information, people rely more heavily on information stored in memory (often stereotypic information) to make a judgment.

Finally, the perceiver's attitudes and behavioral response depend on how the observed behavior is attributed. To the extent that the behavior is attributed to a cause familiar to the perceiver, the response behavior can also be scripted. However, if the observed behavior does not fit an existing category, a new script to guide behavior may have to be created.

The reaction by the perceiver begins another interaction sequence. Variations of this behavioral sequence play themselves out in numerous inter-cultural interactions in a variety of settings. In the following, we draw on this fundamental sequence of behavior, perception, attribution and response, to examine the influence of specific aspects of Chinese culture. While we have outlined this interaction sequence in a way that suggests a universal process, we do not slavishly adhere to the sequence outlined nor do we rule out the possibility (discussed ahead) that individuals from different cultures might differ significantly in their cognitive processes (Nisbett, Peng, Choi, & Norenzayan, 2001; Ji, Lam, & Guo, this volume). Rather, using this idea as a touchstone, we examine the specifics of the Chinese case. Also, in order to be complete in our analysis of the interaction sequence, we must consider the motives of the participants and the demands of the situation.

The demands of the situation can be defined and classified according to the extent to which the situation varies with regard to information from the environment, the characteristics of the task at hand, physical features, and social norms (Hattrup & Jackson, 1996). More broadly, these characteristics combine to form situations that are psychologically 'strong' or 'weak' (Mischel, 1977). Strong situations are well defined and have a high degree of structure, and therefore provide salient cues for behavior, more likely to be socially shared. Weak situations are ambiguous and unstructured in comparison, and thus offer fewer cues for behavior. Thus, in strong situations we would expect less interpersonal variation in behavior as compared to weak situations which are more influenced by dispositional factors. And, in weak, ambiguous situations individuals will fill in the gaps (reduce uncertainty) with reference to information held in memory, such as well learned scripts or stereotypic expectations of the other person (or people from his or her cultural group) in the interaction. Completing the situational matrix is the consideration of whether the interaction is taking place within or across cultures, the later being the focus of this chapter. Thus, as shown in Figure 39.2, we can identify four possible conditions that can be compared with regard to situational influence. While it is the inter-cultural cells that are of most interest here, it is important to consider the within-culture situation for comparison purposes.

Strong situation Intra-cultural	Strong situation Inter-cultural
Weak situation Intra-cultural	Weak situation Inter-cultural

Fig. 39.2 Four interaction contexts.

Selective perception

Research on perception has consistently found that people can be presented with the same stimulus, but perceive it differently. Different priorities for stimuli to which we attend are formed by the internalization of cultural patterns over time (Forgas & Bond, 1985; Markus & Kitayama, 1991). A fundamental cognitive difference thought to exist between Chinese and Westerners is the orientation toward holistic versus analytic thought (Peng & Nisbett, 1999; see also Ji et al., this volume). Holistic thought involves attention to context or the field as a whole, while analytic thought involves detachment of the object from its context (de-contextualizing) and categorization based on its attributes. That is, the Chinese view of the world is that it is a collection of interrelated substances, while a Western view is that it consists of objects that have properties. According to Nisbett et al. (2001), the distinction between holistic and analytic thought stems from deeply embedded differences in philosophical and social systems. This distinction is consistent with notions of *field dependence* and *field independence* with regard to perception (e.g. Witkin & Goodenough, 1977) and *high* versus *low context* communication styles (Gudykunst, Ting-Toomey, & Chua, 1988; Hall, 1976).

A number of studies have documented the holistic versus analytic distinction, and the differences in person perception also extend past the individual to social situations. For example, Abel and Hsu (1949) found that Chinese Americans were more likely to respond to Rorschach cards by giving a description of the whole card as compared to European Americans who focused on a single aspect of the card. Park, Nisbett, and Hedden (1999) reported a similar result in which Chinese but not Americans had better recall for words printed on the back of a card describing a social situation, suggesting that the social background information (context) served as aide to retrieval from memory about the objects in that context. And, while contradictory results exist with regard to field dependence (Bagley, 1995), some recent evidence points to the fact that people with an interdependent self-construal are more field dependent (find it harder to separate an object from its field) than are those with independent self-concepts (Kühnen & Oyserman, 2002). Also, the observation that high-context (indirect) communication styles are associated with collectivist cultures such as China, while low-context communication is associated with individualist cultures (Gudykunst, 2001) is receiving some empirical support (e.g. Park & Kim, 2008). This evidence indicates that Chinese people pay more attention to situational clues in both physical environment and social interactions (see Ji et al., this volume; Kwan, Hui, & McGee, this volume).

In addition to holistic perspective, Chinese also construct social events with dimensions different to those used by Westerners. For example, Forgas and Bond (1985) found that the dimensions Chinese students used to judge social episodes (recurring interaction sequences about which people generally agree, such as meeting someone for lunch or visiting a doctor) reflected the collectivist cultural value of interpersonal connection, social usefulness, and respect to authorities, whereas Australian students relied on dimensions reflecting the individualist cultural value of self-confidence, competitiveness, and freedom. Another important element of person perception, then, is the resultant social categorization of the other culture's participant in an intercultural interaction. That is, persons of different cultures may well believe that they are encountering a different social situation involving them both.

In-group/out-group categorization

Identifying ourselves with a particular cultural group places boundaries around our group (the in-group) and defines non-members as members of out-groups. The in-group and out-group distinction has proven useful in describing attitudes and behavior both within and across cultural group boundaries (see Gudykunst & Bond, 1997). For example, research has shown that, compared to Americans, Hong Kong Chinese students were more likely to share rewards equally with friends (Leung & Bond, 1984), and less likely to have a conflict with close friends (Leung, 1988). Our membership in a cultural group helps to determine how we perceive ourselves, our self-identity as well as how we perceive others. It is the simple categorization of people into different groups that results in a number of assumptions about in-group and out-group members. That is, when categorized as members of a group, individuals are thought to be more similar in their beliefs and behavior, their behavior conveys less information about them as individuals, and the group is believed to be a more important cause of their behavior than are their individual characteristics (Wilder, 1986; see also Leung & Au, this volume).

This in-group versus out-group categorization plays a significant role in Chinese communication. Chinese culture has been identified as an exemplar of collectivist culture, in which people are integrated into their in-groups (Hofstede, 1980; 2001). Members from typically individualist cultures, such as the United States and the United Kingdom, tend to distinguish themselves from other individuals. In comparison, Chinese people draw a sharp distinction between in- and out-groups, view the group as opposed to the individual as a basic unit, and are loyal to their in-groups. Since Chinese integrate the in-group as part of their self-concept, it is not surprising that they are inclined to treat others based on their group memberships (see also Liu, Li, & Yue, this volume).

Although one's social identity derives from one's in-group, the way in which individuals form their social identities differs across cultures (Brewer & Yuki, 2007; Yuki, 2003). Specifically, social identities are formed based on depersonalized membership in individualist cultures and on interpersonal relationships in collectivist cultures. This suggests that people would react differently to others who have the potential to become in-group members either through shared membership or interpersonal connections. In one study (Buchan, Croson, & Johnson, 2003), researchers created an arbitrary category boundary to participants unknown to each other in order to introduce a social identity based on depersonalized membership. They found that Americans increased their levels of trust towards these others, whereas Chinese did not show this in-group bias. This finding suggests that Chinese people do not distinguish strangers from in-group members based on shared membership (e.g. a club), but rather on the location of that person in their social networks (e.g. sister's high school friend). Therefore it is possible for a stranger to be accepted as an in-group member if he or she finds a channel to connect interpersonally to the target Chinese person.

The more holistic cognitive orientation of Chinese people has a number of implications for the person perception associated with our model of inter-cultural interactions. One of the most interesting of these is the influence that holistic cognitive processing has on in-group out-group categorization and stereotyping. Intuitively, one might predict that because Chinese are more likely to take a holistic approach they would be more likely to perceive a group as a collective sharing similar traits and goals instead of a gathering of random individuals. In line with this prediction, recent work by Spencer-Rodgers et al. (2007) found that Chinese viewed social groups as more entitative (regarded as an entity, apart from attendant circumstances) than did Americans. As a result, they were more likely to infer personality traits on the basis of group membership (stereotype) than were Americans.

The perceptual biases of Chinese people, such as the greater tendency to see wholes as opposed to parts, to more readily perceive relationships among elements in the perceptual field, and to view social groups as more entitative have implications for the attribution of cause for the observed behavior of the other, discussed next.

Differential attributions

Attribution helps people to understand and react to their environment by linking the observation of an event to its causes. The extent to which Chinese make sense of their social world (in particular, of culturally different others) influences the intercultural interaction process outlined in Figure 39.1. While the general process of attribution may operate similarly across cultures (Schuster, Fosterlung, & Weiner, 1989), the notion that preferences for causal processes are universal (e.g. the fundamental attribution error, Ross, 1977) is mistaken (e.g. Morris & Peng, 1994; Ross & Nisbett, 1991). In addition to differences in preferences for situational versus dispositional explanations for behavior, discussed ahead, new evidence is providing insight into the way in which culture influences the cognitive process (automatic versus controlled process) of attribution (e.g. Knowles, Morris, Chiu,

& Hong, 2008). Both the preferences for and the way in which Chinese attribute the cause for the behavior of the culturally different others they encounter has implications for intercultural interactions.

Based on the previous discussion of perceptual differences, it seems reasonable to assume that individuals are more likely to attribute causality to elements of the situation that they attend to. That is, if Chinese are more likely to attend to the context (field) and the target's relationship with the context, they are more likely to attribute causality to context and situations. A number of studies provide evidence in support of this position. For example, when showed cartoon depictions of fish moving in relationship to each other in various ways Chinese participants were more likely to attribute the behavior of individual fish to external factors as compared to Americans (Hong, Chiu, & Kung, 1997; Morris & Peng, 1994). Important to our discussion, this attribution preference extends to social situations. For example, in one study Chinese were found to be more likely to explain murders in terms of situational or social factors, whereas Americans attributed the cause to characteristics of the perpetrators (Morris & Peng, 1994). This attention to context also suggests that Chinese may make broader and more complex casual attributions, which extends to differences in the perceptions of the consequences of events. For example, Maddux and Yuki (2006) found that East Asians were more aware of the indirect and distal consequences of events than were Americans.

A holistic versus analytic orientation also seems to influence implicit theories of attribution. In three studies, Menon, Morris, Chiu, and Hong (1999) found that East Asians were more likely to attribute scandals in organizations to groups as opposed to Americans who attributed relatively more to individuals. Similarly, in another study Chiu, Morris, Hong, and Menon (2000) found that Americans blamed the pharmacist who filled the wrong prescription for causing several patients to be sick, while Chinese regarded the pharmacy as a whole to be cause of the event.

Not only do people attribute causality to elements to which they attend, but, in the absence of sufficient information, they attribute causality to implicit theories which are easily accessible. For example, Americans have an easily accessible theory about individuals as autonomous agents, whereas Chinese have a similarly accessible theory of groups as agents (Menon et al., 1999). That is, Chinese perceivers, relative to North Americans, are more likely to focus attention on collective agents when presented with an outcome for which the agent is ambiguous, and the reluctance of Chinese to make disposition attributions for the behavior of individuals does not extend to groups. Said otherwise, Chinese assume groups are autonomous, whereas Americans assume that individuals are autonomous.

Considering attribution as a dual-stage process sheds even more light on the possible differences between Chinese and Westerners. Dual-process models of attribution (Lieberman, Gaunt, Gilbert, & Trope, 2002) suggest that attribution begins with an automatic goal-linked inference about causality, but that the attribution is subsequently corrected by a theory-driven process. In a series of five studies, Lieberman, Jarcho, and Obayashi (2005) found that East Asians (from China, Hong Kong, Korea, and Japan) differed from Americans with regard to their attributions when under different conditions of cognitive load. Under cognitive load both groups made similar automatic attributions consistent with the inference goals. However, in the no-load condition East Asians tended toward situational attributions, while Americans tended toward dispositional. This contrast is consistent with other research that shows that individuals with a high need for closure exhibit cultural bias in attributions (e.g. Chiu et al., 2000), and that when primed with images of Chinese culture, bicultural (Chinese-American) participants skewed attributions in a direction predicted by Chinese social norms (Hong, Morris, Chiu, & Benet-Martínez, 2000). However Lieberman et al. (2005) also found that American no-load participants, when compared to American cognitive load participants, corrected their attributions normatively to information provided in the situation, while East Asian no-load participants corrected in the direction of a situational attribution, even when the content of the information provided suggested a dispositional inference. That is, there seems to be a 'situationalist error' among East Asians that overlooks the specific content presented by the situation.

Attribution for the cause of behavior is influenced by whether the behavior is being exhibited by a member of our own cultural group. Because we derive part of our identity from our association with our cultural group, we are favorably biased toward that group. Research with Western participants is consistent in the finding that individuals are more likely to attribute desirable behavior by members of our in-group to dispositions but more likely to attribute desirable behavior by out-group members to transient external causes (e.g. Hewstone, 1990). Research with several cultural groups has supported this group-serving bias in attributions (see Thomas, 2008). However, attempts to replicate this finding with Chinese have not been successful (Hewstone & Ward, 1985; Morris & Peng, 1994). There are a number of possible causes for these unexpected findings. First, in some case it may not be possible for members of a cultural group to find a positive basis on which to compare their group with another (Tajfel, 1981). Also, in the vertical, collectivist Chinese culture, disadvantaged groups might accept as legitimate the higher status of other groups (Smith & Bond, 1999, ch. 6). Third, because their self-identity derives from group membership, Chinese tend to emphasize self-improvement more than self-enhancement. Therefore, it is also possible that Chinese make attributions in ways that promote group-improvement instead of group-enhancement (see also Kwan et al., this volume).

In summary, bias with regard to dispositional versus situational attributions for behavior seems to be a culture-bound phenomenon. While some research suggests that dispositional tendencies are a largely Western perspective (e.g. Shweder & Bourne, 1982), it seems likely that while Chinese do attribute behavior to individuals they are relatively biased toward situational and group-agentic explanations (e.g. Knowles, Morris, Chiu, & Hong, 2001). Another generalization about Chinese attribution patterns related to our intercultural interaction model is that Chinese are less likely to make self-enhancing attributions for achievement than for affiliation events (Crittenden, 1996). And, a final complicating factor with regard to attributions among Chinese is the existence of indigenous causal categories, such as *yuan* (Yang, 1988; Leung, this volume). *Yuan* is grounded in Buddhist beliefs concerning predestination and determines relationships among persons. As an external causal category with both stable and variable forms, it underscores the Chinese propensity toward situational explanations.

Behavioral norms

The application of our intercultural interaction model to the specific situation of Chinese interacting with culturally different others has led thus far to a consideration of perceptual and attribution processes of Chinese. In order to articulate the behavior of Chinese in an intercultural interaction, it is first necessary to give attention to distinctive Chinese norms and motives in social interaction. Societal norms are of special importance in so-called *tight* societies. China has been classified as well above average in terms of societal tightness (M. J. Gelfand, personal communication, 2009). In these societies the number and strength of social norms are high and there is low tolerance for deviance from norms (Gelfand, Nishii, & Raver, 2006).

Societal tightness is hypothesized to have a number of effects on individuals relevant to our discussion here. For example, according to Gelfand et al. (2006), tightness is thought to lead to the feeling that one's actions are subject to evaluation and that there are potential punishments for such evaluations, called felt accountability (Tetlock, 1985); to a higher cognitive accessibility to normative requirements; to a guiding normative focus of not making mistakes; and to a preference for problem-solving styles that emphasize established procedures. Thus, societal tightness gives rise to an enhanced role for the distinctive norms of Chinese society as a guide to behavior in inter-cultural interactions.

It is of course not possible in a short chapter to do justice to the wide range of social norms for behavior that might influence the intercultural interaction sequence (see Chan, Ng, & Hui, this volume; Cheng, Lo, & Chio, this volume; Leung & Au, this volume; Shi & Feng, this volume; Tang, this volume). Therefore our discussion centers on two sets of behaviors influenced by Confucian concepts that are most divergent with Western norms. We have labeled these relational personalism, and harmony and face-work (Gabrenya & Hwang, 1996; Hwang & Han, this volume). We conclude this section with a brief discussion of the related issue of the Chinese self-concept and its relationship to motives in social interaction.

Relational personalism

Yang (1992) suggests that Chinese make a fundamental distinction among people who are *sheng* ('raw', that is, outsiders), *shu* ('cooked', that is, insiders) and *jia* (family). This distinction parallels the categories of relationships described by Hwang (1987) as instrumental, mixed, or expressive, respectively. Expressive ties are reserved for family members, while mixed ties refer to relationships with close friends, and instrumental ties relate to out-group members with whom one has no long-term relationship. Every Chinese is born into a network of family members and acquires other in-group members through education, occupation, place of residence, and so on. These complex relationships (*guanxi*) persist over person's lifetime. The relative permanence of *guanxi* contributes to the calculus informing exchange norms in Chinese society (Gabrenya & Hwang, 1996). As opposed to short-term, symmetrical, and reciprocal exchange employed by people in the West, Chinese employ different exchange rules based on the nature of the particular relationship (Hwang, 1987). With family members, *need* underlies the basis of exchange, while with other in-group members the complicated rules associated with *guanxi* are dominant. Relationships in this so-called mixed-tie category involve the rule of *renqing* (Hwang, 1987; see also Hwang & Han, this volume). That is, *renqing* has both affective and instrumental characteristics which prescribe the nature of social exchange. While *renqing* involves a norm of reciprocity, the nature of this reciprocity differs significantly from that prescribed by the equity or need rule. With out-group members, the relationship is temporary and anonymous and is embarked upon solely to attain immediate, personal goals. Interaction with out-groups members, as opposed to the complex set of norms associated with in-group members, is thus more instrumental and less informed by normative considerations (Bond & Wang, 1983).

Harmony and face-work

Integrally related to the concept of *guanxi* is the concept of *mainzi* (face). Lin (1939) called face, favor and fate 'the three Muses ruling over China' (p. 191). Hu (1944) identified two categories of face in Chinese culture, *lian* and *mianzi*. *Lian* can be maintained by faithful compliance with social norms; whereas *mianzi* is more closely related to the Western concept of prestige, and is a reputation that one achieves. Face functions to maintain order in groups and plays an important role in regulating interpersonal relationships (e.g. Bond & Lee, 1981; Hwang, 1997-1998; Redding & Ng, 1982; Ting-Toomey, 1988). Not giving face to another is extremely rude in China and hurting another's face would seriously damage the relationship between the two people involved (Kam & Bond, 2008). Ho (1974) identified saving others' *mianzi* in conflict situations as a key social skill in Chinese society. According to Gabrenya and Hwang (1996), even defeated adversaries should be left with face (*liu mianzi*). The concept of 'face-work' is very much akin to Western notions of impression management with the goal of instilling a favorable image in the minds of others (e.g. Schlenker, 1980). An individual's *mianzi* is a function of perceived position in the social network, but can also be derived from socially ascribed status, physical appearance, family background, and so on. It may arise from achieved status obtained either from personal qualities, such as knowledge, strength, integrity, etc., or non-personal factors, such as wealth, positional authority, social connections, family background and so on (Ho, 1976).

However, doing face-work is more than maintaining *mianzi*. It also involves enhancing *minazi* for another, which can involve avoiding criticism of others, especially superiors in public, and giving greater rewards to those skilled at preserving face for others (Hwang, 1987). Oetzel et al. (2001) compared facework across China, Germany, Japan, and United States and found that persons from collectivist, high-power distance cultures (e.g. China) had more other-face concern, more avoidance facework, and less dominating facework than did persons from individualist, low-power distance cultures. Leung and Chan (2003) identified (through factor analysis of facework statements) four dimensions of face-work that they labeled reciprocity, response, respect, and reputation. They found that Hong Kong negotiators manipulated the four dimensions to build connections with powerful

Chinese parties. In this way, doing facework is part of a complicated power game that is undertaken in part to maintain harmony in a relationship-oriented society.

Gabrenya and Hwang (1996) suggest that 'harmony within hierarchy' is the phrase that most aptly describes the orientation of social behaviors in Chinese society. Bond and Hwang (1986) termed this process doing the proper things, with the right people, in the appropriate relationships. *Mianzi*-enhancing behaviors designed to strengthen a person's position in the hierarchy are normative, because hierarchy is a key consideration in making evaluative judgments of performances in social settings (e.g. Bond, Wan, Leung, & Giacalone, 1985). Confucian doctrine prescribes harmony, hierarchy and conformity in relationships (King & Bond, 1985). Members of high context societies, such as China, attend more to facework as a means of avoiding open conflict, if at all possible (Ting-Toomey, 1988). That is, facework is a mediating factor between collectivist conceptions of self (described ahead) and the management of conflict situations to maintain order (Oetzel, & Ting-Toomey, 2003).

Empirical evidence supports the fact that Chinese engage in conflict resolution behaviors, such as obliging, avoiding, compromising, and integrating, more than do Americans (Trubisky, Ting-Toomey, & Lin, 1991). Harmony within hierarchy also influences Chinese norms for communication behavior, and include emotional restraint, politeness, and avoidance of aggressive persuasion (Shenkar & Ronen, 1987; Shi & Feng, this volume). Gao, Ting-Toomey, & Gudykunst (1996) suggest five major characteristics of Chinese communication behavior. These are *hanxu* (implicit communication), *tinghua* (listening centeredness), *keqi* (politeness), *zijiren* (focus on insiders), and *mianzi* (face-directed communication strategies), each of which may contribute to inter-cultural difficulties for persons socialized under different social traditions and logic. And, as suggested by Gelfand et al. (2006), the tight societal structure characteristic of Chinese culture fosters a socialization with highly developed systems of monitoring and sanctioning behavior, underscoring the importance these normative behaviors in social interaction.

Chinese self-identity

Individuals in all cultures have an understanding of themselves as physically distinct and separate from others (Hallowell, 1955). However, people also have an inner or private self that consists of thoughts and feelings that cannot be directly known by others. A key distinction is the extent to which people regard themselves as separate from others or as connected with others (Markus & Kitayama, 1991). When culture emphasizes independent, goal-oriented, instrumental practices and ideas in social relations, individuals see themselves as autonomous individuals with unique attributes whose behavior is organized and made meaningful by reference to their internal thoughts and feelings (Kitayama, Duffy, & Uchida, 2007). In contrast, when a culture emphasizes interdependent, other-oriented communal practices and ideas in social relationships, individuals socialized into those cultures regard themselves as less differentiated and more connected to others, with their own behavior determined, contingent on, and to a large extent organized by the thoughts, feelings and actions of others in the larger social unit (Markus & Kitayama, 1991).

Bochner (1994) studied self-concepts using the Twenty Statement Test, and found that people from collectivist cultures reported more group-category statements. In line with the discussion above, members from collectivist cultures are likely to integrate their group membership into their self-identity (see also Ip & Bond, 1995). Updating a position espoused by Hsu (1971), Yang (2006, p. 342) describes the Chinese self-concept in the following way:

> The self is not construed as a solid thing, or even a concept, but a term paired with other collective terms to represent many/whole part relationships. The most important aspect of the self from this perspective is that the self is always at the center (*of concentric circles*) and is surrounded by other people connected to one.

In our model of intercultural interactions the most important implication of this view of self is for the motivation of behavior. Fundamentally, the self serves to motivate behavior by directing behavior to reduce personal dissonance (Kitayama et al., 2007). For those with interdependent self-concepts as described here, individuals experience dissonance when their behavioral choice poses a threat to the public self-image they wish to maintain. Also, it may be that choices made by in-group members engage this intrinsic motivation for the individual. This is consistent with descriptions of achievement motivation among Chinese as involving feelings of indebtedness to parents, combined with the desire to meet prescribed social obligations and return favors received, especially from in-group members (Yang, 1986).

This emphasis contrasts with the self-enhancement motives of those with independent self-concepts, and has resulted in labeling the motives of East Asians as *self-improving* as opposed to *self-enhancing* (Kitayama, Markus, Matsumoto, & Noraskkunkit, 1997; see also Kwan et al., this volume). Recently, Heine and Hamamura (2007) argued that being a good person is a universal motivation, but that a constant focus on self-improvement serves this goal in East Asian society, where maintaining face is important to the members. All the evidence shows that Chinese people integrate in-group and collectivist cultural requirements into their self-concepts. Instead of identifying themselves as separate individuals, Chinese people see themselves as part of a larger relationship net composed of complex inter-connections, mutually influencing one another.

Situational context

Returning to our model of intercultural interactions, it is thus possible to examine those Chinese norms, motives, and mechanisms that apply to the general interaction sequence identified previously. In particular, we are concerned with differences between strong and weak situations in intercultural interactions. In strong situations, the context indicates appropriate behavior, and Chinese are very likely to conform to situational cues. However, when interacting with people from other cultures Chinese are, in the absence of contextual information that otherwise guides them, likely to be motivated by concerns of harmony within hierarchy and norms associated with self-improvement. Their behavior in intercultural interactions is highly influenced by the categorization of the other participant(s) as an in-group or an out-group member. And, they are likely to have a situational bias with regard to perception and attribution as a result of more holistic cognitive processing. These characteristics create difficulty for Chinese in dealing with out-group members (strangers). That is, the clear distinctions between in-group members and out-group members and the highly specific norms for in-group interaction, but lack of norms for out-group interaction create an uncertain situation for most Chinese (Gao et al., 1996).

Applications

The utility of our sequential model of intercultural interactions in understanding the Chinese case can be seen in an examination of Chinese interactions in cross-cultural communication and negotiation, and in multicultural teams. In each of these situations, Chinese confront out-group members. So, an examination of the interaction process involving cognitive, motivational, and contextual elements provides a lens for understanding the ensuing processes in a way not available through the examination of any single element.

Cross-cultural communication and negotiation. All negotiations share the fact that they involve communication between two or more parties who have conflicting interests, but a common need to reach an agreement (Hofstede & Usunier, 1996). Cross-cultural communication is significantly more demanding than communication within a single culture. An obvious consideration is the language being used; individuals must find a common language that both can use effectively. In practice this means that at least one of the two parties must use a second language. Because Americans (who dominate business transactions) are typically monolingual and the fact that English is often used as a bridge language (Ferraro, 2006), cross-cultural communication for Chinese often involves communicating in English. Recent research has indicated that the willingness of Chinese to communicate in an intercultural interaction was dependent on self-perceived language competence, whereas this effect was not present for Americans (Lu & Hsu, 2008). The authors attribute this result to the sensitivity of Chinese to the judgment of others associated with potential loss of face (see Ho, 1976).

In addition to language considerations, the intercultural interaction brings those aspects of communication that transcend the language being spoken into focus. That is, culturally based rules govern the style, conventions, and practice of language usage. For example, direct communication is typically associated with individualist cultures and indirectness with collectivist cultures (Sanchez-Burks et al., 2003). Yeung (2000) compared the participative decision-making discourse between Hong Kong Chinese and Australians and partially confirmed the long-believed indirect style of Chinese communication. Consistent with this view, Yeung found that Chinese subordinates frequently used question forms to ask for permission which defer the answer or decision to the other person, and usually omitted the subject 'I'. These two characteristics of speech combined to give the self-effacing and indirect impression of Chinese communication. However, contrary to expectations, Chinese subordinates expressed explicit and blunt disagreements with each other and the manager, while Australians hedged their disagreements much more. The implications of these cultural differences for inter-cultural communication are considerable.

Research has also found nonverbal aspects of communication in which Chinese people differ from native English speakers. In a series of studies, Li (2001; 2004; 2006) compared the interruptions, gaze and backchannel responses in intra- and inter-cultural communications. Results from the three studies converged to show a consistent picture: people place different meanings on nonverbal cues, which could lead to misunderstandings in intercultural communications. For example, during intra-cultural communications, Chinese dyads showed more cooperative interruptions (Li, 2001), gazed less frequently and in shorter durations (Li, 2004), and gave more backchannel responses (short utterances used by the listener which do not disturb or take over the floor from the current speaker) than the Canadian dyads (Li, 2006).

However, the communication process changed in the inter-cultural context. Li (2004) found more intrusive and unsuccessful interruptions in Chinese-Canadian communication. Also, Li (2006) reported backchannel responses functioned differently in intra- and inter-cultural contexts. When both parties were Chinese or Canadians, backchannel responses were positively correlated with listener's recall scores, suggesting those responses increased the effectiveness of communication. However, the correlation was negative when the two parties came from different cultures, which suggested that people misunderstood the backchannel responses from a culturally different person and the misleading feedback hindered the exchange of information. Further, the results supported an accommodation in intercultural discourses by showing that Chinese-Chinese discourse had the highest backchannel responses and least gaze, followed by Chinese-Canadian dyads, then by Canadian-Canadian discourses.

An important extension of cross-cultural communication issues is that of face-to-face negotiation. Efforts to understand cross-cultural negotiations have included descriptive approaches documenting the differences in negotiating processes and behaviors in different cultures; a cultural dimensions approach in which cultural effects are attributed to cultural values and norms; and of late, more holistic approaches that consider both the knowledge structures of the participants and the context in which the negotiation takes place (Brett & Crotty, 2008). It is this third approach in which the value of an interactionist approach can be most clearly detected.

Many studies have documented the negotiating styles of people from different cultures, with differences recorded for initial bargaining positions and concession patterns, styles of persuasion, and patterns of conflict resolution (e.g. Leung & Wu, 1990). The Chinese case is no exception, with a significant amount of attention having been paid to styles of Chinese negotiation (e.g. Fang, 1997; Pye, 1982). Although some studies have used indigenous Chinese concepts such as *guanxi* and *face* to explain Chinese negotiation styles, they provide little information about the more fundamental basis for the differences observed, and even less about negotiation in specific inter-cultural contexts.

Research that relates dimensions of cultures such as individualism and collectivism or power distance to negotiation improves our ability to explain and predict the effect of culture on negotiations. For example, results suggest that collectivists, such as Chinese, prefer bargaining and mediation as conflict resolution strategies, whereas individualists prefer adversarial, adjudicative procedures (Leung, 1987). A rational for this finding can be constructed to suggest that, while collectivists might actually prefer an adversarial procedure, the confrontation and competitiveness inherent in the procedure are so inconsistent with Chinese norms governing social interaction that their preference for this procedure is reduced (see Bond, Leung, & Schwartz, 1992; see also Leung & Au, this volume). In another study, Graham, Kim, Lin, and Robinson (1988) found that Chinese negotiators who used less of a problem-solving approach (i.e. more competitive strategies) gained more individual profits in a buyer-seller simulation. Although it is commonly agreed that Chinese people try to avoid conflict and maintain harmony in social interactions, research also suggests a different behavioral pattern is adopted by Chinese depending on the goals of the particular situation.

Cultural dimensions have been related to differences in cognitive processes related to negotiation, such as perceptions of conflict (Gelfand et al., 2001) and egocentric perceptions of fairness (Gelfand et al., 2002; Tinsley & Pillutla, 1998). Cultural dimensions have also been drawn upon to understand the communications used during negotiation. For example, negotiators from high-context cultures have been found to engage in more direct information sharing and affective influence through a negotiation, whereas negotiators from low-context cultures engaged in more direct information exchange and rational influence early in the process (Adair & Brett, 2004; Brett & Crotty, 2008).

The cultural dimensions approach does little, however, to help us understand what happens when negotiating with a member of a *different* culture. For example, Chinese, when trying to resolve a disagreement, used tactics designed to embarrass a Chinese counterpart, but tried to resolve the situation and preserve the relationship when negotiating with people from the United States (Weldon et al., 1996, cited in Smith and Bond, 1999). However, in another study of Canadian and Chinese negotiators, neither group altered its negotiating strategy when negotiating across cultures (Tse, Francis, & Walls, 1994). These examples point to the need for a more interactionsist perspective on the intercultural interaction involved in negotiating across cultural lines.

The recently proposed, dynamic constructivist approach (Hong et al., 2000) investigates the interaction between the person and situation. They argued that culture is stored in people's mind as knowledge structures. Once activated by situational cues, cultural knowledge will influence behavior. That is, people rely on their internalized cultural norms only when certain cultural knowledge structures are cued. This approach explains why the same person would behave differently across situations where he or she receives different social stimuli, especially those involving the cultural identity of their counterpart in the interaction.

Guided by this approach, some recent research has taken a more complex approach that incorporates a consideration of the type of interaction sequence proposed here. For example, Gelfand and Cai (2004) outline how the cultural structuring of the social context of a negotiation can influence the negotiating behavior of participants within culture. For example, the extent to which negotiators believe they are accountable for the negotiation outcomes interacts with cultural norms to influence their behavior. In this case, previous research has generally found that accountability makes negotiators react more competitively. However, recent research has found that accountability influenced negotiators to behave more in line with cultural norms (Gelfand & Realo, 1999). Specifically, independent negotiators became more competitive, whereas interdependent negotiators become more cooperative under high accountability pressure.

Also, the level of negotiators' need for closure influences the extent to which negotiators behave in a culturally prototypical manner (Fu, Morris et al., 2007). As predicted, Fu and her colleagues (2007) found that the higher need-for-closure Chinese preferred to work through a relationally connected third party and tended to seek conciliation-related information, while their American counterparts preferred a relationally unconnected third party (an objective source), and tended to seek investigation-related information. The properties of social context (high accountability pressure) and the individual (need for closure) are two among three sets of the factors affecting the process of activating knowledge structures (Morris & Fu, 2001).

Other than the dynamic constructivist approach focusing on knowledge structures, several studies have identified the interaction between culture and situational factors. Drake (2001) argued that the effect of culture on both communication behaviors and outcomes may differ as a result of the negotiator role. There is evidence that roles for dyads are somewhat differently construed between Chinese and other cultural groups (McAuley, Bond, & Kashima, 2002). Consistent with this general finding, Cai, Wilson, & Drake (2000) found that *seller* collectivism had a more constant effect on communication behavior and joint outcomes than did *buyer* collectivism. Another related example for the Chinese case is provided in a study by Brett, Tinsley, Shapiro, and Okumura (2007) in which they found that cultural norms for resolving a dispute were influenced by whether or not the decision maker was a superior or a peer of the disputants for Chinese, but not for the Japanese or Americans (see also Bond et al., 1985). Clearly the norms governing social interaction that result from perceiving the other party through the hierarchical lens of Chinese culture influenced the subsequent behavior.

During intercultural negotiations, people bring their own cultural norms and rules to the conversation. When they differ, the interesting question is whose norm dominates the other. One indicator of whose rules to play by is provided by adaptation. Since adaptation means sacrificing one's own principles and accommodating to anothers' rules, the central question is which party should adapt. A primary condition for adaptation is knowing the behaviors regarded as normative in the other culture in order to take appropriate actions. Therefore, Weiss (1994) argued that the party with more knowledge about the other's culture should adapt. Some cultures may have equipped individuals with the tendency to adapt, facilitating this process. For example, since collectivistic cultures value social obligations and group harmony, members socialized in these cultures may be more sensitive to variations in interaction norms and more willing to accommodate (Adair & Brett, 2004).

Findings with Japanese negotiators may shed some light on the Chinese case. During a negotiation between Americans and Japanese, Adair et al. (2001) found that Japanese negotiators, but not Americans, adapted their behaviors. An important aspect of their study was that both Japanese and American participants were working in the United States. Thus, the Japanese participants were assumed to know how to behave appropriately in American culture, while American participants were presumed to lack the knowledge about Japanese culture. Similarly it may be reasonable to expect that Chinese people, who are similarly socialized, would be likely to adapt in the same type of intercultural context. What would happen should the Chinese be in their 'home' cultural context awaits future study.

The tendency to follow the local norm when Chinese enter into a novel environment is reflected by idioms such as 'when in a country, follow its customs' and 'guests follow their hosts' convenience'. Examining those idioms closely, however, one may find that being a guest in a new environment is a condition for Chinese people to adapt. That is, Chinese may vary their behavior according to the larger social context when interacting with a person from another culture. For example, when a Chinese businessman goes to North America, he may try to fit into the North American culture. However, when the same person hosts his American business partner in China, he would expect the American to adapt to Chinese culture and thus would not change, but expect culturally typical behaviors from his business partner. Indeed, anecdotal evidence suggests that Chinese are tough negotiators on their home territory (Pye, 1982)!

Negotiation is perhaps the clearest articulation of the need for an interactionist perspective to understanding the influence of culture on inter-cultural encounters. It is evident that, to explain and predict behavior in intercultural negotiations, consideration must be given to more than just the culturally normative behavior of the participants. That is, we must attend to perceptions and categorization of the other party and understand normative behavior specific to that context as well as the motives and roles of the participants.

Multi-cultural work groups. The understanding of cultural influence in work groups provides an additional opportunity to demonstrate the utility of an interactionist approach for examining cultural influence in general and the Chinese case in particular. When people must work together in groups to perform a task, the cultural differences between group members becomes more apparent. Work groups have several distinctive characteristics (Hackman, 1991) that enhance their utility as an exemplar. First, they are social systems that have boundaries with members who have differentiated inter-dependent roles, and they have a task to perform.

The cultural composition of work groups affects the way they function through three types of mechanism (Thomas, 2008): first are the orientations socialized by the specific cultures represented in the group toward the functioning of groups (cultural *norms* or *scripts*); second is the variety of different cultures represented in the group (cultural *diversity*) and their relative balance; third is the extent to which group members are culturally different from each other (*relative cultural distance*). While these mechanisms relate to the interaction sequence previously described, each affects the way groups operate in different ways.

Different cultures have very different orientations toward what is appropriate in work groups with regard to how a group should be structured and how it should function (e.g. Thomas, Ravlin, & Wallace, 1996). For example, as noted previously, Chinese believe that maintaining as sense of harmony is extremely important in interpersonal interactions. This contrasts dramatically with notions of constructive conflict and devil's advocacy popular in the United States, arising from the Western idealization of Athenian democracy. Recent studies have demonstrated that these cultural norms for group structure and function influence how people think about group behavior. For example, Gibson and Zellmer-Bruhn (2001) found that individualistic metaphors for teams reflected clear team objectives (i.e. there is no need to ask 'what are we doing here?', since the obvious goal is to win the game) and voluntary membership, such as occurs in Western sports teams, whereas metaphors in collectivist cultures, such as China, emphasize a broad scope of activity and clear member roles, such as in families.

A number of studies shows that people bring mental representations (metaphors or scripts) to work groups which they then use to interpret events, behaviors, expectations, and other group members (e.g. Bettenhausen & Murnighan, 1991). There is also evidence suggesting that Chinese have different views as to what is appropriate with regard to group process. For example, Earley (1989) in a comparison of Chinese and American participants found that the social loafing prevalent among the Americans was all but non-existent in the Chinese sample, reflecting the Chinese norm for relational personalism described previously. However, in a follow-up study, Earley (1993) found that social loafing did not occur among Chinese when they worked in the context of an in-group, but that it did occur when they were participating with out-group members. Thus, Chinese reacted to their perception of and categorization of the group as members of an out-group by suspending their in-group norms for behavior and employing a more utilitarian interaction norm (see also Leung & Au, this volume).

A second influence on work groups is the cultural diversity of the group. In general, the evidence suggests both positive and negative effects of cultural diversity in work groups (see Thomas, 2008). That is, culturally diverse groups are likely to suffer more process losses resulting from different perceptions and communications patterns, and thus have lower group performance than homogeneous groups. Alternatively, because of the different perspectives of group members, cultural diversity should result in more creative and higher-quality group decisions (see Earley & Mosakowski, 2000; Elron, 1997; McLeod, Lobel & Cox, 1996).

Much of the study of cultural diversity in work groups has compared diverse with homogeneous groups without reference to the specific cultures involved. However, one stream of research is relevant to the Chinese case. That is, when group members fall into two, non-overlapping cultural categories, as opposed to coming from many cultures, individuals sometimes identify more strongly with their cultural sub-group than with the task group as a whole. This causes subgroup favoritism and negatively affects information flow across subgroup boundaries or *faultlines* (Lau & Murnighan, 1998; 2005). The importance of the in-group versus out-group categorization and their associated norms for interpersonal interactions seems relevant here. That is, the interactions among a Chinese sub-group with an overall task group should reflect a much more complex set of interaction norms than would an instrumental interaction across the faultline. We would thus expect significantly different within and between sub-group interactions depending on the cultural composition of sub-groups within a larger task group.

A third way in which culture influences group process is through the extent to which each individual in the group is culturally different from the other group members. Culturally different group members are aware that they are different, and the salience of this awareness causes them to compare themselves to other group members (Bochner & Ohsako, 1997; Bochner & Perks, 1971). Based on this comparison, they evaluate the appropriateness of their behavior in relationship to their status in the work group (Mullen, 1987; Mullen & Baumeister, 1987). The relative difference perceived by individuals from other group members also influences the extent to which they identify with the task group versus their own cultural group.

In general, group members' willingness to participate depends on the salience of the task group identity versus that of their cultural group (e.g. Wit & Kerr, 2002). Greater cultural distance between Chinese and other group members has been shown to influence their perception of conflict in the group and the Chinese willingness to express their ideas (Thomas, 1999). For Chinese, the establishment of a common group identity among out-group members may be more difficult than the activation of concepts of *mianzi* and *renqing* among in-group members.

In summary, the influence of culture is evident through the three mechanisms of culturally based norms, the cultural diversity of the group, and the relative cultural distance of group members. Understanding the Chinese case is facilitated by reference to the interactionist perspective of behavior, perception, attribution and response as well as to specific Chinese norms and motives in social behavior in the context of groups.

Conclusion

We began this chapter by identifying a general model of cultural influence in inter-cultural interactions. This model presents a behavioral sequence between culturally different actors that involves a number of conduits which are influenced by specific aspects of Chinese culture, such as the salience of situational cues, culturally based scripts and expectations, selective perception, out-group identification and attitudes toward out-groups, the situational context, and the motivational influence of the self-concept. We then demonstrated the utility of examining cross-cultural interactions in this way by examining the specific case of Chinese interactions in cross-cultural negotiation and in multicultural groups.

In so doing we highlighted the fact that in any intercultural interaction we must keep in mind that there are at least two cultures involved. Our understanding is thus much improved by a consideration of the effects of selective perception across cultures influenced by attention to context, differential attribution and the culture-specific norms for social interaction which are determined with reference to the culturally different others and the social context.

Authors' note

Correspondence concerning this chapter should be addressed to the authors, Segal Graduate School of Business, Simon Fraser University, 500 Granville Street, Vancouver, BC, V6C 1W6, Canada. Email: dcthomas@sfu.ca; yuan_liao@sfu.ca.

References

Abel, T. M. & Hsu, F. I. (1949). Some aspects of personality of Chinese as revealed by the Rorschach Test. *Journal of Projective Techniques, 13*, 285–301.

Adair, W. L. & Brett, J. M. (2004). Culture and negotiation process. In M. J. Gelfand & J. M. Brett (eds), *The handbook of negotiation and culture* (pp. 158 – 176). Stanford, CA: Stanford University Press.

Bagley, C. (1995). Field independence in children in group-oriented cultures: Comparisons from China, Japan, and North America. *Journal of Social Psychology, 135*, 523–525.

Bettenhausen, K. L. & Murnighan, J. K. (1991). The development of an intragroup norm and the effects of interpersonal and structural changes. *Administrative Science Quarterly, 36*, 20–35.

Bochner, S. & Ohsako, T. (1977). Ethnic role salience in racially homogeneous and heterogeneous societies. *Journal of Cross-Cultural Psychology, 8*, 477–492.

Bochner, S. & Perks, R. W. (1971). National role evocation as a function of cross-national interaction. *Journal of Cross-Cultural Psychology, 2*, 157–164.

Bond, M. H. & Forgas, J. (1984). Linking person perception to behavior intention across cultures: The role of cultural collectivism. *Journal of Cross-Cultural Psychology, 15*, 337–352.

Bond, M. H. & Hwang, K. K. (1986). The social psychology of the Chinese people. In M. H. Bond (ed.), *The psychology of the Chinese people* (pp. 213–266). Hong Kong: Oxford University Press.

Bond, M. H. & Lee, P. W. H. (1981). Face saving in Chinese culture: A discussion and experimental study of Hong Kong students. In A. Y. C. King & R. P. L. Lee (eds), *Social life and development in Hong Kong* (pp. 289–304). Hong Kong: Chinese University Press.

Bond, M. H., Leung, K., & Schwartz, S. (1992). Explaining choices in procedural and distributive justice across cultures. *International Journal of Psychology, 27*, 211–225.

Bond, M. H., Wan, K. C., Leung, K. & Giacolone, R. A. (1985). How are responses to verbal insult related to cultural collectivism and power distance? *Journal of Cross-Cultural Psychology, 16*, 111–127.

Bond, M. H. & Wang, S. H. (1983). Aggressive behavior in Chinese society: The problem of maintaining order and harmony. In A. P. Goldstein & M. Segall (eds), *Global perspectives on aggression* (pp. 58–74). New York: Pergamon.

Brett, J. & Crotty, S. (2008) Culture and negotiation. In P. B. Smith, M. F. Peterson, & D. C. Thomas (eds), *Handbook of cross-cultural management research* (pp. 269–284). Thousand Oaks, CA: Sage.

Brett, J. M., Tinsley, C. H., Shapiro, D. L., & Okumura, T. (2007). Intervening in employee disputes: How and when will managers from China, Japan, and the U. S. act differently? *Management & Organization Review, 3*, 183–204.

Buchan, N. R., Croson, R., & Dawes, R. M. (2002). Swift neighbors and persistent strangers: A cross-cultural investigation of trust and reciprocity in social exchange. *American Journal of Sociology, 108*, 168–206.

Cai, D., Wilson, S. R., & Drake, L. (2000). Culture in the context of intercultural negotiation: Individualism–Collectivism and paths to integrative agreements. *Human Communication Research, 26*, 591–617.

Chiu, C., Morris, M. W., Hong, Y., & Menon, T. (2000). Motivated cultural cognition: The impact of implicit cultural theories on dispositional attribution varies as a function of need fro closure. *Journal of Personality and Social Psychology, 78*, 247–259.

Crittenden, K. S. (1996). Causal attribution processes among the Chinese. In M. H. Bond (ed.), *The handbook of Chinese psychology* (pp. 263–279). Hong Kong: Oxford University Press.

Drake, L. (2001). The culture–negotiation link: Integrative and distributive bargaining through an intercultural communication lens. *Human Communication Research, 27*, 317–349.

Earley, P. C. (1989). Social loafing and collectivism: A comparison of the US and the People's Republic of China. *Administrative Science Quarterly, 34*, 565–581.

Earley, P. C. (1993). East meets West meets Mid-East: Further explorations of collectivist and individualist work groups. *Academy of Management Journal, 36*, 319–348.

Earley, P. C. & Mosakowski, E. (2000). Creating hybrid team cultures: An empirical test of transnational team functioning. *Academy of Management Journal, 43*, 26–49.

Elron, E. (1997). Top management teams within multinational corporations: Effects of cultural heterogeneity. *Leadership Quarterly, 8*, 393–412.

Fang, T. (1997). *Chinese business negotiating style: A socio-cultural approach.* Linköping University Press: Linköping, Sweden.

Ferraro, G. P. (2006). *The cultural dimension of international business.* Englewood Cliffs, NJ: Prentice Hall.

Forgas, J. P. & Bond, M. H. (1985). Cultural influences on the perception of interaction episodes. *Personality and Social Psychology Bulletin, 11*, 75–88.

Fu, H., Morris, M. W., Lee, S., Chao, M., Chiu, C., & Hong, H. (2007). Epistemic motives and cultural conformity: Need for closure, culture and context as determinants of conflict judgments. *Journal of Personality and Social Psychology, 92*, 191–197.

Gabrenya, W. K. & Hwang, K.-K. (1996). Chinese social interaction: Harmony and hierarchy on the good earth. In M. H. Bond (ed.), *The handbook of Chinese psychology* (pp. 309–321). Hong Kong: Oxford University Press.

Gao, G., Ting-Toomey, S., & Gudykunst, W. B. (1996). Chinese communication process. In M. H. Bond (ed.), *The handbook of Chinese psychology* (pp. 280–293). Hong Kong: Oxford University Press.

Gelfand, M. J. & Cai, D. A. (2004). Cultural structuring of the social context of negotiation. In M. J. Gelfand & J. M. Brett (eds), The *handbook of negotiation and culture* (pp. 238–257). Stanford, CA: Stanford University Press.

Gelfand, M. J., Higgins, M., Nishii, L. H., Raver, J. L., Dominguez, A. Murakami, F., Yamaguchi, S., & Toyama, M. (2002). Culture and egocentric perceptions of fairness in conflict and negotiation. *Journal of Applied Psychology, 87*, 833–856.

Gelfand, M. J., Nishii, L. H., Holcombe, K. M., Dyer, N., Ohbuchi, K., & Fukuno, M. (2001). Cultural influences on cognitive representations of conflict: Interpretations of conflict episodes in the United Sates and Japan. *Journal of Applied Psychology, 86*, 1059–1074.

Gelfand, M. J., Nishii, L. H., & Raver, J. L. (2006). On the nature and importance of cultural tightness–looseness. *Journal of Applied Psychology, 91*, 1225–1244.

Gelfand, M. J. & Realo, A. (1999). Individualism–collectivism and accountability in intergroup negotiations. *Journal of Applied Psychology, 84*, 721–736.

Gibson, C. B. & Zellmer-Bruhn, M. E. (2001). Metaphors and meaning: An intercultural analysis of the concept of teamwork. *Administrative Science Quarterly, 46*, 274–303.

Graham, J. L., Kim, D. K., Lin, C.-Y., & Robinson, M. (1988). Buyer–seller negotiations around the Pacific rim: Differences in fundamental exchange process. *Journal of Consumer Research, 15*, 48–54.

Gudykunst, W. B. (2001). *Asian American ethnicity and communication.* Thousand Oaks, CA: Sage.

Gudykunst, W. B., & Bond, M. H. (1997). Intergroup relations across cultures. In J. Berry, M. Segall, & Ç. Kağıtçıbaşı (eds), *Handbook of cross-cultural psychology, Vol. 3* (pp. 119–161). Needham Heights, MA: Allyn & Bacon.

Gudykunst, W. B., Ting-Toomey, S. & Chua, E. (1988). *Culture and interpersonal communication.* Newbury Park, CA: Sage.

Hackman, J. R. (1991). *Groups that work (and those that don't).* San Francisco, CA: Jossey Bass.

Hall, E. T. (1976). *Beyond culture.* New York: Doubleday.

Hallowell, A. I. (1955). *Culture and experience.* Philadelphia, PA: University of Pennsylvania Press.

Hattrup, K. & Jackson, S. E. (1996). Learning about individual differences by taking situations seriously. In K. R. Murphy (ed.), *Individual differences and behavior in organizations* (pp. 507–547). San Francisco, CA: Jossey-Bass.

Hewstone, M. (1990). The 'ultimate attribution error'? A review of the literature on intergroup causal attribution. *European Journal of Social Psychology, 20*, 614–623.

Hewstone, M. & Ward, C. (1985). Ethnocentrism and casual attribution in Southeast Asia. *Journal of Personality and Social Psychology, 48*, 614–623.

Ho, D. (1976). On the concept of face. *The American Journal of Sociology,81*, 867–884.

Hofstede, G. (1980). *Culture's consequences: International differences in work-related values.* Beverly Hills, CA: Sage.

Hofstede, G. (2001). *Culture's consequences: Comparing values, behaviors, institutions and organizations across nations.* Thousand Oaks, CA: Sage Publications.

Hofstede, G. & Usunier, J. C. (1996). Hofstede's dimensions of culture and their influence on internatiuonal business negotiations. In P. Ghauri & J. C. Usunier (eds), *International business negotiations* (pp. 119–129). Oxford, England: Pergamon.

Hong, Y., Chiu, C., & Kung, T. (1997). Bringing culture out in front: Effects of cultural meaning system activation on social cognition. In K. Leung, Y. Kashima, U. Kim, & S. Yamaguchi (eds), *Progress in Asian social psychology* (vol. 1, pp. 135–146). Singapore: Wiley.

Hong, Y., Morris, M. W., Chiu, C., & Benet-Martínez, V. (2000). Multicultural minds: A dynamic constructivist approach to culture and cognition. *American Psychologist, 55*, 709–720.

Hsu, F. L. K. (1971). Psychological homeostasis and *jen*: Conceptual tools for advancing psychological anthropology. *American Anthropologist, 73*, 23–44.

Hu, H. C. (1944). The Chinese concept of 'face'. *American Anthropologist, 46*, 45–64.

Hwang, K. K. (1987). Face and favor: The Chinese power game. *American Journal of Sociology, 92*, 944–974.

Hwang, K. K. (1987). Human emotion and *mien-tzu*: The Chinese power game. In K. S. Yang (ed.), *The psychology of the Chinese* (pp. 289–318). Taipei, Taiwan: Kui-Kuan Books, Inc. (in Chinese)

Hwang, K. K. (1997–8). *Guanxi* and *mientze*: Conflict resolution in Chinese society. *Intercultural Communication Studies, 7*, 17–42.

Ip, G. W. M. & Bond, M. H. (1995). Culture, values, and the spontaneous self-concept. *Asian Journal of Psychology, 1*, 30–36.

Kam, C. C. S. & Bond, M. H. (2008). The role of emotions and behavioral responses in mediating the impact of face loss on relationship deterioration: Are Chinese more face-sensitive than Americans? *Asian Journal of Social Psychology, 11*, 175–184.

Kashima, Y. (2001). Culture and social cognition: Toward a social psychology of cultural dynamics. In D. Matsumoto (ed.), *The handbook of culture and psychology* (pp. 325–360). New York: Oxford University Press.

Kashima, Y., Yamaguchi, S., & Kim, U. (1995). Culture, gender, and self: A perspective from individualism–collectivism research. *Journal of Personality and Social Psychology, 69*, 925–937.

King, A. Y. C. & Bond, M. H. (1985). The Confucian paradigm of man. In W. S. Tseng & D. Y. H. Wu (eds), *Chinese culture and mental health: An overview* (pp. 29–45). Orlando, FL: Academic Press.

Kitayama, S., Duffy, S., & Uchida, Y. (2007). Self as a cultural mode of being. In S. Kitayama & D. Cohen (eds), *Handbook of cultural psychology* (pp 136–174). New York: Guilford.

Kitayama, S., Markus, H. R., Matsumoto, H., & Norasakkunkit, V. (1997). Individual and collective process in the construction of the self: Self-enhancement in the United States and self-deprecation in Japan. *Journal of Personality and Social Psychology, 72*, 1245–1267.

Knowles, E. D., Morris, M. W., Chiu, C., & Hong, Y. (2001). Culture and the process of person perception: Evidence for automaticity among East Asians in correcting for situational influences on behavior. *Personality and Social Psychology Bulletin, 27*, 1344–1356.

Kühnen, U. & Oyserman, D. (2002). Thinking about the self influences thinking in general: Cognitive consequences of salient self-concept. *Journal of Experimental Social Psychology, 38*, 492–499.

Lau, D. C. & Murnighan, J. K. (1998). Demographic diversity and faultlines: The compositional dynamics of organizational groups. *Academy of Management Review, 23*, 325–340.

Leung, K. (1987). Some determinants of reactions to procedural models of conflict resolution: A cross-national study. *Journal of Personality and Social Psychology, 53*, 898–908.

Leung, K. (1988). Some determinants of conflict avoidance. *Journal of Cross-Cultural Psychology, 19*, 125–136.

Leung, K. & Bond, M. H. (1984). The impact of cultural collectivism on reward allocation. *Journal of Personality and Social Psychology, 47,* 793–804.

Leung, K. & Wu, P.-G. (1990). Dispute processing: A cross-cultural analysis. In R. Brislin (ed.), *Applied cross-cultural psychology* (Vol. 14, pp. 209–231). Newbury Park, CA: Sage.

Leung, T. K. P. & Chan, R. K. K. (2003). Face, favour and positioning – a Chinese power game. *European Journal of Marketing, 37,* 1575–1598.

Li, H. Z. (2001). Co-operative and intrusive interruptions in inter- and intra-cultural dyadic discourse. *Journal of Language and Social Psychology, 20,* 259–284.

Li, H. Z. (2004). Gaze and mutual gaze in inter- and intra-cultural conversation in simulated physician–patient conversations. *International Journal of Language and Communication, 20,* 3–26.

Li, H. Z. (2006). Backchannel responses as misleading feedback in intercultural discourse. *Journal of Intercultural Communication Research, 35,* 99–116.

Lieberman, M. D., Jarcho, J. M., & Obayashi, J. (2005). Attributional inference across cultures: Similar automatic attributions and different controlled corrections. *Personality and Social Psychology Bulletin, 31,* 889–901.

Lieberman, M. D., Ochsner, K. N., Gilbert, D. T., & Trope, Y. (2002). Reflection and reflexion: A social-cognitive neuroscience approach to attributional inference. *Advances in Experimental Social Psychology, 34,* 199–249.

Lu, Y. & Hsu, C.-F. (2008). Willingness to communicate in intercultural interactions between Chinese and Americans. *Journal of Intercultural Communication Reserarch, 37,* 75–88.

Maddox, W. W. & Yuki, M. (2006). The 'ripple effect': Cultural differences in perceptions of the consequences of events. *Personality and Social Psychology Bulletin, 32,* 669–683.

Markus, H. (1977). Self-schemata and processing information about the self. *Journal of Personality and Social Psychology, 35,* 63–78.

Markus, H. R. & Kitayama, S. (1991). Culture and the self: Implications for cognition, emotion, and motivation. *Psychological Review, 98,* 224–253.

McAuley, P., Bond, M. H., & Kashima, E. (2002). Towards defining situations objectively: A culture-level analysis of role dyads in Hong Kong and Australia. *Journal of Cross-Cultural Psychology, 33,* 363–380.

McLeod, P. L., Lobel, S. A., & Cox, T. H. (1996). Ethnic diversity and creativity in small groups. *Small Group Research, 27(2),* 248–264.

Menon, T., Morris, M. W., Chiu, C., & Hong, Y. (1999). Culture and the construal of agency: Attribution to individual versus group dispositions. *Journal of Personality and Social Psychology, 76,* 701–717.

Mischel, W. (1977). The interaction of person and situation. In D. Magnusson & N. S. Endler (eds), *Personality at the crossroads: Current issues in interactional psychology* (pp. 333–352). Hillsdale, NJ: Lawrence Erlbaum Associates.

Morris, M. W. & Fu, H.-Y. (2001). How does culture influence conflict resolution? A dynamic constructivist analysis. *Social Cognition, 19,* 324–349.

Morris, M. W. & Peng, K. (1994). Culture and cause: American and Chinese attributions for social and psychical events. *Journal of Personality and Social Psychology, 67,* 949–971.

Mullen, B. (1987). Self-attention theory: The effects of group composition on the individual. In B. Mullen & G. R. Goethals (eds), *Theories of group behaviour* (pp. 125–46). New York: Springer-Verlag.

Mullen, B. & Baumeister R. F. (1987). Groups effects on self-attention and performance: Social loafing, social facilitation, and social impairment. In C. Hendrick (ed.), *Review of personality and social psychology* (pp. 189–206). Newbury Park, CA: Sage.

Nisbett, R. E., Peng, K., Choi, I., & Norenzayan, A. (2001). Culture and systems of thought: Holistic versus analytic cognition. *Psychological Review, 108,* 291–310.

Oetzel, J. G. & Ting-Toomey, S. (2003). Face concerns in interpersonal conflict: A cross-cultural empirical test of face-negotiation theory. *Communication Research, 30,* 599–624.

Park, D. C., Nisbett, R. E., & Hedden, T. (1999). Culture, cognition, and aging. *Journal of Gerontology 54,* 75–84.

Park, Y. S. & Kim, B. S. K. (2008). Asian and European cultural values and communication styles among Asian American and European American college students. *Cultural Diversity and Ethnic Minority Psychology, 14,* 47–56.

Peng, K. & Nisbett, R. E. (1999). Culture, dialectics, and reasoning about contradiction. *American Psychologist, 54,* 741–754.

Pye, L. (1982). *Chinese commercial negotiating style.* Cambridge, MA: Oelgeschlager.

Ross, L. (1977). The intuitive psychologist and his shortcomings. In L. Berkowitz (ed.), *Advances in experimental social psychology* (Vol. 10, pp. 173–220). New York: Academic Press.

Ross, L. & Nisbett, R. E. (1991). *The person and the situation: Perspectives of social psychology.* Philadelphia, PA: Temple University Press.

Redding, S. G. & Ng, M. (1982). The role of 'face' in the organizational perceptions of Chinese managers. *Organization Studies, 3,* 201–219.

Sanchez-Burks, Lee, F., Choi, I., Nisbett, R. Zhao, S., & Koo, J. (2003). Conversing across cultures: East–West communication styles in work and nonwork contexts. *Journal of Personality and Social Psychology, 85,* 363–372.

Schuster, B., Fosterlung, F., & Weiner, B. (1989). Perceiving the causes of success and failure. *Journal of Cross-Cultural Psychology, 20,* 191–213.

Shaw, J. B. (1990). A cognitive categorization model for the study of intercultural management. *Academy of Management Review, 15,* 626–645.

Shenkar, O. & Ronen, S. (1987). The cultural context of negotiations: The implications of Chinese interpersonal norms. *Journal of Applied Behavioral Science, 23*, 263–275.

Shweder, R. A. & Bourne, E. J. (1984). Does the concept of the person vary cross-culturally? In R. A. Shweder & R. A. LeVine (eds), *Culture theory* (pp. 158–199). Cambridge, England: Cambridge University Press.

Smith, P. B. & Bond, M. H. (1999). *Social psychology across cultures.* Boston, MA: Allyn and Bacon.

Spencer-Rodgers, J., Williams, M. J., Hamilton, D. L., Peng, K., & Wang, L. (2007). Culture and group perception: Dispositional and stereotypic inferences about novel and national groups. *Journal of Personality and Social Psychology, 93*, 525–543.

Tajfel, H. (1981). *Human groups and social categories.* Cambridge, England: Cambridge University Press.

Tetlock, P. E. (1985). Accountability: The neglected social context of judgment and choice. In L. L. Cummings & B. M. Staw (eds), *Research in organizational behavior* (vol. 7, pp. 297–332). Greenwich, CT: JAI Press.

Thomas, D. C. (1999). Cultural diversity and work group effectiveness: An experimental study. *Journal of Cross-Cultural Psychology, 30*, 242–263.

Thomas, D. C. (2002). *Essentials of international management: A cross-cultural perspective.* Thousand Oaks, CA: Sage.

Thomas, D. C. (2008). *Cross-cultural management: Essential concepts.* Thousand Oaks, CA: Sage.

Thomas, D. C., Ravlin, E. C., & Wallace, A. W. (1996). Effect of cultural diversity in work groups. *Research in Sociology of Organizations, 14*, 1–33.

Ting-Toomey, S (1988). Intercultural conflict styles. In Y. Y. Kim & W. B. Gudykunst (eds), *Theories in intercultural communication* (pp. 213–238). Beverly Hills, CA: Sage.

Ting-Toomey, S. (1988). A face-negotiation theory. In Y. Y. Kim & W. B. Gudykunst (eds), *Theory in intercultural communication.* Newbury Park, CA: Sage.

Trubisky, P., Ting-Toomey, S., & Lin, S. (1991). The influence of individualism–collectivism and self-monitoring on conflict styles. *International Journal of Intercultural Relations, 15*, 65–84.

Tse, D. K., Francis, J., & Walls, J. (1994). Cultural differences in conducting intra- and inter-cultural negotiations: A Sino–Canadian comparison. *Journal of International Business Studies, 25*, 537–555.

Wilder, D. A. (1986). Social categorization: Implications for creation and reduction of intergroup bias. In L. Berkowitz (ed.), *Advances in Experimental Social Psychology* (Vol. 19, pp. 291–355). New York: Academic Press.

Wit, A. P. & Kerr, N. L. (2002). 'Me versus just us versus us all' categorization and cooperation in nested social dilemmas. *Journal of Personality and Social Psychology, 83*, 616–637.

Witkin, H. A. & Goodenough, D. R. (1977). Field dependence and interpersonal behavior. *Psychological Bulletin, 84*, 661–689.

Yang, C.-F. (2006). The Chinese conception of self: Toward a person-making perspective. In U. Kim, K.-S. Yang, & K.-K. Hwang (eds), *Indigenous and cultural psychology* (pp. 327–356). New York: Springer.

Yang, K. S. (1988). Will societal modernization eventually eliminate cross-cultural psychological difference? In M H. Bond (ed.), *The cross-cultural challenge to social psychology* (pp. 67–85), Newbury Park, CA: Sage.

Yang, K. S. (1992). The social orientation of Chinese. In K. S. Yang & A. B. Yu (eds), *Chinese psychology and behaviors: Methods and concepts* (pp. 67–85). Taipei, Taiwan: Gui Guan. (in Chinese)

Yeung, L. N.-T. (2000). The question of Chinese indirectness: A comparison of Chinese and English participative decision-making discourse. *Multilingua, 19*, 221–264.

CHAPTER 40

On the distinctiveness of Chinese psychology; or: Are we all Chinese?

Peter B. Smith

The basic framework for research in many areas of psychology has derived principally from the extensive range of studies conducted over the past hundred years on and by that small proportion of the world's population that resides in North America. The publication of the second edition of this handbook provides an unrivalled opportunity to evaluate the extent to which the results of psychological investigation would have been different if contemporary psychology had derived instead primarily from studies of Chinese persons.

This chapter briefly identifies some of the key areas in which it has thus far been argued that there is something different or distinctive about the psychology of ethnic Chinese. In other chapters within this handbook there is extensive discussion as to whether the Chinese have, for instance, distinctive ways of thinking, different values, different beliefs, a different structure of personality, different forms of influence, distinctive family dynamics, a preoccupation with relationship harmony, and a distinctive conception of face. The major part of this chapter will be focused on examining the extent to which studies conducted in other parts of the world have also identified some of these supposedly distinctive Chinese attributes.

Preliminary issues

In order to address these matters, some preliminary clarifications are in order. Firstly, if we say that a psychological phenomenon is distinctively Chinese, does this mean that it is must be absent from other cultural contexts, or does it just mean that the effect is more strongly present among Chinese, but to some degree universally present? Secondly, how shall the concept of Chineseness be defined operationally? Is a distinctively Chinese phenomenon established if it is found to be present solely within the People's Republic of China, or must it also be present within other nations with predominantly Chinese ethnicity, and among Chinese who are citizens of nations that are not predominantly Chinese? As Hong, Yang and Chiu (this volume) note, answers to these questions are important, but not easily established.

Thirdly, how shall we know whether an effect is distinctive or not? Researchers with a universalistic orientation have mostly employed 'imposed-etic' research designs (Berry, 1969), assuming that their measures are valid everywhere until evidence emerges that they are not. On the other hand, indigenous researchers have built 'emic' models of locally salient phenomena, but have rarely examined whether these phenomena are also salient or useful in other cultural contexts. It is difficult to integrate these two perspectives, because they often differ not only in terms of substance but also in terms of preferred way of conducting an investigation. Where there is some convergence of research method, the presence of distinctiveness can be tested. For instance, Katigbak, Church, Guanzon-Lapena, Carlota, and del Pilar (2002) compared the Big Five personality inventory (Costa & McCrae, 1992) with indigenously developed Filipino personality inventories. Substantial overlap was found. More frequently, tests for distinctiveness have been made by translating and transporting measures from one location to another. For instance, Ayçiçegi (1993) administered an instrument addressing distinctive Mexican beliefs to Turkish respondents in Turkey and found that all items were also strongly endorsed by Turks. This latter approach provides a first test of distinctiveness, but is weaker than the former because it includes no locally constructed measure.

The predominant motive of many of the researchers engaged in indigenous approaches to psychology has understandably been to find ways of addressing local priorities and concerns most adequately, rather than of contributing to a global psychology (Allwood & Berry, 2005; Yang, this volume). Where indigenous psychology has been particularly strongly developed, for instance in Taiwan, some consequent difficulties have arisen in integrating the perspectives and career paths of locally-trained and foreign-trained psychologists (Gabrenya, Kung, & Chen, 2006). Taiwanese indigenous psychologists prefer to publish in Chinese, but the Taiwan Ministry of Education favors publication in international journals. Foreign-trained Taiwanese psychologists tend to have internalized US criteria for evaluating the worth of a project and are sometimes dismissive of the indigenous perspective.

The perspective of the present chapter follows the often-cited assertion by Kluckhohn and Murray (1948): 'Every man is in certain respects (a) like all other men, (b) like some other men, (c) like no other man' (p. 53). Thus at the broadest level there is no reason to expect that Chinese persons differ from the rest of humankind. At increasingly specific levels of analysis, however, it becomes more and more likely that distinctive effects will become apparent. It is these latter effects upon which indigenous psychologists have most frequently focused. Where evidence of distinctiveness is found, the responsibility falls to cross-cultural psychologists to advance theories that might explain why these effects are found. If appropriate theories can achieve this goal, then effects that are locally distinctive can also contribute to a more adequately global psychology than is provided currently by the fruits of what has so far been an essentially North American indigenous psychology.

Theorizing by cross-cultural psychologists has largely been driven by the identification of dimensions of cultural variation by Hofstede (1980), Schwartz (2004) and others. The classification of national cultures along the dimensions of individualism-collectivism and power distance has been particularly influential. Chinese cultures are found to be collectivist and high on power distance (Bond, 1996; Hofstede, 2001), or in terms of more recent data, high on embeddedness and hierarchy (Schwartz, 2004). Consequently, the primary question to be addressed is whether phenomena reported to be distinctively Chinese are also found in other national contexts that have a similar cultural profile. A second question concerns the extent to which the cultural similarities and differences that are found should be thought of as deep-seated and immutable, or as adaptations that are likely to change as circumstances change.

Indigenous Chinese phenomena

Ho, Peng, Lai, and Chan (2001) identify relatedness between persons as the central focus of indigenous Chinese psychology. They note that the self in Confucian thought is essentially relational, whereas in Hindu, Dao and Buddhist writings it is not (see also Hwang & Han, this volume). Thus, relatedness may be characteristic of Confucian cultures such as those found in China, Japan and Korea, but is not to be equated with the broader concept of collectivism. In their view, the study of relatedness requires a relational methodology. This entails the study of role relationships rather than the study of individuals. Examples within the existing literature include taxonomies of role relationships (McAuley, Bond, & Kashima, 2002), conceptualizations of face (Ting-Toomey, 1988; Hwang &

Han, this volume), of *guanxi* relationships (Hwang & Han, this volume; Liu, Li, & Yue, this volume), of relationship harmony (Kwan, Bond, & Singelis, 1997) and of socially-oriented achievement orientation (Hau, this volume; Yu, 1996).

The interrelatedness of the Confucian cultures of East Asia is also emphasized within a separate strand of conceptualization. Markus and Kitayama's (1991) focus on the interdependence of individuals within Japan rather than the independence of US individuals has led to an extensive series of studies of contrasts between East-Asian and North-American cognition. East Asians are said to think holistically, while North Americans are said to think analytically (Ji, Lam, & Guo, this volume; Nisbett, Peng, Choi, & Norenzayan, 2000).

A third set of studies comprises emic investigations conducted within China that have made no specific prior assumptions as to what phenomena will be identified, but which have employed traditional survey methodology. Here we find for instance, the Chinese Personality Assessment Inventory (Cheung, Cheung, Leung, Ward & Leong, 2003), the Chinese Classification of Mental Disorders (Stewart, Lee, & Tao, this volume; Young, 1989), and studies of paternalistic leadership (Chen & Farh, this volume; Cheng, Chou, Huang, Wu, & Farh, 2004).

Types of distinctiveness

In the remainder of this chapter, evidence for and against two types of Chinese distinctiveness is explored. Firstly, what evidence is there that similar phenomena to those listed above are present in collectivist cultures outside of East Asia? Secondly what evidence is there that the phenomena listed above can be found, or at least elicited in more individualistic cultural contexts?

Values and beliefs in collectivistic cultures

In his modeling of the structure of human values, Schwartz (1992) proposed that members of all cultures face three fundamental problems: provision for biological needs, coordination of individuals' interactions with one another, and the survival and welfare of groups. In addressing these needs, members of a culture prioritize differing sets of values, dependent on the salience of each set of needs. In collectivistic cultures, embeddedness and hierarchy are more strongly valued than elsewhere and autonomy is less valued than elsewhere. Bond (1996) reported a cluster analysis of 36 nation-level value profiles derived from teachers within Schwartz's (1994) dataset. The four Chinese samples within this set were derived from China, Hong Kong, Taiwan and Singapore. The Chinese samples did not cluster together, each resembling more closely the profiles from quite different nations. Hong Kong values resembled those from Israel, those from Singapore resembled Malaysia and mainland China came closest to the data from Zimbabwe. The Taiwan profile was particularly distinct from the other three Chinese profiles.

One could argue that the Chinese samples do not cluster together because the imposed etic nature of the Schwartz Value Survey fails to tap distinctive Chinese values. However, Bond (1996) reported a similar cluster analysis using the individual-level data from students in 21 nations to his Chinese Values Survey (Bond, 1988). The Chinese samples were once again shown to be diverse. A similar procedure was also followed by Leung and Bond (2004), clustering the profiles of beliefs endorsed by students in 40 nations. Here some similarity was found in the profiles for Hong Kong, China and Singapore, but Taiwan was again rather separate.

These findings do not deny that there are similarities between national cultures that are ethnically Chinese. However, they emphasize that Chinese cultures also have a good deal in common with cultures that are neither Confucian nor Asian. Values and beliefs are expressed in relatively generalized, situation-free ways. It may be possible to identify greater degrees of cultural distinctiveness by focusing on how these values and beliefs are operationalized by specific behaviours. There are possible candidates in relation to each of the major issues identified by Schwartz (1992). Let us consider first the universal goal identified by Schwartz as group survival and welfare.

Achieving harmony

The achievement of harmony within Chinese culture has been emphasized by many researchers. Chinese life satisfaction is distinctively linked with relationship harmony (Kwan et al., 1997; Lu, this volume). The question to be addressed is whether Chinese paths to harmony are distinctive. Four aspects can be considered:

Face. Extensive discussions and analyses of the concept of face within Chinese culture are available (Hwang & Han, this volume). The giving, maintaining, and promoting of face involves the exercise of role-appropriate behaviour. However almost all published comparative studies of face have involved contrasts between Chinese and American respondents. We have only anecdotal evidence of the management of face within non-Chinese collectivist cultures. Within Chinese culture, a major distinction has long been noted between *lian* (perceived moral rectitude) and *mianzi* (social reputation in a given setting) (see also Cheng, Lo, & Chio, this volume).

A similar distinction exists within the languages spoken in many non-Chinese Asian nations. Choi and Lee (2002) identify *chemyon* (face) as a key concept within Korean society, also differentiable into moral and success components. They propose that *chemyon, mianzi* and the Japanese concept of *mentsu* refer to closely similar concepts and processes. In Thailand, the system of values favoring harmony gives emphasis to individual responsibility for acting appropriately (*kreng jai*) and interpersonal obligation (*bunkhun*, 'indebted goodness') (Komin, 1990). These concerns also suggest parallels with Chinese *lian* and *mianzi.* Among the Malay population in Malaysia, we find a distinction between individual responsibility (*adab*) and interpersonal obligation (*budi*) (Abdullah, 1996). *Budi* entails a continuing set of reciprocal obligations that may even be passed to the next generation. Thus, linguistic distinctions resembling those that have been explored within Chinese culture also exist within neighbouring national cultures within which Chinese persons are present only as a minority.

Communication style. If we spread the net more widely, harmony is also a highly esteemed value in many other collectivist nations. Indeed values such as 'reciprocation of favors' and 'protection of my public face' contributed to the definition of Schwartz's (2004) definition of Embeddedness, which approximates to collectivism. While giving and maintaining face preserves harmony, it can also be maintained through indirect communication, especially within the in-group. Hall (1966) first proposed a distinction between high-context and low-context cultures. Within high-context cultures, he suggested that role relationships between persons are typically well established, and that there is therefore less need to spell out directly and explicitly what is to be communicated. Kim (1994) elaborated a model of what she termed the conversational constraints that might be found within high-context cultures. These include constraining oneself not to hurt the feelings of the other party and not to impose oneself on others (see Cheng et al., this volume; Xu, this volume).

The recent survey of emotional display rules across 32 nations (Matsumoto, Yoo, Fontaine et al., 2008) provides an opportunity to evaluate the distinctiveness of Chinese communicative style. Two Chinese samples were included in this study. Hong Kong respondents were found to be less emotionally expressive than those from any of the other nations. However, the data from China was placed in the midrange. Respondents from 13 other nations reported greater constraint in expressing emotions than did the Chinese (see also Wong, Bond, & Rodriguez Mosquera, 2008). The measures employed by Matsumoto et al. detected no difference among their respondents between constraint in expressing positive emotions and negative emotions, as might have been surmised from previous work on the expression of emotions in Chinese culture (Bond, 1993).

In order to discern the degree to which Chinese ways of maintaining harmony are distinctive, it may be necessary to differentiate between types of emotional expression and to compare the intensity with which different emotions are expressed. Harmony in Latin American cultures rests on the creation and maintenance of *simpatía* between the parties interacting with one another (Triandis, Lisansky, Marin, & Betancourt, 1984). No empirical studies are available, but it appears that the state of *simpatía* within in-group relationships involves the constraint of negative emotional expression and overt expression of positive emotions. Similar possibilities of differentiated expression across social contexts are worthy of investigation within Chinese cultural groups.

Modesty. Hwang and Han (this volume) report studies showing that their Taiwanese respondents had greater fear of losing face through behaving in ways that rendered them vertically distinctive than through behaving ways that made them horizontally distinctive. This effect relates to current debates as to whether self-enhancement is a universal motive or whether it is absent or weaker in East Asian cultures. Heine, Lehman, Markus, and Kitayama (1999) presented evidence suggesting that East Asians do not seek to present themselves in self-enhancing ways. Sedikides, Gaertner, and Toguchi (2003) countered with evidence favoring the universal need for self-enhancement, but they used a different research method. Kwan, Kwang, and Hui (in press) have also recently shown that Chinese students score higher on a measure of narcissism than US students.

Several studies now suggest a resolution of this debate (Sedikides, Gaertner, & Vevea, 2005). Gaertner, Sedikides, and Chang (2008) showed that Taiwanese respondents did show self-enhancement when ask to rate themselves on attributes related to collectivism, but not when they rated themselves on individualistic attributes. Kurman (2003) compared self-enhancement by Singapore Chinese and Israeli high school students. In both nations those who rated themselves *low* were those who also rated themselves high on the importance of appearing modest. Modesty is also positively valued in Western nations (Sedikides, Gregg, & Hart, 2007), but it is the link between high valuation of modesty and low self-enhancement that appears to be distinctive to East Asian nations. In a study in Japan, Muramoto (2003) asked students to rate how others would evaluate them if they were to present themselves in a modest fashion. She found that her respondents expected that others would think more highly of them if they were modest. Thus, Muramoto's results confirm the view that East-Asian modesty has a distinctive link with the universal need for self-regard (see also Kwan, Hui, & McGee, this volume).

Group honor. In their discussion of face, Hwang and Han (this volume) also identify a distinction between 'small face' and 'big face'. Big face refers to the reputation of one's group, particularly one's family. One may gain or lose big face through the achievements or moral shortcomings of other members of one's family. This formulation is reminiscent of recent studies of honor cultures in non-Chinese, collectivist cultures. Mosquera, Manstead and Fischer (2000) compared students' and adults' descriptions of responses to situations referring to honor in the Netherlands and Spain. In the more collectivist culture of Spain, honor was considered more important and more strongly linked to one's family than in the Netherlands. Loss or gain of family honor was associated with pride, shame, and anger.

Existing studies of honor cultures have laid considerable emphasis on the obligation of group members to take revenge on those who have impugned the honor of one's group (e.g. Vandello & Cohen, 2003). This emphasis has not been very fully explored among Chinese respondents. However, Brockner, Chen, and Chen (2002) showed that when experimental groups of Chinese students were informed that their group had done less well than another group, they rated the other group more negatively than did Americans in the same circumstances. Tinsley and Weldon (2002) found that in situations of conflict Chinese managers showed a stronger desire to shame and teach a moral lesson to the other party than American managers did. These studies provide some support for the view that Chinese do give strong emphasis to the preservation of the honor and reputation of their in-group.

Achieving harmony: summary. It appears that interpersonal harmony is strongly valued within many collectivist cultures. Although Ho et al. (2001) propose that relationalism is uniquely derived from Confucianism, there is no compelling reason why a preference for harmony should have only one historical root. The nature of social relationships in collectivist cultures outside of East Asia has been much less fully investigated. It is therefore currently only possible to speculate as to the relative distinctiveness of face, indirectness, modesty, and honor as contributors toward in-group harmony.

Getting things done

A second universal goal identified by Schwartz (1992) was that of achieving coordination between individuals to achieve shared goals. There has been frequent discussion of the importance of relationships based on *guanxi* ('connections') in organizations within Chinese cultures (Nathan, 1993; Chen & Chen, 2004; Hwang & Han, this volume). Park and Luo (2001) summarize *guanxi* relationships as reciprocal, intangible, utilitarian, and transferable among parties that share a common connection. Some studies are now available that move beyond simple description. For instance, Farh, Tsui, Xin, and Cheng (1998) surveyed pairs of organizational superiors and subordinates in Taiwan. Where there was agreement that *guanxi* existed, trust was strongest if the relationship was based upon being a relative or a former neighbor. When these authors sampled peer relationships, the presence of *guanxi* was again associated with trust. In a more recent survey, Chen, Chen, and Xin (2004) studied attitudes toward others' use of *guanxi*. They found that Chinese business students would trust someone less who had been appointed to a job on the basis of *guanxi*, if this appointment derived from a family relationship or living in the same town. However, they would not distrust a new appointee if the *guanxi* derived from being a schoolmate or close friend. This suggests that the employment selection procedures based on *guanxi* relationships that are approved within the context of contemporary Chinese organizations are those in which there is some preexisting link with those selected, perhaps because such appointments are more expected and normative.

There is no doubt that *guanxi* relationships are an important attribute of Chinese cultures. However, there is room for some doubt as to how distinctive to Chinese culture their importance is. Within other East Asian cultures, Hitt, Lee, and Yucel (2002) have identified the salience of similar types of relationship based on *inmak* in Korea and *kankei* in Japan. Park and Luo (2001) suggest that the use of social networks to achieve benefit and favors is universal, but may take different forms in particular cultural contexts. Yahiaoui and Zoubir (2006) suggest that the use of *guanxi* relationships to achieve one's goals is essentially similar to influence processes based on *wasta* in Arab cultures. So, in order to determine the cultural specificity of *guanxi*, it will be necessary to move beyond comparison of descriptive accounts and undertake studies in which respondents from differing cultural backgrounds evaluate scenarios draw from differing cultural contexts.

An initial step in this direction was taken by Smith, Huang, Harb, & Torres (2009). Students from China, Lebanon, Brazil and the UK were asked to evaluate influence scenarios describing events from each of these four locations, but with the origin of each set of scenarios concealed. Chinese respondents did rate the scenarios of Chinese origin as more representative of *guanxi* than were the scenarios from elsewhere. However, they rated the scenarios derived from UK as equally typical of events that they experience in everyday life. More notably, both the Brazilian and the Lebanese respondents rated the *guanxi* scenarios as significantly more typical of what occurs in their own country than they rated the locally constructed scenarios. This suggests that processes akin to *guanxi* are also prevalent in other collectivist, high power distance cultures.

Influence relationships in China have also been studied in the context of formal leadership (Chen & Farh, this volume). A more distinctively relational approach has been explored through Cheng et al's (2004) model of paternalistic leadership. Cheng et al. did find evidence for the effectiveness of aspects of a paternalistic leader style within China that would certainly not be found in Western nations. However, paternalistic leadership has also been found to show positive effects in non-Chinese cultures that are also high on collectivism and power distance, such as Turkey, Iran, and the Philippines (Aycan, 2008).

Guan. A further area in which distinctive Chinese ways of getting things done has been proposed concerns parenting practices. Chao (1994) proposed that the emphasis that Chinese parents place on explicitly training their children (*guan*) accounts for effects that are additional to those explained by dimensions of parental behaviour identified by US researchers. However, studies that have included both measures of *guan* and measures of parental authoritarianism and authoritativeness have not found independent effects that are attributable to *guan* (Wang & Chang, this volume). Furthermore, *guan* has been found to correlate with parental warmth not just in China but also in Pakistan, and the United States (Stewart, Bond, Kennard et al., 2002).

Getting things done: summary. Influence in Chinese cultures is relational, in other words it is embedded within the requirements and norms informing specific sets of role relationships. We lack evidence as to whether this statement is more true of Chinese cultures than of other cultures high in collectivism and high in power distance. Fu and Liu (2008) suggest that the ubiquity of *guanxi* relationships may make Chinese culture more relationally interdependent than others, but multi-cultural, comparative evidence to confirm that claim is currently lacking.

Individual attributes

Schwartz's (1992) third universal need is simply described as survival. In relation to the present discussion, this refers to the qualities of individuals that best enhance their chances of their own and their own group's survival. This issue can be considered in terms of the ways that people think and in terms of the personality attributes that best meet survival needs in their cultural-ecological setting.

Holistic thinking. We have extensive evidence that Chinese, like other East Asians, address experimental tasks by thinking more holistically than analytically (Ji, Lam, & Guo, this volume; Nisbett et al., 2001). They attend to the context of a stimulus, rather than considering the stimulus in isolation. Another way to phrase this effect would be to say that just as earlier sections of this chapter have emphasized the relational nature of Chinese interpersonal relations, so these studies emphasize the relational nature of their thinking.

It is beyond the scope of this chapter to discuss fully why this predisposition has arisen. However, we can note the way in which Ho (this volume) finds that it is the relational quality of the Chinese language that is distinctively problematic for those who have difficulty in learning to read. Kashima and Kashima (1998) have reported the association between aspects of language structure (such as use of first person pronouns) and the strength of cultural individualism and collectivism in differing parts of the world. Our repeated daily use of a given language, like Chinese with its distinctive set of features (see McBride, Lin, Fong, & Shu, this volume; Him, this volume), may be continually priming its users to particular ways of thinking.

Experimental studies can also help to clarify the status of differences between those who engage in holistic versus analytic thinking. For instance, Ji, Peng, and Nisbett (2000) compared how Koreans and Americans explained behaviour in scenario episodes that were presented to them. Americans more often attributed the causes of behaviour to the actor's personality, whereas Koreans made more attributions to the effects of context. However, when no information about the context was presented, Koreans made just as many person attributions as the Americans. Thus, differences in holistic versus analytic thinking are better thought of as well established situational response habits, rather than deeply rooted aspects of cognition. Most people can think in either way if the circumstances press them to do so.

Personality. Cheung, Zhang, and Cheung (this volume) have described the development of the Chinese Personality Assessment Inventory, and its subsequent use cross-culturally. It is notable that the indigenously identified factor of Interpersonal Relatedness comprises facets that tap several of the aspects of Chinese social relationships discussed earlier in this chapter. The most striking aspect of this impressive project for the purpose of the present discussion is the discovery of the replicability of the Interpersonal Relatedness factor in samples outside the PRC. The factor remained intact among Chinese in Singapore (Cheung, Cheung, Leung, Ward, & Leong, 2003), even when the CPAI items were factored together with the US-derived NEO-FFI items. It also emerged among a sample of Caucasian US students (Cheung et al., 2003) and among non-Chinese Singaporeans (Cheung, Cheung, Howard, & Lim, 2006).

Establishing validated dimensions of Chinese personality also provides confirmation that the relational nature of Chinese culture does not preclude the likelihood that Chinese persons can and do think of themselves and others in terms of individual qualities. Kashima, Kashima, Chiu et al. (2005) found that students from eight nations all perceived individuals as having more fixed and unchangeable qualities than did groups. Respondents from Hong Kong, Japan and Korea differed from those elsewhere only in their belief that groups are equally as able to initiate action as are individuals.

Happiness. Happiness and well-being are typically thought of as having an individual trait-like basis, akin to the fundamental emotions identified by Ekman, Friesen, O'Sullivan et al. (1987).

Lu (this volume) proposes that happiness within Chinese cultures is based more on fulfillment of one's morally-derived role obligations and that these obligations include the requirement not to strive too strongly for personal satisfaction. Cross-national surveys have confirmed that persons from the Confucian nations of East Asia are less concerned as to whether they are happy or not, and spend less time thinking about it (Suh, 2000).

However, individual-level analyses of the relation between life satisfaction and measures of self-construal (Singelis, Triandis et al., 2005) in each of 39 nations have provided no support for the distinctiveness of effects within Chinese cultures (Oishi, 2000). Life satisfaction in Taiwan was predicted by horizontal collectivism, as one might predict on the basis of a role-oriented basis for satisfaction. A similar but weak effect was found in China. Within Singapore high satisfaction was associated with low vertical collectivism and in Hong Kong there were no significant predictors. Self-construal measures do not tap moral obligation, but the variation in these effects between Chinese cultures suggests that other factors are more salient in determining life satisfaction. As Kwan et al. (1997) showed, the effects of self-construal on life satisfaction are differentially moderated by both self-esteem and relationship harmony.

Achievement. There is also continuing debate about the distinctiveness of Chinese attitudes toward achievement. While Yu (1996) emphasized the socially-oriented nature of Chinese achievement motivation, Hau (this volume) reports a more complex set of findings. Attitudes toward achievement have mostly been addressed in ways that take insufficient account of context. As in other cultures, there may be some contexts in which the social norms favour individual striving, and others in which personal achievement enhances the honor of the group. The studies reviewed by Hau (this volume) target the distinctive domain of student achievement. We know much less about attitudes that prevail within other life domains.

Discussion

This chapter began by discussing the criteria that are needed for assessing the distinctiveness of Chinese psychology. Sampling of the beliefs and values endorsed within the four primarily Chinese societies in the world in relation to non-Chinese societies indicates substantial psychological variability within the domain of Chinese ethnicity. The differential history of these four societies over past two centuries provides ample reason to anticipate their increasing diversity. No doubt there is also substantial variability within a society so numerous, so ethnically diverse and so geographically extended as the PRC.

Chinese migration to other parts of the world also provides opportunities to evaluate the extent to which the patterns of relationship found with Chinese societies remain intact within other cultural contexts. Rosenthal and Feldman (1992) compared first, second and third generation Chinese migrants to Australia and the US. They found a decline in Chinese family practices among first generation migrants, but no further decline among later generations. They also recorded much stronger persistence of Chinese practices in the US, where there were more, and more substantial Chinatowns than in Australia. This study is superior to many other studies of migrant acculturation, because it also contained a control group of non-migrants, against whom changes in the migrants could be more validly evaluated. Evidently, Chinese ethnicity has a continuing importance, wherever one lives (see also Ward & Lin, this volume).

The appearance of the second edition of this handbook is an indicator of the very substantial progress that has been achieved in the study of Chinese societies in the past two decades. Cross-cultural psychology during this period has been dominated by comparisons between North America and East Asia (Smith, Bond, & Kağıtçıbaşı, 2006). For this reason, it is easiest to form views as to the distinctiveness of Chinese psychology within East Asia, and in contrast with North America. It is clear, however, that there are substantial similarities between Chinese societies within East Asia and at least some of the predominantly non-Chinese ones.

It is much more difficult to evaluate the degree to which the processes identified within Chinese cultures differ from those that prevail within other collectivist, high power distance nations in South

America, Africa, South Asia, and the Arab region. Direct comparisons between social processes in China and in any of these regions are rare. Examples do exist of parallel conceptualization. For instance, Cheng et al's (2004) analysis of paternalistic leadership in China parallels the work of Aycan (2008) in Turkey and elsewhere. Furthermore, Cheng's distinction between authoritarian leadership and authoritative leadership is also found in studies of parental domination versus order-keeping in China (Lau, Lew, Hau et al., 1990), and in Dwairy, Achoui, Abouserie et al's (2006) studies of authoritarian versus authoritative parenting in Arab cultures. However, until equivalence of measurement is achieved between such studies, we cannot be sure that they are studying equivalent phenomena (see Stewart & Bond, 2002).

Comparative studies between individualist and Chinese societies have rather frequently identified significant differences in the frequency or strength of given phenomena. However, variations in frequency or strength do not make a strong case for distinctiveness. For instance, the study by Kurman (2003) discussed above found that endorsement of modesty could explain levels of self-enhancement, or its opposite, self-effacement, in both Israel and Singapore. Self-enhancement is stronger in Israel, but the process leading to self-enhancement is the same in both cultures. The case for a global psychology is strengthened when it is found that similar explanatory variables can be employed in both locations to explain a given phenomenon.

The replicability of Cheung et al's (2003) personality dimension of interpersonal relatedness within the US can be thought of in the same way - its relatively lower salience in the US may have caused it to be overlooked in prior work. It is necessary next to determine whether endorsement of relatedness can explain phenomena in different cultures in the same way as in China (see e.g. Zhang & Bond, 1993). Does it serve similar interpersonal and other functions elsewhere? If that proves to be the case, it will be one of the few instances in which a variable identified as indigenous has so far been shown to contribute value beyond the borders within which it was first established. An earlier example is Kwan et al's (1997) study of relationship harmony. Although relationship harmony was a particularly distinctive predictor of Chinese life satisfaction, this variable did also account for significant additional variance among US respondents. In a future psychology, we can anticipate that identification of psychological phenomena that are particularly salient in one location can help to elucidate their significance in settings where they have not been previously noted, but are present in more muted but still functional form.

So, is it useful to consider Chinese psychology as distinctive, or as a contribution to the globalization of psychology? I would conclude both, depending on one's immediate purpose. It would be good in the future to read handbooks of Indian, Arab, African, or Latin American psychology that are as fully documented as this one. It would be equally good to read handbooks focused on discrete research topics that succeed in addressing their topic in a way that shows how cultural variations can explicate the universal underlying principles that define humanity and characterize its behavior.

Author's note

I am grateful to Constantine Sedikides for helpful comments on an earlier draft of this chapter.

References

Abdullah, A. (1996). *Going glocal: Cultural dimensions in Malaysian management.* Kuala Lumpur, Malaysia: Malaysian Institute of Management.

Allwood, C. M. & Berry, J. W. (2005). Origins and development of indigenous psychologies. *International Journal of Psychology, 40,* 1–26.

Aycan, Z. (2008). Cross-cultural approaches to leadership. In P. B. Smith, M. F. Peterson, & D. C. Thomas (eds), *Handbook of cross-cultural management research* (pp. 219–238). Thousand Oaks, CA: Sage.

Ayçiçegi, A. (1993). *The effects of the mother training program.* Unpublished master's thesis, Bogaziçi University, Istanbul, Turkey.

Berry, J. W. (1969). On cross-cultural comparability. *International Journal of Psychology, 4,* 119–128.

Bond, M. H. (1988). Finding universal dimensions of individual variation in multi-cultural surveys of values: The Rokeach and Chinese value surveys. *Journal of Personality and Social Psychology, 55,* 1009–1015.

Bond, M. H. (1993). Emotions and their expression in Chinese culture. *Journal of Nonverbal Behavior, 17*, 245–262.

Bond, M. H. (1996). Chinese values. In M. H. Bond (ed.), *The handbook of Chinese psychology* (pp. 208–226). Hong Kong: Oxford University Press.

Brockner, J., Chen, Y. R., & Chen, X. P. (2002). Individual–collective primacy and in-group favoritism: Enhancement and protection effects. *Journal of Experimental Social Psychology, 38*, 482–491.

Chao, R. K. (1994). Beyond parental control and authoritarian parenting: Understanding Chinese parenting through the cultural notion of training. *Child Development, 65*, 1111–1119.

Chen, C. C., Chen, Y. R., & Xin, K. R. (2004). *Guanxi* practices and trust in management: A procedural justice perspective. *Organization Science, 15*, 200–209.

Chen, X. P. & Chen, C. C. (2004). On the intricacies of the Chinese *guanxi*: A process model of *guanxi* development. *Asia Pacific journal of Management, 21*, 305–324.

Cheng, B. S., Chou, L. F., Huang, M. P., Wu, T. Y., & Farh, J. L. (2004). Paternalistic leadership and subordinate reverence: Establishing a leadership model in Chinese organizations. *Asian Journal of Social Psychology, 7*, 89–117.

Cheung, F. M., Cheung, S. F., Leung, K., Ward, C., & Leong, F. (2003). The English version of the Chinese Personality Assessment Inventory. *Journal of Cross-Cultural Psychology, 34*, 433–452.

Cheung, S. F., Cheung, F. M., Howard, R., & Lim, Y. H. (2006). Personality across ethnic divide in Singapore. *Personality and Individual Differences, 41*, 467–477.

Choi, S. C. & Lee, S. J. (2002). Two-component model of *chemyon*-oriented behaviors in Korea: Constructive and defensive *chemyon*. *Journal of Cross-Cultural Psychology, 33*, 332–345.

Costa, P. T., Jr & McCrae, R. R. (1992). *Revised NEO Personality Inventory (NEO-PI—R) and NEO Five Factor Inventory (NEO–FFI)*. Odessa, FL: Psychological Assessment Resources.

Dwairy, M., Achoui, M., Abouserie, R., Farah, A. et al. (2006). Parenting styles in Arab societies: A first cross-regional study. *Journal of Cross-Cultural Psychology, 37*, 230–247.

Ekman, P., Friesen, W. V., O'Sullivan, M. et al. (1987). Universals and cultural differences in the judgment of facial expressions of emotion. *Journal of Personality and Social Psychology, 53*, 712–717.

Farh, J. L., Tsui, A.S., Xin, K., & Cheng, B. S. (1998). The influence of relational demography and *guanxi*: The Chinese case. *Organization Science, 9*, 471–498.

Fu, P. P. & Liu, J. (2008). Cross-cultural influence styles and power sources. In P. B. Smith, M. F. Peterson & D. C. Thomas (eds), *Handbook of cross-cultural management research* (pp. 239–252). Thousand Oaks, CA: Sage.

Gabrenya, W. K., Kung, M. C., & Chen, L. Y. (2006). Understanding the Taiwan indigenous psychology movement: A sociology of science approach. *Journal of Cross-Cultural Psychology, 37*, 597–622.

Gaertner, L., Sedikides, C., & Chang, K. (2008). On pancultural self-enhancement: Well-adjusted Taiwanese self-enhance on personally valued traits. *Journal of Cross-Cultural Psychology, 39*, 463–477.

Hall, E. T. (1966). *The hidden dimension*. New York: Doubleday.

Heine, S. J., Lehman, D. R., Markus, H. R. & Kitayama, S. (1999). Is there a universal need for self-regard? *Psychological Review, 106*, 766–794.

Hitt, M. A., Lee, H. U., & Yucel, E. (2002). The importance of social capital to the management of multinational enterprises: Relational networks among Asian and Western firms. *Asia Pacific Journal of Management, 19*, 353–372.

Ho, D. Y. F., Peng, S. Q., Lai, A. C., & Chan, S. F. F. (2001). Indigenization and beyond: Methodological relationalism in the study of personality across cultural traditions. *Journal of Personality, 69*, 925–953.

Hofstede, G. (1980). *Culture's consequences: International differences in work-related values*. Beverly Hills, CA: Sage.

Hofstede, G. (2001). *Culture's consequences: Comparing values, behaviors, institutions and organizations across nations* (2nd edn). Thousand Oaks, CA: Sage.

Ji, L. J., Peng, K. P., & Nisbett, R. E. (2000). Culture, control and perception of relationships in the environment. *Journal of Personality and Social Psychology, 78*, 943–955.

Kashima, Y. & Kashima, E. (1998). Culture and language: The case of cultural dimensions and personal pronoun use. *Journal of Cross-Cultural Psychology, 29*, 461–486.

Kashima, Y., Kashima, E., Chiu, C. Y. et al. (2005). Culture, essentialism and agency: Are individuals universally believed to be more real entities than groups? *European Journal of Social Psychology, 35*, 147–170.

Katigbak, M. S., Church, A. T., Guanzon-Lapena, M. A., Carlota, A. J. & del Pilar, G. H. (2002). Are indigenous personality dimensions culture specific? Philippine inventories and the five factor model. *Journal of Personality and Social Psychology, 82*, 89–101.

Kim, M. S. (1994). Cross-cultural comparisons of the perceived importance of interactive constraints. *Human Communication Research, 21*, 128–151.

Kluckhohn, C. & Murray, H. A. (1948). *Personality in nature, culture and society*. New York: Knopf.

Komin, S. (1990). Culture and work-related values in Thai organizations. *International Journal of Psychology, 25*, 681–704.

Kurman, J. (2003). Why is self-enhancement low in certain collectivist cultures? An investigation of two competing explanations. *Journal of Cross-Cultural Psychology, 34*, 496–510.

Kwan, V. S. Y., Bond, M. H., & Singelis, T. M. (1997). Pancultural explanations for life satisfaction: Adding relationship harmony to self-esteem. *Journal of Personality and Social Psychology, 73*, 1038–1051.

Kwan, V. S. Y, Kwang, L. L. & Hui, N. H. H. (in press). Identifying the sources of self-esteem: The mixed medley of benevolence, merit and bias. *Self and Identity*.

Lau, S., Lew, W. J., Hau, K. T., Cheung P. C., & Berndt, T. J. (1990). Relations among perceived parental control, warmth, indulgence and family harmony of Chinese in Mainland China. *Developmental Psychology, 26*, 674–677.

Leung, K. & Bond, M. H. (2004). Social axioms: A model of social beliefs in multi–cultural perspective. In M. P. Zanna (ed.), *Advances in Experimental Social Psychology* (Vol. 36, 119-197). San Diego, CA: Elsevier Academic Press.

Markus, H. R. & Kitayama, S. (1991). Culture and the self: Implications for cognition, emotion, and motivation. *Psychological Review, 98*, 224-253.

Matsumoto, D., Yoo, S. H., Fontaine, J., & 58 co-authors (2008). Mapping expressive differences around the world: The relationship between emotional display rules and individualism versus collectivism. *Journal of Cross-Cultural Psychology, 39*, 55-74.

McAuley, P., Bond, M. H., & Kashima, E. (2002). Towards defining situations objectively: A culture-level analysis of role dyads in Hong Kong and Australia. *Journal of Cross-Cultural Psychology, 33*, 363-380.

Mosquera, P. M. R., Manstead, A. S. R., & Fischer, A. H. (2000). The role of honor-related values in the elicitation, communication and experience of pride, shame and anger: Spain and the Netherlands compared. *Personality and Social Psychology Bulletin, 26*, 833-844.

Muramoto, Y. (2003). An indirect enhancement in relationship among Japanese. *Journal of Cross-Cultural Psychology, 34*, 552-566.

Nathan, A. J. (1993). Is Chinese culture distinctive: A review article. *Journal of Asian Studies, 52*, 923-936.

Nisbett, R. E., Peng, K. P., Choi, I., & Norenzayan, A. (2000). Culture and systems of thought: Holistic versus analytic cognition. *Psychological Review, 108*, 291-310.

Oishi, S. (2000). Goals as cornerstones of subjective well-being: Linking individuals and cultures. In E. Diener & E. M. Suh (eds), *Culture and subjective well-being* (pp. 87-112). Cambridge, MA: MIT Press.

Park, S. H. & Luo, Y. D. (2001). *Guanxi* and organizational dynamics: Organizational networking in Chinese firms. *Strategic Management Journal, 22*, 455-477.

Rosenthal, D. A. & Feldman, S. S. (1992). The nature and stability of ethnic identity in Chinese youth: The effects of length of residence in two cultural contexts. *Journal of Cross-Cultural Psychology, 23*, 214-227.

Schwartz, S. H. (1992). Universals in the content and structure of values: Theoretical advances and empirical tests in 20 countries. In M. P. Zanna (ed.), *Advances in experimental social psychology* (Vol. 25, pp 1-65). Orlando, FL: Academic Press.

Schwartz, S. H. (1994). Beyond individualism and collectivism: New cultural dimensions of values. In U. Kim, H. C. Triandis, Ç. Kagitçibasi, S. C. Choi, & G. Yoon (eds), *Individualism and collectivism: Theory, method and applications* (pp. 85-119). Thousand Oaks, CA: Sage.

Schwartz, S. H. (2004). Mapping and interpreting cultural differences around the world. In H. Vinken, J. Soeters, & P. Ester (eds) *Comparing cultures: Dimensions of culture in a comparative perspective* (pp. 43-73). Leiden, Netherlands: Brill.

Sedikides, C., Gaertner, J., & Toguchi, Y. (2003). Pan-cultural self-enhancement. *Journal of Personality and Social Psychology, 84*, 60-79.

Sedikides, C., Gaertner, J., & Vevea, J. L. (2003). Pan-cultural self-enhancement reloaded: A meta-analytic reply to Heine (2005). *Journal of Personality and Social Psychology, 89*, 539-551.

Sedikides, C., Gregg, A. P., & Hart, C. M. (2007). The importance of being modest. In C. Sedikides & S. Spencer (eds), *The self: Frontiers in social psychology* (pp. 163-184). New York: Psychology Press.

Singelis, T. M., Triandis, H. C., Bhawuk, D., & Gelfand, M. (1995). Horizontal and vertical dimensions of individualism and collectivism: A theoretical and measurement refinement. *Cross-Cultural Research, 29*, 240-275.

Smith, P. B., Bond, M. H., & Kagitçibasi, Ç. (2006). *Understanding social psychology across cultures: Living and working in a changing world*. London: Sage.

Smith, P. B., Huang, H. J., Harb, C., & Torres, C. (2009). How distinctive are indigenous ways of achieving influence? A comparative study of *guanxi, wasta, jeitinho* and pulling strings. Paper in preparation.

Stewart, S. M. & Bond, M. H. (2002). A critical look at parenting research from the mainstream: Problems uncovered while adapting Western research to non-western countries. *British Journal of Developmental Psychology, 20*, 379-392.

Stewart, S. M., Bond, M. H., Kennard, B. D., Ho, L. M., & Zaman, R. M. (2002). Does the Chinese construct of guan export to the West? *International Journal of Psychology, 37*, 74-82.

Suh, E. M. (2000). Self, the hyphen between culture and subjective well-being. In E. Diener & E. M. Suh (eds), *Culture and subjective well-being* (pp. 63-86). Cambridge, MA: MIT Press.

Ting-Toomey, S. (1988). A face negotiation theory. In Y. Y. Kim & W. B. Gudykunst (eds) *Theory in intercultural communication* (pp. 215-35). Newbury Park, CA: Sage.

Tinsley, C. H. & Weldon, E. (2002).Responses to a normative conflict among American and Chinese managers. Unpublished paper: http://ssrn.com/abstract=332880.

Triandis, H. C., Lisansky, J., Marin, G., & Betancourt, H. (1984). *Simpatía* as a cultural script for Hispanics. *Journal of Personality and Social Psychology, 47*, 1363-1375.

Vandello, J. A. & Cohen, D. (2003). Male honor and female infidelity: Implicit scripts that perpetuate domestic violence. *Journal of Personality and Social Psychology, 84*, 997-1010.

Wong, S., Bond, M. H., & Rodriguez Mosquera, P. M. (2008). The influence of cultural value orientations on self-reported emotional expression across cultures. *Journal of Cross-Cultural Psychology, 39*, 224-229.

Yahiaoui, D. & Zoubir, Y. H. (2006). HRM in Tunisia. In P. S. Budhwar & K. Mellahi (eds), *Managing human resources in the Middle East* (pp. 233-249). London: Routledge.

Young, D. (1989). *Chinese diagnostic criteria and case examples of mental disorders.* Hunan, China: Hunan University Press.

Yu, A. B. (1996). Ultimate life concerns, self and Chinese achievement motivation. In M. H. Bond (ed.) *The handbook of Chinese psychology* (pp. 227-246). New York: Oxford University Press.

Zhang, J. & Bond, M. H. (1998). Personality and filial piety among college students in two Chinese societies: The added value of indigenous constructs. *Journal of Cross-Cultural Psychology, 29,* 402-417.

CHAPTER 41

Moving the scientific study of Chinese psychology into our twenty-first century: some ways forward

Michael Harris Bond

I write this conclusion to our *Oxford handbook of Chinese psychology* in March of 2009, having helped to finalize almost all the 40 commissioned chapters that you now hold in your hands. As a result of reviewing the work of so many distinguished researchers covering such diverse areas of Chinese psychology, I have a solid understanding of where we have reached in the current stage of our academic development in this now-small tide pool of intellectual activity. I propose to use what I have gleaned from this editorship to offer some bold assessments of the state of our art and its prospects for contributing to our planetary capital. I will focus on the how of doing Chinese psychology, not the content of what will be done. In appreciation of your intellectual labors in reaching this point of this handbook, I will be brief ...

Rising to the scientific challenge

In 1993, Nathan addressed the question 'Is Chinese culture distinctive?' by responding, 'Although anyone who studies it must be convinced that it is, we have far to go to state clearly how it is distinctive and to prove it empirically' (Nathan, 1993, p. 936). In assessing the potential of social sciences in responding to claims for Chinese distinctiveness, Nathan answered, 'What is required is to demonstrate that such distinctiveness exists, what it consists of, and what influence it has on the performance of societies' (Nathan, 1993, p. 923).

As a political scientist, Nathan was focusing on the performance of societies; as psychologists, we focus on the performance of individuals. Even a cursory reading of this handbook would prove that Nathan's question has been answered in the affirmative. Numerous differences in the levels of psychological constructs and the processes linking those constructs abound, certainly when Western populations are the comparison groups. These differences have been established in compliance with Nathan's warning that 'To test a hypothesis about the effect of culture on a social outcome, it is necessary to define cultural attributes in a way that is cross-culturally valid in principle' (Nathan, 1993, p. 933).

In general, we have observed the strictures of scientific measurement and methodology necessary to establish the corpus of cultural group differences proving that there is a cultural case to answer. This is assuredly the case when manuscripts are submitted to international journals for editorial review, as these outlets provide stricter quality assurance.

Chinese people are different, i.e. higher or lower in their *mean scores on measured variables*, than persons of other, mostly geographically separate, cultural groups, most of the time. More occasionally, cultural differences have also been shown for the *strength of linkage among these measured constructs* (e.g. Bond & Forgas, 1984; Liao & Bond, in press). It is rare, indeed, that a linkage among constructs is present in the Chinese group, but absent in a comparison cultural group (however, see Bond & Forgas, 1984; Hui & Bond, 2009). Whether they will be different in these two ways from more proximate cultural groups sharing more historical continuity is, of course, a matter for future research to address.

Are Chinese people distinctive?

Scientific demonstrations of empirical differences, be they frequent or occasional, do not constitute evidence for distinctiveness. In life, every thing and every event is distinctive; in science, nothing is distinctive. To the scientist, things or events, be they particles in a cloud chamber, evolving social systems, or two people touching, are exemplars of underlying constructs, and the processes that represent relationships among these constructs. For psychologists, these are psychological constructs working in concert within a given cultural context to yield observable individual outcomes, called behaviors or responses.

As long as psychologists can legitimately compare across persons and events in their cultural settings, there will be many unique occurrences, but no scientific distinctiveness; all occurrences will be united by the formulas, the equations, and the models developed by scientists to explain the processes by which the constructs operate in the revealed world. Each Chinese person and his or her life course will be unique, as for any person from any culture. But, the way by which each becomes a person and lives his or her life will be describable and explicable by the same constructs and processes everywhere and at any time. Chinese culture is unique, but not distinctive; each Chinese person is unique, but not distinctive. As Confucius put it, 'Within the four seas, all men are brothers'; in this academic context, we might rather say, 'Persons from all cultures are united in their shared humanness'. As cross-cultural psychologists, we strive to demonstrate that unity scientifically.

The role of indigenous contributions to psychological science

As the center of psychological gravity shifts away from the West, it is inevitable that the repertoire of concepts and models of human behavior will be refined and will grow. Presented in the language of their origin by their proponents from cultural systems new to psychological discourse, they will appear distinctive, even unique (see e.g. Hwang & Han, this volume). However, if we are doing science and measuring these constructs and their inter-relationships, then the question of whether and how far indigenous inputs are distinctive remains to be established (see Smith, this volume).

To date, I would venture to say that Interpersonal Relatedness, Holism, the Dialectical Self, Relationship Harmony, Paternalistic Leadership, and concern with the other's face have been adequately demonstrated to be distinctive constructs adduced from a dedicated and disciplined examination of Chinese culture, to identify the most prominent (see Cheung, Zhang, & Cheung; Ji, Lee, & Guo; Kwan, Hui, & McGee; Kwan et al; Chen & Farh; Hwang & Han, this volume, respectively). These constructs may, however, be extracted from responses of persons from other cultural groups to the appropriately designed and translated instruments (see the above chapters, and Smith, this volume). Of course, they will be less salient to members of these cultural groups, and they may prove to be less powerful in predicting relevant psychological outcomes in the 'importing' cultures (see e.g. Hui & Bond, in press, on face loss and forgiveness in Hong Kong and America). Nonetheless, these constructs are present and usually functional when careful scientific testing is conducted.

The role of indigenous theorizing, then, is to enlarge our repertoire of constructs and theories in describing and explaining the human condition using scientific best practice. Their ultimate function is to demonstrate how, 'Within the fours seas, all men are brothers'. Non-mainstream cultural groups like the Chinese can enlarge our conceptual ambit, and ground psychology in the whole of human reality, not just their Western, usually American, versions (Arnett, 2008). Many believe that this expanded disciplinary compass will emerge from Asian psychological science (e.g. Miller, 2006).

Moving beyond the demonstration of cultural differences

How is an interest in other cultural realities provoked? In people's experience, it is the encounter with difference. Among those so inclined, this encounter can lead to the discovery of new tools of thought and a re-organization of their construct system, leading to changed interpersonal functioning (see Bond, 1997). Among behavioral scientists so inclined, this encounter can likewise lead to an identification of new constructs for analyzing social functioning and the development of new or expanded theories to explain that functioning.

Much Chinese psychology derives from this dynamic of demonstrating difference; many chapters in this handbook document these differences across a wide range of human functioning. Such compendiums present a case to be addressed and answered. These answers come in two ways:

From categorical comparisons to unpackaging studies examining process. In the discourse of psychological science, those answers must come from the identification of those constructs and processes that explain the 'Chineseness' of these differences. This is a process of cultural 'unpackaging', of penetrating the categorical differences to reveal the underlying psychological processes that drive them (Bond & van de Vijver, in press). In a sense, cross-cultural psychologists are trying to make the categorical differences 'disappear' by demonstrating that underlying variables may be used to position the Chinese relative to persons of other groups, and lead to the observed difference in the outcome of current interest. So, Chinese and persons from other cultural groups are united in being exemplars of pancultural psychological processes that explain human behavior in all cultural groups assessed. There are two variants to this approach:

1. *Studies of mean difference.* Of course, it does not always work out that we unpackage the difference between the cultural groups. When the difference lies in the mean level of a construct, e.g. the empathetic embarrassability of Singelis, Bond, Sharkey, & Lai (1999), the cultural difference may not be fully explained by the proposed construct, in this case self-construals. That outcome will then provoke further thinking to elaborate the mechanisms responsible for the unexplained difference. Perhaps the facet of 'face' from Cheung et al's (this volume) personality dimension of Interpersonal Relatedness will do the job. An appropriately designed study would reveal the answer.

   And so the scientific endeavor continues. Much of the research reported in this handbook, especially those studies done by earlier cohorts, will be enriched by attempts to build process models for the many outcome differences found between Chinese and other peoples in their content domains. Successful unpackaging will support the proposed models, and render the research of broader interest to scientists whose focus is on humanity, not merely on the Chinese.

2. *Studies of difference in linkage strength.* Once unpackaging studies are tried, a new kind of cultural difference may emerge, viz. the cultural difference involving the Chinese may be a difference in the strength of the linkage between a predictor variable and its outcome. So, for example, Singelis et al. (1999) found that an independent self-construal did a better job of predicting self-embarrassability for the Americans than it did for the Chinese. However, this shortfall in explaining the relative strength of self-embarrassability for the Chinese would likewise stimulate the development of theories about cultural dynamics to explain why an independent self-construal was relatively weaker in its effects within some cultural groups than within others.

   Scientifically defensible and theoretically informative attempts, however, would require an enlargement of cultural groups beyond the initial two-culture comparison that identified the variation in the construct's impact on the outcome of interest. Such work is described and rationalized next.

From categorical contrasts to multi-cultural dimensionalizing. Some psychologists, like some laypersons, have an understandably greater interest in some cultural groups that in others. This interest usually focuses on one's own cultural group, and can only be illuminated in contrast to some other group. In psychology, this comparison group is usually the Americans from the United States, for various historical reasons described by Blowers (this volume). Despite constituting only about 5 per cent of the world's population, they produce about 80 per cent of its theory, measures of constructs, and data (Arnett, 2008). If culture matters, and results suggest that it frequently does (e.g. Smith, Bond, & Kağıtçıbaşı, 2006), then this imbalance must be rectified by building *models of culture of use to psychologists* (see e.g. Bond, 2004).

Scientifically, these models of culture require the identification of dimensions across which cultures may be compared and along which they may be ordered with respect to one another. This dimensionalizing requires many more than two cultural groups, and the more the better; no comparison between any two cultural groups can evince such a dimension, only suggest some plausible candidates. In that respect, Chinese–American comparisons, which form the bulk of this handbook, may be provocative and stimulating—they help generate ideas.

Eventually, however, multi-cultural contrasts are needed. Hofstede's (1980) 40-nation study lead off the quest, and has been extended many times with respect to the countries and cultures assessed, the kinds of psychological constructs measured, and levels at which the data are analyzed (nation-level or individual-level). This empirical, multicultural work is described in Smith et al. (2006, chs. 3 & 4), and frequently involves Chinese persons from more than one socio-political entity, viz. Singapore, Taiwan, the Mainland, and Hong Kong.

Various dimensions may be teased out of such data sets, and achieve benefits for Chinese psychology. First, they locate various Chinese societies and their citizens relative to one another and to other societies and their members. Typically, Chinese societies and their citizens are found to be located in different positions and do not cluster together (see Kulich & Zhang; Leung, this volume), revealing that in respect of some cultural or psychological constructs, there is no Chinese monolith. Instead, these Chinese societies and their members instantiate different positions on underlying societal or psychological constructs.

These constructs may be used in building sophisticated models for individual behavior that incorporate cultural variables. So, a second benefit of dimensions extracted from multicultural studies lies in enabling sophisticated, multi-level studies where individual-level processes are explored across cultural groups using HLM analyses. These studies allow us to see both mean differences and linkage differences simultaneously in the same study. Sometimes these studies show differences across the cultural groups involved, and that the culture-level variables modify or moderate the individual level processes being examined (e.g. Fu et al., 2004; Liao & Bond, in press); sometimes not (e.g. Wong, Bond, & Rodriguez Mosquera, 2008). Regardless of outcome, such studies allow social scientists to begin exploring the universality of psychological processes empirically. Surely, this is the next goal for all cross-cultural psychological work (Bond, 2009).

My debt to Chinese culture and Chinese people

These insights, such as they are, have been gleaned from 35 years of doing psychological research in Hong Kong, mostly with Chinese psychologists. Much of this research has been described in the present handbook. Without participating in doing this research from its early, humble beginnings, none of these understandings would have been possible for me. Of course, they are hardly mine alone, but are now widely shared within the sub-discipline of which I, the authors in this handbook, and others around the planet constitute a large part.

I am stunned to realize the extent of my debt to my fellow Chinese psychologists and to the educational environment in Hong Kong culture and in other parts of the Chinese polity that has enabled me to do this work. I have been provided with a resourceful and sustaining job environment, a cooperative network of competent, enthusiastic colleagues, and service-oriented support staff. I have written appreciations of these happy circumstances elsewhere (Bond, 1997, 2003), but wish to close this handbook by thanking its contributing authors and reiterating my lifelong gratitude.

When drinking from a stream, remember its source.

Chinese adage from a song by Yu Hsin.

References

Arnett, J. J. (2008). The neglected 95 per cent: Why American psychology needs to become less American. *American Psychologist, 63*, 602–614.

Bond, M. H. (1997). Preface: The psychology of working at the interface of cultures. In M. H. Bond (ed.), *Working at the interface of cultures: 18 lives in social science* (pp. XI–XIX). London: Routledge.

Bond, M. H. (1997). Two decades of chasing the dragon: A Canadian psychologist assesses his career in Hong Kong. In M. H. Bond (ed.), *Working at the interface of cultures: 18 lives in social science* (pp. 179–190). London: Routledge.

Bond, M. H. (1999). The psychology of the Chinese people: A Marco Polo returns to Italy. *Psychologia Italiana, 17*, 29–33.

Bond, M. H. (2003). Marrying the Dragon to the Phoenix: Twenty-eight years of doing a psychology of the Chinese people. *Journal of Psychology in Chinese Societies, 4*, No. 2, 269–283.

Bond, M. H. (2004). Culture and aggression – from context to coercion. *Personality and Social Psychology Review, 8*, 62–78.

Bond, M. H. (2009). Circumnavigating the psychological globe: From *yin* and *yang* to starry, starry night ... In A. Aksu-Koc & S. Beckman (eds), *Perspectives on human development, family and culture* (pp. 31–49). Cambridge, England: Cambridge University Press.

Bond, M. H. & van de Vijver, F. (in press). Making scientific sense of cultural differences in psychological outcomes: Unpackaging the *magnum mysterium*. In D. Matsumoto & F. van de Vijver (eds), *Cross-cultural research methods.* New York: Oxford University Press.

Fu, P. P., Kennedy, J., Tata, J., Yukl, G., Bond, M. H. and 10 other co-authors. (2004). The impact of societal cultural values and individual social beliefs on the perceived effectiveness of managerial influence strategies: A meso approach. *Journal of International Business Studies, 35*, 284–305.

Hui, V. K. Y. & Bond, M. H. (2009). Target's face loss, motivations, and forgiveness following relational transgression: Comparing Chinese and US cultures. *Journal of Social and Personal Relationships, 26*, 123–140.

Liao, Y. & Bond, M. H. (in press) The dynamics of face loss following interpersonal harm for Chinese and Americans. *Journal of Cross-Cultural Psychology.*

Miller, G. (2006). The Asian future of evolutionary psychology. *Evolutionary Psychology, 4*, 107–119.

Nathan, A. J. (1993). Is Chinese culture distinctive?—A review article. *The Journal of Asian Studies, 52*, 923–936.

Singelis, T. M., Bond, M. H., Sharkey, W. F., & Lai, C. S. Y. (1999). Unpackaging culture's influence on self-esteem and embarrassability: The role of self-construals. *Journal of Cross-Cultural Psychology, 30*, 315–341.

Smith, P. B., Bond, M. H., & Kağıtçıbaşı, Ç. (2006). *Understanding social psychology across cultures.* London: Sage.

Wong, S., Bond, M. H., & Rodriguez Mosquera, P. M. (2008). The influence of cultural value orientations on self-reported emotional expression across cultures. *Journal of Cross-Cultural Psychology, 39*, 224–229.

Index